Contents

A Guide to the Major Trusts

2005/2006 edition

Volume 2
A further 1,200 trusts

Dave Griffiths
Chris McGuire
Rebecca Ryland
Emma Jepson

DIRECTORY OF SOCIAL CHANGE

A Guide to the Major Trusts
Volume 2
2005/2006 edition

Published by
Directory of Social Change
24 Stephenson Way
London NW1 2DP
Tel: 020 7391 4800; Fax: 020 7391 4804
e-mail: info@dsc.org.uk
www.dsc.org.uk
from whom further copies and a full publications list are available.

Directory of Social Change is a Registered Charity no. 800517

First Published 1993
Second edition 1995
Third edition 1997
Fourth edition 1999
Fifth edition 2001
Sixth edition 2003
Seventh edition 2005

ISBN 1 903991 56 0

British Library Cataloguing in Publication Data

A catalogue record for this book is available from the British Library

Cover designed by Keith Shaw
Text designed by Lenn Darroux and Linda Parker
Typeset by Tradespools
Printed out and bound by Page Bros., Norwich

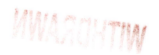

Directory of Social Change Northern Office:
Federation House, Hope Street, Liverpool L1 9BW
Tel: 0151 708 0136; Fax: 0151 708 0139
e-mail: north@dsc.org.uk

Introduction

Welcome to *A Guide to Major Trusts Volume 2.* This guide contains 1,200 UK trusts, following on from the 400 largest detailed in *Volume 1.* As regular users will note, the guide has expanded from 700 trusts, and now features trusts previously contained in *Volume 3* (*Volume 1* has also expanded from 300 trusts). The trusts in this book collectively give about £159 million a year (trusts in *Volume 1* gave a total of £2.1 billion).

The guide's main aim is to help people raise money from trusts. We aim to provide as much information as we can to enable fundraisers to locate relevant trusts and produce suitable applications. There is also a secondary aim: to be a survey of the work of grant-making trusts, to show where trust money is going and for what purposes.

What trusts do we include?

Our criteria are as follows: trusts must have the potential to give at least £30,000 a year in grants, and these grants should go to organisations in the UK. Many give far more than this, with over 500 giving at least £100,000. There are actually about 75 trusts giving £300,000 or more, which appear large enough to be included in *Volume 1.* However, in most cases the income of the trust was lower than the total given in grants for the latest financial year and the level of giving by such trusts may well decrease in future. Other reasons for *Volume 2* inclusion were that the majority of the trust's grants were distributed overseas, or that the trust receives its funds from a parent company with less than £300,000 of its grant total produced by charitable sources and the remainder from company donations. For a full list of the trusts in size order see page ix. A small number of trusts were included regardless of the fact that they gave less than £30,000 as they have the potential to increase this grant total in the future.

What is excluded?

Trusts which appear large enough to warrant inclusion in this guide may be excluded for the following reasons:

- some or all of their money is given to individuals, so that £30,000 a year is not available for organisations. The following two guides provide information on trusts which support individuals: *A Guide to Grants for Individuals in Need* and *The Educational Grants Directory.*
- they give exclusively, or predominantly, to local causes in a particular geographical area of England. There are many very large trusts which restrict their grant-making in this way. So if a trust restricts its giving to a single county or city (or smaller geographical area) it is generally excluded. In this way we hope that *Volume 2* remains a national directory and therefore relevant to more people. For information on local trusts, see our four local guides: *A Guide to Local Trusts in London; A Guide to Local Trusts in the Midlands; A Guide to Local Trusts in the North of England; A Guide to Local Trusts in the South of England; A Guide to the Scottish Trusts;* or *The Welsh Funding Guide* (details of local trusts in Northern Ireland are available at www.dsc.org.uk).
- they only, or predominantly, support international charities. Such trusts were previously included in this guide, but information on these trusts can now be found in *The Directory of Grant Making Trusts.*
- they are company trusts, established as a vehicle for a company's charitable giving. These are detailed in *The Guide to UK Company Giving 2005*; or www.companygiving.org.uk.

The layout of this book

The layout of the entries is similar to that established in the previous editions of *Volumes 1* and *2,* illustrated on page viii. Please also see page vii for other information on how to use this guide.

We have used the word chair in preference to Chairman unless specifically requested to do so by the trust. We have also rounded off the financial figures to allow for easier reading of the guide, which explains why in some places the totals do not add up exactly.

Indexes

The trusts are listed alphabetically in this guide. To help you locate the most relevant trusts there are two indexes, which are a useful starting point.

- Subject index (page 408). This can be useful for identifying trusts with a particular preference for your cause. However, there are many trusts which have general charitable purposes (either exclusively or as well as other specific criteria) but there is no general category in the indexes. It would include so many trusts as to be useless. The index therefore should not be used as the definitive guide to finding the right trusts to apply to.
- Geographical index (page 427). Although trusts limiting their support to one particular area have been excluded, there are many which have some preference for one or more areas. These are listed in this index. Again, in a similar way to the subject index, care is needed. Many trusts state their beneficial area as UK so are not included in this index.

It is important to note that the trusts which appear under a particular index may have other criteria which exclude you. Please always read the entry carefully so you can be sure you fit in with all the trust's criteria. Don't just use the index as a mailing list.

How the guide was compiled

The following are the practical guidelines that were followed to produce this guide:

- concentrates on what the trust does in practice rather than the wider objects permitted by its formal trust deed
- provide extensive information which will be of the most use to readers i.e. publish the trust's criteria and guidelines for applicants in full, where available
- include, where possible, details of the organisations which have received grants, to give the reader an idea of what the trust supports and the amounts it usually gives
- provide the most up-to-date information available at the time of the research
- include all trusts which meet our criteria for inclusion.

Availability of information

We believe that charities are public bodies not private ones and that charities should be publicly accountable. This view is backed up by Charity Commission regulations and the SORP (Statement of Recommended Practice).

Many trusts recognise the importance of providing good, clear information about the work they do. However, there are some that wish to believe they are private bodies and ignore their statutory obligation to provide information to the public. Information held at the Charity Commission on them is sometimes many years out of date. For further details about trust's legal requirements please refer to the introduction of *Volume 1*.

Failing to supply accounts on request

Charities are required to send their annual report and accounts to the Charity Commission and also to any member of the public who requests it in writing. They are obliged to send the information within two months of the request although they can make a 'reasonable charge' for this (i.e. the costs of photo-copying and postage).

Failure to disclose grants

The SORP requires trusts to detail at least 50 grants (if these are for £1,000 or more). This should be accompanied by a proper analysis and explanation of their grant-making in the narrative report (see below).

Failure to provide a narrative report

All trusts should provide a narrative report describing the work of the trust. It is here the trust should give an account of their work during the year with an explanation and analysis of the grants they have made. Many trust's reports are extremely brief giving very little away about their activities.

Good trust reports

On a positive note, there are some trusts which provide excellent reports. When they have been particularly interesting or informative for applicants we have reproduced them in the entries.

What's new?

There are 430 trusts which are new to the series. There have also been trusts added from the previous edition of *Volume 1* as they are no longer large enough to fit into the top 400, and some from the last edition of this guide have grown so they now warrant an entry in *Volume 1*. Others are newly established, or newly discovered. Prominent new trusts include: Capital Charities, the umbrella name for the amalgamation of all of the local funders in the Capital Radio Network; The Sir Steve Redgrave Charitable Trust, established in 2001 by Britain's greatest ever Olympian after his retirement from rowing to raise funds for children's charities through fundraising events and The Austin and Hope Pilkington Trust which, in a refreshing change from conventional practice, changes its areas of support fields each year.

Applying to trusts

There is a lot of competition for grants. Many trusts in this guide receive more applications than they can support. Typically only 1 in 4 applications are successful. The point therefore is to do the research: read the trust's criteria carefully and target the right trusts. This can only lead to a higher success rate and save you a lot of time on writing applications which are destined only for the bin. Applying to inappropriate trusts is bad practice and, as well as annoying trusts, can potentially cause problems for future applicants. Trusts tell us that around half of the applications they receive are from outside their stated areas of support.

Unsolicited applications

A number of trusts do not want to receive applications (and usually therefore do not want to appear in the guide). There can be good reasons for this. For example, the trust may do its own research, or support the same list of charities each year. There are some trusts, however, which believe they are a 'private' trust. No registered charity is a private body. We believe trusts should not resent applications but be committed to finding those charities most eligible for assistance.

We include these trusts for two reasons. Firstly they can state 'no unsolicited applications' simply as a deterrent, in an effort to reduce the number of applications they receive, but will still consider the applications they receive. The second reason relates to the secondary purpose of the guide; to act as a survey of grant-making trusts.

If you choose to write to one of these trusts, do so with caution, and only write to those where your organisation very clearly fits the trust's criteria. We would advise you not to include a stamped addressed envelope and to state that you do not expect a response unless you are eligible. If they do not reply, do not chase them.

Further Information

Unfortunately there are a number of trusts included in this guide which made payments to its trustees. In cases of paying reasonable, out of pocket expenses, then this upholds the principle of volunteers donating their time and knowledge with no financial loss. However, in many cases trusts in this guide have gone against this principal of trustees receiving no personal benefit from their trusteeship. In some cases, this involves trustees contracting work to businesses in which they have an interest, thus making the firms more profitable and increasing the value of their stake in the enterprise. Whilst this may appear a minor point, there is at least one firm of solicitors which receives an income of £100,000 a year from administering trusts a partner is a trustee of. More worrying issues surrounds those trusts which make payments to family members of the trustees. Whilst there is no reason why a deserving individual should be prevented from accessing charitable funds just because a family member is a trustee, such decisions should be made without the relations voicing an opinion. However, our research has uncovered some trusts which give payments to family members without supporting other individuals. These editors feel such payments should be avoided to maintain the reputation of the sector. Whilst we have not found any signs of mispractice, it is easy to see how the process of making a payment to a trust receiving Gift Aid, and then passing it on to a family member could having damaging consequences for the sector should this prevail.

Finally ...

The research has been conducted as efficiently and carefully as possible. Many thanks to those have made this easier; trust officers, trustees and others who have helped us. We send draft entries to all the relevant trusts and their comments are noted, although the text and any mistakes within it remain ours and not theirs.

We are also extremely grateful to all at the Liverpool office of the Charity Commission who have ordered an endless number of files to help us with our research.

We are aware that some of this information is incomplete or will become out of date. We are equally sure we will have missed some relevant charities. We apologise for these imperfections. If a reader comes across any omissions or mistakes please let us know so they can be rectified in the future. We can be contacted at the Liverpool Office Research Department at the Directory of Social Change either by phone on 0151 708 0136 or by e-mail: north@dsc.org.uk.

The most up to date information will be available on our subscription website *www.trustfunding.org.uk*, which contains all the information that we publish in any of our trust directories. We update as soon as we find new information.

To end on a positive note, there are more potential funders out there than you think, and some do not even receive enough relevant applications. Several trusts in this guide even had unspent surpluses – many complain that they don't receive enough really good interesting applications. We hope this gives you extra encouragement and wish you success in your fundraising.

How to use this guide

The contents

The entries are in alphabetical order describing the work of 1,200 trusts. Many of the trusts listed have a grant total of £30,000 or more, with two thirds having the potential of giving over £60,000. The entries are preceded by a listing of the trusts in order of size and are followed by a subject index and geographical index. There is also an alphabetical index at the back of the guide.

Finding the trusts you need

There are three basic ways of using this guide:

(a) You can simply read the entries through from A – Z (a rather time-consuming activity).

(b) You can look through the trust ranking table which starts on page ix and use the box provided to tick trusts which might be relevant to you (starting with the biggest).

(c) You can use the subject or geographical indices starting on pages 408 and 427 respectively. Each has an introduction explaining how to use them.

If you use approaches (b) or (c), once you have identified enough trusts to be going on with, read each entry very carefully before deciding whether to apply. Very often their interest in your field will be limited and specific, and may require an application specifically tailored to their needs – or, indeed, no application at all.

Sending off applications which show that the available information has not been read antagonises trusts and brings charities into disrepute within the trust world. Carefully targeted applications, on the other hand, are welcomed by most trusts and usually have a reasonably high rate of success.

A typical trust entry

The Fictitious Trust

Welfare

£180,000 (2003)

Beneficial area UK

The Old Barn, Main Street, New Town ZC48 2QQ

Correspondent Ms A Grant, Appeals Secretary

Trustees *Trustees Lord Great; Lady Good; A T Home; T Rust; D Prest.*

Charity Commission no. 123456

Information available Full accounts were on file at the Charity Commission.

General The trust supports welfare charities in general, with emphasis on disability, homelessness and ethnic minorities. The trustees will support both captial and revenue projects. 'Specific projects are preferred to general running costs.'

In 2003 the trust had assets of £2.3 million and an income of £187,000. Over 200 grants were given totalling £180,000. Grants ranged from £100 to £20,000, with about half given in New Town. The largest grants were to: New Town Disability Group (£20,000), Homelessness UK (£18,000) and Asian Family Support (£15,000). There were 10 grants of £2,000 to £10,000 including those to the Charity Workers Benevolent Society, Children without Families, New Town CAB and Refugee Support Group.

Smaller grants were given to a variety of local charities, local branches of national charities and a few UK welfare charities.

Exclusions

No grants to non-registered charities, individuals or religious organisations.

Applications

Applications In writing to the correspondent. Trustees meet in March and September each year. Applications should be received by the end of January and the end of July respectively.

Applications should include a brief description of the project and audited accounts. Unsuccessful applicants will not be informed unless a sae is provided.

Name of the charity

Summary of main activities
What the trust will do in practice rather than what its trust deed allows it to do.

Grant total (not income) for the most recent year available

Geographical area of grant-giving including where the trust can legally give and where it gives in practice.

Contact address; telephone and fax numbers; e-mail and website addresses if available

Contact person

Trustees

Sources of information we used and which are available to the applicant.

Background/summary of activities
A quick indicator of the policy to show whether it is worth reading the rest of the entry.

Financial information
We try to note the assets, ordinary income and grant total, and comment on unusual figures.

Typical grants range to indicate what a successful applicant can expect to receive.

Large grants to indicate where the main money is going, often the clearest indication of trust priorities.

Other examples of grants – listing typical beneficiaries, and where possible the purpose of the grant. We also indicate whether the trust gives one-off or recurrent grants.

Exclusions – listing any area, subjects or types of grant the trust will not consider.

Applications including how to apply and when to submit an application.

The ranked by grant total

Trust	*Grants*	*Main grant areas*
☐ **DG Charitable Trust**	**£4,300,000**	General
☐ **Capital Charities**	**£1,900,000**	Children and young people
☐ **The National Gardens Scheme Charitable Trust**	**£1,800,000**	Nursing, welfare, gardening
☐ **The Edith Murphy Foundation**	**£1,200,000**	General
☐ **Roger Vere Foundation**	**£939,000**	General
☐ **Tomchei Torah Charitable Trust**	**£850,000**	Jewish educational institutions
☐ **The Nigel Moores Family Charitable Trust**	**£826,000**	Arts
☐ **The Harry Crook Foundation**	**£709,000**	Education, general
☐ **The Catherine Cookson Charitable Trust**	**£702,000**	General
☐ **The Avenue Charitable Trust**	**£670,000**	General
☐ **The Gur Trust**	**£669,000**	Jewish causes
☐ **The Victor Adda Foundation**	**£657,000**	Fan Museum
☐ **The Francis Winham Foundation**	**£651,000**	Welfare of older people
☐ **The Maurice Wohl Charitable Foundation**	**£651,000**	Jewish, health and welfare
☐ **The Fidelity UK Foundation**	**£644,000**	General
☐ **The Ralph Levy Charitable Company Ltd**	**£564,000**	Educational, medical, general
☐ **The Pet Plan Charitable Trust**	**£563,000**	Dogs, cats and horses
☐ **Rowanville Ltd**	**£552,000**	Orthodox Jewish
☐ **Truedene Co. Ltd**	**£547,000**	Jewish
☐ **R and S Cohen Fondation**	**£536,000**	Education, relief in need and the arts worldwide
☐ **The M Bourne Charitable Trust**	**£518,000**	Jewish and cancer related
☐ **Morgan Williams Charitable Trust**	**£518,000**	Christian
☐ **The Artemis Charitable Trust**	**£513,000**	Psychotherapy, parent education
☐ **Alglen Ltd**	**£509,000**	Jewish causes
☐ **TJH Foundation**	**£498,000**	General
☐ **The Normanby Charitable Trust**	**£485,000**	Social welfare, disability, general
☐ **The George John Livanos Charitable Trust**	**£479,000**	Health, maritime charities, general
☐ **The Ingram Trust**	**£474,000**	General
☐ **Lloyd's Charities Trust**	**£468,000**	General
☐ **The Mole Charitable Trust**	**£468,000**	Jewish, general
☐ **Heathside Charitable Trust**	**£464,000**	General, Jewish
☐ **Premierquote Ltd**	**£457,000**	Jewish, general
☐ **Ford of Britain Trust**	**£454,000**	General
☐ **The Stanley Cohen Charitable Trust**	**£443,000**	Jewish, general
☐ **The Moss Spiro Will Charitable Foundation**	**£438,000**	Jewish welfare
☐ **Friends of Wiznitz Limited**	**£410,000**	Jewish education
☐ **Sino-British Fellowship Trust**	**£410,000**	Education
☐ **BP Conservation Programme**	**£400,000**	Wildlife and conservation.
☐ **Vyoel Moshe Charitable Trust**	**£400,000**	Education, relief of poverty
☐ **The Sir Steve Redgrave Charitable Trust**	**£400,000**	Children and young people up to the age of 18 worldwide
☐ **Joint Committee of St John & Red Cross Society**	**£400,000**	Human services
☐ **Lewis Family Charitable Trust**	**£399,000**	Medical research, health, education, Jewish charities
☐ **The Grace Charitable Trust**	**£396,000**	Christian
☐ **The Swire Charitable Trust**	**£391,000**	General
☐ **Apple Charity (UK) Ltd**	**£378,000**	General

☐ **The Leverhulme Trade Charities Trust**	**£374,000**	Commercial travellers, grocers or chemists
☐ **Michael Marks Charitable Trust**	**£371,000**	Arts, environment
☐ **D D McPhail Charitable Settlement**	**£371,000**	Medical research, disability, older people
☐ **H & L Cantor Trust**	**£365,000**	Jewish, general
☐ **Elshore Ltd**	**£365,000**	Jewish

☐ **Gwyneth Forrester Trust**	**£365,000**	General see below
☐ **The Robert McAlpine Foundation**	**£365,000**	Child disability, older people, medical research, welfare
☐ **The Barnabas Trust**	**£363,000**	Evangelical Christianity
☐ **James Glyn Charitable Trust**	**£358,000**	Jewish
☐ **The George & Esme Pollitzer Charitable Settlement**	**£358,000**	Jewish, health, social welfare, general
☐ **The Thornton Foundation**	**£357,000**	General
☐ **The Radcliffe Trust**	**£355,000**	Music, crafts, conservation
☐ **Melow Charitable Trust**	**£351,000**	Jewish
☐ **The Austin & Hope Pilkington Trust**	**£350,000**	Music, arts, overseas (2005); community, disability (2006)
☐ **Joshua and Michelle Rowe Charitable Trust**	**£341,000**	Jewish

☐ **The Whitley Animal Protection Trust**	**£340,000**	Protection and conservation of animals and their environments
☐ **The Rothermere Foundation**	**£338,000**	Education, general
☐ **The Archbishop of Canterbury's Charitable Trust**	**£336,000**	Christianity, welfare
☐ **The Tufton Charitable Trust**	**£336,000**	Christian
☐ **The Cotton Trust**	**£330,000**	Welfare
☐ **Seamen's Hospital Society**	**£324,000**	Seafarers
☐ **The Daiwa Anglo-Japanese Foundation**	**£314,000**	Anglo-Japanese relations
☐ **The Sir Sigmund Sternberg Charitable Foundation**	**£314,000**	Jewish, inter-faith causes, general
☐ **Solev Co Ltd**	**£313,000**	Jewish charities
☐ **St James' Trust Settlement**	**£313,000**	General

☐ **John Coates Charitable Trust**	**£307,000**	Arts, children, environment, medical, general
☐ **Saint Sarkis Charity Trust**	**£303,000**	Armenian churches and welfare, disability, general
☐ **Lancashire Environmental Fund**	**£301,000**	Environmental
☐ **Fordeve Ltd**	**£300,000**	Jewish, general
☐ **The Platinum Trust**	**£300,000**	Disability
☐ **The Russell Trust**	**£300,000**	General
☐ **R H Southern Trust**	**£296,000**	Education, disability, relief of poverty, environment, conservation
☐ **The Edith Winifred Hall Charitable Trust**	**£295,000**	General
☐ **The Linda Marcus Charitable Trust**	**£295,000**	General
☐ **The Woo Charitable Foundation**	**£295,000**	Education in the arts

☐ **The Palgrave Brown Foundation**	**£291,000**	Education, medical
☐ **The Philip Green Memorial Trust**	**£290,000**	Young and older people, people with disabilities, people in need
☐ **The Ayrton Senna Foundation**	**£290,000**	Children's health and education
☐ **The Vandervell Foundation**	**£288,000**	General
☐ **The R V W Trust**	**£287,000**	Music education and appreciation, relief of need for musicians
☐ **The John Swire (1989) Charitable Trust**	**£279,000**	General
☐ **The True Colours Trust**	**£278,000**	Learning/sensory difficulties, palliative care, young carers, HIV/Aids
☐ **The Evergreen Foundation**	**£277,000**	General
☐ **The M J C Stone Charitable Trust**	**£277,000**	General
☐ **Anglo-German Foundation for the Study of Industrial Society**	**£275,000**	Academics and research workers

☐ **The Alan Sugar Foundation**	**£273,000**	Jewish charities, general
☐ **The Boltons Trust**	**£272,000**	Social welfare, medicine, education
☐ **The Norman Family Charitable Trust**	**£272,000**	General
☐ **The Bernard Kahn Charitable Trust**	**£270,000**	Jewish

☐ **The Hugh & Ruby Sykes Charitable Trust**	**£270,000**	General, medical, education, employment
☐ **Sue Hammerson's Charitable Trust**	**£268,000**	Medical research, relief in need
☐ **The Lillie Johnson Charitable Trust**	**£268,000**	Children, young people who are blind or deaf, medical
☐ **The Cecil Rosen Foundation**	**£267,000**	Welfare
☐ **The Fowler, Smith and Jones Charitable Trust**	**£265,000**	Social welfare
☐ **Florence's Charitable Trust**	**£264,000**	Education, welfare, sick and infirm, general
☐ **The Lister Charitable Trust**	**£264,000**	Water-based activities for young people who are disadvantaged
☐ **The Michael & Morven Heller Charitable Foundation**	**£263,000**	University and medical research projects, the arts
☐ **The Constance Travis Charitable Trust**	**£262,000**	General
☐ **The Dennis Curry Charitable Trust**	**£261,000**	Conservation, general
☐ **The Anton Jurgens Charitable Trust**	**£261,000**	Welfare, general
☐ **The Millichope Foundation**	**£261,000**	General
☐ **The Weinstock Fund**	**£260,000**	General
☐ **The Privy Purse Charitable Trust**	**£259,000**	General
☐ **The Bestway Foundation**	**£255,000**	Education, welfare, medical
☐ **Mrs Waterhouse Charitable Trust**	**£254,000**	Medical, health, welfare, environment, wildlife, churches, heritage
☐ **The George Cadbury Trust**	**£253,000**	General
☐ **The Emerging Markets Charity for Children**	**£253,000**	Children
☐ **The Inman Charity**	**£252,000**	Social welfare, disability, older people, hospices
☐ **The Joseph & Annie Cattle Trust**	**£250,000**	General
☐ **Davidson Charitable Trust**	**£250,000**	Jewish
☐ **The Dellal Foundation**	**£250,000**	General, Jewish
☐ **The M A Hawe Settlement**	**£250,000**	General
☐ **The Panacea Society**	**£250,000**	Christian religion, relief of sickness
☐ **Dr Mortimer and Theresa Sackler Foundation**	**£250,000**	Arts, hospitals
☐ **Bernard van Leer Foundation**	**€414,000**	Development of young children who are disadvantaged
☐ **The David Lean Foundation**	**£249,000**	Film production
☐ **The Toy Trust**	**£245,000**	Children
☐ **The Sylvia Aitken Charitable Trust**	**£244,000**	Medical research and welfare, general
☐ **The Stanley Kalms Foundation**	**£244,000**	Jewish charities, general
☐ **Mercury Phoenix Trust**	**£243,000**	AIDS, HIV
☐ **The Steinberg Family Charitable Trust**	**£243,000**	Jewish, health
☐ **The Barbara Ward Children's Foundation**	**£243,000**	Children, mental disability
☐ **The Homelands Charitable Trust**	**£242,000**	The New Church, health, social welfare
☐ **The Lynn Foundation**	**£242,000**	General
☐ **The Madeline Mabey Trust**	**£324,000**	Medical research, children's welfare
☐ **The Rock Foundation**	**£242,000**	Christian ministries
☐ **The Wakefield Trust**	**£242,000**	General
☐ **The Weinberg Foundation**	**£242,000**	General
☐ **The Ellerdale Trust**	**£240,000**	Children
☐ **Norwood & Newton Settlement**	**£240,000**	Christian
☐ **The Elsie Pilkington Charitable Trust**	**£240,000**	Equine animals, welfare
☐ **Elizabeth & Prince Zaiger Trust**	**£240,000**	Welfare, health, general
☐ **The Sammermar Trust**	**£238,000**	General
☐ **The Coppings Trust**	**£238,000**	General
☐ **Largsmount Ltd**	**£237,000**	Jewish
☐ **Salo Bordon Charitable Trust**	**£234,000**	Jewish, some health-related
☐ **The Christopher Laing Foundation**	**£234,000**	General
☐ **Spar Charitable Fund**	**£234,000**	Children
☐ **Alcohol Education and Research Council**	**£232,000**	Educational and research projects concerning alcohol misuse
☐ **Rees Jeffreys Road Fund**	**£231,000**	Road and transport research and education
☐ **The A H & E Boulton Trust**	**£230,000**	Evangelical Christianity
☐ **Highmoor Hall Charitable Trust**	**£230,000**	Christian mission societies and agencies

☐ **The Tanner Trust**	**£228,000**	General
☐ **The J G Hogg Charitable Trust**	**£227,000**	Welfare, animal welfare, general
☐ **The Edwina Mountbatten Trust**	**£227,000**	Medical
☐ **Coutts & Co. Charitable Trust**	**£226,000**	General
☐ **The Neil Kreitman Foundation**	**£224,000**	Culture, education, health, welfare
☐ **Wychville Ltd**	**£224,000**	Jewish, education, general
☐ **The Duke of Devonshire's Charitable Trust**	**£223,000**	General
☐ **The H & M Charitable Trust**	**£223,000**	Seafaring
☐ **The Iliffe Family Charitable Trust**	**£222,000**	Medical, disability, heritage, education
☐ **The Yapp Charitable Trust**	**£222,000**	Social welfare
☐ **Nathan Charitable Trust**	**£221,000**	Christianity
☐ **L H Silver Charitable Trust**	**£221,000**	Jewish, general
☐ **Woodlands Green Ltd**	**£221,000**	Jewish
☐ **The Sidney & Elizabeth Corob Charitable Trust**	**£220,000**	General
☐ **The Ward Blenkinsop Trust**	**£220,000**	Medicine, social welfare, general
☐ **The Moss Charitable Trust**	**£219,000**	Christian, education, poverty, health
☐ **The McKenna Charitable Trust**	**£218,000**	Welfare, education, children, general
☐ **Old Possum's Practical Trust**	**£218,000**	General
☐ **Brushmill Ltd**	**£217,000**	Jewish
☐ **The Family Foundations Trust**	**£217,000**	General, Jewish
☐ **Help the Hospices**	**£217,000**	Hospices
☐ **The Children's Research Fund**	**£216,000**	Child health research
☐ **The Batchworth Trust**	**£215,000**	Medical, social welfare, general
☐ **The Alan Evans Memorial Trust**	**£215,000**	Preservation, conservation
☐ **The Matt 6.3 Charitable Trust**	**£215,000**	Christian
☐ **The George W Cadbury Charitable Trust**	**£214,000**	Population control, conservation, general
☐ **Gordon Cook Foundation**	**£214,000**	Education and training
☐ **The Edgar E Lawley Foundation**	**£214,000**	Older people, disability, children
☐ **The Rock Solid Trust**	**£214,000**	Christian worldwide
☐ **The Arup Foundation**	**£213,000**	Construction education and research
☐ **The British Council for Prevention of Blindness**	**£213,000**	Prevention and treatment of blindness
☐ **The Ulverscroft Foundation**	**£213,000**	People who are sick and visually impaired, ophthalmic research
☐ **The Kennel Club Charitable Trust**	**£212,000**	Dogs
☐ **The Laura Ashley Foundation**	**£211,000**	Art and design, higher education, local projects in mid-rural Wales
☐ **The Primrose Trust**	**£211,000**	General
☐ **Ranworth Trust**	**£211,000**	General
☐ **Children's Liver Disease Foundation**	**£210,000**	Medical research
☐ **The Ruzin Sadagora Trust**	**£210,000**	Jewish
☐ **The Grahame Charitable Foundation**	**£209,000**	Jewish
☐ **The Law Society Charity**	**£209,000**	Law and justice, worldwide
☐ **The Cyril & Betty Stein Charitable Trust**	**£209,000**	Jewish causes
☐ **The Constance Green Foundation**	**£208,000**	Social welfare, medicine, health, general
☐ **Marbeh Torah Trust**	**£208,000**	Jewish
☐ **The Norman Whiteley Trust**	**£208,000**	Evangelical Christianity, welfare, education
☐ **The Elizabeth Casson Trust**	**£206,000**	Occupational therapy
☐ **The Alderman Norman's Foundation**	**£206,000**	Education
☐ **The Persula Foundation**	**£206,000**	Welfare
☐ **The Craps Charitable Trust**	**£205,000**	Jewish, general
☐ **The Eleanor Rathbone Charitable Trust**	**£205,000**	Merseyside, women, unpopular causes
☐ **The Roger Raymond Charitable Trust**	**£205,000**	Older people, education, medical
☐ **The Stella and Alexander Margulies Charitable Trust**	**£204,000**	Jewish, general
☐ **The Holst Foundation**	**£203,000**	Arts
☐ **The Thames Wharf Charity**	**£203,000**	General

☐ **The Whitaker Charitable Trust**	**£203,000**	Education, environment, music, personal development
☐ **The Inland Waterways Association**	**£202,000**	Inland waterways
☐ **The Oakdale Trust**	**£202,000**	Social work, medical, general
☐ **Oizer Dalim Trust**	**£201,000**	General
☐ **The W G Edwards Charitable Foundation**	**£201,000**	Care of older people
☐ **The Mark Leonard Trust**	**£201,000**	Environmental education, youth, general
☐ **The Simon Heller Charitable Settlement**	**£200,000**	Medical research, science and educational research
☐ **The Incorporated Church Building Society**	**£200,000**	Anglican churches
☐ **Lindale Educational Foundation**	**£200,000**	Roman Catholic
☐ **Ian Mactaggart Trust**	**£200,000**	Education & training, culture, welfare and disability
☐ **Sinclair Charitable Trust**	**£200,000**	Jewish learning, welfare
☐ **The John Slater Foundation**	**£200,000**	Medical, animal welfare, general
☐ **The Norman Evershed Trust**	**£196,000**	Christian, famine relief
☐ **Farthing Trust**	**£199,000**	Christian, general
☐ **Vision Charity**	**£199,000**	Children who are blind, visually impaired or dyslexic
☐ **The Delves Charitable Trust**	**£198,000**	Environment, conservation, medical, general
☐ **The Priory Foundation**	**£198,000**	Health and social welfare, especially children
☐ **The International Foundation for Arts and Culture**	**£197,000**	Music
☐ **The D W T Cargill Fund**	**£196,000**	General
☐ **The A B Charitable Trust**	**£195,000**	Promotion and defence of human dignity
☐ **The Coltstaple Trust**	**£195,000**	Relief in need
☐ **T F C Frost Charitable Trust**	**£195,000**	Medical
☐ **The Truemark Trust**	**£195,000**	General
☐ **The Bowerman Charitable Trust**	**£194,000**	General
☐ **The Bernhard Heuberger Charitable Trust**	**£194,000**	Jewish
☐ **The Holly Hill Charitable Trust**	**£193,000**	Environmental education, conservation and wildlife
☐ **The Music Sound Foundation**	**£193,000**	Music education
☐ **The Altajir Trust**	**£192,000**	Islam, education, science and research
☐ **Epilepsy Research Foundation**	**£192,000**	Epilepsy
☐ **The Second Joseph Aaron Littman Foundation**	**£191,000**	General
☐ **The Scouloudi Foundation**	**£191,000**	General
☐ **Laing's Charitable Trust**	**£190,000**	General
☐ **The Chevras Ezras Nitzrochim Trust**	**£190,000**	Jewish
☐ **The Tay Charitable Trust**	**£190,000**	General
☐ **AF Trust Company**	**£189,000**	Higher education
☐ **Alexandra Rose Day**	**£189,000**	Fundraising partnerships with 'people-caring' charities
☐ **The C A Redfern Charitable Foundation**	**£189,000**	General
☐ **REMEDI**	**£189,000**	Research into disability
☐ **Clover Trust**	**£190,000**	Older people, young people
☐ **The George Elias Charitable Trust**	**£187,000**	Jewish, general
☐ **The Hilda & Samuel Marks Foundation**	**£187,000**	Jewish, general
☐ **The Fred & Della Worms Charitable Trust**	**£187,000**	Jewish, education, arts
☐ **The A Bornstein Charitable Settlement**	**£186,000**	Jewish
☐ **P H Holt Charitable Trust**	**£186,000**	General
☐ **Riverside Charitable Trust Limited**	**£186,000**	Health, welfare, older people, education, general
☐ **G R Waters Charitable Trust 2000**	**£186,000**	General
☐ **Lawrence Atwell's Charity**	**£185,000**	Education, young people
☐ **The Patrick Frost Foundation**	**£185,000**	General
☐ **Ruth and Conrad Morris Charitable Trust**	**£185,000**	Jewish, general
☐ **The Bluston Charitable Settlement**	**£184,000**	Jewish, general
☐ **The Arnold James Burton 1956 Charitable Settlement**	**£183,000**	General
☐ **The Tangent Charitable Trust**	**£183,000**	Jewish, general
☐ **The Broadfield Trust**	**£182,000**	Education
☐ **The Ellinson Foundation Ltd**	**£182,000**	Jewish

☐ **The Irish Youth Foundation (UK) Ltd**	**£182,000**	Irish young people
☐ **Menuchar Ltd**	**£182,000**	Jewish
☐ **Songdale Ltd**	**£182,000**	Jewish
☐ **The Van Neste Foundation**	**£182,000**	Welfare, Christian, developing world
☐ **J A Clark Charitable Trust**	**£181,000**	Health, education, peace, preservation of the earth, the arts
☐ **The H F Johnson Trust**	**£181,000**	Christian education
☐ **The Ratcliff Foundation**	**£181,000**	General
☐ **The Stone-Mallabar Charitable Foundation**	**£181,000**	Medical, education
☐ **The I A Ziff Charitable Foundation**	**£181,000**	General, education, Jewish, arts, youth, older people, medicine
☐ **Alvor Charitbale Trust**	**£180,000**	Christian, humanitarian, 'social change'
☐ **The Thornton Trust**	**£180,000**	Evangelical Christianity, education, relief of sickness and poverty
☐ **The Yamanouchi European Foundation**	**US$265,000**	Medical
☐ **The Keith & Freda Abraham Charitable Trust**	**£179,000**	General
☐ **All Saints' Educational Trust**	**£179,000**	Education, Anglican religious work, home economics
☐ **The Leslie Smith Foundation**	**£179,000**	General
☐ **Warbeck Fund Ltd**	**£179,000**	Jewish, the arts, general
☐ **The Cooks Charity**	**£178,000**	Catering
☐ **Nicholas & Judith Goodison's Charitable Settlement**	**£178,000**	Arts, arts education
☐ **The GRP Charitable Trust**	**£178,000**	Jewish, general
☐ **Child Growth Foundation**	**£177,000**	Growth disorders
☐ **Dromintree Trust**	**£177,000**	General
☐ **The Worwin UK Foundation**	**£177,000**	General
☐ **The Vivienne & Samuel Cohen Charitable Trust**	**£176,000**	Jewish, education, health, medical research and welfare
☐ **The Armourers and Brasiers' Gauntlet Trust**	**£175,000**	General
☐ **E & E Kernkraut Charities Limited**	**£174,000**	General, education, Jewish
☐ **The Rowlands Trust**	**£175,000**	General
☐ **The J B Rubens Charitable Foundation**	**£175,000**	Mainly Jewish causes
☐ **The South Square Trust**	**£175,000**	General
☐ **The Almond Trust**	**£174,000**	Christian
☐ **The Arnold Burton 1998 Charitable Trust**	**£174,000**	Jewish, medical research, education, social welfare, heritage
☐ **Peter De Haan Charitable Trust**	**£174,000**	Youth, general
☐ **The John Jarrold Trust**	**£173,000**	General
☐ **Sumner Wilson Charitable Trust**	**£172,000**	General
☐ **The Andrew Anderson Trust**	**£171,000**	Christian, social welfare
☐ **The English Schools' Football Association**	**£171,000**	Association football
☐ **Miss K M Harbinson's Charitable Trust**	**£171,000**	General
☐ **The Jean Sainsbury Animal Welfare Trust**	**£171,000**	Animal welfare
☐ **The Union of Orthodox Hebrew Congregation**	**£171,000**	Jewish
☐ **The Jack Goldhill Charitable Trust**	**£170,000**	Jewish, general
☐ **Onaway Trust**	**£170,000**	General
☐ **The Billmeir Charitable Trust**	**£101,000**	General, health and medical
☐ **The Gough Charitable Trust**	**£36,000**	Youth, Church of England, countryside, social welfare
☐ **SMILES**	**£169,000**	Children, young people
☐ **The Thomas Sivewright Catto Charitable Settlement**	**£168,000**	General
☐ **The Philanthropic Trust**	**£167,000**	Welfare, environment, homelessness
☐ **The Rayne Trust**	**£167,000**	Jewish, general
☐ **The Catholic Trust for England and Wales**	**£166,000**	Catholic welfare
☐ **The Park House Charitable Trust**	**£166,000**	Education, social welfare, ecclesiastical
☐ **The David and Elaine Potter Charitable Foundation**	**£166,000**	The advancement of education and scientific research
☐ **The SMB Charitable Trust**	**£166,000**	Christian, general
☐ **The Breast Cancer Research Trust**	**£165,000**	Research into breast cancer
☐ **Keren Mitzvah Trust**	**£165,000**	General
☐ **The Harbour Charitable Trust**	**£164,000**	General

☐ **Garvan Limited**	**£163,000**	Jewish
☐ **Tegham Limited**	**£163,000**	Orthodox Jewish faith, welfare
☐ **Lord Barnby's Foundation**	**£162,000**	General
☐ **The Sydney Black Charitable Trust**	**£162,000**	Evangelical Christianity, welfare
☐ **The Owen Family Trust**	**£162,000**	Christian, general
☐ **The James Weir Foundation**	**£162,000**	Welfare, education, general
☐ **The Forte Charitable Trust**	**£161,000**	Education, disability, Roman Catholic, Jewish, general
☐ **The Miller Foundation**	**£161,000**	General, animal welfare
☐ **The River Trust**	**£161,000**	Christian
☐ **The Michael Sacher Charitable Trust**	**£161,000**	General
☐ **The Indigo Trust**	**£160,000**	Offenders, core skills, homelessness, women
☐ **Melodor Ltd**	**£160,000**	Jewish, general
☐ **The Ashe Park Charitable Trust**	**£159,000**	Possible preference for child-related hospitals and hospices.
☐ **The Chapman Charitable Trust**	**£159,000**	Welfare, general
☐ **The Emmandjay Charitable Trust**	**£159,000**	Social welfare, medicine, youth
☐ **R S Charitable Trust**	**£159,000**	Jewish, welfare
☐ **Marc Fitch Fund**	**£158,000**	Humanities
☐ **The Hawthorne Charitable Trust**	**£158,000**	General
☐ **The Cecil Pilkington Charitable Trust**	**£158,000**	Conservation, medical research, general on Merseyside
☐ **The Bassil Shippam and Alsford Trust**	**£158,000**	Welfare, health, education, learning disabilities, Christian
☐ **Access 4 Trust**	**£157,000**	Children, welfare
☐ **The Roger Brooke Charitable Trust**	**£157,000**	General
☐ **The Carpenters' Company Charitable Trust**	**£157,000**	Education, general
☐ **Hockerill Educational Foundation**	**£157,000**	Education, especially Christian education
☐ **The Naggar Charitable Trust**	**£157,000**	Jewish, general
☐ **The Bay Tree Charitable Trust**	**£155,000**	Development work, general
☐ **C B & H H Taylor 1984 Trust**	**£155,000**	Quaker, general
☐ **The Three Oaks Trust**	**£155,000**	Welfare
☐ **The Burden Trust**	**£154,000**	Christian, welfare, medical research, general
☐ **Salters' Charities**	**£155,000**	General
☐ **Talteg Ltd**	**£153,000**	Jewish, welfare
☐ **The Anglian Water Trust Fund**	**£152,000**	Money advice provision/individuals in need
☐ **The Bulldog Trust**	**£152,000**	Arts, medical, youth, general
☐ **Mariapolis Limited**	**£152,000**	Unity, ecumenism
☐ **G M Morrison Charitable Trust**	**£152,000**	Medical, education, welfare
☐ **The Dyers' Company Charitable Trust**	**£151,000**	General
☐ **Newby Trust Limited**	**£150,000**	Welfare
☐ **The Sir Cliff Richard Charitable Trust**	**£150,000**	Spiritual and social welfare
☐ **The Sheldon Trust**	**£150,000**	General
☐ **Thackray Medical Research Trust**	**£150,000**	History of medical products and of their supply trade
☐ **The R D Turner Charitable Trust**	**£150,000**	General
☐ **The Gordon Fraser Charitable Trust**	**£149,000**	Children, young people, environment, arts
☐ **The Sir James Roll Charitable Trust**	**£149,000**	General
☐ **Stervon Ltd**	**£149,000**	Jewish
☐ **The Astor Foundation**	**£148,000**	General
☐ **East Kent Provincial Charities**	**£148,000**	General, education, younger and older people in the UK
☐ **The Charles Littlewood Hill Trust**	**£148,000**	Health, disability, service, children (including schools)
☐ **The Gerald Palmer Trust**	**£148,000**	Education, medical research, religion
☐ **Leslie Sell Charitable Trust**	**£148,000**	Uniformed youth groups
☐ **The Football Association National Sports Centre Trust**	**£147,000**	Play areas, community sports facilities
☐ **MYA Charitable Trust**	**£147,000**	Jewish
☐ **The Kasner Charitable Trust**	**£146,000**	Jewish
☐ **Kermaville Ltd**	**£146,000**	Jewish
☐ **The Elizabeth Clark Charitable Trust**	**£145,000**	Palliative care

☐ **Edith & Ferdinand Porjes Charitable Trust**	**£145,000**	Jewish, general
☐ **The Star Charitable Trust**	**£145,000**	General
☐ **The Weavers' Company Benevolent Fund**	**£145,000**	Offenders, ex-offenders and those at-risk
☐ **London Law Trust**	**£144,000**	Health and personal development of children and young people
☐ **SFIA Educational Trust Limited**	**£144,000**	Education
☐ **The Sir Jack Lyons Charitable Trust**	**£143,000**	Jewish, arts, education
☐ **The Spear Charitable Trust**	**£142,000**	General
☐ **Hospital Saturday Fund Charitable Trust**	**£141,000**	Medical, health
☐ **The Ian Karten Charitable Trust**	**£141,000**	Technology centres for people who are disabled
☐ **The Bisgood Charitable Trust**	**£140,000**	Roman Catholic purposes, older people
☐ **The John Harrison Charitable Trust**	**£140,000**	Multiple Sclerosis
☐ **Carlee Ltd**	**£139,000**	Jewish
☐ **The Kathleen Trust**	**£139,000**	Musicians
☐ **The Sue Thomson Foundation**	**£139,000**	Christ's Hospital School, education
☐ **Trumros Limited**	**£139,000**	Jewish
☐ **The Doris Field Charitable Trust**	**£138,000**	General
☐ **May Hearnshaw's Charity**	**£138,000**	General
☐ **Stuart Hine Trust**	**£138,000**	Evangelical Christianity
☐ **The C S Kaufman Charitable Trust**	**£138,000**	Jewish
☐ **The Lauffer Family Charitable Foundation**	**£138,000**	Jewish, general
☐ **The Erich Markus Charitable Foundation**	**£138,000**	Welfare, hospices, medical, general
☐ **The Woodroffe Benton Foundation**	**£138,000**	General
☐ **Adenfirst Ltd**	**£137,000**	Jewish
☐ **The Wilfrid Bruce Davis Charitable Trust**	**£137,000**	Health
☐ **National Committee of The Women's World Day of Prayer for England, Wales, and Northern Ireland**	**£137,000**	Christian education and literature
☐ **The Haydan Charitable Trust**	**£136,000**	Jewish, general
☐ **The Fawcett Charitable Trust**	**£135,000**	Disability
☐ **The Odin Charitable Trust**	**£135,000**	General
☐ **The Archie Sherman Cardiff Charitable Foundation**	**£135,000**	Health, education, Jewish
☐ **The Mason Porter Charitable Trust**	**£134,000**	Christian
☐ **The Scott Bader Commonwealth Ltd**	**£134,000**	General
☐ **The Bristol Charities**	**£133,000**	General
☐ **The Michael & Ilse Katz Foundation**	**£133,000**	Jewish, music, medical, general
☐ **Quercus Trust**	**£133,000**	Arts, general
☐ **Coral Samuel Charitable Trust**	**£133,000**	General, health, the arts
☐ **The Maurice Wohl Charitable Trust**	**£133,000**	Health, welfare, arts, education
☐ **Buckingham Trust**	**£132,000**	Christian, general
☐ **C & F Charitable Trust**	**£132,000**	Orthodox Jewish charities
☐ **The Lord Faringdon Charitable Trust**	**£132,000**	Medical, general
☐ **The Ruth & Michael Phillips Charitable Trust**	**£132,000**	General, Jewish
☐ **Anona Winn Charitable Trust**	**£132,000**	Health, medical, welfare
☐ **The William Allen Young Charitable Trust**	**£132,000**	General
☐ **The Loftus Charitable Trust**	**£131,000**	Jewish
☐ **The M D & S Charitable Trust**	**£131,000**	Jewish
☐ **The Janet Nash Charitable Trust**	**£131,000**	Medical, general
☐ **The Colonel W H Whitbread Charitable Trust**	**£131,000**	Health, welfare, general
☐ **The Richard Desmond Charitable Trust**	**£130,000**	General
☐ **The A M Fenton Trust**	**£130,000**	General
☐ **The Bluff Field Charitable Trust**	**£130,000**	General
☐ **The Kidani Memorial Trust**	**£130,000**	Cancer related charities, research, welfare, education, training, guide dogs
☐ **A M Pilkington's Charitable Trust**	**£130,000**	General
☐ **Rosalyn and Nicholas Springer Charitable Trust**	**£130,000**	Welfare, Jewish, education, general

☐ **Maranatha Christian Trust**	**£129,000**	Christian
☐ **Newpier Charity Ltd**	**£129,000**	Jewish, general
☐ **The Florence Turner Trust**	**£129,000**	General
☐ **The Carmichael-Montgomery Charitable Trust**	**£128,000**	United Reformed Church, general
☐ **The M & C Trust**	**£128,000**	Jewish, social welfare
☐ **The Sir Harry Pilkington Trust**	**£128,000**	General
☐ **British Institute of Archaeology at Ankara**	**£127,000**	Arts, humanities and social sciences of countries surrounding the Black Sea
☐ **The Joanna Herbert-Stepney Charitable Settlement**	**£127,000**	General
☐ **The Earl & Countess of Wessex Charitable Trust**	**£127,000**	General
☐ **The Felicity Wilde Charitable Trust**	**£127,000**	Children, medical research
☐ **The Almshouse Association**	**£126,500**	Almshouses
☐ **Bud Flanagan Leukaemia Fund**	**£126,000**	Leukaemia research and treatment.
☐ **The Harbour Foundation**	**£126,000**	Jewish, general
☐ **The Raymond & Blanche Lawson Charitable Trust**	**£126,000**	General
☐ **The Mrs C S Heber Percy Charitable Trust**	**£126,000**	General
☐ **Wychdale Ltd**	**£126,000**	Jewish
☐ **Bear Mordechai Ltd**	**£125,000**	Jewish
☐ **The Neville & Elaine Blond Charitable Trust**	**£125,000**	Jewish, education, general
☐ **Houblon-Norman Fund**	**£125,000**	Finance
☐ **The Patricia and Donald Shepherd Trust**	**£125,000**	General
☐ **The Amanda Smith Charitable Trust**	**£125,000**	General
☐ **The Geoff and Fiona Squire Foundation**	**£125,000**	General
☐ **The Fulmer Charitable Trust**	**£124,000**	Developing world, general
☐ **The Edward Sydney Hogg Charitable Settlement**	**£124,000**	General
☐ **J I Charitable Trust**	**£124,000**	General
☐ **The Moulton Charitable Trust**	**£124,000**	Asthma, medical
☐ **The Leslie Mary Carter Charitable Trust**	**£123,000**	Conservation/environment, welfare
☐ **Cuby Charitable Trust**	**£123,000**	Jewish.
☐ **The Marsh Christian Trust**	**£123,000**	General
☐ **The Shipwrights' Company Charitable Fund**	**£123,000**	Maritime or waterborne connected charities
☐ **The Association of Colleges Charitable Trust**	**£122,000**	Further education colleges
☐ **The Crescent Trust**	**£122,000**	Museums and the arts, occasionally health and education
☐ **The Gibbs Charitable Trust**	**£122,000**	Methodism, international, arts
☐ **The Muriel Edith Rickman Trust**	**£122,000**	Medical research, education
☐ **Richard Rogers Charitable Settlement**	**£122,000**	Housing, homelessness
☐ **The J R S S T Charitable Trust**	**£121,000**	Democracy and social justice
☐ **Sir Samuel Scott of Yews Trust**	**£121,000**	Medical research
☐ **The Stanley Smith UK Horticultural Trust**	**£121,000**	Horticulture
☐ **The Sutasoma Trust**	**£121,000**	Education, general
☐ **The Barbers' Company General Charities**	**£120,000**	Medical and nursing education
☐ **The Misses Barrie Charitable Trust**	**£120,000**	Medical, general
☐ **The Benham Charitable Settlement**	**£120,000**	Youth, general
☐ **The Francis Coales Charitable Foundation**	**£120,000**	Historical
☐ **The Haymills Charitable Trust**	**£120,000**	Education, medicine, welfare, youth
☐ **The Lind Trust**	**£120,000**	Christianity
☐ **The Ruth & Stuart Lipton Charitable Trust**	**£120,000**	Jewish, general
☐ **The William & Katherine Longman Trust**	**£120,000**	General
☐ **George A Moore Foundation**	**£120,000**	General
☐ **The Sir Peter O'Sullevan Charitable Trust**	**£120,000**	Animals worldwide
☐ **Scopus Jewish Educational Trust**	**£120,000**	Jewish education
☐ **Triodos Foundation**	**£120,000**	Overseas development, organics, community development
☐ **The Cross Trust**	**£119,000**	Christian work
☐ **The Hope Trust**	**£119,000**	Temperance, Reformed Protestant churches
☐ **The Hudson Foundation**	**£119,000**	Older people, general

☐ **The Geoffrey John Kaye Charitable Foundation**	**£119,000**	Jewish, general
☐ **Lifeline 4 Kids**	**£119,000**	Equipment for children with disabilities
☐ **The Samuel Storey Family Charitable Trust**	**£119,000**	General

☐ **The Christina Mary Hendrie Trust for Scottish & Canadian Charities**	**£119,000**	Youth, people who are elderly, general
☐ **The McDougall Trust**	**£118,000**	Political and economic research.
☐ **The N Smith Charitable Trust**	**£118,000**	General
☐ **The Michael Bishop Foundation**	**£117,000**	General
☐ **The Idlewild Trust**	**£117,000**	Performing arts, culture, restoration & conservation, occasional arts education
☐ **The Millfield House Foundation**	**£117,000**	Social disadvantage, social policy
☐ **Sueberry Ltd**	**£117,000**	Jewish, welfare
☐ **The Thompson Family Charitable Trust**	**£117,000**	Medical, veterinary, education, general
☐ **The Ashworth Charitable Trust**	**£116,000**	Welfare
☐ **The Harry Bottom Charitable Trust**	**£116,000**	Religion, education, medical

☐ **The DLM Charitable Trust**	**£116,000**	General
☐ **The Dorus Trust**	**£116,000**	Health, welfare, environment
☐ **The Ogle Christian Trust**	**£116,000**	Evangelical Christianity
☐ **The Peggy Ramsay Foundation**	**£116,000**	Writers and writing for the stage
☐ **The Weinstein Foundation**	**£116,000**	Jewish, medical, welfare
☐ **The Cleopatra Trust**	**£115,000**	Health and welfare, environment
☐ **The Langley Charitable Trust**	**£115,000**	Christian, general
☐ **The Locker Foundation**	**£115,000**	Jewish
☐ **Oppenheim Foundation**	**£115,000**	General
☐ **The Forest Hill Charitable Trust**	**£114,000**	Mainly Christian causes and relief work in the UK and overseas

☐ **Matliwala Family Charitable Trust**	**£114,000**	Islam, general
☐ **Princess Anne's Charities**	**£114,000**	Children, medical, welfare, general
☐ **The Worshipful Company of Chartered Accountants General Charitable Trust**	**£114,000**	General, education
☐ **The Lord Cozens-Hardy Trust**	**£113,000**	Medicine, health, welfare, general
☐ **The Timothy Franey Charitable Foundation**	**£112,000**	Children, health, education, arts
☐ **The Peter Samuel Charitable Trust**	**£112,000**	Health, welfare, conservation, Jewish care
☐ **Golden Charitable Trust**	**£111,000**	Preservation, conservation
☐ **The Cripps Foundation**	**£110,000**	Education, healthcare and churches in Northamptonshire, Cambridge University
☐ **The Epigoni Trust**	**£110,000**	Health, welfare, environment
☐ **The Fitton Trust**	**£110,000**	Social welfare, medical

☐ **The Forbes Charitable Foundation**	**£110,000**	Adults with learning disabilities
☐ **The Inlight Trust**	**£110,000**	Religion
☐ **The Lyndhurst Trust**	**£110,000**	Christian
☐ **SEM Charitable Trust**	**£110,000**	Disability, general, Jewish
☐ **The Carron Charitable Trust**	**£109,000**	Environment, education, medicine
☐ **The Bishop of Guildford's Foundation**	**£109,000**	General
☐ **The Powell Foundation**	**£109,000**	Elderly, disability
☐ **Royal Masonic Trust for Girls and Boys**	**£109,000**	Children, young people
☐ **The Eventhall Family Charitable Trust**	**£108,000**	General
☐ **Servite Sisters' Charitable Trust Fund**	**£108,000**	Women, refugees

☐ **St Michael's and All Saints' Charities**	**£108,000**	Health, welfare
☐ **The H P Charitable Trust**	**£107,000**	Orthodox Jewish
☐ **The Schreiber Charitable Trust**	**£107,000**	Jewish
☐ **The R J Harris Charitable Settlement**	**£106,000**	General
☐ **The Langdale Trust**	**£106,000**	Social welfare, Christian, medical, general
☐ **Macdonald-Buchanan Charitable Trust**	**£106,000**	General
☐ **The Victor Mishcon Charitable Trust**	**£106,000**	Jewish, social welfare

☐ **The Stanley Foundation Ltd**	**£106,000**	Older people, medical, education, social welfare
☐ **Airways Charitable Trust Limited**	**£105,000**	Welfare, health
☐ **The Paul Bassham Charitable Trust**	**£105,000**	General
☐ **The Graham Kirkham Foundation**	**£105,000**	General
☐ **The Licensed Trade Charities Trust**	**£105,000**	Licensed trade
☐ **The Joseph & Lena Randall Charitable Trust**	**£105,000**	General
☐ **Armenian General Benevolent Union London Trust**	**£105,000**	Armenian education, culture and welfare
☐ **The Blair Foundation**	**£104,000**	Wildlife, access to countryside, general
☐ **The Laurence Misener Charitable Trust**	**£104,000**	Jewish, general
☐ **The Oliver Morland Charitable Trust**	**£104,000**	Quakers, general
☐ **Search**	**£104,000**	Medical research, medicine, health
☐ **The Viznitz Foundation**	**£104,000**	General
☐ **The Roger & Sarah Bancroft Clark Charitable Trust**	**£103,000**	Quaker, general
☐ **Garrick Charitable Trust**	**£103,000**	Theatre, music, literature, dance
☐ **The John Spedan Lewis Foundation**	**£103,000**	Natural sciences, particularly horticulture, ornithology, entomology
☐ **The Charlotte Marshall Charitable Trust**	**£103,000**	Roman Catholic, general
☐ **Mazars Charitable Trust**	**£103,000**	General
☐ **Rokach Family Charitable Trust**	**£103,000**	Jewish, general
☐ **Peter Storrs Trust**	**£103,000**	Education
☐ **The Benjamin Winegarten Charitable Trust**	**£103,000**	Jewish
☐ **The Noon Foundation**	**£102,000**	General
☐ **Prairie Trust**	**£102,000**	Third world development, the environment, conflict prevention
☐ **The Rainford Trust**	**£101,000**	Social welfare, general
☐ **Altamont Ltd**	**£100,000**	Jewish causes
☐ **Barclays Stockbrokers Charitable Trust**	**£100,000**	General
☐ **John Coldman Charitable Trust**	**£100,000**	General, Christian
☐ **The Hammonds Charitable Trust**	**£100,000**	General
☐ **The Harding Trust**	**£100,000**	Arts, welfare
☐ **The J E Joseph Charitable Fund**	**£100,000**	Jewish
☐ **The R J Larg Family Charitable Trust**	**£100,000**	Education, health, medical research, arts
☐ **The Laufer Charitable Trust**	**£100,000**	Jewish
☐ **Marr-Munning Trust**	**£100,000**	Overseas aid
☐ **The Samuel & Freda Parkinson Charitable Trust**	**£100,000**	General
☐ **The Andrew Salvesen Charitable Trust**	**£100,000**	General
☐ **The Stanley Charitable Trust**	**£100,000**	Jewish
☐ **Ulting Overseas Trust**	**£100,000**	Theological training
☐ **The Bertie Black Foundation**	**£99,000**	Jewish, general
☐ **The Edward & Dorothy Cadbury Trust (1928)**	**£99,000**	Health, education, arts
☐ **Hinchley Charitable Trust**	**£99,000**	Mainly evangelical Christian
☐ **The Sir Edward Lewis Foundation**	**£99,000**	General
☐ **The Willie & Mabel Morris Charitable Trust**	**£99,000**	Medical, general
☐ **The Duke of Cornwall's Benevolent Fund**	**£98,000**	General
☐ **The Paragon Trust**	**£98,000**	General
☐ **The Tisbury Telegraph Trust**	**£98,000**	Christian, overseas aid, general
☐ **The Dumbreck Charity**	**£97,000**	General
☐ **Mageni Trust**	**£97,000**	Arts
☐ **The Rest Harrow Trust**	**£97,000**	Jewish, general
☐ **The Beaverbrook Foundation**	**£96,000**	General
☐ **The Cotton Industry War Memorial Trust**	**£96,000**	Textiles
☐ **The Leach Fourteenth Trust**	**£96,000**	Disability, general
☐ **Trust Sixty Three**	**£96,000**	Disability, overseas aid, famine relief, general
☐ **The Dorothy Gertrude Allen Memorial Fund**	**£95,000**	General
☐ **The Wilfrid & Constance Cave Foundation**	**£95,000**	Conservation, animal welfare, health, welfare

☐ **The Walter Guinness Charitable Trust**	**£95,000**	General
☐ **The Jessie Spencer Trust**	**£95,000**	General
☐ **The Matthews Wrightson Charity Trust**	**£95,000**	Caring and Christian charities
☐ **The Ian Askew Charitable Trust**	**£94,000**	General
☐ **Belvedere Trust**	**£94,000**	Arts education, children at risk and conservation projects worldwide
☐ **EAGA Partnership Charitable Trust**	**£94,000**	Fuel poverty
☐ **The Mayfield Valley Arts Trust**	**£94,000**	Arts, especially chamber music
☐ **The Saintbury Trust**	**£94,000**	General
☐ **Sellata Ltd**	**£94,000**	Jewish, welfare
☐ **SFIA Educational Trust**	**£94,000**	Education
☐ **St Gabriel's Trust**	**£94,000**	Higher and further religious education
☐ **Beauland Ltd**	**£93,000**	Jewish
☐ **Jacqueline and Michael Gee Charitable Trust**	**£93,000**	Health, education (including Jewish)
☐ **The Martin Laing Foundation**	**£93,000**	General
☐ **The Little Foundation**	**£93,000**	Neurodevelopmental disorders
☐ **The Marchday Charitable Fund**	**£93,000**	Education, health, social welfare, support groups, overseas aid
☐ **The E H Smith Charitable Trust**	**£93,000**	General
☐ **The Wyseliot Charitable Trust**	**£93,000**	Medical, welfare, general
☐ **The Kyte Charitable Trust**	**£92,000**	Medical, disadvantaged and socially isolated people
☐ **The Lambert Charitable Trust**	**£92,000**	Health, welfare, Jewish, arts
☐ **The Westcroft Trust**	**£92,000**	International understanding, overseas aid, Quaker, Shropshire
☐ **The Mrs F B Laurence Charitable Trust**	**£91,000**	Social welfare, medical, disability, environment
☐ **Morris Leigh Foundation**	**£91,000**	Jewish, general
☐ **Penny in the Pound Fund Charitable Trust**	**£91,000**	Hospitals, health-related charities
☐ **Philip Smith's Charitable Trust**	**£91,000**	Welfare, older people, children
☐ **W W Spooner Charitable Trust**	**£91,000**	General
☐ **The Stewards' Charitable Trust**	**£91,000**	Rowing
☐ **Henry Lumley Charitable Trust**	**£91,000**	Medical, education
☐ **The Carvill Trust**	**£90,000**	General
☐ **The Casey Trust**	**£90,000**	Children and young people, Jewish
☐ **The Andrew Cohen Charitable Trust**	**£90,000**	Jewish, children
☐ **The Beryl Evetts & Robert Luff Animal Welfare Trust**	**£90,000**	Animal welfare
☐ **The Forman Hardy Charitable Trust**	**£90,000**	Arts, Christian, medical, welfare
☐ **Localtrent Ltd**	**£90,000**	Jewish, educational, religion
☐ **The Puebla Charitable Trust**	**£90,000**	Community development work, relief of poverty
☐ **British Humane Association**	**£89,000**	Welfare
☐ **The Harebell Centenary Fund**	**£89,000**	General, education, medical research, animal welfare
☐ **The Pyke Charity Trust**	**£89,000**	Prisoners and disadvantaged communities
☐ **The Chownes Foundation**	**£88,000**	General
☐ **The Corona Charitable Trust**	**£88,000**	Jewish
☐ **The Augustine Courtauld Trust**	**£88,000**	General
☐ **The Grand Order of Water Rats' Charities Fund**	**£88,000**	Theatrical, medical equipment
☐ **The Lawson-Beckman Charitable Trust**	**£88,000**	Jewish, welfare, education, arts
☐ **Mountbatten Festival of Music**	**£88,000**	Royal Marines and Royal Navy charities
☐ **The Sir Jeremiah Colman Gift Trust**	**£87,000**	General
☐ **The Lawlor Foundation**	**£87,000**	Social welfare, education, general
☐ **Limoges Charitable Trust**	**£87,000**	Animals, services, general
☐ **The Max Reinhardt Charitable Trust**	**£87,000**	Deafness, fine arts promotion
☐ **The Saints & Sinners Trust**	**£87,000**	Welfare, medical
☐ **The Ampelos Trust**	**£86,000**	General
☐ **The Bill Butlin Charity Trust**	**£86,000**	General

☐ **H and M Castang Charitable Trust**	**£86,000**	Medical
☐ **The B G S Cayzer Charitable Trust**	**£86,000**	General
☐ **The Dugdale Charitable Trust**	**£86,000**	Christian education
☐ **Diana and Allan Morgenthau Charitable Trust**	**£86,000**	Jewish, health and educational charities worldwide
☐ **The Susanna Peake Charitable Trust**	**£86,000**	General
☐ **WH Smith Group Charitable Trust**	**£86,000**	General
☐ **The Barnsbury Charitable Trust**	**£85,000**	General
☐ **The Amelia Chadwick Trust**	**£85,000**	General
☐ **Grimmitt Trust**	**£85,000**	General
☐ **The Arnold Lee Charitable Trust**	**£85,000**	Jewish, educational, health
☐ **Elizabeth Wolfson Peltz Trust**	**£85,000**	Arts and humanities, education and culture, health and welfare, Jewish
☐ **The Seedfield Trust**	**£84,000**	Christian, relief of poverty
☐ **Blyth Watson Charitable Trust**	**£85,000**	General, UK based humanitarian organisations
☐ **P G & N J Boulton Trust**	**£84,000**	Christian
☐ **The Cayo Foundation**	**£84,000**	Crime, medical research, children
☐ **The Ireland Fund of Great Britain**	**£84,000**	Welfare, community, education, peace and reconciliation, the arts
☐ **The Jephcott Charitable Trust**	**£84,000**	Alleviation of poverty in developing countries, general
☐ **The Homestead Charitable Trust**	**£83,000**	See below
☐ **The Leche Trust**	**£83,000**	Georgian art, music and architecture
☐ **Truemart Limited**	**£83,000**	General, Judaism, welfare
☐ **The Animal Defence Trust**	**£82,000**	Animal welfare
☐ **The Craignish Trust**	**£82,000**	Arts, education, environment, general
☐ **The Gilbert & Eileen Edgar Foundation**	**£82,000**	General - see below
☐ **The Noel Buxton Trust**	**£82,000**	Child and family welfare, penal matters, Africa
☐ **The Helen Roll Charitable Trust**	**£82,000**	General
☐ **Tudor Rose Ltd**	**£82,000**	Jewish
☐ **The Marjorie Coote Animal Charity Fund**	**£81,000**	Wildlife and animal welfare
☐ **Famos Foundation Trust**	**£81,000**	Jewish
☐ **The Worshipful Company of Innholders General Charity Fund**	**£81,000**	General
☐ **The Shanti Charitable Trust**	**£81,000**	General, Christian, international development
☐ **Dixie Rose Findlay Charitable Trust**	**£80,000**	Children, seafarers, blindness, multiple sclerosis
☐ **Foundation for Management Education**	**£80,000**	Management studies
☐ **The Jenour Foundation**	**£80,000**	General
☐ **The John Oldacre Foundation**	**£80,000**	Research and education in agricultural sciences
☐ **The Ouseley Trust**	**£80,000**	Choral services and choir schools
☐ **The Charlotte Bonham-Carter Charitable Trust**	**£79,000**	General
☐ **The Leopold De Rothschild Charitable Trust**	**£79,000**	Arts, Jewish, general
☐ **The Morris Charitable Trust**	**£79,000**	Relief of need, education, community support and development
☐ **The Pestalozzi Overseas Children's Trust**	**£79,000**	Children
☐ **The Salamander Charitable Trust**	**£79,000**	Christian, general
☐ **The A B Strom & R Strom Charitable Trust**	**£79,000**	Jewish, general
☐ **The Conservation Foundation**	**£78,000**	Environmental and conservation
☐ **The Rose Flatau Charitable Trust**	**£78,000**	Jewish, general
☐ **The Kohn Foundation**	**£78,000**	Scientific and medical projects, the arts, education, Jewish charities
☐ **The Nyda and Oliver Prenn Foundation**	**£78,000**	Arts, education, health
☐ **Star Foundation Trust**	**£78,000**	General in the UK
☐ **The Tabeel Trust**	**£78,000**	Evangelical Christian
☐ **A H and B C Whiteley Charitable Trust**	**£78,000**	Art, environment, general
☐ **The Michael and Anna Wix Charitable Trust**	**£78,000**	Welfare, Jewish
☐ **Women at Risk**	**£78,000**	Women

☐ **The GNC Trust**	**£77,000**	General
☐ **Peltz Trust**	**£77,000**	Arts and humanities, education and culture, health and welfare, Jewish
☐ **The Helene Sebba Charitable Trust**	**£77,000**	Disability, medical, Jewish
☐ **The Educational Charity of the Stationers' and Newspaper Makers' Company**	**£77,000**	Printing education
☐ **Kirschel Foundation**	**£76,000**	Jewish, medical
☐ **The Millfield Trust**	**£76,000**	Christian
☐ **The National Manuscripts Conservation Trust**	**£76,000**	Conserving manuscripts
☐ **The Llysdinam Trust**	**£75,000**	General
☐ **Gerald Micklem Charitable Trust**	**£75,000**	General, health
☐ **The Richard Newitt Fund**	**£75,000**	Education
☐ **The Audrey Sacher Charitable Trust**	**£75,000**	Arts, medical, care
☐ **The William and Ellen Vinten Trust**	**£75,000**	Industrial education, training and welfare
☐ **The Atlantic Foundation**	**£74,000**	Education, medical, general
☐ **Veta Bailey Charitable Trust**	**£74,000**	Training of doctors and other medical personnel.
☐ **The Harold and Alice Bridges Charity**	**£74,000**	General
☐ **The Sir William Coxen Trust Fund**	**£74,000**	Orthopaedic hospitals or other hospitals or charities doing orthopaedic work
☐ **The Willie Nagel Charitable Trust**	**£74,000**	Jewish, general
☐ **The Phillips Family Charitable Trust**	**£74,000**	Jewish charities, welfare, general
☐ **The Rootstein Hopkins Foundation**	**£74,000**	Arts
☐ **The Spurrell Charitable Trust**	**£74,000**	General
☐ **The Treeside Trust**	**£74,000**	General
☐ **The Henry & Grete Abrahams Second Charitable Foundation**	**£73,000**	Jewish, medical welfare, general
☐ **A J H Ashby Will Trust**	**£73,000**	Birds, wildlife, education and children
☐ **Calleva Foundation**	**£73,000**	General
☐ **The Holden Charitable Trust**	**£73,000**	Jewish
☐ **The Ironmongers' Quincentenary Charitable Fund**	**£73,000**	General
☐ **The Linmardon Trust**	**£73,000**	General
☐ **The C L Loyd Charitable Trust**	**£73,000**	General
☐ **The E L Rathbone Charitable Trust**	**£73,000**	Education and welfare of women, alleviation of poverty
☐ **Ryklow Charitable Trust 1992**	**£73,000**	Education, health and welfare
☐ **The TUUT Charitable Trust**	**£73,000**	General, but with a bias towards trade-union-favoured causes
☐ **The Richard Cadbury Charitable Trust**	**£72,000**	General
☐ **The Mr and Mrs F C Freeman Charitable Trust**	**£72,000**	General
☐ **The Annie Schiff Charitable Trust**	**£72,000**	Orthodox Jewish education
☐ **The Simpson Education & Conservation Trust**	**£72,000**	Environmental conservation
☐ **The Late St Patrick White Charitable Trust**	**£72,000**	General
☐ **The Simon Whitbread Charitable Trust**	**£72,000**	Education, family welfare, medicine, preservation
☐ **The Acacia Charitable Trust**	**£71,000**	Jewish, education, general
☐ **Blakes Benevolent Trust**	**£71,000**	General
☐ **The Cooper Charitable Trust**	**£71,000**	Medical, disability, Jewish
☐ **The Violet and Milo Cripps Charitable Trust**	**£71,000**	General
☐ **The Demigryphon Trust**	**£71,000**	Medical, education, children, general
☐ **The Emerton-Christie Charity**	**£71,000**	Health, welfare, disability, arts
☐ **The Charles Henry Foyle Trust**	**£71,000**	General
☐ **Gableholt Limited**	**£71,000**	Jewish
☐ **Minge's Gift and The Pooled Charities**	**£71,000**	Medical, education, disadvantage, disability
☐ **The Fanny Rapaport Charitable Settlement**	**£71,000**	Jewish, general
☐ **Dame Violet Wills Charitable Trust**	**£71,000**	Evangelical Christianity
☐ **Bill Brown's Charitable Settlement**	**£70,000**	Health, social welfare
☐ **The Christopher Cadbury Charitable Trust**	**£70,000**	Nature conservation, general
☐ **The Follett Trust**	**£70,000**	Welfare, education, arts

☐ **Friends of Biala Ltd**	**£70,000**	Jewish
☐ **Harbo Charities Limited**	**£70,000**	General, education, religion
☐ **The P & C Hickinbotham Charitable Trust**	**£70,000**	Social welfare
☐ **The Linden Charitable Trust**	**£70,000**	General
☐ **The Lyons Charitable Trust**	**£70,000**	Health, medical research, children
☐ **The Ann & David Marks Foundation**	**£70,000**	Jewish charities
☐ **The Mutual Trust Group**	**£70,000**	Religion, education
☐ **Prison Service Charity Fund**	**£70,000**	General
☐ **Lisa Thaxter Trust**	**£70,000**	Children and adolescents with cancer in the UK
☐ **The Aurelius Charitable Trust**	**£69,000**	Conservation of culture and the humanities
☐ **Barchester Healthcare Foundation**	**£69,000**	Health and social care
☐ **Finnart House School Trust**	**£69,000**	Jewish children and young people in need of care
☐ **The Jewish Youth Fund**	**£69,000**	Jewish youth work
☐ **The Seven Fifty Trust**	**£69,000**	Christian
☐ **Roama Spears Charitable Settlement**	**£69,000**	Welfare causes
☐ **The Weldon UK Charitable Trust**	**£69,000**	Major arts-related projects
☐ **The Equity Trust Fund**	**£68,000**	Theatre
☐ **The Joyce Fletcher Charitable Trust**	**£68,000**	Music, children's welfare
☐ **The Humanitarian Trust**	**£68,000**	Education, health, social welfare, Jewish
☐ **The Kreditor Charitable Trust**	**£68,000**	Jewish, welfare, education
☐ **The Richard Langhorn Trust**	**£68,000**	Sport for children
☐ **Meningitis Trust**	**£68,000**	Meningitis in the UK
☐ **The Millward Charitable Trust**	**£68,000**	Christian, general
☐ **The Earl of Northampton's Charity**	**£68,000**	Welfare
☐ **The Violet M Richards Charity**	**£68,000**	Older people, sickness, medical research and education
☐ **Unity Charitable Trust**	**£68,000**	General
☐ **The Albert Van Den Bergh Charitable Trust**	**£68,000**	Medical/disability, welfare
☐ **The Mary Webb Trust**	**£68,000**	General
☐ **Ashburnham Thanksgiving Trust**	**£67,000**	Christian
☐ **The William Brake Charitable Trust**	**£67,000**	General
☐ **Briggs Animal Welfare Trust**	**£67,000**	Animal welfare
☐ **The David Brooke Charity**	**£67,000**	Youth, medical
☐ **The Ronald Cruickshanks Foundation**	**£67,000**	Welfare.
☐ **Rachel & Jack Lass Charities Ltd**	**£67,000**	Jewish, children, education, medical research
☐ **The P Leigh-Bramwell Trust 'E'**	**£67,000**	Methodist, general
☐ **The J S F Pollitzer Charitable Settlement**	**£67,000**	General
☐ **The Scarfe Charitable Trust**	**£67,000**	Environment, churches, arts
☐ **The Searchlight Electric Charitable Trust**	**£67,000**	General
☐ **The Cyril Shack Trust**	**£67,000**	Jewish, general
☐ **The Thriplow Charitable Trust**	**£67,000**	Higher education and research
☐ **The Geoffrey Woods Charitable Foundation**	**£67,000**	Young people, education, disability, health
☐ **Michael and Leslie Bennett Charitable Trust**	**£66,000**	Jewish
☐ **R M Burton 1998 Charitable Settlement**	**£66,000**	Jewish charities, social welfare, education, the arts
☐ **The Michael and Shirley Hunt Charitable Trust**	**£66,000**	Prisoners' families, animal welfare
☐ **International Bar Association Educational Trust**	**£66,000**	Legal profession
☐ **The Charles Shorto Charitable Trust**	**£66,000**	General
☐ **The Nigel Vinson Charitable Trust**	**£66,000**	General
☐ **The Wilkinson Charitable Foundation**	**£66,000**	Scientific research, education
☐ **The Pat Allsop Charitable Trust**	**£65,000**	Education, medical research, children, relief of poverty
☐ **The Eric Anker-Petersen Charity**	**£65,000**	Conservation of classic films, theatre
☐ **The C J M Charitable Trust**	**£65,000**	Social entrepreneurship
☐ **Highcroft Charitable Trust**	**£65,000**	Jewish, poverty
☐ **The David Laing Foundation**	**£65,000**	Youth, disability, mental health, the arts, general
☐ **Jack Livingstone Charitable Trust**	**£65,000**	Jewish, general
☐ **Pearson's Holiday Fund**	**£65,000**	Young people who are disadvantaged

☐ **The Clive Richards Charity Ltd**	**£65,000**	Disability, poverty
☐ **The Swan Trust**	**£65,000**	General, arts, culture
☐ **The Sylvanus Charitable Trust**	**£65,000**	Animal welfare, Roman Catholic
☐ **The John Young Charitable Settlement**	**£65,000**	Wildlife, general
☐ **Harry Bacon Foundation**	**£64,000**	Medical, animal welfare
☐ **Samuel William Farmer's Trust**	**£64,000**	Education, health, social welfare
☐ **The Thomas J Horne Memorial Trust**	**£64,000**	Hospices
☐ **The Morel Charitable Trust**	**£64,000**	Arts, race, inner-city, developing world
☐ **Oppenheimer Charitable Trust**	**£64,000**	General
☐ **The Raydan Charitable Trust**	**£64,000**	Jewish
☐ **The Scurrah Wainwright Charity**	**£64,000**	Social reform, root causes of poverty and injustice
☐ **The Edinburgh Trust, No 2 Account**	**£63,000**	Education, service, scientific expeditions
☐ **Grand Charitable Trust of the Order of Women Freemasons**	**£63,000**	General in the UK and overseas
☐ **Mrs H R Greene Charitable Settlement**	**£63,000**	General, particularly at risk-groups, poverty, social isolation
☐ **The Kessler Foundation**	**£63,000**	General, Jewish
☐ **The Kathleen Laurence Trust**	**£63,000**	Heart disease, arthritis, children with disabilities
☐ **Nesswall Ltd**	**£63,000**	Jewish
☐ **The Albert Reckitt Charitable Trust**	**£63,000**	General
☐ **The Linley Shaw Foundation**	**£63,000**	Conservation
☐ **Annie Tranmer Charitable Trust**	**£63,000**	General, young people
☐ **The Lionel Wigram Memorial Trust**	**£63,000**	General
☐ **The Barber Charitable Trust**	**£62,000**	Evangelical Christian causes, churches
☐ **The Doughty Charity Trust**	**£62,000**	Orthodox Jewish, religious education, relief of poverty
☐ **The Vernon N Ely Charitable Trust**	**£62,000**	Christian, welfare, disability, children and youth, overseas
☐ **The B & P Glasser Charitable Trust**	**£62,000**	Health, disability, Jewish, welfare
☐ **The Anthony and Elizabeth Mellows Charitable Settlement**	**£62,000**	National heritage, Church of England churches
☐ **The Thompson Fund**	**£62,000**	Medical, welfare, education, general
☐ **The Bagri Foundation**	**£61,000**	General
☐ **Peter Barker-Mill Memorial Charity**	**£61,000**	General
☐ **The Beaufort House Trust**	**£61,000**	Christian, education
☐ **The John & Celia Bonham Christie Charitable Trust**	**£61,000**	Local and national organisations
☐ **The British Dietetic Association General and Education Trust Fund**	**£61,000**	Dietary and nutritional issues
☐ **The Construction Industry Trust for Youth**	**£61,000**	Building projects benefiting young people
☐ **The Jill Franklin Trust**	**£61,000**	Overseas, welfare, prisons, church restoration
☐ **The Ripple Effect Foundation**	**£61,000**	General
☐ **The Wesleyan Charitable Trust**	**£61,000**	General
☐ **The Anchor Foundation**	**£60,000**	Christian
☐ **R S Brownless Charitable Trust**	**£60,000**	Disabled, disadvantage, serious illness
☐ **Candide Charitable Trust**	**£60,000**	Music, visual arts
☐ **The Denise Cohen Charitable Trust**	**£60,000**	Health, welfare, arts, humanities, education, culture, Jewish
☐ **The Earl Fitzwilliam Charitable Trust**	**£60,000**	General
☐ **The Gamma Trust**	**£60,000**	General
☐ **The Golsoncott Foundation**	**£60,000**	The arts
☐ **The Gould Charitable Trust**	**£60,000**	General
☐ **The Gunter Charitable Trust**	**£60,000**	General
☐ **The Cuthbert Horn Trust**	**£60,000**	Environment, people with disability/special needs, older people
☐ **The Dorothy Jacobs Charity**	**£60,000**	Jewish care, medical
☐ **The Marjorie and Geoffrey Jones Charitable Trust**	**£60,000**	General
☐ **Brian Mercer Charitable Trust**	**£60,000**	Welfare, medical in UK and overseas
☐ **The Ragdoll Foundation**	**£60,000**	Children and the arts
☐ **Rosanna Taylor's 1987 Charity Trust**	**£60,000**	General

☐ **Mabel Cooper Charity**	**£59,000**	General
☐ **Double O Charity Ltd**	**£59,000**	General

☐ **The Hyde Charitable Trust**	**£59,000**	Disadvantaged children and young people
☐ **The Inverclyde Bequest Fund**	**£59,000**	Sailors' charities
☐ **The David & Ruth Behrend Fund**	**£58,000**	General
☐ **The Buckingham & Gawcott Charitable Trust**	**£42,000**	General
☐ **The Chetwode Foundation**	**£58,000**	Education, churches, general
☐ **The Elephant Trust**	**£58,000**	Visual arts
☐ **The Elaine & Angus Lloyd Charitable Trust**	**£58,000**	General
☐ **The Oikonomia Trust**	**£58,000**	Christian
☐ **Harold Smith Charitable Trust**	**£58,000**	General
☐ **The Beacon Trust**	**£57,000**	Christian

☐ **The Muriel and Gershon Coren Charitable Foundation**	**£57,000**	Jewish, welfare, general
☐ **Criffel Charitable Trust**	**£57,000**	Christianity, welfare, health
☐ **The Sandy Dewhirst Charitable Trust**	**£57,000**	General
☐ **The Euroclydon Trust**	**£57,000**	Christian
☐ **Forbesville Limited**	**£57,000**	Jewish, education
☐ **The Barry Green Memorial Fund**	**£57,000**	Animal welfare
☐ **The Marina Kleinwort Charitable Trust**	**£57,000**	Arts
☐ **The Schmidt-Bodner Charitable Trust**	**£57,000**	Jewish, general
☐ **The David Uri Memorial Trust**	**£57,000**	Jewish, general
☐ **The Dwek Family Charitable Trust**	**£56,000**	General

☐ **The Inverforth Charitable Trust**	**£56,000**	General
☐ **The Edgar Milward Charity**	**£56,000**	Christian, humanitarian
☐ **The F H Muirhead Charitable Trust**	**£56,000**	Hospitals, medical research institutes
☐ **The Searle Charitable Trust**	**£56,000**	Sailing
☐ **Society for the Assistance of Ladies in Reduced Circumstances**	**£56,000**	Women in need
☐ **The Stephen R and Philippa H Southall Charitable Trust**	**£56,000**	General
☐ **The Tory Family Foundation**	**£56,000**	Education, Christian, medical
☐ **The Peter Beckwith Charitable Trust**	**£55,000**	Medical, welfare
☐ **The Busenhart Morgan-Evans Foundation**	**£55,000**	Music, opera, general
☐ **The Daily Prayer Union Charitable Trust Ltd**	**£55,000**	Evangelical Christian

☐ **The Fairway Trust**	**£55,000**	General
☐ **The Joseph & Queenie Gold Charitable Trust**	**£55,000**	Jewish, general
☐ **The Lord and Lady Haskel Charitable Foundation**	**£55,000**	Jewish, social-policy research, arts, education
☐ **Kinsurdy Charitable Trust**	**£55,000**	General
☐ **The Millhouses Charitable Trust**	**£55,000**	Christian, overseas aid, general
☐ **The Daniel Rivlin Charitable Trust**	**£55,000**	Jewish, general
☐ **The Charles Skey Charitable Trust**	**£55,000**	General
☐ **The Loke Wan Tho Memorial Foundation**	**£55,000**	Environment, medical
☐ **The Company of Actuaries' Charitable Trust Fund**	**£54,000**	Actuaries, medical research, young and older people, disability, general
☐ **The Adnams Charity**	**£54,000**	General

☐ **The Air Charities Trust**	**£54,000**	Guild of Air Pilots and Air Navigators of the City of London
☐ **CLA Charitable Trust**	**£54,000**	Disabled facilities and training
☐ **Elman Charitable Trust**	**£54,000**	Jewish charities
☐ **The Horace & Marjorie Gale Charitable Trust**	**£54,000**	General
☐ **The Good Neighbours Trust**	**£54,000**	People with mental or physical disabilities
☐ **The Mackey & Brewer Charitable Trust**	**£54,000**	General
☐ **The Nadezhda Charitable Trust**	**£54,000**	Christian
☐ **The Monica Rabagliati Charitable Trust**	**£54,000**	Human and animal welfare, education, medical
☐ **The Alex Roberts-Miller Foundation**	**£54,000**	

☐ **Royal Artillery Charitable Fund**	**£54,000**	Service charities
☐ **The Schapira Charitable Trust**	**£54,000**	Jewish
☐ **The Aviezer Wolfson Charitable Trust**	**£53,000**	Jewish
☐ **The Adamson Trust**	**£53,000**	Children, under 16, who are physically or mentally disabled
☐ **The Bartlett Taylor Charitable Trust**	**£53,000**	General
☐ **GMC Trust**	**£53,000**	Medical research, healthcare, general
☐ **Percy Hedley 1990 Charitable Trust**	**£53,000**	General
☐ **The G D Herbert Charitable Trust**	**£53,000**	Medicine, health, welfare, environmental resources
☐ **The Hesed Trust**	**£53,000**	Christian
☐ **R G Hills Charitable Trust**	**£53,000**	General
☐ **The Hinrichsen Foundation**	**£53,000**	Music
☐ **The James Trust**	**£53,000**	Christianity
☐ **Panahpur Charitable Trust**	**£53,000**	Missionaries, general
☐ **The Pennycress Trust**	**£53,000**	General
☐ **Rofeh Trust**	**£53,000**	General, religious activities
☐ **Peter Stormonth Darling Charitable Trust**	**£53,000**	Heritage, medical research, sport
☐ **The Alabaster Trust**	**£52,000**	Christian Church and related activities
☐ **Sir Alec Black's Charity**	**£52,000**	Hospices
☐ **The Britten Foundation**	**£52,000**	Disaster relief, education, general
☐ **The Cazenove Charitable Trust**	**£52,000**	General
☐ **The Dinwoodie Settlement**	**£52,000**	Postgraduate medical education and research
☐ **The Eagle Charity Trust**	**£52,000**	General, international, medicine, welfare
☐ **West London Synagogue Charitable Fund**	**£52,000**	Jewish, general
☐ **The Elmgrant Trust**	**£51,000**	General charitable purposes, education, arts, social sciences
☐ **The Evangelical Covenants Trust**	**£51,000**	Christian evangelism
☐ **The Exilarch's Foundation**	**£51,000**	Jewish
☐ **The Hobart Charitable Trust**	**£51,000**	General
☐ **The Clifford Howarth Charity Settlement**	**£51,000**	General
☐ **The Invicta Trust**	**£51,000**	Jewish educational and general
☐ **The Adrienne and Leslie Sussman Charitable Trust**	**£51,000**	Jewish, general
☐ **ATP Charitable Trust**	**£50,000**	Jewish, education, medical
☐ **The Balney Charitable Trust**	**£50,000**	Preservation, conservation, welfare, service charities
☐ **The Dickie Bird Foundation**	**£50,000**	Sport
☐ **The Classic FM Charitable Trust**	**£50,000**	Music and education; music and health
☐ **Coats Foundation Trust**	**£50,000**	Textile and thread-related training courses and research
☐ **Col-Reno Ltd**	**£50,000**	Jewish
☐ **The John & Freda Coleman Charitable Trust**	**£50,000**	People with disabilities, technical education for young people
☐ **Ann and Shelia Diamond Charitable Trust**	**£50,000**	Jewish, general
☐ **The Ebenezer Trust**	**£50,000**	Evangelical Christianity, welfare
☐ **The EOS Foundation**	**£50,000**	Money advice provision/individuals in need
☐ **The Gerald Fogel Charitable Trust**	**£50,000**	Jewish, general
☐ **The Isaac and Freda Frankel Memorial Charitable Trust**	**£50,000**	Jewish, general
☐ **The Hare of Steep Charitable Trust**	**£50,000**	General
☐ **Philip Henman Trust**	**£50,000**	General
☐ **The India Foundation (UK)**	**£50,000**	Developmental and healthcare education projects for Indian communities
☐ **J A R Charitable Trust**	**£50,000**	Roman Catholic, education, welfare
☐ **The Mathilda and Terence Kennedy Charitable Trust**	**£50,000**	General
☐ **Land Aid Charitable Trust**	**£50,000**	Homelessness, escape from poverty
☐ **The Luck-Hille Foundation**	**£50,000**	Education, health, welfare
☐ **Mandeville Trust**	**£50,000**	Cancer, young people and children
☐ **The Minos Trust**	**£50,000**	Christian, general
☐ **The Peter Morrison Charitable Foundation**	**£50,000**	Jewish, general

☐ **The Pallant Charitable Trust**	**£50,000**	Church music
☐ **Saint Luke's College Foundation**	**£50,000**	See below
☐ **The Green & Lilian F M Ainsworth & Family Benevolent Fund**	**£49,000**	Youth, disability, health, medical research, disadvantage, older people, general
☐ **The Cumber Family Charitable Trust**	**£49,000**	General
☐ **William Dean Countryside and Educational Trust**	**£49,000**	Education in natural history, ecology and conservation
☐ **The Laduma Dhamecha Charitable Trust**	**£49,000**	General
☐ **DLA Charitable Trust**	**£49,000**	General
☐ **The P Y N & B Hyams Trust**	**£49,000**	Jewish, general
☐ **The Jonathan Joels Charitable Trust**	**£49,000**	General
☐ **The Boris Karloff Charitable Foundation**	**£49,000**	General
☐ **The Emmanuel Kaye Foundation**	**£49,000**	Medical research, welfare and Jewish organisations.
☐ **The Mizpah Trust**	**£49,000**	General
☐ **The Park Hill Trust**	**£49,000**	Older people
☐ **The Bernard Piggott Trust**	**£49,000**	General
☐ **Edwin George Robinson Charitable Trust**	**£49,000**	Medical research
☐ **The Ernest William Slaughter Charitable Trust**	**£49,000**	Health, older people
☐ **The Whitecourt Charitable Trust**	**£49,000**	Christian, general
☐ **AM Charitable Trust**	**£48,000**	Jewish, general
☐ **The Bacta Charitable Trust**	**£48,000**	General
☐ **Moshal Charitable Trust**	**£48,000**	Jewish
☐ **The Penny Charitable Trust**	**£48,000**	Photographic archival projects
☐ **Social Education Trust**	**£48,000**	Young people
☐ **David Solomons Charitable Trust**	**£48,000**	Disability
☐ **The E C Sosnow Charitable Trust**	**£48,000**	Arts, education
☐ **David Young Charitable Trust**	**£48,000**	Mainly Jewish
☐ **The Annandale Charitable Trust**	**£47,000**	Major UK charities
☐ **The Bothwell Charitable Trust**	**£47,000**	Disability, health, older people, conservation
☐ **The Tony Bramall Charitable Trust**	**£47,000**	Children, medical research, sickness
☐ **The Louis and Valerie Freedman Charitable Settlement**	**£47,000**	General
☐ **The David Pickford Charitable Foundation**	**£47,000**	Christian, general
☐ **Premishlaner Charitable Trust**	**£47,000**	Jewish
☐ **Mrs M H Allen Trust**	**£46,000**	Military charities
☐ **The Astor of Hever Trust**	**£46,000**	Youth, medical research, education
☐ **The Bedfordshire & Hertfordshire Historic Churches Trust**	**£46,000**	Churches
☐ **Elizabeth Hardie Ferguson Charitable Trust Fund**	**£46,000**	Children, medical research, health, hospices
☐ **Ruth & Lionel Jacobson Trust (Second Fund) No 2**	**£46,000**	Jewish, medical, children, disability
☐ **Vivdale Ltd**	**£46,000**	Jewish
☐ **The Catalyst Charitable Trust**	**£45,000**	Medical, general
☐ **Cowley Charitable Foundation**	**£45,000**	Registered charities
☐ **Dischma Charitable Trust**	**£45,000**	General
☐ **Mildred Duveen Charitable Trust**	**£45,000**	General
☐ **The Sydney & Phyllis Goldberg Memorial Charitable Trust**	**£45,000**	Medical research, welfare, disability
☐ **Mary Homfray Charitable Trust**	**£45,000**	General
☐ **The Geoffrey C Hughes Charitable Trust**	**£45,000**	Nature conservation, environment, performing arts
☐ **The Huxham Charitable Trust**	**£45,000**	Christianity, churches and organisations, development work in Albania and Kosova
☐ **The Life Insurance Association Charitable Foundation**	**£45,000**	General
☐ **The Barbara A Shuttleworth Memorial Trust**	**£45,000**	Disability
☐ **The F J Wallis Charitable Settlement**	**£45,000**	General
☐ **The A & R Woolf Charitable Trust**	**£45,000**	General
☐ **Miss E B Wrightson's Charitable Settlement**	**£45,000**	Music education, inshore rescue, recreation

☐ **The Birmingham Hospital Saturday Fund Medical Charity & Welfare Trust**	**£44,000**	Medical
☐ **The Oliver Ford Charitable Trust**	**£44,000**	Mental disability, housing
☐ **The Nicholas Joels Charitable Trust**	**£44,000**	Jewish, medical welfare, general
☐ **The Richard Kirkman Charitable Trust**	**£44,000**	General
☐ **William Arthur Rudd Memorial Trust**	**£44,000**	General in the UK, and certain Spanish charities
☐ **The Sharon Trust**	**£44,000**	Christian
☐ **Belsize Charitable Trust No. 1**	**£43,000**	Envrionment, conservation, heritage in the UK
☐ **Thomas Betton's Charity for Pensions and Relief-in-Need**	**£43,000**	General, disadvantage
☐ **Bois Rochel Dsatmar Charitable Trust**	**£43,000**	Jewish
☐ **C J Cadbury Charitable Trust**	**£43,000**	General
☐ **The Hamamelis Trust**	**£43,000**	Ecological conservation, medical research
☐ **The Hellenic Foundation**	**£43,000**	Greek, general
☐ **The S Hodgkiss Charitable Trust**	**£43,000**	General, arts
☐ **The Loseley & Guildway Charitable Trust**	**£43,000**	General
☐ **Morris Family Israel Trust**	**£43,000**	Jewish
☐ **Mr and Mrs F E F Newman Charitable Trust**	**£43,000**	Christian, overseas aid and development
☐ **The Old Broad Street Charity Trust**	**£43,000**	General
☐ **Eric Abrams Charitable Trust**	**£42,000**	Jewish/Israeli
☐ **The Ardwick Trust**	**£42,000**	Jewish, welfare, general
☐ **The Cemlyn-Jones Trust**	**£42,000**	General
☐ **The Friarsgate Trust**	**£42,000**	Health and welfare of young and older people
☐ **The Hollick Family Charitable Trust**	**£42,000**	General
☐ **The ISA Charity**	**£42,000**	General
☐ **The JMK Charitable Trust**	**£42,000**	Children's health
☐ **LSA Charitable Trust**	**£42,000**	Horticulture
☐ **The Magen Charitable Trust**	**£42,000**	Education, Jewish
☐ **The A M McGreevy No 5 Charitable Settlement**	**£42,000**	General
☐ **The Primrose Hill Trust**	**£42,000**	Prison welfare
☐ **Willy Russell Charitable Trust**	**£42,000**	General, arts
☐ **The AS Charitable Trust**	**£41,000**	Chrisitan, development, social concern
☐ **The Baltic Charitable Fund**	**£41,000**	General, service, seafarers, fishermen
☐ **The Burry Charitable Trust**	**£41,000**	Medicine, health
☐ **The David Finnie & Alan Emery Charitable Trust**	**£41,000**	Welfare, health, education, personal development
☐ **The Frognal Trust**	**£41,000**	General
☐ **Help the Homeless Ltd**	**£41,000**	Homelessness
☐ **The Lawson Charitable Foundation**	**£41,000**	Jewish, general
☐ **Lord and Lady Lurgan Trust**	**£41,000**	Medical, older people and the arts
☐ **Brian Abrams Charitable Trust**	**£40,000**	Jewish/Israeli
☐ **The Carpenter Charitable Trust**	**£40,000**	Humanitarian and Christian outreach
☐ **The Chandris Foundation**	**£40,000**	Greek, shipping
☐ **The Coates Charitable Settlement**	**£40,000**	Medical, health, welfare, education
☐ **The Manny Cussins Foundation**	**£40,000**	Older people, children, health, Jewish, general
☐ **The Diamond Industry Educational Charity**	**£40,000**	Diamond industry, education, general
☐ **The Dickon Trust**	**£40,000**	General
☐ **The Harold Joels Charitable Trust**	**£40,000**	Jewish
☐ **The M Miller Charitable Trust**	**£40,000**	Jewish, general
☐ **The Red Rose Charitable Trust**	**£40,000**	People who are elderly, disability
☐ **The Cyril Taylor Charitable Trust**	**£40,000**	Education
☐ **Mrs Maud Van Norden's Charitable Foundation**	**£40,000**	General
☐ **The Catholic Charitable Trust**	**£39,000**	Catholic organisations
☐ **Gilbert Edgar Trust**	**£39,000**	General
☐ **The Ericson Trust**	**£39,000**	Welfare
☐ **The Nancy Kenyon Charitable Trust**	**£39,000**	General

☐ **The Ruth & Jack Lunzer Charitable Trust**	**£39,000**	Jewish; children, young adults and students; education
☐ **Padwa Charitable Foundation**	**£39,000**	Education, religion, general
☐ **Arthur James Paterson Charitable Trust**	**£39,000**	Medical research, welfare of older people and children
☐ **The Smith Charitable Trust**	**£39,000**	General
☐ **The Tillett Trust**	**£39,000**	Classical music
☐ **D G Albright Charitable Trust**	**£38,000**	General
☐ **Sir John & Lady Amory's Charitable Trust**	**£38,000**	General
☐ **The Andre Christian Trust**	**£38,000**	Christian organisations.
☐ **The T B H Brunner Charitable Settlement**	**£38,000**	Heritage, arts, general
☐ **Datnow Limited**	**£38,000**	Jewish, general
☐ **The Eeman Charitable Trust**	**£38,000**	General
☐ **Lord Forte Foundation**	**£38,000**	Hospitality
☐ **The Glanrose Trust**	**£38,000**	General
☐ **The Grimsdale Charitable Trust**	**£38,000**	Christian religion, education, poverty
☐ **The Moette Charitable Trust**	**£38,000**	Education
☐ **The John Pryor Charitable Trust**	**£38,000**	Medical research, homelessness
☐ **Rita and David Slowe Charitable Trust**	**£38,000**	General
☐ **Stanley Spooner Deceased Charitable Trust**	**£38,000**	Children, general
☐ **The Diana Edgson Wright Charitable Trust**	**£38,000**	Animal conservation, welfare, general
☐ **The Dennis Alan Yardy Charitable Trust**	**£38,000**	General
☐ **William P Bancroft (No 2) Charitable Trust and Jenepher Gillett Trust**	**£37,000**	Quaker
☐ **The Delius Trust**	**£37,000**	Organisations benefiting young adults, older people and musicians; individuals.
☐ **The Harry Dunn Charitable Trust**	**£37,000**	Medical, general
☐ **Audrey Earle Charitable Trust**	**£37,000**	General, with some preference for animal welfare and conservation charities
☐ **The Earth Love Fund**	**£37,000**	Community-based rainforest conservation projects, Artists for the Environment (AFTE) Festival
☐ **The Isaacs Charitable Trust**	**£37,000**	Jewish, medical, general
☐ **The Ratcliffe Charitable Trust**	**£37,000**	General
☐ **The Frank Russell Charitable Trust**	**£37,000**	Not known
☐ **The R H Scholes Charitable Trust**	**£37,000**	Children and young people who are disabled or disadvantaged
☐ **Wakeham Trust**	**£37,000**	Community development, education, community service by young people
☐ **The Kay Williams Charitable Foundation**	**£37,000**	Medical research, disability, general
☐ **The Goldschmied Charitable Settlement**	**£101,000**	Education, general
☐ **The Geoffrey Burton Charitable Trust**	**£30,000**	General
☐ **Cardy Beaver Foundation**	**£36,000**	General
☐ **The Pamela Champion Foundation**	**£36,000**	General, disability
☐ **The Robert Clutterbuck Charitable Trust**	**£36,000**	Service, sport and recreation, natural history, animal welfare and protection
☐ **Cobb Charity**	**£36,000**	Sustainable development, green initiatives and related education
☐ **The John Feeney Charitable Bequest**	**£36,000**	Arts, general
☐ **The Dorothy Holmes Charitable Trust**	**£36,000**	General
☐ **The N B Johnson Charitable Settlement**	**£36,000**	Education, older people
☐ **The Katzauer Charitable Settlement**	**£36,000**	Jewish
☐ **Malcolm Lyons Foundation**	**£36,000**	Jewish
☐ **The E M MacAndrew Trust**	**£36,000**	Medical, children, general
☐ **The Music Sales Charitable Trust**	**£36,000**	Children and youth, musical education; see below
☐ **The Pedmore Trust**	**£36,000**	Christian
☐ **The Rhododendron Trust**	**£36,000**	Welfare, overseas aid and development, culture, wildlife
☐ **Daisie Rich Trust**	**£36,000**	General

☐ **The John Ritblat Charitable Trust No. 1**	**£36,000**	Jewish, general
☐ **The Camilla Samuel Fund**	**£36,000**	Medical research
☐ **Angus Allnatt Charitable Foundation**	**£35,000**	Music and water-based activities for young people
☐ **James and Grace Anderson Trust**	**£35,000**	Cerebral palsy
☐ **The Berkeley Reafforestation Trust**	**£35,000**	Reafforestation projects
☐ **The Bintaub Charitable Trust**	**£35,000**	Jewish, health, education, children
☐ **Peter Black Charitable Trust**	**£35,000**	General, particularly Jewish
☐ **The Britto Foundation**	**£35,000**	General, Children, Israel
☐ **The Buckinghamshire Masonic Centenary Fund**	**£35,000**	General
☐ **The Cheruby Trust**	**£35,000**	Welfare, education, general
☐ **Miss V L Clore's 1967 Charitable Trust**	**£35,000**	General
☐ **The Iris Darnton Foundation**	**£35,000**	Educational and research projects
☐ **The Dorcas Trust**	**£35,000**	Christian, general
☐ **The R M Douglas Charitable Trust**	**£35,000**	General
☐ **The Ian Fleming Charitable Trust**	**£35,000**	Disability, medical
☐ **The Flow Foundation**	**£35,000**	Welfare, education, environment, medical
☐ **Leonard Gordon Charitable Trust**	**£35,000**	Jewish religious, educational and welfare organisations
☐ **The Metropolitan Drinking Fountain and Cattle Trough Association**	**£35,000**	Provision of pure drinking water
☐ **The Mitchell Charitable Trust**	**£35,000**	Jewish, general
☐ **The D C Moncrieff Charitable Trust**	**£35,000**	Social welfare, environment
☐ **The W L Pratt Charitable Trust**	**£35,000**	General
☐ **The Rawlings Charitable Trust**	**£35,000**	General
☐ **The Baker Charitable Trust**	**£34,000**	Mainly Jewish, older people, sickness and disability, medical research
☐ **Birthday House Trust**	**£34,000**	General
☐ **The Canning Trust**	**£34,000**	General
☐ **The Alderman Joe Davidson Memorial Trust**	**£34,000**	Jewish, general
☐ **Ralph and Muriel Emanuel Charity Trust**	**£34,000**	General in the UK
☐ **The Florian Charitable Trust**	**£34,000**	General
☐ **The Huggard Charitable Trust**	**£34,000**	General
☐ **The Modiano Charitable Trust**	**£34,000**	Jewish, general
☐ **The Elani Nakou Foundation**	**£34,000**	Education, international understanding
☐ **The Norton Foundation**	**£34,000**	Young people under 25 years of age
☐ **G S Plaut Charitable Trust**	**£34,000**	Sickness, disability, Jewish, elderly, Christian, general
☐ **The John M Archer Charitable Trust**	**£33,000**	General charitable purposes.
☐ **The Geoffrey Berger Charitable Trust**	**£33,000**	General
☐ **The Oliver Borthwick Memorial Trust**	**£33,000**	Homelessness
☐ **The Carlton House Charitable Trust**	**£33,000**	Bursaries, Jewish, general
☐ **Lance Coates Charitable Trust 1969**	**£33,000**	Biological and ecological approach to food production
☐ **The Emily Fraser Trust**	**£33,000**	Specific trades, older people
☐ **The Horace Moore Charitable Trust**	**£33,000**	General
☐ **S C and M E Morland's Charitable Trust**	**£33,000**	Quaker, sickness, welfare, peace and development overseas
☐ **The Mount 'A' Charity Trust**	**£33,000**	General, children, arts
☐ **The Mount 'B' Charity Trust**	**£33,000**	General, children, arts
☐ **The Mushroom Fund**	**£33,000**	General
☐ **The Duncan Norman Trust Fund**	**£33,000**	General
☐ **The Late Barbara May Paul Charitable Trust**	**£33,000**	Older people, young people, medical care and research, preservation of buildings
☐ **The Col W W Pilkington Will Trusts**	**£33,000**	Welfare
☐ **The Rivendell Trust**	**£33,000**	Sickness, disability, family problems, education, music
☐ **Jimmy Savile Charitable Trust**	**£33,000**	General
☐ **The Lili Tapper Charitable Foundation**	**£33,000**	Jewish
☐ **The Alexis Trust**	**£32,000**	Christian
☐ **The Ashby Charitable Trust**	**£32,000**	Medical research, education, business start-up/expansion

☐ **The Viscountess Boyd Charitable Trust**	**£32,000**	Conservation, horticulture, education and preservation
☐ **The Calpe Trust**	**£32,000**	Relief work
☐ **Ellador Ltd**	**£32,000**	Jewish
☐ **Sydney E Franklin Deceased's New Second Charity**	**£32,000**	Development
☐ **The Halecat Trust**	**£32,000**	General
☐ **The Kass Charitable Trust**	**£32,000**	Welfare, nursing homes, older people, education, cancer, Jewish
☐ **Martin McLaren Memorial Trust**	**£32,000**	General
☐ **The Mountbatten Memorial Trust**	**£32,000**	Technological research in aid of disabilities
☐ **Nazareth Trust Fund**	**£32,000**	Christian, in the UK and developing countries
☐ **The Simone Prendergast Charitable Settlement**	**£32,000**	General
☐ **Ambika Paul Foundation**	**£31,000**	Education, young people
☐ **The Sir Leon Bagrit Memorial Trust**	**£31,000**	Educational, general
☐ **The C B Trust**	**£31,000**	General, Jewish
☐ **Henry T and Lucy B Cadbury Charitable Trust**	**£31,000**	Quaker, health, homelessness, support groups, developing World
☐ **The Malcolm Chick Charity**	**£31,000**	General
☐ **The Angela Gallagher Memorial Fund**	**£31,000**	Children and youth, Christian, humanitarian, education
☐ **D K A Hackney Charitable Trust**	**£31,000**	General
☐ **The Dorothy Hay-Bolton Charitable Trust**	**£31,000**	Deaf, blind
☐ **Paul Lunn-Rockliffe Charitable Trust**	**£31,000**	General
☐ **The New Durlston Trust**	**£31,000**	Christian, overseas development
☐ **St Andrew Animal Fund Ltd**	**£31,000**	Animal welfare
☐ **The Lady Tangye Charitable Trust**	**£31,000**	Catholic, overseas aid, general
☐ **The Thistle Trust**	**£31,000**	Arts, general
☐ **The Barbara Welby Trust**	**£31,000**	Animal welfare, medical, general
☐ **The Appletree Trust**	**£30,000**	Disability, sickness, poverty
☐ **Belljoe Tzedoko Ltd**	**£30,000**	Jewish
☐ **Billingsgate Christian Mission Charitable Trust**	**£30,000**	Fishing industry-related, medical research
☐ **The Derek Crowson Charitable Settlement**	**£30,000**	General
☐ **Michael Davies Charitable Settlement**	**£30,000**	General
☐ **The Helen and Geoffrey de Freitas Charitable Trust**	**£30,000**	Preservation of wildlife, conservation and environment, cultural heritage
☐ **The Edith M Ellis 1985 Charitable Trust**	**£30,000**	Quaker, ecumenical, education, peace and international affairs, general
☐ **Gerald Finzi Charitable Trust**	**£30,000**	Music
☐ **Hartnett Charitable Trust**	**£30,000**	Environmental issues
☐ **Heagerty Charitable Trust**	**£30,000**	Catholic, general
☐ **The Lanvern Foundation**	**£30,000**	Education and health, especially relating to children
☐ **The Leonard Trust**	**£30,000**	Christian, overseas aid
☐ **The Macfarlane Walker Trust**	**£30,000**	Education, the arts, social welfare, general
☐ **The Maximillian Trust**	**£30,000**	Medical research, education, social welfare, heritage
☐ **The Colin Montgomerie Charitable Foundation**	**£30,000**	General
☐ **The Oak Trust**	**£30,000**	General
☐ **The John Rayner Charitable Trust**	**£30,000**	General
☐ **The Rowing Foundation**	**£30,000**	Water sports
☐ **The Rural Trust**	**£30,000**	Countryside
☐ **The Huntly & Margery Sinclair Charitable Trust**	**£30,000**	Medical, general
☐ **The Solo Charitable Settlement**	**£30,000**	Jewish, general
☐ **The Worshipful Company of Spectacle Makers Charity**	**£30,000**	Visual impairment, City of London, general
☐ **Webb Memorial Trust**	**£30,000**	Higher education furthering of democracy and human rights
☐ **Mrs S K West's Charitable Trust**	**£30,000**	General
☐ **The John Apthorp Charitable Trust**	**£29,000**	General
☐ **The Tunnell Trust**	**£29,000**	Chamber music
☐ **Zephyr Charitable Trust**	**£29,000**	Housing, health, environment, third world

☐ **The Boughton Trust**	**£28,000**	Elderly people, disability, youth groups, conservation projects
☐ **Beatrice Hankey Foundation Ltd**	**£28,000**	Christian
☐ **Maurice Fry Charitable Trust**	**£28,000**	General
☐ **The Ormsby Charitable Trust**	**£28,000**	General
☐ **The Constance Paterson Charitable Trust**	**£28,000**	Medical research, health, welfare of children, older people, service people
☐ **The Peter Stebbings Memorial Charity**	**£28,000**	General
☐ **Misselbrook Trust**	**£27,000**	General
☐ **Panton Trust**	**£27,000**	Animal wildlife worldwide; environment UK
☐ **Miss Doreen Stanford Trust**	**£27,000**	General
☐ **Murphy-Newmann Charity Company Limited**	**£26,000**	People who are older, very young have disabilities
☐ **Miss S M Tutton**	**£26,000**	Music
☐ **B E Perl Charitable Trust**	**£25,000**	Jewish, general
☐ **The Gretna Charitable Trust**	**£23,000**	General
☐ **The King/Cullimore Charitable Trust**	**£22,000**	General
☐ **The Theodore Trust**	**£6,500**	Christian education

The A B Charitable Trust

Promotion and defence of human dignity

£195,000 (2002/03)

Beneficial area UK and developing world.

12 Addison Avenue, London W11 4QR

Tel. 020 7371 4374

Correspondent T M Denham, Secretary

Trustees *Y J M Bonavero; D Boehm; Mrs A G M-L Bonavero; Miss C Bonavero; Miss S Bonavero; O Bonavero; P Bonavero.*

CC Number 1000147

Information available Accounts were on file at the Charity Commission.

General The trust gives grants for the promotion and defence of human dignity. It is the trust's aim to make 'medium-sized' grants for a three-year period, subject to satisfactory reports and reapplication to the trustees.

In 2002/03 the trust had assets of £332,000 and an income of £206,000. Grants totalled £195,000.

From 507 applications received, grants to 51 organisations were made generally ranging from £500 to £5,000. The exceptions being £12,000 to Prison Reform Trust, £7,500 to a Kurdish human rights project and £6,000 to Link Community Development.

Other beneficiaries included Amber, Bethany Project, Detention Advice Service, Forth Sector, Holy Cross Centre Trust, Howard League for Penal Reform, Mustard Tree New Bridge, Portland College and Scottish Refugee Council (£5,000 each), Nurses' Welfare Trust (£4,000), Cancer Resource Centre, Kemp Hospice and Wells for India (£3,000 each), Ark Trust, Find Your Feet, Headway, Kurdish Cultural Centre, Rethink Disability and Theresa's House in Peterborough (£2,500 each), Gingerbread Centre and Voices for Ballet (£2,000) and St Mary's Church in Ilfracombe (£500).

Exclusions No support for medical research, animal welfare, expeditions, scholarships, conservation and environment.

Applications In writing to the secretary, up to a maximum of four A4 pages if appropriate, plus the most recent detailed audited accounts. The trustees meet on a quarterly basis in March, June, September and December. Applications should be from UK registered charities only.

The Keith & Freda Abraham Charitable Trust

General

£179,000 (2004)

Beneficial area UK, and local organisations in north Devon.

Church Farm, Yelland Road, Fremington, Devon EX32 3BU

Tel. 01271 345326

Correspondent C J Bartlett, Secretary

Trustees *K N Abraham; H J Purnell; C D Squire; C T Mill; G L Watts; J Sunderland; M R A Ford.*

CC Number 288672

Information available Information was provided by the trust

General The trust only supports major UK charities with which the trustees sympathise and local projects in north Devon.

In 2004 the trust had an income of £71,000 and assets of £140,000. Grants totalled £179,000 for the year. The trustees have been accumulating income over the last few years while considering support for some major projects. Having grown considerably due to investments, most of this income was donated in 2004 to North Devon Hospice Care Trust (£100,000) and Barnstaple & Pilton Cricket Club (£70,000).

Other beneficiaries included Breast Cancer Campaign, North Devon Maritime Museum and Samaritans (£2,000 each), Radio Devon Chestnut Appeal and Stroke Association (£1,000 each), Children's Summer Club (£500), Barnstaple Poverty Action Group, Barnstaple Swimming Club and Park School (£250 each) and Age Concern and Royal British Legion (£100 each).

Applications In writing to the correspondent.

The Henry & Grete Abrahams Second Charitable Foundation

Jewish, medical welfare, general

£73,000 (2000/01)

Beneficial area UK.

Hill Dickinson, 66–67 Cornhill, London EC3V 3RN

Tel. 020 7695 1048 **Fax** 020 7695 1001

Correspondent D Maislish, Trustee

Trustees *Grete Abrahams; David Maislish; Mark Gluckstein.*

CC Number 298240

Information available Full accounts were on file at the Charity Commission.

General Established in 1987 by Henry and Grete Abrahams, the foundation supports a variety of medical and health organisations. In the past there has also been a preference for Jewish and London-based organisations. In 2002/03 the trust had an income of £46,000 and a total expenditure of £29,000. Further information for this year was not available.

However previous information stated in 2000/01 it had assets of £167,000 and an income of £53,000. Grants were made to 29 organisations and totalled £73,000.

Donations ranged from £100 to £13,000. The largest grants were £13,000 to Wizo Charitable Foundation and £10,000 each to St John's Hospice and Wingate Youth Trust.

Other beneficiaries receiving £1,000 or more were Liberal Jewish Synagogue (£6,000), Trustees of the London Clinic and Lewis Hammerson Charitable Trust (£5,000 each), Gurkha Welfare Trust (£4,000), Marie Curie Cancer Care, Elimination of Leukaemia Fund and Children Nationwide Medical Research Fund (£2,000 each), Great Ormond Street Hospital Children's Charity (£1,500) and Boys Town Jerusalem, Food Lifeline, Nightingale House, United Jewish Israel Appeal, Brainwave, Imperial Cancer Research Fund, Royal Alexander Hospital for Sick Children, Roy Castle Lung Cancer Research Fund, King's Medical Research Trust, Universal Beneficent Society and Cancer Research Campaign (£1,000 each).

Grants under £1,000 were made to Friends of St George's Hospital, Wlodowa Charitable Reconciliation Trust and Beis Malka Girls' School (£500 each), Police Foundation and JNF (£250 each) and Sense (£100).

Exclusions No grants to individuals or non-registered charities.

Applications The trust states: 'We are fully committed to a number of charities for the next few years, therefore cannot undertake any more appeals'. The trustees meet in November.

Eric Abrams Charitable Trust

Jewish/Israeli

£42,000 (1999/2000)

Beneficial area UK and Israel.

130–132 Nantwich Road, Crewe CW2 6AZ

Tel. 01270 213475

Correspondent Robert Talyor

Trustees *Brian Abrams; Eric Abrams; Steven Abrams.*

CC Number 275939

Information available Limited information was available on file at the Charity Commission.

General The only recent information available on this trust comes from the Charity Commission website, which states that in 2002/03 it had an income of £54,000 and a total expenditure of £35,000.

Despite the information clearly having been filed for more recent years, the most up-to-date accounts stored in the public files at the Charity Commission in December 2004 were for 1999/2000. In that year, it had assets of £1.2 million, an income of £50,000 and gave grants totalling £42,000. Unfortunately a grants list was not included in those accounts.

Exclusions No grants to individuals.

Applications The trust has previously stated that its funds are fully committed and applications are not invited.

Brian Abrams Charitable Trust

Jewish/Israeli

£40,000 (1998/99)

Beneficial area UK and Israel.

130–132 Nantwich Road, Crewe CW2 6AZ

Tel. 01270 213475

Correspondent Robert Taylor

Trustees *Betty Abrams; Brian Abrams; Eric Abrams; Gail Gabbie.*

CC Number 275941

Information available Limited information was available on file at the Charity Commission.

General The only recent information available on this trust comes from the Charity Commission website, which states that in 2002/03 it had an income of £54,000 and a total expenditure of £35,000.

Despite the information clearly having been filed for more recent years, the most up-to-date accounts stored in the public files at the Charity Commission in December 2004 were for 1998/99. In that year, it had assets of £993,000, an income of £45,000 and gave grants totalling £40,000. Unfortunately a grants list was not included in those accounts.

Exclusions No grants to individuals.

Applications The trust has previously stated that its funds are fully committed and applications are not invited.

The Acacia Charitable Trust

Jewish, education, general

£71,000 (2002/03)

Beneficial area UK and Israel.

5 Clarke's Mews, London W1G 6QN

Tel. 020 7486 1884 **Fax** 020 7487 4171

Correspondent Mrs Nora Howland, Secretary

Trustees *K D Rubens; Mrs A G Rubens; S A Rubens.*

CC Number 274275

Information available Full accounts were on file at the Charity Commission.

General In 2002/03 the trust had assets of £1.3 million and an income of £87,000. Grants were given in the categories of education, overseas aid, UK charities and Jewish charities (other than education), and totalled £71,000. Grants ranged from £20 to £36,000, although most were for under £1,000, and were given to 37 organisations. About half of the grants were recurrent.

The largest beneficiary continued to be University of Reading, which received £36,000 to provide a lectureship in Land Management. Other larger grants were to ORT Trust (£27,000), World Jewish Relief (£12,000), Community Security Trust (£10,000), Jewish Museum (£9,000), Centre for Theology and Society and Jewish Care (£2,000 each) and Spanish and Portuguese Jews Congregation (£1,600). Grants of £1,000 each went to British Museum Development Trust, Institute for Jewish Policy Research, Norwood Ltd, JJCT, NSPCC, Royal National Theatre and Spanish and Portugese Jews' Home for the Aged.

Beneficiaries receiving £500 or less included British Friends of Haifa University, Big Issue Foundation, St John's Hospice, Nightingale House, Care International, Shelter and Jewish Women's Week.

Exclusions No grants to individuals.

Applications In writing to the correspondent.

Access 4 Trust

Children, welfare

£157,000 (2001/02)

Beneficial area UK, Bangladesh, Ghana and Uganda.

Slater Maidment, 7 St James's Square, London SW1Y 4JU

Tel. 020 7930 7621

Correspondent C Sadlow

Trustees *Miss S M Wates; J R F Lulham.*

CC Number 267017

Information available Full accounts were on file at the Charity Commission.

General Most grants, as in previous years, were to assist families in need with funds also going overseas to developing countries.

The assets in 2001/02 stood at £450,000. The income was £169,000 and grants totalled £157,000. Larger grants, above

£10,000, included: £30,000 to Womankind – West Africa Programme; £23,000 to Post-Adoption Centre; £19,000 to Entebbe All-Christian Women's Association; £17,000 to Action on Disability and Development; and £13,000 to Friends of the Centre for the Rehabilitation of the Paralysed.

Other grants included: £9,200 to Barnabus Tinkasmire – Uganda; £5,000 each to Child Advocacy International and UNIFAT School – Uganda; £3,000 to Newham Bengali Community Trust; £2,000 to Concern Universal; £1,600 to Girls Growth and Development; £1,300 to Bawku Women's Development Association; and £1,000 to Acid Survivors Foundation, Kuga Fong Community Association and Prisoners Abroad. Grants below £1,000 totalled £3,700.

Many of the beneficiaries had received support in the previous year.

Exclusions No grants to individuals or sponsorships.

Applications In writing to the correspondent.

The Company of Actuaries' Charitable Trust Fund

Actuaries, medical research, young and older people, disability, general

£54,000 to organisations (2002/03)

Beneficial area UK and overseas, with a preference for the City of London.

34 Howe Drive, Beaconsfield, Buckinghamshire HP9 2BD

Tel. 01494 673451

Correspondent Graham Lockwood, Almoner

Trustees *R Squires, Chair; E S Thomas; G G Bannerman; A Benke; R Cobley; J Jolliffe.*

CC Number 280702

Information available Full accounts were provided by the trust.

General The trust gives grants under the four following areas:

- medical research and support
- young people
- people who are elderly or disabled
- general.

The trust believes that charities should be run efficiently and an indicator of efficiency is the level of administration expenses as a percentage of gross income. Therefore charities which can demonstrate effective expenditure will be preferred, with the ratio of volunteers to paid staff seen as an indicator of effectiveness.

There is also a preference for smaller charities where a comparatively small donation can be of real help, and for charities having a substantial connection with the City of London or surrounding boroughs.

In 2002/03 it had assets of £202,000 and an income of £61,000. Grants to organisations totalled £54,000.

Up to 20% of the funds are given solely at the discretion of the Master of the Company each year. In 2002/03 grants totalling £8,500 were approved to 12 organisations. These were £2,000 to Abbeyfield, £1,000 each to Corinne Burton Memorial Fund, Corpus Christi College – Oxford and University College London Development Fund for the J J Sylvester Scholarship Fund and £500 each to seven charities included Foot and Mouth Painters, Karen Morris Memorial Trust, North London Hospice and Tuberous Sclerosis Association.

Under the research category, £8,500 went to The Chronic Disease Research Fellowship. Other grants were broken down into those in the City of London and those with no connection to the area. In total, seven City charities were supported. £2,000 went to Lord Mayor's Appeal for Save the Children with £500 each to Brokerage Citylink, City and Guilds of London Institute, Federation of London Youth Clubs, Mansion House Scholarship Scheme, Royal British Legion for the City Poppy Appeal and Sheriffs' and Recorders' Fund.

Other grants went to 55 charities and totalled £29,000. Aside from the £1,000 each to Cancer Research UK, Royal Marsden Cancer Campaign and Stoke Damerel Community College, the grants were of £500 each. Beneficiaries included Avon Sexual Abuse Centre, Brent Centre for Young People, Colchester Furniture Project, Epilepsy Research Foundation, Help the Hospices, INSPIRE Foundation, Kiloran Trust, Livewire Youth Project, Matthew Trust, Mersey Region Epilepsy Association, Nepal Leprosy Trust, Remedi, Shooting Star Trust, Sustrans and Universal Beneficent Society.

Exclusions No grants for the propagation of religious or political beliefs, the maintenance of historic buildings or for conservation. The trustees do not usually support an organisation which has received a grant in the previous 24 months.

Applications In writing to the correspondent, including a copy of the most recent audited accounts, aims and purposes of the charity and details of the purposes for which the grant is needed.

The Adamson Trust

Children, under 16, who are physically or mentally disabled

£53,000 to organisations (2002/03)

Beneficial area UK, but preference will be given to requests on behalf of Scottish children.

Barnshaw, Comrie Street, Crieff, Perthshire PH7 4BQ

Tel. 01764 656048

Correspondent K B Devine

Trustees *A R Muir; R C Farrell; J Allen; Dr H Kirkwood.*

SC Number SC016517

Information available Full accounts were provided by the trust.

General Formerly known as Miss Agnes Gilchrist Adamson's Trust, grants are made to organisations providing holidays for children under 16 who are mentally or physically disabled. Donations are usually one-off.

In 2002/03 it had assets of £1.3 million and an income of £61,000. Grants totalled £56,000, of which a total of £53,000 was made to 38 organisations and £2,500 to 12 individuals.

Beneficiaries to recieve grants of £1,000 or above included: Barnardos Dundee Family Support Team, Children's Hospice Association Scotland, Lady Hoare Trust for Physically Disabled Children and Scottish Spina Bifida Association (£5,000 each); React and Sense Scotland (£3,000 each); Peak

Holidays (£2,500); Hopscotch Holidays, Over the Wall Gang Group, Scotland Yard Adventure Centre and Special Needs Adventure Play Ground (£2,000 each); and Lothian Autistic, St Nicholas' Special School – Edinburgh and Trefoil House (£1,000 each). Grants under £1,000 totalled £8,700.

Exclusions Unsolicited applications.

Applications On a form available from the correspondent. A copy of the latest audited accounts should be included together with details of the organisation, the number of children who would benefit and the proposed holiday. Applications are considered in January, May and September.

The Victor Adda Foundation

Fan Museum

£657,000 (2002/03)

Beneficial area UK, but in practice Greenwich.

c/o Kleinwort Benson Trustees, PO Box 191, 10 Fenchurch Street, London EC3M 3LB

Tel. 020 7475 5093

Correspondent C Gilbert

Trustees *Mrs H E Alexander; R J Gluckstein; A Mossen*

CC Number 291456

Information available Accounts were provided by the trust.

General Virtually since it was set up in 1984, the foundation has been a stalwart supporter of the Fan Museum in Greenwich. Both the foundation and the museum share a majority of the same trustees; the foundation also owns the property in which the museum is sited and has granted it a 999-year lease. In addition the foundation has made a loan of £573,000 to the trust.

In 2002/03 the trust had an income of £35,000 and made grants totalling £657,000. Consequently, the trust assets have decreased to £911,000 (£1.9 million in 2001/02). As in previous years, the Fan Museum received nearly all of the grant total. Only one other small grant was made to Children's Trust (£500).

Applications In writing to the correspondent. Only successful applications are notified of a decision.

Adenfirst Ltd

Jewish

£137,000 (2001)

Beneficial area Worldwide.

479 Holloway Road, London N7 6LE

Tel. 020 7272 2255

Correspondent I M Cymerman, Governor

Trustees *Mrs H F Bondi; I M Cymerman; Mrs R Cymerman.*

CC Number 291647

Information available Information was on file at the Charity Commission.

General The trust supports mostly Jewish organisations, with a preference for education and social welfare. In 2001 grants totalled £137,000.

The largest grants were £18,000 to Ichud Mosdos Gur and £10,000 each to Beis Yankov Institutions, Centre for Torah Education Trust and Friends of Harim Establishments.

Other beneficiaries included Ponevez Beth Hamedrash, Yad Eliezer and Yeshiva Gedola Zichron Michoel (£7,000 each), Craven Walk Charity Trust (£6,000), Pardes Chama Institutions (£5,000), Ner Shimri Binyarnina (£4,000), Rehabilitation Trust and Yesodei Hatprah Schools (£2,000). Miscellaneous payments of less than £1,000 each totalled £1,000.

Applications In writing to the correspondent.

The Adnams Charity

General

£54,000 (2001/02)

Beneficial area Southwold in Suffolk, and the area within 25 miles of Southwold Church, excluding Ipswich and Norwich.

Sole Bay Brewery, Southwold, Suffolk IP18 6JW

Tel. 01502 727200 **Fax** 01502 727267

Correspondent Rebecca Abrahall, Charity Administrator

Trustees *Simon Loftus, Chair; Jonathan Adnams; Melvyn Horn; Andrew Wood; Robert Chase; Emma Hibbert; Guy Heald.*

CC Number 1000203

Information available Report, accounts and detailed grants list provided by the trust.

General Set up in 1990 the charity gives support to a wide variety of organisations including those involved with social welfare, education, recreation, the arts and historic buildings. The trust 'aims to make a real difference to the work of dozens of local organisations which have difficulty in attracting funds from elsewhere' and it prefers to give 'small sums to achieve specific ends'.

In 2003/04 the trust had an income of £53,000. Grants for this year totalled £50,000.

In 2001/02 grants totalled £54,000 and were distributed to 64 organisations. They were broken down as follows:

Historic buildings – 4 grants totalling £2,600

These went to All Saints' Church – Easton for porch window repair (£870), St Michael and All Angels' Church – Cookley for preservation of ancient graffiti found on its lead (£650), Church of St Catherine Pettaugh for repairs to the church roof (£610) and St Cross Church for repairs to the oak louvres of the bell sound openings (£550).

Social welfare – 18 grants totalling £17,000

Beneficiaries included Waveney Counselling Service for its general work (£2,000), Framlington and District Volunteer Centre for a new photocopier (£1,400), Headway – Great Yarmouth for equipment (£1,000), Friends of the Priory Paddocks – Leiston for a voice amplifier (£700) and St Barnabas for improved disability access (£500).

Education – 9 grants totalling £14,000

The largest grant was £5,000 to Bungay High School to help its quest to gain specialist status in science. Other recipients included Kirkley High School for a counselling service (£1,600), Gunton County Primary School for nursery equipment (£1,000) and Ways with Words for workshops to encourage the pleasures of reading and creative writing amongst children (£500).

Health – 2 grants totalling £2,800

Both of these grants were towards automated defibrillators, with Darsham Response Team receiving £1,800 and Aldeburgh Lay Responders £1,000.

Recreation – 20 grants totalling £9,000

Beneficiaries included Slaughen Sailing Clubhouse and Training Project for installation of a wheelchair ramp (£1,500), Clopton Village Hall for goalposts (£800), Pakefield Rosebud Playgroup for child-height tables (£500), Wrentham Youth Football Club for footballs for a year for the scheme which aids over 500 children (£250), St Andrews' Playgroup – Lowestoft to cover the fees of a child with health problems (£85) and Edgar Sewtar Playschool – Halesworth for toys which are both fun and educational (£50).

Local History and Conservation – 4 grants totalling £3,500

Excelsior Trust received £2,000 towards a new engine which will allow an 80-year vessel to continue to operator. Other beneficiaries were Woodland Trust Great Glenham for the planting of two hedges to preserve the wildlife in the area (£680). Blythburgh Society for a publication containing 30 essays by 16 authors on the history of the region (£500) and a joint project by five museums in Southwold to produce a joint brochure to increase visitor numbers (£250).

Arts – 2 grants totalling £1,100

East Anglian Traditional Music Trust received £750 for the tutorial costs of a song event whilst Beccles Choral Society was given £230 to purchase vocal scores which are not available for hire.

Robinson Fund – 4 grants totalling £3,800

Old Warren House, which works with children who have difficulties with mainstream education, received £1,500 for a computer to enable teachers to project images onto the whiteboard. Breakout was given £1,200 towards achieving ISO9001 accreditation to open further channels of funding for its work with young people who are disaffected or socially excluded. They were also helped by another grant from this fund, as the trust gave FWA £500 for a front door on the condition that it was made by Breakout. The other grant, of £530, went to Budden Trust to cover an insurance payment for its work with people with learning difficulties or other mental health problems.

Exclusions No grants for UK organisations unless they are a local branch in the area of benefit. No grants to individuals.

Applications In writing to the correspondent. Trustees meet quarterly.

AF Trust Company

Higher education

£189,000 (2000/01)

Beneficial area England.

34 Chapel Street, Thatcham, Berkshire RG18 4QL

Correspondent P D Welch, Secretary

Trustees *Anthony J Knapp; Jane Ross; Denise Everitt; Miles S Hodge; Roger Clayton; Alison A Reid; Colin R Showell; Keith R Blanshard; Richard A Clarke; Martin Wynne-Jones; David C L Savage.*

CC Number 1060319

Information available Information was provided by the trust. Accounts were on file at the Charity Commission, with an incomplete list of grants.

General Support is given for charitable purposes connected with the provision of higher education in England. The company currently provides property services and leasing facilities to educational establishments on an at arms length basis.

In 2000/01 it had assets of £208,000. The total income was £5.6 million with its total expenditure £5.3 million. However, it is worth noting that this relates to the funds used to lease buildings from educational establishments and then enter into lease-back arrangements rather than describing the size of funds available. Grants were made totalling £189,000.

The largest grants were £44,000 to University of Nottingham, £34,000 to Imperial College, £27,000 to Southampton University, £22,000 to University of Reading and £14,000 to University of Surrey.

Exclusions No grants to individuals.

Applications In writing to the correspondent. However, unsolicited applications are only accepted from higher education institutions within England.

The Green & Lilian F M Ainsworth & Family Benevolent Fund

Youth, disability, health, medical research, disadvantage, older people, general

£49,000 (2001/02)

Beneficial area UK, with some preference for north west England.

Royal Bank of Scotland plc, Trust Estate Services, Capital House, 2 Festival Square, Edinburgh EH3 9SU

Tel. 0131 523 2679

Correspondent The Trustees

Trustee *The Royal Bank of Scotland plc.*

CC Number 267577

Information available Full accounts were on file at the Charity Commission.

General The trust states that each year it selects to support UK charities covering a wide range of interests mainly involving people of all ages who are disadvantaged by either health or other circumstances.

In 2001/02 the trust had assets of £833,000 and an income of £39,000. Grants to 42 organisations totalled £49,000. Beneficiaries included Claire House Children's Hospice, Kinder Mountain Rescue Team and Autistic Society – Greater Manchester (£2,000 each), Princess Trust – North West and Deafblind UK (£1,500 each), Brain Injury Rehabilitation & Development (£1,200), ChildLine – North West, Weston Spirit – Merseyside, North West Air Ambulance, Merseyside Children's Holidays Foundation and Mustard Tree (£1,000 each), Cancer Care (£800) and City Escape (£500).

Exclusions No grants to individuals or non-registered charities.

Applications In writing to the correspondent.

The Air Charities Trust

Charities linked with the work of the Guild of Air Pilots and Air Navigators of the City of London

£54,000 (2001/02)

Beneficial area UK and City of London.

Cobham House, 9 Warwick Court, Grays Inn, London WC1R 5DJ

Tel. 020 7404 4032 **Fax** 020 7404 4035

Email gapan@gapan.org

Website www.gapan.org

Correspondent Capt. Christopher Hodgkinson

Trustees *The Master of the Guild of Air Pilots and Air Navigators; Sir Michael Cobham; Capt. Christopher Hodgkinson; Capt. Robert Owens.*

CC Number 286915

Information available Information was provided by the trust.

General The trust supports the advancement of education in all branches of aviation, especially the promotion of safety. It is the practice of the trust to make grants only to charities linked with the work of the Guild of Air Pilots and Air Navigators of the City of London.

In 2001/02 it had an income of £54,000, all of which was given in grants. Each year the trust's funds are divided between Air Safety Trust and Guild of Air Pilots.

Applications In writing to the correspondent.

Airways Charitable Trust Limited

Welfare, health

£105,000 (1999/2000)

Beneficial area UK.

The Gate House, 2 Park Street, Windsor, Berkshire SL4 1LU

Tel. 01753 753900 **Fax** 01753 753901

Email sandra.fletcher@actg.co.uk

Website www.actg.co.uk

Correspondent Sandra Fletcher, Grants Coordinator

Trustees *E P Gostling, Chair; D P Dugard; J J O'Sullivan; D N Taylor; M Street; P Nield.*

CC Number 1068617

Information available Accounts were on file at the Charity Commission.

General The charity has several wholly owned trading subsidiaries. The companies donate profits to the charity under the Gift Aid scheme. The trust's assets total some £30 million.

The trust stated in 2002 that it had pledged a grant totalling £4 million, to be made over three or more years, towards building sheltered accommodation.

In 2000/01 the trust had an income of £1.2 million with an expenditure of £1.4 million. No further information was available.

In 1999/2000 grants totalling £105,000 were made to organisations and £46,000 was given to 19 individuals. Grants to organisations included £27,000 to Shepperton Parish Church, £15,000 to Woodlands School – Guildford, £10,000 to CONNECT, £9,800 to Spelthorne Farm, £9,000 to Royal Schools for the Deaf, £5,000 to Age Concern, £4,100 to Guildford Voluntary Services, £4,000 to Hillington Autistic Care and Support and £3,500 to National Benevolent Fund for the Aged.

Applications In writing to the correspondent, stating: the name of your organisation and what you do; what you want the grant for; how much you want; how much of the grant total you have already raised; and who else you are approaching for funds. Individual applicants should contact the correspondent to request an application form.

The Sylvia Aitken Charitable Trust

Medical research and welfare, general

£244,000 (2002/03)

Beneficial area UK, with a preference for Scotland.

Fergusons Chartered Accountants, 24 Woodside, Houston, Renfrewshire PA6 7DD

Tel. 01505 610412 **Fax** 01505 614944

Correspondent Mrs N Ferguson, Trust Administrator

Trustees *Mrs S M Aitken; Mrs M Harkis; J Ferguson.*

SC Number SC010556

Information available Full accounts were provided by the trust.

General Whilst this trust has a preference for medical projects, it has general charitable purposes, making small grants to a wide range of small local organisations throughout the UK, particularly those in Scotland.

In 2002/03 the trust had assets of £3 million and an income of £140,000. Grants were made to organisations totalling £244,000. A payment of £27,000 was paid to a firm of chartered accountants, of which one of the trustees is a partner, for 'day to day management of the trust and professional advice'. Even though wholly legal, these editors always regret such payments unless, to use the words of the Charity Commission, 'there is no realistic alternative'.

The largest grant by far was £115,000 to University of Glasgow for the Myeloma Cancer Project. Other grants included £5,000 each to YMCA and Rainbow Club, £4,000 to Friends of the Lake District, £3,000 to I–Can, £2,500 to Variety Club, £2,000 each to Association for International Cancer Research and Skye View Animal Home, £1,500 each to Chest, Heart & Stroke and Scottish Spina Bifida and £1,000 each to Animal Concern, Botton Village, Deafblind, International League for the Protection of Horses.

Grants below £1,000 included £750 to Sense Scotland, £500 each to Alzheimer's Society, Solent Multiple Sclerosis Society and Woodlands Trust, £400 to Children's Adventure Farm Trust and £200 each to Acorn Centre Youth Project, Angels, Down's Syndrome Scotland, Edinburgh Young Carers Project, Friends of Park Lane, Kaimes Special School Association, Kingsway Christian Fellowship, Renfrewshire Care & Repair, Sensory Impaired Support Group, Trinity Tots Under 5's and Visual Impairment Services South East Scotland.

Exclusions No grants to individuals: the trust can only support UK registered charities.

Applications In writing to the correspondent. Applicants should outline the charity's objectives and current projects for which funding may be required. The trustees meet at least twice a year, usually in March/April and September/October. The trust stated in December 2003 that its funds were usually fully committed.

The Alabaster Trust

Christian Church and related activities

£52,000 (2001/02)

Beneficial area UK and overseas.

1 The Avenue, Eastbourne, East Sussex BN21 3YA

Tel. 01323 644579 **Fax** 01323 417643

Email john@caladine.co.uk

Correspondent J R Caladine, Accountant

Trustees *G A Kendrick; M Buchanan; Mrs J Kendrick; Mrs A Sheldrake.*

CC Number 1050568

Information available Accounts were on file at the Charity Commission, without a list of grants.

General This trust was set up to make grants to evangelical Christian organisations in the UK and abroad. In 2001/02 it had an income of £59,000, mostly derived from Gift Aid donations. Total assets were £67,000 and grants totalled £52,000. Further information was not available.

Exclusions No grants to individuals.

Applications In writing to the correspondent. The trustees meet to consider grants quarterly, in March, June, September and December.

D G Albright Charitable Trust

General

About £38,000 (2002/03)

Beneficial area UK, with a preference for Gloucestershire.

Old Church School, Hollow Street, Great Somerford, Chippenham, Wiltshire SN15 5JD

Tel. 01249 720 760

Correspondent Richard G Wood, Trustee

Trustees *Hon. Dr G Greenall; R G Wood.*

CC Number 277367

Information available Information provided by the trust.

General In 2002/03 this trust had an income of £36,000. Grants were made totalling around £38,000 and the total assets were £840,000.

Beneficiaries of donations in this year included £4,000 to St. Lukes Hospital for the Clergy, £3,000 each to St. Mary's School Bromesberrow After School Care Club and The Children's Society, £2,500 each to Bromesberrow Parochial Church Council and Mission Aviation Fellowship, £2,000 each to Dean and Chapter Gloucester, Gloucester Family Support (G.D.V.S.A.P.), Gloucester Macmillan Cancer Service, Leonard Cheshire Foundation and Pershore Theatre Arts Association.

Exclusions Grants are not usually made to individuals.

Applications In writing to the correspondent.

Alcohol Education and Research Council

Educational and research projects concerning alcohol misuse

£232,000 (2002/03)

Beneficial area UK.

Room 408, Horseferry House, Dean Ryle Street, London SW1P 2AW

Tel. 020 7271 8896 **Fax** 020 7271 8847

Email len.hay@aerc.org.uk

Website www.aerc.org.uk

Correspondent Andrea Tilouche

Trustees *Dr Noel Olsen, Chair; David Rae; Mrs Daljit Sidebottom; Prof. Robin Davidson; John Bennett; Prof. Ilana Crome; Dr Jonathan Chick; Ms Perminder Dhillon; Henry Fairweather; Peter Harraway; Ms Rhoda Emlyn-Jones; Dr John Kemm; Gaye Pedlow; Dr Betsy Thom; Prof Richard Velleman.*

CC Number 284748

Information available Annual report was available from the council's website but without a list of beneficiaries.

General The council states in their 2002/03 accounts that 'the council seeks to increase awareness of alcohol issues, to facilitate a reducation in alcohol–related harm in society and to encourage best practice. Our aim is to make a positive difference to the ways in which society understands and uses alcohol.'

The aims of council are:

(a) The education of the public as to the causes and effects of, and means of preventing excessive consumption of alcohol.

(b) The care and rehabilitation of persons convicted of offences involving drunkenness.

(c) The provision of treatment and other help for persons dependent on alcohol or given to excessive consumption of alcohol.

(d) Research into matters relevant to any of the purposes mentioned in (a) to (c), and the publication of the results of such research.

The council provides four types of grant:

- Research grants
- People and organisation development grants
- Small grants (up to £5,000)
- Studentship grants, to support fees and expenses linked to taught courses.

Full information about grant application procedures is available on the council's website.

In 2002/03 it had assets of £8.7 million and an income of £649,000. Grants totalled £232,000, of which studentships totalled £120,000, research and action projects totalled £93,000 and miscellaneous grants amounted to £18,000.

A list of beneficiaries was not provided in the council's accounts. Previous recipients have included Addictions Forum to fund conference bursaries, Alcohol & Health Research Centre, Edinburgh for epidemiological survey on drug use amongst European students, Centre for Alcohol & Drug Studies, Newcastle upon Tyne to carry out research and develop strategy for implementing brief interventions in primary health care, National Federation of Young Farmers' Clubs for Theatre-in-Education project on sensible drinking,

TACADE to develop educational materials, University of Bath for research on work with relatives of alcohol and drug misusers, University College Medical School for an alcohol epidemiological project and University of Nottingham for epidemiological research.

Exclusions No grants to statutory authorities or for service provision.

Applications An application form is available on request and can be downloaded from the website.

Alexandra Rose Day

Fundraising partnerships with 'people-caring' charities

£189,000 (2001/02)

Beneficial area UK.

5 Mead Lane, Farmhan, Surrey GU9 7DY

Tel. 0870 7700 275 **Fax** 0870 7700 276

Email enquiries@alexandraroseday.org.uk

Website www.alexandraroseday.org.uk

Correspondent The National Director

Trustees *The Council: Rt Hon. Lord Wakeham, Chairman; Andrew Mitchell; Lady Grade; Lady Heald; Lord King of Wartnaby; Mrs Aubrey Beckham; Peter Beckham; Ms Cecily Engle; Stephen King; Mrs Katheryn Langridge; Mrs Morton Neal; Sir Ian Rankin; Peter Russell-Wood; Raymond Salisbury-Jones; Mrs Diane Sillem; Mrs Domonic Tayler.*

CC Number 211535

Information available Information was provided by the trust.

General Alexandra Rose Day was founded in 1912 by Queen Alexandra, as a practical way of marking the fiftieth anniversary of her first arrival in the UK from Denmark. The charity offers partnership in fundraising and other forms of support for smaller, people-caring charities. Its activities include an annual national Flag Day (Alexandra Rose Day) and regular raffles.

For Flag Days, this charity makes the arrangements and supplies equipment whilst the partner charity provides the flag sellers. Alexandra Rose Day makes an immediate grant to the partner equivalent to 70% of its gross collection. For raffles, Alexandra Rose Day organises the prizes and prints the tickets, which the partner charity sells and receives 70% of all gross sales.

Small charities are also offered access to value-for-money insurance, printing and other services. The Rose Ball is the largest of the two or three major fundraising events the charity organises each year, the surplus of which is donated through the special appeal fund, an annual programme of grants designed to bring immediate, practical benefits to people-caring charities and voluntary groups.

In 2001/02 the trust had assets of £543,000 and an income of £379,000. Grants were made during the year totalling £189,000.

Beneficiaries included League of Friends – St Helier Hospital (£6,000), Shooting Star Trust (£4,000), SPHERE (£3,000), Bishop Creighton House (£2,500), Norfolk Association for the Disabled, League of Friends – Rutland Hospital and Friends of Abbeyfield (Orpington) Society (£2,000 each) and Friends of Royal Brompton Hospital and Shaftsbury Society (£1,000 each).

Exclusions Only charities participating in Flag Days or raffles are eligible to apply. Grants are not made to individuals or charities operating overseas.

Applications In writing to the correspondent.

The Alexis Trust

Christian

£32,000 (2001/02)

Beneficial area UK and overseas.

14 Broadfield Way, Buckhurst Hill, Essex IG9 5AG

Correspondent Prof. D W Vere, Trustee

Trustees *Prof. D W Vere; C P Harwood; Mrs E M Harwood; Mrs V Vere.*

CC Number 262861

Information available The information for this entry was provided by the trust.

General Support is given to a variety of causes, principally Christian. In 2001/02 the trust gave grants totalling £32,000 from an income of £35,000. No further information was available.

Exclusions No grants for building appeals, or to individuals for education.

Applications In writing to the correspondent, although the trust states that most of the funds are regularly committed.

Alglen Ltd

Jewish causes

£509,000 (1999/2000)

Beneficial area Worldwide.

Felds, Trustees' Accountants, 5 North End Road, London NW11 7RJ

Tel. 020 8455 6789 **Fax** 020 8455 2277

Correspondent Mrs R Lipschitz, Governor

Trustees *D Schreiber; Mrs E Stieglitz; Mrs R Lipschitz; J A Brunner.*

CC Number 287544

Information available Annual report and accounts, though not in up-to-date form, on file at the Charity Commission.

General The trust's object is 'the promotion of the Orthodox Jewish Faith and the relief of poverty'.

In 2002/03 the trust had assets of £176,000, an income of £22,000 and a total expenditure of £41,000. Neither a grant total or grants list was available on file at the Charity Commission.

Previous grant beneficiaries have included Torah Vemmunah Charity Trust, Torah Vechased Le'ezra Vesad, Beis Yaacov, SOFT, Gur Trust, Emuno Educational Centre Ltd, Ponevez Yeshivah, Friends of Harim Establishments, Friends of Achiezer and Hachnasas Kalloh Fund Aguda.

Applications In writing to the correspondent.

All Saints' Educational Trust

Education, Anglican religious work, home economics

£179,000 to organisations (2001/02)

Beneficial area UK.

St Katherine Cree Church, 86 Leadenhall Street, London EC3A 3DH

Tel. 020 7283 4485 **Fax** 020 7621 9758

Email enquiries@aset.org.uk

Website www.aset.org.uk

Correspondent The Clerk

Trustees *The Rt Revd & Rt Hon. Richard Chartres, Bishop of London, Chair; Revd Prebendary Swan; Mrs M R Behenna; P Chandler; T L Guiver; Revd Canon P Hartley; Dr D W Lankshear; Ms D McCrea; Miss A Philpott; Revd K G Riglin; Mrs A Rose; D Trillo; Ven C Chessun; Mrs B Harvey; J K Hoskin; G King.*

CC Number 312934

Information available Information was provided by the trust.

General This trust was established from the proceeds of the closure of two teacher training colleges in London, one of which worked within a Christian framework and the other of which specialised in domestic science (now home economics and technology). Keeping in line with the former colleges, the trust's objects are advancing higher or further education by:

- allowing individuals to attend a further education institute, or otherwise pursue a course of study to enable them to gain teaching qualifications
- promoting in other ways education and training
- promoting research and development of education, particularly in religious studies and home economics and similar subjects.

It achieves these aims by providing financial assistance to 'institutions that seek to undertake imaginative projects that enhance higher and further education', with the trustees distributing their grants in the way they feel will make the maximum possible difference to the institutions and their respective communities or spheres of influence. (For further information on the grants made to individuals and how to apply, please see *The Educational Grants Directory*, also published by DSC.)

In terms of grants to organisations, the trustees are keen to support proactive projects that promote the development of education, particularly in the areas of religious education, home economics and related areas, such as multi-cultural or inter-faith education. Priority is given to projects where teachers (particularly of religious studies, home economics or related areas) are helped directly or indirectly. Preference is given to 'pump-priming' projects and those which which 'make a difference' through the intrinsic quality of new ideas or approach being put forward, or through the quantity of teachers and/or pupils who will benefit from it.

In 2001/02 the trust had assets totalling £8.7 million (£11 million in 2000/01), which generated an income of £431,000. Grants to 14 organisations totalled £179,000, and to 60 individuals £281,000.

The largest grants were £35,000 each to RSA 'Focus on Food' Campaign for an issue of a new magazine to be distributed free to 28,000 schools in the UK and Association of Church College Trusts for an extension to the RETRI project, and £33,000 to The Patrick V Saxton Fellowship Award for a University of Stirling student to continue her research.

Other large grants went to: The Society for Promoting Christian Knowledge for the final year towards the establishment of a website to provide updated Christian material for use in school assemblies (£15,000); The Wulugu Project for an educational project in Northern Ghana which involved 'twinning' with UK schools and establishing a science curriculum which is relevant to girls in a developing country (£10,000); Guildhall School of Music and Drama for bursary funds to be awarded to two students selected by the school on a postgraduate music therapy course (£9,000); London Diocesan Board for Schools for the final of three grants for a 'Preparation for Headship' course for staff in church schools (£8,600); and Exchange for the continuation of a research and communication network (£8,500).

Smaller grants included those to: Southwark Cathedral Education Trust towards the salary and associated costs of an educational officer (£5,000 for three years); Churches' Action for Racial Equality as the last of three grants to enable research and the preparation of teaching materials on 'holy people of the African diaspora' (£3,000); and Ockenden International to provide textbooks, training materials and other supplies to 240 teachers in Sudan (£2,500).

Exclusions The trust cannot support:

- general or core funds
- public appeals
- school buildings, equipment or supplies
- the establishment of courses or departments in universities or colleges
- general bursary funds.

Applications For applications from organisations (not individuals): applicants are invited to discuss their ideas informally with the clerk before requesting an application form. In some cases, a 'link trustee' is appointed to assist the organisation in preparing the application and who will act in a liaison role with the trust. Completed applications are put before the awards committee in February or May, with final decisions made in June.

The Dorothy Gertrude Allen Memorial Fund

General

£95,000 (2003)

Beneficial area UK.

Teigncombe Barn, Chagford, Devon TQ13 8ET

Tel. 01647 433235

Email dgallen.memorialfund@btinternet.com

Website www.peter.shone.btinternet.co.uk

Correspondent Peter B Shone, Trustee

Trustees *Miss Heather B Allen; Peter B Shone.*

CC Number 290676

Information available Full accounts were provided by the trust.

General Grants range from £1,000 to £5,000 (typically £2,000 to £3,000) and can be recurring or one-off, and for revenue or capital purposes. Priority is given to charities which have been supported in the past. The trust also states that they have no restrictions as to the kinds of project or the areas supported, and are generally prepared to consider any field. Intending applicants should note that organisations that have received grants in the past should not be taken as indicative of a geographical or other bias.

In 2003 it had assets of £687,000 and an income of £99,000. From 643 application, grants were made to 48 organisations totalling £95,000. They were broken down as follows:

Arts – 2 grants totalling £2,000

These were £1,000 each to Petersfield Youth Theatre and Pimlico Opera.

Blindness – 5 grants totalling £7,000
British Blind Sport and National Eye Research Centre each received £2,000, whilst £1,000 each went to Calibre, Cue and Review Recording Service and Talking Newspaper Association.

Carers/elderly – 1 grant of £2,000
This went to Crossroads Caring for Carers.

Children/young people – 7 grants totalling £14,000
The largest grants, of £3,000 each, went to ChildHope UK for work with street children and Rural Youth Trust. Other grants were £2,000 each to Chicks, Children First and National Playbus Association and £1,000 each to Scout Holiday Homes Trust and Sussex Snowdrop Trust.

Disabled – 4 grants totalling £9,000
Beneficiaries were Bath Institute of Medical Engineering and Canine Partners for Independence (£3,000 each), Queen Elizabeth's Foundation for Disabled People (£2,000) and British Amputee and Les Autres Sports Association (£1,000).

Education/schools – 1 grant of £1,000
This went to Farming and Countryside Education.

Environment/wildlife – 11 grants totalling £21,000
The largest were £4,000 to International Otter Survival Fund, £3,000 each to Royal Society for the Protection of Birds and Wildfowl and Wetlands Trust and £2,000 each to Barn Owl Trust, Cornwall Wildlife Trust and Farm Animal Sanctuary. The remaining grants were of £1,000 each.

General community – 5 grants totalling £8,000
These were £2,000 each to Crimestoppers Trust, MedicAlert Foundation and Prisoners Abroad and £1,000 each to National Playing Fields Association and Penrose.

Housing/homelessness – 2 grants totalling £4,000
St Petroc's Society was given £3,000 whilst £1,000 went to St Giles Trust.

Medical conditions/research/ hospitals – 9 grants totalling £21,000

The largest were £5,000 to Blond McIndoe Centre and £3,000 each to British Home and Hospital for Incurables and Rainbow Trust Children's Charity. Other grants were £2,000 each to Royal Hospital for Neuro-disability and Sargent Cancer Care for Children and £1,000 each to Changing Faces, Migraine Trust and Myasthenia Gravis Association.

Overseas aid/international – 3 grants totalling £6,000
These went to Send a Cow for Africa (£3,000), Gurkha Welfare Trust (£2,000) and Britain-Nepal Medical Trust (£1,000).

Exclusions No grants to individuals (including gap-year students) or to organisations which are not UK-registered charities.

Applications In writing to the correspondent, including the latest annual report and accounts. Applications should be received by October for consideration in November/December. Due to an increasing number of appeals (the number rose from 180 in 1996, and over 400 in 2001, to 643 in 2003) the trustees do not acknowledge them. Applicants are contacted usually only when they are successful or where further information is required.

Mrs M H Allen Trust

Military charities

£46,000 (2002/03)

Beneficial area UK.

West Field, Gelt Road, Brampton, Cumbria CA8 1QH

Tel. 01697 72833 **Fax** 01697 72833

Correspondent Col. A F Niekirk, Trustee

Trustees *Col. A F Niekirk; Capt. A P C Niekirk; Maj. W D Niekirk.*

CC Number 211529

Information available Full accounts were provided by the trust.

General The trust can only support military charities or institutions. The trustees currently prefer to support service charities that assist people rather than support buildings or property.

In 2002/03 it had assets of £863,000, which generated an income of £40,000. Grants totalling £46,000 were made to 22 organisations, 13 of which were also supported in the previous year.

The largest grants were £5,000 to a joint appeal by Army Benevolent Fund and Lord Kitchener National Memorial Fund, £4,500 to King Edward VII's Hospital Sister Agnes and £3,000 each to Gurkha Welfare Trust and St David's Nursing Home.

The remaining grants were £2,500 each to British Limbless Ex-Servicemen's Association, Erskine Hospital, Ex-Services Mental Welfare Society for Combat Stress, Gordon Highlanders London Association Benevolent Fund, Royal Star and Garter Home, St Dunstan's, Scottish National Institute for the War Blinded and Scottish Veteran's Residences, £2,000 to SSAFA Forces Help – Cumbria, £1,000 each to Army Museums Ogilby Trust, Broughton House, Ex-Services Fellowship Centres, Gurkha Welfare Trust, League of Rememberance, Royal Northumberland Fusiliers Common Investment Fund, Sandes Soldiers and Sailors Centres and Winged Fellowship and £250 to Army Cadet Force Association.

Exclusions No grants to any non-naval or military charities, individuals, scholarships or education generally.

Applications In writing to the correspondent at any time, preferably on one side of A4.

Angus Allnatt Charitable Foundation

Music and water-based activities for young people

£28,000 (2003)

Beneficial area UK.

c/o 2 The Court, High Street, Harwell, Oxfordshire OX11 0EY

Correspondent Marian Durban, Trustee

Trustees *David Briggs; Rodney Dartnall; Marian Durban; Calton Younger.*

CC Number 1019793

Information available Information was provided by the trust.

General Established in 1993 this trust makes grants to organisations which provide music or water-based activities, such as canoeing or sailing, for young people aged 13 to 25. Grants are usually for between £250 and £1,000, with grants of up to £2,000 in special cases.

In 2003 it had assets of £457,000 and an income of £24,000. Grants were made to

41 organisations totalling £28,000, broken down as follows:

Music – 30 grants totalling £21,000

The largest grants, of £1,000 each, went to Edinburgh Youth Orchestra for a tour, Jackdaws Educational Trusts for a workshop in the schools programme, Oundle International Festival for a bursary fund, Ulster Orchestra for ensemble performances in Belfast schools and Vivace Charitable Trust for four workshops.

Other beneficiaries included Royal Northern College of Music for two full-sized violins (£900), Sounds New for an educational programme (£860), Guildhall School Trust for musical instruments (£600), National Youth Orchestra for a new contra bassoon (£500), Aberdeen International Youth festival for a bursary fund (£400), Hereford International Summer School for the bursary scheme (£350) and Salvation Army for bursaries for young medical students on a residential week (£310).

Water – 11 grants totalling £6,800

Grants of £1,000 each went to 2nd Warwick Sea Scouts for a rescue boat for safety cover and Helensburgh Sea Cadet Unit for a new 4.4 metre rib. Other grants were £750 to UK Atlantic Challenge to prepare and enter the Northern Ireland Gig, £700 each to Endeavour Training for canoeing equipment and Essex Association of Boys' Clubs for a new bell boat, £580 to Chester-le-Street Sea Cadets for a winch, £530 to Nancy Oldfield Trust for a small size Canadian canoe and £500 to Morning Star Trust for refit costs, Reach Out Projects for mooring lighting and Sussex Clubs for Young People for a canoe test.

Exclusions No grants to individuals, and none to organisations which use music or water-based activities primarily for therapeutic or social purposes.

Applications In writing to the correspondent. Trustees meet three times a year to consider applications. The trust has no staff and no telephone. Appeals falling outside the guidelines will not be considered.

The Pat Allsop Charitable Trust

Education, medical research, children, relief of poverty

£65,000 (1998/99)

Beneficial area UK.

c/o Monier Williams & Boxalls, 71 Lincoln's Inn Fields, London WC2A 3JF

Tel. 020 7405 6195 **Fax** 020 7405 1453

Correspondent J P G Randel, Trustee

CC Number 1030950

Information available Full accounts were on file at the Charity Commission, with a detailed narrative report. The trust has historical connections with surveying and estate management.

General A number of educational grants are made each year, e.g. towards research and organising educational events. The founder of the trust was a partner in Allsop & Co. Chartered Surveyors, Auctioneers and Property Managers, therefore the trust favours supporting those educational projects and charities which have connections with surveying and property management professions.

In 2000/01 the trust had an income of £53,000 with an expenditure of £63,000. No further information was available.

In 1998/99 grants were made totalling £65,000. The largest grant was £10,000 to Annigton Trust. Grants of £1,000 or more were made to 17 organisations, including Babes in Arms, Centrepoint, Cottage Homes Charity, Jewish Care, National Schizophrenia Fellowship, Norwood Ravenswood, NSPCC, Sparks and Story of Christmas.

The remaining grants were mostly for less than £500 and the range of organisations was similar to those listed above.

Exclusions No grants to individuals.

Applications In writing to the correspondent, but please note, the trust does not accept unsolicited applications.

The Almond Trust

Christian

£174,000 (2002/03)

Beneficial area UK and worldwide.

19 West Square, London SE11 4SN

Correspondent J L Cooke, Trustee

CC Number 328583

Information available Full accounts were provided by the trust.

General The trust's aims are the support of evangelistic Christian projects, Christian evangelism and the translation, reading, study and teaching of the Bible.

In 2002/03 it had assets of £416,000, which generated an income of £43,000. Grants were made to 15 organisations totalling £174,000. There was a deficit at the end of the year of £131,000. However, in the previous year it had an income of £299,000 and a total expenditure of £220,000, mostly gained through receiving donations of £289,000 (compared to £32,000 in 2002/03). This provides a number of possible reasons for the large deficit in the year, although as no reasons are given in the accounts these can only be speculative.

The largest grants were £50,000 to Christian Youth and Schools Charitable Company, £30,000 to London Institute for Contemporary Christianity, £20,000 each to Haggai Institution and Oasis Trust and £10,000 each to Christians in Sport, St Mary's – Warbleton and Wycliffe Bible Translators.

Other beneficiaries included Agape, Operation Mobilisation, Overseas Missionary Fellowship and St Peter's Trust (£5,000 each), Friends of St Ebbe's Trust (£2,000) and Lawyers' Christian Fellowship (£1,000).

Applications In writing to the correspondent, but please note that the trust states it rarely responds to uninvited applications.

The Almshouse Association

Almshouses

£126,500 (1999)

Beneficial area UK.

Billingbear Lodge, Carters Hill, Wokingham, Berkshire RG40 5RU

Tel. 01344 452922 **Fax** 01344 862062

Email naa@almshouses.org.uk

Correspondent Anthony De Ritter

Trustee *Executive Committee.*

CC Number 245668

Information available Annual report and quarterly Almshouse Gazette.

General The association makes grants and loans to almshouse charities after full advantage has been taken of statutory aid.

In 2003 the trust had an income of £576,000 and a total expenditure of £464,000. Further information for this year was unavailable.

In 1999 grants totalled £126,500 including: £38,000 to Dixon's Almshouses, Christleton (Cheshire); £7,500 to Eight Men of Broadclyst, Devon; £5,200 to Wadham Almshouses, Ilton (Somerset); £5,000 each to Almshouses of Thomas Bell, Kingerby (Lincolnshire), Friskney United Charities (Leicestershire), and Hebden Wright Almshouse Charity, Keighley; £2,500 to Tibbenham Almshouse Charity, Norfolk; and £1,800 to Portsmouth & District Friendly Societies Homes, Milton (Hampshire).

Exclusions No grants to individuals.

Applications In writing to the director at any time.

The Altajir Trust

Islam, education, science and research

£192,000 to organisations (2002)

Beneficial area UK and Arab or Islamic states.

11 Elvaston Place, London SW7 5QG

Tel. 020 7581 3522 **Fax** 020 7584 1977

Correspondent D Haldaney, Director

Trustees *Sir John Moberly, Chair; Peter Tripp; Prof. Alan Jones; Dr Roger Williams; Dr Charles Tripp.*

CC Number 284116

Information available Accounts were on file at the Charity Commission.

General This trust makes grants for the advancement of science, education and research which is beneficial to the community in Britain or any Arab or Islamic state. Support is also given to students at universities in the UK, USA and Bahrain, and conferences and exhibitions are sponsored which promote understanding and the study of Islamic culture and arts throughout the world. Grants are made to both individuals and organisations.

In 2002 the trust had assets of £285,000 and an income of £824,000. Direct charitable expenditure totalled £192,000 of which £74,250 went to welfare, £72,300 on educational grants & scholars, £33,800 on exhibition support, £10,000 on medical aid and £1,160 on travel.

Beneficiaries of these grants were Arab Women's Association (£50,000), York University (£45,000), Trustees of British Museum (£30,000), Dar Al Hekma (£24,000), School of Oriental & African Studies (Research Fellowship) (£20,000), other smaller grants came to £12,500 and finally Medical Aid for Palestine received £10,000.

Applications The trust states that its resources are fully used without receiving applications.

Altamont Ltd

Jewish causes

£100,000 (2002/03)

Beneficial area Worldwide.

18 Green Walk, London NW4 2AJ

Tel. 020 7247 8376

Correspondent David Last

Trustees *D Last; H Last; Mrs H Kon; Mrs S Adler; Mrs G Wiesenfeld.*

CC Number 273971

Information available Accounts on file at the Charity Commission.

General In 2002/03 the trust had an income of £138,000 and made grants totalling £100,000. The beneficiaries were Claimworth Ltd, Fordeve Ltd, Meadowgold Ltd and Naltas Trust whom all received a grant of £25,000.

Applications In writing to the correspondent.

Alvor Charitable Trust

Christian, humanitarian, 'social change'

£180,000 (2002/03)

Beneficial area UK, with a preference for Sussex, Norfolk and north east Scotland.

9 Chequer Grange, Forest Row, East Sussex RH18 5AD

Correspondent I Wilkins, Chair

Trustees *Clive Wills; Mrs Wills; Mark Atherton; Mrs Atherton; I Wilkins; Mrs Wilkins.*

CC Number 1093890

Information available Accounts were on file at the Charity Commission.

General Established in August 2002, this Christian and humanitarian charity predominately supports Christian social change projects in the UK and overseas. A proportion of its target funding goes to local projects around Sussex, Norfolk and north east Scotland where the trust has personal interests. The trust tends to support smaller projects where the grant will meet a specific need. It typically makes one large donation each year (£175,000 in 2003/04) and a number of smaller grants (around £25,000 to £50,000 in 2003/04).

In 2002/03 it had an income of £11,000; it funded three projects with grants totalling £180,000. Assets stood at about £2 million. Towards the end of the financial year 2003/04 it had given around £250,000 to five organisations; beneficiaries included Amos Trust, Care for the Family, Kenward Trust and NSPCC.

Exclusions The trust does not look to support animal charities or medical charities outside of the geographic areas mentioned above.

Applications In writing to the correspondent.

AM Charitable Trust

Jewish, general

£48,000 (2002/03)

Beneficial area UK and overseas.

Kleinwort Benson Trustees Ltd, The Trustees Department, 10 Fenchurch Street, London EC3M 3LB

Tel. 020 7475 5086 **Fax** 020 7475 5558

Correspondent The Secretary

Trustee *Kleinwort Benson Trustees Ltd.*

CC Number 256283

Information available Full accounts were provided by the trust.

General This trust supports a range of causes, particularly Jewish organisations but also medical, welfare, arts and conservation charities. Certain charities are supported for more than one year, although no commitment is usually given to the recipient. Grants range between £50 and £5,000 each, but are mostly of £200 to £400.

In 2002/03 it had assets of £1.6 million and an income of £103,000. Grants were made to 43 organisations totalling £48,000.

Larger donations were £5,000 each to British Friends of Boys' Town Jerusalem, British ORT, Magen David Adom UK, Weizmann Institute Foundation and Youth Aliyah Child Rescue.

Other beneficiaries of grants over £1,000 included Friends of the Hebrew University at Jerusalem (£4,000), Cancer Research UK and West London Synagogue Charitable Fund (£2,500 each), British Heart Foundation and SEM Charitable Trust (£2,000 each) and Blond McIndoe Centre of Medical Research (£1,500).

Beneficiaries of the smaller grants included Ability UK, Academy of Ancient Music, Alcohol Recovery Project, Barkingside Jewish Youth Centre, Bradford Police Club for Young People, Bud Flanagan Leukaemia Fund, Community Drug Project, Contact with the Elderly, Contemporary Dance Trust, Coram Family, Deafblind UK, Disabled Housing Trust, Elizabeth Finn Trust, Flip's Fund, Foundation for the Education of the Underachieving and Dyslexic, Iris Fund, JNF Charitable Trust, KIDS, Leonard Cheshire Foundation, National Music for the Blind, National Trust, Rape Counselling and Research Project, Royal Air Force and Dependants Disabled Holiday Trust, Royal Air Force Association, Royal National Institute for Deaf People, Shelter, St John of Jerusalem Eye Hospital, St Loye's Foundation, UK Friends of AWIS, UK Society for the Protection of Nature in Israel and Visceral.

Exclusions No grants to individuals.

Applications Unsolicited applications are not welcomed. The trust stated that its funds are fully committed and only a small percentage of its income is allocated to new beneficiaries. Only successful applications are notified of the trustees' decision. Trustees meet in March and applications need to be received by January.

Ambika Paul Foundation

Education, young people

£31,000 (2002/03)

Beneficial area UK and India.

Caparo House, 103 Baker Street, London W1U 6LN

Tel. 020 7486 1417

Correspondent Lord Paul

Trustees *Lord Paul; Lady Paul; Hon. Angad Paul; Hon. Anjli Punn.*

CC Number 276127

Information available Full accounts were on file at the Charity Commission.

General The trust supports large organisations, registered charities, colleges and universities benefiting children, young adults and students in the UK and India. Main areas of interest are to do with young people and education. Grants usually range from £100 to £3,000.

In 2002/03 it had an income of £440,000, mostly from donations received. Grants were made totalling £31,000. At the end of the year there was a surplus of £371,000 which was transferred to assets, a similar amount to what was carried over in the previous year.

The largest grants were £11,000 to Jennifer Brown Research Fund, £5,000 each to Leukaemia Research Fund, PiggyBankKids and Shine, £2,000 to Family Services Unit, £1,500 to Shaila Welfare Trust and £1,000 to Asian Women of Achievement. Of these, only Shine was supported in the previous year.

Exclusions Grants are only available to children and young people's charities. No funding for individuals or DSS requests, nor for individuals' salaries/running costs. Applications from individuals, including students, are mainly ineligible. Funding for scholarships are made direct to colleges/universities, not to individuals. No expeditions.

Applications In writing to the trustees at the address above. Acknowledgements are sent if an sae is enclosed. However, the trust has no paid employees and the enormous number of requests it receives creates administrative difficulties.

Sir John & Lady Amory's Charitable Trust

General

£38,000 to organisations (2003/04)

Beneficial area Devon, and elsewhere in the UK.

The Island, Lowman Green, Tiverton, Devon EX16 4LA

Tel. 01884 254 899

Correspondent Lady Heathcoat Amory, Trustee

Trustees *Sir Ian Heathcoat Amory; Lady Heathcoat Amory and William Heathcoat Amory.*

CC Number 203970

Information available Full accounts were provided by the trust.

General In 2003/04 the trust had assets of £1.4 million and an income of £46,000. Grants were made to organisations totalling £38,000, with a further £1,900 paid to individuals. They included £8,000 to National Trust, £3,700 to Blundells School and £3,200 to Relief for the Elderly and Infirm.

Applications In writing to the correspondent.

The Ampelos Trust

General

£86,000 (2001/02)

Beneficial area UK.

9 Trinity Street, Colchester, Essex CO1 1JN

Tel. 01206 544434

Correspondent G W N Stewart, Secretary

Trustees *G W N Stewart; Baroness Rendell of Babergh; A M Witt.*

CC Number 1048778

Information available Accounts were on file at the Charity Commission.

General In 2001/02 the trust had assets of £232,000 and an income of £202,000, mostly made up of a donation of just under £200,000.

Grants totalled £86,000 with beneficiaries including Chester Zoo (£11,000), Institute Trust Fund, RNIB and World Trade Disaster Fund (£10,000 each), Ethiopaid (£7,000), Medical Foundation, Red Cross Afghanistan Appeal, Shelter and Teenage Cancer Trust (£5,000 each) and Macmillan (£2,000).

Applications In writing to the correspondent.

The Anchor Foundation

Christian

About £60,000 (2001/02)

Beneficial area UK.

PO Box 21107, Alloa FK12 5WA

Website www.theanchorfoundation.org.uk

Correspondent The Secretary

Trustees *Prudence Thimbleby; Michael Mitton; Catherine Middleton; Revd Anker-Petersen.*

CC Number 1082485

Information available Information was provided by the foundation.

General The foundation was registered with the Charity Commission in September 2000, it supports Christian charities concerned with social inclusion, particularly through ministries of healing and the arts. The grant range for a project is between £500 and £12,000. It is not the normal practice of the charity to support the same project for more than three years.

In its first year of operation it received capital of £4.9 million. In 2001/02 it had an income of £199,000 and a total expenditure of £62,000; most of this was given in grants. Unfortunately, no examples of beneficiaries were available.

Applications Application forms and information for applicants is available in pdf format on the foundation's website. A copy of the applying organisation's constitution and most recent accounts should be included. Other supporting information, documentation and budgets may also be attached.

Applications are considered at twice yearly trustees' meetings in April and October and need to be received by 28 February or 31 August each year. Please note that incorrectly or partially completed applications will not be considered.

The foundation regrets that applications cannot be acknowledged. Successful applicants will be notified as soon as possible after trustees' meetings.

The Andrew Anderson Trust

Christian, social welfare

£171,000 to organisations (2002/03)

Beneficial area UK and overseas.

84 Uphill Road, Mill Hill, London NW7 4QE

Correspondent The Trustees

Trustees *Miss A A Anderson; Miss M S Anderson; Revd A R Anderson; Mrs M L Anderson.*

CC Number 212170

Information available Full accounts were provided by the trust.

General The trust states in its trustees' report that it provides support to a wide range of charitable causes. Most of its money appears to go to evangelical organisations and churches, but it also makes a large number of small grants to health, disability and social welfare charities.

In 2002/03 it had assets of £6.1 million and an income of £226,000. Grants went to 280 organisations totalling £171,000. A further £33,000 was given in welfare grants and £2,000 to theology students.

The largest grants were £9,000 to Cornhill Training Course, £5,100 to Mission Aviation Fellowship, £5,000 each to Belgian Evangelical Mission, Evangelical Theological College of Wales, Great St Helen's Trust, St Luke's College and Swanage Christian Centre, £3,700 to Latin Link, £3,300 each to Echoes of Service, Universities and Colleges Christian Fellowship and Watford New Hope and £3,000 each to Christian Medical Fellowship and St Giles' Christian Mission.

Other large grants included £2,500 to Armagh Baptist Church, £2,000 to Credit Action, International Student Christian Services and World in Need, £1,600 to John Grooms Association for Disabled People, £1,500 to Proclamation Trust, £1,100 to London Bible School and £1,000 each to Bibles for Children, Grosvenor Road Baptist Church and St Peter's Church – Cape Town.

Most of the grants were for much smaller amounts than these. They included £660 to Retired Missionary Aid Fund, £500 to Medical Missionary News, £450 to Overseas Missionary Fellowship, £420 to Counties Evangelistic Work, £330 to Society for Distributing Hebrew Scriptures, £270 to Slavic Gospel Association, £260 to War on Want, £240 to FEBA Radio, £230 to Moorlands College, £220 to National Autistic Society, £210 to Brain Research Trust, £190 to Motability, £150 to Christian Family Concern, £130 to Activenture and £120 to Rock Foundation.

Exclusions Individuals should not apply for travel or education.

Applications In writing to the correspondent. The trust states 'we prefer to honour existing commitments and initiate new ones through our own contacts rather than respond to applications'.

James and Grace Anderson Trust

Cerebral palsy

£35,000 (2001/02)

Beneficial area UK.

32 Wardie Road, Edinburgh EH5 3LG

Tel. 0131 552 4062 **Fax** 0131 467 1333

Email tim.straton@virgin.net

Correspondent T D Straton, Trustee

Trustees *W A Souter; J Donald; J D M Urquhart; T D Straton.*

SC Number SC004172

Information available Accounts were provided by the trust.

General The trust was established in 1974 and currently funds research with a view to alleviating conditions arising from cerebral palsy. In 2001/02 the trust had assets amounting to £648,000 and an income of £27,000.

During the year the trust continued to support research in gait analysis with a view to alleviating the conditions arising from cerebral palsy.

Grants in the year were £30,000 to Lothian Primary Care NHS Trust towards Gait Analysis Projects, £3,800 to Craighalbert Centre and £1,000 to Bobath Scotland. The sum of £500 was given to an individual for a Bobath Paediatric Course.

Exclusions No grants are made: to individuals who do not have cerebral palsy; to projects not directly related to research into cure or alleviation of cerebral palsy; or as sponsorship of individuals.

Applications In writing to the correspondent. Trustees meet in May and October. Applications should be received by the previous month.

The André Christian Trust

Christian organisations.

£38,000 (2001)

Beneficial area UK.

15 West Hill, Sanderstead, South Croydon, Surrey CR2 0SB

Tel. 020 8657 1207

Correspondent Christopher M Mowll, Secretary to the Trustees

Trustees *Christopher M Mowll; Andrew K Mowll.*

CC Number 248466

Information available Full accounts were on file at the Charity Commission.

General The trust makes grants towards the advancement of Christianity, either through printing and distributing Bible scriptures or through evangelistic work. A number of charities are listed in the trust deed, and they are its principle beneficiaries. Grants appear to mainly be ongoing.

In 2002 the trust had an income of £38,000 with an expenditure of £1,500. No further information was available.

Grants totalled £38,000 in 2001. Larger grants, of £5,000 each, were given to: CARE for the Family, Overseas Missionary Fellowship, Open Air Campaigners (West Country), Scripture Gift Mission, Scripture Union International, Strangers' Rest Mission, and Universities and Colleges Christian Fellowship.

Applications In writing to the correspondent. However, the trust states: 'Applications are discouraged since grants are principally made to those organisations which are listed in the trust deed.' Funds are therefore fully committed and unsolicited requests cannot be supported.

The Anglian Water Trust Fund

Money advice provision/ individuals in need

£152,000 to organisations (2002/ 03)

Beneficial area Anglian Water region (Cambridgeshire, Lincolnshire, Norfolk, Suffolk, Peterborough, Milton Keynes and Hartlepool plus parts of Bedford, Buckinghamshire, Essex, Hertfordshire, Leicestershire, Northamptonshire, and Rutland).

PO Box 42, Peterborough PE3 8XH

Tel. 01733 331177 **Fax** 01733 334344

Email admin@awtf.org.uk

Website www.awtf.org.uk

Correspondent The Trustees

Trustees *Graham Blagden, Chair; Barbara Ruffell; Norman Guffick; Elizabeth Ingram; Stuart de Prochnow; John Sansby; Stephen Harrap; Valerie Mansfield.*

CC Number 1054026

Information available Information was provided by the trust.

General The trust 'exists for the relief of those persons who are in condition of need, poverty, hardship or distress and aims to make a significant and sustainable improvement to quality of life throughout the Anglian and Hartlepool Water regions'.

The trust currently receives an annual grant of £1 million from Anglian Water plc, £12,000 from Tendring Hundred Water and £7,000 from Three Valleys Water.

In 2002/03 grants totalled £876,000, of which £152,000 went to organisations. Beneficiaries included Basildon CAB, Buckingham CAB, Castle Point CAB, Great Yarmouth CAB, Huntingdon Independent Advice Centre, Lowestoft CAB, Mancroft Advice Projects, Norfolk Money Advice, Welfare Rights Advice Service – Northampton and Wymondham CAB.

The trust states that although it has been able to fund organisations wishing to install or improve money audit services, due to its commitment to currently funded projects, coupled with a reduction of available funding, there is no new money available to organisations to fund new projects.

The trust also operates a programme of grants to individuals and families in need, within the beneficial areas, helping them with arears of water/sewerage charges, other priority bills and the purchase of essential household items. In 2002/03 grants to individuals and families totalled £724,000.

Exclusions No grants for: fines for criminal offences; educational or training needs; debts to central government departments; medical equipment, aids and adaptations; holidays; business debts; catalogues; credit cards; personal loans; deposits for secure accommodation; or overpayment of benefits.

Applications Organisational grants: no applications from organisations can be considered due to commitments to individuals and families. Up-to-date information can be found on the trust's website. Individual grants: applications can be submitted throughout the year. Applications must be made on a standard application form which can be obtained from local advice centres such as citizen's advice bureaux or by writing to the trust.

Anglo-German Foundation for the Study of Industrial Society

Academics and research workers

£275,000 (2003)

Beneficial area UK and Germany.

34 Belgrave Square, London SW1 8DZ
Tel. 020 7823 1123 **Fax** 020 7823 2324
Email info@agf.org.uk
Website www.agf.org.uk
Correspondent Dr Ray Cunningham, Director

Trustees *Bryan Rigby, Chair; Lord Croham; Simon Broadbent; Prof. Dorothy Wedderburn; Prof. Robert Leicht; Prof. Dr Anita B Pfaff; Dr Jürgen Ruhfus; Prof. Dr Carl-Christian von Weizsacker; John Edmonds; Dr Erika Mezger; Peter von Siemens; Dr Andrew Sentence; Dr Jurgen Oesterhelt.*

CC Number 266844

Information available Publication list available on request.

General Currently, the trust's priority areas are: research/meetings concerned with employment and unemployment; public spending and taxation; the future of the welfare state; adjustment to European and global economic change; the environment. Strong preference is given to binational (British-German) comparisons.

In 2003 the trust had assets of just under £7 million and an income of £22,000. The trust awarded 35 grants totalling £275,000. Beneficiaries included the following projects: The Search for Solutions: Policy Learning in Britain and Germany (Ango-German Foundation), Employment and Social Policies for an Ageing Society (University Dortmund and University of Sheffield), Employment, Wage Structure and Economic Cycle: Differences between immigrants and natives (Institution for Employment Research Nurnberg and University College London), Labour Market Policies for Older Workers (University Dortmund and University of Cambridge), Reconciling Demand for Labour Migration with Public Concerns about Immigration (Hamburgisches Welt-Wirtschafts-Archiv and Royal Institute of International Affairs) and Is it easier to be a Turk in Berlin or a Pakistani in Bradford? (The Times and Der Tagesspiegel).

Exclusions The Foundation does not provide grants of any kind for undergraduate or postgraduate study or fund academic posts, or pay overheads.

Applications In the first instance by letter. Two page outline required before the formal application is submitted.

The Animal Defence Trust

Animal welfare

£82,000 (2000/01)

Beneficial area UK.

PO Box 44, Plymouth, Devon PL7 5YW
Tel. 01295 811888
Email ba@kingssuttonfreeserve.co.uk
Correspondent The Trustees

Trustees *Marion Saunders; Alan A Meyer; Vivien McIrvine; Carole Bowles; Paddy Newton.*

CC Number 263095

Information available Accounts were on file at the Charity Commission.

General The trust makes grants for capital projects purely to animal welfare charities. In 2000/01 it had assets totalling £1.5 million and an income of £52,000, including £21,000 from donations and legacies. Grants were made to 27 organisations, including 16 that have previously been supported, totalling £82,000.

Grants of £6,000 each were made to Celia Hammond Animal Trust, International League for the Protection of Horses – Glenda Spooner Farm, Ferne Animal Sanctuary and Thoroughbred Rehabilitation Centre. Other beneficiaries included Society for the Welfare of Horses and Ponies (£4,000), Dartmoor Livestock Protection Society, Brooke Hospital for Animals, Cat Abuse Treatment Society, International Otter Foundation, People and Dogs Society and Essex Horse and Pony Protection Society (£2,500), Devon Horse and Pony Sanctuary (£2,000), Prevent Unwanted Pups (£1,500) and Birmingham Dogs Home (£500).

Exclusions No grants to individuals.

Applications In writing to the correspondent.

The Eric Anker-Petersen Charity

Conservation of classic films, theatre

£65,000 (2001/02)

Beneficial area UK.

8–10 New Fetter Lane, London EC4A 1RS
Tel. 020 7203 5000
Correspondent D E Long

Trustees *George Lindsay Duncan; Eric Anker-Petersen; Shan Warnock-Smith; David Eric Long.*

CC Number 1061428

Information available Full accounts were on file at the Charity Commission.

General The trust makes grants mostly towards the conservation of classic films. It will only consider grants to charitable causes in the fields of screen and stage.

In 2001/02 it had assets of £792,000 and an income of £15,000 (after adjusting for the costs of generating these funds). The management and administration fees totalled £20,000, which means the trust is costing more to operate than it receives in income. This is a particularly worrying situation as these fees are paid to firms in which trustees are partners. Whilst wholly legal, these editors always regret such payments unless, in the words of the Charity Commission, 'there is no realistic alternative'.

Five grants were made totalling £65,000. Four of these were for projects at the Imperial War Museum, namely the films *The British Atomic Trials at Maralinga* (£24,000), *Everybody's Business* (£14,000) and *The Women's Portion* (£5,500) and the book *This Film is Dangerous* (£15,000). The other grant was £6,000 to Theatrical Ladies Guild for running costs.

Exclusions No grants to individuals or for non-charitable purposes.

Applications In writing to the correspondent. The trust has previously wished to emphasise that it is always looking for projects to support which meet its criteria, outlined above. However, it replied to our request for information with a standard letter rejecting our application for assistance; hopefully real appeals will be read more attentively.

The Annandale Charitable Trust

Major UK charities

£47,000 (2001/2002)

Beneficial area UK.

HSBC Trust Services, Norwich House, Nelson Gate, Commercial Road, Southampton SO15 1GX

Tel. 023 8072 2244

Correspondent A T Fryers, Trust Officer

Trustees *Mrs S M Blofeld; Mrs A Lee; HSBC Trust Company (UK) Ltd.*

CC Number 1049193

Information available Accounts on file at Charity Commission.

General The trust supports a range of major UK charities. In 2001/02 the trust had an income of £93,000 and made grants totalling £47,000.

Beneficiaries included Oxfam (£11,000), British Red Cross and Mossburn Animal Sanctuary (£5,000 each), Motor Neurone Disease (£4,000), ILPH and Southern Africa Crisis Appeal (£3,000 each) and Macmillan Nurses, NSPCC, Save the Children Fund and Victim Support (£2,000 each).

Applications In writing to the correspondent. The trust stated that it has an ongoing programme of funding for specific charities and all its funds are fully committed.

Apple Charity (UK) Ltd

General

£378,000 (2000/01)

Beneficial area UK.

27 Ovington Square, London SW3 1LJ

Tel. 020 7761 9600 **Fax** 020 7225 0661

Correspondent N S Aspinall, Trustee/ Director

Trustees *N S Aspinall; B M Capocciama; S Tenenbaum.*

CC Number 1067560

Information available Accounts were on file at the Charity Commission.

General Established in 1998 this charity is a company limited by guarantee. In 2000/01 it had assets of £685,000 and an income of £150,000. Grants to four organisations totalled £378,000, three of these were based in the UK: UK Garland Appeal (£120,000); Lotus Foundation (£118,000); and Leander Trust (£20,000). A US-based organisation, Memorial Sloan-Kettering Cancer Centre received the fourth and final grant of £120,000.

Applications In writing to the correspondent.

The Appletree Trust

Disability, sickness, poverty

£30,000 (2003)

Beneficial area UK and overseas, with a preference for Scotland and the north east Fife district.

Royal Bank of Scotland plc, Private Trust & Taxation, 2 Festival Square, Edinburgh EH3 9SU

Tel. 0131 523 2648 **Fax** 0131 228 9889

Correspondent Eileen Kidd

Trustees *The Royal Bank of Scotland plc; Revd W McKane; Revd Dr J D Martin; Revd L R Brown.*

SC Number SC004851

Information available Information was provided by the trust.

General This trust was established in the will of the late William Brown Moncour in 1982 to relieve disability, sickness and poverty. The settlor recommended that Action Research for the Crippled Child, British Heart Foundation and National Society for Cancer Relief should receive funding from his trust, particularly for their work in the north east Fife district.

In 2003 the trust had an income of £60,000 and made grants totalling £30,000. Large grants were made to Home-Start (£6,000) and British Heart Foundation, Children's Hospice Association, Marie Curie Cancer Care and Rymonth Housing Association (£5,000 each). Other beneficiaries included Arthritis Care – Scotland (£2,400), Prince's Trust (£2,100) and British Wireless for the Blind (£2,000).

Exclusions No grants to individuals.

Applications In writing to the correspondent. Trustees meet to consider grants in April.

The John Apthorp Charitable Trust

General

£29,000 (2003/04)

Beneficial area UK, with an interest in Greater London.

BDO Stoy Hayward, 8 Baker Street, London W1U 3LL

Tel. 020 7486 5888

Correspondent The Trustees Accountant

Trustees *John Dorrington Apthorp; Dr D Arnold.*

CC Number 289713

Information available Accounts were provided by the trust.

General The trust was established by its eponymous settlor in 1983. In 2003/04 it had assets of £6,600 had an income of £32,000. Grants totalled £29,000. Beneficiaries were Tay Foundation (£10,000), Radlett Choral Society and Radlett Music Club (£5,000 each), Radlett Art Society (£4,000), Radlett Rotary Club (£1,800), Citizens Advice in Hertsmere, Rotary Club of Elstree and Borehamwood (£1,000 each) and De Morgan Centre (£300).

Applications Unsolicited appeals are not welcome and will not be answered. The trustees carry out their own research into prospective grant areas.

The Archbishop of Canterbury's Charitable Trust

Christianity, welfare

£336,000 to individuals and organisations (2002)

Beneficial area Worldwide.

1 The Sanctuary, Westminster, London SW1P 3JT

Tel. 020 7222 5381

Correspondent P F B Beesley, Registrar

Trustees *Archbishop of Canterbury; Miss Sheila Cameron; Rt Revd Richard Llewellin; Jeremy Harris.*

CC Number 287967

Information available Accounts were on file at the Charity Commission.

General This trust was established in 1983 by the former Archbishop of Canterbury, Lord Runcie, to advance the Christian religion and Christian education, in particular the objects and principles of the Church of England, as well as supporting individuals working towards these goals. The trust deed states that trustees should hold particular interest towards:

- people training for the ministry and church work
- ministers, teachers and the church workers who are in need, and their dependants
- the extension of education in, and knowledge of, the faith and practice of the Church of England
- the development of work of any church, union of churches, denominations or sects which will further the Christian religion generally.

A proportion of the trust's funds are distributed through the Archbishop of Canterbury Trinity Church Fund, which can give support worldwide to Anglican projects at the discretion of the Archbishop of Canterbury. However, the correspondent states that there is much call on these funds and therefore the success rate of applications is very small.

There are also three smaller, restricted funds which are administered as part of this trust. The Michael Ramsey Chair Fund finances the Michael Ramsey Chair in Anglican and Ecumenical Theology at the University of Kent. Dick and Sheila Stallard Fund supports church-related work in China and the Far East, rarely supporting work in the Middle East. Living Memory Rogers Harrison Lozo Relief Fund supports British-born retired Anglican bishops and priests, and their wives and widows living in England, as well as supporting people who are poor, blind, elderly or disabled in Greater London.

In 2002 the trust had assets of £1.7 million. The total income was £268,000, including £198,000 in donations received. After low management and administration expenses of £7,000, grants were made totalling £336,000 and were broken down as follows.

General fund	£326,000
Dick and Sheila Stallard Fund	£6,000
Living Memory Rogers Harrison Lozo Relief Fund	£2,500
The Michael Ramsey Chair Fund	£1,400

Beneficiaries included Coventry Cathedral (£26,000), Aid Relief for Projects in the Congo and Diocese of Bukava – Congo (£17,000), Christchurch – Conneticut (£16,000), Malawi Famine (£14,000), Diocese of Burundi and Norwich Cathedral (£10,000 each), Diocese of Ghana (£9,500), Christian Muslim Listening (£8,000), Dagenham Parish Church (£7,000), Anglican Council UN Observer (£5,000), St Andrew's Ecumenical (£4,500), Anglican Renewal Ministries (£3,000), St John's College and Tantur Ecumenical Centre (£2,000 each) and Decade Evangelism (£1,000).

Applications Funds are allocated for several years ahead, therefore no new applications can be considered.

The John M Archer Charitable Trust

General charitable purposes.

£33,000 (2003/04)

Beneficial area UK and overseas.

12 Broughton Place, Edinburgh EH1 3RX

Tel. 0131 556 4518

Correspondent Mrs Elizabeth Grant, Secretary

Trustees *G B Archer; Mrs I Morrison; Mrs A Morgan; Mrs W Grant; Mrs C Fraser; Mrs I C Smith.*

SC Number SC010583

Information available Full accounts were available from the trust.

General The trust supports local, national and international organisations, in particular those concerned with:

- prevention or relief of individuals in need
- welfare of people who are sick, distressed or afflicted
- alleviation of need
- advancement of education
- advancement of religious or missionary work
- advancement of medical or scientific research and discovery
- preservation of Scottish heritage and the advancement of associated cultural activities.

In 2003/04 the trust had assets of £659,000 and an income of £49,000 with 145 grants made totalling £33,000.

Included among the donations during the year were £5,000 to The Usher Hall Conservation Trust, £3,000 to the Merchants' Trust for university student bursaries, £2,500 each to Castlebrae School Entrepreneurial Spirit Project and Royal Liverpool University Hospital for macular degeneration research, £2,000 to Mercy Corps Scotland and £1,500 to Castlebrae School Tutoring Programme. No other donations exceeded £1,000.

Applications In writing to the correspondent.

The Ardwick Trust

Jewish, welfare, general

£203,000 (2001/02)

Beneficial area UK, Israel and the developing world.

c/o Knox Cropper, 24 Petworth Road, Haslemere, Surrey GU27 2HR

Correspondent Janet Bloch, Trustee

Trustees *Mrs J B Bloch; Dominic Flynn; Miss Judith Portrait.*

CC Number 266981

Information available Full accounts were on file at the Charity Commission.

General The trust supports Jewish welfare, along with a wide band of non-Jewish causes to include social welfare, health, education (especially special schools), older people, conservation and the environment, child welfare, disability and medical research. Although the largest grants made by the trust are to Jewish organisations, the majority of recipients are non-Jewish.

In 2001/02 it had assets of £839,000 and an income of £110,000. Grants were made to 195 organisations. Despite the large number of grants made, the management and administration charges were low at just £3,700. However, this included a payment of £750 plus VAT to a firm of solicitors in which one of the trustees is a partner. Whilst wholly legal, these editors always regret such payments unless, in the words of the Charity Commission, 'there is no realistic alternative'.

The main beneficiary, as in recent years, was Nightgale House which received three grants totalling £165,000. These were for the refurbishment of the first floor of one of its buildings (£150,000), an Alzheimer's wing (£10,000) and the Howard Bloch Training Fund (£5,000).

The next largest grants were £2,000 each to Jewish Care and World Jewish Relief and £1,000 each to British Sjorgens Syndrome Association, British Technion Society, Friends of the Hebrew University in Jerusalem, Headway, Norwood, United Jewish Appeal and Weizmann Institute Foundation.

The remaining grants consisted of 10 of £500 each, 3 of £250 each, 32 of £200 each and 140 of £100 each; there was no noticable pattern amongst which organisations received larger amounts and which received smaller. Beneficiaries included Action on Elder Abuse, Age Concern, Beth Shalom Holocaust Memorial Centre, British Heart Foundation, British Ski Club for the Disabled, Farm Africa, Galapagos Conservation Trust, Institute for Jewish Policy Research, Jewish Child's Day, Jubilee Sailing Trust, Magen David Amon UK, National Back Pain Association, North London Hospice, Ockenden International, Royal British Legion, SSAFA Forces Help, Toynbee Hall, World Emergency Fund, World Medical Fund and Youth Aliyah.

Exclusions No grants to individuals.

Applications In writing to the correspondent.

Armenian General Benevolent Union London Trust

Armenian education, culture and welfare

£108,000 (2002)

Beneficial area UK and overseas.

Armenian House, 25 Cheniston Gardens, London W8 6TG

Tel. 0207 964 5386

Correspondent The Chair

Trustees *G S Kurkjian; L Simone; B Setrakian; A R E Topalian; H Hamparzounian; S Pattie; H Aghajanian.*

CC Number 282070

Information available Information was provided by the trust.

General The purpose of the trust is to advance education among Armenians, particularly those in the UK, and to promote the study of Armenian history, literature, language, culture and religion. The trustees may:

(a) provide grants and scholarships to needy students

(b) assist other Armenian institutions which are registered as exclusively charitable institutions

(c) establish charitable schools and provide facilities for the physical education of those people attending such schools

(d) establish charitable educational institutes, cultural centres and clinics, and other medical institutions, and provide assistance in the running of such institutions.

In 2002 it had assets of almost £2.5 million and an income of £164,000. Grants were made to organisations totalling £108,000 broken down as follows: £38,000 as student loans and grants; £28,000 for humanitarian and medical aid to Armenia; £4,900 for Armenian culture; £3,900 to AGBU London Branch; £1,300 to CAIA Elderly Persons' Activities; and £1,000 to Armenian House London. A further £35,000 went to individuals in need.

Exclusions No support for projects of a commercial nature or for education for individual students.

Applications In writing to the correspondent. Applications are considered all year around.

The Armourers and Brasiers' Gauntlet Trust

Organisations benefiting young adults, academics, research workers and students; general

£175,000 (2003)

Beneficial area UK, with some preference for London.

Armourers' Hall, 81 Coleman Street, London EC2R 5BJ

Tel. 020 7374 4000 **Fax** 202 7606 7481

Correspondent The Secretary

Trustees *Ven. C J H Wagstaff, Chair; Revd P E de D Warburton; R A Crabb; R N Lay; A M R Pontifex; J H Chatfield-Roberts.*

CC Number 279204

Information available Full accounts were provided by the trust.

General The trust, which provides the charitable outlet for the Worshipful Company of Armourers and Brasiers, was set up in 1979. Three-quarters of charitable giving is directed towards materials science education, supporting students and also teachers. The remaining funds are therefore quite limited and are directed towards 'people' rather than 'things', with the emphasis on youth and community projects. Grants are given in single payments, not on an ongoing basis. However organisations can still apply for grants each year.

In 2003 the trust had assets of £4 million and an income of £322,000, including £123,000 in donations received. Grants totalling £175,000 were broken down as follows:

Armourers' Alcan Scheme - 13 grants totalling £55,000

Beneficiaries at school level received £6,400, at undergraduate level £42,000 and at research student level £6,300.

Armourers' Corus Scheme - 7 grants totalling £20,000

Beneficiaries at school level received £7,500, at undergraduate level £6,500 and at research student level £5,970.

Charitable grants towards materials sciences (excluding both above schemes) – 46 grants totalling £51,000

Beneficiaries at school level received £18,000, at undergraduate level £12,000, at research student level £9,000 and other awards £12,000.

Armed services: prizes – 4 grants totalling £700

Beneficiaries included Royal Air Force and Royal Navy (£200 each).

Armed services: grants – 3 grants totalling £700

£300 each went to Inns of Court & City Yeomanry and VC & GC Association and £100 to Alexander Forsyth Award.

Children/Youth – 2 grants totalling £4,300

STA received £3,300 for voyages and £1,000 to Lord Mayor's Appeal.

Community and Social Care – 26 grants totalling £10,000

The largest grants were £750 each to St Botolph's Project and Tower Hamlets

Mission. Other grants included £500 each to 3H Fund, Church Housing Trust, Dolphin Society, Family Holiday Association, Listening Books, St Giles Trust, St Martin-in-the-Fields, Support Dogs and The Police Rehabilitation Trust.

Children/youth – 24 grants totalling £13,000

These included Boys' Brigade, Spitalfield City Farm, Foyer Federation, Hornsey Trust and Westminster Children's Society (£500 each). Other beneficiaries were Freightliners City Farm, Cardinal Hulme Centre and Matthew Trust (£400 each) and DELTA and Epping Forest Centenary Trust (£300 each).

Medical/health – 21 grants totalling £9,000

These included £800 each to Helen Arkell Dyslexia Centre and Mental Aid Projects. Other beneficiaries were Action for Tinnitus Research (£700), Marfan Association UK (£600) and Alzheimer's Research Trust, Mental Aid Projects, Miscarriage Association, Rehab UK, Link Centre for Deafened People and Tuberous Sclerosis Association (£500 each).

The Arts – 6 grants totalling £2,000

These included Guildhall School Trust, Churchill Memorial – Missouri (£500 each) and Guild Church of St Katherine Cree and London Festival of Chamber Music (£250 each).

Arms and armour – 1 grant of £1,000

This went to an individual for research.

Armed forces – 6 grants totalling £2,500

Beneficiaries were the Victoria Cross Memorial Appeal (£700), British Commonwealth Ex-Services personnel and Gurkha Welfare Trust (£500 each), Broughton House Home for Ex-Services Personnel, Sailors' Families' Society (£250 each) and Honourable Artillery Company (£200).

Christian Mission – 3 grants totalling £2,000

Recipients were the Spire Trust (£1,000) and St Margaret's Church, Thornbury and Felsted School Mission (£500 each).

Exclusions In general grants are not made to:

- organisations or groups which are not registered
- individuals
- organisations or groups whose main object is to fund or support other charitable bodies which are in direct relief of any reduction of financial support from public funds
- charities with a turnover of over £4 million
- charities which spend over 10% of their income on fundraising activities
- organisations whose accounts disclose substantial financial reserves.

Nor towards general maintenance, repair or restoration of buildings, including ecclesiastical buildings, unless there is a long standing connection with the Armourers and Brasiers' Company or unless of outstanding importance to the national heritage.

Applications In writing to the correspondent, with a copy of the latest annual report and audited accounts. Applications are considered quarterly.

The Artemis Charitable Trust

Psychotherapy, parent education, and related activities

£513,000 to institutions (2001/02)

Beneficial area UK.

Brook House, Quay Meadow, Bosham, West Sussex PO18 8LY

Tel. 01243 573475

Correspondent Richard Evans, Trustee

Trustees *Richard Evans; Joyce Gai Evans.*

CC Number 291328

Information available Annual report and accounts were provided by the trust.

General The trust was set up in 1985 by Richard and Gail Evans to make 'grants to aid the provision of counselling, psychotherapy, parenting, human relationship training and related activities'. They do this, on the whole, proactively, seeking out organisations and programmes to which they give long-term support. Only two or three grants to new beneficiaries are awarded each year, usually for less than £5,000, but they can be for more than £200,000 if made to an organisation working in the trust's specialised field of counselling, psychotherapy or parenting.

The trust categorised its grants as follows:

	2001/02	*1999/2000*
Research	£166,000	£148,000
Social welfare	£347,000	£386,000

The largest grants went to the following organisations, which all receive funding on an annual basis:

	2001/02	*1999/2000*
Counselling in Primary Care Trust	£206,000	£140,000
Metanoia Institute	£166,000	£140,000
Parents in Partnership (for Parent Infant Network)	£84,000	£111,000

All grants for over £1,000 were listed, and only two of the recipients had not received grants the previous year. These new recipients were WPF Counselling (£5,000) and Core Systems Trust (£2,000). The trust's annual report noted that it 'continued to provide resources for the Parenting Education and Support Forum which arose out of the International Year of the Family'.

Applications The trust can only give grants to registered charities. 'We cannot entertain applications either from individuals or from organisations which are not registered charities. Applicants should also be aware that most of the trust's funds are committed to a number of major ongoing projects and that spare funds available to meet new applications are very limited.'

The Arup Foundation

Construction – education and research

£213,000 (2002/03)

Beneficial area Unrestricted

13 Fitzroy Street, London W1T 4BQ

Tel. 020 7755 3298

Website www.theovearupfoundation.com

Correspondent The Trustees

Trustees *M Shears; D Michael; R F Emmerson; R B Haryott; C Cole; R Hough; T O'Brien; R Yau.*

CC Number 328138

Information available Full accounts were provided by the trust

General The trust was established in 1989 with the principal objective of supporting education in matters associated with the built environment, including construction-related academic research. The trustees are appointed by the board of the Ove Arup Partnership. It gives grants for research and projects, including start-up and feasibility costs.

In 2002/03 the foundation had assets of £1.8 million and an income of £33,000. Grants were made to 18 organisations totalling £213,000.

The largest grants were £88,000 to University of Hong Kong and £50,000 to London School of Economics. Other recipients included University of London (£28,000), Imperial College (£25,000), Barbican Education and Foundation for Art & Creative Technology (£5,000), XL Wales (£4,000), Royal Institute of British Architects and Space Link Learning Foundation (£2,000 each) and The New Wells Initiative (£1,500).

Exclusions No grants to individuals, including students.

Applications In writing to the correspondent, with brief supporting financial information. Trustees meet quarterly to consider applications (March, June, September and December).

The AS Charitable Trust

Chrisitan, development, social concern

£41,000 (2000/01)

Beneficial area UK and developing countries.

Bixbottom Farm, Bix, Henley-on-Thames RG9 6BH

Tel. 01491 577745

Correspondent The Administrator

Trustees *R Calvocoressi; C W Brocklebank.*

CC Number 242190

Information available Full accounts were on file at the Charity Commission.

General This trust makes grants in particular to projects which combine the advancement of the Christian religion, with Christian lay leadership, with third world development, with peacemaking and reconciliation or with other areas of social concern.

In 2001/02 the trust had an income of £174,000 with an expenditure of £61,000. No further information was available.

Grants were made totalling £41,000 in 2000/01. The largest grant was £30,000 to Christian International Peace Service. A grant of £1,500 went to War on Want with £1,100 each going to Barnabas Fund and St Matthew Housing. The remaining four grants were of £1,000 each and went to Christian Engineers in Development, Corrymeela Community, St Michael's Church – Chester Square and Traidcraft Exchange.

Exclusions Grants to individuals or large charities are very rare. Such applications are discouraged.

Applications In writing to the correspondent.

Ashburnham Thanksgiving Trust

Christian

£67,000 to organisations and individuals (2002/03)

Beneficial area UK and worldwide.

Agmerhurst House, Ashburnham, Battle, East Sussex TN33 9NB

Tel. 01424 892253

Email att@lookingforward.biz

Correspondent The Trustees

Trustees *Mrs M Bickersteth; Mrs E M Habershon; E R Bickersteth; R D Bickersteth.*

CC Number 249109

Information available Full accounts were on file at the Charity Commission.

General The trust supports a wide range of Christian mission organisations and other Christian organisations which are known to the trustees, in the UK and worldwide. Individuals are also supported.

In 2002/03 the trust's assets, including properties owned, totalled £4.8 million, and generated an income of £141,000. A total of £67,000 was distributed, of which £48,000 went to organisations. Further monies were distributed in restricted grants and grants to individuals.

The largest grants were £3,000 to Genesis Arts Trust, £2,300 to Ashburnham and Penhurst Churches, £2,000 to Christian Overseas Service Trust, £1,500 each to Open Doors and Wycliffe Bible Translators, £1,400 to Interserve, £1,100 to Overseas Mission Fellowship and £1,000 each to Lawrence Barham Memorial Trust, Release International, Stewards Trust, Titus Trust and Youth With A Mission.

Smaller grants included The Micah Trust (£900), St Stephen's Society (£800), International Nepal Fellowship (£510), Christian Renewal Centre (£400), Edinburgh Medical Missionary Society (£240) and United Christian Broadcasters (£200).

Exclusions No grants for buildings.

Applications By e-mail only; potential applicants should not send anything by post. The trust has stated that its funds are fully committed to current beneficiaries. Unfortunately it receives far more applications than it is able to deal with.

The Ashby Charitable Trust

Medical research, education, business start-up/expansion

£32,000 (2001/02)

Beneficial area Derbyshire or with a Derbyshire connection.

c/o The Old Vicarage, 226 Ashbourne Road, Turnditch, Belper, Derbyshire DE56 2LH

Correspondent B A Ashby

Trustees *Brian Ashby, Chair; Mrs I Ashby; D R Ashby; C Clements.*

CC Number 276497

Information available Accounts were on file at the Charity Commission.

General Grants are made to individuals and organisations. With regard to both, particular emphasis is placed on a connection with Derbyshire.

In particular, the trust funds:

- educational awards to educational establishments and to individuals, especially to mature students ineligible for state support
- other registered charities to fund research or help for people with cancer, leukaemia, heart disease, multiple sclerosis or spina bifida.

In 2001/02 the trust's income was £109,000 and it made grants totalling £32,000. Assets totalled £783,000 at the year end.

Grants included 'sponsorship of the employment costs of Derbyshire Community Foundation' – an ongoing beneficiary. Short-term loans were made to young entrepreneurs through the

Derbyshire branch of The Prince's Youth Business Trust.

Applications In writing to the correspondent. Applications are considered throughout the year.

A J H Ashby Will Trust

Birds, wildlife, education and children

£73,000 (2002)

Beneficial area UK, especially Lea Valley area of Hertfordshire.

HSBC Trust Company (UK) Ltd – Trust Services, Norwich House, Nelson Gate, Commercial Road, Southampton, Hampshire SO15 1GX

Tel. 023 8072 2243

Correspondent S J Gladwell, Trust Manager

CC Number 803291

Information available Accounts were on file at the Charity Commission.

General The trust was established in 1990 to support birds and wildlife throughout the UK, as well as education projects and young people specifically in the Lea Valley area of Hertfordshire.

In 2002 it had assets of £1.3 million and an income of £73,000. Grants totalled £73,000. Previous recipients of support include Brookland School, Goffs Oak Junior Mixed Infant and Nursery School, Rolelands Primary School, RSPB, St Michaels Church of England School and Victim Support.

Exclusions No grants to individuals or students.

Applications In writing to the correspondent.

The Ashe Park Charitable Trust

Possible preference for child-related hospitals and hospices.

£159,000 (2001)

Beneficial area UK, with a possible preference for Hampshire, Isle of Wight and West Sussex.

Ashe Park, Steventon, Basingstoke, Hampshire RG25 3AZ

Tel. 01256 771689

Correspondent Mrs Jan Scott

Trustees *P J Scott; Mrs J M T Scott.*

CC Number 297647

Information available Accounts were on file at the Charity Commission.

General In 2002 the trust had an income of £58,000 and a total expenditure of £56,000. Further information for this year was not available.

Previous information gathered stated in 2001 the trust generated an income of £289,000, mainly derived from fundraising events, including £118,000 from the value of donated goods to auction, £93,000 from ticket sales and £35,000 from sponsorships. After fundraising costs of £147,000, four grants were made to the following beneficiaries: Prince's Foundation Trust (£75,000); Chase Children's Hospice Services (£69,000); Winchester Theatre Fund (£15,000); and Get Kids Going Local Charity (£250).

Exclusions No funding towards salaries.

Applications In writing to the correspondent.

The Laura Ashley Foundation

Art and design, higher education, local projects in mid-rural Wales

£211,000 to organisations (2002/03)

Beneficial area Mostly Wales, other areas considered.

3 Cromwell Place, London SW7 2JE

Tel. 020 7581 4662 **Fax** 020 7584 3617

Email jane@laf.uk.net

Website www.laf.uk.net

Correspondent Jane Ashley

Trustees *Jane Ashley, Chair; Prof. Susan Golombok; Martyn C Gowar; Martin Jones; Emma Shuckburgh; Marquis of Queensbury; Helena Appio.*

CC Number 288099

Information available Information was provided by the trust.

General The foundation was set up in 1986 in memory of Laura Ashley by her family. It has a strong commitment to art and design and also to Wales, particularly Powys, where the Ashley business was first established.

The foundation is constantly reviewing its funding policies. Potential applicants are advised to check the website for the latest details and recent grants made.

The main areas of activity are:

Projects in mid-rural Wales

- to enhance the lives of families and communities
- rural regeneration
- adult education
- music or art & design projects.

Education

Special bursaries have been set up through institutions of the trustees' choice:

- music conservatoires – bursaries for talented musicians
- LSE – scholarship for a mature anthropology MA student
- Royal College of Art – scholarship for mature textile student.

The Arts in London

A pilot project set up by Jane Ashley called SLATE – a network of documentary film makers to encourage wider use of their talents.

In 2002/03 the trust had an income from investments of £295,000. Grants to 35 organisations totalled £211,000.

Donations in 2003/04 included: £15,000 to Montgomeryshire Crossroads to fund their short breaks respite care; £10,000 each to Beacon of Hope, Aberystwyth towards their respite care and Over the Wall Gang Camps to provide holidays for children with or recovering from serious illness or injury; £7,000 to Awards for Young Musicians to provide bursaries for Welsh students; £5,400 to Music in Hospitals to provide a programme of concerts in Powys; £5,000 each to National Eisteddfod to commission an artwork in memory of Iorwerth Peate, founder of the Welsh Folk Museum, St Fagan's and Llanfyllin Music Festival towards costs; £4,000 to South Montgomery Volunteer Bureau towards programme costs; £3,500 to Hafan Day Centre, Rhayader towards programme costs; £3,000 to Green Man Festival; £2,500 to Radnorshire Wildlife Trust towards their Education Programme; £2,000 each to Opera School Wales towards scholarship fund and Volunteering in Powys towards costs; and £430 to Tower Art Group Brecon to pay their venue rent.

Exclusions The foundation does not fund the following:

- individuals
- new buildings
- medical research
- overseas travel/exchange visits
- private education
- purchase cost of property/land
- restoration of historic buildings or churches
- university or similar research
- projects concerned with domestic violence
- penal affairs
- sport
- youth clubs/projects concerned with 'youth at risk'
- general funds
- taking projects into schools
- outward bound type courses
- newspapers/journals/publications/ information packs
- video projects
- safety devices
- theatre, dances, shows/touring
- internet-related projects.

Applications Potential applicants are encouraged to telephone the trust to discuss eligibility before submitting an application. An initial application should be made in writing to the correspondent. It should include a summary of your activities and work, outline the actual project and for what specific purpose the grant is required and what funds have already been raised. It should be typed on one side of headed note paper.

The Ashworth Charitable Trust

Welfare

£116,000 to organisations (2002/03)

Beneficial area UK and worldwide, with some preference for certain specific needs in Ottery St Mary, Honiton and Sidmouth in Devon.

Foot Anstey Sargent, 4–6 Barnfield Crescent, Exeter, Devon EX1 1RF

Tel. 01392 411221 **Fax** 01392 685220

Email ajt@foot-ansteys.co.uk

Correspondent Alison Tancock, Administrative Correspondent

Trustees *C F Bennett, Chair; Miss S E Crabtree; Mrs K A Gray; G D R Cockram.*

CC Number 1045492

Information available Accounts were on file at the Charity Commission.

General The trust currently supports:

- Ironbridge Gorge Museum Trust
- people living in the areas covered by the medical practices in Ottery St Mary, Honiton and Sidmouth (such grants are to be paid only for particularly acute needs)
- humanitarian projects.

In 2002/03 the trust had assets of £2.7 million and an income of £109,000. Management and administration charges were high at £125,000. Grants totalled £116,000.

As in the previous year the largest grants of £10,000 each went to Ironbridge Gorge Museum Trust and Hospiscare. Other larger grants included those made to Esther Benjamins Trust (£4,000) and Douglas House, Impact, Life Education Centres, Micro Loan Foundation, Rhys Daniels Trust, Support Dogs and Who Cares Trust (£3,000 each).

Smaller grants of £1,000 or under were made to various charities including Bag Books, Exeter Women's Aid, FSN and Torbay Citizens Advice Bureau (£500 each). Grants to individuals totalled £815.

Exclusions No grants for:

- research-based charities
- animal charities
- 'heritage charities' such as National Trust or other organisations whose aim is the preservation of a building, museum, library and so on (with the exception of the Ironbridge Gorge Museum).
- 'faith-based' charities, unless the project is for primarily humanitarian purposes and is neither exclusive to those of that particular faith or evangelical in its purpose.

Grants to individuals are strictly limited to the geographical area and purpose specified in the general section.

Applications In writing to the correspondent.

The Ian Askew Charitable Trust

General

£94,000 to organisations and individuals (2001/02)

Beneficial area UK, with a preference for Sussex, and overseas.

Hanover House, 18 Mount Ephraim Road, Tunbridge Wells, Kent TN1 1ED

Tel. 01892 511944

Correspondent Richard Lewis

Trustees *J R Rank; Mrs C Pengelley; R A R Askew; R J Wainwright; G B Ackery.*

CC Number 264515

Information available Accounts were on file at the Charity Commission.

General Grants are given to a wide variety of charitable bodies through the country with a preference for those connected with the county of Sussex. In 2001/02 the trust had assets of £5.9 million and an income of £210,000. Grants totalled £94,000, of which £9,600 was given to individuals and £3,500 was donated to British Trust for Conservation Volunteers through the trust's educational sub fund.

The majority of grants to organisations were for £500 or less, with 18 for £1,000 or more. These included: £20,000 to East Sussex Farmers' Benevolent Fund; £2,500 to Ringmer Village Hall Fundraising Appeal; £2,000 each to Harry Field Memorial Trust, National Art Collection Fund and Sussex Heritage Trust; and £1,500 each to ARC Addington Fund and Church of the Good Shepherd. Beneficiaries receiving £1,000 each included Carthusian Society Charitable Fund, Dame Vera Lynn Trust for

Children with Cerebral Palsy, Foundling Museum and Glyndebourne Arts Trust.

Applications In writing to the correspondent. Applications are considered monthly.

The Association of Colleges Charitable Trust

Further education colleges

£122,000 (2002/03)

Beneficial area UK.

5th Floor, Centre Point, 103 New Oxford Street, London WC1A 1RG

Tel. 020 7827 4600 **Fax** 020 7827 4645

Email alice_thiagaraj@aoc.co.uk

Website www.aoc.co.uk

Correspondent Alice Thiagaraj, Trust Manager

Trustee *Association of Colleges.*

CC Number 1040631

Information available Full accounts and a prospectus were provided by the trust.

General This trust is responsible for administering four programmes. The largest of these is the Beacon Awards, which provide monetary grants to specific initiatives within further education (FE) colleges. The other programmes that operate within the trust are the Gold Awards and the Work Shadowing Scheme.

Established in 1994, the Beacon Awards recognise and promote the interdependence of further education colleges and business, professional and voluntary sector organisations to their mutual advantage. Its aims are to:

- give recognition annually to outstanding teaching and learning practice across the further education curriculum
- highlight the breadth and quality of further education throughout the UK
- support learning and continuous improvement through the dissemination of award-bearing practice
- raise awareness and increase understanding of the colleges' contribution to and role within the UK economy.

The following general criteria must be fulfilled:

- the application may be for a programme, course, or project or for some other aspect of college provision – teaching, learning, guidance or support
- institutions can only submit one application to a specific award each year, but may apply for as many of the different award programmes as are relevant
- it must meet the criteria of the particular award
- it must be subject to evaluation and quality assurance
- it must have been running for at least one academic session before the deadline
- it must promote effective teaching and learning
- it must benefit one or more groups of students or trainees who should be identified and described in the application
- it must have wider relevance and applicability to other colleges as an example of good practice and innovation.

Each award has separate criteria in the interests of the area of work of the sponsor. They range from broad educational development to the promotion of particular courses or subjects, covering most aspects of further education. Programmes in 2002/03 included:

- The Basic Skills Agency Award for ESOL/EAL, which is open to all departments in further education colleges in England and Wales demonstrating best practice in the development and management of ESOL/EAL programmes that meet a range of local needs
- The Churches' Award for Sustainable Community Development, which supports the college in the UK which has been seen as most effectively fostering a broad and sustainable sense of self-worth in a marginalised group, whilst recognising the diversity and opportunities in the locality
- The Edexcel Award for Lifelong Learning, which supports sixth form and further education colleges with effective and imaginative approaches of motivating adults back into education
- The Protocol Professional Award for Art and Design, which is open to all educational institutions providing training in art and design, media studies, publishing, journalism, design and crafts or fine art which encourage students' creativity, learning and transferable skills.

Other schemes operated by the trust are: The Gold Awards for Further Education Alumni, which reward former members of further education colleges who have since excelled in their chosen field or profession; the International Churchill Society Awards for Fine Art Painting, which are given to promising students nominated by their college; and The Work Shadowing Scheme, which provides an opportunity for senior managers to update their skills by spending time in industry.

In 2002/03 the trust had assets of £122,000. Total income was £193,000, of which £92,000 came from Beacon Awards donations received and a further £80,000 from Beacon Awards administrative donations. Total expenditure for the year was £256,000, including £122,000 in 34 Beacon Awards and £1,000 in general donations.

Organisations to receive support included Plymouth College of FE (£8,400 in two grants), Beacon Awards included Bedford College, Coleg Llandrillo, Hull College, John Leggott College and Strode College (£4,200 each), South Birmingham College (£4,000), Bourneville College (£3,500), Pembrokeshire College (£2,800) and Cornwall College, Loreto College and Tameside College (£2,100 each).

Exclusions Applications from individuals. Grants are only awarded through Beacon Awards, which are soley open to further education colleges.

Applications Potential applicants are advised to look at the Beacon Awards Charitable Trust Zone at the Association of College's website, or contact the Beacon Awards office for a prospectus.

Applications should be made in writing to the correspondent, with three copies of each application sent. There is an annual deadline, usually in early summer. Contact should be made solely with the trust's office; the individual sponsors should never be approached.

The following is taken from the 2002/03 Beacon Awards Prospectus:

'Your application should address all of the criteria and should be made in a statement of no more than 3,000 words. The statement should be made by a senior member of staff who has had close contact with the initiative. Written evidence from beneficiaries should be included in the word limit. You may make reference to other materials (i.e. multimedia material, college documents etc.) which the assessors can request, should they wish to do so.

'Your submissions should be structured, as far as possible, under the following headings:

- The Project: Planning and Purpose – include a description of the initiative and how it was set up or developed. Also include a clear description of target group, including numbers.
- Aims and Objectives – outline how aims and objectives were established and how the initiative evolved to meet them.
- Monitoring Procedures – demonstrate how quality assurance was used to improve the initiative.
- Outcomes and Benefits – show how the initiative has benefited the students/trainees and others involved with the project – this should be supported by written evidence from beneficiaries who may be students, trainees, employers or, in some cases, parents.
- Dissemination and the Future – indicate how the initiative could be of benefit to other colleges and how you perceive it developing in the future.

'The statement needs to be accompanied by a completed application form [available on the back of the prospectus or the website] and must be signed by the principal/chief executive.

'All applications will be treated as strictly confidential by the steering group, assessors and Beacon Awards manager. Material from any application will only be made public with the express approval of the college concerned.

'Each application will be sent an acknowledgement addressed to the principal/chief executive. Your college will be subsequently contacted only if the project is shortlisted.'

The Astor Foundation

General

£148,000 (2000/01)

Beneficial area UK.

2 Kew Gardens, Shalbourne, Wiltshire SN8 3QW

Tel. 01672 870733 **Fax** 01672 870926

Email pam.garroway@which.net

Correspondent Mrs Pam Garraway, Secretary

Trustees *J R Astor, Chair; Sir William Slack; Lord Astor of Hever; Dr H Swanton; R H Astor; C Money-Coutts.*

CC Number 225708

Information available Full accounts were on file at the Charity Commission.

General The trust supports a variety of causes, particularly disability, health and medical research. The grants list also shows some preference for conservation projects. In the past the trust has not favoured giving large grants for building projects although they are not excluded.

In 2001/02 the trust had an income of £148,000 with an expenditure of £172,000. No further information was available.

Grants were made totalling £148,000 in 2000/01. By far the largest grant was £25,000 to Royal Free University College Medical School. Other grants included those to League of Friends – Middlesex Hospital (£4,500), Help the Hospices (£3,500), Samaritans (£3,000) and Aidis Trust, Jubilee Sailing Trust, RNLI and Royal National College for the Blind (£2,500 each).

The remainder of grants were mainly for amounts of £2,000, £1,500, £1,000 or £500 each. Beneficiaries included: Born Free Foundation, Demand, Gurkha Welfare Trust and Memorial Gates Trust (£2,000 each); British Stammering Association, British Wheelchair Sports Foundation, Catholic Housing Aid Society, DEBRA and National Library for the Blind (£1,500 each); Action for Kids, Children's Country Holidays Fund, Fight for Sight and Memorial Gates Trust (£1,000 each); and Age Concern, Greenwich Healthcare Trust, National Eye Research Centre and Pelican Centre (£500 each).

Exclusions No grants to individuals or towards salaries. Grants are given to registered charities only.

Applications There are no deadline dates; applications should be in writing to the correspondent. If the appeal arrives too late for one meeting it will automatically be carried over for consideration at the following meeting. The trustees meet twice a year, in March and October. A reply will always be sent irrespective of whether an appeal is successful.

This entry was not confirmed by the trust, but is correct according to information on file at the Charity Commission.

The Astor of Hever Trust

Youth, medical research, education

£48,000 (2001/02)

Beneficial area UK and worldwide, with a preference for Kent and the Grampian region of Scotland.

Frenchstreet House, Westerham, Kent TN16 1PW

Tel. 01959 565070 **Fax** 01959 561286

Correspondent Lord Astor of Hever, Trustee

Trustees *John Jacob, Third Baron Astor of Hever; Irene, Lady Astor of Hever; Hon. Philip D P Astor.*

CC Number 264134

Information available Accounts were on file at the Charity Commission.

General The trust gives grants UK-wide and internationally. It states that there is a preference for Kent and the Grampian region of Scotland, although the preference for Kent is much stronger.

When Gavin Astor, second Baron Astor of Hever, founded the trust in 1955, its main areas of support were arts, medicine, religion, education, conservation, youth and sport. Reflecting the settlor's wishes, the trust makes grants to local youth organisations, medical research and educational programmes. Most beneficiaries are UK-wide charities or a local branch.

In 2002/03 the trust had an income of £35,000 and a total expenditure of £56,000. Further information for this year was not available, instead we refer to previous information collated stating in 2001/02 it had assets of £985,000 and an income of £39,000. Grants totalled £48,000.

Some of the larger grants were: £5,000 to Migvie Church; £3,500 to Household Cavelry Museum; £3,000 to Trustees of Uppingham School; and £1,000 each to Commonwealth Press Union Education and Training Trust, Hospice in the Weald, Jubilee Appeal of Commonwealth Veterans, RAFT and St Mary's Church Restoration Appeal (Westerham, Kent).

Smaller grants in Kent and Scotland included: £500 each to British Red Cross – Kent and Cromar & District Horticultural and Industrial Society – Scotland; and £100 each to National Youth Orchestra of Scotland and Mental Health Foundation – Kent.

Exclusions No grants to individuals.

Applications In writing to the correspondent. Unsuccessful applications are not acknowledged.

The Atlantic Foundation

Education, medical, general

£74,000 (2002/03)

Beneficial area Worldwide, though with some preference for Wales.

7–8 Raleigh Walk, Atlantic Wharf, Cardiff CF10 4LN

Tel. 029 2054 5680

Correspondent Mrs B L Thomas, Trustee

Trustees *P Thomas; Mrs B L Thomas.*

CC Number 328499

Information available Full accounts were on file at the Charity Commission.

General The trust supports a range of causes, with a strong interest in Wales. In 2002/03 it had assets of £17,000, an income of £73,000 and made grants totalling £74,000 broken down as follows:

Independent schools and colleges	£35,000
Registered charities	£17,000
Community aid	£17,000
Medical appeals and support	£400
Local authority support	£4,000
Religious foundations	£1,000

In total 43 charitable donations were made by the trust with beneficiaries including Afrikids, Barnardos, DeafBlind, Marie Curie Cancer Care and Starlight Children's Foundation (£1,000 each), Dial-A-Ride (£650) and Brittle Bone Society, CURSE Bereavement Centre, Joshua Foundation and Mobility Trust (£500 each).

Applications In writing to the correspondent. Applications are considered throughout the year.

ATP Charitable Trust

Jewish, education, medical

£50,000 (2001/02)

Beneficial area Worldwide.

Heath Cottage, 1 Constable Close, London NW11 6UA

Correspondent M R Bentata, Trustee

Trustees *M R Bentata; J A Bentata; Mrs S Bentata.*

CC Number 328408

Information available Full accounts were on file at the Charity Commission.

General In 2001/02 the trust had assets of £82,000 and an income of £54,000 of which £50,000 came from Gift Aid. Grants to 15 organisations were made totalling £50,000.

The largest were £15,000 to Jewish Care and £10,000 each to Centre for Jewish Education and Givat Haviva. Other beneficiaries included Nightingale House (£5,300), Bar Ilan University (£3,000), J M Trust (£2,300), Brighton Jewish Film Festival (£1,300), Hammerson House (£1,000), Textile Conservation Centre and Worldwide Volunteers (£500) and Imperial College, London School of Jewish Studies and University of Edinburgh (£250).

Exclusions Expeditions are not funded.

Applications In writing to the correspondent. Individuals who apply must include two personal references and a current CV. Applications are considered throughout the year.

This entry was not confirmed by the trust but was correct according to information on file at the Charity Commission.

Lawrence Atwell's Charity

Education, young people

£185,000 to organisations (2002/03)

Beneficial area UK-wide.

The Skinners' Company, Skinners' Hall, 8 Dowgate Hill, London EC4R 2SP

Tel. 020 7213 0561 **Fax** 0207 236 6590

Correspondent The Atwell Administrator

Trustee *The Worshipful Company of Skinner's.*

CC Number 210773

Information available Information was provided by the trust.

General The purpose of the charity is to promote the education, including social and physical training, of young people who have reached the age of 16, but who are under the age of 27. Grants are made to schools, institutions and charities that undertake training and support with disadvantaged young people. The trust states that they do not publicise their grantmaking to organisations as they only give to organisations that they proactively contact.

In 2002/03 the charity had an income of £536,000 and a total expenditure of £565,000. Vocational grants were made to individuals totalling £272,000 and a further £185,000 was distributed to organisations, a large proportion of which was given to the Skinners' Company Schools. A list of further beneficiaries was not available.

Exclusions No unsolicited applications.

Applications The trust states that they only give to organisations they proactively contact. Applications will therefore not be considered.

The Aurelius Charitable Trust

Conservation of culture and the humanities

£69,000 (2002/03)

Beneficial area UK.

Briarsmead, Old Road, Buckland, Betchworth, Surrey RH3 7DU

Tel. 01737 842186

Email haynes@knowall.co.uk

Correspondent P E Haynes, Trustee

Trustees *W J Wallis; P E Haynes.*

CC Number 271333

Information available Information was provided by the trust.

General During the settlor's lifetime, the income of the trust was distributed broadly to reflect his interests in the conservation of culture inherited from the past, and the dissemination of knowledge, particularly in the humanities field. Since the settlor's death in April 1994, the trustees have continued with this policy.

Donations are for seed-corn or completion funding not otherwise available. They are usually one-off and range from £500 to £3,000.

In 2002/03 it has assets of £1.5 million, which generated an income of £72,000. Donations were made to 21 organisations totalling £69,000.

The largest were £10,000 to IHR Trust for the Victoria County History, £7,500 to British Academy for a centenary collection of fellow's bibliographies, £6,000 to University of Leicester for a national electronic atlas and £5,000 each to Trustees of the British Museum for a Sasanian coin database, Bromley House Library – Nottingham for an early books conservation project, Fenland Archaeological Trust for the Flag Fen project and University of Surrey – Roehampton for the Hearth Tax Centre.

Other beneficiaries included University of Portsmouth for an ancient parishes of England database (£3,000), Royal Society for the Encouragement of Arts, Manufactures and Commerce for restoration of the library and research rooms (£2,500), The Voltaire Foundation at Oxford University for preparation of a volume of his works (£1,800) and Royal West of England Academy for conservation of murals and Strathclyde Building Preservation Trust for building preservation (£1,000 each).

Exclusions No grants to individuals.

Applications In writing to the correspondent. Donations are generally made on the recommendation of the trust's board of advisors. Unsolicited applications will only be responded to if an sae is included. Trustees meet twice a year, in January and July, and applications need to be received by May and November.

The Avenue Charitable Trust

General

£670,000 (2001/02)

Beneficial area Worldwide.

c/o Messrs Sayers Butterworth, 18 Bentinck Street, London W1M 5RL

Tel. 020 7935 8504 **Fax** 020 7487 5621

Correspondent Susan Simmons

Trustees *R D L Astor; The Hon. Mrs B A Astor; S G Kemp.*

CC Number 264804

Information available Accounts were on file at the Charity Commission.

General In 2001/02 the trust had assets of £1.5 million with an income of £23,000 and grants totalling £670,000.

The largest grants were £150,000 Blanes Trust, £144,000 to Oil Depletion Analysis Centre and £50,000 each to Connectus Komonia Trust, Elm Tree Trust, Meadowbrook Trust, Neuro Psychoanalysis Fund, Primrose Trust and Pravo Trust.

Other substantial grants include £26,000 to Prisons Video Trust, £20,000 to Brandon Centre, £15,000 to Matthew Trust, £8,000 each to Koostler Award Trust and St Johns Wood, £5,000 to Presswise Trust and £3,000 each to Sutton Courtenay PCC and Anti Slavery International.

Grants of £1,000 or less include Redress Trust, Replay Trust, SANE Foundation, St Brides Church, St Mungo's, St Vincent de Paul, Bourne Trust, Medical Foundation, New School Butterstone, Toynbee Hall, YMCA for Ex-Offenders, Age Concern Westminster, Breast Cancer Campaign, Cassell Hospital Families Centre Appeal, Child Psychotherapy Trust, Cobden Trust, Council for the Preservation of Rural England, Emmaus UK, ITDG, Irish Charitable Trust, The Kingswood Trust, Macmillan Cancer Relief, NACRO, New Era Schools, Order of St Johns, Parkinson's Disease Society and Polish Institute Sikorski Museum.

Applications The trust has previously stated that all available income is now committed to existing beneficiaries.

Harry Bacon Foundation

Medical, animal welfare

£64,000 (2002)

Beneficial area UK.

NatWest Bank plc, 153 Preston Road, Brighton BN1 6BD

Tel. 01273 545035 **Fax** 01273 545141

Correspondent The Manager

Trustee *NatWest Bank plc.*

CC Number 1056500

Information available Accounts were on file at the Charity Commission.

General In 2003/04 the trust had an income of £61,000 and a total expenditure of £84,000.

The trust made major grants in 2002 of £7,950 each to: Arthritis Research Campaign, British Heart Foundation, Imperial Cancer Research, Peoples Dispensary for Sick Animals, Royal National Lifeboat Institution, Donkey Sanctuary, ILPH and Arthritis Research Campaign.

Applications In writing to the correspondent.

The Bacta Charitable Trust

General

£48,000 (2000/01)

Beneficial area UK.

Bacta House, Regents Wharf, 6 All Saints Street, London N1 9RQ

Tel. 020 7713 7144 **Fax** 020 7713 0446

Correspondent Linda Malcolm, Clerk

Trustees *N Harding, Chair; R D Withers; S I Meaden; M C Henry; R Higgins; M Horwood; K Smith.*

CC Number 328668

Information available Information on file at the Charity Commission.

General The trust only supports charities recommended by Bacta members. Bacta is the Trade Association for the Coin Operated Amusement Industry.

The trust's principal fundraising takes place at the annual Bacta Charity Ball through a prize raffle and pledges made by guests.

In 2000/01 the trust had assets of £102,000, an income of £110,000 and a grant total of £48,000. Grant beneficiaries included RNID (£26,000), MacMillan Windmill Fund (£10,000) and South West Region Matched Funds (£3,000).

Beneficiaries receiving £1,000 were Age Concern, Diabetes UK, Children's Wish Foundation, Luke White Appeal, Marie Curie Cancer Care, National Deaf Children's Society and NSPCC.

Exclusions No grants for overseas charities or religious purposes.

Applications In writing to the correspondent, but via a Bacta member. Applications should be submitted by January, April or August, for trustees' meetings in February, May or September.

The Bagri Foundation

General

£61,000 to organisations (2001/02)

Beneficial area Worldwide.

Metdist Limited, 3rd Floor, 80 Cannon Street, London EC4N 6EJ

Tel. 020 7280 0000

Correspondent The Trustees

Trustees *Lord Bagri; Hon. A Bagri; Lady Bagri; R J Gatehouse.*

CC Number 1000219

Information available Accounts were on file at the Charity Commission, but without a list of grants.

General This trust was set up in 1990 with general charitable purposes. In 2001/02 it had assets of £2.3 million and an income of £95,000. Grants to organisations totalled £61,000, with a further £27,000 given to individuals. No further information was available, and a grants list was not on file at the Charity Commission.

Applications In writing to the correspondent.

The Sir Leon Bagrit Memorial Trust

Educational, general

£31,000 (1999)

Beneficial area UK.

66 Lincoln's Inn Fields, London WC2A 3LH

Tel. 020 7242 2022

Correspondent Hon. Mark T Bridges, Trustee

Trustees *Lady Sarah Bagrit; Sir Matthew Farrer; Hon. Mark T Bridges; Lord Rees-Mogg; Lady Rees-Mogg; Lawrence P Fielding.*

CC Number 298075

Information available Accounts were on file at the Charity Commission.

General In 1991 the trust established The Bagrit Centre for The Department of Biological and Medical Systems at Imperial College. In the 1999 report the trust states that it is 'primarily concerned with continuing to support scholarships to the college', although it did not appear to make grants to this end in this year.

In 2001 the trust had an income of £23,000 with an expenditure of £61,500. No further information was available.

In 1999 it had an income of £24,000, assets of £755,000 and gave five grants totalling £31,000. These went to World Jewish Relief (£25,000), Royal College Radiologists (£3,000) and Charing Cross Holiday Dialysis Trust, Help the Hospices and Yehudi Menuhin Memorial Trust (£1,000 each).

Exclusions No grants to individuals.

Applications In writing to the correspondent, although the trust states that it does not respond to unsolicited applications.

Veta Bailey Charitable Trust

Training of doctors and other medical personnel.

£82,000 (2004)

Beneficial area Developing countries (generally those with GNP less than US$1,000 a head), or UK for work in developing countries.

The Cottage, Tiltups End, Horsley, Stroud, Gloucestershire GL6 0QE

Tel. 01453 834914

Correspondent B L Worth, Trustee

Trustees *Brian Worth; Dr Elizabeth McClatchey; John Humphreys; Sue Yates; Dr Madura Gupta; Davod Trim.*

CC Number 1007411

Information available Full accounts are on file at the Charity Commission.

General The trust supports the training of doctors and other medical personnel and the development of good healthcare practices in Third World and developing countries.

In 2004 the trust had assets of £206,000 generating an income of £23,000. Grants for the year totalled £82,000.

Previous beneficiaries have included Voluntary Service Overseas, LEPRA, Centre for Caribbean Medicine, Africa Now, International Nepal Fellowship, Mildmay, UNA International Service, Tearfund, Ockenden Ventrue, a local organisation for work in Cameroon, and a local organisation for work in Kenya.

Exclusions No grants to individuals.

Applications In writing to the correspondent by June, for consideration at a trustees' meeting in August.

The Baker Charitable Trust

Mainly Jewish, older people, sickness and disability, medical research

£34,000 (2002/03)

Beneficial area UK and overseas.

16 Sheldon Avenue, Highgate, London N6 4JT

Tel. 020 8340 5970 **Fax** 020 8347 7017

Correspondent Dr Harvey Baker, Trustee

Trustees *Dr Harvey Baker; Dr Adrienne Baker.*

CC Number 273629

Information available Full accounts were provided by the trust.

General The trust makes grants in the areas of people who are elderly, chronic sickness or disability and people who have had limited educational opportunity. The trust also supports medical research related to the above groups. There is a preference for Jewish organisations.

In 2002/03 it had assets of £1.1 million and an income of £39,000. Grants to 27 organisations totalled £34,000.

The largest grants were £7,500 to Norwood, £5,800 to United Jewish Israel Appeal, £4,300 to Chai Cancer Care, £3,000 to Community Security Trust, £2,500 to British Council Shaare Zedek Medical Centre and £1,000 each to Friends of Magen David Adom in Great Britain, Hillel Foundation, Institute of Jewish Policy Research, National Society for Epilepsy and United Synagogue for a young people's project.

Other beneficiaries included Marie Curie Cancer Care, Jewish Women's Aid and World Jewish Relief (500 each), St John's Hospice (£350), Disabled Living Foundation (£300) and Beth Shalom and Winged Fellowship (£250 each).

Exclusions No grants to individuals or non-registered charities.

Applications In writing to the correspondent. The trustees meet to consider applications in January, April, July and October.

The Balney Charitable Trust

Preservation, conservation, welfare, service charities

£50,000 (2001/02)

Beneficial area UK, with a preference for north Buckinghamshire and north Bedfordshire.

The Balney Charity, Bartlemas Office, Pavenham, Bedford MK43 7PF

Tel. 01234 823663 **Fax** 01234 825058

Correspondent G C W Beazley, Clerk

Trustees *Maj. J G B Chester; R Rucke-Keene.*

CC Number 288575

Information available Information was provided by the trust.

General The trust has a preference for local causes in north Buckinghamshire and north Bedfordshire, and ex-servicemen and women's institutions. Regular donations by standing order range from £25 to £500 a year and are given to 15 organisations. Other donations are mostly one-off.

In 2001/02 the trust had assets of £785,000 and a gross income of £61,000 (mainly rents). Grants totalled £50,000. The largest grant was to Willen Hospice which received £5,000. Other larger grants were £2,000 to Macmillan Milton Keynes Appeal and £1,000 to both Emmaus Village and Gurkha Welfare Trust.

Exclusions Local community organisations and individuals outside north Buckinghamshire and north Bedfordshire.

Applications In writing to the correspondent. Applications are acknowledged if an sae is enclosed, otherwise if the charity has not received a reply within six weeks the application has not been successful.

The Baltic Charitable Fund

Registered charities benefiting residents of the City of London, seafarers, fishermen, ex-service and service people.

£41,000 (2002/03)

Beneficial area UK, with a preference for the City of London.

The Baltic Exchange, 38 St Mary Axe, London EC3A 8BH

Tel. 020 7623 5501

Correspondent Mark Soutter, Company Secretary

Trustee

CC Number 279194

Information available Full accounts were on file at the Charity Commission.

General The trust aims to support applications relating to the sea, including training for professionals and children, the City of London, Forces charities and for sponsorship for Baltic Exchange members.

In 2002/03 the trust had assets of £950,000 and an income of £58,000. Grants totalled £41,000, of which the largest grants (£1,000 and over) were £6,000 each to City of London School for Boys and City of London School for Girls, £5,300 to Save the Children Fund, £3,500 to City University Business School, £2,600 to Lloyds Officer Cadet Scholarship and £1,000 each to Jubilee Sailing Trust, Reeds School Foundation Appeal and Sail Training Association. An individual also received a grant of £9,500.

Smaller grants included £500 each to Challenge Adventure Charities and Jubilant Trust and £250 to Aid International, Bobarth Children, Diabetics UK, Merlin Bazley Cancer Care for Children and Teenage Cancer Trust and Hellenic Centre.

Exclusions No support for advertising or charity dinners, and so on.

Applications Since 2001 the fund has supported a set list of charities and funds have been fully committed, however support for new beneficiaries is available from 2005. Unsolicited applications are not considered.

William P Bancroft (No 2) Charitable Trust and Jenepher Gillett Trust

Quaker

£37,000 available (2004)

Beneficial area UK and overseas.

Fernroyd, St Margaret's Road, Altrincham, Cheshire WA14 2AW

Tel. 0161 928 5112 **Fax** 0161 928 5112

Correspondent Dr Roger Gillett

Trustees *R Gillett; G T Gillett; D S Gillett; J Moseley; A J Yelloly; C E Gardiner.*

CC Number 288968

Information available Full accounts were provided by the trust.

General This trust is unusual as it consists of two separate trusts which are operated as one. For historical reasons there is a William P Bancroft trust giving in the UK and a Jenepher Gillet trust giving in Delaware, USA which shared a common settlor/joint-settlor; the two trusts are now being run jointly with the same trustees and joint finances.

It makes grants towards charitable purposes connected with the Religious Society of Friends, supporting Quaker conferences, colleges and Friends' homes for older people.

In 2003 it had an income of £47,000 and gave 21 grants totalling £46,000. However, reduced income recently has limited the available funds, which totalled just £37,000 for 2004.

A total of £23,000 was given in nine grants through the William P Bancroft branch. These were £5,000 to BYM, £4,500 to Sibford School for bursaries, £2,000 to Chaigley Educational Centre, £1,000 each to Howard League for Penal Reform, Ramallah Friends' School,

Swarthmore Lecture 2004 and Ulster Quaker Service Committee and £500 each to Alternatives to Violence and Friends of Hope.

A total of £24,000 was given in 10 grants through the Jenepher Gillet branch. These were £11,000 to Charney Manor for Quaker courses, £2,000 each to Quaker Council for European Affairs and Quaker Social Action, £1,500 each to Cape Town Quaker Peace Centre and Pendle Hill, £1,000 each to Bootham School, Leaveners, Mount School York Foundation, Plymouth Quakers and Quaker Voluntary Action and £500 to *Friends Quarterly.*

Exclusions No appeals unconnected with Quakers. No support for individual or student grant applications.

Applications In writing to the correspondent. Trustees meet in May, applications must be received no later than April.

The Barber Charitable Trust

Evangelical Christian causes, churches

£62,000 (2002/03)

Beneficial area UK, with some preference for West Sussex, and overseas.

Tortington Cottage, Tortington, Arundel, West Sussex BN18 0BG

Tel. 01903 882337 **Fax** 01903 882337

Correspondent E E Barber, Trustee

Trustees *E E Barber; Mrs D H Barber.*

CC Number 269544

Information available Accounts were on file at the Charity Commission.

General The trust makes grants to churches and Christian charities for evangelical Christian causes. It also makes a few grants to individual missionaries and Christian workers personally known to the trustees.

In 2002/03 the trust's assets totalled £48,000 and it had an income of £64,000, mostly from donations. Grants totalled £62,000, with over 50 organisations and churches supported, principally for evangelical causes, in the UK and overseas.

Grants over £1,000 were made to 19 organisations, 17 of which received grants in the previous year, although of different amounts. Beneficiaries included Arundel Baptist Church (£9,000); Hope Now Ministries (£5,500); Africa Inland Mission (£5,000); Gideons International (£4,500); Scripture Union International (£4,000); Christian Ministries (£2,500); and Missionary Aviation Fellowship, SASRA and Scripture Gift Mission (£2,000 each).

Projects supported included:

- Bible distribution in the British Isles and overseas
- Christian workers in Africa, Madagascar, Romania and Albania (personally known to the trustees)
- training of Christian leaders in developing countries
- training of students in Bible colleges (personally known to the trustees)
- a mission hospital, two hospices and children's work in Madagascar
- ministry and evangelism in the UK, Ukraine and South Africa.

Exclusions Requests from students are not considered unless personally known by the trustees. Requests from non-registered charities are not considered. Requests for building construction or renovation are generally not considered.

Applications In writing to the correspondent. Funds tend to be committed several years in advance and therefore unsolicited applications are unlikely to be considered or acknowledged.

The Barbers' Company General Charities

Medical and nursing education

See below

Beneficial area UK.

1 Monkwell Square, Wood Street, London EC2Y 5BL

Correspondent The Clerk

Trustees *A J Missen, Chair; A M Denney; J A H Bootes; Sir B Jackson; Prof. J W Last; J C Bach; C W Sprague; F N Read; H M Harris Hughes.*

CC Number 265579

Information available Information was provided by the trust.

General The charities were registered in May 1973; grants are made to organisations and individuals. It no longer has direct contact with the hairdressing fraternity. However, a small amount is given each year to satisfy its historical links. Causes supported include those related to medicine education and nursing.

In 2002/03 it had assets of £923,000, an income of £134,000 and a total expenditure of £145,000. No further details were available for this year.

Applications The charities do not welcome unsolicited applications.

Barchester Healthcare Foundation (formerly Westminster Health Care Foundation)

Health and social care

£69,000 to organisations and individuals (2003)

Beneficial area England, Scotland and Wales.

Westminister House, Randalls Way, Leatherhead, Surrey KT22 7TZ

Tel. 01372 860390 **Fax** 01372 860333

Email info@whcfoundation.org.uk

Website www.whcfoundation.org.uk

Correspondent The Administrator

Trustees *Tony Heywood; Prof. Malcolm Johnson; Robert Lewis; Elizabeth Mills; Chris Vellenoweth; Chris Hodgson.*

CC Number 1083272

Information available Information is available on the foundation's website.

General The foundation was established by Westminster Health Care (UK) Ltd. It announced in February 2005 that it was changing its name from Westminster Health Care Foundation. Due to this change, it is likely that the foundation's website, e-mail and literature will be changing at some point in the future.

The foundation is a registered charity with independent trustees. The fund was set up with an initial grant of over £250,000. Recently a further £70,000 was donated to the foundation by Westminster Health Care (UK) Ltd. This represents funds received to date from Westminster Health Care (UK) Ltd. It is hoped that others will continue to contribute.

The foundation's objective is to support identified health and social care needs in the community that cannot be met by statutory funds. The emphasis is on supporting practical solutions that provide direct support to people in need. The foundation attaches importance to the assessment and dissemination of the results of work it has funded, so that others might benefit.

Grants are available for work supporting:

- older people
- adults with physical disabilities
- adults with mental disabilities.

Examples of instances where the foundation will provide funding include:

- to support small community groups who provide activities and support for older people or disabled adults
- where an individual is living with visual impairment or loss of hearing which causes a severe impediment to their quality of life
- to provide specialist care equipment.

The foundation can provide grants of any amount, up to a maximum of £10,000.

In 2003 the trust had assets of £260,000 and an income of £79,000. A total of 25 grants were awarded amounting to £69,000. Beneficiaries included: Glen Devon Day Club (£10,000 to extend the opening hours of their day club for people with dementia); MS Society Eastbourne (£10,000 to fund disability adaptations in a new central Resource/ Information Centre for people with multiple sclerosis in East Sussex); The Oxford Auditory Verbal UK (£1,900 to pay for video camera and accessories); Stanningley and Swinnow Live at Home scheme (£1,000 to buy new chairs for elderly members attending social activities); and Middleton Elderly Aid in Leeds (£900 to buy collapsible tables and chairs for its centre for older people).

Applications are welcomed from organisations, small groups or from individual applicants on behalf of the person who would benefit. They are not normally accepted from someone applying on their own behalf.

Exclusions The foundation will not normally provide ongoing support for a project following an initial grant. A further application for the same project will only be considered after a period of three years. Funds cannot be used to provide any services normally offered in a care home operated by the parent company or by any other group, nor to provide services for which the health and social care authorities have statutory responsibility.

Applications An online application form is available on the foundation's website. No additional documentation is required. A decision usually takes approximately eight-twelve weeks from the date of application.

Barclays Stockbrokers Charitable Trust

General

£100,000 (2003/04)

Beneficial area UK.

Barclays Bank Trust Co. Ltd, Osborne Court, Gadbrook Park, Rudheath, Northwich, Cheshire CW9 7UE

Correspondent Miss M Y Bertenshaw, Trust Officer

Trustee *Barclays Bank Trust Company Ltd.*

CC Number 1093833

Information available Information was provided by the trust.

General Established in 2002, this charity makes grants to registered and exempt charities only. Preference is given to small and medium-sized charities and local branches of UK charities. Support is only given for capital projects and specific programmes rather than funding core or revenue costs.

Applications are considered in the following categories:

- physical and mental disability
- older people
- ill health/relief in need
- children/youth
- family and social welfare
- education and training
- blind/deaf
- poverty/homelessness.

Only one-off grants are made, grants are usually in the range of £10,000 and £50,000. Support will only be given for capital projects or specific programmes rather than core or revenue costs.

In 2003/04 the trust had an income and expenditure of £100,000, all of which was given in grants. Beneficiaries were £30,000 to BASIC, £15,000 to Rainbow Trust Childrens' Charity, £10,000 to Hospice in the Weald, £9,800 to Venture Trust, £9,000 to Hastings & Rother Citizens Advice, £8,800 to Ryder, £7,300 to East Radnorshire Day Centre, £5,800 to Henshaws Society for the Blind and £5,000 to Age Concern – Camden.

Exclusions The following categories will not be considered for funding:

- large national charities
- individuals
- schools/colleges/universities
- religion/church buildings
- overseas charities/projects
- medical research
- animal welfare
- expenses that have already been incurred.

Applications In writing to the correspondent. Appeals are considered quarterly at trustees' meetings held at the end of February, May, August and November. If eligibility is established following receipt of an appeal letter, then an application form will be sent.

Peter Barker-Mill Memorial Charity

General

£61,000 (2001/02)

Beneficial area UK, with a preference for Hampshire, including Southampton.

Longdown Management Ltd, The Estate Office, Longdown, Marchwood, Southampton, Hampshire SO40 4UH

Tel. 023 8029 2107

Correspondent Mrs Annette Todhunter, Administrator

Trustees *G N Knowles, Chair; C Gwyn-Evans; T Jobling.*

CC Number 1045479

Information available Full accounts were on file at the Charity Commission.

General In 2001/02 the trust had assets of £2.4 million and an income of £86,000. Expenditure totalled £97,000, which included two payments of £6,600 and £5,000 to firms which have trustees as the directors. Grants totalled £61,000 of which £15,000 was distributed in grants to three individuals for financial assistance to tenant farmers due to foot and mouth restrictions.

Grants to organisations were as follows: £10,000 to Magpie Cancer Campaign for the cancer centre appeal; £8,000 to Royal Botanic Gardens for a publication of the works of Ruth Vollner; £5,300 to St Martin's College for computer equipment for research; £5,000 each to Armac Films New Forest Trust for a film about life in the New Forest and Tug Tender Clashot Trust for a restoration project; £2,500 to Students Exploring Marriage Trust for general funding; and £2,400 to Centre for Applied Research for development of psychoanalytical research.

Donations of £1,000 or below included: £1,000 to Youth Cancer Trust for holiday accommodation; £500 each to Totton and Eling Carnival as a donation to funds and Wessex Cancer Trust Children Fund for research; and £240 to St Boniface Church for insuring the Barker–Mill monument.

Exclusions No grants to individuals.

Applications In writing to the correspondent.

The Barnabas Trust

Evangelical Christianity

About £194,000 to organisations (2003/04)

Beneficial area UK and overseas. Overseas projects are supported only if they are personally known by the trustees.

63 Wolsey Drive, Walton-on-Thames, Surrey KT12 3BB

Tel. 01932 220622

Correspondent Mrs Doris Edwards, Secretary

Trustees *K C Griffiths, Chair; D S Helden; N Brown.*

CC Number 284511

Information available Full accounts were on file at the Charity Commission.

General In 2003/04 the trust had an income of £175,000 and a total expenditure of £194,000, most of which probably went in grants. No further information was available for the year.

In 2000/01 the trust had assets of £4.1 million generating an income of £208,000. Grants to 108 organisations totalled £363,000, to 16 individuals for education £13,000, with a further £7,000 to six individuals for Christian missionary work. Grants were split into the following categories:

Community welfare: 29 grants totalled £90,000

Grants were given to local, UK and international medical institutions and charities concerned with the welfare of children, older people, prisoners, people experiencing poverty and the general community. Beneficiaries included Shaftesbury Society (£12,000), Princess Alice Hospice (£8,000), Medical Missionary News and Yeldall Manor (£6,000 each), Bethany Children's Trust and International Fellowship of Evangelical Students (£5,000 each) and Torch Trust for the Blind (£2,500).

Educational: 33 grants to organisations totalled £65,000

Grants were given to establishments in the UK and overseas, and general educational charities, including religious education. Beneficiaries included Schools Outreach and Haggai Institute (£6,000 each), Redcliffe College (£4,000), National Bible Society of Scotland (£2,500), Danoka Training College – Kenya and Medina Valley Centre (£2,000 each) and National Bible Study Group (£1,000).

Christian mission overseas: 23 grants to organisations totalled £146,000

The largest grants were £90,000 to SGM International. Other grants were of £1,000 to £6,000 (although one grant of £75 was also given) and beneficiaries included Echoes of Service, High Adventure Ministries, Naval, Military and Air Force Bible Society, Nigeria Evangelical Missionary Institute, SGM International – Pavement Project (£5,000 each) and Operation Mobilisation and Latin Link (£3,000 each).

Christian mission in the UK: 27 grants totalled £43,000

Grants included £5,000 each to Counties Evangelical Trust and Message to Schools Trust, £3,000 to Scripture Union, £1,500 each to Manchester City Mission and Careforce and £1,000 each to Campaigners Scotland, Warrington Youth for Christ and St Mary's Church, Lemmington Spa. Smaller grants were also given.

Exclusions 'The trust is no longer able to help with building, refurbishment or equipment for any church, since to be of any value grants need to be large.' On-going revenue costs such as salaries are not supported.

Applications In writing to the correspondent, giving as much detail as possible, and enclosing a copy of the latest audited accounts, if applicable. The trust states: 'Much of the available funds generated by this trust are allocated to existing donees. The trustees are willing to consider new applications, providing they refer to a project which is overtly evangelical in nature.' If in doubt about whether to submit an application, please telephone the secretary to the trust for guidance.

The trustees meet four times a year, or more often as required, and applications will be put before the next available meeting.

Lord Barnby's Foundation

General

£162,000 (2000/01)

Beneficial area UK.

PO Box 71, Plymstock, Plymouth PL8 2YP

Correspondent Mrs J A Lethbridge, Secretary

Trustees *Sir John Lowther; Lord Newall; Sir Michael Farquhar; Hon. George Lopes; Countess Peel.*

CC Number 251016

Information available Accounts were available at the Charity Commission, with only a brief narrative report.

General The foundation has established a permanent list of charities that it supports each year, with the remaining funds then distributed to other charities. The grants list does not indicate which charities are on the permanent list.

Its priority areas include the the following:

- heritage; the preservation of the environment; and the countryside and ancient buildings, particularly the 'great Anglican cathedrals'
- charities benefiting people who are ex-service and service, Polish, disabled or refugees
- welfare of horses and people who look after them
- youth and other local organisations in Ashtead – Surrey, Blyth –

Nottinghamshire and Bradford – Yorkshire
- technical education for the woolen industry.

In 2001/02 it had an income of £146,000 with an expenditure of £136,000. No further information was available.

In 2000/01 the trust made grants totalling £162,000. By far the largest donation was £40,000 to Therfield School. Beneficiaries of other grants over £5,000 each included Country Trust (£15,000), Atlantic College (£14,000) and Animal Health Trust, Ashtead Rotary Club, Fairbridge, Ghurkha Welfare Trust, Langford Trust, Royal Commonwealth Society for the Blind and Volunteer Reading Help (£5,000 each).

Smaller grants in the range of a few hundred pounds to £2,000 included those to Raleigh International, Royal Star and Garter Home (£2,000 each), All Hallows Development Trust and Racing Welfare Charities (£1,000 each), Cedar Trust, Sick Children's Trust, Teenage Cancer Trust and Tetbury Hospital Trust (£500 each), Game Conservancy Trust (£400) and Spinal Research Trust (£250).

Exclusions No grants to individuals.

Applications Applications will only be considered if received in writing accompanied by a set of the latest accounts. Applicants do not need to send an sae. Appeals are considered three times a year, in February, June and November.

The Barnsbury Charitable Trust

General

£85,000 (2001/02)

Beneficial area UK, but no local charities outside Oxfordshire.

26 Norham Road, Oxford OX2 6SF

Tel. 01865 316431

Correspondent H L J Brunner, Trustee

Trustees *H L J Brunner; M R Brunner; T E Yates.*

CC Number 241383

Information available Accounts were on file at the Charity Commission.

General In 2002/03 the trust had an income of £31,000 and a total expenditure of £115,000. Further information for this year was unavailable, however previous information gathered stated that in 2001/02 the trust had assets of £1.4 million and generated an income of £32,000. Grants totalling £85,000 were given in 58 donations, with over half of these given in Oxfordshire.

The largest donations given in the year were £10,000 each to Hebridean Trust and Brookes University. Other grants ranged from £25 to £5,500, beneficiaries included: Vale of White Horse District Charities (£5,500); Chipping Norton Theatre Trust, OCVYS, Oxford Chamber Music Festival, Oxford Community Foundation, Oxfordshire Victoria County History Trust and Volunteer Reading Help (£5,000 each); Friends of St Giles' – Oxford, See Saw and Wheatley Windmill Restoration Society (£2,500); and Deafblind UK, Kids at Art Relate Oxfordshire and University of Oxford Development Trust (£2,000 each).

Smaller grants of £1,000 and below included: Common Purpose UK and Oxford Christian Institute for Counselling (£1,000 each); Home–Start Oxford (£500); Mencap – Oxford (£400); Oxfordshire Historic Churches Trust (£200); Oxford Sleep–out (£160); Dorchester Abbey Preservation Trust and Oxford Oratory (£100 each); and Burford Church PCC (£25).

Exclusions No grants to individuals.

Applications In writing to the correspondent.

The Misses Barrie Charitable Trust

Medical, general

£120,000 (2003/04)

Beneficial area UK.

Messrs Raymond Carter & Co, 1b Haling Road, South Croydon CR2 6HS

Tel. 020 8686 1686

Correspondent Raymond Carter, Trustee

Trustees *R G Carter; R S Waddell; R S Ogg; Mrs R Fraser.*

CC Number 279459

Information available Full accounts were on file at the Charity Commission.

General In 2003/04 the income of the trust was £212,000 and grants to 80 organisations totalled £120,000; assets stood at £4.7 million.

The largest grant was £10,000 to University of Oxford Weatherall Institute of Molecular Medicine. Other larger grants went to Princess Royal Trust for Carers (£5,000), Surrey Cricket Board (£3,200) and University of Dundee Biomedical Research Centre (£3,000). All of these organisations have been supported in previous years.

Remaining donations were for £2,000 (24), £1,000 (50) or £500 (2). Beneficiaries included Action for Blind People, Broadway Parish Council, Canterbury Oast Trust, Crimestoppers Trust, Daisy Chain Trust, Gurkha Welfare Trust, High Blood Pressure Foundation, Life Education Centres - Surrey, Sports Aid Trust, Sparks, Vision Aid and Victim Support - Gloucestershire.

An amount of £60,000 has also been set aside by the trust towards an ultimate grant of a much larger sum to the Royal National Lifeboat Institution.

Exclusions No grants to individuals.

Applications In writing to the correspondent. Trustees meet three times a year, in April, August and December.

The Bartlett Taylor Charitable Trust

General

£53,000 (2002/03)

Beneficial area Preference for Oxfordshire.

24 Church Green, Witney, Oxfordshire OX8 6AT

Tel. 01993 703941 **Fax** 01993 776 071

Correspondent I Welch, Trustee

Trustees *I O Welch; Mrs B Cook; R Bartlett; P A Burchett; Mrs R Warner; J W Dingle.*

CC Number 285249

Information available Information was provided by the trust.

General In 2002/03 the trust had assets of £1.3 million and an income of £52,000. Grants were made totalling £53,000. Over one-third of the total number of grants were made to individuals.

There were 133 grants awarded during the year which were covered in the following categories:

International charities
2 grants were made of £350 and £1,000 each.

UK national charities
Medical: 7 grants were made in the range of £250 to £500 totalling £3,000

Educational: 2 grants were made totalling £1,000

Other: 14 grants were made in the range of £250 to £1,000 totalling £6,800

Local organisations
Community projects: 33 grants were made in the range of £100 to £1,000 totalling £12,000

Medical: 12 grants made in the range of £250 to £1,000 totalling £6,800

Educational: 9 grants were made in the range of £100 to £500 totalling £3,300

Other: 10 grants were made in the range of £100 to £500 totalling £3,400

Individuals
Educational: 17 grants were made ranging between £100 and £350 totalling £3,300

Relief: 24 grants ranging between £100 and £1,400 totalling £12,000

Medical: 3 grants were made in the range of £500 to £1,500 totalling £3,000.

Applications In writing to the correspondent. Trustees meet bi-monthly.

The Paul Bassham Charitable Trust

General

£105,000 (2001/02)

Beneficial area UK, mainly Norfolk.

Howes Percival, The Guildyard, 51 Colegate, Norwich NR3 1DD

Tel. 01603 762103

Correspondent R Lovett, Trustee

Trustees *R Lovett; R J Jacob.*

CC Number 266842

Information available Full accounts were provided by the trust.

General This trust was established in the early 1970s and in 2001/02 had assets of £4.5 million and an income of £122,000. During the year 159 donations were made totalling £105,000 (£162,000 in 2000/01).

Beneficiaries for the year 2001/02 included: Norwich School and Inspire (£10,000 each); Norfolk Youth Projects and The Prince's Trust (£5,000 each) and Nancy Oldfield Trust (£3,000). All other grants listed ranged between £1,000 and £2,000. Beneficaries included: Norfolk County Scout Council, St. William's Primary School and 35th Norwich Sea Scouts (£2,000 each) and Norwich Cathedral Millennium Appeal, Samaritans, The Hamlets Centre Trust and United Reformed Church (£1,000 each).

In addition the trust have pledged £52,000 to organisations, including Theatre Royal's Youth Project (£25,000), Hewett School (£12,000), Norwich & Norfolk Association for the Blind (£10,000) and Rotary House (£4,000).

The trustees state that although they can give support to appeals from national charities, in practice all grants are given for work that has an involvement in Norfolk.

Exclusions Grant payments will not be made directly in favour of individuals.

Applications In writing to the correspondent – no formal application forms issued. Telephone enquiries are not invited because of administrative costs. 'The trustees meet quarterly (March, June, September, December) to consider general applications although additional meetings or discussions are held where major projects are the subject of an application or where there is some degree of urgency.'

The Batchworth Trust

Medical, social welfare, general

£215,000 (2001/02)

Beneficial area Worldwide.

33–35 Bell Street, Reigate, Surrey RH2 7AW

Tel. 01737 221311

Correspondent M R Neve, Administrative Executive

Trustee *Lockwell Trustees Ltd.*

CC Number 245061

Information available Accounts were on file at the Charity Commission.

General The trust mainly supports nationally-recognised charities, in the categories shown below.

In 2003/04 the trust had an income of £275,000 and a total expenditure of £278,000. Further information for this year was unavailable.

In 2001/02 it made 36 grants totalling £215,000, broken down as follows:

	2001/02	*2000/01*
Social welfare	48%	44%
Medical	22%	20%
Foreign aid	15%	22%
Youth & education	13%	13%
Environment	2%	1%

Grants ranged from £2,000 to £10,000, but were mainly for amounts of £5,000 or less. The largest, £15,000, went to International Red Cross with eight grants of £1,000 each going to Alzheimer's Society, Médicins Sans Frontiéres, New Hall College, Prisoners of Conscience, RNID, Restore, Royal Commonwealth Society for the Blind and Schizophrenia Research.

Smaller grants included those to Action for Kids, Anchor Society, Farm Africa, Garsington Opera, Haddo Arts Trust, Royal Agricultural Benevolent Trust, Waterside Trust and Youth Clubs UK.

Exclusions No applications from individuals can be considered.

Applications In writing to the correspondent. An sae should be included if a reply is required.

The Bay Tree Charitable Trust

Development work, general

£155,000 (2001)

Beneficial area UK and overseas.

10 New Square, London WC2A 3QG

Tel. 0207 465 4300

Correspondent c/o Payne Hicks Beach

Trustees *I M P Benton; Miss E L Benton; P H Benton.*

CC Number 1044091

Information available Accounts were provided by the trust.

General In 2002 the trust had an income of £142,000 with an expenditure of £110,000. No further information was available.

Previous beneficiaries have included Crusaid, Tree Aid, Wateraid, British Red Cross, Fair Trial Abroad, Save the Children, Cotswold Riding for the Disabled, Médecins Sans Frontières and Youth Care Initiative.

Exclusions No grants to individuals.

Applications In writing to the correspondent. No acknowledgements will be made to unsuccessful applications.

The Beacon Trust

Christian

£57,000 (1999/2000)

Beneficial area Mainly UK, but also some overseas (usually in the British Commonwealth) and Spain and Portugal.

Unit 3, Newhouse Farm, Old Crawley Road, Faygate, Horsham, West Sussex RH12 4RU

Tel. 01293 851 715

Correspondent Mr G Scofield

Trustees *Mrs D J Spink; Miss J M Spink; M Spink.*

CC Number 230087

Information available Accounts were on file at the Charity Commission, but with a very brief report and without a list of grants.

General The trust's objects are 'to advance the Christian faith, relieve poverty and advance education'.

In 2000/01 the trust had an income of £117,000 with an expenditure of £177,000. No further information was available.

The emphasis of the trust's support is on Christian work overseas, particularly amongst students, although the trust does not support individuals. The trust has previously stated that it has a list of charities that it supports in most years. This leaves very little funds available for unsolicited applications.

Exclusions Applications from individuals are not considered.

Applications In writing to the correspondent. The trustees normally meet once a year in December and all applications are generally dealt with at that meeting.

Bear Mordechai Ltd

Jewish

£125,000 (2001/02)

Beneficial area Worldwide.

136 Holmleigh Road, London N16 5PY

Correspondent Mrs Leah Benedikt, Secretary

Trustees *Y Benedikt; C Benedikt; E S Benedikt.*

CC Number 286806

Information available Accounts were on file at the Charity Commission.

General Grants are made to Jewish organisations. The trust states that religious, educational and other charitable institutions are supported.

In 2001/02 this trust had assets of £776,000, an income of £73,000 and made grants totalling £125,000.

Grant beneficiaries included Agudat Yad Yemin Jerusalem (£64,500), Kollel Bear Mordechy (£20,000), Zedokoh Bechol Eis (£15,700), Almat Limited (£5,800), Anpride Limited (£5,000), Hod Yurushalaim Educational Centre (£3,300), Lolev Charitable Trust (£1,900), Craven Walk Charities Trust (£1,600), Kollel Ohel E Limelech (£1,500) and Mesifta Talmudical College (£1,300).

Applications In writing to the correspondent.

The Beaufort House Trust

Christian, education

£61,000 to individuals and organisations (2003)

Beneficial area UK.

Beaufort House, Brunswick Road, Gloucester GL1 1JZ

Tel. 01452 528533 **Fax** 01452 308860

Website www.allchurches.co.uk

Correspondent Mrs R J Hall, Company Secretary

Trustees *Sir Alan McLintock, Chair; M R Cornwall-Jones; B V Day; Viscount Churchill; Rt. Revd D G Shelgrove; W H Yates; Mrs S B S Homersham; Hon N Assheton.*

CC Number 286606

Information available Full accounts were provided by the trust.

General The trustees make grants to promote the furtherance of education and the Christian religion. Appeals are considered from schools, colleges, universities or any other charitable body involved in this work. It receives an annual payment from the Ecclesiastical Insurance Group plc.

In 2003 the trust had assets of £123,000 and an income of £512,000, including £462,000 from their school fees scheme. After school fees were paid totalling £435,000, the sum of £61,000 was distributed in grants. In total 15 grants were given to educational organisations totalling £17,000 and 41 to individual bursaries totalling £44,000.

The largest grants were given to Ministry Bursary Awards (£42,000). Donations over £1,000 each were to: King Edward's School – Surrey (£5,000), National Star College – Gloucestershire (£3,000), Dyson Perrins C of E High School – Worcestershire, Moorlands College – Dorset and St William Foundation (£2,000 each) and St John's College – Nottingham (£1,000).

Beneficiaries of smaller grants included: Finchamstead C of E Primary School – Berkshire (£250), Hatherley Infants School – Gloucester and St Nicholas' Church of England Junior School – Devon (£200 each), St Mark's Elm Tree C of E Primary School – Devon (£150) and South Street Primary School – Bristol (£100).

Exclusions No grants are made to organisations with political associations, UK wide charities or individuals.

Applications In writing to the correspondent detailing: the objectives of the charity; the appeal target; how the funds are to be utilised; funds raised to date; and previous support received from the trust.

Beauland Ltd

Jewish

£93,000 (2001/02)

Beneficial area Worldwide, possibly with a preference for the Manchester area.

32 Stanley Road, Salford M7 4ES

Correspondent M Neumann

Trustees *F Neuman; H Neuman; M Friedlander; H Roseman; J Bleir; R Delange; M Neuman; P Neuman; E Neuman; E Henry.*

CC Number 511374

Information available Accounts were on file at the Charity Commission.

General The trust's objects are the advancement of the Jewish religion in accordance with the Orthodox Jewish faith and the relief of poverty. It gives grants to 'religious, educational and similar bodies'.

In 2001/02 it had assets of £1.6 million and an income of £295,000, of which £188,000 came from donations. Grants totalled £93,000, mostly given to Jewish organisations.

The accounts listed 20 donations made over £1,000 each. Grants inlcuded £16,000 to Yeshiva L'Zeirim, £6,000 to Chested L'Yisroel, £5,500 to Manchester Yeshiva Kollel, £2,500 to Jewish High School, £1,700 to Pnevez, £1,900 to Jewish Day School and £1,100 to Broom Foundation.

Applications In writing to the correspondent.

This entry was not confirmed by the trust but was correct according to information on file at the Charity Commission.

The Beaverbrook Foundation

General

£96,000 to organisations (1999/2000)

Beneficial area UK and Canada.

Wytham Court, 11 West Way, Oxford OX2 0JB

Website www.beaverbrookfoundation.org

Correspondent Sarah Way

Trustees *Lord Beaverbrook, Chair; Lady Beaverbrook; Lady Aitken; T M Aitken; Laura Levi; J E A Kidd; M F Aitken.*

CC Number 310003

Information available Accounts were on file at the Charity Commission with an inadequate report and without a list of grants.

General This trust mostly supports its own work in the preservation and renovation of Cherkley Court. Grants are also made to other organisations as funds allow. The most recent financial information available from a grant-making year is from 1999/2000, when the trust had assets of £18 million and an income of £519,000. Grants to organisations totalled £96,000. Other expenditure included £209,000 on management and administration, presumably related to managing the trust's properties and £466,000 on renovations to Cherkley Court, which is owned by the trust.

The trust has, in recent years, spent most of its funds on a major redevelopment project, which was expected to be completed in March 2005.

Exclusions Only registered charities are supported.

Applications In writing to the correspondent with an sae. Trustees meet in May and November.

The Peter Beckwith Charitable Trust

Medical, welfare

£55,000 (2002/03)

Beneficial area UK.

Hill Place House, 55a High Street, Wimbledon Village, London SW19 5BA

Tel. 020 8944 1288

Correspondent P M Beckwith, Trustee

Trustees *P M Beckwith; Mrs P Beckwith; Mrs A Peppiatt.*

CC Number 802113

Information available Accounts were on file at the Charity Commission but without a list of grants.

General This trust was established in 1989. In 2002/03 it received an income of £44,000 mostly from donations. Assets at the year end totalled £10,000. In this year grants came to £55,000 but, unfortunately, no list of grants was included with the accounts that were on file at the Charity Commission.

In previous years beneficiaries have included Burnbake Trust, Cara Trust, Carousel, Dartington International Summer School, Handy Aid to Independent Living, Queen Elizabeth Foundation for Disabled People, REAC, Royal School for Deaf Children and Rugby Mayday Trust.

Applications In writing to the correspondent.

The Bedfordshire & Hertfordshire Historic Churches Trust

Churches

£46,000 (2003/04)

Beneficial area Bedfordshire and Hertfordshire.

31 Ivel Gardens, Biggleswade, Bedfordshire SG18 0AN

Tel. 01767 314513

Correspondent S A Russell, Grants Secretary

Trustees *A A I Jenkins; S C Y Farmbourgh; C P Green; B A Hunt; P F D Lepper; P A Lomax; A J Philpott; S A Russell; R H Tomlins.*

CC Number 1005697

Information available Information provided by the trust.

General The trust gives grants for the restoration, preservation, repair and maintenance of churches in Bedfordshire and Hertfordshire.

The aims of the trust are as follows:

- 'maintain a large, supportive membership whose annual, committed income from subscriptions and donations will give the firm basis upon which to conduct its affairs
- foster an informed appreciation of the history, architecture and beauty of the churches and chapels in the two counties and so provide a way for the wider community to help to maintain that irreplaceable hertitage

- raise substantial amounts of money, primarily through the annual sponsored bicycle ride, an event promoted by the trust and supported by other county trusts.'

In 2003/04 the trust had assets of £132,000 and an income of £115,000. Grants totalled £46,000.

In 2001/02 grants totalling £47,000 were made to 17 churches. Donations were broken down by geographical area as follows: £5,000 in Ware; £4,000 each in Benington, Houghton Regis, Knebworth, Sundon and Walkern; £3,500 in Westoning; £3,000 in Broxbourne; £2,500 in Stapleford; £1,500 each in Hexton and Stotfold; and £1,000 to Buntingford URC.

In previous years funds were given for roof repairs, window repairs, flint work on a tower, pointing and stonework repairs.

Exclusions No grants to individuals.

Applications In writing to the correspondent.

The David & Ruth Behrend Fund

General

£58,000 (2001/02)

Beneficial area UK, with a preference for Merseyside.

c/o Liverpool Council of Social Service (Inc.), 14 Castle Street, Liverpool L2 0NJ

Tel. 0151 236 7728 **Fax** 0151 258 1153

Correspondent The Secretary

Trustee *Liverpool Council of Social Service (Inc).*

CC Number 261567

Information available Information was provided by the trust.

General This trust was established in 1969 and appears to give exclusively in Merseyside. The trust states that grants are only made to charities known to the settlors; unsolicited applications are not considered.

In 2001/02 it had assets of £1.3 million and an income of £59,000. Grants totalled £58,000.

Grants of £1,000 or more were made to 18 organisations. These were Merseyside Development Foundation (£12,000), Amelia Chadwick Trust (£4,000), Chara Trust, PSS and Remisus (£2,500 each), Liverpool Family Service Unit and Refugee Council (£1,800 each), Liverpool Somali Youth Association (£1,500), Bankfield House, British Red Cross Society, Christian Aid, Energywise Recycling, Furniture Resource Centre, Kind, Knowsley Counselling Agency, Merseyside Holiday Service, Merseyside Sexual Assault Centre and The Missionary Training Service (£1,000 each).

Smaller grants totalled £19,000.

Exclusions Anyone not known to the settlors.

Applications This trust states that it does not respond to unsolicited applications.

Belljoe Tzedoko Ltd

Jewish

About £30,000 (2003)

Beneficial area UK.

27 Fairholt Road, London N16 5EW

Tel. 020 8800 4384

Correspondent H J Lobenstein, Trustee

Trustees *H J Lobenstein; Mrs B Lobenstein; D Lobenstein; M Lobenstein.*

CC Number 282726

Information available Accounts were on file at the Charity Commission, but without a list of grants.

General The trust's objects are 'the advancement of religion in accordance with the orthodox Jewish faith and the relief of poverty'.

In 2003 the trust had a gross income of £32,000 with a total expenditure of £31,000. Unfortunately no other financial information was provided.

The most recent grants list available in the Charity Commission file was for 1995 when grants totalled £76,000. They ranged from £10 to £8,600 and were made to 87 Jewish organisations. The three largest were £8,600 to Marbeh Torah Trust, £7,500 to Society of Friends of the Torah and £5,500 to Yesodey Hatorah School.

Applications In writing to the correspondent.

Belsize Charitable Trust No. 1

Envrionment, conservation, heritage in the UK

£43,000 (2001/02)

Beneficial area UK.

Lloyds TSB Private Banking Ltd., UK Trust Centre, The Clock House, 22–26 Ock Street, Abingdon, Oxfordshire OX14 5DW

Correspondent The Trustees

Trustee *Lloyds TSB Private Banking Ltd.*

CC Number 262535

Information available Accounts are on file at the Charity Commission.

General Established in 1971, in 2001/02 the trust had an income of £25,000 and made grants totalling £43,000. Beneficiaries included: St Loye's Foundation – Exeter (£12,000); Salvation Army (£8,000); Mission to Seafarers and Somerset Rural Youth Project (£5,000 each); National Trust (£4,000); and Cumbria Wildlife Trust and National Memorial Arboretum (£3,000 each).

Applications In writing to the correspondent.

Belvedere Trust

Arts education, children at risk and conservation projects worldwide

£94,000 (2002)

Beneficial area Worldwide

The Belvedere, 2 Back Lane, London NW3 1HL

Tel. 020 7433 3600

Correspondent Mervyn Hughes

Trustees *Richard Mervyn Hughes; Irene Josephene Ann Cerini; Mary Ellen Marziale; Stella Prince-Wright.*

CC Number 1078667

Information available Accounts were on file at the Charity Commission.

General Established in December 1999, priority areas for grants include:

- arts education

- children at risk, particularly primary school children
- conservation.

In 2002 the trust had assets of £62,000, an income of £10,000 and made grants totalling £94,000. Grants included:

Children at risk

Coram Mentoring Programme – towards childcare costs and residential weekend costs (£16,000)

Chance UK – towards trainers and volunteer expenses (£6,000)

Out of School Hours Learning – for study support materials (£5,000)

SADA - towards a holiday scheme (£5,000)

Friends United Network – towards volunteer expenses/ a Christmas party (£3,500)

Support for children who are chronically and terminally ill

Starlight Children's Foundation – towards two fun centres at hospitals (£6,000)

Arts for young people in state schools

Charm – towards general costs (£20,000)

Donmar Theatre – Education Double Initiative (£10,000)

Donmar Theatre –towards captioned performances for people who are deaf or hearing impaired (£6,500)

Donmar Theatre – Write Now project (£3,500)

Impact Theatre – towards a group visit to Walt Disney Studios in Paris

Tower Hamlets Youth and Community Band – towards core costs (£1,500)

Applications In writing to the correspondent.

The Benham Charitable Settlement

Youth, general

£120,000 (2003/04)

Beneficial area UK, with very strong emphasis on Northamptonshire.

Hurstbourne, Portnall Drive, Virginia Water, Surrey GU25 4NR

Correspondent Mrs M Tittle, Managing Trustee

Trustees *Mrs M M Tittle; Lady Hutton; E N Langley.*

CC Number 239371

Information available Full accounts were provided by the trust.

General The settlement was founded in 1964 by the late Cedric Benham and his wife Hilda, then resident in Northamptonshire, 'to benefit charities and for divers good causes and considerations'.

'The object of the charity is the support of registered charities working in many different fields – including charities involved in medical research, disability, elderly people, children and young people, disadvantaged people, overseas aid, missions to seamen, the welfare of ex-servicemen, wildlife, the environment, and the arts. The trust also supports the Church of England, and the work of Christian mission throughout the world. Special emphasis is placed upon those churches and charitable organisations within the county of Northamptonshire [especially as far as new applicants are concerned].'

'In recent years the settlement has made a series of substantial donations, exceeding £1.6 million, to the Northamptonshire Association of Youth Clubs.' These donations were principally for the purchase of a freehold site and to facilitate the financing and construction of an indoor sports arena. The trust stated its intention to continue to support certain operations of the association on a selected basis.

In 2002/03 the trust had assets of £3.6 million which generated an income of £122,000. A total of £120,000 was given in 199 grants. These ranged from £50 to £35,000, although most were for £400 or less. Northamptonshire Association of Youth Clubs received the largest grant, of £35,000. Other larger grants included £3,000 to Coworth Park School, £2,000 to Northampton Symphony Orchestra, £1,500 to Holy Trinity Sunningdale and £1,000 to Victoria County Library.

Beneficiaries receiving £500 or less included 1st Burton Latimer Scout Group, Abbey Centre User's Association, Bibles for Children, Care, Combat Stress, Defeating Deafness, Dreams Come True Charity, Finedon Community Centre, Helen House, Iris Trust, Kettering and Corby Sick Pilgrims Trust, Messengers of Love, Newton in the Willows Trust, Northampton Grammar School, Paul Bevan Cancer Foundation, Royal Star & Garter Home, Seaman's Christian Friend Society, Thames Valley Hospice, Traidcraft, Ventures Search & Rescue, Whale and Dolphin Conservation and Woodland Trust.

Exclusions No grants to individuals.

Applications The trust stated in January 2005 that it 'cannot consider any new applications, of any sort, for at least the next two years'.

Michael and Leslie Bennett Charitable Trust

Jewish

£66,000 (2002/03)

Beneficial area UK.

c/o 69–77 Paul Street, London EC2A 4PN

Tel. 0208 458 4945

Correspondent Michael Bennett

Trustees *Michael Bennett; Lesley V Bennett.*

CC Number 1047611

Information available Full accounts were on file at the Charity Commission.

General The trust supports a range of causes, but the largest donations were to Jewish organisations. In 2002/03 the trust had assets of £351,000, an income of £12,000 mostly from investments and made grants totalling £66,000.

Those grants to Jewish organisations included £10,000 each to Jewish Care and World Jewish Relief, £7,500 to Norwood, £5,000 each to Nightingale and UJIA. Other donations included £320 to The Disability Foundation, £250 to British ORT and £100 each to Barnet Hospital (Maternity Trust Fund) and Alzheimers Trust.

Applications In writing to the correspondent.

The Geoffrey Berger Charitable Trust

General

£34,000 (2001/02)

Beneficial area UK and overseas.

PO Box 12162, London NW11 7WR
Tel. 0208 731 7799
Correspondent G D Berger, Trustee
Trustees *G D Berger; N J Berger; Mrs A Berger.*
CC Number 1059991
Information available Accounts were on file at the Charity Commission, but without a list of grants.

General This trust had an income in 2001/2, of £28,000 and assets totalled £12,000. Its total expenditure on grants was £34,000. Information about how much was given in grants was not available for that year.

Exclusions No grants to individuals.

Applications The trust has stated that its funds are fully committed and that it does not accept unsolicited applications.

The Berkeley Reafforestation Trust

Reafforestation projects

£35,000 (2001/02)

Beneficial area Worldwide

3 Harley Gardens, London SW10 9SW
Tel. 020 7370 1965
Correspondent R J B Portman, Trustee
Trustees *Rodney Portman; Loulou Cooke; Nicholas Foster; Rozzie Portman.*
CC Number 297982
Information available Acounts were on file at the Charity Commission.

General The trust's aims are:

- the relief of poverty by promoting tree planting and effective tree management internationally as means of combating land erosion and degradation, rural poverty and ecological and environmental deterioration
- the advancement of education in the importance of the role of forestry and in tree planting and tree management.

It states that it largely supports ongoing projects in Kenya, Zimbabwe, Niger and the Himalayan region of India. It also trials the Global Circle of Knowledge educational software in UK schools.

In 2001/02 it had assets of £37,000. Total income was £28,000, including £26,000 in donations received. Grants were made totalling £35,000. Other expenditure totalled £20,000, including fundraising events, newsletters, videos and computer software.

The largest grant was £24,000 to CHIRAG in India. SOS Sahel in Niger received £5,000 while MPT in Kenya was given £2,800. A total of £1,300 was spent on the Trees for Life project for Global Circle of Knowledge.

Applications In writing to the correspondent, although please note, the trust states that it 'does not solicit applications'.

The Bestway Foundation

Education, welfare, medical

£255,000 (2001/02)

Beneficial area UK and overseas.

Bestway Cash & Carry Ltd, 2 Abbey Road, Park Royal, London NW10 7BW
Correspondent A K Bhatti
Trustees *A K Bhatti; A K Chaudhary; M Y Sheikh; Z M Chaudrey; M A Pervez; Z U H Khan.*
CC Number 297178
Information available Brief information was supplied by the trust.

General The trust supports:

- the education of schoolchildren and students of Indian, Pakistani, Bangladeshi or Sri Lankan origin, in the UK and overseas
- the relief of sickness and preservation and protection of health in the UK and overseas (especially Indian, Pakistan, Bangladesh and Sri Lanka) by supporting existing and new hospitals, clinics and medical research establishments
- UK charities working with people who are elderly, disabled or otherwise in need.

In 2001/02 it had assets of £2.9 million and an income of £565,000, mostly from donations received. a total of 19 grants were made totalling £255,000. A breakdown of these was listed as follows:

UK registered charities	£60,000
Non-registered UK charities	£114,000
Foreign charities – Individuals	£80,000

The largest grants were £50,000 to May Lane School, £45,000 to Duke of Edinburgh Awards, £25,000 to Rodillion School and £19,000 to Trustees of the UN.

Exclusions No grants for trips/travel abroad.

Applications In writing to the correspondent, enclosing an sae. Applications are considered in March/April. Telephone calls are not welcome.

Thomas Betton's Charity for Pensions and Relief-in-Need

General, disadvantage

£43,000 to organisations (2002/03)

Beneficial area UK.

Ironmongers' Hall, Barbican, London EC2Y 8AA
Tel. 020 7776 2311
Website www.ironhall.co.uk
Correspondent The Charities Administrator
Trustee *The Worshipful Company of Ironmongers.*
CC Number 280143
Information available Information was provided by the trust.

General In 2002/03 the trust had assets of £602,000 and an income of £51,000, including £29,000 from Thomas Betton's Estate Charity and £22,000 from investments. Grants totalled £43,000 and £2,800 was also spent on pensions to individuals.

The trust makes a block grant to Housing the Homeless which allocates grants to individuals, which totalled £19,000 in 2001/02. Other grants during that year were £3,500 to Phoenix Lodge, £2,500 to Spitalfields Farm Association, £2,200 to British Red Cross, £2,000 each to National Autistic Society, RNIB, Royal Metal Trades' Benevolent Society, RPS Rainer, Sheriffs' and Recorders' Fund, Thrive and YMCA – London, £1,000 to Alone in London and £900 given in smaller donations.

Exclusions Applications for grants to individuals are accepted only from registered social workers or other agencies, not directly from individuals.

Applications In writing to the correspondent.

Billingsgate Christian Mission Charitable Trust

Fishing industry-related, medical research

£30,000 (2002)

Beneficial area UK.

Fishmongers' Company, Fishmongers' Hall, London Bridge, London EC4R 9EL

Tel. 020 7626 3531 **Fax** 020 7929 1389

Correspondent K S Waters, Clerk

Trustee *The Clerk, Assistant Clerk and the Court of the Fishmongers' Company.*

CC Number 1013851

Information available Full accounts were provided by the trust.

General The trust states its aims in the guidelines as:

- to relieve poverty, distress and sickness among persons engaged in the Fish and Fishing Industries in the UK
- to advance religious and social work in accordance with the Christian faith among persons engaged in the Fish and Fishing Industries in the UK
- to advance medical science, particularly by way of grants for scholarships.

In 2003 it had assets of £583,000, which generated an income of £15,000, all of which was given in grants. These were broken down as follows:

Fishery-related charities

Grants of £5,000 each went to The Fishermen's Mission and Fishmongers' and Poulterers' Institute, both of which were also supported in the previous year.

Medical-related charities

The only grant was of £5,000 and went to St Peter's Trust. In the previous year five grants were made totalling £20,000. These were of £2,500 or £5,000 each and went to Dermatitis and Allied Diseases, International Glaucoma Trust, Marfan Trust, Meningitis Trust and St George's Hospital.

Exclusions No grants to individuals.

Applications In writing to the correspondent, including the latest annual accounts. Trustees meet three times a year.

The Billmeir Charitable Trust

General, health and medical

£101,000 (2002/03)

Beneficial area UK, with a preference for the Surrey area, specifically Elstead, Tilford, Farnham and Frensham.

Messrs Moore Stephens, 1 Snow Hill, London EC1A 2EN

Tel. 020 7334 9191

Correspondent T T Cripps, Accountant

Trustees *B C Whitaker; M R Macfadyen; S Marriott; J Whitaker.*

CC Number 208561

Information available Full accounts were provided by the trust.

General The trust states it supports a wide variety of causes. About a quarter of the grants are given to health and medical charities and about a third of the grants are given to local organisations in Surrey, especially the Farnham, Frensham, Elstead and Tilford areas.

In 2002/03 the trust's assets were £2.8 million and it had an income of £125,000. Donations were given to 24 charities totalling £101,000. Of those supported, 18 had received a grant in the previous year.

The largest grants went to Reeds School – Cobham (£10,000) and Arundel Castle Cricket Foundation, Blaser, Lord Mayor Treloar School and Meath Home (£7,000 each). Other donations included Marlborough College (£6,000), Parochial Church Council of St James – Elstead, Woodlarks Campsite Trust and Youth Sport Trust (£5,000 each), Alzheimer's Society, Checkendon Parochial Church Council and Grove School (£2,000 each) and Music in Hospitals (£1,000).

Applications The trust states that it does not request applications and that its funds are fully committed.

The Bintaub Charitable Trust

Jewish, health, education, children

About £35,000 (2001/02)

Beneficial area Greater London, national and international.

89 Rechovbayitzegan, Jerusalem 96426

Tel. 020 8455 1874 **Fax** 020 8209 1831

Correspondent The Trustees

Trustees *James Frohwein; Tania Frohwein; Daniel Frohwein.*

CC Number 1003915

Information available Accounts were on file at the Charity Commission.

General This trust was set up in 1991 and provides grants to mainly London organisations, towards 'the advancement of education in and the religion of the orthodox Jewish faith'. Grants are also given for other charitable causes, mainly towards medical and children's work. In 2003/04 it had an income of £48,000 and a total expenditure of £52,000.

In previous years it has made numerous grants ranging from £10 to £930, averaging just £66 each. Beneficiaries have included Finchley Road Synagogue, Great Ormond Street Hospital, Horden Centre for Arthritis, London Friends of Care for the Needy, London Jewish Academy, North West London Talmudical College, North London Hospice, Norwood Child Care and West London Action for Children.

Applications In writing to the correspondent. However, the correspondent stated previously that new applications are not being accepted.

The Dickie Bird Foundation

Sport

Unknown

Beneficial area UK/wide.

Jefferson House, Orchard Lane, Guiseley, Leeds LS20 9HZ

Tel. 01943 873482 **Fax** 01943 871873

Email info@thedickiebirdfoundation.org

Website www.thedickiebirdfoundation.org

Correspondent The The Clerk to the Trustees

Trustees *Harold Dennis 'Dickie' Bird; Sidney Fielden; Dayal Sharma.*

CC Number 1104646

Information available Information was taken from the foundation's website.

General The foundation was established by legendary cricket umpire Dickie Bird in March 2004 with the aim of helping disadvantaged young people, nationwide, to participate in sport. Grants are expected to range from between £500 to £5,000.

Its objective is:

'To provide or assist the provision of facilities which enable young people in schools, universities and other educational establishments, local clubs and community groups to participate in sporting activities in the interests of healthy recreation or the advancement of physical education.

'It is our fervent hope that, through our efforts and the grants we make, more young people will be able to access sport and fulfil their ambitions as sportsmen whilst at the same time improving their prospects in life.

'If you feel you, a young person you know, or your school, club, university/ college sporting society or sports association would meet our criteria, please ask for an application form. Every application will be given fair and equal consideration.'

At the time this entry was researched, the trust had not completed its first financial year. It was not known how much was expected to be given away in grants each year.

Applications Application forms and eligibility requirements can be downloaded from the foundation's website. Applicants need to show that they are unable to raise the necessary finance required as a result of impoverished circumstance and that funds cannot be rasied through any other means.

The Birmingham Hospital Saturday Fund Medical Charity & Welfare Trust

Medical

£44,000 (2003)

Beneficial area UK, but mostly centred around the West Midlands and Birmingham area.

Gamgee House, 2 Darnley Road, Birmingham B16 8TE

Tel. 0121 454 3601

Correspondent Kate Lister, Appeals Administrator

Trustees *Dr R P Kanas; S G Hall; E S Hickman; M Malone; D J Read; J Salmons.*

CC Number 502428

Information available Information was provided by the trust.

General This trust supports the relief of sickness, with the trustees also holding an interest in medical research. The trustees continue to give priority to charities that benefit those living in the West Midlands area with some interest in the south west for historical reasons. The trust no longer receives an income from the parent company and so the trustees are now working purely with reserves and the interest from them. This has resulted in a more critical look at projects at each meeting and donations are now generally less than £2,000. Projects that are appropriate and reflect well thought through projects with realistic cost breakdowns are given greater consideration.

In 2003 it had assets of £593,000 and an income of £24,000. Grants totalled £44,000. The largest donation was £10,000 to School of Medicine – University of Birmingham for Gamgee Bursary Awards for 2004/05 and 2005/ 06. Other donations included: £5,000 to Action Research – Sussex for a research project for sickle cell disease; £3,400 to NHS West Midlands for two nurse travel scholarships; £2,500 to Warwickshire Domestic Violence Support Services – Stratford-upon-Avon; £2,000 to Shakespeare Hospice – Stratford-upon-Avon; £1,300 to Institute of Ageing and Health for Excellent Care awards for 2004; £1,100 to Movement Foundation – Shropshire for refurbishment costs for mobility equipment for children; £1,000 to Birmingham Centre for Arts Therapies for therapy sessions of those with learning and behavioural problems; £550 to Alzheimer's Society – Birmingham for delegate packs for conference on dementia care; £400 to Ladywood Day Centre – Birmingham for equipment and materials for therapeutic arts and crafts; and £200 to William Rathbone Fundraisers – Birmingham for entertainment for older people.

Exclusions The trust will not generally fund: direct appeals from individuals or students; administration expenditure including salaries; bank loans/deficits/ mortgages; items or services which should normally be publicly funded; large general appeals; vehicle operating costs; or motor vehicles for infrequent use and where subsidised vehicle share schemes are available to charitable organisations.

Applications On a form available from the correspondent. The form requires basic information and should be submitted with financial details. Evidence should be provided that the project has been adequately considered through the provision of quotes or supporting documents, although the trust dislikes applications which provide too much general information or have long-winded descriptions of projects. Applicants should take great care to read the guidance notes on the application form. The trustees meet four times a year and deadlines are given when application forms are sent out.

Birthday House Trust

General

£34,000 (2002/03)

Beneficial area England and Wales.

Dickinson Trust Ltd, Pollen House, 10–12 Cork Street, London W1S 3LW

Tel. 020 7439 9061

Correspondent Alan Winborn

Trustee *Dickinson Trust Ltd.*

CC Number 248028

Information available Full accounts were provided by the trust.

General Established in 1966, the main work of this trust is engaged with the running of a residential home for people who are elderly in Midhurst, West

Sussex. In 2002/03 it had assets of £4.6 million and an income of £161,000. Out of a total expenditure of £190,000, grants to 22 organisations totalled £34,000 and grants to 12 pensioners totalled £52,000.

The largest grant was £20,000 to Prince of Wales's Charitable Foundation. Other grants were £5,000 to Oxford Research Group, £2,000 to U Can Do I.T., £1,300 to Chichester Cathedral Restoration and Development Trust and £1,000 each to Midhurst Parochial Church Council and Selham Parochial Church Council.

All other donations were of £500 or less. Beneficiaries included Canine Partners for Independence and Fire Services National Benevolent Fund (£500 each), Camphill Village Trust Limited (£450), Music Sound Foundation and Save the Rhino (£250 each), Royal United Kingdom Beneficient Association and Murray Downland Trust (£50).

Exclusions No applications will be considered from individuals or non-charitable organisations.

Applications In writing to the correspondent, including a sae. No application forms are issued and there is no deadline. Only successful applicants are acknowledged.

The Bisgood Charitable Trust (registered as The Miss Jeanne Bisgood's Charitable Trust)

Roman Catholic purposes, older people

£140,000 (2002/03)

Beneficial area UK, overseas and locally in Bournemouth and Dorset, especially Poole.

12 Waters Edge, Brudenell Road, Poole BH13 7NN

Tel. 01202 708460

Correspondent Miss J M Bisgood, Trustee

Trustees *Miss J M Bisgood; P Schulte; P J K Bisgood.*

CC Number 208714

Information available The information for this entry was provided by the trust. Full accounts were on file at the Charity Commission.

General This trust has emerged following a recent amalgamation of The Bisgood Trust with The Miss Jeanne Bisgood's Charitable Trust. Both trusts had the same objects. It now operates a sub-fund, The Bertram Fund (see below).

The General Fund has the following priorities:

1. Roman Catholic charities

2. Charities benefiting people in Poole, Bournemouth and the county of Dorset

3. National charities for the benefit of older people.

No grants are made to local charities which do not fall under categories 1 or 2. Many health and welfare charities are supported as well as charities working in relief and development overseas.

The trust was given 12 paintings to be held as part of the trust funds. Most of the paintings were sold and the proceeds were placed in a new fund, The Bertram Fund, established in 1998, the income of which is purely for Roman Catholic causes. It is intended that it will primarily support major capital projects.

In 2002/03 the trust had total assets of £3.8 million and an income of £165,000. Grants totalled £140,000, of which £83,000 were made from the Bertram Fund and £57,000 from the General Fund. The largest grants made from the general fund included £2,500 to ITDG, £2,000 each to Apex Trust, Impact and Sight Savers International and £1,500 each to St Barnabas' Society and St Francis Leprosy Guild.

Most of The Bertram Fund grants are made anonymously.

Exclusions Grants are not given to local charities not fitting categories 1 or 2 above. Individuals and non-registered charities are not supported.

Applications In writing to the correspondent, quoting the UK registration number and registered title of the charity. A copy of the most recent accounts should also be enclosed. Applications should NOT be made directly to the Bertram Fund. Applications for capital projects 'should provide brief details of the main purposes, the total target and the current state of the appeal'. The trustees regret that they are unable to acknowledge appeals. The trustees normally meet in late February/early March and September.

The Michael Bishop Foundation

General

£117,000 (2001/02)

Beneficial area Worldwide with a preference for Birmingham and the Midlands.

Donington Hall, Castle Donington, Derby DE74 2SB

Tel. 0161 904 8300

Correspondent Mrs P Robinson

Trustees *Sir Michael Bishop, Chair; Grahame N Elliott; John T Wolfe; John S Coulson.*

CC Number 297627

Information available Full accounts were on file at the Charity Commission.

General Sir Michael Bishop of British Midland set up the foundation in 1987 by giving almost £1 million of shares in Airlines of Britain (Holdings) plc, the parent company of British Midland. A further sum was given in 1992.

In 2001/02 the trust had assets of £3 million, which generated an income of £141,000. Grants were made to 21 organisations and totalled £117,000.

By far the largest grant was £50,000 to D'Oyly Carte Opera Trust, of which the settlor is a trustee. Other large grants included £25,000 to Derby Grammar School and £13,000 to Atlantic Council of the UK. Other beneficiaries included Isle of Wight International Oboe Competition and Shooting Star Trust (£5,000 each), Christie Hospital – Manchester and Friends of Norwich Cathedral (£2,500 each), SAAF Adoption and Fostering (£2,000), Kola Youth Theatre Production (£1,500) and Derbyshire Collections Appeal (£1,000).

Applications In writing to the correspondent. However, the long-term commitment mentioned above means that new applicants are not supported at present.

The Sydney Black Charitable Trust

Evangelical Christianity, social welfare, young people, older people and people who are disabled

About £162,000 (2002/03)

Beneficial area UK.

6 Leopold Road, London SW19 7BD

Tel. 020 8947 1041

Correspondent M B Pilcher, Secretary

Trustees *Mrs J D Crabtree; Mrs H J Dickenson; S J Crabtree; P M Crabtree.*

CC Number 219855

Information available Accounts were filed at the Charity Commission, without a grants list.

General In 2001 The Edna Black Charitable Trust and The Cyril Black Charitable Trust were incorporated into this trust. For the latest year the report stated that support is given to youth organisations, religious, medical and other institutions, such as those helping people who are disadvantaged or disabled.

In 2002/03 the trust had an income of £106,000 and total assets were £2.8 million. Charitable donations were made to Endevour (£18,000), others were at £144,000 and grants between £125 and £200 were made to approx. 700 institutions.

Applications Applications, made in writing to the correspondent, will be considered by the appropriate trust.

Peter Black Charitable Trust

General, particularly Jewish

£35,000 (2001/02)

Beneficial area UK and overseas.

Peter Black Holdings Ltd, Airedale Mill, Lawkholme Lane, Keighley, West Yorkshire BD21 3BB

Correspondent Kathleen M Bell

Trustees *T S S Black; G L Black; A S Black.*

CC Number 264279

Information available Accounts and grants list were provided by the trust.

General In 2001/02 the trust had an unusually high income of £402,000 due to a large donation of £400,000. The trust used this donation money to increase the value of its assets to £406,000, compared to £39,000 in the previous year. Grants totalling £35,000 were made to 51 organisations.

The largest grants went to Abbeyfield Ilkely Society, Imperial Cancer Research Fund and Martin House Hospice (£5,000 each), Home from Home and One to One Project (£3,000 each), Yorkshire Ballet Seminars (£2,000) and Church On The Way – Poland Project, Craven Trust Dales Recovery Appeal and Macmillan Cancer Relief (£1,000 each).

Beneficiaries under £1,000 included SPARKS (£950), Samaritans and Weizmann Institute (£500 each), Anthony Nolan Bone Marrow Trust and Homestart (£300 each), Bristol Cancer Health Centre, Cotswold Care Hospice and Social Exclusion Trust (£250 each), ASPIRE, Chernobyl Children's Project and Royal Humane Society (£100 each), A Safe Place, City Escape and Diabetes UK (£50 each) and Bradford Benevolent Society (£10).

Exclusions No grants to individuals.

Applications In writing to the correspondent.

The Bertie Black Foundation

Jewish, general

£99,000 (2001/02)

Beneficial area UK, Israel.

Abbots House, 198 Lower High Street, Watford WDI7 2FG

Correspondent Mrs I R Broido, Trustee

Trustees *I B Black; Mrs D Black; H S Black; Mrs I R Broido.*

CC Number 245207

Information available Full accounts were on file at the Charity Commission.

General The trust tends to support organisations which are known to the trustees or where long-term commitments have been entered into. Grants can be given over a three-year period towards major projects.

In 2001/02 it had assets of £2.4 million and an income of £132,000. Grants were made to 16 organisations totalling £99,000.

The largest grants were £20,000 to Youth Aliyah, £15,000 to Friends of Ilan and £10,000 to Jewish Care. Other beneficiaries were Magen David Adom UK (£9,000), Community Security Trusts, FMRC Charitable Trust and Norwood (£5,000 each), Jewish Blind and Disabled (£3,000), Lubavitch UK and UK Friends of AWIS (£2,000 each), United Jewish Israel Appeal (£1,500) and British Friends of Assaf Harofeh Medical Centre, Laniardo Hospital and UJS Hillel.

Applications The trust states it 'supports causes known to the trustees' and that they 'do not respond to unsolicited requests'.

Sir Alec Black's Charity

Hospices

£52,000 to individuals and organisations (2003/04)

Beneficial area UK, with a preference for Grimsby.

Messrs Wilson Sharpe & Co., 17–19 Osborne Street, Grimsby, North East Lincolnshire DN31 1HA

Tel. 01472 348315

Correspondent Stewart Wilson, Trustee

Trustees *J N Harrison; P A Mounfield; G H Taylor; Dr D F Wilson; S Wilson.*

CC Number 220295

Information available Information was provided by the trust.

General The primary purposes of the trust are:

- the purchase and distribution of bed linen and down pillows to charitable organisations caring for people who are sick or infirm
- the provision of pensions and grants to people employed by Sir Alec Black during his lifetime
- the benefit of sick, poor fishermen from the borough of Grimsby.

In 2003/04 it had assets of £1.2 million and an income of £82,000. Grants to former employees of the settlor totalled

£18,000. A further £34,000 went in other grants to individuals and organisations.

Applications In writing to the correspondent. Trustees meet in May and November; applications need to be received in March or September.

The Blair Foundation

Wildlife, access to countryside, general

£104,000 (2002/03)

Beneficial area UK and overseas.

Smith & Williamson, 1 Bishops Wharf, Walnut Tree Close, Guildford, Surrey GU1 4RA

Tel. 01483 407100 **Fax** 01483 407194

Correspondent Graham Healy, Trustee

Trustees *Robert Thornton; Jennifer Thornton; Graham Healy; Alan Thornton; Philippa Thornton.*

CC Number 801755

Information available Full accounts were provided by the trust, with a detailed narrative report.

General This foundation was originally established to create environmental conditions in which wildlife can prosper, as well as improving disability access to such areas. This work is focused on Scotland and southern England. However, it has since widened its scope and aims to provide at least £100,000 to other charities in addition to its wildlife work.

In 2002/03 it had assets of £1.4 million, which generated an income of £62,000. Grants totalled £104,000.

By far the largest grant, of £27,000, went to Ayrshire Wildlife Services, which also received a grant of £8,000. The next largest were £6,000 each to Dailly Amateur Football Club and Raleigh International, £5,000 each to Girvan Youth Trust and Home Farm Trust and £4,000 to Sense.

Other beneficiaries included National Trust for Scotland (£2,600), Ayrshire Fiddler Orchestra (£2,000), Culzean Community Park, Royal School of Art (£1,500) and Blairquhan (£1,100), with £1,000 each to Guideposts Trust, Help the Aged, Motor Neurone Disease Association, Scottish Society for Autism, United World College of the Atlantic and Water of Leith Conservation Trust.

Exclusions Charities that have objectives the trustees consider harmful to the environment are not supported.

Applications In writing to the correspondent, for consideration at trustees' meetings held at least once a year. A receipt for donations is requested from all donees. The correspondent stated: 'I have been inundated with appeals for help, which far exceed the resources available. The costs of administration are now becoming disproportionate to the funds available.'

Blakes Benevolent Trust

General

£71,000 to organisations (2002/03)

Beneficial area UK.

Carrickness, Oldfield Drive, Heswell, Wirral CH60 6SS

Tel. 0151 342 3103

Correspondent Norman Silk, Trustee

Trustees *N K Silk; B Ball; P M Davies.*

CC Number 225268

Information available Accounts are on file at the Charity Commission, but with only a brief narrative report and without a grants list.

General In 2002/03 the trust had assets of £1.7 million and an income of £83,000. Grants were given to organisations totalling £71,000, with individuals receiving £21,000.

Five grants were delivered to beneficiaries: £25,000 to Motor Trade Benevolent Fund, and £5,000 each to Crisis, Front Line, Liverpool City Mission and Salvation Army.

Applications In writing to the correspondent. However, please note that the trust stated that it only gives to 'private beneficiaries'.

The Neville & Elaine Blond Charitable Trust

Jewish, education, general

£125,000 (2001/02)

Beneficial area Worldwide.

c/o H W Fisher & Co, Chartered Accountants, Acre House, 11–15 William Road, London NW1 3ER

Tel. 020 7388 7000

Correspondent The Trustees

Trustees *Dame Simone Prendergast; Peter Blond; Mrs A E Susman; S N Susman; Mrs J Skidmore.*

CC Number 206319

Information available Full accounts were on file at the Charity Commission.

General In 2001/02 the trust had assets of £1.4 million and an income of £74,000. Grants totalling £125,000 were made to 13 organisations, 11 of which had been supported in the previous year. The main beneficiary was British WIZO which received £55,000. Other larger grants were £30,000 to JPAIME and £10,000 each to Weizmann Institute Foundation and World Jewish Relief.

The remaining grants were in the range of £1,000 to £7,000 and included those to GRET (£7,000), Halle Orchestra (£4,000) and Jerusalem Foundation (£2,500). Five grants of £1,000 each were made to British ORT, Chicken Shed Theatre, Fulcrum Challenge, Institute of Child Health, Jewish Lads' and Girls' Brigade and Westminster Children's Society.

Exclusions Only registered charities are supported.

Applications In writing to the correspondent. Applications should arrive by 31 January for consideration in late spring.

The Bluston Charitable Settlement

Jewish, general

£184,000 (2001/02)

Beneficial area Mostly UK.

BDO Stoy Hayward, 8 Baker Street, London W1U 3LL

Tel. 020 7486 5888

Correspondent The Trustees

Trustees *D Dover; M D Paisner.*

CC Number 256691

Information available Full accounts were on file at the Charity Commission.

General The trust has general charitable purposes, although in practice most grants are given to Jewish organisations.

In 2001/02 the trust had assets of £5.6 million, an income of £1.7 million and made grants totalling £184,000. Grant beneficiaries included Jewish Free School and Variety Club (£50,000 each), Nightingale House and Norwood Ravenswood (£25,000 each), Family Welfare Association (£7,000), Jewish Women's Aid (£6,000), New Israel Fund (£5,000), St John and Elizabeth Hospice (£2,500) and Federation of London Youth Clubs and Larchers (£2,000 each).

Exclusions No grants to individuals.

Applications In writing to the correspondent. The trustees meet annually in March.

Bois Rochel Dsatmar Charitable Trust

Jewish

£43,000 (2002)

Beneficial area UK.

21 Warwick Grove, London E5 9HX

Tel. 020 8806 1549

Correspondent The Trustees

Trustees *W Low; J Low; J Frankel.*

CC Number 281371

Information available Full accounts were on file at the Charity Commission.

General The trust makes grants towards the advancement of the Jewish religion in general and in particular towards the maintenance of a school that provides Jewish and secular education.

In 2002 the trust's assets totalled £1.3 million and it had an income of £636,000. Grants totalled £43,000 and a further £614,000 was given to the above-mentioned school towards its running expenses. A grant of £38,000 was given to BRYL (Beis Rochel Yetev Lev). Information listing other grant beneficiaries was not available.

Applications In writing to the correspondent.

The Boltons Trust

Social welfare, medicine, education

£272,000 (2000/01)

Beneficial area Unrestricted.

1st Floor , Lynton House, 7–12 Tavistock Square, London WC1 H9LT

Tel. 020 7388 3577

Correspondent Clive Marks, Trustee

Trustees *Clive Marks; Henry B Levin; Mrs C Albuquerque.*

CC Number 257951

Information available Report and accounts on file at the Charity Commission.

General The main aims of the trust are:

- 'the pursuit of peace and understanding throughout the world, and the reduction of innocent suffering
- 'to support education'.

The policy of the trust is to select and support a strictly limited number of projects, and it is at pains to deter unsolicited applications, emphasising its request for 'absolutely no personal callers or telephone enquiries', and stating that 'unsolicited applications are unlikely to be successful'.

In 2000/01 the trust had assets of £2.4 million, an income of £75,000 and made grants totalling £247,000. Donations included £50,000 each to Conciliation Resources and Power; £30,000 to Spiro Institute; £20,000 each to Friends of Israel Education Trust and Nightingale House; £10,000 each to Dartington International Summer School, Human Rights Watch and Prisoners Abroad; £5,000 to Family Welfare Association; and £2,000 to Macmillan Cancer Relief Fund.

Applications 'Sadly, the trust can no longer respond to unsolicited applications.'

The John & Celia Bonham Christie Charitable Trust

Local and national organisations

£61,000 to organisations (2000/01)

Beneficial area UK, with some preference for the former county of Avon.

Charitable Trust 326296, Po Box 6, Bath BA1 2YH

Tel. 01258 480 666

Correspondent P R Fitzgerald, Trustees

Trustees *Mrs J R Bonham Christie; Richard Bonham Christie; Mrs Rosemary Kerr; P R Fitzgerald; Robert Bonham Christie.*

CC Number 326296

Information available Full accounts were on file at the Charity Commission.

General In 2000/01 the trust had assets of £1.1 million and an income of £37,000. In total 94 grants were made amounting to £61,000, of which 2 individuals received grants totalling £600.

The largest grants were: £4,000 to Cassell Foundation; £2,000 to Jubilee Sailing Trust; £1,500 to RTYC Youth Sailing Academy; and £1,000 each to to Action on Addiction, Blackie Foundation, Blue House Frome, Frome Memorial Hospital, Look Forward, Raft, Tenovus and Winston's Wish

Donations under £1,000 included: £800 each to Headway, Open Door Foundation and Rheumatology; £600 each to Alzheimer's Disease Society and Care and Repair; £500 each to Frome Mencap and Frome RDA; £400 each to Bath Abbey, British Wheelchair Sports Association, Friends of Howtown, Southmead Hospital and Hatch Camphill Community; £300 each to Bath Area Play Project, Camphill Community,

Searchlight Project and Street Scene; £250 each to Taunton Hospital and The Ladybird Appeal; £200 to Youth Club Hampshire; and £120 to Regional Development Agency – Somerset.

Exclusions No grants to individuals.

Applications In writing to the correspondent. The trustees regret that the income is fully allocated for the foreseeable future. Only a small number of new applications are supported each year.

This entry was not confirmed by the trust, but was correct according to information on file at the Charity Commission.

The Charlotte Bonham-Carter Charitable Trust

General

£79,000 (2002/03)

Beneficial area UK, with some emphasis on Hampshire.

66 Lincoln's Inn Fields, London WC2A 3LH

Tel. 020 7917 7331 **Fax** 020 7831 6301

Correspondent Sir Matthew Farrer, Trustee

Trustees *Sir Matthew Farrer; Norman Bonham-Carter; Nicolas Wickham-Irving.*

CC Number 292839

Information available Full accounts were provided by the trust.

General The trust is principally concerned to support charitable bodies and purposes which were of particular concern to Lady Bonham-Carter during her lifetime or are within the county of Hampshire.

In 2002/03 the trust had assets of £2.7 million, which generated an income of £105,000. It gave £79,000 in 53 grants, ranging from £200 to £15,000. Of the grants made, 9 were recurrent from the previous year. The largest went to National Trust (£15,000), Fitzwilliam Museum (£10,000) and Ashmolean Museum (£5,000 each).

Other recipients included TATE (£4,000), British Museum (£3,000), Lyric Theatre Hammersmith and Wordsworth Trust (£2,500 each), Rambert Dance Company (£2,000), Gilbert White Museum (£1,500), Awards for Young Musicians, Clifton College, Lennox Berkeley Society (£1,000 each), Harvest Trust (£900), Ditchling Museum (£750), Binsted C E Primary School, Council for National Parks, Fort Cancer Charity, KUDOS Employment, People's Trust for Endangered Species, Royal West of England Academy, St Andrew's Church and Windsor Parish Church (£500 each) and Romsey Choral Society (£250).

Exclusions No grants to individuals or non-registered charities.

Applications In writing to the correspondent, although the trust states that 'unsolicited general applications are unlikely to be successful and only increase the cost of administration'. There are no application forms. Trustees meet in January and July; applications need to be received by May or November.

Salo Bordon Charitable Trust

Jewish, some health-related

£234,000 (2002/03)

Beneficial area Worldwide.

78 Corringham Road, London NW11 7EB

Tel. 020 8458 5842

Correspondent S Bordon, Trustee

Trustees *S Bordon; Mrs L Bordon.*

CC Number 266439

Information available Full accounts were on file at the Charity Commission.

General This trust makes grants mainly to Jewish organisations, for social welfare and religious education. In 2002/03 it had assets amounting to £7 million and an income of £260,000. Grants were made totalling £234,000.

Grants of over £1,000 each were listed in the accounts. The largest were £8,500 each to Agudas Israel Housing Association Ltd and MIR Charitable Trust, £5,300 to Gateshead Foundation for Torah and £5,000 each to Gateshead Jewish Primary School, North West London Communal Mikvah and Shaarei Torah Buildings Ltd. Other listed beneficiaries included Golders Green Beth Hamedrash Congregation (£4,900), Institute for Higher Rabbinical Studies (£4,300), Parsha Ltd (£4,400), Yad Eliezer (£3,000), Talmudic Research Centre (£2,000) and AB Foundation (£1,000).

Applications In writing to the correspondent.

The A Bornstein Charitable Settlement

Jewish

£186,000 (2000/01)

Beneficial area UK and Israel.

HLB AV Audit plc, 66 Wigmore Street, London W1H 2HQ

Tel. 020 7467 4000 **Fax** 020 7467 4040

Correspondent Peter Musgrave

Trustees *N P Bornstein; M Hollander.*

CC Number 262472

Information available Information was on file at the Charity Commission.

General In 2002/03 the trust had an income of £13,000 with an expenditure of £507,500. No further information was available.

In 2000/01 it made grants totalling £186,000. The largest grant was given to Shaare Zedek Hospital in Israel, which received £115,000. Other beneficiaries were British Olim Society Charitable Trust (£23,000), UJA Federation (£15,000), Friends of Care of the Needy of Jerusalem (£12,500), Friends of Yad Sarah (£7,500), National Foundation for Jewish Culture (£5,000), Chabad House (£2,000) and Chai Lifeline Cancer Care (£500). Six of these beneficiaries were supported in the previous year.

Exclusions No grants for non-Jewish organisations.

Applications In writing to the correspondent.

The Oliver Borthwick Memorial Trust

Homelessness

£33,000 (2001/02)

Beneficial area UK.

Donor Grants Department, Charities Aid Foundation, Kings Hill, West Malling, Kent ME19 4TA

Tel. 01732 520082 **Fax** 01732 520001

Correspondent Sue David, Donor Grants Officer

Trustees *Earl Bathurst; R Marriott; H L de Quetteville; M H R Bretherton; R A Graham; J MacDonald; J R Marriott; Mrs V Wrigley; Mrs J S Mace.*

CC Number 256206

Information available The information for this entry was provided by the trust.

General The intention of the trust is to provide shelter and help the homeless. The trustees welcome applications from small but viable charities where they are able to make a significant contribution to the practical work of the charity, especially in disadvantaged inner-city areas.

In 2001/02 it had assets of £838,000, which generated an income of £37,000. Grants totalling £33,000 were made to 20 organisations, only one of which was supported in the previous year.

Aside from the £5,000 to Almshouse Charities of Matthew Chubb and Others and the £1,000 to Almshouse Association, the grants were of £1,500 each. Beneficiaries included Ace of Clubs – Clapham, Byker Bridge Housing Association, E C Roberts Centre, Exeter Community Umbrella Ltd, Framework Housing Association, Homerton Space Project, Mission in Hounslow Trust, Parish of East Ham for a night shelter, Southend Night Shelter for the Homeless and St George Dragon Trust.

Exclusions No grants to individuals, including people working temporarily overseas for a charity where the request is for living expenses, together with applications relating to health, disability and those from non-registered charitable organisations.

Applications Letters should be set out on a maximum of two sides of A4, giving full details of the project with costs, who the project will serve and the anticipated outcome of the project. Meetings take place once a year in May. Applications should be received no later than April.

The Bothwell Charitable Trust

Disability, health, older people, conservation

£47,000 (2002/03)

Beneficial area England, particularly the South East.

14 Kirkly Close, Sanderstead, Surrey CR2 0ET

Tel. 020 8657 3369

Correspondent Angela Bothwell, Chair of Trustees

Trustees *Mrs Angela J Bothwell, Chair; Paul James; Crispian M P Howard.*

CC Number 299056

Information available Full accounts were provided by the trust.

General The trust makes grants towards health, disability, conservation and older people's causes. It also supports conservation projects. In 2002/03 it had an income of £42,000 and gave £47,000 in total to 24 organisations.

The largest grants, of £2,500 each, went to Arthritis Research Campaign, Blackthorn Trust, British Heart Foundation, British Home and Hospital for Incurables, ECHO International Health Services Ltd, Family Holiday Association, Friends of the Elderly, Invalid Children's Aid Nationwide, Leukaemia Research Fund, Macmillan Cancer Relief, Parkinson's Disease Society, St Christopher's Hospice, Sight Savers International and Winged Fellowship Trust. The remaining grants were of £1,000 each.

Exclusions No grants for animal charities, overseas causes, individuals, or charities not registered with the Charity Commission.

Applications In writing to the correspondent. Distributions are usually made in March each year.

The Harry Bottom Charitable Trust

Religion, education, medical

£116,000 (2002/03)

Beneficial area UK, with a preference for Yorkshire and Derbyshire.

Westons, Queen's Buildings, 55 Queen Street, Sheffield S1 2DX

Tel. 0114 273 8341 **Fax** 0114 272 5116

Correspondent D R Proctor

Trustees *J G Potter; J M Kilner; I G Rennie.*

CC Number 204675

Information available Accounts were on file at the Charity Commission.

General The trust states that support is divided roughly equally between religion, education and medical causes. Within these categories grants are given to:

- religion – small local appeals and cathedral appeals
- education – universities and schools
- medical – equipment for hospitals and charities concerned with disability.

In 2002/03 the trust had assets of £3.3 million. It had an income of £134,000, of which £55,000 came from investments and £77,000 from rent. After administration costs of £25,000 and property expenditure of £23,000, grants totalled £116,000 and were broken down as follows:

Medical

29 grants ranging from £250 to £5,500 totalled £48,000. Beneficiaries included University of Sheffield School of Medicine (£5,500), Children's Hospital (£5,000), St Luke's Hospice (£4,500), Cavendish Hip Foundation (£3,000), Sheffield Mencap (£2,800), Association for Spina Bifida (£1,800), Delta (£1,000), Heartline (£780), Multiple Sclerosis Therapy Centre (£500) and Age Concern Sheffield (£250).

Religious

13 grants ranging from £500 to £25,000 totalled £33,000. Beneficiaries included South Yorkshire Baptist Association (£25,000), Industrial Mission of South Yorkshire (£2,000 in two donations), St Chad's (£1,000) and Bank Street Methodist Church, Castleton Methodist Church, Hallam Methodist Church and St Helen's Church – Grindleford (£500).

Education and other
42 grants ranging from £200 to £3,300 totalled £35,000. Beneficiaries included Cherry Tree Children's Home (£3,300), RNLI (£3,000), Whirlow Hall Farm (£2,000), Boy's Brigade (£1,800), YMCA (£1,300), Sheffield Family Holiday Fund (£1,000), Spurgeon's Child Care (£750), Barnardo's Rowan Centre and North Centre Handicap Association (£500 each), Oakdale House (£250) and Hurlfield Agewell + 60 (£200).

Exclusions No grants to individuals.

Applications In writing to the correspondent at any time.

The Boughton Trust

Elderly people, disability, youth groups, conservation projects

£28,000 (2000/01)

Beneficial area UK.

c/o Kidd Rapinet, Solicitors, 14 and 15 Craven Street, London WC2N 5AD

Tel. 0207 925 0303

Correspondent R D A Sweeting, Clerk to the Trustees

Trustees *P M Williams; G J M Wilding; C J T Harris.*

CC Number 261413

Information available Information was provided by the trust.

General The trust makes grants to organisations known to the trustees, benefiting elderly people, people with disabilities and environmental charities.

In 2000/01 the trust's assets totalled £620,000 and it had an income of £36,600. Grants were made totalling £28,000.

Grants given in this year included, £4,000 to Winston Churchill Memorial Trust Fellowship, £3,000 each to The Royal Agricultural Benevolent Institution and The Royal Star and Garter House for Disabled Soldiers, £2,750 to British Wheelchair Sports Foundation, £2,500 to Paignton Zoo, £1,000 each to The Haselmere 2000 Project, Family Line Surrey and The National Trust For Scotland (sole Trading Appeal) and £750 each to The Cherry Trees Project Limited, Crisis and Seven Springs & Cheshire Homes.

Exclusions No individuals would be sponsored by the charity. Registered charities only.

Applications In writing only to the correspondent.

The A H & E Boulton Trust

Evangelical Christian

£230,000 (2002/03)

Beneficial area Worldwide.

Moore Stephens, 47–49 North John Street, Liverpool L2 6TG

Tel. 0151 236 9044

Correspondent J Glasby

Trustees *Mrs J R Gopsill; F P Gopsill.*

CC Number 225328

Information available Accounts were on file at the Charity Commission.

General The trust mainly supports the erection and maintenance of buildings to be used for preaching the Christian gospel, and teaching its doctrines. The trustees can also support other Christian institutions, especially missions in the UK and developing world.

In 2002/03 the trust had assets of £3.1 million and an income of £109,000. Grants totalled £230,000.

The largest beneficiaries were Liverpool City Mission (£60,000), Echoes of Service (£50,000) and Charles Thompson Mission (£45,000). Other beneficiaries included Holy Trinity Chiurch and Bridge Street Chapel (£15,000 each), Open Air Mission (£6,000) and Pocket Testament League, Salvation Army and Home Evangelism (£4,000 each).

A number of smaller grants were also made totalling £12,800.

Applications In writing to the correspondent. The trust tends to support a set list of charities and applications are very unlikely to be successful.

P G & N J Boulton Trust

Christian

£84,000 (2003/04)

Beneficial area Worldwide.

PO BOX 72, Wirral, Merseyside CH28 9AE

Email email@boultontrust.org.uk

Website www.boultontrust.org.uk

Correspondent Mr Andrew L Perry, Trustee

Trustees *Miss N J Boulton, Chair; Miss L M Butchart; A L Perry; Mrs S Perry.*

CC Number 272525

Information available Information was provided by the trust and available on its website.

General The trust's 2002/03 annual report stated:

'The aims of the trust, as set out in the deed, are to provide assistance to the victims of disaster and to any charitable cause that the trustees consider worthy. The trustees are free to distribute both the capital and income of the trust as they see fit.

'The trustees fulfil these aims by making donations to other charities and by minimising administration costs. The trustees aim to target smaller charities, to whom a relatively small gift can make a significant difference.

Whilst a substantial proportion of donations is allocated to Christian missionary work in accordance with the interests of the trustees, a wider interest is maintained by covering other areas such as poverty relief, medical research, healthcare and disability relief.'

In 2003/04 grants totalled £84,000, broken down as follows:

Christian missionary work	39.7%
Specialised Christian ministries	32.8%
Combined Christian missionary/relief work	23.3%
Poverty relief (UK)	1.8%
Disability relief and care of the elderly	0.6%
Other	1.8%

The largest grants were £17,000 to Intecessors for Britain, £15,000 to Elim Pentecostal Church, £5,500 to Shalom Christian Trust, £4,500 to Just Care, £2,500 to Christian Witness to Israel, £1,500 each to Cedars School and Children Alone and £1,300 to SAO – Cambodia.

In 2002/03 it had assets of £2.2 million, which generated an income of £85,000. Grants were made totalling £98,000, broken down as follows:

Christian missionary work	29.3%
Specialised Christian ministries	28.7%
Combined Christian missionary/relief work	26.1%
Medical research and healthcare	4.7%
Disability relief and care of elderly	3.7%
Poverty relief (UK)	1.8%
Poverty/disaster relief (overseas)	1.6%
Other	4.1%

Exclusions No grants to individuals or towards environment/conservation, culture, heritage, sports, leisure, church building repairs or animal welfare.

Applications In writing to the correspondent. Owing to the number of applications received the trustees cannot acknowledge all of them. Successful applicants will be contacted within two months.

The M Bourne Charitable Trust

Jewish and cancer related

£518,000 (2002/03)

Beneficial area UK.

9 Lanark, London E14 9RE

Tel. 0207 536 6360

Correspondent David Morein, Trustee

Trustees *C J Bourne; Mrs J H Bourne; D M Morein.*

CC Number 290620

Information available Full accounts were on file at the Charity Commission.

General The trust makes grants to Jewish individuals and institutions benefiting them. In 2002/03 the trust's assets totalled £2.5 million and it had an income of £359,000. Grants were made totalling £518,000.

The largest grants were £500,000 to Melbourne Community Academy, £7,400 to PCCT and £3,500 to Jewish Care. Other grants included £900 to Jewish Museum, £350 to Norwood Ravenswood, £200 to Teenage Cancer Trust and £100 to Jewish Womans Aid.

Applications In writing to the correspondent.

The Bowerman Charitable Trust

General

£194,000 to organisations (2002/03)

Beneficial area UK, with a preference for West Sussex.

Champs Hill, Coldwatham, Pulborough, West Sussex RH20 1LY

Tel. 01798 831205

Correspondent D W Bowerman, Trustee

Trustees *D W Bowerman; Mrs C M Bowerman; Mrs J M Taylor; Miss K E Bowerman; Mrs A M Downham; J M Capper.*

CC Number 289446

Information available Full accounts were on file at the Charity Commission.

General The trust makes grants towards:

- church activities
- the arts, particularly music
- medical charities
- youth work
- charities concerned with relief of poverty and the resettlement of offenders.

In 2002/03 the trust had assets of £1.4 million and an income of £228,000. Donations were made amounting to £194,000.

Large grants were £32,000 to English Chamber Orchestra Musical Society' £25,000 to University of St Andrews' £19,000 to Royal Philharmonic Society' £18,000 to Elgar Foundation; £17,000 to Music at Boxgrove and £15,000 to Chichester Catherdral Trust. Grants under £10,000 included those to Royal College of Music (£8,000), Chelsea Festival and Williams Syndrome (£7,000 each), Crime Reduction Initiative (£6,500), National Gardens Scheme (£5,000), Medici Trust (£3,000) and British Youth Opera, Malvern Concert Club and NSPCC (£1,000 each).

Applications In writing to the correspondent. The trustees said that they are bombarded with applications and unsolicited applications will not be considered.

The Viscountess Boyd Charitable Trust

Conservation, horticulture, education and preservation

£32,000 (2002/03)

Beneficial area Worldwide, with a bias towards south west England, Devon and Cornwall.

Ince Castle, Saltash, Cornwall PL12 4QZ

Tel. 01752 842249 **Fax** 01752 847134

Email boydince@aol.com

Correspondent The Administrator

Trustees *The Iveagh Trustees Ltd; Viscount Boyd; Viscountess Boyd; Hon. Dr Charlotte M Mitchell.*

CC Number 284270

Information available Full accounts were on file at the Charity Commission.

General In 2002/03 the trust had an income of £24,000 and a total expenditure of £48,000. Grants for this year totalled £32,000.

Previous beneficiaries have included Abbey Restoration Fund (Onslow Tomb), Delaware Playgroup, East Cornwall Bach Festival, Eden Project, El Shaddai Trust, Gardeners' Benevolent Society, Historic Chapels Trust, Landulph Church, National Trust, Lichfield Cathedral Music Campaign, Mihai Eminescu Trust, National Asthma Campaign, Oxford Radcliffe Hospitals Charitable Fund, Parish Church of St Sampson Golant, St German's Under Fives, World Cancer Research Fund.

Exclusions No grants to individuals.

Applications In writing to the correspondent; no application form is used. Please enclose an sae to ensure a reply. Applications are considered four times a year.

BP Conservation Programme

Wildlife and conservation.

£400,000 (2004)

Beneficial area Expeditions to and from anywhere in the world.

Birdlife International/FFI, Wellbrook Court, Girton Road, Cambridge CB3 0NA

Tel. 01223 277318 **Fax** 01223 277200

Email bp-conservation-programme@birdlife.org

Website http://conservation.bp.com

Correspondent Marianne Dunn, BP Conservation Programme Manager

Trustees *The Council: Dr Enrique Bucher (Argentina); Dr Jon Fjeldsa (Denmark); S A Hussain (India); Petar Iankov (Bulgaria); Anastasios P Leventis (UK); Prof. Yaa Ntiamoa-Baidu (Ghana); Baroness Young of Old Scone (UK).*

CC Number 1042125

Information available Information was provided by the trust.

General International conservation projects involving teams of interested students, which address globally recognised priorities at a local level; projects must involve local counterparts. The programme is a partnership between Birdlife International, Fauna and Flora International, Conservation International, The Wildlife Conservation Society and BP.

In 2004 the trust had an income of £1 million and a grant total of £400,000 donated to various projects protecting endangered species and habitats.

Examples of grants in 2000 include: £20,000 to Project Tutururu, Tahiti; £13,000 for Bat Surveys, Madagascar; £12,000 for Operation Tortoise, Malaysia; £10,000 for Chinese Grouse project; £7,000 for Iguana Conservation, Fiji; £5,000 each to Andinoheps 2000 (Ecuador), Amphibian Monitoring (Hungary), Conservation Education (Ecuador), Conservation of Kerita Forest (Kenya), and Wetlands Survey (Madagascar).

Exclusions Only an entire expedition team will be funded: no applications will be considered from individuals applying for funding to join an expedition.

Applications Contact the programme manager for guidelines for applicants and application forms, or alternatively this can be found on the company website.

The William Brake Charitable Trust

General

£67,000 (2001/02)

Beneficial area UK, with a preference for Kent.

Gill Turner & Tucker, Colman House, King Street, Maidstone, Kent ME14 1JE

Tel. 01622 759051 **Fax** 01622 762792

Correspondent B Rylands, Solicitor

Trustees *Bruce Rylands; Michael Philpott; David Richardson; Philip Wilson.*

CC Number 1023244

Information available Full accounts were on file at the Charity Commission.

General The assets of this trust consist mostly of shares in Brake Brothers plc with a market value of £1 million in 2001/02. During this year an income of £39,000 was received and the charity made donations totalling £67,000 to 19 charitable institutions.

The largest grant awarded was to St Bartholomews and Royal London Charitable Foundation which received £25,000. Other donations included: £5,000 each to Christina Noble Children's Foundation and Elimination of Leukaemia and Barts Cancer Centre; £3,250 to Macmillan Cancer Relief; £2,500 to Wooden Spoon Society; £2,000 each to Heart of Kent Hospice, Samaritans and The Dorothy Kerin Trust; and £1,000 each to Sea Cadets Corps and Richard House Trust.

Applications In writing to the correspondent.

The Tony Bramall Charitable Trust

Children, medical research, sickness

£47,000 (2001/02)

Beneficial area UK, with some preference for Yorkshire.

Harlow Court, Beckwis Knowle, Otley Road, Harrogate HG3 1PU

Tel. 01423 537616

Correspondent D C A Bramall

Trustees *D C A Bramall; Mrs K S Bramall Odgen; Mrs M J Foody; G M Tate; Miss A Bramall.*

CC Number 1001522

Information available Full accounts were on file at the Charity Commission.

General The trust was established with investments totalling £600,000 in Cilva Holdings plc. The trust makes grants towards 'charities where there is an objective to support children in need or medical research or causes endeavouring to improve the welfare of those who are sick or suffering with infirmities and who are unable to help themselves sufficiently'.

The trust originally had a strong preference for local charities, although this has decreased as the company has expanded to other parts of the UK.

In 2001/02 it had assets of £588,000 and an income of £57,000. Grants were made totalling £47,000.

In 1998/99 the trust gave 22 grants totalling £23,000. Grants ranged from £100 to £3,500 with 13 under £1,000. The largest two grants, both of £3,500 were to Bradford Millennium Scanner Appeal. Other grants included £1,000 each to Marie Curie Bradford Appeal and Wakefield Hospice.

Applications In writing to the correspondent.

The Breast Cancer Research Trust

Research into breast cancer

£165,000 (2003)

Beneficial area UK.

48 Wayneflete Tower Avenue, Esher, Surrey KT10 8QG

Tel. 01372 463235 (Gazet); 01243 583143 (Sutcliffe) **Fax** 01372 463235

Email bcrtrust@aol.com

Correspondent J C Gazet, Trustee or R Sutcliffe, Secretary

Trustees *Vera Lynn; Jean-Claude Gazet.*

CC Number 272214

Information available Information was provided by the trust.

General The trust supports medical research at a scientific and laboratory level within a recognised UK medical unit into the causation and diagnosis of breast cancer. Grants can be given for up to three years, ranging up to £35,000 a year.

In 2003 it had assets of £900,000 and an income of £263,000. Grants totalled £165,000.

The largest went to Imperial College for two projects (£73,000), Royal Hampshire County Hospital (£42,000), Marie Curie Cancer Care for Mount Vernon Hospital (£35,000), University Hospital Glasgow (£9,500) and Royal Marsden Hospital for equipment (£5,400).

Exclusions No grants to students.

Applications On a form available from the correspondent.

The Harold and Alice Bridges Charity

General

£74,000 (2001/02)

Beneficial area South Cumbria and North Lancashire (as far south as Preston)

Messrs Senior Calveley & Hardy Solicitors, 8 Hastings Place, Lytham FY8 5NA

Tel. 01253 733333 **Fax** 01253 794430

Email rnh@seniorslaw.co.uk

Correspondent Richard N Hardy, Trustee

Trustees *Richard N Hardy; Jeffrey W Greenwood.*

CC Number 236654

Information available Information was provided by the trust.

General The trust concentrates its giving almost exclusively on projects operating in Lancashire from north of the Ribble Valley to the South Lakes. The trustees also favour locally-based projects with a strong element of community benefit and participation, where there has been a degree of fundraising from other community sources. They prefer to contribute to capital costs rather than running expenses.

In 2001/02 the trust had an income of £79,000 and a total expenditure of £85,000. Grants totalled £74,000. No further information was available for this year.

In 1998/99 the trust had assets of £2.1 million and an income of £99,000, including £22,000 transferred from The Wayfarers Trust. Grants to 60 charities totalled £73,000.

The largest grants were £5,000 to St Martin's College – Lancashire, £2,000 each to Eden Valley Hospice Carlisle Ltd, Heart of Lancashire Trust, Macmillan Cancer Relief – Furness Appeal, Penwortham Grammar School Foundation, RNLI, St Catherine's Hospice, St Peter's Parish Church and £1,600 to St John's Church for their churchyard maintenance fund.

Other grants included £1,500 each to 1st Lytham St Anne's (St Cuthbert's) Sea Scout Group, Charnock Richard Cricket Club, Hale Village Hall, Ingleton Swimming Pool and St Peter's Church of England Primary School, £1,000 each to Disabled Living, Over Kellet Parish Council, Manley and Mouldsworth Pre-school, Spurgeon's Child Care, Warton Pre-School Playgroup and West Lancashire County Scout Council, £500 each to Abbeyfield Seascale & District Society, Manic Depression Fellowship North West, South Lakeland Support Group for the Disabled and Warton Village Hall Management Committee with £200 to Wigan Girls' Under 16s Rugby League Team.

Exclusions No grants to individuals.

Applications In writing to the correspondent, followed by completion of a standard application form.

Briggs Animal Welfare Trust

Animal welfare

£67,000 (2002/03)

Beneficial area UK and overseas.

Belmoredean, Maplehurst Road, West Grinstead, West Sussex RH13 6RN

Correspondent Mrs A J Hartnett

Trustee *Miss L M Hartnett and Mrs F Mathers.*

CC Number 276459

Information available Full accounts were on file at the Charity Commission. Only one of the specified charities appeared to receive support, although many charities appear to receive regular support.

General This trust derives most of its income from shares in the company Eurotherm International plc. Although the original objects of the trust were general, but with particular support for animal welfare, the trust's policy is to support only animal–welfare causes. There are five named beneficiaries in the trust deed: RSPCA, Reystede Animal Sanctuary Ringmer, Brooke Hospital for Animals Cairo, Care of British Columbia House and the Society for the Protection of Animals in North Africa.

In 2002/03, the trust had assets of £853,000 and made grants totalling £67,000. No other information was available for this year.

In 1998/99 grants distributed were 30 of £1,000 and one grant of £2,000. Only one of the specified charities appeared to receive support. The largest grant was £2,000 to Society for the Welfare of Horses and Ponies. Other causes supported included Bleakholt Animal Sanctuary, Friends of Bristol Horses Society, Sebakwe Black Rhino Trust, Thoroughbred Rehabilitation Centre and Woodgreen Animal Shelters. Many charities appear to receive regular support.

Applications In writing to the correspondent. This entry was not confirmed by the trust, but the information was correct according to the trust's file at the Charity Commission.

The Bristol Charities

General

£133,000 to organisations (2001/02)

Beneficial area Within a 10-mile radius of Bristol city centre.

17 St Augustines Parade, Bristol BS1 4UL

Tel. 0117 9300 301

Email info@bristolcharities.org.uk

Website www.bristolcharities.org.uk

Correspondent D W Jones, Chief Executive

Trustees *B R England, Chair; J Ackland; A K Bonham; J Cottrell; C A Halton; D W P Lewis; J G Mason; M Sisman; V H W Stevenson; V L Stone; C E Sweet; D B Tedder; S W Thomas; D L J Watts.*

CC Number 204665

Information available Accounts were on file at the Charity Commission.

General In July 2004 the charities stated that: 'The organisation is focusing upon its activities for Bristol's older people, through the provision of day services and housing – it currently manages a residential/nursing home and six of the city's almshouses, providing accommodation for 120 people. It is also developing a pioneering £7 million Very Sheltered Housing scheme.

'It operates a day service provision, for older people, at the Beehive Day Centre in the St George's area of the city. This provides valuable day care services and activities for 120 older people per week. Plans are being developed for a network of similar services across the city.

'Bristol Charities also administers a number of major grant-giving charities for the relief of people in need, as well as educational charities. Over £400,000 is awarded annually in over 1,500 grants. [The organisation also] administers £29 million worth of endowment funds for many historic charities [and] provides management services to a variety of local charities.

'In recent times, Bristol Charities has assumed the management responsibility for other charities, including the Bristol and Anchor Almshouse Charity and the Lady Haberfield's Almshouse Charity. It has worked with other charities who were encountering difficulties and has enabled their activities to continue. An example is First Help Project. When British Mencap ceased operation, Bristol Charities accepted transfer of their advice worker, who continues to offer the service to families.

'[The organisation also] works with individuals who wish to establish permanent endowment for specific grant-giving or other charitable activities.'

In 2001/02 the charities had property assets including almshouses and schools valued at £8.7 million and an income of £1.3 million. Grants totalled £393,000, of which £133,000 went to organisations and £261,000 went to individuals (see *A Guide to Grants for Individuals in Need* and *The Educational Grants Directory*).

The largest grants of £1,000 or above were £65,000 to Bristol Grammar School and £13,000 to Orchard Homes, both had received support in previous years. Other donations of £1,000 or more were: £10,000 each to Bristol Care and Repair and Bristol Drugs Project; £2,900 to Bristol Centre for the Deaf; £2,100 to Young Bristol; £1,900 to Temple Hospital; £1,600 to Bristol Children's Hospital – Social Work Department; £1,400 to Stranger's Friend; £1,200 each to Hooks Mills Diocese of Bristol and Southmead Hospital; £1,200 to St Peter's Hospice; and £1,000 to Florence Brown School.

Applications In writing to the correspondent.

The British Council for Prevention of Blindness

Prevention and treatment of blindness

£213,000 (2002/03)

Beneficial area Worldwide.

29b Montague Street, London WC1B 5BW

Tel. 020 7631 5100

Email info@bcpb.org

Website www.bcpb.org

Correspondent Jackie Webber

Trustees *Prof. Andrew Elkington (Chair); Rolf Blach; William Weisblatt; Mark Thompson; Prof. Alistair Fielder; Lady Wilson; Richard Porter; Jackie Boulter; Margaret Hallendorff; Richard Titley; Cpt. Ray Hazan; M Hallendorf; R Titley.*

CC Number 270941

Information available Full accounts were on file at the Charity Commission.

General The BCPB's mission statement is 'to help prevent blindness and restore sight in the UK and developing world by:

- funding research in UK hospitals and universities into the causes and treatments of the major eye diseases
- supporting practical treatment programmes and research in the developing world
- promoting vital skills, leadership, awareness and demand for the expansion of community eye health in the developing world through the education of doctors and nurses within communities.'

The trust's policy is to divide its support equally between projects in the UK and abroad. Grants are given to hospitals, universities and health centres both in the UK and in developing countries. Grants are also given to individuals through the Boulter Fellowship Awards (see below). Grants are usually for a maximum of £40,000 and given for a maximum of three years.

In 2002/03 the trust had assets of £234,000. It had an income of £243,000. Grants totalled £214,000.

In this year there were only five beneficiaries but they all received substantial amounts as grants. £136,000 to ICEH (for eye-screening programmes for children in Tanzania), £38,000 to University of London (Pathogenesis of Acanthamoeba Keratisis), £20,000 to British Ophthalmological Sureveillance Unit (one of its purposes is Survey of Incidence of Fungal Keratisis), £15,000 to Bootler Fellowship Awards (which gives Awards to Individuals from developing countries to study community eye health) and £5,000 to Institute of Child Health-British Opthalmological Surveillance Unit (Study on retinochoroiditis in children with particular emphasis on congenital toxoplasmosis).

Exclusions 'We do NOT deal with the individual welfare of blind people in the UK.'

Applications Applications can be made throughout the year. Please note that the charity is currently reviewing its grant-making policy with new guidelines published in the latter part of 2004.

The British Dietetic Association General and Education Trust Fund

Dietary and nutritional issues

£61,000 (2001/02)

Beneficial area UK.

5th Floor, Charles House, 148–149 Great Charles Street, Queensway, Birmingham B3 3HT

Tel. 0121 200 8080 **Fax** 0121 800 8081

Email info@bda.uk.com

Website www.bda.uk.com

Correspondent A D Burman, Secretary to the Trustees

Trustees *P Brindley; Dame Barbara Clayton; Mrs S Jones; Mrs Carol Leverkus; Miss E T Elliot; W T Seddon.*

CC Number 282553

Information available Information was provided by the trust.

General The trust supports the development of the scientific knowledge base for the discipline of dietetics through funding of relevant research; support to the profession's development of pre- and post-registration education structures and standards; an annual travel bursary for students and newly-qualified dietitians.

In 2001/02 it had assets of £1.2 million and an income of £629,000. Grants were made totalling £61,000.

Beneficiaries included British Dietetic Association as the final payment towards a clinical effectiveness project and towards an expert patient programme for people with Type II diabetes (£20,000 in total), Community Nutrition Group as the second of two payments to produce, print and mail-out the 'From Bottle to Cup' action pack (£14,000) a study in using dietetic assistants to improve the dietary intake, nutritional status and outcome of hip fracture (£9,500), London Region Dietetic Manager's Group for the production of a video and CD-Rom to help student dietitians (£2,300).

Exclusions Direct support of dietetic students in training or postgraduate qualifications for individuals, i.e. the trust will not pay postgraduate fees/ expenses, or elective/MSc study for doctors.

Applications Guidelines, the grant-giving policy and an application form are sent to prospective applicants. All applications are acknowledged.

British Humane Association

Welfare

£89,000 (2001)

Beneficial area UK.

24 Craddocks Avenue, Ashtead, Surrey KT21 1PB

Tel. 01372 813717

Correspondent C A E Butler

Trustees *C Campbell-Johnston, Chair; Sir David Floyd Ewin; B Campbell-Johnston; H Gould; A C W Lee; Sir Anthony Grant; J M Huntington-Whiteley; Richard Walduck.*

CC Number 207120

Information available Information was provided by the association.

General In 2002 the trust had an income of £114,000 with an expenditure of £82,000. No further information was available.

Grants were made totalling £89,000 in 2001. Beneficiaries included: £20,000 each to Medical Foundation and Professional Classes Aid Council; £7,500 to Craighead Centre; £7,000 to Ophthalmic Hospital Jerusalem; £5,000 each to Friends of the Elderly, Guild of Aid for Gentlepeople and St Luke's Hospital for Clergy; and £2,500 each to Church Lad's and Girl's Brigade and Greater London Central Scout County.

Applications In writing to the correspondent; however, the trust only supports one new cause each year and applications are unlikely to be successful.

British Institute of Archaeology at Ankara

Arts, humanities and social sciences of countries surrounding the Black Sea

£127,000 (2002)

Beneficial area UK, Turkey and the Black Sea region.

10 Carlton House Terrace, London SW1Y 5AH

Tel. 020 7969 5204 **Fax** 020 7969 5401

Email biaa@britac.ac.uk

Website www.biaa.ac.uk

Correspondent Gina Coulthard

Trustee *Council of Management.*

CC Number 313940

Information available Information was available on the institute's website.

General The charity describes its work by stating that it 'supports, promotes and publishes British research focused on Turkey and the Black Sea littoral in all academic disciplines within the arts, humanities and social sciences, whilst maintaining a centre of excellence in Ankara focused on the archaeology and related subjects of Turkey'.

As well as performing its own research and having a large research library in Ankara, the charity also proves a number of grants to individuals and organisations to undertake this work. In 2002 it gave grants totalling £127,000 from an income of £367,000. The following programmes are open to group applications:

BIAA Research Grants

These annual research grants support excavation, survey, other fieldwork, museum/library-based and institute-based projects. The institute is keen to encourage novel and imaginative projects which make use of its equipment, research collections and Ankara-based facilities.

Conference grants

These are small grants of up to £500 to support conferences, day schools or seminars on the archaeology, history and related subjects of Turkey and surrounding regions. They are intended to pay the travel expenses of speakers who would not otherwise be able to attend these conferences.

Applications Initial telephone calls welcome. Application forms and guidelines are available on the website, along with exact deadlines.

The Britten Foundation

Disaster relief, education, general

£52,000 (2001/02)

Beneficial area UK and overseas.

PO Box 8, Chobham, Woking, Surrey GU24 8YE

Correspondent The Trustees

Trustees *J F Britten; Mrs D M Britten; Miss S S Britten.*

CC Number 1040558

Information available Accounts were on file at the Charity Commission.

General The trust has two main areas of interest:

- relief for people in need, hardship or distress as a result of local, national or international disaster, or for other welfare needs
- the furtherance of education for children and young people at all levels, whether they are permanently resident in the UK or only temporarily.

Other general causes are also supported by the trust.

In practice, the trust stated it is a 'private charity with specific objects and does not consider unsolicited applications'.

In 2001/02 the trust had assets of £1.2 million and a very low income of only £6,000. Management and admistration fees were high at £4,800 and the grant total was £52,000. It made eight grants in this financial year, £50,000 to Institute of Cancer Research, £1,000 to New Horizon Youth Centre, £500 to Ethiopia Aid, £400 to General Aviation Awareness Council, £300 to Royal Marsden Hospital Charity, £40 to Compassion in World Farming, £30 to SP Ancient Buildings and £25 to Royal School for the Deaf.

Applications The trust says it only supports charities it knows. Speculative applications have no possibility whatsoever of being successful.

The Britto Foundation

General, Children, Israel

£35,000 (1999/2000)

Beneficial area UK.

14a Eccleston Street, London SW1W 9LT

Correspondent The Trustees

Trustees *J C Y P Gommes; C L Corman; H K Lewis; T Gommes.*

CC Number 1010897

Information available Full accounts were on file at the Charity Commission.

General In 2000/01 the foundation had an income of £40,000 with an expenditure of £33,000. No further information was available.

In 1999/2000 grants were made totalling £35,000. Larger grants were to Israeli organisations, as follows: £16,000 to Tel Aviv Fund, £9,000 to Keshet Eilon, £2,000 to B'nai B'rith Hillel Foundation, £1,600 to UK Friends for Further Education in Israel, £1,300 to Israel Philharmonic Orchestra Fund, £1,000 to Friends of MDA in GB and £700 to Buxington.

The remaining grants ranged from £100 to £500 and included those to Chicken Shed Theatre Company, Council of Christians and Jews, Duslinn Aid Charity, Designer Crafts Foundation, Sporting Chance Appeal and Whizz-Kidz.

Applications The trustees stated: 'Applications are not sought at this time – trustees choose causes.' They were also keen to point out that these causes were 'Israeli' rather than 'Jewish'.

The Broadfield Trust

Education

£182,000 (2002/03)

Beneficial area UK.

c/o Baker Tilly, Elgar House, Holmer Road, Hereford HR4 9SF

Tel. 01432 352222

Correspondent Peter Johnston

Trustees *Hon. E R H Wills; J R Henderson; Sir Ashley Ponsonby; P N H Gibbs; C A H Wills; P J H Wills.*

CC Number 206623

Information available Accounts were on file at the Charity Commission.

General In 2002/03 the trust had assets of £4.7 million and an income of £186,000. Management and administration costs totalled £141,000.

Grants were made totalling £182,000 to two regular beneficiaries; the Farmington Trust (£168,000) and Rendcomb College (£14,000).

Exclusions No grants to individuals.

Applications In writing to the correspondent.

The Roger Brooke Charitable Trust

General

£157,000 (2001/02)

Beneficial area UK, with a preference for Hampshire.

Withers, 16 Old Bailey, London EC4M 7EY

Correspondent J P Arnold, Trustee

Trustees *J P Arnold; C R E Brooke; N B Brooke; J R Rousso; S H R Brooke.*

CC Number 1071250

Information available Accounts were provided by the trust.

General Established in 1998, this trust has general charitable purposes, including medical research, support for carers and social action.

In 2001/02 it had assets of £882,000 and an income of £34,000. Grants were made totalling £157,000. Unfortunately there were no further details on the size or number of beneficiaries.

Exclusions In general, individuals are not supported.

Applications In writing to the correspondent. Applications will only be acknowledged if successful.

The David Brooke Charity

Youth, medical

£67,000 (2002/03)

Beneficial area UK.

Billings House, Singers Lane, Henley-on-Thames, Oxfordshire RG9 1HB

Tel. 01491 573 411

Correspondent D J Rusman, Trustee

Trustees *D Brooke; D J Rusman; P M Hutt; N A Brooke.*

CC Number 283658

Information available Accounts were on file at the Charity Commission.

General The trust supports youth causes, favouring disadvantaged young people, particularly through causes providing self-help programmes and outdoor-activity training. Grants are also given to medical organisations.

In 2002/03 the trust had assets of £1.5 million generating an income of £73,000. After administration and management costs of £15,000, grants were given to 30 organisations and totalled £77,000.

Grants were given to a variety of UK and local groups concerned with children's welfare, the largest of which was £3,500 to Great Ormond St Hospital. Other grants were in the range of £500 to £3,000 and included those to Barnardos, British Stammering Association, Camphill Village Trust, Children's Society, Finchdale Training College, Fortune Centre of Riding Therapy, Kennet & Avon Canal Trust, NSPCC, RNIB, RNLI, Salvation Army, Unicef, Who Cares Trust and Yorkshire Dales Millennium Trust.

Applications The correspondent stated that the trust's annual income is not for general distribution as it is committed to a limited number of charities on a long-term basis.

The Palgrave Brown Foundation

Education, medical

£291,000 (2001/02)

Beneficial area UK, with a preference for the south of England.

c/o PB Forestry Lands Ltd, 24 Bedford Row, London WC1R 4EH

Tel. 020 7831 6393

Correspondent D Dooley, Trustees' Correspondent

Trustees *A P Brown; I P Brown.*

CC Number 267848

Information available Information was provided by the trust.

General Grants are given primarily to educational and medical organisations and generally range from £2,000 to £50,000 each.

In 2001/02 it had assets of £3.5 million and an income of £324,000. Grants totalled £291,000. The largest were £125,000 to Shrewsbury School Foundation, £50,000 to The Fettes Foundation and £40,000 to University of Cambridge School of Clinical Medicine.

Other grants included £10,000 each to Macmillan Cancer Relief and Prostate Cancer Charity and £5,000 each to British Limbless Ex-Servicemen's Association, Marie Curie Cancer Care, Greensleeves House Trust and Tapping House Hospice.

Exclusions No grants to individuals.

Applications Unsolicited applications are not accepted under any circumstances and will not be responded to.

Bill Brown's Charitable Settlement

Health, social welfare

£70,000 (2002/03)

Beneficial area UK.

Payne Hicks Beach, 10 New Square, Lincoln's Inn, London WC2A 3QG

Tel. 020 7465 4300

Correspondent G S Brown, Trustee

Trustees *P W E Brown; G S Brown; A J Barnett.*

CC Number 801756

Information available Full accounts were on file at the Charity Commission.

General This settlement support health and welfare causes, including those for older people.

In 2002/03 the trust had assets of £950,000 generating an income of £67,000. Grants totalling £70,000 were made to 20 organisations, a number of which were recurrent. Administration and management costs totalled £10,000.

Grants of £10,000 went to Salvation Army, £7,000 to Macmillan Cancer Relief, and £5,000 each to Alzheimer's Disease Society, Disability Challengers, National Association for Colitis and Crohn's Disease, Parkinson Disease Society and The Princess Alice Hospice. Other grants included £4,000 to Scout Association, £3,000 to Linden Lodge Charitable Trust and £2,500 to Cancer Research UK.

Applications In writing to the correspondent, including as much detail as possible. Applications are considered every six months. The trust states that nearly all of its funds are allocated to charities known to the trust and new applications have little chance of receiving grants.

R S Brownless Charitable Trust

Disabled, disadvantage, serious illness

£60,000 (2002/03)

Beneficial area Mainly UK and occasionally overseas.

Hennerton Holt, Wargrave, Reading RG10 8PD

Tel. 01189 404029

Correspondent Mrs P M A Nicolai, Trustee

Trustees *Mrs F A Plummer; Mrs P M Nicolai.*

CC Number 1000320

Information available Full accounts were on file at the Charity Commission.

General The trust makes grants to causes that benefit people who are disabled, disadvantaged or seriously ill.

Charities working in the fields of accommodation and housing, education, job creation and voluntary work are also supported. Grants are usually one-off, ranging between £100 and £2,000.

In 2002/03 it had assets of £34,000 and an income of £61,000. Grants totalled £60,000. Further information for this year was unavailable.

In 1999/2000 the trust's assets totalled £1.7 million, it had an income of £67,000 and grants were made totalling £46,000. The largest grants were: £4,000 to Camp Mohawk for maintenance and running costs, £3,500 to UNICEF for Mozambique and Venezuela, £3,000 to Prader-Willi Foundation for research and support, £1,500 to Wargrave PCC for cemetery maintenance, £1,000 each to Casa Allianza UK, Foundation for Study of Infant Deaths, St Andrew's Hall (for maintenance) and Witham on the Hill PCC and £500 each to Alzheimer's Society and Crisis.

Exclusions Grants are rarely given to individuals for educational projects or to education or conservation causes or overseas aid.

Applications In writing to the correspondent. The trustees meet twice a year, but in special circumstances will meet at other times. The trust is unable to acknowledge all requests.

The T B H Brunner Charitable Settlement

Heritage, arts, general

£38,000 (2001/02)

Beneficial area UK.

2 Inverness Gardens, London W8 4RN

Tel. 020 7727 6277

Correspondent T B H Brunner, Trustee

Trustees *T B H Brunner; Mrs H U Brunner.*

CC Number 260604

Information available Accounts were on file at the Charity Commission.

General In 2001/02 this trust had an income of £33,000. A total of 74 grants were made totalling £38,000.

Of the donations made, nine were to Rotherfield Greys PCC. Collectively these grants totalled over £7,500. Other larger grants included those to The University of Maryland (£3,400), The Royal British Legion - Poppy Day Appeal (£2,300), Family Welfare Association, Live Music Now!, St Mary Abbots Church and York Early Music Restival (£1,000 each).

Other smaller grants were between £100 and £800. Beneficiaries included I M S Prussia Cove (£500), Chinese Lantern Dinner (£250), Greater London Fund for the Blind (£150), Church of England Children's Society, The Friends of Covent Garden and The Oxfordshire Historic Churches Fund (£100 each).

Applications In writing to the correspondent.

Brushmill Ltd

Jewish

£217,000 (1995/96)

Beneficial area Worldwide.

Cohen Arnold & Co., New Burlington House, 1075 Finchley Road, London NW11 0PU

Tel. 020 8731 0777 **Fax** 020 8731 0778

Correspondent Stanley Davis

Trustees *J Weinberger; Y Getter; Mrs E Weinberger.*

CC Number 285420

Information available Information was on file at the Charity Commission.

General In 2000/01 the trust had an income of £281,000 with an expenditure of £261,000. No further information was available.

In 1995/96 the trust had an income of £134,000, virtually all from Gift Aid. Grants totalled £217,000, but no grants list was available.

In 1991/92 the trust had an income of £158,000, down from £283,000 the previous year. Grants totalled £186,000, a slight rise from £167,000 the previous year. All the recipients were Jewish organisations with the largest grants going to Bais Rochel (£34,000), Friends of Yeshivas Shaar Hashomaim (£15,000) and Holmleigh Trust (£14,000).

Applications In writing to the correspondent.

The Buckingham & Gawcott Charitable Trust

General

£42,000 (2003/04)

Beneficial area Buckingham and Gawcott.

30A Little Horwood Road, Great Horwood, Milton Keynes MK17 0QE

Correspondent David Bolton, Clerk to the Trust

Trustees *H Cadd; H Carey; R Lehman; P Collins; T Mills; D Rowlands; Mrs B Martin; P Dealey; R Stuchbury; P Strain-Clarke.*

CC Number 1010071

Information available Accounts were on file at the Charity Commission, but without a list of grants.

General The trust supports the 'preservation, improvement and enhancement of Buckingham and Gawcott and the amenities thereof for the benefit of the inhabitants'.

In 2003/04 the trust had assets of £160,000 and an income of £14,000. It made grants totalling £42,000. No further information was provided for this year.

In 2000/01 the trust stated in the accounts that over the future years a further £30,000 had been committed in support of the Buckingham Church project.

Exclusions No grants to individuals or for projects which would normally be a statutory responsibility.

Applications In writing to the correspondent.

Buckingham Trust

Christian, general

£155,000 to organisations (2001)

Beneficial area UK and worldwide.

Farthings, Hillcrest Drive, Tunbridge Wells, Kent TN2 3AG

Correspondent Philip Rennie Edwards

Trustees *Philip R Edwards; David J Hanes; Richard W D Foot.*

CC Number 237350

Information available Full accounts were on file at the Charity Commission.

General In 2001 the trust had assets of £838,000 and an income of £221,000. A total of £155,000 was given in 56 grants.

In 1999/2000 it had an income of £170,000 and gave £160,000 in grants. This included £8,400 in over 30 grants to individuals. Grants to organisations were broken down as follows:

Churches – 47 grants totalling £64,000

Beneficiaries included Pembury Free Church (£15,000), Sewardstone Church (£6,300), St Thomas's – Lancaster (£5,100), All Saints' Church (£4,500), New Life Church – Tunbridge Wells (£3,100) and Tonbridge Baptist Church (£1,200).

Charities – 250 grants totalling £87,000

Recipients included African Revival (£9,600), Tearfund (£9,100), New Frontiers International (£3,600), Dorothy Kerin Trust (£3,000), Relationships Foundation and Waltham Forest Youth for Christ (£2,000 each) and Bible Society and Burrswood Golden Jubilee Appeal (£1,200).

Applications In writing to the correspondent. However, the trust stated its beneficiaries are all determined by the trustees in advance and unsolicited applicants are simply rejected.

The Buckinghamshire Masonic Centenary Fund

General

£35,000 (2004)

Beneficial area Buckinghamshire.

51 Townside, Haddenham, Aylesbury, Buckinghamshire HP17 8AW

Tel. 01844 291275

Correspondent A R Watkins, Hon. Secretary

Trustees *D G Varney; J H Parkin; Lord Burnham; R Reed.*

CC Number 1007193

Information available Information was provided by the trust.

General This trust was set up in 1992, to make grants to charities in Buckinghamshire. In 2004 the trust had an income of £36,000 and made grants totalling £35,000.

Grants included £4,200 to Chamberlain Road Enterprises; £4,000 to Mediation in Buckinghamshire; £2,600 to Association for the Blind in Buckinghamshire; £2,400 to Youth Enquiring Service and £1,000 each to Heron's Lodge Guide Centre and Marie Curie Cancer Care.

Exclusions No grants to individuals for expeditions or for youth work overseas. Larger charities which have national appeal capability are unlikely to receive funding.

Applications In writing to the correspondent, setting out aims and objectives on one page of A4 with a copy of the latest audited annual report and accounts if available. Details should be supplied of the specific facilities or projects for which funding is sought. The trustees meet three or four times a year to consider applications. The trust states that some grants are made after the organisation has been visited by a committee member.

The Bulldog Trust

Arts, medical, youth, general

£152,000 (2000/01)

Beneficial area Worldwide, with a preference for the south of England.

2 Temple Place, London WC2 3BB

Tel. 020 7353 4522

Correspondent Richard Hoare, Trustee

Trustees *Richard Hoare; Messrs Hoare Trustees; Martin Rupert Riley.*

CC Number 326292

Information available Full accounts were provided by the trust.

General The objects of the trust are general, but it focuses on education and the arts, the environment and the support of excellence and enterprise, particularly in the young.

The total income for the year 2000/01 was almost £2.4 million, with £1.9 million being donated to the endowment funds. The assets stood at almost £6.6 million at the year end. Ordinary income came from several sources: donations (£210,000), trading activities (£162,000), rent (£60,000) and investments (£47,000).

Expenditure totalled £567,000, of which £152,000 was given in grants. These were classified as follows:

Education	£77,000
Performing arts	£18,000
Medical	£5,000
Social welfare	£49,000
Sport	£1,200
Religion	£2,000

The largest grants were £22,000 to Chamraj Children's Home (India), £15,000 to Royal British Legion, £14,000 to Hampshire County Council Project Tahir and £10,000 to Hampshire Gardens Trust. A further 38 causes received £1,000 to £5,000 including nine schools (from Rugby School to St Mary's Primary), and three universities. Others to receive grants in this range included Army Benevolent Fund, Chicken Shed Theatre Company, National Theatre, Rescue a Child, Royal Veterinary College, Trinity College of Music and Winchester Music Festival. Smaller grants of less than £1,000 totalled almost £15,000.

Exclusions No grants are given to individuals or to unsolicited applications.

Applications In writing to the correspondent; there are no application forms. However, please note that unsolicited applications are not acknowledged and are unlikely to be successful.

The Burden Trust

Christian, welfare, medical research, general

£154,000 (2002/03)

Beneficial area UK and overseas.

51 Downs Park West, Westbury Park, Bristol BS6 7QL

Tel. 0117 962 8611 **Fax** 0117 962 8611

Email p.oconor@netgates.co.uk

Correspondent Patrick O'Conor

Trustees *Dr M G Barker, Chair; R E J Bernays; A C Miles; Prof. G M Stirrat; Bishop of Southwell.*

CC Number 235859

Information available Full accounts were provided by the trust.

General The trust operates in accordance with various trust deeds dating back to 1913. These deeds provide for grants for medical research, hospitals, retirement homes, schools and training institutions, homes and care for the young and people in need. The trust operates with an adherence to the tenets and principles of the Church of England.

In 2002/03 it had assets of £3.1 million, which generated an income of £160,000. Grants totalled £154,000, broken down as follows:

Neurological research – 1 grant of £45,000
This went to Burden Neurological Institute.

Homes and care for aged, infirm and disabled – 1 grant of £6,000
This went to Brunelcare.

Clergy families' welfare – 2 grants totalling £3,000
£2,000 went to Society of Mary and Martha with £1,000 to St Luke's Hospital for the Clergy.

Schools and training institutions – 13 grants totalling £92,000
The largest grants were £18,000 to Trinity House, £15,000 to Langham Research Scholarships, £12,000 to Oxford Centre for Mission Studies and £10,000 each to Association for Theological Education by Extension – Bangladesh and Union Biblical Seminary – Pune. All of those grants went to organisations supported in the previous year; indeed, the only three grants to new beneficiaries in this category were £2,500 to Redcliffe College, £2,000 to Bristol Cathedral Trust and £1,000 to Tyndale House.

Other beneficiaries included Theological College – Vaux-sur-Seine (£9,000), Home Farm Trust (£4,000), St Paul's Divinity College – Kenya (£3,000) and All Nations Christian College (£2,500).

Organisations for care and training of young people – 1 grant of £4,000
This went to Easton Christian Family Centre, which received the same amount in the previous year.

Relief for necessitous persons – 2 grants totalling £4,000
These were £3,000 to Julian House – Bath and £1,000 to Crisis Centre Ministries.

Human research and curative care
No grants were made in this category during the year, although two grants (of £5,000 and £1,000 each) were made in the previous year.

Exclusions No grants to individuals.

Applications In writing to the correspondent to be received before 31 March each year. Financial information is required in support of the project for which help is requested. No application is responded to without an sae. Recipients of recurring grants are notified each year that grants are not automatic and must be applied for annually. Applications are considered at the annual trustees meeting.

The Burry Charitable Trust

Medicine, health

£41,000 (2001/02)

Beneficial area UK, with a preference for Hampshire.

261 Lymington Road, Highcliffe, Christchurch, Dorset BH23 5EE

Tel. 01590 682366

Correspondent R J Burry

Trustees *R J Burry; Mrs J A Knight; A J Osman.*

CC Number 281045

Information available Accounts were on file at the Charity Commission.

General In 2002/03 the trust had an income of £36,000 and a total expenditure of £37,000. Further information for this year was unavailable.

In 2001/02 grants totalled £41,000. A total of 13 organisations received donations including: Oakhaven Hospice Trust (£15,000); Life Education Centre Dorset, Tahir Project and Wessex Heartbeat (£5,000 each); New Milton Heath Centre (£2,700); Salvation Army (£2,500); John Grooms Association – Disabled People and Wessex Autistic Society (£1,000 each); Julia Perks Foundation (£500); and Mudeford Junior Cricket Club (£250). One individual received a grant of £75.

Exclusions No grants to individuals or students.

Applications This trust states that it does not respond to unsolicited applications.

The Arnold James Burton 1956 Charitable Settlement

General

£183,000 (2001/02)

Beneficial area UK and overseas, with preferences for Yorkshire and Israel.

Trustee Management Limited, 19 Cookridge Street, Leeds LS2 3AG

Correspondent Keith Pailing

Trustees *A J Burton; J J Burton; M T Burton.*

CC Number 1020986

Information available Full accounts were on file at the Charity Commission.

General Although donations are made at the discretion of the trustees, special consideration will be given to registered institutions relating to Jewish charities, medical research, education, social welfare and heritage.

In 2001/02 the trust had assets of £4.5 million which generated an income of £195,000. Grants to 67 organisations totalled £183,000. The main grant categories were as follows:

Health – 24 grants totalling £45,000
Recipients included Marie Stopes International (£10,000), Corda (£5,000), Breakthrough Breast Cancer (£2,000) and Disability Action – Yorkshire, Fight for Sight, Fund for Epilepsy, Richard Jackson Charitable Trust and Well Being (£1,000 each).

Jewish – 4 grants totalling £33,000
These were JNF Charitable Trust (£27,000), Community Security Trust (£4,000) and Harrogate Hebrew Congregation and National Jewish Chaplaincy (£1,000 each).

Social welfare – 18 grants totalling £33,000
Beneficiaries included Leeds Jewish Housing Association (£10,000), Children in Crisis (£3,000), RNIB and YMCA (£2,500 each), NSPCC (£1,100) and

Botton Village Appeals Trust, Centrepoint, Inkind Direct, National Association of Clubs and Renton Foundation (£1,000 each).

Education/arts – 16 grants totalling £21,000
Beneficiaries included Leeds College of Music (£2,300), British ORT (£2,000), York Festival Trust (£1,500) and Early Mines Research Group Museum Trust, Inspire Foundation and Yorkshire Arts (£1,000 each).

Overseas/developing countries – 5 grants totalling £11,000
Recipients were World Jewish Relief (£6,200), AMREF (£2,000) and Care International, Survival International and UNICEF (£1,000 each).

Exclusions No grants to individuals.

Applications In writing to the trust managers. The trust states that its funds are fully committed to charities already known to the trustees and new applications are not invited. Unsuccessful appeals will not necessarily be acknowledged.

R M Burton 1998 Charitable Settlement

Jewish charities, social welfare, education, the arts

£66,000 (2002/03)

Beneficial area England, with a preference for the Yorkshire and Humber area, particularly Leeds; also Israel.

c/o Trustee Management Ltd, 19 Cookridge Street, Leeds LS2 3AG

Correspondent The Trustees

Trustees *Raymond M Burton; Arnold Burton.*

CC Number 1070588

Information available Accounts were on file at the Charity Commission, but without a list of grants.

General The trust has general charitable purposes, with particular interests in Jewish charities, social welfare, education and the arts, particularly in Yorkshire. Grants are given to national and international organisations as well as local charities in Yorkshire and London. Many of the beneficiaries appear on the grants list each year, with the trust not wishing to add organisations to the list which provide the same services as those that have received funding in the past.

In 2002/03 it had assets of £1 million and an income of £48,000. Grants were made totalling £66,000. A grants list was not included in the accounts.

In 2000/01 it had assets of £1.2 million and an income of £124,000. Grants made to organisations totalled £84,000. There was also £500,000 spent on 'Capital appropriated', comprised of £250,000 each to Harriet Burton Charitable Trust and The Calmcott Trust.

The largest grant made was £10,000 to Dean and Chapter of York. Other large grants went to Community Security Trust (£5,500) and Harrogate Community House Trust and Yorkshire Archaeological Society (£5,000 each).

Other grants in the Yorkshire area included £2,000 to Yorkshire and Humberside Arts and £1,000 each to Boothby Road Community Project, Hull Jewish Community Care, Leeds Jewish Welfare Board and St George's Crypt.

Other beneficiaries elsewhere included Weizmann Institute (£3,500), The Woodland Trust (£2,000), Royal Opera House Trust (£1,500) with £1,000 each to Aidis Trust, British Heart Foundation, Norwood, Prince's Trust, RNIB, St John Ambulance, Textile Industry Children's Trust, UJIA and University of Cambridge.

Exclusions Grants are not given to local charities outside Yorkshire or London, individuals or to new charities where their work overlaps with already established organisations that are supported by the trust.

Applications In writing to the correspondent at any time. The trustees try to make a decision within a month. Negative decisions are not necessarily communicated.

The Arnold Burton 1998 Charitable Trust

Jewish, medical research, education, social welfare, heritage

£174,000 (2000/01)

Beneficial area Worldwide.

Trustee Management Ltd, 19 Cookridge Street, Leeds LS2 3AG

Correspondent The Trust Managers

Trustees *A J Burton; J J Burton; N A Burton; M T Burton*

CC Number 1074633

Information available Accounts were on file at the Charity Commission.

General Established in 1998, this trust gives special consideration to appeals from Jewish charities and projects related to medical research, education, social welfare and heritage. No grants are made to individuals. In 2000/01 it had assets of £48,000, an income of £127,000 and made grants totalling £174,000.

A total of 14 donations were made, the largest of which were £50,000 each to Royal Geographical Society and UJIA. Other beneficiaries included: Berkshire School (£15,000); Leeds Jewish Housing Association and Royal College of Surgeons (£10,000 each); Jewish Aid Committee, UNICEF and World Jewish Relief (£5,000 each); and Balfour Diamond Jubilee Trust (£1,000).

Applications In writing to the trust managers. Unsuccessful appeals will not necessarily be acknowledged.

The Geoffrey Burton Charitable Trust

General

£30,000 (2003/04)

Beneficial area UK, especially Suffolk.

Salix House, Falkenham, Ipswich IP10 0QY

Tel. 01394 448339 **Fax** 01394 448339

Email ericmaule@hotmail.com

Correspondent Eric Maule, Trustee

Trustees *E de B Nash; E E Maule.*

CC Number 290854

Information available Information was provided by the trust.

General In 2003/04 the trust had assets of £635,000 and an income of £42,000. Grants for the year totalled £30,000 and went to a wide range of organisations. Beneficiaries included the Green Light Trust (£4,000), RSPB (£3,000), University of Manchester (£1,700), East Anglia Children's Hospice, DanceEast, Red Rose Chain Theatre and Mid-Suffolk Citizens Advice (£1,000 each).

Exclusions No grants to individuals.

Applications In writing to the correspondent.

The Busenhart Morgan-Evans Foundation

Music, opera, general

£55,000 (2003/04)

Beneficial area England.

Brambletye, 455 Woodham Lane, Woodham, Addlestone, Surrey KT15 3QQ

Tel. 01932 344806

Correspondent John F Bedford, Trustee

Trustees *John F Bedford; C J Morgan-Evans; J B Morgan-Evans.*

CC Number 1062453

Information available Information was taken from the Charity Commission's database.

General Set up in 1997, the main objects of the foundation are the support of music, opera and young musicians at the outset of their professional careers, and help in the local community. It also makes an annual award for a young musician to continue postgraduate studies, on the recommendation of the Worshipful Company of Musicians.

In 2003/04 grants totalled £55,000. Further details were not available, however previous beneficiaries have included BACUP, English National Opera, Mind, Shelter and St Martin's-in-the-Fields.

Applications In writing to the correspondent. There are no formal application procedures and each application is considered on its merits within the above objectives. Candidates for the annual Young Musician Award should be made through the Principal of a University Music Department or Conservatoire to the Worshipful Company of Musicians.

The Bill Butlin Charity Trust

General

£86,000 (2002/03)

Beneficial area UK.

Eagle House, 110 Jermyn Street, London SW1Y 6RH

Tel. 020 7451 9000

Correspondent The Secretary

Trustees *Robert F Butlin; Lady Sheila Butlin; Peter A Hetherington; Trevor Watts; Frederick T Devine; Sonia I Meaden; Terence H North.*

CC Number 228233

Information available Full accounts were provided by the trust.

General This trust was established by Sir William E Butlin in 1963. It has a preference for organisations working with children, especially those with disabilities and older people. The trust has a list of regular beneficiaries, to which only a few charities may be added each year.

In 2002/03 it had assets of £2 million, which generated an income of £94,000. Grants were made totalling £86,000. Management and administration charges, including the costs of generating the funds, were high at £11,000. Grants totalling £86,000 were made to 25 organisations, of which 11 were also supported in the previous year.

The largest grants, of £15,000 each, went to Canadian Veterans Association of the UK and University of Southampton for cancer research. Other larger grants were £5,000 each to Dame Vera Lynn Trust for Children with Cerebral Palsy and NSPCC for the Full Stop Appeal, £4,000 to The Harbour, £3,000 each to Chagford Young Person's Educational Trust, Children's Hospice South West, Cup of Kindness Fund and MS Society and £2,500 each to Chichester Cathedral Restoration and Development Trust, Chicks and Sea Cadet Association.

The remaining grants were £2,000 each to BIBIC, Changing Faces, Finton House Educational Trust, Flying Scholarship for the Disabled, Grand Order of Water Rats, Saints and Sinners Club of London, South Buckinghamshire Riding for the Disabled, St George's Field – Fulmer and Story of Christmas 2002, £1,000 each to Bud Flanagan Leukaemia Fund, Entertainment Artistes Benevolent Fund, National Centre for Young People with Epilepsy and Tusk Trust and £500 to Royal Marsden Hospital.

Applications In writing to the correspondent. Trustees usually meet twice a year.

The C B Trust

General, Jewish

£31,000 (2002/03)

Beneficial area UK.

HSBC Trust Company UK Ltd, Trust Services, Norwich House, Nelson Gate, Southampton SO15 1GX

Tel. 023 8072 2229

Correspondent Steve Gladwell

Trustees *Harold S Klug; Naomi S Klug; HSBC Trust Co. Ltd.*

CC Number 287180

Information available Full accounts were on file at the Charity Commission.

General In 2002/03 the trust's assets totalled £460,000, the income £25,000 and grants £31,000. A range of organisations are supported, including a number of Jewish charities.

Grants were: £15,000 to Genesis Osteopathic Foundation, £10,000 to Charities Aid Foundation, £1,000 to The New North London Synagogue and £1,000 to British Friends of Neve Shalom.

Applications In writing to the correspondent.

C & F Charitable Trust

Orthodox Jewish charities

£132,000 (2002/03)

Beneficial area UK and overseas.

c/o New Burlington House, 1075 Finchley House Road, London NW11 0PU

Correspondent C S Kaufman, Trustee

Trustees *C S Kaufman; F H Kaufman; S Kaufman.*

CC Number 274529

Information available Accounts on file at the Charity Commission.

General The trust income derives mainly from investment properties and other investments. Grants are made to Orthodox Jewish charities.

In 2002/03 the trust had assets of £1 million, an income of £171,000 and made grants totalling £132,000. Beneficiaries included Yetev Lev Jerusalem Trust (£125,000), Kollel Shaarei Shlomo (£5,000), Community Council of Gateshead (£1,000), Ezras Nitrochim (£750), Gur Trust (£100) and SOFT (£50).

Exclusions Registered charities only.

Applications In writing to the correspondent.

The C J M Charitable Trust

Social entrepreneurship

£65,000 (2000/01)

Beneficial area UK and overseas.

Messrs Farrer and Co., 66 Lincoln's Inn Fields, London WC2A 3LH

Tel. 020 7242 2022

Correspondent Mrs Jane Leighton

Trustees *Christopher James Marks; Timothy John Marks; William Robert Marks; Rupert Philip Marks; Mary Elizabeth Falk.*

CC Number 802325

Information available Full accounts were on file at the Charity Commission.

General In 2000/01 this trust had an income of £23,000 and assets totalled £400,000. Grants totalled £65,000.

Beneficiaries were Network Foundation (£47,000), Mulberry Trst (£10,000), Dance United (£5,000), Ashoka (UK) Trust (£2,000) and Charities Aid Foundation (£500).

Applications In writing to the correspondent.

The Richard Cadbury Charitable Trust

General

£74,000 (2003)

Beneficial area UK, but mainly Birmingham, Coventry and Worcester.

26 Randall Road, Kenilworth, Warwickshire CV8 1JY

Tel. 01926 857793

Correspondent Mrs M M Eardley, Administrator

Trustees *R B Cadbury; Mrs M M Eardley; D G Slora; J A Slora.*

CC Number 224348

Information available Information was provided by the trust.

General The correspondent stated that the trust is 'people orientated' and supports projects such as playgroups, helping homeless people and the like and not arts and heritage-type causes. Grants range from £400 to £1,000 and are one-off. Grants are only given towards projects.

In 2003 the trust had assets of £600,000, an income of £27,000 and it gave grants totalling £74,000. No beneficiaries list was available from 2003 and the following is taken from the 2002 accounts:

The largest grant was £1,500 to Centrepoint. Other grants included £1,000 each to Birmingham Settlement, ChildLine, Children's Society, Friends of Swanirvar, Help the Aged, Little Sisters of the Poor, National Children's Home, Oxfam, Salvation Army, VSO and YMCA, £750 each to MIND, Population Concern and RNID and £500 each to Adventure Holidays, Billersley Primary School, Cathedral Camps, Cornerstone, Edward's Trust, Headway, Iris Fund, Listening Books, One Parent Families, Royal British Legion, St Chad's and Warwickshire Association of Boy's Clubs.

Exclusions Grants are only given to organisations with charitable status and not to individuals and students. No grants for running costs.

Applications In writing to the correspondent giving reasons why a grant is needed and including a copy of the latest accounts if possible. Meetings are held in February, June and October.

The Christopher Cadbury Charitable Trust

Nature conservation, general

£70,000 (2003/04)

Beneficial area UK, with a strong preference for the Midlands.

New Guild House, 45 Great Charles Street, Queensway, Birmingham B3 2LX

Tel. 0121 212 2222

Correspondent Roger Harriman, Administrator

Trustees *Roger V J Cadbury; Dr C James Cadbury; Mrs V B Reekie; Dr T N D Peet; P H G Cadbury; Mrs C V E Benfield.*

CC Number 231859

Information available Information was provided by the trust.

General In 2003/04 the trust had assets with a market value of £1.6 million and an income of £78,000. Grants totalled £70,000. The trustees have drawn up a schedule of commitments covering 15 charities which they have chosen to support. These charities can receive up to a maximum of £51,000 in any one year. Any surplus funds will be given to six other grant-making charitable trusts.

The largest grants included those to Croft Trust (£11,000), Royal Society for Nature Conservation (£10,000), Playthings Past Museum Trust (£8,500), Devon Wildlife Trust (£6,000) and Norfolk Wildlife Trust (£5,000).

Beneficiaries in the Midlands included Worcestershire Wildlife Trust (£4,000), Guide Association Beaconfield Campsites (£3,000), Edith Cadbury Nursery School and Ironbridge Gorge Museum Trust (£1,000 each), Avoncroft Arts Society and Selly Oak Nursery Schoool (£500 each), St Augustine's Church – Edgbaston (£250) and St Anne's Church – Wyre Piddle (£200).

Exclusions No support for individuals.

Applications The trustees have fully committed funds for projects presently supported and cannot respond positively to any further applications. Unsolicited applications are unlikely to be successful.

The George W Cadbury Charitable Trust

Population control, conservation, general

£214,000 (2002/03)

Beneficial area Worldwide.

New Guild House, 45 Great Charles Street, Queensway, Birmingham B3 2LX

Tel. 0121 212 2222 **Fax** 0121 212 2300

Correspondent Roger Harriman, Trust Administrator

Trustees *M/s C A Woodroffe; M/s L E Boal; P C Boal; M/s J C Boal; N B Woodroffe; M/s J L Woodroffe.*

CC Number 231861

Information available Information was provided by the trust.

General In 2002/03 the trust had assets of £4.4 million, generating an income of £203,000. Grants totalled £214,000, given in the following geographical areas:

UK	47%	£100,000
USA	47%	£102,000
Canada	6%	£12,000

The trust has general charitable purposes with a bias towards population control and family planning, welfare causes and conservation.

Altogether 83 grants were given, with 18 of £5,000 and above. The largest were £16,000 to Professional Children's School, £15,000 to Cancer Counselling Trust and £13,000 each to New York City Ballet Combinations Fund and Westchester Children's Association.

Exclusions No grants to individuals or non-registered charities, or for scholarships.

Applications In writing to the correspondent. However, it should be noted that trustees' current commitments are such that no unsolicited applications can be considered at present.

C J Cadbury Charitable Trust

General

£43,000 (2002/03)

Beneficial area UK.

Martineau Johnson, St Philips House, St Philips Place, Birmingham B3 2PP

Tel. 0121 200 3300

Correspondent H B Carslake, Trustee

Trustees *H B Carslake; Mrs Joy Cadbury; P H G Cadbury.*

CC Number 270609

Information available Accounts were on file at the Charity Commission.

General In 2002/03 the trust had assets of £451,000 and an income of £36,000. Grants to 30 organisations totalled £43,000.

The main beneficiaries were Royal Society for Nature Conservation (£18,000 in four grants), Goodenough College (£5,800 in three grants), Cortauld Institute (£2,900), Kingfisher's Bridge Wetland Creation Centre (£2,000) and Devon Wildlife Trust (£1,100).

Applications In writing to the correspondent. However, the trust stated in the summer of 2004 that it was not accepting any applications at present.

Henry T and Lucy B Cadbury Charitable Trust

Quaker causes and institutions, health, homelessness, support groups, Third World

£30,000 (2002)

Beneficial area Mainly UK, but also the developing world.

B C M, Box 2024, London WC1N 3XX

Correspondent Tamsin Yates, Trustee

Trustees *E Rawlins; M B Gillett; C Carolan; C R Charity; V Franks; T Yates; T Hambly.*

CC Number 280314

Information available Full accounts were on file at the Charity Commission.

General In the administration of this trust the trustees take it in turns to carry out the roles of the chair and secretary. Different trustees take responsibility for each area of concern to which grants are made. Each trustee is also separately allocated £1,500 in total to distribute to usually one to three charities, which relate to issues they are currently interested in.

In 2002 the trust had assets of £519,000, an income of £24,000 and made grants totalling £30,000. Beneficiaries which were the personal choice of one of the six trustees were £1,500 each to Dodford Children's Holiday Farm and Family Help, £1,000 to Battle Against Tranquillisers and £500 each to Action for ME, Anaphylaxis Campaign, Bhopal Medical Appeal, Medical Foundation for Victims of Torture, Prisoners of Conscience, Quaker Opportunity Playgroup, Riverside Community Project, Tools for Self-Reliance and Womankind Worldwide for Afghan Women.

The remaining 'general donations' were listed under the following headings:

Quaker

Grants were £1,500 to Quaker Peace and Social Witness, £1,000 to Quaker Social Action and £500 to Ulster Quaker Service.

Homeless

Grants were £1,000 each to Community Self Build and Turntable Furniture Project and £500 each to Kennet Action for Single Homeless and People's Kitchen.

Health

Donations were £1,000 to Riverside Community Health Project and £500 each to Bedfordshire and Northamptonshire MS Therapy Centre, Manic Depression Fellowship – Scotland and Macmillan Cancer Relief – Durham.

Support groups

Donations were £1,000 each to CAB, Newham Monitoring Project and Youth at Risk, £750 to Body and Soul and £500 each to Age Concern – Eastbourne, Hand Partnership, HIV–Aids Carers and Family Support Group, Medical Foundation, Prisoners of Conscience and Victim Support.

Overseas

Grants were £1,000 each to Action for Disability and Development, Centre for Peacemaking and Community Development, Jubilee Plus, Ockenden International and Tools for Self-Reliance and £500 to Basic Needs.

Exclusions No grants to non-registered charities.

Applications The trust's income is committed each year and so unsolicited applications are not normally accepted. The trustees meet in March to consider applications.

The George Cadbury Trust

General

£253,000 (2003/04)

Beneficial area Preference for the West Midlands, Hampshire and Gloucestershire.

New Guild House, 45 Great Charles Street, Queensway, Birmingham B3 2LX

Tel. 0121 212 2222 **Fax** 0121 212 2300

Correspondent Roger Harriman, Trust Administrator

Trustees *Peter E Cadbury; Annette L K Cadbury; R N Cadbury; Sir Adrian Cadbury; Roger V J Cadbury.*

CC Number 1040999

Information available Information was provided by the trust.

General The trust was set up in 1924 and maintains a strong financial interest in the Cadbury company. In 2003/04 the trust had assets of £7.8 million and an income of £320,000. Grants were made to 225 beneficiaries totalling £253,000.

The largest grants went to National Youth Ballet of Great Britain (£22,000), St John Ophthalmic Trust (£20,000), Serbian Church of St Hangar (£13,000), Artificial Heart Fund (£8,000) and Avoncroft Museum of Buildings (£7,500).

Other larger grants of £6,000 each went to Bower Trust and a number of grantmaking trusts: PHG Cadbury Charitable Trust, RVJ Cadbury Charitable Trust, RA & VB Reekie Charitable Trust, Sarnia Charitable Trust and C James Cadbury Charitable Trust.

It also gave 54 grants of £5,000 each, 5 grants of between £1,000 and £5,000 and 156 of £1,000 or less. Many beneficiaries have been supported in previous years.

Exclusions No support for individuals for projects, courses of study, expeditions or sporting tours. No support for overseas appeals.

Applications In writing to the correspondent to be considered quarterly. Please note that very few new applications are supported due to ongoing and alternative commitments.

The Edward & Dorothy Cadbury Trust (1928)

Health, education, arts

£99,000 (2003/04)

Beneficial area Preference for the West Midlands area.

Rokesley, University of Birmingham Selly Oak, Bristol Road, Selly Oak, Birmingham B29 6QF

Tel. 0121 472 1838 **Fax** 0121 472 7013

Correspondent Miss Susan Anderson, Trust Manager

Trustees *Mrs P A Gillett, Chair; Dr C M Elliott; Mrs P S Ward.*

CC Number 221441

Information available Full accounts were provided by the trust.

General The trust has general charitable purposes in the West Midlands, with areas of work funded including music and the arts, children's charities, disadvantaged groups and support for the voluntary sector. Although grants have been given up to £10,000, most are for £500 or less, with very few over £1,000.

In 2003/04 it had assets of £3.4 million, which generated an income of £114,000. Grants were made to 98 organisations and totalled £99,000. Donations were broken down as follows:

Arts and culture – 15 grants totalling £16,000

Donations included £5,000 to Elmhurst School for Dance, £3,800 to Bromsgrove Festival, £1,000 each to Avon Arts Society, Bromsgrove Operatic Society and Gloucester Three Choirs Festival, £750 to Birmingham Music Festival and £500 to Birmingham Centre for Arts Therapies. Grants of less than £500 totalled £1,500.

Community projects and integration – 27 donations amounting to £23,000

Grants included £10,000 to Girlguiding UK, £3,500 to Birmingham Settlement, £1,000 each to Kids Creche Service in Birmingham and National Playbus Association, £600 to Summerfield Friends of the Elderly, City Hospital – Birmingham and £500 each to Ackers Trust – Birmingham, St Martin's Youth and Community Centre – Birmingham and Willow Trust. Grants of less than £500 amounted to £3,800.

Compassionate Support – 38 grants amounting to £38,000

Donations included £10,000 to Acorns Children's Hospice, £5,000 each to Age Concern Bromsgrove and District and Birmingham Children's Hospital, £4,000 to Bromsgrove Bereavement Counselling, £1,000 to Care International UK, £850 to MS Mercia Therapy Centre – Coventry, £750 to John Grooms, £600 to Relate – Birmingham and £500 each to Children's Heart Foundation and City Hospital Neo-Natal Unit – Birmingham. Grants of less than £500 totalled £5,700.

Conservation and environment – One grant of £200

Education and training – 8 donations totalled £18,000

Grants of £500 and over were £7,000 to Camphill Village Trust, Community Centre – Birmingham, £5,000 to Cape Town, £4,000 to Dodford Children's Holiday Farm and £500 each to Calibre Cassette Library, CBSO Education and Outreach Department – Birmingham, Foundation for Conductive Education – Birmingham and Raddlebarn School – Birmingham. One grant of less than £500 was made totalling £250.

Research – 4 grants totalling £2,500

Donations were £1,000 to Wellchild Children's Research Centre, Birmingham and £500 each to Iris Fund for the Prevention of Blindness, Staffordshire University, Robotic Aid to Independent Living Project and Wellbeing.

Exclusions No grants to individuals.

Applications In writing to the correspondent, giving clear, relevant information concerning the project's aims and its benefits, an outline budget and how the project is to be funded initially and in the future. Up-to-date accounts and annual reports, where available, should be included. Applications can be submitted at any time but three months should be allowed for a response. Applications that do not come within the policy as stated above may not be considered or acknowledged.

Calleva Foundation

General

£73,000 (2002)

Beneficial area UK and worldwide.

PO Box 22554, London W8 5GN

Correspondent The Trustees

Trustees *S C Butt; C Butt.*

CC Number 1078808

Information available Accounts were on file at the Charity Commission.

General Registered with the Charity Commission in January 2000, this trust can give in the UK and worldwide for the benefit of 'local communities'.

In 2002 it had assets of £63,000 and an income of £130,000. Grants totalled £90,000, broken down as follows:

Education	£64,000
Children's holidays and social services	£800
Ecological	£2,300
Medical equipment	£180
Social services	£7,200
Medical research	£7,800
Animal welfare	£500
Medical care	£2,000
Respite care	£3,000
Art	£100
Overseas help	£2,200

Information on the size or type of grants, of the names of beneficiaries.

Applications In writing to the correspondent.

The Calpe Trust

Relief work

£32,000 (2002/03)

Beneficial area Worldwide.

The Hideaway, Hatford Down, Faringdon, Oxfordshire SN7 8JH

Tel. 01367 870665 **Fax** 01367 870500

Email reg.nort@rmplc.co.uk

Correspondent R H Norton, Trustee

Trustees *R H L R Norton, Chair; B E M Norton; E R H Parks.*

CC Number 1004193

Information available Information was provided by the trust.

General The trust makes grants towards registered charities benefiting people in need including refugees, homeless people, people who are socially disadvantaged, victims of war, victims of disasters and so on.

In 2002/03 it made 57 grants totalling £32,000. The largest were £5,000 in two grants to Anti-Slavery International, £1,000 to Hardman Trust, Pax Christi, Religious Society of Friends and Trocaire.

Aside from the £300 to Orfa Reyes Montalban and £250 to Orbis, all the remaining grants were of £500 each. Recipients included Cambodia Trust, Children in Crisis, ChildLine, Christian Ecology Link for Operation Noah, Eating Disorders Association, Family Holiday Association, Howard League for Penal Reform, Mulberry Bush School, One World Trust, Tuberous Sclerosis Association and Wells for India.

Exclusions No grants towards animal welfare or to individuals.

Applications In writing to the correspondent. Applicants must contact the trust before making an application.

Candide Charitable Trust

Music, visual arts

£60,000 (2002/03)

Beneficial area Worldwide

S G Kellys LLP, 52 Newtown , Lickfield, East Sussex TN22 5DE

Tel. 0182 5S H74 6888

Correspondent Christopher Stebbing

Trustees *S H Schaefer; O Ma; A Clark; M Kay.*

CC Number 1081134

Information available Accounts were on file at the Charity Commission.

General Established in 2000 this trust supports education and the advancement of promising young artists in the fields of visual arts and music by making grants and scholarships.

In 2002/03 the trust had an income of £46,000 mainly from donations. Grants totalled £60,000. The trust's annual report stated that it hoped to maintain a level of giving at £60,000 per year for the foreseeable future.

There were 10 grants made during the year. Beneficiaries were: Mariinsky Theatre Library (£17,000); Mikkeli Music Festival (£10,000); London Symphony Orchestra – scholarships (£8,300); London Philharmonic Youth Orchestra, National Youth Orchestra of Scotland, Royal Opera House – 'Chance to Dance' and Young Concert Artists' Trust (£5,000 each); Mariinsky Academy Scholarships (£4,000); University of Natal – opera scholarships (£3,000); and Prince of Wales 'Trust (£2,000).

Applications In writing to the correspondent.

The Canning Trust

General

£34,000 (2002/03)

Beneficial area UK and the developing world.

10 Knaresborough Place, London SW5 0TG

Correspondent The Trustees

Trustees *A J MacDonald; Mrs R R Pooley; Mrs R Griffiths.*

CC Number 292675

Information available Full accounts are on file at the Charity Commission.

General This trust only makes donations to causes proposed internally by staff members.

In 2002/03 it had an income of £7,000 and a total expenditure of £35,000. Total assets were £190,000. Grants totalled £34,000.

Beneficiaries included: £5,000 each to Emmanuel Hospital, Imani Esva, Nchima Trust, Society for Motivational Training, Stansberry Children's Home and Village Water. A grant of £4,000 was given to Wells for India.

Applications Unsolicited applications are not considered. The trust states that it generally only makes grants to charities which staff, ex-staff and friends are directly involved with.

H & L Cantor Trust

Jewish, general

£365,000 (2001/02)

Beneficial area UK, with some preference for Sheffield.

Massada, 478 Ecclesall Road South, Sheffield S11 9PZ

Tel. 0114 230 6354

Correspondent Mrs Lilly Cantor, Trustee

Trustees *H Cantor; L Cantor.*

CC Number 220300

Information available Information was on file at the Charity Commission.

General The trust has a preference for making grants to Jewish charities, but makes a small number of grants to other organisations.

In 2002/03 the trust had an income of £41,000 and a total expenditure of £72,000.

In the previous year it had assets of £1.3 million generating an income of £64,000. Grants to 66 charities totalled £365,000 with the trust making a number of major grants. This is a significant increase from the previous year when grants totalled £28,000. The trust usually has a yearly surplus of around £60,000 and it is likely that this surplus accounts for the unusually high grant total.

By far the largest grant was £250,000 to Sheffield Hallam University. Other major grants included National Yad Vashem Charity (£50,000), Royal Star and Garter Home (£21,000), Sheffield Botanical Garden Trust (£15,000) and United Jewish Israel Appeal Charities (£10,000). Other beneficiaries receiving £1,000 or more included Sheffield Jewish Congregation Centre (£1,600), Friends of Alyn (£1,500) and Cavendish Centre for Cancer, Royal Academy Trust and St Luke's Hospice (£1,000 each).

Smaller grants included West Riding Masonic Charities (£630), Cancer Research UK, Norwood Ltd and Youth Aliyah Child Rescue (£500 each), Ben Gurion University Foundation and Friends of Hebrew University (£250 each), Council of National Parks, Jewish Museum, Sheffield Furniture Trade Benevolent Association, Sheffield Hillel Association, Sheffield Hospital Sunday Fund and Sheffield Jewish Blind Society (£100 each) and Sheffield Synagogue Ladies' Guild (£15).

Applications Unsolicited applications are not invited.

Capital Charities

Children and young people

Around £1.9 million (2003)

Beneficial area The broadcast area of Red Dragon FM; the Red Rose radio franchise area; the transmission area of Century radio (effectively north east England); Edinburgh, Lothians and Fife; South Yorkshire and North Midlands; London, specifically the 95.8 Capital FM transmission area.

c/o Capital Radio, 30 Leicester Square, London WC2H 7LA

Tel. 020 7766 6203/6536 **Fax** 020 7766 6195

Email annabel.durling@capitalradiogroup.com

Website www.capitalfm.com

Correspondent Annabel Durling

Trustee

CC Number 1091657b

Information available Information was available on the Charity Commission website.

General This trust is an amalgamation of all of the local funders in the Capital Radio Network. Help a London Child is large enough to warrant an entry in Volume One of this guide. An entry for the combined charities is included in this volume to reflect the size and scope of funds available. Whilst it may effectively be a collective of local funders, the potential beneficial area is certainly wider than the actual giving of many UK-wide funders.

Capital Charities run the following appeals through Capital Radio Group's stations across the UK. These are:

- 'Help a London Child' at Capital Radio
- 'Help a South Wales Child' at Red Dragon FM,
- 'Help a Local Child' in Sussex at Southern FM,
- 'Help a Local Child' in Kent at Invicta FM,
- 'Help a Local Child' in Hampshire at Power FM,
- 'Help a Local Child' in the West Midlands at BRMB FM
- 'Help a Local Child' in Oxfordshire at FOX FM
- '21st Century Kids' in Nottingham, Manchester and Newcastle at 106 Century FM, 105.4 Century FM and 100–102 Century FM.

Each branch of the charity seeks to allocate grants to children and young people who experience disadvantage in the above regions and cities.

This trust raises all the money it allocates. It does this through a combination of fundraising activities, auctions, charity balls and treks. It has two rounds of funding per year.

The categories of organisations that may be supported are:

- Community groups
- Playgroups
- Refuge/homelessness projects
- Social/leisure groups
- Special needs/health projects
- Youth
- Language and literacy

The trust will consider funding:

- sessional posts
- capital costs, for example play, sports and special needs equipment
- key core running costs, for example rent, project telephone bills, postage costs
- projects run by local branches of national/regional organisations
- trips or holidays in the UK
- construction costs only for safety surfacing, storage and installation of equipment
- volunteer costs
- booklets, publications and information leaflets targeted at children and young people.

The panel look most favourably on projects that directly benefit children. It invites applications from any group which has a written constitution and child protection policy as well as a management committee. Non-registered charities can still apply, but must have its application endorsed by a registered group willing to accept the grant on its behalf.

Reapplications are encouraged. Organisations can be funded repeatedly for three years or more as long as they can show new aspects of the project and particularly, how the previous grant has enabled the project to develop. Organisations applying for a fourth year in a row will be given less priority than other applicants.

In 2002/03 the charities had an income of just under £1 million and a total expenditure of £1.9 million, the majority of which was distributed in grants by the Help a London Child branch. The charity has branches throughout the UK, due to the concentration of grants within the Greater London area, our narrative will be placed specifically on the Help a London Child branch.

In 2002/03 Help A London Child made 524 grants totalling £731,000, benefitting over 100,000 of London's less advantaged and most vulnerable children and young people.

HALC aims to give opportunities to the Capital's children and young people who:

- experience poverty and disadvantage
- have/are experiencing abuse, neglect, homelessness, violence, crime
- have an illness or disability.

Community groups – 32 grants

- Playschemes and activities organised by, and equipment for: community centres, after-school clubs, residents' associations, adventure playgrounds.
- Cultural activities and projects addressing the needs of children from local ethnic communities.
- London branches of welfare groups (i.e. Gingerbread, Homestart, WelCare).

Language and literacy projects – 8 grants

- Groups addressing non-statutory educational needs such as local branches of Volunteer Reading Help.
- Supplementary and mother tongue schools.

Playgroups and toy libraries – 10 grants

- Projects offering primary play facilities to children from disadvantaged backgrounds ages five and under.

Refuge/homeless projects – 6 grants

- Organisations running refuges for children affected by domestic violence (i.e. London Women's Aid and refuge groups).
- Projects focusing on homeless families with young children, and youth homelessness.

Social/leisure groups – 19 grants

- Arts, drama, music, and sports clubs for less advantaged young people.

Special needs/health projects – 33 grants

- Equipment, activities and playschemes for groups supporting children and young people with disabilities and/or special needs.
- Projects for young people dealing with health issues (i.e. alcohol, drug and physical abuse, bullying, sexual health).

Youth - 12 grants

- Clubs and projects focused on young people aged 11 to 18.

Exclusions Each individual branch has specific exclusions, generally however the charities will not fund:

- individual children or families
- retrospective funding
- statutory Funding, such as schools and hospitals
- salaried posts
- deficit funding
- medical research
- purchase of minibuses
- trips abroad
- distribution to other organisations
- distribution to individuals
- religious activities
- political groups
- general structural changes to buildings
- projects which are part of a larger charity organisation and not separately constituted
- core funding for a national or regional charity.

Applications Please contact Annabel Durling at Capital Charities on 020 7766 6536 for more details, or email annabel.durling@capitalradiogroup.com

Grants are awarded twice a year, with closing dates in June for funding starting in October, and October for funding starting in February.

Cardy Beaver Foundation

General

£36,000 (2001/02)

Beneficial area UK.

Brannans, 63 Stowe Road, London, W12 8BE

Tel. 020 8749 2575

Correspondent G R Coia, Trustee

Trustees *M G Cardy; G R Coia.*

CC Number 265763

Information available Accounts were on file at the Charity Commission.

General Registered with the Charity Commission in May 1973, in 2001/02 the foundation had assets of almost £2 million and an income of £126,000. Grants totalled £36,000. The foundation's annual report stated that it supports 'national and local charities'.

During the year 25 grants were made. All were for £1,500 each, bar one. Beneficiaries included Action Research, Battle Hospital Cardiac Unit, British Red Cross, Daisy's Dream, NSPCC, Prostrate Cancer Research, Scope, See Ability, Thames Valley Air Ambulance, Treloar Trust and Macmillan Cancer Relief – West Berkshire.

Applications In writing to the correspondent.

The D W T Cargill Fund

General

£196,000 (2000/01)

Beneficial area UK, with a preference for the west of Scotland.

Miller Beckett & Jackson, 190 St Vincent Street, Glasgow G2 5SP

Tel. 0141 204 2833

Correspondent Norman A Fyfe, Trustee

Trustees *A C Fyfe; W G Peacock; N A Fyfe; Mirren Elizabeth Graham.*

SC Number SC012703

Information available Accounts were previously provided by the trust.

General This trust has the same address and trustees as two other trusts, W A Cargill Charitable Trust and W A Cargill Fund, although they all operate independently.

This trust supports 'any hospitals, institutions, societies or others whose work in the opinion of the trustees is likely to be beneficial to the community'.

In 2000/01 it had assets of £6.3 million and an income of £194,000. Grants to organisations totalled £196,000, broken down as annual grants and appeals.

Annual – 35 grants totalling £161,000

The largest grants, as in the previous year, were £35,000 to Ardgowan Hospice and £15,000 to RUKBA. Other notable grants included £9,000 to Marie Curie Cancer Care – Hunter's Hill, £8,000 to Greenock Medical Aid Society, £7,500 to City of Glasgow Society of Social Service, £7,000 to Quarriers Village and £6,000 to Glasgow and West of Scotland Society for the Blind.

Other beneficiaries included Scottish Maritime Museum – Irvine and Scottish Episcopal Church and Eventide Homes (£5,000 each), The Thistle Foundation, Muscular Dystrophy Group and Enable (£4,000 each), Colquhoun Bequest Fund for Incurables (£3,000), Glasgow City Mission and Scottish Motor Neurone Disease Association (£2,000 each) and Bethesda Nursing Home and Hospice – Stornoway and Earl Haig Fund (£1,000 each).

Appeals – 11 grants totalling £35,000

David Cargill House received four grants, £20,000 for operating deficits, £1,300 for residents' Christmas outings, £1,100 for staff Christmas outing and £1,000 for staff gift vouchers. Other beneficiaries were Kilmacolm Community Transport New Bus Fund (£3,000), David Cargill Club (£2,000 for rewiring), St Mary's Episcopal Cathedral, Lead Scotland, Three Towns Blind Bowling/Social Club, North Glasgow Community Forum, Crathie Opportunity Holidays and The Pavillion Youth Cafe (£1,000 each), Alzheimer Scotland Action on Dementia and Kennyhill School (£500 each).

Exclusions No grants are made to individuals.

Applications In writing to the correspondent, supported by up-to-date accounts. Trustees meet quarterly.

Carlee Ltd

Jewish

£139,000 to organisations and individuals (2001/02)

Beneficial area Worldwide.

32 Pagent Road, London N16 5NQ

Correspondent The Secretary

Trustees *Hershel Grunhut; Mrs Pearl Grunhut; Bernard Dor Stroh; Mrs Blima Stroh.*

CC Number 282873

Information available Full accounts were on file at the Charity Commission.

General The trust's principal activity is 'Jewish charitable purposes in the advancement of religion and the relief of need of persons, such as Talmudical students, widows and their families'.

In 2001/02 it had assets of £796,000 and an income of £140,000. Grants were made totalling £139,000 to individuals and organisations.

The largest grants were £18,000 to Tevini, £13,000 to Antryvale Ltd, £10,000 each to Asos Cheshed, Glasgow Kollel and Union of Hebrew Congregations, £9,500 to YHTC, £9,000 to Egerton Road Building Fund, £7,200 to Rav Chesed Trust and £7,000 each to HTVC and YHS.

Applications In writing to the correspondent.

This entry was not confirmed by the trust, but the address was correct according to the Charity Commission database.

The Carlton House Charitable Trust

Bursaries, Jewish, general

£33,000 (2002/03)

Beneficial area UK and overseas.

Craven House, 121 Kingsway, London WC2B 6PA

Tel. 020 7242 5283 **Fax** 020 7831 1162

Email stewartcohen@carltonconsultants.com

Correspondent Stewart S Cohen, Trustee

Trustees *Stewart S Cohen; Pearl C Cohen; Fiona A Stein.*

CC Number 296791

Information available Information was provided by the trust.

General In 2002/03 it had assets of £614,000, which generated an income of £34,000. Grants were made to 35 organisations totalling £33,000.

The largest grants were £11,000 to B'nai B'rith United Kingdom, £4,900 to Westminster Advocacy Service for Senior Residents, £4,500 to Western Marble Arch Synagogue, £2,500 to British WIZO, £1,500 to Community Security Trust and £1,000 each to Magen David Adom and Sayser Charity.

The next largest grants, of £500 each, went to Emunah, Friends of Lubacitch UK, Jewish Museum, National Trust, St James's Conservation Trust and United Jewish Israel Appeal.

Most of the grants were in the region of £50 to £200 each. These included £200 each to Board of Deputies Charitable Trust and Shaare Zedek UK, £170 to B'nai B'rith First Lodge of England Charitable Trust, £100 each to Association of Cancer Research, Institute of Jewish Policy Research, PDSA and Tel Aviv University Trust and £50 each to Cosgrove Care and National Patients Support Trust.

Applications In writing to the correspondent.

The Carmichael-Montgomery Charitable Trust

United Reformed Church, general

£128,000 (2002/03)

Beneficial area England and Wales.

3 Bear Close, Henley-in-Arden, Warwickshire B95 5HS

Tel. 01564 793561

Correspondent Mrs N Johnson, Trustee

Trustees *Mrs B J Baker; D J Carmichael; The Revd B Exley; K Forrest; D M Johnson; Mrs N Johnson; Revd M G Hanson; P J Maskell; Mrs S Nicholson.*

CC Number 200842

Information available Accounts were on file at the Charity Commission, but without a grants list since those for 1995/96.

General The main purpose of this trust is to make grants to United Reformed churches. Grants are normally for capital expenditure and not usually for 'running' expenses, or salaries. In addition, the trustees make small grants to individual young people, who are known either to the trustees or their contacts. The trust would only support organisations which fall outside its criteria if there is a personal contact with one of the trustees.

In 2002/03 it had assets of £1.3 million and an income of £62,000. Grants totalled £128,000. A list of beneficiaries for the year was not provided.

In 1999/2000 the trust gave 42 grants totalling £62,000, broken down as follows: 24 grants to United Reform churches totalled £41,000; 10 grants to trusts and societies ranging from £250 to £5,000 totalled £14,000; and 8 grants to individuals totalled £7,100. Unfortunately, further information for this year was not available.

The latest grants list available was for 1995/96 when £49,000 was given in 39 grants. Grants totalling £28,000 were given to 16 different United Reformed churches. Other grants ranged from £200 to £5,000. Beneficiaries included several churches and also Harry Guntrip Memorial Trust (£5,000), The Oasis Appeal (£2,000), The Sports Centre – Moussa Conteh for a project in Sierra Leone (£1,000) and Newcastle College Chaplaincy (£500).

Three clergymen received grants totalling about £4,000 and grants to other individuals totalled £600.

Exclusions Grants are not generally made to medical charities or individuals.

Applications The trustees normally meet in April and October to consider applications submitted in March and September. However, the trust stated in January 2005 that it would not be in a position to make any grants during 2005 or 2006. An sae is not necessary, since the trust does not acknowledge ineligible applications.

The Carpenter Charitable Trust

Humanitarian and Christian outreach

Around £40,000 per annum

Beneficial area UK and overseas.

The Old Vicarage, Hitchin Road, Kimpton, Hitchin, Hertfordshire SG4 8EF

Email michael.carpenter4@btinernet.com

Correspondent M S E Carpenter, Trustee

Trustees *M S E Carpenter; Mrs G M L Carpenter.*

CC Number 280692

Information available Full accounts were provided by the trust.

General During 2003/04 the trustees undertook a critical review of their grant–making pattern in part to reflect difficult investment conditions which have prevailed. As a result the trustees have reduced the number of grants available and in some cases they will now only support one charity rather than several. The number of grants is likely to be around 30 a year, with up to 5 grants of £5,000, 10 of £1,000 and the balance at £500.

The range of charity selected to receive grants is quite wide but a preference is shown to charities with a Christian bias, whether this involves relief of hardship or Christian outreach through education or otherwise. The trustees are happy to contribute to core funding or to special projects (but are concerned that special projects will enhance the charitable services to beneficiaries and can be properly funded in the longer run without dilution to the core provision).

In 2002/03 the trust's assets totalled £743,000 and it received an income of £30,000. A total of 330 applications were received, 56 of which were accepted. Grants totalled £78,000. This included one exceptional donation of £50,000, made to the Millennium Room at Kimpton Church. The trustees stated that it is unlikely that a grant of this magnitude will be considered again.

Donations included: £2,000 to Mission Aviation Fellowship; £1,500 to UNICEF; £1,000 each to Christians Against Poverty, Landmark Trust and Merlin; £750 each to Relationship Foundation and Save The Children Fund; £500 each to Crusaders, Carrymeera Community, Habit For Humanity, In-kind Direct, Tower Hamlets Mission and Traidcraft Exchange; £250 each to All Nations Christian College, Contact The Elderly, Fight For Sight and Macmillan Cancer Relief; and £100 each to Covent Garden Cancer Research Trust, Derma Trust, Highland Theological College and People's Dispensary For Sick Animals.

Exclusions No grants to individuals or to repair local churches. Overseas applications are not considered.

Applications In writing to the correspondent including sufficient details to enable a decision to be made. However, as about half the donations made are repeat grants, the amount available for unsolicited applications remains small.

The Carpenters' Company Charitable Trust

Education, general

£157,000 to organisations and individuals (2002/03)

Beneficial area UK.

Carpenters' Hall, 1 Throgmorton Avenue, London EC2N 2JJ

Tel. 020 7588 7001

Correspondent The Clerk

Trustees *V F Browne; M R Francis; P C Osborne; M I Montague-Smith.*

CC Number 276996

Information available Full accounts were on file at the Charity Commission.

General This trust's income is mainly comprised of donations from the Carpenters' Company. In 2002/03 it had an income of £2.2 million and made grants totalling £157,000 to organisations and individuals.

The trust makes grants in the areas listed below:

Educational grants, scholarships and prizes

'Craft grants' were given to 38 individuals and totalled £30,000, about half of which was given to individuals at Building Crafts College. Other organisations which also received support; City of London Schools (£3,000), King Edward's School, Witley (£2,000), City University (£1,500) and Henry Osborne Award (£1,000)

Other donations and gifts

The largest grant was to Carpenters and Dockland Centre, which received £20,000, and is supported each year. £17,000 went to Wood Awards 2003 and £12,500 to Institute of Carpenters. Further grants of £2,000 were made to Action for Kids Charitable Trust, Heritage Information Trust, Sheriff's & Recorder's Fund and St Paul's Cathedral. Grants of £1,000 went to All Hallows Church, Defeating Deafness, LUPUS (UK), Purley Park Trust and Scout Council.

Applications In writing to the correspondent, although the trust states that unsolicited applications are not invited.

The Carron Charitable Trust

Environment, education, medicine

£109,000 (2003)

Beneficial area UK and overseas.

Messrs Rothman Pantall & Co., 10 Romsey Road, Eastleigh, Hampshire SO50 9AL

Tel. 023 8061 4555

Correspondent Mrs C S Cox

Trustees *P G Fowler; Mrs J Wells; W M Allen; D L Morgan.*

CC Number 289164

Information available Full accounts were on file at the Charity Commission.

General Applications from charities linked to wildlife, education, medicine, the countryside, printing and publishing will be considered, including charities working in the fields of health professional bodies, health campaigning and advocacy, conservation, wildlife parks and sanctuaries, natural history, endangered species, education and training, costs of study and academic research. Organisations benefiting academics, medical professionals, nurses and doctors, research workers and students are supported.

Grants are towards projects, research, running costs and salaries.

In 2003 the trust's income was £128,000 and it made grants totalling £109,000. Assets totalled £256,000 at the year end. Grants included £34,900 to St Brides Church Appeal, £27,100 to National Missing Persons Helpline, £13,500 Imperial College of Science & Medicine and £12,100 to Covent Garden Research Trust.

Other grants were £5,000 to Battle Hospital, £3,400 to Highland Clearances Memorial Centre, £2,700 to Friends of Boyton Church, £1,300 Bath Clinic, £1,000 each Leading the Fight Against Cancer Brochure, KCC Foundation, Kyle Fishery and National Academy of Writing.

Exclusions No grants to individuals.

Applications Almost all of the charity's funds are committed for the foreseeable future and the trustees therefore do not invite applications from the general public.

The Leslie Mary Carter Charitable Trust

Conservation/ environment, welfare

£123,000 (2001)

Beneficial area UK, with a preference for Norfolk, Suffolk, Uttlesford, Braintree, Colchester and Tendring.

Birketts, 24–26 Museum Street, Ipswich IP1 1HZ

Tel. 01473 232300

Correspondent Daniel Agar

Trustees *Miss L M Carter; S R M Wilson.*

CC Number 284782

Information available Information was on file at the Charity Commission.

General The trust has a preference for welfare organisations and conservation/ environment causes, with an emphasis on local projects including those in Suffolk, Norfolk and North Essex. Grants generally range from £500 to £5,000, but larger grants sometimes considered. In 2003 it had an income of £102,000 and a total expenditure of £108,000. Further details for this year were not available.

In 2001 the trust had assets of £4.4 million and an income of £169,000. Grants totalled £123,000. They included £10,000 each to Multiple Sclerosis Society, Raleigh International, Royal Agricultural Benevolent Institution, Save the Children Fund, Soil Association and YWCA, £7,500 to WWF – UK, £6,000 each to British Trust for Ornithology and Macmillian Cancer Relief, £5,000 each to Greenpeace Environmental Trust and SSAFA Forces Help in East Anglia, £3,000 to St John's Church – Great Clacton and £2,500 to Council for Protection of Rural England.

Exclusions No grants to individuals.

Applications In writing to the correspondent. Telephone calls are not welcome. There is no need to enclose an sae unless applicants wish to have materials returned.

The Carvill Trust

General

£90,000 (2002/03)

Beneficial area UK.

5th Floor, Minories House, 2–5 Minories, London EC3N 1BJ

Tel. 020 7780 6900

Correspondent K D Tuson, Trustee

Trustees *R K Carvill; R E Pooley; K D Tuson.*

CC Number 1036420

Information available Accounts were on file at the Charity Commission.

General In 2002/03 the trust had assets of £472,000 an income of £123,000 and grants totalled £90,000.

Grants were £20,000 to War Child, £13,000 to Ocean Reef Academy, £11,000 to Irish Youth Foundation, £ 10,000 to Electronics For The Blind, £ 5,000 each to Action for the Blind, Delta, LINK, Lloyds Patriotic Fund, Royal London Society for Blind and Sense, £3,000 to Linmara Trust, £2,600 to Treloar Trust, £500 to St Saviour's Church and £75 to The Lord's Taverners.

Applications In writing to the correspondent, although the trust states that it only supports beneficiaries known to or connected with the trustees. Unsolicited applications from individuals will not be supported.

The Casey Trust

Children and young people, Jewish

Over £90,000 to UK causes (2002/03)

Beneficial area UK and developing countries.

27 Arkwright Road, London NW3 6BJ

Correspondent Ken Howard, Trustee

Trustees *Kenneth Howard; Edwin Green; Judge Leonard Krikler.*

CC Number 1055726

Information available Full accounts were on file at the Charity Commission.

General This trust was established to help children and young people in the UK and developing countries by supporting new projects, in a variety of countries. Set up in 1996, it had an initial income of £2.2 million in 1996/97, comprising mainly funds transferred from the estate of the late Mrs Beatrice Howard.

In 2002/03 the trust's income was £124,000 and its assets totalled £2.3 million. Grants were made totalling £90,000.

Grants given in the UK included: £19,000 to World Medical Fund, £7,000 to Family Wefare Association, £6,500 to Norwood, £5,300 to Challenge, £5,000 each to ACORNS and ChildHope UK, £4,000 to Family Services Unit, £3,000 each to Books Abroad, Esther Benjamin Trust, Henshaws Society for the Blind, Hope and Homes for Children, Homesy Trust and Joshua Foundation and £2,500 to Norman Laud Association.

Exclusions Grants are not given to 'individual applicants requesting funds to continue studies or travel'.

Applications In writing to the correspondent. This entry was not confirmed by the trust, but the information was correct according to the trust's file at the Charity Commission.

The Elizabeth Casson Trust

Oxford Brookes University, other occupational therapy schools and departments, and individual occupational therapists.

£206,000 (2003/04)

Beneficial area UK.

20 Chaundy Road, Tackley, Kidlington, Oxfordshire OX5 3BJ

Tel. 01869 331379

Email bernard.davies@btinternet.com

Correspondent B A Davies, Secretary

Trustees *B M Mandlebrote; K D Grevling; Mrs C Rutland; Prof. D T Wade; Mrs J S Croft; Mrs C A G Gray; Dr P L Agulnic; G A Paine; Mrs R Hallam.*

CC Number 227166

Information available The trust was founded in 1930 as Dorset House School of Occupational Therapy (a registered company). In 1948 the founder Dr Elizabeth Casson, registered this trust and an associated trust, the Casson Trust, under the same number at the Charity Commission. In 1992 Dorset House site was leased to Oxford Brookes University and in 1993 the company changed its name to the Elizabeth Casson Trust.

General Grants are divided: 75% to support Oxford Brookes University occupational therapy courses; and 25% to support other occupational therapy schools/departments and individual occupational therapists.

In 2003/04, the trust had assets of £5.2 million and an income of £215,000. Grants totalled £206,000 the largest of which were: £55,000 to Oxford Brookes University School of Healthcare; £22,000 for a one-year scholarship at Tufts University, Boston, USA; £5,000 to University of Greenwich for wheelchair course accreditation; £1,000 towards MSc course fees.

Exclusions No support for anything other than occupational therapy education and training.

Applications On the trust's application form which can be obtained from the address below.

H and M Castang Charitable Trust

Medical professionals, research workers and people with physical or mental disabilities.

£86,000 (2001/02)

Beneficial area UK.

Carmelite House, 50 Victoria Embankment, Blackfriars, London EC4Y 0LS

Tel. 020 7842 8000

Correspondent I A Burman, Trustee

Trustees *I A Burman; M B Glynn; Dr I St J Kemm.*

CC Number 1003867

Information available Information was on file at the Charity Commission.

General In 2001/02 the trust had assets of £2.5 million and an income of £103,000. Grant total for this year was £86,000. No further details were available for this year.

In 1998/99 grants totalled £46,000. The largest grants were: £40,000 to The Little Foundation for a research project relating to cerebral palsy (£30,000) and for general purposes (£10,000); £5,200 to Neurology and Orthopaedic Development Fund – Royal Hospital for Sick Children Edinburgh for a part-time study assistant for a cerebral palsy study' £600 for travelling expenses for a doctor to attend a meeting at the International Federation of Placental Associations and £500 to fund a trip to Tubingen for a doctor.

Applications In writing to the correspondent.

The Catalyst Charitable Trust (formerly the Buckle Family Charitable Trust)

Medical, general

£45,000 to organisations (2001/02)

Beneficial area Mainly Suffolk and Essex.

9 Trinity Street, Colchester, Essex CO1 1JN

Tel. 01206 544434

Correspondent G W N Stewart, Trustee

Trustees *Gillian Margaret Lecky Buckle; James Kennedy Buckle; Joanna Lecky Thomson; Gavin William Nicol Stewart.*

CC Number 1001962

Information available Accounts were on file at the Charity Commission.

General This trust has an interest in supporting small charities in the Suffolk/ Essex area. It also funds a research fellowship at Charing Cross and Westminster Hospital.

In 2001/02 the trust had an income of £64,000 and gave grants totalling £51,000, of which £6,000 was given to individuals. Donations were made to a variety of charitable organisations and projects, with the largest recipients being Imperial College of Science and Medicine (£20,000) and the Oundle Schools Foundation (£10,000).

Further examples of beneficiaries were not available for this year, however previous recipients have included 2nd Hadleigh Scouts Group, Hadleigh Farmers' Agricultural Association, Hadleigh High School and Nettlestead PCC.

Applications In writing to the correspondent although beneficiaries are normally selected through personal contact.

The Catholic Charitable Trust

Catholic organisations

£39,000 (2002)

Beneficial area America and Europe.

Messrs Vernor, Miles & Noble, 5 Raymond Buildings, Gray's Inn, London WC1R 5DD

Tel. 020 7242 8688

Correspondent J C Vernor Miles, Trustee

Trustees *J C Vernor Miles; R D D Orr; W E Vernor Miles.*

CC Number 215553

Information available Full accounts were provided by the trust.

General The trust supports traditional Catholic organisations in America and Europe.

In 2002 it had assets of £1.1 million, which generated an income of £37,000. Grants were made to 11 organisations totalling £39,000. Management and administration expenses were high at £6,500, mostly to firms in which at least one of the trustees is a partner. Whilst wholly legal, these editors always regret such payments unless, in the words of the Charity Commission, 'there is no realistic alternative'.

By far the largest grant, of £15,000, went to Society of Saint Pius X. Other beneficiaries were Worth School (two grants totalling £6,500), Little Sisters of the Poor (£5,000), Oratorian Community Monterey California (£3,200), White Fathers and White Sisters (£2,500 each), Society of the Grail (£2,000) and Bar Convent Trust (£1,000), with £500 each to Quarr Abbey, Society of St Gregory and Traditional Congregation for the Most Holy Redeemer.

Exclusions The trust does not normally support a charity unless it is known to the trustees. Grants are not made to individuals.

Applications Applications can only be accepted from registered charities and should be in writing to the correspondent. In order to save administration costs replies are not sent to unsuccessful applicants. For the most part funds are fully committed.

The Catholic Trust for England and Wales (formerly National Catholic Fund)

Catholic welfare

£166,000 (2001)

Beneficial area England and Wales.

39 Eccleston Square, London SW1V 1BX

Tel. 020 7901 4810 **Fax** 020 7901 4819

Email secretariat@cbcew.org.uk

Website www.catholic-ew.org.uk

Correspondent Monsignor Andrew Summersgill

Trustees *Archcardinal Cormac Murphy O'Connor; Archbishop Michael Bowen; Archbishop Vincent Nicholls; Archbishop Peter Smith; Robin Smith; Monsignor Michael McKenna; John Gibbs.*

CC Number 257239

Information available Information was provided by the trust.

General The fund, formerly New Pentecost Fund, was established in 1968 and is concerned with 'the advancement of the Roman Catholic religion in England & Wales'. The trust achieves its objectives through the work of 23 Committees of the Bishops' conference and various agencies such as the Catholic Communications Service. Each committee is concerned with a different area of work of the Church. Grants are only given to organisations which benefit England and Wales as a whole, rather than local projects.

In 2001 the trust had assets of £1.8 million and an income of £1.6 million, £950,000 of which was from diocesan assessments. The majority of its income was spent on running the General Secretariat and the Catholic Communications Service but £166,000 was also spent on Christian organisations (£185,000 in 2000). A total of 29 grants were awarded ranging from £200 to £30,000. These grants were broken down as follows:

Grants to organisations

19 grants totalling £166,000 ranging from £200 to £30,000. Recipients of larger grants included: Young Christian Workers (£30,000), National Board of Catholic Women (£18,000), Diocesan Vocational Service and Movement of Christian Workers (£16,000 each), National Conference of Priests (£11,000) and Linacre Centre (£10,000). Other beneficiaries included Catholic Housing Aid Society and Catholic Student Council.

National expenses

10 grants totalling £33,000 ranging from £100 to £14,000. Recipients included Churches Commission on Mission (£14,000), Universities (£6,500), CTBI Interfaith (£4,700) and CCEE (£4,100).

Exclusions No grants to individuals, local projects or projects not immediately advancing the Roman Catholic religion in England and Wales.

Applications In writing to the correspondent before June.

The Joseph & Annie Cattle Trust

General

£250,000 (2001/02)

Beneficial area Worldwide, with a preference for Hull and East Yorkshire.

Morpeth House, 114 Spring Bank, Hull HU3 1QJ

Tel. 01482 211198 **Fax** 01482 219772

Correspondent Roger Waudby, Administrator

Trustees *J A Collier; M T Gyte; P A Robins.*

CC Number 262011

Information available Full accounts were on file at the Charity Commission.

General The object of the charity is to provide for general charitable purposes by making grants, principally to applicants in the Hull area. Older people and people who are disabled or underprivileged are assisted wherever possible, and there is a particular emphasis on giving aid to children with dyslexia.

In 2001/02 the trust had assets of £7.1 million and an income of £300,000. Grants totalled £250,000 and were broken down into three main categories.

Church and Missions

Beneficiaries included Toll Gravel United Church (£2,200), Holy Trinity Church,

Newland Church Rooms Restoration Fund and Tower Hill Methodist Church Redevelopment Fund (£2,000 each) and St Matthew's Church (£1,000).

Local Societies and Activities

The largest grants went to Dyslexia Institute (£17,000), Sobriety Project (£7,500) and Linnaeus Street Community Project and Wilton Lodge (£5,000 each). Other recipients included Godfrey Robinson Home for the Disabled (£4,000), Hull and East Riding Institute for the Blind (£3,000), Cottingham Young Persons' Sports Foundation, Dove House Hospice and Joseph Antcliff Trust (£2,000 each) and Hull and East Yorkshire Council for Drug Problems, Mires Beck Nursery, Samaritans, Sailors' Families' Society, Woodlands Respite Care Centre and Yorkshire Air Ambulance (£1,000 each).

National Societies

Recipients included Laser Trust Fund (£10,000), Marie Curie Cancer Centre (£3,000), Martin House, Martin House Teenager Unit and Stepping Stones (£2,000 each) and Avocet Trust, Botton Village Appeal Fund, British Red Cross, National Eve Research Centre and The Retreat (£1,000 each).

Exclusions Grants are very rarely given to individuals and are only supported through social services or relevant charitable or welfare organisations.

Applications In writing to the correspondent. Meetings are usually held on the third Monday of each month.

The Thomas Sivewright Catto Charitable Settlement

General

£168,000 (2002/03)

Beneficial area Unrestricted, for UK-based registered charities.

PO Box 47408, London N21 1YW

Correspondent Miss Ann Uwins

Trustees *Lord Catto; Mrs Olivia Marchant; Miss Zoe Richmond-Watson.*

CC Number 279549

Information available Full accounts were provided by the trust.

General This trust has general charitable purposes, making a large number of smaller grants to a wide range of organisations and a few larger grants of up to £20,000. Despite the large number of grants made, there appears to be no strong preference for any causes or geographical areas.

In 2002/03 the trust had assets of £6.7 million, almost entirely composed of shares in Yule Catto & Co. plc, which produced an income of £260,000. Grants totalled £168,000.

The largest grants were £20,000 to Oxfam Partners Against Poverty, £10,000 each to King Edward VII's Hospital and London Immunotherapy Cancer Trust and £5,000 each to Haddo House Choral & Operatic Society, London Immunotherapy Cancer Trust, Royal Scottish Academy of Music and Drama, YWCA and World YWCA.

Other grants included: £3,000 to Royal Scottish National Orchestra; £2,000 each to British Museum and Lizard Island Reef Research Foundation; £1,000 each to Edinburgh & Leith Age Concern, Fovant Badges Society Appeal, Romsey Hospital Appeal, St Peter's Church – Grange Park and Wiltshire Air Ambulance; and £500 each to Alone in London, British Liver Trust, Gordon Renal Dialysis, Lifetrain Trust, Parents for Children, Pestalozzi Children's Village Trust, Tools for Self Reliance and Women's Aid Federation of England.

Exclusions The trust does not support non-registered charities, expeditions, travel bursaries and so on, or unsolicited applications from churches of any denomination. Grants are unlikely to be considered in the areas of community care, playschemes and drug abuse, or for local branches of national organisations.

Applications In writing to the correspondent, including a first or second class stamped addressed envelope.

The Wilfrid & Constance Cave Foundation

Conservation, animal welfare, health, welfare

£95,000 (2002)

Beneficial area UK, with preference for Berkshire, Cornwall, Devon, Dorset, Hampshire, Oxfordshire, Somerset, Warwickshire and Wiltshire.

New Lodge Farm, Drift Road, Winkfield, Windsor SL4 4QQ

Tel. 01344 890351

Email l.olsen@cavefoundation.fsnet.co.uk

Correspondent Mrs Lorraine Olsen, Secretary

Trustees *F Jones, Chair; Mrs T Jones; Mrs J Pickin; M D A Pickin; Mrs N Thompson; Mrs J Archer; R Walker; Mrs M Waterworth.*

CC Number 241900

Information available Accounts were on file at the Charity Commission.

General The trust supports local and UK–wide organisations for general charitable purposes.

In 2002 it had assets of £2.5 million which generated an income of £93,000. Grants to 40 organisations totalled £95,000, of which the majority ranged between £1,000 or £2,000 each.

The largest grants were given to Nuneaton Equestrian Centre (£12,000), Farmers' Club Pinnacle Award (£8,000) and Exmooor Trust Recovery Fund (£6,000). Other beneficiaries included Rare Breeds Society (£5,000), Take-a-Break and All Saints' Church Ratcliffe Culley (£3,000 each) and St Margarets' Hospice – Taunton (£1,000).

Exclusions No grants to individuals.

Applications In writing to the correspondent a month before the trustees' meetings held twice each year, in May and October.

The Cayo Foundation

Crime, medical research, children

£84,000 (2000/01)

Beneficial area UK.

7 Cowley Street, London SW1P 3NB

Tel. 020 7248 6700

Correspondent Angela E McCarville

Trustees *Mrs Angela E McCarville; Stewart A Harris.*

CC Number 1080607

Information available Full accounts were on file at the Charity Commission.

General The trust supports the fight against crime, medical research and training and children's charities.

In 2000/01 it had assets of £117,000. The income was £201,000, almost entirely from donations received. Grants to 12 organisations totalled £84,000.

The largest grants were £25,000 to Allen and Overy Foundation, £19,000 to Juvenile Diabetes Research Foundation, £13,000 to Crimestoppers Trust, £10,000 to Barnardo's, £5,000 each to British Empire and Commonwealth Museum and Prostate Cancer Charity, £2,500 to WellBeing, £2,000 to Friends of War Memorials and £1,000 to Volunteer Reading Help.

Applications In writing to the correspondent.

The B G S Cayzer Charitable Trust

General

£86,000 (2001/02)

Beneficial area UK.

Cayzer House, 30 Buckingham Gate, London SW1E 6NN

Tel. 020 7802 8080

Correspondent Ms Jeanne Cook

Trustees *Peter N Buckley; Peter R Davies.*

CC Number 286063

Information available Full accounts were on file at the Charity Commission.

General In 2001/02 the trust had assets of £2 million with an income of £82,000 and grants totalling £86,000.

The largest grant of £25,000 was awarded to Feathers Club Association.

Other grants include £5,000 to Westerkirk Parish Trust, Hilier Arboretum, Game Conservancy, Castle Howard Arboretum and Ethelburga's Centre, £2,500 to Mind in Bracknell, £1,300 to St Christopher's Hospice, £1,000 each to MSF Charity, Paddington Farm Trust and Square Trust.

Grants of under £1,000 awarded totalled £6,000.

Exclusions No grants to organisations outside the UK. Unsolicited appeals will not be supported.

Applications In writing to the correspondent, although the trust tends to support only people/projects known to the Cayzer family or the trustees.

The Cazenove Charitable Trust

General

£52,000 (2003)

Beneficial area UK.

20 Moorgate, London EC2R 6DA

Email bernard.cazenove@cazenove.com

Correspondent Bernard Cazenove

Trustees *Bernard Michael De Lerisson Cazenove; Charles Richard Maurice Bishop; Simon Robert Maurice Baynes.*

CC Number 1086899

Information available Information was provided by the trust.

General Established in 1969, this trust is connected to Cazenove Group plc. In addition to making its own direct charitable distributions, in 2001 and 2002 the company donated almost £800,000 in total to this trust; no donation was received in 2003.

In 2003 the sum of £52,000 was distributed by the trust (£344,000 in 2002). No information was available on beneficiaries or the size or number of grants.

Applications In writing to the correspondent.

The Cemlyn-Jones Trust

See below

£42,000 (2001/02)

Beneficial area North Wales and Anglesey.

59 Madoc Street, Llandudno LL30 2TW

Tel. 01492 874391

Correspondent P G Brown, Trustee

Trustees *P G Brown; Mrs J E Lea; Mrs E G Jones.*

CC Number 1039164

Information available Full accounts were on file at the Charity Commission. An annual report is available.

General This trust was registered in 1994, and has a welcome preference for making grants to small local projects in North Wales and Anglesey. Its objects, listed in the annual report, are:

a) conservation and protection of general public amenities, historic or public interests in Wales

b) medical research

c) protection and welfare of animals and birds

d) study and promotion of music

e) activities and requirements of religious and educational bodies.

In 2001/02 the trust's assets totalled £91,000, it received an income of £412,000 and grants were made totalling £42,000. Larger grants were: £40,000 to University of Wales, Bangor, Development Trust, £1,300 to Moelfre–Arts & Play and £1,000 to Anglesey Music Trust.

Exclusions No grants to individuals or non-charitable organisations.

Applications In writing to the correspondent.

The Amelia Chadwick Trust

General

£85,000 (2001/02)

Beneficial area UK, especially Merseyside.

Guy Williams Layton, Pacific Chambers, 11–13 Victoria Street, Liverpool L2 5QQ

Tel. 0151 236 7171 **Fax** 0151 236 1129

Correspondent J R McGibbon

Trustees *J R McGibbon; J C H Bibby.*

CC Number 213795

Information available Full accounts were on file at the Charity Commission.

General The trust supports a wide range of charities, especially welfare causes. Although grants are given throughout the UK, there is a strong preference for Merseyside.

In 2001/02 the trust had an income of £97,000 and a total expenditure of £92,000. Grants totalled £85,000.

The largest grants were £27,000 to Merseyside Development Foundation, £11,000 to St Helens Women's Aid and £7,500 to Liverpool PSS. Other grants for £1,000 or more included Sheila Kay

Fund (£2,600), Volunteer Reading Help (£2,500), Centrepoint, Liverpool Dyslexia Association, Oxfam, Sue Ryder Home and Sylvia's Fund (£2,000 each), British Red Cross and Merseyside Holiday Service (£1,500 each), European Playwork Association (£1,200) and Alzheimer's Disease Society, Council for the Protection of Rural England, Kensington Housing Trust, Liverpool One-Parent Families, Oxfordshire Dyslexia Association and Prostate Research Campaign (£1,000 each)

Beneficiaries under £1,000 included Age Concern and Salvation Army (£750 each), Royal Liverpool Philharmonic (£700), Shrewsbury House (£500), Liverpool Housing Association (£300), Brainwave (£250) and Fair Play for Children (£150).

Applications All donations are made through Liverpool Council for Social Services. Grants are only made to charities known to the trustees, and unsolicited applications are not considered.

The Pamela Champion Foundation

General, disability

£36,000 (2002)

Beneficial area UK, with a preference for Kent.

Wiltons, Newnham Lane, Eastling, Faversham, Kent ME13 0AS

Tel. 01795 890 233

Correspondent The Trustees

Trustees *Miss M Stanlake; Mrs C Winser; Mrs E Bell; P M Williams.*

CC Number 268819

Information available The information for this entry was provided by the trust.

General Grants are made to all or any of the following: National Council for the Single Woman and Her Dependants, The Salvation Army, Church Army, Royal United Kingdom Beneficent Association, Wood Green Animal Shelter, Help the Aged, NSPCC, Marie Curie Memorial Foundation, and other charitable causes.

In 2002 the foundation had assets of £546,000. Its income was £36,000, all of which was given in grants.

Other grants include £2,000 each to Ghurkha Trust, Macmillan Nurses, British Horse Society, Faversham Gym and Disability Challenge, £1,000 each to Riding for the Disabled, Fortune Centre, Autism Society, Friends of Kent Churches, Merlin, Royal British Legion and Oxfam.

Exclusions No grants to non-registered charities.

Applications In writing to the correspondent.

The Chandris Foundation

Greek, shipping

Around £23,000 (2003)

Beneficial area UK and Greece.

Chandris Foundation Trustees Ltd, 17 Old Park Lane, London W1K 1QT

Tel. 020 7412 3922

Correspondent R H Hall, Director

Trustee *Chandris Foundation Trustees Ltd.*

CC Number 280559

Information available Full accounts were on file at the Charity Commission.

General The trust makes grants mainly to Greek charities and secondarily in the area of shipping, reflecting respectively the nationality of the Chandris family and the core business of the connected company Chandris England Ltd. Smaller preference is given to other charities such as medical and health-related and Greek Orthodox organisations. Most beneficiaries are UK organisations, but Greek organisations elsewhere may also be considered.

In 2003 the trust made grants totalling £23,000. Unfortunately no further information was available for this year. In 2002 it had assets of £647,000, an income of £74,000 and made grants totalling £40,000. Donations were broken down as follows:

Greek charities – 11 grants totalling £24,000

Beneficiaries included Hellenic College of London (£20,000), Greek Cathedral Agia Sophia (£2,000), St Sophia's School Benevolent Fund (£500), Greek Orthodox Community of Cheltenham (£300), London Hellenic Society (£150) and St Nicholas' Catherdral (£100).

Blind charities – 1 grant of £250

The recipient was National Federation of the Blind.

Children's charities – 19 donations totalling £4,700

Beneficiaries included Great Ormond Street Hospital Children's Charity (£800), Guy's and St Thomas' Hospital Trust (£500), Children with Leukemia (£400), Barnardos (£250), London Ambulance Service for a child safety programme and NSPCC (£200 each) and Ostepathic Centre for Children (£150.)

Cancer relief charities – 3 grants totalling £1,000

Recipients were Royal Marsden Hospital Charity (£500), Christian Lewis Children's Cancer Care (£300) and Breast Cancer Campaign (£200).

Maritime Charities – 5 grants totalling £2,700

Beneficiaries were RNLI (£1,200), Jubilee Sailing Trust (£1,000), King George's Fund for Sailors (£250) and Mercy Ships and Sailor's Families Society (£100).

Sundry – 25 grants totalling £8,000

Recipients included Lifeline Humanitarian Organisation (£2,500), Action in Addiction and Royal Free Hospital Kidney Patients Association (£500 each), National Eczema Society (£300), Bendrigg Trust, British Wheelchair Sports Association and RADAR (£250 each), Scope (£200), Anglian Benedicitine Community of St Mary at the Cross (£150), Little Sisters of the Poor and Mentor Foundation (£100), Dementia Relief Trust (£50) and Friends of Africa Foundation (£25).

Exclusions No grants to individuals.

Applications The trustees allocate grants mainly to their existing beneficiaries, and prefer to seek new beneficiaries through their own research.

The Chapman Charitable Trust

Welfare, general

£159,000 (2002/03)

Beneficial area Eastern and south east England, including London, and Wales.

Benedict McQueen, 62 Wilson Street , London EC2A 2BU

Tel. 020 7782 0007 **Fax** 020 7782 0939

Email cct@crouchchapman.co.uk

Correspondent Roger S Chapman, Trustee

Trustees *Roger S Chapman; Richard J Chapman; Bruce D Chapman; Guy J A Chapman.*

CC Number 232791

Information available Full accounts were provided by the trust.

General Established in 1963 with general charitable purposes, the trust mainly supports culture and recreation, education and research, health, social services, environment and heritage causes.

In 2002/03 the trust had assets of £4.5 million, which generated an income of £162,000. Grants were made totalling £159,000, broken down as shown in the table below.

The largest grants were £15,000 to Aldeburgh Productions and £10,000 each to Methodist Homes – MHA Care Group, NCH Action for Children, Pesticide Action Network UK, Queen Alexandra Hospital Home and St Bridget's Cheshire Home. All of these grants were made in two payments.

Other large grants included £5,000 to A Rocha, £4,000 to Fragile X Society, £3,000 to Royal Cambrian Academy, £2,000 each to Yateley Industries, British Epilepsy Association, Cystic Fibrosis Trust, Motability, National Back Pain Association, National Schizoprenia Society and National Youth Orchestra of Great Britian.

There were also 26 grants of £1,000 each, 63 grants of £500 each and 1 grant of £250. Beneficiaries of £1,000 included Association of Wheelchair Children, Cherry Trees, Colon Cancer Concern, Criccieth Arts Association, Huntington's Diseases Society, Lupus UK, National Rheumatoid Arthritis Society, Parkinson's Diseases Society, Sustrans, Winged Fellowships and Yateley Industries. Recipients of £500 included AbilityNet, Braille Chess Association, Canine Partners, Dyslexia Computer Training Charity, Equipment for independent Living, Iris Fund, Kent Wildlife Trust, Perthes Association for children with osteochondritis, Resources for Autism, Shaw Trust and Woodland Trust and £250 was received by Porthmadog.

Exclusions No grants to or for the benefit of individuals, local branches of UK charities, animal welfare, sports tours or sponsored adventure holidays.

Applications In writing at any time. The trustees currently meet to consider grants twice a year at the end of September and in February. They receive a large number of applications and regret that they cannot acknowledge receipt of them. The absence of any communication for six months would mean that an application must have been unsuccessful.

THE CHAPMAN CHARITABLE TRUST
Grants in 2002/03

	Local		*National*		*Total*	
	total	*No.*	*total*	*No.*	*total*	*No.*
Culture and recreation	£6,000	3	£21,000	8	£27,000	11
Education and research	£1,500	3	–	–	£1,500	3
Health	–	–	£12,000	10	£12,000	10
Social services	£44,000	32	£67,000	55	£111,000	87
Environment and heritage	£2,000	4	£6,500	3	£8,000	7

The Cheruby Trust

Welfare, education, general

£35,000 (2002/03)

Beneficial area UK and worldwide.

62 Grosvenor Street, London W1K 3JF

Tel. 020 7499 4301

Correspondent Mrs Sylvia Berg, Trustee

Trustees *A L Corob; L E Corob; T A Corob; Mrs S P Berg.*

CC Number 327069

Information available Full accounts were on file at the Charity Commission.

General The trust's charitable objectives are the relief of poverty, the advancement of education and such other charitable purposes as the trustees see fit.

In 2002/03 the trust had assets of £146,000, an income of £78,000 and made 12 grants totalling £35,000. Beneficiaries included International Centre for Enhancement of Learning (£10,000), Disasters Emerency Committee (£5,000), British Humanitarian Aid, Wateraid and World Medical Fund (£3,000 each), Family Holiday Association and The Hornsey Trust (£2,500 each), Brain & Spine and Friends of Amma (£2,000 each), Books Abroad and Trees for Life (£1,000 each) and April Charity (£500).

Applications In writing to the correspondent.

The Chetwode Foundation

Education, churches, general

£58,000 (2002/03)

Beneficial area UK, with a preference for Nottinghamshire, Leicestershire and Derby.

Samworth Brothers (Holdings) Ltd, Chetwode House, 1 Samworth Way, Leicester Road, Melton Mowbray, Leicestershire LE13 1GA

Tel. 01664 414500

Correspondent J G Ellis

Trustees *J G Ellis; R N J S Price.*

CC Number 265950

Information available Full accounts were on file at the Charity Commission.

General This trust has general charitable purposes, giving without exclusion across the UK. Whilst it has preferences for education, churches and work in Nottinghamshire, Leicestershire and Derby, this is not at the expense of other causes.

In 2002/03 the trust had assets of £1 million, which generated an income of £58,000. Grants totalling £58,000 were made to 13 organisations.

The largest grants were £25,000 to Uppingham School and £10,000 each to The Abbeyfield Nottingham Society and University of Nottingham.

Other beneficiaries were Cropwell Butler PCC (£5,000), Tythby & Cropwell Butler PCC and Winged Fellowship Trust (£2,000 each), Newark & Nottinghamshire Agricultural Society (£1,375), Rupert Earl (£1,000), Nottinghamshire Farming and Wildlife Advisory Group and Rutland House School for Parents (£500 each), St Peter's Church Whetstone and Thomas Harley's Charities (£250 each) and RNLI (£95).

Applications In writing to the correspondent.

The Malcolm Chick Charity

General

£31,000 (2000/01)

Beneficial area England only.

White Horse Court, 25c North Street, Bishops Stortford, Hertfordshire CM23 2LD

Email charities@pothecary.co.uk

Correspondent The Trust Administrator

CC Number 327732

Information available Full accounts were provided by the trust.

General This trust has been in existence for some time with the trustees making small grants to organisations they were familiar with. On the death of one of the trustees, Malcolm Chick, the trust received part of his estate and has grown in size.

Grants are made throughout England, in the following fields:

Youth character building
There is an emphasis on grants towards sailing training.

Armed service charities
Grants are limited to those charities supporting ex-army personnel and to charities providing direct care for ex-army personnel, for example grants to homes and charities providing welfare services for such persons.

Medical research and care
Grants are made towards research into causes and treatment of heart disease and for buying equipment suitable for the treatment and care of people recovering from coronary heart disease.

Grants for 2000/01 amounted to £31,000, but the trust had not yet received the accounts for the year.

In 1999/2000 grants totalled £17,000. It was noted that grants were down on the previous year due to the trustees meeting date being altered. Grants were given to 10 organisations including £4,000 each to The Cord Blood Charity and the Children's Heart Foundation, £3,700 to Fairbridge – Freespirit Bursary Scheme and £1,000 to Barrow and District Council for Voluntary Service Voyager.

Applications In the first place, applicants should write to ask for a copy of the criteria and application forms. Telephone calls are not welcomed. The trustees meet to consider applications in November and completed forms must be returned by the middle of October. There is a separate application form and guidance notes for individual applicants.

Child Growth Foundation

Institutions researching child/adult growth disorders, and people with such diseases.

£177,000 (1998/99)

Beneficial area UK.

2 Mayfield Avenue, Chiswick W4 1PY

Tel. 020 8995 0257 **Fax** 020 8995 9075

Email cfglondon@aol.com

Correspondent T Fry, Hon. Chair

Trustees *Tam Fry, Chair; plus one representative from each condition group the foundation supports, e.g. Growth Hormone Deficiency, Premature Sexual Maturation, Turner Syndrome, Sotos Syndrome and Bone Dysplasias.*

CC Number 274325

Information available Patient information booklets, newsletters.

General The foundation seeks to: (a) ensure that the growth of every UK child is regularly assessed and that any child growing excessively slowly or fast is referred for medical attention as soon as possible; (b) ensure that no child will be denied the drugs they need to correct their stature; (c) support institutions researching the cause/cures of growth conditions; (d) maintain a network of families to offer support/advice for any family concerned/diagnosed with a growth problem.

In 2002/03 the trust had an income of £459,000 and a total expenditure of £456,000. Further information for this year was not available.

In 1998/99 it had an income of £533,000 and gave grants totalling £177,000. The largest were: £45,000 to Imperial College; £34,500 to University of Wales; £22,000 to University of Wales, £21,000 to Institute of Child Health, £19,000 to Edinburgh Hospital for Sick Children, £18,000 to Endocrine Research Nurse – Imperial College £17,000 to Institute of Child Health, £16,000 to Middlesex Hospital, £8,000 to British Society for Paediatric Endocrinology & Diabetes and £6,000 to Sheffield Children's Hospital.

Applications In writing to the correspondent.

Children's Liver Disease Foundation

Organisations benefiting children (0–18 years) with liver disease; medical professionals; research workers and scientists.

£210,000 (2003/04)

Beneficial area UK.

36 Great Charles Street, Queensway, Birmingham B3 3JY

Tel. 0121 212 3839 **Fax** 0121 212 4300

Email info@childliverdisease.org

Website www.childliverdisease.org

Correspondent Mrs C Arkley, Chief Executive

Trustees *Robert J Benton; Thomas Ross, Chair; Dr H Richard Maltby; Mrs Ann Mowat; Mrs Michele Hunter; Andrew Sparrow.*

CC Number 1067331

Information available The foundation is a member of the Association of Medical Research Charities (AMRC), and adheres to their guidelines. An annual report is available. Delivery magazine published twice yearly.

General The foundation funds medical research into all aspects of paediatric liver disease and disease of the biliary tract.

In 2003/04 the foundation had assets of £494,000 and an income of £624,000. Grants were made to 7 organisations totalling £210,000. The largest grant was £86,000 to King's College Hospital. Other beneficiaries included University of Southampton (£39,000), Birmingham University Hospital (£35,000), University of Newcastle upon Tyne (£20,000) and Biliary Atresia Research (£14,000).

Exclusions No grants to individuals, whether medical professionals or patients. No grants for travel or personal education.

Applications Applicants are advised to telephone prior to making an application. Research grants can be applied for via an application form. All grant requests are subject to peer review and are assessed by the Medical Advisory Committee before submission to the trustees.

The Children's Research Fund

Child health research

£216,000 (1998/99)

Beneficial area UK.

668 India Buildings, Water Street, Liverpool L2 0RA

Tel. 0151 236 2844 **Fax** 0151 258 1606

Website www.crfund.org

Correspondent H Greenwood, Chair

Trustees *H Greenwood, Chair; G W Inkin; Dr G J Piller; H E Greenwood; Prof. J Lister; Lord Morris; Elizabeth Theobald.*

CC Number 226128

Information available Full accounts were on file at the Charity Commission.

General The trust supports research into children's diseases, child health and prevention of illness in children, carried out at institutes and university departments of child health. The policy is to award grants, usually over several years, to centres of research. It will also support any charitable project associated with the well being of children.

In 2002/03 the trust had an income of £265,000 and a total expenditure of £285,000. Further information for this year was not available.

In 2000/01 it had an income of £219,000 and a total expenditure of £234,000. This information was taken from the Charity Commission database; unfortunately no further details were available for this year.

In 1998/99 it had assets of £1.3 million and an income of £198,000. A total of £216,000 was given in 11 grants. The largest grants were £45,000 to University of Liverpool – Department of Paediatrics, £32,000 to Great Ormond Street Hospital and £25,000 each to the Great Ormond Street Hospital Institute of Child Health and University of Southampton – Therapist course. The remaining grants were all to different UK universities, ranging from £650 to £23,000. Five of the grants were recurrent.

Exclusions No grants for capital projects.

Applications Applicants from child health research units and university departments are invited to send in an initial outline of their proposal; if it is eligible they will then be sent an application form. Applications are considered in March and November.

The Chownes Foundation

General

£88,000 (2001/02)

Beneficial area UK.

The Courtyard, Beeding Court, Shoreham Road, Steyning, West Sussex BN44 3TN

Tel. 01903 816699

Email sjs.russellnew@btconnect.com

Correspondent Sylvia Spencer, Secretary

Trustees *Charles Stonor; the Abbot of Worth; Mrs U Hazeel.*

CC Number 327451

Information available Accounts were on file at the Charity Commission.

General The objectives of this trust are the advancement of religion, the advancement of education among the young, the amelioration of social problems, and the relief of poverty amongst older people and the former members of Sound Diffusion PLC who lost their pensions when the company went into receivership.

In 2001/02 the foundation had an income of £70,000 and made grants totalling £88,000. Grants were broken down as follows:

	No.	*Total*
Grants to institutions	13	£28,000
Grants to individuals	30	£60,000

A further breakdown of these grants was not available. In the past most beneficiaries have been based in the south of England.

Exclusions Applicant organisations must fit into the above criteria.

Applications In writing to the correspondent.

CLA Charitable Trust

Disabled facilities and training

£54,000 (2002/03)

Beneficial area England and Wales only.

Caunton Grange, Caunton, Newark, Nottinghamshire NG23 6AB

Tel. 01636 636171 **Fax** 01636 636171

Website www.clacharitabletrust.org

Correspondent Peter Geldart

Trustees *A Duckworth-Chad; A H Duberly; G E Lee-Strong; G N Mainwaring.*

CC Number 280264

Information available Information was provided by the trust.

General The trust was founded in 1980. Its work includes support for education projects in the countryside (a) to provide sport and recreation facilities for disabled people, and (b) for children and young people with learning difficulties or who are disadvantaged.

It prefers to support smaller projects where a grant from the trust can make a 'real contribution to the success of the project'. It gives grants for specific projects or items rather than for ongoing running costs.

In 2002/03 it had assets of £316,000 and an income of £75,000. Grants totalled £54,000. The largest were £2,500 to Swift Research, £2,200 to Swallows and Amazons – Wirral, £2,100 to Portland College – Mansfield, £2,000 to Sailability – Grafham Water and £1,800 to John Grooms Association.

Exclusions No grants to individuals.

Applications In writing to the correspondent. Trustees meet four times a year.

J A Clark Charitable Trust

Health, education, peace, preservation of the earth, the arts

£181,000 (2002/03)

Beneficial area UK, with a preference for South West England.

PO Box 1704, Glastonbury, Somerset BA16 0YB

Email jactrust@ukonline.co.uk

Correspondent Mrs P Grant, Secretary

Trustees *Lance Clark; Cyrus Clark; Tom Clark; William Pym; Aidan Pelly.*

CC Number 1010520

Information available Full accounts were on file at the Charity Commission.

General The trust was established in 1992. It is concerned with projects oriented towards social change in areas of health, education, peace, preservation of the earth and the arts. Quaker organisations are also well supported. The trustees are particularly interested in supporting the work of small, new or innovative projects.

In 2002/03 the trust had assets of £9.4 million, an income of £313,000 and made grants totalling £181,000. Grant beneficiaries included Eucalyptus Charitable Foundation (£33,000), New Economics Foundation (£30,000), Inner City Scholarship Fund (£14,000), Ashoka UK, Quaker Intenational Education Trust, Sponsored Arts for Education and Street Theatre Workshop Trust (£10,000 each), Student Partnerships Worldwide (£7,000), Clark Bursary Fund and Greenbank Swimming Pool (£6,000 each), Women Against Violence in Israel (£5,000) Creative Health Network (£3,000), Addiction Recovery Agency (£2,000) and Ukraine Environmental Project (£1,000).

Exclusions No support for individuals, independent schools (unless they are for special needs) or towards the conservation of buildings.

Applications The trust is fundamentally restructuring itself towards the objective of supporting exclusively one or two innovative projects, and so is 'absolutely unable to respond to any unsolicited appeals at this point in time'.

The Roger & Sarah Bancroft Clark Charitable Trust

Quaker, general

£103,000 to organisations (2001)

Beneficial area UK and overseas, with preference for Somerset and Scotland.

40 High Street, Street, Somerset BA16 0YA

Email lynette.cooper@clarks.com

Correspondent Mrs Lynette Cooper, Secretary

Trustees *Eleanor C Robertson; Mary P Lovell; Stephen Clark; S Caroline Gould; Roger S Goldby.*

CC Number 211513

Information available Full accounts were on file at the Charity Commission.

General The objects of the trust are general charitable purposes with particular reference to:

- Religious Society of Friends and associated bodies
- charities connected with Somerset
- education (for individuals).

For historical reasons the accounts for this trust were split into two separate funds, although it is administered as one. This entry will break the trust down into the two funds, even though they are essentially the same.

ECR Fund

In 2001 this fund had assets of £723,000, which generated an income of £25,000. Grants totalled £25,000.

The largest were £2,000 to Religious Society of Friends, £1,200 to Edinburgh Competition Festival Organisation and £1,000 each to Buildings of Scotland, Prisoners of Conscience, Refugee Council and Scottish Women's Aid.

Other beneficiaries included Amnesty International Charitable Trust (£600), Shelter (£500), Women's International Centre (£400), Scottish Churches' Housing Agency (£300), Salvation Army (£200), Herschel House Museum (£50), Friends of the Royal Scottish Academy (£15) and Friends of the Talbot Rice Art Centre (£5).

SBC Fund

In 2001 it had assets of £3 million, which generated an income of £109,000. Grants were made to 110 organisations totalling £78,000 and to 106 individuals totalling £26,000.

Grants included £7,100 to Hickman Retirement Home, £5,000 each to Newnham College and Sibford College, £3,000 to Long Sutton Court House, £2,500 each to QSRE Friends School Joint Benevolent Fund, QSRE Higher Education Awards and Quaker Peace and Service, £2,000 to Society for the Protection of Ancient Buildings, £1,500 to Retreat Benevolent Fund, £1,100 to Cope Environmental Centre and £1,000 each to Bootham School Trust Bursary Fund and Historic Chapels Trust.

Applications In writing to the correspondent. There is no application form and telephone calls are not accepted. Trustees meet about three times a year. Applications will be acknowledged if an sae is enclosed or email address given.

The Elizabeth Clark Charitable Trust

Palliative care

£145,000 (2003/04)

Beneficial area UK.

Allington House, 1st Floor, 150 Victoria Street, London SW1E 5AE

Tel. 020 7410 0330 **Fax** 020 7410 0332

Email info@sfct.org.uk

Correspondent Michael Pattison, Director

Trustees *Miss Judith Portrait; Dr Jane Davy; Dr Gillian Ford.*

CC Number 265206

Information available Full accounts were provided by the trust.

General This is the smallest of the 18 Sainsbury Family Charitable Trusts, which collectively give over £54 million a year. It describes its work as follows in the 2003/04 annual report:

'Trustees are free to apply funds for any charitable purpose. Bearing in mind the settlor's wish to bring about improvements in nursing, the trustees have decided to concentrate on supporting development of good practice in palliative care. Trustees do not generally support capital or revenue appeals from hospices and research bodies nor make grants to individuals. They have a proactive approach to their grantmaking and unsolicited appeals are unlikely to succeed, particularly now that the resources of the charity are predominately earmarked for a single programme as discussed below under Review of the Year.'

The following text is taken from the 'Review of the Year' section:

'Breathlessness is a major symptom for many patients with end-stage disease. For some time [the] trustees have been keen to support an innovative breathlessness project, and this year they approved a grant to Addenbrooke's NHS Trust (now Cambridge University Hospitals NHS Foundation Trust) of £120,000 over two years towards a pilot for a community-based, multidisciplinary breathlessness service for both cancer and non-cancer patients.

'As noted in previous annual reports, the trustees are supporting a major project at the University of Sheffield Department of Palliative Medicine. This project aims to design and test a general assessment and referral tool for palliative care which can be used in all care settings. Trustees consider that progress in the concluding stages of the first phrase of this project has been good. Trustees plan to look at the case for supporting a second phrase in due course, and are unlikely to make other significant awards until they have decided whether to offer further support to this project.'

In 2003/04 it had assets of £472,000 and an income of £27,000. Management and administration charges for the year were high at £4,500, including payments totalling £1,900 to a firm of solicitors in which one of the trustees is a partner. Whilst wholly legal, these editors always regret such payments unless, in the words of the Charity Commission, 'there is no realistic alternative'.

Grants totalled £145,000. Aside from the £120,000 to Addenbrooke's NHS Trust, £25,000 went to St Michael's Hospice.

Applications The 18 Sainsbury Family Charitable Trusts are jointly administered and follow the same application precedure. An application to one trust is considered as an application to them all. However, 'applications' are probably not the best way forward to gaining funding from these trusts. More sensible might be to write briefly and say what is being done or planned, on the assumption that, if one or more of the trusts is indeed interested in that area of work, they will want to know about what you are doing. A telephone call to do the same is fine. Staff are polite, but wary of people seeking to talk about money rather than issues.

More generally, the trusts are involved in a number of networks, with which they maintain long-term contact. Charities doing work relevant to the interests of these trusts may find that if they are not a part of these networks (which may not be inclusive and most of which are probably London-based) they may get limited Sainsbury attention.

The most inappropriate approach would often be from a fundraiser. Staff, and in many cases trustees, are knowledgeable and experienced in their fields, and expect to talk to others in the same position.

The Classic FM Charitable Trust

Music and education; music and health

About £50,000 (2001/02)

Beneficial area UK.

Eltham College, Grove Park Road, London SE9 4QF

Tel. 020 8857 7360

Email bursar@eltham-college.org.uk

Correspondent Danny Cooper

Trustees *Mrs V L Duffield; Prof. Stanley Glasser; Robert O'Dowd; John McLaren; Robin Ray; John Spearman; Douglas Thackway; Andrew Tuckey.*

CC Number 1028531

Information available Accounts were on file at the Charity Commission.

General The trust states that it will support national, established organisations involved with 'music and education' and 'music and health'. In practice, the trustees make one grant per year associated with music.

In 2001/02 the trust had an income of £60,000 and a total expenditure of £53,000. Grants totalled about £50,000. In the previous year the trust made one grant of £60,000 to the Master Class Charity, towards the production of a video for the Federation of Music Teachers.

Exclusions No grants to individuals.

Applications In writing to the correspondent.

The Cleopatra Trust

Health and welfare, disability, homelessness, addiction, children who are disadvantaged, environment

£115,000 (2002)

Beneficial area Mainly UK.

Charities Aid Foundation, King's Hill, West Malling, Kent ME19 4TA

Tel. 01732 520083 **Fax** 01732 520159

Correspondent Mrs Sue David, Donor Grants Officer

Trustees *Charles Peacock; Mrs Bettine Bond; Dr Clare Sellers.*

CC Number 1004551

Information available Full accounts were provided by the trust.

General The trust has common trustees with two other trusts, Dorus Trust and Epigoni Trust (see separate entries), with which it also shares the same aims and polices. All three trusts are administered by Charities Aid Foundation. Generally the trusts support different organisations each year.

The trust makes grants in the following areas:

- mental health
- cancer welfare/education – not research
- diabetes
- physical disability – not research
- homelessness
- addiction
- children who are disadvantaged.

There is also some preference for environmental causes. It only gives grants for specific projects and does not give grants for running costs or general appeals. Support is only given to national organisations, not for local areas or initiatives.

In 2002 it had assets of £2.9 million, which generated an income of £105,000. Grants were made to 27 organisations totalling £115,000.

The largest were £10,000 each to National Children's Home and Sick Children's Trust, £7,000 each to Association for Rehabilitation of Communication and Oral Skills, National Library for the Blind and Springhead Trust, £6,000 to Foyer Foundation and £5,000 each to Jubilee Sailing Trust, National Meningitis Trust,

Riverpoint Single Homeless, Treloar Trust and UK Youth.

Other beneficiaries included Brain and Spine Foundation (£4,000), Lupus UK and National Centre for Young People with Epilepsy (£3,000 each), Cardinal Hume Centre and Vitiligo Society (£2,000 each) and Changing Faces and Norwood (£1,000 each).

Exclusions No grants to individuals, expeditions, research, scholarships, charities with a local focus, local branches of UK-wide charities or towards running costs.

Applications On a 'funding proposal form' available from the correspondent. Applications should include a copy of the latest audited annual report and accounts. They are considered twice a year in mid-summer and mid-winter. Organisations which have received grants from this trust, Dorus Trust or the Epigoni Trust should not reapply in the following two years. Usually, funding will be considered by only one of these trusts.

Miss V L Clore's 1967 Charitable Trust

General

£35,000 (2002/03)

Beneficial area UK.

Unit 3 Chelsea Manor Studios, Flood Street, London SW3 5SR

Tel. 020 7351 6061 **Fax** 020 7351 5308

Email info@cloreduffield.org.uk

Correspondent Sally Bacon

CC Number 253660

Information available Information was provided by the trust.

General The trust has general charitable purposes, but broadly speaking is concerned with the performing arts, education, social welfare, health and disability. Grants range from £500 to £6,000. It is administrated alongside the much larger Clore Duffield Foundation, which gives well over 100 times more funds a year in grants.

In 2002/03 grants were made to 22 organisations totalling £35,000. The annual report did not state any income or expenditure figure but did state that it is administered alongside the much larger Clore Duffield Foundation and that they received 2,981 applications between them. However, the relationship between the trusts was not further explained, especially regarding if an application to one trust is automatically considered by the other.

The largest grants were £6,000 to Chain of Hope, £5,000 to Friends of the Hebrew University of Jerusalem, £3,000 to SMART, £2,000 each to Chelsea Festival and Elias Ashmole Trust and £1,500 to Cancer Research UK.

Grants of £1,000 each went to 14 organisations, including British Friends of the Arts Museums of Israel, Chai Cancer Care, English National Ballet, Facial Surgery Research Foundation, Anglo-Russian Opera and Ballet Trust, Women's UJIA and Young Persons Concert Foundation. The remaining grants, of £500 each, went to Animal Health Trust and Music Theatre Wales.

Exclusions No grants are given to individuals.

Applications In writing to the correspondent on one to two sides of A4, enclosing an sae.

Clover Trust

Older people, young people

£190,000 (2002)

Beneficial area UK, and occasionally overseas, with a slight preference for West Dorset.

c/o Suite 7, Messrs Herbert Pepper and Rudland, Accurist House, 44 Baker Street, London W1U 7BD

Tel. 020 7486 5535

Correspondent Nicholas C Haydon, Trustee

CC Number 213578

Information available Full accounts were provided by the trust.

General This trust supports organisations concerned with health, disability, children and Catholic activities. However, most grants are given to a 'core list' of beneficiaries and the trust states: 'the chances of a successful application from a new applicant are very slight, since the bulk of the income is earmarked for the regular beneficiaries, with the object of increasing the grants over time rather than adding to the number of beneficiaries.'

Grants are given towards general running costs, although no grants are given towards building work. Unsolicited applications which impress the trustees are given one-off grants, although only a tiny percentage of the many applications are successful.

In 2002 the trust had assets of £3.8 million and an income of £225,000. Grants to 42 organisations totalled £190,000. Grants were in the range of £1,000 to £18,500, but were mainly for amounts under £5,000. Beneficiaries included: Friends of Orphanages in Romania (£18,000); National Society for the Prevention of Cruelty to Children (£15,000); CAFOD, Cotswold Care and Action Research for the Crippled Child (£10,000 each); Dorset Association for the Disabled, Cardinal Hume Centre and Lady Margaret Beaufort Appeal (£5,000 each); St Gregory's Jericho Appeal, Crohn's in Childhood Research Association and Invalids at Home (£2,000 each); Blandford R.C. Parish, PCC of Farnham and Uphill Ski Club of Great Britain (£1,000); and FRSF (£500).

Exclusions The arts, monuments and non-registered charities are not supported.

Applications In writing to the correspondent. Replies are not given to unsuccessful applications.

The Robert Clutterbuck Charitable Trust

Service, sport and recreation, natural history, animal welfare and protection

£36,000 (2003/04)

Beneficial area Mainly UK, with preference for Cheshire and Hertfordshire.

28 Brookfields, Calver, Hope Valley, Derbyshire S32 3XB

Tel. 01433 631308 **Fax** 0870 133 3198

Email geowolfe@onetel.com
Website www.clutterbucktrust.org.uk
Correspondent G A Wolfe, Secretary
Trustees *Maj. R G Clutterbuck; I A Pearson; R J Pincham.*
CC Number 1010559
Information available Information was provided by the trust.

General The trust normally only makes grants to registered charities in the following areas: personnel and charitable activities within the armed forces, and ex-service men and women; charities associated with the counties of Cheshire and Hertfordshire; sport and recreational activities in Cheshire and Hertfordshire; natural history and wildlife; and the welfare and protection of domestic animal life.

In 2003/04 the trust had assets of £965,000 and an income of £36,000. Grants totalled £36,000. The trust prefers to make grants towards buying specific items.

The largest grants were £5,300 to Royal Star and Garter, £2,800 to Watford Council for Voluntary Service, £2,400 to Children's Adventure Farm Trust, £2,000 each to RNIB and South Manchester Gymnastics Centre, £1,800 to Chantry Trust, £1,500 to RVC Animal Care Trust, £1,200 each to Lytham St Anne's Sea Cadets and Manchester Regiment Museum and £1,000 each to Broughton House, Riding for the Disabled – Digswell Place, St Mary's Church – Rosetherne and Turnford School.

Other grants were £800 to Sir John Deane College, £600 each to Army Cadet Force Association and North West Army Cadet Force, £530 to International Otter Survival and £500 each to 18 organisations including British Forces Foundation, Harpenden Lions Club, Manchester Dogs Home, Rainforest Concern, Shopmobility – Stockport and Watford and Three Rivers Furniture Recycling Scheme.

Exclusions No grants to individuals.

Applications In writing to the correspondent. There are no application forms. Applications are acknowledged and considered by the trustees twice a year.

The Francis Coales Charitable Foundation

Historical

£120,000 (2003)

Beneficial area UK, with a preference for Bedfordshire, Buckinghamshire, Hertfordshire and Northamptonshire.

The Bays, Hillcote, Bleadon Hill, Weston-super-Mare, Somerset BS24 9JS
Tel. 01934 814009 **Fax** 01934 814009
Email fccf45@hotmail.com
Correspondent T H Parker, Administrator
Trustees *J Coales, Chair; H G M Leighton; A G Harding; Revd B H Wilcox; H M Stuchfield.*
CC Number 270718
Information available An information leaflet was provided by the trust. Full accounts were on file at the Charity Commission.

General The 2001 trustees' report stated: 'In 1885 Francis Coales and his son, Walter John Coales, acquired a corn merchant's business in Newport Pagnell, Buckinghamshire. Over the years similar businesses were acquired, but after a major fire it was decided to close down the business. From the winding-up was established The Francis Coales Charitable Trust in 1975.

'The nature of the foundation is to assist with grants for the repair of old buildings which are open to the public, for the conservation of monuments, tombs, hatchments, memorial brasses, etc., also towards the cost of archaeological research and related causes, the purchase of documents or items for record offices and museums, and the publication of architectural and archaeological books or papers. Assistance for structural repairs is normally given to churches and their contents in Buckinghamshire, Bedfordshire, Northamptonshire and Hertfordshire where most of the business of Francis Coales and Son was carried out with farmers. However, no territorial restriction is placed upon church monuments, etc.'

In 2003 it had assets of £1.7 million, an income of £98,000 and gave £120,000 in grants. Larger grants included £10,000 to Northamptonshire V C H Trust for research, £6,000 to Society of Antiquaries for conservation of records, £5,000 to Stoneleigh – Warks for the conservation of a monument, £4,000 to Cranfield – Bedfordshire for exterior stonework, £2,500 to Whaddon – Buckinghamshire for tower stonework and roof leadwork and £2,000 to Beaconsfield – Buckinghamshire.

Donations of £1,500 or below included £1,500 to Cheddington – Buckinghamshire, £1,000 each to Lincoln Catherdal Library to clean and refurbish books and Maids Moreton – Buckinghamshire for tower roof and stonework, £750 to Stutton – Suffolk for conservation of five brasses, £500 each to Bishop's Stortford – Hertfordshire to rectify damp, Radwell – Hertfordshire to conserve brasses and Thornborough Baptist – Buckinghamshire for general fabric, £300 to Cheswardine – Shropshire, £250 to Lidlington History Society – Bedfordshire and £100 to Barton-le-Clay – Bedfordshire for tower and lead roofs.

Exclusions No grants for buildings built after 1875, hospitals or hospices. Ecclesiastical buildings cannot receive grants for 'domestic' items such as electrical wiring, heating, improvements or re-ordering.

Applications On a form available from the correspondent.

Applications should include a quotation for the work or the estimated cost, details of the amount of funds already raised and details of funds applied for and other bodies approached. Applications for buildings or contents should include a copy of the relevant part of the architect/conservator's specification showing the actual work proposed. 'Photographs showing details of the problems often speak louder than words.'

The trust also states that receiving six copies of any leaflet or statement of finance is helpful so that each trustee can have a copy in advance of the meeting. Trustees normally meet three times a year to consider grants.

The Coates Charitable Settlement

Medical, health, welfare, education

£40,000 (2002/03)

Beneficial area UK, with a preference for Leicestershire.

KPMG, Peat House, 1 Waterloo Way, Leicester LE1 6LP

Tel. 0116 256 6000

Correspondent M A Chamberlain, Trustee

Trustees *W C Coates; Mrs B M Coates; M A Chamberlain.*

CC Number 1015659

Information available Accounts were on file at the Charity Commission.

General The trust was established in 1992. It supports medical, health, welfare and educational causes.

In 2002/03 the trust had assets of £378,000 with an income of £14,000 and grants totalling £40,000. Unfortunately there was no available grants list for recent years.

Previous beneficiaries have included Leicester Action on Domestic Violence, Leicester Children's Asthma Centre and Leicester Royal Infirmary Coronary Care Unit.

Exclusions No support for individuals.

Applications In writing to the correspondent.

John Coates Charitable Trust

Arts, children, environment, medical, general

£307,000 (2001/02)

Beneficial area UK, mainly southern England.

40 Stanford Road, London W8 5PZ

Tel. 020 7938 1944 **Fax** 020 7938 2390

Correspondent Mrs P L Youngman, Trustee

Trustees *Mrs McGregor; Mrs Kesley; Mrs Lawes; Mrs Youngman.*

CC Number 262057

Information available Full accounts were provided by the trust.

General This trust has general charitable purposes. Grants are made to large UK–wide charities, or small charities of personal or local interest to the trustees.

In 2001/02 the trust had assets of £8.7 million, which generated an income of £286,000. Management and administration charges were very high at £53,000, largely due to a stockbroker's management fee of £46,000. Grants totalling £307,000 were made to 59 organisations, of which 31 were also supported in the previous year.

The largest grants were £15,000 each to OPTIMA and South Bank Centre for the Royal Festival Hall. Grants of £10,000 each went to British Wheelchair Sports Foundation, Cleft Lip and Palate Association, English National Opera, Girton College – Cambridge, Handel House Museum, Jubilee Sailing Trust, NASS, National Trust, NSPCC, Painshill Park Trust, Royal Albert Hall Trust, Royal Hospital for Neuro-disability, Scope, Shakespeare Globe Trust and Tommy's The Baby Charity.

Other donations included £5,000 each to Dulwich Picture Gallery and St Bride's Church; £3,000 each to Canine Partners for Independence and The Sixteen; £2,500 to National Back Pain Association; £2,000 to Wey and Arun Canal Trust; £1,500 each to High School of Dundee and Queen Elizabeth's Foundation; £1,000 each to Chichester Cathedral Trust and Worldwide Volunteering for Young People; £500 each to Barn Owl Trust and RNLI; and £50 to All Saints' Church – Fulham.

Exclusions Grants are given to individuals only in exceptional circumstances.

Applications In writing to the correspondent. Small local charities are visited by the trust.

Lance Coates Charitable Trust 1969

Biological and ecological approach to food production

£33,000 (2002/03)

Beneficial area UK.

Sanilles, Ctra de Lles, Lles de Cerdanya, 25726 Lerida

Email ecomundi@teleline.es / info@sanilles.com

Correspondent H L T Coates, Trustee

Trustees *H L T Coates; E P Serjeant.*

CC Number 261521

Information available Accounts were on file at the Charity Commission.

General The trust supports the promotion of ecological and integrated healthcare initiatives and practical holistic research projects. Projects deemed most important by the trust are funded on an annual basis with smaller grants given on a one-off basis.

In 2002/03 the trust had assets of £734,000, an income of £25,000 and a grant total of £33,000. Grant beneficiaries included International Therapeutic Institute (UK) Ltd (£20,000), Country Trust (£12,500), Farm Africa, Hearing Research Trust, Lawrence Home Nursing Team Trust and Westcare (£250 each).

Exclusions No grants to individuals.

Applications In writing to the correspondent including a summary of proposal.

Coats Foundation Trust

Textile and thread-related training courses and research

£50,000 (2002/03)

Beneficial area UK.

Coats Ltd, Pacific House, 70 Wellington Street, Glasgow G2 6UB

Tel. 0141 207 6821 **Fax** 0141 207 6856

Email jenny.mcfarlane@coats.com

Correspondent Jenny McFarlane

Trustees *S Dow; A H Macdiamid; C Healy; Jonathon Lea.*

CC Number 268735

Information available Basic information was provided by the trust.

General Preference is given, but not specifically restricted, to applicants from textile and thread-related training courses.

In 2002/03 the foundation had assets of £1.5 million. It receives an annual income of £70,000 from Coats Ltd. Grants were made during the year totalling £50,000. Unfortunately a list of recent beneficiaries was not available.

Applications Please write, enclosing a cv and an sae, giving details of circumstances and the nature and amount of funding required. There is no formal application form. Only applicants enclosing an sae will receive a reply. Applications are considered four times a year.

Cobb Charity

Sustainable development, green initiatives and related education

£36,000 (2002/03)

Beneficial area UK.

108 Leamington Road, Kenilworth, Warwickshire CV8 2AA

Correspondent Eleanor Allitt, Trustee

Trustees *E Allitt; C Cochran; E Cochran; M Wells.*

CC Number 248030

Information available Accounts were on file at the Charity Commission.

General The trust supports organisations involved in:

- Encouraging eco-friendly technology and appreciation of our natural environment, such as appropriate technology for the developing world, and cycle routes.
- Research for projects such as looking into the connection between food and health and the encouragement of organic gardening and food production.
- The preservation of tribal homelands and the preservation of country and traditional skills closer to home.
- Sustainable energy and recycling projects.

Funding is available for more than three years and can be for capital and core costs, feasibility studies, one-off projects, other projects, research, running costs, recurring costs, salaries and start-up costs.

Most beneficiaries are nationally based charities, but there are exceptions.

In 2002/03 it had assets of £428,000 and an income of £23,000. Grants were made totalling £37,000. Further information was not available.

Exclusions Grants are given to registered charities only, not to individuals. No support for medical organisations, student expeditions or building restorations.

Applications Funds are fully committed. New applications cannot be met.

The Andrew Cohen Charitable Trust

Jewish, children

£90,000 (2001/02)

Beneficial area UK

c/o Wood Hall Securities Ltd, Wood Hall Lane, Shenley, Hertfordshire WD7 9AA

Tel. 01923 289999

Email alc@woodhall.com

Correspondent Mr & Mrs Cohen

Trustees *Andrew L Cohen; Wendy P Cohen.*

CC Number 1033283

Information available Basic accounts were on file at the Charity Commission, without a grants list or a narrative report.

General In 2003/04 the trust had an income of £125,000 and a total expenditure of £25,000. Further information for this year was not available.

The most up-to-date grants total available was £90,000 for 2001/02. Previous grants have been given to JIA, Oxford University L'Chaim Society, Scope Jewish Trust and Imperial Cancer Research.

Applications The trust stated in January 2005 that the trust was set up to allow the settlors to provide support to organisations which are close to their hearts. Regular support is given each year based on these personal interests and therefore applications for funding will not be considered.

The Vivienne & Samuel Cohen Charitable Trust

Jewish, education, health, medical research and welfare

£176,000 (2002/03)

Beneficial area UK and Israel.

9 Heathcroft, Hampstead Way, London NW11 7HH

Correspondent Dr Vivienne Cohen, Trustee

Trustees *Dr Vivienne Cohen; M Y Ben-Gershon; G Cohen; D H J Cohen; J S Lauffer.*

CC Number 255496

Information available Full accounts were on file at the Charity Commission.

General The majority of the trust's support is to Jewish organisations. In 2002/03 the trust had assets of £2 million and an income of £143,000. Grants totalled £176,000 and were donated to charities concerned with general charitable purposes.

Beneficiaries included London School of Jewish Studies (five grants totalling £75,000), Immanuel College (£15,000), Chai Lifeline (three grants totalling £11,000), Yeshivas Be'er Hatorah School (£8,000), Variety Club (two grants totalling £7,000), Maaleh Hatorah School and World Jewish Relief (£5,000 each), B'Nei B'Rith and Jewish Care (£3,000 each) and Queen Mary and Westfield College (£2,500).

Exclusions No grants to individuals.

Applications In writing only, to the correspondent.

The Denise Cohen Charitable Trust

Health, welfare, arts, humanities, education, culture, Jewish

£60,000 (2000/01)

Beneficial area UK.

Berwin Leighton & Paisner, Bouverie House, 154 Fleet Street, London EC4A 2JD

Tel. 020 7353 0299 **Fax** 020 7583 4897

Email martin.paisner@blplaw.com

Correspondent Martin D Paisner, Trustee

Trustees *Mrs Denise Cohen; M D Paisner; Sara Cohen.*

CC Number 276439

Information available Full accounts were on file at the Charity Commission.

General In 2000/01 the trust had assets totalling £902,000 and an income of £48,000. Grants were made to 90 charities totalling £60,000. Most grants were for under £600. No recent accounts have been submitted to the Charity Commission.

Grants have previously been listed under the categories of health and welfare, arts and humanities, education and culture.

The largest grants were given to Norwood Ravenswood Foundation (£10,000), Royal Opera House Trust (£8,000) and Nightingale House (£5,500).

Other grants included those to Donmar (£2,000), National Gallery Trust (£1,500), Jewish Care (£1,300), Ben Gurion University Foundation, Almedia Theatre Company and Western Marble Arch Synagogue (£1,200 each), British EMUNAH Child Resettlement Fund (£1,100), Imperial Cancer Research Fund, British Technion Society, Macmillan Cancer Relief, Royal Academy Exhibition Patrons Group and Royal National Theatre Board (£1,000 each).

Smaller grants included those to Lifeline for the Old, Mind, React, Sargent Cancer Care and World Jewish Relief.

Applications In writing to the correspondent.

The Stanley Cohen Charitable Trust

Jewish, general

£443,000 (2000/01)

Beneficial area UK.

RSM Robson Rhodes, Centre City Tower, 7 Hill Street, Birmingham B5 4UU

Tel. 0121 697 6000 **Fax** 0121 697 6111/2

Correspondent R Hale

Trustees *Joy Audrey Cohen; Stanley Cohen; David John Brecher; Susan Rubin.*

CC Number 1065470

Information available Accounts were on file at the Charity Commission.

General This trust was established in March 1997 and gives support to Jewish and UK charities. In 2002/03 the trust had an income of £3,300 and a total expenditure of £347,000. This low income and very large overspend has been a feature of the trust's work in recent years and it may be in the process of winding up. Further information was not available.

In 2000/01 it had assets amounting to £1.2 million and an income of £29,000. Grants were made to 50 organisations totalling £433,000.

Recipients of the largest grants were: Nightingale House and UJIA (£100,000 each); Duke of Edinburgh Award (£85,000); and Outward Bound Trust (£50,000). Other smaller beneficiaries included: Scopus (£20,000); Community Security Trust (£5,000), Welfare Works Charitable Trust (£1,500); Welsh National Opera (£1,000); Salvation Army (£50); and Samaritans (£25).

Applications In writing to the correspondent.

R and S Cohen Fondation

Education, relief in need and the arts worldwide

£536,000 (2000/01)

Beneficial area Worldwide.

Apax Partners & Co. Ltd, 15 Portland Place, London W1B 1PT

Tel. 020 7872 6302 **Fax** 020 7872 6440

Email tony.halls@apax.com

Correspondent Tony Halls

Trustees *Sir Ronald Cohen; Lady Cohen; Clive Sherling.*

CC Number 1078225

Information available Accounts were on file at the Charity Commission.

General In 2000/01 the foundation had assets of £4.2 million with an income of £1.7 million and grants totalling £536,000.

For this period the foundation concentrated its funding on two main categories, which are listed below with examples of grants awarded.

Education

£150,000 to Jews Free School, £25,000 to City University Business School, £10,000 each to Institute for Strategic Studies and Prince's Trust, £3,500 to Weizman Institute Foundation, £2,500 to Chicks, £2,000 to Tel Aviv University Trust and £1,000 to Holocaust Educational Trust.

Relief in need

£47,000 to UJIA, £25,000 to Bevis Marks Synagogue, £17,500 to Lord Ashdown Charitable Trust, £15,000 to Community Security Trust, £12,500 to Jewish Policy Research, £11,400 to Macmillan Cancer Relief, £10,000 each to Alzheimer's Society, B'Nai B'RithHillel Foundation, Cancer Research Campaign, Jewish Care, Labour Friends of Israel and Refuge, £9,000 to Community Links, £5,000 each to Human Rights Watch, Royal National Institute for the Blind and Save the Children Fund, £4,000 to West London Synagogue, £3,000 each to Association for the Well-Being of Israel's Soldiers, Jo's Trust and Unite for the Future Fund, £2,500 to Camphill Village Trust, £1,700 to Mencap, £1,000 each to Cancerkin, Kensington & Chelsea WIZO, Magen David Adom UK, Royal Marsden Hospital and Soldiers, Sailors, Airmen and Families Association.

Applications In writing to the correspondent.

Col-Reno Ltd

Jewish

About £50,000 (2001/02)

Beneficial area UK, Israel, USA.

15 Shirehall Gardens, Hendon, London NW4 2QT

Tel. 020 8202 7013

Correspondent Mrs C Stern, Trustee

Trustees *M H Stern; A E Stern; Mrs C Stern.*

CC Number 274896

Information available accounts were on file at the Charity Commission.

General The trust appears to support only Jewish organisations, with a preference for medical aid organisations and education.

In 2001/02 it had an income of £78,000. Grants probably totalled about £50,000. No information on recent beneficiaries was available.

Previous beneficiaries included Agudas Yisroel – California, JSSM, Friends of Yeshivas Beis Yisroel and SOFOT.

Applications In writing to the correspondent.

John Coldman Charitable Trust

General, Christian

About £100,000 (2002/03)

Beneficial area UK, with a preference for Edenbridge in Kent.

Polebrook, Hever, Edenbridge, Kent TN8 7NJ

Tel. 020 7578 7000

Correspondent D Coldman, Trustee

Trustees *D J Coldman; G E Coldman; C J Warner.*

CC Number 1050110

Information available Information was on file at the Charity Commission.

General The trust gives grants to community and Christian groups in Edenbridge, Kent and UK organisations whose work benefits that community such as children's and medical charities.

This trust appears to have grown significantly over the last two years. In 2002/03 it had an income of £180,000 and a total expenditure of £191,000. Grants usually total about £100,000. Unfortunately no further information was available on beneficiaries during the year.

Previous beneficiaries included British Liver Trust, Care and Action for Children with Handicaps, Croydon Colorectal Cancer Appeal, Cypress Junior School, League of Friends – Edenbridge Hospital, Marie Curie Cancer Care, NSPCC, Oasis Trust India and St Peter's Church – Hever.

Applications In writing to the correspondent.

The John & Freda Coleman Charitable Trust

People with disabilities, technical education for young people

About £50,000

Beneficial area Woking and its surrounding area.

Headway House, Crisby Way, Farnham, Surrey GL19 7XG

Tel. 01483 283 649

Email roundjohnround@aol.com

Correspondent Paul Coleman, Administrator

Trustees *P B Spark; Mrs F M K Coleman; L P Fernandez; A J Coleman; P H Coleman; B R Coleman.*

CC Number 278223

Information available Information was on file at the Charity Commission

General The trust aims to provide: 'an alternative to an essentially academic education, to encourage and further the aspirations of young people with talents to develop manual skills and relevant technical knowledge to fit them for satisfying careers and useful employment. The aim is to develop the self-confidence of individuals to succeed within established organisations or on their own account and to impress upon them the importance of service to the community, honesty, good manners and self discipline'.

The trust also noted that 'as a small family charitable trust we only help those who are based near our base in Woking'.

In 2003/04 the trust had an income of £33,000 and a total expenditure of £58,000. Further information from this year was not available.

Previous beneficiaries have included Guildford YMCA, Parity for Disabled, Royal National Institution for the Blind, Sayers Croft Trust, Skillway, Surrey SATRO, Surrey Scholars Scheme, Surrey Science and Technology, Treloar Trust, Waverley Youth Project, White Lodge Centre and Woking Hospice.

Exclusions No grants are made to students.

Applications In writing to the correspondent. Telephone calls are not welcome.

The Sir Jeremiah Colman Gift Trust

General

£87,000 (2002/03)

Beneficial area UK, with a preference for Hampshire, especially Basingstoke.

Malshanger, Basingstoke, Hampshire RG23 7EY

Correspondent Sir Michael Colman, Trustee

Trustees *Sir Michael Colman; Lady Judith Colman; Oliver J Colman; Cynthia Colman; Jeremiah M Colman.*

CC Number 229553

Information available Accounts were provided by the trust.

General The trust has special regard to:

- advancement of education and literary scientific knowledge
- moral and social improvement of people
- maintenance of churches of the Church of England and gifts and offerings to church work
- financial assistance to past and present employees/members of Sir Jeremiah Colman at Gatton Park, J & J Colman Ltd or other clubs and institutions associated with Sir Jeremiah Colman.

In 2002/03 the trust had assets of £2.1 million and an income of £88,000. Grants totalled £87,000 and were broken down as follows:

Annual grants	£54,000
Extra grants	£830
Special grants	£32,000

In 2001/02: The largest grant was given to Ark Facility, which received a final instalment of £5,000 (£25,000 in total over the last five years); The Margaret Mee Fellowship Programme received

£3,000. All other grants were for £2,500 or less, with most under £1,000.

The trust made 165 'annual' grants, with all the beneficiaries being supported in the previous year. Of these, just eight were for £1,000 or more. These were to National Art Collections Fund (£2,000), Basingstoke & North Hampshire Medical Trust and Church of England Pensions Fund (£1,500 each), Bridges International (£1,300) and National Trust, Skinners Company School for Girls, Wootton St Lawrence Church and Youth for Christ (£1,000 each).

Other beneficiaries included Action Research, Age Concern – Basingstoke & Dean, Basingstoke Samaritans, British Deaf Association, British Sailors Society, Careforce, Children's Society – Southern, Divert Trust, Endeavour Training, FWA, Gatton Park Educational Trust, Hamilton Lodge School for Deaf Children, Handicapped Adventure Playground Association, Independent Adoption Society, Living Waters, Multiple Sclerosis Society, National Council for One Parent Families, Prison Reform Trust, Royal Naval Museum, Spinal Injuries Association and YWCA.

During the year, 43 'special' grants were made, including nine which were part of a long-term payments scheme. Examples of 'special' grants include those to The Anvil and Basingstoke Sports Centre (£2,500 each), CARE (£1,000), The Grub Institute and UK Youth Parliament (£750 each) and YMCA Norwich and YWAM – Restore (£500 each).

Just one 'extra' grant was awarded during the year to MNDA Schroder (£300).

Exclusions Grants are not made to individuals requiring support for personal education, or to individual families for welfare purposes.

Applications The funds of the trust are fully committed. The trust stated that unsolicited applications are therefore unlikely to be successful.

The Coltstaple Trust

Relief in need

£195,000 (2002/03)

Beneficial area Worldwide.

c/o Pollen House, 10–12 Cork Street, London W15 3NP

Correspondent Lord Oakshott of Seagrove Bay

Trustees *Lord Oakshott of Seagrove Bay; Dr P Oakshott; Lord Newby of Rothwell; B R M Stoneham; Mrs E G Colville.*

CC Number 1085500

Information available In writing to the correspondent.

General In 2002/03 the trust had assets of £2.1 million with an income of £159,000 and grants totalling £195,000.

The five grants issued over this period were £115,000 to Oxfam, £40,000 to Opportunity International, £20,000 to St Mungo's and £10,000 each to Langley House Trust and Beacon Youth Trust.

Applications In writing to the correspondent.

The Conservation Foundation

Environmental and conservation

Around £78,000 (2003)

Beneficial area UK and overseas.

Lowther Lodge, 1 Kensington Gore, London SW7 2AR

Tel. 020 7591 3111 **Fax** 020 7591 3110

Email info@conservationfoundation.co.uk

Website www.conservationfoundation.co.uk

Correspondent W F Moloney, Trustee

Trustees *J Senior, Chair; D A Shreeve; G W Arthur; Dr B Baxter; Prof. D J Bellamy; J B Curtis; W F Moloney.*

CC Number 284656

Information available Information was available on the trust's website.

General The foundation is involved in the creation and management of environmental and conservation orientated projects funded by sponsorship. Income is generated to pay for the costs of managing charitable projects and supporting activities.

In 2003 the foudation had an income of £281,000 and a total expenditure of £250,000. Grants have previously totalled around £78,000. Information about the foundation's current projects can be found on its website.

Applications In writing to the address below.

The Construction Industry Trust for Youth

Building projects benefiting young people

£61,000 to individuals and organisations (2002/03)

Beneficial area UK.

55 Tufton Street, London SW1P 3QL

Tel. 020 7608 5184/5147 **Fax** 020 7608 5001

Email city@thecc.org.uk

Website www.constructionyouth.org.uk

Correspondent The Company Secretary

Trustees *Rod Bennion, Chair; Norman Critchlow; Doug Barrat; Michael Brown; John Carpenter; Martin Davis; Anthony Furlong; Richard Haryott; Richard Laudy; Rob Oldham; Martin Scarth; Ray Squires; John Taylor; Alistair Voaden; Sir Michael Latham.*

CC Number 1094323

Information available Information was provided by the trust.

General The trust aims to increase access by young people to construction training and skills opportunity, with a particular focus on overcoming disadvantage and alleviating disadvantage. It achieves this through providing bursaries and scholarships to individuals and by funding voluntary projects.

It supports projects which arose from the initiative of local communities or charitable bodies. Consideration is given to local community trusts to initiate programmes of work placements and training with regeneration contractors. Training and placements should ideally be for people aged between 16 and 30, although applications for vocational skills training to disaffected 14 and 15 year olds will also be considered.

In 2002/03 it had assets of £96,000 and an income of £138,000, mostly from donations received. Grants totalled £62,000, with a further £83,000 spent on its own work. Details on the beneficiaries, or a breakdown of donations, was not available.

Exclusions Training outside of the construction industry and its associated trades and professions is not considered. Applications for build grants or the refurbishment of youth centres are not considered.

Applications In writing, or via e-mail, to the correspondent for an application form, with an outline of the request. Forms can be downloaded from the trust's website.

Gordon Cook Foundation

Education and training

£214,000 (2000)

Beneficial area UK.

3 Chattan Place, Aberdeen AB10 6RB

Tel. 01224 571010 **Fax** 01224 571010

Email i.b.brown@gordoncook.org.uk

Website www.gordoncook.org.uk

Correspondent Mrs Irene B Brown, Foundation Secretary

Trustees *G Ross, Chair; D A Adams; Prof. B J McGettrick; Dr P Clarke; Dr W Gatherer; J Marshall; C P Skene.*

SC Number SC017455

Information available Information was provided by the trust.

General This foundation was set up in 1974 and is dedicated to the advancement and promotion of all aspects of education and training which are likely to promote 'character development' and 'citizenship'. The following information is taken from the foundation's own leaflet.

'In recent years, the foundation has adopted the term 'Values Education' to denote the wide range of activity it seeks to support. This includes:

- the promotion of good citizenship in its widest terms, including aspects of moral, ethical and aesthetic education, youth work, cooperation between home and school, and coordinating work in school with leisure time pursuits
- the promotion of health education as it relates to values education
- supporting relevant aspects of moral and religious education
- helping parents, teachers and others to enhance the personal development of pupils and young people
- supporting developments in the school curriculum subjects which relate to values education
- helping pupils and young people to develop commitment to the value of work, industry and enterprise generally
- disseminating the significant results of relevant research and development.'

The view of the trustees is that the work of the foundation should:

- invest in people and in effective organisations
- have an optimum impact on the educational and training system, and consequently on children and young people in life and work.

The trust would not provide a copy of its latest annual accounts and the following information is taken from the 2000 accounts. In this year the trust's assets stood at £9 million generating an income of around £285,000 each year. The foundation states that it currently supports a number of projects, including 'Consultations' organised by Institute of Global Ethics, Professional Ethics, Business Ethics, Enterprise Ethics and Values Education in the Four Home Nations.

Grants to 28 projects totalled £214,000. They ranged from £1,000 to £30,000. Larger grants included those to Norham Foundation (£30,000), Health Education Board for Scotland (£20,000), Citizen Foundation (£14,000) and North Lanarkshire Council and Northern College (£10,000 each).

Exclusions Individuals are unlikely to be funded.

Applications The trustees are proactive in looking for projects to support; however, unsolicited applications may be considered if they fall within the foundation's criteria and are in accordance with current programmes. Forms may be obtained from the correspondent.

The Cooks Charity

Catering

£178,000 (2000/01)

Beneficial area UK, especially City of London.

The Old Deanery, Deans Court, London EC4V 5AA

Tel. 01428 606670

Correspondent M C Thatcher, Clerk and Solicitor

Trustees *M V Kenyon; A W Murdoch; H F Thornton.*

CC Number 297913

Information available Accounts were on file at the Charity Commission.

General The trust was established in 1989 to support educational and welfare projects concerned with people involved in catering, and then any charitable purposes (with some sort of catering connection) in the City of London.

In 2002/03 the trust had an income of £269,000 and a total expenditure of £110,000. Further information for this year was not available.

In 2000/01 it had assets of £3 million and an income of £224,000, of which £80,000 came from investments and £62,000 from Gift Aid.

Grants were given to Hackney College (£98,000) and Bournemouth University (£51,000), both of which appear to be receiving ongoing support. Other beneficiaries were Academy of Culinary Arts (£20,000), Cooks Benefactors Charity (£7,500), St Lawrence Jewry (£1,000) and City of London Sea Cadets (£800). In previous years other beneficiaries have included British Heart Foundation, Broderers Trust, Constable Trust, Friends of Highgate Cemetery, HCBA, St John Ambulance and PM Club.

Applications In writing to the correspondent. Applications are considered in spring and autumn.

The Catherine Cookson Charitable Trust

General

£702,000 (2001/02)

Beneficial area Worldwide with a possible preference for the North East of England.

Thomas Magnay & Co, 13 Regent Terrace, Gateshead, Tyne and Wear NE8 1LU

Tel. 0191 488 7459

Email whickham@magnay.u-net.com

Correspondent Peter Magnay

Trustees *J E Ravenscroft; W R Brien; H F Marshall; P Magnay; D S S Hawkins.*

CC Number 272895

Information available Accounts had been filed at the Charity Commission.

General This trust was registered with the Charity Commission in February 1977. As well as supporting general charitable purposes, its objects are:

- the relief of poverty
- the advancement of education
- the advancement of religion.

In 2001/02 it had assets of £18 million and an income of £1.6 million, including £497,000 in royalties. Grants totalling £702,000 were made to 135 organisations.

The largest grant was £100,000 to Royal Agricultural Benevolent Association. Other major grants went to St Chad's Community Project (£81,000), Children's Foundation (£57,000), Parkinson's Disease Society and University of Newcastle-Upon-Tyne and Percy Headley Foundation (£50,000 each), Calvert Trust Kielder (£47,000), Bubble Appeal (£30,000), St Oswald's Hospice Jigsaw Appeal (£20,000) and Brainwave Centre, Historic Hexham Trust and NSPCC (£10,000 each).

The remaining grants were mainly for under £8,000 and given in amounts of £1000, £500 or £250. Beneficiaries included Breakthrough Breast Cancer and RNIB (£5,000 each), Shelter (£2,000), Newcastle-Upon-Tyne Chaucer Music Society and Salvation Army (£1,000 each), Weardale Museum (£600), East Cleveland Youth Housing, Holy Trinity Church Wingate, Northumberland Association of Clubs for Young People and Trinity House Social Care (£500 each) and Breakthrough North and Young Minds (£250 each).

Applications In writing to the correspondent.

The Cooper Charitable Trust

Medical, disability, Jewish

£71,000 (2002/03)

Beneficial area UK.

c/o Portrait Solicitors, 1 Chancery Lane, London WC2A 1LF

Tel. 020 7320 3890

Correspondent Miss J S Portrait, Trustee

Trustees *Mrs S Roter; Miss Judith Portrait; T Roter; Miss A Roter.*

CC Number 206772

Information available Information was provided by the trust.

General The trust was originally endowed with shares in Lee Cooper plc, which was taken over by Vivat Holdings plc. These shares were sold in 1990/91 and the assets of the trust are now invested in government stocks.

In 2002/03 it had assets of £2 million and income of £146,000. Grants ranging between £250 and £5,000 totalled £71,000. The largest grant by far was £57,000 to David Tolkien Trust for Stoke Mandeville. Other grants included: £5,000 each to Ferry Country Centre, Great Ormond Street Hospitals Children's Charity and Jewish Blind and Disabled; £4,000 each to Evelina Children's Hospital Appeal Guys, St Thomas' Charitable Foundation and University of Glasgow Leukaemia Research Fund Centre; £3,000 each to Bobath Centre, Children's Trust – Tadworth, Covent Garden Cancer Research Trust and National Eye Research Centre Yorkshire; £2,000 each to Action for Kids Charitable Trust, North London Hospice, React and Shooting Star Trust; £1,000 to BIME, Communicability, Dressability and Jubilee Sailing Trust; and £250 to Whizz-Kidz.

Exclusions No grants to individuals.

Applications In writing to the correspondent; applications are not acknowledged.

Mabel Cooper Charity

General

Around £59,000 (2001/02)

Beneficial area UK, with a possible interest in South Devon.

Lambury Cottage, East Portlemouth, Salcombe, Devon TQ8 8PU

Tel. 01548 842118

Correspondent A E M Harbottle, Secretary

Trustees *A E M Harbottle; J Harbottle; I A Harbottle.*

CC Number 264621

Information available Accounts were on file at the Charity Commission.

General In 2002/03 the trust had an income of £44,000 and a total expenditure of £27,000. Further information for this year was not available.

In 2001/02 it had an income of £71,000 and made grants totalling around £59,000. No further information was available for the year.

In previous years beneficiaries have included Age Concern, Christian Aid, Crisis, Grateful Society, Kingsbridge Methodist Church Building Foundation, Kingsbridge Swimming Pool Building Foundation, Plantlife, Red Cross, RSPCA, Sidney Hill Cottage Houses and St Martin's BBC Christmas Appeal. Many of these organisations have received recurring support.

Exclusions No grants to individuals.

Applications In writing to the correspondent, although the trust states that it does not welcome, or reply to, unsolicited applications.

The Marjorie Coote Animal Charity Fund

Wildlife and animal welfare

£81,000 (2002/03)

Beneficial area Worldwide.

Barn Cottage, Lindrick Common, Worksop, Nottinghamshire S81 8BA

Correspondent Sir Hugh Neill, Trustee

Trustees *Sir Hugh Neill; Mrs J P Holah; N H N Coote.*

CC Number 208493

Information available Information was provided by the trust.

General The trust was established in 1954 for the benefit of five named charities and any other charitable organisation which has as its main purpose the care and protection of horses, dogs or other animals or birds.

The trustees concentrate on research into animal health problems and on the protection of the species, whilst applying a small proportion of the income to general animal welfare, including sanctuaries.

In 2002/03 it had assets of £2.3 million and an income of £103,000. Grants to 35 organisations ranged from £500 to £7,000 each and totalled £81,000.

20 of the grants went to regular beneficiaries, totalling £65,000. The largest were £7,000 each to Friends of Conservation and PDSA, £6,000 each to Guide Dogs for the Blind and World Wildlife Fund for Nature and £5,000 to FRAME.

Other regular beneficiaries included Whitley Wildlife Conservation Trust (£4,000), Dian Fossey Gorilla Fund and Tusk Trust (£2,500 each), Ada Cole Rescue Stables (£2,000), Shalpa Animal Sanctuary (£1,500) and SPANA (£1,000).

One-off grants were to 15 organisations and totalled £17,000. The largest were £3,000 each to Brooke Hospital for Animals, Dr Hadwen Trust and £1,000 each to Environmental Investigation Agency, Fauna and Flora International, Help in Suffering, Horses and Ponies Protection Association, Nottinghamshire Wildlife Trust, Sheffield Wildlife Trust, Veteran Horse Society and Yorkshire Wildlife.

The remaining one-off grants were of £500 each and went to Animals Asia Foundation, Animal Concern Advice Line, National Canine Defence League, Prevent Unwanted Pets and Wigtownshire Animal Welfare Association.

Exclusions No grants to individuals.

Applications In writing to the correspondent. Applications should reach the correspondent during September for consideration in October/ November.

The Coppings Trust

General

£238,000 (2002/03)

Beneficial area UK.

1st Floor, Lynton House, 7/12 Tavistock Square, London WC1H 9LT

Tel. 0207 388 3577

Correspondent Clive M Marks, Trustee

Trustees *Clive Marks; Dr R M E Stone; T P Bevan.*

CC Number 1015435

Information available Accounts were on file at the Charity Commission.

General This trust does not respond to unsolicited applications as its funds are fully allocated in advance.

The trust states: 'The principal aims and objectives ... are centred around human rights, be it for immigrants' aid, the welfare of prisoners, or the victims of torture and anti-personnel mines. Care for disadvantaged youths, the aged and refugees are also the concern of the trustees. The trust also supports the literary and educational interests of the late settlor.'

In 2002/03 the trust had an assets of £953,000, an income of £14,000 and an expenditure of £238,000 which was broken down as follows:

Arts/Literature	£30,000
Children/Youth	£250
Community	£42,000
Disability	£250
Education	£250
Hospices/Aged	£1,800
Individual	£250
Interfaith	£85,000

Beneficiaries included Uniting Britain Trust (£70,000), Ebony Steel Band (£30,000), Jewish Council for Racial Equality (£20,000), Brighton Islamic Mission and Community Security Trust (£15,000 each), Power (£5,000), Heathland (£1,800) and Jewish Lads' and Girls' Brigade (£1,000).

Various other beneficiaries received smaller grants totalling £1,750.

Applications In 2004 the trust stated: 'Not being a re-active trust it is regretted that the trustees are unable to respond to the many requests for assistance. In order to reduce our costs, the trustees only respond where charitable institutions are known to the trustees.'

The Muriel and Gershon Coren Charitable Foundation

Jewish, welfare, general

£57,000 (2000/01)

Beneficial area UK and the developing world.

2 Tavistock Place, London WC1H 9SS

Tel. 020 7833 2033

Correspondent G Coren, Trustee

Trustees *G Coren; Mrs M Coren; A Coren.*

CC Number 257615

Information available Full accounts were on file at the Charity Commission.

General The trust supports registered charities, particularly Jewish organisations. In 2000/01 its assets totalled around £2 million and it recieved an income of £85,000. Grants to 44 organisations totalled £57,000.

The largest were £5,500 to Gategi Village Self Help Group, £5,000 to Friends of the United Institute of Arad, £3,000 to Hydra Water Wells (K) Ltd – Kenya, £2,500 each to Gategi Girls Secondary Schools, Jewish Blind and Disabled and Yesoday Hatorah School, £2,000 to Magen David Adom, £1,500 to Joint Jewish Charitable Trust, £1,200 to Boys Town Jerusalem and £1,100 to Norwood.

Other grants included £1,000 each to Action for Blind People, British Emunah, Greenpeace, India Earthquake Appeal, King's Cross Homelessness Project and UJIA, £500 each to ChildLine, Delamere Forest School, Sue Harris Bone Marrow Trust, Macmillan Cancer Relief and Shaare Zedek Hospital, £260 each to Parkinson's Disease Society and Woodstock Sinclair Trust, £250 to Hatzola N West and £60 to Friends of R F H Projects.

Applications In writing to the correspondent.

The Duke of Cornwall's Benevolent Fund

General

£98,000 (2002/03)

Beneficial area UK, with a number of grants made in the Cornwall area.

10 Buckingham Gate, London SW1E 6LA

Tel. 020 7834 7346 **Fax** 020 7931 9541

Correspondent Robert Mitchell

Trustees *Hon. James Leigh-Pemberton; W R A Ross.*

CC Number 269183

Information available Full accounts were on file at the Charity Commission.

General The fund receives donations from the Duke of Cornwall (Prince Charles) based on amounts received by the Duke as Bona Vacantia (the casual profits of estates of deceased intestates dying domiciled in Cornwall without kin) after allowing for costs and ex-gratia payments made by the Duke in relation to claims on any estate.

The fund's objectives are the relief of people in need, provision of almshouses, homes of rest, hospitals and convalescent homes, advancement of education, advancement of religion, advancement of the arts and preservation for the benefit of the public of lands and buildings.

In 2002/03 the fund had assets of £2.1 million with an income of £277,000 and grants totalling £98,000.

Substantial grants were £25,000 to Isles of Scilly Wildlife Trust, £15,000 to Small Woods Association, £6,000 to Trustees of the Edington Foundation, £5,000 each to Gloucester Cathedral and Devon & Canons of Windsor Special College Fund, £4,500 to Cornwall Wildlife Trust, £4,000 to Soil Association and £2,000 to Lifebuoy Charitable Trust.

Grants of £1,000 went to Truro Young Women's Centre, Hereford Three Choir Festival, Civic Trust, St Andrew's Church, Plantlife, St Wenappa's PCC, Stanton Prior PCC, Stoke Climsland Sports & Social Club, Liskeard School & Community College and Devon County Agricultural Association.

Applications In writing to the correspondent. Applicants should give as much detail as possible, especially information on how much money has been raised to date, what the target is and how it will be achieved. Applications can be made at any time.

The Sidney & Elizabeth Corob Charitable Trust

General

£220,000 (2001/02)

Beneficial area UK.

62 Grosvenor Street, London W1K 3JF

Tel. 020 7499 4301

Correspondent Stephen Wiseman, Trustee

Trustees *S Corob; E Corob; C J Cook; J V Hajnal; Ms S A Wechsler; S Wiseman.*

CC Number 266606

Information available Full accounts were on file at the Charity Commission.

General The trust has general charitable purposes, supporting a range of causes including education, arts, welfare and Jewish charities.

In 2001/02 the trust had assets of £1.5 million with an income of £64,000 and grants totalling £220,000.

The largest grants were £40,000 to Oxford Centre, £27,000 to University College London, £10,000 each to HOPE and London Jewish Cultural Centre and £7,000 to CST.

Other grants include £5,000 each to EJPS, Royal National Theatre, Norwood Ravenswood, British ORT, British Museum Development Trust, Jewish Care, Chief Rabbivate Trust and UKJAID, £4,500 to University of Cambridge, £3,000 to UJIA Dinner, £2,500 each to Group Relations Educational Trust, Speech Language and Hearing Centre and B'Nai Brith, £2,000 each to United Jewish Israel Appeal, British Technion Society, Immanuel College and Centre for Innovation in Voluntary Action.

Grants of £1,000 were awarded to Friends of the Sick, ICCJ, Scopus Jewish Educational Trust, United Synagogue, Oxford Jewish Centre, Yad Voezer, Friends of Israel Educational Trust, Yakar and Limmud.

Exclusions No grants to individuals or non-registered charities.

Applications Due to funds being fully committed the trust cannot accept any further applications for at least the next 12, possibly 24, months.

The Corona Charitable Trust

Jewish

£88,000 (2001/02)

Beneficial area UK and overseas.

16 Mayfield Gardens, Hendon, London NW4 2QA

Tel. 020 7405 3041

Correspondent A Levy, Trustee and Secretary

Trustees *A Levy; A Levy; B Levy.*

CC Number 1064320

Information available Accounts were on file at the Charity Commission, with a brief narrative report and a list of grants of over £1,000.

General In 2001/02 the trust had an income of £96,000 and made grants totalling £88,000. The surplus was transferred into the trust's capital account, which resulted in assets totalling £110,000 at the year end.

In 2001/02 the grants appear to have been made to Jewish organisations. Grants included £20,000 to Cosmos Belz Limited, £10,000 to Kisharon, £8,400 to Torah & Chesed Limited Menorah Foundation School, £7,600 to Neve Yerushalayim-Michlete Esth, £5,000 to Friends of JSSM Trust, £4,800 to Achisomach Aid Co., £3,900 to Menorah Foundation School, £3,000 to Yosis Olaich Charitable Trust, £1,225 to Hasmonean High School and £1,000 to London Academy of Jewish Studies.

Applications In writing to the correspondent.

The Cotton Industry War Memorial Trust

Textiles

£96,000 to organisations (2002/03)

Beneficial area UK.

5 Brampton Close, Platt Bridge, Wigan WN2 5HS

Tel. 01942 735097

Correspondent Robert G Morrow

Trustees *Peter J R Booth; Christopher R Trotter; Prof. Albert P Lockett; Keith D Lloyd; Keith R Garbett; Mrs Hilda Ball; Peter Reid; Dennis Babbs.*

CC Number 242721

Information available Full accounts were on file at the Charity Commission.

General This trust makes grants to educational bodies to assist eligible students in furtherance of their textile studies, to other bodies which encourage recruitment into or efficiency in the industry or organisations otherwise researching or benefiting the cotton industry.

In 2002/03 it had assets of £5.2 million and an income of £137,000. Grants to five organisations totalled £96,000, with a further £2,200 given in grants to individuals.

Beneficiaries were Adventure Farm Trust (£30,000), Texprint and Museum of Science and Industry (£25,000 each), Textile Institute for its scholarship fund (£10,000) and Bolton Institute (£5,500).

Applications In writing to the correspondent.

The Cotton Trust

Relief of suffering, elimination and control of disease, people who are disabled and disadvantaged

£330,000 (2002–04)

Beneficial area UK and overseas.

PO Box 6895, Earl Shilton, Leicester LE9 8ZE

Tel. 01455 440917 **Fax** 01455 440917

Correspondent Mrs J B Congdon, Trustee

Trustees *Mrs J B Congdon; Mrs T E Dingle; Ms E S Cotton.*

CC Number 1094776

Information available Accounts were provided by the trust, but without a narrative report or a list of grants.

General The trust's policy is: the relief of suffering; the elimination and control of diseases; and helping people of any age who are disabled or disadvantaged. Grants are given for defined capital projects (excluding building construction and the purchase of new buildings). Running costs can be funded where there are identified projects. About 100 grants are awarded to UK registered charities working both at home and overseas each year, ranging between £250 and £5,000.

The financial information provided by the trust accounted for an 18–month period (October 2002–April 2004). In 2002–04 the trust had assets of £4.7 million, an income of £242,000 and made grants totalling £330,000.

Grant beneficiaries included Leicester Charity Link (£45,000), The Pace Centre and UNICEF (£20,000 each), British Red Cross (£15,000), Merlin (£10,000), Impact Foundation (£8,000), The Cambodia Trust (£7,000) and Care International UK, Crisis and Tree Aid (£5,000 each).

Exclusions Grants are only given to UK-registered charities that have been registered for at least one year. No grants to animal charities, individuals, students, further education, travel, expeditions, conservation, environment, arts, new building construction, the purchase of new buildings or 'circular' appeals. The trustees will only support the purchase of computer systems and equipment if it is to be directly used by people who are disadvantaged or have disabilities, but not general IT equipment for the running of organisations.

Applications In writing to the correspondent with latest accounts, evidence of charitable status, detailed budget, timetable and details of funds raised.

Guidelines are available with an sae. Deadlines for applications are the end of July and the end of January, with successful applicants being notified within three months of these dates. It is regretted that only successful applications can be answered. The trustees only accept one application in a 12-month period.

The Augustine Courtauld Trust

General

£88,000 to organisations (2002/03)

Beneficial area UK, with a preference for Essex.

Red House, Colchester Road, Halstead, Essex CO9 2DZ

Tel. 01787 272200

Website www.augustinecourtauldtrust.org

Correspondent Richard Long, Clerk

Trustees *Lord Bishop of Chelmsford; Lord Lieutenant of Essex; Revd A C C Courtauld; Lord Braybrooke; J Courtauld; Lady Braybrooke; Derek Fordham.*

CC Number 226217

Information available Information was provided by the trust.

General This trust was founded in 1956 by Augustine Courtauld, an Arctic explorer who was proud of his Essex roots. His charitable purpose was simple: 'my idea is to make available something that will do some good.' Among the main areas of work supported before his death in 1959 were young people, people with disabilities, the countryside, certain churches, Arctic exploration and the RNLI. The current guidelines are to support organisations that are:

- working within the historical boundaries of the county of Essex
- involved in expeditions to the Arctic and Antarctic regions
- known to one of the trustees.

Within Essex, the preference is to support disadvantaged young people, conservation projects and certain charities that the founder specifically wanted to help. Grants range from £500 to £2,000 for projects and core costs and can be for multiple years, but only if the charity applies for a grant in consecutive years.

In 2002/03 the trust had an income of £78,000. Grants were made totalling £88,000 and were given to 71 organisations.

The largest grants were £8,000 to Friends of Essex Churches, £4,000 to Essex Association of Boys' Clubs, £3,000 each to Cirdan Sailing Trust, Dawns Hall Trust, Chelmsford Branch YMCA, Farleigh Hospice – Chelmsford and Bishop of Chelmsford for overseas aid, £2,500 each to Bishop of Chelmsford's Discretionary Fund and Lord Lieutenant's Discretionary Fund, £2,000 each to Prader-Willi Syndrome and Youth at Risk, £1,500 each to College of St Marks' – Audley End, East Anglian Children's Hospice, Infocus and Little Haven Children's Hospice and £1,400 to Rural Community Council of Essex for the Augustine Courtauld Award (including £400 for administration expenses).

Smaller grants included £1,000 each to Chafford Hundred Church Development Project, Deafblind UK, Essex Heritage Trust and a project for drug counselling in Saffron Walden Deanery, £500 each to Fishermen's Mission, North Avenue Youth Centre – Chelmsford and Prison Fellowship and £250 each to Colchester Women's Aid, Conservation Foundation, Havering Womens Aid and Joseph Clarke School Trust – London.

The trust also supported four expedition projects totalling £9,300. Beneficiaries included £7,000 to Gino Watkins Memorial Fund, £1,000 each to British Schools Exploring Society towards the expenses of the Footsteps of Shackleton Project 2003/04 and Friends of the Scott Polar Research Institute and £300 to Arctic Norway Expedition.

Exclusions No grants to individuals. No grants to individual churches for fabric repairs or maintenance.

Applications In writing to the correspondent, or online via the trust's website. Applications are considered in spring.

Coutts & Co. Charitable Trust

General

£226,000 (2001/02)

Beneficial area UK, specifically London.

440 Strand, London WC2R 0QS

Tel. 020 7753 1000 **Fax** 020 7753 1066

Email carole.attwater@coutts.com

Correspondent Mrs C Attwater, Administrator

Trustees *The Earl of Home; Nigel G C P Banbury; Mrs Sally Doyle; Paul Richardson.*

CC Number 1000135

Information available Information was provided by the trust.

General The trust was set up by the company Coutts and Co. which provides banking and allied services. It is funded by the bank under a deed of covenant equivalent to one half of 1% of the bank's pre-tax profit with a minimum of £50,000. In 2001/02 it gave donations totalling £226,000.

Grants are given to UK organisations only and the trust prefers to support organisations in areas where the bank has a presence, mainly London.

The trust summarised its donations as follows:

Aged	£5,200
Alcohol/drug addiction	£3,300
Animal welfare	£500
Arts/culture	£1,300
Blind	£2,300
Cancer care	£6,600
Cancer research	£3,700
Children	£9,100
Children/youth	£22,000
Deaf	£5,500
Disabled physical/mental	£5,700
Education	£12,000
Environment	£250
Heritage	£4,300
Homeless	£13,000
Hospices	£3,700
Hospitals	£7,000
Housing	£250
International fellowship	£650
Law & order	£2,700
Medical research	£13,000
Mental health	£850
Mentally handicapped	£750
Physically disabled	£5,400
Prison aid	£1,000
Rehabilitating offenders	£1,200
Religious	£52,000
Service charities	£4,000
Social welfare	£19,000
Sports and recreation	£500
Sundry	£4,200
Wildlife Conservation	£250
Youth organisations	£5,300

Exclusions No response to circular appeals. No support for appeals from individuals or overseas projects.

Applications In writing to the correspondent, at any time. Applications should include clear details of the purpose for which the grant is required. Grants are made regularly where amounts of £500 or less are felt to be appropriate. The trustees meet quarterly to consider larger donations.

Cowley Charitable Foundation

Registered charities

£45,000 (2003/04)

Beneficial area Worldwide.

140 Trustee Co. Ltd , 36 Broadway, London SW1H 0BH

Correspondent 140 Trustee Co. Ltd

Trustees *The 140 Trustee Co. Ltd; Mrs H M M Cullen.*

CC Number 270682

Information available Information was provided by the trust.

General In 2003/04 the trust had assets of £958,000 and an income of £42,000. Grants to 29 organisations totalled £45,000.

The largest grants were £10,000 to International Dark Sky Association, £9,500 to Thinking Foundation, £5,000 to Action Aid for Lepers' Children of Calcutta, £3,000 each to Friends of War Memorials and Sharegift and £1,000 each to Age Concern Buckinghamshire, Alzheimer's Society, Medicin sans Frontiere and Wordsworth Trust.

The remaining grants were for £500 or less and beneficiaries included Association for International Cancer Research, Friends of War Memorials, Nina Lawrence Trust, Salvation Army, Save the Children, Trinity Hospice and Woodland Trust (£500 each), Hemihelp (£100) and MacMillan Cancer Relief (£50).

Exclusions No grants to non-registered charities. No grants to individuals, or for causes supposed to be serviced by public funds or with a scope considered to be too narrow.

Applications The trust states that unsolicited applications are not invited, and that the trustees carry out their own research into charities.

The Sir William Coxen Trust Fund

Orthopaedic hospitals or other hospitals or charities doing orthopaedic work

£74,000 (2001/02)

Beneficial area England.

The Town Clerk's Office, Corporation of London, PO Box 270, Guildhall, London EC2P 2EJ

Tel. 020 7332 1432

Email david.haddon@corpoflondon.gov.uk

Correspondent The Trustees

Trustee *Six Aldermen appointed by the Court of Aldermen, together with the Lord Mayor.*

CC Number 206936

Information available Accounts were on file at the Charity Commission.

General This trust was established following a bequest from the late Sir William Coxen in 1940. Expenditure is mainly applied for the support of orthopaedic hospitals or other hospitals or charities doing orthopaedic work.

In 2001/02 the trust had assets of £1.6 million and an income of £66,000. Grants were made to nine organisations totalling £74,000. By far the largest grant was £34,000 to St Bartholomew's Foundation to fund a fellowship. The remaining eight beneficiaries each received £5,000; these were Brittle Bones Society, Claire House, Jennifer Trust, Medical Engineering Resource Unit, Osteopathic Centre for Children, Handicapped Children's Action Group, Brainwave and Simon Paul Foundation.

Exclusions No grants to individuals or non-charitable institutions.

Applications In writing to the correspondent.

The Lord Cozens-Hardy Trust

Medicine, health, welfare, general

£113,000 (2001/02)

Beneficial area Merseyside and Norfolk.

PO Box 29, Fakenham, Norfolk NR21 9LJ

Correspondent The Trustees

Trustees *Hon. Beryl Cozens-Hardy; J E V Phelps; Mrs L F Phelps; J J P Ripman.*

CC Number 264237

Information available Full accounts were on file at the Charity Commission.

General The trust supports a few UK charities in the fields of medicine, health and welfare and local groups in Merseyside and Norfolk. It gives both one-off and recurrent grants.

In 2001/02 it had assets of £1.9 million and an income of £105,000. Grants were made to 162 organisations and totalled £113,000.

Girl Guide Association received £20,000 for the construction of 'Group Adventures', leadership training, group outings and general funding. BMA Medical Education Trust Fund was given £10,000 to donate to medical students of its choosing. Other large grants were £6,000 to British Disabled Sailing Team for general expenses and £5,000 to Extracare Charitable Trust for the St Helens Village Appeal to construct housing for local people who are disadvantaged.

Other Merseyside grants included £1,000 each to Claire House Children's Hospice and Liverpool School of Tropical Medicine, £500 each to Age Concern St Helens, League of Friends of St Helens Hospital, Liverpool City Environment Centre, Liverpool Voluntary Society for the Blind, Merseyside Rescue Services Ltd and St Helens District CVS, £400 to Cardiothoracic Centre, £250 each to Friends of Liverpool Cathedral and L'Arche – Liverpool and £200 to Mersey Park Playgroup.

Grants in Norfolk included £1,400 to Letheringsett PCC, £1,000 to Norfolk and Norwich Association for the Blind, £900 to Norwich Community Workshop Trust, £750 each to Musical Keys Norwich and Norfolk Wildlife Trust, £500 each to Crisis UK for the Norfolk Appeal, East Anglia Children's Hospice, Glaven District Caring Committee, Kelling Hospital, Norfolk and Norwich Families House, Norfolk Churches Trust, Norfolk Youth Trust, St John Ambulance and Theatre Royal (Norwich) Trust for a schools project, £400 each to Blakeney PCC, Leeway Norwich Women's Refuge and Thetford Counselling Service, £250 to Age Concern Norfolk, Anglia Girl Guides, Friends of Norwich Cathedral, Norfolk Scout Association and Samaritans – Norwich and £100 to Gunthope Parish Church.

Amongst the grants to organisations not identifiably in these areas were £1,400 to Sue Ryder Care, £1,300 to Raleigh International Trust, £1,000 each to Canine Partners for Independence, Cardiac Risk in the Young and Salvation Army, £750 to RNIB, £500 each to Cancer Research Campaign, Deafblind UK, International Spinal Research Trust, Let's Face It, Migraine Trust and St John Ambulance branches in Greater Manchester and Lancashire, £400 each to Benjamin Foundation, National Library for the Blind and Victim Support, £300 each to Meningitis Research Foundation and University of Oxford and £250 each to Blue Cross, Intermediate Technology Development Group, Music Therapy Charity, Orbis International, PDSA, RUKBA and Women's Royal Voluntary Service.

Applications In writing to the correspondent. Applications are not acknowledged and are considered twice a year. Telephone calls are not invited.

The Craignish Trust

Arts, education, environment, general

£82,000 (2000/01)

Beneficial area UK, with a preference for Scotland.

Messrs Geoghegan & Co, 6 St Colme Street, Edinburgh EH3 6AD

Tel. 0131 225 4681 **Fax** 0131 220 1132

Correspondent The Secretaries

Trustees *Clifford Hastings; Ms Caroline Younger; Ms Margaret Matheson.*

SC Number SC016882

Information available Full accounts were provided by the trust.

General Established in 1961 by the late Sir William McEwan Younger, the 2000/01 accounts summarised the funding criteria as follows:

- no large national charities
- Scottish bias, but not exclusively
- arts, particularly where innovative and/or involved in the community
- education
- environment
- of particular interest to a trustee.

In 2000/01 the trust had assets of £4.1 million, which generated an income of £151,000. From a total expenditure of £117,000, grants were given to 48 organisations totalling £82,000. Nine of the beneficiaries were also supported in the previous year.

The largest grants were £5,000 each to Henley Symphony Orchestra and Institute of Economic Affairs, £4,000 to Autonomic Disorders Association and £3,500 to John Muir Trust Appeal. Other grants included £2,500 each to Boilerhouse Theatre Group, Drug Prevention Group, Edinburgh Common Purpose and Friends of the Earth Scotland, £2,000 each to Edinburgh Cyrenians and Sustrans, £1,500 to Cannongate Youth Project, £1,000 each to Braendam Link, ChildLine Scotland, Edinburgh Youth Orchestra Society, Reality at Work in Scotland and Visible Fictions Theatre Company, £500 each to Edinburgh Sitters and Working for Environmental Community Action and £250 to Orcadia Creative Learning Centre.

Exclusions Running costs are not normally supported.

Applications There is no formal application form; applicants should write to the correspondent. Details of the project should be included together with a copy of the most recent annual report and accounts.

The Craps Charitable Trust

Jewish, general

£205,000 (2002/03)

Beneficial area UK, Israel.

3rd Floor, Bryanston Court, Selden Hill, Hemel Hempstead, Hertfordshire HP2 4TN

Correspondent The Trustees

Trustees *J P M Dent; C S Dent; L R Dent.*

CC Number 271492

Information available Information was provided by the trust.

General This trust supports mostly Jewish charities, although medical and other organisations are also supported. There is a list of eight charities mentioned in the trust deed, although not all of these are supported every year and other groups in the UK and overseas can be supported.

In 2002 it had assets of £2.7 million, which generated an income of £235,000. Grants totalling £205,000 were made during the year.

The largest grants were: £30,000 to British Technion Society; £20,000 to Jewish Care; £16,000 each to Friends of the Federation of Women Zionists and Home for Aged Jews; and £11,000 to Jerusalem Foundation.

Applications The trust states that 'funds of the trust are fully committed and the trust does not invite applications for its funds'.

The Crescent Trust

Museums and the arts, occasionally health and education

£122,000 (2002/03)

Beneficial area UK.

9 Queripel House, 1 Duke of York Square, London SW3 4LY

Tel. 020 7730 5420

Correspondent Ms C Akehurst

Trustees *J C S Tham; R A F Lascelles.*

CC Number 327644

Information available Information was provided by the trust.

General The trust concentrates on arts (especially larger museums), heritage and ecology. Smaller grants are mainly given in the medical field. Only specific charities of which the trustees have personal knowledge are supported.

In 2002/03 the trust had assets of £223,000, an income of £8,000 and made grants totalling £122,000.

Grants were made to 16 organisations ranging between £250 and £43,000.

Beneficiaries included The Wallace Collection (£43,000), Burlington Magazine (£30,000), Donhead St Mary Village Hall (£21,000), The Attingham Trust (£11,000), Addaction (£5,000), Victoria and Albert Museum (£3,500), P.M.S.A (£3,000), The National Society for Epilepsy (£2,000), Wiltshire Wild Life Appeal (£1,000) and The Royal Collection Trust (£650).

Applications This trust states that it does not respond to unsolicited applications.

Criffel Charitable Trust

Christianity, welfare, health

£57,000 (2002/03)

Beneficial area UK and overseas.

Hillfield, 4 Wentworth Road, Sutton Coldfield, West Midlands B74 2SG

Correspondent Mr & Mrs J C Lees, Trustees

Trustees *J C Lees; Mrs J E Lees; Mrs J I Harvey.*

CC Number 1040680

Information available Accounts were provided by the trust, but without a list of grants or a full narrative report.

General The objectives of the trust are the advancement of Christianity and the relief of poverty, sickness and other needs. In 2002/03 it had assets of £753,000 and an income of £44,000. Grants totalled £57,000 and were broken down as follows:

Advancement of Christianity	£31,000
Relief of poor and needy	£13,000
Relief of sickness	£11,000
Miscellaneous	£2,000

Details of the beneficiaries and size or type of grants was not available.

Exclusions No grants to individuals.

Applications All funds are fully committed. The trust states that no applications are considered or acknowledged. Please do not apply.

The Violet and Milo Cripps Charitable Trust

General

About £20,000 (2001/02)

Beneficial area UK.

2 Lambs Passage, London EC1Y 8BB

Correspondent Fiona Burtt

Trustees *Lord Parmoor; Anthony J R Newhouse; Richard J Lithenthal.*

CC Number 289404

Information available Full accounts were on file at the Charity Commission.

General The trust supports large prison and human rights organisations.

In 2001/02 the trust had an income of £8,000 and a total expenditure of £26,000. Grants totalled about £20,000. No further information was available for this year.

In 1998/99 the trust had assets of £240,000 and an income of £15,000. Grants to 11 organisations totalled £71,000. The trust often gives more in grants than it receives in income.

The largest grants were £20,000 each to Howard League and Prison Reform Trust, both of which have received similar grants in recent years. Other large grants were given to Amnesty International (£10,000) and Multi A Ltd (£5,000). Grants ranging from £1,000 to £3,000 included those to Sutton Veny CE School (£3,000), Finecell Work (£2,500) and Order of Malta Volunteers (£1,000).

Applications The trust states that unsolicited applications will not receive a response.

This entry was not confirmed by the trust but was correct according to information on file at the Charity Commission.

The Cripps Foundation

Education, healthcare and churches in Northamptonshire, Cambridge University

£110,000 (2002/03)

Beneficial area Northamptonshire, diocese of Peterborough and University of Cambridge.

CLB, 8th Floor Aldwych House, 81 Aldwych, London WC2B 4HP

Tel. 020 7242 2444

Correspondent Ken Clarke, Secretary

CC Number 212285

Information available Accounts were on file at the Charity Commission.

General The foundation mainly supports schools and churches in Northamptonshire and colleges of Cambridge University. Almost all the money is given in a few very large awards to organisations. A minimal amount is reportedly available to unsolicited applications from organisations in Northamptonshire.

In 2002/03 the trust had an income of £22,000 and made grants totalling £110,000.

The largest beneficiary during the year was Peterborough Cathedral which received £80,000. Other beneficiaries included Uppingham Parish Church and Northampton Volunteer Bureau (£3,000 each).

In previous years major beneficiaries included the Northampton School for Boys (£5 million over three years up to 1999) and Magdalene College, Cambridge.

Exclusions No grants are made to individual applicants or to organisations based outside the beneficial area.

Applications Applications should be by letter or by direct approach to the trustees. The trustees have a number of projects to which the majority of their funds are committed, but there is a relatively small amount open to unsolicited applications. Applications are filtered by assessing whether or not they strictly fit the areas of interest: Is it local? Is it a religious charity? Is it an educational charity? Suitable applications are then passed on to the council of management (the trustees) for consideration. Both applicants and recipients are visited by the foundation, particularly in the case of larger projects.

The Harry Crook Foundation

Education, general

£709,000 (2001/02)

Beneficial area Bristol.

Veale Wasbrough Solicitors, Orchard Court, Orchard Lane, Bristol BS1 5WS

Tel. 0117 925 2020 **Fax** 0117 925 2025

Correspondent The Trustees

CC Number 231470

Information available Full accounts were on file at the Charity Commission.

General 'The trustees of the foundation consider it to be their primary duty to continue to maintain and support those causes which were dear to Harry Crook's heart.' Dr Crook, who set up the foundation in 1962, endowed it with shares in his Kleen-E-Zee Brush Co Ltd, famed for its door to door brush salesmen. He had served Bristol City Council as an alderman for 25 years and in 1955 was its Lord Mayor. During his lifetime he had supported a wide number of charities in the city. The policy of the trustees is to follow in the founder's footsteps and support charities which 'serve the city of Bristol, or its immediate environs or are personally known to the trustees'.

The foundation's report states it is mainly concerned with elderly, homeless, education and youth charities. It can also make grants to support other specific projects, and small donations for a wide range of charitable purposes. With few exceptions grants are made to charities within the City of Bristol only and applications from charities outside the area from UK or international charities are general.

In 2001/02 it had assets of £1.8 million and an income of £65,000 from investments and bank deposits. Grants totalled £709,000 and were broken down by the trust into four categories, shown here with examples of grants.

Annual Commitments – £49,000 (22 grants in the range of £400 to £5,000)

Beneficiaries included: Boy's Brigade (£5,000); NSPCC – Bristol branch (£3,000); Fairbridge West and Young Bristol (£1,000 each); Pensioners' Voice Soundwell Branch (£500); and Avon Outward Bound Association (£400)

Discretionary Grants £5,000 and over – £635,000 (7 grants in the range of £5,000 and £180,000)

Organisations to benefit were: Clifton College (£180,000); The Vassall Centre Development Project (£163,000); University of Bristol for deaf studies (£140,000); Bristol 5 Club for Young People (£130,000); Espoir (£10,000); and Rotary Club of Chelwood (£5,000).

Discretionary Grants under £5,000 – £25,000 (23 grants in the range of £100 to £3,700)

Grant recipients included: Summerhill Club (£3,700); Dolphin Trust (£2,500); Friends of All Saints' Pusey (£1,800); Colston Society and St Mary's Church (£1,000 each); Network, Rotary Club of Kingswood and Young Enterprise west of England (£500 each); and Bristol Children's Playhouse and Hartcliffe Club for Young People (£100 each).

Adventurers – £1,400 (8 grants in the range of £100 to £500)

Among those to benefit were: Raleigh International (£500); Oasis Trust (£200); and GAP Activities Project, Project Trust and Teaching and Projects Abroad (£100 each).

Exclusions Medical research charities and charities serving need outside the boundaries of the City of Bristol. No grants to individuals.

Applications In writing to the correspondent. The trustees meet twice a year in November and July, but applications can be sent at any time as there is a vetting process prior to the trustees' meetings.

The Cross Trust

Christian work

£119,000 to organisations and individuals (2002/03)

Beneficial area UK and overseas.

Cansdales, Bourbon Court, Nightingale Corner, Little Chalfont, Buckinghamshire HP7 9QS

Tel. 01494 765428

Correspondent The Trustees

Trustees *M S Farmer; Mrs J D Farmer; D J Olsen.*

CC Number 298472

Information available Full accounts were provided by the trust.

General The trust's objects are:

- work for the furtherance of religious and secular education
- advancement of the Christian faith in the UK and overseas
- relief of Christian workers, their dependants, and other people who are poor, sick, elderly or otherwise in need
- support for any religious or charitable institution.

In 2002/03 the trust had assets of £134,000 and an income of £106,000. Grants were made totalling £119,000, of which 8 were made to organisations totalling £80,000 and 16 were given to individuals totalling £38,000.

Donations included £25,000 each to Oak Hill College for a bursary fund and Proclamation Trust Media, £10,000 to Cornhill Training Courses for overseas students' fees, £5,000 each to Emmanuel Church Northwood and Nine Thirty Eight for students for full time gospel work, £4,000 each to International Students Christian Services for support for foreign student ministry and Navigators Support of Sherwood Ministry, £1,500 to MET Clinic and £1,000 to Rock Foundation.

Applications No unsolicited applications are supported, with funds already fully committed.

The Derek Crowson Charitable Settlement

General

£30,000 (2000/01)

Beneficial area UK.

39–40 High Street, Lewes, East Sussex BN7 2LU

Correspondent J R Hughes, Trustee

Trustees *D C Crowson, Chair; J R Hughes; J E Eden.*

CC Number 1027486

Information available Accounts were on file at the Charity Commission, but without a full narrative report.

General In 2000/01 the trust had assets of £14,000 and an income of £15,000. Grants totalled £30,000. Beneficiaries included St Giles' Church (£18,000), St Giles' School towards a computer room (£10,000) and Comic Relief and Plumpton College Charity Fair (£500 each).

Applications In writing to the correspondent.

The Ronald Cruickshanks Foundation

Welfare.

£67,000 (2001/02)

Beneficial area UK, with some preference for Folkestone, Faversham and the surrounding area.

34 Cheriton Gardens, Folkestone, Kent CT20 2AX

Tel. 01303 251742 **Fax** 01303 258039

Correspondent I F Cloke, Trustee

Trustees *I F Cloke, Chair; Jan Siemen Schilder; Mrs S Cloke.*

CC Number 296075

Information available Full accounts were on file at the Charity Commission.

General The settlor of this trust died in 1995 leaving his shareholding in Howe Properties Ltd to the foundation, under the terms of his will. The trust's objects are to make grants to UK organisations and local organisations in Folkestone, Faversham and the surrounding area, for the benefit of people in financial and other need. Over the years the trust has been operating, many charities appear to have received ongoing support.

In 2001/02 the trust had an income of £185,000 and made grants totalling £67,000. Beneficiaries included: Pilgrim's Hospice (£4,000); Salvation Army, Kent Air Ambulance and Age Concern – Folkestone (£3,000 each); and Arthritis Research Campaign, Cancer Research UK, British Heart Foundation, Barnado's, RNLI and British Red Cross (£1,000 each). Grants were also given to various local churches.

Applications In writing to the correspondent. Applications should be received by the end of September for consideration on a date coinciding closely with the anniversary of the death of the founder, which was 7 December.

Cuby Charitable Trust

Jewish.

£123,000 (1999/2000)

Beneficial area UK, overseas.

16 Mowbray Road, Edgware, Middlesex HA8 8JQ

Tel. 020 7563 6868

Correspondent S S Cuby, Chair

Trustees *S S Cuby; Mrs C B Cuby.*

CC Number 328585

Information available Accounts are on file at the Charity Commission, but without a list of grants.

General 'The main objectives of this charitable trust are providing charitable assistance in any part of the world and in particular for the advancement of Orthodox Jewish religious education'.

In 2002/03 the trust had assets of £121,000, an income of £144,000 and a total expenditure of £148,000. Further information including a list of grant beneficiaries was not available.

Applications In writing to the correspondent.

The Cumber Family Charitable Trust

General

£49,000 (2003/04)

Beneficial area Worldwide, with a preference for the developing world and Berkshire and Oxfordshire.

Manor Farm, Marcham, Abingdon, Oxfordshire OX13 6NZ

Tel. 01865 391327/ 391840 **Fax** 01865 391164

Correspondent Mrs M E Tearney, Trustee

Trustees *Miss M Cumber; A R Davey; W Cumber; Mrs M J Cumber; Mrs M J Freeman; Mrs M E Tearney.*

CC Number 291009

Information available Information provided by the trust.

General This trust has a preference for UK-wide needs, developing countries and local organisations in Oxfordshire and Berkshire. It favours the following causes: health, homeless, disability, welfare, rural development, housing, overseas aid, Christian aid, agricultural development, youth and children's welfare and education. Usually a single grant is given and not repeated within three years, although occasionally project support can be given for up to three years.

In 2003/04 a total of £49,000 was given in 67 grants. The largest were £2,500 to Hillforts of the Ridgeway Archaeological Project for an education officer and £2,000 to Oxford Children's Hospital Campaign.

A total of 26 grants were in the range of £1,000 to £2,000 each. Beneficiaries included Action on Addiction, Amity, Biblelands, Deafblind UK, Feed the Minds, Invalids at Home, New Bridge, Prisoners of Conscience, Send a Cow and Trinity Church – Abingdon for a youth worker.

Smaller grants included those to Anwab, Bees Abroad, Busoga Trust, ChildLine, Crosslinks, Dressability, Ingliston Development Trust, Micro-Loan Foundation, Oxford Youthworks, Reading Disabled Society, Reading Single Homeless Project, Riders for Health, Toybox Charity and Wells for India.

Exclusions No grants for animal welfare. Only very few to individuals with local connections and who are personally known to the trustees are supported. Local appeals outside Berkshire and Oxfordshire are not usually supported.

Applications In writing to the correspondent. Applications are considered in February and September. Accounts are requested from new applicants.

The Dennis Curry Charitable Trust

Conservation, general

£261,000 (2001/02)

Beneficial area UK.

Messrs Alliotts, 5th Floor, 9 Kingsway, London WC2B 6XF

Tel. 020 7240 9971

Correspondent N J Armstrong, Secretary to the Trust

Trustees *M Curry; Mrs A S Curry; Mrs M Curry-Jones; Mrs P Edmond.*

CC Number 263952

Information available Information was provided by the trust.

General The trust has general charitable objects with special interest in the environment and education; occasional support is given to churches and cathedrals.

In 2001/02 it had assets of £2.8 million and an income of £110,000. Grants were made totalling £261,000.

In the previous year, it had an income of £125,000 and a total of £90,000 was given in 19 grants. The largest grants were of £10,000 each and went to three organisations: Council for National Parks, Durrell Wildlife Conservation Society and Galopagos Trust. Other grants included £9,400 to Earth Science Teachers' Association, £5,000 each to Friends of Ludlow Museum, National Youth Wind Orchestra of Great Britian and South Buckinghamshire NHS Trust, £2,000 to Forest Stewardship Council, £1,000 to Project Trust and £500 each to International Scientific Support Trust and Rainforest Concern.

Applications In writing to the correspondent.

The Manny Cussins Foundation

Older people, children, health, Jewish, general

About £40,000 (2001/02)

Beneficial area Mainly UK, with some emphasis on Yorkshire.

c/o Freedman Ross, 9 Lisbon Square, Leeds LS1 4LY

Tel. 0113 243 3022

Correspondent Arnold Reuben, Chair

Trustees *A Reuben, Chair; A Cussins; A J Cussins; J R Cussins; Mrs A Reuben.*

CC Number 219661

Information available Full accounts were on file at the Charity Commission.

General The trust's objects are as follows: to support the welfare and care of the elderly; welfare and care of children at risk; health care in the Yorkshire region and abroad; charities in Yorkshire and the former county of Humberside; charitable need amongst Jewish communities in the UK and abroad; and general charitable purposes.

In 2001/02 the trust had an income of £59,000 and a total expenditure of £48,000. Grants totalled about £40,000. Grants usually range from £20 to £8,000, although most are for under £1,000. Unfortunately no information was available on recent beneficiaries.

Previous beneficiaries have included Manny Cussins House, which usually receives the largest grant, Angels International, Bramley & Rodley Community, British Heart Foundation, The Community Shop Trust, Cot Death Society, Hadassah Lodge, Jewish National Fund – Charitable Trust, Leeds Jewish Welfare Board, Lifeline for the Old, Manny Cussins Diabetics Centre, St Gemma's Hospice, St George's Crypt, Whizz Kidz, World Jewish Relief, Yorkshire and Humberside Chaplaincy Board.

Exclusions Applications for the benefit of individuals are not supported.

Applications The correspondent states that applications are not sought as the trustees carry out their own research.

The Daily Prayer Union Charitable Trust Ltd

Evangelical Christian

Around £57,000 a year.

Beneficial area UK.

10 Belitha Villas, London N1 1PD

Correspondent Sir Timothy Hoare, Trustee

Trustees *Revd G C Grinham; Canon J Tiller; Sir T Hoare; Mrs E Bridger; Mrs A Thompson; Mrs F M Ashton; Mrs R K Harley; Revd D Jackman; R M Horn; Mrs A J I Lines.*

CC Number 284857

Information available Accounts were on file at the Charity Commission, but without a list of grants.

General The trust supports evangelical Christian causes. Grants ranged from £1,000 to £7,000. In 2003/04 it had an income of £59,000 and a total expenditure of £60,000. Further information for this year was not available.

Previous beneficiaries have included Monkton School, Fan Fare – New Generation, IFES, Oak Hill College and Society for International Mission and Dagenham Church.

Exclusions No grants for bricks and mortar.

Applications The trust supports causes already known to the trustees. Unsolicited applications are unlikely to be successful. Trustees meet at different times throughout the year, usually around March, June and October.

The Daiwa Anglo-Japanese Foundation

Anglo-Japanese relations

£314,000 to organisations and individuals (1999/2000)

Beneficial area UK, Japan.

Daiwa Foundation, Japan House, 13/14 Cornwall Terrace, London NW1 4QP

Tel. 020 7486 4348 **Fax** 020 7486 2914

Email office@dajf.org.uk

Website www.dajf.org.uk

Correspondent Prof. Marie Conte-Helm, Director General

Trustees *Sir David Wright; Yoshitoki Chino; Lady Adrian; Prof. Sir Alec Broers; Lord Carrington; Nicholas Clegg; Hiroaki Fujii; Tomoaki Kusuda; Lord Roll of Opsden.*

CC Number 299955

Information available An information leaflet was available from the foundation. Full accounts were on file at the Charity Commission.

General The foundation was established in 1988, through a donation made by Daiwa Securities, to promote understanding between the UK and Japan in the cultural, professional, academic and artistic fields.

The foundation has three objectives:

- advancement of UK and Japanese citizens' understanding of each other's peoples and culture
- award of scholarships and maintenance allowances for UK or Japanese students to travel abroad to pursue education
- grants to institutions involved in promoting education in the UK or Japan, or research into cultural, historical, medical and scientific subjects and publication of such research.

In 1999/2000 the trust had assets of £40 million and an income of £1.6 million. Charitable expenditure totalled £1.1 million and administration and management fees £234,000, spent on the centre's library and holding seminars and conferences. Grants totalled £314,000.

The grants list was divided into the following catergories:

Grants given in the UK

Japanese Language: £12,000 in four grants, including £5,000 to Association for Language and Learning (ALL) to fund the first two years of the newly established Japanese Language Committee and £1,500 to British Association for Teachers of Japanese (BATJ) to cover the costs of printing the BATJ journal.

Japanese Studies: £97,000 in 20 grants, the largest was £15,000 to Birbeck College, London, towards a lectureship in Japanese History (last instalment of a five-year grant). There were 14 grants of £1,000 each for annual student exchanges at schools. The foundation has entered into an arrangement with Connect Youth International (part of the British Council), which now processes applications for school and youth exchanges related to Japan.

Professional and academic exchanges: £56,000 in 18 grants, including £7,500 to the UK/Japan Research and Development Group for Ageing, Disability and Rehabilitation (RADGADAR) in order to advance areas of development in relation to ageing and £5,000 to Links Japan towards the costs of a week long visit by a delegation from the Shimin (civil) Forum 21 Non Profit Organisation centre to study the structure of the voluntary sector in the UK.

Art: £53,000 in 31 grants, including £2,000 each to Tate Gallery towards the costs of a pilot scheme to send two British Artists on three month residencies in Japan, to World Haiku Festival and to West Country Craftsmen of UK–Japan for members to travel to Japan to put on an exhibition in Okayama and to acquire experience of Japanese traditional crafts.

Grants given in Japan

Professional and academic exchanges: £63,000 in 27 grants of between £1,000 and £3,000, to allow Japanese citizens to visit the UK for academic or medical research.

Art: £32,000 in 15 grants, including £1,000 each towards the visit a Kabuki actor to London for a public discussion at the Globe Theatre and to Theatre Planning Network Kansai to hold a workshop on the Alexander Technique.

The foundation also awards the Daiwa Adrian Prizes every three years to joint teams of British and Japanese scientists engaged in collaborative research. (In December 1998 four prizes totalled £50,000.)

Applications Forms are available online at www.dajf.org.uk. Deadlines for applications are 31 March and 30 September.

Applications originating from the UK should be sent to the address below. Applications originating from Japan should be sent to The Daiwa Anglo-Japanese Foundation, TBR Bldg. 810, Nagat-cho2–10–2, Chiyoda-ku, Tokyo 100–0014.

Oizer Dalim Trust

General

£201,000 (2002/03)

Beneficial area UK.

68 Osbaldeston Road, London N16 7DR

Correspondent M Cik

Trustees *B Berger; M Freund; N Weinberger.*

CC Number 1045296

Information available Accounts were on file at the Charity Commission, but without a list of grants.

General The trust has previously supported a wide range of charities throughout the UK, but without having been able to see a recent grants list we are unable to confirm this is still true.

In 2002/03 the trust had assets of £15,000, an income of £193,000 and made grants totalling £201,000. A list of grant beneficiaries was not available.

Applications In writing to the correspondent.

The Iris Darnton Foundation

Educational and research projects

£35,000 (2001/02)

Beneficial area UK, but preference for overseas.

Hadcow Place, Three Elm Lane, Tonbridge, Kent TN11 0BW

Tel. 0797 321 1548

Email hdt@hadlow.com

Correspondent Harry Teacher

Trustees *J Teacher, Chair; Miss A D Darnton; Hon. Sara Morrison; Harry Teacher; Matt Darby.*

CC Number 252576

Information available Full accounts are on file at the Charity Commission.

General Support is given to educational and research projects only, such as research into habitat and species protection and conservation. The trust aims to promote by educational means the aesthetic appreciation of flora and fauna, and to promote public morality and advancement of humanitarian principles in relation to wildlife and its preservation.

In 2001/02 it had assets of £568,000 and an income of £19,000. Grants were made to 12 organisations totalling £35,000.

One-off grants went to two organisations; £5,000 to Ezo Kongiwa Wildlife Services and £2,000 to Royal Botanical Gardens – Edinburgh. The rest of the funds went in continuing grants, as follows: £5,000 each to Oxford Wildlife Conservation Research Unit, Whitley Darnton Award and World Wildlife Fund for basking shark research, £2,500 to Galapagos Conservation Trust, £2,000 each to Mauritian Wildlife Foundation and National Pony Society and £1,000 each to Exmoor Pony Society and New Forest Pony Breeding and Cattle Breeding Society.

Exclusions No grants for expeditions, scholarships or individuals.

Applications No written or telephone applications will be accepted. The trust states that new applicants are only considered if proposed by World Wildlife Fund for Nature.

Datnow Limited

Jewish, general

£38,000 (2002/03)

Beneficial area UK and overseas.

130 Holland Park Avenue, London W11 4UE

Tel. 020 7243 2416

Correspondent A D Datnow, Trustee

Trustees *Mrs E M Datnow; E L Datnow; J A Datnow; A D Datnow.*

CC Number 247183

Information available Full accounts were on file at the Charity Commission.

General The trust has general objects, but in practice appears to have a very strong preference for Jewish related causes. In 2002/03 the trust had assets of £302,000, an income of £9,000 and a grant total of £38,000.

Grant beneficiaries included Worldwide Evangelism (£8,500), Durham University (£6,000), NSE (£4,200), West London Synagogue and Westminster Synagogue (£2,300 each), Community Security Trust (£1,750) and Charities Aid Foundation, King's College Cambridge and The Holocaust Educational Trust (£1,000 each). Other grants less than £1,000 totalled £9,500.

Applications In writing to the correspondent, but replies will not be sent to unsuccessful applicants.

Davidson Charitable Trust

Jewish

£250,000 (2002/03)

Beneficial area UK.

58 Queen Anne Street, London W1G 8HW

Tel. 020 7224 1030

Correspondent Mrs E Winer, Trustee

Trustees *G A Davidson; M Y Davidson; Mrs E Winer.*

CC Number 262937

Information available Accounts were on file at the Charity Commission.

General In 2002/03 this Jewish charity had assets of £67,000 and an income of £226,000. After very low adminstration costs of just £176, grants totalled £250,000, although a grants list was not included in the trust's annual report for that year.

Previous beneficiaries include British Friends of CBI, Imperial War Museum's Holocaust Project, Joint Jewish Charitable Trust, Norwood Ravenswood, World Jewish Relief.

Applications In writing to the correspondent.

The Alderman Joe Davidson Memorial Trust

Jewish, general

£33,000 (2002/03)

Beneficial area UK, with a preference for Hampshire.

Chief Executive's Office, Civic Offices, Portsmouth PO1 2AL

Tel. 023 9283 4060 **Fax** 023 9283 4076

Email saskia.kiernan@portsmouthcc.gov.uk

Correspondent Saskia Kiernan, Secretary to the Trustees

Trustees *Ald. Mrs M B E Leonard; C Davidson; P Gooch; Miss M A Ashton; K J Veness; J Klein; K Crabbe; M Thomas.*

CC Number 202591

Information available Accounts were on file at the Charity Commission.

General The trust was established in 1958 for 'dwellings for persons over 70 in necessitous circumstances'. Grants are also given to local and national charities which are named in the trust deed, deserving poor people (ten of whom should be Jewish) and for the provision of Christmas parties. The trust also presents watches to school children for regular attendance. Grants to organisations which are not named in the trust deed are limited.

In 2002/03 the trust had an income of about £35,000. Grants to 28 organisations totalled £33,000, and were listed in two schedules and the Trust Deed. Information on the size of the grants was unavailable.

Schedule 1

Grants are made each year to the same 15 organisations, and they receive a similar share of the grant total each year. Beneficiaries included Barnardo's, Hampshire County Council for Children's Cottage Homes, Portsmouth Council of Community Service, Hampshire Association for the Care & Resettlement of Offenders, Portsmouth Association for the Welfare of the Deaf & Dumb, Portsea Methodist Mission, Portsmouth Cathedral Council, Portsmouth Family Welfare Association, Sussex Unity Lodge 4150 and Tibet Relief Fund for the UK.

Schedule 2

In schedule 2, 13 organisations receive ongoing grants, representing a similar proportion of the grant total each year. All the grants were to Jewish organisations including Portsmouth & Southsea Hebrew Congregation which received the largest grant.

Applications Applications are not accepted if not a regular beneficiary.

Michael Davies Charitable Settlement

General

£30,000 (2002/03)

Beneficial area UK.

Lee Associates, Thames Wharf Studios, Rainville Road, London WC1A 2DA

Tel. 020 7025 4600

Correspondent K Hawkins

Trustees *M J P Davies; G H Camamile.*

CC Number 1000574

Information available Accounts were on file at the Charity Commission, but without a grants list.

General In 2002/03 the trust had assets of £466,000 and an income of £122,000. The total amount given in grants was £30,000.

The largest grant was £10,000 to Arkwright Arts Trust and then £7,000 each was given to Age Concern, Bartlett School of Architecture, The Everest Memorial Fund, North London Hospice, Royal Albert Dock Trust, Unicorn Children's Centre and Village Education Project.

Smaller grants were £5,000 to Goldsmiths College and £2,500 to Medecins du Monde.

Applications In writing to the correspondent.

The Wilfrid Bruce Davis Charitable Trust

Health

£137,000 (2003/04)

Beneficial area UK, but mainly Cornwall; India.

La Feock Grange, Feock, Truro, Cornwall TR3 6RG

Tel. 01872 862795

Email wbdfeock@aol.com

Correspondent W B Davis, Trustee

Trustees *W B Davis; Mrs D F Davis; Mrs D S Dickens; Mrs C A S Pierce.*

CC Number 265421

Information available Accounts were provided by the trust.

General The trust was set up in 1967, the objects being 'such charities as the settlor in his lifetime and the trustees after his death shall determine'. The trust presently concentrates on 'improving the quality of life for those who are physically disadvantaged and their carers'. The geographical area covered is almost exclusively Cornwall, however the main thrust of the trust activities is now focused on India.

The trust operates a 5 year lease on a cottage on Portameor Reach, St Ives for holidays for people who have cancer and their carers. All bookings are through the Macmillan Cancer Relief Fund in London with patients being referred by Macmillan nurses throughout the country.

In 2003/04 the trust had assets of £394,000 and an income of £47,000. A total of £137,000 was distributed in grants. The three largest grants were to Pain and Palliative Care Society (£73,000), Royal Cornwall Hospital's Trust (£38,000) and Guwahati Pain Clinic (£20,000).

Other beneficiaries were Cornwall Community Foundation (£5,000), Pathway (£2,000), Scope Camborne Project (£1,500), Cornwall Macmillan Service (£1,000) and Jubilee Sailing Trust and St Teresa's Cheshire Home (£500 each). A further £360 was also given in smaller grants of £200 or less to registered charities.

The trust is fully committed to its beneficiaries, as for example further grants have been pledged to support the ongoing costs of a hospice built in Kerala in India.

Exclusions No applications from individuals are considered.

Applications No replies are made to unsolicited applications. The correspondent has stated that the budget for many years to come is fully committed and that the trust receives hundreds of applications, none of which can be supported.

The Helen and Geoffrey de Freitas Charitable Trust

Preservation of wildlife and rural England, conservation and environment, cultural heritage

£30,000 (2002/03)

Beneficial area UK.

PO Box 18667, London NW3 5WB

Correspondent The Trustees

Trustees *R C Kirby; Frances de Freitas; Roger de Freitas.*

CC Number 258597

Information available Full accounts were provided by the trust.

General Most of the trust's income is designated for the conservation of countryside and environment in rural Britain, for the preservation of Britain's cultural heritage and for the assistance of disadvantaged people through community facilities and services, advice centres, community arts and recreation.

Grants are usually one-off for feasibility studies, project and start-up costs and range from £500 to £5,000 each.

In 2002/03 it had assets of £419,000 and an income of £18,000. Grants totalled £30,000.

Beneficiaries included Ramblers Association for a social inclusion programme (£3,000), Gloucestershire Wildlife Trust towards acquiring a farm for wildlife conservation and Skippo Arts Team for creative visual arts work with community groups (£2,500 each), Friends of St Peter's – Sibton towards the creation of community facilities within the parish church (£2,000), Hanworth Park Preservation Trust for railing to protect the play area which is in a conservation area (£1,000) and Brighton Unemployed Workers Project for outings for the children of refugees (£500).

Exclusions No grants to non-registered charities, individuals, or to charities on behalf of individuals. Definitely no support for charities concerned with medical or health matters, or with physical, mental or sensory impairments.

Applications In writing to the correspondent. No application form or guidelines are available. No sae required. All applications are acknowledged by postcard. Trustees meet four times a year. Unsuccessful applicants are not notified.

Peter De Haan Charitable Trust

Youth, general

£174,000 (2000/01)

Beneficial area UK.

1C China Wharf, 29 Mill Street, London SE1 2BQ

Tel. 020 7232 5477

Email stusontaylor@opus-trust.com

Correspondent Mrs Sam Tuson Taylor

Trustees *Peter Charles De Haan; Katherine Cockburn De Haan; Sallie Donaldson; David Peter Davies.*

CC Number 1077005

Information available Accounts were on file at the Charity Commission.

General As well as having general charitable purposes, this trust makes a number of grants to charities connected with children and young people.

In 2002/03 the trust had an income of £23.8 million with an expenditure of £950,000. No further information was available.

Grants totalled £174,000 in 2000/01. By far the largest grants were £40,000 to Brandon Centre, £30,000 to Rainbow Centre, £25,000 to National Missing Persons Helpline, £20,000 to CHAS Housing Aid Centre and £15,000 to Kids Company.

Other grants included £8,000 to League of Friends of Hazelhurst Resource Centre, £5,000 each to Apex Leicester and Tenterden Day Care Centre, £4,800 to KCA, £2,500 to Princes Trust and £2,000 to Demelza House.

Smaller grants in the range of £50 to £1,000 included those to Children's Aid Direct, Anthony Nolan Bone Marrow Trust, Victoria Hospital League of Friends and Youth Call Centre.

Applications In writing to the correspondent.

The Leopold De Rothschild Charitable Trust

Arts, Jewish, general

About £40,000 (2001/02)

Beneficial area UK.

Rothschild Trust Corporation Ltd, New Court, St Swithin's Lane, London EC4P 4DU

Correspondent Miss Norma Watson

Trustee *Rothschild Trust Corporation Ltd.*

CC Number 212611

Information available Accounts were on file at the Charity Commission.

General The trust gives most of its support to the arts and has some preference for Jewish organisations, with limited support to other causes covering heritage, welfare, medical and children.

In 2001/02 this trust had an income of £47,000 and a total expenditure of £42,000. This information was taken from the Charity Commission database; unfortunately no further details were available for this year.

Previous grant beneficiaries have included English Chamber Orchestra and Music Society, American Museum in Britain, Child Southbank Foundation, Jewish Childrens Day and Sadlers Wells.

Applications In writing to the correspondent.

William Dean Countryside and Educational Trust

Education in natural history, ecology and conservation

£49,000 (2003)

Beneficial area Principally Cheshire; also Derbyshire, Lancashire, Staffordshire and the Wirral.

St Mary's Cottage, School Lane, Astbury, Congleton, Cheshire CW12 4RG

Tel. 01260 290194

Email bellstmarys@hotmail.com

Correspondent Mrs Brenda Bell

Trustees *David Daniel, Chair; William Crawford; John Ward; David Crawford; Margaret Williamson.*

CC Number 1044567

Information available Information was provided by the trust.

General This trust gives grants towards enterprises in its immediate locality which promote education in natural history, ecology and the conservation of the natural environment.

In 2003 it had assets of £1 million, an income of £49,000 and made grants totalling £48,000. The largest grant was £25,000 to Cheshire Wildlife Trust. There were nine further grants made of £1,000 each or over including those to: Astbury Mere Trust (£5,000), Derbyshire Wildlife Trust, Douglas MacMillan Hospice and Sandbach School (£2,000 each), Astbury St Mary's Primary School, Fairfield Junior School, Friends of Gunside, Halton Borough Council, Palace Fields Primary School and St Mary's Primary School (£1,000 each)

Other beneficiaries included Chester Festival of Flowers (£850) and Wheelock County Primary School and Record (£750 each).

Exclusions The trust stated that education is not funded, unless directly associated with one of the eligible categories.

Applications In writing to the correspondent.

The Delius Trust

Organisations benefiting young adults, older people and musicians; individuals.

£37,000 (2002)

Beneficial area UK and overseas.

16 Ogle Street, London W1P 6JA

Tel. 020 7436 4816 **Fax** 020 7637 4307

Email DeliusTrust@mbf.org.uk

Website www.delius.org.uk

Correspondent Marjorie Dickinson, Secretary to the Trust

Trustees *Musicians' Benevolent Fund (Representative: Helen Faulkner); David Lloyd-Jones; Martin Williams.*

CC Number 207324

Information available *A Descriptive Catalogue of the Works of Frederick Delius* **by Robert Threlfall.** *A Descriptive Catalogue with Checklists of the Letters and Related Documents in the Delius Collection of the Grainger Museum, University of Melbourne, Australia* **by Rachel Lowe. A supplementary catalogue by Robert Threlfall,** *The Collected Edition of the works of Frederick Delius.* **Brochure** – *Delius, 1862–1934: A Short Guide to his Life and Works.*

General Promoting the music of Delius by financing recordings; by giving grants for performances where the making of profit is not an object; by financing the issue of a uniform edition of Delius' music; acquiring material for the trust's archives; preserving and making available to the public, improving, and diffusing knowledge of his life and works.

In 2002 the trust had an income of £152,000 and made grants totalling £37,000. Grants made during the year can be grouped under the following headings including examples of beneficiaries:

Publications £7,900

Performing material - A Village Romeo and Juliet (£2,000) and Hiawatha tone poem towards the publication of existing deficient score (£5,000)

Delius's stage works check list of published editions (£1,000)

Performances £14,000

Delius Society - Annual Grant (£3,400)

Derby Bach Choir - Performance of Sea Drift (£3,200)

Haverhill Sinfonia- Performance of In a Summer Garden (£1,000)

Rose Theatre Trust- Showing of Ken Russell's film, A Song of Summer (£750)

Books, manuscripts etc £5,900

Boydell & Brewer- Five copies of Parry to Finzi by Trevor Hold £170

The Delius Society- Six copies of Ken Russell's film, A Song of Summer £90

Edwin Mellor Press- Two copies of Max Chop on Delius by Philip Jones £50

Lady Beecham- Purchase of Negro Songs MS

Mrs Jane Brabyn- Two letters from Delius to Sir Thomas Beecham £3,000

Publications etc purchased for Archive £2,500

Extended object £3,500

Royal Philarmonic Society- Contribution to Composition Prize 2002 £3,500

Applications In writing for consideration by the trustees and the advisers (Felix Aprahamian, Dr Lional Carley, Robert Montgomery, Robert Threlfall). Notes on application procedure are available from the secretary.

The Dellal Foundation

General, Jewish

£250,000 (2002/03)

Beneficial area UK.

25 Harley Street, London W1G 9BR

Tel. 020 7299 1400

Correspondent S Hosier, Administrator

Trustees *J Dellal; E Azouz; J Azouz; G Dellal.*

CC Number 265506

Information available Full accounts were on file at the Charity Commission, but with only a brief narrative report.

General The trust states that it continues to give 'a significant proportion of the grants towards charities whose aim is the welfare and benefit of Jewish people'.

In 2002/03 the trust had assets of £1.9 million and an income of £72,000. A total of £250,000 was given in grants.

There were two exceptionally large grants, of £50,000 each to ARK and Westminster Synagogue. Other grants of £25,000 went to Dove House Hospice, £22,500 to The Suzanne Dellal Centre, £14,460 to The Chemical Dependency Ltd, £11,000 to Chicken Shed, £10,000 each to Rescue a Child and Sargent Cancer Care for Children, £8,500 to Norwood Ravenswood and £5,000 each to British Friends of the Art Museums of Israel, Jubilee Action and The Philip Green Memorial Trust.

Smaller grants of £3,000 to £500 included those to Jewish Association of Business Ethics (£3,000), Leonard Cheshire (£2,500), Bishopgate School & Great Ormond St Hospital Children's Charity (£1,000), Bikur Cholim (£700) and The Institute for Jewish Policy Research (£500).

Exclusions No grants to individuals.

Applications In writing to the correspondent.

The Delves Charitable Trust

Environment, conservation, medical, general

£198,000 (2001/02)

Beneficial area UK.

New Guild House, 45 Great Charles Street, Queensway, Birmingham B3 2LX

Tel. 0121 212 2222 **Fax** 0121 212 2300

Correspondent Roger Harriman, Trust Administrator

Trustees *Mary Breeze; John Breeze; George Breeze; Dr Charles Breeze; Elizabeth Breeze; Roger Harriman.*

CC Number 231860

Information available Information was provided by the trust.

General This trust has a list of 32 organisations that receive an annual subscription from the trust, and also provides a small number of grants to other organisations.

In 2002/03 the trust had assets of £4.2 million, which generated an income of £188,000. Management and administration for the year totalled £25,000. Grants totalled £198,000, broken down as follows:

Subscriptions – 32 totalling £192,000

The largest were £25,000 to British Heart Foundation, £10,000 each to Macmillan Cancer Relief, Sequel WaterAid, Liverpool School of Tropical Medicine and Quaker Peace and Social Witness and Survival International.

Donations – 4 totalling £5,500

Survival International received £5,000 from this category as well as £5,000 from the subscriptions list. These were £3,000 to Selly Oak Nursery School, £1,000 each to Compassion and Survival and £500 to Friends of Friendless Churches.

Exclusions The trust does not give sponsorships or personal educational grants.

Applications 'The funds of the trust are currently fully committed and no unsolicited requests can therefore be considered by the trustees.' Trustees meet in July and applications should therefore be received by the end of May in years when funds may be available. This will not be until after 5 April 2005 at the earliest.

The Demigryphon Trust

Medical, education, children, general

£71,000 to organisations (2002/03)

Beneficial area UK, with a preference for Scotland.

Pollen House, 10–12 Cork Street, London W1S 3LW

Tel. 020 7439 9061

Correspondent Alan Winborn, Secretary

Trustee *The Cowdray Trust Ltd.*

CC Number 275821

Information available Information was provided by the trust.

General The trust supports a wide range of organisations and appears to have a preference for education, medical, children and Scottish organisations.

In 2003/04 the trust had an income of £79,000 and a total expenditure of £115,000. Further information from this year was not available. However, we do know that in 2002/03 it had assets of £1.9 million and an income of £84,000. Grants were made totalling £71,000, ranging from between £100 and £18,000 each.

The largest grant of £18,000 went to Game Conservancy. Other grants included: £10,000 to Conifers School Limited, £5,000 to Tillington Parochial Church Council, £2,000 to St Richards Charitable Trust, £1,300 to Brise Community Trust; £1,000 to Midhurst Parochial Church Council and £500 each to Midhurst Primary School, Royal Northern Countryside Initiative and Royal Scottish Agricultural Benevolent Institution. Recipients of smaller grants included Strathdee Music Club, Projectchild and Royal British Legion.

In addition, payments totalling £30,000 were made to 30 older people.

Exclusions No grants to individuals; only registered charities are supported.

Applications In writing to the correspondent, including an sae. No application forms or guidelines are issued and there is no deadline. Only successful applications are acknowledged.

The Richard Desmond Charitable Trust

General

About £130,000 (2001)

Beneficial area Worldwide.

The Northern and Shell Tower, Ludgate House, 245 Blackfriars Road, London SE1 9UX

Tel. 020 7579 4580

Correspondent Gary Suckling

Trustees *R C Desmond; Mrs J Desmond.*

CC Number 1014352

Information available Information was provided by the trust

General The trust gives one-off and recurrent grants for core, capital and project funding for general charitable purposes, especially for the relief of poverty and sickness amongst children.

In 2001 the trust had an income of £144,000 and gave £138,000 in grants. Beneficiaries included Disability Foundation, Variety Club Educational Trust and World Jewish Relief.

Applications In writing to the correspondent.

The Duke of Devonshire's Charitable Trust

General

£223,000 (2002/03)

Beneficial area UK, with a preference for Derbyshire.

Currey & Co, 21 Buckingham Gate, London SW1E 6LS

Tel. 020 7802 2700 **Fax** 020 7828 5049

Correspondent The Trustee Manager

Trustees *Marquess of Hartington; Sir Richard Beckett; Nicholas W Smith.*

CC Number 213519

Information available Full accounts were provided by the trust.

General This trust has general charitable purposes giving grants ranging from £50 to £55,000 to a wide range of organisations, with a preference for those working in Derbyshire.

In 2002/03 the trust had assets of £7.6 million, which generated an income of £288,000. Grants were made to 127 organisations totalling £223,000. Management and administration expenditure was high at £32,000, including £14,000 in administration fees to a firm of solicitors in which one of the trustees is a parter. Whilst wholly legal, these editors always regret such payments unless, in the words of the Charity Commission, 'there is no realistic alternative'.

The largest grant was £55,000 to Pilsley Church of England School. Other large grants included those to the Museum of Garden History, Royal Society of Edinburgh and NSPCC (£10,000 each); with £5,000 each to Chaseley Trust, Abbeyfield Society Eastbourne and Martin House Jospice.

Grants in Derbyshire included those to Derbyshire Association for the Blind (£2,500), with £1,000 each donated to Derbyshire Wildlife Trust and Hillstown Miners Welfare Scheme.

Other beneficiaries included St Mary's Collegiate Church (£7,800) and Listening Books (£1,350).

Exclusions Grants are only given to registered charities and not to individuals.

Applications In writing to the correspondent.

The Sandy Dewhirst Charitable Trust

General

£57,000 (2002)

Beneficial area UK, with a strong preference for East and North Yorkshire.

Sovereign House, Sovereign Street, Leeds LS1 1HQ

Tel. 0113 209 2000

Correspondent Paul J Howell, Trustees' Solicitor

Trustees *T C Dewhirst; P J Howell; J A R Dewhirst.*

CC Number 279161

Information available Full accounts were on file at the Charity Commission.

General The trust was established in 1979, firstly for the welfare of people connected through employment with I J Dewhirst Holdings Ltd or the settlor of the trust and secondly for general charitable purposes, with a strong preference for East and North Yorkshire.

In 2002 the trust had assets of £984,000 generating an income of £62,000. Grants totalled £57,000. The largest grant was £7,500 to York Minister Fund. Other grants ranged from £500 to £2,000. Further information for this year was not available.

Previous beneficiaries have included Burma Star Association – Bridlington branch, Cleveland Alzheimer's Residential Centre, Driffield PCC, Hull Sea Cadets, RNIB, Salvation Army, University of Hull Concert Fund and YMCA.

Applications In writing to the correspondent. The trust does not accept unsolicited applications.

DG Charitable Trust

General

£4.3 million (2001/02)

Beneficial area UK.

PO Box 62, Heathfield, East Sussex TN21 8ZE

Tel. 01435 867604 **Fax** 01435 863287

Correspondent Joanna Nelson

Trustees *D J Gilmour; P Grafton-Green; Ms P A Samson.*

CC Number 1040778

Information available Accounts are on file at the Charity Commission.

General This trust makes regular donations to a fixed list of charities. In 2001/02 the trust had assets of £147,000 and an income of £3.6 million. Grants totalled £4.3 million with all except four beneficiaries also receiving support in the previous year.

Beneficiaries were: Crisis (£3.6 million), Notting Hill Housing Trust (£300,000), Amnesty International, Environment Investigation Agency Charitable Trust, Medical Foundation for Victims of Torture and Shelter (£50,000 each), Oxfam (£25,000), Age Concern and Greenpeace (£20,000), Terrence Higgins Trust (£17,000), St Richard's Hospital, Great Ormond Street Hospital, Help the Hospices, Imperial Cancer Research Fund and Prisoners of Conscience Appeal Fund (£10,000 each), Prisoners Abroad (£7,500), Keppleway Trust and Prince of Wales' Trust (£5,000 each) and Battersea Home for Dogs (£1,000).

Applications This trust does not consider unsolicited applications.

The Laduma Dhamecha Charitable Trust

General

£49,000 (2002/03)

Beneficial area UK and overseas.

Dhamecha Foods Ltd, Wembley Stadium Industrial Estate, First Way, Wembley, Middlesex HA9 0TU

Tel. 020 8903 8181

Correspondent Pradip Dhamecha, Trustee

Trustees *K R Dhamecha; S R Dhamecha; P K Dhamecha.*

CC Number 328678

Information available Accounts were on file at the Charity Commission.

General The trust supports a wide range of organisations in the UK and overseas. The aims of the trust are listed in the annual report as being:

- to provide relief of sickness by the provision of medical equipment and the establishing or improvement of facilties at hospitals
- to provide an educational establishment in rural areas to make children self-sufficient in the long term
- other general charitable purposes.

In 2002/03 the trust had assets of £1 million, an income of £227,000 and made grants totalling £49,000. No information was available on the size or number of beneficiaries during this year or the previous one.

Applications In writing to the correspondent.

Alan and Sheila Diamond Charitable Trust

Jewish, general

About £50,000 (2003/04)

Beneficial area UK.

Bright Grahame Murray, 124–130 Seymour Place, London W1H 1BG

Tel. 020 7402 5201

Email peterrodney@bgm.co.uk

Correspondent Peter Rodney, Trustee

Trustees *A Diamond, Chair; Mrs S Diamond; P Rodney; J Kropman.*

CC Number 274312

Information available Accounts were on file at the Charity Commission but without a description of the trust's policy.

General About two-thirds of the trust's grant-making is to Jewish organisations. The trust supports the same organisations each year which are listed in its trust deed, and cannot consider other applications.

In 2003/04 the trust made grants totalling £50,000.

Regular beneficiaries include Community Centre in Israel Project, Youth Aliyah, Girton College – Cambridge, British School of Osteopathy, Anglo Israel Association, Jewish Care, Norwood Ravenswood, Community Security Trust and Holocaust Educational Trust.

Exclusions No grants to individuals.

Applications The trust states that it will not consider unsolicited applications. No preliminary telephone calls. There are no regular trustees' meetings. The trustees frequently decide how the funds should be allocated. The trustees have their own guidelines, which are not published.

The Diamond Industry Educational Charity

Diamond industry, education, general

£40,000 (2000/01)

Beneficial area UK and overseas.

1 Charterhouse Street, London EC1P 1BL

Tel. 020 7404 4444

Correspondent Nicholas Stacey

Trustees *Sir Christopher Collet; G L S Rothschild; G I Watson; Alasdair Adamson.*

CC Number 277447

Information available Accounts were on file at the Charity Commission.

General Up to three-quarters of the income and capital in any year can be put towards the secondary educational needs of children of those currently or formerly employed in the mining, cutting, polishing, marketing or brokering of diamonds. Apart from scholarships, the trustees will also consider applications for educational projects. Other small grants are made to educational establishments.

In 2000/01 the trust had an income of £50,000 and made grants totalling £40,000. No further information was available on the size or number of beneficiaries during the year.

Previous beneficiaries include Friends of Guys Hospital, Harrow School, King Edward's School, Jesus College Cambridge, Cobham Hall, Modern School in New Delhi, Charutar Arogya Mandal, London School of Hygiene and Tropical Medicine and Churchill College.

Applications In writing to the correspondent, preferably between October and December.

The Dickon Trust

General

£40,000 (2003/04)

Beneficial area North East England, Scotland and overseas.

Dickinson Dees, St Anne's Wharf, 112 Quayside, Newcastle NE99 1SB

Tel. 0191 279 9698

Correspondent Helen Tavroges

Trustees *J R Barrett; Mrs D L Barrett; Major-General R V Brims; R Y Barrett; M L Robson.*

CC Number 327202

Information available Information was provided by the trust.

General The trust has general charitable purposes, giving grants, as the trustees in their absolute discretion determine, to local groups in North East England (from the Tees in the south to Cumbria in the west), Scotland and organisations working overseas.

In 2003/04 the trust had assets of £1 million and an income of £47,000. Grants totalled £40,000.

Grants included £1,000 to Sight Savers International and £500 to St Oswalds Hospice.

Exclusions No support for individuals, unregistered charities or churches.

Applications In writing to the correspondent.

The Dinwoodie Settlement

Postgraduate medical education and research

£52,000 (2002/03)

Beneficial area UK.

c/o Thomas Eggar, The Corn Exchange, Baffins Lane, Chichester, West Sussex PO19 1GK

Tel. 01243 786111

Correspondent The Clerk

Trustees *William A Fairbairn; Dr John M Fowler; Miss Christian Webster; Ewan W Gillison; Rodney B N Fisher.*

CC Number 255495

Information available Full accounts were provided by the trust.

General The trustees set out to 'assist ... postgraduate medical education, primarily by improvements to the buildings of independently controlled Postgraduate Medical Centres (PMCs) and by enabling a limited number of postgraduates to widen their knowledge through medical research and by obtaining appropriate experience in hospitals overseas'. They also state that they will continue their 'policy of identifying and supporting significant projects in the field of medical education and research'. The trust only gives grants to projects in England.

The maximum grant towards a PMC project in any one area is normally £1 million. Medical research is for no more than the salary of two research workers in any one year.

In 2002/03 the trust had assets of £3.2 million and an income of £399,000. Declared grants for the year totalled £52,000. Projects receiving funding were Postgraduate Centre, Royal Shrewsbury Hospital (£1 million) and St George's Hospital Medical School for Research Fellowships (£43,000). The figures in brackets refer to the trust's total commitment to each project.

Please note that: Annual figures for grants versus income may vary substantially as payments towards building costs of each project usually absorb more than one year's available income.

Exclusions Anything falling outside the main areas of work referred to above. The trustees do not expect to fund consumable or equipment costs or relieve the NHS of its financial responsibilities.

Applications In writing to the correspondent. The trustees state they are proactive rather than reactive in their grant-giving. Negotiating for new PMCs and monitoring their construction invariably takes a number of years. The trust's funds can be committed for three years when supporting major projects. The accounts contain detailed reports on the development of centres under consideration.

Dischma Charitable Trust

General

£45,000 (2001/02)

Beneficial area Worldwide.

Rathbone Trust Company Ltd, c/o 159 New Bond Street, London W15 2UD

Tel. 0207 399 0820

Correspondent The Secretary

Trustees *Simon Manwaring Robertson; Edward Manwaring Robertson; Lorna Manwaring Robertson; Virginia Stewart Robertson; Selina Manwaring Robertson; Arabella Brooke.*

CC Number 1077501

Information available Accounts were on file at the Charity Commission.

General Registered with the Charity Commission in September 1999, in 2001/02 the trust had an income of £110,000 from investments. Grants to 18 organisations totalled £45,000. There was one donation of £10,000 to Treloars and two of £5,000 each to Meadow School and Trees for Life. Other beneficiaries included Starlight Children's Fund, St Giles Trust, Book Power, NCH Action for Children, Sculpture Academy and Volunteer Reading Help.

Applications The trustees meet half-yearly to review applications for funding. Only successful applicants are notified of the trustees' decision. Certain charities are supported annually, although no commitment is given.

DLA Charitable Trust

General

£49,000 (2002)

Beneficial area UK.

DLA, Fountain Precinct, Balm Green, Sheffield S1 1RZ

Tel. 0114 267 5594 **Fax** 0114 276 3176

Email godfrey.smallman@wrigleys.co.uk

Correspondent G J Smallman, Secretary

Trustees *N G Knowles; P Rooney.*

CC Number 327280

Information available Full accounts were provided by the trust.

General This trust was formerly called Dibb Lupton Alsop Charitable Trust, changing its name to reflect the change in the company's name. In 2002 it had an income of £76,000 and gave £49,000 in grants.

Large grants included £5,600 to Solicitors' Benevolent Fund, £3,200 to Birmingham Children's Hospital, £2,500 to Aldegate Freedom Foundation, £1,200 to RCJ Advice Bureau and £1,000 each to Africa Mercy School, Bootstrap Project and Coast to Coast Challenge. A further £25,000 was distributed to 93 organisations in donations of less than £1,000.

Exclusions No grants to individuals.

Applications In writing to the correspondent, for consideration every three months.

The DLM Charitable Trust

General

£116,000 (2002/03)

Beneficial area UK, especially the Oxford area.

Messrs Cloke & Co., Warnford Court, Throgmorton Street, London EC2N 2AT

Tel. 020 7638 8992

Correspondent J A Cloke, Trustee

Trustees *Dr E A de la Mare; Mrs P Sawyer; J A Cloke; J E Sawyer.*

CC Number 328520

Information available Full accounts were on file at the Charity Commission.

General The trust was established in 1990, after R D A de la Mare left 25% of the residue of his estate for charitable purposes. It supports charities that were supported by the settlor and local Oxford organisations 'where normal fundraising methods may not be successful'.

In 2002/03 the trust had assets of £3.3 million with an income of £112,000 and grants totalling £116,000.

The largest grants were £35,000 to University Oxford Public Health Department, £15,000 to Lay Community and £11,000 to See Saw.

Other grants include £5,000 each to Macintyre House, Harriet Davis Trust, Wildlife Conservation Trust and Royal National College for the Blind, £4,000 to Nightingales Children's project, £3,000 to Whizz Kidz, £2,000 each to Homeshare, Church Housing Trust and Action Against Breast Cancer.

Grants of £1,000 or less were awarded to Abingdon Young People's Drop-In Centres, Ace Centre Advisory Trust, Alzheimer's Research Trust, Oxford Crossroads Caring for Carers, Dogs for the Disabled, Earthwatch Institute, Oxford Samaritans, Happy Days, Dream Holidays, Macmillan Cancer Relief, Orbis, Oxfordshire Group Downs Syndrome Association, Parkinson's Disease Society, S.T.E.P.S, Family Naturing Network, Woodland Trust, Society for Mucopolysaccharide Disease, Talking Newspapers Association, Hinksey Kids Club, Cot Death Society and Prison Phoenix Trust.

Exclusions No grants to individuals.

Applications In writing to the correspondent. Trustees meet in February, July and November to consider applications.

The Dorcas Trust

Christian, general

£35,000 (2001/02)

Beneficial area UK.

Port of Liverpool Building, Pier Head, Liverpool L3 1NW

Tel. 0151 236 6666

Correspondent I Taylor

Trustees *J C L Broad; J D Broad; P L Butler.*

CC Number 275494

Information available Accounts were on file at the Charity Commission.

General The trust has a preference for Christian causes, although other charities have also been supported.

In 2001/02 the trust had an income of £25,000. Grants were made totalling £35,000.

Regular beneficiaries include Navigators, Krila Riding, Shaftesbury Society, Macmillan Cancer Relief, Newmarket Day Centre, Treasures in Heaven Trust, Botton Village, Church Army, Help the Aged, Mildmay Mission and Jubilee Trust.

Applications In writing to the correspondent, although the trust stated that applications cannot be considered as funds are already committed.

The Dorus Trust

Health and welfare, disability, homelessness, addiction, children who are disadvantaged, environment

£116,000 (2002)

Beneficial area Mainly UK.

Charities Aid Foundation, Kings Hill, West Malling, Kent ME19 4TA

Tel. 01732 520083 **Fax** 01732 520159

Correspondent Mrs Sue David, Donor Grants Officer

Trustees *C H Peacock; Mrs Bettine Bond; A M Bond.*

CC Number 328724

Information available Full accounts were provided by the trust.

General The trust has common trustees with two other trusts, The Cleopatra Trust and The Epigoni Trust (see separate entries) with which it also shares the same aims and polices. All three trusts are administered by Charities Aid Foundation. Generally the trusts support different organisations each year.

The trust makes grants in the following areas:

- mental health
- cancer welfare/education – not research
- diabetes
- physical disability – not research
- homelessness
- addiction
- children who are disadvantaged.

There is also some preference for environmental causes. It only gives grants for specific projects and does not give grants for running costs or general appeals. Support is only given to national organisations, not local areas or initiatives.

In 2002 it had assets of £2.9 million, which generated an income of £104,000. Grants were made to 30 organisations totalling £116,000.

The largest were £10,000 each to Brainwave, British Commonwealth Ex-services League and Cancer Research UK, £6,000 each to Foundation for Conductive Education and Royal Scottish Society for the Prevention of Cruelty to Children and £5,000 each to British Liver Trust, Roy Castle Lung Cancer Foundation, Hearing Research Trust, National ME Centre, Northern Friends of Arms and Thyroid Eye Disease Association.

Other beneficiaries included Royal Blind Society for the UK (£4,000), Royal Star and Garter Home (£3,700), Dogs for the Disabled (£3,600), Medic Alert Foundation and National Missing Persons Helpline (£3,000 each), Ehlers Danlos Support Group (£1,100), Nehemiah Project (£1,000) and Living Paintings Trust (£700).

Exclusions No grants to individuals, expeditions, research, scholarships, charities with a local focus, local branches of UK charities or towards running costs.

Applications On a 'funding proposal form' available from the correspondent. Applications should include a copy of the latest audited annual report and accounts. They are considered twice a year in mid-summer and mid-winter. Organisations which have received grants from this trust, The Cleopatra Trust or The Epigoni Trust should not reapply in the following two years. Usually, funding will be considered from only one of these trusts.

Double 'O' Charity Ltd

General

£59,000 (2003)

Beneficial area UK and overseas.

1 Conduit Street, London W1S 2XA

Correspondent The Trustees

Trustees *P D B Townshend; Mrs K Townshend.*

CC Number 271681

Information available Accounts were on file at the Charity Commission, only up to 1998/99.

General The primary objective of the trust is to make grants towards the relief of poverty, preservation of health and the advancement of religion. The trust considers all requests for aid.

In 2003 the charity had assets of £223,000 with an income of £254,000 and grants totalling £59,000.

Grants include £32,000 to Avatar Meher Baba PPC Trust, £7,800 to Priory Hospital, £5,500 to Mawnan Smith Junior Playing Field Trust, £5,000 to Waterford School Trust and £3,100 to Providence Project.

In the period of 2003 over £4,000 was awarded to individuals.

Exclusions No grants to individuals towards education or for their involvement in overseas charity work.

Applications In writing to the correspondent. This entry was not confirmed by the trust, but the information was correct according to the trust's file at the Charity Commission.

The Doughty Charity Trust

Orthodox Jewish, religious education, relief of poverty

£62,000 (2002)

Beneficial area England, Israel.

22 Ravenscroft Avenue, Golders Green, London NW11 0RY

Tel. 020 8209 0500

Correspondent Gerald B Halibard, Trustee

Trustees *G Halibard, Chair; Mrs M Halibard.*

CC Number 274977

Information available Full accounts were on file at the Charity Commission.

General This trust appears to confine its giving to Orthodox Jewish causes.

In 2002 the trust had assets of £40,000 with an income of £60,000 and grants totalling £62,000.

The largest grants were £11,500 to Tomchei Shaarei Zion, £8,000 to Ezra Nitzrochim, £5,000 each to Ponevez Talmudical Studies, Boboy Institutions and Sharrei Torrah and £3,000 each to Wst and Ofakim.

Other grants include £2,700 to Sinai Synagogue, £2,000 to Friends of Mir, £1,000 each to G Tallmundical C, Kisharon, Chinuch Atzmai, J R Charitable Trust, NW London Mikvch and Finchley Synagogue.

Grants of less than £1,000 were awarded to Office of the Rabbinate, Jewish Relief and Rescue, Menorah Primary, Yissocher Dov, Friends of Kapath hour, Ohei Sarah, BSD Trust, Marbai Torah Trust and Gateshead Academy for Jewish Girls.

Exclusions No grants to individuals.

Applications In writing to the correspondent. This entry was not confirmed by the trust, but the information was correct according to the trust's file at the Charity Commission.

The R M Douglas Charitable Trust

General

About £35,000 to organisations (2002/03)

Beneficial area UK, preference for Staffordshire.

68 Liverpool Road, Stoke-on-Trent ST4 1BG

Correspondent The Administrator

Trustees *J R T Douglas; Mrs J E Lees; F W Carder.*

CC Number 248775

Information available Information was provided by the trust.

General The trust was set up for relief of poverty (including provision of pensions) especially for present and past employees (and their families) of Robert M Douglas (Contractors) Ltd, and for general charitable purposes especially in the parish of St Mary, Dunstall. In practice grants are only given to organisations previously supported by the trust. Grants range from £200 to £5,000, although only a few are for over £500.

In 2002/03 it had assets of £560,000 and an income of £52,000. Grants were made totalling £50,000, including about £15,000 in pensions and other grants to individuals.

Previous beneficiaries have included Bible Explorer for Christian outreach, British Red Cross for general purposes, Burton Graduate Medical College to equip a new lecture theatre, Four Oaks Methodist Church for its centenary appeal, Lichfield Diocesan Urban Fund for Christian mission, St Giles Hospice – Lichfield for development, SAT-7 Trust for Christian outreach and John Taylor High School – Barton in Needwood for a performing arts block.

Applications The trust states that its funds are fully committed and applications 'are not being sought for the time being'.

Dromintree Trust

General

£177,000 (2002/03)

Beneficial area Worldwide.

The Manor House, Main Street, Thurnby, Leicester LE7 9PN

Correspondent Hugh Murphy, Trustee

Trustees *Hugh Murphy; Margaret Murphy; Robert Smith; Paul Tiernan.*

CC Number 1053956

Information available Accounts were on file at the Charity Commission.

General Established in March 1996, in 2002/03 the trust had an income of £136,000 mainly from donations and gifts. Grants to five organisations totalled £177,000. The beneficiary of by far the largest grant was University College London, receiving £140,000. Other beneficiaries were: CAFOD (£20,000); Intercare (£10,000); Shelter and World Medical Fund (£3,000 each); and Breast Cancer Campaign (£1,000).

Applications In writing to the correspondent.

The Dugdale Charitable Trust

Christian education, the advancement of Methodist education and the Catholic religion

£86,000 (2001/02)

Beneficial area UK, with a preference for Hampshire and West Sussex, and overseas.

Harmsworth Farm, Botley Road, Curbridge, Hampshire SO30 2HB

Tel. 01489 788 343

Correspondent R Dugdale, Trustee

Trustees *R A Dugdale; Mrs B Dugdale.*

CC Number 1052941

Information available Full accounts were on file at the Charity Commission.

General As well as having general charitable purposes, this trust supports the advancement of the Methodist religion and Christian education. In 2001/02 it had assets of £495,000 and an income of £65,000. Grants totalled £86,000.

Beneficiaries included: Kings School Fair Oak (£25,000); Winchester Family Church (£20,000); Waltham Chase Methodist Church (£6,900); Imperial Cancer Research (£60); and Shipton Gift Mission (£50).

Overseas beneficiaries included: Nambikkai Foundation (£26,000); Maranatha Family Village (£10,000); OMS International (£5,200); Africa Evangelical Fellowship (£2,000); and Freemantle India (£250).

Applications This trust only supports causes known personally to the trustees. Unsolicited applications are not considered.

The Dumbreck Charity

General

£97,000 (2002/03)

Beneficial area Worldwide, especially the Midlands.

Church House, North Piddle, Worcestershire WR7 4PR

Correspondent A C S Hordern, Trustee

Trustees *A C S Hordern; H B Carslake; Mrs J E Melling.*

CC Number 273070

Information available Full accounts were on file at the Charity Commission.

General In 2002/03 the charity had assets of £2.4 million and an income of £87,000. Grants to organisations totalled £97,000, and were of between £500 and £3,000. Although the trust gives worldwide, new grants are only made in the Midlands.

Animal welfare/conservation

International/UK: 15 grants totalled £14,300, including Brooke Hospital for Animals – Cairo (£3,000), International League for Protection of Horses (£2,000), Greek Animal Welfare Fund and People's Dispensary for Sick Animals (£1,000 each) and Donkey Sanctuary, RSPB and World Wildlife Fund (£500 each).

Local: Seven grants totalled £6,500. Beneficiaries were Spear (£2,000), Birmingham Dogs Home and Pet Care (£1,000 each), Rugby Animal Trust and Worcester Farming and Wildlife Advisory Group (£750 each) and Avon Cats Home and Warwickshire Nature Conservation Trust (£500 each).

Children's welfare

UK: Five grants totalling £3,500, including NSPCC and Save the Children Fund (£1,000 each) and Childline and Farms for City Children (£500 each).

Local: Five grants totalling £4,000, including Lemington Boy's Club and Warwickshire Association of Boys' Clubs (£1,000 each) and Dr Barnado's and West Midlands Autistic Society (£500 each).

Elderly people and people with mental/physical disabilities

International/UK: 11 Grants totalling £7,300, including Injured Jockeys' Fund and Royal Agricultural Benevolent Institution (£1,000 each), Listening Books (£750) and Deafblind UK, Electronic Aids for the Blind and Royal Star and Garter Home (£500 each).

Local: 19 grants totalled £15,500, including Myton Hospice (£2,000), Warwickshire Association for the Blind (£1,500), Dogs of Disabled and Helen Ley Charitable Trust (£1,000 each), TOCH (£750) and Birmingham Settlement, Coventry and Warwickshire Association for the Deaf, Mencap – Warwick and Warwick Talking Newspaper (£500 each).

Medical

UK: Three grants totalled £2,500, including Breast Cancer Campaign (£1,000) and Marie Curie Cancer Care (£500).

Local: Nine grants totalled £8,300 including British Red Cross Association – Hereford and Worcester Branch (£1,000), National Association for Crohns and Colitis and Stoke Mandeville Hospital Charitable Fund (£750 each) and Meningitis Trust (£500).

Miscellaneous

International/UK: Six grants totalled £5,800, including Countryside Alliance (£2,000), Council for Protection of Rural England and Hunt Servants' Benefit Society (£1,000 each) Leonard Cheshire Foundation (£750) and SSAFA (£500).

Local: 16 grants totalled £12,000, including Elgar School of Music (£2,500), Pershore Theatre Arts Association and Worcester Three Choirs Festival (£1,000 each), Mayor of Leamington Christmas Fund, Roundabout and Suzy Lamplugh Trust (£750) and Hanbury Church Restoration Appeal and National Memorial Arboretum (£500 each) .

Exclusions No grants to individuals.

Applications In writing to the correspondent. The trustees meet annually in April/May. Unsuccessful applications will not be acknowledged.

The Harry Dunn Charitable Trust

Medical, general

£37,000 (2001/02)

Beneficial area UK, with a strong preference for Nottinghamshire.

Rushcliffe Developments, 13–15 Rectory Road, West Bridgford, Nottingham NG2 6BE

Tel. 0115 945 5300

Correspondent P Robinson

Trustees *A H Dunn; N A Dunn; R M Dunn.*

CC Number 297389

Information available Full accounts were on file at the Charity Commission.

General This trust supports health, multiple sclerosis research, conservation, ecology and general community and voluntary organisations.

In 2001/02 it had assets of £1.1 million and a total income of £79,000, including £33,000 in donations received. Grants totalling £37,000 were made to 29 organisations, only 4 of which were not also supported in the previous year.

The largest grants were £3,000 to Nottingham MS Therapy Centre, £2,500 to Disability Aid, £2,000 to Winged Fellowship and £1,500 each to Holme Lodge Cheshire Home, Medical Oncology Research Fund, Multiple Sclerosis Trust, Nottinghamshire Hospice, RNLI and Wildfowl and Wetlands Trust.

Aside from the £500 to Yoga for Health Foundation, all other grants were of £1,000 each. Beneficiaries included Haywood House Cancer Care Trust, Nottingham City Hospital Trust Fund for urological research, Macmillan Cancer Relief, Motor Neurone Disease Association and St Peter's Church for the Nottingham Tower Appeal.

Exclusions Only organisations known to the trustees are supported. No grants to individuals.

Applications In writing to the correspondent.

Mildred Duveen Charitable Trust

General

£45,000 (2001/02)

Beneficial area Worldwide.

Devonshire House, 60 Goswell Road, London EC1M 7AD

Tel. 020 7566 4000

Correspondent Peter Holgate, Trustee

Trustees *P Holgate; A Houlstoun; P Loose; J Shelford.*

CC Number 1059355

Information available Accounts were on file at the Charity Commission.

General Registered with the Charity Commission in November 1996, in 1999/2000 this trust received a substantial income of £1.3 million. In 2001/02 its assets stood at £1.2 million, generating an income of £29,000. After management and administration costs of £16,000, grants totalled £45,000.

There were 19 donations made in the range of £1,000 and £5,000. Beneficiaries included: Child Psychotherapy Trust (£5,000); Westminster Refugee Consortium (£3,000); Friends of the Lake District and Royal Agricultural Benevolent Institute (£2,000 each); CHIPS and Charlie Waller Memorial Trust (£1,500 each); and Abbeyfield North Down Extra Care Society, Breast Cancer Campaign and Sussex Multiple Scelrosis Treatment Centre (£1,000 each).

Applications In writing to the correspondent.

The Dwek Family Charitable Trust

General

About £56,000 (2003/04)

Beneficial area UK, with a preference for the Greater Manchester area.

Suite One, Courthill House, 66 Water Lane, Wilmslow, Cheshire SK9 5AP

Tel. 01625 549081 **Fax** 01625 530791

Correspondent J C Dwek, Trustee

Trustees *J C Dwek; J V Dwek; A J Leon.*

CC Number 1001456

Information available Brief accounts, with no grants list, narrative report or details of the address or trustees, were supplied by the trust.

General In 2003/04 the trust had an unusually high income of £476,000, due to a donation of shares totalling £430,000. The trust had a total expenditure of £56,000, all of which was distributed in grants. No further information was available.

Applications In writing to the correpondent.

The Dyers' Company Charitable Trust

General

£151,000 (2002)

Beneficial area UK.

Dyers Hall, Dowgate Hill, London EC4R 2ST

Tel. 020 7236 7197

Correspondent The Clerk

Trustee *The court of The Dyers' Company.*

CC Number 289547

Information available Full accounts were on file at the Charity Commission.

General In 2002 the trust had assets of £3.3 million generating an income of £157,000. Grants to 100 organisations totalled £151,000 and were given in the following categories:

Crafts

Eight grants of between £500 and £9,000 totalled £27,000. They were given towards education and training in the crafts and included £9,000 to Heriot-Watt University – Galashiels, £7,500 to Leeds University – Colour Chemistry Department, £3,000 to Textile Conservation Centre, £1,000 to City University and £500 to Royal School of Needlework.

Education and young people

12 grants of between £500 and £23,000 totalled £34,000. Support was given towards the development of young people, largely in the form of grants to educational establishments and youth organisations. These included £23,000 to Norwich School, £2,500 to Hyde Park Nursery School, £1,000 each to All Saints School – Datchworth and Young Enterprise, £700 to Camp & Trek and £500 each to Arkwright Scholarships and Connection.

Health and welfare

32 grants of between £250 and £2,000 totalled £26,000. Recipients included Camphill Village Trust (£2,000), Abbots Langley Community Centre Appeal, Help a Neighbour in Distress Scheme and Hospice of St Francis – Berkhamsted (£1,500 each), AbilityNet, Sara May Fund and Starlight Children's Foundation (£1,000 each), Listening Books (£750), DEBRA and Fight for Sight (£500 each) and Changing Faces (£250).

Local community city/inner London

17 grants of between £250 and £9,600 totalled £38,000. Larger grants were given to educational establishments including St Saviour's and St Olave's Secondary School – Southwark (£9,600), Boutcher CE Primary School – Bermondsey (£8,400) and Homerton College of Technoloy (£6,800). Other grants included those to St James Church – Garlickhythe (£2,000), College of Arms Trust (£1,000), Centre 70 (£750) and Charterhouse in Southwark and Sheriffs' and Recorder's Fund (£500 each).

The arts

14 grants of between £500 and £1,500 totalled £12,000. Suport was given towards musical development and museums, including Royal Over – Seas League Music Competition (£1,500), Chelsea Opera Group, Heritage of London Trust and Riding Lights Theatre Company (£1,000 each), Ironbridge Gorge Museum Development Trust (£750) and Chiltern Open Air Museum (£500).

Services

Three grants were made to Ulysses Trust (£2,500), Royal British Legion Poppy Appeal (£250) and Airborne Forces Charities (£100).

The church

Six grants of between £500 and £2,000 totalled £5,000. Beneficiaries included St Albans Cathedral Campaign (£2,000), St Peter's Church – Guestwick (£1,000) and Norwich Cathderal Appeal (£500).

Other Appeals

Eight grants of between £500 and £2,000 were made in this category and totalled £8,000. Beneficiaries included Swan Sanctuary – Egham (£2,000), Jubilee Sailing Trust (£1,500), Chelsea Physic Garden (£1,000) and Comeback, Sail

Training Association and Thames Salmon Trust (£500 each).

Exclusions No grants to individuals.

Applications The trust does not welcome unsolicited applications.

EAGA Partnership Charitable Trust

Fuel poverty

£94,000 (2002/03)

Beneficial area UK.

23 Macadam Gardens, Penrith, Cumbria CA11 9HS

Tel. 01768 210220 **Fax** 01768 210220

Email eagact@aol.com

Website www.eaga.co.uk

Correspondent Dr Naomi Brown, Trust Administrator

Trustees *Prof. J H Chesshire; J Clough; V Graham; A Harvey; E Jones; Prof. G Manners; G Ritzema; Dr J Wade; G White; P Wilkinson.*

CC Number 1088361

Information available Information was provided by the trust.

General The trust supports projects and research which help to clarify the nature, extent and consequences of fuel poverty; and offer insights into opportunities for the energy-efficient and cost-effective relief of fuel poverty in the UK.

The work funded by the trust can be divided into four categories:

- rigorous, policy-related research
- action projects (such as practical, community based initiatives which have wider applicability)
- the promotion of good practice (such as tool kits and workshops)
- practical resource materials and events (such as training and education resources)

In 2002/03 the trust had assets of £1.2 million, an income of £83,000 and made grants totalling £94,000. The largest grant was donated to National Heart Forum (£26,000). Luton Borough Council, in conjuction with four other councils, received a total of £20,000 for work on a project entitled Tackling Fuel Poverty (A Beacon Council Toolkit for Local Authorities); Plymouth & South Devon RDSU received £17,000 towards The Riviera Housing and Health Survey; Forum for the Future was given £13,000; National Right to Fuel Campaign and Trevor Davidson Employment & Training Consultant received £5,000 each.

Exclusions No grants to individuals. No grants for general fund-raising appeals; no grants for projects that comprise solely of capital works; no retrospective funding; no funding for energy advice provision materials and no funding towards the maintenance of websites.

Applications In writing to the correspondent. Trustees assess grant applications three times a year. The administrator can supply application deadlines and an information pack, including guidelines.

The Eagle Charity Trust

General, international, medicine, welfare

£52,000 (2002)

Beneficial area UK, in particular Manchester, and overseas.

Messrs Nairne Son & Green, 477 Chester Road, Cornbrook, Manchester M16 9HF

Tel. 0161 872 1701

Correspondent C Roberts, Accountant

Trustees *Mrs L A Gifford; Miss D Gifford; Mrs E Y Williams; Mrs S A Nowakowski; R M E Gifford.*

CC Number 802134

Information available Full accounts were on file at the Charity Commission.

General The trust stated it supports a wide variety of charities, including UK and international charities and local charities in Manchester. There is a preference for those concerned with medicine and welfare. In 2002 the trust had assets of £709,000, which, after administration costs of just £470, generated an income of £48,000. Grants totalling £52,000 were made to 35 organisations.

The largest grants went to South Africa Crisis Appeal (£8,000), Oxfam (£4,000) and Independent Options Ltd (£3,500). Other beneficiaries receiving £1,000 or more included British Red Cross (£2,500), Amnesty International, Salvation Army, Save the Children and UNICEF (£2,000 each), Francis House, Henshaws Society and Goma Volcano Appeal (£1,500 each) and Alzheimer's Society, Help the Aged, SCOPE, Turning Point and World Wildlife Fund (£1,000 each).

Grants under £1,000 included those to Cancer Help Centre, Claire House, People's Dispensary for Sick Animals, RNLI, RUKBA, Samaritans and Winged Fellowship Trust (£500 each) and Inside/Out Trust (£300).

Applications In writing to the correspondent. However, please note, unsolicited applications are not invited.

Audrey Earle Charitable Trust

General, with some preference for animal welfare and conservation charities

£37,000 (2002/03)

Beneficial area UK.

24 Bloomsbury Square, London WC1A 2PL

Tel. 020 7637 0661 **Fax** 020 7436 4663

Correspondent Paul Sheils

Trustees *John Francis Russell Smith; Paul Andrew Shields; Roger James Weetch.*

CC Number 290028

Information available Accounts were on file at the Charity Commission.

General In 2002/03 this trust had an income of £1.2 million, including. Grants were made to 30 organisations totalling £36,500. Most of the beneficiaries are supported year after year. At the year end the trust's assets totalled £1.2 million.

Larger grants were £3,000 to British Red Cross, £2,000 each to The League of Friends of Wells & District Hospital, Burnham Market & Norton Village Hall, St Clement's Church Fabric Fund, RSPCA Norfolk Wildlife Hospital and The Royal British Legion.

Other grants ranged between £500 and £1,500 and beneficiaries included: Age Concern, Animal Health Trust, Battersea Dogs' Home Battersea, The Blue Cross, John Grooms Association for Disabled People, The Salvation Army and Sense.

Applications In writing to the correspondent.

The Earth Love Fund

Community-based rainforest conservation projects, Artists for the Environment (AFTE) Festival

£37,000 (2000/01)

Beneficial area UK and overseas.

9 Market Place, Grenchester, Gloucestershire GL7 2NX

Tel. 01285 643111 **Fax** 01285 643222

Email mail@pauldenby.com

Website www.unisong.com/elf

Correspondent Paul Antony Denby

Trustees *Nicholas H Glennie-Smith; Ivan Hattingh; Ed Posey.*

CC Number 328137

Information available Full accounts were on file at the Charity Commission.

General The trust is a UK-based charity which works through the arts to raise awareness and funds for community-based rainforest conservation projects worldwide. The fund was set up in 1989 by three individuals from the music fraternity; the founders' contacts have enabled them to gain the support of top international artists. In 1996 the ELF was awarded the United Nations Global 500 Award for outstanding practical achievements in the protection and improvement of the environment.

The fund also coordinates Artists for the Environment (AFTE), an awareness-raising programme, through which small grants of up to £500 are offered to local community arts throughout the UK for the annual AFTE Festival.

In 2000/01 the trust had an income of £33,000, including £21,000 from donations and newsletter subscriptions. A total of £37,000 was distributed in 17 grants, of which the 5 over £3,000 were listed in the accounts. Beneficiaries were Bona Vista Project – Brazil (£15,000), Rainforest Alliance (£11,000), Amazon Watch and Gurukula Botanical Project (£3,000 each) and Kayapo Land Management (£1,500). Unlisted grants totalled £3,900.

Applications Applications should be made in writing to the correspondent.

This entry was not confirmed by the trust but is correct according to information on file at the Charity Commission.

East Kent Provincial Charities

General, education, younger and older people in the UK

£148,000 (2001/02)

Beneficial area UK, with a preference for Kent.

Masonic Centre, Tovil, Maidstone, Kent ME15 6QS

Tel. 01622 766212

Correspondent Geoffrey Hugh Pierce, Secretary

Trustees *Noel Grout, Chair; Graham Smith; John Edmondson; John Grumbridge; David Mander; Peter Daniels.*

CC Number 1023859

Information available Accounts were on file at the Charity Commission, but without a list of beneficiaries.

General In 2001/02 the trust had an income of £123,000 and made grants to individuals and organisations totalling £148,000. Donations were broken down as follows:

	2002	*2001*
The relief of poverty of children and older people	£45,000	£351
The advancement of education	£86,000	£97,000
The care of people who are sick and older people	£2,600	£11,000
General charitable purposes	£15,000	£22,000
Total	£148,000	£130,000

Unfortunately a list of beneficiaries was not provided in the accounts.

Applications In writing to the correspondent.

The Ebenezer Trust

Evangelical Christianity, welfare

About £50,000 (2000/01)

Beneficial area UK and overseas.

180 Strand, London, Essex WC2R 1BL

Tel. 020 7936 3000

Email nigel.davey@deloitte.co.uk

Correspondent N T Davey, Trustee

Trustees *Nigel Davey; Ruth Davey.*

CC Number 272574

Information available Accounts are on file at the Charity Commission.

General The trust gives grants to Evangelical Christian charities for education, medical, religion and welfare purposes.

In 2000/01 the trust had an income of £124,000 and a total expenditure of £60,000. No further information was available.

Previous beneficiaries include Brentwood Baptist Church, Tearfund, 'Pilgrims' Hatch Baptist Church, Scripture Union, Servants Fellowship International, Medical Foundation for the Victims of Torture, Word of Life and Treasures in Heaven Trust.

Exclusions No grants to individuals.

Applications The trust states that they 'are most unlikely to consider unsolicited requests for grants'.

The Gilbert & Eileen Edgar Foundation

General – see below

£82,000 (2002)

Beneficial area UK (and a few international appeals).

c/o Chantrey Vellacott DFK, Prospect House, 58 Queens Road, Reading RG1 4RP

Tel. 0118 952 4700

Website www.cvdfk.com

Correspondent Penny Tyson

Trustees *A E Gentilli; J G Matthews.*

CC Number 241736

Information available Full accounts were on file at the Charity Commission.

General The settlor expressed the desire that preference be given to the following objects:

- the promotion of medical and surgical science in all forms
- helping people who are young, old or in need
- raising artistic taste of the public in music, drama, opera, painting, sculpture and the fine arts
- the promotion of education in the fine arts
- the promotion of academic education
- the promotion of religion
- the promotion of conservation and heritage, facilities for recreation and other leisure-time activities.

There is a preference for smaller organisations 'where even a limited grant may be of real value'. The majority of grants are around £500 each. Many of the organisations supported are regular beneficiaries.

In 2002 the foundation had assets of £1.5 million and an income of £75,000. Grants were made totalling £82,000 and were broken down as follows:

Category	*No*	*Total*
Medical and surgical research	24	£11,000
Care and support	75	£37,000
Fine arts	7	£6,300
Education in fine arts	4	£20,000
Academic education	4	£2,500
Religion and recreation, including conservation and heritage	13	£5,500

Care and support was further broken down:

Children and young people	26	£12,000
Older People	10	£7,000
People with special needs	39	£18,000.

This category receives the most applications. Its areas of support are quite broad and can include disability, people with chronic medical disorders, refugees and people who have experienced war, homelessness, natural disasters or poverty.

Examples of grants given under each category are shown below.

Medical and surgical research

Most grants were for £500 each, including those to Breast Cancer Campaign and Leukaemia Research Fund. Smaller grants included Cardiac Fund – Battle Hospital (£300) and Meningitis Research Foundation (£250).

Care and support

Children and young people: The largest grant was £1,000 to Operation New World. A further 19 grants of £500 each included those to Aberlour Childcare Trust, ChildLine and Women Caring Trust for Children in Northern Ireland. The remaining grants were £250 each, for example, to Breakout Children's Holidays.

Older people: Grants ranging from £250 to £500 included those to Alzheimers Scotland, Council and Care for the Elderly and New Horizon Trust.

People with special needs: One grant of £1,000 went to National Missing Perssons Helpline. 29 grants of £500 each included those to Action for Blind People and DEMAND – Design & Manufacture for Disability. The remaining grants were of £250 each, beneficiaries included Arthritis Care and Disability Law Service.

Fine Arts

Larger grants were given under this category with £3,000 to Royal National Theatre and £1,000 to English National Ballet. Smaller grants of £250 or £500 included those to Artists General Benevolent Institution and Lincoln Cathedral.

Education in fine arts

Scholarships were given, one of £18,000 to Royal College of Music, two for £5,000 each to Royal Academy of Arts and Royal Academy of Dramatic Art and one for £1,000 to Elizabeth Harwood Memorial Trust.

Academic education

Four grants went to Wolverhampton Grammar School (£1,500), Royal National College for the Blind (£500) and £250 each to St Loye's College Foundation and Royal School for the Blind, Leatherhead. They were all recurrent.

Religion and recreation, including conservation

Nine grants of £500 each included those to Atlantic Salmon Trust, Fauna and Flora International and Survival for Tribes People. Five grants of £250 each included those to Jubilee Sailing Trust and Northamptonshire Association of Youth Clubs.

Exclusions Grants for education in the fine arts are made by way of scholarships awarded by academies and no grants are made directly to individuals in this regard.

Applications In writing to the correspondent. There are no application forms.

Gilbert Edgar Trust

See below

£39,000 (2001/02)

Beneficial area Predominantly UK, limited overseas.

c/o Cave Harper & Co., North Lee House, 66 Northfield End, Henley-on-Thames, Oxfordshire RG9 2BE

Tel. 01491 572565

Correspondent The Trustees

CC Number 213630

Information available Accounts were on file at the Charity Commission.

General In 2001/02, the trust had assets of £930,000, an income of £45,000 and made grants totalling £39,000 towards the causes listed below with examples of grants:

Homeless – 6 grants totalling £4,900

Grants of £1,000 were made to Centrepoint (Solo), Mind, Notting Hill Housing Trust and Shelter. The remaining grants were for £400 and £500.

Hospice – 6 grants of £500 each

Beneficiaries included Myton Hamlet Hospice and St Luke's Hospice.

Medical – 8 grants totalling £3,900

Grants included £1,000 to Cancer Relief Macmillan Fund and £500 to Multiple Sclerosis Society. Six grants of £400 were made to, for example, Quest for Test for Cancer and Scope.

Overseas – 5 grants totalling £2,800

Grants were £1,000 to British Red Cross, £500 each to Save the Children Fund and Impact Foundation and £400 to both Echo and Prisoners Abroad.

Research – 10 grants totalling £4,000

Grants included £400 each made to, for example, National Prostate Cancer Research to ME Association and Schizophrenia Association.

Social – 9 grants totalling £3,750

Grants were £1,000 to Samaritans, £500 to Police Foundation and St John's Ambulance, £400 each to Homelife (DGAA), New Bridge, Prison Reform Trust, RABI and St John's Ambulance, and £250 to Hambleden Church Council.

Youth – 3 grants totalling £1,300
Grants were £500 to YMCA and £400 each to National Association of Boys Clubs and Venturers' Search and Rescue.

Children – 12 grants totalling £6,100
Grants included £1,000 to NSPCC and National Institute of Conductive Education, and £500 to Babes in Arms. Others were all for £400 including Action Research, Early Bird Fund and National Playbus Association.

Disabled – 3 grants totalling £1,300
Grants went to Disabled Housing Trust (£500) and £400 each to Robert Owen Foundation and Woodcraft Folk.

Deaf/Blind – 3 grants of £400 each
Grants went to Cambridge Learning Trust, Iris Fund and Sense.

Drug Abuse – 5 grants of £400 each
Grants included those to Accept Clinic, Re–Solv and Rhoserchan Project.

Handicapped – 11 grants totalling £4,600
Grants of £500 each were made to HAPA, Home Farm Trust Fund. All other grants were for £400 each.

Exclusions No grants to individuals or non-registered charities.

Applications In writing to the correspondent, with a copy of a brochure describing your work.

The Edinburgh Trust, No 2 Account

Education, service, scientific expeditions

£63,000 (2002/03)

Beneficial area UK and worldwide.

Buckingham Place, London SW1A 1AA

Tel. 020 7930 4832

Correspondent Paul Hughes, Secretary

Trustees *Sir Brian McGrath; C Woodhouse; M Hunt-Davis.*

CC Number 227897

Information available Full accounts were on file at the Charity Commission.

General Grants are mostly given towards the armed services, education and 'scientific expeditions'. The trust appears to favour the areas of wildlife and nature conservation, preservation of historic buildings, youth and outdoor pursuits, and in some cases medical and health-related causes.

In 2002/03 it had assets of £1 million and an income of £64,000. Grants were made to 25 organisations and totalled £63,000, broken down as follows:

Armed service	£15,000
Education	£6,200
General	£42,000

The largest were £2,800 to Edwina Mountbatten Trust, £2,500 each to The Award Scheme, British Commonwealth Ex-serviceman's League, Federation of London Youth Clubs, King George Fund for Sailors, Outeard Bound Trust and Royal Marines General Fund and £2,000 each to International Sacred Literature Trust and PP Trust for Windsor and Maidenhead.

Other grants were £1,800 to King Edward VII Hospital for Officers, £1,500 each to Burma Star Association, Game Conservancy Trust, The Maritime Trust, Friends of the National Maritime Museum, National Playing Fields Association, Population Concern, Royal Life Saving Society, Sail Training Association, SSAFA Forces Help, St George's House, WWF and Zoological Society of London, £1,300 to Romsey Abbey and £1,000 each to Cheam School and Countryside Foundation.

Exclusions No grants to individuals; only scientific expeditions are considered with the backing of a major society. No grants to non-registered charities.

Applications In writing to the correspondent. The trustees meet to consider grants in April each year. Applications must be submitted by January.

The W G Edwards Charitable Foundation

Care of older people

£201,000 (2001/02)

Beneficial area UK.

Wedge Property Co. Ltd, 123a Station Road, Oxted, Surrey RH8 0QE

Tel. 01883 714412 **Fax** 01883 714433

Email janetbrown@wgedwardscharitablefoundation.org.uk

Website www.wgedwardscharitablefoundation.org.uk

Correspondent Janet Brown, Clerk to the Trustees

Trustees *Mrs Margaret E Offley Edwards; Prof. Wendy D Savage; Mrs G Shepherd Coates.*

CC Number 293312

Information available Information was provided by the trust, without a list of grants.

General The foundation assists with the provision of care for older people through existing registered charities, principally with capital projects but also supporting innovative schemes involved in ongoing care. The average size of a grant made is £5 to £10,000 per charity.

In 2002 grants were made to around 30 charities totalling £201,000. No further information was available on the size of grants given or who received them.

In 2000/01 the foundation had an income of £82,000 and a total expenditure of £40,000.

The foundation has previously made large donations to Lillian Faithful Homes, Age Concern in Tower Hamlets and Friends of the Elderly.

Exclusions No grants to individuals.

Applications In writing to the correspondent. There are no forms or deadlines for applications but the Trustees usually meet in January, April, July and November.

The Eeman Charitable Trust

General

£38,000 (2001/02)

Beneficial area UK and overseas.

Green Cottage, Ward Green, Old Newton, Stowmarket, Suffolk IP14 4EZ

Tel. 01449 673650

Correspondent R Hutchinson

CC Number 261972

Information available Accounts were on file at the Charity Commisison.

General The trust supports established national charities and international emergencies, whilst maintaining the interest in theological projects with which the settlor or her advisor had already established connection.

In 2001/02 the trust had an income of £73,000 and gave grants totalling £38,000.

The trust gave grants to the following beneficiaries Monastery of Iberan (Mt Athos) (£10,000), British Red Cross (£8,000), Hermitage of St Charalambos (£3,000), Task Brazil Trust (£2,000), Community of St John the Baptsit (£1,500), St Luke's Hospital for the Clergy and St Mary's Church, Old Newton (£1,250 each), Children with Leukaemia and Lagan College (£1,000 each) and Citizen's Advice Bureau (£530).

Applications In writing to the correspondent.

This entry was not confirmed by the trust, but the information was correct according to the Charity Commission file.

The Elephant Trust

Visual arts

£58,000 to organisations and individuals (2003/04)

Beneficial area UK.

Bankside Lofts, 65 Hopton Street, London SE1 9GZ

Tel. 020 7922 1160

Email ruth@elephanttrust.org.uk

Website www.elephanttrust.org.uk

Correspondent Ruth Rattenbury

Trustees *Dawn Ades; Antony Forwood; Matthew Slotover; Tony Penrose; Richard Wentworth; Sarah Whitfield, Chair.*

CC Number 269615

Information available Information was provided by the trust

General The trust makes grants to individual artists, arts organisations and publications concerned with the visual arts. It aims to extend the frontiers of creative endeavour, to promote the unconventional and the imaginative and, within its limited resources, to make it possible for artists and arts organisations to realise and complete specific projects.

In 2003/04 the trust's assets totalled £1.4 million and it received an income of £60,000. Grants ranging from £800 to £5,000 were awarded to 4 individuals, 7 galleries and 8 institutions. Galleries supported included Artangel, Cubitt, Drawing Room, Gasworks, the Standpoint Gallery and the Showroom. Organisations supported included Architecture Association, Camden Arts Centre, Mead Gallery, Oxford Museum of Modern Art and Whitechapel Gallery.

The trust also administers the George Melhuish Bequest, which has similar objectives.

Exclusions No education or other study grants.

Applications In writing to the correspondent. Guidelines are available. The trustees meet four times a year.

The George Elias Charitable Trust

Jewish, general

£187,000 (2001/02)

Beneficial area Some preference for Manchester.

Elitex House, 1 Ashley Road, Hale, Altrincham, Cheshire WA14 2DT

Tel. 0161 928 7171

Correspondent N G Denton, Charity Accountant

Trustees *G H Elias; Mrs D Elias; E C Elias; S E Elias.*

CC Number 273993

Information available Accounts were on file at the Charity Commission but without a list of grants

General This trust states it gives grants to charities supporting educational needs and the fight against poverty as well as organisations promoting the Jewish faith.

In 2001/02 the trust had assets of £293,000 and an income of £167,000, of which £151,000 came from gift aid. Grants totalled £187,000. Further information from this year was not available.

Previous beneficiaries have included Aish Hatorah, Association Chested, Bet Hatfusot, Hoba, Manchester Beth Din, Manchester Charitable Trust, Manchester Jewish Federation, Neve Jerusalem, Parkhill Charity Trust, Ponovez Congregation, South Manchester Mikva Trust, Yad Eli Ezer and YSCCR.

Applications In writing to the correspondent. Trustees meet monthly.

Ellador Ltd

Jewish

£32,000 (2002/03)

Beneficial area UK.

Ellador Ltd, 20 Ashstead Road, London E5 9BH

Tel. 020 7242 3580

Correspondent J Schrieber, Trustee & Governor

Trustees *J Schrieber; S Schrieber; Mrs H Schrieber; Mrs R Schrieber.*

CC Number 283202

Information available Accounts were on file at the Charity Commission, but without a grants list.

General The trust supports organisations benefiting Jewish people and also Jewish individuals. In 2002/03 its assets totalled £378,000 and it received an income of £46,000. Grants totalled £32,000. Types of charities which benefit from donations are educational, religious and other charitable organisations. Unfortunately a list of grants was not included in the accounts for this year.

Applications In writing to the correspondent.

The Ellerdale Trust

Children

£240,000 (2002/03)

Beneficial area Worldwide.

c/o Macfarlane & Co., Cunard Building, Water Street, Liverpool L3 1DS

Tel. 0151 236 6161

Correspondent The Trustees

Trustees *Simon Moores; Alistaire Macc; Paul Kurthausen.*

CC Number 1073376

Information available Accounts were on file at the Charity Commission.

General This trust was established to relieve poverty, distress or suffering in any part of the world particularly children who are disadvantaged or in need.

In 2002/03 the trust had assets of £4.4 million with an income of £224,000 and grants totalling £240,000.

The largest grants were £100,000 to NSPCC, £30,000 to Action for Kids, £20,000 each to Rainbow Centre, Psychiatric Research Trust and Mind, £15,000 to Barnardo's, £7,000 each to Martin House, Break and Childhope International, £3,000 each to National Association of Toys and Leisure, British Blind Sport, Angels International and Brainwave and £2,000 to National Deaf Children's Society.

Applications The trust's report stated that: 'The trustees are currently in the process of developing a distribution policy which will enable them to identify appropriate causes for support.'

The Ellinson Foundation Ltd

Jewish

£182,000 (2002/03)

Beneficial area Worldwide.

Messrs Robson Laidler & Co, Fernwood House, Fernwood Road, Jesmond, Newcastle upon Tyne NE2 1TJ

Tel. 0191 281 8191

Email ellinsonestates@aol.com

Correspondent Gerry Crichton

Trustees *C O Ellinson; Mrs E Ellinson; A Ellinson; A Z Ellinson; U Ellinson.*

CC Number 252018

Information available Full accounts were on file at the Charity Commission.

General The trust supports hospitals, education and homelessness in the UK and overseas, usually with a Jewish-teaching aspect. The trust regularly supports organisations such as boarding schools for boys and girls teaching the Torah.

In 2002/03 the trust had assets of £802,000 and an income of £370,000. Grants totalled £182,000.

Grants included £29,000 to Kollel Rabbi Yechiel (Ezras Torah), £18,000 to Gateshead Yeshiva L'Zeirim and £16,000 each to Friends of Neve Yurusholayim and Friends of Yeshivas Brisk.

Beneficiaries of £10,000 and under included Aish Hatorah Uk and World Jewish Relief (£10,000 each), Gateshead Hebrew Congregation and Society of Friends Torah (£9,000 each) and Beis Yaacov Matesdorf JLM and British Friends of Chazon Ish Institutions (£7,000 each).

Exclusions No grants to individuals.

Applications In writing to the correspondent. However, the trust generally supports the same organisations each year and unsolicited applications are not welcome.

The Edith M Ellis 1985 Charitable Trust

Quaker, ecumenical, education, peace and international affairs, general

About £30,000

Beneficial area UK, Ireland and overseas.

c/o Field Fisher Waterhouse, 35 Vine Street, London EC3N 2AA

Tel. 020 7481 4841

Correspondent The Clerk

Trustees *A P Honigmann; E H Milligan.*

CC Number 292835

Information available Accounts are on file at the Charity Commission but only up until 1996/97.

General The trust supports general charitable purposes including religious and educational projects (but not personal grants for religious or secular education nor grants for church buildings) and projects in international fields especially related to economic, social and humanitarian aid to developing countries. Ecumenical and Quaker interests.

Unfortunately only information up to 1996/97 is available from the Charity Commission, when the trust had an income of £49,000 and a total expenditure of £35,000. Research confirms that the trust still exists. Grants appear to total about £30,000 each year. A recent beneficiary of this trust was University of Southampton Faculty of Law which received a contribution towards a conference entitled 'Restorative and Community Justice: Inspiring the Future'.

Exclusions No grants to individuals.

Applications In writing to the correspondent. Telephone enquiries are not invited.

Elman Charitable Trust

Jewish charities

£54,000 (2002/03)

Beneficial area UK and Israel.

Laurence Homes (Eastern) Limited c/o, 14 Ruskin Close, Chilton Hall, Stowmarket, Suffolk IP14 1TY

Tel. 01449 771177

Correspondent Kenneth Elman, Trustee

Trustees *Charles Elman; Kenneth Elman; Colin Elman.*

CC Number 261733

Information available Basic accounts but no narrative report on file at the Charity Commission.

General The majority of the grants are given in Israel to organisations such as schools and hospitals. Jewish charities in the UK are also supported. In 2002/03 the trust gave grants totalling £54,000.

By far the largest grants were £10,000 to Shai Society and £7,500 to Norwood.

Other beneficiaries included Atidemi Fund, Neve Michael Children's Village and North London Hospice (£5,000 each), Joint Jewish Charitable Trust (£4,000), Wells Cathedral School (£2,000), Beth Ulpana–Torah Study Centre and British WIZO (£1,500 each) and Holocaust Educational Trust (£1,000).

Exclusions Grants are not usually given to individuals.

Applications In writing to the correspondent.

The Elmgrant Trust

General charitable purposes, education, arts, social sciences

£51,000 to organisations (2002/03)

Beneficial area UK, with a preference for the south west of England, occasionally abroad.

The Elmhirst Centre, Dartington Hall, Totnes, Devon TQ9 6EL

Tel. 01803 863160

Correspondent Angela Taylor, Secretary

Trustees *Marian Ash, Chair; Sophie Young; Paul Elmhirst; David Young; Mark Sharman.*

CC Number 313398

Information available Full accounts were provided by the trust.

General This trust has general charitable purposes, but in particular aims to encourage local life through education, the arts and social sciences. Although there is a preference for south west England, grants to organisations are awarded throughout the UK.

In 2002/03 the trust had assets of £1.7 million and an income of £74,000. Grants totalled £59,000, of which £51,000 was given to 64 organisations and £7,500 to 14 individuals. Grants were broken down as follows:

	2002/03	*2001/02*
Retraining grants	£24,000	£29,000
Education and educational research	£17,000	£16,000
Arts and arts research	£7,300	£7,000
Social sciences and scientific grants	£5,900	£17,000
Pension, donations and compassionate grants	£4,400	£5,000

The largest beneficiary receiving £25,000 was Devon and Cornwall Second Chance Trust (formerly Elmgrant Fellowships). Other beneficiaries included £2,000 each to Awards for Young Musicians, Rudolph Steiner School and Sands School, £1,300 to Curnow Community Special School and £1,000 each to Bicton College of Agriculture and Mounts Bay Luger Association.

Exclusions The following are not supported: large scale UK organisations; postgraduate study, overseas student grants, expeditions and travel and study projects overseas; counselling courses; renewed requests from the same (successful) applicant within a two-year period.

Applications In writing to the correspondent, giving full financial details and, where possible, a letter of support. Initial telephone calls are welcome if advice is needed. There are no application forms. Guidelines are issued. An sae would be very helpful, although this is not obligatory. Currently, meetings are held three times a year in March, June and October. Applications need to be received one clear month prior to meeting.

Elshore Ltd

Jewish

£365,000 (2002/03)

Beneficial area Worldwide.

10 West Avenue, London NW4 2LY

Tel. 020 8203 1726

Correspondent H Lerner, Trustee

Trustees *H M Lerner; A Lerner; S Yanofsky.*

CC Number 287469

Information available Accounts were on file at the Charity Commission, but without a full written report or a grants list.

General This trust appears to make grants solely to Jewish organisations. In 2002/03 it had an income of £60,000. Grants were made totalling £365,000. The trust's assets came to £74,000. A grants list was not included with the accounts for this year.

Further information has been unavailable since 1994/95, when grants to 40 beneficiaries totalled £178,000. The larger grants were £26,000 to Eminor Educational Centre and £20,000 to Cosmon Belz. Grants of £10,000 were given to 10 organisations, including Gur Trust and Marbe Torah Trust. Most other grants were less than £1,000, although some were for up to £8,000.

Applications In writing to the correspondent.

The Vernon N Ely Charitable Trust

Christian, welfare, disability, children and youth, overseas

£62,000 (2001/02)

Beneficial area Worldwide, with a preference for London borough of Merton.

Grosvenor Gardens House, 35–37 Grosvenor Gardens, London SW1W 0BY

Tel. 020 7828 3156 **Fax** 020 7630 7451

Correspondent Derek Howorth, Trustee

Trustees *J S Moyle; D P Howorth; R S Main.*

CC Number 230033

Information available Accounts were on file at the Charity Commission, but without a list of grants.

General The trust makes grants to Christian, welfare, disability, children, youth and overseas charities. Its 1997/98 annual report stated that the trust's policy had been reviewed during the year and it had been decided that the number of beneficiaries each year would be reduced, with larger grants being made.

In 2001/02 the trust had assets of £1.3 million and an income of £56,000. Grants were made totalling £62,000. Information regarding the size or number of beneficiaries was not available, except that a payment of £3,000 went to Helmores CA.

Exclusions No grants to individuals.

Applications In writing to the correspondent. Please note that the trust has previously stated that no funds are available.

Ralph and Muriel Emanuel Charity Trust

General in the UK

About £34,000 (2001/02)

Beneficial area UK.

61 Redington Road, London NW3 7RP

Correspondent Ralph N Emanuel, Trustee

Trustees *Ralph Neville Emanuel; Muriel Helena Emanuel; Maurice Seymour Emanuel; Sara Jane Emanuel.*

CC Number 266944

Information available Accounts were on file at the Charity Commission.

General This trust was established in 1974; grants are made at the trustees' discretion. In 2001/02 it had assets amounting to £293,000 and an income of £28,000. Grants totalled about £34,000, unfortunately, no list of grants was included with the accounts on file at the Charity Commission for that year.

In the previous year about 70 grants were made totalling more than £30,000, they were mainly for £250 or less. Beneficiaries included Age Concern – Camden, Almedia Theatre, Brighton Jewish Film Festival, Hampstead and Highgate Festival, Institute of Jewish Studies, Jewish Care, Manchester Jewish Museum, Royal College of Music, University of the Third Age and Youth Aliyah.

Applications In writing to the correspondent.

This entry was not confirmed by the trust, but the information was correct according to the Charity Commission.

The Emerging Markets Charity for Children

Children

£253,000 (2001)

Beneficial area Worldwide, with a preference for the developing world.

13 Clareville Grove, London SW7 5AU

Tel. 020 7244 9007

Correspondent Stephanie Field, Director

Trustees *S Field; E Littlefield; H Snell; A McLeod.*

CC Number 1030666

Information available Accounts are on file at the Charity Commission, but without a list of grants.

General The trust makes grants worldwide, with a preference for 'emerging markets' – probably the developing world. Grants are made for:

- relief of poverty, deprivation and distress
- advancement of education and training including establishing scholarships, prizes etc.
- other charitable causes.

In 2001 it had assets of £58,000 and a total income of £310,000. Grants totalled £253,000.

Applications In writing to the correspondent.

The Emerton-Christie Charity

Health, welfare, disability, arts

£74,000 (2001/02)

Beneficial area UK.

c/o Cartmell Shepherd, Viaduct House, Carlisle CA3 8EZ

Tel. 01228 516666

Correspondent The Trustees

Trustees *A F Niekirk; D G Richards; Dr N A Walker.*

CC Number 262837

Information available Full accounts were provided by the trust.

General The Emerton Charitable Settlement was established in 1971 by Maud Emerton, with additional funds subsequently added by Vera Bishop Emerton. In April 1996, it became the Emerton-Christie Charity following a merger with another trust, The Mrs C M S Christie Will Trust.

In 2001/02 it had assets totalling £2.1 million and an income of £69,000. Grants totalled £74,000.

Grants included £5,000 each to Eastleach PCC to help a youth worker and Knights of the Round Table Benevolent Fund for general purposes, £4,000 to Royal Academy of Music for General Purposes, £3,500 to Royal College of Music for educational bursaries and £2,000 each to Cambridge Arthritis Research, Hope and Homes for Children, Missions to Seafarers, RNLI and Sue Ryder Home – Ely, all for general purposes.

Exclusions Generally no grants to: individuals; religious organisations; restoration or extension of buildings; start-up costs; animal welfare and research; cultural heritage; or environmental projects.

Applications In writing to the correspondent. A demonstration of need based on budgetary principles is required and applications will not be acknowledged unless accompanied by an sae. Trustees normally meet once a year in the autumn to select charities to benefit.

The Emmandjay Charitable Trust

Social welfare, medicine, youth

£159,000 (2001/02)

Beneficial area UK, with a special interest in West Yorkshire.

PO Box 88, Otley, West Yorkshire LS21 3TE

Correspondent Mrs A E Bancroft, Administrator

Trustees *Mrs Sylvia Clegg; John A Clegg; Mrs S L Worthington; Mrs E A Riddell.*

CC Number 212279

Information available Full accounts were on file at the Charity Commission, but without a grants list.

General The trust was established in 1962 by Frederick Moore, his wife Elsie, and their daughter and son-in-law, Sylvia and John Clegg 'as a token of gratitude for the happiness given to them by their late daughter and grand-daughter'. It is a time charity: all remaining capital will be distributed to the descendants of the family in 50 years from 1962, or 21 years from the death of the last survivor of the descendants of George V, whichever is the sooner.

The trust gives 'most particularly to help disadvantaged people, but many different projects are supported – caring for the disabled, physically and mentally handicapped and terminally ill, work with young people and medical research. The trust likes projects which reach a lot of people. The trustees are keen that grants are actually spent'.

In 2001/02 the trust had assets of £3.4 million generating an income of £205,000. Grants totalled £159,000.

No grants list was included in the accounts, although it contained a breakdown of the areas in which it gives grants as follows:

Hospices, terminally ill, care	£33,000	£70,000
Youth activities, schools	£22,000	£17,000
Medical research	£6,000	£17,000
National charities	£51,000	£47,000
Special overseas appeals	£5,000	£5,000
Special schemes, workshops, disability	£12,000	£12,000
Homeless	£9,600	£15,000
Local community groups	£11,000	£11,000
Hospital appeals	Nil	£3,300
Social services, probation services	£3,300	£4,600
Counselling services	£1,000	£1,100
Children's charities and care	£500	£11,000
Housing associations	Nil	£10,000
Advice centres	£1,800	£600
Church, religious activities	£2,400	£1,500

Exclusions 'The trust does not pay debts, does not make grants to individual students, and does not respond to circulars.' Grants are only given, via social services, to individuals if they live in Bradford.

Applications In writing to the correspondent.

This entry was not confirmed by the trust but was correct according to information on file at the Charity Commission.

The English Schools' Football Association

Association football

£171,000 (2003)

Beneficial area England.

1–2 Eastgate Street, Stafford ST16 2NQ

Tel. 01785 251142 **Fax** 01785 255485

Email dawn.howard@schoolsfa.com

Website www.esfa.co.uk

Correspondent Ms D Howard

Trustees *G Smith; M R Duffield; P J Harding Chair.*

CC Number 306003

Information available Accounts and information provided by the association. Referees' charts, Guide to Teaching Soccer in Schools' International Honours List, History of ESFA and Handbooks are available.

General Support is given for the mental, moral and physical development and improvement of schoolchildren and students up to twenty years of age through the medium of association football. Assistance to teacher charities. General charitable purposes.

In 2003 the association had an income of £794,000 and a total expenditure of £864,000. A total of £171,000 was spent on sponsorships and tournament expenses.

Exclusions Grants are restricted to membership and teacher charities.

Applications In writing to the correspondent.

The EOS Foundation

Money advice provision/ individuals in need

Not known

Beneficial area England and Wales.

PO Box 42, Peterborough PE3 8XH

Tel. 01733 331177 **Fax** 01733 334344

Correspondent The Trustees

Trustees *Graham Blagden, Chair; Barbara Ruffell; Norman Guffick; Elizabeth Ingram; Stuart de Prochnow; John Sansby; Stephen Harrap; Valerie Mansfield.*

CC Number 1101072

Information available Information was provided by the trust.

General The foundation can help by giving grants to customers of the following companies Bournemouth and West Hampshire Water, Folkestone and Dover Water, Mid Kent Water, Portsmouth Water, South East Water and Tendring Hundred Water.

It can give grants to:

- clear or reduce arrears of domestic water charges
- help towards other essential domestic bills and costs. It is possible to apply for such help without applying for help with water charges.

Organisational grant programmes are also available. The direction of such programmes is dependent upon the availability of funds and the length of the commitment from doner companies. Many of the grants are awarded for money advice and debt management projects.

Exclusions No grants for: fines for criminal offences; educational or training needs; debts to central government departments; medical equipment, aids and adaptations; holidays; business debts; catalogues; credit cards; personal loans; deposits for secure accommodation; or overpayment of benefits.

Applications In writing to the correspondent.

The Epigoni Trust

Health & welfare, disability, homelessness, addiction, children who are disadvantaged, environment

£110,000 (2002)

Beneficial area UK.

Charities Aid Foundation, King's Hill, West Malling, Kent ME19 4TA

Tel. 01732 520083 **Fax** 01732 520159

Correspondent Mrs Sue David, Donor Grants Officer

Trustees *H Peacock; Mrs Bettine Bond; A M Bond.*

CC Number 328700

Information available Full accounts were provided by the trust.

General The trust has common trustees with two other trusts, Cleopatra Trust and Dorus Trust (see separate entries) with which it also shares the same aims and policies. All three trusts are administered by Charities Aid Foundation. Generally the trusts support different organisations.

The trust makes grants in the following areas:

- mental health
- cancer welfare/education – not research
- diabetes
- physical disability – not research
- homelessness
- addiction
- children who are disadvantaged.

There is also some preference for environmental causes. It only gives grants for specific projects and does not give grants for running costs or general appeals. Support is only given to national projects, not local areas or initiatives.

In 2002 it had assets of £3 million, which generated an income of £106,000. Grants to 33 organisations totalled £110,000.

The largest were £10,000 to Council of Milton Abbey School, £6,000 to Royal National Institute for Deaf People, £5,000 each to Action on Elder Abuse, Care Alliance, Family Nurturing Network, Listening Books, National Asthma Campaign, Roundhouse Trust, St Richard's Hospital Charitable Trust and Starlight Children's Foundation and £4,000 each to Marie Curie Cancer Care and Lifeline Project.

Other beneficiaries included Cystic Fibrosis Trust and Manic Depression Fellowship (£3,000 each), Weston Spirit (£2,800), Victim Support (£2,500), Contact a Family and National Blind Children's Society (£2,000 each), Reality at Work in Scotland (£1,000) and Harvest Trust (£540).

Exclusions No grants to individuals, expeditions, research, scholarships, charities with a local focus, local branches of UK charities or towards running costs.

Applications On an application form available from the correspondent. Applications should include a copy of the latest audited annual report and accounts. They are considered twice a year in mid-summer and mid-autumn. Organisations which have received grants from this trust, Cleopatra Trust or Dorus Trust should not reapply in the following two years. Usually, funding will be considered from only one of these trusts.

Epilepsy Research Foundation

Epilepsy.

£192,000 (2002)

Beneficial area UK.

PO Box 3004, London W4 4XT

Tel. 020 8995 4781 **Fax** 020 8995 4781

Email info@erf.org.uk

Website www.erf.org.uk

Correspondent Isabella von Holstein, Research and Information Executive

Trustees *B Akin; Prof. F Besag; Prof. C Binnie; Prof. S Brown; Mrs J Cochrane; Dr H Cross; Prof. G Harding; Dr J Mumford; Dr J Oxley; Prof. A Richens; M Stevens.*

CC Number 326836

Information available A newsletter, annual report and synopsis of research funded to date are available.

General The trust supports researchers conducting studies that will benefit people with epilepsy. Grants are available only for basic and clinical scientific research in the field of epilepsy.

In 2002 the trust had assets of £524,000 and an income of £350,000. Grants totalled £192,000 and included: £57,000 to an individual at King's College for research into neuronal discharge patterns in human symptomatic epilepsy; £52,000 (over two years) to an individual at the Institute of Child Health, London for research into speech and language after hemispherectomy in childhood: a combined neuropsychological and neuroimaging investigation; £3,000 to Great Ormond Street Hospital for equipment to enable a comparison of wireless protocols with cable-based techniques for EEG telemetry for epilepsy.

Exclusions Research not undertaken within a recognised institute in the UK.

Applications Applications for the annual grant round are invited in October. Full details are available on www.erf.org.uk

The Equity Trust Fund

Theatre

£68,000 to organisations (2003/04)

Beneficial area UK.

222 Africa House, 64 Kingsway, London WC2B 6AH

Tel. 020 7404 6041 **Fax** 020 7831 4953

Email keith@equitytrustfund.freeserve.co.uk

Correspondent Keith Carter, Secretary

Trustees *Milton Johns; Jeffrey Wickham; Nigel Davenport; Gillian Raine; Peter Plouviez; Derek Bond; Frank Williams; Ian McGarry; Colin Baker; Barbara Hyslop; Annie Bright; Graham Hamilton; Harry Landis; Frederik Pyne; Rosalind Shanks; Johnny Worthy; Frank Hitchman; James Bolam; Imogen Claire; John Rubinstein; Ian Talbot; Josephine Tewson; Robin Browne; Oliver Ford Davies; Jean Rogers.*

CC Number 328103

Information available Information was provided by the trust.

General The charity is a benevolent fund for professional performers and stage managers and their dependants. It offers help with welfare rights, gives free debt counselling and information and can offer financial assistance to those in genuine need. It also has an education fund to help members of the profession with further training provided they have at least 10 years' professional adult experience. It also makes grants and loans to professional theatres or theatre companies.

In 2003/04 the trust had assets of £7.5 million and an income of £350,000. Grants to organisations totalled £68,000 and a further £159,000 was given in 112 grants to individuals.

Exclusions No grants to non-professional performers, drama students, non-professional theatre companies, multi-arts venues, community projects or projects with no connection to the professional theatre.

Applications In the first instance please call the office to ascertain if the application is relevant. Failing that, submit a brief letter outlining the application. A meeting takes place about every six to eight weeks. Ring for precise dates. Applications are required at least two weeks beforehand.

The Ericson Trust

See below

£39,000 (2002/03)

Beneficial area UK, developing countries, Eastern and Central Europe.

Flat 2, 53 Carleton Road, London N7 0ET

Tel. 020 7607 8333

Correspondent Ms C Cotton, Trustee

Trustees *Miss R C Cotton; Mrs V J Barrow; Mrs A M C Cotton.*

CC Number 219762

Information available Full accounts were on file at the Charity Commission.

General The trust provides grants to previously supported organisations in the following fields: (a) older people; (b) community projects/local interest groups, including arts; (c) prisons, prison reform, mentoring projects, as well as research in this area; (d) refugees; (e) mental health; (f) environmental projects and research; and (g) aid to developing countries provided by a UK-registered charity.

In 2002/03 it had assets of £475,000 and an income of £21,000. Grants were made to 15 organisations and totalled £39,000.

These were £4,000 each to Ashram International, Minority Rights Group International and Psychiatric Rehabilitation Association, £3,900 to Relatives and Residents Association, £3,000 each to CAMFED, Development Organisation of Rural Sichuan, One World Action and Quaker Social Action, £2,000 each to Anti-Slavery International, Geese Theatre Company, Howard League for Penal Reform, Praxis Community Projects and Tools for Self-Reliance, £1,000 to Tools for Self-Reliance – Middlesbrough and £500 to Koestler Award Trust.

Exclusions No grants to individuals or to non-registered charities. Applications from the following areas are generally not considered unless closely connected with one of the above: children's and young people's clubs, centres and so on; schools; charities dealing with illness or disability (except psychiatric); or religious institutions, except in their social projects.

Applications Unsolicited applications cannot be considered as the trust has no funds available. The correspondent stated: 'We are increasing worried by the waste of applicants' resources when they send expensive brochures at a time when we are unable to consider any new appeals and have, indeed, reduced some of our long standing grants due to the bad economic situation. It is particularly sad when we receive requests from small charities in Africa and Asia.'

The Euroclydon Trust

Christian

£57,000 (2002/03)

Beneficial area UK and worldwide.

UKET, PO Box 99, Loughton, Essex LG10 3QJ

Correspondent Stewardship Services

Trustees *United Kingdom Evangelical Trust (UKET); Leslie Lucas.*

CC Number 290382

Information available Full accounts were provided by the trust.

General In 2002/03 this trust had assets of £1.6 million, which generated an income of £67,000. Grants were made totalling £57,000.

By far the largest grant, of £20,000, went to Missionary Aviation Fellowship. Other beneficiaries included Covenantors with Christ (£9,400), Ambassadors for Christ (£4,500), Timothy Trust (£4,200), Echoes of Service (£4,000), London Institute of Contemporary Christianity (£2,800), Langham Trust (£2,400), Mill Grove Children's Home and Prison Fellowship (£1,900 each), Yeldhall Christian Centre (£1,700), Jubilee Care (£1,400), The 40–3 Trust (£1,300), Tearfund (£1,100) and Evangelical Alliance (£750).

Applications The trust states that applications are not invited.

The Evangelical Covenants Trust

Christian evangelism

£51,000 (2001/02)

Beneficial area UK, with a preference for Devon.

Mardon, 188b Exeter Road, Exmouth, Devon EX8 3DZ

Tel. 01392 273287

Email ect@tarrings.freeserve.co.uk

Correspondent Alfred W Tarring, Trustee

Trustees *C Desmond Gahan; Alfred W Tarring; Kathleen M Tarring.*

CC Number 285224

Information available Accounts were provided by the trust, but without a list of grants.

General The objects of this trust is to distribute funds to Christian organisations of an evangelical nature, although any charitable cause will be considered. In 2001/02 the trust had assets of £15,000 and an income of £51,000, coming mostly from covenants and Gift Aid donations. A total of £51,000 was given in grants.

Grants are distributed on a UK basis, but with the majority of donors living in Devon – in 2001/02 42% of all gifts were distributed to churches in the county. Unfortunately no further details were available on beneficiaries.

Applications Unsolicited applications are not considered: 'Grants are made only on the request and recommendation of donors of the trust.'

The Alan Evans Memorial Trust

Preservation, conservation

£215,000 (2002/03)

Beneficial area UK.

Coutts & Co., Trustee Department, PO Box 1236, 6 High Street, Chelmsford, Essex CM13 1BQ

Tel. 0207 753 1000

Correspondent The Trust Manager

Trustees *Coutts & Co.; D J Halfhead; Mrs D Moss.*

CC Number 326263

Information available Full accounts were on file at the Charity Commission.

General The objects of the trust 'are to promote the permanent preservation, for the benefit of the nation, of lands and tenements (including buildings) of beauty or historic interest and as regards land, the preservation (so far as practicable) of the natural aspect, features and animal and plant life'.

In 2002/03 the trust had assets of £2.5 million and an income of £125,000. After administration and management costs of £55,000, grants totalled £215,000.

A total of 123 grants, ranging from £6,250 to £1,000, were given to various UK and local countryside, environmental and restoration organisations. Beneficiaries included St Mary's Church (£6,250), Church of All Saints (£5,000), Sheffield Cathedral and Green Light Trust (£3,000 each), Kent Wildlife Trust, Merchant House Trust and Norfolk Wildlife Trust (£2,000 each).

Over half the grants made ranged between £1,500 and £1,000 and were mainly given to a number of church and cathedrals throughout the country. Other beneficiaries included Dorset Wildlife Trust, Gaia Trust, Gordon Community Woodland Association, Purbeck Vineyard, Ripon Museum Trust and RSPB (£1,000 each).

Charitable payments less than £1,000 totalled £18,000 and beneficiaries are not listed in the accounts.

Exclusions No grants to individuals or for management or running expenses, although favourable consideration is given in respect of the purchase of land and restoration of buildings. Grants are given to registered charities only. Appeals will not be acknowledged.

Applications There is no formal application form, but appeals should be made in writing to the correspondent, stating why the funds are required, what funds have been promised from other sources (for example, English Heritage) and the amount outstanding. The trust also told us that it would be helpful when making applications to provide a photograph of the project. Trustees normally meet four times a year, although in urgent cases decisions can be made between meetings.

The Eventhall Family Charitable Trust

General

£108,000 (2002/03)

Beneficial area Preference for north west England.

PO Box 490, Altrincham WA14 22T

Correspondent The Trustees

Trustees *Julia Eventhall; David Eventhall.*

CC Number 803178

Information available Accounts were on file at the Charity Commission, but without a grants list.

General In 2002/03 the trust had assets of £1.8 million and an income of £217,000. Grants to 80 charities totalled £108,000. The largest grant went to Bowdon Synagogue Trust. Further information for this year was not available.

In previous years other beneficiaries have included Aish Hatorah, ChildLine, Clitheroe Wolves Football Club, Community Security Trust, Greibach Memorial, Guide Dogs for the Blind, Heathlands Village, International Wildlife Coalition, JJCT, MB Foundation Charity, Only Foals and Horses Sanctuary, Red Nose Day, RNLI, Sale Ladies Society, Shelter and South Manchester Synagogue.

Exclusions No grants to students.

Applications In writing to the correspondent. Please note, however, that the trust stated it only has a very limited amount of funds available. Telephone calls are not accepted by the trust. Trustees meet monthly to consider grants. A pre-addressed envelope is appreciated (stamp not necessary). Unsuccessful applicants will not receive a reply.

The Evergreen Foundation

General

£277,000 (2000/01)

Beneficial area UK and North America.

14 Park Place Villas, London W2 1SP

Tel. 020 7627 3373

Email warner@shonda.demon.co.uk

Correspondent Ms S K Warner, Chair

Trustees *Ms S K Warner, Chair; N Losse.*

CC Number 1072519

Information available Accounts are on file at the Charity Commission.

General In 2000/01 the trust had assets of £709,000 and an income of £16,000. Grants totalled £277,000. Unlike the previous year which saw the trust make donations to 15 beneficiaries, in 2001 there was one recipient, the John Armitage Charitable Trust.

Applications In writing to the correspondent.

The Norman Evershed Trust

Christian, famine relief

£196,000 (2002/03)

Beneficial area UK and overseas.

35 Lemsford Road, St Albans, Hertfordshire AL1 3PP

Tel. 01727 852019

Correspondent Mrs C A Evershed, Trustee

Trustees *Mrs J S Evershed; R J Evershed; Mrs C A Evershed; G P Smith.*

CC Number 271318

Information available Full accounts were on file at the Charity Commission.

General The trust supports organisations which are known to the trustees in the fields of Christian work, disaster relief, developing countries, drug and alcohol abuse, cancer research and mental disability. The 2002/03 accounts stated that the trustees were intending to distribute all the funds and close the trust by April 2008.

In 2002/03 it had assets of £747,000, which generated an income of £3,300. Grants to 19 organisations totalled £196,000. A further £1,500 was given in total to four individuals.

The largest grants were £35,000 each to Christchurch Harpenden and Evangelicals Now and £20,000 to Radstock Ministries. Other large grants were £11,000 to Woodlands School and £10,000 each to Compass Christian Centre, Spicer Street International Chapel and UCCF for the Life Project.

Smaller grants were £3,000 each to Gideons International, London Bible College, UCCF and Wycliffe Bible Translators, £2,000 to Sight Savers International and £1,000 each to All Nations Christian College, Beeston Evangelical Free Church, Christians in Sport for the Golf Ministry, Hope Now Ministry, Mission to Seafarers, Oak Hill Theological College and Romanian Missionary Society.

Applications In writing to the correspondent. However, the trust states: 'No applications should be made: the funds are all committed.'

The Beryl Evetts & Robert Luff Animal Welfare Trust

Animal welfare

£90,000 (2001/02)

Beneficial area UK.

294 Earls Court Road, London SW5 9BB

Tel. 020 8954 2727

Correspondent The Administrator

Trustees *Sir R Johnson; Revd M Tomlinson; Mrs J Tomlinson; R P J Price; B Nicholson; Lady Johnson; Ms G Favot.*

CC Number 283944

Information available Full accounts were on file at the Charity Commission.

General The principal objective of the trust is the funding of veterinary research and the care and welfare of animals. It appears to make substantial commitments to a few organisations over several years, whether to build up capital funds or to establish fellowships. The trust gives priority to research projects and bursaries. In practice, the trust supports the same beneficiaries each year.

In 2001/02 the trust had assets of £1.3 million with an income of £67,000 and grants totalling £90,000.

Grants include £35,000 each to Animal Health Trust (Grant payment) and Royal Veterinary College and £10,000 each to Animal Health Trust and Mayhew Trust.

Applications 'No applications, thank you.' The trust gives grants to the same beneficiaries each year and funds are often allocated two years in advance.

The Exilarch's Foundation

Jewish

£51,000 (2002)

Beneficial area Mainly UK.

4 Carlos Place, Mayfair, London W1K 3AW

Tel. 020 7399 0850 **Fax** 020 7399 0860

Correspondent His Highness the Exilarch , Trustees

Trustees *N E Dangoor; D A Dangoor; E B Dangoor; R D Dangoor; M J Dangoor.*

CC Number 275919

Information available Information was on file at the Charity Commission.

General In 2002 the trust had significantly increased assets of £28 million (£17 million) and it had an income of £5.5 million, comprising mainly donations (£3.6 million) and investment income (£1.9 million). The trust seems to be currently using most of its income to increase its assets and after management and administration costs of £16,000, grants were made totalling £51,000 (£408,000 in 2000).

Beneficiaries included Friends of Hazon Yeshaya (£6,800), Spanish and Portuguese Jews Congregation (£3,700), Cambridge University Jewish Society (£3,000), Youth Aliyah Child Rescue (£2,000) and Jewish Child's Day (£1,000). A further £20,000 was given in grants less than £1,000 each.

Applications The trust stated that it does not respond to unsolicited applications for grants.

The Fairway Trust

General

About £55,000 (2001/02)

Beneficial area UK and worldwide.

The Gate House, Coombe Wood Road, Kingston-upon-Thames, Surrey KT2 7JY

Correspondent Mrs J Grimstone, Trustee

Trustees *Mrs Janet Grimstone; Ms K V M Suenson-Taylor.*

CC Number 272227

Information available Accounts were on file at the Charity Commission.

General The trust's objects are to support:

- universities, colleges and schools in the UK and overseas
- religious purposes (including the promotion of religion and supporting clergy)
- clubs and recreational facilities for children and young people
- preservation and maintenance of buildings of particular historical, artistic and architectural interest
- scholarships and grants to postgraduates and undergraduates.

Social welfare charities are also supported.

In 2001/02 the trust had an income of £36,000 and a total expenditure of £58,000. Most of its total expenditure is usually spent on grants. No information was available on the size or number of beneficiaries during the year.

The trust has previously had a slight preference for north-west England. Previous beneficiaries include British and International Sailors' Society, Family Education Trust and Riverside Housing Association. Many of the organisations receiving large grants have previously been supported by the trust.

Exclusions No grants to medical charities.

Applications In writing to the correspondent, althought the trust states 'as funds and office resources are limited it cannot be guaranteed that unsolicited applications will be answered'.

The Family Foundations Trust (also known as Mintz Family Foundation)

General, Jewish

£217,000 (2002/03)

Beneficial area UK.

Gerald Edelman, 25 Harley Street, London W1G 9BR

Tel. 020 7299 1400

Correspondent Simon Hosier, Accountant to the Trustees

Trustees *R B Mintz; P G Mintz.*

CC Number 264014

Information available Full accounts were on file at the Charity Commission.

General In 2002/03 the trust's assets totalled £629,000 and it had an income of £208,000. Grants to 47 organisations totalled £217,000. Beneficiaries were mainly Jewish organisations.

The largest grants were £50,000 to JFS General Charitable Trust, £35,000 to Bar Ilan University, £27,000 to United Jewish Israel Appeal, £20,500 to Jewish Care, £13,000 to Community Security Trust and £10,000 to Chief Rabbi Charitable Trust.

Other larger grants included £6,800 to Western Marble Arch Synagogue, £5,400 to Lubavitch Foundation, £5300 to World Jewish Relief and £5,000 to British ORT.

There were a further 37 grants made of under £5,000 each.

Applications In writing to the correspondent.

Famos Foundation Trust

Jewish

£81,000 (2002/03)

Beneficial area UK and overseas.

4 Hanover Gardens, Salford, Lancashire M7 4FQ

Correspondent Rabbi S M Kupetz, Trustee

Trustees *Rabbi S M Kupetz; Mrs F Kupetz.*

CC Number 271211

Information available Information was provided by the trust.

General The trust supports a wide range of Jewish organisations, including those concerned with education and the relief of poverty. Many grants are recurrent and are of up to £5,000 each. In 2002/03 it had assets of £884,000 and an income of £83,000. Grants totalled £81,000. Unfortunately further information was not available.

Exclusions No grants to individuals.

Applications In writing to the correspondent, at any time. The trust does not accept telephone enquiries.

The Lord Faringdon Charitable Trust

Medical, general

£132,000 (2002/03)

Beneficial area UK.

The Estate Office, Buscot Park, Oxfordshire SN7 8BU

Tel. 01367 240786 **Fax** 01367 241794

Correspondent J R Waters, Secretary to the Trustees

Trustees *A D A W Forbes, Chair; Hon. J H Henderson; R P Trotter.*

CC Number 1084690

Information available Full accounts were provided by the trust.

General This trust was formed in 2000 by the amalgamation of the Lord Faringdon first and second trusts. It supports:

- educational objectives
- hospitals and the provision of medical treatment for the sick
- purchase of antiques and artistic objects for museums and collections that have public access
- care and assistance of people who are elderly or infirm
- development and assistance of arts and sciences, physical recreation and drama
- research into matters of public interest
- relief of poverty
- support of matters of public interest
- maintaining and improving the Faringdon Collection.

In 2002/03 it had assets of £3.9 million, which generated an income of £147,000. Grants to 45 organisations totalled £132,000.

The largest were £36,000 to Oxford's Youth Music Trust, £15,000 to Faringdon Collection Trust, £10,000 to National Trust Centenary and Millennium Fund, Oxford Diocesan Board of Finance, £6,300 to Royal Opera House Foundation and £5,000 each to Faringdon Pre-School, Farmors School – Fairford and Stowe House Preservation Trust.

Smaller grants included £2,500 to Sir Harold Hillier Gardens and Arboretum, £2,000 each to British Wheelchair Sports Foundation, Burlington Magazine and Wonderful Beast, £1,500 to Book Aid International, £1,000 each to Chelsea Physic Garden, Milbrook County Primary School, Oxford Philomusica Trust and Oxford Radcliffe Hospital Charitable Trust, £500 each to Artificial Heart Fund, Fairford Youth Orchestra, Guideposts Trust and Thamesdown Hydrotherapy Pool Association and £250 to Macmillan Cancer Relief – Berkshire.

Exclusions No grants to individuals, just to registered charities.

Applications In writing to the correspondent.

Samuel William Farmer's Trust

Education, health, social welfare

£64,000 (2002)

Beneficial area Mainly Wiltshire.

Tanglewood, 33 The Fairway, Devizes, Wiltshire SN10 5DX

Correspondent Mrs J Simpson

Trustees *Mrs J A Liddiard; W J Rendell; P G Fox-Andrews; B J Waight; D Brockis.*

CC Number 258459

Information available Accounts were provided by the Trust.

General The trust was established in 1928 for: the benefit of poor people who through ill health or old age are unable to earn their own livelihood; for educational purposes; and for the benefit of hospitals, nursing and convalescent homes or other similar objects. The trustees apply a modern interpretation of these aims when assesing applications, supporting both individuals and organisations.

In 2002 the trust had assets of £1.6 million and an income of £76,000. Grants for this year totalled £64,000, of which £7,000 were annual grants given to 3 organisations including Royal Agricultural Benevolent Institution and Royal United Kingdom Beneficent Association (£3,000 each) and Barnardos (£1,000).

Special grants went to 19 organisations, 6 of which had received grants in previous years. The largest beneficaries included Dauntseys School Biology Block Appeal (£15,000), Wiltshire & Swindon Community Foundation (£10,000) and Wiltshire Air Ambulance Association (£9,000). Other beneficaries included St Mary's Almshouses – Devizes and Prospect Hospice (£3,000 each), Larkrise Community Farm and Enford Youth Club (£2,000 each), Motor Neurone Disease Association, Dauntsey's School Foundation and Stroke Association (£1,000 each) and Enford PCC (£250).

Exclusions No grants to students, or for schools and colleges, endowments, inner-city welfare or housing.

Applications In writing to the correspondent. Trustees meet in April and October.

Farthing Trust

Christian, general

£199,000 to organisations (2001/02)

Beneficial area UK and overseas.

48 Ten Mile Bank, Littleport, Ely, Cambridgeshire CB6 1EF

Tel. 01353 860 586

Correspondent The Trustees

Trustees *C H Martin; Mrs E Martin; Miss J Martin; Mrs A White.*

CC Number 268066

Information available Accounts were on file at the Charity Commission.

General In 2001/02 the trust had a grant total of £199,000. Further information was unavailable. Grants were broken down as follows:

Christian workers (active)	£32,000
Christian workers (retired)	£3,400
Christian organisations (overseas)	£28,000
Christian organisations (UK)	£52,000
General causes (UK)	£6,600
Local causes	£4,400
"Individuals in need" (UK & Overseas)	£72,000

Organisations supported included Arab World Ministries, Books Abroad, CARE, City Farms & Thetford garden, Good News + Prison Aid, KatweStreetChildren, Message Tribe Trust, OpenDoors, Prisoners Abroad, TELIT and World Focus.

Applications Applications and enquiries should be made in writing to the correspondent. Applicants, and any others requesting information, will only receive a response if an sae is enclosed. There would seem little point in applying unless a personal contact with a trustee is established.

The Fawcett Charitable Trust

Disability

£135,000 (2002/03)

Beneficial area UK, but preference given to Hampshire and West Sussex.

Blake Lapthorn, Harbour Court, Compass Road, North Harbour, Portsmouth, Hampshire PO6 4ST

Tel. 023 9222 1122

Correspondent Céline Lecomte

Trustees *D J Fawcett; Mrs F P Fawcett; D W Russell.*

CC Number 1013167

Information available Information was provided by the trust.

General The trust was set up in 1991 by Derek and Frances Fawcett with an endowment of shares in their company with an initial value of £1.6 million. In recent years the annual income from the fund has averaged about £100,000.

According to the trust, it supports work aimed at increasing the quality of life of disabled people by facilitating and providing recreation opportunities. Preference is normally given to organisations and projects located in Hampshire and West Sussex. Outstanding deserving UK initiatives are also supported such as Sense.

The trust is, however, currently devoting its charitable support to RYA Sailability and funds are not available to other organisations.

In 2002/03 it had assets of £1.5 million, an income of about £80,000 and gave £135,000 in grants, presumably all to RYA Sailability.

Exclusions Large national charities are excluded as a rule.

Applications Until further notice the trust is closed to new applications for the reasons given in the general section.

The John Feeney Charitable Bequest

Arts, general

£36,000 (2004)

Beneficial area Birmingham.

Cobbetts Solicitors, One Colmore Square, Birmingham B4 6AJ

Tel. 0845 404 2404

Correspondent M J Woodward, Secretary

Trustees *Mrs M Martineau; Charles R King-Farlow; Derek M P Lea; S J Lloyd; P W Welch; Mrs M F Lloyd; H B Carslake; Ms A Bhalla; J R Smith; M S Darby; Mrs S R Wright.*

CC Number 214486

Information available Information was provided by the trust.

General The trust was set up in 1907 when John Feeney directed that one tenth of his residue estate be invested and the income used for the benefit of public charities in the city of Birmingham, for the promotion and cultivation of art in the city and for the acquisition and maintenance of parks, recreation grounds or open spaces in or near the city.

In 2004 it gave grants totalling £36,000, broken down as follows:

Arts – 6 grants totalling £3,600

These grants went towards a book on the Feeney family (£1,250), Royal Birmingham Society of Artists Development Fund (£1,000), Birmingham Arts Marketing (£500) and Adeoti Arts & Crafts, Big Brum Theatre in Education Co and Hocus Pocus Theatre Group (£300 each).

Music – 5 grants totalling £5,100

CBSO Schools' Roadshow and City of Birmingham Choir (£1,500 each), Birmingham Bach Choir (£1,000), Midland Youth Orchestra (£600) and Birmingham Music Festival (£500).

Open spaces – 1 grant totalling £500

Castle Bromwich Hall Gardens Trust (£500)

Children and young people: Medical – 4 grants totalling £2,500

Edward's Trust (£1,000) and Arthritis Research Campaign, Edgbaston, Foundation for Conductive Education and Pioneer Centre (£500 each)

Children and young people: General – 10 grants totalling £6,600

Birmingham Federation of Clubs for Young People, Chrysalis Club 2000 and King Edward VI School Handsworth and Second City-Second Chance Care (£1,000 each), Birmingham Phab Camps, ComAc Kids Adventure-BUGS, Dodford Children's Holiday Farm and Priority Area Playgroups (£500 each) and Birmingham Guiding Association and St Martin's Youth and Community Centre (£300 each).

General: Medical – 7 grants totalling £5,500

These were £1,000 to BID Services with Deaf People, Cope Black Mental Health Foundation, Queen Alexandra College and St Mary's Hospice (£1,000 each) and Autism West Midlands, MSA and STIRF (£500 each).

General – General: 9 grants totalling £12,000

Birmingham Settlement (£5,000), St Paul's Church Appeal (£2,000), Birmingham Conservation Trust and East Birmingham Family Service Unit (£1,000 each), Cruse Bereavement Care (£800) and Birmingham & District African Caribbean Community, City of Birmingham Special Olympics, Phoenix Sheltered Workshop and Summerfield Care and Repair Project (£500).

Exclusions No support for causes which could be considered as political or denominational.

Applications In writing to the correspondent by March of each year.

There is no application form and no sae is required.

The A M Fenton Trust

General

£130,000 (2002)

Beneficial area UK, preference for North Yorkshire, and overseas.

14 Beech Grove, Harrogate, North Yorkshire HG2 0EX

Correspondent J L Fenton, Trustee

Trustees *J L Fenton; C M Fenton.*

CC Number 270353

Information available Full accounts were on file at the Charity Commission.

General The trust was created by Alexander Miller Fenton in 1975. After his death in 1977, the residue of his estate was transferred to the trust.

In 2002 the trust had assets of £2.9 million and an income of £128,000. Grants totalled £130,000. The largest grant was £20,000 to Yorkshire County Cricket Club Charitable Youth Trust. Grants of £10,000 each went to Cancer Research UK, Hipperholme Grammar School and Ripon Cathedral Development. Other beneficiaries included Dewsbury League of Friendship (£7,500), Order of St John and St Thomas the Apostle – Batley (£5,000 each), Disability Action Yorkshire (£4,000) and Tweed Foundation and Woodhead Mountain Rescue Team (£3,000 each).

Smaller grants were made to British Heart Foundation, Crime Stoppers Trust and Horticap (£1,000 each), Harold Styan Charity for Youth (£750), Royal National Lifeboat Institute, Age Concern Knaresborough and Help at Home Scheme (£500 each) and Song Bird Survival (£200).

A small number of grants are given to individuals, usually for educational purposes. The trust stated, however, that it is unlikely to fund student gap years.

Exclusions The trust is unlikely to support local appeals, unless they are close to where the trust is based.

Applications In writing to the correspondent.

Elizabeth Hardie Ferguson Charitable Trust Fund

Children, medical research, health, hospices

£46,000 (1998/99)

Beneficial area UK, with some interest in Scotland.

6 Union Row, Aberdeen AB10 1DQ

Correspondent Ted Way, Secretary

Trustees *Sir Alex Ferguson; Cathy Ferguson; Huw Roberts; Ted Way; Les Dalgarno.*

SC Number SC026240

Information available Information was provided by the trust.

General Unfortunately we were unable to contact this trust and entry is repeated from previous research.

This trust was created by Sir Alex Ferguson in 1998 in memory of his mother. It supports a range of children's and medical charities. In 1998/99 the trust gave £46,000 to children's charities, medical research and hospices. Grants range from £250 to £10,000 and can be recurrent. Various high-profile events, including concerts by Simply Red, premieres of 'Spiceworld the Movie' in Glasgow and Manchester, and a dinner hosted by Chinese chef Ken Hom have contributed to the trust's income. Grants are distributed in the areas where the income is raised.

Charities supported by the founder in his home town of Govan will be continued to be supported through the trust. Recent beneficiaries have included The Govan Initiative and The Harmony Row Boys' Club in Govan.

Exclusions Non-registered charities and individuals are not supported. The trust does not make grants overseas.

Applications An application form and guidelines should be requested in writing from the correspondent. The committee meets to consider grants at the end of January and July. Applications should be received by December and June respectively.

The Fidelity UK Foundation

General

£644,000 (2003)

Beneficial area Particular preference is given to projects in Kent, Surrey, London and continental Europe, where Fidelity Investments has an office.

Oakhill House, 130 Tonbridge Road, Hildenborough, Tonbridge, Kent TN11 9DZ

Tel. 01732 361144 **Fax** 01732 838143

Website www.fidelityukfoundation.org

Correspondent Miss Jacqueline Guthrie

Trustees *Edward C Johnson; Barry Bateman; Anthony Bolton; Martin Cambridge; Robert Milotte; Richard Millar.*

CC Number 327899

Information available Guidelines for applications and accounts were provided by the trust.

General The trust aims to encourage the highest standards of management and long-term self-reliance in non-profit organisations. It gives to registered charities and some exempt charities, such as certain schools. Particular preference is given to projects in Kent, Surrey, London and continental Europe, where Fidelity Investments have offices. Giving is primarily allocated to the following sectors: community development, health, arts and culture, and education.

The trust seeks to support projects undertaken by organisations to increase proficiency, achieve goals and reach long-term self-sufficiency. Most often this entails major projects such as capital improvements, technology upgrades, organisational development and planning initiatives. The trust will assess an organisation to determine whether its collaboration and investment can add value. Among the factors considered are:

- the organisation's financial health
- the strength of its management team and board
- evidence of an overall strategic plan.

It also looks at the size and scope of an organisation, evaluating its position within the context of its market and the needs of the constituents it serves. The trust ultimately seeks to understand the potential returns of a project and seeks evidence of:

- instrumental commitment to the project on behalf of the organisation's board
- a realistic project budget
- a thorough implementation plan, including a plan for performance measurement
- net value to the organisation and the community it serves
- significant support from other funders.

In 2003 the trust had assets of £24.6 million and an income of £4.9 million. After management and administration costs of £159,000 grants were made totalling £644,000 and were broken down as follows:

Community – 13 grants totalling £284,000

Large grants were to Number One Twin Communities Trust and The Samaritans (£50,000 each), Special Olympics (£45,000), Grange (£40,000), Who Cares Trust (£30,000), All Saints' Benhilton Granfers and RPS Rainer (£15,000 each) and Council for Voluntary Services, ((£10,000). Other beneficiaries included Surrey Oaks NHS Trust and Furniture New (£5,000 each), Remap (£4,500), Defeating Deafness (£3,500), Age Concern (£2,000) and Kent Wildlife Trust (£1,000).

Education – 6 grants totalling £73,000

Beneficiaries were Chicken Shed Theatre (£25,000), Worldwide Volunteering (£20,000), New Philanthropy Capital (£15,000), London Sinfonietta (£6,000), Tower Hamlets Education Business Partnership (£5,000) and Clarendon School (£2,000)

Arts and Culture – 6 grants totalling £230,000

Beneficiaries were Bletchley Park Trust (£75,000), Camden Arts Centre (£60,000), Museum of London (£50,000), Sir John Soane's Museum (£25,000), London Musici and Edinburgh Botanical Gardens (£10,000 each)

Health – 3 grants totalling £57,000

Grants went to Bromley Autistic Trust and Trinity Hospice (£20,000 each), Hospice in the Weald (£13,000) and St Joseph's Hospice (£4,400).

Exclusions Grants are not made for sponsorships or benefit events, scholarships, corporate membership, advertising and promotional projects or exhibitions.

Grants are not generally made to: start-up cost, sectarian, or political organisations; private schools and colleges or universities; or individuals.

Generally grants are not made for running costs, but may be considered on an individual basis through the foundation's small grant scheme. Grants will not normally cover the entire cost of a project, or support an organisation in successive years.

Applications In writing to the correspondent. Applications should include the Fidelity UK summary form, organisation history and objectives, itemised project budget, a list of other funders and the status of each request, a list of directors and trustees with their backgrounds, current operating budget and most recently audited financial statements. A description of the request and rationale should also be included addressing the following:

- how the project fits into the larger strategic plan of the organisation
- what a grant will allow the organisation to achieve
- how a grant will change or improve the long-term potential of the organisation
- what the implementation plan and timeline for the project is and who is responsible
- how the project will be evaluated.

Applications will receive an initial response within three months.

The foundation receives many more applications for grants than it is able to fund so not all applications that fall within the guidelines will receive grants.

The Doris Field Charitable Trust

General

£138,000 (2001/02)

Beneficial area UK, with a preference for Oxfordshire.

Morgan Cole Solicitors, Buxton Court, 3 West Way, Oxford OX2 0SZ

Tel. 01865 262183 **Fax** 01865 262623

Correspondent Helen Fanyinka

Trustees *N A Harper; J Cole; Mrs W Church.*

CC Number 328687

Information available Information was provided by the trust.

General One-off and recurrent grants are given to large UK organisations and small local projects for a wide variety of causes. The trust states that it favours playgroups and local causes in Oxfordshire.

In 2001/02 it had assets of £5 million and an income of £248,000. Grants were made to 93 organisations and 1 individual totalling £138,000. Management and administration charges were very high at £35,000, even after £40,000 had been spent on generating the income. This included payments totalling £56,000 to two firms which have one of the trustees as a partner. Whilst wholly legal, these editors always regret such payments unless, in the words of the Charity Commission, 'there is no realistic alternative'.

The largest grants were £10,000 to Douglas Home, £5,500 to Waste Recycling Group, £5,000 each to Dogs for the Disabled, Everest Memorial Trust and RSPB, £4,000 to Alastair Parkinson Trust, £3,300 to Ridgefield Road Scout Hut and £3,200 to King's School.

Other grants include £2,500 each to Cord Blood Charity, £2,000 to Hook Norton Sports and Social Committee, £1,000 each to Addiction, Grandpont Nursery School, Lion Clubs of Oxfordshire and 1st Standlake Sea Scouts, £800 to Eyeless Trust, £500 each to East Oxford Community Association and Lupus UK, £300 to Lake Street Community Playgroup, £200 to Merton Parent and Toddler Group, £150 to Cheney School and £100 to Bartons' Open Door Amenities Account.

Exclusions It is unlikely that grants would be made for overseas projects or to individuals for higher education.

Applications On a form available from the correspondent. Applications are considered three times a year.

The Bluff Field Charitable Trust

General

£130,000 (2001)

Beneficial area UK.

Risk Publications, Haymarket House, 28–29 Haymarket, London SW1Y 4RX

Correspondent Peter Field, Trustee

Trustees *Peter Field; Michael Frost; Sonia Field.*

CC Number 1057993

Information available Accounts were on file at the Charity Commission.

General Established in 1996, in 2001 this trust had assets of £39,000. Its income of £121,000 came mainly from donations and Gift Aid. Grants totalled £130,000.

There were eight grants made during the year, the major beneficiary was St George's Hospital Medical School, receiving two grants totalling over £100,000. Other beneficiaries included: Wigmore Hall Trust (£5,000); Risk Waters' World Trade Centre UK Appeal (£1,000); Emmanuel Church Billericay (£200); and Leukemia Research Fund (£100).

Applications In writing to the correspondent.

This entry was not confirmed by the trust, but the information was correct according to information filed publicly at the Charity Commission.

Dixie Rose Findlay Charitable Trust

Children, seafarers, blindness, multiple sclerosis

£80,000 available (2004)

Beneficial area UK.

HSBC Trust Co. (UK) Ltd, 15–17 Cumberland House, Southampton SO15 2UY

Correspondent Colin Bould

Trustees *HSBC Trust Co. (UK) Ltd; Miss D R Findlay.*

CC Number 251661

Information available Information was provided by the trust.

General This trust is concerned with children, seafarers, blindness, multiple sclerosis and similar conditions. It had £80,000 available for grants in 2004. Beneficiaries have included Cassel Hospital, The Children's Society, Glen Arun, Leukaemia Research, Mission to Seamen and St Johns' Wood Church.

Applications In writing to the correspondent.

Finnart House School Trust

Jewish children and young people in need of care

£69,000 to organisations (2002/03)

Beneficial area Worldwide.

5th Floor, 707 High Road, North Finchley, London N12 0BT

Tel. 020 8445 1670 **Fax** 020 8446 7370

Email finnart@anjy.org

Correspondent Peter Shaw, Clerk

Trustees *Dr Louis Marks, Chair; Robert Cohen; Lady Grabiner; Hilary Norton; David Fobel; Lilian Hochhauser; Jane Leaver; Dr Amanda Kirby; Mark Sebba; Linda Peterson; Sue Leifer.*

CC Number 220917

Information available Full accounts were provided by the trust.

General The trust supports the relief of children and young people who are of the Jewish faith and aged 21 and under. Bursaries and scholarships are given to Jewish secondary school pupils and university entrants who are capable of achieving, but would probably not do so because of family and economic pressures. Also supported is work concerned with people who are disaffected, disadvantaged socially and economically through illness or neglect or in need of care and education.

In 2002/03 it had assets of £3.3 million, which generated an income of £160,000. Grants were made to 19 organisations totalling £69,000. A further £149,000 was given in total in 17 scholarships to individuals (please see *The Educational Grants Directory*, also published by DSC, for further information).

The largest grants were £9,000 to Hasmonean High School, £5,700 to Association for Research into Stammering in Childhood, £5,000 each to British Friends of Jerusalem College of Technology, Cosgrove Care and JFS School, £4,800 each to Beit Miriam and Gimmel Foundation, £4,200 to Manchester Jewish Federation and £4,000 to Hamifal.

Other grants were £3,000 each to Nitzan, Peace Child Israel and Yoav Association, £2,500 to Eran Centre, £2,000 each to Akim, Eliya, Fun Lodge and Interlink Foundation and £1,000 each to Jewish Women's Aid and Mercaz Harmony.

Applications There is an application form, which needs to be submitted together with a copy of the latest annual report and accounts.

The David Finnie & Alan Emery Charitable Trust

Welfare, health, education, personal development

£41,000 to organisations (2002/03)

Beneficial area UK.

4 De Grosmont Close, Abergavenny, Monmouthshire NP7 9JN

Tel. 01873 851048

Correspondent J A C Buck, Trustee

Trustees *J A C Buck; R J Emery; Mrs S A Hyde.*

CC Number 258749

Information available Information was provided by the trust.

General The trust supports: the advancement of education; personal achievement and development; temporary relief of hardship; and national organisations working in health, welfare and education and training fields. Local organisations are also funded.

In 2002/03 it had assets of £1.6 million and an income of £75,000. Grants were made to 27 individuals totalling £20,000 and to 34 organisations totalling £41,000, broken down as follows:

Benevolent funds	3	£4,000
Carers	1	£1,500
Children/youth	8	£8,600
Education	2	£1,200
Hospice and Aged	10	£11,000
Medical	4	£6,000
Welfare of people in need	4	£6,800
Disability	2	£1,500

The largest grants were £2,500 each to Salvation Army and Samaritans, £2,000 each to Age Concern, NSPCC and St Joseph's Hospice and £1,500 each to Alzheimer's Disease Society, British Heart Foundation, Cancer Research UK, Diabetes UK, Merton Crossroads Care Attendants Scheme, Royal Star and Garter Home and Scottish Chartered Accountants' Benevolent Fund.

Other beneficiaries included Fairbridge de Cymru (£1,300), Royal School for the Deaf – Manchester and Welsh Association of Youth Clubs (£1,000), Francis Drake Fellowship (£750), St Anne's Hospice (£580), Weston Spirit (£560) and Universal Beneficent Society (£500).

Exclusions No grants where alternative funding was or should be made available by other agencies, government or otherwise. No support for: loans and non-specific cash sums; expeditions, conference attendance and seminars; general cases of hardship falling outside the stated criteria; requests for holiday trips, family reunions and the like; debts of any kind; house removal or funeral expenses; TV, car and animal licences; nursing and/or residential care fees (including for homeless people); furniture and fixtures; treatment that should be provided by the NHS; overseas funding; religious purposes; or building work of any nature.

Applications In writing to the correspondent. Trustees usually meet in April, July and October each year to consider grants. Replies will be sent to applicants who include an sae and cases considered of merit will generally be forwarded a grant application form for completion.

Gerald Finzi Charitable Trust

Music

About £30,000 (1998/99)

Beneficial area UK.

Hillcroft, Shucknall Hill, Hereford HR1 3SL

Correspondent Elizabeth Pooley

Trustees *Christopher Finzi; Nigel Finzi; Jean Finzi; Andrew Burn; Robert Gower; J Dale Roberts; Paul Spicer; Michael Salmon; Christian Alexander.*

CC Number 313047

Information available Information was on file at the Charity Commission.

General The trustees aim to reflect the ambitions and philosophy of the composer Gerald Finzi (1901–56), which included the general promotion of 20th-century British music through assisting and promoting festivals, recordings and performances of British music. A limited number of modest grants are also offered to young musicians towards musical training.

In 2002/03 the trust had an income of £90,000 and a total expenditure of £59,000. Further information for this year was not available.

In 1998/99 it had an income of £71,000 and a total expenditure of £32,000. This information was taken from the Charity Commission. No further details were available.

Applications In writing to the correspondent.

Marc Fitch Fund

Humanities

£158,000 to organisations (2002/03)

Beneficial area UK.

PO Box 207, Chipping Norton OX7 3ZQ

Tel. 01608 811944

Email admin@marcfitchfund.org.uk

Website www.marcfitchfund.org.uk

Correspondent The Executive Secretary

Trustees *A S Bell, Chair; Hon. Nicholas Assheton; Prof. J P Barron; Dr J I Kermode; Prof. D M Palliser; J Porteous; Dr J Blair; Dr H Forde; A Murison; Dr G Worsley.*

CC Number 313303

Information available Information was provided by the trust.

General The trust makes grants to organisations and individuals for 'publication and research in archaeology, historical geography, history of art and architecture, heraldry, genealogy, surnames, catalogues of and use of archives (especially ecclesiastical), conservation of artefacts and other antiquarian, archaeological or historical studies'. Emphasis is on the local and regional history of the British Isles.

In 2002/03 it had assets of almost £4 million and an income of £215,000. Grants to organisations totalled £158,000, whilst £57,000 was given in research grants to individuals.

Beneficiaries included Holburne Museum (£7,500), Yorkshire Country Houses Project (£2,000), Survey of Lincoln (£1,500), Medieval Pottery Research Group (£1,000) and Hertfordshire Record Society (£600).

Exclusions No grants are given towards foreign travel or for research outside the British Isles, unless the circumstances are very exceptional; or people reading full-time higher degrees.

Applications In writing to the correspondent. The trustees meet twice a year to consider applications.

The Fitton Trust

Social welfare, medical

£110,000 (2002/03)

Beneficial area UK.

Phoenix House, 9 London Road, Newbury, Berkshire RG14 1DH

Tel. 01635571000

Email Fitton.Trust@virgin.net

Correspondent The Secretary

Trustees *Dr R P A Rivers; D M Lumsden; D V Brand.*

CC Number 208758

Information available Accounts were on file at the Charity Commission, but without a list of grants.

General In 2002/03 the trust had an income of £110,000 and total assets came to £1.4 million. The total amount given in 425 grants came to £110,000. The majority of beneficiaries received £100–£250. Only three grants amounted to £1,000 or more, to King's Medical Research Trust (£2,100), Whizz-Kids (£1,200) and Young Peoples Trust for the Environment (£1,000).

Exclusions No grants to individuals.

Applications In writing to correspondent. The trust states: 'No application considered unless accompanied by fully audited accounts. No replies will be sent to unsolicited applications whether from individuals, charities or other bodies.'

The Earl Fitzwilliam Charitable Trust

General

£60,000 (2001/02)

Beneficial area UK, with a preference for areas with historical family connections, chiefly in

Cambridgeshire, Northamptonshire and Yorkshire.

Estate Office, Milton Park, Peterborough PE6 7AH

Correspondent J M S Thompson, Secretary to the Trustees

Trustees *Sir Philip Naylor-Leyland; Lady Isabella Naylor-Leyland.*

CC Number 269388

Information available Full accounts were provided by the trust.

General The trust tends to favour charities that benefit rural communities, especially those with a connection to Cambridgeshire, Peterborough, South Yorkshire and Malton in North Yorkshire where the Fitzwilliam family have held their landed estates for many centuries.

It was established in 1975 by the Rt Hon. Earl Fitzwilliam and has since had various capital sums and property gifted to it. In 2002/03 it had an income of £186,000 and a total expenditure of £169,000. Further information for this year was not available.

In the previous year assets totalled £5.1 million and grants totalled £60,000.

Past beneficiaries have included Brathay Hall Trust, Cambridgeshire Life Education Centre, High Sherriff's Award Scheme, National Autistic Society, Peterborough Diocesan Family Care, Rural Minds, Sheffield Galleries and Museum Trust and The Wildside Trust.

Exclusions No grants to individuals.

Applications In writing to the correspondent. Trustees meet about every three months.

Bud Flanagan Leukaemia Fund

Leukaemia research and treatment.

£126,000 (2002)

Beneficial area UK.

40 Redwood Glade, Leighton Buzzard, Bedfordshire LU7 3JT

Tel. 01525 376550 **Fax** 01525 376550

Website www.bflf.org.uk

Correspondent J Bernard Jones

Trustees *B Coral; S Coventry; R Powles; Countess of Normanton; K Kaye; A Rowden; A Kitcherside; J Goodman; G Till.*

CC Number 1092540

Information available Information was provided by the trust.

General Established in 1969 from the estate of the late Bud Flanagan, the principle objects of the fund are 'the promotion of clinical research into the treatment and possible cure of leukaemia and allied diseases and the publication of the results of all such research'. The fund makes grants to hospitals and research institutions for research into the causes, diagnosis and treatment of leukaemia.

In 2002 it had assets totalling £486,000 and an income of £93,000, from interest, donations and fundraising events. Grants were made during the year totalling £126,000.

The main beneficiary of the trust has been Royal Marsden Hospital in Sutton, which received £1 million for the Bud Flannigan ward, £101,000 for a multicolour FISH system for use in the understanding and use of the genetic code in leukaemia cells as a marker of disease activity and response and £100,000 for a research fellowship for two years intensive research trials testing new drugs.

Other recent grants have included £100,000 to Fergus Maclay Leukaemia Database to upgrade a unique database for eventual dissemination on the internet, £98,000 to Institute of Cancer Research for research into the human genome and the genetic susceptibility to acute myelod leukaemia, £50,000 to Northwick Park Hospital to equip a leukaemia cubicle in a new children's ward and £6,500 to Bath Cancer Research towards a vacuum concentrator for use in drug-sensitivity testing.

Exclusions The fund does not normally make grants to welfare charities or to individuals.

Applications In writing to the correspondent.

The Rose Flatau Charitable Trust

Jewish, general

£78,000 (2002/03)

Beneficial area UK.

5 Knott Park House, Wrens Hill, Oxshott, Leatherhead KT22 0HW

Tel. 01372 843082

Correspondent M E G Prince, Trustee

Trustees *M E G Prince; A E Woolf; N L Woolf.*

CC Number 210492

Information available Full accounts were provided by the trust.

General The trust supports Jewish organisations, although it also supports other organisations which particularly attract the interest of the trustees.

In 2002/03 it had assets of £1.1 million, which generated an income of £48,000. Grants were made to 23 organisations totalling £78,000.

The largest grants, of £5,000 each, went to Anglo-Jewish Association, Barntwood Trust, Cherry Trees, Cancer Research Campaign, Jewish Care, MS Society, Norwood, Queen Elizabeth Foundation for the Disabled, Queen Mary's Clothing Fund, United Jewish Israel and World Jewish Relief.

Other grants were £2,000 each to Bernhard Baron Settlement, Pelican Cancer Foundation, Jewish Lads and Girls Brigade, Jewish Child's Day and Talking Newspapers, £1,500 to Royal Masonic Benevolent Association, £1,000 each to British Red Cross and Listening Books and £120 to United Synagogues.

Exclusions No grants to individuals.

Applications The trust stated: 'Our funds are fully committed to the foreseeable future'. Speculative applications will therefore be fruitless.

The Ian Fleming Charitable Trust

Disability, medical

£35,000 to organisations (2002/03)

Beneficial area UK.

haysmacintyre, Fairfax House, 15 Fulwood Place, London WC1V 6AY

Tel. 020 7969 5500 **Fax** 020 7696 5600

Correspondent A A I Fleming, Trustee

Trustees *A A I Fleming; N A M McDonald; A W W Baldwin; A H Isaacs.*

CC Number 263327

Information available Full accounts were provided by the trust.

General This trust's income is allocated equally between: (a) UK charities actively operating for the support, relief and welfare of men, women and children who are disabled or otherwise in need of help, care and attention, and charities actively engaged in research on human diseases; and (b) Music Education Awards under a scheme administered by the Musicians Benevolent Fund and advised by a committee of experts in the field of music.

In 2002/03 it had assets of £2.1 million, which generated an income of £92,000. Grants were made totalling £78,000, of which £35,000 was given in 23 grants to organisations and £43,000 in 12 music awards to individuals.

The largest grants, of £2,000 each, went to Arthritis Care, British Red Cross, Erskine Hospital, Jubilee Sailing Trust, King George's Fund for Sailors, Parkinson's Disease Society, Royal Blind and Asylum School – Edinburgh, Royal Star and Garter Home and Stroke Association.

The remaining grants were £1,500 each to ASBAH, Marie Curie Cancer Care, Disabled Living Foundation, Lupus UK, National Asthma Campaign and Samaritans and £1,000 each to Anthony Nolan Trust, Charterhouse-in-Southwark, Fight for Sight, Headway, Mental Health Foundation, National Benevolent Fund for the Aged, Rainbow Trust and RYA Sailability.

Exclusions No grants to individuals except under the music education award scheme. No grants to purely local charities.

Applications In writing to the correspondent.

The Joyce Fletcher Charitable Trust

Music, children's welfare

£68,000 (2003/04)

Beneficial area England, with a preference for the South West.

17 Westmead Gardens, Upper Weston, Bath BA1 4EZ

Tel. 01225 314355

Correspondent R A Fletcher, Trustee

Trustees *R A Fletcher; W D R Fletcher; S C Sharp; S P Fletcher.*

CC Number 297901

Information available Information was provided by the trust.

General The policy of the trust is to support institutions and organisations, usually registered charities, specialising in music in a social or therapeutic context, music and special needs, and children and young people's welfare. Other organisations which are supported outside these areas are usually known to the trustees.

In 2003/04 the trust had an income of £70,000 and made grants totalling £68,000. Grant beneficiaries included Live Music Now! (£12,000), Share Music (£6,000), Welsh National Opera (£3,000), Buxton Festival, Children's Hospice South West, For Ever Friends Appeal – RUH, Holburne Museum in Bath, Holtwood Methodist Chapel in Dorset, National Youth Orchestra of GB and Wiltshire Music Centre (£2,000 each).

Exclusions Grants to individuals and students are exceptionally rare. No support for areas which are the responsibility of the local authority. No support is given to purely professional music/arts promotions.

Applications In writing to the correspondent before 1 November each year. There are no application forms. Applications should include the purpose for the grant, an indication of the history and viability of the organisation and a summary of accounts. Preliminary telephone calls are accepted. Acknowledgements are only given if the application is being considered or if an sae is sent.

Florence's Charitable Trust

Education, welfare, sick and infirm, general

£264,000 (2002/03)

Beneficial area UK, with a preference for Rossendale in Lancashire

E Suttons & Sons, PO Box 2, Riverside, Bacup, Lancashire OL13 0DT

Tel. 01706 874961 **Fax** 01706 879268

Email ronnie@esutton.co.uk

Correspondent R Barker, Secretary to the Trustees

Trustees *C C Harrison, Chair; R Barker; A Connearn; G D Low; J Mellows; R D Uttley; K Duffy.*

CC Number 265754

Information available Information was provided by the trust.

General In autumn 2003 the trust stated that: 'for a number of years, the resources expended have exceeded the annual income of the charity. The trustees are now taking steps to rebuild the investment core to raise income levels in order to compensate for the fall in world stock markets. This will allow the trust to facilitate substantial charitable support for the future.'

In 2003/04 the trust had an income of £56,000 and a total expenditure of £151,000. Further information from this year was not available.

In 2002/03 the trust had assets of £798,000, an income of £128,000 and made grants totalling £264,000.

Grants were mainly recurrent. They are categorised under four main headings: support for aged (£12,000), education (£70,000), sick and infirm (£30,000) and other charitable public benefits (£152,000).

Two awards were made in the 'support for aged' category with the largest being £10,000 to Lancashire Constabulary Over 55's Burglary Fightback Project.

There were 42 grants given in the 'education' category. The largest grant went to All Saint's School to support their 'special school status'. The rest were mainly annual grants although they were reduced in amount from previous years.

The 'sick and infirm' category included 25 grants. The two largest grants, of £5,000 each went, to North West Air Ambulance and Mencap Gateway Awards.

In the 'other charitable public benefits' category 30 grants were made. The largest two grants totalled £115,000 for CCTV monitoring. Many of the other grants were recurrent and included five donations to local branches of the Samaritans.

Exclusions No grants to individuals educational fees, exchange visits or gap year activities.

Applications In writing only to the correspondent (no telephone calls allowed). To save on administration costs, unsuccessful applications will not be acknowledged even if an sae is provided. The trust states that funds are fully committed until 2006.

The Florian Charitable Trust

General

£34,000 (2001/02)

Beneficial area UK.

Lawrence Graham, 190 Strand, London WC2R 1JN

Tel. 020 7379 0000 **Fax** 020 7393 6854

Correspondent Richard Wood, Trustee

Trustees *V J Treasure; Mrs G W Treasure; G A Treasure; R W Wood.*

CC Number 1043523

Information available Accounts were on file at the Charity Commission.

General This trust seems to have an interest in supporting medical causes and disabled children.

In 2001/02 the trust had assets of £1.1 million with an income of £79,000 and grants totalling £34,000.

Grants of £2,000 were awarded to Royal National Lifeboat Institution, Sussex Autistic Society, National Homeless Alliance, Hertfordshire MS Therapy Centre, International Spinal Research Trust, Motor Neurone Disease Association, West Sussex Deaf and Hard of Hearing Association, Shipley Windmill Charitable Trust and Headway.

Grants of £1,500 or less include Starlight Children's Foundation, Weston Spirit & YP.UK, Alzheimer's Society, Arthritis Care, Marie Curie Cancer Care, Brainwave, Braille Chess Association, Dermatrust, Multiple Sclerosis Society, St John Ambulance and Sussex Autistic Society.

Applications In writing to the correspondent. The trust says: 'Whilst the trustees have been prepared to look at all applications received during the six months prior to the biannual trustees' meeting, particular emphasis has been placed on funding specific projects.'

The Flow Foundation

Welfare, education, environment, medical

£35,000 (2001/02)

Beneficial area UK.

Suite A, 15 Portman Square, London W1H 6LJ

Tel. 020 7224 0077

Correspondent Mrs Nita Sowerbutts

Trustees *Mrs N Shashou; Mrs Nina Sowerbutts; H Woolf; Mrs J Woolf.*

CC Number 328274

Information available Full accounts were on file at the Charity Commission.

General In 2001/02 it had assets of £989,000, which generated an income of £50,000. Grants totalling £35,000 were made to 22 organisations, half of which were also supported in the previous year.

The largest beneficiaries were Norwood (£9,000 in two grants), Chicken Shed Theatre Company (£5,000), Weizmann Institute Foundation (£3,500), British Friends of Haifa University (£2,500), After Adoption (£2,200) and Survivors of the Shak Visual History Foundation (£2,000).

Other grants were £1,000 each to Brain Research Trust, British ORT, Tate Gallery Foundation, Toynbee Hall Foundation, Unite for the Future, Variety Club Children's Charity and West London Synagogue, £690 to Friends of Covent Garden, £500 each to Honey Pot Charity, Intenational Centre for Child Studies, Jewish Care, Royal Pharmaceutical Society and Royal Star and Garter and £450 in total in three smaller grants.

Applications In writing to the correspondent on one sheet of paper only.

The Gerald Fogel Charitable Trust

Jewish, general

About £50,000

Beneficial area UK.

Morley & Scott, Lynton House, 7–12 Tavistock Square, London WC1H 9LT

Tel. 020 7387 5868

Email clayj@morley-scott.co.uk

Correspondent J Clay, Accountant

Trustees *J G Fogel; B Fogel; S Fogel; D Fogel.*

CC Number 1004451

Information available Accounts were on file at the Charity Commission.

General The trust stated in its annual report that its policy is 'to make a wide spread of grants'. In practice it appears to support mainly Jewish organisations.

In 2002/03 the trust had an income of £74,000 and a total expenditure of £84,000. Further information for this year was not available.

Previous beneficiaries include Jewish Care, Norwood Ravenswood, Jewish Child's Day, The Constable Educational Trust, Jewish Marriage Council, Imperial Cancer Research, Jack's Pack, King Edward VII's Hospital for Officers, Macmillan Cancer Relief, Marie Curie Cancer Care, St John's Hospice and Variety Club.

Exclusions No grants to individuals or non-registered charities.

Applications In writing to the correspondent.

The Follett Trust

Welfare, education, arts

£70,000 (2001/02)

Beneficial area UK and overseas.

17 Chescombe Road, Yatton, North Somerset BS49 4EE

Tel. 01934 838337

Correspondent M D Follett, Trustee

Trustees *Martin Follett; Ken Follett; Barbara Follett.*

CC Number 328638

Information available Accounts were on file at the Charity Commission.

General The trust's policy is to: give financial assistance to organisations in the field of education and individual students in higher education including theatre; support organisations concerned with disability and health; support trusts involved with writers and publishing; respond to world crisis appeals for help.

In 2003/04 the trust had an income of £59,000 and a total expenditure of £105,000. Further information from this year was not available.

In 2001/02 the trust had an income of £72,000 and made grants totalling £70,000. For its income the trust relies almost entirely on regular donations from its trustees. Grants ranged from £50 to £20,000.

Beneficiaries during the year included Dyslexia Institute, Canon Collins Trust, University College London Development Fund, Stevenage CAB, Oxfam, Amnesty

International, Artsline, Community Heart, New Horizon Youth Centre, Roebuck Junior School, Save the Rhino International, Gwent Cancer Support, Hertfordshire and Bedfordshire Pastoral Foundation and Parkinson's Disease Society.

Applications The trust states, 'A high proportion of donees come to the attention of the trustees through personal knowledge and contact rather than by written application. Where the trustees find it impossible to make a donation they rarely respond to the applicant unless a stamped addressed envelope is provided'.

The Football Association National Sports Centre Trust

Play areas, community sports facilities

£147,000 (2003)

Beneficial area UK.

25 Soho Square, London W1D 4FA

Tel. 020 7745 4589 **Fax** 020 7745 5589

Email mike.appleby@TheFA.com

Correspondent Mike Appleby, Secretary to the Trustees

Trustees *G Thompson; W T Annable; R G Berridge; B W Bright; M M Armstrong.*

CC Number 265132

Information available Full accounts were provided by the trust.

General The trust supports the provision, maintenance and improvement of facilities for use in recreational and leisure activities. Grants are made to county football associations, football clubs and other sports associations.

In 2003 the trust received a donation of £2 million from The Football Association. It also generated £15,000 through its own investments. Grants were made totalling £147,000. By the end of the year, the assets rose from £531,000 to £2.4 million. The accounts stated that despite this large donation, the trust was in a position to retain its independence from The Football Association.

A total of six grants were made towards hard surface play areas or multi-use game areas, totalling £114,000. The remaining £33,000 was given in eight grants (of up to £6,000 each) for grassroots football clubs.

These grants were £25,000 each to Exeter City Council, Knowsley MBC and Somerset County Council, £21,000 to St Cleer Parish Council, £13,000 to London Borough of Lambeth, £7,600 in two grants to Woolmer Green Parish Council, £6,000 to Mevagissey Playing Fields Trust, £5,600 to Hitchin Town FC, £5,000 each to Ashtead FC, Hanwell Town FC and Kibworth Football and Sports Association, £2,100 to Acton Ealing Whistlers FC and £1,900 to Bolton County AFC.

Applications In writing to the correspondent.

The Forbes Charitable Foundation

Adults with learning disabilities

£110,000 (2002/03)

Beneficial area UK.

9 Weir Road, Kibworth, Leicestershire LE8 0LQ

Tel. 0116 279 3225 **Fax** 0116 279 6384

Email j.shepherd@care-international.co.uk

Website www.care-ltd.co.uk

Correspondent J B Shepherd, Secretary to the Trustees

Trustees *Colonel R G Wilkes, Chair; Major Gen. R L S Green; I Johnson; J C V Lang; C G Packham; N J Townsend; J M Waite; R Warburton.*

CC Number 326476

Information available Full accounts were provided by the trust.

General The trust supports charities involved with the care of adults with learning difficulties. It prefers to support capital rather than revenue projects.

In 2002/03 it had assets of £1.4 million, which generated an income of £67,000. Grants to two organisations totalled £110,000. CARE Fund received £100,000 for the Hand-in-Hand appeal whilst £10,000 went to Robert Owen Community.

In the previous year grants were made to nine organisations totalling £60,000. Again this mostly went to CARE Fund, which received £50,000.

Applications In writing to the correspondent. Applications are considered in June and November.

Forbesville Limited

Jewish, education

£57,000 (2002)

Beneficial area UK and overseas.

Holborn House, 219 Golders Green Road, London NW11 9DD

Tel. 020 8209 0355

Correspondent M Berger, Chair

Trustees *M Berger, Chair; Mrs J S Kritzler; D B Kritzler.*

CC Number 269898

Information available Brief information for this trust was available at the Charity Commission.

General The trust makes grants to Orthodox Jewish organisations, educational and charitable institutions.

In 2002 the trust had assets of £19,000 with an income of £110,000 and grants totalling £57,000. Unfortunately no grants list was available for this period.

Applications In writing to the correspondent.

The Oliver Ford Charitable Trust

Mental disability, housing

£44,000 to organisations (2002/03)

Beneficial area UK.

Messrs Macfarlanes, 10 Norwich Street, London EC4A 1BD

Tel. 020 7831 9222 **Fax** 020 7831 9607

Correspondent Matthew Pintus

Trustees *Derek Hayes; Lady Wakeham; Martin Levy.*

CC Number 1026551

Information available Information was provided by the trust.

General The objects of the trust are to educate the public and advance knowledge of the history and techniques of interior decoration, the designs of fabric and other decorative materials and landscape gardening with particular reference to Oliver Ford's own work. Income not used for these purposes is used for the Anthroposophical Society of Great Britain, Camphill Village Trust, Norwood or any other village or home for people with mental disabilities which is not state-subsidised.

Grants are given each year to students on the Victoria and Albert Museum/ Royal College of Art MA course in the History of Design. From 2003 a grant has been given to students on the Wisley Diploma in Practical Horticulture run by Royal Horticultural Society.

In 2002/03 it had assets of £1.7 million, which generated an income of £91,000. Grants were made totalling £63,000, of which £19,000 went to students and £44,000 to 11 organisations. Management and administration expenses were very high at £15,000, representing 16% of the income for the year.

By far the largest grant, of £20,000, went to Purley Park Trust. Other beneficiaries were Rose Road Association (£5,000), Oakfield (Eastern Maudit) Limited (£4,000), Martha Trust (£3,500), Spadework Limited (£2,600), John Grooms Nottingham Nursery (£2,300), Nottingham Regional Society for Autistic Children and University of Manchester for the Whitworth Art Gallery (£2,000 each), L'arche Inverness Community and Parchment Trust (£1,000) and L'arche Preston (£600).

Applications In writing to the correspondent. Trustees meet in March and October.

Ford of Britain Trust

Arts, community service, education, environment, disability, diversity, hospitals, professional and trade, schools, special schools, youth

£454,000 (2001/02)

Beneficial area Local to the areas where the company is situated, namely Dagenham/East London, Croydon, Essex, Merseyside, South Wales, Southampton, Daventry and Leamington Spa.

Room 1/619, Ford Motor Company, Central Office, Eagle Way, Brentwood, Essex CM13 3BW

Tel. 01277 252551

Website www.ford.co.uk

Correspondent Phil Taylor

Trustees *R G Putnam, Chair; W G F Brooks; M J Callaghan; Prof. S Hochgreb; S McIlveen; I G McAllister; J H M Norris; P G Knight.*

CC Number 269410

Information available Information was provided by the trust.

General The objects of the trust are the 'advancement of education, and other purposes beneficial to the community'. The trust supports organisations in the areas where the Ford Motor Company is based. When this is a town it will support the surrounding area, i.e. where the employees are likely to be living. There is also a preference for charities where a member of staff is involved. Grants are typically one-off. They normally range from £50 to £5,000 but some larger grants are made. The trust prefers to support projects run by registered charities.

Applications for new Ford vehicles are considered when two-thirds of the purchase price is available from other sources. These grants are not usually more than £1,500, but registered charities may be able to arrange a reduction from the recommended retail price. Grants are not available for second-hand vehicles.

The trust's income consists of donations from the company, and interest earned on these donations. In 2001/02 the trust had assets of £1.2 million and an income of £689,000. Grants were made totalling £454,000. No further information was available on the size or number of beneficiaries during the year.

In 2000/01 the trust had assets of £1.2 million and an income of £694,000. Grants totalled £490,000. An analysis of the grants for this year by regional area is as follows:

Area	£	%
Merseyside	£93,000	19
Essex & South East (includes London)	£231,000	47
South Wales	£76,000	16
Northern Ireland	£23,000	5
Southampton	£41,000	8
Midlands	£24,000	5
Croydon	£2,000	1
Enfield	nil	0
Total	£490,000	100

The grants were also categorised according to the area of work:

Category	£	%
Arts	£2,000	1
Community Service	£141,000	29
Education	£11,000	2
Environment	£400	
Disability	£74,000	15
Hospitals	£4,100	1
Professional and trade	nil	0
Race relations	£5,500	1
Schools	£166,000	34
Special schools	£30,000	6
Youth	£56,000	11
Other	£1,000	

The proportions given in each category are similar to previous years.

Exclusions Organisations outside the beneficial area and national charities are rarely assisted, except for specific projects in Ford areas. Applications in respect of individuals (including students), charities requiring funds for overseas projects, and wholly religious or politically orientated projects are ineligible. Major building projects and research projects (including medical) are rarely assisted.

Applications In writing to the correspondent. Applications should include the following:

- purpose of the project
- whom it is intended to help and how
- why the project is important and necessary (how things were done before)
- how the project is to be carried out
- the project's proposed starting time and time of completion
- total cost of the project
- how much has been raised so far, sources of funding obtained and expected
- examples of fundraising activities by the organisation for the project
- the amount being asked for.

A brief resumé of the background of the charity is appreciated. Where appropriate copies of accounts should be provided.

Trustees meet in March, July and November each year. Applications are considered in order of receipt and it may take several months before an application is considered. The trust receives many more applications than it can help; it received 1,300 in 2001/02.

Fordeve Ltd

Jewish, general

See below

Beneficial area UK.

c/o Gerald Kreditor & Co., Tudor House, 1 Holesworth Road, London NW2 2AQ

Tel. 020 8209 1535 **Fax** 020 8209 1923

Correspondent J Kon, Trustee

Trustees *J Kon; Mrs H Kon.*

CC Number 1011612

Information available Information was on file at the Charity Commission

General The trust makes grants to Jewish causes and for the relief of need. In 2003/04 it had an income of £356,000 and a total expenditure of £322,000. Further details were not available.

Applications In writing to the correspondent.

The Forest Hill Charitable Trust

Mainly Christian causes and relief work in the UK and overseas

£114,000 to organisations (2003)

Beneficial area UK and overseas.

104 Summercourt Way, Brixham, Devon TQ5 0RB

Tel. 01803 872857

Correspondent Mrs P J Pile, Secretary to the Trustees

Trustees *H F Pile, Chair; Mrs P J Pile; R S Pile; Mrs M S Tapper; M Thomas.*

CC Number 1050862

Information available Full accounts were provided by the trust.

General This trust gives grants mainly to Christain causes and for relief work (80%), although support is given to agencies helping people who are disabled, in need or sick.

In 2003 the trust had assets of £1.5 million and an income of £77,000. Grants to organisations were made totalling £114,000. Over 100 charities were supported, each receiving a regular monthly donation. Two exceptional large donations were made in the year to Linx for £20,000 and Great Parkes Chapel for £6,000. Other larger donations were £2,000 each to Barnabas Fund and Home Evangelism and £1,600 to CR2EE.

On average grants are for £1,000 or below, beneficiaries in the year included: Dentaid, Harvest Trust, Local Context, Prison Fellowship, SASRA and St Loyers' Foundation (£1,000 each); Ark Youth Trust, Redcliffe College and World Villages Children (£800 each); Crossroad Carers and Plymstock Chapel (£600 each); Acorn, Straight Street, Time for Families and Visions of Glory (£500 each); and Barnabas House and Cross Border Arts (£400 each).

Applications In April 2004 the trustees stated that their aim is to maintain regular and consistent support to the charities they are currently supporting. New requests for funding are therefore very unlikely to succeed.

The Forman Hardy Charitable Trust

Arts, Christian, medical, welfare

£90,000 (2001/02)

Beneficial area Mostly Nottinghamshire.

64 St James' Street, Nottingham NG1 6FJ

Tel. 0115 950 8580

Correspondent N J Forman Hardy, Trustee

Trustees *N J Forman Hardy; J M Forman Hardy; C R Bennion; Canon J E M Neale.*

CC Number 1000687

Information available Full accounts were on file at the Charity Commission.

General The trust exists to benefit a wide range of charitable activities but primarily focuses on the charitable needs of the city of Nottingham and the county of Nottinghamshire.

In 2001/02 the trust had assets of £1.5 million and an income of £34,000. Grants totalled £90,000.

The two main beneficiaries were Nottingham University (£75,000) and Aysgarth School (£25,000), which also received most of the grant total in the previous year although the grants were reversed.

Other beneficiaries included Concert 2000 (£5,000), Mencap (£2,000), Millennium Millions (£1,600) and Galleries of Justice (£1,000).

Exclusions No grants are made to individuals.

Applications In writing to the correspondent.

Gwyneth Forrester Trust

General see below

£365,000 (2001/02)

Beneficial area England and Wales.

231 Linden Hall, 162–168 Regent Street, London W1B 5TB

Correspondent Ms B G Ward

Trustees *W J Forrester; A J Smee; M B Jones.*

CC Number 1080921

Information available Information was on file at the Charity Commission.

General Established in May 2000, the trustees plan to support a specific charitable sector each year. In 2003/04 it had an income of £478,000 and a total expenditure of £485,000. Unfortunately further details for this year were not available.

In 2001/02 this trust's assets stood at almost £20 million and it had an income of £555,000 mainly from investments, but including £100,000 from Gift Aid. After management and administration costs of £101,000, grants totalled £365,000. Donations were made to age-related charities.

Beneficiaries included: Research Institute for the Care of the Elderly (£50,000); 2 Care, Age Concern England and Friends of the Elderly (£25,000 each); and British Geriatrics Society (£15,000).

Applications 'Applications for aid cannot be considered.'

The Forte Charitable Trust

Education, disability, Roman Catholic, Jewish, general

£161,000 (2002/03)

Beneficial area UK and overseas.

Lowndes House, Lowndes Place, Belgrave Square, London SW1X 8DB

Tel. 020 7235 6244 **Fax** 020 7259 5149

Correspondent Mrs Heather McConville

Trustees *Hon. Sir Rocco Forte; Hon. Mrs Olga Polizzi di Sorrentino; G F L Proctor.*

CC Number 326038

Information available Full accounts were provided by the trust.

General The trust supports community-based projects and national organisations benefiting primarily children, young adults, people with disabilities, Roman Catholics and Jewish people.

In 2002/03 it had assets of £2.2 million, which generated an income of £71,000. Grants totalled £160,000.

The largest grants were £18,000 to University of Houston, £15,000 to The Bar Convent Trust and £11,000 to Strathclyde University Development Fund.

Other large grants went to English National Ballet School (£9,600), National Catholic Fund (£9,000), St Mary's Hospital Special Trustees (£7,500), KIDS (£6,000), with £5,000 each to British Commonwealth Ex-Services League, Cardinal Hume Centre, Hearing Dogs for Deaf People, Institute of Economic Affairs, Institute for Policy Research, SPECeast and St Patrick's Church.

Smaller grants included those to British Food Trust (£4,000), Shooting Star Children's Hospice Appeal (£3,000), Ripple Down House Trust (£2,500), CHICKS and Westminster Cathedral (£2,000 each), Community Jewish Trust (£1,300) and Holocaust Education Trust and Young Persons Concert Foundation (£1,000 each).

Applications In writing to the correspondent.

Lord Forte Foundation

Hospitality

£38,000 to organisations (2002/03)

Beneficial area UK.

Lowndes House, Lowndes Place, Belgrave Square, London SW1X 8DB

Tel. 020 7235 6244 **Fax** 020 7259 5149

Correspondent Mrs Heather McConville

Trustees *Lord Janner; Hon. Sir Rocco Forte; Hon. Mrs Olga Polizzi di Sorrentino; Lord Montagu of Beaulieu; Viscount Montgomery; Sir Chips Keswick; G F L Proctor.*

CC Number 298100

Information available Full accounts were provided by the trust.

General This trust was set up in 1987, 'to encourage excellence in the fields of hospitality encompassing the hotel, catering, travel and tourism industries'. It does this by giving grants directly to educational establishments which provide training courses or carry out research projects in these fields.

In 2002/03 it had assets of £1.2 million, which generated an income of £46,000. Grants were made totalling £38,000. Payments of £15,000 each went to British Food Trust and Springboard, with £7,500 going to St Loye's Foundation. A grant of £920 went to an individual.

Applications In writing to the correspondent.

Foundation for Management Education

Management studies

£80,000 (2000/01)

Beneficial area UK.

Westwards, 42 Mount Road, Higher Bebington, Wirral, Merseyside CH63 5PL

Tel. 0151 608 3193

Email fme@online.net

Correspondent Dr Brian A W Redfern, Director & Secretary

CC Number 313388

Information available Accounts were on file at the Charity Commission.

General In 2000/01 the trust had assets of £1.4 million and an income of £69,000. Charitable expenditure amounted to £80,000, broken down into grants totalling £21,000 and support costs of £59,000. Grant beneficiaries included Aston University (£10,000), University of Lancaster (£9,800) and University of London (£900).

Exclusions Individual applications for further studies cannot be supported.

Applications Unsolicited applications are not encouraged.

The Fowler, Smith and Jones Charitable Trust

Social welfare

£265,000 (2002/03)

Beneficial area Essex, occasionally elsewhere.

c/o Messrs Tolhurst & Fisher, Malbrough House, Victoria Road South, Chelmsford, Essex CM1 1LN

Tel. 01245 216123

Correspondent Mrs A Mason, Secretary

Trustees *P J Tolhurst, Chair; W J Tolhurst; E C Watson.*

CC Number 259917

Information available Full accounts were provided by the trust.

General This trust has retained the Charity Commission registration of The Albert and Florence Smith Memorial Trust, but has amalgamated with The Fowler Memorial Trust and The Edward and Cecil Jones Charitable Settlement. The following entry details the work of The Albert and Florence Smith Memorial Trust in 2002/03; but it is worth considering that given the other two trusts gave £86,000 and £107,000 respectively in the year it is worth considering that the grant total may increase in future years.

The trust supports nominated charities on an annual basis, with the balance given to local charities in Essex. It has now been decided to concentrate its giving as follows:

- charities nominated by the original benefactors

- overseas projects jointly with CAFOD and Raleigh International
- church projects
- other Essex-related projects.

There is a fundamental criterion that any funding made must be matched by other funding or contributions.

In 2002/03 The Albert and Florence Smith Memorial Trust had assets of £4.2 million, which generated an income of £307,000. Grants were made totalling £265,000. Donations of £1,000 or more were listed in the accounts and were broken down as follows:

Essex Community Foundation

Received a grant of £14,000.

Churches

Beneficiaries included: Our Lady of the Assumption – Norfleet (£25,000); Langham Parish Council (£5,000); Wesley Street Methodist Church (£3,000); Fullbridge Evangelical and St Michael's Church – Great Sampford (£2,000 each); Church of All Saints – High Roding and St Mary's Church – Chigwell (£1,500 each); and St John's Church – Great Calow (£1,000).

Local

Recipients were: Colchester Night Shelter and Farriers Barn Bures (£5,000 each); Essex Association of Boys' Clubs (£3,000); Business Enterprise Advice and Training and Maldon (Essex) Mind (£2,500 each); Hearing Help – Essex (£2,000); and Endeavour Trust – Leigh on Sea and Emmaus – Colchester (£1,500 each).

National

The largest donations were £50,000 to Helen Rollason Cancer Appeal and £25,000 to Raleigh International, which also received £30,000 in the previous year. Other organisation to receive grants included: Royal British Legion (£6,000); Barnardos and Prince's Trust (£5,000 each); RNIB (£3,500); National Association of Clubs for Young People and RNLI (£2,500 each); U Can Do It (£1,500); and One Parent Families and WRVS (£1,000 each).

International

One grant was made over £1,000 to Gonda Health Project (£1,500).

Exclusions No grants to individuals.

Applications In writing to the correspondent.

The Charles Henry Foyle Trust

General

£71,000 (2002/03)

Beneficial area UK, particularly south west Birmingham and north east Worcestershire.

Imex Spaces Business Centre, Oxleasow, East Moons Moat, Redditch, Worcestershire B98 ORE

Tel. 01527 830532 **Fax** 01527 830533

Email admin@foyletrust.org.uk

Correspondent Mrs P Elvins, Trust Administrator

Trustees *Michael Francis, Chair; Roger K Booth; Mrs Bridget Morris; Prof. Rae Mackay; Paul R Booth.*

CC Number 220446

Information available Information was provided by the trust.

General The trust aims to promote and support social, cultural and educational projects, particularly those of a pioneering nature.

In 2002/03 grants totalled £71,000. The largest donation was £23,000 to The Ironbridge Gorge Museum Trust. Other grants included: £6,500 to Stitched Textile Award; £4,600 to St Basil's – Birmingham; £3,000 to Acorns Children's Hospice; £2,500 to Highgate Family Support Centre; £2,000 each to Break–a–Leg Theatre Group and Whizz Kidz; £1,600 to RNID; £1,500 each to BID and Friends of Victoria School; £1,300 to Worcestershire Wildlife Trust; and £1,000 each to Big Brum Theatre in Education Company, Birmingham Settlement, Care and Counselling India and Jebet Beverley Cheserem.

Exclusions Generally no grants are given outside the beneficial area with the exception of medical degrees which are considered nationally (for two years pre-clinical/intercalated/elective periods only).

Applications In writing to the correspondent or via email.

The Timothy Franey Charitable Foundation

Children, health, education, arts

£112,000 (2002/03)

Beneficial area Mainly UK, although approximately 10% goes on overseas support. There is a small preference for south east London.

32 Herne Hill, London SE24 9QS

Email info@franeyfoundation.com

Correspondent T Franey, Trustee

Trustees *Timothy Franey; Wendy Ann Franey; Samantha Richmond.*

CC Number 802189

Information available Information was provided by the trust.

General The trust helps children who are sick or underprivileged and supports causes in south east London concerned with health, education and the arts.

In 2002/03 it had assets of £270,000 and an income of £20,000. Grants totalled £112,000. No grants list was included in the accounts.

Previous beneficiaries have included Anita Goulden Trust, NCH Action for Children, Dulwich College Bursary Appeal, Hope and Homes for Children, King's Appeal and Malcolm Sargent Cancer Fund for Children.

The trust has decided that, because of the large amount of applications it receives and the resulting administration burden and costs, it will now only support charities which it has worked with in the past.

Exclusions No grants to individuals. The trust stated 'we mainly support registered charities, or work with them in funding specific situations and projects'.

Applications Application by e-mail only. Further information will be requested by the trust if required. Applications in writing or by phone will not be considered.

The Isaac and Freda Frankel Memorial Charitable Trust

Jewish, general

About £50,000

Beneficial area UK and overseas, particularly Israel.

c/o Messrs Davis Frankel Mead, 33 Welbeck Street, London W1G 8LX

Tel. 020 7872 0023

Correspondent M D Frankel, Secretary

Trustees *M D Frankel; G Frankel; G J Frankel.*

CC Number 1003732

Information available Accounts were on file at the Charity Commission.

General The Isaac and Freda Frankel Memorial Charitable Trust was established in July 1991 by members of the Frankel family to support mainly Jewish causes.

In 2002/03 the trust had an income of £52,000 and a total expenditure of £63,000. Further information for this year was not available.

Grants have previously totalled about £50,000.

Exclusions No grants to individuals or students, for expeditions or scholarships.

Applications In writing to the correspondent.

Sydney E Franklin Deceased's New Second Charity

Development

£32,000 (2001/02)

Beneficial area Worldwide. Priority, but not exclusively, to developing world projects.

c/o 39 Westleigh Avenue, London SW15 6RQ

Correspondent Dr R C G Franklin, Trustee

Trustees *Dr R C G Franklin; Ms T N Franklin; Ms C Holliday.*

CC Number 272047

Information available Information was provided by the trust.

General The trust supports small charities with low overheads, focusing on developing world self-help projects, endangered species and people disadvantaged by poverty.

In 2001/02 the trust had assets of £632,000 and an income of £28,000. Grants totalled £32,000. The largest grants were £4,000 to Kerala Federation for the Blind for a South Indian group helping people who are blind; £2,500 to Womenkind Worldwide to support women's rights globally; £2,000 to Water for Kids for water/sanitation to developing world children; £1,000 each to Survival International to support indigenous peoples, Tree Aid, Children of the Andes, and Approriate Technology for Tibel, Books Abroad – all supporting projects to improve the lives of people in poverty in the developing world.

Exclusions No grants to individuals or for scholarships. No grants to large or umbrella charities. No grants to religious sectarism specific charities.

Applications Donations may only be requested by letter, and these are placed before the trustees at their meeting which is normally held at the end of each year. Applications are not acknowledged.

The Jill Franklin Trust

Welfare, church restoration

£61,000 (2002/03)

Beneficial area Worldwide.

78 Lawn Road, London NW3 2XB

Tel. 020 7722 4543 **Fax** 020 7722 4543

Email info@jill-franklin-trust.org.uk

Website www.jill-franklin-trust.org.uk

Correspondent N Franklin, Trustee

Trustees *Andrew Franklin; Norman Franklin; Sally Franklin; Sam Franklin; Tom Franklin.*

CC Number 1000175

Information available Full accounts were provided by the trust.

General The trust states it has about £70,000 a year to spend, including committed funds. Grants are given in the following areas:

- advice, training, employment and self-help groups to support people with a mental illness or learning difficulties, and their carers
- respite care and holidays (UK only). Grants for holidays are only given where there is a large element of respite care, and are given to registered charities only, not individuals
- the restoration (not improvement) of churches of architectural importance.

Grants are also given towards the resettlement of offenders including young offenders, and work with prisoners and their families. Grants of up to £150 are also given towards the education and training of prisoners. For these grants, the prisoners themselves should apply.

Grants are made worldwide, although overseas organisations are only supported if they have a correspondent in London.

In 2002/03 the trust had assets of £1.3 million and a total income of £59,000. Grants were made totalling £61,000 and were broken down as follows.

Category	*No.*	*Total*	*Percentage*
Bereavement Counselling	1	£9,000	15%
Church restoration, etc	20	£10,000	16%
Mental Health & Learning Difficulties	14	£8,500	14%
Overseas	16	£8,000	13%
Prisoners, for Education	94	£11,000	17%
Refugees	19	£9,500	16%
Respite/Holiday	10	£5,500	9%

The largest grants were £9,000 to Camden City Islington & Westminster Bereavement Services, £2,000 to Mencap and £1,000 each to Respite Association, HMP Albany, Princess Royal Trust and Support for Asylum Seekers. A further 76 grants of £500 each were given to unknown beneficiaries.

Exclusions Grants are not given to:

- both branches of a UK organisation and its centre (unless it is a specific grant, probably for training in the branches)
- building appeals or endowment funds
- encourage the 'contract culture', particularly where authorities are not funding the contract adequately
- religious organisations set up for welfare, education and so on, of whatever religion, unless the users of the service are from all

denominations, and there is no attempt whatsoever to conduct any credal propaganda or religious rituals
- restoration
- 'heritage schemes'
- animals
- students or any individuals or for overseas travel
- medical research.

Applications In writing to the correspondent, including the latest annual report, accounts and budget, and a clear statement of purpose. The trustees tend to look more favourably on an appeal which is simply and economically prepared rather than glossy, 'prestige' and mailsorted brochures. Many worthy applications are rejected simply due to a lack of funds. No acknowledgement is given to unsolicited enquiries, except where an sae is enclosed.

The Gordon Fraser Charitable Trust

Children, young people, environment, arts

£149,000 (2003/04)

Beneficial area UK, with some preference for Scotland.

Holmhurst, Westerton Drive, Bridge of Allan, Stirling FK9 4QL

Correspondent Mrs M A Moss, Trustee

Trustees *Mrs M A Moss; W F T Anderson.*

CC Number 260869

Information available Full accounts were provided by the trust.

General Currently the trustees are particularly interested in supporting children/young people in need, the environment and visual arts (including performance arts). Most grants are given within these categories. The trust states that 'applications from or for Scotland will receive favourable consideration, but not to the exclusion of applications from elsewhere'.

In 2003/04 the trust had assets of nearly £2.2 million and an income of £108,000. After administration costs of £21,000 a total of £149,000 was given in grants. Most grants were for less than £1,000, with 37 for £1,000 or more.

The largest grant was given to Scottish International Piano Competition (£15,000). Others included those to Ballet West (£7,000), Scottish Museums Council (£6,000), Aberlour Child Care Trust (£6,500), Kelvingrove Refurbishment Appeal and Lochaber Music Charitable Trust (£5,000 each), Girl guides Scotland (£4,000), London Children's Flower Society and Royal Scottish National Orchestra (£3,500 each), Scottish Society for Autism (£3,000), Scottish Opera, Queen's Hall and Waverley Care Trust (£2,000 each), Edinburgh Festival Society, Fairbridge in Scotland, and Scottish Ensemble (£1,500 each) and Council for Music in Hospitals, Edinburgh Headway Group, Hebrides Ensemble, Innerpeffray Library, John Muir Trust, Koestler Award Trust, Mansfield Traquair Trust, Music as Therapy, National Youth Choir of Scotland, National Youth Orchestras of Scotland, St Mary's Music School, St Mungo Community Housing Association, Trades Hall of Glasgow Trust, Usher Hall Conservation Trust and Voice of Carers Across Lothian (£1,000 each).

Smaller grants of less than £1,000 were given to a wide range of charities, both national and local, throughout Scotland. Beneficiaries included Aberdeen Cyrenians, Books Abroad, Cathedral Camps, Crisis, Ecas, Firsthand, Inverness Women's Aid, Lydia Project, Orkney Heritage Society, Pilton Retreat, Rock Trust, Stirling City Choir and Woodland Trust.

Exclusions No grants are made to organisations which are not recognised charities, or to individuals.

Applications In writing to the correspondent. Applications are considered in January, April, July and October. Grants towards national or international emergencies can be considered at any time. All applicants are acknowledged; an sae would, therefore, be appreciated.

The Emily Fraser Trust

Specific trades, older people

£33,000 to organisations (2002/03)

Beneficial area UK, with a preference for Scotland.

Turcan Connell, Princes Exchange, 1 Earl Grey Street, Edinburgh EH3 9EE

Tel. 0131 228 8111 **Fax** 0131 228 8118

Email ink@turcanconnell.com

Correspondent Heather Thompson, Trust Administrator

Trustees *Dr Kenneth Chrystie, Chair; The Hon. Miss Ann Fraser; Patricia Fraser; Blair Smith.*

SC Number SC007288

Information available Information was provided by the trust.

General The trust makes grants mainly to people in Scotland and their dependants who were or are engaged in the drapery and allied trades and the printing, publishing, books and stationery, newspaper and allied trades. Preference is given to people who are or were employed by House of Fraser Limited, Scottish Universal Investments Limited and Paisleys.

Grants are also made to Scottish organisations caring for older and infirm people with connections in the fields described above. It prefers to support small, community organisations which find it difficult to raise funds. It also prefers to support organisations in areas where there is little local funding available. The trustees 'consider that grants to large highly publicised national appeals are not likely to be as effective a use of funds as grants to smaller and more focused charitable appeals'.

In 2002/03 it had assets of £1.6 million and an income of £80,000. Grants to 19 organisations totalled £33,000, with a further £41,000 given to individuals.

The largest grants were £4,800 to Stobhill Kidney Kids' Association and £4,000 each to Colon Cancer Concern and St Andrew's Hospice. Other grants included £2,400 to Dundee City Council and £2,000 each to Leonard Cheshire Homes, DEBRA, Enable, Queen's Nursing Institute and St David's Cottage Day Centre.

Exclusions Applicants already receiving grants from the Hugh Fraser Foundation (see separate entry) will not be eligible.

Applications In writing to the correspondent. The trustees meet quarterly to consider applications. In 2003 the meetings were held in January, April, July and October. The trustees of this trust are also the trustees of the Hugh Fraser Foundation and applications are allocated to one or other of the trusts as appears appropriate.

The Louis and Valerie Freedman Charitable Settlement

General

£47,000 (2001/02)

Beneficial area UK, especially Burnham in Buckinghamshire.

c/o Bridge House, 11 Creek Road, East Molesey, Surrey KT8 9BE

Tel. 0208 941 4455

Correspondent F H Hughes, Trustee

Trustees *M A G Ferrier; F H Hughes.*

CC Number 271067

Information available Information was provided by the trust.

General The trust supports health, welfare and equine interests in which the Freedman family have a particular interest. Local education and youth charities in Burnham are also supported.

In 2003/04 it had an income of £103,000 and a total expenditure of £65,000. Further information for this year was not available.

In 2001/02 the trust had assets of £2.9 million and an income of £95,000. Grants were made totalling £47,000, including £15,000 each to Tavistock Trust for Aphasia and Winged Fellowship.

Exclusions No grants to individuals. Only registered charities are considered for support.

Applications There is no application form. Applications should be in writing to the correspondent and they will not be acknowledged. Notification of a failed application will only be given if a sae is enclosed

The Mr and Mrs F C Freeman Charitable Trust

General in the UK

£72,000 (2001/02)

Beneficial area UK.

United Trusts, PO Box 14, Liverpool L69 7AA

Tel. 0151 709 8252 **Fax** 0151 708 5621

Correspondent F C Freeman, Trust Patron and Secretary

Trustees *J B Bibby; R S Freeman; J R McGibbon.*

CC Number 326462

Information available Accounts were on file at the Charity Commission.

General This trust was registered with the Charity Commission in November 1983. It has general charitable purposes. The trust stated in the summer of 2004 that 'it is likely that distributions will exceed income in future years'.

In 2001/02 it had assets of £460,000 generating an income of £52,000. Grants totalling £72,000 were made to four organisations. Beneficiaries included United Way (£35,000), United Trusts (£33,000), Institute for the Study of Hierological Values (£3,000) and Invalids at Home (£1,000).

Applications In writing to the correspondent.

The Friarsgate Trust

Health and welfare of young and older people

£42,000 (2002/03)

Beneficial area UK, with a strong preference for West Sussex, especially Chichester.

The Corn Exchange, Bassins Lane, Chichester, West Sussex PO19 1GE

Tel. 01243 786111

Correspondent Miss Amanda King-Jones, Trustee

Trustees *A C Colenutt; T J Bastow.*

CC Number 220762

Information available Information was provided by the trust.

General The trust was established to support education of children whose parents are in need (including support for camps, playing fields and so on), orphans and the welfare of people in need, older people and other charitable causes. UK charities and local organisations are supported; in practice there is strong preference for East and West Sussex, especially Chichester.

In 2002/03 the trust had an income of £90,000 and assets came to £1.8 million. Grants totalled £42,000.

The largest grant by far of £5,000 was made to Fordwater School. Other donations included: £1,200 to Winged Fellowship Trust. There were 15 donations of £1,000 some beneficiaries were Air Training Corps (Chichester), Alzheimer's Society, Burgess Hill Girl Guide Hall Committee, Chichester Youth Adventure Trust, Mrs J Hardy (for Mandy), Macmillan Cancer Relief and The Sussex Autistic Society.

Other grants were between £250 and £750 and example beneficiaries are Chestnut Tree House (St Barnabas Hospice), Field Lane and Hastings Furniture Service.

Exclusions Local organisations outside Sussex are unlikely to be supported.

Applications In writing to the correspondent. Applicants are welcome to telephone first to check they fit the trust's criteria.

Friends of Biala Ltd

Jewish

About £70,000 (2001/02)

Beneficial area UK and overseas.

c/o 5 Rodsley Avenue, Gateshead NE8 4JY

Correspondent The Secretary

Trustees *B Z Rabinovitch; Mrs T Weinberg.*

CC Number 271377

Information available Accounts were on file at the Charity Commission, but without a list of grants.

General The trust supports religious education in accordance with the orthodox Jewish faith and registered welfare charities. In 2001/02 the trust had an income of £565,000 and a total expenditure of £79,000. Funds are raised by the trustees and volunteers. Grants totalled about £70,000. A list of beneficiaries was unfortunately unavailable.

Applications In writing to the correspondent. This entry was not confirmed by the trust but the information was correct according to the Charity Commission.

Friends of Wiznitz Limited

Jewish education

£410,000 (2002/03)

Beneficial area UK and overseas.

8 Jessam Avenue, London E5 9UD

Correspondent E Gottesfeld

Trustees *H Feldman; E Kahan; R Bergmann; S Feldman.*

CC Number 255685

Information available Grants were on file at the Charity Commission.

General This trust supports major educational projects being carried out by orthodox Jewish institutions.

In 2002/03 the trust had assets of £447,000, an income of £493,000 and made grants totalling £410,000.

Larger grants were £179,000 to Wiznitz Institution Israel, £50,000 to Yehivat Wiznitz, £36,000 to Congregation Tzemach Tzadik USA and £30,000 each to Mifal Chesed Tzemach Tzadik Israel and CMZ.

Other grants included £15,000 to Ahavat Israel Synagogue, £11,000 each to Kollel Aron Yisroel and Beth Harnidrash Wiznitz Israel, £10,000 each to Shemtov Charitable Trust and Imrei Chaim – Israel, £8,000 to Wiznitz Institution Belgium, £5,000 to Chasidei Wiznitz Antwerp, £4,000 each to Kollel Ateres Yeshiva and Wiznitz Synagogue and £2,000 to CMA Trust.

Applications In writing to the correspondent.

This entry was not confirmed by the trust but was correct according to information on file at the Charity Commission.

The Frognal Trust

Older people, disability, blindness/ ophthalmological research, environmental heritage, youth development

£41,000 (2002/03)

Beneficial area UK.

Charities Aid Foundation, King's Hill, West Malling, Kent ME19 4TA

Tel. 01732 520083 **Fax** 01732 520159

Correspondent Mrs Sue David, Donor Grants Officer

Trustees *Philippa Blake-Roberts; J P Van Montagu; P Fraser.*

CC Number 244444

Information available Full accounts were provided by the trust.

General The trust supports smaller charities rather than national organisations or local branches of large national charities.

In 2002/03 it had assets of £1.4 million, which generated an income of £59,000. Grants were made to 90 organisations totalling £41,000.

The largest grants, of £1,000 each, went to Alzheimer's Research Trust, Barnet Old People's Welfare Committee, Bovey Tracy Activities Trust, Canniesburn Research Trust, Dermatitis and Allied Diseases Research Trust, Elimination of Leukaemia Fund, Hartlepool Alzheimer's Trust, Ladybarn Community Association, Lancashire Wildlife Trust, Prince of Wales Foundation for Integrated Medicine, Royal Liverpool and Broadgreen University Hospitals NHS Trust and Wiltshire Wildlife Trust.

Other grants, more typical of the size given, included £500 each to Nottinghamshire Wildlife Trust and Shared Earth Trust, £450 to Meningitis Research Foundation, £440 to Dukes Barn Company, £400 each to East Grinstead Medical Research Trust and National Children's Orchestra, £350 each to Action for Blind People and Dolphin Society, £300 each to GlosAid Youth Action and Rutland House Community Trust, £250 to Joseph Clarke School Trust, £200 to Birmingham Young Volunteers Association and Edinburgh Sitters and £100 to Cheshire Deaf Society.

Exclusions The trust does not support:

- any animal charities
- the advancement of religion
- charities for the benefit of people outside the UK
- educational or research trips
- branches of national charities
- general appeals
- individuals.

Applications In writing to the correspondent. Applications should be received by February, May, August and November, for consideration at the trustees' meeting the following month.

T F C Frost Charitable Trust

Medical

About £195,000 (2002/03)

Beneficial area UK and overseas.

Holmes & Co Accountants, 10 Torrington Road, Claygate, Esher, Surrey KT10 0SA

Tel. 01372 465378

Correspondent The Trustees

Trustees *Mrs S E Frost; T A F Frost; M D Sanders; M H Miller.*

CC Number 256590

Information available Information was provided by the trust.

General The trust supports research associates of recognised centres of excellence in ophthalmology, individuals and organisations benefiting academics, medical professionals, research workers and people with sight loss.

In 2002/03 it had an income of £109,000. Grants totalled about £195,000 and assets totalled £2 million.

'Our Founders, wish in establishing the Frost Charitable Trust was to foster research into the prevention of blindness by supporting programmes submitted by senior trainees and by enhancing their horizons by underwriting the costs of educational or research periods of training at home or abroad at recognised centres.'

Donations in this year included £64,000 to Institute of Ophthalmology and Schepens Eye Research Institute Boston USA, £50,000 to Institute of Ophthalmology, £34,000 to The Rayne Institute St. Thomas' Hospital, £33,000 to University College London, £11,000 to Department of Optanetry and Vision

Sciences Cardiff University and £6,000 to University of Lancaster.

Exclusions There are no available resources for the relief of blind people or people suffering from diseases of the eye.

Applications In writing to the correspondent. Trustees meet twice a year.

The Patrick Frost Foundation

General

£185,000 (2002/03)

Beneficial area Worldwide, but only through UK charities.

c/o Trowers & Hamlins, Sceptre Court, 40 Tower Hill, London EC3N 4DX

Tel. 020 7423 8000 **Fax** 020 7423 8001

Correspondent Mrs H Frost, Trustee

Trustees *Mrs Helena Frost; Donald Jones; Luke Valner; John Chedzoy.*

CC Number 1005505

Information available Full accounts were provided by the foundation.

General The foundation makes general welfare grants to organisations and grants to help small charities that rely on a considerable amount of self-help and voluntary effort.

In 2002/03 the foundation's assets totalled £4.6 million, a high figure due to a large Gift Aid donation received in the previous year. The foundation had an income of £226,000 and grants were made to 24 organisations totalling £185,000. Legal and professional fees amounted to £22,000 to a firm in which one of the trustees is a partner. Even though wholly legal, these editors regret such payments unless, to use the words of the Charity Commission, 'there is no realistic alternative'.

The largest grants were £25,000 to Motivation Charitable Trust, £20,000 to St Joseph's Pastoral Centre and £10,000 each to Camphill Village Trust, Acorn Christian Foundation, Family Holiday Association, Trinity Hospice, Write Away and Worthing & District Animal Rescue Service.

The remaining beneficiaries each received £5,000. They included Ability Net, Chance for Children Trust, Contact the Elderly, Demand, Gurkha Welfare Trust, London Narrow Boat Project, Naomi House, Tools for Self Reliance, Tree Aid, Ty-Agored Animal Sanctuary and Reach.

A number of the above beneficiaries have been supported in previous years.

Exclusions No grants to individuals or non-UK charities.

Applications In writing to the correspondent, accompanied by the last set of audited accounts. The trustees regret that due to the large number of applications they receive, they are unable to acknowledge unsuccessful applications.

Maurice Fry Charitable Trust

Medicine, health, welfare, humanities, environmental resources, international

£28,000 (2002)

Beneficial area UK and overseas.

98 Savernake Road, London NW3 2JR

Tel. 020 7267 4969

Correspondent L Fry, Trustee

Trustees *L E A Fry; Miss A Fry; Mrs F Cooklin; Mrs L Weaks.*

CC Number 327934

Information available The information for this entry was provided by the trust.

General The trust's main areas of interest are welfare, humanities, environmental resources and international causes, but it is not restricted to these. Grants range between £500 and £2,500. Grants total about £25,000 a year, to about 30 charities.

In 2002 the trust had assets of £776,000 and a total income of £28,000. Grants to 26 organisations totalled £28,000. The largest grants were £2,500 to Island Trust and £2,250 to Womens' Aid Federation of Britain. Other beneficiaries included Charterhouse in Southwark, Intermediate Technology and NSPCC (£1,500 each), Alone in London, Borders Talking Newspaper, National Childbirth Trust, National Trust for Scotland and Tree Aid (£1,000 each) and Berwick Youth Project, Friends of Quetta Hospital, Life 50 Plus, National Missing Persons Helpline, Raleigh International and St John Association of South East Scotland (£500 each).

Exclusions No grants to individuals.

Applications The trust states that it does not respond to unsolicited applications.

The Fulmer Charitable Trust

Developing world, general

£124,000 (2002)

Beneficial area Worldwide, especially the developing world and Wiltshire.

Estate Office, Street Farm, Compton Bassett, Calne, Wiltshire SN11 8SW

Tel. 01249 760219

Correspondent J S Reis, Chair

Trustees *S A Reis; C M Mytum.*

CC Number 1070428

Information available Accounts were on file at the Charity Commission.

General Most of the support is given in the developing world, although UK charities are also supported, especially those working in Wiltshire.

In 2002/03 the trust had an income of £162,000 and a total expenditure of £138,000. Further information for this year was not available.

In the previous year it had assets of £1.7 million and an income of £159,000. Grants totalled £124,000 and ranged between £190 and £5,000.

Beneficiaries included: United Methodist Foundation (£5,000); UNICEF (£4,500); Care International (£5,000); Intermediate Technology Development Group (£3,500); Children in Distress, Church Mission Society, Ethiopaid, Sight Savers International, Tearfund and Traidcraft (£3,000 each); Salvation Army and Wiltshire Community Foundation (£2,500 each); Amnesty International, Church Army, Medical Foundation, Mercy Ships, NCH Action for Children and Project Rachel (£2,000 each); SOS Children's Village (£1,500); and Aid for the Aged in Distress, Church Housing Trust, Imperial Cancer Research, National Missing Persons Helpline and Wiltshire Air Ambulance (£1,000 each).

Recipients of smaller grants included; Abbeyfield Homes, Rotary Club of

Norwich and Shelter and Youth Action Wilshire (£500 each); and Wiltshire Ambulance Service Service Trust (£190).

Exclusions No support for gap year requests.

Applications In writing to the correspondent.

Gableholt Limited

Jewish

£71,000 (1999/2000)

Beneficial area UK.

115 Craven Park Road, London N15 6BL

Correspondent M A Vemitt, Governor

Trustees *S Noe; Mrs E Noe; C Lerner; P Noe.*

CC Number 276250

Information available Accounts were on file at the Charity Commission.

General Set up as a limited company in 1978, the trust gives practically all of its funds to Jewish institutions, particularly those working in accordance with the Orthodox Jewish faith.

In 2002/03 the trust had an income of £2 million and a total expenditure of £335,000. Further information for this year was not available.

In 1999/2000 it had assets of £3.5 million and an income of £344,000, of which £194,00 came from donations. Grants to organisations and individuals totalled £71,000.

Unfortunately no information on grants was included with the trust's accounts that were on file at the Charity Commission. In previous years beneficiaries have included: Afula Society, Child Resettlement, Friends of Harim Establishment, Friends of the Sick, Gur Trust, Mengrah Grammar School, Rachel Charitable Trust and Torah Venchased Le'Ezra Vasad.

Applications In the past this trust has stated that 'in the governors' view, true charitable giving should always be coupled with virtual anonymity' and for this reason they are most reluctant to be a party to any publicity. Along with suggesting that the listed beneficiaries might also want to remain unidentified, they also state that the nature of the giving (to orthodox Jewish organisations) means the information is unlikely to be of much interest to anyone else. Potential applicants would be strongly advised to take heed of these comments.

The Horace & Marjorie Gale Charitable Trust

General

£54,000 (2002/03)

Beneficial area UK, mainly Bedfordshire.

Garner Associates, 138 Bromham Road, Bedford MK40 2QW

Tel. 01234 354508

Correspondent Gerry Garner

Trustees *G D Payne, Chair; J Tyley; J Williams; P H Tyley; K Fletcher.*

CC Number 289212

Information available Full accounts were on file at the Charity Commission.

General The trust gives support in three areas:

- for churches and church ministries, with emphasis on Bunyan Meeting Free Church in Bedford and the ministries of the Baptist Union in England and Wales
- donations to charities and organisations active in the community life of Bedford and Bedfordshire
- donations to UK charities and organisations active in community life.

In 2002/03 the trust had assets of £1.9 million and an income of £65,000. After management and administration costs of £12,000, grants were made totalling £54,000. Donations were broken down as follows:

Churches – 9 grants totalling £26,000

By far the largest donation of £9,000 was made to Bunyan Meeting Free Church. Other grants included: £7,000 to The Baptist Union – Home Mission Fund; £4,000 to St Paul's Church, Bedford, £1,000 each to St Andrew's Church Bedford, St James Church Biddenham and St Peter's Church Bedford.

Local charities – 20 donations amounting to £21,000

Grants included: £2,000 each to North Bedfordshire Hospice and Sarah Burrow, £1,000 each to Bedford Playing Fields Association, Bedford Philharmonic Orchestra, Beds & Northants MS Therapy Centre, Befordshire Rural Communities Charity, Mayday Trust and Motor Neurone Disease Association and £500 to Cotton End Lower School,

General charities – 8 grants totalling £8,000

Beneficiaries each to recieve a grant of £1,000 were Arthritis Care, Brainwave, Coronary Prevention Group, Headway, Meningitis Research Foundation, National Blind Children's Society, Starlight Children's Foundation, The Wishbone Trust and Warboys Orphanage project.

Exclusions Grants are rarely given to individuals.

Applications In writing to the correspondent. Grants are distributed once a year and applications should be made by May for consideration in June.

The Angela Gallagher Memorial Fund

Children and youth, Christian, humanitarian, education

£31,000 (2001)

Beneficial area UK and international organisations based in the UK.

Church Cott, The Green, Mirey Lane, Woodbury, Nr Exeter, Devon EX5 1LT

Correspondent Mrs D R Moss, Secretary

Trustees *N A Maxwell-Lawford; P Mostyn; P A Wolrige Gordon; A Swan.*

CC Number 800739

Information available Full accounts are on file at the Charity Commission.

General The aim of the fund is to help children within the UK. The fund will also consider Christian, humanitarian and educational projects worldwide, although international disasters are only aided through British Red Cross or CAFOD. Small charities which do not have access to large corporate donors are given priority.

In 2003 the trust had an income of £30,000. A grant total or list of beneficiaries was not provided. However, we do know that in 1999, when grants totalled £45,000, CAFOD received three grants of £1,000 for disasters and emergencies. Other grants included £3,000 to Grace & Compassion Benedictines for Indian project and £1,000 each to AMREF for general work in Africa, Autism – Bedfordshire for general funding, C-Far for general funding, Lady Hoare Trust, Christina Noble Children's Fund for general funding, Novo Futuro for Portuguese Child Project, St Loye's Foundation and Uganda Disabled Children.

Exclusions Donations will not be made to the following: older people; scientific research; hospitals and hospices; artistic and cultural appeals; animal welfare; or building and equipment appeals. No grants to individuals.

Applications In writing to the correspondent, for consideration at trustees' meetings twice a year. Applicants must include a set of accounts or the appeal will not be considered. Applications are not acknowledged without an sae.

The Gamma Trust

General

About £60,000

Beneficial area UK, with a possible preference for Scotland.

Clydesdale Bank, Trust & Executry Unit, Brunswick House, 51 Wilson Street, Glasgow G1 1UZ

Tel. 0141 223 2507

Correspondent The Manager

SC Number SC004330

Information available Information was provided by the trust.

General This trust has general charitable purposes. It appears that new grants are only given to UK-wide organisations although most grants are ongoing commitments to local organisations in Scotland. It has a grant total of about £60,000 a year.

Beneficiaries in 2003 included £4,000 to British Red Cross and £3,000 each to British Heart Foundation, Cancer Research Campaign and Erskine Hospital.

Exclusions No grants to individuals.

Applications In writing to the correspondent for consideration quarterly.

Garrick Charitable Trust

Theatre, music, literature, dance

£103,000 (2001/02)

Beneficial area UK.

15 Garrick Street, London WC2E 9AY

Tel. 020 7836 1737 **Fax** 020 7379 5966

Correspondent The Secretary

Trustees *Revd G Reddington, Chair; N Willcox; N Newton; A Hammond; G Palmer.*

CC Number 1071279

Information available Information was provided by the trust.

General The trust was established by the members of the Garrick Club in London in 1998. It was expected to be endowed with about £4 million from the proceeds of selling the Winnie the Pooh copyright to the Disney organisation.

The trust is able to spend interest on capital and it is expected that it will support institutions which are seeking to further the profession of theatre (including dance), literature or music.

In 2001/02 the trust had assets of £4.1 million and an income of £4.2 million, almost entirely from donations. Grants totalled £103,000. Donations included: £10,000 each to Actors Professional Centre Ltd and Royal National Theatre Board; £7,500 to Chicken Shed Theatre Company; £5,000 each to Bath Festivals Trust, Freehand Theatre amd National Academy of Writing; and £2,500 to Bards Bash Celebrating Shakespeare, Rude Mechanical Theatre Company and Young Actors' Company.

Applications Initial approaches should be made in writing to the correspondent. Since it was established the trust has been receiving applications so there is likely to be high competition for funds.

Garvan Limited

Jewish

£163,000 (2002/03)

Beneficial area UK.

Flat 9, Windsor Court, Golders Green Road, London NW11 9PP

Correspondent S Ebert

Trustees *A Ebert; L Ebert.*

CC Number 286110

Information available Accounts were on file at the Charity Commission, but without a list of grants.

General This trust makes grants to Jewish organisations. In 2002/03 it had assets of £474,000 and an income of £245,000. Grants totalled £163,000. Unfortunately, no further information was available on the size or number of beneficiaries for this year.

Applications In writing to the correspondent.

Jacqueline and Michael Gee Charitable Trust

Health, education (including Jewish)

£93,000 (2002/03)

Beneficial area UK.

27 Berkeley House, Hay Hill, London W1J 8NS

Tel. 020 7493 1904 **Fax** 020 7499 1470

Email trust@sherman.co.uk

Correspondent Michael J Gee, Trustee

Trustees *M J Gee; J S Gee.*

CC Number 1062566

Information available Accounts were provided by the trust.

General This charity's policy is to benefit almost exclusively health and educational charities. In practice this includes many Jewish organisations.

It was created in 1997 by the settlement of £50 from the Archie Sherman Charitable Trust. In 2002/03 the trust had assets of £17,000, an income of £84,000 made up mostly from grants and made donations totalling £93,000.

Grants were broken down as follows:

Education and Training	£55,690
Arts and Culture	£22,000
Medical, Health and Sickness	£9,200
General Charitable Purposes	£2,300
Relief of Poverty	£1,500

Grant beneficiaries included Friends of the Hebrew University of Jerusalem (£15,000), Purcell School (£10,400), British Wizo (£9,250), BF of IPO, Garsington Opera, Manor House Trust, The Royal Academy of Arts and The Hall

School CT (£5,000 each), LJCC (£2,500) and Frank Foley Fair (£2,000).

Applications In writing to the correspondent.

The Gibbs Charitable Trust

Methodism, international, arts

£122,000 (2002/03)

Beneficial area UK, occasionally elsewhere.

8 Victoria Square, Clifton, Bristol BS8 4ET

Tel. 0117 973 6615 **Fax** 0117 974 4137

Website www.thegibbscharitabletrust.org.uk

Correspondent Dr James M Gibbs, Trustee

Trustees *Dr J N Gibbs; A G Gibbs; Dr J M Gibbs; W M Gibbs; Dr J E Gibbs; Mrs C Gibbs; Mrs E Gibbs; Mrs P Gibbs; Ms R N Gibbs; Ms J F Gibbs; Mrs J Gibbs.*

CC Number 207997

Information available Full accounts were provided by the trust.

General The trust supports innovative Methodist work, other Christian causes (especially those of an ecumenical nature) and creative arts, education and international causes. It has a slight preference for projects which can be easily visited by the trustees and it also occasionally supports overseas applications.

In 2002/03 it had assets of £1.6 million, which generated an income of £73,000. Grants were made totalling £122,000, broken down as follows:

Methodist churches, circuit and districts – 12 grants totalling £13,000

The largest were £4,000 to Alton Methodist Church, £3,000 to Penarth Circuit and £1,000 each to Evesham Methodist Church, Knowle Methodist Church and Pool Methodist Church. Aside from the £200 to Emsworth Methodist Church, all remaining grants were of £500 each.

Other Methodist initiatives – 8 grants totalling £24,000

These went to Jasperian Theatre Company (£8,000), Methodist Church Collection of Modern Christian Art (£7,500), Amelia Trust Farm (£3,000), Wesleyana Exhibition (£2,000), British Methodist Choir and MIH Bristol (£1,000), Essays in Methodism (£750) and National Methodist Youth Brass Band (£500).

Other Christian Initiatives – 7 grants totalling £5,500

Grants were £2,000 to Arthur Rank Centre, £1,000 to Oasis and £500 each to Bristol Cathedral for the Connect Appeal, Christians Abroad, Riding Lights, SCM Conference and Urbankaos.

International – 16 grants totalling £41,000

The largest were £13,000 to Christian Aid and £8,000 to Child to Child. Other beneficiaries included Sight Savers International – Sierra Leone and Traidcraft (£2,500 each), Intercare and Oxfam – Afghanistan (£2,000 each), Dabou Hospital – Ivory Coast (£1,000), Salt River Project – South Africa (£500) and Jama Koro Foundation (£200).

Arts and drama – 7 grants totalling £7,500

£5,000 went to Washington Gallery – Penarth. Other grants were £500 each to Builth Community Play, Circomedia, Cornwall Arts Trust and National Theatre, £250 to St John's – Waterloo and £200 to Puppets in Pomeroy.

Social and medical need – 4 grants totalling £2,500

These were £1,000 to Prisons Video Magazine and £500 each to L'Arche, St Briavels and Womankind.

Designated fund – 1 grant of £30,000

This went to Methodist Church Fund for ministerial training.

Exclusions A large number of requests are received by the trust from churches undertaking improvement, refurbishment and development projects, but only a few of these can be helped. In general, Methodist churches are selected, sometimes those the trustees have particular knowledge of.

Individuals and animal charities are not supported.

Applications The trust has no application forms, although an application cover sheet is available on the trust's website along with a policy and guidelines page. Requests should be made in writing to the correspondent. The trustees meet three times a year, at Christmas, Easter and late summer. Unsuccessful applicants are not normally notified. The trustees do not encourage telephone enquiries or speculative applications. They also state that they are not impressed by applicants that send a huge amount of paperwork.

The Glanrose Trust

General

£38,000 (2001/02)

Beneficial area UK.

HSBC, Norwich House, Nelson Gate, Commercial Road, Southampton SO15 1GX

Tel. 023 8072 2231 **Fax** 023 8072 2250

Correspondent Mr C Bould

Trustees *Wyn Howell Hughes; Margaret Theodora James; HSBC Trust Co. (UK) Ltd.*

CC Number 1079498

Information available Accounts were on file at the Charity Commission.

General Registered with the Charity Commission in February 2000, in 2001/02 the trust had assets of £643,000 and an income of £36,000. After management and administration costs of £4,500, grants totalled £38,000.

There were 12 grants made during the year to three organisations: BRC for Ethiopian famine relief, Barnardos and Salvation Army.

Applications In writing to the correspondent.

The B & P Glasser Charitable Trust

Health, disability, Jewish, welfare

About £62,000 (2001/02)

Beneficial area UK and worldwide.

Stafford Young Jones, The Old Rectory, 29 Martin Lane, London EC4R 0AU

Tel. 020 7623 9490

Correspondent B S Christer

Trustees *H Glasser; J C Belfrage; J D H Cullingham; M J Glasser; J A Glasser.*

CC Number 326571

Information available Accounts were on file at the Charity Commission, but without a full narrative report.

General This trust makes grants mainly to health and disability-related charities and Jewish charites, but also for other social-welfare purposes.

In 2001/02 the trust had an income of £77,000. Grants totalled around £62,000 and assets came to £1.1 million.

Beneficiaries included Nightingale House (£8,000), Jewish Care and Royal National Institute for the Blind (£5,000 each), Sight Savers International and UNICEF (£3,000 each), British Council Share Zadek Medical Centre, Friends of Magen David Adam, ITDG and Macmillan Cancer Relief (Hertfordshire) (£2,000 each) and Abbeyfield (Buckinghamshire) Society, Barnardo's, British Foundation, Help The Aged, Royal National Lifeboat Institute, and The Samaritans (Chiltern Branch) (£1,000 each).

Exclusions No grant to individuals or students.

Applications In writing to the correspondent. To keep administrative costs to a minimum the trust is unable to reply to unsuccessful applicants.

James Glyn Charitable Trust

Jewish

£358,000 (2000/01)

Beneficial area UK and Israel.

4 Harley Street, London W1G 9TB

Tel. 020 7631 0020

Correspondent J Glyn, Trustee

Trustees *J Glyn; Mrs S C Glyn; S Glyn; T M Glyn.*

CC Number 266245

Information available Information was collated from the Charity Commission.

General In 2000/01 the trust had assets of £2,000, an income of £13,000 and made grants totalling £358,000.

Grant beneficiaries included James and Sarah Glyn Fund (£305,000), Lubavitch Foundation (£12,500), Jewish Care (£10,300), British WIZO (£4,900), Joint Jewish Charitable Trust–UJIA (£5,100), Western Marble Arch Synagogue (£3,000), British Friends of the Jaffa Institute and British Ort (£2,850 each), Community Security Trust (£2,700) and World Jewish Relief (£1,900).

Exclusions No grants to individuals.

Applications In writing to the correspondent.

GMC Trust

Medical research, healthcare, general

£53,000 (2004)

Beneficial area UK, predominantly in the West Midlands.

4 Fairways, 1240 Warwick Road, Knowle, Solihull, West Midlands B93 9LL

Tel. 01564 779971 **Fax** 01564 770499

Correspondent Rodney Pitts, Secretary

Trustees *Sir Adrian Cadbury; B E S Cadbury; M J Cadbury.*

CC Number 288418

Information available Full accounts from the trust.

General The trust supports medical research and causes related to inner city disadvantage. Income is substantially committed to a range of existing beneficiaries.

In 2004 the trust had assets of £1.8 million and an income of £62,000. Grants totalled £53,000.

The largest were: £10,000 each to Cancer Research (Birmingham) and Mental Health Foundation. Other beneficiaries included Acorns Children's Hospice (£6,000); Birmingham Settlement (£5,000); Runnymede Trust (£2,500); and Alzheimer's Research Trust, Friend's of Nelson Mandela Children's Fund, Listening Books, Prisoners of Conscience Appeal and Rehab UK (£1,000 each).

Exclusions No grants to individuals, or to local or regional appeals outside the West Midlands. The trust does not respond to national appeals, except where there are established links.

Applications In writing to the correspondent. The trust will only consider written applications, and applications outside the trust's remit will not be acknowledged.

The GNC Trust

General

£77,000 (2001/02)

Beneficial area UK, with preferences for Midlands, Cornwall and Hampshire.

c/o Messrs PricewaterhouseCoopers, Temple Court, Bull Street, Birmingham B4 6JT

Tel. 0121 265 5000 **Fax** 0121 265 5450

Correspondent R Hardy, Agent to the Trustees

Trustees *G T E Cadbury; R Cadbury; Mrs J E B Yelloly.*

CC Number 211533

Information available Full accounts were on file at the Charity Commission.

General In 2001/02 the trust had assets of £166,000 with an income of £83,000 and grants totalling £77,000.

The largest grants were £20,000 to Downing College, £10,000 to National Institute of Conductive Education and £8,000 to Charnoy Manor (Society of Friends).

Other grants included £5,600 to Brooke Hospital for Animals, £5,000 to Meridian Trust Association and £4,000 to Britain Yearly Meeting (Society of Friends).

Grants of £1,000 of or less were awarded to St John Eye Hospital, Association for Spinabifida and Hydrocephalus, Birmingham Symphony Hall, Action Aid, Miracles, Women's Link, Age Concern, Alzheimers Society, Birmingham Settlement, British Cancer Help Centre and Children of the Andes.

Exclusions Only very occasionally are grants made to individuals. National appeals are not favoured, nor are most London-based charities.

Applications In writing to the correspondent at any time. There are no application forms and applications are not acknowledged.

The Joseph & Queenie Gold Charitable Trust

Jewish, general

£55,000 (2002/03)

Beneficial area UK.

Phredella House, Hyver Hill, Mill Hill, London NW7 4HU

Tel. 020 8959 2300

Correspondent Mrs Queenie Gold, Trustee

Trustees *Mrs Queenie Gold; Mrs Carol Djanogly.*

CC Number 286351

Information available Full accounts were on file at the Charity Commission.

General The trust makes grants mainly to Jewish organisations, although other charities are also occasionally supported.

In 2002/03 the trust had assets of £471,000 with an income of £27,000 and grants totaling £55,000.

The largest grants were £25,000 to Jewish Free School General Charitable Trust and £10,000 each to JJA Victim Support Aid and VJJA.

Other grants include £3,000 to Community Security Trust, £1,150 to Friends of Barla University, £1,000 each to BW Elstree Synagogue for Mikvah, Jewish Care, JAMI and Youth Aliyah.

Grants of less than £1,000 were awarded to Seopus, Save the Children, Friends of Alyn Hospital, Hospice St John's, Beth Shalom, World Cancer Research, Shaare Sedek Hospital, BBC Children in Need, United Jewish Israel Appeal and Salvation Army.

Exclusions No grants to individuals.

Applications In writing to the correspondent. This entry was not confirmed by the trust, but the information was correct according to the trust's file at the Charity Commission.

The Sydney & Phyllis Goldberg Memorial Charitable Trust

Medical research, welfare, disability

£45,000 (2002/03)

Beneficial area UK.

Coulthards Mackenzie, 17 Park Street, Camberley, Surrey GU15 3PQ

Tel. 01276 65470

Correspondent M J Church, Trustee

Trustees *H G Vowles; M J Church; C J Pexton.*

CC Number 291835

Information available Full accounts were on file at the Charity Commission.

General The income for the trust comes from its investments which are mainly held in Syona Investments Limited. Phyllis Goldberg initially bequeathed her shareholding in Syona Investments Limited to the trust and since then the trust has bought the balance of the shares.

In 2002/03 the trust had assets of £1.8 million with an income of £41,500 and grants totalling £45,000.

Grants include £6,000 each to Prostate Cancer Charity, Queen Alexander Hospital Portsmouth, Children of St Mary's Intensive Care Department of Child Health, Children with Special Needs Foundation, Dystonia Society and British Stammering Association.

Grants of £3,000 were made to Isaac Goldberg Charity Trust, Kidsactive and Cystic Fibrosis Trust.

Applications In writing to the correspondent. Telephone requests are not appreciated. Applicants are advised to apply towards the end of the calendar year.

Golden Charitable Trust

Preservation, conservation

£111,000 (2001/02)

Beneficial area UK with a preference for West Sussex.

Little Leith Gate, Angel Street, Petworth, West Sussex GU28 0BG

Tel. 01798 342434

Correspondent Lewis Golden, Secretary to the Trustees

Trustees *Mrs S J F Solnick; J M F Golden.*

CC Number 263916

Information available Information was on file at the Charity Commission.

General The trust appears to have a preference in its grantmaking for organisations in West Sussex in the field of the preservation and conservation of historic articles and materials.

In 2003/04 the trust had an income of £200,000 and a total expenditure of £78,000. Further details for this year were not available.

In 2001/02 it had assets of £390,000 and an income of £100,000, including £84,000 from donations. After minimal expenses of £118, grants were made to 13 organisations totalling £111,000. By far the largest was £100,000 to Westminster Synagogue. Other beneficiaries included British ORT (£5,000), Petworth Festival (£1,500), Friends of King Edward Hospital – Midhurst (£1,400), National Trust (£1,000), Chichester Cathedral Restoration and Development Trust (£700), Whizz-Kidz (£500) and Petworth Cottage Nursing Home (£450).

Exclusions No grants to individuals.

Applications In writing to the correspondent.

The Jack Goldhill Charitable Trust

Jewish, general

£170,000 (2002)

Beneficial area UK.

85 Kensington Heights, Campden Hill Road, London W8 7BD

Correspondent Jack Goldhill, Trustee

Trustees *G Goldhill; J A Goldhill; M L Goldhill.*

CC Number 267018

Information available Accounts were on file at the Charity Commission.

General In 2002 the trust had assets of £503,000 with an income of £80,000 and grants totalling £170,000. Unfortunately no grants list was provided for recent years.

In 1999 the trust had assets of £596,000 and an income of £80,000, including £25,000 in donations received. Grants totalled £84,000.

The largest grants were £27,000 to Jack Goldhill Award Fund and £18,000 to Jewish Care, both of which are regularly supported by the trust.

Other grants included £3,500 to CST, £3,000 to Royal London Hospital, £2,300 to Joint Jewish Charitable Trust, £2,000 each to Inclusion, Tate Gallery and Tricycle Theatre Co., £1,500 to West London Synagogue and £1,000 each to Atlantic College, City and Guilds of London School of Art, JNF Charitable Trust, Nightingale House and Royal Academy of Arts.

Exclusions No support for individuals or new applications.

Applications The trustees have a restricted list of charities to whom they are committed and no unsolicited applications can be considered.

The Goldschmied Charitable Settlement

Education, general

£101,000 (1999/2000)

Beneficial area UK.

Lee Associates, 5 Southampton Place, London WC1A 2DA

Tel. 020 7025 4600

Correspondent K A Hawkins

Trustees *A Goldschmied; M L S Goldschmied.*

CC Number 283250

Information available Accounts were on file at the Charity Commission, but without a narrative report or grants list.

General In 2001/02 the trust had an income of £182,000 and a total expenditure of £122,000. Further information was not available.

In 1999/2000 the trust's assets totalled £124,000 and its income was £17,000. Charitable expenditure was split into two categories – money given as charitable donations, which totalled £37,000, and money given for educational purposes, which totalled £64,000.

The annual report states the trust's objectives as the support of general charitable activities. It also stated that 'following the failure of the Ancient Egyptian Cultural Centre to attract sufficient students, the charity is seeking to dispose of the property that was acquired'.

There was no list of grants in the public files at the Charity Commission, but in 1997/98 beneficiaries were Architectural Association Building Fund (£4,400), Egyptian Cultural Centre (£2,300), St James Bursary Fund (£1,500) and St James Independent School (£114). In that year grants totalled only £8,400.

Applications In writing to the correspondent.

This entry was not confirmed by the trust, but the information was correct according to the trust's file at the Charity Commission.

The Golsoncott Foundation

The arts

£60,000 (2002/03)

Beneficial area UK.

31 Danes Road, Exeter EX4 4LS

Tel. 01392 252855 **Fax** 01392 252855

Correspondent Hal Bishop, Administrator

Trustees *Penelope Lively, Chair; Josephine Lively; Stephen Wick; Diana Hinds; Dr Harriet Harvey Wood.*

CC Number 1070885

Information available Full accounts were provided by the trust.

General The trust states its objects as follows: 'to promote, maintain, improve and advance the education of the public in the arts generally and in particular the fine arts and music. The fostering of the practice and appreciation of the arts, especially amongst young people and new audiences, is a further specific objective.

'Grants vary according to context and are not subject to an inflexible limit, but they are unlikely to exceed £5,000 and are normally given on a non-recurrent basis.'

In 2002/03 the foundation had assets of £1.4 million and an income of £60,000. Grants to 32 organisations totalled £60,000. Larger grants were: £5,000 each to Geffrye Museum, National Youth Orchestra and Scottish Opera, £4,000 to Gladstonbury Festival for the Dollis Hill House restoration; £3,500 to Philharmonic Orchestra; £3,000 to Ledbury Poetry Festival; and £2,500 each to Ballet West and Sarum Chamber Orchestra.

Other grants £2,000 and below included: £2,000 each to Britten Sinfonia, Peter Darrell Trust and Tabula Rasa; £1,500 each to Painting in Hospitals – Scotland and Words Live Literature Festival; £1,300 to Concerts for Rodhuish Church; £1,000 each to Oglander Roman Trust, Royal Schools for the Deaf and South West Academy of Arts; £580 to Hand & Eye Press; and £500 each to National Youth Orchestra and Second World War Experience Centre.

Exclusions No grants to individuals.

Applications The trustees meet quarterly to consider applications, in February, May, August and November. Applications should be sent to the correspondent by the end of the month preceding the month of the trustees meeting. They should include the following:

- 'A clear and concise statement of the project, whether the award sought will be for the whole project or a component part. Is the applicant organisation of charitable status?
- 'Evidence that there is a clear benefit to the public, i.e. does the project conform with the declared object of the trust.
- 'The amount requested should be specified, or a band indicated. Is this the only source of funding being sought? All other sources of funding should be indicated, including those that have refused funding.
- 'If the grant requested is part of the match-funding required by the Heritage Lottery Foundation (HLF) following an award, state the amount of that award and the percentage of match-funding required by the HLF and the completion date.
- 'Wherever possible an annual report and accounts should accompany the application, as may other supporting information deemed relevant.

'Second or further applications will not be considered until a minimum of 12 months has elapsed since determination of the previous application, whether successful or not.'

The Good Neighbours Trust

People with mental or physical disabilities

£54,000 (2003)

Beneficial area UK, with preference for Bristol, Somerset and Gloucestershire.

16 Westway, Nailsea, Bristol BS48 2NA

Correspondent P S Broderick, Secretary

Trustees *G V Arter, Chair; J C Gurney; P S Broderick.*

CC Number 201794

Information available Information was provided by the trust.

General The present policy of the trust is to principally support registered charities whose activities benefit people who are physically or mentally disabled. It mainly gives one-off grants for low-cost specific projects such as purchase of equipment or UK holidays for people with disabilities.

In 2003 the trust had assets of £2 million and an income of £75,000. Grants totalling £54,000 were made to 117 organisations and were broken down as follows.

Local Grants – 42 grants were made totalling £19,000

Beneficiaries included £1,000 to RNID – Bath, £500 each to Bath Opportunity Pre School, Jackdaws Educational Trust – Frome, Jessie May Trust – Bristol, National Eye Research Centre – Bristol, Spring Centre Trust Fund – Gloucestershire and Taunton Opportunity Group – Taunton and £250 each to Anchor Society – Bristol, Gloucester MS Information Centre, North Wilts Holiday Club – Chippenham and Tripscope – Bristol.

National Grants – 75 grants were made totalling £36,000

Beneficiaries included £2,500 to Help the Hospices and £1,000 each to Ace Centre Advisory Trust, Ataxia Telangiectasia Society, Curnow Special School – Cornwall, Deafblind UK, Eyeless Trust, Pace Centre, Royal National Institute for the Deaf and West of England School & College for Young People with Little or No Sight.

Exclusions Support is not given: for overseas projects; general community projects*; individuals; general education projects*; religious and ethnic projects*; projects for unemployment and related training schemes*; projects on behalf of offenders and ex-offenders; projects concerned with the abuse of drugs and/or alcohol; wildlife and conservation schemes*; and general restoration and preservation of buildings, purely for historical and/or architectural reasons.

* If these projects are mainly or wholly for the benefit of people who have disabilities then they will be considered.

Ongoing support is not given, and grants are not usually given for running costs, salaries, research and items requiring major funding. Loans are not given.

Applications The trust does not have an official application form. Appeals should be made in writing to the secretary and the trust asks that the following is carefully considered before submitting an application:

Appeals must:

- be from registered charities
- include a copy of the latest audited accounts available (for newly registered charities a copy of provisional accounts showing estimated income and expenditure for the current financial year)
- show that the project is 'both feasible and viable' and, if relevant, give the starting date of the project and the anticipated date of completion
- include the estimated cost of the project, together with the appeal's target-figure and details of what funds have already been raised and any fundraising schemes for the project.

The trustees state that 'where applicable, due consideration will be given to evidence of voluntary and self-help (both in practical and fundraising terms) and to the number of people expected to benefit from the project'. They also comment that their decision is final and 'no reason for a decision, whether favourable or otherwise, need be given' and that 'the award and acceptance of a grant will not involve the trustees in any other commitment'.

Appeals are dealt with on an ongoing basis, but the trustees meet formally four times per year in March, June, September and December.

Nicholas & Judith Goodison's Charitable Settlement

Arts, arts education

£178,000 (2002/03)

Beneficial area UK.

PO Box 2512, London W1A 5ZP

Correspondent Sir N Goodison, Trustee

Trustees *Sir Nicholas Goodison; Lady Judith Goodison; Miss Katharine Goodison.*

CC Number 1004124

Information available Full accounts were provided by the trust.

General The trust supports registered charities in the field of the arts and arts education. Grants are also given to institutions in instalments over several years towards capital projects.

In 2002/03 it had assets of £1.1 million, which generated an income of £277,000. Grants were made to 26 organisations totalling £178,000. Management and administration expenses for the year were very low at just £590.

The largest grants were £51,000 to Tate Gallery, £33,000 to Fitzwilliam Museum and £28,000 to English National Opera.

Other large grants were £17,000 to British Museum, £11,000 to Courtauld Institute of Art, £8,000 to Worshipful Company of Clockmakers, £7,000 to Dulwich Picture Gallery, £5,500 to Wigmore Hall, £5,000 to National Life Story Collection, £2,000 to National Art Collections Fund, £1,500 to World Monuments Fund and £1,000 each to Aldeburgh Productions, Handel House Trust, Royal Academy Exhibitions, Movern Parish Church, Museum of London and Victoria and Albert Museum.

Smaller grants were £650 to Ashmolean Museum, £500 each to Academy of Ancient Music, Miriam Dean Refugee Trust, King Edward VII Hospital, Methodist Church Collections of Art and Westminster Cathedral, £320 to Albanian Musicians' Trust, £250 to Heritage of London Trust and £200 to King's College Supplementary Exhibition Fund.

Exclusions No grants to individuals.

Applications The trust states that it cannot respond to unsolicited applications.

Leonard Gordon Charitable Trust

Jewish religious, educational and welfare organisations

£35,000 (2001/02)

Beneficial area England and Wales.

17 Park Street, Salford M7 4NJ

Tel. 0161 792 3421

Correspondent Leonard Gordon, Chair

Trustees *Leonard Gordon, Chair; Geoffrey Robert Marks.*

CC Number 1075185

Information available Information was on file with the charity Commission.

General Established in 1999, in 2003/04 this trust had an income of £17,000 and a total expenditure of £53,000. Further information for this year was not available.

In 2001/02 it had an income of £41,000, including £32,000 in a donation from the settlor. Grants were made totalling £35,000. No list of donations was included with the accounts.

Applications In writing to the correspondent.

This entry was not confirmed by the trust, but was correct according to information on file at the Charity Commission.

The Gough Charitable Trust

Youth, Episcopal and Church of England, preservation of the countryside, social welfare

£36,000 available (2003/04)

Beneficial area UK, with a possible preference for Scotland.

Lloyds TSB Private Banking Ltd, UK Trust Centre, 22–26 Ock Street, Abingdon OX14 5SW

Correspondent Mrs E Osborn-King, Trust Manager

Trustees *Lloyds Bank plc; N de L Harvie.*

CC Number 262355

Information available Accounts were on file at the Charity Commission.

Information available

General In 2003/04 the trust had an income of £36,000 and a total expenditure of £77,000. Although the trust have updated their financial status with the Charity Commission, full accounts for 2003/04 were not available.

Instead we refer to 2003/04 in which the trust had an income of £48,000 and an expenditure of £45,000. Charitable payments totalling £40,000 were made, leaving over £128,000 carried forward to the following year. The trust has previously shown a preference for Scotland, however it is not clear if this is still the case.

Beneficiaries in 2000/01 included St Luke with Holy Trinity Charlton (£15,000), RNLI (£10,000), Wykeham Crown and Manor Trust and 999 Club (£5,000 each). Small grants of £100 to £200 were given to National Army Development Trust, Lifeboat Service, Trinity Hospice, Household Brigade Lodge Benevolent Fund, The Prince of Wales Lodge Benevolent Fund, Irish Guards' Fund, Lloyds' Benevolent Fund and Lloyds' Charities Fund.

Exclusions No support for non-registered charities and individuals including students.

Applications In writing to the correspondent at any time. No application forms are available; no acknowledgements are sent. Applications are considered quarterly.

The Gould Charitable Trust

General

£60,000 (2002/03)

Beneficial area UK.

Cervantes, Pinner Hill, Pinner, Middlesex HA5 3XU

Correspondent S Gould, Trustee

Trustees *Mrs J B Gould; L J Gould; M S Gould; S Gould; S H Gould.*

CC Number 1035453

Information available Accounts were on file at the Charity Commission.

General In 2002/03 the trust had an income of £72,000 and made grants totalling £60,000.

By far the largest grant was £25,000 to JPAIME. Other grants over £1,000 included LMT (£4,000), Childhope Asia Philippines and Diabetes UK (£3,300 each), Friends of Philharmonica, Medecins sans Frontieres and Pattan (£2,000 each), National Medicines Society (£1,500) and World Jewish Relief (£1,100).

Most grants were for under £1,000 and beneficiaries included JNF (£830), Friends of Hebrew University and Youth Aliyah (£400), SOS Child Village (£300), St Catherine's College (£200), Arthritis Research, Hackney Quest, New Israel Fund, Palace Theatre and Westminster Pastoral (£100 each).

Exclusions No support for non-registered charities. No grants to individuals.

Applications In writing to the correspondent, although the trust states: 'We never give donations to unsolicited requests on principle.'

The Grace Charitable Trust

Christian

£396,000 (2002/03)

Beneficial area UK.

Rhuallt House, Rhuallt, St Asaph, Sir Ddinbych LL17 0TG

Tel. 01745 583141 **Fax** 01745 585243

Correspondent Mrs G J R Payne, Trustee

Trustees *Mrs G J R Payne; E Payne; Mrs G M Snaith; R B M Quayle.*

CC Number 292984

Information available Information was provided by the trust and accounts were on file at the Charity Commission. However, a grants list was not available.

General In 2002/03 the trust had assets of £4.8 million and an income of £208,000, mostly from investments. After management and administration costs of £1,500, grants to organisations totalled £396,000.

Whilst no information on beneficiaries was available, the trust confirmed it give grants generally of £1,000 to £10,000 each with a preference for Christian organisations. The only known recipient in recent years is OAC Ministries, which received £2,000 in 2001/02.

Applications The trust states: 'Grants are made only to charities known to the settlors and unsolicited applications are, therefore, not considered.'

The Grahame Charitable Foundation

Jewish

£209,000 (2002)

Beneficial area UK and worldwide.

5 Spencer Walk, Hampstead High Street, London NW3 1QZ

Tel. 020 7794 5281 **Fax** 020 7794 0094

Correspondent Mrs S Brooks

Trustees *Gitte Grahame; Jeffrey Greenwood.*

CC Number 259864

Information available Accounts were on file at the Charity Commission, but without a grants list.

General The trust's objects are to advance education, relieve poverty and advance religion anywhere in the world. In practice, it appears to make grants to these ends mainly to Jewish charities. Each year small grants are made to a handful of non-Jewish welfare and medical charities.

In 2002 the trust's assets totalled £359,000. It had an income of £208,000, including £141,000 in covenants and donations and £61,000 in rent. Grants totalled £209,000. Unfortunately, for several years now, the trust has not provided a grants list.

The last information available on grants related to 1996, when the trust made 120 grants totalling £81,000. The largest grants were £15,000 to Child Resettlement Fund, £10,000 to Jerusalem College and £5,000 each to Bais Ruzin Trust and Share Zedek. Most grants were for £500 or less. The only non-Jewish beneficiaries were Operation Wheelchairs (£150) with £100 each to Sue Harris Bone Marrow Transplant, The Samaritans and Scope.

Exclusions No grants to individuals.

Applications In writing to the correspondent. Funds are fully committed for the next four to five years. The trustees allocate funds on a long-term basis and therefore have none available for other applicants.

Grand Charitable Trust of the Order of Women Freemasons

General in the UK and overseas

£63,000 to non-Masonic charities (2001/02)

Beneficial area UK and overseas.

27 Pembridge Gardens, London W2 4EF

Tel. 020 7229 2368

Correspondent Mrs Joan Sylvia Brown, Trustee

Trustees *B I Fleming-Taylor; M J P Masters; B I Whittingham; H I Naldrett; J S Brown; I M Boggia-Black.*

CC Number 1059151

Information available Accounts were on file at the Charity Commission, but without a list of beneficiaries.

General This trust donates about half its grant total to causes related to the Order of Women Freemasons, including individual members and their dependants. The remaining half is donated to external charities.

In 2001/02 it had assets of £532,000 and an income of £157,000. A payment of £47,000 went to Adelaide Litten Charitable Trust, who provides support to individual Masons who are in need. Grants to other organisations totalled £63,000 while a total of £5,600 went directly to individuals.

Unfortunately there was no grants list included in the trust's accounts which makes it difficult to know which non-Masonic charities are supported, although the trust has previously stated that it helped a number of hospices during 1999/2000. The trust refused to send us a copy of their annual report and accounts, stating their policy of only supplying them to the Charity Commission and members of the Order of Women Freemasons. This is despite an obligation to supply them to any member of the public who requests them.

Applications In writing to the correspondent. Applications should be submitted by the end of July each year for consideration by the trustees.

The Grand Order of Water Rats' Charities Fund

Theatrical, medical equipment

£88,000 (2001)

Beneficial area UK.

328 Gray's Inn Road, London WC1X 8BZ

Tel. 020 7407 8007 **Fax** 020 7403 8610

Email gowr4adrian@aol.com

Website www.gowr.net

Correspondent John Adrian, Secretary

Trustees *Wyn Calvin; Declan Cluskey; Roy Hudd; Kaplan Kaye; Keith Simmons.*

CC Number 292201

Information available Accounts were provided by the trust but without a list of grants. Updated information was not available at the Charity Commission.

General The trust was established to assist members of the variety and light entertainment profession and their dependants who, due to illness or age, are in need. The fund also buys medical equipment for certain institutions and also for individuals who have worked with or who have been closely connected with the same profession.

In 2001 the trust had an income of £130,000 and a total expenditure of £137,000. The income mainly comes from the profit gained from functions organised by the members of the Grand Order of Water Rats. The assets at the year-end stood at £896,000. Grants totalled £88,000, which included £48,000 listed as donations, £38,000 in monthly allowances, grants and gifts, and £2,700 for fruit and flowers.

In 1997, the last year in which grant information was available, the largest grants went to Cause for Hope (£11,000), Bud Flanagan Leukaemia Fund (£6,700) and Queen Elizabeth Hospital for Children (£3,000). There were six grants of between £1,000 and £2,000 including those to Actors Church Union, British Legion Wales and Northwick Park Hospital.

Exclusions No grants to students.

Applications In writing to the correspondent. The trustees meet once a month.

The Constance Green Foundation

Social welfare, medicine, health, general

£208,000 (2002/03)

Beneficial area England, with a preference for West Yorkshire.

ASL House, 12–14 Davis Place, St Helier, Jersey JE2 4TD

Tel. 01534 560100

Email management@asl-jersey.com

Correspondent The Trustees

Trustees *M Collinson; Col. H R Hall; Mrs M L Hall; Mrs S Collinson.*

CC Number 270775

Information available Report and accounts were provided by the trust.

General The foundation makes grants mainly in the fields of social welfare and medicine. There is a special emphasis on the needs of young people and people who are mentally or physically disabled. In 2002/03 it had assets of £6.2 million generating an income of £362,000. Out of 761 eligible applications received, 65 grants were made to organisations totalling £208,000. From this figure 70% (in value) was given to charities operating within the UK and 30% to those outside the UK. Within the UK, 52% (£108,000) was given to charities either operating in, or with projects focused on, various parts of Yorkshire. Grants were broken down as follows:

Medical and social care, including terminal care for children and young people 11%

People who are disabled, both physically and mentally 6.5%

People who are homeless 10.5%

Children and young people, including those who are disadvantaged 42%

Medical, including facilities and equipment 10%

Church and community projects 20%

Most grants were made to assist special projects, rather than to provide core funding.

The accounts stated: 'During the year the Trustees agreed in principal to provide major financial support to Disability Action Yorkshire in connection with their redevelopment project at St George's House, Harrogate, which is expected to take place in 2003/04. No formal offer to provide this financial assistance has yet been made, but the trustees considered it necessary to reserve some part of the 2002/03 accruing income to meet this potential commitment.'

The largest grant was £20,000 to Nidderdale Swimming Pool Appeal. Other major beneficiaries were First Steps – Scarborough (£15,000), UK Scout Association (£13,000) and Friends of GOVI, Leeds Teaching Hospitals NHS Trust – Eye Research Centre and Rift Valley Futures (£10,000 each).

Grants under £10,000 included Africa Equipment for Schools, Boys' and Girls' Welfare Society, Children in Distress, Eureka, Halifax Learning Zone, Operation Smile and Save The Children (£5,000 each), Children's Heart Federation (£3,500), National Playing Fields Association and St Gemma's Hospice (£2,500 each), Esther Benjamin's Trust and Whizz Kids (£2,000 each) and Extra – Care Charitable Trust, Night Stop UK and Rainbow Centre (£1,000 each).

Grants of £500 included those to ACT, Bradford District Autistic Support Group, Centre Point, GlosAid, Peter Pan Nursery – Newcastle, Seven Springs Foundation and York Women's Aid.

Exclusions Sponsorship of individuals is not supported.

Applications At any time in writing to the correspondent (no special form of application required). Applications should include clear details of the need the intended project is designed to meet, plus an outline budget. All applications meeting the foundation's criteria are acknowledged.

The Barry Green Memorial Fund

Animal welfare

£57,000 (2002/03)

Beneficial area UK, with a preference for Yorkshire and Lancashire.

Claro Chambers, Horsefair, Boroughbridge, York YO51 9LD

Correspondent The Clerk to the Trustees

Trustees *Richard Fitzgerald-Hart; Mark Fitzgerald-Hart.*

CC Number 1000492

Information available Information was provided by the trust.

General The trust was created under the Will of Mrs E M Green. It supports animal welfare charities concerned with the rescue, maintenance and benefit of cruelly treated animals and also the prevention of cruelty to animals. There is a preference for small charities.

In 2002/03 the trust had assets of £1.2 million and an income of £180,000. Management and administration costs totalled £71,000. Grants to 48 organisations totalled £57,000, including 17 that were supported in the previous year. The grant total is a significant reduction from the previous year when £137,000 was given although the trust anticipates making a much larger total of grants in 2003/04. Grants ranged from £200 to £4,000, although most were for £1,000 or less.

Beneficiaries included Royal Veterinary College (£4,000), Assisi Animal Sanctuary, Vale Wildlife Rescue and Wildlife in Need (£3,000 each), Eden Animal Rescue, Society for the Welfare of Horses & Ponies, South West Equine Protection and Westport Wildlife Rescue (£2,000 each) and Brooke Hospital for Animals, Labrador Rescue Trust, Proteous Reptile Trust, Tyddyn Cat Rescue Centre and HADA Golden Oldies (£1,000 each).

Beneficiaries receiving £500 or less included Cats Protection League, Cotton Tails Sanctuary, Island Farm Donkey Sanctuary and Sattburn Animal Rescue Association (£500 each), Buchanan Veterinary Group, Hennley Veterinary Group and Lincolnshire Trust for Cats (£250 each) and Famborough Pets to Vets (£200).

This trust has stated that a large proportion of the applications it receives bear no relation to its objects.

Exclusions No expeditions, scholarships, work outside the UK or individuals.

Applications In writing to the correspondent including a copy of the accounts.

The Philip Green Memorial Trust

Young and older people, people with disabilities, people in need

£290,000 (2003/04)

Beneficial area UK.

301 Trafalgar House, Grenville Place, Mill Hill, London NW7 3SA

Tel. 020 8906 8732 **Fax** 020 8906 8574

Email info@pgmt.org.uk

Website www.pgmt.org.uk

Correspondent The Trustees

CC Number 293156

Information available Accounts were provided by the trust.

General The trust's 2003/04 set of accounts states that the objectives of the charity are 'raising money to help young people, older people, people with disabilities, and the needy in the community at large'.

It had assets of £2.5 million and received donations totalling £564,000 of which £557,000 was raised through means such as annual dinners, a quiz night and the London Marathon.

The beneficiary of the largest grant was CHAS Trading (Scotish Hospice) who received £127,000. Other grant beneficiaries included Community Security Trust, Glen Family Centre and The Stephen and Lorraine Trust (£10,000), PACE Centre (£7,000), Edgware and District Reform Synagogue (£6,500), St Joan of Ark School (£6,400), Jewish Care (£5,000), Best of Morocco Ltd (£4,000) and London Ex-Boxers Association (£1,000).

Applications In writing to the correspondent.

Mrs H R Greene Charitable Settlement

General, particularly at risk-groups, poverty, social isolation

About £63,000 to organisations (2002/03)

Beneficial area UK, with a preference for Norfolk and Wistanstow in Shropshire.

Eversheds, Holland Court, The Close, Norwich NR1 4DX

Tel. 01603 272727

Correspondent N G Sparrow

Trustees *A C Boston; Revd J B Boston; D A Moore.*

CC Number 1050812

Information available Accounts were on file at the Charity Commission.

General The founder of this trust lived in Wistanstow in Shropshire and the principal trustee was for many years based in Norwich. Both these factors influence the grant-making of the trust, with several grants given in both the parish of Wistanstow and in the Norfolk area. The trust has an additional preference for supporting organisations helping at-risk groups and people who are disadvantaged by poverty or socially isolated.

In 2002/03 the trust had an income of £60,000 and its assets totalled £1.2 million. The total amount given in grants was £63,000. This is the only information available for this year. The most recent grants list available comes from 1997/98, when it had an income of £61,000, a total expenditure of £72,000 and gave £60,000 in grants. This includes £6,700 given to individuals, plus £3,500 in Christmas gifts and poultry. The rest was given to 43 organisations, in grants ranging between £170 and £6,000.

The largest grant in 1997/98 was £6,000 to St Michael's Hospital Bartestree, followed by a grant of £2,500 to Norfolk and Norwich Clergymen's Widows' and Children's Charity. Grants of £2,000 were given to Brittle Bone Society, Children's Food Fund, Landau, Macmillan Cancer Relief, Muscular Dystrophy Group and Orbis.

The grants list did not mention the geographical location of most of the charities. It was possible to distinguish that some are based in Norfolk, as follows: Beeston Church Organ (£1,000), Friends of Norwich Cathedral (£500), Horsford and St Faith's Scout Group (£400) and Litcham Parochial Church Council (£300); also see the second largest grant, above. It was not obvious from the grants list that the trust gave any grants in Wistanstow, Shropshire in 1997/98, although a couple of charities appeared on the grants list that were in the bordering county of Herefordshire (such as the largest grant).

Applications The trust states that it does not respond to unsolicited applications.

The Gretna Charitable Trust

General

£23,000 (2000/01)

Beneficial area UK, with a preference for Hertfordshire and London.

c/o Director's Office, Imperial London Hotel Limited, Russell Square, London WC1 B5BB

Tel. 020 7837 3074 **Fax** 020 7278 0469

Correspondent H R Walduck, Trustee

Trustees *H R Walduck; Mrs S M C Walduck; A H E P Walduck; C B Bowles.*

CC Number 1020533

Information available Full accounts were on file at the Charity Commission.

General This trust gives grants to a wide range of voluntary organisations in the UK, with a preference for Hertfordshire.

In 2002/03 the trust had an income of £76,000 and a total expenditure of £41,000. Further information for this year was not available.

In 2000/01 it had assets totalling £703,000 and an income of £95,000. Grants totalled £23,000. Beneficiaries included: St John Ambulance (£2,600); University of Hertfordshire (£2,500); Action for Blind People, Emmaus St Albans for the homeless appeal, Hertfordshire Community Foundation, High Sheriffs' Fund – Hertfordshire, Museum of Garden History and Paul Kossoff Foundation (£1,000 each); Garden House Hospice and Hertfordshire Action on Disability (£500 each); Hertfordshire Gardens' Trust (£250); and St Luke's Church and Stevenage Museum (£100 each).

Exclusions The trust will not provide support to fund salaries or administration costs.

Applications This trust does not encourage applications.

Grimmitt Trust

General

£85,000 (2002/03)

Beneficial area Birmingham and district and areas where trustees have a personal connection.

c/o Welconstruct Group Limited, Woodgate Business Park, Kettles Wood Drive, Birmingham B32 3GH

Tel. 0121 421 7000 **Fax** 0121 421 9848

Correspondent Catherine E Chase

Trustees *P W Welch; Mrs M E Welch; Revd C Hughes Smith; C Humphreys; Dr C Kenrick; Dr A D Owen; Mrs S L Day; A Reeve.*

CC Number 801975

Information available Full accounts were on file at the Charity Commission.

General Grants are given to organisations in the Birmingham area. Local branches of UK organisations are supported, but larger UK appeals are not. Over half of the grant total is given in grants of less than £500 each.

In 2002/03 it had assets of £373,000 and an income of £34,000, including £4,800 in donations received. Grants were made totalling £85,000, broken down as follows:

Cultural and educational	£17,000
Community	£35,000
Children and youth	£17,000
Medical and health	£10,000
Elderly	£1,100
Overseas	£2,100
Benevolent	£2,200
Other small grants	£150

The largest grants were £6,000 to Barnardo's, £5,000 each to Scripture Union – Lozells and Support Awareness Dyslexia Information and £4,500 to Canterbury Festival. Other beneficiaries included NCH Action for Children (£2,200), City of Birmingham Symphony Orchestra (£1,500), Dorrington Primary School (£1,200), Frontier Youth Trust (£800), St David's Theatre Company (£750), 870 House and The Durazano Project (£700 each), Walk Thru the Bible Ministries (£600), Bishop of Birmingham Lent Appeal (£550) and Queen Alexander College (£500).

The accounts stated that £100,000 remained in a designated fund to build a statue of two Christian martyrs, one Catholic and one Protestant, meeting each other in the Bull Ring centre.

Applications In writing to the correspondent.

The Grimsdale Charitable Trust

Christian religion, education, poverty

£38,000 (2001/02)

Beneficial area UK, with a preference for east and west Sussex, and overseas.

25 The Uplands, Gerrards Cross, Buckinghamshire SL9 7JQ

Tel. 01753 885391

Correspondent Martin Grimsdale, Trustee

Trustees *Mrs M Grimsdale, Chair; B Holt; Martin Grimsdale.*

CC Number 327118

Information available Full accounts were on file at the Charity Commission.

General Mrs Margaret Grimsdale, a trustee, is a Minister in the Methodist Church and this is reflected in the trust's grant-making, with some preference for Methodist and other Christian charities. The trust also states that it has a preference for supporting 'reasonably local things' – it will therefore probably not support local organisations outside of east or west Sussex and the surrounding area.

In 2001/02 the trust had assets of £909,000 and an income of £34,000. Donations totalling £38,000 were distributed throughout the year to religious and secular charities. Beneficiaries included: Lee Abbey and St Margaret's Hospice – Yeovil (£5,000 each); Intermediate Technology Development and Water Aid (£2,500 each); Compassionate Friends (£1,300); Methodist Church Castle Cary (£1,200); and Christians Against Poverty, Filwood Hope Centre, Hope and Homes for Children, National Children's Home and Medical Missionary Association (£1,000 each).

Exclusions No grants to individuals.

Applications In writing to the correspondent.

The GRP Charitable Trust

Jewish, general

£178,000 (2002/03)

Beneficial area UK.

Kleinwort Benson Trustees Ltd, PO Box 191, 10 Fenchurch Street, London EC3M 3LB

Tel. 020 7475 5086 **Fax** 020 7475 5558

Correspondent The Secretary

Trustee *Kleinwort Benson Trustees Ltd.*

CC Number 255733

Information available Full accounts were on file at the Charity Commission.

General The G R P of the title stands for the settlor, George Richard Pinto, a London banker who set up the trust in 1968. Most of the grants are given to Jewish organisations.

In 2002/03 the trust had assets of £3.8 million and an income of £227,000, of which £110,000 came from donations. A total of £178,000 was given in 36 grants, broken down as follows:

Jewish causes – 26 grants totalling £159,000

The largest were £41,000 to Oxford Centre for Hebrew and Jewish Studies (which has also received a large proportion of the grant total in previous years), £29,000 to Jerusalem Foundation and £10,000 each to British Technion Society, Jewish Care, United Jewish Israel Appeal and World Jewish Relief.

Other beneficiaries included Anglo-Israel Association (£8,100), Friends of the Hebrew University of Jerusalem and Magen David Adom UK (£5,000 each), Community Security Trust (£2,500), British Friends of Israel Free Loan Association (£2,000), Israel Disapora Trust (£1,500), Institute for Jewish Policy Research (£1,200), Reform Synagogue of Great Britain (£1,000), British Friends of Gesher, Haifa University and Oxford Jewish Centre Building Appeal (£500 each) and Tel Aviv Foundation (£200).

General – 10 grants totalling £19,000

The largest were £5,000 each to Council of Christians and Jews and National Gallery Trust, £4,000 to Royal Opera House Foundation, £2,000 to English Chamber Orchestra and Music Society and £1,000 each to Friends of Courtauld Institute of Art and Gurkha Regimental Trust. Other grants were £500 to Tusk Trust, £300 to Chicken Shed Theatre Company and £100 each to Artists' General Benevolent Institution and King Edward VII Hospital Sister Agnes.

Exclusions No grants to individuals.

Applications In writing to the correspondent. However, the trustees prefer to provide medium-term support for a number of charities already known to them, and unsolicited applications are not acknowledged. Trustees meet annually in March.

The Bishop of Guildford's Foundation

General

£109,000 (2001/02)

Beneficial area The Diocese of Guildford.

Diocesan House, Quarry Street, Guildford, Surrey GU1 3XG

Tel. 01483 304000 **Fax** 01483 790333

Email jane.schofield@cofeguildford.org.uk

Website www.bgf.co.uk

Correspondent Mrs Jane Schofield

Trustees *Bishop of Guildford; Lord Lane of Horsell; Michael Young; Alan Foster; Ian Brackley.*

CC Number 1017385

Information available Information was provided by the trust.

General This trust gives to independent organisations which fund the relief of poverty and isolation, the advancement of education and other charitable purposes beneficial to the community. In 2001/02 the trust had assets of £105,000 and an income of £164,000. A total of £109,000 was awarded in grants. The largest donations included £30,000 to Partnership of Growth, £19,000 to Farmers Appeal and £17,000 to Indian Earthquake Appeal.

Other grants included: £5,000 to Rainbow Trust; £2,200 to Stillway CC; £1,000 each to Disability Challenge and Waverley Youth; £920 to Mental After Care; and £120 to North Guildford Reading Recovery.

Exclusions The total cost of the project will not be funded. No grants to individuals.

Applications An information pack with guidelines for applicants is issued by the trust.

The Walter Guinness Charitable Trust

General

£95,000 (2002/03)

Beneficial area UK and overseas, with a preference for Wiltshire and Hampshire.

Biddesden House, Andover, Hampshire SP11 9DN

Correspondent The Secretary

Trustees *Hon. F B Guinness; Hon. Mrs R Mulji; Hon. Catriona Guinness.*

CC Number 205375

Information available Accounts were on file at the Charity Commission.

General The trust was established in 1961 by Bryan Walter, the second Lord Moyne, in memory of his father, the first Lord Moyne. Most grants are given to a number of charities which the trust has been consistently supporting for many years. In 2002/03 the trust had assets of £3 million, an income of £119,000 and made grants totalling £95,000.

Grants were broken down as follows:

	No.	*Total*
Children	5	£3,500
Communities/Community	11	£5,500
Culture	10	£6,500
Disability	15	£7,000
Ecology	6	£7,800
Education	9	£5,000
Elderly	4	£2,000
General	2	£1,000
Medical	28	£21,000
Mental Health	6	£5,000
Overseas	19	£16,000
Prisoners	4	£2,000
Refugees	2	£1,000
Research	1	£500
Youth	11	£11,000

Grant beneficiaries included Fairbridge and Hawk and Owl Trust (£5,000 each), British Red Cross, Ockenden International, Oxfam and Oxford Medical Students Elective Trust (£3,000 each), Andover Mind (£2,500), Rainbow Trust (£2,000), Youth With A Mission (£1,800) and Alternative Theatre Company (£1,000).

Exclusions No grants to individuals.

Applications In writing to the correspondent. Replies are only sent when there is a positive decision. Initial telephone calls are not welcome. There are no application forms, guidelines or deadlines. No sae is required.

The Gunter Charitable Trust

General

£60,000 (2002/03)

Beneficial area UK.

c/o Forsters, 67 Grosvenor Street, London W1K 3JN

Tel. 0207 863 8333

Correspondent Rupert Meicle

Trustees *J de C Findlay; H R D Billson.*

CC Number 268346

Information available Full accounts were on file at the Charity Commission.

General The trust gives grants to a wide range of local and UK organisations, including countryside, medical and wildlife causes.

In 2002/03 the trust had assets of £2 million, an income of £91,000 and made grants totalling £60,000.

The largest grants were £9,240 to Liverpool School of Tropical Medicine,

£5,500 to Dandelion trust and £4,500 to Hunter trust.

Other beneficiaries included £2,000 each to UNICEF and Royal British Legion, £1,300 to Friends of the Elderly and £1,000 to Survival International.

Smaller grants of £500 or less went to Age Concern, Alzheimers Society, Association for the Preservation of Rural Scotland, CPRE, Camphill Village Trust, Care International, Children with Leukaemia Foundation, Council for Music in Hospitals, Council for the Protection of Rural England, Friends of the Earth, Greenpeace, Help the Aged, Save the Children, Children's Hospice, Africa Foundation, World Village for Children, Small School and Scottish Wildlife Trust.

Exclusions No support for unsolicited applications.

Applications No unsolicited applications are accepted by the trustees. All such applications are immediately returned to the applicant.

The Gur Trust

Jewish causes

£669,000 to organisations (2000/01)

Beneficial area Worldwide.

479 Holloway Road, London N7 6LD

Tel. 020 8880 8911

Email sugerwhite.accts@rtalk21.com

Correspondent The Trustees

Trustees *I M Cymerman; M Mandel; S Morgenstern*

CC Number 283423

Information available Annual report and accounts on file at the Charity Commission.

General In 2002/03 the trust had an income of £44,000 and a total expenditure of £29,000. A grant total and list of beneficiaries was unavailable; instead we refer to 2000/01 in which the trust had assets of £1.4 million and an income of £805,000. Grants totalled £696,000 with £669,000 donated to charitable organisations and the remainder (£27,000) distributed to individuals.

Grants included £239,000 to Gur Talmudical College, £66,000 Kollel Arad, £57,000 to Beis Yaacov Casidic Seminary, £44,000 to Central Charity Fund, £42,000 to Yeshiva Lezeirim, £27,000 to Beth Yaacov Town, £26,000 to Bnei Emes Institutions, £24,000 to Pri Gidulim,, £19,000 to Mifal Gevura Shecehessed and £15,000 to Maala.

Applications In writing to the correspondent. The brief annual report also states the following:

'Funds are raised by the trustees. All calls for help are carefully considered and help is given according to circumstances and funds then available.'

The H & M Charitable Trust

Seafaring

£223,000 (2001/02)

Beneficial area UK, with some preference for Kent.

c/o Brooks Green, Chartered Accountants, Abbey House, 342 Regents Park Road, London N3 2LJ

Correspondent D Harris, Trustee

Trustees *I C S Lewis, Chair; Mrs P M Lister; D Harris.*

CC Number 272391

Information available Information was on file at the Charity Commission.

General The trust supports charities concerned with seamanship, divided between educational and welfare causes. In 2003/04 it had an income of £415,000 and a total expenditure of £72,000.

In 2001/02 it had assets of £2.1 million and an income of £21,000. Grants totalled £223,000 and were broken down as follows:

Charitable grants

Donations totalled £195,000 and were distributed to Arethus Venture Centre (£105,000), Royal Star and Garter Home (£80,000) and Royal Star and Garter (£10,000).

Educational grants

Grants were made totalling £28,000. Beneficairies included Arethus Trainee Centre (£20,000) and Sea Cadets Association (£6,000).

The trust has previously stated that 'resources are committed on a regular annual basis to organisations who have come to rely upon us for their funding'. It is likely, therefore, that some of the 2001/02 recipients receive donations on an annual basis.

Applications The trustees said they do not wish their trust to be included in this guide since it leads to disappointment for applicants. Unsolicited applications will not be successful.

The H P Charitable Trust

Orthodox Jewish

£107,000 (2001/02)

Beneficial area UK.

26 Lingwood Road, London E5 9BN

Tel. 020 8806 2432

Correspondent Aron Piller, Trustee

Trustees *A Piller; Mrs H Piller.*

CC Number 278006

Information available Accounts were on file at the Charity Commission, but without a grants list.

General The H P Charitable Trust was created by Hannah Piller in 1979 and makes grants to orthodox Jewish charities. In 2001/02 its assets totalled £1.9 million and it had an income of £235,000. Grants totalled £107,000.

The trust gave out 7 grants and smaller beneficiaries received £1,000 altogether. The largest grant was to Yetev Lev at £50,000, then Yad Eliezer received £20,000, Ponivez £17,000, Craven Walk Charities £10,000, Gur Trust £2,800, Emuno Educational Centre Ltd £2,500 and lastly Yeshuas Caim Synagogue £1,300.

Applications In writing to the correspondent.

D K A Hackney Charitable Trust (also known as Katharine Hackney Trust)

General

£31,000 (2002/03)

Beneficial area UK.

Thomson Snell & Passmore, 3 Lonsdale Gardens, Tunbridge Wells, Kent TN1 1NX

Tel. 01892 510000

Correspondent Mrs Janet Mills

Trustees *Mrs D K A Hackney; Mrs D P M Schiffer; J C Passmore.*

CC Number 1021109

Information available Accounts were on file at the Charity Commission.

General In 2002/03 the trust's assets totalled £45,000. It received an income of £5,000 and grants totalled £31,000.

In this year the trust gave out 10 grants at £3,100. The beneficiaries were Barnado's, Help the Aged, London City Mission, The Lucas Trust, OXFAM, Save the Children, Scripture Union, Shelter, South American Mission Society, The Sunshine Fund and St Mary's Church.

Applications The trust responded to our request for background information with a standard letter stating: 'The trustees have their own policy for the application of their funds, which is not in any way influenced by appeal literature. We are sorry that you have been put to the trouble of writing, but regret that we cannot offer any assistance now or in the future.' Applicants are unlikely to receive anything other than their own version of the letter we received.

The Halecat Trust

General

£32,000 (2002)

Beneficial area UK, with a preference for north west England.

Witherslack, Grange-over-Sands, Cumbria LA11 6RU

Correspondent Jeremy Major

Trustee *Smith Trustee Company Limited*

CC Number 258157

Information available Accounts were on file at the Charity Commission.

General Grants are given to a wide range of UK and local organisations throughout the UK, although there was a slight preference for north-west England.

In 2002 it had assets of £222,000 and an income of £27,000. Grants to 57 organisations totalled £32,000. By far the largest donation was £17,000 to Bristol University – Institute of Child Health. There were six further grants over £1,000 each to, beneficiaries including Charing Cross Holiday Dialysis Trust (£5,000) and CT Scanner Appeal, Cliburn Public Hall and Royal Academy Trust (£1,000 each).

Other beneficiaries included British Red Cross, Cumbria Wildlife Trust, Friends of Carlisle Cathedral, Glyndebourne Festival, North West Cancer Research Fund and St Andrews House and Club. The majority of grants were recurrent.

Applications In writing to the correspondent.

The Edith Winifred Hall Charitable Trust

General

£295,000 (2002/03)

Beneficial area UK.

Numerica Business Services Ltd, Stoughton House, Harborough Road, Oadby, Leicester LE2 4LP

Tel. 01295 204000

Correspondent D Endicott, Trustee

Trustees *D Reynolds; D Endicott; J R N Lowe; P P Reynolds; L C Burgess-Lumsden.*

CC Number 1057032

Information available Full accounts were on file at the Charity Commission.

General This trust has stated that it wants its funds to make a difference. It prefers to make a small number of large grants.

In 2002/03 the trust had assets of just under £3 million and an income of £119,000. Grants totalled £295,000. Beneficiaries included Elizabeth Anne Hasling's Music Endowment Fund for Peterborough Cathedral Choir, Peterborough Cathedral towards its nave ceiling restoration and lighting appeal, Peterborough Cathedral towards its fire repair appeal, Leicester and Rutland Crimebeat, St Marys Little Harrowden Heritage Trust towards major refurbishment of church roof and boundary wall), Jo's Trust to develop and promote a cervical cancer advice website, Oxford Children's Hospital, Order of St John to purchase ambulances and Action for Youth towards the High Sheriff's initiative.

Applications In writing to the correspondent.

The Hamamelis Trust

Ecological conservation, medical research

£43,000 (2002/03)

Beneficial area UK, but with a special interest in the Godalming and Surrey areas.

c/o Penningtons, Highfield, Brighton Road, Godalming, Surrey GU7 1NS

Tel. 01483 791800

Correspondent Michael Fellingham

Trustees *Michael Fellingham; Dr A F M Stone; Mr R Rippengal.*

CC Number 280938

Information available Information was provided by the trust.

General The trust was set up in 1980 by John Ashley Slocock and enhanced on his death in 1986. The main areas of work are medical research and ecological conservation. Grants are distributed to these areas of work equally. Occasionally grants are made to other projects. Preference is given to projects in the Godalming and Surrey areas.

In 2002/03 it had assets of £2 million and an income of £72,000. Grants totalled £43,000.

Grants were £3,000 to Normandy Community Therapy Garden, £2,500 each to Association for Spina Bifida and Hydrocephalus, Friends of Bedgebury Pinetum, Brainwave, Covent Garden Cancer Research Trust, Cumbria Wildlife Trust, Dermatrust, Devon Wildlife Trust, Lifeblood, Progressive Farming Trust, Progressive Supra-Nuclear Palsy Association, Royal Hospital for Neuro-Disability, Trees for Life, Wildlife Conservation Research Unit, Woodland Trust and Worcestershire Acute Hospitals NHS Trust and £1,300 each to Countryside Venture and Lochaber and District Fisheries Trust.

Exclusions Projects outside the UK are not considered. No grants to individuals.

Applications In writing to the correspondent. All applicants are asked to include a short summary of the application along with any published material and references. Unsuccessful appeals will not be acknowledged.

Medical applications are assessed by Dr Adam Stone, one of the trustees, who is medically qualified.

Sue Hammerson's Charitable Trust

Medical research, relief in need

£268,000 (2002/03)

Beneficial area UK, with a slight preference for London.

H W Fisher & Co, Acre House, 11–15 William Road, London NW1 3ER

Tel. 020 7388 7000

Correspondent T D Brown

Trustees *Sir Gavin Lightman; A J Thompson; A J Bernstein; Mrs P A Beecham; D B Hammerson; P S Hammerson.*

CC Number 235196

Information available Information was provided by the trust.

General The objects of this trust are to advance medical learning and research and the relief of sickness and poverty; it also supports a range of other charities including a number of Jewish and arts organisations.

In 2002/03 it had assets of £5.8 million and an income of £211,000. Grants were made to 176 organisations totalling £268,000. Only 75 of the beneficiaries were not also supported in the previous year.

By far the largest grant was £208,000 to Lewis W Hammerson Memorial Home, which also received the largest grant in the previous year (£150,000).

Other large grants went to Royal Opera House (£3,800); English National Opera (£3,300); Tommy's Campaign (£2,500); Army Benevolent Fund and Marie Curie Cancer Care (£2,000 each); West London Synagogue (£1,900); UJIA and New Shakespeare Co. Ltd (£1,500 each); and £1,000 each to Cheltenham College, Children's Trust, National Children's Home, National Trust, Tate Gallery – London and Unicorn Children's Centre.

The remaining grants ranged between £50 and £850, with most being for less than £500. Beneficiaries included Action Research, British Heart Foundation, Crusaid, Dementia Relief Trust, Fitzwilliam College, Honeypot, Jewish Blind and Disabled, Kids, Leukaemia Research Fund, Motability, National Hospital, Oxfam, PDSA, RSPCA, Spinal Injuries Association, Women at Risk and Zoological Society of London.

Exclusions No grants to individuals.

Applications In writing to the correspondent. The trust states, however, that its funds are fully committed.

The Hammonds Charitable Trust

General

About £100,000 (2001/02)

Beneficial area Mainly Birmingham, London, Leeds, Bradford and Manchester.

Hammonds, 7 Devonshire Square, Cutlers Gardens, London EC2M 4YH

Tel. 0870 839 0000 **Fax** 0870 839 1001

Email dawn.sariko@hammonds.com

Correspondent Dawn Sariko

Trustees *Paul Cliff; Stephen Tupper; Noel Hutton; Chris Marks; John Heller; Mike Shepherd; Simon Gordon.*

CC Number 1064028

Information available Full accounts were on file at the Charity Commission.

General This trust (formerly known as The Hammond Suddards Edge Charitable Trust) usually makes donations to charitable organisations based locally to the trust. While the trust has general charitable purposes, a number appear from the grants list to be health and disability charities, particularly cancer related. Several children's charities also benefited. In 2002/03 the trust had an income of £73,000.

Previous information stated that out of around 100 applications received each month, about 10 or 12 are successful. In 2001/02 it had an income of £93,000 and a total expenditure of £117,000, more than three times the usual expenditure of the trust.

Beneficiaries have included Acorns Children's Hospice, After Adoption, Barnardo's Trek Trust, Business in the Community, Edward's Trust, Holborn Scout and Guide Group, Home Farm Trust, KIDS, Parents for Children, St Mary's Hospice and Sense.

Applications In writing to the correspondent.

Beatrice Hankey Foundation Ltd

Christian

£28,000 (2002)

Beneficial area UK and overseas.

11 Staverton Road, Werrington, Peterborough, Cambridgeshire PE4 6LY

Correspondent Mrs M Churchill, Secretary

Trustees *P H W Dannowski; Mrs A M Dawe; Rev Canon P Gompertz; Mrs C H Mentink-Zuiderweg; Rev Sister L R Morris; Mrs D Sampson; Rev D Savill; Mrs A Y Stewart; Mrs H Walker.*

CC Number 211093

Information available Accounts on file at the Charity Commission.

General Grants are made to individuals and groups known personally to the foundation members and carrying out activities which will promote the values of Christian teaching. It gives small grants of between £50 and £500 each.

In 2002 the trust had assets of £843,000, an income of £36,000 and a grant total of £28,000.

Grant beneficiaries included Lagan College (£12,500), St Alfege Schools Project (£5,000), Corrymeela Community (£2,500), Tema Diocese Methodist Church in Ghana (£1,500), Medical Foundation for the Relief of Victims of Torture and Village Services Trust (£1,250 each), Holy Land Institute for the Deaf (£1,000), Cornerstone Community (£500) and Onkhojang Children's Home in Bangladesh and Pastor Children Education Fund in Rwanda (£360 each).

Exclusions No grants for buildings or equipment.

Applications Unsolicited applications cannot be considered.

Miss K M Harbinson's Charitable Trust

General

£171,000 (1994)

Beneficial area UK and developing countries.

190 St Vincent Street, Glasgow G2 5SP

Tel. 0141 204 2833

Correspondent The Secretary

Trustees *A Maguire; G L Harbinson; R Harbinson.*

Information available Very little information is available on this trust.

General The trust supports development organisations, giving grants ranging from £1,000 to £9,000, often in two instalments during the year. In 1993/94 grants included £9,000 each to ActionAid, Intermediate Technology, Marie Stopes International and Oxfam, £8,000 each to British Red Cross and Worldwide Fund for Nature, £4,000 each to Breadline Africa, Care Britain, Ethopiaid and UNICEF, £3,000 to Romanian Orphanage Trust and £2,000 to Sight Savers International.

Up-to-date information was unavailable.

Applications In writing to the correspondent.

Harbo Charities Limited

General, education, religion

£70,000 (2002/03)

Beneficial area UK.

Cohen Arnold & Co., New Burlington House, 1075 Finchley Road, London NW11 0PU

Tel. 020 8731 0777 **Fax** 020 8731 0778

Correspondent J Schwarz

Trustees *Harry Stern; Barbara J Stern; Harold Gluck.*

CC Number 282262

Information available Accounts were on file at the Charity Commission, but without a grants list.

General In 2002/03 the trust had assets of £739,000 with an income of £118,000 and grants totalling £70,000.

Grants include £8,800 to Chevras Maoz Ladol, £6,000 to Craven Walk Charitable Trust, £4,500 each to Beis Chinuch Lebonos Girls School and Beth Rochel d'Satmar, £3,300 each to Tevini Limited and Tomchei Shabbos, £2,300 to Bobov Trust, £1,800 to Yeshiva Chachmay Tsorphat, £1,700 to Yad Eliezer, £1,500 each to Yesode Ha Torah School and Edgware Yeshiva Trust and £1,000 each to Keren Yesomim and Kollel Shomrei HaChomoth.

Applications In writing to the correspondent.

The Harbour Charitable Trust

General

£164,000 (2002/03)

Beneficial area UK.

c/o Blevins Frank, Barbican House, 26–34 Old Street, London EC1V 9QQ

Tel. 020 7935 7422

Correspondent The Trustees

Trustees *Mrs B B Green; Mrs Z S Blackman; Mrs T Elsenstat; Mrs E Knobil.*

CC Number 234268

Information available Accounts were on file at the Charity Commission, but without a list of grants.

General The trust makes grants for the benefit of childcare, education and health research and to various other charitable organisations. In 2002/03 it had assets of £3.1 million and an income of £160,000. Grants were made totalling £164,000. These were categorised by the trust as follows:

Healthcare	£34,000
Joint Jewish Charitable Trust	£48,000
Education	£45,000
Other	£35,000
Childcare	£2,000

No further information was available on the charities supported.

Exclusions Grants are given to registered charities only.

Applications In writing to the correspondent.

The Harbour Foundation

Jewish, general

£126,000 (2001/02)

Beneficial area Worldwide, with a preference for London.

The Courtyard Building, 11 Curtain Road, London EC2A 3LT

Tel. 020 7456 8180

Correspondent The Trustees

Trustees *S R Harbour; A C Humphries; Mrs Z S Blackman; S Green; B B Green.*

CC Number 264927

Information available Accounts were on file at the Charity Commission, but without a grants list.

General The principal activities of the trust are providing relief among refugees and people who are homeless, the advancement of education, learning and research, and to make donations to any institution established for charitable purposes throughout the world.

In 2002/03 the foundation had a high income of £1.2 million and a total expenditure of £289,000.

The following is taken from the 2001/02 trustee's report:

'The main thrust of the foundation's current and future charitable programme comprises two areas of activities which are, to some extent, complementary.

'The first is the support and development of technology-based education for the community. This support is directed both to university level and to those who have been failed by the educational system especially in the inner boroughs of London. Rapid and continual innovation in this field and the attraction and retention of highly qualified teaching staff necessitate a high level of financial support on a consistent and ongoing basis. A carefully phased release of donations by the foundation to education providers at the leading edge acts as an incentive for them to maximise performance and enables them to plan ahead with some degree of confidence. It is therefore essential to continue to build up reserves of the foundation to a level sufficient to ensure a reliable high level of financial support to such providers.

'The second strand of activity is also mainly aimed at the inner boroughs of London where it is intended to provide funds to improve the physical environment in deprived areas. This will be directed to the development of run down space, both open and constructed, for community use. Again this activity will require a high level of financial support and, therefore, also necessitates an expansion of the foundation's reserves.'

In 2001/02 the trust had assets of £7 million and an income of £814,000. Grants totalled £126,000. Despite having a detailed and comprehensive narrative report, the trust provides no grants list or details of type or size of grants in their accounts.

Applications In writing to the correspondent. Applications need to be received by February, as trustees meet in March.

The Harding Trust

Arts, welfare

Possibly about £100,000 (2002/03)

Beneficial area Mainly, but not exclusively, north Staffordshire and surrounding areas.

Brabners Chaffe Street, 1 Dale Street, Liverpool L2 2ET

Tel. 0151 236 5821 **Fax** 0151 600 3333

Correspondent The Administrator

Trustees *J S McAllester; G G Wall; J P C Fowell; M N Lloyd.*

CC Number 328182

Information available Information was on file at the Charity Commission.

General The aims of this trust is 'to promote, improve, develop and maintain public education in, and appreciation of, the art and science of music, by sponsoring or by otherwise supporting public concerts, recitals and performances by amateur and professional organisations'. In 2002/03 it had an income of £104,000 and a total expenditure of £118,000.

Previous beneficiaries have included Civit Hills Opera, Clonter Farm Music Trust, English Haydn Festival at Bridgnorth, Katherine House Hospice, London Mozart Players, Staffordshire County Youth Orchestra, Stoke and Newcastle Festival and Zenith Ensemble.

Applications In writing to the correspondent. The trustees meet annually in spring/early summer.

Accounts are needed for recurrent applications.

The Hare of Steep Charitable Trust

General

£50,000 (2004)

Beneficial area UK, with preference for the south of England, especially Petersfield and East Hampshire.

56 Heath Road, Petersfield Hants, Hampshire GU31 4EJ

Correspondent Mrs S M Fowler

Trustees *P L F Baillon; V R Jackson; J R F Fowler; S M Fowler; S E R Johnson-Hill.*

CC Number 297308

Information available Information was provided by the trust.

General In 2004 the trust had assets of £873,000 and an income of £47,000. Grants were made to 51 organisations and totalled £50,000. There were no donations greater than 5% of the total distibuted. There is a preference for local charities and other community projects in the south of England particularly in East Hampshire. Unfortunately an exact breakdown of the grant beneficiaries was not provided by the trust.

Exclusions No funding for overseas charities, students, visits abroad or political causes.

Applications 'The trustees already support as many charities as they could wish and would certainly not welcome any appeals from others. Unsolicited requests are not acknowledged.'

The Harebell Centenary Fund

General, education, medical research, animal welfare

£89,000 (2002)

Beneficial area UK.

50 Broadway, London SW1H 0BL

Tel. 020 7227 7000

Correspondent Ms P J Chapman

Trustees *J M Denker; M I Goodbody; F M Reed.*

CC Number 1003552

Information available Full accounts were provided by the trust.

General Established in 1991, this trust provides funding towards the promotion of neurological and neurosurgical research and the relief of sickness and suffering amongst animals, as well as holding an interest in the education of young people.

The current policy of the trustees is to concentrate on making donations to charities that do not receive widespread public support and to keep administrative expenses to a minimum. For this reason the trustees have decided to make donations only to registered charities and not to individuals.

In 2002 it had assets of £1.6 million, which generated an income of £72,000. Grants totalling £89,000 were made to 22 organisations, half of which were also supported in the previous year. Management and administration fees were high at £20,000, including payments to firms in which at least one of the trustees is a partner. Whilst wholly legal, these editors always regret such payments unless, in the words of the Charity Commission, 'there is no realistic alternative'.

The largest grants were £7,500 to Hebridean Trust for the Treshnish Isles and £5,000 each to Abilitynet, Blackie Foundation, Canine Partners for Independence, Demand, Ferriers Barn, Motor Neurone Disease Society, National Library for the Blind, REMAP and Royal Hospital for Neurodisability.

Other grants included £3,900 to National Trust for School – Pitmedden, £3,000 each to Little Haven Children's Hospice, Message in a Bottle and St Joseph's Hospice – Hackney and £2,500 to Crathie School.

Exclusions No grants are made towards infrastructure or to individuals.

Applications In writing to the correspondent. Unsolicited applications are not requested, as the trustees prefer to make donations to charities whose work they have come across through their own research.

The R J Harris Charitable Settlement

General

£106,000 to organisations (2002/03)

Beneficial area UK, with a preference for west Wiltshire, with particular emphasis on Trowbridge – north Wiltshire south of the M4 verging into Bath and environs.

Messrs Thring Townsend, Midland Bridge, Bath BA1 2HQ

Tel. 01225 340098

Correspondent S M Nutt, Secretary

Trustees *H M Newton-Clare, Chair; J L Rogers; A Pitt; C I W Hignett; J J Thring.*

CC Number 258973

Information available Accounts were provided by the trust, but without a list of grants or a full narrative report. A brief information sheet for applicants was also provided.

General This trust has general charitable purposes, supporting both individuals and organisations. Support is focused on west Wiltshire, with particular emphasis on Trowbridge – North Wiltshire south of the M4 verging into the environs of Bath. The main areas of work are social welfare, the arts, education, medical, mental health, conservation, environmental and youth organisations and projects.

In 2002/03 it had assets of £1.2 million, which generated an income of £50,000. Grants were made to 69 organisations totalling £106,000, with a further £8,400 given in total to 11 individuals. Information on beneficiaries was not included in the accounts.

Applications In writing to the correspondent. Trustees meet three times each year. An sae is required.

The John Harrison Charitable Trust

Multiple Sclerosis

£140,000 (2002/03)

Beneficial area UK.

PO Box 326, Bedford MK40 3XU

Tel. 01234 266657

Correspondent David Hull

Trustees *Judy Sebba; Iris Sebba; Sian Crookes.*

CC Number 277956

Information available Accounts were on file at the Charity Commission.

General Established in 1979, in 2002/03 the trust had assets amounting to £1.1 million and an income of £20,000. Grants totalled £140,000. In its annual report the trust stated that the trustees were developing plans to expend an accumulate the income of the charity in a continuing programme of grants in the field of Multiple Sclerosis support and research.

Applications In writing to the correspondent.

Hartnett Charitable Trust

Environmental issues

Possibly about £30,000 a year.

Beneficial area UK.

Ivorys Farm, Burnt House Lane, Cowfold, Horsham, West Sussex RH13 8DQ

Tel. 01903 234094

Correspondent Dr David Hartnett

Trustees *Mrs M Hartnett; D W Hartnett.*

CC Number 276460

Information available Information was taken from the Charity Commission's website.

General The trust stated it supports environmental issues. In 2002/03 it had an income of £31,000 and an expenditure of £47,000. Unfortunately it was not known how much of this was given in grants. However, we do know that beneficiaries included Battlefields Trust, Mary Rose Trust and Friends of War Memorials.

Exclusions No grants to individuals.

Applications In writing to the correspondent, enclosing an sae.

The Lord and Lady Haskel Charitable Foundation

Jewish, social–policy research, arts, education

£55,000 (2000)

Beneficial area UK.

58–60 Berners Street, London W1T 3JS

Tel. 020 7637 4121

Correspondent The Trustees

Trustees *A M Davis; J Haskel; M Nutman; Lord Haskel.*

CC Number 1039969

Information available Full accounts were on file at the Charity Commission.

General The charity funds projects concerned with social–policy research, Jewish communal life, arts and education.

In 2003 the trust had an income of £61,000 and a total expenditure of £26,000. Further information for this year was not available.

In 2000 it had assets of £416,000 and an income of £313,000, including £280,000 in donations received. Grants totalled £55,000 and were: £25,000 to Kingston Synagogue, £22,000 to Institute for Jewish Policy Research, £3,500 to Britten–Pears Bursary Fund, £2,000 to Orange Tree Theatre, £1,000 to Chronic Disease Research Foundation, and £500 each to Holocaust Education Trust, New Israel Fund and Science Line.

Applications This trust states that it does not respond to unsolicited applications.

The M A Hawe Settlement

General

£250,000 (2001/02)

Beneficial area UK, with a preference for the north west of England, particularly the Fylde coast area.

94 Park View Road, Lytham St Annes, Lancashire FY8 4JF

Tel. 01253 796888

Correspondent M A Hawe, Trustee

Trustees *M A Hawe; Mrs G Hawe; Marc G Hawe.*

CC Number 327827

Information available Information was provided by the trust.

General In 2001/02 the trust had an income of £289,000 and a total expenditure of £286,000. Grants totalled £250,000.

As usual, the largest grant was to Kensington House Trust Ltd, which received £240,000. This company was established to run a property bought by the trust in 1993, as accommodation on a short-stay basis for young homeless people. It now also provides furniture and equipment to people in need, shelter for victims of domestic violence and holidays for children who are deprived.

The remaining grants ranged between £100 to £1,000. A list of recipients was not available. Previous beneficiaries have included Change for Charity, DVU, Foetal Anti-Convulsent Syndrome Association, Holy Cross Church and Soup Kitchen, Home-Start, Mereside School and Women's Refuge.

Applications In writing to the correspondent.

The Hawthorne Charitable Trust

General

£158,000 (2003/04)

Beneficial area UK, especially Hereford and Worcester.

c/o Messrs Baker Tilly, 2 Bloomsbury Street, London WC1B 3ST

Tel. 020 7413 5100

Correspondent Roger Clark, Trustee

Trustees *Mrs A S C Berington; R J Clark.*

CC Number 233921

Information available Full accounts were on file at the Charity Commission.

General The trust supports a wide range of organisations, particularly health and welfare causes but also charities concerned with animal welfare, disability, heritage and young people.

In 2003/04 it had assets of £5.5 million, which generated an income of £192,000. After management and administration costs of £17,000, grants to 68 organisations totalled £158,000.

The largest grant was £15,000 to Society of Friends of Little Malvern Priory. Large grants also went to Downside Abbey Trustees for St Wulstan's (£5,000) and Acorn Children's Hospice Trust (£3,000).

Most of the grants were either for £1,000 or £2,500. Recipients of £2,500 included Abbeyfield Society, Alzheimer's Research Trust, Brain Research Trust, Canine Partners for Independence, Hearing Concern, Iris Fund, National Meningitis Trust, Royal Albert Hall Trust and Universal Beneficent Society. Beneficiaries of £1,000 each included Age Concern, Army Benevolent Fund, Dogs Trust, Malvern Hills Citizen's Advice, Malvern Sea Cadets, Noah's Ark Trust and Worcestershire Acute Hospitals NHS Trust Charitable Fund.

Recipients of other amounts were SSAFA – Worcestershire (£2,000), Acquired Asphasia Trust (£1,500), Samaritans – Worcester (£1,300) and Special Olympics – Worcestershire.

A number of the above beneficiaries have been supported in previous years.

Exclusions Grants are given to registered charities only. No grants to individuals.

Applications In writing to the correspondent, including up-to-date accounts. Applications should be received by October for consideration in November.

The Dorothy Hay-Bolton Charitable Trust

Deaf, blind

£31,000 (2001/02)

Beneficial area UK, with a preference for the south-east of England and overseas.

F W Stephens & Co., 10 Charterhouse Square, London EC1M 6LQ

Tel. 020 7251 4434

Correspondent Brian E Carter, Trustee

Trustees *Brian E Carter; Stephen J Gallico.*

CC Number 1010438

Information available Full accounts were on file at the Charity Commission.

General The trust makes grants towards charities working with people who are deaf or blind, particularly children and young people. In 2001/02 the trust had assets of £897,000, an income of £29,000 and made grants totalling £31,000.

Beneficiaries included: British Wireless for the Blind, Falconer Trust and Hearing Dogs for the Deaf (£2,500 each), Telephones for the Blind and Brighton Society for the Blind (£2,000 each), Threshers Day Nursey and Country Holidays for Inner City Kids (£1,500 each), NCH Action for Children – Pastens and Sense (£1,300 each), and Darrick Wood Impaired Hearing Support Unit and Helping Sense Limited (£1,000 each).

Exclusions The trust states that it does not generally give to individuals.

Applications In writing to the correspondent.

The Haydan Charitable Trust

Jewish, general

£136,000 (2000)

Beneficial area UK.

4th Floor, 1 Knightsbridge, London SW1X 7LX

Tel. 020 7823 2200

Correspondent Jenny Kelly

Trustees *Christopher Smith; Irene Smith; Anthony Winter.*

CC Number 1003801

Information available Full accounts were on file at the Charity Commission.

General This trust was set up in 1990 it has a clear relationship with its namesake company, Haydan Holdings Ltd.

In 2003 the trust had an income of £42,000 and a total expenditure of £37,000. Further information for this year was not available.

In 2000 it had assets of just £450 with its income of £158,000 coming mainly from Gift Aid. Grants totalled £136,000. The charity expected to receive a Gift Aid donation from Haydan Holdings Ltd in the period to 30 June 2001.

The trust states that it gives recurrent grants to a few organisations and does not invite applications. In 2000 the three largest grants were £50,000 to Nordoff

Robbins Music Therapy Centre, £25,000 to Cedar School and £10,000 to Tommy's Campaign. A further 15 grants were listed in the accounts including those to Babes in Arms (£8,000), Wessex Children's Heart Circle, Wessex Heartbeat and Whizz Kidz (£5,000 each), Children with Leukaemia, Leukaemia Research Fund and Nightingale House (£2,500 each), and Beating Bowel Cancer and Sheffield Children's Hospital (£1,000 each). Unlisted miscellaneous grants totalled £3,000.

Exclusions No grants are given for projects overseas.

Applications Unsolicited applications are not considered.

The Haymills Charitable Trust

Education, medicine, welfare, youth

£120,000 to organisations and individuals (2001/02)

Beneficial area UK, but particularly the west of London and Suffolk, where the Haymills group is sited.

Wesley House, 1–7 Wesley Avenue, London NW10 7BZ

Tel. 020 8951 9700

Correspondent I W Ferres, Secretary

Trustees *W G Underwood, Chair; E F C Drake; I W Ferres; A M H Jackson; K C Perryman; J A Sharpe; J L Wosner.*

CC Number 277761

Information available Accounts were on file at the Charity Commission, but without a list of grants.

General 'The trustees regularly review their policy, aiming to make the best use of the funds available by donating varying amounts to projects which they believe are not widely known and thus are likely to be inadequately supported. Their main support is to registered charities operating in areas known to them, especially those lying in and to the west of London and in Suffolk.

'Grants fall into four main categories:

Education: grants to schools, colleges and universities

Medicine: grants to hospitals and associated institutions and to medical research

Welfare: primarily to include former Haymills' staff, and to those who are considered to be in necessitous circumstances or who are otherwise distressed or disadvantaged

Youth: support for training schemes to assist in the education, welfare and training of young people.

'No personal applications for support will be considered unless endorsed by a university, a college or other appropriate authority. Each year, a limited number of applicants can be considered who can show that they are committed to further education and training preferably for employment in the construction industry.'

In 2001/02 it had assets of £4.3 million and an income of £2.7 million, largely from a bequest of £2.6 million which was transferred to assets. Grants totalled £120,000 and were broken down as follows:

Youth and welfare	£87,000
Medical	£25,000
Education	£8,300

Unfortunately no list of grants was included with the accounts on file at the Charity Commission, although they did state that it has agreed a five-year scholarship at Merchant Taylor's School, of £5,000 in the first year and increasing cumulatively in each of the following years.

In 1999/2000 beneficiaries in the three categories included the following:

Educational

Grants were given to various educational establishments, especially towards bursaries, prizes and scholarships. Grants included those to: Merchant Taylor's Company for the Dudley Cox Bursary Fund and the Dudley Cox Awards for engineering, design and technology; Anglia Polytechnic University for the Haymills Building Management Scholarship; Suffolk College; and Hammersmith and West London College.

Medical

Grants were mainly given to hospitals and hospital appeals, although grants were also given towards research. Beneficiaries included Central Middlesex Hospital League of Friends, Ealing Hospital League of Friends, Great Ormond Street Children's Hospital and Royal London Hospital.

Youth and welfare

Beneficiaries included Children's Hospice Eastern Region, East Suffolk Association for the Blind, Dyslexia Association, Friends of Samaritans – Ealing, Greater London Central Scout County, London Bible College, Macmillan Cancer Relief, Middlesex Young People's Clubs, Queen Elizabeth Hospital Children's Fund and West London Action for Children.

Exclusions No personal applications will be considered unless endorsed by a university, college or other appropriate authority.

Applications In writing to the correspondent, but note the comments in the general section. Trustees meet at least twice a year, usually in March and October. Applications are not acknowledged.

Heagerty Charitable Trust

Catholic, general

£30,000 (2002/03)

Beneficial area UK.

Walstead Grange, Lindfield, Surrey RH16 2QQ

Correspondent J S Heagerty, Trustee

Trustees *J S Heagerty; Miss P Smith; P J P Heagerty; Mrs V C M Heagerty.*

CC Number 1033543

Information available Accounts were on file at the Charity Commission.

General In 2002/03 the trust had assets of £618,000 and an income of £33,000. Grants were made to 12 organisations totalling £30,000.

Beneficiaries were Hope in the Valley Riding Group (£6,000), Bridge Trust (£3,500), CAFOD, Grace & Compassion Benedictines, London Children's Ballet and Michael Palin Centre for Stammering Children (£3,000 each), Action Aid (£2,500), Crawley Open House (£2,000) and Changing Faces, NCH Palmeira Project, RNIB Talking Books and Woodland Trust (£1,000 each).

Applications The trust says it identifies causes it wishes to support itself and unsolicited applications are not considered.

May Hearnshaw's Charity

General

£138,000 (2002/03)

Beneficial area UK, particularly north Midlands and South Yorkshire.

35–47 North Church Street, Sheffield S1 2DH

Tel. 0114 275 2888 **Fax** 0114 273 0108

Correspondent The Trustees

Trustees *David Law; Jack Rowan.*

CC Number 1008638

Information available Full accounts were on file at the Charity Commission.

General This trust was set up by the will of the late May Hearnshaw who died in 1988. It was her wish that the trust be used for the promotion of education, advancement of religion and relief of poverty and sickness. Support is mostly given to children's organisations within these themes. Grants are made to UK-wide charities or local charities working in the South Yorkshire or north Midlands area.

In 2002/03 it had assets of £1.6 million and an income of £85,000. Grants totalled £138,000, with about half of these recurrent.

Beneficiaries included Cavendish Centre (£8,000), Cherry Tree Orphanage (£5,000), Children's Appeal and Mind (£3,000 each), St Gemma's Hospice (£2,500) Age Concern, Leonard Cheshire Foundation and Sheffield Kidney Research (£2,000 each), Aspire – Sheffield, Cavendish Hip Foundation, Corda, MS Trust, South Yorkshire & Hallams Clubs (£1,000 each) and British Epilepsy Association (£500).

Applications 'The trustees usually decide on and make grants to charitable organisations twice a year but may decide to make grants at any time. They do not include in their consideration appeals received direct from individuals.'

Heathside Charitable Trust

General, Jewish

£464,000 (2001)

Beneficial area UK.

Hillsdown House, 32 Hampstead High Street, London NW3 1QD

Tel. 020 7431 7739

Correspondent Sir Harry Solomon, Trustee

Trustees *Sir Harry Solomon; Lady Judith Solomon; G R Jayson; R C Taylor.*

CC Number 326959

Information available Full accounts were on file at the Charity Commission.

General This trust has general charitable purposes, with a preference for Jewish organisations.

In 2001 it had assets of just under £3 million, which generated an income of £38,000. Grants totalled £464,000; however, a list of grant beneficiaries was not available.

In 2000, the largest grant was £141,000 to Joint Jewish Charitable Trust. Large grants also went to Raft (£35,000), Jewish Education Defence Trust (£25,000), Community Security Trust (£25,000), Jewish Care (£15,000), with £10,000 each to British Friends of Jaffa Institute, GRET and Motivation.

Other beneficiaries included Holocaust Educational Trust (£8,500), First Cheque 2000 and Royal London Institute (£5,000 each), Royal National Theatre (£4,500), Jewish Museum (£3,300), Cancerkin and King Solomon High School (£2,500), Babes in Arms (£2,000), and Marie Curie Cancer Care and Weitzmann Institute (£1,000 each).

Applications In writing to the correspondent, at any time.

Percy Hedley 1990 Charitable Trust

General

£53,000 (2001/02)

Beneficial area UK with a preference for Northumberland and Tyne and Wear.

c/o Dickinson Dees, St Ann's Wharf, 112 Quayside, Newcastle upon Tyne NE99 1SB

Tel. 0191 279 9000

Correspondent G W Meikle, Trustee

Trustees *G W Meikle; J R Armstrong; Mrs F M Ruffman.*

CC Number 1000033

Information available Accounts were on file at the Charity Commission.

General In 2001/02 this trust had assets of £1.3 million and an income of £48,000. After management and administration costs of £15,000, grants to 64 organisations were made totalling £53,000 (41 of these were supported in the previous year). The largest grant in the year was £7,000 to Percy Hedley Foundation.

Other beneficiaries of larger grants over £1,000 each included: Anaphylaxis Campaign, Marie Stopes International, St Oswald Hospice and Samaritans of Tyneside (£2,000 each); and British Heart Foundation, Meningitis Research, NSPCC, Northumberland Playing Fields Association and University of Newcastle Cancer Research (£1,000 each).

Grants in the range of £200 and £500 included those to Dementia Care Initiative, North East Children's Society, Finchdale Training College, Henshaws Society for the Blind, Imperial Cancer Research Fund, National Trust of Scotland, Newcastle Toy and Leisure Library, Northumberland Touring Theatre Co., Quaker Opportunity Group, Royal Star and Garter Homes, Robert Stephenson Trust, Sustrans, Woodland Trust and YMCA.

Applications In writing to the correspondent. Trustees meet twice a year.

The Hellenic Foundation

Greek, general

£43,000 (2001)

Beneficial area UK.

St Paul's House, Warwick Lane, London EC4P 4BN

Tel. 020 7251 5100

Correspondent S J Fafalios, Honorary Secretary

Trustees *George A Tsavliris, Chair; Nicos H Sideris; Irene M Monios; Stamos J Fafalios; Tryphon Kedros; Dr Eleni Yannakakis; Zenon K Mouskos; Constantinos I Caroussis; Mary Bromley; Irene J Fafalios-Zannas; Costas N Hadjipateras; Angela K Kulukundis; George A Lemos; George D Lemos; Louisa Williamson; Despina M Moschos; Anna S Polemis-Alisafakis.*

CC Number 326301

Information available Full accounts were on file at the Charity Commission.

General The foundation was set up in 1982 to 'advance and propagate education and learning in Great Britain in the cultural tradition and heritage of Greece and particularly in the subjects involving education, research, music and dance, books and library facilities and university symposia'.

In 2001, the trust's assets totalled £505,000 and it had an income of £39,000. Grants totalled £43,000 distributed to 30 charitable organisations including Notos Theatre Company of Athens (£3,000), Anglo Hellenic League, Theatro Technis and Queens University Belfast – The Institute of Byzantine Studies (£2,000 each), St Cross College Hellenic Fellowship (£1,700), Oxford University and Somerville College Oxford (£1,500 each), Icarus Productions, Exeter College and Worcester College Oxford (£1,000 each).

Exclusions The foundation is unable to offer scholarships or grants to cover tuition fees and living expenses.

Applications In writing to the correspondent.

The Michael & Morven Heller Charitable Foundation

University and medical research projects, the arts

£263,000 (2001/02)

Beneficial area Worldwide.

8–10 New Fetter Lane, London EC4A 1NQ

Tel. 020 7415 5000 **Fax** 020 7415 0611

Correspondent The Trustees

Trustees *Michael Heller; Morven Heller; Pearl Livingstone.*

CC Number 327832

Information available Accounts and a separate grants list were on file at the Charity Commission.

General This trust was established in 1972, and funds specific projects relating to medical research, science and educational research. This usually involves making large grants to universities for research purposes, particularly medical research. In practice, there appears to be some preference for Jewish organisations.

In 2001/02 the trust had assets of £3.2 million and an income of £242,000. Grants during the year totalled £263,000. No further information was available for the year.

In 2000/01 the trust had assets of £2.4 million and an income of £220,000. Grants totalled £153,000, with 30 grants of over £1,000 each being listed in the accounts. St Catherine's College received four grants totalling £29,000. Other recipients of awards over £10,000 each were Hampstead Theatre and London Jewish Cultural Centre (£15,000 each) and Norwood Ltd (£12,000).

Other beneficiaries included Beth Shalom (£7,500), Community Security Trust and Jewish Marriage Council (£5,000 each), Ben Uri Gallery (£2,500), Sense (£2,000), New End Theatre (£1,500), Institute for Jewish Policy Research, Royal Academy of Art and Sheffield Jewish Congregation (£1,000 each).

Exclusions No support for individuals.

Applications In writing to the correspondent.

The Simon Heller Charitable Settlement

Medical research, science and educational research

£200,000 (2001/02)

Beneficial area Worldwide.

8–10 New Fetter Lane, London EC4A 1NQ

Tel. 020 7415 5000 **Fax** 020 7415 0611

Correspondent The Trustees

Trustees *M A Heller; Morven Heller; W S Trustee Company Limited.*

CC Number 265405

Information available Accounts were on file at the Charity Commission.

General This trust was established in 1972, and funds specific projects relating to medical research, science and educational research. This usually involves making large grants to universities for research purposes, particularly medical research. In practice, there appears to be some preference for Jewish organisations.

In 2001/02 the trust had assets of £4.7 million and an income of £294,000. Grants were made totalling £200,000.

In the previous year, grants totalled £192,000 and were broken down by the trust as follows:

Education	£67,000
Research	£50,000
Humanitarian	£75,000

The 2000/01 accounts listed 19 grants over £1,000 each. UJIA received the largest single grant of £35,000 with Institute for Jewish Policy Research receiving the same amount in two grants of £25,000 and £10,000. Other major beneficiaries were Jewish Care (£30,000), Aish Hatora (£15,000 in two grants), Spiro Institute (£13,000), Scopus (£12,000 in two grants) and Chief Rabbinate Charitable Trust (£10,000).

Other beneficiaries were British ORT, Common Denominator and Community Charity Trust (£5,000 each), Shvut Ami (£2,500) and Israel Diaspora Trust (£2,000).

Exclusions No grants to individuals.

Applications In writing to the correspondent.

Help the Homeless Ltd

Homelessness

£41,000 (2002/03)

Beneficial area UK.

5th Floor, Babmaes House, 2 Babmaes Street, London SW1Y 6HD

Tel. 020 7925 2582 **Fax** 020 7925 2583

Correspondent T Kenny

Trustees *F J Bergin; T S Cookson; L A Bains; M McIntyre; T Rogers; R Reed; P Fullerton.*

CC Number 271988

Information available Full accounts were provided by the trust.

General The trust makes small grants to smaller or new voluntary organisations, who are registered charities, for items of capital expenditure directly related to the provision of housing for people who are single and homeless. Grants do not normally exceed £3,000.

In 2001/02 the trust had assets of £817,000 and an income of £68,000. Grants were made to 19 beneficiaries totalling £41,000. Support, management and administration costs totalled £15,000.

Donations in the year included: £3,000 each to Alone in London, BOSCO Society, Ipswich Women's Aid, Warrington Action and West London Church; £2,400 each to Macedon and Society of St James; £2,000 each to Aberdeen Cyrenaina, Ark Trust, Finsbury Park Street Drinkers and Victory Outreach; £1,900 to Homerton Space; £1,300 to Steer Mental Health; £1,000 to Ripon YMCA; and St John's Hackney.

Exclusions Charities with substantial funds are not supported. No grants for revenue expenditure such as ongoing running costs or salaries, and so on.

Applications The trust has a specific application form that must be completed, which states that: 'you need to provide us with information about your organisation, its aims, how it works and how it intends to continue to meet those aims in the future. You will also be asked to send us a copy of your most recent audited reports and accounts'. Unformatted applications will not be considered.

Trustees meet to consider grants four times a year. There should be a minimum period of two years between the receipt of a grant and a subsequent application.

Help the Hospices

Hospices

Around £217,000 (2003/04)

Beneficial area UK.

34–44 Britannia Street, London WC1 9JG

Tel. 020 7520 8200 **Fax** 020 7278 1021

Email grants@helpthehospices.org.uk

Website www.helpthehospices.org.uk

Correspondent David Praill, Chief Executive

Trustees *Rt Hon. Lord Newton of Braintree, Chair; Ron Giffin; John Cherry; Dr Helen Clayson; Ms Suzy Croft; Robin Eve; Dr Andrew Hoy; Mrs Ann Lee; Ms Terry Maggee; Miss Agnes Malone; Mrs Hilary McNair; George Miall; Hugh Scurfield.*

CC Number 1014851

Information available Full accounts and guidelines were provided by the trust.

General The objects of the charity are to:

- help hospices deliver high standards of care, relief and treatment of terminally ill patients, and support for their families and carers
- support the development and sustainability of independent voluntary hospices
- facilitate working relationshi ps and shared expertise amongst providers and other supports of palliative care, both in the UK and overseas
- promote public education about end of life issues
- raise public support, resources and sufficient funds to enable the achievement of, and add value to, the strategic objectives.

These objectives are met by providing education and training as well as funding hospices and palliative care units through the following programmes:

Major grants

The major grants programme provides financial support for special projects in independent voluntary hospices on an annual basis. Funding for these awards is usually received from other charitable trusts and therefore specific criteria apply each year. Details of current awards can be found on the trust's website.

Regional and outreach training awards

These are available to individual hospices or groups of hospices, as well as professional associations, to help subsidise the cost of their education and training initiatives which:

- encourage increased collaboration, sharing of knowledge and good practice amongst palliative care staff
- satisfy unmet education and training needs cost-effectively within hospices' immediate or wider 'region' (such as a loose geographical area not related to health regions)
- develop closer local control of specialist education and training provision and its evaluation
- improve patient care.

Worldwide Grants Programme

The trust has established two grant programmes with the aim of developing palliative care provision in resource poor countries.

These programmes are:

Worldwide Education Grants – the aim of which is to increase and improve the provision of palliative care in resource poor countries through the support of education and training programmes for professionals involved in the development and provision of palliative care services in these countries.

Worldwide Project Grants – grants are available for small and innovative projects that would make a tangible difference to patients in need of palliative care and their families/carers in resource poor countries.

Ellerman Awards

The John Ellerman Foundation supports hospices through this awards programme. Awards are dedicated to special projects in independent voluntary hospices – up to a maximum of £15,000. Projects should make a discernable difference to patients, and their families and carers, to the individual unit and to palliative care generally.

Rank Foundation Awards

Between 2002 and 2004 the Rank Foundation has provided £100,000 per annum to support special capital projects in independent voluntary hospices. Awards were between £10,000 and £20,000 each and applications were considered for new buildings, extensions, ward conversions, and renovations.

St James's Place Foundation – non cancer projects
The aim of the programme is to inspire and fund small and innovative projects in the UK that will make a tangible difference to patients dying of a condition other than cancer and their families/carers.

Carer's Grants (Time to Care Awards)
The aim of the Carers Project Grant is two-fold:

- to explore and develop support strategies for carers of people with terminal illness
- to support new elements of an existing service which will effectively develop a new aspect and therefore enhance the existing service.

Emergency Support
Assistance is also available for consultancy help for hospices facing urgent financial programmes.

The trust also provides support in the form of professional development grants and a volunteer grants programme. Information for these two, and all of the other grant programmes list is available on the trust's website.

In 2003/04 the trust had an income of just under £4 million and a total expenditure of £4 million.

Those to benefit from grants distributed via the St James's Place Foundation included St Christopher's Hospice, Ardgowan Hospice, Ellenor Foundation in Dartford and Tapping House Hospice (£25,000 each), St John's Hospice in London (£22,700), Katharine House Hospice and Overgate Hospice (£22,500 each), St Nicholas' Hospice (£20,000), St Catherine's Hospice in Scarborough (£17,600).

Applications Generally on a form available from the Grants Officer, from whom further information is also available. For major grant programmes, potential applicants should request details first as policies change. The trust's website contains detailed information of the grant-making policy and should be viewed before an application is considered. For emergency grants, applicants should write directly to the chief executive.

The Christina Mary Hendrie Trust for Scottish & Canadian Charities

Youth, people who are elderly, general

£119,000 (2002/03)

Beneficial area Scotland and Canada.

1 Rutland Court, Edinburgh EH3 8EY

Tel. 0131 270 7700 **Fax** 0131 270 7788

Correspondent George R Russell

Trustees *Mrs A D H Irwin; C R B Cox; J K Scott Moncrieff; Miss C Irwin; Maj. Gen. A S H Irwin; R N Cox; A G Cox.*

SC Number SC014514

Information available Full accounts were provided by the trust.

General The trust was established in 1975 following the death in Scotland of Christina Mary Hendrie. The funds constituting the trust originated in Canada. Grants are distributed to charities throughout Scotland and Canada, although the majority is now given in Scotland. There is a preference for charities connected with young or older people, although other groups to receive grants include cancer charities.

In 2002/03 it had assets of £201,000, which generated an income of £92,000. Grants to 25 organisations totalled £119,000.

The largest grants were £20,000 to Boys' Brigade Carronvale for its development appeal and £10,000 each to Macmillan Cancer Relief and Princess Royal Trust for Carers.

Other beneficiaries included Crossroads Scotland and Gowanbank Historic Village (£7,000 each), Falkland Employment Access Trust (£6,700), Aberlour Childcare Trust (£6,000), Ardgowan Hospice (£5,000), Youth Without Shelter (£4,000), Aberlour Childcare Trust (£3,000), Association for the Protection of Rural Scotland and Inverpeffray Library (£2,000 each), Church of Scotland Board of Social Responsibility (£1,500), Dundas Foundation and Storytelling Scotland (£1,000 each) and Columba 1400 (£500).

Exclusions Grants are not given to individuals.

Applications In writing to the correspondent. The trustees meet twice a year to consider grants, usually in March and November.

Philip Henman Trust

General

About £50,000 (2001/02)

Beneficial area Worldwide.

16 Pembury Road, Tonbridge TN9 2HX

Tel. 01732 362227

Email info@pht.org.uk

Website www.pht.org.uk

Correspondent D J Clark, Trustee

Trustees *J C Clark; D J Clark; J Duffy.*

CC Number 1054707

Information available Information was provided by the trust, including comprehensive guidelines for applicants, most of which are reproduced below.

General The trust's guidelines state 'The trust was set up in 1986 with equity left by the late Philip Henman. The original aim was to continue funding causes supported by Philip Henman during his lifetime. After ten years the trustees felt a need to restructure the trust and a consultant was brought in to recommend more effective grant-giving'.

The trust makes grants towards a range of causes and splits its grant-making as follows:

80% to long-term grants

20% to one-off grants

Long-term grants
The trust makes grants: 'to UK-based overseas aid organisations requiring partnership funding for projects lasting between three and five years. These grants are split into annual payments (normally between £3,000 and £5,000 a year) with a maximum total of £25,000. Once the grant has been approved the organisation will be guaranteed an annual grant for the duration of the project, as long as receipts and reports are sent back to the trust.

'The trust only has resources to guarantee an average of two new long-term grants a year, and therefore it is important to be sure any project fits our criteria before applying. Successful applications are normally those that prove the following, that the:

- project is being run professionally by an established UK-registered charity
- project will start and finish within five years
- funding from the trust is important to the project
- project will provide a lasting beneficial impact to the people or environment it seeks to help
- project is being partly funded by other sources. Voluntary work and central office administration costs can be counted as other source funding.

One-off grants
'One-off grants of up to £1,000 are made and aimed at projects benefiting young people in the UK. Once a grant has been given the individual or organisation is then not eligible to apply for a further one-off grant for five years.

'Successful applications are normally those that prove the following, that the:

- application is specific about the way the grant will be used
- grant will make a substantial difference to the project
- applicant can prove an ability to make the project work
- project will make lasting positive changes to the people or environment it involves
- project is not entirely funded by the grant. Voluntary work and office administration costs count as alternative funding.'

The trust gives an annual grant to Folly Gallery, a community arts centre setup in part using funds left by Philip Henman.

In 2001/02 the trust had an income of £65,000 and gave £50,000 in grants. Beneficiaries included Winged Fellowship, Jubilee Sailing Trust, Wateraid, NCH Action for Children, Anti Slavery, AMIE, Traidcraft Exchange, Sight Savers, International Care and Relief and Childhope. Grants ranged from £800 to £5,000 totalling about £50,000.

Exclusions 'There are no restrictions on which organisations can apply as long as they are a UK-registered charity.'

Applications The trust stated it can now only accept online applications. Materials should not be sent by post. Further details about the compiling of the application form is available on the website.

The trustees meet twice a year in March and October. Applications for long-term grants should be sent before 10 September for consideration at the October meeting and applications for one-off grants should be sent before 10 February for consideration at the March meeting. 'All applications will receive an acknowledgement that their application has been received a further note to indicate whether the application was successful or not. The trust receives far more worthy applications than it has funds available and therefore encourages applicants to make simple low cost project descriptions.'

The G D Herbert Charitable Trust

Medicine, health, welfare, environmental resources

£53,000 (2002/03)

Beneficial area UK.

Tweedie & Prideaux Solicitors, 5 Lincoln's Inn Fields, London WC2A 3BT

Tel. 020 7405 1234

Correspondent J J H Burden, Trustee

Trustees *M E Beaumont; J J H Burden.*

CC Number 295998

Information available Full accounts were on file at the Charity Commission.

General The trust makes grants in the areas of medicine, health, welfare and environmental resources. It mainly gives regular grants to a set list of charities, with a few one-off grants given each year.

In 2002/03 this trust had assets of £1.3 million, an income of £49,000 and made 27 regular donations totalling £53,000.

Grant beneficiaries included The National Trust (£4,000), Abbeyfield Development Trust, Aged in Distress, Anston – Mansfield, Canterbury Oast Trust Appeal, 2Care, Children's Country Holiday Fund, Council for the Protection of Rural England, Friends for the Elderly and Marie Curie Cancer Care (£2,000 each).

Applications In writing to the correspondent. No applications are invited other than from those charities currently supported by the trust.

The Joanna Herbert-Stepney Charitable Settlement (also known as The Paget Charitable Trust)

General – see below

£127,000 (2001/02)

Beneficial area Worldwide, with an interest in Loughborough.

Old Village Stores, Dippenhall Street, Crondall, Farnham, Surrey GU10 5NZ

Tel. 01252 850253

Correspondent Joanna Herbert-Stepney, Trustee

Trustees *Joanna Herbert-Stepney; Lesley Mary Blood; Meg Williams.*

CC Number 327402

Information available Information was on file at the Charity Commission.

General The trust supports both UK and local charities for general charitable purposes. Prioritiies include international aid and development, children who are disadvantaged, older people, animal welfare and environmental projects. The trust states that there is a preference for the 'unglamorous' and 'projects where a little money goes a long way'. In many cases ongoing support is given to organisations.

In 2002/03 the trust had an income of £119,000 and a total expenditure of £170,000.

In 2001/02 it had assets of £3.4 million and an income of £165,000. Grants were made to 126 organisations and totalled £127,000. This was well down on the £253,000 given in the previous year, when some of the capital funds were distributed.

Royal Agricultural Benevolent Fund received two grants totalling £7,500. Other large grants were £6,000 to Oxfam, £4,500 to Royal Scottish Agricultural Benevolent Fund, £2,500 to Soil Association and £3,000 each to Charnwood CVS and Family Holiday Association.

Other overseas beneficiaries included Ethiopiaid, Global Cancer Concern and Pattaya Orphanage Trust (£2,000 each), Churches Commission on Overseas Students (£1,500), ApTibeT and Vision Aid Overseas (£1,000 each), Calcutta Rescue Fund and Relief Fund for Romania (£750), Trek Aid (£500) and Moon Bear Rescue (£300).

Local beneficiaries included Leicestershire Care at Home Scheme (£2,000), ChildLine Midlands and Dove Cottage Day Hospital (£1,000 each), MS Society - Loughborough (£750) and Rockingham Estate Play Association and Victim Support – Loughborough and District (£500 each) and Hind Leys Pre-School Playgroup (£100).

Other recipients included Stepney Children's Fund (£2,000), Hartlepool and District CVS and Southwark Community Education Council (£1,000), Katherine House Hospice (£750) and Humane Slaughter Association (£500).

Exclusions The trust states that 'sheer need is paramount, in practice, nothing else is considered'. Grants are only given to registered UK charities. Overseas projects can only be funded via UK charities; no money can be sent overseas. The trust does not support individuals (including students), projects for people with mental disabilities, medical research or AIDS/HIV projects.

Applications In writing to the correspondent; there is no application form. The trustees meet in spring and autumn. The trust regrets that it cannot respond to all applications.

The Hesed Trust

Christian

£53,000 (2001/02)

Beneficial area UK and overseas.

14 Chiltern Avenue, Cosby, Leicestershire LE9 1UF

Tel. 0116 286 2990

Correspondent G Rawlings, Secretary

Trustees *P Briggs; R Eagle; G Rawlings; J C Smith.*

CC Number 1000489

Information available Accounts were on file at the Charity Commission, but without a narrative report or a list of grants.

General The trust's objectives are:

- the advancement of the Christian faith
- the relief of persons who are in conditions of need, hardship or distress or who are aged or sick
- the provision of instruction the Christian faith at any educational establishment
- the provision of facilities for recreation for persons in need of, for the benefit of the public at large with the object of improving the conditions of life for such persons.

In 2001/02 the trust had an income of £83,000 and gave grants to the sum of £53,000. Its assets totalled £40,000. Ministry support totalled £29,000, with £25,000 given in charitable gifts.

Exclusions No support for expeditions and individual requests.

Applications The trust states that no applications are now being considered.

The Bernhard Heuberger Charitable Trust

Jewish

£194,000 (2002/03)

Beneficial area Worldwide.

12 Sherwood Road, London NW4 1AD

Correspondent H Heuberger, Secretary

Trustees *D H Heuberger; S N Heuberger.*

CC Number 294378

Information available Accounts were on file at the Charity Commission, but without a narrative report.

General This trust was established in 1986. In 2002/03 the Trust had assets of £3 million with an income of £166,000 and grants totalling £194,000.

The largest grants were £100,000 to North West London Communal Mikvah, £22,000 to Magen David Adom UK and £20,000 to Beth Yisochor Dov Limited.

Other grants include £6,000 to Service to the Aged, £5,000 each to Kemble Charitable Trust, Hachzokas Torah Vechesed Charity and Kolel Shomrei Hachomoth, £3,000 each to Aish, British Friends of Shalva and Share Zedek, £2,000 each to Kahal Imrei Chaim Ltd and Ezer North West, £1,000 each to Beis Brucha, Institute of Higher Rabinical Studies, Hampstead Garden Suburb Emunah and JNF.

Other small charitable donations totaled £8,600.

Applications In writing to the correspondent.

The P & C Hickinbotham Charitable Trust

Social welfare

£70,000 (2001/02)

Beneficial area UK, with a preference for Leicestershire and Rutland.

69 Main Street, Bushby, Leicester LE7 9PL

Tel. 0116 243 1152

Correspondent Mrs C R Hickinbotham, Trustee

Trustees *Mrs C R Hickinbotham; P F J Hickinbotham; R P Hickinbotham.*

CC Number 216432

Information available Full accounts were on file at the Charity Commission.

General Grants are generally not recurrent and are largely to social welfare organisations, with some churches and Quaker meetings also receiving support. Grants are mainly under £500, with some smaller grants made to a variety of registered charities. The trust gives occasional, one-off larger grants usually between £5,000 and £20,000.

In 2001/02 it had assets of £2.1 million, which generated an income of £59,000. Grants were made totalling £70,000.

By far the largest grant was £50,000 to Age Concern – Leicester for Catherine House. Other grants of £1,000 or more went to Winifred Matthews Day Centre (£10,000), Leicester Preparative Meeting Society of Friends (£1,200) and Cope for the Laura Centre (£1,000).

Exclusions No grants to individuals applying for bursary-type assistance or to large UK charities.

Applications In writing to the correspondent, giving a brief outline of the purpose of the grant. Replies will not be sent to unsuccessful applicants.

Highcroft Charitable Trust

Jewish, poverty

£65,000 (2001/02)

Beneficial area UK and overseas.

15 Highcroft Gardens, London NW11 0LY

Tel. 020 8458 5382

Correspondent Rabbi R Fischer, Trustee

Trustees *Rabbi R Fischer; S L Fischer.*

CC Number 272684

Information available Accounts were on file at the Charity Commission.

General The trust supports the advancement and study of the Jewish faith and the Torah, and also the relief of poverty and advancement of education among people of the Jewish faith. Grants range between £148 and £5,000.

In 2001/02 the trust had assets of £264,000 and an income of £112,000 with grants totalling £65,000.

The largest grants were £11,000 to Jewish Learning Exchange, £8,600 to Tevini Limited and £7,500 each to Kolel Divrei Shir and FCCE.

Other grants include £5,000 each to Yeshiva Marbeh Torah, Union Orthodox Hebrew Congregation and Institute for Higher Rabbinical Studies, £2,500 to Society of the Friends of Torah, £2,000 to Hachzokas Torah Veched Charity, £1,500 to Yeshiva Wolozin, £750 each to Yeshiva Horomoh and Beth Jacob Grammar School, and £100 each to Beis Hatalmud Gateshead and Kisharon.

Applications In writing to the correspondent.

Highmoor Hall Charitable Trust

Christian mission societies and agencies

£230,000 (2001/02)

Beneficial area UK and overseas.

Long Meadow, Dark Lane, Chearsley, Aylesbury, Buckinghamshire HP18 0DA

Correspondent P D Persson, Trustee

Trustees *P D Persson; Mrs A D Persson; J P G Persson; A S J Persson.*

CC Number 289027

Information available Basic accounts were on file at the Charity Commission.

General This trust makes grants to Christian mission societies and agencies. In 2001/02 it had an income of £156,000 and a total expenditure of £239,000. In the previous year charitable expenditure was divided into three categories: home missions, overseas missions and 'other charities'.

About two thirds of its charitable expenditure has previously gone to 'other charities'; during this year that percentage was around £159,000.

No further information was available on the size or number of beneficiaries.

Exclusions No grants to non-registered charities.

Applications The trust states that it does not respond to unsolicited applications. Telephone calls are not welcome.

This entry was not confirmed by the trust but was correct according to information on file at the Charity Commission.

The Holly Hill Charitable Trust

Environmental education, conservation and wildlife

£193,000 (2002/03)

Beneficial area UK.

Flat 5, 89 Onslow Square, London SW7 3LT

Tel. 020 7589 2651

Correspondent M D Stanley, Trustee

Trustees *M D Stanley; A Lewis.*

CC Number 1044510

Information available Full accounts were provided by the trust.

General This trust was established in 1995 to support environmental education, conservation and wildlife organisations.

In 2002/03 it had assets of £1 million and an income of £165,000, mostly from donations received. Grants were made to 14 organisations totalling £193,000.

The largest grants were £43,000 to Plymouth University, £35,000 to Rain Forest Concern and £25,000 each to Devon Wildlife Trust and Somerset Wildlife Trust.

Smaller grants were £13,000 to Sussex Wildlife Trust, £10,000 each to CASA, PTES and Soil Association, £5,400 each to Ecology Project International and Hereford Hospital, £5,200 to Fund Cuencas Limon, £4,000 to Aberdeen University, £2,000 to Nottingham University and £1,000 to Global Young Leaders.

Exclusions No grants to individuals.

Applications In writing to the correspondent. Applications need to be received in April and September, and trustees meet in June and November.

The Charles Littlewood Hill Trust

Health, disability, service, children (including schools)

£148,000 (2003)

Beneficial area UK, with a preference for Nottinghamshire and Norfolk.

Eversheds, 1 Royal Standard Place, Nottingham NG1 6FZ

Tel. 0115 950 7000 **Fax** 0115 950 7111

Correspondent W F Whysall, Trustee

Trustees *C W L Barratt; W F Whysall; T H Farr; N R Savory.*

CC Number 286350

Information available Information was provided by the trust

General The trust supports schools, disability, health, service and children's organisations. It gives UK-wide, although particular preference is given to applications from Norfolk and Nottinghamshire.

In 2003 it had assets of £3.1 million, which generated an income of £146,000. Grants amounted to £148,000 and those of £1,000 or over were broken down as follows:

Nottinghamshire – 18 grants totalling £44,000

The largest grants were £5,000 each to Bassetlaw Hospice of the Good Shepherd, Dove Cottage Day Hospice, Fundays in Nottinghamshire and Peter Le Marchant Trust. Other beneficiaries included Relate – Nottinghamshire (£3,000), Nottingham Sea Cadet Unit, St John Ambulance Retford and Stonebridge City Farm (£2,000 each) and Carlton Life-Saving Club, Dyspraxia Connexion, Kirklington Village Hall and Self Help Nottingham (£1,000 each).

Norfolk – 14 grants totalling £67,000

The largest grants were £25,000 to Victim Support – Norfolk, £10,000 to Horstead Centre and £5,000 each to Great Hospital, Norfolk Churches Trust, St Margaret's Church – Swannington and We Care 2000 Appeal. Other beneficiaries included Norfolk Eating Disorders Association (£3,000), Norfolk Wildlife Trust (£2,500) and Hand Partnership, How Hill Trust, Sue Ryder Care and Tapping House Hospice (£1,000).

Elsewhere – 20 grants totalling £25,000

Beneficiaries included British Epilepsy Association (£3,000), Bramford Road New Community Centre Project, DARE Foundation and Royal Leicestershire Regiment Museum Appeal (£2,000 each) and Army Cadet Force Association, British Wheelchair Sports Foundation, Cleft Lip and Palate Foundation, Gurkha Welfare Trust, National Autistic Society, Police Foundation, Prostate Cancer Charity, Spinal Injuries Association and St Loyes Foundation (£1,000 each).

Exclusions Applications from individuals are not considered. Grants are seldom made for repairs of parish churches outside Nottinghamshire.

Applications In writing to the correspondent, including the latest set of audited accounts, at least one month before trustees' meetings in March, July and November. Unsuccessful applications will not be notified.

R G Hills Charitable Trust

General

£53,000 (2002/03)

Beneficial area UK and overseas.

Furley Page, 39 St Margaret's Street, Canterbury, Kent CT1 2TX

Tel. 01227 763939

Correspondent Mr Barton

CC Number 1008914

Information available Full accounts are on file at the Charity Commission.

General This trust was dormant until Mrs E M Hill's death in March 1996, when she left three-quarters of the residue of her estate to the trust. The balance was received in June 1999.

In 2002/03 the trust had assets of £2 million, an income of £83,000 and made grants totalling £53,000.

Grant beneficiaries were: Demelza House (£4,000), British Executive Service Overseas, Bud Flanigan Leukaemia Fund, The Children's Trust, Coronary Artery Disease Research, Ex Services Mental Welfare Society, Greater London Fund for the Blind, Kent Air Ambulance, King George Fund for Sailors, Salvation Army and Spinal Injuries Association (£3,000) and Deaf Education through Listening and Talking, Hope UK, Impact Foundation, RNLI, RUKBA, Unicef and Wingate Special Children's Trust (£2,000 each).

Applications In writing to the correspondent.

Hinchley Charitable Trust

Mainly evangelical Christian

£99,000 (2001)

Beneficial area UK and overseas.

Watersmeet, 56 Barton Road, Haslingfield, Cambridge CB3 7LL

Tel. 01223 741120

Email bs217@cam.ac.uk

Correspondent Dr Brian Stanley, Trustee

CC Number 281178

Information available Accounts were on file at the Charity Commission, but without a full narrative report.

General In 2002/03 the trust had an income of £125,000 and a total expenditure of £130,000. Further information for this year was not available.

In 2001 the trust's assets totalled £1.9 million following substantial income of £1.4 million during the year. Grants were made totalling £99,000.

Larger grants were: £12,000 to Tearfund for Christian relief and development work, £11,000 each to Associated Bus Ministries for evangelistic work and Mildmay Hospital for general expenses, £10,000 to Crusader's Union for Christian youth work, £5,000 each to Epsom and Ewell Boys' Club for youth work and Spurgeon's College for theological training, £2,500 to Arbury Road Baptist Church, Cambridge for church work and £1,500 to Church Pastoral Aid Society for church work.

Applications The trust states that it does not respond to unsolicited applications. Replies will rarely, if ever, be made to applications for grants by post or on the telephone, as existing funds are all fully committed to charities which are regularly supported.

Stuart Hine Trust

Evangelical Christianity

£138,000 (2003/04)

Beneficial area UK and overseas.

'Cherith', 23 Derwent Close, Hailsham, East Sussex BN27 3DA

Tel. 01323 843948

Correspondent Raymond Bodkin, Trustee

CC Number 326941

Information available Information was supplied by the trust.

General The trust gives grants to evangelical Christian organisations that have been supported by the trustees or by the settlor during his lifetime and that are known to the trustees. In 2003/04 the trust had an income of £121,000 and gave grants totalling £138,000.

A detailed grants list was not available, although the trust did inform us that the bulk of the grant total was given to Wycliff Bible Translators (£95,000).

Applications In writing to the correspondent. Please note, the trust states that 'unsolicited requests for funds will not be considered'. Funds are basically distributed in accordance with the wishes of the settlor.

The Hinrichsen Foundation

Music

£53,000 (2002/03)

Beneficial area UK.

10–12 Baches Street, London N1 6DN

Correspondent Mrs Lesley E Adamson, Secretary

Trustees *Mrs C E Hinrichsen; P Strang; K Potter; P Standford; Prof. S Walsh; Dr J Cross; Dr Linda Hirst; M Williams; T Berg; S Lubbock; T Estell.*

CC Number 272389

Information available Full accounts were provided by the trust.

General The trust states: 'The Hinrichsen Foundation is a charity devoted to the promotion of music. Although the objects of the trust are widely drawn, the trustees have decided for the time being to concentrate on assisting in the written areas of music, that is, assisting contemporary composition and its performance and musical research'.

The trust supports the public performance of living composers; grants include those to performing ensembles for concerts and festivals. Grants are not made retrospectively. Organisations supported include both UK organsiations and local groups throughout the UK.

In 2002/03 it had assets of £83,000 and an income of £108,000, almost entirely from donations received. Grants were approved to 45 organisations totalling £47,000. A total of £6,000 was given in 10 grants to individuals.

The largest grants were £20,000 in two grants to Huddersfield Contemporary Music Festival, £10,000 in three grants to Kettles Yard, £2,000 each to Bath Festival, London Sinfonietta, Music Theatre Wales and Opera Circus and £1,500 to British Contemporary Piano Competition, Goldberg Ensemble, Kokoro, Mr McFall's Chamber, Psappha, St Mary de Haura Church – Storeham and Spitalfields Festival.

Other beneficiaries included Cheltenham Contemporary Concerts and York Late Music Festival (£1,000 each), Apartment House and Continuum Ensemble (£750 each), BT Scottish Ensemble (£700) and Adur Arts Forum and Corrado Canonici (£500 each).

Exclusions The trust does not support study courses, including those at postgraduate level. Grants are not given for instruments, equipment or recordings.

Applications On a form available from the correspondent. Grants are paid after the completion of the project, whenever that is. The trustees meet to consider grants four times a year, usually in February, April, July and October.

The Hobart Charitable Trust

General

£51,000 (2003/04)

Beneficial area UK, prioritising Hampshire.

140 Trustee Company, 36 Broadway, London SW1H 0BH

Correspondent The Trustees

Trustees *N G McNair Scott; Hon. Mrs Denise Berry; Mrs Kate Andrews.*

CC Number 800750

Information available Information was provided by the trust.

General In 2003/04 the trust had assets of £317,000 and an income of £12,000. Grants totalled £51,000, consisting of £50,000 to North Hampshire Medical Foundation and £1,000 to Battle of Britain Monument Fund.

Exclusions No grants to individuals.

Applications Applications are not invited.

Hockerill Educational Foundation

Education, especially Christian education

£157,000 (2001/02)

Beneficial area UK, with a preference for the dioceses of Chelmsford and St Albans.

16 Hagsdell Road, Hertford, Hertfordshire SG13 8AG

Tel. 01992 303053 **Fax** 01992 425950

Correspondent C R Broomfield, Secretary

Trustees *Dr S Hunter, Chair; Rt Revd Lord Bishop of Chelmsford; Rt Revd Lord Bishop of St Albans; Rt Revd Bishop of Bedford; Rt Revd Bishop of Bradwell; Ven. T P Jones; Ven. P Taylor; Prof. B J Aylett; Revd P Hartley; Mrs M L Helmore; H Marsh; Mrs H Potter; J O Reynolds; R Woods.*

CC Number 311018

Information available Full accounts, guidelines and an information leaflet were provided by the trust.

General The foundation was established in 1978 following the closure of Hockerill College, which was established in 1852 to train women teachers who 'would go to schools in the service of humanity'. When the Secretary of State for Education and Science decided in 1976 to wind down Hockerill College, the proceeds of the sale of its assets were given to this foundation to use for the purposes for which the college was created. The foundation's priorities are:

- education and training of teachers and others involved in education (particularly religious education)
- research and development of religious education
- support for students in further and higher education (normally only to first degree level)
- those involved in non-statutory education, including adult and Christian education.

These grants are made to individuals wishing to train as teachers and to existing teachers who wish to improve their qualifications, particularly with regards to education. For further information, please see *The Educational Grants Directory* (published by DSC).

Grants are also made to organisations for projects and research likely to enhance the Church of England's contribution to higher and further education or religious education in schools. The trust's *Guidance for Applicants* states:

'The trustees will normally consider applications from corporate bodies or institutions associated with education on Christian principles. There is a religious dimension to all education, but the trustees would expect any activity, course, project or research supported to be of real benefit to religious education and/or the church's educational work. They will give priority to imaginative new projects which will enhance the Church of England's contribution to higher and further education and/or promote aspects of religious education in schools.

'Recurrent grants may be made, normally for up to three years and for a maximum of five years. Grants for the funding of research or appointment of individuals will be paid termly or quarterly and subject to funds being available. The trustees will wish to make suitable arrangements to monitor research or the progress of a project, and will ask for a report on the progress of any course or project they are funding. They shall also be entitled to ask for a line of credit in the final line of a research project.'

The foundation also arranges the annual Hockerill Lecture, which was given in 2001 by the Rt Revd Alan Chesters, Chair of the Church of England Board of Education, on the subject *'Distinctive or Divisive? The Role of Church Schools'*.

In 2001/02 the trust had assets of £5.1 million and an income of £206,000. Grants were made totalling £157,000.

The largest grants were £61,000 to Chelmsford Diocesan Board of Finance in six grants towards employment and travel costs of a Further Education Officer, salary of children's officer and related costs, expenses of children's work advisor, salary costs of staff at St Mark's College, resources for school visits and towards the costs of the Diocesan early years advisor, and £49,000 to St Albans Diocesan Board of Education in five grants towards salaries of a Religious Education support teacher and youth outreach worker, resources for the Diocesan Religious Education Centre in Welwyn Garden City and children's projects concerned with IT and spirituality.

Other grants included £5,000 to Faculty of Initial Education – St Andrew's Paraguay for student bursaries (second of five annual grants), £4,500 to Luton Grassroots Programme to promote interfaith dialogue (third of three annual grants), £3,000 to St Albans Cathedral Music Trust to help develop the choirs at the cathedral (second of three grants) and £2,000 each to Bedford Chaplaincy Committee to support the ecumenical chaplaincy at De Montfort (Bedford) University (third of three annual grants) and St Albans DBF Youth Services Account to subsidise the provision of 'Enable Holidays' canal boat holidays for young people with special needs.

Exclusions Grants are not given for general appeals for funds, 'bricks and mortar' building projects or purposes that are the clear responsibility of another body.

With regard to individuals, grants will not normally be considered for:

- teachers who intend to move out of the profession
- those in training for ordination or for other kinds of mission
- clergy who wish to improve their own qualifications, unless they are already engaged in teaching in schools and/or intend to teach in the future
- students of counselling, therapy or social work
- undergraduates or people training for other professions, such as accountancy, business, law or medicine
- people doing courses or visits abroad, including 'gap' year courses (except as an integral part of a course, or a necessary part of research)
- children at primary or secondary school.

Applications On a form available from the correspondent and submitted by 1 March each year. Results of applications will be communicated in early April. Receipt of applications are not acknowledged. Applications which do not fit the criteria would not normally receive a reply. Further information on the grants to individuals can be found in *The Educational Grants Directory published by DSC.*

This entry was not confirmed by the trust but was correct according to information on file at the Charity Commission.

The S Hodgkiss Charitable Trust

General, arts

£43,000 (2001/02)

Beneficial area UK with a preference for Greater Manchester.

57 The Woodlands, Lostock, Bolton BL6 4JD

Correspondent Joseph Swift, Trustee

Trustees *Joseph John Swift; Susan Katrina Hodgkiss.*

CC Number 1077803

Information available Accounts were on file at the Charity Commission.

General Established in October 1999, in 2001/02 this trust had an income of £71,000, including £56,000 from Gift Aid. Its assets stood at £68,000. Grants to 13 organisations totalled £43,000.

Beneficiaries included Broughton House (£10,000), Chetham's School of Music and Octagon Theatre Trust (£5,000 each), Christies' Hospital (£2,000), Big Issue (£1,600) and BESO (£1,000).

Applications This trust does accept unsolicited applications.

The Edward Sydney Hogg Charitable Settlement

General

£124,000 (2002/03)

Beneficial area UK.

Messrs Hoare Trustees, 37 Fleet Street, London EC4P 4DQ

Tel. 020 7353 4522

Correspondent The Secretary

Trustee *Messrs Hoare Trustees.*

CC Number 280138

Information available Full accounts were on file at the Charity Commission.

General In 2002/03 the trust had assets of £2.6 million with an income of £99,000 and grant totalling £124,000.

Grants include £10,000 each to Dementia Centre at the University of Stirling, Action Research and Leicester Theatre Trust, £7,000 to Orbis Charitable Trust, £6,000 to Guild of Air Pilots and Navigators, £5,000 each to Relate Kent Educational Training Service, Royal British Legion, Harrow Development Trust, Borders 1996 Company Ltd and Our Lady's Manor, £3,000 each to Quaker Social Action and St George's Community Children's Project, £2,000 each to Muscular Dystrophy Association, Game Conservancy Scottish Research Trust, Living Paintings Trust, Wiltshire Wildlife Trust, Sussex Young Cricketers Educational Trust and £1,000 each to Foundation for Skin Research and Rye Health & Care Ltd.

Applications In writing to the correspondent. Trustees meet monthly.

The J G Hogg Charitable Trust

Welfare, animal welfare, general

£227,000 (2001/02)

Beneficial area Worldwide.

Chantrey Vellacott DFK, Russell Square House, 10 –12 Russell Square, London WC1B 5LF

Tel. 020 7509 9000

Correspondent C M Jones, Trustees' Accountant

Trustees *Sarah Jane Houldsworth; Joanna Wynfreda Turvey.*

CC Number 299042

Information available Accounts were provided by the trust.

General The trust states that it has no set policy on the type of charity supported, but would give favourable consideration to those based primarily in the UK that support the relief of human and animal suffering.

In 2001/02 the trust had an income of £215,000 and made grants totalling £226,500 distributed in 35 individual donations.

The largest grants were made to Oxfam (£29,000), Students Exploring Marriage Trust (£13,500), Canine Partners for Independence (£11,000), Pets Placement and The Chemical Dependency Centre (£10,000 each).

Other grants were of £7,000 or less and included Trust for Chernobyl Children (£7,000), Quest, Royal Ballet School, Sue Ryder and Care Variety Club of Great Britain (£6,000 each).

Exclusions No grants to individuals. Registered charities only are supported.

Applications In writing to the correspondent. To keep administration costs to a minimum, the trust is unable to reply to unsuccessful applicants.

The Holden Charitable Trust

Jewish

£70,000 a year

Beneficial area UK, with a preference for the Manchester area.

c/o Lopian Gross Barnett & Co., Cardinal House, 20 St Mary Parsonage, Manchester M3 2IG

Tel. 0161 832 8721

Correspondent The Clerk

Trustees *David Lopian; Marion Lopian.*

CC Number 264185

Information available Accounts were on file at the Charity Commission, but without a list of grants since 1993/94.

General The trust has general charitable purposes, although it appears to support exclusively Jewish causes. In 2002/03 it had an income of £187,000 and a total expenditure of £107,000.

Grants total about £70,000 annually. Past beneficiaries have included Binoh Manchester, Broughton Jewish Primary School, Manchester Jewish Grammar School, North Cheshire Jewish Primary School and North Salford Synagogue.

Applications In writing to the correspondent.

The Hollick Family Charitable Trust

General

£42,000 (2000/01)

Beneficial area UK and overseas.

30 St James's Street, London SW1A 1HB

Tel. 020 7930 6225

Correspondent D W Beech, Solicitor

Trustees *Lord Hollick; Lady Hollick; C D Hollick; C M Kemp; D W Beech; G L Hollick; A M Hollick.*

CC Number 1060228

Information available Full accounts were on file at the Charity Commission.

General The trust makes grants for general purposes. The trust's policy is to make a number of relatively small but significant donations to a range of charities each year and also to identify one cause to give more substantial funding to. In 2000/01 the trust's assets totalled £950,000 and it received an income of £36,000. Grants totalled £42,000.

Altogether 21 grants were given over the year, ranging from £1,000 to £7,000. The largest grant of £7,000 went to The Portobello Trust. Other large grants included £5,000 to The Medical Foundation, £3,570 to Tampa Crossroads, USA, £2,500 to English National Opera, £2,000 each to National Portrait Gallery and Saving Faces, £1,500 each to Writers & Scholars Educational Trust and St Christopher's Fellowship, £1,000 each to SHAPE London and Theatre Royal Stratford East.

Applications In writing to the correspondent.

The Dorothy Holmes Charitable Trust

General

£36,000 (2001/02)

Beneficial area UK, with a preference for Dorset.

Moorfield Cody & Co, 5 Harley Place, Harley Street, London W1G 8QD

Tel. 020 7631 4574

Correspondent Margaret Cody

Trustees *D G Roberts; B M Cody; Miss M E A Cody; S C Roberts.*

CC Number 237213

Information available Information was provided by the trust.

General The trust's policy is to make a substantial number of relatively small donations to groups working in many charitable fields – including those involved in medical research, disability, older people, children and young people, churches, the disadvantaged, the environment and the arts. The trust can give throughout the UK but has a preference for Dorset, especially Poole. In practice nearly all grants are given to either national charities or those based in Dorset.

In 2001/02 the trust had an income of £31,000 and an expenditure of £57,000. Grants totalled £36,000. Donations generally range from between £200 to £500, however some larger grants, up to £1,000, are made. Further information for this year was not available. Previous beneficiaries have included Crisis at Christmas, Friends of Stanstead School, RAFT, St John's School – Wallingford and St Wilfrid's Hospice – Chichester.

Exclusions Only applications from registered charities will be considered.

Applications In writing to the correspondent.

The Holst Foundation

Arts

£203,000 to individuals and organisations (2002/03)

Beneficial area UK.

43 Alderbrook Road, London SW12 8AD

Tel. 020 8673 4215

Correspondent The Grants Administrator

Trustees *Rosamund Strode, Chair; Noel Periton; Prof. Arnold Whittall; Peter Carter; Andrew Clements; Julian Anderson; Dr Colin Matthews; Bayan Northcott.*

CC Number 283668

Information available Full accounts were provided by the trust.

General The trust has two objects: firstly, to promote public appreciation of the musical works of Gustav and Imogen Holst; and secondly, to encourage the study and practice of the arts.

In practice the trust tends to be proactive. Funds are available almost exclusively for the performance of music by living composers. The trust has historical links with Aldeburgh in Suffolk and is a major funder of new music at the annual Aldeburgh Festival. It also promotes the recording of new music by means of substantial funding to the recording label NMC, which the foundation also provided the funds to set up.

In 2002/03 it had assets of £1.5 million and an income of £258,000. Grants totalling £203,000 were made to 94 individuals and organisations.

By far the largest donation, of £105,000, went to NMC Recordings. Aldeburgh Productions received two grants totalling £16,000.

Other beneficiaries included BMIC (£6,000), Park Lane Group (£5,000), Huddersfield Festival (£2,500), Dartington International Summer School (£2,300), Bath Festivals Trust (£2,000), Cheltenham International Festival (£1,800), Music Theatre - Wales (£1,500) and Conservational Concert and Yorke Trust (£1,000).

Exclusions No support for the recordings or works of Holst that are already well supported. No grants to individuals for educational purposes.

Applications In writing to: The Grants Administrator, 43 Alderbrook Road, London SW12 8AD. Trustees meet four times a year. There is no application form. Seven copies of the application should be sent. Applications should contain full financial details and be as concise as possible. Funding is not given retrospectively.

P H Holt Charitable Trust

General

£186,000 (2002/03)

Beneficial area UK, with a preference for Merseyside.

India Buildings, Liverpool L2 0RB

Tel. 0151 473 4693

Correspondent Roger Morris, Secretary

Trustees *K Wright, Chair; John Utley; Derek Morris; Tilly Boyce; Neil Kemsley.*

CC Number 217332

Information available Full accounts were provided by the trust.

General The trust makes a large number of mostly small grants, about three quarters of them in Merseyside. This trust is a welcome and exceptional example of Liverpool shipping money staying in and around the city. It continues to organise its giving in three established grant programmes concerned with Merseyside, 'Holt tradition' and elsewhere.

In 2002/03 the trust had assets of £8.5 million, an income of £323,000 and a total expenditure of £320,000. Grants were made totalling £186,000.

The trust summarised its activities and the categories supported in 2002/03 as shown in the tables. A full list of grants was provided by the trust, with brief descriptions of the purpose of the larger grants made.

Payments in 2002/03 were categorised as follows:

	Total	*Merseyside*	*'Holt tradition'*
Community	£55,000	£47,000	£4,100
Welfare	£52,000	£48,000	£3,900
Education	£15,000	£14,000	£500
Arts	£41,000	£39,000	£1,500
Heritage	£2,500	£1,500	£1,000
Environment	£19,000	£18,000	£1,000
Medicine	£1,500	£1,500	nil
Total	£186,000	£170,000	£16,000

Merseyside grants – one-off

Three large grants were made to Emmaus (£20,000), and to FACT and the Mersey Basin Trust (£15,000 each). Other beneficiaries included HFT (£7,500), Arts Council England – North West (£6,800), For-J Development Trust (£4,000), Maritime CDA and Women's Enterprising Breakthrough (£3,000 each), The Greenbank Project (£2,000), Partnership for Racial Equality (£1,500), Anne Frank Trust UK, Bronte Youth and Community Centre, RSPB and Wirral Holistic Care Services (£1,000 each), MYPT (£750), Liverpool Yemeni Arabic Club (£500), Project Trust (£200) and Student Partnerships Worldwide (£100).

Merseyside grants – regular donations

Routine gifts to organisations with which the trust is in regular contact included those to PSS (£10,000), Liverpool Council of Social Service (£7,500), Local solutions (£5,000), Liverpool School of Tropical Medicine (£1,500), Birkenhead School and Liverpool College (£1,000 each), Merseyside Play Action Council (£250) and Merseyside Civic Society (£100).

The 'Holt Tradition' – one-off

One-off grants were given to 3 organisations, with the largest of £5,000 being made to the Children & Families

P H HOLT CHARITABLE TRUST
Activity 2002/03

	Merseyside	*'Holt tradition'*	*Elsewhere*
No. of applications received	287	48	222
No. of grants made	82	27	0
of which			
recipients previously supported	58	26	
recipients supported for the first time	19	1	
consortium projects	5	0	
total value of grants	£170,000	£16,000	

of the Far East Prisoners of War. The remaining two went in support of Liverpool Domestic Society (£1,000) and Anti-Slavery International (£500).

The 'Holt Tradition' – regular donations

Regular annual subscriptions included those to King George's Fund for Sailors (£2,000), Outward Bound Trust (£1,000), Friends of the Royal Academy (£750), Runnymede Trust (£500), John Muir Trust (£250) and Historic Churches Preservation Trust and Society for the Protection of Ancient Buildings (£200 each).

Exclusions No grants to individuals. Grants are not usually given to organisations outside Merseyside.

Applications In writing to the correspondent at any time.

The Homelands Charitable Trust

The New Church, health, social welfare

£242,000 (2001/02)

Beneficial area UK.

c/o Alliotts, Ingersoll House, 5th Floor, 9 Kingsway, London WC2B 6XF

Tel. 020 7240 9971

Correspondent N J Armstrong, Trustee

Trustees *D G W Ballard; N J Armstrong; Revd C Curry.*

CC Number 214322

Information available Information was on file at the Charity Commission.

General This trust was established in 1962, the settlors were four members of the Curry family and the original endowment was in the form of shares in the Curry company.

In 2002/03 the trust had an income of £251,000 and a total expenditure of £242,000.

In 2001/02 it had assets of £5.7 million and a total income of £266,000. Grants were made totalling £242,000. Management and administration charges remained low at £10,000, including payments of £7,500 to a firm which had a trustee amongst its partners. Whilst wholly legal, these editors always regret such payments unless, in the words of the Charity Commission, 'there is no realistic alternative'.

No grants information was included in the accounts, although the following was included under the heading 'Future plans and commitments':

'The trustees intend to continue supporting registered charities with a bais towards:

1) General Conference of the New Church

2) medical research

3) care and protection of children

4) hospices.

'The trustees are aware of the proposed extension and refurbishment of the New Church Residential Centre in the Midlands at an estimated cost of £1.5 million and are considering a substantial donation towards this project.'

Exclusions No grants to individuals.

Applications In writing to the correspondent.

The Homestead Charitable Trust

See below

£83,000 (2002/03)

Beneficial area UK.

Flat 7, Clarence Gate Gardens, Glentworth Street, London NW1 6AY

Tel. 0207 258 1051

Correspondent Lady Nina Bracewell-Smith, Trustee

Trustees *Sir C Bracewell-Smith; Lady N Bracewell-Smith.*

CC Number 293979

Information available Information was provided by the trust.

General This trust makes grants towards medical, health and welfare, animal welfare, Christianity and the arts.

In 2002/03 it had an income of £154,000 and a total expenditure of £100,000. Grants given to individuals and institutions totalled £83,000. The total assets at the end of the year were £2.6 million.

The largest grant was £14,000 to Help the Aged along with £10,000 each to Medecins sans Frontiere, Orbis Eye Charity and Unicef – Afghanistan Appeal.

Other grants were between £50 and £5,000. Some beneficiaries were Banyan Hospital (£5,000), Fight for Sight (£3,000), The Order of Carthissians (£1,000), Aftermath (£500), Royal British Legion (£100) and Water Aid (£50).

Applications In writing to the correspondent

Mary Homfray Charitable Trust

General

£45,000 (2001/02)

Beneficial area UK, with a preference for Wales.

c/o Deloitte and Touche, Private Clients Ltd, Blenheim House, Fitzalan Court, Newport Road, Cardiff CF24 0TS

Tel. 029 2048 1111

Correspondent Mrs A M Homfray, Trustee

Trustees *Mrs A M Homfray; G C S Gibson.*

CC Number 273564

Information available Information was provided by the trust.

General The trust supports a wide range of organisations, including many in Wales.

In 2001/02 it had assets of £2 million and an income of £69,000. Grants were made to 25 organisations totalling £45,000. The only three organisations which were not also supported in the previous year were League of Friends of Fairford Hospital (£2,200), Meningitis Cymru (£2,000) and United Kingdom Antartic Heritage Trust (£1,000).

Aside from the £500 each to Maes-y-Dyfan, National Museum of Wales and RSPB, all the other grants were of £2,000 each. Beneficiaries included Age Concern, British Heart Foundation, Centrepoint, Danybryn Cheshire Home, National Children's Home, PDSA, Shelter Cymru, Urdd Gobaith Cymru and YMCA.

Applications In writing to the correspondent. Applications should be made towards the end of the year, for consideration at the trustees' meeting in February or March each year.

The Hope Trust

Temperance, Reformed Protestant churches

£119,000 (2000)

Beneficial area Worldwide, with a preference for Scotland.

Drummond Miller, 32 Moray Place, Edinburgh EH3 6BZ

Tel. 0131 226 5151

Correspondent Robert P Miller, Secretary

Trustees *Prof. G M Newlands; Prof. D A S Ferguson; Revd G R Barr; Revd Dr Lyall; Carole Hope.*

SC Number SC000987

Information available Information was provided by the trust.

General This trust was established to promote the ideals of temperance in the areas of drink and drugs, and Protestant church reform through education and the distribution of literature. In 2000 its income was £174,000. Grants towards temperance causes totalled £15,000, and other grants to causes related to the Protestant Reformed tradition in Scotland and worldwide totalled £104,000. PhD students of theology studying at Scottish universities were also supported.

Larger grants included those to Church of Scotland Priority Areas Fund (£11,000), World Alliance of Reformed Churches (£10,000), National Bible Society for Scotland (£4,000) and Feed the Minds and Waldensian Mission Aid (£3,000 each).

Exclusions No grants to gap year students, scholarship schemes or to any individuals, with the sole exception of PhD students of theology studying at Scottish universities. No grants for the refurbishment of property.

Applications In writing to the correspondent. The trustees meet to consider applications in June and December each year. Applications should be submitted by mid-May or mid-November each year.

The Cuthbert Horn Trust

Environment, people with disability/special needs, older people

£60,000 (2001)

Beneficial area UK.

Capita Trust Company Limited, Phoenix House, 18 King William Street, London EC4N 7HE

Tel. 020 7800 4188 **Fax** 020 7800 4180

Correspondent L A Anderson

Trustees *Alliance Assurance Company Ltd; A H Flint.*

CC Number 291465

Information available Information was taken from the Charity Commission.

General The trust's main aims are to support charities helping older people and charities undertaking practical work in supporting the conservation and preservation of the environment.

In 2003 the trust had an income of £75,000 and a total expenditure of £76,000. This information was taken from the Charity Commission database. Unfortunately no further details were available for this year.

In 2001 the trust had assets of £1.2 million and a total income of £215,000. Grants were made totalling £60,000. The largest grants were £8,000 to Counsel & Care for the Elderly, £6,000 to Soil Association and £5,000 to Ability Net. Other beneficiaries included Henry Doubleday Research Association, Farms for City Children and Pesticide Action Network UK (£4,000 each), Cotswold Canals Trust, Island Trust, Norwegian Locomotive Trust and St John's RC School (£3,000 each) and Bulgaria Project, Cancer Bacup, Green Alliance, International Bee Research Association and Wildfowl & Wetlands Trust (£2,000 each).

Exclusions No grants are made to individuals.

Applications There are no application forms to complete; applicants should provide in writing as much background about their charity or cause as possible. Applications need to be received by December as the trustees meet as soon as possible after the financial year end. Only successful applications will be notified.

The Thomas J Horne Memorial Trust

Hospices

£64,000 (2002/03)

Beneficial area UK and the developing world.

Kingsdown, Warmlake Road, Chart Sutton, Maidstone, Kent ME17 3RP

Email postmaster@horne-trust.org.uk

Correspondent J T Horne, Trustee

Trustees *Mrs M Horne; J T Horne; J L Horne; N J Camamile.*

CC Number 1010625

Information available Information was provided by the trust.

General The trust supports homelessness charities and hospices, particularly children's hospices. Grants can also be given to medical support charities and organisations helping to develop self-reliant technology in Africa and the developing world.

In 2002/03 it had an income of £41,000. Grants ranging from £500 to £5,000 each went to 25 organisations and totalled £64,000. Further information was not available.

Applications Normally in writing to the correspondent, although the trust has stated that currently unsolicited applications cannot be supported.

Hospital Saturday Fund Charitable Trust

Medical, health

£141,000 to organisations (2002/03)

Beneficial area UK, the Republic of Ireland and overseas.

24 Upper Ground, London SE1 9PD

Tel. 020 7928 6662 **Fax** 020 7928 0558

Email trust@hsf.co.uk

Correspondent K R Bradley, Administrator

Trustees *K R Bradley, Chair; D C Barnes; L I Fellman; P P Groat; Miss I Racher; A F Tierney; Mrs L M C Warner.*

CC Number 327693

Information available Full accounts were on file at the Charity Commission.

General The Hospital Saturday Fund is a healthcare cash plan organisation, which was founded in 1873. In 1987 it established a charitable trust to support a wide range of hospitals, hospices and medical charities for care and research, as well as welfare organisations providing similar services. The trustees are now trying to provide more support to smaller, lesser-known charities connected with diseases and disabilities about which there is little public awareness. Individuals can also be supported by the trust, usually for special equipment to relieve their condition or in cases where their health has contributed to their financial hardship, although sponsorship can be given to people studying for a medically-related career.

In 2002/03 it had assets of £112,000 and an income of £160,000, mostly through donations from its parent company. Grants were made to organisations totalling £141,000 and to individuals totalling £7,700 (of which £4,500 was for welfare and £3,200 to medical electives). Grants to organisations were broken down geographically, as follows:

National – 55 grants totalling £31,000

The largest grant, of £2,500, went to Variety Club. Aside of this, it gave 11 grants of £750 and 43 grants of £500 each. Recipients included Action on Addiction, British Liver Trust, Children Nationwide, Coronary Prevention Group, Elimination of Leukaemia Fund, International Spinal Research Trust, Listening Books, Myasthenia Gravis Association, National Association for the Relief of Paget's Disease, Prostate Research Campaign UK, Rethink, Royal Hospital for Neuro-Disability, Sick Children's Trust, Sign and Walsingham Community Homes.

South East and London – 41 grants totalling £25,000

These included 7 grants of £1,000 each to hospices and 16 grants of £500 each to hospitals. Other grants were £750 to Berkshire Multiple Sclerosis Therapy Centre, Foley House Residential Home for Deaf People, Molesey and Dittons Housework Scheme and St Joseph's Pastoral Centre and £500 each to 14 organisations including Canterbury Oast Trust, Community Housing and Therapy – London, Disability Challengers – Guildford, Kingston Bereavement Service and Tadworth Children's Trust.

South West and Wales – 15 grants totalling £8,300

These were £1,000 each to three hospices, £750 to North Wiltshire Holiday Club and £500 each to Robert Owen Communities – Totnes, Wiltshire Air Ambulance and nine hospitals.

Midlands and North – 26 grants totalling £17,000

These included £1,000 each to 7 hospices and £500 each to 10 hospitals. Other grants were £750 each to Disability Care Enterprise, Nightingale Nursing Fund and Noah's Ark Trust and £500 each to Break – Norfolk, MS Therapy Centre – Bedfordshire and Northamptonshire, New Thresholds – Suffolk, Royal School for the Blind – Liverpool, Royal School for the Deaf – Manchester and Sue Ryder Care – Manorlands in Keighley.

Scotland – 23 grants totalling £22,000

These were £750 to Borders Talking Newspaper and £500 each to Edinburgh Young Carers Project, Enable, Glasgow City Council Cleansing Charity, Lothian Regional Transport Handicapped Children's Fund, Scottish Motor Neurone Disease Association and Scottish Society for Autism, 5 grants to hospices of £1,000 each and 11 grants to hospitals totalling £6,100.

Ireland – 40 grants totalling £30,000

These were £750 each to 10 hospitals, 7 hospices and 23 charities, including Amputee Ireland, Cheshire Foundation, Children's Leukaemia Research Project, Coeliac Society of Ireland, Eating Disorders Association – Ireland, Enable, Hospitaller Order of St John of God – Stillorgan, Irish Haemophilia Society, Irish Raynaud's and Scleroderma Society, Irish Sudden Infant Death Association, MS Ireland and RehabCare.

Overseas – 4 grants totalling £2,300

These were £750 to Merlin Health Care in Crises and £500 each to Komso Children's Hospital – Russia, Relief Fund for Romania and Royal Commonwealth Society for the Blind.

Exclusions Unless there are exceptional circumstances, organisations are not supported in successive years.

Applications Hospitals, hospices and medically-related charities are invited to write detailed letters or to send a brochure with an accompanying letter. There is a form for individuals to complete available from the personal assistant to the trust administrator.

Houblon-Norman Fund

Finance

£125,000 (2002/03)

Beneficial area UK.

MA Business Support Unit HO-2, Bank of England, Threadneedle Street, London EC2R 8AH

Tel. 020 7601 5213 **Fax** 020 7601 4423

Email laura.edmunds@bankofengland.co.uk

Website www.bankofengland.co.uk/houblonnorman/

Correspondent Ms Laura Edmunds, Secretary

Trustees *Sir Andrew McLoed Brooks Large, Chair; Sir Jeremy Morse; Kathleen Anne O'Donovan*

CC Number 213168

Information available Information was provided by the trust.

General The trust supports research into the interaction and function of financial and business institutions, the economic conditions affecting them, and the dissemination of knowledge thereof. Fellowships are tenable at the Bank of England. The research work to be undertaken is intended to be full-time work, and teaching or other paid work must not be undertaken during the tenure of the fellowship, without the specific consent of the trustees. In considering applications the trustees will pay particular regard to the relevance of the research to current problems in economics and finance.

In 2002/03 the trust had assets of £1.4 million, an income of £83,000 and made grants totalling £125,000 in the form of the granting of four fellowships.

Applications On an application form available from the website.

The Clifford Howarth Charity Settlement

General

£51,000 (2003/04)

Beneficial area UK, with a preference for Lancashire (Burnley/Rossendale).

14A Hall Garth, Kelbeck, Barrow in Furness, Cumbria LA13 0QT

Tel. 01229 812 844

Correspondent James Howarth, Trustee

Trustees *James Clifford Howarth; Miss Elizabeth Howarth; Mary Fenton.*

CC Number 264890

Information available Information was provided by the trust.

General The trust has general charitable purposes assisting local and UK charities supported by the founder. This is generally for work within Burnley and Rossendale.

In 2003/04 the trust had an income of £42,000 and a total expenditure of £60,000. Grants totalled £51,000 distributed to ten charities, with funds being committed up until the end of year period of 5 April 2005.

Grant beneficiaries included Barrow (rampside) Hall (£15,000), BRGS Community Sports Hall Fund (£10,000), Religious Society of Friends, Rossendale Hospice and Salford Church (£5,000 each), Sion Church (£3,000), St Nicholas Church, Duddon Inshore Rescue, Treloar and Whitworth School Projector (£2,000 each).

Exclusions Only registered charities will be supported. No grants to individuals, for scholarships or for non-local special projects.

Applications In writing to the correspondent. Grants are distributed in February/March.

The Hudson Foundation

Older people, general

£119,000 (2001/02)

Beneficial area UK, with a preference for the Wisbech area.

12–13 The Crescent, Wisbech, Cambridge PE13 1EP

Correspondent A D Salmon, Trustee

Trustees *P A Turner, Chair; M A Bunting; H A Godfrey; A D Salmon.*

CC Number 280332

Information available Full accounts were on file at the Charity Commission.

General The trust makes grants for general charitable purposes, although in practice groups caring for people who are elderly or infirm are more favoured. Grants are given mostly to organisations in the Wisbech area.

In 2001/02 the trust had assets of £2 million and an income of £631,000. Grants were made to 17 organisations and totalled £119,000.

The largest grants were £23,000 to Wisbech Grammar School, £19,000 to Wishbone Trust, £11,000 to Methodist Homes for the Aged and £10,000 to Wisbech St. Mary PCC. Beneficiaries receiving under £10,000 included Wisbech Angles Theatre Trust (£7,600), Wisbech Swimming Club (£5,700), Royal Naval Benevolent Trust and Tapping House Hospice (£5,000 each), Fens Pageant Youth Trust and Ely Diocesan School Fund (£2,000 each), Wisbech St Augustines PCC (£1,000) and Wisbech St Mary Luncheon Club (£750).

Applications In writing to the correspondent. Applications are considered throughout the year.

The Huggard Charitable Trust

General

£34,000 (2002/03)

Beneficial area UK, with a preference for South Wales.

Blacklands Farm, Five Mile Lane, Bonvilston, Cardiff CF5 6TQ

Correspondent S J Thomas, Trustee

Trustees *Mrs E M Huggard; T R W Davies; S J Thomas.*

CC Number 327501

Information available Accounts were on file at the Charity Commission.

General In 2002/03 the trust had assets of £1.7 million and an income of £49,000. Grants to organisations totalled £34,000 (£97,000 in 2000/01).

The main beneficiary during the year were donations under £2,000 which totalled £15,900. Other beneficiaries were Amelia Methodist Trust, Vale of Glamorgan and Whitton Rosser Trust, Vale of Glamorgan, which both received £9,000 each. A smaller grant was made to Nazareth House, Cardiff at £600.

The trust has previously stated that it has supported a wide variety of organisations, including some major projects in South Wales which have received substantial funding. These have included the Amelia Trust Farm in the Vale of Glamorgan, Penrhys Community Partnership in the Rhondda Valley and Cardiff Action for the Single Homeless. For the future the trustees wish to concentrate on a specific list of organisations (about 80) whom they will support, and therefore do not seek applications from others.

Applications The trustees are not inviting applications for funds.

The Geoffrey C Hughes Charitable Trust

Nature conservation, environment, performing arts

About £60,000 (2001/02)

Beneficial area UK.

Beachcroft Wansbroughs, 100 Fetter Lane, London EC4A 1BN

Tel. 020 7242 1011

Correspondent P C M Solon, Trustee

Trustees *J R Young; P C M Solon; R Hillman.*

CC Number 1010079

Information available Basic accounts are on file at the Charity Commission.

General This trust is essentially interested in two areas: nature conservation/environment and performing arts, particularly ballet or opera with a bias towards modern work.

The latest information on the Charity Commission database stated that the income of the trust in 2001/02 was just over £34,000, with expenditure totalling £68,000.

Exclusions No grants to individuals.

Applications In writing to the correspondent.

The Humanitarian Trust

Education, health, social welfare, Jewish

£68,000 to organisations (2002/03)

Beneficial area Worldwide, mainly Israel.

27 St James' Place, London SW1A 1NR

Correspondent Mrs M Myers, Secretary

Trustees *M Jacques Gunsbourg; P Halban; A Lerman.*

CC Number 208575

Information available Accounts were on file at the Charity Commission, but without a list of grants.

General The trust was founded in 1946. In the early years donations were made overwhelmingly to educational causes in Israel. Nowadays the trust is giving to a wider range of causes, still mainly Jewish, but some smaller grants are given to non-Jewish organisations.

In 2002/03 it had assets of £2.8 million and an income of £79,000. Grants to organisations totalled £68,000, with a further £1,800 given to individuals. Further information for this year was not available.

In 2000/01 the trust had assets of £584,000 and an income of £76,000. Grants were made totalling £62,000. The largest were £10,000 to Friends of the Hebrew University of Jerusalem, around £5,000 to Jerusalem Foundation, £3,000 to Michaelson Institute for the Prevention of Blindness – Hadassah, £2,000 to Ben Gurion University and £1,500 to Shaare Zedek Medical Centre.

Exclusions Awards are not given for travel, overseas courses, fieldwork or the arts (such as theatre, dance, music, fashion, journalism and so on), but for academic purposes only. They are intended only as one-off grants to individuals up to a maximum of £200 as a final top-up for fees, not as domestic funding.

Applications In writing to the correspondent for consideration at trustees' meetings in March and November.

The Michael and Shirley Hunt Charitable Trust

Prisoners' families, animal welfare

£66,000 (2002/03)

Beneficial area UK and overseas.

Ansty House, Henfield Road, Small Dole, West Sussex BN5 9XH

Tel. 01903 817116 **Fax** 01903 879995

Correspondent Mrs D S Jenkins, Trustee

Trustees *W J Baker; C J Hunt; S E Hunt; D S Jenkins; K D Mayberry.*

CC Number 1063418

Information available Information was provided by the trust.

General The trust makes grants for the benefit of prisoners' families, and also animals which are unwanted, sick or ill-treated. Grants ranged between £20 and £6,000, averaging £600 each.

In 2002/03 it had assets of £3.6 million and an income of £213,000. Grants were made totalling £66,000.

Beneficiaries included Christine Noble Children's Foundation for Mongolian Children's Prison (£6,000), NEPACS and Prisoners Abroad (£5,000 each), Federation of Prisoners' Families Supports Groups (£2,500) and Corrymeela Community – Belfast (£2,000). Other beneficiaries included animal welfare organisations and prisoners' families.

Exclusions No grants for fines, bail, legal costs, rent deposits and so on.

Applications In writing to the correspondent.

The Huxham Charitable Trust

Christianity, churches and organisations, development work in Albania and Kosova

£45,000 to individuals and organisations (2001/02)

Beneficial area UK and Eastern Europe, especially Albania and Kosova.

Thatcher Brake, 37 Whidborne Avenue, Torquay TQ1 2PG

Tel. 01803 380399

Correspondent Adrian W Huxham

Trustee *Revd Deryck Markham.*

CC Number 1000179

Information available Accounts were on file at the Charity Commission.

General In 2001/02 the trust had an income of £36,000. £45,000 was given in grants.

The trust divided its grants as follows:

- £2,900 to individuals for Christian and development work
- £1,300 to UK charities
- £14,000 towards UK education
- £950 towards UK older people and poor people
- £1,400 to humanitarian and medical-aid mission to Eastern Europe
- £2,200 towards costs incurred by a young refugee fleeing Albania
- £9,200 to an Albanian church
- £150 to support of UK charity-Project 58
- £1,700 to support for TELL TORBAY-a christian mission outreach in Torbay, UK

Applications The trust stated it is has been unable to support any new organisations in recent years.

The P Y N & B Hyams Trust

Jewish, general

£49,000 (2002/03)

Beneficial area Worldwide.

610 Clive Court, Maida Vale, London W9 1SG

Tel. 020 7266 5747

Correspondent N J Hyams, Trustee

Trustees *N Hyams; Mrs M Hyams; D Levy; L Shebson.*

CC Number 268129

Information available Accounts were on file at the Charity Commission, but without a narrative report or a list of grants.

General In 2002/03 the trust had assets of £1 million and an income of £84,000. Grants to organisations totalled £49,000.

The accounts for 2002/03 provided no grants list.

In previous years, grants have been mostly given to Jewish organisations, although other causes are also funded.

Applications In writing to the correspondent, but please note, the trust states that funds are fully committed and unsolicited applications are not welcomed.

The Hyde Charitable Trust

Disadvantaged children and young people

£59,000 (2003/04)

Beneficial area The areas in which Hyde Housing operates (currently South East England, especially London, Kent, Hampshire and Sussex).

Youth Plus London Regional Office, Hollingsworth House, 181 Lewisham High Street, London SE13 6AA

Tel. 020 8297 7575/
020 8927 7552 **Fax** 020 8297 7565

Email info@youthplus.co.uk

Website www.youthplus.co.uk

Correspondent Kate Morris or Mallia Young

Trustees *D Small, Chair; B Bishop; P Breathwick; R Finlinson; J Fitzmaurice; R Collins.*

CC Number 289888

Information available Information was provided by the trust.

General Applications will be considered from projects that are specifically benefiting young people, including some young tenants of Hyde Housing property who are aged 26 or under and live in disadvantaged areas.

The trust's School Roots programme offers grants of up to £1,000 each to schools around the areas in which Hyde Housing operates. Residents in Hyde property liaise with schoold in their area and 'sponsor' project ideas. Funding can be given towards setting up environmental projects, improvements to play facilities or for pre- or after-school activities. Grants of up to £500 each can also be made to young residents for education or development training and equipment.

In 2003/04 grants to six organisations totalled £59,000. Beneficiaries were Sports Inquiry for research into the barriers preventing young people in London from accessing sport and cultural activities (£25,000), Northam 521 Group – Southampton for a multi-purpose games areas on an estate to faciliate youth development work (£13,000), Dorset Road Community Centre – Stockwell/Oval, South London for part-time youth workers to run a youth club for 9 to 19 year olds (£8,300), Inside Out Training and Consultancy – Stonebridge for part-time workers to provide training and support for young people aged 9 to 15 (£6,000), Somerville Adventure Playground – Kender for improvements to the playground and a roof (£5,300) and Newtown Football Club towards kits and equipment for young people to play football after school and in the school holidays (£1,000).

Exclusions No grants to individuals, medical research, hospices, residential homes for older people, and any other projects the trustees decide fall outside the main criteria.

Applications In writing to the correspondent, or by completing an Expression of Interest available on the website. Full application forms are then sent to all suitable candidates. However, for the School Roots project a separate form is used which is available from the trust.

The Idlewild Trust

Performing arts, culture, restoration & conservation, occasional arts education

£117,000 (2003)

Beneficial area UK.

1a Taylors Yard, 67 Alderbrook Street, London SW12 8AD

Tel. 020 8772 3155

Email idlewildtrust@lineone.net

Correspondent Mrs Angela Freestone, Administrator

Trustees *Lady Judith Goodison, Chair; Mrs A S Bucks; J C Gale; Mrs A C Grellier; J A Ford; M Wilson.*

CC Number 268124

Information available Full accounts and annual report were provided by the trust.

General The trust was founded in 1974 by Peter Brissault Minet. Its policy is to support charities concerned with the encouragement of performing and fine arts and preservation for the benefit of the public of lands, buildings and other objects of beauty or historic interest. Occasionally support is given to bodies for educational bursaries in these fields or for conservation of the natural environment. The trust prefers to support UK-charities and it is unlikely to support a project of local interest only.

In 2003 the trust had assets of £3.5 million, an income of £138,000 and made grants totalling £117,000.

Grants were categorised in the trust's annual report as follows:

Category	*No.*	*Total*
Education in the arts	9	£21,000
Performing arts	12	£21,000
Museum and galleries	10	£25,000
Preservation and restoration	17	£38,000
Fine art	2	£3,500
Nature/conservation	4	£8,500

Grant beneficiaries included Royal School of Needlework (£5,000), St Paul's PCC in Deptford and Green College Oxford (£3,500) and Birmingham Contemporary Music Group, Bowes Museum, Buxton Festival, National Museums Liverpool, Pleasance Theatre Festival Ltd, Society for the Promotion of New Music, The British Library, The Landmark Trust and Victoria and Albert Museum (£3,000 each).

Exclusions Grants to registered charities only. No grants are made to individuals. The trust will not give to:

- repetitive UK-wide appeals by large charities
- appeals where all, or most, of the beneficiaries live outside the UK
- local appeals unless the artistic significance of the project is of more than local importance
- appeals whose sole or main purpose is to make grants from the funds collected
- endowment or deficit funding.

Applications On a form available from the correspondent, which can be sent via post or e-mailed as a Microsoft Word file. Applications should include the following information:

- budget breakdown (one page)
- most recent audited accounts
- a list of other sponsors, including those applied to
- other relevant information.

Potential applicants are welcome to telephone the trust on Tuesdays or Wednesdays between 10am and 4pm to discuss their application and check eligibility. Trustees meet twice a year in March and November.

All eligible applications, which are put forward to the trustees, are acknowledged; other applications will not be acknowledged unless an sae is enclosed. Applications from organisations within 18 months of a previous grant will not be considered.

The Iliffe Family Charitable Trust

Medical, disability, heritage, education

£222,000 (2002/03)

Beneficial area UK and Worldwide.

Barn Close, Yattendon, Berkshire RG18 0UX

Tel. 01635 203 929

Correspondent Miss Julia Peel, Secretary to the Trustees

Trustees *N G E Petter; G A Bremner; Lord Iliffe; Hon. Edward Iliffe.*

CC Number 273437

Information available Full accounts were on file at the Charity Commission.

General The trust gives grants towards groups concerned with medical causes, disability, heritage and education. The bulk of the grants made are to charities already known to the trustees, to which funds are committed from year to year. Other donations are made for a wide range of charitable purposes in which the trust has a special interest.

In 2002/03 the trust had assets of £1.7 million and an income of £160,000 with grants totalling £222,000.

The largest grants were £80,000 to Oxford Diocesan Board of Education (Yettendon School) and £25,000 to Sherborne School Foundation.

Other grants included £13,000 to Covent Garden Cancer Research Trust, £10,000 each to Bradfield Foundation, Jubilee Sailing Trust and University of Cambridge Veterinary School Trust, £8,800 to Berkshire Community Foundation, £5,000 each to Sporting Chance Appeal, Green Island Holiday Trust and John Simonds Trust, £1,500 each to Commonwealth Press Union and Yattendon & Frilsham Christian Stewardship and £1,000 each to Friends of Conservation, The Dolphin Trust, Farm Africa, Summer Fields School and RNLI Crew Training Appeal.

Exclusions No grants to individuals and rarely to non-registered charities.

Applications In writing to the correspondent. Only successful applications will be acknowleged. Grants are considered at ad hoc meetings of the trustees, held throughout the year.

The Incorporated Church Building Society

'Living churches benefiting Anglicans'

£200,000 (2003)

Beneficial area England, Wales, Isle of Man and the Channel Islands.

The Historic Churches Preservation Trust, 31 Newbury Street, London EC1A 7HU

Tel. 020 7600 6090 **Fax** 020 7796 2442

Email grants@historicchurches.org.uk

Website www.historicchurches.org.uk

Correspondent James Blott, Director

Trustee *The Committee of Clergy and Laymen.*

CC Number 212752

Information available Full accounts were provided by the trust.

General Grants and interest-free loans, repayable over four years, are made to Anglican churches, of any age. In 2003 it gave £200,000 in grants and distributed a further £25,000 in loans.

In 2002 it had assets of £981,000 and an income of £56,000. Grants were made to 40 churches and totalled £157,000. These ranged from £1,000 to £10,000 each and included churches in Berkshire, Cheshire, Cumbria, East Sussex, Herefordshire, Kent, Lincolnshire, Norfolk, North Yorkshire, Somerset, Suffolk and Warwickshire. A further £82,000 was given in 14 loans.

Exclusions Aid is limited to actual church and chapel buildings. Repairs are limited to essential fabric repairs. Enlarging is restricted to the worship area.

Applications In writing to the correspondent.

The India Foundation (UK)

Developmental and healthcare education projects for Indian communities

£73,000 (1999/2000)

Beneficial area UK and India.

26 Lightwoods Hill, Warley, West Midlands B67 5EA

Tel. 07802288182

Email drkiranpatel@hotmail.com

Correspondent Dr Kiran C R Patel, Chair

Trustees *Dr Kiran C R Patel, Chair; Dr Pankaj Sharma; Mahesh Kothari; Chandrakant D Patel.*

CC Number 1073178

Information available The information for this entry was provided by the trust.

General The trust supports developmental and healthcare education projects for Indian communities in the UK and India. It said that a major focus in 1999/2000 would be health promotion and education in ethnic communities in the UK.

In 2000/01 the foundation had an income of £77,500 with an expenditure of £86,000. No further information was available.

Grants totalled £73,000 in 1999/2000. Beneficiaries included West Bromwich Community Hall Project, which received £60,000 towards rebuilding following an arson attack, and Manav Kalyan Trust which received a donation of £4,000 for a school in India for children who are deaf.

Exclusions No grants to individuals.

Applications In writing to the correspondent.

The Indigo Trust

Offenders, core skills, homelessness, women

£160,000 (2003/04)

Beneficial area UK and overseas.

Allington House, 1st Floor, 150 Victoria Street, London SW1E 5AE

Tel. 020 7410 0330 **Fax** 020 7410 0332

Email info@sfct.org.uk

Correspondent Michael Pattison, Director

Trustees *Miss F E Sainsbury; C T S Stone; Miss J S Portrait.*

CC Number 1075920

Information available Full accounts were provided by the trust.

General This is one of the 18 Sainsbury Family Charitable Trusts, which collectively give over £54 million a year.

'During the year, the trustees have continued to support projects in the following areas of interest:

- improvement of education, learning and mental health care in young offenders institutions and prisons
- supporting the development of core skills, especially literacy, in children, women and disadvantaged groups
- homelessness, particularly among young people and ex-armed services personnel
- women's issues, particularly raising awareness of domestic violence.

'Grants are likely to be made to a small number of pilot projects which have the potential to develop into larger programmes. The trustees are also likely to consider support for projects that assist in raising awareness and the development of high quality educational materials. The trustees prefer to support innovative schemes that can be successfully replicated or become self-sustaining.

'Proposals are generally invited by the trustees or initiated at their request. Unsolicited applications are not encouraged and are unlikely to be successful. Grants are not normally made to individuals.'

In 2003/04 it had assets of £2.4 million and an income of £2.6 million, almost all of which came from donations received. Management and administration charges included payments totalling £3,663 to a firm of solicitors in which one of the trustees is a partner. Whilst wholly legal, these editors always regret such payments unless, in the words of the Charity Commission, 'there is no realistic alternative'. Grants were approved to four organisations totalling £180,000. These were categorised under four separate headings, which did not include the homelessness category from the previous year.

Clean Break Theatre Company received £35,000 in the Young Offenders category. This was for the 'Women and Anger' anger-management programme for women who are prisoners, ex-offenders or detained under the Mental Health Act.

Women's Education in Building was given £42,000 in the Women's Issues categories, for teaching costs for a pilot English course for Somali women.

Refugees into Jobs received £93,000 in the Literacy and Basic Skills category. This was for an access to work scheme for refugee teachers in West London.

Under the General category, Ashden Awards for Sustainable Energy received £10,000 towards its 2004 awards.

Applications The 18 Sainsbury Family Charitable Trusts are jointly administered and follow the same application precedure. An application to one trust is considered as an application to them all. However, 'applications' are probably not the best way forward to gaining funding from these trusts. More sensible might be to write briefly and say what is being done or planned, on the assumption that, if one or more of the trusts is indeed interested in that area of work, they will want to know about what you are doing. A telephone call to do the same is fine. Staff are polite, but wary of people seeking to talk about money rather than issues.

More generally, the trusts are involved in a number of networks, with which they maintain long-term contact. Charities doing work relevant to the interests of these trusts may find that if they are not a part of these networks (which may not be inclusive and most of which are probably London-based) they may get limited Sainsbury attention.

The most inappropriate approach would often be from a fundraiser. Staff, and in many cases trustees, are knowledgeable and experienced in their fields, and expect to talk to others in the same position.

The Ingram Trust

General

£474,000 (2002/03)

Beneficial area UK and overseas, especially Surrey.

c/o 8th Floor, 101 Wigmore Street, London W1U 1QU

Correspondent Joan Major, Administrator

Trustees *C J Ingram; Mrs J E Ingram; Ms C M Maurice.*

CC Number 1040194

Information available Accounts were provided by the trust.

General The trust's policies are as follows:

- it selects a limited number of charities which it commits itself to support for three to five years
- it prefers to support specific projects which can include identifiable costs for special services provided by the charity or equipment that is required
- beneficiaries will generally be major UK–wide or international charities together with some local ones in the county of Surrey
- the majority of grants will be made for periods of three – four years at a time in order to better assess grant applications and monitor progess
- the only overseas aid charities which are considered are those dedicated to encouraging self-help and providing more permanent solutions to problems

- no animal charities are considered except those concerned with wildlife conservation.

In 2002/03 the trust had assets of £10 million and an income of £417,000. It received an income of £6.5 million in the previous year from donations and recoverable income tax. Grants were made totalling £474,000, including some carried over from the previous year.

In 2001/02 the trust's assets totalled £12 million and it had an income of £6.7 million. A total of £289,000 was given in grants to 23 organisation, generally ranging between £500 and £7,000. By far the largest grant of £108,000 was donated to WWF (UK) for their climate control and arctic programmes; the project was also committed £8,000 for the following two years.

The following examples were provided by the trust to illustrated the causes in line with the charity's objectives that were supported in the year:

National

- NSPCC were awarded the third of four payments of £7,000 to the West Sussex Children's Services Team. This team works with children and their families including group work for children and mothers who have experienced domestic violence.
- RNIB received £6,000 as the second of four annual payments to promote the better education, training, employment and well being of people who are blind and to promote their interests.

Local

- CHASE received £5,000 as the second of three annual payments towards the building of a children's hospice at Loseley Park – Guildford and the subsequent wide ranging care services for children with limited life expectancy.
- Prostate Project was given a grant of £4,000 as the second of three annual payments towards an appeal by the Royal Surrey Hospital and St Lukes Cancer Centre – Guildford to aid prostate cancer awareness, detection and treatment.

Overseas

- ActionAid received £5,000 as the third of four annual payments to assist its programme in the Dominican Republic working with employees of the sugar plantations, one of the poorest sections of the population.
- LEPRA received a final grant of £5,000 to support the charities Koralep Project in India, which will extend beyond leprosy to the related diseases of Aids/HIV, with an emphasis on education and rehabilitation.

The trust committed £95,000 to 19 organisations to be made in subsequent years.

Exclusions No grants to non-registered charities or to individuals. No charities specialising in overseas aid are considered except those dedicated to encouraging self help or providing more permanent solutions. No animal charities except those concerned with wildlife conservation.

Applications In writing to the correspondent, although the trust states that it receives far more worthy applications than it is able to support.

The Inland Waterways Association

Inland waterways

£202,000 (2002)

Beneficial area UK and Ireland.

c/o IWA Head Office, PO Box 114, Rickmansworth WD3 1ZY

Tel. 01923 711114 **Fax** 01923 897000

Email iwa@waterways.org.uk

Website www.waterways.org.uk

Correspondent The Chairman of the IWA Restoration Committee

Trustee *The Council of the Association.*

CC Number 212342

Information available Accounts were on file at the Charity Commission.

General The trust supports organisations promoting the restoration of inland waterways (i.e. canal and river navigations).

It makes grants for:

(a) construction, especially works relating to the restoration of navigation such as locks, bridges, aquaducts, culverts, weirs, pumps, excavation, dredging, lining and so on

(b) administration – support for a particular purpose, such as a project officer, a funding appeal or for promotional literature or events

(c) professional services, such as funding of feasibility studies or detailed work on engineering, economic or environmental issues

(d) land purchase

(e) research on matters affecting waterway restoration, including original research, reviews of research undertaken by others and literature reviews

(f) education, such as providing information to local authorities or agencies to promote the nature and benefits of waterway restoration.

In 2002 the trust had assets of £1.3 million, an income of just over £1 million and made grants totalling £202,000.

Grant beneficiaries included Droitwich Canals Trust (£83,000), Lichfield and Hatherton Canals Restoration Trust and Wendover Arm Trust (£20,000 each), Wey and Arun Canal Trust (£15,000), Surrey and Hants Canal Society (£12,000), Waterway Recovery Group (£6,500), British Waterways (£5,000), South Lakeland District Council (£3,500), London Canal Museum (£2,000) and Anderton Boat Lift Appeal (£1,000).

Exclusions No grants to individuals. No retrospective grants for projects where expenditure has already been incurred or committed.

Applications In writing to the correspondent. Applications should comply with the 'Guidelines for Applicants', also available from the correspondent. Each applicant should provide a full description of its proposal, show that the organisation can maintain a satisfactory financial position and demonstrate that it is capable of undertaking the proposed project.

Applications for up to £2,000 are assessed under a simplified procedure – each application should demonstrate that the grant would be used to initiate or sustain a restoration scheme or significantly benefit a specific small project.

Applications for over £2,000 should demonstrate that the grant would be applied to one of the types of projects (a–f). Applicants should also demonstrate the extent to which the project satisfies one or more of the following conditions:

- the grant would unlock (lever) a grant several times larger from another body
- the grant would not replace grants available from other sources
- the project does not qualify for grants from major funding sources
- the grant would enable a key project to be undertaken which would have a significant effect on the prospect of advancing the restoration and gaining

funds from other sources for further restoration projects
- the result of the project would have a major influence over the progress of a number of other restoration projects
- The Inland Waterways Association Restoration Committee would have a major influence in the management of the project, including monitoring of expenditure.

The Inlight Trust

Religion

£110,000 (2002/03)

Beneficial area UK.

P O Box 2, Liss, Hampshire GU33 6YP

Correspondent Mrs Judy Hayward

Trustees *Sir Thomas Lucas; Wendy Collett; Michael Collishaw; Michael Meakin; Stuart Neil; Richard Wolfe.*

CC Number 236782

Information available Full accounts were provided by the trust.

General The trust makes grants for the advancement of religion only. It states that its funding priorities are: 'To make donations on an undenominational basis to charities providing valuable contributions to spiritual development and charities concerned with spiritual healing and spiritual growth through religious retreats.'

Grants are usually one-off for a specific project or part of a project. Bursary schemes may also be supported. Core funding and/or salaries are rarely considered.

In 2002/03 it had assets of £3.2 million, which generated an income of £107,000 (after rental expenses). Grants were made to 12 organisations totalling £110,000.

The main beneficiaries were White Eagle Lodge – Liss (£32,000 in two grants), Holy Island Project – Dumfriesshire (£26,000 in two grants) and Hamblin Religious Centre – Bosham (£10,000).

Other grants were £6,000 to Dhanakosa Retreat Centre – Balquhidder, £5,000 each to Acorn Christian Foundation – Bordon, Dharma Cloud Trust – Newport, Holy Island Women's Retreat Fund – Dumfriesshire, Impersonal Enlightenment Fellowship – London, Samantabhadra Centre – Birmingham and Tharpapland Kadampa Retreat Centre – Dumfriesshire and £3,000 each to Time & Space – Birkenhead and Gyaltsabje Buddhist Centre – Sheffield.

Exclusions Grants are made to registered charities only. Applications from individuals, including students, are ineligible. No grants are made in response to general appeals from large national organisations. Grants are seldom available for church buildings.

Applications In writing to the correspondent including details of the need the intended project is designed to meet plus an outline budget and the most recent available annual accounts of the charity. Only applications from eligible bodies are acknowledged. Applications must be accompanied by a copy of your trust deed or of your entry in the Charity Commission register. They are considered four times a year. Only successful applicants are informed.

The Inman Charity

Social welfare, disability, older people, hospices

£252,000 (2000)

Beneficial area UK.

Payne Hicks Beech, 10 New Square, Lincoln's Inn, London WC2A 3QG

Correspondent The Trustees

Trustees *A L Walker; Miss B M A Strother; M R Matthews; Prof. J D Langdon.*

CC Number 261366

Information available Full accounts were on file at the Charity Commission.

General The trust states: 'The trust maintains a list of charitable organisations which it regularly supports and the list is reviewed half-yearly at the meeting of the directors. Surplus income funds are distributed to other charitable organisations during the year.' The trust aims to disburse £250,000 a year, including an annual bursary to Uppingham School (£14,000). This grant stands outside its main areas for support – disability, medical, research, older people and hospices.

In 2003 the charity had a gross income of £199,000 with a total expenditure of £229,000. Unfortunately no other financial information was available.

In 2000 it had assets of £5.3 million generating an income of £228,000. Grants to 63 organisations totalled £252,000. After the grant of £14,000 to Uppingham School – Victor Inman Bursary Fund, remaining grants were in the range of £1,000 to £7,500. Beneficiaries of larger grants Deafblind UK (£11,000) and Counsel and Care for the Elderly, Gurkha Welfare Trust, National Benevolent Fund for the Aged, Queen Elizabeth's Foundation for the Disabled, Samaritans and Winged Fellowship (£7,500 each).

Most other grants were for £3,000 or less. Beneficiaries included Cancer Resource Centre, Guideposts Trust, New Bridge, Reach, Reading YMCA, Iain Rennie Hospice at Home, Women's Link, Shaftesbury Society, Thrift Urban Housing and REMAP.

Exclusions No grants to individuals.

Applications In writing only to the correspondent, including up-to-date reports and accounts. Trustees meet half-yearly, usually in March and September.

The Worshipful Company of Innholders General Charity Fund

General

£81,000 (2002/03)

Beneficial area UK.

Innholders' Hall, 30 College Street, London EC4R 2RH

Tel. 020 7236 6703 **Fax** 020 7236 0059

Email mail@innholders.co.uk

Correspondent The Clerk

Trustee *The Worshipful Company of Innholders.*

CC Number 270948

Information available Full accounts were provided by the trust.

General This trust supports children and young people, older people and education and training, particularly regarding the hotel industry.

In 2002/03 it had assets of £328,000 and an income of £36,000, which included £20,000 in donations received. Grants were made totalling £81,000.

Most of the funds were given in two substantial grants; £35,000 to City of London Schools for scholarships and £34,000 to Master Innholders' Charitable Trust for scholarships. Other beneficiaries included 31st Signals Regiment (£5,300), Master Innholders' Charitable Trust (£3,500), City University (£2,000) and Lord Mayor's Appeal (£1,500).

Exclusions No grants to individuals.

Applications In writing to the correspondent, including the reason for applying and current financial statements and so on.

International Bar Association Educational Trust

Legal profession

£66,000 (2002)

Beneficial area UK and developing countries.

271 Regent Street, London W1R 7PA

Email educationaltrust@int-bar.org

Website www.ibanet.org

Correspondent Elaine Owen, Executive Assistant

Trustees *Francis Neate; Andrew Primrose; Richard Turnor; Dianna Kempe; Fernando Pombo; Julie Onslow-Cole; Linda Packard.*

CC Number 287324

Information available Accounts were provided by the trust.

General The trust's objects are to advance legal education, to promote the study of law, and to promote research into common legal problems and disseminate useful results, with an emphasis on grants to developing countries.

In 2002 the trust had assets of £169,000 and an income of £91,000. A total of 15 grants were made amounting to £66,000. Donations included £10,000 each to IBA Distance Based Learning Programme, Legalbrief Africa (an electronic publication) and University of Cape Town Trust, £4,800 to Book Aid International and £4,200 to CLEAR Kenya.

In the 2002 annual report and accounts the trust stated that it is continuing to concentrate its focus on assisting legal education and development, usually in the developing world. Example of types of projects the trust wishes to support include:

- 'Provision of legal textbooks for courts and Bar libraries in the developing world.
- 'Financial assistance to the International Bar Association's Distance Based Learning Programme.
- 'Scholarships for the International Bar Association's Distance Based Learning Programme.
- 'The development of *Africa Legalbrief* a hugely successful newsletter circulated across the African continent (and beyond) via email.'

Exclusions No grants to individuals.

Applications In writing to the correspondent. The trustees meet three times a year, usually at the time of the Council and Management Committee meetings, to consider applications.

The International Foundation for Arts and Culture

Music

£197,000 (2001)

Beneficial area UK.

36 High Street, Cobham, Surrey KT11 3EB

Tel. 01932 589 060

Correspondent M Randerson, Trustee

Trustees *H Handa, Chair; M Randerson; N Osaki; J Szepietowski; Dr J L Breen.*

CC Number 1064735

Information available Accounts were on file at the Charity Commission.

General Established in October 1997, the objects of the foundation are to advance the education of the public in music.

In 2001 the foundation had assets of £189,000 with an income of £366,000 and grants totalling £197,000.

The largest grants were £85,000 to SOAS/SISJAC, £67,500 to RNIB, Funding of Music Scholarships totalled £19,500, £15,500 to Theatre of Royal Holloway College and £6,300 to St John Smith Square Concert Costs.

The foundation stated that in recent years major support had been given to Soundscape.

Applications This trust does not accept unsolicited applications.

The Inverclyde Bequest Fund

Sailors' charities

£59,000 (2003)

Beneficial area UK and USA, with a preference for Glasgow and the west of Scotland.

Merchants' House of Glasgow, 7 West George Street, Glasgow G2 1BA

Tel. 0141 221 8272

Correspondent Jimmy Dykes, Assistant Collector

Trustee *The Directors of the Merchants' House of Glasgow.*

Information available Information was supplied by the trust.

General The trust supports seamen's missions. Forty per cent of the fund's income is distributed in Glasgow and the West of Scotland. Due to the decline in the shipping industry there are fewer missions and the trust states that most grants are recurrent. It prefers to support long-established missions. In 2003 it gave grants totalling £59,000. Grants range from £500 to £15,000.

Exclusions The fund does not give grants to individuals.

Applications In writing to the correspondent, including your annual report and audited accounts.

The Inverforth Charitable Trust

General

£56,000 (2003)

Beneficial area UK (as a whole).

The Farm, Northington, Alresford, Hampshire SO24 9TH

Correspondent E A M Lee, Secretary and Treasurer

Trustees *Elizabeth Lady Inverforth; Lord Inverforth; Hon. Mrs Jonathan Kane; Michael Gee.*

CC Number 274132

Information available Full accounts were provided by the trust.

General The trust supports national charities only, especially 'small nationals'. A wide variety of causes are supported, including music, the arts, religion, heritage, health, youth, older people, education and disability. It has a core list of 25 organisations that receive grants each year. The trust usually supports around 100 other applicants annually. Since a recent change of policy, the trust now only makes grants of £500 which can be spent generally, including covering core costs, rather than for projects or specific items, with the number of beneficiaries being reduced.

In 2002/03 it had assets of £3.1 million, which generated an income of £94,000. Grants were made to 112 organisations totalling £56,000, broken down as shown in the table below.

Beneficiaries, all of which received £500 each, included AFASIC, Arkwright Scholarships Trust, Bampton Classical Opera, Book Aid International, British Deaf Association, British Lung Foundation, Brook Advisory Centres, Charity Search, ChildLine, Coventry Cathedral, Dyslexia Institute, Friends of the Elderly, Haemophilia Society, Iris Fund for Prevention of Blindness, Katie's Ski Tracks, Live Music Now!, Mission to Seafarers, Money Advice Trust, National Opera Studio, National Sports Medicine Institute of the United Kingdom, No Panic, Pain Relief Foundation, Psoriasis Association, Research into Ageing, Richard House Children's Hospice, St Mungo's, Support Society for Children of High Intelligence, Trestle Theatre Company, VSO, WellBeing and Youth Sport Trust.

Exclusions No grants are made to:

- local churches, village halls, schools and so on
- animal charities
- branches, affiliates or subsidiary charities
- individuals
- advertisers or fundraising events
- organisations that have been supported (or had an application rejected) in the last 12 months
- individuals
- small local charities
- charities which are not registered in the UK

NB. Charities with the word 'community' or a relevant place name in their title are unlikely to be considered by the trust as a national charity.

Applications In writing to the correspondent at least one month before meetings. No special forms are necessary, although accounts are desirable. A summary is prepared for the trustees, who meet quarterly in March, June, September and early December. Replies are normally sent to all applicants; allow up to four months for an answer or grant. Over 1,000 applications are received each year, producing a high failure rate for new applicants. The trust has stated that nearly half of all applicants are ineligible for support, so potential applicants should read 'exclusions' above carefully. Telephone calls are discouraged, particularly from ineligible applicants or people enquiring to see if they are eligible.

THE INVERFORTH CHARITABLE TRUST
Grants in 2002/03

Category	*2003*		*2002*	
Music and the arts	£6,500	12%	£8,500	19%
Churches, heritage etc.	£2,500	5%	£1,500	3%
Physical and mental health	£14,000	25%	£11,000	24%
Hospices	£4,000	1%	£3,000	7%
Youth and education	£7,500	13%	£6,000	14%
Handicapped and elderly	£11,000	18%	£6,500	15%
Sundry (including international)	£12,000	21%	£8,000	18%

The Invicta Trust

Jewish educational and general

£51,000 (2000/01)

Beneficial area Worldwide.

817 Finchley Road, London NW11 8AJ

Tel. 02084554732

Correspondent Mrs F H Hirsch, Trustee

Trustees *Mrs F H Hirsch; E H Feingold; Mrs N Silber.*

CC Number 327039

Information available Accounts were on file at the Charity Commission.

General The charity makes grants for orthodox Jewish educational and general purposes. In 2000/01 its assets totalled £528,000 and it received an income of £54,000. Grants totalled £51,000.

There were fourteen grants listed in the annual report. Those listed were Beth Hamedrash Ponevez (£8,000), Craven Walk Charities Trust (£7,000), Torah Learning Centre and Wlodowa Charity & Rehabilitation Trust (£4,000 each), Before Trust and UTA (£3,500 each), Beis Chinuch Lebonos, UTA, Vyoel Moshe Charitable Trust and Yad Eliezer (£3,000 each), and various charities amounts not exceeding £180 (£3,952).

Applications In writing to the correspondent.

The Ireland Fund of Great Britain

Welfare, community, education, peace and reconciliation, the arts

£84,000 (2002)

Beneficial area Ireland and Great Britain.

2nd Floor, Wigglesworth House, 69 Southwark Bridge Road, London SE1 9HH

Tel. 020 7378 8373 **Fax** 020 7378 8376

Email greatbritain@irlfunds.org

Website www.irlfunds.org/great_britain

Correspondent Aileen Ross, Director

Trustees *Josephine Hart; Hon. Kevin Pakenham; Dr Anthony O'Reilly; John Riordan; Gavin O'Reilly; Stanley Watson; Peter Sutherland, Chair; Kingsley Aikihj; Bryan Hays; Susan Wildman.*

CC Number 327889

Information available Full accounts and other information was provided by the fund.

General The trust's grant application leaflet states: 'The Ireland Funds are a confederation of concern, connecting people around the world with Ireland, north and south. Through the generosity of those linked to Ireland in interest, ancestry and compassion, the organisation assists groups in Ireland whose initiatives serve the people of the island directly. The Ireland Funds are non-political and non-sectarian.

'Each year, The Ireland Fund supports hundreds of projects, north and south, which promote peace and reconciliation, arts and culture, community development and education. Grants range from a few hundred pounds to several thousand. For many projects, a seed grant from the funds provides the leverage necessary to qualify for additional monies from government agencies and other organisations.

'Founded in 1976 by Sir Anthony O'Reilly and a number of key American businessmen. The Ireland Funds now operate in 11 countries, i.e. Australia, Canada, France, Germany, Great Britain, Ireland, Japan, Mexico, Monaco, New Zealand and the United States.

'All of the funds' monies are secured from private sources, either by donors making contributions directly to the funds or by attending its many events. In 2001, for instance, the funds held approximately 65 events in 11 countries involving 25,000 people. The funds are growing rapidly as they translate the real affection and concern for Ireland worldwide into practical help and support.'

The following eligibility criteria for each programme is taken from the trust's website:

Arts and culture
'The funds wish to support excellence and innovation in arts activities within communities across the island and especially projects which make the arts more accessible to the wider community. In particular, The Ireland Funds will focus on the following:

- arts applied in settings of socio-economic disadvantage
- arts applied in educational or health settings
- arts promoting tolerance and reconciliation.

Community development
'Ireland is undergoing tremendous economic, social and cultural changes. The Ireland Funds are seeking ways to promote an inclusive and integrated society and to ensure the regeneration of marginalised urban and rural communities. The Funds see the following areas as priorities:

- increasing the capacity of the social economy
- support of rural development initiatives
- promotion of social inclusion
- promotion of tolerance and diversity.

Education
'Investment in education is investment in Ireland's future. Economic and social development depends on a well educated population. For this reason, The Ireland Funds will focus on programmes promoting and supporting:

- access and progression from second level to third level
- lifelong learning
- tolerance through education.

Peace and reconciliation
'The Ireland Funds are seeking to support communities in Northern Ireland working together and towards a shared future. The skills and culture of negotiation and compromise need to be honed politically and organisationally within and between communities. To this end, programmes supporting the following areas have been prioritised for assistance:

- citizenship and participation
- a greater understanding of cultural identity within and between communities
- social inclusion
- support for those affected by the troubles.

What The Ireland Funds are looking for
'When assessing the merits of each application, The Ireland Funds' Advisory Committee shall be looking for the following:

- Is the application form fully completed? Is it clear what the group is proposing?
- Does the proposal address a particular problem? Has it been well researched and planned?
- What impact will the proposal have?
- Is the proposal creative and innovative?
- Is the project sustainable?
- Are the financial figures provided accurate? Is the proposal offering good value for money?
- What benefits does the organisation bring to the community? Is the Community involved in the planning and implementation stages of the proposal?
- Does the organisation have a good track record?'

In 2002 the trust had assets of £384,000 and income of £539,000, including £348,000 from functions and £147,000 in donations received. It made grants totalling £84,000 broken down as follows:

Education - 3 grants totalling £46,000
Beneficiaries were Newman Institute (£25,000), All Hallows College (£19,000) and Belvedere College (£2,000).

Community development - 10 grants totalling £16,000
Beneficiaries included ICAP Immigration Counselling & Psychotherapy (£3,000), St Michael's Irish Centre (£2,500) and St John Bosco Youth Clubs, Birmingham Irish Community Forum, London Irish Centre and London Irish Centre Community Welfare Service (£1,000 each).

Exclusions Grants are generally not given for: general appeals; purchase of buildings or land; major construction or repairs to buildings; other grant-making trusts; individuals; purchase of vehicles; debt repayment; tuition or student expenses; travel or transport costs; commercial trading businesses; replacement of statutory funding; medical research; or general administration.

Applications On a form available from the correspondent. In Ireland, applications are welcome between 1 October and 31 January, with successful applicants notified in early June. In Great Britain, the deadline for receipt of applications is 15 August with grants distributed in December/January.

'Notification of outcome will be by letter. In the meantime we would ask you not to contact the office, due to our small staff number. Lobbying will disqualify.'

There is a stringent application of the guidelines and exclusions criteria. Applicants must submit copies of their constitution and audited accounts before receiving funding. Projects supported must make regular reports of progress and monitoring as well as providing promotional material and publicity.

The Irish Youth Foundation (UK) Ltd

Irish young people

£182,000 (2002/03)

Beneficial area UK.

The Irish Centre, Blacks Road, Hammersmith, London W6 9DT

Tel. 020 8748 9640 **Fax** 020 8748 7386

Email info@iyf.org.uk

Website www.iyf.org.uk

Correspondent Linda Tanner, Administrator

Trustees *J O'Hara; Mary Clancy; F Hucker; P Kelly; D Murray; John O'Neill, Chair; Nessa O'Neill; John Power; Colin McNicholas; Sean O'Neill; John Dwyer.*

CC Number 328265

Information available Full accounts, guidelines and other information was provided by the trust.

General This trust supports organisations anywhere in the UK working with young Irish people aged up to 25 who are socially, educationally or culturally disadvantaged. The foundation gets its annual income from fundraising events it stages, including golf days, lunches and an annual ball.

Funding is available for a wide range of projects, including training, counselling, drug rehabilitation, advice, advocacy, youth work, homelessness, education, cultural and social activities, disability and travellers. The trust will support projects or capacity building, recognising that improving resources and personnel is often the best way for projects to develop.

For applicants in England, Scotland and Wales, there are three categories of grant given. Small grants are of £2,500 or less and medium grants are for larger amounts which are less than £12,000; applications forms A or B should be used respectively. Large grants range from £12,000 to £25,000 and can be recurrent; they should be applied for using form C, which requests detailed information on the organisation, project, breakdown of beneficiaries, monitoring, budget and coordination with other services.

There is a separate programme for organisations based in Northern Ireland to those based on the British mainland funded jointly by the Irish Youth Foundation (UK) and Irish Youth Foundation (Ireland). Grants are one-off of up to £5,000 each and can be used to extend an existing activity, to employ additional staff, to purchase equipment, undertake an evaluation, publish a report, improve organisational capacity or try something new and different.

In 2002/03 the trust had assets of £6,000, an income of £184,000 and made grants totalling £182,000. Grants were awarded to 41 projects 'representing the largest voluntary contribution to Irish youth projects in the UK'.

In 2004 grants totalled £200,000 and were made to Bristol Playbus (£18,000), St Michael's Irish Centre and London Irish Centre (£15,000 each), Bias Brent Irish Advisory Service and Irish Commission for Prisoners Overseas (£12,000 each), Irish Community Care (£10,000), Solas Anois (£9,500), An Teach Irish Housing Association (£8,000) and The Connection at St Martin's andWest Midlands Schools Gaelic Athletic Association (£6,000 each).

Exclusions The foundation generally does not support: projects which cater for people over 25 years of age; individuals; general appeals; work in the arts, museums, or of an environmental nature; grants for academic research; educational bursaries; to substitute state support; alleviation of deficits already incurred; services run by statutory/public authorities; and major capital appeals.

Applications In writing to the correspondent, requesting an application form. The application period is short, with forms being available early September to be returned early October. Applicants should photocopy and send six copies of the completed form if they are in Northern Ireland and seven copies if they are applying from elsewhere. Applications are considered in January and all applicants notified in February. Applications are assessed on the following requirements: need; continuity; track record/evaluation; disadvantaged young people; innovativeness; funding sources; and budgetary control. Faxed or emailed applications are not considered.

The Ironmongers' Quincentenary Charitable Fund

General

£73,000 (2000/01)

Beneficial area UK.

Ironmongers' Hall, Barbican, London EC2Y 8AA

Tel. 020 7776 2311

Website www.ironhall.co.uk

Correspondent Ms H Sant, Charities Administrator

Trustee *Worshipful Ironmongers' Company.*

CC Number 238256

Information available Accounts were on file at the Charity Commission.

General Set up under trust deed in 1964, the fund had an income of £109,000 in 2002/03. No other information was provided for this year, however we do know that in 2000/01 its assets stood at £1.9 million. Its income for that year was £177,000 and grants totalled £73,000. The accounts listed beneficiaries in receipt of awards over £1,000 each, divided as follows:

Crafts – £9,400

The major beneficiary was Surrey Institute of Art and Design, which received funding towards travel bursaries (£2,200), equipment (£2,500) and an artist in residence (£2,500).

Universities and industry – £13,000

Four universities were supported, each receiving £2,700. A grant of £1,800 was also made towards the Foundry Industry Jubilee Award.

National Trust and other restoration – £32,000

The National Trust received a grant of £19,000. Grants for other restoration totalled £14,000 and included those to St John's School – Leatherhead (£5,000), Goose Green Centre (£2,000), Thornhill Primary School (£1,500) and St Christopher's Hospice (£1,300).

Other organisations – £18,000

Beneficiaries included Lord Mayor's Appeal (£5,000), Arkwright Scholarship (£3,800), Guildhall School of Music and Drama (£2,100) and Army Cadets (£1,100).

Applications In writing to the correspondent by 31 March each year, for consideration in May. Applications should include: details of the property, ironwork and the work required (if appropriate); a full breakdown of the costs, including specific elements for which a grant can be made; proposed start and completion date; details of funds already raised and details of applications to other funders for the project; conservation plans/craftsman's drawings; public access arrangements and visitor numbers (where appropriate); and any other information or photographs which might be helpful.

The ISA Charity

General

£42,000 (2001/02)

Beneficial area UK.

ISA (Holdings) Ltd, 29–35 Rathbone Street, London W1P 1NJ

Tel. 020 7636 4301

Correspondent R Paice, Trustee

Trustees *R Paice; Mrs M Paice; Miss A Paice.*

CC Number 326882

Information available Accounts were on file at the Charity Commission, but without a list of grants.

General This charity was created in 1985 and makes grants to a wide range of registered charities. In 2001/02 the charity had assets of £1 million, an income of £44,000 and made grants totalling £42,000. A list of beneficiaries was not available for this or any other recent year.

Applications The trust states that all funds have been allocated for several years ahead. The trust states that unsolicited applications cannot be considered nor responded to.

The Isaacs Charitable Trust

Jewish, medical, general

£37,000 (2001/02)

Beneficial area UK and Israel.

11 Grantham Close, Edgware, Middlesex HA8 8DL

Tel. 020 8958 7854

Correspondent Nathan David Isaacs, Trustee

Trustees *J E Isaacs; N D Isaacs; M C Sefton-Green.*

CC Number 264590

Information available Accounts were on file at the Charity Commission, but without a narrative report.

General The trust gives its largest grants to Jewish causes but also supports other charities, especially medical related. Grants can be one-off and recurrent.

In 2001/02 the trust had assets of £201,000 with an income of £201,000 and grants totalling £37,000.

The largest grants were £6,000 to Jewish Care, £4,000 to Rachel Charitable Trust and £2,500 each to The Child Resettlement Fund and British Friends of Laniado Hospital.

Other grants include £2,000 each to Norwood Ravenswood and British Friends of the New Synagogue of Netanya, £1,500 each to SCOPE, Marie Curie Foundation, Nightingale House, British Heart Foundation and Rosh Pinah Jewish Preparatory School Trust, £1,000 each to Friends of Magen David Adom, London School of Jewish Studies, Imperial Cancer Research Fund and Joint Jewish Charitable Trust.

Grants of less than £1,000 were awarded to British Friends of Israeli War Disabled, Jewish Child's Day, St John's Ambulance, Jewish Marriage Council, British Aid Committee Jewish Institute for the Blind Jerusalem, LBC-CJE, Royal National Lifeboat Institution and Friends of Slough Hospital.

Applications This trust's income is fully committed to its current list of donees. New applications are not considered.

J A R Charitable Trust

Roman Catholic, education, welfare

£50,000 (2002/03)

Beneficial area Worldwide.

c/o Vernor Miles & Noble, 5 Raymond Buildings, Gray's Inn, London WC1R 5DD

Tel. 020 7242 8688

Correspondent Philip R Noble, Trustee

Trustees *Philip R Noble; Revd William Young; Revd Paschal Ryan.*

CC Number 248418

Information available Full accounts were provided by the trust.

General The trust states in its annual report that it makes grants towards: Roman Catholic missionaries, churches and other causes; education for people under 30; and food and clothing for people over 55 who are in need. In practice, the trust gives regular grants to support mainly Roman Catholic organisations.

In 2002/03 the trust had assets of £1.6 million, which generated an income of £58,000. Grants were made to 30 organisations totalling £50,000.

The largest grants were £4,000 to Westminster Cathedral, £2,800 to United Westminster Schools and £2,500 to St Teresa's Youth Pilgrimage Fund. The remaining grants were for either £1,000 or £2,000 and included those to Archdiocese of Liverpool, Basis – Gascoigne, Bourne Trust, Cardinal Hume Centre, Diocese of Middlesbrough, Jesuit Missions, Marriage Care, The Passage, St Barnabas Society, St James's Spanish Place, St Joseph's Hospice – Hackney, Tongabezi Trust School and White Sisters.

Exclusions The trust does not normally support a charity unless it is known to the trustees and it does not support individuals.

Applications In writing to the correspondent. Please note that the trust's funds are fully committed to regular beneficiaries and it states that there is very little, if any, for unsolicited appeals. In order to save administration costs replies are not sent to unsuccessful applicants.

J I Charitable Trust

General

£124,000 (2003)

Beneficial area England and Wales.

20 Tudor Close, Woodford Green, Essex IG8 0LF

Tel. 020 8505 5699

Correspondent P Katz

CC Number 1059865

Information available Accounts were on file at the Charity Commission, without a list of grant beneficiaries.

General In 2003 this trust had an income of £195,000. The assests of the trust totalled £257,000 and the total grants given in this year came to £124,000.

Eight charities received grants in 2003, the largest being £50,000 to Community Security Trust, £32,880 to Lehman Bros. Foundation, £15,000 to Lubavitch, £5,600 to Marc Fumer Trust, £3,880 to CFF Greater NI Chapter, £3,100 to NSPCC, £3,000 to North London Hospice and £2,000 to Children Youth Foundation. A total amount of three grants went to individuals and totalled £4,150.

Applications In writing to the correspondent.

The J R S S T Charitable Trust

Democracy and social justice

£121,000 (2003)

Beneficial area UK.

The Garden House, Water End, York YO30 6WQ

Tel. 01904 625744 **Fax** 01904 651502

Email info@jrrt.org.uk

Website www.jrrt.org.uk

Correspondent Tina Walker

Trustees *Archibald J Kirkwood, Chair; Trevor A Smith (Lord Smith of Clifton); Christine J Day; Christopher J Greenfield; Diana E Scott; David T Shutt (Lord Shutt of Greetland); Paedar Cremin; Mandy Cormack.*

CC Number 247498

Information available Information was provided by the trust.

General The trust was originally endowed by the non-charitable Joseph Rowntree Reform Trust Ltd. It will consider and sometimes instigate charitable projects which relate specifically to the work of The Joseph Rowntree Reform Trust Ltd in supporting the development of an increasingly democratic and socially-just society in Great Britain.

In 2003 the trust had assets of £3.1 million and an income of £205,000. Grants totalled £121,000.

Exclusions No student grants are funded.

Applications The trustees meet quarterly. They do not invite applications.

The Dorothy Jacobs Charity

Jewish care, medical

£60,000 (2002)

Beneficial area UK.

Heywards, 6th Floor, Remo House, 310–312 Regent Street, London W1B 3BS

Tel. 020 7299 8150

Correspondent R H Moss, Trustee

Trustees *R H Moss; A M Alexander.*

CC Number 328430

Information available Accounts were on file at the Charity Commission, but without a grants list or a narrative report.

General The trust was established in 1989 to provide 'relief of sickness by provision of medical aid and undertaking of medical research, advancement of education and relief of the elderly and infirm'.

The trust can only support the 15 nominated charities which are listed in the trust deed – three hospitals, four Jewish charities, three cancer-related charities and five others: Arthritis and Rheumatism Council, BBC Children in Need, British Red Cross, Oxfam and Scope. Other charities cannot be supported.

In 2002 the trust had assets of £455,000, which generated an income of £19,000. Grants totalled £60,000.

Exclusions Any charity that is not listed in the trust deed.

Applications The trust states that it cannot accept unsolicited applications.

The Ruth & Lionel Jacobson Trust (Second Fund) No 2

Jewish, medical, children, disability

£46,000 (2003/04)

Beneficial area UK, with a preference for north east England

High Wray, 35 Montagu Avenue, Newcastle upon Tyne NE3 4JH

Correspondent Mrs I R Jacobson, Trustee

Trustees *Irene Ruth Jacobson; Malcolm Jacobson.*

CC Number 326665

Information available Accounts were on file at the Charity Commission.

General The trust supports UK charities and organisations based in the North East. The trust states that it supports the advancement of Jewish religious education and healthcare charities. The trust states that it receives many more applications than it is able to support. Local charities outside the North East are supported whenever possible.

In 2003/04 the trust had an income of £39,000 and made grants totalling £46,000.

The main grants made were £13,000 to United Jewish Israel Appeal, £4,300 to Multiple Sclerosis Society, £2,000 to National Kidney Research Centre, £1,200 to Defeating Deafness and £1,000 each to Coping with Cancer, Gateshead Jewish Boarding School, Pamela Peterson Charitable Trust and Valerie Freedman Trust.

The remaining grants were mainly for amounts under £500 each, some were for as low as £50.

Beneficiaries in the north east included Fairbridge in Tyne & Wear, Great North Air Ambulance Service, Newcastle CVS, Newcastle Society for Blind People, Sunderland Mind, Tyne & Wear Autistic Association and University of Sunderland Development Trust.

Jewish organisations to benefit included Gateshead Jewish Boarding School, Jewish Blind and Disabled, Jewish Deaf Association, United Jewish Israel Appeal and Youth Aliyah.

Other UK organisations to benefit, which may have been local branches, included Barnado's, British Cancer Campaign, Help the Aged, Macmillan Cancer Relief, Scope and Variety Club Childrens' Charity.

Exclusions No grants for individuals. Only registered charities will be supported.

Applications In writing to the correspondent. Please enclose an sae. Applications are considered every other month.

The James Trust

Christianity

£53,000 (2003)

Beneficial area UK and overseas.

27 Radway Road, Upper Shirley, Southampton, Hampshire SO15 7PL

Tel. 023 8078 8249

Correspondent R J Todd, Trustee

Trustees *R J Todd; P Smith.*

CC Number 800774

Information available Information was provided by the trust.

General Principally, the trust has a preference for supporting Christian organisations. It operates primarily as a channel for the giving of a small group of donors. Grants are primarily to churches and Christian organisations involved in overseas development and work with young people.

In 2003 grants totalled £53,000, broken down as follows:

Churches	£19,000
Development and relief	£15,000
UK organisations	£15,000
Overseas organisations	£4,300

Exclusions No grants to individuals not personally known to the trustees.

Applications In writing to the correspondent. Unsolicited applications are not acknowledged.

The John Jarrold Trust

Arts, churches, environment/ conservation, Developing World, social welfare, medical research

£173,000 (2001/02)

Beneficial area UK and overseas, but mostly Norfolk.

Jarrold and Sons Ltd, Whitefriars, Norwich NR3 1SH

Tel. 01603 660211

Correspondent Caroline Jarrold, Secretary

Trustees *A C Jarrold, Chair; R E Jarrold; P J Jarrold; Mrs D J Jarrold; Mrs J Jarrold; Mrs A G Jarrold; Mrs W A L Jarrold.*

CC Number 242029

Information available Full accounts were on file at the Charity Commission.

General The trust supports a wide range of organisations including churches, medical, arts, environment/ conservation, welfare and overseas aid. It prefers to support specific projects, rather than contribute to general funding. In practice, most of the funds are given in Norfolk.

In 2001/02 the trust had assets of £1.5 million, which generated an income of £107,000. Grants were made to 274 organisations totalling £173,000 and were broken down as follows:

The arts – 37 grants totalling £43,000

The largest grants were £11,000 to Northern Ballet Theatre, £10,000 to Broadland Music Festival and £5,000 to Christopher Hepworth Organs Trust. Other grants included: £2,000 to Theatre Royal Norfolk Schools Project, £1,000 to Norwich Arts Centre, £500 each to History of Advertising Trust and Pilgrim Players, £250 each to Folk Norfolk, Musical Keys and Norwich School of Art and Design, £150 to Frontier Publishing and £100 each to Rig-a-jig-jig and National Youth Music Theatre.

Schools/education – 29 grants totalling £6,500

These included 17 school prizes of £25 each. Other grants included £2,000 to UEA School of English and American Studies, £1,000 to Thorpe St Andrew School, £750 to Arkwright Scholarship Trust, £250 to Harford Manor School, £100 to Oriel High School and £50 to Cawston VC Primary School.

Social welfare and community – 92 grants totalling £48,000

Donations included £8,000 to UEA Sports Park, £3,000 to The Hamlet Centre, £2,500 to Norwich Mark Place Ideas Competition, £2,000 to Prince's Trust, £1,000 each to Salvation Army and Tapping House Hospice, £500 each to Cathedral Camps, Escape Artists, Families House and RSPCA, £250 each to Army Benevolent Fund, ChildLine and Mid Norfolk Railway Preservation Trust, £200 to Buckingham Emergency Food Appeal, £100 each to Royal British Legion and Norfolk Junior Chess and £60 to Norwich Sea Cadets.

Medical – 27 grants totalling £27,000

These included £5,000 to East Anglian Air Ambulance, £2,000 each to Cancer Care Society, National Asthma Campaign and Wheelchair Children Association, £1,000 each to Alzheimer's Society, Break, National Autistic Society and Royal College of Surgeons, £500 each to Orchid Cancer Appeal and Starlight Children's Trust and £250 to Access Partnership.

Developing Countries – 27 grants totalling £10,000

Farm Africa and Leprosy Mission both received two grants, one of £1,000 and one of £500. Other grants included £1,000 each to Concern, Feed the Minds and Sight Savers International and £100 to Otjiwaranjo Veterinary Clinic.

Ecclesiastical – 29 grants totalling £28,000

By far the largest grant was £12,000 to Norwich Cathedral Trust. Other donations included £2,000 to St Peter's Church – Cringleford, £1,500 to Octagon Organ Appeal, £1,000 each to Chelmsford Cathedral and Peterborough Cathedral Trust, £500 each to Diss Methodist Church and Holy Innocents Church – Foulsham and £100 to RC Diocese of East Anglia.

Environment – 9 grants totalling £9,500

Norfolk Wildlife Trust received three grants totalling £6,300. Other recipients to receive grants included £1,000 each to National Trust for the Neptune coastline and Plantation Garden Preservation Trust, £500 each to The Green Quay and Plantlife and £100 to ACF Wilderness Expedition – South Africa and Benjamin Britten High School.

Exclusions Educational purposes that should be supported by the state will not be helped by the trust. Local groups outside Norfolk are very unlikely to be supported unless there is a personal connection to the trust. Individual educational programmes and gap year projects are not supported.

Applications Trustees meet in January and June each year and applications should be made in writing by the end of November and April respectively. Grants of up to £250 can be made between meetings.

Rees Jeffreys Road Fund

Road and transport research and education

£231,000 (2003)

Beneficial area UK.

13 The Avenue, Chichester, West Sussex PO19 5PX

Tel. 01243 787013

Minicom 01243 790622

Correspondent B Fieldhouse, Secretary

Trustees *D Bayliss, Chair; Prof. S Glaiser; M N T Cottell; Mrs June Bridgeman; Sir James Duncan; M J Kendrick; Prof. J Wootton.*

CC Number 217771

Information available Report and accounts with full grants list, explanation of grants, and descriptions of the trust's history and objects provided by the trust.

General This trust was established in 1950 by the late William Rees Jeffreys. Mr Rees Jeffreys was a 'road enthusiast' and was described by Lloyd George as 'the greatest authority on roads in the United Kingdom and one of the greatest in the world'. The fund is just one legacy of a life time dedicated to the improvement of roads; Rees Jeffreys was the author of an historical and autobiographical record of sixty years of road improvement (The King's Highway, published 1949) which is introduced by the words 'I early knew my mission in life'. Ironically, given the conquering of the roads by the petrol engine and cycling's shift off-road, he was also a very keen cyclist.

The fund 'gives financial support for research to improve the quality and efficiency of roads and their use by vehicles, cyclists, pedestrians and public transport'.

The trust's priorities are:

- Education of transport professionals, largely through financial support for teaching staff and bursaries for postgraduate studies. The trust is concerned about the supply of trained professionals and has launched a study of future requirements.
- Stimulating research into all aspects of roads, road usage and road traffic – this commands a large share of the trust's budget. The trust develops its own research programmes as well as responding to proposals from recognised agencies and researchers. Proposals are assessed against prevailing transport issues, such as environmental questions, congestion, modal choice and resource development.
- Roadside environment. Applications for the provision of roadside rests are welcome, while support for the work of country wildlife trusts for improving land adjoining main roads is also maintained. The trust is not normally able to buy land or to fund improvements to roads, footpaths or cycle tracks.

The trust will support projects and pump-priming for longer-term ventures for up to a maximum of five years. Operational or administrative staff costs are rarely supported. In almost all cases applicants are expected to provide or arrange match funding.

In 2003 the fund had assets of £5.7 million and an income of £178,000. Grants in the range of £140 to £56,000 totalled £231,000, divided as follows:

Research and general	£132,000
Education	£76,000
Physical projects	£23,000

Research and other projects

Grants were given to 12 organisations, ranging from £1,000 to £56,000. A grant of £56,000 was given to TRL/ITS Leeds towards the Enhancing the Road Travel Experience Project (Year 2). Other beneficiaries included PACTS for Road Traffic Police Enforcement and towards new technologies (£20,000); British Red Cross towards materials for Road Safety and First Aid Campaign and ITC towards Road Pricing and Investment Phase II (£15,000 each); IHT - Contribution to new guidelines on Accident Investigation and Prevention (£10,000); TPSI towards web-based work experience scheme, Young Transnet - 16+ Portal including careers option (£8,000 each); Imperial College for a conference on congestion charging, Life Cycle UK Take a Stand Project and TPSI for the Where Are You Headed? 2003 Edition (£3,000 each).

Education

This category included £52,000 for academic posts and studentships; £30,000 in support of PhD research.

Physical projects

Grants to organisations ranged from £2,500 to £5,000. The largest grant was £5,000 given to Birmingham and Black Countries WLT (for access improvements at Park Hall Farm). Others grants included: £4,000 each to Greensand Trust (for a feasibility study for the next stage of Deadman's Hill Layby improvements) and Norfolk WLT (for Rakenford and Knowstone Moors towards scrub control and removal of debris); £3,500 each to Devon DLT (for Rakenford and Knowstone Moors - scrub control and removal of debris) and Suffolk DLT (for car park improvements at Foxburrow Farm) and £2,500 to Surrey WLT (for picnic tables and paths at Newlands Corner).

Exclusions Operational and administrative staff costs are rarely considered. Grants are not given to environmental projects not related to highways, individual works for cycle tracks or works of only local application.

Applications There is no set form of application for grants. Brief details should be submitted initially. Replies are sent to all applicants. A preliminary telephone call is helpful but not essential. The trustees meet five times in the year, usually in January, April, July, September and November.

The Jenour Foundation

General

£80,000 (2002/03)

Beneficial area UK, with a special interest in Wales.

Deloitte & Touche, Blenhein House, Fitzalan Court, Newport Road, Cardiff CF24 0TS

Tel. 029 2048 1111

Correspondent Steve Allen, Trustee

Trustees *Sir P J Phillips; G R Camfield; D M Jones.*

CC Number 256637

Information available Full accounts were on file at the Charity Commission.

General This foundation has general charitable purposes, with a preference for Welsh causes.

In 2002/03 the foundation had assets of £1.9 million with an income of £93,000 and grants totalling £80,000.

The largest grants were £6,000 each to Atlantic College and Welsh National Opera, £5,000 each to British Heart Foundation and Cancer Research Wales and £4,000 to Macmillan Cancer Care Fund.

Other grants included £3,000 each to Bath Institute of Medical Engineering, Children's Hospital for Wales, Barnardo's, Provincial Grand Lodge of Monmouth, SCOPE and Wales Council for the Blind and £2,000 each to British Deaf Association, British Limbless Ex-Servicemen's Association, Holy Cross Church, Multiple Sclerosis Society, Representative Body of the Church in Wales, RNLI Welsh District, Salvation Army and Samaritans.

Grants of £1,000 or less were awarded to Gurkha Welfare Trust, High Sheriffs Youth Awards, Parish of Llanishen, Princes Trust Bro, Physiotherapy Training Fund, Society for Welfare of Horses & Ponies, St John's Ambulance in Wales and Welsh St Donat's Art.

Exclusions No support for individuals.

Applications Applications should be in writing and reach the correspondent by February for the trustees' meeting in March.

The Jephcott Charitable Trust

Alleviation of poverty in developing countries, general

£84,000 (2002/03)

Beneficial area UK, developing countries.

Cotley, Streatham Rise, Exeter, Devon EX4 4PE

Website www.jephcottcharitabletrust.org.uk

Correspondent Mrs Meg Harris, Secretary

Trustees *Mrs M Jephcott, Chair; Judge A North; H Wolley; K Morgan; J Bunnell; Mrs C Thomas.*

CC Number 240915

Information available Accounts were provided by the trust.

General The trust's 2002/03 annual report states that its priorities are directed towards population control, education, health and the environment. It stated that the trustees have a particular interest in making grants to organisations requiring start-up funds to enable projects to commence. Both UK and overseas projects are funded.

The trustees are flexible in their approach, but take the following into account when considering a project:

- the ability to evaluate a project, (with overseas projects local involvement is thought to be essential for on-going success)
- the involvement of a third party such as ODA, NGOs, National Heritage
- financial: level of administration costs, reserves held within the group and so on
- whether the project is basic or palliative
- whether it is one-off or on-going
- to what extent the organisation helped themselves.

In 2002/03 the trust's assets stood at £4.6 million with an income of £260,000. A total of £84,000 was given in 16 grants, ranging from £1,000 to £23,000.

By far the largest grant was £23,000 to HOESO in Uganda. Other grants included £7,000 each to CEC in Sierra Leone and Aloysius Lubega Memorial School, £6,000 each to Appropriate Technology, Goedgedacht Trust and Mozambique Schools Fund, £5,000 each to Farms for City Children and Haven Housing Trust, £3,500 to The Maforga Mission and £2,000 to ADC Theatre.

Exclusions No grants to individuals, including students, or for medical research. No response to general appeals from large, UK organisations nor from organisations concerned with poverty and education in the UK. Core funding and/or salaries are rarely considered.

Applications Guidelines and application forms are available on request and receipt of an sae or via the trust's website. Applications can be made in writing at any time to the correspondent. Trustees meet twice a year (in April and October) and must have detailed financial information about each project before they will make a decision. Only applications from eligible bodies are acknowledged, when further information about the project may be requested. Monitoring of grant expenditure is usually required.

The Jewish Youth Fund

Jewish youth work

£69,000 (2001/02)

Beneficial area UK.

5th Floor, 707 High Road, North Finchley, London N12 0BT

Tel. 020 8445 1670 **Fax** 020 8446 7370

Email jyf@anjy.org

Correspondent Peter Shaw, Secretary

Trustees *Jonathan Gestetner; Richard McGratty; Lady Morris of Kenwood; Miss Wendy F Pollecoff.*

CC Number 251902

Information available Full accounts were on file at the Charity Commission.

General The fund's objectives are to promote and protect religious, moral, educational, physical and social interests of young members of the Jewish community in the UK.

In 2001/02 the trust had assets of £1.8 million and an income of £109,000. Grants totalling £69,000 went to 17 organisations, 8 of which were also supported in the previous year.

The largest grants were £10,000 to Liverpool Jewish Youth and Community Centre, £5,400 to Redbridge Jewish Youth and Community Centre and £5,000 each to Belmont Synagogue, Jewish Experience for Teens, Noam Masorti Youth, North Manchester Jewish Youth Project and Reform Synagogue Youth Netzer.

Other beneficiaries were Brady Maccabi Youth & Community Centre (£4,000), Habonim Dror (£3,750), Ezra Youth Movement (£3,500), B'nai Brith Youth Organisation, Bushey Youth Scene, Chigwell & Hainault Jewish Youth Club and Hanoar Hatzioni (£3,000 each), Friends of Zionist Youth (£2,800), Friends of Jewish Servicemen (£1,500) and Chaverim South Tottenham Jewish Trust (£1,450).

Exclusions Grants are not made in response to general appeals. Formal education is not supported.

Applications On an application form available from the correspondent, enclosing a copy of the latest accounts and an annual report.

The JMK Charitable Trust

Children's health

£42,000 (2002/03)

Beneficial area Worldwide.

Messrs Chantrey Vellacott DFK, Prospect House, 58 Queen's Road, Reading, Berkshire RG1 4RP

Tel. 0118 959 5432

Correspondent The Trustees

Trustees *Mrs J M Karaviotis; J Karaviotis; R S Parker.*

CC Number 274576

Information available Accounts were on file at the Charity Commission.

General This trust supports registered charities, with a preference for those concerned with children's health.

In 2002/03 the trust had assets of £1.5 million with an income of £66,000 and grants totalling £42,000.

The two largest grants include £24,000 to Royal College of Music and £12,000 to Royal Academy of Arts.

Other grants include £1,500 each to Tower Hamlets Old People's Welfare and Royal Opera House, £1,000 each to World Jewish Relief and Royal National Theatre, £500 to Royal Albert Hall Trust, £250 to Royal College of Arts, £200 each to Elizabeth Finn Trust and Flood Relief Fund Prague and £100 each to West London Synagogue and Alice Model Trust Fund.

Applications In writing to the correspondent. No acknowledgement of receipt is given.

The Harold Joels Charitable Trust

Jewish

£40,000 (2002/03)

Beneficial area UK and overseas.

Grunberg & Co, 13 Accommodation Road, London NW11 8ED

Tel. 020 8458 0083

Correspondent R A Lipman

Trustees *H Joels; Dr N Joels; Mrs V Joels; N E Joels.*

CC Number 206326

Information available Full accounts were on file at the Charity Commission.

General The trust makes grants to Jewish organisations in the UK and US.

In 2002/03 the trust had assets of £732,000 and an income of £24,000. Donations totalling £40,000 were made to 61 organisations.

In the UK, 41 grants totalling £22,000 were made. Beneficiaries included World Jewish Relief (£5,300), Jewish Care (£4,000), Royal National Theatre (£2,000), Royal Academy Trust (£1,300), Friends of the Hebrew University of Jerusalem (£1,200), United Synagogue (£820), JNF Charitable Trust (£600), British WIZO and University of Cambridge (£500 each), Tricycle Theatre Co (£300), Jewish Blind and Disabled (£150) and Community Security Trust, Jewish Child's Day and Nightingale (£100 each).

In the US, 20 grants totalling £18,000 were made. Beneficiaries receiving over £1,000 were Women's Resource Centre of Sarasota County (£8,600), Temple Beth Shalom (£4,100) and Flonda Studio Theatre (£1,400).

Applications In writing to the correspondent.

The Jonathan Joels Charitable Trust

General

£49,000 (2001/02)

Beneficial area UK and overseas.

EBK Partnership, 311 Ballards Lane, Finchley, London N12 8LY

Tel. 020 8446 6026

Correspondent The Trustees

Trustees *J Joels; N E Joels; H Joels.*

CC Number 278408

Information available Accounts were on file at the Charity Commission.

General This trust supports general charitable purposes, making grants to registered charities only.

In 2001/02 the trust had an income of £427,000 with grants totalling £49,000. No financial information on the Trust's assets were provided for this period.

The figures provided by the trust on grants awarded are quoted in US dollars and include $34,800 to UJA Federation of Bergen County & North Hudson, $8,500 to Congregation Ahavath Torah, $8,000 to Moriah School of Englewood, $6,700 to Ramaz School, $3,600 to Ramaz Special Educational Fund, $3,300 to Jewish Community Center on the Palisades, $2,200 to Emunah of America and $1,900 to Shaare Zedek Medical Center in Jerusalem.

Grants of less than $1,000 include Sinai Special Needs Institute, Jewish Home and Rehabilitation Center, Boys Town Jerusalem Foundation of America, Jewish Family Service, East Hill Synagogue, United Lifeline/Kav Lachayim, Yeshiva Chanoch Lenaar, Yeshiva Ohr Hatalmud of Englewood, Chai Lifeline, AZTUM, League for the Hard of Hearing, National Jewish Council for the Disabled, SCAT, Keser Dovid Inc, Chabad Center of Fort Lee, Friends of the Israeli Defense Forces, Lakewood Cheder School and Friends of the Lubavitch of Bergen County.

Applications In writing only, to the address below.

The Nicholas Joels Charitable Trust

Jewish, medical welfare, general

£44,000 (2001/02)

Beneficial area UK and overseas.

20 Copse Wood Way, Northwood, Middlesex HA6 2UF

Correspondent N Joels, Trustee

Trustees *N E Joels; J Joels; H Joels; Ms Carolyn Avril Joels*

CC Number 278409

Information available Full accounts were on file at the Charity Commission.

General The trust makes grants to registered charities only, and from the list of beneficiaries it appears to support Jewish causes and medical and welfare charities. In 2001/02 it had an income of £18,000 and a total assets were £619,000. The grant total was £44,000

The largest grants were £16,000 to United Jewish Israel appeal, £6,000 to Aspire and £5,000 to St Helans School, £2,250 to World Jewish Relief, £1,250 to Youth Aliyah Child Rescue, £1,150 to Habad Orphan Aid Society and £1,125 to Weizmann Institute.

The rest of the grants were for between £25 and £900 and included £900 to Norwood Ravenswood, £780 to JNF Charitable Trust, £500 to Great Ormond Street Hospital, £200 to Multiple Sclerosis and £25 to CMZ Trust.

Applications In writing to the correspondent.

The N B Johnson Charitable Settlement

Education, older people

£36,000 (2002/03)

Beneficial area UK, with a preference for Greater Manchester.

PO Box 165, Manchester M45 7XD

Correspondent Leslie Hyman

CC Number 277237

Information available Full accounts were on file at the Charity Commission.

General In 2002/03 the trust had an assets of £6,000, an income of £32,000 and made grants totalling £36,000. A list of grant beneficiaries was not available.

In 2000/01 beneficiaries included Heathlands (£5,100), Whitefield Hebrew Congregation (£3,500), Community Security Trust (£3,000), Manchester Charitable Trust (£2,000), Elliott Levy Memorial (£1,500) and Whitefield Kollel and Lubavitch Manchester (£1,000 each).

Smaller grants included those to Delamere School and League of Jewish Women (£500 each) and Bay Community and JNF (£250 each).

Applications In writing to the correspondent. The trust has previously stated that unsolicited applications are not invited.

The Lillie Johnson Charitable Trust

Children, young people who are blind or deaf, medical

£268,000 (2001/02)

Beneficial area UK, with a preference for the West Midlands.

Heathcote House, 136 Hagley Road, Edgbaston, Birmingham B16 9PN

Tel. 0121 454 4141

Correspondent Victor M C Lyttle, Trustee

Trustees *Victor Lyttle; Peter Adams.*

CC Number 326761

Information available Information was on file at the Charity Commission.

General In 2003/04 the trust had an income of £176,000 and a total expenditure of £175,000. Further information for this year was not available.

In 2001/02 it had assets of £4.4 million and an income of £202,000. Grants were made totalling £268,000. By far the largest grant, of £101,000, went to Jobs Close.

The next largest grants were £40,000 to Primrose Trust, £20,000 to Web Care, £16,000 to CRAB and £10,000 to Heir A Recreational Trust. Other beneficiaries included BMOS Youth Theatre (£6,400), Lady Katherine Leveson Foundation and Muscular Dystrophy Campaign (£5,000 each), Macmillan Cancer Relief (£4,500), Pulse (£4,000), Coughton Church of England Primary School and Rotary Club of Edgbaston (£2,500 each), Birmingham and District Theatre Guild (£2,000), Solihull Basketball Club (£1,500) and Harborne Carnival and Northfield Operatic Society (£1,000 each).

Exclusions No support for individuals.

Applications Applications are only considered from charities which are traditionally supported by the trust. The trust stated that it is inundated with applications it cannot support and feels obliged to respond to all of these.

The H F Johnson Trust

Christian education

£181,000 (2002/03)

Beneficial area Worldwide, but mainly the UK.

PO Box 300, Kingstown Broadway, Carlisle, Cumbria CA3 0QS

Correspondent David Ryan

Trustees *Keith Danby; David Ryan; Libby Kelly; Ian Waterfield.*

CC Number 1050966

Information available Information was provided by the trust.

General Established by trust deed in 1962, the trust's main object is the advancement of the Christian faith. Most of the funds are given towards distributing Bibles and Christian books to state schools where teachers or heads are concerned with the promotion of good educational reading materials.

In 2003 it had assets of £1.1 million and an income of £166,000. Grants were made totalling £181,000, of which £125,000 was donated to the Challenge Literature Fellowship Ltd (a Christian charity that was established for the purpose of advancing Christian faith with an emphasis on literature) and the remainding £56,000 was spent on supplying bibles and books to schools and Christian organisations that work with schoolchildren.

Applications The trust stated that applications must be in writing enclosing a sae. Applicants should have direct involvement with the school for which the application is being made.

The Marjorie and Geoffrey Jones Charitable Trust

General

£60,000 (2003/04)

Beneficial area UK, preference south west of England.

Carlton House, 30 The Terrace, Torquay, Devon TQ1 1BS

Tel. 01803 213251 **Fax** 01803 296871

Correspondent The Trustees

Trustees *N J Wollen; W F Coplestone Boughey; P M Kay.*

CC Number 1051031

Information available Full accounts were on file at the Charity Commission.

General This trust was set up under the terms of the will of Rose Marjorie Jones, who died in 1995, leaving the gross of her estate amounting to £2.2 million for grantmaking purposes. In her will she donated amounts of £15,000 and £10,000 to charities based in Devon, such as The Donkey Sanctuary – Sidmouth, Paignton Zoological and Botanical Gardens Limited, The Rowcroft Hospital – Torquay, The Torbay Hospital League of Friends and RNIB – Torquay. Other organisations named in the will were UK-wide, such as RNLI, RSPCA and NSPCC – although grants were probably given to local branches.

In 2003/04 the trust had assets of £1.6 million and an income of £71,000. After management and administration costs of £23,000, grants to 21 organisations totalled £60,000. The largest grants were £5,000 each to Dartington Hall Trust, Devon and Cornwall Care Trust, Groundwork – Brewery Park Project, Home Farm Trust, Leonard Cheshire Foundation, National Trust and Torquay Child Contact Centre. Other beneficiaries were Coldharbour Mill, Torbay Civic Society and Woodland Trust (£3,000 each), Newton Carenet, Stroke Association, Towersay Foundation, Trinity Sailing Foundation and Wessex Autistic Society (£2,000 each) and Barn Owl Trust, Beacons Wheelchair Dancers, Belgrave Torbay Scout Group, Braille Chess Association, DELTA and Macular Disease Society – Barnstaple (£1,000 each).

Applications In writing to the correspondent. The trustees meet four times a year to consider applications.

The J E Joseph Charitable Fund

Jewish

See below

Beneficial area London, Manchester, Israel, India and Hong Kong.

Flat 1, Burham Court, 33 Marsh Lane, Stanmore, Middlesex HA7 4HQ

Tel. 020 8289 2573

Correspondent Roger J Leon, Secretary

Trustees *F D A Mocatta, Chair; D Silas; J H Corre; P S Gourgey; J S Horesh; S Frosh.*

CC Number 209058

Information available Information was on file at the Charity Commission.

General The trust was established for the benefit of Jewish communities for any puposes, including welfare, educational and religious causes. In 2003/04 it had an income of £125,000 and a total expenditure of £131,000. Further information from this year was not available.

The trust had previously stated that 'The trustees believe it inappropriate to disclose the names of grantees, being other charities and individuals.'

Exclusions No grants to individuals.

Applications In writing to the correspondent, including a copy of the latest. The trustees respond to all applications which are first vetted by the secretary. The trust stated that many applications are unsuccessful as the number of appeals exceeds the amount available from limited income.

The Anton Jurgens Charitable Trust

Welfare, general

£261,000 (2001/02)

Beneficial area UK.

Saffrey Champness, Lion House, 72–75 Red Lion Street, London WC1R 4GB

Tel. 020 7841 4000 **Fax** 020 7841 4100

Correspondent Michael J Jurgens, Trustee

Trustees *C V M Jurgens, Chair; J F M Jurgens; B W M Jurgens; E Deckers; M J Jurgens; F A V Jurgens.*

CC Number 259885

Information available Full accounts were on file at the Charity Commission.

General This trust has general charitable purposes, although welfare and children's groups feature prominently in the grants, as do organisations based in the south east of England.

In 2001/02 the trust had assets of £6.7 million and an income of £373,000. Grants were made totalling £261,000.

The largest grants were £15,000 to Ashram International, St John's RC Special School, £10,000 each to Combat Stress, St John Ambulance – Berkshire, Princes Trust – Young Offenders Initiative, Understanding Industry and Voice for the Child in Care, £7,000 to Abbeyfield – Wey Valley, £6,000 to Percy Hedley Foundation and £5,000 each to Avocet Trust, Fairbridge, Filey Sea Cadets, Listening Books, Youth at Risk – Coaching for Success and Youth Outreach – West Cumbria.

Smaller grants went to Centrepoint and Chailey Heritage School – Sussex, Enham Trust and NANSA Scope (£4,000 each), Advance Housing & Support, Blackwater Valley Scope, Dukes Barn, Marie Curie Cancer Care, New Cares Community Church (£3,000 each), Alexandra House – Plymouth, Granville Bear Appeal, Interact Reading Service, Royal School for the Deaf and Woodlands Respite Care Centre – York (£2,000 each), Kingsclere Community Association and Woodley Age Concern (£1,500 each) and Brainwave, Children's Adventure Farm Trust – Cheshire, John Simonds Trust, Scope, Sea Cadets – Northumberland, Samaritans Llandrodnod Wells and Shefield Children's Hospital. (£1,000 each).

Applications In writing to the correspondent. The trustees meet twice a year in the spring and the autumn. It is recommended that applications be submitted by 31 March for consideration at the spring meeting and by 31 August for the autumn meeting. The trustees do not enter into correspondence concerning grant applications beyond notifying successful applicants.

The Bernard Kahn Charitable Trust

Jewish

£270,000 (2002/03)

Beneficial area UK and Israel.

18 Gresham Gardens, London NW11 8PD

Correspondent The Trustees

Trustees *Mrs C B Kahn; S Fuehrer, Y E Kahn.*

CC Number 249130

Information available Accounts were on file at the Charity Commission.

General In 2002/03 the trust had assets of £2.2 million and an income of £164,000, including £77,000 in donations. Grants were made to organisations totalling £270,000.

The largest grants were £45,000 to Jewish Education Trust, £30,000 to Margenita D'avraham, £25,000 to Orthodox Council of Jerusalem, £24,000 to Gateshead Academy for Torah Studies, £20,000 to UCL Hospital, £16,000 to Achisomoch Aid Co. Ltd, £15,000 to Gevurath Ari Torah Academy Trust, £12,500 to Marbeh Torah Trust and £10,000 to Telz Talmudical Academy Trust.

Other grants included £8,000 to Hasmonean High School, £7,000 to Gateshead Primary School, £6,000 to North West London Communal Mikvah, £4,000 to Lubavitch Yeshiva Gedola, £2,500 to Friends of Religious Settlements, £2,000 to Yeshivah L'zeirim, £1,500 to Dyslexic Institute and Ulpanit Bnei Akosh and £1,000 to Knessseth.

Around half the grants were of under £1,000.

Applications In writing to the correspondent.

The Stanley Kalms Foundation

Jewish charities, general

£244,000 (2001/02)

Beneficial area UK and overseas.

Dixons Group plc, 29 Farm Street, London W1J 5RL

Tel. 020 7499 3494

Correspondent Mrs Jane Hunt-Cooke

Trustees *Sir Stanley Kalms; Pamela Kalms; Stephen Kalms.*

CC Number 328368

Information available Accounts were on file at the Charity Commission.

General Established in 1989 by Sir Stanley Kalms, the president of Dixons Group plc, this charity states its objectives as the encouragement of Jewish education in the UK and Israel. Other activities include support for the arts and media and other programmes, both secular and religious.

In 2001/02 the foundation had assets of £1.2 million and an income of £64,000. Grants were made totalling £244,000.

Grants were mainly to Jewish organisations (social and educational) with grants also going to the arts, education and health. Donations over £1,000 each were listed in the accounts and went to 31 organisations. The largest included those to Business for Sterling (£75,000), Royal Opera House Trust (£40,000), Institute for Policy Research (£20,000), Pluto Productions (£11,000) and Oxford Centre for Jewish and Hebrew Studies and St Jame's Conservation Centre (£10,000 each).

Other grants included £9,700 to Norwood Ltd, £6,000 each to Keren Klita and Holocaust Education Trust, £5,000 to Festival of Jewish Arts and Culture, £3,200 to British Friends of Haifa University, £2,000 to Jewish Music Institute and £1,000 each to Commonwealth Jewish Trust, Jewish Museum and One to One Children's Fund.

Unlisted donations under £1,000 each totalled £5,900.

Applications In writing to the correspondent, but note that most of the trust's funds are committed to projects supported for a number of years.

The Boris Karloff Charitable Foundation

General

£49,000 (2001/02)

Beneficial area Worldwide.

Peachey & Co., 95 Aldwych, London WC2B 4JF

Correspondent The Trustees

Trustees *Ian D Wilson; P A Williamson; O M Lewis.*

CC Number 326898

Information available Full accounts were on file at the Charity Commission.

General This foundation was set up in 1985, by Evelyn Pratt (Karloff), wife of the famous horror actor, Boris Karloff (whose real name was William Henry Pratt). When Evelyn Pratt died in June 1993, she bequeathed over £1.4 million to the assets of the foundation.

In 2001/02 the trust had assets of £1.7 million and an income of £62,000. Grants totalled £49,000. grants included £20,000 to Green Croft New Alliance, £10,000 to Royal Theatrical Fund, £5,000 to Bromley CAB, Cinema and Television Benevolent Fund and Rose Road Association and £1,000 each to Action for Blind People, Amnesty International, Cancer Bacup, Cancer Vaccine Institute, Mental Health Foundation and Royal Blind Asylum and School.

Exclusions Charities with large resources are not supported.

Applications In writing to the correspondent.

The Ian Karten Charitable Trust

Technology centres for people who are disabled

£141,000 to organisations (2003/04)

Beneficial area Great Britain and Israel, with some local interest in Surrey and London.

The Mill House, Newark Lane, Ripley, Surrey GU23 6DP

Tel. 01483 225020 **Fax** 01483 222420

Email iankarten@aol.com

Correspondent Angela Hobbs

Trustees *Ian H Karten, Chair; Mrs Mildred Karten; Tim Simon; Ellen Fraenkel.*

CC Number 281721

Information available Full accounts were provided by the trust.

General The trusts states its objects in its 2003/04 thus:

'The objects of the trust are to carry out legally charitable purposes for the relief of poverty, the advancement of education or religion or otherwise for the benefit of the community.

'The trust currently concentrates on:

- 'improving the quality of life and independence of people with severe physical, sensory, cognitive disability or mental health problems by providing for them Centres for Computer-aided Training, Education and Communication (CTEC Centres). These are typically established by and located in colleges of further education or (mainly residential) host charities concerned with rehabilitation and education, especially vocational, of people with one or more of the above mentioned disabilities.
- 'the support of higher education by funding studentships for postgraduate studies and research at universities in the UK.

'The trust also has a separate modest budget from which it makes small donations to other selected registered charities, mostly local to the trust (London or Surrey).'

In 2003/04 it had assets of £5.9 million and an income of £377,000. Grants to individuals totalled £3,900. Grants to organisations totalled £141,000, broken down as follows:

Scholarships to institutions – 9 grants totalling £102,000

These went to AJA (£40,000), University College London (£25,000), Centre for Jewish Christian Relations (£11,000), Southampton University (£10,000), Hafia University (£6,000), ALEH, Ohr Torah and Tel Aviv University (£3,000 each) and Jerusalem Hebrew University (£1,000).

CTEC Centres – 1 grant of £10,000

This went to Cedar Foundation (NICOD).

Other charities – grants totalled £29,000

All grants of £500 or larger were listed in the accounts. These were £10,000 to

Norwood, £1,500 to Jewish Care, £1,000 each to Commonwealth Jewish Trust, Disability Aid Fund, Speech Language and Hearing Centre, Spiro Ark, UJIA Foundation for Education and World Jewish Relief, £750 each to Anne Frank Educational Trust, Community Security Trust, Simon Marks Jewish Primary School Trust and Surrey Care Trust and £500 each to Institute for Jewish Policy Research and Refugee Council.

Exclusions No grants to individuals.

Applications Those interested in the CTEC programme should contact Angela Hobbs. Students should approach their university. Applications for other grants should be accompanied by recent accounts and other material about the charity's activity.

The Kasner Charitable Trust

Jewish

£146,000 (2001/02)

Beneficial area UK and Israel.

Kimberley House, 172 Billet Road, London E17 5DT

Tel. 020 8342 0211

Correspondent Josef Kasner, Trustee

Trustees *Mrs Elfreda Erlich; Baruch Erlich; Josef Kasner.*

CC Number 267510

Information available Full accounts were on file at the Charity Commission.

General In 2001/02 the trust had assets of £840,000 with an income of £50,000 and grants totalling £146,000.

The largest grants were £18,000 to Telz Academy Trust, £16,000 to Gevurath Ari, £11,000 to Ponevez, £10,000 each to Law of Truth, CWC Trust and Beis Eliyahu.

Other grants were £6,000 to Rav Chesed Trust, £5,000 to Gateshead Academy for Torah Studies, £4,000 each to Emunah Educational Centre and New Rachmastrivke Synagogue Trust, £3,000 each to United Jewish Israel Appeal and Gateshead Talmudical College, £2,000 to Beth Sholom Synagogue, £1,000 each to British Friends of Bnei Brak Hospital, Friends of Bar Ilan University, Friends of Lubavitch, Torah Temimah Primary School and Yesoday Hatorah School.

Grants of less than £1,000 were awarded to Academy of Rabbinical Research, Akim, Avigdor, Boys Town Jerusalem, British ORT, Chinuch Atzman, Craven Walk Charitable Trust, Friends of Hebrew University Jerusalem, Food Life Line, Delamere Forest School, Friends of Mir, Friends of the Sick, Ichud Hayeshivot, JNF Charitable Trust, Kisharon, Kolel Gur, MFPA, Lelov, Moreshet Hatorah, Operation Wheelchair, Otzar Hatorah, KTV Trust, Schonfeld Square Foundation, Services for the Aged, Yad Torah Trust, UNICEF and Yeshivat Kol Torah.

Applications In writing to the correspondent.

The Kass Charitable Trust

Welfare, nursing homes, older people, education, cancer, Jewish

£30,000 (2002/03)

Beneficial area UK.

13 Haslemere Avenue, London NW4 2PU

Tel. 020 8202 9655

Correspondent D E Kass, Trustee

Trustees *David Elliot Kass; Samuel Simcha Bunimkass; Mrs Shulamith Malkah Sandler.*

CC Number 1006296

Information available Accounts were on file at the Charity Commission, but without a list of grants.

General The trust supports:

- provision of financial assistance without regard to any religious denominations to those who are in need or are experiencing hardship.
- provision and maintenance of nursing homes and other facilities for the benefit of older and infirm people.
- promotion of education
- promotion of research into the causes of and cure for cancer and similar diseases
- promotion and advancement of the Jewish religion including the preservation and maintenance of Jewish cemeteries.

In 2002/03 the trust's assets comprised £4,200 held in cash in the bank. Its income was £49,000 mostly from donations received. Grants totalled £30,000.

Unfortunately a list of grant beneficiaries was not included with the accounts for 2002/03.

Applications In writing to the correspondent.

The Kathleen Trust

Musicians

£139,000 (2002)

Beneficial area UK, with a preference for London.

Currey & Co, 21 Buckingham Gate, London SW1E 6LS

Tel. 020 7828 4091 **Fax** 020 7828 5049

Correspondent E R H Perks, Trustee

Trustees *E R H Perks; Sir O C A Scott; Lady P A Scott; Mrs C N Withington.*

CC Number 1064516

Information available Information was provided by the trust.

General Established in 1997, it is the policy of the trustees to 'assist young and impecunious musicians'. After an additional settlement of £113,000 the trust has assets of £1.1 million and an income of £144,000 of which £139,000 was given in grants. Largest grant was awarded to N Clein Cello Trust (£100,000). Other beneficiaries were Oxford Chamber Music Festival (£10,000), Richard Harwood and Royal College of Music Awards Fund (£9,000 each), Dulwich College and Sounds Great (£4,000 each), Guildhall School of Music and Dance (£1,000).

Applications In writing to the correspondent.

The Michael & Ilse Katz Foundation

Jewish, music, medical, general

£133,000 (2002/03)

Beneficial area Worldwide.

The Counting House, Trelill, Bodmin, Cornwall PL30 3HZ

Tel. 01208 851814 **Fax** 01208 851813

Email osman.azis@virgin.net

Correspondent Osman Azis, Trustee

Trustees *Norris Gilbert; Osman Azis.*

CC Number 263726

Information available Full accounts were on file at the Charity Commission.

General Established in 1971, this foundation supports many Jewish organisations, although musical and medical charities also received funds.

In 2002/03 its assets totalled £917,000 and generated an income of £23,000. After high management and administration professional expenses of £14,600, grants were made totalling £133,000.

Large grants were made to Poole Arts Trust Ltd (£20,000), Jewish Care (£16,000), Bournemouth Orchestral Society (£15,500) and UK Friends of the Association for the Wellbeing of Israel's Soldiers (£10,000). Other beneficiaries included Community Security Trust (£8,000), Norwood-Ravenswood (£7,000), Leo Baeck College (£5,000), Hillel Foundation and Holocaust Educational Trust (£3,000 each), WIZO (£2,500), Beth Shalom Memorial Centre and British ORT (£2,000 each) and Jewish Child's Day, Sharre Zedik Medical Centre and Tel Aviv Sourasky Medical Centre (£1,000 each). A further £25,000 was given in grants under £1,000.

Applications In writing to the correspondent.

The Katzauer Charitable Settlement

Jewish

£36,000 (2002/03)

Beneficial area UK, but mainly Israel.

c/o Devonshire House, 1 Devonshire Street, London W1W 5DR

Tel. 020 7304 2000

Correspondent Gordon Smith, Trustee

Trustees *G C Smith; A Katzauer; H G Kramer.*

CC Number 275110

Information available Full accounts were on file at the Charity Commission.

General In 2002/03 the trust had assets of £805,000 with an income of £78,000 which was mainly derived from donations and investment income. Grants totalling £36,000 were issued for this period.

The largest grants were £8,000 to Moria Synagogue, £3,000 each to Kollel Ra'anana and Nahalat Yehiel, £2,000 each to World Jewish Relief, British Friends of Mercaz Hatorah and Germach Yaron, £1,000 each to Chatam Memorial Synagogue and Friends of Lubavitch UK.

Other grants of less than £1,000 were awarded to Jewish Disabled & Blind Association, Lubavitch Scotland, British ORT, Kollel Haifa, Beit Issi Shapiro, Nightingale House, Beit Knesset Gan Vealiya, Kol Torah Rabbinical College, Kollel Yad Sarah, Jewish Children's Holiday Fund, Beit Midrash Gavoha, Shaare Zedek Hospital, Yeshivat Pressburg, Micha Society, Limudei Hashem, Shivtei Yisrael, Keren Gernah Leesra Refuit, Yeshivat Ofakim, Esra Community Fund and Jewish Academy Trust.

Grants of under £150 totalled £2,300.

Applications In writing to the correspondent.

The C S Kaufman Charitable Trust

Jewish

£138,000 (2002/03)

Beneficial area UK

162 Whitehall Road, Gateshead, Tyne & Wear NE8 1TP

Correspondent C S Kaufman

Trustees *I I Kaufman; J Kaufman.*

CC Number 253194

Information available Accounts were on file at the Charity Commission.

General In 2002/03 this trust had an income of £71,000 and a grant total of £138,000. Grant beneficiaries included Yetev Lev Yerusholayim (£25,000), Yeshiva Shaarei Zion-Turda (£20,000), Society of Friends of Torah (£16,000), Gateshead Academy for Torah Studies (£10,000), Gateshead Foundation for Torah and UTA (£5,500 each), Ponevez (£5,000), Tevini (£2,300), Colel Hibath Yerusholayim (£1,700) and Kupat Ha'ir (£1,600).

Exclusions No grants to individuals.

Applications In writing to the correspondent.

This entry was not confirmed by the trust but was correct according to information on file at the Charity Commission.

The Geoffrey John Kaye Charitable Foundation

Jewish, general

£119,000 (2001/02)

Beneficial area UK and overseas.

PEG, 54 Welbeck Street, London W1G 9XS

Tel. 020 7935 1339

Correspondent R J Freebody, Accountant

Trustees *G J Kaye; Mrs S Rose; J Pears.*

CC Number 262547

Information available Accounts are on file at the Charity Commission.

General In 2001/02 the trust had assets of just over £1 million, an income of £91,000 and made grants totalling £119,000. Grants are largely recurrent and are made to Jewish organisations.

Beneficiaries included Animal Shelter AC (£40,000), JJCT Beersheva Project (£35,000), Consejo de Colaboracion (£11,000), Friends of Nightgale House (£10,000), Lubavitch Foundation (£6,000), The Ashten Trust (£3,500), Holocaust Educational Trust (£1,000) and Cruz Roja Mexicana (£700).

Exclusions The funds for the charity are fully committed for the forseeable future.

Applications In writing to the correspondent, but note the comments above.

The Emmanuel Kaye Foundation

Medical research, welfare and Jewish organisations.

£49,000 (2002/03)

Beneficial area UK and overseas.

Hart House, Hartley Wintney, Hampshire RG27 8PE

Tel. 01252 843773

Correspondent John Forster

Trustees *David Kaye; Lady Kaye; John Forster; Michael Cutler.*

CC Number 280281

Information available Full accounts were provided by the trust.

General The trust supports organisations benefiting medical professionals, research workers, scientists, Jewish people, at risk groups, people who are disadvantaged by poverty and socially isolated people.

In 2002/03 it had assets of £1 million, which generated an income of £36,000. Grants totalled £49,000.

The largest were £25,000 to Thrombosis Research Institute, £5,000 each to Imperial College London and Schools J Link, £3,500 to St Michael's Hospice – North Hampshire, £2,000 to Almeida Theatre Company Limited, £1,500 to Caius House and £1,000 to Age Concern. Smaller grants totalled £6,200.

Exclusions Organisations not registered with the Charity Commission are not supported.

Applications In writing to the correspondent.

The Mathilda and Terence Kennedy Charitable Trust

General

£50,000 (2001/2002)

Beneficial area UK.

H W Fisher & Co., Acre House, 11–15 William Road, London NW1 3ER

Tel. 020 7388 7000

Correspondent The Trustees

Trustees *Hon. Amanda Sieff; John O'Neill; Mrs L Sieff; J Henderson.*

CC Number 206330

Information available Accounts were on file at the Charity Commission.

General The trust makes grants to a range of organisations. In 2001/02 the trust had assets of £578,000. an income of £24,000 and a grant total of £50,000.

Grant beneficiaries included Royal Ballet School (£20,000), Stonewall Iris Trust (£10,000), British WIZO (£5,000), Future Trust Foundation-Lullabye Project, M & TK Institute of Rheumatology (£3,500 each), The Trussel Trust (£2,500), Alternative Theatre Company Limited-Bush Theatre, London Connection and Rough Magic Theatre Company (£1,500 each) and The Art Dance Company (£750).

Applications Grants are mainly made to charities known personally to the trustees, rather than as a result of unsolicited applications. Unsuccessful applications will not receive a reply.

The Kennel Club Charitable Trust

Dogs

£212,000 (2003)

Beneficial area UK.

1–5 Clarges Street, Piccadilly, London W1J 8AB

Tel. 020 7518 1029 **Fax** 020 7518 1050

Email mwetherell@the-kennel-club.org.uk

Website www.the-kennel-club.org.uk

Correspondent Mrs Mary Wetherell, Secretary

Trustees *Brig. R J Clifford; W R Irving; M Townsend, Chair; M Herrtage; W H King; Mrs I E Terry*

CC Number 327802

Information available Full accounts and guidance notes were provided by the trust.

General The trust describes its objects as 'science, sentiment and support'. It supports the furthering of research into canine diseases and hereditary disorders of dogs and also organisations concerned with the welfare of dogs in need and those which aim to improve the quality of life of humans by promoting dogs as practical or therapeutic aids. The trust gives both ongoing and one-off grants.

At December 2003 the trust had assets of £1.2 million of which £900,000 was unrestricted. The trust's income amounted to £457,000, of which £439,000 was from donations. Grants totalled £212,000 and were divided into 'scientific and research project support' which received £154,000 and 'donations' totalling £58,000.

Animal Health Trust received a total of £65,000 (£40,000 for KC Genetics and £25,000 for epidemiology). Other large grants were £47,000 to University of Glasgow – genetics of cardiomyopathy and a total of £35,000 to University of Cambridge (£11,000 to Veterinary School Trust, £9,000 to genetics of hyperparathyroidism, £8,000 to genetics of PRA and £7,000 to Department of Clinical Medicine).

The largest non-research grant was £8,000 to Breeders' Helpline. Other larger donations included £7,500 to RVC Animal Care Trust, £5,200 to Battersea Dogs Home and £5,000 each to Canine Partners, Hearing Dogs for Deaf People, Dogs for the Disabled, Bath Cats and Dogs Home and Mid Antrim Animal Sanctuary. There were a further 11 smaller donations.

Exclusions The trust does not give grants directly to individuals; veterinary nurses can apply to the British Veterinary Nursing Association where bursaries are available. The trustees tend not to favour funding the costs of building work.

Applications In writing to the correspondent, including latest accounts. Please state clearly details of the costs for which you are requesting funding, and for what purpose and over what period the funding is required. The trustees meet three or four times a year.

The Nancy Kenyon Charitable Trust

General

£39,000 (2001/02)

Beneficial area UK.

c/o Mercer and Hole, Gloucester House, 72 London Road, St Albans, Hertfordshire AL1 1NS

Tel. 01727 869141 **Fax** 01727 869149

Correspondent R G Brown, Trustee

Trustees *C M Kenyon; R B Kenyon; R G Brown; L S Bee Phipps; S M Kenyon.*

CC Number 265359

Information available Accounts are on file at the Charity Commission.

General The trust makes grants primarily for people and causes known to the trustees.

In 2001/02 the trust's assets totalled around £1.3 million. It had an income totalling £41,000 and made grants totalling £39,000.

Grants for this year were £21,000 to Nancy Oldfield Trust, £3,000 to Cheltenham Youth for Christ, £1,000 each to Benjamin Foundation, Breakthrough Breast Cancer, Cheltenham Open Door, The Fifth Trust, Operation New World, Sense, Women's Health Concern and The Wynd Centre.

Exclusions No grants to individuals.

Applications In writing to the correspondent at any time. Applications for causes not known to the trustees are considered annually in December.

Kermaville Ltd

Jewish

£146,000 (2002/03)

Beneficial area UK.

5 Windus Road, London N16 6UT

Tel. 020 8880 8910

Correspondent Mr Sugarwhite

Trustee *L Rabinowitz.*

CC Number 266075

Information available Accounts were on file at the Charity Commission, but without a list of grants or a description of its grant-making policy.

General The trust makes grants to Jewish organisations and towards those concerned with general charitable purposes.

In 2002/03 the trust had assets of £389,000 and an income of £96,000. Grants totalled £146,000 with beneficiaries including Telz Academy Trust (£100,000), American Friends of Viznitz (£15,000), Bais Rochel D'Satmar (£12,000), Keren Tzedaka V'Chesed and Wlodowa Charity Trust (£5,000 each), BH Panovez (£3,500), Yetev Lev Jerusalem (£2,000), Midrash Shmuel (£1,900), Yeshivas Toras Moshe (£1,000) and Beis Brucha (£700).

Applications In writing to the correspondent.

E & E Kernkraut Charities Limited

General, education, Jewish

£174,000 (2001/02)

Beneficial area UK.

The Knoll, Fountayne Road, London N16 7EA

Tel. 020 8806 7947

Correspondent E Kernkraut, Chair

Trustees *E Kernkraut, Chair; Mrs E Kernkraut; Joseph Kernkraut; Jacob Kernkraut.*

CC Number 275636

Information available Accounts were on file at the Charity Commission, but without a list of grants.

General The trust states that it makes grants for educational, Jewish and other charitable purposes. It did not provide a list of grants with its accounts or further detail of its grant-making criteria, so we were unable to tell what type of educational charity is likely to be supported by this trust.

In 2003/04 the trust had an income of £225,000 and a total expenditure of £193,000. Further information for this year was not available.

In 2001/02 it had assets of £111,000 and received an income of £145,000, mainly from dontions. Grants exceeded the income at £174,000.

Applications In writing to the correspondent.

The Kessler Foundation

General, Jewish

£63,000 (2002/03)

Beneficial area UK.

The Jewish Chronicle, 25 Furnival Street, London EC4A 1JT

Tel. 020 7415 1500 **Fax** 020 7405 0278

Email kesslerfoundation@thejc.com

Correspondent Richard A Fass, Secretary

Trustees *Mrs J Jacobs; L Blackstone, Chair; R A Fass; Prof. M Geller; Lady Susan Gilbert; Mrs J F Mayers; P Morgenstern; E J Temko.*

CC Number 290759

Information available Full accounts provided by the trust.

General The foundation makes grants for general charitable causes, with particular emphasis on supporting Jewish organisations. Generally the trust will support relatively small institutions (with an income of less than £100,000 a year) which do not attract funds from the larger charities. In exceptional circumstances grants to individuals will be considered. The foundation's funds depend upon dividends from its shareholdings in the Jewish Chronicle and grants made by the newspaper. Grants generally range from £250 to £1,000 each, mostly at the lower end of this scale.

The foundation will assist organisations which may be devoted to:

- the advancement of Jewish religion, learning, education and culture
- the improvement of inter-faith, community and race relations, and the combating of prejudice
- the alleviation of the problems of minority and disadvantaged groups
- the protection, maintenance and monitoring of human rights
- the promotion of health and welfare
- the protection and preservation of records and objects with special significance to the Jewish and general community
- the encouragement of arts, literature and science including archaeology, natural history and protection of the environment with special reference to the Jewish community.

In 2002/03 the foundation had assets of £306,000 and an income of £26,000. Grants were made to 61 organisations totalling £63,000.

By far the largest grant was the £26,000 given to Festival of Jewish Arts and Culture. The next in size were £1,500 to The Jewish Museum, £1,300 to Jewish Book Week and £1,000 each to 12 organisations including AJEX, Bath Recital Artists Group, Association of Jewish Sixth Formers, Peace Child Israel, Spitalfields Centre and Small Communities Jewish Memorial Council.

Other grants included £900 to JCORE, £800 to Birmingham Jewish Youth Trust, £750 to British Friends of the Forgotten People Fund, Delamere Forest School and MAKOR, £500 each to Avigdor Primary School Charitable Trust, Barnet Multicultural Community Centre, Berkeley Street Club, Exiled Writers Ink!, Joshua Gilbert Rhabdomyosarcoma Appeal, Hull Jewish Community Centre, Menorah School PTA, North Manchester Jewish Youth Project, Tzivos Hasham Craft Workshops, £300 to Women's Rabbi's Conference and £250 to Bedford Council of Faiths.

Exclusions In general the foundation will not support the larger well-known charities with an income in excess of £100,000, and will not provide grants for social, medical and welfare projects which are the responsibility of local or national government.

Applications On a form available from the correspondent. The trustees meet at least twice a year in June and December. Applicants will be notified of decisions as soon as possible after then.

The Kidani Memorial Trust

Cancer related charities, research, welfare, education, training, guide dogs

£130,000 (2002)

Beneficial area UK and Japan.

Galsworthy & Stones, PO Box 145, Hawksford House, Caledonia Place, St Helier, Jersey JE4 8QP

Tel. 01534 836800 **Fax** 01534 836999

Email mail@galsworthy.com

Website www.galsworthy.com

Correspondent Peter Milner, Trustee

Trustees *DW Trustees Limited; Peter Milner; James Howes.*

Information available Information was provided by the trust.

General The trust was established in 1999 to support organisations specialising in cancer research, or those that support people who are disabled. In addition to funding research fellowships, the trust provides funds to organisations which provide information, care and support to people who have cancer and their families.

Grants included £11,000 to the Momiji Project, an Anglo-Japanese Young People's Exchange Programme. The contribution represented one third of the total cost incurred in funding a trip to Japan by a team of five wheelchair bound football players to compete in an Anglo-Japanese football tournament.

Applications In writing to the correspondent.

The King/ Cullimore Charitable Trust

General

£22,000 (2001/02) but see below

Beneficial area UK.

52 Ledborough Lane, Beaconsfield, Buckinghamshire HP9 2DF

Correspondent P A Cullimore, Trustee

Trustees *P A Cullimore; A G Cullimore; C J King; A G McKechnie.*

CC Number 1074928

Information available Accounts were on file at the Charity Commission.

General This trust has general charitable purposes and was registered with the Charity Commission on 30 March 1999. The trust stated in 2004 that its approximated assets for the year were £4.5 million and that they had an income of £185,000. No further details were available for this year and the following is taken from the 2001/02 accounts:

In 2001/02 it had assets amounting to £6.4 million. It had an income of £1.2 million, including a legacy of £1 million comprising 50,000 GlaxoSmithKline shares. Grants were made totalling £22,000, to Crisis and YMCA (£10,000 each) with the remainder going to one individual. The trust's report stated that since the year end a further £1 million had been donated to various charities and that the trustees were researching possible future beneficiaries.

Previous grant recipients have included British Red Cross, Child Bereavement Trust, National Asthma Campaign, National Society for Epilepsy, NSPCC and Ian Rennie Hospice.

Applications In writing to the correspondent.

Kinsurdy Charitable Trust

General in the UK

£55,000 (2001/02)

Beneficial area UK.

UBS Laing and Cruickshank, 1 Curzon Street, London W1J 5UB

Correspondent The Trustees

Trustees *R P Tullett; A H Bartlett.*

CC Number 1076085

Information available Information was provided by the trust.

General Registered in June 1999, in 2003/04 this trust had an income of £53,000 and a total expenditure of just £920.

In 2001/02 this trust had assets of £835,000 and an income of £139,000 including £82,000 from donations and £53,000 from investments.

Grants totalled £55,000 and were made to nine organisations: National Trust and RNLI (£10,000 each); and Age Concern, British Red Cross, Help the Aged, Marwell Preservation Trust, RABI, RNLI, Samaritans and WWF-UK (£5,000 each).

Applications In writing to the corresponent.

The Graham Kirkham Foundation

General

£124,000 (2001/02)

Beneficial area UK and Ireland.

1 Rockingham Way, Red House, Interchange, Adwick Le Street, Doncaster, South Yorkshire DN6 7NA

Tel. 01302 330365

Correspondent Barry Todhunter

Trustees *Lord G Kirkham; Lady P Kirkham; M Kirkham.*

CC Number 1002390

Information available Information was on file at the Charity Commission.

General The objectives of the foundation are:

- promotion or development of the study and/or appreciation of literature, art, music or science
- advancement of education of people of any age
- advancement of physical education among young people at school or university
- relief of poverty or hardship by providing financial assistance and accommodation for people who are disadvantaged
- relief of illness and disease through provision of treatment, financial assistance or accommodation
- support of research into treatment and prevention of illness
- relief of suffering of animals and birds through support or rescue homes, hospitals, sanctuaries and so on
- relief of poverty, hardship and distress amongst members of the armed services, and their dependants
- provision of support or protection for people with drugs problems, or in danger of becoming dependent on drugs
- provision of facilities for public recreation
- protection and preservation of buildings of architectural interest or sites of historical interest or natural beauty.

In 2002/03 the foundation had an income of just £3,500 and a total expenditure of £25,000.

These figures are much reduced from the previous year when the foundation had an income of £198,000 and grants totalled £124,000. By far the largest grant was £69,000 to Animal Health Trust. London Immunotherapy also received a grant for £5,000. The remaining £50,000 was distributed to 'outward bound' causes.

Applications In writing to the correspondent.

The Richard Kirkman Charitable Trust

General

£44,000 (2001/02)

Beneficial area UK, with a preference for Hampshire.

Ashton House, 12 The Precinct, Wincester Road, Chandlers Ford, Eastleigh, Hampshire F053 2GB

Tel. 023 8027 4555

Correspondent M Howson-Green, Trustee

Trustees *M Howson-Green; Mrs F O Kirkman.*

CC Number 327972

Information available Accounts were on file at the Charity Commission.

General This trust supports a range of causes with a preference for Hampshire, especially Southampton. The trustees have stated that they are considering financing various plans for alleviating drug addiction.

In 2001/02 the trust had an income of £42,000 and made grants totalling £44,000. Beneficiaries included: BLESMA (£3,500); Wessex Children's Hospice Trust, Aidis Trust and Salvation Army (£1,000 each); and Hampshire and Isle of Wight Association for the Deaf, Leukaemia Busters, NSPCC and Rose Road Association (£500 each).

Applications The trust carries out its own research for beneficiaries and does not respond to applications by post or telephone.

Kirschel Foundation

Jewish, medical

£76,000 (2001/02)

Beneficial area UK.

171 Wardour Street, London W1F 8WS

Tel. 020 7437 4372

Correspondent John Hoare, Trustee

Trustees *Laurence Grant Kirschel; John Hoare.*

CC Number 1067672

Information available Accounts were on file at the Charity Commission.

General This trust states its aims and objectives are 'to provide benefits to underprivileged persons, who may be either handicapped or lacking resources'. In practice this includes many Jewish organisations.

In 2001/02 the foundation had assets of £52,000 with an income of £125,000 and grants totalling £76,000.

Substantial grants were £20,000 to Friends of Ohr Somayach, £15,500 to Lubavitch Foundation of Scotland and £10,000 to Aish Hatorah UK.

Other beneficiaries include £9,000 to Notwood Ravenswood, £6,000 to Gateshead Academy for Torah Studies, £5,000 to British Friends of Ohr Chadash, £3,000 to Rabbi YY Peritz Charitable trust, £2,000 each to Festival of Jewish Arts and Culture and Life Neurological Reasearch trust, £1,000 to Palace for All.

Grants under £1,000 were to Lolev charitable trust, Marc Fisher trust, Cancer Research UK, North London Hospice, Youth Aliyah Child Rescue, IFAW, Jewish Blind and Disabled, Dyslexia Research trust, British Friends of Ohel Sarah and Friends of Ella & Ridley Jacobs House.

Applications In writing to the correspondent.

The Marina Kleinwort Charitable Trust

Arts

£57,000 (2002/03)

Beneficial area UK.

PO Box 191, 10 Fenchurch Street, London EC3M 3LB

Tel. 020 7475 6246

Correspondent The Secretary

Trustees *Miss Marina Rose Kleinwort, Chair; David James Roper Robinson; Miss Zenaida Yanowsky.*

CC Number 1081825

Information available Full accounts were provided by the trust.

General In 2002/03 it had assets of £1.2 million and an income of £51,000. Grants totalling £57,000 were made to six organisations, four of which were also supported in the previous year.

Interestingly the two new beneficiaries received the largest grants. These were £25,000 to Almeida Theatre Co Ltd and £16,000 to Fondation & Faveur De L'Art Choregraphique. Other beneficiaries were Rambert Dance Company (£10,000), Endymion Ensemble (£3,000), Royal Ballet School (£2,500) and Ackroyd Trust (£1,000).

Exclusions No grants to individuals.

Applications In writing to the correspondent.

The Kohn Foundation

Scientific and medical projects, the arts – particularly music, education, Jewish charities

£78,000 (2000)

Beneficial area UK.

100 Fetter Lane, London EC4A 1BN

Correspondent Dr R Kohn, Chair to the Trustees

Trustees *Dr Ralph Kohn, Chair; Zahava Kohn; Anthony A Forwood.*

CC Number 1003951

Information available Full accounts were on file at the Charity Commission.

General The foundation supports advancement of scientific and medical research, promotion of the arts – particularly music, general educational projects and Jewish charities.

In 2001 the foundation had an income of £140,000 with an expenditure of £367,000. No further information was available.

In 2000 grants were made totalling £78,000. By far the largest grant was £145,000 to Monteverdi Choir and Orchestra Ltd. Other large grants were £50,000 to Royal Society and £25,000 to Wigmore Hall International Song Contest.

Other grants listed in the accounts were £10,000 each to National Osteoporosis Society and Vega Science Trust, £6,000 to Hasmonean High School, £5,000 each to Jewish Music Institute and Liver Research Trust, £2,000 to Rudolf Kempe Society, £1,300 to United Jewish Israel Appeal and £1,000 each to Collel Chibath Yerushalayim and North West London Jewish Day School. Smaller grants totalled £8,400.

Applications In writing to the correspondent.

The Kreditor Charitable Trust

Jewish, welfare, education

£68,000 (2002)

Beneficial area UK, with preferences for London and North East England.

Gerald Kreditor & Co., Chartered Accountants, Hallswater House, 1 Hallswater Road, London NW11 0DH

Tel. 020 8209 1535 **Fax** 020 8209 1923

Correspondent P M Kreditor, Trustee

Trustees *P M Kreditor; Merle Kreditor.*

CC Number 292649

Information available Accounts are on file at the Charity Commission, but only up to 1998/99.

General In 2002 the trust had assets of £56,000 with an income of £48,000 and grants totalling £68,000. Unfortunately no grants list was available for this period.

In previous years, grants have been mostly for less than £100 and have been given mainly to Jewish organisations working in education and social and medical welfare. Beneficiaries have been scattered across London and the north-east of England. The vast majority of grants were for less than £100. Recipients have included: Fordeve Ltd, London Academy of Jewish Studies, Jerusalem Ladies Society, NW London Talmudical College, Ravenswood, Academy for Rabbinical Research, British Friends of Israel War Disabled, Kosher Meals on Wheels, Jewish Marriage Council and Jewish Care. Non-Jewish organisations supported included RNID, UNICEF UK and British Diabetic Association.

Applications In writing to the correspondent.

The Neil Kreitman Foundation

Culture, education, health, welfare

£224,000 (2001/02)

Beneficial area UK and Israel.

Citroen Wells (Chartered Accountants), Devonshire House, 1 Devonshire Street, London W1W 5DR

Tel. 020 7304 2000

Correspondent Eric Charles, Trustee

Trustees *N R Kreitman; Mrs S I Kreitman; G C Smith.*

CC Number 267171

Information available Full accounts were on file at the Charity Commission.

General The foundation supports cultural, educational, health and welfare organisations.

In 2001/02 it an income of £249,000 and a total expenditure of £263,000. Grants were made totalling £224,000.

The largest grant was £137,000 to Ashmolean Museum at Oxford University, which was promised in December 1998 eight annual grants of £100,000 each.

Other large grants were £30,000 to British Library, £15,000 to Ancient India and Iran Trust, £14,000 to Corpus Inscriptionium Iranicarum and £10,000 each to British Museum, Onaway Trust, Release Legal Emergency and Drugs

Service, SE Cross College Development Fund, and Victoria and Albert Museum.

Other beneficiaries included Hindu Kush Conservation Association and International PEN Foundation (£5,000 each), Royal Numismatic Society (£4,000), British Heart Foundation, NSPCC and Save the Children Fund (£2,000 each) and ApTibeT and Henry Spink Foundation (£1,000 each).

The only three beneficiaries not also supported in the previous received the smallest grants. They were Anti-Slavery International and Royal National College for the Blind (£1,000 each) and School of Oriental and African Studies (£500).

Exclusions No grants to individuals.

Applications In writing to the correspondent.

The Kyte Charitable Trust

Medical, disadvantaged and socially isolated people

About £90,000 (2002/03)

Beneficial area UK.

Business Design Centre, 52 Upper Street, London N1 0QH

Tel. 020 7390 7777

Correspondent The Trustees

Trustees *D M Kyte; T M Kyte; A H Kyte.*

CC Number 1035886

Information available Information was on file at the Charity Commission.

General The trust supports organisations benefiting medical professionals and research workers. Support may go to organisations working with at- risk groups, and people who are disadvantaged by poverty or socially isolated.

In 2002/03 the trust had an income of £102,000 and a total expenditure of £92,000. Further information from this year was not availlable.

In the previous year, the trust had an expenditure of £85,000, all of which was distributed in grants.

Applications In writing to the correspondent.

The Christopher Laing Foundation

Social welfare, environment, culture, health and medicine throughout the UK; general in Hertfordshire

£234,000 (2001/02)

Beneficial area UK, with an interest in Hertfordshire.

c/o Ernst & Young, 400 Capability Green, Luton LU1 3LU

Tel. 01582 643128

Correspondent Mrs Margaret R White, Senior Trust Consultant

Trustees *Donald G Stradling; Peter S Jackson; Christopher M Laing; Diana C Laing.*

CC Number 278460

Information available Full accounts were provided by the trust, at the cost of £10.

General In 2001/02 the trust had assets of £4.6 million, which generated an income of £171,000. Management, administration and investment manager's charges totalled £23,000. Grants were made totalling £234,000. Of this, £40,000 was given to Charities Aid Foundation for disbursement amongst smaller charities. Other grants were broken down as follows:

Animal welfare – one grant of £3,000
This went to Royal Veterinary College Animal Care Trust.

Child & youth – six grants totalling £57,000
The Lords' Taverners and NPFA both received £25,000. Other beneficiaries were Youth Centre (£3,500), Stevenage Sea Cadets (£2,000), Make-A-Wish Foundation (£1,000) and Award Events Ltd (£880).

Cultural & environmental – three grants totalling £6,500
These went to Bunbury ESCA Festival (£5,000), Hertfordshire Gardens Trust (£1,200) and Fund for the Future (£250).

Health and medicine – seven grants totalling £109,000
The largest grant during the year was £102,000 to Tyingham Foundation, which also received a loan of £300,000. Other grants went to Marie Curie Cancer Care (£2,500), St John Ambulance (£2,000), GUTS and Rowan Breast Cancer Unit (£1,000 each), Diabetes UK (£250) and ICRF Trading Ltd (£150).

Social welfare – 13 grants totalling £19,000
High Sheriff's Fund received £10,000. Other grants were £2,500 to Hertfordshire Action on Disability, £2,000 to Army Benevolent Fund, £1,500 to Garden House Hospice, £500 to Luton Women's Aid and £250 each to nine organisations including Hertfordshire Hearing Advisory Service, Isabel Hospice, Relate, Stevenage Community Trust and Watford New Hope Trust.

Exclusions Donations are only made to registered charities.

Applications In writing to the correspondent.

The Martin Laing Foundation

General

£93,000 (2001/02)

Beneficial area UK and worldwide.

c/o Ernst & Young, 400 Capability Green, Luton LU1 3LU

Tel. 01582 643128 **Fax** 01582 643006

Correspondent Mrs Margaret R White, Senior Trust Consultant

Trustees *Sir John Martin Laing; Donald Stradling; Brian O Chilver; Edward Charles Laing.*

CC Number 278461

Information available Full accounts were provided by the foundation, at the cost of £10.

General This trust makes a large number of small grants, given through the Charities Aid Foundation. Most of the support is given to organisations and projects with which the trustees have a personal connection. A small number of larger grants are also made.

In 2002/03 the foundation had an income of £172,000 and a total expenditure of £221,000.

In the previous year it had assets of £4.3 million, which generated an income of £195,000. Management and administration charges totalled £17,000, while the investment manager's charges totalled £9,100. Grants were made to 69 organisations totalling £93,000.

£30,000 was distributed through CAF to 62 organisations, which received between £75 and £10,000 each. Two organisations of which Sir Martin Laing is a vice president were among the recipients of the seven grants made directly by the trust, which were broken down as follows:

- Cultural and environmental – Ponds Conservation Trust received £13,000.
- Education and training – Princess Helena College received £10,000.
- Health and medicine – Three grants were made; £10,000 to Action for ME, £5,500 to Westminster Pastoral Foundation and £5,000 to Macmillan Cancer Relief.
- Overseas aid – £10,000 to British Executive Service Overseas.
- Social welfare – £10,000 to Business in the Community.

Applications The trust states: 'The trustees receive an enormous and increasing number of requests for help. Unfortunately the trustees are only able to help a small proportion of the requests and consequently they limit their support to those charities where they have a personal connection or interest in their activities.'

The David Laing Foundation

Youth, disability, mental health, the arts, general

£65,000 (2002)

Beneficial area Worldwide.

The Studio, Mackerye End, Harpenden, Hertfordshire AL5 5DR

Correspondent David E Laing, Trustee

Trustees *David Eric Laing; John Stuart Lewis; Richard Francis Dudley Barlow; Frances Mary Laing.*

CC Number 278462

Information available Information was provided by the trust.

General This trust has general charitable purposes, with emphasis on youth, disability, mental health and the arts. It makes large grants to a wide and varied number of organisations as well as donating smaller grants through Charities Aid Foundation.

In 2002 the foundation had assets of £349,000 and an income of £122,000 with grants totalling £65,000.

The largest grants were £4,000 to London Pro Arte Orchestra, £3,500 to Lord Taverners and £2,500 to Youth Sport UK Charitable Trust.

Other grants include £2,100 to Game Conservancy Trust, £2,000 each to Airshaft Trust, Ataxia Telangiectasia Society, Cheltenham Arts Festivals Ltd, Hertfordshire Gardens Trust and Sports Aid Trust, £1,500 each to International Students House, Greensong Productions and Mind in St Albans District and £1,000 each to Sparks Charity, Send a Cow Ltd, Royal Scottish Academy of Music and Drama, National Sports Medicine Institute of the United Kingdom and Flamstead Pony Club.

Exclusions No grants to individuals.

Applications In writing to the correspondent. Trustees meet in March, June, October and December, although applications are reviewed weekly. Due to the large number of applications received, and the relatively small number of grants made, the trust is not able to respond to all requests.

Laing's Charitable Trust

General

£190,000 to organisations (2003)

Beneficial area UK.

The Waterfront, Elstree Road, Elstree, Herts WD6 3BS

Tel. 020 8236 8821

Email michael.a.hamilton@laing.com

Correspondent Michael Hamilton, Secretary

Trustees *C Laing; Sir Martin Laing; D C Madden; R I Sumner; G D Gibson; D Whipp.*

CC Number 236852

Information available Annual report provided by the trust.

General 'The first priority of the trust is to support existing and former employees of John Laing plc who face hardship. The second is to make general donations to organisations, not individuals, and in particular to support those organisations dealing with homelessness, disadvantaged young people, education and the environment'.

In 2003 the trust had an income of £1.4 million. The trust made grants totalling £190,000 to organisations, with a further £814,000 distributed to 850 individuals whom were either current or former employees of John Laing plc.

The largest grant of £20,000 was given to The Children's Society. Other beneficiaries included: Atlantic College (£15,000); Hertfordshire Groundwork (£13,000); CEDC/Education Extra and Homeless Link (£10,000 each); Business in the Community and Emmaus (£7,500 each); and Church Action on Homelessness, CRASH and Groundswell (£5,000 each).

Exclusions No grants to individuals (other than to Laing employees and/or their dependants).

Applications In writing to the correspondent. The trust says that all applications are acknowledged.

The Lambert Charitable Trust

Health, welfare, Jewish, arts

£92,000 (2002/03)

Beneficial area UK and Israel.

Mercer & Hole, 72 London Road, St Albans, Hertfordshire AL1 1NS

Tel. 020 7353 1597 **Fax** 020 7353 1748

Correspondent Mrs Lynne Wright

Trustees *M Lambert; Prof. H P Lambert; H Alexander-Passe; Jane Lambert; O E Lambert.*

CC Number 257803

Information available Full accounts were on file at the Charity Commission.

General This trust usually uses half of its funds supporting Jewish and Israeli causes and half for medical, welfare and arts causes.

In 2002/03 the trust had assets of £2 million with an income of £91,000 and grants totalling £92,000.

The largest grants were £12,000 to Jewish Care, £5,000 to New Horizon Youth Club and £2,000 to Meningitis Research Foundation.

Grants of £1,000 were awarded to Boys Town Jerusalem, British Council of the Shaare Zedek Medical Centre, Friends of the Hebrew University of Jerusalem, Operation Wheelchairs Committee,

Sanhedria Children's Home & Educational Centre, Camp Aguda, Food Line, Jewish Aid Committee, Jewish Marriage Council, Kisharon Day School, London School of Jewish Studies, Action for Addiction, Action Research, Anxiety Care, ASPIRE, Association for Post natal Illness, Breast Cancer Campaign, Children Nationwide, Defeating Deafness, East Anglia's Children's Hospices, Friends of War Memorials, Headway, ICAN, KIDS and Multiple Sclerosis Society.

Grants of less than £1,000 were awarded to Young Vic Theatre Company, Winged Fellowship, Well Being, Victim Support, 3H Fund, St. Giles Trust, St Christophers, Sports Aid, Side by Side, Royal London Society for the Blind, No Panic, Action for Kids, Aids Trust, ARP, British Blind Sport, Fight for Sight, British EMUNAH, Camp Gan Israel, Anne Frank Trust UK, Jewish Children's Holidays Fund and Jewish Child's Day.

Applications In writing to the correspondent before July for payment by 1 September.

Lancashire Environmental Fund

Environmental

£301,000 (2003)

Beneficial area UK, particularly Lancashire.

The Barn, Berkeley Drive, Bamber Bridge, Preston, Lancashire PR5 6BY

Tel. 01772 317247/ 324129 **Fax** 01772 628849

Email lef@lancswt.cix.co.uk

Website www.lancsenvfund.org.uk

Correspondent Karen Gardener, Administration Officer

Trustees *Brian Johnson; Peter Greijenberg; David Tattersall; John Leaver.*

CC Number 1074983

Information available Annual review was supplied by the trust, on a CD-Rom.

General This fund was established in June 1998 from a partnership of four organisations: SITA (Lancashire) Ltd, Lancashire County Council, The Wildlife Trust for Lancashire, Manchester and North Merseyside and Community Futures. The fund enables community groups and organisations throughout the country to take advantage of the funding opportunities offered by landfill tax credits. It achieves this by supporting organisations and projects based within Lancashire, or nationwide research or development with a relevance to Lancashire, which are managed by an Enrolled Environmental Body, as recognised by Entrust.

Areas of support are:

- reclamation of contaminated land, remediation and restoration
- prevention or removal of pollution
- providing and maintaining public amenities and parks
- provision, conservation, restoration or enhancement of a natural habitat, maintenance or recovery of a species
- repair, restoration and maintenance of religious and historical buildings.

In 2003 it had assets of £1.6 million and an income of £1.5 million. This was well down on the previous year, when the total income was over £3 million. Grants were made totalling £301,000, broken down as follows:

Community facility improvements	11%
Environmental education	1%
General environmental improvements	18%
Habitat creation and management	17%
Bio-diversity	8%
Parks, gardens and open spaces	17%
Play areas and recreational facilities	26%
Ponds, canals and rivers	2%

Beneficiaries included Leisure in Hyndburn to replace a dated athletics track (£50,000), Groundwork East Lancashire for the development of a demostration garden which provided training for local people (£30,000), Wildfowl and Wetlands Trust for a nature trail at Martin Mere (£17,000), Euxton PCC for landscaping of a seated area and inclusion of disability parking and Lord's House Farm for development of a quarry (£7,500 each), Wildlife Trust for Lancashire Manchester and North Merseyside and Wildfowl and Wetlands Trust for a joint project to improve the habitat of Jenning's proboscis worms (£7,000), and Wildlife Trust for Lancashire Manchester and North Merseyside for developments at an environmental education centre (£6,500).

Exclusions All projects must satisfy at least one objective of the Landfill Tax Credit Scheme. For more information about the scheme contact Entrust, the regulatory body, by visiting their website at www.entrust.org.uk or telephoning 0161 972 0044.

Applications On a form available from the correspondent or the website. Completed forms should contain all possible relevant material including maps, photographs, plans, etc. if relevant. The board meets quarterly.

Staff are willing to have informal discussions before an application is made. Potential applicants are strongly advised to visit the website before contacting the trust.

Land Aid Charitable Trust

Homelessness, escape from poverty

£50,000 available (2004/05)

Beneficial area England.

11–15 Farm Street, London W1J 5RS

Website www.landaid.org

Correspondent The Grants Committee

Trustees *Abi Broom; Neil Richmond; Steven Ossack.*

CC Number 295157

Information available Detailed information was provided by the trust.

General Land Aid's mission is to support homeless people by raising funds to help:

- provide accommodation
- assist with refurbishment projects
- run training and life skills programme
- give start-up funding for schemes that might not otherwise get of the ground.

In 2004/05 it wished to distribute £50,000 to appropriate specialist agencies. Applications are invited for awards ranging from £1,000 to £50,000. The trustees will then consider whether to award several grants of different sizes or a single grant for the full amount available for an exceptional project.

Previous grants have included £40,000 to Look Ahead Housing and Care for the refurbishment of fire-damaged rooms, £10,000 to St John's Hackney to provide day centre services to people disadvantaged by poverty and £5,000 each to CRASH to support a training kitchen to allow people who are homeless to develop skills to care for themselves and Homeless in Barnet to prevent the closure of a local facility.

Exclusions No grants to individuals.

Applications In writing to the correspondent, setting out the aims, objectives, outputs and outcomes of the project in no more than 500 words.

Applications should be submitted between 1 November and 31 December each year. They must be marked 'application for funding' on the envelope.

The Langdale Trust

Social welfare, Christian, medical, general

About £100,000 (2002/03)

Beneficial area Worldwide, but with a special interest in Birmingham.

c/o Cobbetts Solicitors, One Colmore Square, Birmingham B4 6AJ

Tel. 0121 236 4477

Correspondent M J Woodward, Trustee

Trustees *T R Wilson; Mrs T Whiting; M J Woodward.*

CC Number 215317

Information available Information was provided by the trust.

General The trust was established in 1960 by the late Antony Langdale Wilson. There is a preference for local charities in the Birmingham area and those in the fields of social welfare and health, especially with a Christian context.

In 2002/03 the trust had an income of £119,000 and a total expenditure of £114,000. Grants probably totalled around £100,000.

In the previous year grants were made totalling £106,000. Beneficiaries included £8,000 to Leprosy Mission, £7,000 to Tree Aid, £6,000 each to Barnardos – Birmingham and Save the Children, £3,000 each to Help the Aged, Mercy Ships, Macmillan Cancer Relief – Birmingham, National Playing Fields Association, National Trust for the Neptune campaign, Oxfam, Relate – Birmingham and St Mary's Hospice and £2,000 each to Field Lane Foundation and Rainforest Concern.

Applications In writing to the correspondent. The trustees meet in September/October.

The Richard Langhorn Trust

Sport for children

£68,000 (2001)

Beneficial area UK and overseas.

Stoop Memorial Ground, Langhorn Drive, Twickenham, Middlesex TW2 7SX

Tel. 020 8410 6030 **Fax** 020 8410 6014

Email polly@rltrust.org

Website www.rltrust.org

Correspondent Polly Wiseman

Trustees *S Langhorn; P Winterbottom.*

CC Number 1046332

Information available Information was provided by the trust and available on its website.

General The trust makes grants towards sports charities for the benefit of children only, particularly in the areas of rugby, sailing, basketball and skiing.

In 2001 it had assets of £181,000 and an income of £27,000. Grants totalled £68,000.

Beneficiaries have included Calvert Trust for wheelchair-accessible self-catering chalets at an outdoor activities centre for people with disabilities, Future Hope for work with street children in Calcutta, Great Britain Wheelchair Basketball Association for the young persons' team, Meridian Trust for two sailing boats for children from disadvantaged areas and Rugby in the Community for various projects.

Applications In writing, or by e-mail, to the correspondent.

The Langley Charitable Trust

Christian, general

£115,000 (2002)

Beneficial area UK, with a preference for the West Midlands, and worldwide.

Wheatmoor Farm, 301 Tamworth Road, Sutton Coldfield, West Midlands B75 6JP

Tel. 0121 308 0165

Correspondent The Trustees

Trustees *J P Gilmour; Mrs S S Gilmour.*

CC Number 280104

Information available Accounts were on file at the Charity Commission, but without a grants list.

General The trust makes grants to evangelical Christian organisations and to other charities in the fields of welfare, medicine and health. It makes grants in the UK and worldwide, but appears to have a small preference for the West Midlands. It operates My Word, a trading book shop and rents out the first floor of its offices to other charities to supplement its income.

In 2002 it had assets of £2.9 million and an income of £722,000. Grants were made totalling £115,000. As well as providing grants totalling £111,000 to institions, the trustees also helped individuals by giving £3,400.

Exclusions No grants to animal or bird charities.

Applications In writing to the correspondent. 'The trustees only reply where they require further information and so on. No telephone calls nor correspondence will be entered into concerning any proposed or declined applications.'

The Lanvern Foundation

Education and health, especially relating to children

£30,000 (2003)

Beneficial area UK.

P O Box 34475, London W6 9YB

Tel. 020 8741 2930

Correspondent J C G Stancliffe, Trustee

Trustees *J C G Stancliffe; A H Isaacs.*

CC Number 295846

Information available Information was provided by the trust.

General The foundation was established in 1986. The trustees state that it supports registered charities working primarily in the fields of education and health, with particular emphasis on children. There are never any grants to individuals.

In 2003 it had an income of £56,000 and an expenditure of £31,000. Grants totalled £30,000. Beneficiaries included Connect, Jet, Ican, Ochre, Peper Harow

Foundation and Winchester Young Carers.

Exclusions Absolutely no grants to individuals.

Applications In writing to the correspondent.

The R J Larg Family Charitable Trust

Education, health, medical research, arts – particularly music

About £100,000 (1999/2000)

Beneficial area UK but generally Scotland, particularly Tayside.

Messrs Thorntons WS, 50 Castle Street, Dundee DD1 3RU

Correspondent N Barclay

Trustees *R W Gibson; D A Brand; Mrs S A Stewart.*

SC Number SC004946

Information available Information was provided by the trust.

General Unfortunately we were unable to contact the trust and this entry is repeated from previous research.

The trust has an annual income of approximately £127,000. Grants, which totalled about £100,000 in 1999/2000, ranged between £250 and £6,000 and were given to a variety of organisations.

These include organisations concerned with cancer research and other medical charities, youth organisations, university students' associations and amateur musical groups.

Beneficiaries of larger grants included: High School, Dundee (£6,000 for the cadet force and £5,000 for the Larg Scholarship Fund), Whitehall Theatre Trust (£4,000), Macmillan Cancer Relief – Dundee and Sense Scotland Children's Hospice (£2,500 each) and £2,000 to Rachel House.

Exclusions Grants are not available for individuals.

Applications In writing to the correspondent. Trustees meet to consider grants in February and August.

Largsmount Ltd

Jewish

£237,000 (2000/01)

Beneficial area UK and overseas.

Cohen Arnold & Co., New Burlington House, 1075 Finchley Road, London NW11 0PU

Tel. 020 8731 0777 **Fax** 020 8731 0778

Correspondent Mrs I R Kaufman, Trustee

Trustees *Z M Kaufman; Mrs I R Kaufman; S Kaufman.*

CC Number 280509

Information available Accounts were on file at the Charity Commission.

General This trust supports Orthodox Jewish charities. In 2002/03 it had an income of £618,000 and a total expenditure of £475,000. Further information for this year was not available.

In 2000/01 the trust had assets of £2.4 million and had an income of £409,000. Out of a total expenditure of £294,000, grants to 40 organisations were made totalling £237,000.

The largest donations were £95,000 to Yetev Lev Jerusalem and £45,000 to Shaarei Zion Turda. A further 14 grants were made for £1,000 or more including those to A & H Pillar Charitable Trust (£27,000), Dushinsky Trust (£25,000), Gateshead Foundation for Torah (£14,000), Tomechi Torah Family Relief (£4,100), Gateshead Jewish High School (£1,800), UTA (£1,400), and Bobov Charities and Kimche de Pische (£1,000 each).

Applications In writing to the correspondent.

Rachel & Jack Lass Charities Ltd

Jewish, children, education, medical research

£67,000 (2002/03)

Beneficial area England, Scotland and Wales.

New Burlington House, 1075 Finchley Road, London NW11 0PU

Tel. 020 8446 8431 **Fax** 020 8446 6019

Correspondent Mrs R Lass, Governor

Trustees *Leonard Lass; Rachelle Lass; Sally Lass.*

CC Number 256514

Information available Full accounts were on file at the Charity Commission.

General We were advised that the trust, which in 2002/03 had an income of £285,000, is in the process of being closed down. However, it is the trustees' intention to establish a new, similar, trust in 2004 for details of which you are asked to contact Leonard Lass. Meanwhile, we repeat below the previous entry for this trust.

The trust gives primarily to Jewish charities, preferring those involved with children, education and medical research.

In 2000/01 it had an income of £82,000, mostly in donations received from four investment companies one of the trustees is the director of. Grants were made totalling £171,000. At the year end, assets totalled £167,000.

The largest grants were £36,000 to Yeshiva Horomo Talmudical College, £20,000 each to Friends of Ilan and Ravenswood Foundation, £15,000 to Tevini Ltd and £10,000 each to Gevurath Ari Torah Academy Trust and Yesodey Hatdlah

Other beneficiaries listed in the accounts were Beth Hamedrash Ponovez, Minister Centre and Yad Eliezer (£5,000 each), United Synagogue (£2,700), Mogen David Adom (£2,000), World Jewish Relief (£1,200) and Jewish Care (£600). A total of £19,000 was given in smaller grants.

Exclusions No grants to individuals for welfare or educational purposes. Only registered charities are considered.

Applications In writing to the correspondent. Grants are paid annually during July/August/September.

The Laufer Charitable Trust

Jewish

About £100,000 (2003)

Beneficial area UK.

15 Leys Gardens, Cockfosters, Herts EN4 9NA

Tel. 020 8449 3432 **Fax** 020 8449 3432

Correspondent S W Laufer, Trustee

Trustees *S W Laufer; Mrs D D Laufer.*

CC Number 275375

Information available Accounts are on file at the Charity Commission only up to 1998/99.

General The trust makes grants mainly to Jewish organisations and has a list of charities which it has a long-term commitment to and supports annually or twice a year. It rarely adds new charities to the list.

In 2003 the trust had assets of £1.3 million with an income of £100,000 and an expenditure of £103,000. Unfortunatley a grants list and grant expenditure were unavailable for this period.

Exclusions No grants to individuals, as grants are only made to registered charities.

Applications New beneficiaries are only considered by the trust in exceptional circumstances, as the income is already allocated for some years to come. In view of this it is suggested that no applications be made.

The Lauffer Family Charitable Foundation

Jewish, general

£138,000 (2002/03)

Beneficial area Commonwealth countries, Israel and USA.

18 Norrice Lea, London N2 0RE

Email bethlauffer@lineone.net

Correspondent J S Lauffer, Trustee

Trustees *Mrs R R Lauffer; J S Lauffer; G L Lauffer; R M Lauffer.*

CC Number 251115

Information available Full accounts were on file at the Charity Commission.

General This trust has general charitable purposes, supporting Jewish causes in the Commonwealth, Israel and USA.

In 2002/03 it had assets of £3.1 million, which generated an income of £145,000. Grants were made totalling £138,000.

Grants were broken down as follows:

Education	£84,000
Religious Activites	£19,000
Environment	£1,100
Welfare and care of children and fFamilies	£9,300
Medical Healthcare	£18,000
Recreation and culture	£6,000

Grant beneficiaries included Spiro Ark (£15,000), British Friends of Sarah Herzog Memorial Hospital (£10,000), Menorah Foundation School (£7,500), Hasmoneon High School (£5,500), British Friends of Schvut Ami, Hendon Adath Y Isroel Congregation, Jewish Learning Exchange and United Jewish Israel Appeal (£5,000 each), United Synagogue (£3,500) and SPNI UK (£3,000).

Exclusions No support for individuals.

Applications In writing to the correspondent; applications are considered once a year.

The Mrs F B Laurence Charitable Trust

Social welfare, medical, disability, environment

£91,000 (2002/03)

Beneficial area Worldwide.

PO Box 28927, London SW14 7WL

Correspondent The Trustees

Trustees *M Tooth; G S Brown; D A G Sarre.*

CC Number 296548

Information available Information was provided by the trust.

General The trust produces guidelines which state: 'Our priority is for the care and/or improvement of conditions of the disadvantaged members of society within the United Kingdom or those overseas to whom the United Kingdom owes a duty of care.

'We mainly support charities that are known to the Trustees, or are established in their field and have a good track record. We do, however, consider small innovative charities with a hands on approach, even if their work may be primarily devoted to a particular locality, or if they are likely to provide a model for wider application.'

This trust gives for general charitable purposes, including many service, medical and welfare charities as well as hospices and environmental groups.

In 2002/03 the trust had assets of £2 million, which generated an income of £81,000. Grants were made totalling £91,000. Management and administration expenses were high at £16,000, including a payment of £12,600 to a firm in which one of the trustees is a partner. Whilst wholly legal, these editors always regret such payments unless, in the words of the Charity Commission, 'there is no realistic alternative'.

Five beneficiaries received grants of £2,500 and beneficiaries included BASIL, Macmillan Cancer Relief and Railway Children. All other grants were for £1,000 or less.

Exclusions No support for individuals. The following applications are unlikely to be considered:

- appeals for endowment or sponsorship
- overseas projects, unless overseen by the charity's own fieldworkers
- maintenance of buildings or landscape
- provision of work or materials that are the responsibility of the state
- where administration expenses, in all their guises, are considered by the trustees to be excessive
- where the fundraising costs in the preceding year have not resulted in an increase in the succeeding years' donations in excess of these costs.

Applications In writing to the correspondent, including the latest set of accounts, as filed with the Charity Commission. The guidelines state: 'Write to us on not more than two sides of A4 paper with the following information:

- who you are
- what you do
- what distinguishes your work from others in your field
- where applicable describe the project that the money you are asking for is going towards and include a business plan/budget
- what funds have already been raised and how
- how much are you seeking from us
- how do you intend to measure the potential benefits of your project or work as a whole.

Trustees usually meet in April and November. Please submit your application by 1 February for the April meeting and by 1 August for the October meeting.

To save on our administration costs, we will only notify the successful applicants.'

The Kathleen Laurence Trust

Heart disease, arthritis, children with disabilities

£63,000 (2002/03)

Beneficial area UK.

Trustee Department, Coutts & Co, P O Box 1236, 6 High St, Chelmsford, Essex CM1 1BQ

Tel. 020 7753 1000 **Fax** 020 7663 6794

Correspondent David Breach, Assistant Trust Manager

Trustee *Coutts & Co.*

CC Number 296461

Information available Full accounts were provided by the trust.

General Donations are given to a wide range of institutions, particularly favouring smaller organisations and those concerned with the treatment and care of individuals and research of heart diseases and arthritis. Organisations concerned with children who are mentally or physically disabled are also considered.

In 2002/03 it had assets of £2.4 million, which generated an income of £56,000. Grants were made to 55 organisations totalling £63,000.

The largest were £9,700 to Battersea Dogs Home, £4,300 each to British Heart Foundation, Elizabeth Finn Trust, Mencap and NSPCC, £2,700 each to Arthritis and Rheumatism and Cancer Research Fund, £2,300 to Selby District Peter Pan Nursery, £1,600 to Arthritis Research Campaign, £1,300 to Wingate Spec Children's Trust and £1,000 to Headway South Bedfordshire.

Smaller grants included £760 each to Bobath Children's Therapy – Wales, Hackney Quest and Martha Trust, £750 each to Association of Wheelchair Children, Children in Crisis, High Blood Pressure Foundation and Mental Health Foundation, £500 each to Age Concern, Barnardos, Children's Transplant Foundation, Lillian Faithfull Homes, Sense, Tiny Tim Centre and Wessex Autistic Society and £250 to Juvenile Diabetes Research.

Exclusions No donations are made for running costs, management expenses or to individuals.

Applications In writing to the correspondent. Trustees meet in January and June.

The Law Society Charity

Law and justice, worldwide

£209,000 to unconnected charities (2002/03)

Beneficial area Worldwide.

113 Chancery Lane, London WC2A 1PL

Tel. 020 7320 5905

Correspondent Bill Bilimoria

Trustee *The Law Society Trustees Ltd.*

CC Number 268736

Information available Full accounts were on file at the Charity Commission.

General As the name suggests, this trust is concerned with causes connected to the legal profession, particularly in advancing legal education and access to legal knowledge. Organisations protecting people's legal rights and lawyers' welfare are also supported, as are law-related projects from charities without an identifiable legal connection.

In 2002/03 the trust had assets of £1.9 million and an income of £2.1 million, including a donation of £1 million from The Law Society of England and Wales. These funds and more were returned to The Law Society, in a grant of £1.1 million for educational purposes. Donations were also made to 14 unconnected organisations, totalling £209,000.

The largest grants were: £78,000 to Solicitors' Benevolent Association, £60,000 to Citizenship Foundation, £18,000 to LawCare Limited and £15,000 to BAILII. Other grants included £6,000 to Fair Trials Abroad, £5,900 to Justice, £5,100 to Book Aid International, £5,000 each to Capital Cases Charitable Trust and Paddington Law Centre, £3,750 to VCC, £3,000 each to Family Rights Group and Legal Action Group and £2,300 to Incorporated Council of Law Reporting.

Applications In writing to the correspondent. Applications are considered at quarterly trustees' meetings, usually held in April, July, September and December.

The Edgar E Lawley Foundation

Older people, disability, children

£214,000 (2003/04)

Beneficial area UK, with a preference for the West Midlands.

Hollyoak, 1 White House Drive, Barnt Green, Birmingham B45 8HF

Tel. 0121 445 3536 **Fax** 0121 445 3536

Email philipjcooke@aol.com

Correspondent Philip J Cooke, Trustee

Trustees *F S Jackson, Chair; Mrs M D Heath; J H Cooke; Mrs G V H Hilton; P J Cooke; Mrs E E Sutcliffe.*

CC Number 201589

Information available Accounts were provided by the trust.

General The trust's primary objects are 'the making of grants to charitable bodies for provision of medical care and services to children and the aged, the advancement of medicine and for educational purposes'. There is a preference for the west Midlands.

In 2003/04 it had assets of £3.1 million, which generated an income of £148,000. Grants were made to 92 organisations totalling £214,000. Administration costs were very low at just £2,100.

Beneficiaries in the west Midlands included Birmingham Habitat for Humanity, Birmingham Rathbone, Birmingham Young Volunteers, Castel Froma – Leamington Spa, Compton Hospice – Wolverhampton, Redditch Association for the Blind, Salvation Army – West Midlands, Shakespeare Hospice, Walsall Society for the Blind and Walsall Street Teams.

Beneficiaries elsewhere included Ataxia UK, Belfast City Mission, Bolton Hospice, Roy Castle Lung Cancer Foundation, Deafblind UK, East Anglia's Children's Hospices, Foundation for the Prevention of Blindness, Kids Konnect, London Narrow Boat Project, Prostate Cancer Charity, Sense, Sobell House and Winged Fellowship Trust.

Exclusions No grants to individuals.

Applications In writing to the correspondent. Applications must be received during April.

The Lawlor Foundation

Social welfare, education, general

£87,000 to organisations (2002/03)

Beneficial area Principally Northern Ireland, also Republic of Ireland, London, the Home Counties and Avon.

37 Downshire Hill, London NW3 1NU

Tel. 020 7317 8103 **Fax** 020 7317 8103

Correspondent Virginia Lawlor, Chairman

CC Number 297219

Information available A comprehensive annual report and accounts was provided by the foundation.

General The following is taken from the 2002/03 annual report:

'There are four principal objectives: support for organisations working with troubled adolescents (these organisations having an identifiable Irish component); the relief of poverty and the advancement of education in Northern Ireland and the Republic of Ireland; educational grants for individual Irish students; projects underpinning the peace process in Ireland.

'From the foundation's earliest days, the trustees have had a particular interest in adolescent problems and in promoting cooperation and mutual understanding between the peoples of Ireland, North and South. Currently the emphasis is on education and the principal beneficiaries include a number of Northern Irish schools and individual students, British-based projects supporting Irish immigrants, and vulnerable young people.

'Grants are made on a one-off or recurring basis and can include core funding and salaries. A substantial proportion of the foundation's income is committed on a long-term basis, which restricts the funds available for new applicants.'

Grants to organisations range between £500 and £10,000 and can be given for a maximum of three years, although beneficiaries may reapply at the end of the grant. Individuals can receive between £100 and £500 each.

The trust aims to be even-handed in its grantmaking across the communal divide in Belfast. Since 1996 the foundation has run the Shankill Education Project to allow children from disadvantaged families in the Greater Shankill area of West Belfast to attend grammar schools, which they would not otherwise be able to afford. 2003 saw the pupils reach their A-levels, of the seven who took them six have gone onto university and the other has taken a job with a bank in Belfast. This project has received funds from other trusts, companies and individual donations. However, due to lack of demand from schools no new students are starting this scheme. Those already on it are being supported through to the completion of their fifth year.

In 2002/03 the foundation had assets of £2 million and an income of £95,000, including £3,000 in donations received. Grants were made totalling £99,000, including £12,000 given to students in the British Isles. Grants to organisations were broken down geographically as follows:

Britain	5	£31,000
Northern Ireland	15	£54,000
Republic of Ireland	1	£2,500

The annual report also broken down the grants into the following categories.

Education

Grants to nine organisations totalled £68,000, which included £14,000 to the aforementioned Shankill Education Project. Most of the grants were given to schools in disadvantaged areas to allow their pupils to take up university places; these included £6,000 each to La Salle Boys' Secondary School – Belfast, St Cecilia's College – Derry, St Mary's Christian Brothers' Boys' Grammar School and St Mary's College – Derry and £2,500 to Tullow Community School – County Carlow. The other two grants were given to institutions to enable Irish students from low income families to take up places there and went to Jesus College – Cambridge (£7,500) and the Irish Studies Centre at London Metropolitan University (£5,000).

Social welfare

Grants to eight organisations totalled £24,000. As in previous years, the largest in this category was £10,000 to Brent Adolescent Centre as a recurrent grant towards core costs for its mental health service for vulnerable young people aged 14 to 21 London-wide. Other beneficiaries included Brandon Centre – London for core costs (£5,000), New Horizon Youth Centre for a peer education training project (£3,000), Habitat for Humanity for a cross-community initiative to train Catholics and Protestants to learn a trade and participate in building houses for themselves and each other (£2,000), Pirates for Peace to provide training and experience of radio recording and broadcasting to young people from all backgrounds and communities (£1,000) and Fishermen's Mission for a project in Kilkeel and Portavogie to support cross-community acceptance and understanding in the face of tragedy at sea (£500).

Peace and reconciliation

Grants to three organisations totalled £2,500. These were £1,300 to Lifeline – Belfast as an annual grant towards running costs, £1,000 to Northern Ireland Children's Holiday Scheme for a youth leader training programme and £250 to Newry Outdoor Bowling Club for general costs of the club which has cross-community and cross-border membership.

Women's interests

The only grant, of £2,000, was the third of three to Creggan Pre-School and Training Association – Derry towards the salary of an education liaison office to work with parents under the age of 24 in a disadvantaged area of Derry, looking at issues such as childcare, health, housing, benefits, career guidance and continuing education.

Exclusions No grants are made in response to general appeals from large organisations or from organisations outside the geographical areas of Ireland, London and the Home Counties. Grants are not normally made to the arts, medicine, the environment, building projects, expeditions, children's projects or national causes.

Applications By letter to the correspondent at any time, with a description of the project and a copy of the latest accounts. Preliminary telephone enquiries are welcomed. Applications will only be acknowledged if they relate to the trust's general interests. The trustees normally meet in January, April, July and October.

Please note that the trust has many ongoing commitments, which restrict the funds available for new applicants.

The Lawson Charitable Foundation

Jewish, education and culture, health and welfare, arts and humanities, general

£41,000 (2001/02)

Beneficial area South of England.

Stilemans, Munstead, Godalming, Surrey GU8 4AB

Correspondent G C H Lawson, Trustee

Trustees *G C H Lawson; M R Lawson; Mrs C Lawson.*

CC Number 259468

Information available Full accounts were on file at the Charity Commission.

General In 2001/02 the trust had assets of £156,000 and an income of £15,000. Grants were made to organisations totalling £41,000. Donations were broken down as follows in the trust's accounts:

General charitable purposes

Grants totalling £9,250 were made to The Neuropathy Trust (£5,000), Central Synagogue (£2,500), B & L Lyons Charitable Trust (£1,250) and British WIZO (£250).

Health and welfare

Donations to 5 organisations totalled £3,300. Recipients included: The King's Appeal (£1,125), Palm Beach Community Chest (£720), and Chase Children's Hospice, Friends of Alyn and Great Ormond Street Hospital (£500 each).

Educational and cultural

Grants to 8 recipients totalled £6,800, including those to: Jewish Foundation at Palm Beach (£2,150), Norwood Ravenswood (£1,500), British Ort and London Symphony Orchestra (£1,000 each), Cranford Job Seekers Club and The Spiro Ark (£500 each).

Art and culture

In total 1 grant was made amounting to £250. The beneficiary was Friends of Israel Opera.

Disability

Grants totalling £3,000 were made to Leonard Cheshire Foundation (£1,500), Mencap, Motor Neuron Disease Association and Sage (£500 each).

Religious Activities

A total of 3 grants were made amounting to £16,800. Beneficiaries were: Live Music Now (£8,000), United Synagogue (£7,800) and Chatham Memorial Synagogue (£1,000).

Sports & Recreation

One grant of £1,000 went to Sports Aid London.

Exclusions No grants to individuals.

Applications In writing to the correspondent, preferably with an sae.

This entry was not confirmed by the trust but was correct according to information on file at the Charity Commission.

The Raymond & Blanche Lawson Charitable Trust

General

£126,000 (2002/03)

Beneficial area UK, with an interest in west Kent and East Sussex.

28 Barden Road, Tonbridge, Kent TN9 1TX

Tel. 01732 352183 **Fax** 01732 352621

Correspondent Mrs P E V Banks, Trustee

Trustees *John V Banks; John A Bertram; Mrs P E V Banks; Mrs Sarah Hill.*

CC Number 281269

Information available Information was provided by the trust.

General The trust has a preference for local organisations and generally supports charities within the following categories:

- scouts, guides, brownies, cubs, and so on.
- preservation of buildings
- hospices
- care in the community
- assistance for people who are blind
- armed forces' benevolent funds.

In 2002/03 the trust had assets of £1.9 million and an income of £149,000 from investments, rents and donations. Grants amounting to £126,000 were awarded to 124 organisations.

The largest grants were given to Bowles Outdoor Centre (£7,500), Spade Works (£5,900), Age Concern and Marden Village Hall (£5,000 each), Happy Faces Pre Play School (£3,600), British Legion Poppy Appeal and Heart of Kent Hospice and Hospice in the Weald (£3,000 each).

Grants in the range of £1,000 and £2,000 were given to 53 organisations. Beneficiaries included Abbeyfield Medway Valley Society, Barts Cancer Centre of Excellence, Cancer Research UK and Royal London Society for the Blind (£2,000 each), John Groom Group, National Trust and St John's Kent (£1,500 each) and Age Concern, Bowles Outdoor Centre, English Heritage, Home Farm Trust, League of Friends – Maidstone Hospital, Royal Seafarers' Society, and YMCA Housing Association (£1,000 each).

Organisations receiving less than £1,000 each included Kent County Scout Group and Tonbridge War Relief Fund (£750 each), Barnabus Trust, Cystic Fibrosis, Martha Trust, National Missing Persons Helpline, Relate – Tunbridge Wells and Singalong Group (£500 each), National Autistic Society, Paula Carr Trust and Royal Lifesavers Society (£250 each) and Chasaley Trust, Fun in Action for Children and Kent Lupus Group (£100 each).

Exclusions No support for churches or individuals.

Applications In writing to the correspondent.

The Lawson-Beckman Charitable Trust

Jewish, welfare, education, arts

£88,000 (2002/03)

Beneficial area UK.

A Beckman plc, 111/113 Great Portland Street, London W1N 5FA

Tel. 020 7637 8412 **Fax** 020 7436 8599

Correspondent Maurice Lawson

Trustees *M A Lawson; J N Beckman.*

CC Number 261378

Information available Full accounts were on file at the Charity Commission.

General The report states that the trust gives grants for the 'relief of poverty, support of the arts and general charitable purposes'. Grants are allocated two years in advance.

In 2002/03 the trust had assets of £1.8 million and an income of £123,000. A total of £88,000 was distributed in grants broken down as follows:

General charitable purposes – £2,800
Central Synagogue General Charities Fund (£1,500), Bernard & Lucy Lyons Charitable Trust (£750) and The Grocery Relief Fund (£500).

Education and training – £6,800
British O.R.T (£3,500), British Friends of Haifa University (£2,000), Orbis (£750) and Mill Hill Aviv and Saatchi Synagogue (£250 each).

Medical, health and sickness – £34,000
Nightgale House (£16,000), Norwood Ravenswood (£11,000), UCH Hospital Charity (£2,500), Who Cares Trust (£2,000), Chai Lifeline Cancer Care (£1,000), Magen David Adom and North London Hospice (£500 each), Aid for Alyn and UCH Special Trust Charity (£250 each) and Noah's Ark (£200).

Disability – £1,500
Harrow MS Therapy Centre (£1,000) and British Friends of Ohel Sarah (£500).

Overseas – £5,000
World Jewish Relief (£5,000)

Accomodation and housing – £11,000
Jewish Care (£11,000)

Religious activities – £27,000
Project SEED (£13,000), Wilbraham Road (Manchester) Trust Ltd (£7,500), Community Security Trust (£5,000), London Jewish Cultural Centre and United Synagogue (£1,000 each) and Hospital Kosher Meals (£250).

Exclusions No grants to individuals.

Applications In writing to the correspondent, but please note that grants are allocated two years in advance.

The Leach Fourteenth Trust

Disability, general

£96,000 (2003/04)

Beneficial area UK, with some preference for south west England and the Home Counties, and overseas.

Nettleton Mill, Castle Combe, Nr Chippenham, Wiltshire SN14 7NJ

Correspondent Roger Murray-Leach, Trustee

Trustees *W J Henderson; Mrs J M M Nash; Roger Murray-Leach.*

CC Number 204844

Information available Information was provided by the trust.

General Although the trust's objectives are general, the trustees mainley support disability organisations. The trust has previously also had a preference for conservation (ecological) organisations. In practice there is a preference for south west England and the Home Counties. In 2003/04 the trust had assets of £2.4 million, an income of £100,000 and gave grants totalling £96,000.

A few charities receive regular donations. The trustees prefer to give single grants for specific projects rather than towards general funding and also favour small organisations or projects.

A list of beneficiaries was only available from 2002/03, when the trust made grants totalling £95,000. Beneficiaries in that year included £10,000 to Fosse Way School, £7,000 to Deafblind UK, £5,300 to Middlesex Hospital Special Trustees RYMD, £4,000 to Dorothy House Foundation, £1,600 to St Michael'Ss Hospice, £1,500 to Julian House – Cancer Bacup and £1,000 each to Alzheimer's Support West Wiltshire, Brunelcare, Exmouth Community College, Eyeless Trust, Invalids at Home, Meningitis Trust and Prostate Cancer Charity.

Exclusions Only registered charities based in the UK are supported (the trust only gives overseas via a UK-based charity). No grants to: individuals, including for gap years or trips abroad; private schools, unless for people with disabilities or learning difficulties; or for pets.

Applications In writing to the correspondent. Applications for a specific item or purpose are favoured. Only successful appeals can expect a reply. A representative of the trust occasionally visits potential beneficiaries. There is an annual meeting of trustees in the autumn, but not necessarily to consider grants. Grants tend to be distributed twice a year.

The David Lean Foundation

Film production

£249,000 (2001/02)

Beneficial area UK and overseas.

Churchill House, Regent House, Stoke-on-Trent ST1 3RQ

Website www.davidleanfoundation.org

Correspondent The Trustees

Trustees *A A Reeves; J G Moore.*

CC Number 1067074

Information available Accounts were on file at the Charity Commission.

General This foundation was registered on 23 December 1997. It receives income derived from the profits to which Sir David Lean was entitled from most of his major films. In 2001/02 the foundation had an income of £474,000 and distributed grants totalling £249,000.

Its objects are to promote and advance education and to cultivate and improve public taste in the visual arts, particularly in the field of film production, including screenplay writing, film direction and editing. The foundation supports scholarships at NFTS, Leighton Park School and other institutions.

The largest grants of the year were: £69,000 to British Film Institute; £62,000 to NFTS; £55,000 to Individual Projects and £27,000 to The David Lean Endowment Fund at BAFTA.

Other beneficiaries included: Leighton Park Scholarships (£18,000); a translation of a biography into French (£5,000); Royal Academy of Arts and Queen's University (£4,000 each); Talamasca Productions (£2,000); and Cacti Films (£1,000).

Applications Application details are available on the foundation's website.

The Leche Trust

Georgian art, music and architecture

£83,000 to organisations (2002/03)

Beneficial area UK.

84 Cicada Road, London SW18 2NZ

Tel. 020 8870 6233 **Fax** 020 8870 6233

Correspondent Mrs Louisa Lawson, Secretary

Trustees *Mrs Primrose Arnander, Chair; Dr Ian Bristow; Mrs Felicity Guinness; Simon Jervis; John Porteous; Sir John Riddell; Simon Wethered.*

CC Number 225659

Information available Full accounts were provided by the trust.

General The trust was founded and endowed by the late Mr Angus Acworth in 1950. It supports the following categories:

- assistance to students from overseas during the last six months of their postgraduate doctorate study in the UK
- assistance to academic, educational or other organisations concerned with music, drama, dance and the arts
- preservation of buildings and their contents and the repair and conservation of church furniture (including such items as monuments, but excluding structural repairs to the fabric) – preference is given to buildings and objects of the Georgian period
- assistance to conservation, including museums
- support with the charitable activities associated with the preservation of rural England
- the promotion of amity and good relations between Britain and developing world or former 'Iron Curtain' countries by financing visits to such countries by teachers or other appropriate persons.

In 2002/03 it had assets of £5.2 million, which generated an income of £239,000. Grants were approved totalling £210,000, broken down as follows:

Historic buildings – 10 grants totalling £39,000

These included £10,000 to Moggerhanger House Preservation Trust to open the oculus and lantern space on the first floor landing, £5,000 to Grecian Valley – Stowe for the restoration of two statue groups from Trent Park and £2,400 to House of St Barnabas in Soho to replace door furniture.

Churches – 18 grants totalling £37,000

The majority of these grants were for the restoration of monuments in churches and tombs in churchyards, including £5,000 to Church of St Mary and St Gabriel in South Harting, West Sussex for the polychrome monument and £2,500 to St Mary Magdalene Church in East Ham, London towards the restoration of wall paintings. There was also a grant of £2,000 to St Oswald's Church – Oswestry for the restoration of a 1730's painted triptych.

Institutions and museums – 6 grants totalling £12,000

Beneficiaries included Victoria and Albert Museum for the restoration of a chair in the Henrietta Street Rooms (£4,500), Holburne Museum of Art – Bath for the publication of a catalogue for an exhibit of portraits (£1,500) and York Castle Museum for the restoration of a dummy board (£900).

Education (individuals) – £52,000

These were mostly given to arts students, as London Academy of Music and Dramatic Art, National Youth Dance Company and National Youth Orchestra. Support was also given to individual musicians for postgraduate courses at music schools in London, and in one case in New York. Grants in this category averaged £2,000 each.

Arts – 25 grants totalling £45,000

This category included bursaries for students to attend music competitions, such as the Oundle International Festival and Summer School for organists and Lionel Tertis International Viola Competition – Isle of Man. It also paid the fare for two teachers to go to Croatia to teach at a summer school.

Overseas students – 34 grants totalling £25,000

Grants went to students from 19 separate countries who were in the final six month of their PhD degrees. The majority of the beneficiaries were from the Indian sub-continent.

Exclusions No grants are made for: religious bodies; overseas missions; schools and school buildings; social welfare; animals; medicine; expeditions; or British students other than music students.

Applications In writing to the secretary. Trustees meet three times a year, in February, June and October; applications need to be received the month before.

The Arnold Lee Charitable Trust

Jewish, educational, health

£85,000 (2001/02)

Beneficial area UK.

47 Orchard Court, Portman Square, London W1H 9PD

Tel. 0207 486 8918

Correspondent A Lee, Trustee

Trustees *Arnold Lee; Helen Lee; Alan Lee.*

CC Number 264437

Information available Full accounts were on file at the Charity Commission, but without an up-to-date grants list.

General The policy of the trustees is to distribute income to 'established charities of high repute' for any charitable purpose or object. The trust supports a large number of Jewish organisations.

In 2001/02 the trust had assets of £1.4 million and an income of £98,000. There were 48 grants made, totalling £85,000. Further information was not available.

The largest grants list filed at the Charity Commission was from 1997/98 when 63 grants were made totalling £89,000. The largest grant went to Joint Jewish Charitable Trust (£34,000). Other recipients of substantial grants included Project SEED (£7,500), Jewish Care (£6,500), Lubavich Foundations (£5,000), The Home of Aged Jews (£2,500) and Yesodey Hatorah School and Friends of Akim (£2,400 each).

Virtually all remaining grants were to Jewish charities and most were for around £500 or less. Recipients included The President's Club (£600), Gesher (£500), British Technion Society and Institute of Higher Rabbinical Studies (£250 each), Bolton Village Appeal Fund (£100) and Society of Friends of the Torah (£50).

Exclusions Grants are rarely made to individuals.

Applications In writing to the correspondent.

Morris Leigh Foundation

Jewish, general

£91,000 (2001/02)

Beneficial area Worldwide.

Adelaide house, London Bridge, London EC4R 9HA

Tel. 020 7353 0299

Correspondent M D Paisner, Trustee

Trustees *Martin D Paisner; Howard D Leigh.*

CC Number 280695

Information available Full accounts were on file at the Charity Commission.

General This foundation has general charitable purposes, mostly supporting Jewish, welfare and arts organisations.

In 2001/02 the foundation had assets of £1.6 million with an income of £71,000 and grants totaling £91,000.

The largest grants include £14,000 to Royal College of Music, £10,000 to London Business School, £7,500 each to Rycolewood College and Institute for Jewish Policy Research, £5,000 each to Ronald Raven Cancer Trust and London Symphony Orchestra.

Other grants include £3,000 each to London Philharmonic Orchestra, Somerset House Arts Fund and Sussex University, £2,000 to Community Service Trust, £1,750 to Chicken Shed Theatre, £1,500 to Holocaust Educational Fund.

Grants of £1,000 or less include British ORT, Cancerkin – Women Gala, Commonwealth Jewish Trust, London Jewish Culture Centre, Reading Hebrew Congregation, UJIA, Medical Foundation and Inspire Foundation.

Applications In writing to the correspondent.

The P Leigh-Bramwell Trust 'E'

Methodist, general

£67,000 (2002/03)

Beneficial area UK, with a preference for Bolton

W & J Leigh & Co., Tower Works, Kestor Street, Bolton BL2 2AL

Tel. 01204 521771

Correspondent P Morrison, Secretary

CC Number 267333

Information available Information was provided by the trust.

General This trust generally supports the same organisations each year, leaving little funds available for unsolicited applications. It has general charitable purposes, with a preference for education and Methodism.

In 2002/03 the trust had an income of £72,000. Grants were made totalling £67,000.

The same beneficiaries are supported each year; these are Leigh-Bramwell Scholarship Fund, for educational purposes, Bolton Hospice, Breightmet Methodist Church, Circuit Methodist Church, Delph Hill Methodist Church, International Scientific Support Trust, RNLI and West London Mission.

Exclusions No grants to individuals.

Applications In writing to the correspondent; however, please note that there is only a small amount of funds available for unsolicited applications and therefore success is unlikely.

The Leonard Trust

Christian, overseas aid

About £30,000 a year

Beneficial area Overseas and UK, with a preference for Hampshire.

18 Edgar Road, Winchester, Hampshire SO23 9TW

Correspondent Tessa Feilden, Trustee

Trustees *Tessa Feilden; Dominic Gold; Carol Gold.*

CC Number 1031723

Information available There was no narrative report and no accounts for the trust on file at the Charity Commission, but bank statements were available there.

General The trust informed us that it makes grants totalling about £30,000 each year, ranging between £1,000 and £5,000 each. It supports Christian and overseas aid organisations. Grants are not made to individuals.

Grants are mainly to national organisations, although the trust possibly has a preference for those in Winchester and the surrounding area. The trust looks favourably on special one-off appeals.

Past beneficiaries have included: ARC – Diamond Jubilee Appeal, Botton Village Appeal Fund, British and Foreign Bible Society, CAF Bulgaria Appeal, The Children's Society, Evangelism Explosion, Frontier Youth Trust, Headway, Lepra, Mental Health Foundation, Salvation Army, The Samaritans, Scripture Union, Shelter, Tearfund, UNICEF, Winchester Cancer Research Trust and Winchester Churches Nightshelter.

Exclusions No grants to individuals. Medical research or building projects are no longer supported.

Applications Unsolicited applications cannot be considered.

The Mark Leonard Trust

Environmental education, youth, general

£201,000 (2003/04)

Beneficial area Worldwide, but mainly UK.

Allington House, 1st Floor, 150 Victoria Street, London SW1E 5AE

Tel. 020 7410 0330 **Fax** 020 7410 0332

Email info@sfct.org.uk

Correspondent Michael Pattison, Director

Trustees *Mrs Z Sainsbury; Miss Judith Portrait; J J Sainsbury; Mark Sainsbury.*

CC Number 1040323

Information available Full accounts were provided by the trust.

General This is one of the 18 Sainsbury Family Charitable Trusts, which collectively give over £54 million a year. It mostly supports environmental causes and youth work, although it also gives towards general charitable purposes. The following descriptions of its more specific work are taken from its 2003/04 annual report:

Environment

'Grants are made for environmental education, particularly to support projects displaying practical ways of involving children and young adults. The trustees rarely support new educational resource packs in isolation from the actual process of learning and discovering. They are more interested in programmes which help pupils and teachers to develop a theme over time (such as renewable energy), perhaps combining IT resources for data gathering and communication, with exchange visits and the sharing of information and ideas between schools.

'The trustees are particularly interested in projects that enable children and young people to develop a sense of ownership of the project over time, and that provide direct support to teachers to deliver exciting and high quality education in the classroom.

'The trustees are also interested in the potential for sustainable transport, energy efficiency and renewable energy in the wider society. In some cases the trustees will consider funding research, but only where there is a clear practical application. Proposals are more likely to be considered when they are testing an idea, model or strategy in practice.'

Youth Work

'The trustees aim to help projects that support the rehabilitation of young people who have become marginalised and involved in anti-social or criminal activities. They wish to apply their grants to overcome social exclusion. They are also interested in extending and adding value to the existing use of school buildings, enhancing links between schools and the community, and encouraging greater involvement of parents, school leavers and volunteers in extra-curricular activities.

The accounts also included the following statement:

'Proposals are generally invited by the trustees or initiated at their request. Unsolicited applications are not encouraged and are unlikely to be successful, even if they fall within an area in which the trustees are interested. The trustees' objective is to support innovative schemes with seed funding, leading projects to achieve sustainability and successful replication. Grants are not normally made to individuals.'

In 2003/04 it had asset of £8.5 million and an income of £881,000. The management and administration charges included payments totalling £3,300 to a firm of solicitors in which one of the trustees is a partner. Whilst wholly legal, these editors always regret such payments unless, in the words of the Charity Commission, 'there is no realistic alternative'. Grants were approved totalling £201,000, broken down as follows:

Environment – 14 grants totalling £111,000

The largest grants were £22,000 to Ashden Awards for Sustainable Energy and £21,000 to Building Exploratory for a new exhibition room on construction and regeneration in Hackney. Other grants included £10,000 to Transport 2000 Trust for core costs, £9,600 to Green Light Trust to setup a forest schools programme in the East of England, £7,000 to Walworth Garden Farm for a part-time community-education coordinator, £4,000 to Sustrans for the national development and dissemination of Travel Smart Initiative pilots and activities, £3,500 to Cyclists' Touring Club for a web-based cycling information facility, £600 to Liverpool City Environment Centre for a feasibility study for an outdoor classroom and renewable energy demonstration facilities.

Youth work – 9 grants totalling £77,000

The largest were £14,000 to WorldWide Volunteering for Young People towards enabling a free postal service for youth volunteering opportunities and £10,000 each to Energy and Vision for a schools-education worker, Resonance 104.4FM for training and outreach posts and the employment of a business-development officer, Shout! towards a mentor coordinator working with performance arts amongst young people at risk of teenage pregnancy or gun crime in Tottenham and Street Dreams towards salary costs.

Other grants were £7,000 to Children's Express for the photojournalism component of a nine-month media course for children in Islington, £5,900 to Groundwork Leeds for two pilot environmental and social-learning courses for 13–14 year-olds and £5,000 each to The Bridge for a training video for people working with young people at risk from drug or alcohol dependency and Hampton Trust for a peer-mentoring project amongst teenagers in south-east Hampshire.

General – 3 grants totalling £28,000

These went to London Borough of Tower Hamlets towards the creation of a Learning Lab at Whitechapel Idea Store (£20,000), Play Ball for All towards the indigenous production of low-cost leather footballs for promoting health and fitness amongst young people in sub-Saharan Africa (£5,800) and St Nicholas's Church – New Romney for emergency repairs (£2,000).

Applications The 18 Sainsbury Family Charitable Trusts are jointly administered and follow the same application precedure. An application to one trust is considered as an application to them all. However, 'applications' are probably not the best way forward to gaining funding from these trusts. More sensible might be to write briefly and say what is being done or planned, on the assumption that, if one or more of the trusts is indeed interested in that area of work, they will want to know about what you are doing. A telephone call to do the same is fine. Staff are polite, but wary of people seeking to talk about money rather than issues.

More generally, the trusts are involved in a number of networks, with which they maintain long-term contact. Charities doing work relevant to the interests of these trusts may find that if they are not a part of these networks (which may not be inclusive and most of which are probably London-based) they may get limited Sainsbury attention.

The most inappropriate approach would often be from a fundraiser. Staff, and in many cases trustees, are knowledgeable and experienced in their fields, and expect to talk to others in the same position.

The Leverhulme Trade Charities Trust

Charities benefiting commercial travellers, grocers or chemists

£374,000 to organisations (2002)

Beneficial area UK.

1 Pemberton Row, London EC4A 3BG

Tel. 020 7822 6915

Correspondent The Secretary

Trustees *Sir Michael Angus, Chair; Sir Michael Perry; N W A Fitzgerald; Dr J I W Anderson; A S Ganguly.*

CC Number 288404

Information available Full accounts were provided by the trust.

General Grants are made only to:

- trade benevolent institutions supporting commercial travellers, grocers or chemists

- schools or universities providing education for them or their children.

The Leverhulme Trade Charities Trust derives from the will of the First Viscount Leverhulme, who died in 1925. He left a proportion of his shares in Lever Brothers Ltd upon trust and specified the income beneficiaries to included certain trade charities. In 1983, the Leverhulme Trade Charities Trust itself was established, with its own shareholding in Unilever, and with grantmaking to be restricted to charities connected with commercial travellers, grocers or chemists, their wives, widows or children. The trust has no full-time employees, but the day-to-day administration is carried out by the director of finance at The Leverhulme Trust.

In 2002 the trust had assets of £33 million, which generated an income of £1 million. Grants to organisations totalled £374,000. A further £225,000 was given in 51 undergraduate bursaries.

The largest grants, of £100,000 each, went to Commercial Travellers' Benevolent Institution and Royal Pinner School Foundation. Other beneficiaries were UCTA Samaritan Fund (£45,000), Girls Day School Trust (£39,000), Royal Pharmaceutical Society (£30,000 for research fellowships and £5,000 for pharmacy practice research), United Reformed Church Schools (£19,000), Provision Trade Benevolent Institution (£17,000), Commercial Travellers of Scotland Benevolent Fund (£13,000) and Royal Wolverhampton School (£6,000).

Exclusions No capital grants. No response is given to general appeals.

Applications By letter to the correspondent. All correspondence is acknowledged. The trustees meet in February and applications need to be received by the preceding October.

Undergraduate bursary applications should be directed to the relevant institution.

The Ralph Levy Charitable Company Ltd

Educational, medical, general

£564,000 (2002/03)

Beneficial area UK, occasionally overseas.

14 Chesterfield Street, London W1J 5JN

Tel. 020 7408 9333 **Fax** 020 7408 9346

Correspondent Christopher Andrews, Trustee

Trustees *S M Levy; D S Levy; C J F Andrews.*

CC Number 200009

Information available Accounts were on file at the Charity Commission, but without a grants list or narrative report.

General This trust has general charitable purposes, with a preference for educational and medical organisations.

In 2002/03 it had an income of £14,000 and made grants totalling £564,000. This saw the assets fall from £954,000 at the start of the end to £314,000 at the year end. There was no list of grants included in the accounts, nor an explanation as to why there was such a dramatic overspend during the year.

Exclusions No educational grants to individuals.

Applications In writing to the correspondent. Written applications must be received three clear months before the commencement of the proposed project.

Lewis Family Charitable Trust

Medical research, health, education, Jewish charities

£399,000 (1998/99)

Beneficial area UK and overseas.

Chelsea House, West Gate, London W5 1DR

Tel. 020 8991 4601

Correspondent David Lewis, Trustee

Trustees *David Lewis; Bernard Lewis.*

CC Number 259892

Information available Accounts were on file at the Charity Commission.

General Grants are made, in particular, to charities involved in the promotion of medical research. In addition, Jewish charities have in the past accounted for a large part of the trust's grant expenditure, but the proportion appears to be decreasing.

In 2002/03 the trust had an income of £604,000 and a total expenditure of £376,000. Further information for this year was not available.

In 2000/01 it had an income of £168,000 and a total expenditure of £418,000. Unfortunately no further details were available for this year. In 1998/99 net assets were £3.3 million but a £500,000 donation saw the trust's income rise to £679,000, up from £206,000 the year before.

Out of 12 organisations receiving grants of over £10,000 (accounting for over three quarters of the total), 10 had been supported in the previous year. Most were medical research organisations receiving repeat awards, many with a long-standing relationship with the trust, including:

- King's College Hospital, £58,500 (£25,500 in 1997/98)
- Birth Defects Foundation, £57,000 (£59,000)
- Association for the Advancement of Cancer Therapy, £42,000 (£25,000)
- University of Nottingham, £19,000 (£25,000)
- Queen Mary and Westfield College Hospital, £19,000 (also funded in 1996/97)
- Imperial Cancer Research, £17,000 (£55,000)

In addition, the British Council received £40,000 for the Lewis Fellowship Fund, while the largest grant to a Jewish organisation was for £21,000 to UJIA/Joint Jewish Charitable Trust, both long-term beneficiaries.

The only apparently new beneficiary receiving a large grant was the Bedford Square Charitable Trust (£30,000).

A further 15 recipients received grants ranging from £1,000 to £3,000. Only Norwood Ravenswood and CACDP had been supported in the previous year, receiving £2,000 and £1,750 respectively.

Others included Chernobyl Children's Lifeline (£3,000); the Multiple Sclerosis Society (£2,000); West London Synagogue (£1,000); Teenage Cancer Trust (£1,000), and the Council for

Christians and Jews (£1,000). Another £15,000 was spent on grants under £1,000.

Exclusions No grants to individuals.

Applications To the correspondent in writing. Grants are normally made only once a year. The trust states: 'Grants are not made on the basis of applications received.'

The John Spedan Lewis Foundation

Natural sciences, particularly horticulture, ornithology, entomology

£103,000 (2002/03)

Beneficial area UK.

171 Victoria Street, London SW1E 5NN

Tel. 020 7828 1000

Email bmfchamberlain@johnlewis.co.uk

Correspondent Ms B M F Chamberlain, Secretary

Trustees *Sir Stuart Hampson; C W F Redmond; Helen Hyde; Dr Vaughan Southgate; Simon Fowler.*

CC Number 240473

Information available Information was provided by the trust.

General The trust makes grants in the areas of horticulture, ornithology and entomology, and to associated educational and research projects.

In 2002/03 it had assets of £1.6 million, which generated an income of £85,000. Grants were made totalling £103,000. Further details were not available.

Exclusions No grants to individuals (including students), local branches of national organisations, or for salaries, medical research, welfare projects, building works or overseas expeditions.

Applications In writing to the correspondent with latest report and accounts and a budget for the proposed project.

The Sir Edward Lewis Foundation

General

£99,000 (2002/03)

Beneficial area UK and overseas, with a preference for Surrey.

Messrs Rawlinson & Hunter, Eagle House, 110 Jermyn Street, London SW1Y 6RH

Tel. 020 7451 9000

Correspondent Mrs Sandra Frankland

Trustees *R A Lewis; K W Dent; Christine Lewis; Sarah Dorin.*

CC Number 264475

Information available Full accounts were on file at the Charity Commission.

General The trust was established in 1972 by Sir Edward Roberts Lewis. By 2002/03 it had assets of £5.7 million producing an income of £153,000. Grants were made totalling £99,000.

The trust has revised its policy and now plans to make one substantial donation every two or three years to an appropriate cause as well as smaller donations on an annual basis. Therefore it will not distribute all its income every year. The trustees prefer to support charities known personally to them and those favoured by the settlor.

There were 93 beneficiaries in this year the largest donations were £7,000 to Accord International and £5,000 each to Ling Edward VII's Hospital and The Solti Foundation.

Smaller donations made totalled £82,200 some of which were £3,000 each to The David Shepherd Wildlife Foundation, Institute of Economic Affairs and Progressive Supranuclear Palsy Association. £2,000 each went to St Bartholomew's Church, Leigh, CRISIS, Gurkha Welfare Trust and National Hospital Development Fund.

Exclusions Grants are only given to charities, projects or people known to the trustees. No grants are given to individuals.

Applications In writing to the correspondent. The trustees meet every six months.

The Licensed Trade Charities Trust

Licensed trade

£105,000 (2001/02)

Beneficial area England and Wales.

Willow Barn, Stalbridge Western, Sturminster Newton DT10 2LA

Tel. 01963 362 068 **Fax** 01306 731169

Correspondent Nicholas Harry Block

Trustees *A G Eadie, Chair; W L Page; S Williams; W P Catesby; T G Cockerell; C Cox; M Curnock Cook; C J Eld; J J Madden; J C Overton; G B Richardson.*

CC Number 282161

Information available Information was provided by the trust.

General The trust supports charitable institutions connected to the licensed trade only.

In 2001/02 the trust had assets of £3 million with an income of £114,000 and grants totalling £105,000.

Grants include £47,000 to Society of Licensed Victuallers, £31,000 to Hospitality Action Licensed Victuallers, £22,000 to Wine and Spirit Trades Benevolent Society and £5,000 to National Homes.

Exclusions No grants to individuals.

Applications New applications are not considered.

The Life Insurance Association Charitable Foundation

General

About £45,000 a year

Beneficial area UK.

Personal Finance Society, 20 Aldermanbury, London EC2V 7HY

Tel. 01923 285333

Website www.lia.co.uk

Correspondent The Trustees

Trustees *K Carby, Chair; M Clarke; S Myers; J Travis; F Weisinger; S Sprung; M Bousfield.*

CC Number 1071492

Information available Accounts were on file at the Charity Commission.

General Established in September 1998, the foundation raises funds for UK-wide and local causes through the efforts of its 35 branches.

In 2002 the foundation had a gross income of £59,000 with a total expenditure of £48,000. Unfortunately no other financial information was available.

In 2000 it had an income of £69,000. Out of a total expenditure of £71,000, the sum of £65,000 was given in grants with £4,100 going on fundraising costs and £2,300 on management and administration costs.

The largest grant in the year was £7,500 to the Royal Marsden Hospital. A further 28 grants were made to local causes throughout the UK.

Applications Beneficiaries are elected by local LIA regions.

Lifeline 4 Kids

Equipment for children with disabilities

£119,000 to individuals and organisations (2002)

Beneficial area Worldwide.

215 West End Lane, London NW6 1XJ

Tel. 020 7794 1161

Email mail@lifeline4kids.org

Website www.lifeline4kids.org

Correspondent Roger Adelman

Trustees *Jeffrey Bonn; Roger Adelman; Paul Maurice; Beverley Emden; Mrs Roberta Harris.*

CC Number 200050

Information available Accounts were on file at the Charity Commission, but without a list of grants. Information was available on its website.

General The following description of the trust is taken from its website:

'We are a London-based children's charity established in 1961. Originally known as the Handicapped Children's Aid Committee, our working name has now been changed to Lifeline 4 Kids. We were formed for one purpose, to provide essential equipment and services to benefit children with disabilities and also to help prevent disability and disease amongst children, irrespective of their race or creed.

'To date we have raised and spent well over £15 million.

'We have no paid staff, paid fund raisers or administrative costs, thus virtually every penny that we are able to raise is spent on the children. Unlike most other charities, our annual operating costs are less than 1% of expenditure.

'Our members work on an entirely voluntary basis to raise money and to decide how it should be spent. Since inception in 1961 our essence and philosophy has been to raise vital funds and directly pay for equipment and services to help improve the quality of life of children with special needs.

'Applications for assistance arrive from many different sources from around the UK and abroad. We are regularly approached for help from hospitals and special schools and from parents and social workers on behalf of individual children.

'Major past projects have included the presentation of specially adapted Heart Scanning Equipment to Professor Yacoub's children's heart transplant unit at Harefield Hospital, at a cost of £70,000. We also spent some £100,000 on equipping a new children's unit at the Royal London Hospital in Whitechapel and we equipped the children's ambulatory unit at Northwick Park Hospital at a cost of £150,000. A further £150,000 has been earmarked towards equipping a brand new state-of-the-art children's ward which is opening this year at Northwick Park Hospital.

'We also help children's hospices, respite care homes and support centres throughout the UK with varying items including soft playrooms and multi-sensory rooms at costs ranging between £12,000 and £15,000.

'Emergency and Welfare appeals are dealt with by a Sub-Committee, which is deputed to give immediate approval within the limits of its authority. As an example, we recently provided special clothing and a more comfortable bed at a cost of £285 for a three-year-old boy with severe eczema and asthma.

'Our work has many facets. We are one of the few UK charities helping the individual disabled child from a low income family with any essential item from a £20 pair of shoes or clothing. We also provide specialised computers, sensory equipment and electric wheelchairs, many costing well over £10,000. We equip hospital neonatal units with the latest incubators and ultrasonic monitors amongst other life saving equipment.'

In 2002 it had assets of £819,000, an income of £141,000 and gave £119,000 in grants.

Exclusions Building projects, research grants and salaries will not be funded.

Applications Initial telephone calls from applicants are not welcome. Application forms and guidelines are available from the correspondent.

Limoges Charitable Trust

Animals, services, general

£87,000 (2001/02)

Beneficial area UK, with a preference for Birmingham.

Tyndallwoods Solicitors, 29 Woodbourne Road, Edgbaston, Birmingham B17 8BY

Tel. 0121 693 2222 **Fax** 0121 693 0844

Correspondent Ms J A Dyke, Trustee

Trustees *Catherine Harriet Mary Bligh St George; Albert Kenneth Dyer; Judy Ann Dyke; Andrew Miller.*

CC Number 1016178

Information available Full accounts were on file at the Charity Commission.

General This trust has general charitable purposes, although there are preferences for animal and service organisations. Many of the beneficiaries are based in Birmingham.

In 2001/02 the trust had assets of £750,000 and an income of £25,000. Grants were made totalling £87,000. Further information for this year was not available, other than that it paid £11,000 in trustees' disbursements, although there was no information provided on how these differed to grants.

In the previous year, when the grant total was at a similar level, Symphony Hall (Birmingham) Ltd received two grants totalling £20,000, including £15,000 for the organ appeal. Many of the other larger grants were also given to Birmingham organisations, including Blue Coat School for the piano appeal (£15,000), University of Birmingham

(£5,000), Birmingham Parish Church (St Martin's) Renewal Campaign (£3,000) and Birmingham Early Music Fund (£2,000).

Smaller Birmingham grants included those to Birmingham and Midland Limbless Ex-Servicemen's Association (£1,400), Royal Marine Association (£1,000), MSA for Midlands People with Cerebral Palsy and Wythall Village Hall (£500 each), Birmingham Dogs Home and West Birmingham Scout Association (£250 each), Edgbaston Rotary Club (£150) and Edgewood Court Day Centre (£50).

Grants made elsewhere included £2,700 to Elizabeth Svendsen Trust, £2,000 each to KGFS and Web Care Services, £1,200 to Edwards Trust, £1,000 each to Arthritis Research Campaign, Dogs for the Disabled, Gloucester Three Choirs Appeal, Hope and Homes for Children and Live Music Now!, £600 to Royal British Legion for the Poppy Appeal, £500 each to Caring for Victims of Torture and When You Wish Upon a Star, £400 to RSPCA, £350 to Canine Partners for Independence, £250 to Rehab UK, £200 to Children Nationwide and £140 to Alexander MacMillan Trust.

Applications In writing to the correspondent.

The Lind Trust

Christianity

£140,000 to organisations (2001/02)

Beneficial area UK.

Tithe Barn, Attlebridge, Norwich NR9 5AA

Tel. 01603 262626

Correspondent Graham Dacre

Trustees *Leslie C Brown; Dr Graham M Dacre; Gavin C Nilcock; Mrs Julia M Dacre.*

CC Number 803174

Information available Accounts were on file at the Charity Commission.

General In 2001/02 this trust had assets of £3.8 million and an income of £269,000. Grants were made totalling £140,000, broken down as follows:

Churches	£102,000
Proclaimers International	£17,000
Other charities	£1,200
Individuals in full-time ministry	£21,000

Applications In writing to the correspondent at any time. However, the trust commits most of its funds in advance, giving the remainder to eligible applicants as received.

Lindale Educational Foundation

Roman Catholic

£200,000 (2001/02)

Beneficial area UK and overseas.

1 Leopold Road, London W5 3PB

Tel. 0207 229 7574

Correspondent J Valero

Trustees *Netherhall Educational Association; Dawliffe Hall Educational Foundation; Greygarth Association.*

CC Number 282758

Information available Information was on file at the Charity Commission.

General This foundation supports the Roman Catholic religion and the advancement of education. Its aims are to:

- train priests
- establish, extend, improve and maintain churches, chapels, oratories and other places of worship
- establish, extend, improve and maintain university halls and halls of residence for students of all nationalities
- arrange and conduct courses, camps, study centres, meetings, conferences and seminars
- provide financial support for education or research by individuals or groups of students
- provide financial support for other individuals or institutions which meet the trust's criteria, including the corporate trustees.

In 2002/03 it had an income of £143,000 and a total expenditure of £134,000.

In 2001/02 the foundation had an income of £180,000, of which £175,000 came from donations received. Assets totalled £6,400. Grants were made totalling £200,000, whilst other expenditure amounted to just £20.

The main emphasis was on the training of priests, with grants being made to Collegio Romano della Santa Croce (four grants totalling £60,000), Fondation Belmont (two grants totalling £55,000) and Collegio Mayor de Humanidades (£2,000 to support seminarians).

The accounts stated: 'LEF was able to help projects run by its charitable trustees, with £12,000 going to the Brixton Baytree Centre, part of Dawliffe Hall Educational Foundation, which itself received a grant of £12,000 for general educational purposes. Wickenden Manor, the Natherhall Educational Association Centre for Retreats and Study Activites received six grants totalling £41,000 and Thornycroft Hall, a centre for similar activities and which is part of the Charity Siddington Trust Limited, received five grants totalling £6,100.'

Other grants were £10,000 to Fundacion para el desarrollo integral (FUDI) for a humanitarian/educational project in Guatemala and £1,000 to a school project in Ghana.

Exclusions No grants to individuals.

Applications In writing to the correspondent, but note that most funds are already committed.

The Linden Charitable Trust

General

About £70,000 a year

Beneficial area UK, with a preference for West Yorkshire

Addleshaw Goddard Booth & Co., Sovereign House, PO Box 8, Sovereign Street, Leeds LS1 1HQ

Tel. 0113 209 2465 **Fax** 0113 209 2611

Correspondent Mrs M E Jones

Trustees *G L Holbrook; Miss M H Pearson; J F H Swales.*

CC Number 326788

Information available Information was provided by the trust.

General This trust supports a wide range of organisations including medical and healthcare charities and those related to the arts. In 2002/03 it had an income of £84,000 and a total expenditure of £83,000. Further information for this year was not available.

Grants in the previous year totalled around £70,000 and large donations were made to Elizabeth Foundation and Leeds Grammar School. Other donations in the range of £500 and £5,000 were made to: Little Sisters of the Poor, Macmillan Cancer Relief, Marie Curie, Mission to Seafarers, Opera North Foundation and Yorkshire Dales Millennium Trust.

Exclusions No grants to individuals.

Applications In writing to the correspondent.

The Linmardon Trust

General

£73,000 (2001/02)

Beneficial area UK, with a preference for the Nottingham area.

HSBC Trust Company Limited, Norwich House, Nelson Gate, Commercial Road, Southampton SO15 1GX

Tel. 023 8072 2218

Correspondent Barry Sims, Trust Manager

Trustee *HSBC Trust Company Limited.*

CC Number 275307

Information available Full accounts were on file at the Charity Commission.

General The trust supports charities in the UK with a preference for those in the Nottingham area. In 2003/04 it had an income of £50,000 and a total expenditure of £59,000. Further information from this year was not available.

In 2001/02 it had assets of £1.3 million and an income of £52,000. Grants totalling £73,000 were made to 78 organisations.

All of the largest 50 grants listed in the accounts were of £1,000 each. Beneficiaries included Baby Lifeline, Bassetlaw Hospice, Bassetlaw Housing Advice Centre, Birmingham Youth for Christ, Breast Cancer Campaign, Brittle Bone Society, Changing Faces, Children's Heart Foundation, DeafBlind UK, Elizabeth Fry Centre, Honeypot Charity, Kilton Youth and Community Centre, Mark Way School, MS Society, Noah's Ark Trust, Nottingham Counselling Service, Nottingham Regional Society, Nottinghamshire Sea Cadet Unit, Nottinghamshire Wildlife Trust, Pace Centre and Papplewick Pre-School.

Exclusions Grants are made to registered charities only. No support to individuals.

Applications In writing to the correspondent. The trustees meet quarterly, generally in February, May, August and November.

The Ruth & Stuart Lipton Charitable Trust

Jewish, general

£120,000 (2002/03)

Beneficial area UK and overseas

Lewis Golden & Co., 40 Queen Ann Street, London W1M 9EL

Tel. 020 7580 7313

Correspondent N W Benson, Trustee

Trustees *Sir S Lipton; Lady Lipton; N W Benson.*

CC Number 266741

Information available Accounts were on file at the Charity Commission.

General This trust was founded by property/art mogul Stuart Lipton and his wife in 1973.

In 2002/03 the trust had assets of £430,000 and an income of £105,000 of which £119,000 was received in Gift Aid. Grants totalled £120,000.

Grant beneficiaries included Winnicot Foundation (£50,000), The Tate Gallery (£33,000), Western Marble Arch Synagogue (£11,600), Royal Opera House (£9,900), Community Security Trust (£5,500), Prostate Cancer Research (£5,250), United Israel Appeal (£850), London Philharmonic (£700) and Nightingale House and The Chai Cancer Care (£500 each).

Exclusions No grants to individuals.

Applications In writing to the correspondent.

The Lister Charitable Trust

Water-based activities for young people who are disadvantaged

£264,000 (2001/02)

Beneficial area UK.

Burkes Court, Burkes Road, Beacon Field, Buckinghamshire HP9 1NZ

Tel. 0149 468 1682

Correspondent Mrs S J Sharkey

Trustees *Noel A V Lister; Benjamin Piers Cussons; Stephen John Chipperfield; D A Collingwood; David J Lister.*

CC Number 288730

Information available Information was provided by the trust.

General This trust aims to help disadvantaged young people through sailing and other water-based activities. Grants are usually one-off for a specific project or part of a project. Core funding and/or salaries are rarely considered. Funding may be given for up to one year.

In 2002/03 the trust had an income of £218,000 and a total expenditure of £243,000. Further information from this year was not available.

In the previous year the trust had assets of £9.5 million and income of £264,000. Grants totalling £264,000 were made to four organisations: Miami Project (£125,000), Bobath Centre (£100,000), UK Sailing Academy (£38,000) and Treasury Cay Community Centre (£1,500).

Exclusions Applications from individuals, including students, are ineligible. No grants are made in response to general appeals from large UK organisations or to smaller bodies working in areas outside its criteria.

Applications In writing to the correspondent. Applications should include clear details of the need the intended project is designed to meet, plus an outline budget. Only applications from eligible bodies are acknowledged, when further information may be requested.

The Little Foundation

Neurodevelopmental disorders

£93,000 (2001/02)

Beneficial area UK.

30 Furnivel Street, London EC4A 1JQ

Tel. 020 7831 4918 **Fax** 020 7405 5365

Correspondent C Robinson, Chair

Trustees *C Robinson, Chair; Prof. M Crawford; Dr K Hameed; Prof. D Harvey; Prof. N Morris; Sara Cooke.*

CC Number 803551

Information available Information was provided by the trust.

General This foundation makes grants to established research bodies which will benefit future generations of children with neurodevelopmental disorders. It favours research projects recommended by its own Scientific Advisory Committee. These projects directly reflect the aims of the foundation to find the primary causes of such disorders and set up research with a view to prevention.

In 2001/02 the foundation had an income of £53,000 and issued grants totalling £93,000. Unfortunately there was no grant list or other supporting financial information for this period.

Exclusions No grants for individuals, training grants or scholarships.

Applications All available funds are committed.

The Second Joseph Aaron Littman Foundation

General

£191,000 (2002)

Beneficial area UK.

190 Strand, London WC2R 1JN

Tel. 020 7379 0000 **Fax** 020 7379 6854

Correspondent Barry Lock

Trustees *Mrs C C Littman; R J Littman.*

CC Number 201892

Information available Information was provided by the trust.

General This trust has general charitable purposes with special preference for acadmeic and medical research. In 2002 it had assets of £2.6 million and an income of £370,000. Grants were made to four organisations totalling £191,000.

The main beneficiary, as usual, was Littmann Library of Jewish Civilisation, which received £182,000. Other beneficiaries were Westminster Synagogue (£5,000), LGH – Warners (£2,000) and Worthing Hospice (£1,000).

Exclusions Applications from individuals are not considered.

Applications The trust's funds are fully committed and no new applications are considered.

The George John Livanos Charitable Trust

Health, maritime charities, general

£479,000 (2001)

Beneficial area UK.

c/o Jeffrey Green Russell, Apollo House, 56 New Bond Street, London W1S 1RG

Tel. 020 7339 7000

Correspondent Philip Harris, Secretary

Trustees *Mrs S D Livanos; P N Harris; A S Holmes.*

CC Number 1002279

Information available Annual report and accounts were provided by the trust.

General The trust gives grants from its income of about £300,000 a year but has also been making substantial awards from capital. Grants are widely spread and the previously reported interest in maritime causes, while still existing, is not as prominent as it was.

The trust says that 'funds are fully committed and unsolicited applications are not requested'.

In 2001 the trust had assets of £5 million, generating a high £297,000 in income. Administration costs have been greatly reduced from their previously high levels.

£479,000 was paid in 47 grants, 15 going to organisations supported with similar amounts in the previous year.

There were three large donations, all repeating similar awards in the previous year, to the Abbeyfield Society (£100,000) and Crimestoppers and Maritime Volunteer Service (£30,000 each). £25,000 each was given in new awards to Macmillan Cancer Relief and Trinity Hospice, and £20,000, for work in Wales, to WhizzKidz.

Organisations receiving repeated smaller grants included City Escape (£2,500) and Wandsworth Cancer Research Centre (£5,0000). New beneficiaries included Alder Hey Children's Hospital, Liverpool (£5,000), Sunrise Cornwall (£10,000), and the Pain Association of Scotland (£3,000).

The trust has a close association with St Mary's Hospital, Paddington in London, where £750,000 has been committed, with payments expected to start in 2002. The trust was also committed to a grant of £70,000 to Oban Hospital's Scanner Appeal.

Exclusions No grants to individuals or non-registered charities.

Applications Unsolicited applications are not requested.

Jack Livingstone Charitable Trust

Jewish, general

About £65,000 (2002/03)

Beneficial area UK and worldwide, with a preference for Manchester.

Westholme, The Springs, Park Road, Bowdon, Altrincham, Cheshire WA14 3JH

Tel. 0161 928 3232 **Fax** 0161 928 3232

Correspondent Mrs Janice Livingstone, Trustee

Trustees *Mrs J V Livingstone; Brian White.*

CC Number 263473

Information available Accounts were on file at the Charity Commission.

General In 2002/03 the trust had an income of £78,000 and a total expenditure of £68,000. Grants totalled about £65,000. A list of beneficiaries was not available.

Grants have previously been given to large Jewish organisations and local groups in Manchester and the north west of England for various purposes including arts and welfare.

Previous beneficiaries include Christie's Against Cancer, UJIA, Royal Exchange Theatre Appeal Fund, Jerusalem Foundation, Community Security Trust, National Councl of YMCAs, Heathlands Village, Manchester Balfour Trust, Ashten Trust, Brookvale Royal Schools for the Deaf and Manchester Jewish Federation.

Applications The trust does not respond to unsolicited applications.

The Elaine & Angus Lloyd Charitable Trust

General

£58,000 to organisations (2001/02)

Beneficial area UK, with a preference for Surrey, Kent and the south of England.

Messrs Badger Hakim Chartered Accountants, 10 Dover Street, London W1S 4LQ

Tel. 020 7493 3166

Correspondent R Badger

Trustees *C R H Lloyd; A S Lloyd; J S Gordon; Sir Michael C Cooper; V E Best; J S Lloyd; P J Lloyd; R J Lloyd.*

CC Number 237250

Information available Full accounts were on file at the Charity Commission.

General In 1992, the Elaine Lloyd Charitable Trust and the Mr Angus Lloyd Charitable Settlement were amalgamated and are now known as the Elaine & Angus Lloyd Charitable Trust. Many grants are recurrent, some may be paid quarterly. Grants are mainly to UK charities and local organisations in the Surrey and Kent area and elsewhere in the south of England. There is a preference for health and welfare charities and churches. Grants are given in practice to those charities known to one or more of the trustees.

In 2003/04 the trust had an income of £73,000 and a total expenditure of £80,000. Further information for this year was not available.

In 2001/02 it had assets of £2.4 million and an income of £75,000. Grants totalled £66,000, of which £8,500 was distributed to individuals.

Donations of £1,000 or more included: £4,700 to Salvation Army; £2,000 to Oxfam; £1,800 to Brighton and Hove Parents' and Childrens' Group; £1,500 each to Barry Vale Community Aid, Medway Cyrenians and Streetwise; £1,300 to Seeability; £1,100 to St Luke's – Chiddingstone; and £1,000 each to Chigwell Riding Trust, St Clement's Church – Sandwich and St Mary's Church – Newport.

Exclusions No support for overseas aid.

Applications In writing to the correspondent. The trustees meet regularly to consider grants.

Lloyd's Charities Trust

General

£468,000 (2002)

Beneficial area UK, with some interest in London.

One Lime Street, London EC3M 7HA

Tel. 020 7327 6075 **Fax** 020 7327 6368

Website www.lloyds.com

Correspondent Mrs Vicky Mirfin, Secretary

Trustees *J L Stace, Chair; H Richie; E Gilmour; N Gooding; J Lowe; Ms B Merry.*

CC Number 207232

Information available Information was on file at the Charity Commission. The trust stated some of the information was incorrect but refused to elaborate on this.

General This charity was set up in 1953, and is the charitable arm of Lloyd's insurance market in London. Originally the trust was funded mainly by covenanted subscriptions from members of Lloyd's. By 1997 the majority of these covenants had expired, having a substantial impact on lowering the income of the trust. The trust in response has adopted a new policy in their grant-giving, described below. Other sources of income are available and Lloyd's have also secured substantial corporation funding.

In 2003 the trust had an income of £448,000 and a total expenditure of £862,000.

In 2002 it had total assets of £2.1 million (including restricted and unrestricted funds), its income was £370,000 and £468,000 was given in grants to organisations. Grants from unrestricted funds were distributed via two methods.

Partner Charities Fund

The trust continued its successful relationship with 3 partner charities, who were selected in 2001. The total grants awarded to the three partner charities are as follows:

Help the Aged – awarded £150,000 over three years for the East London (Hackney) Handy Van Scheme and safety devices for older people

Save the Children – awarded £75,000 over three years for an HIV/AIDS project with young children in Africa

Addaction – awarded £45,000 over three years for the Impact Project – based in Camden and Islington for young children and prevention of drug abuse.

Two additional major grants of £25,000 each were made to Alzheimer's Research Trust and Hope and Homes for Children.

General grants

The 2002 report stated that the trustees were able to continue to support a number of ad-hoc appeals. In total, 18 from over 1,000 appeals were supported, totalling £139,000. Grants were mainly to support work in the fields of social welfare, national medical projects and schemes benefiting children and young people and were broken down as follows:

	No.	*Total*
Environmental	2	£23,000
Social welfare	7	£51,000
National medical	6	£49,000
Children and youth	3	£16,000

The trust also supports two projects from its restricted funds:

Lloyd's Community Programme

The principal elements of this programme are support for projects in the fields of education, training and enterprise. The funds are raised predominantly by subscription from member companies from the Lloyd's market and are used to support organisations with which Lloyd's has had long working relationships.

In 2002 grants totalled £81,000, and were given mainly to London-based charities. The largest grant was £41,000 to Tower Hamlets Education Business Partnership (this included £15,000 towards core funding and £15,000 in respect of Lloyd's sponsorship of the business mentoring scheme). East London Small Business Centre received £20,000 (which included £10,000 towards the cost of administering Lloyd's Loan Fund, £5,000 to fund training courses and a further £5,000 was granted to support the Portal Administration). At the end of the year an amount of £46,000 remained to be carried forward to 2003.

Cuthbert Health Centenary Fund

This fund provides bursaries at nine schools, each are allocated £6,500 a year. The nine participating schools are Aldenham, Bishops Stortford, Bradfield, Brighton, Charterhouse, Felsted, Reeds, Queenswood and Westminster. The cost of funding the bursaries during the year amounted to £58,000.

Capital Funds
Sums of £350,000 remain allocated to The Rising Sun Project – Newcastle upon Tyne for the purpose of building a new visitors centre at the Rising Sun country park. North Tyneside Challenge in conjunction with the local borough council is managing the overall project.

The trustees have also agreed to part fund the Idea Store in Tower Hamlets, a new concept offering art learning and library services in an accessible retail environment, with a grant of £300,000. The project is being managed in conjunction with Tower Hamlets Borough Council.

Exclusions No grants for any appeal where it is likely that the grant would be used for sectarian purposes or to local or regional branches of charities where it is possible to support the UK organisation. Support is not given to individuals.

Applications The trust stated in January 2005 that: 'Lloyds Charities Trust changed its policy on charitable giving a number of years ago and now works in partnerships with a small number of charities over a three-year period. Funds are therefore committed and we are unable to respond positively to the numerous appeals we receive.' They went on to state they wished to be removed from this guide to avoid wasting the time of fundraisers. This entry has been included for reasons of comprehension.

The Llysdinam Trust

General

£75,000 (2003/04)

Beneficial area Wales.

Rees Richards & Partners, Managing Agents, Druslyn House, De La Beche Street, Swansea, West Glamorgan SA1 3HH

Tel. 01792 650705 **Fax** 01792 468384

Email post@reesrichards.co.uk

Correspondent The Trustees

CC Number 255528

Information available Full accounts were on file at the Charity Commission.

General In 2003/04 the trust had an income of £165,000 and a total expenditure of £160,000. Grants totalled around £75,000. Further information for this year was not available.

Previous beneficiaries include Brecon & District Disabled Club, Friends of St Andrews Church, Llandovery College 150th Anniversary Fund, Penclacwydd Wildlife & Wetlands Centre, Radnorshire Macmillan Nurse Appeal, Swansea Rugby Foundation and University of Wales.

Exclusions No grants to individuals.

Applications The trust stated that it was overloaded with applications and does not welcome unsolicited applications.

Localtrent Ltd

Jewish, educational, religion

About £90,000

Beneficial area UK, with some preference for Manchester.

Lopian Gross Barnett & Co., Harvester House, 37 Peter Street, Manchester M2 5QD

Tel. 0161 832 8721

Correspondent Mrs M Weiss, Secretary

Trustees *Mrs M Weiss; B Weiss; J L Weiss; P Weiss; Mrs J J Weissmandl; Mrs R Sofer.*

CC Number 326329

Information available Full accounts were on file at the Charity Commission.

General The trust was established in 1983 for the distribution of funds to religious, educational and similar charities for the advancement of the Jewish religion.

In 2002/03 it had an income of £73,000 and a total expenditure of £91,000, most of which was distributed in grants. Further information for this year were not available.

In the previous year grants totalled £92,000. Two large grants were made to Chasdei Yoel Charitable Trust (£35,000) and Beis Minchas Yitzchok (£20,000). Other beneficiaries included UTA (£5,700) and Mosdos Beis (£3,500).

Applications In writing to the correspondent. Please note the trust stated in autumn 2003 that its funds were committed to refurbishing a local hospital for the foreseeable future.

The Locker Foundation

Jewish

£115,000 (2001/02)

Beneficial area UK and overseas.

28 High Road, East Finchley, London N2 9PJ

Tel. 020 8455 9280

Correspondent The Trustees

Trustees *I Carter; M Carter; Mrs S Segal.*

CC Number 264180

Information available Full accounts were on file at the Charity Commission.

General This trust mainly supports Jewish organisations. In 2001/02 it had assets of £1.7 million and an income of £235,000. It made nine grants totalling £215,000.

The largest grant was £34,000 to Kahal Chassidim Bobov. Grants of £22,000 went to Friends of Magon David Adom, £10,000 to Jewish Care, £7,600 to Norwood Ravenswood and £6,000 to British Friends of Israel War Disabled.

Seven grants of £5,000 each went to British Friends of Yad Sarah, Community Security Trust, Jewish Association for Mentally Ill, Jewish Blind and Disabled, Norris Lea Charitable Settlement, Save the Children and Society of Friends of Torah.

Other smaller grants between £75 to £300 were made' some of which went to Jewish National Fund and New Israel Fund.

Applications In writing to the correspondent.

The Loftus Charitable Trust

Jewish

£131,000 (2001/02)

Beneficial area UK and overseas.

48 George Street, London W1U 7DY

Tel. 020 7486 2969

Correspondent A Loftus, Trustee

Trustees *R I Loftus; A L Loftus; A D Loftus.*

CC Number 297664

Information available Accounts were on file at the Charity Commission.

General The trust was established in 1987 by Richard Ian Loftus. Its objects are the:

- advancement of the Jewish religion
- advancement of Jewish education and the education of Jewish people
- relief of the Jewish poor.

In 2001/02 the trust had an income of £93,000. Grants were made totalling £131,000.

The largest grants were £32,000 to Jewish Care and £25,000 to Lubavitch Foundation. Other large grants went to Community Security Trust (£13,000), Chief Rabbinate Trust (£6,500) and Ambrion Aviation (£6,000).

Other beneficiaries included United Synagogue (£4,000), Norwood and United Israel Appeal (£3,000 each) and Jewish Learning, Hasmoneon School, (£2,500 each).

Applications The trustees state that all funds are committed and unsolicited applications are not welcome.

London Law Trust

Health and personal development of children and young people

£144,000 (2001/02)

Beneficial area UK.

Messrs Hunters, 9 New Square, Lincoln's Inn, London WC2A 3QN

Tel. 020 7412 0050

Correspondent G D Ogilvie, Secretary

Trustees *Prof. Anthony R Mellows; R A Pellant; Sir Michael Hobbs; Sir Ian Gainsford.*

CC Number 255924

Information available Information was on file at the Charity Commission.

General The trust's aims are to:

- prevent and cure illness and disability in children and young people
- alleviate or reduce the causes or likelihood of illness and disability in children and young people
- encourage and develop, in young people, the qualities of leadership and service to the community.

Within these guidelines, the trust favours seedcorn grants, small research projects and new ventures. Grants generally range from £500 to £5,000 and are typically of about £2,500 each.

In 2002/03 the trust had income of £131,000 and a total expenditure of £198,000.

In the previous year it had assets of £3.4 million and an income of £135,000. Grants were made totalling £144,000. They included £5,000 to Michael Palin Center for Stammering Children, £3,000 to Young Minds, £2,500 each to Association of Wheelchair Users, Soundabout and West Wiltshire Portage Service and £1,000 each to Angus Special Play Scheme, Circus Eruption and Hereditary Extosis Support Group.

Exclusions Applications from individuals, including students, are ineligible.

Applications In writing to the correspondent. The trustees employ a grant advisor whose job is to evaluate applications. Grant applicants are requested to supply detailed information in support of their applications. The grant advisor makes on-site visits to almost all applicants.

The trustees meet twice a year to consider the grant advisor's reports. Most grants are awarded in the autumn.

The William & Katherine Longman Trust

General

£120,000 (2002/03)

Beneficial area UK.

Charles Russell, 8–10 New Fetter Lane, London EC4A 1RS

Tel. 020 7203 5000

Correspondent W P Harriman, Trustee

Trustees *W P Harriman; J B Talbot; A C O Bell.*

CC Number 800785

Information available Full accounts were provided by the trust.

General The trust supports a wide range of organisations with grants ranging from £500 to £18,000 each, mostly at the lower end of the scale.

In 2002/03 it had assets of £2.6 million, which generated an income of £81,000. Grants were made totalling £120,000. Management and administration charges were high at £25,000. This included £22,000 paid to firms in which a trustee is a partner. Whilst wholly legal, these editors always regret such payments unless, in the words of the Charity Commission, 'there is no realistic alternative'.

The largest grants were £18,000 to Coventry Cathedral Development Trust and £10,000 to World Vision UK. Other grants included £7,500 to Care, £5,000 to Royal British Legion, £4,000 each to Chelsea Festival and Sargent Cancer Care for Children, £3,000 each to British Kidney Patients Association and Trinity Hospice, £2,500 each to King Edward VII Hospital, Oxford Kilburn Boys' Club and RSPCA for Harmsworth Hospital, £2,000 each to Helen Arkell Dyslexia Centre, Care International, Shelter and Youth Sport UK and £500 to Chelsea Old Church.

Exclusions Grants are only made to registered charities.

Applications The trustees believe in taking a proactive approach in deciding which charities to support and it is their policy not to respond to unsolicited appeals.

The Loseley & Guildway Charitable Trust

General

£43,000 (2003/04)

Beneficial area International and UK, with an interest in Guildford.

The Estate Offices, Loseley Park, Guildford, Surrey GU3 1HS

Tel. 01483 304440 **Fax** 01483 302036

Correspondent Miss Nicola Cheriton-Sutton, Secretary

Trustees *Maj. James More-Molyneux, Chair; Mrs Susan More-Molyneux; Michael More-Molyneux; Adrian Abbott; Glye Hodson.*

CC Number 267178

Information available Information was on file at the Charity Commission.

General The trust was founded in 1973, when 'the More-Molyneux family injected private capital and transferred five of their own properties to the trust'. The rent of these properties provides about half the trust's present income.

Two of these properties have now been sold in order to finance the purchase of land on which Christopher's (a hospice for life limited children) has been built.

The trust states its objects as follows:

- compassionate causes
- charities with which various members of the More-Molyneux family and trustees are associated such as cancer charities (including Macmillan Cancer Relief and Marie Curie Cancer Care); Queen Elizabeth's Foundation for Disabled People; Children's Hospice Association for the South East; Challengers (Disability Challenge); and Harriet Davis Seaside Holiday Trust for Disabled Children
- local charities
- some environmental causes
- emergency/disaster appeals worldwide.

In 2003/04 it had assets of £1 million and an income of £46,000. Grants were made totalling £43,000. These included £5,000 to Challengers and £1,000 each to Gurkha Welfare Trust and King George Fund for Sailors.

Exclusions No grants to individuals or non-registered charities.

Applications In writing to the correspondent. The trustees meet in February, May and September to consider applications. However, due to commitments, new applications for any causes are unlikely to be successful.

The C L Loyd Charitable Trust

General

£73,000 (2001/02)

Beneficial area UK, with a preference for Berkshire and Oxfordshire.

Lockinge, Wantage, Oxfordshire OX12 8QL

Tel. 01235 833265

Correspondent C L Loyd, Trustee

Trustees *C L Loyd; T C Loyd.*

CC Number 265076

Information available Full accounts were on file at the Charity Commission.

General The trust supports UK charities and local charities (in Berkshire and Oxfordshire) involved in welfare, animals, churches, medical/disability, children/youth and education.

In 2001/02 the assets of the trust stood at £2.35 million generating an income of £115,000. Grants totalled £73,000. The largest grant made was £31,000 to Wm Rowden Charitable Trust.

Donations of £1,000 or above included: £3,500 each to Ardington and Lockinge Church and Ardington and Lockinge Parochial Church Council; £3,000 each to Countryside Buildings Protection Trust and King Alfred's Educational Charity; £2,000 to Ardington and Lockinge Relief-in-Need; and £1,000 to Wantage Counselling Service.

Smaller donations included: £500 to Cumbria Community Recovery Fund; £250 each to Amber Foundation and Animals in War Memorial Fund; £200 each to Brendoncare Foundation and Ryder-Cheshire Foundation; £100 each to Berks Clergy Charity, Enham Trust, Oxfordshire Animal Sanctuary, St Mary's Church – Banbury and St Peter's Church – Hook Norton; £50 each to Bibles for Children and Donkey Sanctuary; £25 to Outward Bound Trust; and £10 each to Ardington and Lockinge British Legion and National Children's Home and Orphanage.

Exclusions No support for individuals or medical research.

Applications In writing to the correspondent. Grants are made several times each month.

LSA Charitable Trust

Horticulture

£42,000 (2002/03)

Beneficial area UK.

c/o Farrer & Co, 66 Lincoln's Inn Fields, London WC2A 3LH

Tel. 020 7242 2022

Correspondent Cheryl Boyce

Trustees *B E G Howe; P Hadley; C F Woodhouse; A M M Ross; S R V Pomeroy.*

CC Number 803671

Information available Information was provided by the trust.

General The trust supports horticultural research, the promotion of horticultural knowledge, and the relief of poverty for ex LSA tennents.

In 2002/03 the trust had assests of £982,000 and an income of £45,000. Grants totalled £42,000 and were broken down as follows:

Individuals and institutions for education – £13,000
Beneficiaries were Nuffield Farming Scholarships Trust (£6,000), RHS Harlow Carr (£5,000) and University of Manchester and Kingston Maurward College (£1,000 each).

Individuals for the relief of poverty – £29,000
Grants were made to 19 individuals.

Applications For organisations: in writing to the correspondent. Grants to individuals for the relief of poverty are made through the Royal Agricultural Benevolent Institution.

The Luck-Hille Foundation

Education, health, welfare

£50,000 (2000/01)

Beneficial area UK.

c/o Citroen Wells, Devonshire House, 1 Devonshire Street, London W1N 2DR

Tel. 020 7304 2000

Correspondent J W Prevezer, Trustee

Trustees *Mrs Jill Luck-Hille; P M Luck-Hille; J W Prevezer.*

CC Number 269046

Information available Accounts were on file at the Charity Commission.

General This trust was established in 1975 as The Jill Kreitman Charitable Trust, daughter of the founders of the much larger trust The Kreitman Foundation. Grants are made to registered and exempt charities in the UK working concerned with education, health and welfare.

In 2003/04 the foundation had an income of £172,000 and a total expenditure of £86,000. Unfortunately, no further information for this year was on file.

In 2000/01 the foundation had assets of £4.4 million which generated an income of £202,000. Grants were made to seven organisations totalling £50,000.

The largest grant was £37,000 to Middlesex University. Due to an agreement in 1998 to construct and refit a real-tennis court on the campus of Middlesex University to a maximum of

£1.5 million, the institution actually received £175,000 from the foundation during the year, most of which was accounted for in previous financial years.

King Alfred School Appeal was given £8,500 whilst Norwood received £3,600. Other grants went to Project Trust (£500), The National Hospital and Raleigh International (£250 each) and Children with Aids Charity (£200).

Exclusions No grants to individuals.

Applications To the correspondent in writing. The trustees seem to have a list of regular beneficiaries and it may be unlikely that any new applications will be successful.

Henry Lumley Charitable Trust

See below

£91,000 (2002)

Beneficial area England and Wales.

Hargraves House, Belmont Road, Maidenhead, Berkshire SL6 6TB

Correspondent Peter Lumley, Trustee

Trustees *Henry Lumley; Peter Lumley; Robert Lumley; James Porter.*

CC Number 1079480

Information available Accounts were on file at the Charity Commission.

General Registered in February 2000, the income of the trust is derived from the dividends and interest received from shares in the private company Edward Lumley Holdings Ltd. Charities supported should be known to at least one trustee. Aside from the founder's initial list of beneficiaries, new charities have been added as funds permit and are usually of a one-off nature to assist medical or educational projects.

In 2002 a total of 22 donations were made totalling £90,500. It had assets of £301,000 and an income of £35,000.

Beneficiaries of the largest grants were: Magdalen College – Student Access and Hardship Fund (£25,000), and Royal Australasian Alzheimer's Society (£10,000).

Other grants for either £1,000, £2,500, £3,000, £4,000 or £5,000 included those to Alzheimer's Society, The Dyslexia Institute, The Mountbatten Community Trust, Parish Church of St Mary the Virgin, Shenfield – The Organ Fund, The Salvation Army and Well Being.

Applications In writing to the correspondent.

Paul Lunn-Rockliffe Charitable Trust

General

£33,000 (2003/04)

Beneficial area UK with a preference for Hampshire.

4a Barnes Close, Winchester, Hampshire SO23 9QX

Tel. 01962 852949 **Fax** 01962 852949

Correspondent Mrs J M Lunn-Rockliffe, Secretary

Trustees *Mrs Jacqueline Lunn-Rockliffe; Victor Lunn-Rockliffe; James Lunn-Rockliffe.*

CC Number 264119

Information available Accounts were provided by the trust.

General The annual report states that the trust gives 'first but not exclusive consideration to charities likely to further Christianity, followed by those connected with the relief of poverty, to help the infirm, and encourage youth organisations'. It prefers to give larger grants to fewer charities (rather than smaller grants to more). It seeks out 'special organisations or projects which may only be known locally to the trustees and members of their families'. Most of the donations are repeated from year to year, but some is kept aside for one-off grants.

In 2003/04 the trust had assets of £704,000 and an income of £136,000. Grants were made totalling £33,000 and donated to 68 organisations, of which around 20 were situated in the Hampshire area. They were broken down as follows:

	No.	*Total*
Aged	1	£500
Children	5	£2,600
Disabled	7	£2,800
Education students	6	£2,700
Family	4	£2,100
Mission	6	£3,300
Needy, drug addicts, homeless, unemployed	11	£6,000
Prisoners	4	£1,900
Radio/ mission	4	£1,900
Third World	9	£4,300
Youth	5	£2,000
Others	6	£2,600

Beneficiaries included: Christians Against Poverty (£1,100); Bible Society (£800); Children's Society, Christian Aid, Church Urban Fund, Hour of Revival and Tearfund (£600 each); British Red Cross, Intermediate Technology, Keston Institute, Life, Prison Fellowship and Spastics Society of India (£500 each); People International, Way to Life, Society of St Dismas and Scripture Union (£400 each); Boys' Brigade, Cre8ted, Damaris and Delta (£300 each); and Oscar (£200).

Exclusions The trustees will not fund individuals; for example, student's expenses and travel grants. Repair and maintenance of historic buildings are also excluded for support.

Applications The trust encourages preliminary phone calls to discuss applications. It will generally only reply to written correspondence if an sae has been included.

The Ruth & Jack Lunzer Charitable Trust

Jewish; children, young adults and students; education

£39,000 (2002/03)

Beneficial area UK.

c/o BDO Stoy Hayward, 8 Baker Street, London W1U 3LL

Tel. 020 7893 2499

Correspondent M D Paisner, Trustee

Trustees *J V Lunzer; M D Paisner.*

CC Number 276201

Information available Accounts were on file at the Charity Commission, but with only a brief narrative report.

General The trust says it makes grants to organisations benefiting children, young adults and students; primarily educational establishments. In practice many such beneficiaries are Jewish organisations.

In 2002/03 the trust had assets of £45,000 and an income of £52,000 with grants totalling £39,000.

The largest grants were £5,000 to Yesoday Hatorah Schools and £3,500 to KKL.

Other grants include £2,400 to GGBH Congregation, £2,000 each to GGBH Ladies Guild and Jewish National Fund

Charitable Trust, £1,500 each to Independent Jewish Day School and Helenslea Charities, £500 each to Project Seed and SAGE, £200 each to Shuva Israel, Oxford University Jewish Society, J & R Charitable Trust, Gateshead Academy for Torah Studies, Craven Walk Charity Trust and Beis Brucha-Mother and Baby Home and £100 each to Agudas Yisroel Women's Group, Friends of Religious Settlements - Yud Benjamin, London Academy of Jewish Studies and Rav Chesed Trust.

Applications In writing to the correspondent.

Lord and Lady Lurgan Trust

Medical, older people and the arts, in the UK and South Africa

£41,000 (2001/02)

Beneficial area UK and South Africa.

Pemberton Greenish (Ref MDB), 45 Pont Street, London SW1X 0BX

Tel. 020 7591 3333 **Fax** 020 7591 3300

Correspondent The Trustees

Trustees *Simon David Howard Ladd Staughton; Andrew John Francis Stebbings; Diana Sarah Graves (partners Pemberton Greenish).*

CC Number 297046

Information available Accounts were on file at the Charity Commission.

General The registered objects of this trust are:

- the relief and medical care of older people
- medical research, in particular cancer research and the publication of the useful results of such research
- the advancement of education including education in the arts for the public benefit by the establishment of educational and artistic bursaries
- other charitable purposes at the discretion of the trustees.

There is also a special interest in South Africa, due to the settlors spending the latter part of their lives there, and in Northern Ireland because of family origins.

In 2001/02 the trust had assets of £1 million with an income of £42,000 and grants totalling £41,000.

Grant distribution is divided into two key areas.

Institutional Grants in the UK

£10,000 to Royal College of Music, £3,000 to Pushkin Prizes, £1,000 each to Aldeburgh Productions, Alzheimer's Society, Arthritis Care, Brain Research Trust, Cancer Research UK, Chelsea Children's Hospital School, Dorset Opera, Foundation for Young Musicians, Help the Aged, Lady Hoare Trust, Magic Lantern, National Autistic Society, POD, Prostate Cancer Society, Royal Marsden Hospital Charity, Royal National Institute for the Blind, Shaftesbury Society, Trinity Hospice and Wellbeing.

South Africa

£400 each to BUSKAID, Cotlands Baby Sanctuary, Deaf Federation of South Africa, Johannesburg Children's Home, Nelson Mandela Children's Fund, Tape Aids forthe Blind, Star Seaside Home, Marilyn Lahana Memorial Award, Forest Town School for Cerebral Palsied Children, OPTIMA (South African National Council for the Blind) and Princess Alice Adoption Home.

Applications In writing to the correspondent.

The Lyndhurst Trust

Christian

£110,000 (2001/02)

Beneficial area UK and overseas, with preferences for north east England and the developing world.

66 High Street, Swainby, Northallerton, North Yorkshire DL6 3DG

Correspondent W P Hinton, Trustee

Trustees *W P C Hinton; J A L Hinton; Dr W J Hinton.*

CC Number 235252

Information available Full accounts were on file at the Charity Commission.

General The 2001/02 accounts stated: 'The trustees have sought opportunities for the promotion and advancement of the Christian religion in any part of the world, in accordance with the trust's deed. The trustees have continued to support opportunities to promote and advance the spreading of the Christian religion in any part of the world. The policy has continued to be to regularly support charities that are promoting the awareness of the Christian gospel, in those areas of the world where people are prevented from hearing it through normal channels of communication. Agencies operating in difficult circumstances are given special consideration.

'The trustees have continued their policy of making funds available to the disadvantaged in the United Kingdom and Europe. Special attention continues to be given to those charities involved in meeting the needs of those with drug and alcohol problems through Christian rehabilitation programmes.'

In 2001/02 the trust had assets of £1.2 million generating an income of £48,000. Grants totalled £110,000, broken down as follows:

	No.	*Total*	*Percent*
North east England	26	£46,000	33%
Third world countries	17	£35,000	37%
UK – general	17	£16,000	17%
Europe and the rest of the world	8	£13,000	13%

Beneficiaries in the north east of England included St Aidan's Community Church (£16,000), North East Youth for Christ (£10,000), New Life Pentecostal Church and Thorntree Apostolic Church (£1,500 each), Emmanuel Prison Ministry (£1,200), Redcar Baptist Church (£1,100), Christian Institute, South Bank Baptist Church and Lightfoot Grove Church (£1,000 each). Recipients of grants of £800 and under included those to All Saints' Church Eaglescliffe, Church of Nazarene, Marton Christian Fellowship, Scripture Union In Schools and South Bank Mission.

Other beneficiaries in the UK included Evangelical Alliance and Prison Christian Fellowship (£1,500 each), Walsall Street Teams (£1,100), Betel International, Link House Trust and Teen Challenge UK – Strahclyde (£1,000 each). Grants of £1,000 and under included those to Boys Brigade, Life Challenge, Pocket Testament League and Twenty Five Trust.

Grants to the developing world included those to OMS International – South Africa (£2,000), Church Missionary Society – Sudan, Operation Mobilisation – India and Valathi Outreach Ministries Trust – India (£1,500 each), Bible Society – Cuba and Tear Fund – Asia (£1,300 each) and Christian Fellowship Ministry – Kenya, Haggi Institute – Ghana and UFM Worldwide – Sierra Leone (£1,000 each).

Beneficiaries in Europe and the rest of the world include European Christian Mission in Romania, Albania and Kosovo (£1,500 each), Albanian Evangelical Trust and Operation Mobilisation – Spain (£1,000 each),

Haggi Institute – Spain, Pocket Testament League – Spain (£500 each).

Exclusions No support for individuals or buildings.

Applications In writing to the correspondent, enclosing an sae if a reply is required. Requests are considered half-yearly.

The Lynn Foundation

General

£242,000 (2003/04)

Beneficial area UK and overseas.

Blackfriars, 17 Lewes Road, Haywards Heath, West Sussex RH17 7SP

Tel. 01444 454773 **Fax** 01444 456192

Correspondent Guy Parsons, Trustee

Trustees *Guy Parsons, Chair; J F Emmott; Dr P E Andry; P R Parsons; Ian Fair.*

CC Number 326944

Information available Information was provided by the trust.

General The trust has previously stated that it supports a very wide range of organisations, including those in the areas of music, the arts, Masonic charities, disability, older people and children.

In 2003/04 the trust had assets of £5.5 million and received an income of £270,000. Grants during the year totalled £242,000.

Recent beneficiaries include Wigmore Hall, Discover - Children's Discovery Centre, London Master Classes, Awards for Young Musicians, The Young Vic, Bath International Music Festival, Northern Rock Festival Group, Oratorio and Jazz Choirs, Bampton Classical Opera, Abbotsbury Music and Listening Books.

Applications In writing to the correspondent.

The Lyons Charitable Trust

Health, medical research, children

£70,000 (1999/2000)

Beneficial area UK.

Field Fisher Waterhouse, 35 Vine Street, London EC3N 2AA

Correspondent Mrs H Fuff

Trustees *M S Gibbon; Nick Noble.*

CC Number 1045650

Information available Accounts were on file at the Charity Commission, but without a recent grants list.

General The trust in particular makes grants in the fields of health, medical research and children in need.

In 1999/2000 it had assets of £1.5 million and an income of £87,000. Administration and accountancy charges for the year were high at £8,000. Grants were made to six organisations totalling £70,000.

As in recent years, there was no grants list included in the 1999/2000 accounts. The most recent available grants information refers to 1994/95, when five grants of £12,000 and one grant of £5,000 were made; the beneficiaries were Great Ormond Street Hospital for Sick Children, Terrence Higgins Trust, Florence Nightingale Fund, Printers Charitable Corporation and WWF.

Applications In writing to the correspondent.

This entry was not confirmed by the trust, but was correct according to information on file at the Charity Commission.

The Sir Jack Lyons Charitable Trust

Jewish, arts, education

£143,000 (2002/03)

Beneficial area UK and overseas.

Sagars, 3rd Floor, Elizabeth House, Queen Street, Leeds LS1 2TW

Tel. 0113 297 6789

Correspondent M J Friedman, Trustee

Trustees *Sir Jack Lyons; Lady Roslyn Marion Lyons; M J Friedman; J E Lyons; D S Lyons.*

CC Number 212148

Information available Full accounts were on file at the Charity Commission.

General This trust shows a particular interest in Jewish charities and also a consistent interest in the arts, particularly music. In 2002/03 the trust had assets of £2.7 million and an income of £174,000. After management and administration costs of £10,000, grants were made to 12 organisations totalling £143,000. Grants ranged from £100 to £100,000.

By far the largest grant was £100,000 to Heslington Foundation. Other large grants were to British Ort and University of York (£15,000 each) and London Symphony Orchestra (£7,800).

Smaller grants were to City University – London (£2,500), UKAWIS (£1,000), Henry Wood Hall and Nightingale House (£500 each), Life Line for the Old Jerusalem (£250) and York Early Music Festival and Institute for the Special Child (£100 each).

Exclusions No grants to individuals.

Applications In writing to the correspondent. In the past the trust has stated: 'In the light of increased pressure for funds, unsolicited appeals are less welcome and would waste much time and money for applicants who were looking for funds which were not available.'

Malcolm Lyons Foundation

Jewish

£36,000 (2002/03)

Beneficial area UK.

BDO Stoy Hayward, 8 Baker Street, London W1U 3LL

Tel. 020 7893 2318

Correspondent J S Newman, Trustee

Trustees *M S Lyons; Mrs J Lyons; D Mendoza; J S Newman.*

CC Number 1050689

Information available Full accounts were on file at the Charity Commission.

General This trust supports Jewish and Israeli organisations. In 2002/03 it had assets of £47,000. Total income was £50,000 and grants totalled £36,000.

The largest grants were £9,600 to Mesorah Heritage Foundation, £5,500 to Lubavitch Foundation and £5,000 to Jewish Care. Other beneficiaries included Kollel Gur Trust (£3,000), North West London Jewish Day Centre (£2,500), United Jewish Israel Appeal (£1,500) and Jewish Learning Exchange and United Synagogue (£1,100 each).

Beneficiaries receiving under £1,000 included Kisharon (£800), Finchley Synagogue (£500), Hampstead Garden Suburb Synagogue (£470) and Craven Walk Charities (£400).

Applications The trust states that it will not consider unsolicited applications.

The M & C Trust

Jewish, social welfare

£128,000 (2002/03)

Beneficial area UK.

c/o Chantrey Vellacott DFK, Russell Square House, 10/12 Russell Square, London WC1B 5LF

Tel. 020 7509 9000 **Fax** 020 7509 9219

Correspondent A C Langridge, Trustee

Trustees *A Bernstein; Mrs J B Kemble; A C Langridge; Elizabeth J Marks; Rachel J Lebus.*

CC Number 265391

Information available Full accounts were provided by the trust.

General Since 1999 the trust's primary charitable objects have been Jewish causes and social welfare.

In 2002/03 the trust had assets of £3.3 million and an income of £110,000. Grants totalled £128,000.

By far the largest grants were donated to Jewish Care and Norwood which received £20,000 each.

Beneficiaries of smaller grants included Connect and Jewish Children's Holiday Fund (£10,000 each), Friends of Israel Educational Trust, Helen House, Nightgale House and Treehouse (£7,500 each) and Break and Community Security Trust (£5,000 each).

The trust is connected with Quercus Trust, being under the same administration and having similar objectives.

Exclusions No grants to individuals.

Applications In writing to the correspondent, but the trust states that funds are currently earmarked for existing projects. In order to keep administration costs to a minimum, they are unable to reply to any unsuccessful applications.

The M D & S Charitable Trust

Jewish

£131,000 (2001/02)

Beneficial area UK and Israel.

479 Holloway Road, London N7 6LE

Tel. 020 7272 2255

Correspondent Martin D Cymerman, Trustee

Trustees *M D Cymerman; Mrs S Cymerman.*

CC Number 273992

Information available Full accounts were on file at the Charity Commission.

General This trust supports Jewish organisations in the UK and has general charitable purposes in Israel.

In 2001/02 the trust had assets of £634,000 and an income of £124,000 with grants totalling £131,000.

The largest grants were £10,000 each to Yashivat Magen Avrohom and Yeshivat Hechel Shimon Volozhin, £6,000 each to Gevurath Ari Academy Trust, Ichud Mosdos Gur, Kolel Ohel Naftali and Yeshivat Breslaw.

Other grants include £5,000 each to Yeshivat Nechomos Isar Yisroel, Yeshivat Nachalat Shay, Yeshivat Dorg, Kolel Breslaw and Mosdos Chassidey Dorg Institutions, £4,000 to Friends of Yeshivat Ponevez, £3,000 to Seminar Ateres Malkah, £2,000 each to Bes Yisroel Benevolent Trust and Yeshivat Meshech Chochmo, £1,700 to Ponevez Aid and Benevolence Fund, £1,400 to Yeshivat Sharei Shimon, £1,200 to Or Mizion Institutions and £1,000 to Yeshivat Strikov.

Applications In writing to the correspondent.

The Madeline Mabey Trust

Medical research, children's welfare

£324,000 (2001/02)

Beneficial area UK, and UK registered international charities.

Mabey House, Floral Mile, Twyford, Reading RG10 9SQ

Correspondent Joanna Singeisen, Trustee

Trustees *Alan G Daliday; Bridget A Nelson; Joanna L Singeisen.*

CC Number 326450

Information available Accounts were on file at the Charity Commission, but without a list of grants, or a full narrative report.

General The 2001/02 trustees report and accounts provided little detail of the nature of this trust, containing no grants list or narrative report. In previous years the trust has stated that it principally, but not exclusively, supports medical research and children's welfare charities. The report states 'a separate analysis of donations is provided to the Charity Commission'; however, one was not available not on file.

In 2001/02 the trust had assets of £300,000, an income of £457,000 and made grants totalling £324,000. No further information was available.

Applications In writing to the correspondent. Please note, unsuccessful applications are not acknowledged.

The Robert McAlpine Foundation

Children with disabilities, older people, medical research, welfare

£365,000 (2001/02)

Beneficial area UK.

Eaton Court, Maylands Avenue, Hemel Hempstead, Hertfordshire HP2 7TR

Tel. 01442 233444

Correspondent Graham Prain

Trustees *Hon. David McAlpine; M H D McAlpine; Kenneth McAlpine; Cullum McAlpine; Adrian N R McAlpine.*

CC Number 226646

Information available Full accounts were on file at the Charity Commission.

General This foundation generally supports causes concerned with children with disabilities, older people, medical research and social welfare. A small number of other charities are also supported, through a long-term connection with the foundation and therefore no new beneficiaries are considered from outside the usual areas.

In 2001/02 it had assets of £3.1 million and an income of £396,000. Grants totalled £365,000. Further information for this year was unavailable unfortunately.

In 1999/2000 Ewing Foundation received £40,000 while £35,000 was donated to Fairbridge. Other grants included £17,000 to Stoke Mandeville Burns and Reconstruction Surgery, £10,000 each to Devas Club and H & F Skills Centre, £7,500 to Brittle Bone Society, £5,000 each to Age Concern, Beamsley Project, Glasgow Old People's Welfare Association, St Briavels Centre for Child Development, Somers Workshop and Thrift Urban Housing, £4,500 to Defeating Deafness, £4,000 to Child & Sound, £3,000 to Side by Side, £2,500 each to Age Concern Wirral, League of Venturers Search and Rescue, Mountsandel Christian Fellowship and Ro-Ro Sailing Project and £1,000 to New Horizons.

Exclusions The trust does not like to fund overheads. No grants to individuals.

Applications In writing to the correspondent at any time. Considered annually, normally in November.

The E M MacAndrew Trust

Medical, children, general

£36,000 (2001/02)

Beneficial area UK.

J P Thornton & Co., The Old Dairy, Adstockfields, Adstock, Buckingham MK18 2JE

Tel. 01296 714886 **Fax** 01296 714711

Correspondent J P Thornton, Administrator

Trustees *A R Nicholson; E P Colquhoun.*

CC Number 290736

Information available Information was on file at the Charity Commission,

General The trust is mainly interested in medical and children's charities. In 2003/04 it had an income of £49,000 and a total expenditure of £39,000. Further details for this year were not available.

In 2001/02 it had assets of £993,000 and an income of £47,000. Grants totalled £36,000. The largest were: £7,000 in two grants to Stoke Mandeville Burns and Reconstructive Surgery Research Trust; and £4,000 in two grants to MERLIN.

Applications The trustees state that they do not respond to any unsolicited applications under any circumstances, as they prefer to make their own decisions as to which charities to support.

Macdonald-Buchanan Charitable Trust

General

£106,000 (2001)

Beneficial area UK, with a slight preference for Northamptonshire.

Rathbone Trust Ltd, 159 New Bond Street, London W1S 2UD

Tel. 020 7399 0820

Correspondent Miss Linda Cousins

Trustees *Capt. John Macdonald-Buchanan; A J Macdonald-Buchanan; A R Macdonald-Buchanan; H J Macdonald-Buchanan; Mrs M C A Philipson.*

CC Number 209994

Information available Full accounts were on file at the Charity Commission.

General The Hon. Catherine Macdonald-Buchanan set up this trust in 1952 for general charitable purposes and endowed it with 40,000 shares in the then Distillers Company.

In 2002 the trust had an income of £113,000 with an expenditure of £119,000. No further information was available.

Grants totalled £106,000 in 2001. Two substantial grants were made during the year: £30,000 to Carrie Jo Charitable Trust and £23,000 to Orrin Charitable Trust. The only other grant of over £1,000 went to Queen Margaret's School (£1,500).

A number of organisations in Northamptonshire were supported. Northamptonshire Association of Youth Clubs received £500 while Clubs for Young People Northamptonshire and YMCA Northamptonshire each received two grants totalling £400. Grants of £250 each went to Northampton and District Mind, Northamptonshire Council for Disabled People and Northamptonshire Association for the Blind.

Other grants included £500 each to British Red Cross, Cot Death Society, East Anglia Children's Hospice, Imperial Cancer Research Fund, National Asthma Association, Anthony Nolan Bone Marrow Trust, Oxfam and Spinal Injuries Association, £200 each to Age Concern, Battersea Central Mission, Canine Partners for the Independence, Ex-Service Mental Welfare Society and Gurkha Welfare Trust, £150 each to Game Conservancy Trust and £25 to Philharmonic Choir.

Exclusions No grants to individuals.

Applications In writing to the correspondent, for consideration once a year. Appeals will not be acknowledged.

The McDougall Trust

Political and economic research.

£118,000 (2000)

Beneficial area UK and overseas.

6 Chancel Street, London SE1 0UX

Tel. 020 7620 1080 **Fax** 020 7928 1528

Email admin@mcdougall.org.uk

Correspondent Paul Wilder, Trust Secretary

Trustees *Prof. David M Farrell, Chair; Elizabeth Bee; Elizabeth Collingridge; Michael Meadowcroft; Nigel Siedever; John Ward; Prof. Paul Webb.*

CC Number 212151

Information available Very little information was available on this trust.

General The trust supports the knowledge, study and research of: political or economic science and functions of government and the services provided to the community by public and voluntary organisations; methods of election of and the selection and government of representative organisations whether national, civic, commercial, industrial or social; and representative democracy, its forms, functions and development and also its associated institutions. Special priority is given to electoral research projects.

In 2000 the trust had an income of £206,000 and made grants totalling £118,000. Recent information on beneficiaries was not available.

Previous beneficiaries include Electoral Reform Society and University of Strathclyde.

Exclusions No grants to any political party or commercial organisation, for an individual's education, for social welfare matters, or for general appeals, expeditions or scholarships.

Applications In writing to the correspondent, including annual accounts. Trustees normally meet quarterly. Brief details of proposal needed. Initial enquiries by telephone accepted. Two deadlines for receipt of applications: 1 May and 1 October. Applications received after a deadline may be held over for consideration at the trustees' discretion.

The Macfarlane Walker Trust

Education, the arts, social welfare, general

£30,000 to organisations and individuals (2003/04)

Beneficial area UK, with priority for Gloucestershire.

50 Courthope Road, London NW3 2LD

Correspondent Mrs S V Walker, Secretary

Trustees *D F Walker; N G Walker.*

CC Number 227890

Information available Accounts and annual report provided by the trust.

General This trust has particular interest in the provision of facilities for recreation and social welfare in Gloucestershire, the relief of poverty and hardship among employees and former employees of Walker Crosweller & Co Ltd, the provision of educational facilities particularly in scientific research and the encouragement of music, drama and the fine arts. The trust also prefers to support small projects were they believe their 'contribution will be significant.'

In 2003/04 the trust had an income of £20,000. Grants to individuals totalled £1,600, with grants to organisations totalling £28,000.

Beneficiaries included the Second World War Experience Centre (£5,000), Vita Nova (£3,000), Blackheath Concert Halls, Carlton Primary School, Charlton Kings Senior Citizens Welfare, Dyslexia Institute, Gloucestershire Association for Mental Health, Gloucestershire Society, Listening Books and National Star College (£2,000 each) Brewery Arts, Perranzabuloe Rotary Club (Permuteran gamelan), St Peters C of E Primary School (£1,000 each) and University of Gloucestershire (£900).

Exclusions No grants for expeditions, medical expenses, nationwide appeals, animal charities or educational fees.

Applications In writing to the correspondent giving the reason for applying, and an outline of the project with a financial forecast. An sae must accompany the initial application.

The A M McGreevy No 5 Charitable Settlement

General

£42,000 (2001/02)

Beneficial area UK, with a preference for the Bristol and Bath area.

KPMG, 100 Temple Street, Bristol BS1 6AG

Tel. 0117 905 4554

Correspondent Sarah Farrow

Trustees *Avon Executor & Trustee Co.; Anthony M McGreevy; Elise McGreevy-Harris; Katrina McGreevy.*

CC Number 280666

Information available Full accounts were on file at the Charity Commission.

General The trust was established in 1979 by Anthony M McGreevy. In previous years there has been a preference for charities based in the former county of Avon.

In 2003/04 the trust had an income of £36,000 and a total expenditure of £36,000. Further information for this year was unavailable. Instead we refer to previous information collated which states in 2001/02 the assets were £1.7 million and the income was £38,000. Grants to six organisations totalled £42,000. Beneficiaries were: St Peter's Church – Camerton (£20,000); Childline (£13,000); GEM Appeal (£5,000); National Missing Persons Helpline (£3,000); and Alzheimer's Society and Stroke Association (£250 each). Over half of the recipients had received support in the previous year.

Exclusions No support for individuals.

Applications In writing to the correspondent.

The McKenna Charitable Trust

Welfare, education, children, general

£218,000 to organisations (2002/03)

Beneficial area England and Wales.

c/o Buzzacoat, 12 New Fetter Lane, London EC4A 1AG

Tel. 020 7556 1200

Correspondent The Trustees

Trustees *P A McKenna; Mrs M E A McKenna; J L Boyton; H R Jones.*

CC Number 1050672

Information available Full accounts were on file at the Charity Commission.

General The trust's aims are to:

- assist with education, medical welfare and relief of need amongst people with disabilities
- provide funds for education as a means of relieving poverty
- make grants to children's charities
- make grants for general charitable purposes.

In 2002/03 it had an income of £200,000 and gave £237,000 in grants. However, this included an exceptional donation to the trust of £200,000, which is also how much was given to the main beneficiary, Young Vic Theatre Company. It appears that this may have been a grant given through the trust rather than by it and the generated income of £7 (from assets at the year end of £239,000) and grant total to other organisations and individuals of £37,000 appears to better describe the nature of this trust.

Aside from the large grant, beneficiaries were Downing College – Cambridge (£10,000), Miracles (£5,000), Breakthrough (£1,000) and North London Hospice (£500). It also gave £20,000 to individuals.

Applications In writing to the correspondent at any time.

The Mackey & Brewer Charitable Trust

General

£54,000 (2001/02)

Beneficial area UK.

c/o HSBC Trust Co. (UK) Ltd, 10th Floor, Norwich House, Nelson Gate, Commercial Road, Southampton SO15 1GX

Tel. 023 8072 2218

Correspondent Miss A C S Brewer, Trustee

Trustees *HSBC Trust Co. (UK) Ltd; Miss A C S Brewer.*

CC Number 1072666

Information available Accounts were on file at the Charity Commission.

General In 2001/02 the trust had assets of £717,000 with an income of £113,000 and grants totalling £54,000.

Grants include £6,000 each to PDSA, Hampshire Association for the Care of the Blind, Marie Curie Cancer Care, National Trust for Scotland, MacMillan Cancer Trust, Salvation Army and St Johns Ambulance, £5,000 to Open Doors with Brother Andrew, £2,000 each to Leprosy Mission, Middle Eastern Christian Outreach and Julia Perks Foundation and £1,000 to Southampton University Hospitals NHS Trust.

Applications In writing to the correspondent.

Martin McLaren Memorial Trust

General

£32,000 (2001/02)

Beneficial area UK.

8–10 New Fetter Lane, London EC4A 1RS

Tel. 020 7203 5000

Correspondent Michael Macfadyen, Trustee

Trustees *Mrs Nancy Gordon McLaren; Nicholas Durlacher; Michael Robert Macfadyen; Revd Richard Francis McLaren; Sir Kenneth Carlisle.*

CC Number 291609

Information available Accounts were on file at the Charity Commission but without a description of the trust's grant-making policy.

General In 2001/02 the trust's assets totalled £629,000 generating an income of £26,000. Grants were £11,900 to Art & Christianity Enquiry Trust, £10,000 to Horticultural Scholarships Fund, £4,800 to European Gardens and £2,000 to St John's Smith Square.

Further grants under £500 were to Combe PCC, ESU Music Scholarship Fund, (£500 each), Queen Mary's Clothing Guild (£200), Macmillan Cancer Relief, The PCC Busbridge Church (£100 each) and Fairbridge Garden Society (£50).

Applications In writing to the correspondent.

D D McPhail Charitable Settlement

Medical research, disability, older people

£371,000 (2003/04)

Beneficial area UK.

PO Box 285, Pinner, Middlesex HA5 3FB

Correspondent Mrs Sheila Watson, Administrator

Trustees *I McPhail; P Cruddas; J K Noble.*

CC Number 267588

Information available Accounts were on file at the Charity Commission.

General This trust has been growing in size since 1997, when it began to receive sums from the Estate of the late Mr D D McPhail. Assets at the end of 1995/96 totalled £223,000 and grants were made in that year of £17,000. By 2003/04 the assets had risen to £7.9 million and it made grants totalling £371,000. In that year the trust had an income of £250,000.

In 2003/04 the largest grant of £123,500 was made to MIND in Harrow, £92,500 went to Newcastle NHS Trust, £74,000 to Community Links, £40,000 to Down's Syndrome Trust, £10,000 to Sir William Burrough School and £9,000 to NSYPE.

Except for £2,500 going to Merry-Go-Round, all other grants were £1,000 some of the beneficiaries were DEMAND, Friends of Northwick Park Hospital, John Groom's Association for the Disabled, National Society for Epilepsy, Riding for the Disabled Association, RNID and The Samaritans – Harrow.

Applications In writing to the correspondent.

This entry was not confirmed by the trust, but is correct according to information on file at the Charity Commission.

Ian Mactaggart Trust

Education & training, culture, welfare and disability

£200,000 (2001/02)

Beneficial area UK, with a possible preference for Scotland.

63a South Audley Street, London W1K 2QS

Tel. 020 7491 2948 **Fax** 020 7629 0414

Correspondent The Trustees

Trustees *Sir John Mactaggart; P A Mactaggart; Jane L Mactaggart; Fiona M Mactaggart; Lady Caroline Mactaggart; Karin T Woodcock; Leora J Armstrong.*

SC Number SC012502

Information available Limited information was available on this trust.

General The trust supports education and training, culture, the relief of people who are poor, sick, in need or disabled. In 2001/02, the trust had an income of £1.1 million and gave 82 grants totalling £200,000. Grants ranged from £100 – £17,000.

Beneficiaries in 2001/02 included: Bobath Scotland £250, Cantilena Festival on Islay £500, Royal One Scotland £1,000, Glasgow Social Work Department £2,000, Islay Pipe Band £3,000 and Greater Glasgow Health Fund £5,000.

Applications In writing to the correspondent. Unsolicited requests for donations are discouraged

The Magen Charitable Trust

Education, Jewish

£42,000 (2002/2003)

Beneficial area UK.

Lopian Gross Barnett & Co., Harvester House, 37 Peter Street, Manchester M2 5QD

Tel. 0161 832 8721

Correspondent The Trustees

Trustees *Jacob Halpern; Mrs Rose Halpern.*

CC Number 326535

Information available Accounts were on file at the Charity Commission, but without a narrative report or list of grants.

General In the accounts the trust's aims were stated as making donations to charitable and educational institutions. In 2002/03 the trust had assets of £1.1 million, an income of £252,000 and made grants totalling £42,000. Unfortunately there was no grants list on file even though the trust's set of accounts states 'A full list of charitable donations were supplied to the Charity Commission'.

Previous beneficiaries have included Manchester Yeshiva Kollel, Talmud Educational Trust, Bnos Yisroel School and Mesifta Tiferes Yisroel.

Applications In writing to the correspondent.

Mageni Trust

Arts

£97,000 (2001/02)

Beneficial area UK.

17 Hawthorne Road, Bromley, Kent BR1 2HN

Tel. 020 8295 0297

Correspondent G L Collins, Trustee

Trustees *G L Collins; Mrs G L Collins; S J Hoare.*

CC Number 1070732

Information available Accounts were on file at the Charity Commission.

General In 2001/02 the trust had assets of £1 million with an income of £57,000 and grants totalling £97,000.

Substantial grants were £10,000 each to VSO, Pearsons Holiday fund, CAF Giftaid and ATI Marathon Appeal.

Other beneficiaries include £5,000 each to League of Friends, South Bank Foundation Limited, Medecins sans Frontieres, Camp and Trek, Oxfam and Unicef, £3,000 to LPO Benefactor Maestoso, £2,000 each to Halifax Charity Gala, LPO Bright Sparks Appeal 2002, Liverpool Phil Schools Project, Royal Albert Hall trust, Concern, Red Cross and Save the Children.

Grants of £1,000 or less were awarded to 123rd Manchester Scouts, Brunel Care, Foundation for young Music, Headway, Ace Centre, Crimestoppers trust, Tools for Self Reliance and London Symphony Orchestra.

Applications In writing to the correspondent.

Mandeville Trust

Cancer, young people and children

£50,000 (2001/02)

Beneficial area UK.

The Hockett, Hockett Lane, Cookham Dean, Berkshire SL6 9UF

Tel. 01628 484272

Correspondent R C Mandeville, Trustee

Trustees *Robert Cartwright Mandeville; Pauline Maude Mandeville; Peter William Murcott; Justin Craigie Mandeville.*

CC Number 1041880

Information available Accounts were on file at the Charity Commission.

General In 2002/03 the trust had an income of £10,000 and similar expenditure. Further information for this year was not available.

In 2001/02 it had an income of £46,500 and made charitable donations totalling £50,000. Grant beneficiaries included University College London towards a research grant (£27,600), Imperial College (£16,000) and The Berkshire Community Foundation (£5,000). Other smaller grants totalled £1,000.

Applications In writing to the correspondent.

Maranatha Christian Trust

Christian

£129,000 (2001/02)

Beneficial area UK and worldwide.

208 Cooden Drive, Bexhill-on-Sea, East Sussex TN39 3AH

Fax 01424 844741

Correspondent G P Ridsdale

Trustees *A C Bell; Revd L Bowring; Rt Hon. Viscount Brentford.*

CC Number 265323

Information available Accounts were on file at the Charity Commission but without a list of grants.

General The trust makes grants towards the advancement of the Christian gospel in the UK and overseas.

In 2001/02 the trust had assets of £1.2 million and an income of £33,000. Grants were made totalling £129,000.

The largest grants were £25,000 to World Vision and £10,000 to Christian Action, Research and Education. Other large grants included those to Kenya Outreach Trust and Relationships Foundation International (£7,500 each), Alpha, Action for ME, Stewards Trust and Twyford Fellowship Group (£5,000 each), Warham Trust (£3,000) and Emmanuel Institute Trust, OK Club and Warwick Leadership Foundation (£2,000 each).

Grants of £1,000 each went to Christians in Entertainment, Label of Love, Mercy is a Person, Mission Aviation Fellowship, Shaftesbury Society and Through the Roof Ministries.

Applications In writing to the correspondent, but please note, the trust does not consider unsolicited applications.

Marbeh Torah Trust

Jewish

£208,000 (2000/01)

Beneficial area UK and Israel.

116 Castlewood Road, London N15 6BE

Correspondent M C Elzas, Trustee

Trustees *Moishe Chaim Elzas; Jacob Naftoli Elzas; Simone Elzas.*

CC Number 292491

Information available Accounts were on file at the Charity Commission, but only up to those for 2000/01 (which did not contain a grants list).

General The trust's objects are to further and support Jewish education and religion as well as the relief of poverty.

In 2000/01 the trust had an income of £214,000, almost entirely comprised of donations received. Grants were made totalling £208,000, leaving assets of £20,000. No further information was available for this year.

In 1999/2000, grants were made to 18 organisations totalling £239,000. The largest were £70,000 to Yeshiva Marbeh Torah, £36,000 to Sharei Shimon Aryeh, £25,000 to Yeshiva Beis Meir, £15,000 to Mishkenos Yakov, £13,000 each to Ezer Mitzion and Nachalat Avrohom and £10,000 each to Knesess Hatorah and Nechomas Isser Yisoroel. The remaining nine grants ranged from £2,800 to £7,500 and included those to Beis Hillel, Kollel Beth Hamedrash and Yeshiva Beis Hillel.

Applications In writing to the correspondent.

The Marchday Charitable Fund

Education, health, social welfare, support groups, overseas aid

£93,000 (2003)

Beneficial area UK, with a preference for south east England.

c/o Marchday Group plc, Allan House, 10 John Princes Street, London W1G 0AH

Tel. 020 7629 8050 **Fax** 020 7629 9204

Correspondent Mrs Rose Leigh

Trustees *Alan Mann; Lyndsey Mann; Dudley Leigh; Rose Leigh; Maureen Postles; Graham Smith; John Orchard; Priyen Gudka.*

CC Number 328438

Information available Full accounts were on file at the Charity Commission.

General The trust was established in 1989 to support charities and projects in a broad spectrum of education, health, social welfare, support groups and overseas aid. The trustees wish to assist small charities where a grant will support a particular project or make a difference to the continuation of the charity. There is a preference for charities in the south east of England. The trust also prefers to commit itself to three year's support rather than give a one-off grant, and revenue funding is preferred. The trustees like to have continual involvement with supported charities.

In 2003 the trust had assets of £268,000 and an income of £326,000. Grants to 17 organisations were made totalling £93,000. The largest grants were £7,500 to the Core Trust for a holistic drug rehabilitation centre, £7,000 each to the Refugee Council for a volunteer coordinator and Pimlico Toy Library towards the running of a toy library, £6,500 to REMAP for providing specialised equipment designed to relieve and rehabilitate disabled persons, £6,200 to Tunbridge Wells Mental Health Resource for a support service and £6,000 each to Alone in London towards the support service for young homeless people and Domestic Violence Matters for a support service for victims of domestic violence. A further 10 grants were made ranging between £5,000 and £3,000.

The majority of the above beneficiaries have been supported in previous years.

Exclusions The trust prefers not to support local organisations outside the south east of England. No grants to individuals or towards building projects or for religious activities.

Applications In writing to the correspondent. Replies cannot be sent to all requests. Trustees meet quarterly.

The Linda Marcus Charitable Trust

General

£295,000 (2002/03)

Beneficial area UK and Israel.

Mount Street Investors Limited, 79 Mount Street, London W1K 2SN

Tel. 020 7616 4700

Correspondent Mrs Sarah Hunt

Trustees *Dame Shirley Porter; Mrs Linda Streit; Peter Green; Steven Nigel Porter.*

CC Number 267173

Information available Information was provided by the trust.

General The trust states that it supports projects concerned with education, culture, the environment and welfare. In practice, most grants are made to Jewish or Israeli organisations.

In 2001/02 it had assets of £8.4 million, which generated an income of only £231,000. Grants were made totalling £295,000.

The main beneficiaries were J'PAIME which received £127,000 in three grants and Tel Aviv University Trust which received six grants totalling £75,000.

Other beneficiaries were Arva Institute for Environmental Studies (£30,000), Foundation for the Advancement of Family Therapy in Israel (£25,000), Israel Philharmonic Orchestra (£17,000), British Fund for World Relief for METUNA (£6,900), International Scholarship Foundation (£6,000), Tel Aviv Foundation for Israel Vocal Arts Institute (£4,000), British Friends of the Israel Opera and Children's Leukaemia Trust (£1,500 each) and Friends of Beit Issie Shapiro (£250).

Exclusions Grants are only made to registered charities. No grants to individuals.

Applications In writing to the correspondent.

The Stella and Alexander Margulies Charitable Trust

Jewish, general

£204,000 (2001/02)

Beneficial area UK.

23 Grosvenor Street, London W1K 4QL

Tel. 020 7416 4160

Correspondent M J Margulies, Trustee

Trustees *Marcus J Margulies; Martin D Paisner; Sir Stuart Lipton.*

CC Number 220441

Information available Accounts were on file at the Charity Commission.

General This trust has general charitable purposes, with a preference for Jewish organisations.

In 2001/02 it had assets of £6.7 million, which generating an income of £441,000. Grants were made to 39 organisations totalling £203,000.

The largest grants given were £175,000 to UJIA, £45,000 to the Royal Opera House and £10,000 to Aish HaTorah UK. Other beneficiaries included the Rain Forest Concern (£5,500), British Friends/Erza Le Morpeh, Nightingale House (£5,000), The Shallom Foundation (£2,700), Central Synangogue, Community Security Trust, YMER (£2,000 each).

Applications In writing to the correspondent.

Mariapolis Limited

Unity, ecumenism

£152,000 (2000/01)

Beneficial area UK and overseas.

57 Twyford Avenue, London W3 9PZ

Tel. 020 8992 7666/020 7373 9808

Correspondent Carlo Poggi, Secretary

Trustees *Timothy M King; Rumold Van Geffen; Bartolomé Mayans.*

CC Number 257912

Information available Accounts are on file at the Charity Commission, but without a grants list.

General This trust promotes the international Focolare Movement in the UK, and grantmaking is only one area of its work. It works towards a united world and its activities focus on peace and cooperation. It has a related interest in ecumenism and also in overseas development. Activities include organising conferences and courses, and publishing books and magazines.

Its 2000/01 annual report stated: 'The charity has links with several projects in the developing world, particularly in Brazil, the Phillipines and the Cameroon Republic. It gives aid to these either directly or through the International Centre Pia Associazione Maschile Opera di Maria (PAMOM) in Rome.'

In 2000/01 it had assets of £941,000 and a total income of £370,000, mostly from various donations received and earned income. Total expenditure was £416,000, of which £152,000 was given in grants.

Applications In writing to the correspondent.

This entry was not confirmed by the trust, but was correct according to information on file at the Charity Commission.

Michael Marks Charitable Trust

Arts, environment

£371,000 (2000/01)

Beneficial area UK and overseas.

5 Elm Tree Road, London NW8 9JY

Tel. 020 7286 4633 **Fax** 020 7289 2173

Correspondent The Secretary

Trustees *Martina, Lady Marks; Prof. Sir Christopher White; Dr D MacDiarmid.*

CC Number 248136

Information available Full accounts were on file at the Charity Commission.

General The trust supports the arts (including galleries and museums), and environmental groups, with grants generally ranging from £150 to £25,000, although larger grants have been given.

In 2003/04 it had an income of £172,000 and a total expenditure of £262,000. Further information was not available.

In 2000/01 it had assets of £3.5 million, which generated an income of £177,000. Grants totalling £371,000 were made to 32 organisations, a quarter of which were also supported in the previous year.

The largest grants were £50,000 to Walton-on-Thames Community Arts Trust, £36,000 to British Museum, £27,000 to Christchurch College – Oxford, £25,000 each to Arc Dance Company, and Victoria and Albert Museum, £20,000 each to British Institute of Florence, British School at Rome, Mauritshuis and Vivat Trust, £15,000 each to Early English Organ Project, National Library of Scotland and Wordsworth Trust, £13,000 to Woodland Trust and £12,000 each to Burlington Magazine and Hellenic Centre.

Other grants ranged from £150 to £5,300, with beneficiaries including English Chamber Choir Society (£5,300), BT Scottish Ensemble and Polish Knights of Malta (£5,000 each), St Pancras Community Centre (£4,800), Patriarchate of Constantinople (£3,000), International Centre for Missing and Exploited Children (£2,000), Anglo Israel Association (£1,000), Ionian Society (£310), Lifeline Humanitarian Organisation (£250) and Lykion ton Hellinidon (150).

Exclusions Grants are given to registered charities only. No grants to individuals or profit organisations.

Applications In writing to the correspondent before July. Applications should include audited accounts, information on other bodies approached and details of funding obtained. Requests will not receive a response unless they have been successful.

The Hilda & Samuel Marks Foundation

Jewish, general

£187,000 (2002/03)

Beneficial area UK and Israel.

1 Ambassador Place, Stockport Road, Altrincham, Cheshire WA15 8DB

Tel. 0161 941 3183 **Fax** 0161 927 7437

Email davidmarks@mutleyproperties.co.uk

Correspondent D L Marks, Trustee

Trustees *S Marks; Mrs H Marks; D L Marks; Mrs R D Selby.*

CC Number 245208

Information available Accounts were provided by the trust.

General This trust mainly gives support to UK charities and to charities based in Israel.

In 2002/03 the assets of the trust stood at £2.6 million with an income of £282,000 (including £135,000 from donations and £147,000 from investments). Grants, which totalled £187,000, were categorised as follows:

Community	£18,000	9.6%
Religious activity	£1,000	0.5%
Education	£47,000	25.2%
Health	£35,000	18.9%
Welfare	£85,000	45.8%

UK charities received £113,000 of the total, with £68,000 to charities in Israel. The largest grant was £28,000 to Chai Lifeline for a new building in Hendon – London. Other large grants went to Emunah Child Resettlement Fund for a project working with dysfunctional children at Even Shmuel – Israel (£26,000), Operation Wheelchairs (£25,000), Heathlands – a residential facility for the elderly in Greater Manchester (£15,000) and Manchester Jewish Federation (£10,000). Support has been given to all these organisations for a number of years.

Exclusions No grants to individuals.

Applications The trust primarily supports projects known to the trustees and its funds are fully committed. Therefore unsolicited applications are not being sought.

The Ann & David Marks Foundation

Jewish charities

£70,000 (2002)

Beneficial area Worldwide with a preference for Manchester.

Mutley House, 1 Ambassador Place, Altrincham, Cheshire WA15 8DB

Tel. 0161 941 3183 **Fax** 0161 927 7437

Email davidmarks@mutleyproperties.co.uk

Correspondent D L Marks, Trustee

Trustees *D L Marks; Mrs A Marks; Dr G E Marks; A H Marks.*

CC Number 326303

Information available Accounts were provided by the trust.

General The trust mainly supports Jewish charities, especially in the Manchester area. It has a number of regular commitments and prefers to distribute to charities known to the trustees.

In 2002 it had an income of £55,000 and made grants totalling £70,000.

Beneficiaries included Emunah (£50,000), Chai Network (£5,000), Manchester Jewish Federation (£2,000), Shaare Zedek Hospital (£1,500) and Heathlands Village (£1,100).

Applications The trust's funds are mostly committed and unsolicited applications are not welcome.

The Erich Markus Charitable Foundation

Welfare, hospices, medical, general

£138,000 (2001)

Beneficial area UK.

Courts & Co, 15 Wimpole Street, London W1G 9SY

Tel. 020 7637 1651

Correspondent The Trustees

Trustee *Erich Markus Charity Trustees Ltd.*

CC Number 283128

Information available Full accounts were provided by the trust.

General Erich Markus died in 1979, leaving half of his residual estate to the trust. The original capital was made up of 355,000 ordinary 25p shares in Office & Electronic Machines Ltd.

In 2003 the foundation had an income of £105,000 and a total expenditure of £125,000. Further information for this year was not available.

In 2001 the foundation had an income of £100,000, had assets at £3.2 million and made 61 grants totalling £138,000. Management and administration costs totalled £23,000.

The largest grants went to Magen David Adom (£15,000), St Francis Hospice and World Jewish Relief (£5,000 each) and St Christopher's Hospice (£4,500). All other grants were of £4,000 or less.

Grants of £4,000 were given to Chai Lifeline Cancer Care, In Kind Direct, Jewish Blind & Disabled, Jewish Care, Kisharon, Lady Hoare Trust, Nightingale House, Norwood, RABI, Samaritans, Spanish & Portuguese Jews' Home for the Aged and Trinity Hospice.

The remaining grants were for either £1,000 or £2,000. Beneficiaries included Action on Elder Abuse, British Blind Sport, Charing Cross Hospital Dialysis Trust, Children with Aids Charity, Headway, Motability, Royal School for the Blind, Weston Spirit and Umbrella.

Exclusions No grants to individuals.

Applications In writing to the correspondent. Applications will only be considered if accompanied by a copy of the latest report and accounts. Trustees meet twice a year, usually in April and October. No telephone enquiries please.

Marr-Munning Trust

Overseas aid

Possibly about £100,000 a year

Beneficial area Worldwide, mainly developing world.

9 Madeley Road, Ealing, London W5 2LA

Tel. 020 8998 7747

Correspondent D Gleeson

Trustees *W Macfarlane; Mary Herbert; J O'Brien; C A Alam; Margaret Lorde; Richard Tomlinson.*

CC Number 261786

Information available Information was on file at the Charity Commission.

General The trust makes grants to overseas aid organisations mainly working in the developing world.

In 2001/02 the trust had an income of £364,000 and a total expenditure of £328,000. Further information for this year was not available.

In 1999/2000 the trust had assets of £2.8 million and an income of £292,000. Total expenditure was £302,000, including £138,000 for maintenance of the trust's properties and £54,000 for management and administration costs. Direct charitable expenditure was just 8.5% more than management and administration costs, totalling £59,000.

No grants were listed in the trust's accounts, however donations were broken down as follows:

Helping natural disaster victims	£30,000
Providing shelter to destitute people	£18,000
Providing healthcare to poor people	£12,000
Providing educational support	£500

Beneficiaries previously listed in the trust's accounts include: Impact, Marr-Munning Ashram, Gram Niyojan, Joe Holman Trust, Nilgiris Adivasi and Village Services, all of which are based in India. Other beneficiaries have included Fund for Human Need – Jamaica, Health Unlimited, Sense, Sound Seekers, UNICEF – North Korea, Cambodia Trust, Save the Children – Vietnam, Africa Now, Aid to Romania, Almsakin Hospital –Pakistan and Hope – Sri Lanka.

Exclusions No grants to individuals.

Applications In writing to the correspondent.

This entry was not confirmed by the trust, but is correct according to information on file at the Charity Commission.

The Marsh Christian Trust

General

£123,000 (2000/01)

Beneficial area UK.

Granville House, 132–135 Sloane Street, London SW1X 9AX

Tel. 020 7730 2626 **Fax** 020 7823 5225

Correspondent Lorraine McMorrow, Administrator

Trustees *B P Marsh; R J C Marsh; N C S Marsh.*

CC Number 284470

Information available Full accounts and a copy of their triennial review were provided by the trust.

General The trust was established in 1981 and has increased steadily in size with each year. In 2000/01 it had an income of £168,000 and assets of £4.3 million. It made 251 grants totalling £123,000, 130 of which went to organisations supported in the previous year. The financial report showed high administration costs of £80,000, but this can be accounted for by the proactive nature of the charity and the large number of small grants made.

Based on the report for 1997–2000 report during which time £336,000 was distributed (£491,000 between 1994 and1997), causes were supported in the following areas (percentage of grant fund allocation is shown in brackets):

Social welfare (20%)

Small donations went to charities helping people with physical and mental disabilities. Charities working amongst the young, the aged, the homeless, alcoholics and drug abusers were all supported as far as is possible, especially those displaying a Christian emphasis in their work. The largest grant given in this area was £1,600.

Environmental causes/animal welfare (15%)

The trust has been a supporter of various organisations devoted to nature conservation and the wellbeing of wildlife, both within Britain and overseas. A particular project, Wildlife Information Network, which was previously an initiative of the Marsh Christian Trust, has now become fully independent and established itself within the Royal Veterinary College. The largest grant was £2,000.

Healthcare and medical research (22.5%)

Much of the money distributed under this category went to hospices and other organisations working with the terminally ill. (The trustees try to avoid giving funds to hospitals in the belief that it is the responsibility of the local and national community to maintain these.) The largest grant was £3,000.

Education and training (9%)

Funding and training for children and adults with disabilities is a part of the trust's programme. The trust regularly makes grants to the Royal College of Music, English Speaking Union, Young Enterprise and Oxford Evangelical Research Trust among others. (The trustees try to avoid giving funds to ordinary schools, colleges or universities in the belief that it is the responsibility of the local and national community to maintain these.) The largest grant was £3,000.

Literature, arts and heritage (22.5%)

The trust gives support to a number of museums and galleries, including the National Portrait Gallery, the V&A Museum and the British Museum. (The trustees try wherever possible to avoid making donations to appeals for individual church buildings or cathedrals, believing that it is the responsibility of individual congregations and the church to maintain these). The largest grant was £3,000.

Overseas appeals (8.5%)

Examples of causes supported during the year include Voluntary Service Overseas, ActionAid and Sight Savers International. The largest grant was £2,000.

Miscellaneous (2.5%)

The Highgate Cemetery, Prisoners Abroad and Population Concern are examples of causes supporting during the period. The largest grant was £1,250.

The Marsh Awards Scheme

Educational, literary, social and animal welfare awards ranging between £600 and £3,500 were also made by the trust; 14 were given out during the period.

The trustees will normally only make grants to registered charities experienced within their chosen field of work. Long-term core funding of appropriate work is the trust's normal approach, taking the form of money given on a recurring annual basis subject to yearly resubmission and review.

The size of donations normally ranges from £250 to £4,000 but can be as low as £10 and as high as £6,000. In 2000/01, 13 grants of £1,000 or over were awarded, the largest going to English Speaking Union (£6,000). Other recipients of larger grants were The Arts Club (£4,700), Wildlife Information Network (£4,000) and Radiological Research Trust (£2,000).

Grants under £1,000 included Sight Savers International (£900), Rare Breeds Survival Trust (£850), The Grubb Institute (£800), Mayday Trust and Crusaid (£750 each), The Aidis Trust (£650), Acorn Christian Foundation (£600), Action Centres UK (£500), Campaign for Learning (£400), Young People's Trust for the Environment (£350), Youth Inclusive (£300), Special Toys Educational Postal Service (£250), Health Unlimited (£200), Rainer Foundation (£150), Nevis Historical and Conservation Society (£100), Small Woods Association (£80), Society of Authors (£75), Society of Friends of the National Army (£50) and Friends of National Maritime Museum (£35).

The trust also offers advice on fundraising and other organisational issues to its active 'customer charities'.

Exclusions No grants can be made to individuals or for sponsorships. No start-up grants. No support for building funds, ordinary schools, colleges, universities or hospitals, or research.

Applications In writing to the correspondent, including a copy of the most recent accounts. The trustees currently receive about 8,000 applications every year, of which 7,800 are new. Decisions are made at monthly trustee meetings.

The trustees attempt to visit each long-term recipient at least once every three years to review the work done, to learn of future plans and renew acquaintance with those responsible for the charity. Advice on fund-raising and other organisational problems is also offered free of charge by the trust.

The Charlotte Marshall Charitable Trust

Roman Catholic, general

£103,000 (2002/03)

Beneficial area UK.

c/o C & C Marshall Limited, 55–65 Castleham Road, Castleham Industrial Estate, Hastings, East Sussex TN38 9NU

Tel. 01424 856058

Correspondent J Pharaoh

Trustees *Miss C C Cirket; E M Cosgrove; J Crosgrove; K B Page; J M Russell.*

CC Number 211941

Information available Information was provided by the trust

General The trust has general charitable purposes in the UK, mainly supporting educational, religious and other charitable purposes for Roman Catholics.

In 2002/03 the trust had assets of £592,000 and an income of £86,000. Grants were given to 33 organisations totalling £103,000.

Catholic beneficiaries included St Richard's Catholic College (£10,000), Sacred Heart Catholic Primary School (£6,000), Catholic Housing Aid Society (£5,000), Catholic Children's Society and Our Lady Catholic High School (£3,000 each) and St Mary Magdalene's Church (£1,800).

Other organisations supported included Concern Universal (£4,000), Sara Lee Trust (£2,000), Alone in London, Arthritis Care, Compaid Trust, Hope House, Motor Neurone Disease Association and Zoe's Place Baby Hospice (£1,000 each) and Children's Heart Foundation (£600).

Exclusions No grants are given to individuals.

Applications On a form available from the correspondent. Completed forms must be returned by 31 December for consideration in March.

The Mason Porter Charitable Trust

Christian

£134,000 (2002/03)

Beneficial area UK.

Liverpool Council of Social Service (Inc.), 14 Castle Street, Liverpool L2 0NJ

Tel. 0151 236 7728

Correspondent The Secretary

Trustees *William Fulton, Chair; David Bebb; Roger Morris; Mark Blundell; Dil Daly; Mike Eastwood; Charles Feeny; Prof. Philip Love; Andrew Lovelady; Shirley Mashiane-Talbot; Sue Newton; Christine Reeves; Hilary Russell.*

CC Number 255545

Information available Full accounts were provided by the trust.

General This trust appears to support Christian causes in the UK, including those which provide relief or missionary work overseas.

In 2002/03 it had assets of £1.7 million, which generated an income of £97,000. Grants were made totalling £134,000.

The largest were £25,000 to St Luke's Development Fund, £20,000 each to Abernethy Trust and Cliffe College, £11,000 to Life Changing Ministries and £10,000 to New Creations.

Other grants large enough to be included in the accounts were £7,500 to Just Care, £5,000 each to New Life Centre, Sisters of Jesus Way and Share Jesus, £2,700 to Links International Trust and £1,000 each to Makuru Promotion Centre for Children of Nairobi, PSS, Riverway Christian Fellowship, St Luke's Methodist Church – Hoylake. Smaller grants totalled £19,000.

Applications The trust states that it only makes grants to charities known to the settlor and unsolicited applications are not considered.

Matliwala Family Charitable Trust

Islam, general

£114,000 (2001/02)

Beneficial area UK and overseas, especially Bharuch – India.

9 Brookview, Fulwood, Preston PR2 8FG

Tel. 01772 706501

Correspondent A V Bux, Trustee

Trustees *Ayub Vali Bux; Usman Salya; Abdul Aziz Vali Patel; Yousuf Bux; Ibrahim Vali Patel.*

CC Number 1012756

Information available Full accounts were on file at the Charity Commission.

General The trust's areas of giving are:

- the advancement of education for pupils at Matliwala School Of Bharuch in Gujerat – India, and other schools, including assisting with the provision of equipment and facilities
- the advancement of the Islamic religion
- the relief of sickness and poverty
- the advancement of education.

In 2002/03 the trust had an income of £173,000 and a total expenditure of £108,000. No further information from this year was available.

In the previous year the trust had assets totalling £1.7 million. Total income was £279,000, including £147,000 in donations received and £123,000 in rents received from a property in Skegness. Management and administration costs for the year were low at £2,700.

Grants were made totalling £114,000. Of this, £70,000 was given to various causes in Bharuch, including hospital care, improvements to water supply, food, oil and housing construction for people who are disadvantaged. Other grants were £14,000 to Jamia Faizanul Quran, £5,000 each to Bharuch Muslim Medical and Welfare Trust and Munshi (Manubarwaia) Educational Trust, £3,400 to Dar-ul-aloom Jamia Habibia and £2,500 each to Islamic Research Institute of Great Britain and Preston Muslim Girls' School.

The accounts also stated that 48 non-material grants were made during the year, totalling £12,000.

Applications In writing to the correspondent.

The Matt 6.3 Charitable Trust

Christian

£215,000 (2002/03)

Beneficial area UK.

c/o PO Box 40, Normanby Road, Scunthorpe, North Lincolnshire DN15 8RQ

Tel. 01724 289 777

Correspondent I H Davey

Trustees *S J Savage; T J Carson; N J Barnett; C R Barnett.*

CC Number 1069985

Information available Accounts were on file at the Charity Commission.

General Established in 1998, this trust mainly supports Christian organisations. In 2002/03 the trust had assets of £992,000 with an income of £87,000 and grants totalling £215,000.

Grants include £91,000 to Christian Centre Limited (Humberside), £78,000 to Don Summers Evangelistic Association, £32,000 to G Littler Esq, £5,000 to St Augustine's Church, £4,000 to Kings Christian Bookshop, £2,500 each to Gunville Methodist Church and Evangelistic Library and £250 to J Fudge Esq.

Applications This trust does not accept unsolicited applications. Funds are committed to ongoing projects.

The Maximillian Trust (formerly known as The N and F Burton Charitable Trust)

Medical research, education, social welfare, heritage

£30,000 (1998/99)

Beneficial area UK.

The Old Rectory, Childrey, Wantage, Oxfordshire OX12 9UP

Tel. 01253 524346

Correspondent N A Burton, Trustee

Trustees *N A Burton; Mrs M F Burton.*

CC Number 326579

Information available Up-to-date information was not available.

General The trust has a preference for supporting medical research, education, social welfare and heritage causes. The trust has not submitted accounts to the Charity Commission since 2000, however no recent information was available on file. In 1998/99 the trust's assets totalled £229,000 and its income was £14,000. Grants totalled £30,000.

Grants were £10,000 each to Action on Disability and Development and Wantage Counselling Service, and £5,000 each to The Porch and Ridgeway School.

Applications In writing to the correspondent, although the trust states that the funds are already over-committed. Unsolicited appeals are unlikely to be successful and unsuccessful appeals will not necessarily be acknowledged.

The Mayfield Valley Arts Trust

Arts, especially chamber music

£94,000 (2001/02)

Beneficial area Unrestricted, but with a special interest in Sheffield and South Yorkshire.

Irwin Mitchell, St Peter's House, Hartshead, Sheffield S1 2EL

Tel. 0870 1500 100 **Fax** 0114 275 3306

Correspondent J M Jelly, Administrator

Trustees *A Thornton; J R Thornton; P M Thornton; D Whelton; D Brown; J R Rider.*

CC Number 327665

Information available Information was on file at the Charity Commission.

General Established in 1987, the objects of this trust are the advancement of education by the encouragement of art and artistic activities of a charitable nature, especially music and the promotion and preservation of concerts and other musical events and activities. In recent years, particular favour has been given towards chamber music. Grants range from £2,000 to £16,000, although more than one grant can be made to an organisation in each year.

In 2003/04 the trust had an income of £112,000 and a total expenditure of £101,000. No further information from this year was available.

In 2001/02 the trust had assets of £2.4 million and grants totalled £94,000.

Sheffield Chamber Music in the Round received a total of £35,000. Other beneficiaries were York Early Music Foundation (£28,000), Wigmore Hall (£15,000), Prussia Cove (£10,000) and Live Music Now! (£7,000).

Exclusions No grants to students.

Applications The trust states that no unsolicited applications are considered.

Mazars Charitable Trust

General

£103,000 (2001/02)

Beneficial area UK, overseas.

1 Cranleigh Gardens, South Croydon, Surrey CR2 9LD

Tel. 020 8657 3053

Correspondent Bryan K H Rogers

Trustees *Peter R Hyatt, Chair; John S Mellows; David E Ryan.*

CC Number 287735

Information available Full accounts were provided by the trust.

General This trust acts as a conduit for the charitable giving of the Mazars firm of chartered accountants (formerly Mazars Neville Russell). Up to 10% of the funds raised from each of the regional branches can be given to local organisations at the discretion of the managing partner; the rest of the funds are given by the trustees for general charitable causes to charities which must be known personally to a trustee or staff member.

Grants are only given to projects which are nominated to the management committee by the partners and staff of Mazars (chartered accountants). The trustees like to give grants which will make a significant impact on the recipient organisation and as such rarely support the largest organisations, while the availability of funding from the local partners make the trustees wary of supporting causes specific to a particular locality. 30% of total funds is directed towards community projects.

In 2001/02 the trust had assets of £41,000 with an income of £119,000 and grants totalling £103,000.

The largest grants were £10,000 each to John Grooms, Maharogi Sewa Samiti and Scargill House, £6,400 to Haven House Children's Hospice, £6,000 to Worldshare, £5,000 each to Chartered Accountants Benevolent Fund, Interserve, KunDE Foundation, Thare Machi, Toybox Charity, Tyndale House – Cambridge, £4,300 to UK Youth, £4000 to Enham, £3,800 to Business in the Community, £3,000 to Marie Curie Cancer Care, £2,500 to Ryder – Cheshire Foundation and £1,300 to Lloyd's Charities Trust.

Grants of £1,000 or less include CARE International UK, Homeless International Himalayan Challenge, Manning School Fund Charity, Sense, City and East London Bereavement Service, Friends of Lloyd's Choir, LGU Graduate Show 2002, Lincoln County Hospital Nocton Ward – Neonatal Unit, St Christopher's Hospice and St Francis Hospice Development Trust.

30 other grants of between £25 and £250 each were made totalling £4,800.

Exclusions Support is not given to an organisation within three years of an earlier grant, and, as such, recurrent grants are not made. No grants are made to individuals.

Applications Unsolicited applications will rarely be considered or acknowledged. Applications will only be considered in respect of charities nominated to the management committee by partners or staff of Mazars.

The Anthony and Elizabeth Mellows Charitable Settlement

National heritage, Church of England churches

£62,000 (2001/02)

Beneficial area UK

22 Devereux Court, Temple Bar, London WC2R 3JR

Tel. 020 7353 6221

Correspondent Prof. A R Mellows, Trustee

Trustees *Prof. Anthony R Mellows; Mrs Elizabeth Mellows.*

CC Number 281229

Information available Full accounts were on file at the Charity Commission.

General This trust gives grants towards arts and national heritage to national institutions and to churches on recommendation from Council for Care of Churches.

In 2003/04 it had both an income and total expenditure of £40,000. Further information for this year was not available.

In 2001/02 grants totalled £62,000. The largest grants went to two regular beneficiaries, Order of St John (£24,000) and Royal Opera House (£14,000).

Other grants included those to St John Ambulance (£1,500), National Art Collections Fund (£1,400), Arc Dance Company (£1,100), Great Hospital – Norwich, National History Museum and The Sixteen (£1,000 each), Matlock PCC for the preservation of 18th century crances (£800), King Edward VII Hospital for Officers (£500) and St John of Jerusalem Eye Hospital (£400).

Exclusions Applications from individuals, including students, are ineligible.

Applications Applications are considered when received, but only from UK institutions. No application forms are used. Grants will be made three times a year when the trustees meet to consider applications.

Melodor Ltd

Jewish, general

£160,000 (1999/2000)

Beneficial area UK and overseas.

148 Bury Old Road, Manchester M7 4SE

Correspondent The Trustees

Trustees *B Weiss; M Weiss; P Weiss; S Weiss; J L Weiss; H Weiss; R Sofer; H Neuman; M Neuman; E Neuman; P Neumann; J Bleier; E Henry; R De Lange; J Weissmandel.*

CC Number 260972

Information available Full accounts were on file at the Charity Commission.

General This trust supports religious, educational and similar causes, with most grants going to Jewish organisations.

In 2001/02 it had assets of £704,000 and an income of £158,000. Grants to organisations totalled £160,000.

The largest grants were £18,700 to Beis Minchas Yitzhok, £16,000 to Yeshiva L'Zeirim, and £10,000 each to Central Charity Funds and Vehodarto Pnei Zokain.

Smaller grants included those to Peri Gedulim (£8,000), Siach Sod and Friends of Harim (£7,500 each), Friends of Maase Tzedokoh (£5,000), Yeshivas Ohel Shimon (4,800) and Belz (£3,550).

Applications In writing to the correspondent.

This entry was not confirmed by the trust, but the address was correct according to the Charity Commission database.

Melow Charitable Trust

Jewish

£351,000 (2001/02)

Beneficial area UK and overseas.

21 Warwick Grove, London E5 9HX

Correspondent J Low

Trustees *M Spitz; E Weiser.*

CC Number 275454

Information available Accounts were on file at the Charity Commission, but with only a brief narrative report.

General This trust makes grants to Jewish charities both in the UK and overseas. In 2001/02 its assets totalled £1.1 million and it had an income of £415,000. Grants totalled £351,000 with many organisations receiving more than one grant.

Grants were broken down as follows:

Assisting the Needy	19	£47,000
Education	23	£159,000
General	9	£13,000
Orphanage	1	£250
Relief of Poverty	55	£252,000
Religious Education	25	£47,000
Synagogues	98	£351,000

Organisations receiving the largest amounts were: Shalom Torah Centres (£69,000 in 2 grants); Yeter Lev Jerusalem (£38,000 in 3 grants), Congregation Yetev Lev (£37,000 in 16 grants), Satmar Gemach (£30,000 in 2 grants), Yesodey Hatorah School (£12,000 in 3 grants), Lolev Charitable Trust (£12,000 in 3 grants) and Oneg Shabbos Youth Club (£11,000 in 2 grants).

Beneficiaries of smaller grants included Belz Institutions Bnei Brak (£7,000), British Jewish Heritage Society (£4,000), Keren Zedakah Foundation (£3,000) and Yeshivas Toras Moshe (£1,200).

Applications In writing to the correspondent.

Meningitis Trust

Meningitis in the UK

£86,000 to organisations (2002/03)

Beneficial area UK.

Fern House, Bath Road, Stroud, Gloucestershire GL5 3TJ

Tel. 01453 768000

Email grants@meningitis-trust.org

Website www.meningitis-trust.org

Correspondent The Trustees

Trustees *Albert Geoffrey Shaw; Basil Edmond; Mrs Bernadette Julia McGhie; Mrs Beryl Anne Sutcliffe; Mrs Gillian Mae Noble; James Willaim Edward Wilson; Dr Jane Wells; Michael Anthony Hall; Peter James Johnson; Robert Johnson; Suzanne Devine.*

CC Number 803016

Information available Information was provided by the trust.

General 'The Meningitis Trust is an international charity with a strong community focus, fighting meningitis through the provision of support, education & awareness and research.'

Since 1986 grants totalling over £4 million have been awarded for funding research into all aspects of the disease.

In 2002/03 the trust had an income of £4.1 million and a total expenditure of £3.2 million. Grants to organisations totalled £86,000. The sum of £123,000 was distributed in 81 grants to individuals.

Applications Application forms are available from the trust.

Menuchar Ltd

Jewish

£182,000 (2002/03)

Beneficial area UK.

Equity House, 128–136 High Street, Edgware HA8 7EL

Correspondent The Trustees

Trustees *N Bude; G Bude.*

CC Number 262782

Information available Accounts were on file at the Charity Commission, but without a list of grants.

General The main objects of the trust are the advancement of religion in accordance with the Orthodox Jewish faith and the relief of people in need.

In 2002/03 the trust had assets of £200,000 and an income of £73,000. Grants totalled £182,000. Unfortunately, a list of beneficiaries was not available.

Exclusions No grants to non-registered charities or to individuals.

Applications In writing to the correspondent.

Brian Mercer Charitable Trust

Welfare, medical in UK and overseas

£60,000 (2002)

Beneficial area UK and overseas.

Central Buildings, Richmond Terrace, Blackburn BB1 7AP

Tel. 01254 686600 **Fax** 01254 682483

Email arowntree@waterworths.co.uk

Correspondent A T Rowntree, Trustee

Trustees *C J Clancy; K F Martin; K J Merrill; A T Rowntree.*

CC Number 1076925

Information available Accounts were on file at the Charity Commission.

General In 2002 the trust had assets of £3 million with an income of £120,000 and a total expenditure of £61,000. Grant beneficiaries were Fight for Sight (£50,000) and Macmillan Cancer Relief and Marie Curie Cancer Care (£5,000 each).

Applications In writing to the correspondent.

Mercury Phoenix Trust

AIDS, HIV

£243,000 (2002/03)

Beneficial area Worldwide.

The Mill, Mill Lane, Cookham, Berkshire SL6 9QT

Tel. 01628 527874

Correspondent Peter Chant

Trustees *M Austin; Jim Beach; B H May; R M Taylor.*

CC Number 1013768

Information available Accounts were on file at the Charity Commission.

General The trust was set up in memory of Freddie Mercury by the remaining members of the rock group, Queen, and their manager. It makes grants to 'help relieve the poverty, sickness and distress of people with AIDS and HIV and to stimulate awareness and education in connection with the disease throughout the world'.

Starting with the Freddie Mercury Tribute Concert for AIDS Awareness, the trust's fundraising activities have been spectacular. Income has been raised from, for example, a fan-initiated annual national street collection, a Queen album and from a ballet which was inspired by the music of Queen and Mozart.

The trust's information leaflet states 'Applications for grants have come in from many counties around the world and collaboration has been realised with groups as far removed as the World Health Organisation, to grass-root organisations run partly by voluntary workers in Uganda, Kenya, South Africa, Zambia, Nepal and India. The trust is following the latest developments in drug therapies and adapting funding policy to the changing needs of those affected by HIV/AIDS in the UK and elsewhere'.

In 2002/03 the trust had assets of £1.5 million and an income of £354,000. Grants were made totalling £243,000.

Overseas beneficiaries included Cape Town Child Welfare (£23,000), Sinai Wildlife – Tanzania (£10,000), Cara – India (£7,500), Dominican Sisters – South Africa, Paradise – Bangladesh and Uganda Mines and Metalwork Union (£5,000 each), Hurama Rehabiliation – Tanzania (£4,000) and Aids Health – Uganda and Mkauzaneni Aids Centre – Zimbabwe (£3,000 each).

UK beneficiaries included Helpage International and Plan International UK (£7,500), British Leprosy Relief, Care and Relief of the Young, Civis Trust, Inter Child Care and Oxfam (£5,000 each), Concern Universal (£4,500), Friends of Hope (£3,000) and Terrence Higgins Trust (£1,400).

Applications In writing to the correspondent.

The Metropolitan Drinking Fountain and Cattle Trough Association

Provision of pure drinking water

£35,000 (2002)

Beneficial area UK, mainly London, and overseas.

Oaklands, 5 Queenborough Gardens, Chislehurst, Kent BR7 6NP

Tel. 020 8467 1261

Email ralph.baber@tesco.net

Correspondent R P Baber, Secretary

Trustees *Executive committee: J E Mills, Chair; I Evans; R P Baber; Mrs S Fuller; J N King; R Sheridan-White; Sir J Smith; M W Elliott; J Barrett; R E T Gurney; A King; M Bear; Mrs L Erith.*

CC Number 207743

Information available Accounts and an annual report are on file at the Charity Commission.

General The objectives of the association are to promote the provision of drinking water for people and animals in the United Kingdom and overseas, and the preservation of the association's archive materials, artefacts, drinking fountains, cattle troughs and other installations.

Over the years the association has recognised a need for supplying fountains to schools throughout the United Kingdom. The association typically gifts a Novus drinking fountain to a school on the condition that the school pays £25 to join the association. Generally one fountain is donated per 100 children. The school is responsible for the installation and the maintenance of the fountain.

In 2003 the trust had an income of £5,000 and a total expenditure of £38,000.

In the previous year the trust had an income of £36,000. Grants totalled £35,000. Management and administration charges were high at £10,000, including £5,500 to a company one of the trustees has an interest in. Whilst wholly legal, these editors always regret such payments unless, in the words of the Charity Commission, 'there is no realistic alternative'. It has provided grants totalling £25,000 to 63 schools to provide 77 drinking fountains it also assists in payments for the restoration of drinking fountains.

Beneficiaries include St John the Baptist Church – Howton (£3,000), Karen Hilltribes Trust (£2,500), Busoga Trust (£2,000) Azafady and Dhaka Ahsania Mission (£1,000 each) and Royal London Society for the Blind (£750).

As of 2002 the total of fountains and troughs supplied, for use both in the UK and overseas by the association were: 4,300 drinking fountains; 930 cattle troughs; 3,700 dog troughs; and 40 water wells/storage tanks.

Applications In writing to the correspondent.

Gerald Micklem Charitable Trust

General, health

About £75,000 (2003)

Beneficial area UK, especially Hampshire.

Bolinge Hill Farm, Buriton, Petersfield, Hampshire GU31 4NN

Tel. 01730 264207 **Fax** 01730 268515

Email ghmicklem.charitabletrust@btinternet.com

Website www.peter.shone.btinternet.co.uk

Correspondent Mrs S J Shone, Trustee

Trustees *Susan J Shone; Joanna L Scott-Dalgleish; Helen Ratcliffe.*

CC Number 802583

Information available Information was on file at the Charity Commission.

General The trust was established in November 1989 with a bequest left in the will of Gerald Micklem. The trust states that it supports 'a wide range of activities' although most grants appear to be to health and welfare charities. Grants can be recurring or one–off and for revenue or capital purposes. Donations are generally for either £2,000 or £3,000.

In 2003 the trust had an income of £96,000 and a total expenditure of £75,000, most of which was distributed in grants.

Previous beneficiaries have included Aigas Trust, Arthritis Care, BRACE, Chicks, Disabilities Trust, Fight for Sight, Hawk and Owl Trust, Harvest Trust (Holidays for Children), Mencap, Place To Be, Research into Ageing, Sustrans, Treloar Trust and Write Away.

Exclusions No grants to non-registered charities or to individuals.

Applications In writing to the correspondent. Interested applicants should note that the organisations which have received grants in the past should not be taken as indicative of a geographical or other bias. The trustees meet informally a few times each year, but the dates are not fixed. They usually meet once only to decide on grants in January or February. Applications can be sent at any time, but preferably not later than the preceding November.

The M Miller Charitable Trust

Jewish, general

Possibly around £40,000 a year

Beneficial area UK.

41 Harrogate Road, Chapel Allerton, Leeds, West Yorkshire LS7 3PD

Tel. 0113 228 4000

Correspondent Richard Ellis, Trustee

Trustees *Matthew Miller; Renee B Miller; Richard Ellis.*

CC Number 1014957

Information available Accounts were on file at the Charity Commission, but without a grants list.

General The M Miller Charitable Trust was set up by Matthew and Renee Miller and Richard Ellis in 1992 with general charitable objects. Unfortunately no financial information has been provided for recent years.

In 1998/99 it had an income of £43,000 and made grants totalling £42,000. The trust had no assets. Grants are directed predominantly at Jewish causes.

Applications In writing to the correspondent.

The Miller Foundation

General, animal welfare

£161,000 (1999)

Beneficial area UK, with a preference for Scotland, especially the West of Scotland.

c/o Maclay Murray & Spens, 151 St Vincent Street, Glasgow G2 5NJ

Tel. 0141 248 5011 **Fax** 0141 248 5819

Correspondent A Biggart, Secretary to the Foundation

Trustees *C Fleming-Brown; G R G Graham; J Simpson; G F R Fleming-Brown.*

SC Number SC008798

Information available Information was provided by the trust.

General The trust supports the following:

- charities in Scotland, especially in the west of Scotland
- UK animal welfare charities.

It will support a wide range of charities in Scotland. Grants range from £500 to £2,000, with the majority of them recurrent. Financial information was only available from 1999 when grants totalled £161,000. A list of beneficiaries was not available.

Exclusions No grants to individuals.

Applications On a form available from the secretary. Trustees meet once a year to consider grants in October. Applications should be received by the end of September. The trust stated in 2003 that its funds are currently fully committed.

The Millfield House Foundation

Social disadvantage, social policy

£117,000 (2003/04)

Beneficial area North-east England particularly Tyne and Wear.

19 The Crescent, Benton Lodge, Newcastle upon Tyne NE7 7ST

Tel. 0191 266 9429 **Fax** 0191 266 9429

Email finley@lineone.net

Website www.newnet.org.uk/mhf

Correspondent Terence Finley, Administrator

Trustees *Grigor McClelland; Rosemary Chubb; Jenifer McClelland; Stephen McClelland; George Hepburn.*

CC Number 271180

Information available Information was provided by the trust.

General This foundation aims to 'tackle poverty, disadvantage and exclusion, and to promote social change in Tyne and Wear. It funds selected initiatives and research that inform debate and influence public policy and attitudes, with the intention of improving social provision and empowering communities.'

Projects supported may, for example:

- Give a voice to excluded groups
- Bring first-hand experience of poverty to opinion formers and policy makers
- Promote social-policy debate in the region
- Campaign on local social issues
- 'The financial resources available to the foundation are a tiny fraction of the total available for charitable activity in Tyne and Wear. The trustees therefore wish to concentrate their resources on objects which most other funding bodies cannot or will not support.
- 'As a charity, the foundation must confine its grants to purposes accepted in law as charitable. However, official guidance makes it clear that charities may include a variety of political and campaigning activities to further their purposes.
- 'The foundation wishes to promote equal opportunities through its grantmaking. It will do its best to ensure that applications are dealt with fairly and that noone is denied access to information or funding on grounds of race, colour, ethnicity or national origin, religious affiliation, gender, sexual orientation, age or disability. If appropriate, the foundation will offer help with the completion of an application.
- 'The foundation welcomes applications from stand-alone projects, from organisations which sponsor or manage projects, or from two or more projects applying jointly.
- 'In certain cases, and strictly subject to compliance of Section 6 of the Charity Commission's guidance on Political Activities and Campaigning (CC9), the foundation may be willing to support proposals which involve non-violent direct action.
- 'The trustees may consider an additional element of grant to allow for support from a consultant, or training of staff, particularly in the skills required for campaigning, lobbying, media and public relations.
- 'The trustees are willing to take some risks in funding projects which strongly reflect the stated priorities. The administrator is available to discuss and give guidance on the submission of innovative proposals.'

The guidance notes go on to state the foundation: 'aims to provide, alone or in partnership with other funders, significant and medium-term support to a small number of carefully selected projects or organisations. MHF is unlikely to have more than about 6–12 grants at any one time and can therefore approve only a small number of new grants in any year. In some cases, the trustees may consider a small grant to support work needed in preparation for an application for a major grant.

An analysis of the foundation's grant distribution over the 1996–2004 time period produced these results:

	No.	Total	Percent
Poverty	8	£133,000	17.9%
Families, Children and Young People	8	£170,000	23.0%
Health and Social Care	7	£98,000	13.2%
Community Development and Regeneration	6	£99,000	32.4%
Regional Development and Governance	8	£240,000	32.2%

In 2003/04 the foundation had an income of £127,000 and made grants totalling £117,000. Grant beneficiaries included Institute of Public Policy Research towards development work and core costs (£60,000) and North East Women's Forum towards increasing women's understanding of regional governance and their participation in it (£33,000 over two years).

Exclusions Applications unconnected to Tyne and Wear are not acknowledged.

Applications Initial outline proposals should be made in writing to the correspondent. If the application meets the stated guidelines the administrator may request further information or arrange a meeting. Applications unconnected to Tyne and Wear are not acknowledged.

The trustees meet twice a year, in May and November' so completed applications should arrive by the end of March or end of September. The administrator is willing to provide guidance for the preparation of final applications, but not without first receiving an outline proposal.

Applications should include:

- contact details, including an e-mail address if possible
- a detailed description of the project, its aims and intended outcomes
- a budget for the project, giving a breakdown of the total expenditure and of any other sources of expected income (where an application is submitted by a sponsoring body, a budget for the organisation as a whole should also be provided for the year(s) the application is made)
- the most recent annual report and audited accounts (if older than six months a signed statement of income and expenditure for the period should also be provided)
- the constitution of the responsible body
- details of the organisation's equal opportunities policy and procedures
- if appropriate, plans for the dissemination of the results of the project
- details of internal and external arrangements for monitoring and evaluation of the project for which a grant is sought, including indicators for measuring its longer-term impact
- a job description if funding is sought for a salaried post
- the names of two independent referees (these may not be taken up in every case).

For further information potential applicants are strongly advised to see the trust's website.

The Millfield Trust

Christian

£76,000 (2002/03)

Beneficial area UK and worldwide.

Millfield House, Bell Lane, Liddington, Swindon, Wiltshire SN4 0HE

Tel. 01793 790181

Correspondent D Bunce, Trustee

Trustees *D Bunce; Mrs R Bunce; P W Bunce; S D Bunce; A C Bunce; R W Bunce.*

CC Number 262406

Information available Full accounts were on file at the Charity Commission.

General This trust was set up to provide grants to Christian organisations, and has supported a number of missionary societies for the last 50 years. Grants are given solely to organisations known to the trust and new applications are not considered.

In 2002/03 the trust had an income of £84,000 and a total expenditure of £76,000. Grants totalled £76,000 and were broken down in the trust's accounts as follows:

Donations to charitable and religious institutions	£66,000
Donations to individual evangelists and missionaries	£9,000
Gifts to older people/widows	£350

In 2000/01 the trust had assets of £142,000 and an income of £79,000 including over £57,000 in Gift Aid donations from two of its trustees. Grants to organisations totalled £67,000. A further £8,000 was given in grants to individual missionaries and evangelists and £350 to older people.

There were 16 grants made over £1,000 each and these were listed in the accounts. The largest grants were £15,000 to Gideons International and £10,000 to Mission to Europe. Other beneficiaries included Mark Gillingham Charitable Trust (£6,000), Tear Fund (£3,300), Ashbury Evangelical Free Church (£3,200), Overseas Council (£2,000), Scripture Union (£1,800) and British Red Cross, Leoprosy Mission, Prospect Hospice and Schools Outreach (£1,000 each).

Remaining grants were mainly for £500 each and included those to Abacus Trust, Action Partners, London City Mission, NSPCC, Revival, Salvation Army, Swindon Churches Together, UFM Worldwide and Willows Counselling Service.

Applications No replies to unsolicited applications.

The Millhouses Charitable Trust

Christian, overseas aid, general

£55,000 (2002/03)

Beneficial area UK and overseas.

c/o MacFarlane & Co., Cunard Building, Water Street, Liverpool L3 1DS

Correspondent The Trustees

Trustees *Revd J S Harcus; Dr A W Harcus.*

CC Number 327773

Information available Information was provided by the trust.

General In 2002/03 the trust had assets of £497,000 and an income of £37,000. Grants totalled £51,000. The beneficiary of the largest grant was Kirton Lindsey Baptist Church (£12,000). Other beneficiaries included Relate (£5,000), Tearfund (£3,500) and Christian Aid, Save the Children, Release International, Barnabas Fund, Unicef, Christian Solidarity and Batah Foundation (£2,500 each).

Exclusions Grants are made to registered charities only; no grants to individuals.

Applications In writing to the correspondent, but note that most of the grants given by this trust are recurrent. If new grants are made, they are usually to organisations known to the trustees.

The Millichope Foundation

General

£261,000 (2001/02)

Beneficial area UK, especially the West Midlands and Shropshire.

Millichope Park, Munslow, Craven Arms, Shropshire SY7 9HA

Tel. 01584 841234 **Fax** 01584 841445

Correspondent Mrs S A Bury, Trustee

Trustees *L C N Bury; Mrs S A Bury; Mrs B Marshall.*

CC Number 282357

Information available Full accounts were on file at the Charity Commission.

General The trust makes donations to a wide range of different organisations including:

- UK charities
- local charities serving Birmingham and Shropshire
- conservation charities.

In 2002/03 it had an income of £299,000 and a total expenditure of £259,000. Further information was not available for this year.

In the previous year it had assets of £5.9 million, which generated an income of £324,000. Grants were made to 170 organisations and totalled £261,000.

The principal beneficiary, as usual, was Fauna and Flora Preservation Society, which received six grants totalling £45,000. The next largest grant was the £21,000 given to Trinity School of Music.

Six grants of £5,000 each were made, to Cumbria Community Foundation, Lady Forester Trust, Sir Harold Hillies, National Trust, Save the Children and Shropshire and Mid Wales Hospice.

Other grants in the Midlands included £2,500 to Where Next Association for Redditch projects, £2,000 to Shrewsbury Homes for All, £1,500 to Shropshire Heritage Trust, £1,000 each to Age Concern branches in Birmingham and Ludlow, Birmingham Royal Ballet Trust, Midland Youth Orchestra, Shropshire Hills Countryside Unit and South Shropshire Volunteer Exchange and £500 each to Shropshire Youth Adventure Trust and South Shropshire Citizen's Advice.

Beneficiaries elsewhere included The Cambridge Foundation (£4,000), Royal Opera House Trust (£3,500), Avron Foundation (£3,000), VSO (£2,500), Drug and Alcohol Foundation (£2,000), British Cancer Help Care (£1,500), National Trust of Scotland (£1,000), Royal Commonwealth Society for the Blind, Mid Wales Opera and Norwood (£500 each), Care for the Wild International (£300), Islay and Jura Advice Centre (£250) and Isle of Jura Music (£100).

Exclusions No grants to individuals or non-registered charities.

Applications In writing to the correspondent.

The Millward Charitable Trust

Christian, general

£68,000 (1999/2000)

Beneficial area UK and overseas

Burgis & Bullock, 2 Chapel Court, Holly Walk, Leamington Spa, Warwickshire CV32 4YS

Tel. 01926 451000 **Fax** 01926 450795

Correspondent John Hulse

Trustees *Maurice Millward; Sheila Millward; Edward Hodgson.*

CC Number 328564

Information available Brief accounts, without a grants list are on file at the Charity Commission.

General This trust has general charitable purposes. In 2002/03 it had an income of £85,000 and a total expenditure of £124,000. Further information for this year was not available.

In 1999/2000 it had assets of £2.5 million, which generated an income of £84,000. Grants were made totalling £68,000. Further information on size of grants or types of beneficiaries was not available.

Applications In writing to the correspondent.

The Edgar Milward Charity

Christian, humanitarian

£56,000 (2001/02)

Beneficial area Worldwide, with a preference for Reading and the surrounding area.

16 Cufelle Close, Chineham, Basingstoke, Hampshire RG24 8RH

Tel. 01256 359590

Correspondent Mrs J C Austin, Trustee

Trustees *J S Milward, Chair; T Pittom; Mrs M V Roberts; G M Fogwill; Mrs J C Austin; Mrs E M Smuts.*

CC Number 281018

Information available Accounts were on file at the Charity Commission.

General In 2002/03 the charity had an income of £59,000 and a total expenditure of £57,000. No further details where available for this year.

In 2001/02 it had an income of £63,000 and made grants totalling £56,000. It distributes its funds as follows, shown here with amounts given and examples of grants:

Christian religion

One half is given for the furtherance of the Christian religion within the UK and throughout the world. Grants to 61 organisations totalled £27,000. Beneficiaries of larger grants were Greyfriars Church – Reading (£5,000) and Christchurch – Chineham, Evangelical Alliance and Veritas College (£1,000 each).

Trustees' discretion

Four-tenths is given at the trustees' discretion. In 2001/02, 55 grants were made totalling £23,000. The largest grant recipients were Southcote Jubilee Project (£2,000), College Samuel and A Roche Trust (£1,500 each) and Interserve and Vine Trust (£1,000 each).

Educational purposes

One-tenth is given for educational purposes within a 15-mile radius of Reading civic centre. Grants to 3 organisations totalling £5,000 included those to Reading Bluecoat School (£2,500) and Old Redingensians Association Ltd (£2,000).

The trustees have an established interest in a range of charities. Few new charities will be added to this list.

Exclusions No new applications will be supported.

Applications Unsolicited applications cannot be considered.

Minge's Gift and The Pooled Charities

Medical, education, disadvantage, disability

£71,000 to organisations (2001/02)

Beneficial area UK.

The Worshipful Company of Cordwainers, 8 Warwick Court, Gray's Inn, London WC1R 5DJ

Tel. 020 7242 4411 **Fax** 020 7242 3366

Correspondent Lt Col. J R Blundell, Clerk

Trustee *The Master and Wardens of the Worshipful Company of Cordwainers.*

CC Number 266073

Information available Accounts were on file at the Charity Commission.

General Registered charities are supported with general charitable purposes as directed by the Master and Wardens of the Cordwainers Company. The income of Minge's Gift is generally allocated for the long-term support of medical and educational establishments and towards disabled and/or disadvantaged young people's organisations.

In 2001/02 Minge's Gift had assets of £649,000 and an income of £89,000. In addition to the £200 paid in to individuals in pensions, grants were made to organisations totalling £60,000, broken down as follows:

Standard grants – 20 totalling £44,000

The largest were £15,000 to Cordwainers Educational Trust, £5,500 to London College of Fashion for scholarships and prizes and £5,000 to University College of Northampton. Other beneficiaries included Royal London Society for the Blind for Dorton House (£2,500), St Dunstan-in-the-West Church (£2,000), Royal Free Hospital for nurses travel bursaries (£1,500), Jubilee Sailing Trust and Lord Mayor's Appeal (£1,000 each), Fairbridge Trust and Royal Hospital for Neuro-disability (£500 each), Ironbridge Gorge Museum (£250), City Red Cross (£200) and Sheriffs' and Recorders' Fund (£100).

Master's gifts – 4 totalling £1,000

These were £500 to Square Smile Charity, £250 to Breast Cancer Charity, £200 to Alan Pinkham Memorial and £60 to The Sea Cadets.

Special grants - 6 totalling £15,000

The largest was £10,000 went to Cordwainers Educational Trust. Other grants were £1,000 each to Lord Mayor's Charity, Royal Albert Hall Trust and St Ethelburga's Centre and £500 each to Church of St Lawrence Jewry and Sports Aid London.

Support for specific beneficiaries - 3 grants totalling £1,200

These were £500 to Royal Free Hospital – Marsden, £250 to Royal London Society for the Blind for meeting room hire with a further £500 given for trophies and engraving.

Also included in the accounts for this trust was details of the giving of The Pooled Trusts, a number grantmaking arm of the Worshipful Company of Cordwainers with similar aims to Minge's Gift. This had assets of £719,000 and an income of £30,000. Pensions to individuals totalled £12,000, whilst a total of £6,300 went to seven organisations.

Grants were £1,100 to King George's Fund for Sailors, £1,000 each to British Commonwealth Ex-servicemen's League for the Golden Jubilee Appeal, Royal Chelsea Hospital, Royal Free Hospital School of Medicine for scholarships and Thiepval Project and £250 to Royal British Legion.

Exclusions Grants to individuals are not supported through Minge's Gift, although student and welfare grants can be made through The Pooled Trusts.

Applications In writing to the correspondent.

The Minos Trust

Christian, general

£50,000 (2002/03)

Beneficial area UK and overseas.

Kleinwort Benson Trustees Ltd, PO Box 191, 10 Fenchurch Street, London EC3M 3LB

Correspondent The Trustees

Trustees *K W Habershon; E M Habershon; Mrs D Irwin-Clark.*

CC Number 265012

Information available Full accounts were provided by the trust.

General The trust gives most of its support to Christian charities in grants ranging up to £15,000. Remaining funds are given to other causes, with a preference for animals and wildlife, although these grants tend to be less than £1,000. Many of the organisations receiving the larger grants are regularly supported by the trust.

In 2002/03 the trust had assets of £277,000 and an income of £23,000. The total amount given as grants was £50,000.

The largest grants were £3,000 each to Care Trust and Tigers Club Project. Other large grants included those to Care Trust (£2,500), Tearfund (£2,000) and Ashburnham Christian Trust (£1,500), with £1,000 each to Bible Society, Friends of the Elderly and Youth with a Mission.

80% of the grants were were under £1,000 and were given to Christian organisations in the UK and overseas including: Africa Christian Press (£400), Aid to Russian Christians (£300) and Gideons International (£100). Other grants included those to Worldwide Fund for Nature (£450) and Sussex Farming Wildlife Advisory Group and RSPB (£50 each).

Applications In writing to the correspondent, for consideration on an ongoing basis.

The Laurence Misener Charitable Trust

Jewish, general

£104,000 (2002/03)

Beneficial area UK.

Messrs Bourner Bullock, Sovereign House, 212–224 Shaftesbury Avenue, London WC2H 8HQ

Tel. 020 7240 5821

Correspondent C A Letts

Trustees *J E Cama; P M Tarsh; Mrs J M Cama.*

CC Number 283460

Information available Accounts were on file at the Charity Commission.

General In 2002/03 the trust had assets of £2.1 million with an income of £136,000 and grants totalling £104,000.

The largest grants were £10,000 to Richard Dimbleby Cancer Fund, £7,500 each to Jewish Care, Jewish Association for Physically Handicapped and Home for Aged Jews – Nightingale House, and £6,000 to Robert Owen Foundation.

Other grants include £4,500 to Imperial Cancer Research Fund, £3,000 each to St George's Church (Dittisham), SSAFA, Multiple Sclerosis Society of Great Britain and Northern Ireland and Age Concern, £2,500 each to Blond McIndoe Centre, Cassel Hospital Families Centre Appeal, Central British Fund – World Jewish Relief, Elimination of Leukaemia Fund, Imperial War Museum Trust, Marilyn Houlton MND Research Trust and St Peter and St James Home & Hospice, £2,000 each to ORHCF Fund, Royal Marsden Hospital and World Ship Trust and £1,400 to Royal National Lifeboat Institution and RNLI – Salcombe Lifeboat.

Applications In writing to the correspondent.

The Victor Mishcon Charitable Trust

Jewish, social welfare

£106,000 (2002/03)

Beneficial area UK.

Summit House, 12 Red Lion Square, London WC1R 4QD

Tel. 020 7440 7000

Correspondent Miss M Grant

Trustees *Lord Mishcon; P A Cohen; P Mishcon; R Mishcon; J Landau.*

CC Number 213165

Information available Full accounts were on file at the Charity Commission.

General The trust supports mainly Jewish charities, but also gives grants to general social welfare and medical/ disability causes, especially children's charities.

In 2002/03 the trust had assets of £1.5 million, which generated an income of £77,000. Grants were made totalling £106,000.

The largest grants were £38,000 to British Council of Shaare Zedak and £3,7000 to United Synagogue.

Many of the other grants were also made to Jewish organisations. Larger grants included those to Nightingale House and Friend's of Lubavitch (£1,500 each), Friends of Alyn (£1,000), Bevis Marks Synagogue (£1,300), Central Synagogue (£800); Smaller grants included, Community Security Trust (£250), Chevras Ezras Nitzrochem (£400), Cambridge University Jewish Society (£100), Institution of Jewish Affairs (£50).

Grants for other charitable purposes included £1,2000 to British On, £750 to BA City of London Police Federation Rupen Fund, £250 each to Acorns Children's Hospice and Aids Ark and £100 each to Arthritis Care, British Blind Sport, Children in Crisis, People's Dispensary for Sick Animals and UBS.

Applications In writing to the correspondent.

The Mitchell Charitable Trust

Jewish, general

£35,000 (2003/04)

Beneficial area UK, with a preference for London.

28 Heath Drive, London NW3 7SB

Tel. 020 7794 5668 **Fax** 020 7794 5680

Correspondent Ashley Mitchell, Trustee

Trustees *Ashley Mitchell; Elizabeth Mitchell; Antonia Mitchell.*

CC Number 290273

Information available Information was provided by the trust.

General The trust was established in 1984. It has general charitable purposes but in practice appears to have a strong preference for welfare charities, Jewish organisations and health charities.

In 2003/04 the trust had assets of £850,000, an income of £37,000 and made grants totalling £35,000. The largest grants were £13,000 to Jewish Care, £6,500 to World Jewish Relief and £5,000 to London School of Economics.

Exclusions No grants to individuals or for research, education, overseas appeals or non-Jewish religious appeals. Applicants from small charities outside London are unlikely to be considered.

Applications In writing to the correspondent. Applications must include financial information. The trust does not reply to any applications unless they choose to support them. Trustees do not meet on a regular basis, thus applicants may not be advised of a grant for a considerable period.

Keren Mitzvah Trust

General

£165,000 (2002)

Beneficial area UK.

c/o Manro Haydan Trading, 1 Knightsbridge, London SW1X 7LX

Tel. 020 7823 2200

Correspondent C Campbel

Trustees *C J Smith; M Weiss; M Weiss.*

CC Number 1041948

Information available Information was provided by the trust.

General In 2003 the trust had an income of £270,000 and a total expenditure of £284,000. No further information was available from this year.

In the previous year grants totalled £165,000. Beneficiaries included Society of Friends of the Torah (£35,000), Yad Yemin (£12,000), Kisharon (£11,000), Friends of the Jewish Secondary School Movement (£10,000), Project Seed (£6,800), Sage (£6,000) and Avigdor Primary School (£5,000).

Applications The trust stated that the trustees support their own personal charities.

The Mizpah Trust

General

£49,000 (2001/02)

Beneficial area UK.

Foresters House, Humbly Grove, South Warnborough, Hook, Hampshire RG29 1RY

Correspondent A C O Bell, Trustee

Trustees *A C O Bell; J E Bell.*

CC Number 287231

Information available Full accounts were on file at the Charity Commission.

General The trust is proactive and makes grants to a wide range of organisations.

In 2001/02 the trust had assets of £50,000 with an income of £18,000 and grants totalling £49,000.

Grants include £25,000 to World Vision, £7,500 to Micah Trust, £5,000 to Stewards Trust, £2,000 each to Church Team Ministries International, Knight Foundation for Cystic Fibrosis and HTB Alpha Partners, £1,500 to P & P Trust, £1,000 each to Warham Trust and Burrswood Golden Jubilee.

Grants of less than £1,000 were awarded to Upton Grey Alpha Course, South Warnborough Golden Jubilee, Joynson – Hick Trust and May Place.

The trust also gave grants totalling £1,000 to individuals.

Applications The trust has stated that 'no applications will be considered'.

This entry was not confirmed by the trust but the information was correct according to the Charity Commission.

The Modiano Charitable Trust

Jewish, general

£34,000 (2001/02)

Beneficial area UK and overseas

Broad Street House, 55 Old Broad Street, London EC2M 1RX

Tel. 020 7377 7550

Correspondent G Modiano, Trustee

Trustees *G Modiano; Mrs B Modiano; L S Modiano.*

CC Number 328372

Information available Accounts are on file at the Charity Commission, but without a narrative report.

General This trust gives between 30% and 40% of its income to Jewish organisations and also supports a number of development organisations, mainly those working with people in need and arts organisations. Grants can be one-off or recurrent. In 2002/03 the trust had an income of £90,000 and a total expenditure of £86,000. Further details for this year were not available.

In 2001/02 it had assets of £44,000. Total income was £50,000, almost all of which came from a single donation. Grants were made to 34 organisations and totalled £34,000.

The largest grants went to Philharmonic Orchestra, South Bank Foundation (first of four), UJIA, Westminster Synagogue and World Jewish Relief.

Other grants included £1,000 each to Help the Aged, Musicians' Benevolent Society and Royal National Theatre.

Applications In writing to the correspondent.

The Moette Charitable Trust

Education

£38,000 (2002/03)

Beneficial area UK.

1 Holden Road, Salford M7 4NL

Tel. 0161 832 8721

Correspondent Simon Lopian, Trustee

Trustees *Simon Lopian; Pearl Lopian; David Haffner.*

CC Number 1068886

Information available A brief accounts sheet was available at the Charity Commission.

General The trust states 'The principal activity of the trust is the provision of support of the poor and needy for educational purposes'.

In 2002/03 the trust's assets comprised cash at the bank totalling £158,000. Its income was £27,000, mostly from donations received. Grants totalled £38,000.

Larger grants to beneficiaries were £15,000 to Finchley Road Synagogue, £2,500 each to King David Schools (Manchester) and Manchester Charitable Trust, £2,000 to The Purim Fund and £1,000 each to Yad Voezer and Yeshivas Lev Aryeh.

Smaller grants included £500 each to Hakalo and London School of Jewish Studies, £400 to Manchester Jewish Federation and £50 to Manchester Seminary for Girls.

Applications In writing to the correspondent.

The Mole Charitable Trust

Jewish, general

£468,000 (2001/02)

Beneficial area UK, with a preference for Manchester.

2 Okeover Road, Salford M7 4JX

Tel. 0161 832 8721

Correspondent Martin Gross

Trustees *M Gross; Mrs L P Gross.*

CC Number 281452

Information available Accounts were on file at the Charity Commission.

General In 2003/04 the trust had an income of £274,000 and a total expenditure of £361,000. Further information for this year was not available.

In 2001/02 it had assets amounting to £2.1 million and grants to 35 organisations totalled £468,000. Beneficiaries of the largest donations were Shaarei Torah Buildings Ltd (£200,000), Manchester Jewish Grammar School (£55,000), Bar Yochai Charitable Trust and Broom Foundation (£50,000 each), Binoh of Manchester (£25,000), Shaarei Chested Trust (£15,000) and Manchester Charitable Trust (£11,000).

Remaining grants were all for £5,000 or less and included those to Community Security Trust, Kisharon, Kollel Rabbi Yechiel, Lubaritch Manchester, Sayser Charity and United Jewish Israel Appeal.

Applications In writing to the correspondent.

The D C Moncrieff Charitable Trust

Social welfare, environment

£35,000 (2003/04)

Beneficial area UK and worldwide, with a preference for Norfolk and Suffolk.

8 Quinnell Way, Lowestoft, Suffolk NR32 4WL

Tel. 01502 564613

Correspondent D J Coleman, Trustee

Trustees *D J Coleman; A S Cunningham; R E James; M F Dunne.*

CC Number 203919

Information available Accounts were provided by the trust.

General The trust was established in 1961. It supports a number of large UK organisations, however it tends to concentrate on charities local to the Norfolk and Suffolk areas.

In 2003/04 the trust had assets of £748,000 and an income of £41,000. Grants were made to 38 organisations totalling £35,500.

Beneficiaries included All Hallows' Hospital (£3,000), Lowestoft Girl Guides Association (£2,500), St Luke's Hospital for Clergy, East Anglian Air Ambulance, Friends of Lothingland Hospital and Send A Cow (£2,000 each), Saxmundham Skateboard Park (£1500) and Caister Lifeboat Appeal and Children's Hospice for the Eastern Region (£1,000 each).

Exclusions No grants for individuals.

Applications In writing to the correspondent. The trust stated in January 2005 that demand for funds exceeded available resources, therefore no further requests are currently invited.

The Colin Montgomerie Charitable Foundation

General

Around £30,000 (2002)

Beneficial area UK.

c/o IMG, Pier House, Strand on the Green, Chiswick, London W4 3NN

Tel. 020 8233 5240

Correspondent John Murray, Trustee

Trustees *Colin Montgomerie; Guy Kinnings; John Murray.*

CC Number 1072388

Information available Information was taken from the Charity Commission's website.

General Set up in November 1998, the foundation aims to support the relief of poverty, the advancement of education and religion, and any other charitable purposes as decided by the trustees.

In 2002 it had an income of £38,000 and an expenditure of £36,000. Grants probably totalled around £30,000. Details on beneficiaries were not available for the year, however previous recipients have included British Lung Foundation, Cancer Vaccine Institute, NSPCC for the Full Stop Campaign and University of Glasgow MRI Scanner Fund.

Applications In writing to the correspondent.

Misselbrook Trust

General

£27,000 (2002/03)

Beneficial area UK with a preference for the Wessex area.

Ashton House, 12 The Precinct, Winchester Road, Chandlers Ford, Eastleigh, Hampshire SO53 2GB

Tel. 023 8027 4555

Correspondent M Howson-Green, Trustee

Trustees *Miss M J Misselbrook; M Howson-Green.*

CC Number 327928

Information available Full accounts were on file at the Charity Commission.

General In 2002/03 the trust had assets of £414,000, an income of £65,000 and made grants totalling £27,000.

Beneficiaries of grants exceeding £500 included Haemophilia Society, Jubilee Sailing Trust, Salvation Army and Southampton Rotary Club Trust Fund (£1,000 each). Grants of £500 or less were donated to 69 institutions totalling £23,000.

Applications In writing to the correspondent.

The Horace Moore Charitable Trust

General

£33,000 (2002/03)

Beneficial area UK.

Mallows Studio, Warreners Lane, Weybridge, Surrey KT13 0LH

Tel. 01932 710 250

Correspondent J A G Leighton, Trustee

Trustees *J A G Leighton; J E A Leighton.*

CC Number 262545

Information available Full accounts were on file at the Charity Commission.

General The priorities of the trust are: ballet, music, opera and theatre; church buildings; animal homes, animal welfare and horse facilities; and heritage. The trust will consider funding: information technology and computers; Christian education and churches; hospices and hospice at home; conservation and environment; purchase of books for education; and community facilities and day centres.

In 2002/03 the trust had assets totalling £112,000 and made grants totalling £33,000 to 44 organisations. Larger grants made were to Canine Partners and St Edward's School Oxford (£4,000 each), Mark Davies Injured Riders Fund, The Royal Marines Benevolent Society, The Royal Airfirce Benevolent Society and St Mary the Virgin Riddleson (£2,000 each), and grants of £1,000 each were made to Brocklands Museum, King George's Fund, Obsessive Action and St Peter's Church Hersham. Other donations were for between £100 and £500.

Applications The trust states that funds are fully committed. Donations are only given to charitable organisations and to those of personal interest to the trustees.

George A Moore Foundation

General

£120,000 (2002/03)

Beneficial area Principally Yorkshire and the Isle of Man but also some major UK appeals.

Mitre House, North Park Road, Harrogate, North Yorkshire HG1 5RX

Correspondent Miss L P Oldham

Trustees *George A Moore; Mrs E Moore; J R Moore; Mrs A L James.*

CC Number 262107

Information available Information and grants list provided by the trust.

General In previous years the trustees of the foundation have selected causes and projects from applications received during the year, as well as using independent research to identify specific objectives where they wish to direct assistance. However, in its 2001/02 report it stated that it plans to follow a more definite policy where particular areas will be targeted and ongoing relationships formed. As a result, fewer funds will become available for unsolicited requests. These changes have resulted in donations for subsequent years being lower than previously.

In 2002/03 the trust had assets of £7.5 million and an income of £492,000. A total of £120,000 was given in 75 grants, over half of which were for £1,000 or less.

Beneficiaries receiving grants of over £5,000 each were: Keighley Sea Cadets (£24,000), Age Concern Knaresborough (£12,000), National Autistic Society (£10,000), Harrogate Alcohol and Drugs Agency (£6,500) and Diabetes UK (£6,000).

Other smaller grants included those to: St John Ambulance (£3,800), York Sea Cadets (£3,400), Dyslexia Institute Bursary Fund (£3,000), 11th Spen Valley Scout Group (£2,000), RNIB (£1,750), Childline Yorkshire & North East and Ryedale Carers Support (£1,500 each), Calibre Cassette Library, Centrepoint, Cerebal Palsy Children's Charity, Dystonia Society, Haemophilia Society, Knaresborough FEVA, Memorial Gates Trust, Northern Ballet Theatre and Queen's Nursing Institute (£1,000 each).

Exclusions No assistance will be given to individuals, courses of study, expeditions, overseas travel, holidays, or for purposes outside the UK. Local appeals for UK charities will only be considered if in the area of interest. Because of present long-term commitments, the foundation is not prepared to consider appeals for religious property or institutions, or for educational purposes.

Applications In writing to the correspondent. No guidelines or application forms are issued. The trustees meet approximately four times a year, on variable dates, and an appropriate response is sent out after the relevant meeting.

The Nigel Moores Family Charitable Trust

Arts

£826,000 paid and committed (2001/02)

Beneficial area UK, but mostly Wales and Liverpool.

c/o Macfarlane & Co., 2nd Floor, Cunard Building, Water Street, Liverpool L3 1DS

Tel. 0151 236 6161 **Fax** 0151 236 1095

Correspondent P Kurthausen, Accountant

Trustees *J C S Moores; Mrs L M White; Mrs P M Kennaway.*

CC Number 1002366

Information available Accounts were on file at the Charity Commission.

General The main focus of this trust is promoting the arts, particularly among the wider community. Outside of this, grants are available towards education, the environment, recreational and leisure-time facilities and the advancement of religion. The grants list indicates most of the beneficiaries are Welsh, although arts organisations in Liverpool often receive large grants, probably due to the Moores family connections.

In 2002/03 the trust had an income of £72,000 and a total expenditure of £258,000. Grants paid and committed totalled £826,000 in 2001/02. Grants paid were £210,000 to the A Foundation (a connected charity), £18,000 to International Society for Ecology and Culture and £10,000 to Super Nova.

Applications In writing to the correspondent.

The Morel Charitable Trust

See below

£64,000 (2001/02)

Beneficial area UK and the developing world.

34 Durand Gardens, London SW9 0PP

Tel. 020 7582 6901

Correspondent S E Gibbs, Trustee

Trustees *J M Gibbs, Chair; W M Gibbs; S E Gibbs; B M O Gibbs; S Gibbs; E Gibbs; Thomas Gibbs.*

CC Number 268943

Information available Full accounts are on file at the Charity Commission.

General This trust supports: the arts, particularly drama; organisations working for improved race relations; inner-city projects and developing-world projects. Also supported are: culture and recreation; health; conservation and environment; education and training; and social care and development.

In 2001/02 the trust had assets of £1.3 million with an income of £81,000 and grants totalling £64,000.

The largest grants were £5,000 each to Child to Child, African Initiatives and Oxfam, £4,000 each to Child to Child (Ecuador) and Action Aid (Peace Building), £3,000 each to Jubilee Plus, Oxfam (BRAC in Bangladesh), Oxfam (Maharashtra), Tree Aid, Walls of Llangynidr and Hope and Homes for Children, £2,000 each to Walworth Methodist Church, Ockenden Ventures, Book Aid International and Sightsavers.

Grants of £1,000 or less were awarded to International Planned Parenthood, Healthlink Worldwide, Ghana School Aid, Achimota Trust, Hospice Care, Mildmay Mission Hospital, Harvest Help, Royal West of England Academy, Northumberland Community Trust, Corrymeela, Pecan, Greenwich Committee Against Racist Attacks, Llangynidr Church Fabric Fund and Rainbow Trust.

Exclusions No grants to individuals.

Applications In writing to the correspondent. The trustees meet three times a year to consider applications.

Morgan Williams Charitable Trust

Christian

£518,000 (2000/01)

Beneficial area UK.

2 Finsbury Avenue, London EC2M 2PP

Tel. 020 7568 2569 **Fax** 020 7568 0912

Email sally.baker@ubsw.com

Correspondent K J Costa, Trustee

Trustees *K J Costa; Mrs A F Costa.*

CC Number 221604

Information available Full accounts were on file at the Charity Commission.

General In 2000/01 the trust had assets of £53,000. The total income was £576,000, mostly from donations. Grants were made totalling £518,000.

The largest grant was £450,000 to Holy Trinity Church, a regular beneficiary.

Other grants were £10,000 to Soul Survivor, £5,000 each to Oasis Trust and Ptuio Trust, £3,400 to Glyndebourne Productions, £2,500 to Joshua Generation and New Life Outreach, and £1,000 to Youth for Christ. Donations to individuals totalled £17,000.

Applications The trust states that only charities personally connected with the trustees are supported and absolutely no applications are either solicited or acknowledged.

Diana and Allan Morgenthau Charitable Trust

Jewish, health and educational charities worldwide

£86,000 (2001/02)

Beneficial area Worldwide.

Flat 27, Berkeley House, 15 Hay Hill, London W1J 8NS

Tel. 020 7493 1904

Correspondent Allan Morgenthau, Trustee

Trustees *Allan Morgenthau; Diana Morgenthau.*

CC Number 1062180

Information available Accounts were on file at the Charity Commission.

General Registered with the Charity Commission in April 1997. In 2001/02 the trust had an income of £68,000 and made grants totalling £86,000.

There were 25 grants in the range of £200 and £20,000. Beneficiaries included: Jaffa Centre (£20,000); Conciliation Resources (£15,000); UJIA (£13,000); Jewish Music Institute (£5,000); Jerusalem Foundation (£2,500); AJR Social Services and Nightingale House (£2,000 each); Aspire and Brent Centre for Young People (£1,000 each); Weizmann Institute (£750); Norwood Ltd (£520); World Jewish Relief (£500); and Soho Theatre (£200).

Applications In writing to the correspondent.

The Oliver Morland Charitable Trust

Quakers, general

£104,000 (2001/02)

Beneficial area UK.

Thomas's House, Stower Row, Shaftesbury, Dorset SP7 0QW

Tel. 01747 853524

Correspondent J M Rutter, Trustee

Trustees *Priscilla Khan; Stephen Rutter; Joseph Rutter; Jennifer Pittard; Kate Lovell; Charlotte Jones; Simon Pittard.*

CC Number 1076213

Information available Accounts were on file at the Charity Commission.

General The trustees state that the majority of funds are given to Quaker projects or Quaker-related projects, which are usually choosen through the personal knowledge of the trustees. In 2001/02 the trust had an income of £89,000 and made grants totalling £104,000.

Grants included £26,000 to Quaker Peace and Service, £7,400 to Quaker Home Service – Children and Young People, £5,000 to Woodbrooke, £2,500 to Pakistan Environmental Protection Foundation, £1,500 to Sightsavers International, £1,000 to Uganda Peace Education, £800 to SOS Sahel International, £300 to Tools for Self Reliance and £200 to Stoneham Housing Association Yeovil.

Exclusions No grants to individuals.

Applications The trustees meet twice a year, probably in May and November. The trust tends to support the same charities each year and only limited funds are available for unsolicited applications.

S C and M E Morland's Charitable Trust

Quaker, sickness, welfare, peace and development overseas

£33,000 (2002/03)

Beneficial area UK.

Gable House, Parbrook, Glastonbury, Somerset BA6 8PB

Tel. 01458 850804

Correspondent J C Morland, Trustee

Trustees *J C Morland; Ms J E Morland; Ms E Boyd; H N Boyd.*

CC Number 201645

Information available Full accounts were provided by the trust.

General This trust has stated that it 'gives to Quaker, local and national charities which have a strong social bias, and also to some UK-based international charities'. The trust later on says that it supports those charities concerned with the relief of poverty and ill health, and those promoting peace and development overseas.

In 2002/03 it had assets of £684,000, which generated an income of £35,000. Grants to 88 charities totalled £33,000. The only one of over £1,000, and therefore large enough to be mentioned in the accounts, was of £6,500 and went to Britain Yearly Meeting, which has often received the largest grant.

Exclusions The trust does not usually give to animal welfare, individuals or medical research.

Applications In writing to the correspondent. The trustees meet two times a year to make grants, in March and December. Applications should be submitted in the month before each meeting.

Ruth and Conrad Morris Charitable Trust

Jewish, general

£185,000 (2001/02)

Beneficial area UK and Israel.

c/o Paul Maurice, MRI Moores Rowland, 3 Sheldon Square, Paddington, London W2 6PS

Tel. 020 7470 0000

Correspondent Conrad Morris, Trustee

Trustees *R S Morris; C J Morris.*

CC Number 276864

Information available Full accounts were on file at the Charity Commission.

General This trust has Jewish charitable purposes. In 2001/02 the trust had assets of £196,000 with an income of £190,000 and grants totalling £185,000.

The largest grants were £48,000 to Bar Ilan, £20,000 to Ohr Torah and £16,000 to Aish Hatorah Jerusalem Fellowships.

Other grants include £9,000 to Menorah Grammar School, £6,600 to Luhavitch, £4,000 each to Ascent, Jewish Care and National Jewish Chaplaincy, £3,000 to UK Friends of AWIS, £2,000 each to BFO Ezer Mitzion, Encounter, Hamayon, Immanuel College, J Link, JLE, Kol Nidre Appeal and UJIA.

Grants of £1,000 or less were awarded to Avigdor School, BFO Ariel Institute, BICC, Child Resettlement Fund, Conference of European Rabbis, Cyril Dennis, Hope, JABE, Jami, JCT UK, London School of Jewish Studies, MDA, Mifal Hatorah, Noam Shabbos, Pardes House, Sage, SAJFID, School J-Link, Scopus, Seed, United Synagogue, Womens Campaign Soviet Jewry and Yad Ezra.

Applications In writing to the correspondent.

The Willie & Mabel Morris Charitable Trust

Medical, general

£99,000 (2001/02)

Beneficial area UK.

Bramfield Place, Church Road, Sutton, Sandy, Bedfordshire SG19 2NB

Tel. 01767262728

Correspondent Angela Tether

Trustees *Michael Macfadyen; Joyce Tether; Peter Tether; Andrew Tether; Angela Tether; Suzanne Marriott.*

CC Number 280554

Information available Full accounts were on file at the Charity Commission.

General The trust was established in 1980 by Mr and Mrs Morris. It was constituted for general charitable purposes and specifically to relieve physical ill-health, particularly cancer, heart trouble, cerebral palsy, arthritis and rheumatism. Grants are usually only given to registered charities.

In 2001/02 the trust had assets of £2.9 million and an income of £116,000. Grants were made totalling £99,000.

Donations were in the range of £250 to £12,000. Beneficiaries of larger grants included St Thomas' Lupus Trust (£12,000), British Heart Foundation (£5,500), Diabetes (UK) (£5,200), Arthritis Reasearch Campaign, J Starmer Smith T Cell Lymphoma Appeal, Motor Neuron Disease Association, The Prostate Cancer Charity, SCOPE and University of Nottingham (£5,000 each).

Smaller grants included £2,500 to Alzheimer's Society, £1,000 to Breast Cancer Campaign, £870 to Friends of Cockayne Hatley Church, £850 to The Royal British Legion, £750 to MAGPAS, £500 to Heartlands Cystic Fibrosis Appeal, £300 to Open Doors, £164 to Friends of Addenbrookes Hospital and £100 each to St John Ambulance Brigade and Thomas' Charity Appeal.

Exclusions No grants for individuals or non-registered charities.

Applications The trustees 'formulate an independent grants policy at regular meetings so that funds are already committed'.

The Morris Charitable Trust

Relief of need, education, community support and development

£79,000 (2001/02)

Beneficial area UK and overseas, with a preference for Islington.

Management Office, Business Design Centre, 52 Upper Street, London N1 0QH

Tel. 020 7288 6436 **Fax** 020 7226 0590

Email info@morrischaritabletrust.com

Website www.morrischaritabletrust.com

Correspondent Linda Morris

Trustees *Mrs G Morris; J A Morris; P B Morris; A R Stenning.*

CC Number 802290

Information available Information was provided by the trust.

General This trust was established in 1989 by the Morris family, owners of a number of businesses in Islington. A proportion of the profits of these businesses, together with investment income, makes up the funds available for grants each year.

The trust has general charitable purposes, placing particular emphasis on alleviating social hardship and deprivation, supporting national, international and local charities. There is a preference for supporting causes within Islington.

In 2002/03 the trust had an income of £126,000 and a total expenditure of £106,000. No further information was available for this year.

In the previous year the trust had assets of £135,000. Total income was £126,000, including £125,000 in donations received. Grants were made to 122 organisations totalling £79,000.

The largest grants were £15,000 to Highbury Quadrant School, £5,000 each to Anne Frank Trust and Sunnyside Garden Project, £3,500 to Dial A Dream, £2,500 each to Community Action Trust and Anna Scher Theatre and £2,000 to Whittington Park Play Centre.

The trust produces an information leaflet, which lists many organisations that have been supported in the past. Beneficiaries in Islington include Angel Association, Archway Festival, Bumpers After School Workshop, ChildLine, Copenhagen Youth Trust, Finsbury Park Action Group, Freightliners City Farm, Highbury Roundhouse, Islington Boat Club, Islington Green School, Leap Theatre Group, Manors Garden Centre, Mayville Community Centre, Safer Islington Trust, Shape, South Sudanese Community Association, Thirty Sunnyside Road and Whittington Festival.

Recipients elsewhere included Age Concern, British Heart Foundation, Children with Leukaemia, Diabetes Foundation, Jewish Care, National Children's Bureau, Norwood, Quidenham Children's Hospice, RNLI, Romanian Orphanage Trust, Shelter and War on Want.

Exclusions No grants for individuals. No repeat donations are made within 12 months.

Applications By application form available from the trust or the website.

Morris Family Israel Trust

Jewish

£43,000 (2001/02)

Beneficial area UK and Israel.

Flat 90, North Gate, Prince Albert Road, London NW8 7EJ

Correspondent Conrad J Morris, Trustee

Trustees *Conrad Morris; Ruth Morris; Sara Jo Ben Zvi; Elisabeth Pushett; David Morris.*

CC Number 1004976

Information available Information was on file at the Charity Commission.

General In 2001/02 the trust had assets of £45,000 and an income of £16,000 from donations. Grants were made to 35 organisations totalling £43,000. Grants ranged from £32 to £5,800, although most were for under £1,000.

The largest grants were £5,800 to Beit Haggai, £5,400 to Machon Zichron Msohe, £4,500 to Pikuch Nefesh, £3,700 to One Jerusalem, £3,200 to Jaffa Institute of Advanced Education, £2,900 to Mosdot Neu Zvia, £2,600 to Chaim Yitxchak Cohen, £2,000 to Efrat Boys Choir and £1,600 each to Keren Malki and Leor Hatamud Rav Kook.

Beneficiaries receiving grants of under £1,000 included Chabad, Forum for Jerusalem, Mevaserett Education Center, Neurim and Yishuv Mezad.

Applications In writing to the correspondent.

The Peter Morrison Charitable Foundation

Jewish, general

£50,000 (2002/03)

Beneficial area UK.

Hope Agar, Chartered Accountants, Epworth House, 25 City Road, London EC1Y 1AR

Tel. 020 7628 5801

Correspondent J Payne

Trustees *M Morrison; I R Morrison.*

CC Number 277202

Information available Full accounts were on file at the Charity Commission.

General In the trust's annual report it states that 'the trustees are concerned to make donations to charitable institutions which in the opinion of the trustees are most in need and which provide a beneficial service to the needy'.

In 2002/03 the trust had an income of £55,000, assets of £1 million and its grant total was £50,000. Administration costs came to £19,000.

The largest grants went to Norwood Ravenswood and World Jewish Relief (£2,500 each), West London Synagogue (£2,300), Emergency Relief for Thouroughbreds (£2,200), Eastbury Village Hall (£2,000), London Philharmonic Orchestra (£1,800), Hampshire CSC, Royal National Institute for the Blind and Royal Albert Hall (£1,500 each) and Lambourne Valley Housing Trust (£1,400). The rest of the grants ranged down to £47 and went to various national and local organisations.

Applications In writing to the correspondent.

G M Morrison Charitable Trust

Medical, education, welfare

£152,000 (2002/03)

Beneficial area UK and worldwide.

Currey & Co, 21 Buckingham Gate, London SW1E 6LS

Correspondent A E Cornick, Trustee

Trustees *G M Morrison, Chair; N W Smith; A E Cornick.*

CC Number 261380

Information available Full accounts were provided by the trust.

General Grants are given to a wide variety of activities in the social welfare, medical and education/training fields. The trust maintains a list of beneficiaries that it has regularly supported.

In 2002/03 the trust had assets of £4.2 million and a total income of £192,000. Grants to 258 organisations were made totalling £152,000. They were in the range of £250 and £10,000, but were mainly for amounts under £1,000; the average grant was £590. The trust produced the following comprehensive summary of the grants made.

G M MORRISON CHARITABLE TRUST
Grants in 2002/03

	No.	*Total*	*Average*
Medical and health			
Medical research and support	67	£36,050	£538
Disabled (mental and physical)	35	£14,200	£406
Professional bodies (medical)	5	£5,900	£1,180
Hospitals/hospices	9	£5,100	£567
Respite care	4	£2,200	£550
Social welfare			
Benevolent associations	14	£6,150	£439
Residential and nursing homes	4	£1,750	£438
Elderly support	8	£4,250	£532
Young people (homes and support)	19	£10,500	£553
Homeless	10	£5,200	£520
Drugs and alcohol	2	£700	£350
Prisoners	3	£1,150	£383
Refugees and immigrants	1	£350	£350
Counselling and advice (social)	4	£1,900	£475
Crime prevention/victim support	2	£700	£350
Holidays	4	£1,950	£488
Housing trusts	3	£1,250	£417
Families	2	£950	£475
Welfare general	1	£350	£350
Education and training			
Universities, colleges and adult education	8	£20,500	£2,563
Schools	6	£4,800	£800
Music and arts	5	£4,400	£880
Spiritual and religious education	5	£1,800	£360
Others			
Overseas aid	16	£8,150	£509
Churches	9	£4,650	£517
Conservation, nature	7	£2,750	£393
Research general	3	£2,950	£983
Sports and recreation	1	£600	£600
Environment/transport	1	£350	£350

The largest grants were £10,000 to University of Aberdeen Development Trust and £6,000 to Wolfson College – Wolfson Course (Police). A further 27 grants were made, of over £1,000 each; beneficiaries included Royal College of Surgeons (£2,200), Royal Society of Arts Endowment Fund and Royal College of Paediatrics and Child Health (£2,000 each), Help the Aged (£1,300), Ninewells Hospital Cancer Campaign – Dundee (£1,200) and Echo International Health Services Ltd, Northwick Park Institute of Medical Research, Royal Academy of Music, SSAFA, St Luke's Hospital for Clergy, Understanding Children and YMCA England (£1,000 each).

The remaining grants were in the range of £250 to £900 and included those to: Alzheimer's Research Trust, Anchor Trust, Bristol Cancer Help Centre, BCTV – Scotland, Brittle Bone Society, Canine Partners for Independence, CORDA, Christian Aid, Cord Blood Charity, Crossroads Care, Elimination of Leukaemia Fund, Friends of King Edward VII Hospital, IBS Appeal, Interact Worldwide, Liverpool School of Tropical Medicine, McCabe Educational Trust, Police Foundation, Possum Trust, RAF Benevolent Fund, Royal Society of Edinburgh, RNLI, RSPB, Samaritans, Save the Children, Sight Savers International, Sustrans, Weston Spirit, Woodland Trust and YWCA of Great Britain.

Exclusions No support for individuals, charities not registered in the UK, schemes or activities which are generally regarded as the responsibility of statutory authorities, short-term projects or one-off capital grants.

Applications In writing to the correspondent. However, grants are normally selected on the basis of trustees' personal knowledge and recommendation. As the trust's grantmaking is of a long-term recurring nature and is restricted by available income, very few new grant applications can be accepted each year. Applications are not acknowledged. Grants are distributed once a year in January. Please note, telephone applications are not considered.

Monitoring is undertaken by assessment of annual reports and accounts which are required from all beneficiaries, and by occasional trustee visits.

Moshal Charitable Trust

Jewish

£48,000 (2002/03)

Beneficial area UK.

c/o Lopian Barnett & Co., Harvester House, 37 Peter Street, Manchester M2 5QP

Correspondent D Z Lopian, Accountant

Trustees *D Halpern; L Halpern.*

CC Number 284448

Information available Accounts were on file at the Charity Commission, but without a narrative report or a grants list, and only up to 1995/96.

General In 2002/03, the trust's assets totalled £95,000, it had an income of £37,000 and grants totalled £48,000. No grants list was available in the file at the Charity Commission for that year.

In 1994/95, grants were made to Jewish charities, ranging between £15 and £3,100 (mostly for less than £500), and totalling £24,000.

Applications In writing to the correspondent. This entry was not confirmed by the trust, but the information was correct according to the trust's file at the Charity Commission.

Vyoel Moshe Charitable Trust

Education, relief of poverty

About £400,000 (2001/02)

Beneficial area UK and overseas.

2–4 Chardmore Road, London N16 6HX

Tel. 020 8806 2598

Correspondent J Weinberger, Secretary

Trustees *Rabbi M Teitelbaum; Rabbi J Meisels; Y Frankel; B Berger; S Seidenfeld.*

CC Number 327054

Information available Accounts were on file at the Charity Commission, but without a list of grants or a narrative report.

General In 2001/02 the trust's assets totalled only about £35,000 and it had an income from donations of £430,000. Grants were made totalling around £400,000. About two thirds to three quarters of donations are made to UK charities. Further information was not available.

Applications In writing to the correspondent.

The Moss Charitable Trust

Christian, education, poverty, health

£219,000 (2002/03)

Beneficial area Worldwide, with an interest in Dorset, Hampshire and Sussex.

7 Church Road, Parkstone, Poole, Dorset BH14 8UF

Tel. 01202 730002

Correspondent P D Malpas

Trustees *J H Simmons; A F Simmons; P L Simmons; D S Olby.*

CC Number 258031

Information available Information was provided by the trust.

General The objects of the trust are to benefit the community in the county borough of Bournemouth and the counties of Hampshire, Dorset and Sussex, and also the advancement of religion in the UK and overseas, the advancement of education and the relief of poverty, disease and sickness. It achieves this by providing facilities for contributors to give under Gift Aid or direct giving and redistributes them according to their recommendations. The trustees also make smaller grants from the general income of the trust.

In 2002/03 it had assets of £634,000 and an income of £133,000. Grants were made totalling £219,000.

Beneficiaries included World Outreach (£25,000), Tearfund (£24,000), Scripture Union (£14,000), Evangelical Literature Distributors (£7,500), Christ Church – Westbourne (£6,000) and Slavic Gospel Association Limited (£5,000).

Applications No funds are available by direct application. Because of the way in which this trust operates it is not open to external applications for grants.

The Moulton Charitable Trust

Asthma, medical

£124,000 (2001/02)

Beneficial area UK, with a preference for Kent.

The Mount, Church Street, Shoreham, Sevenoaks, Kent TN14 7SD

Tel. 01959 524008

Correspondent J P Moulton, Trustee

Trustees *J P Moulton; P M Moulton.*

CC Number 1033119

Information available Accounts were on file at the Charity Commission, but without a list of grants.

General The trust supports established organisations benefiting people with asthma. In 2002/03 the trust had an income of £82,000 and a total expenditure of £251,000. Further information for this year was not available.

In the previous year grants totalled £124,000. A list of beneficiaries was not provided in the trust's accounts but previous research has shown that one-off grants of £5,000 or more are made, towards buildings, capital, core costs, project, research, recurring costs and running costs.

Exclusions No grants for individuals, students or animal charities.

Applications In writing to the correspondent.

The Mount 'A' Charity Trust

General, children, arts

£33,000 (2002/03)

Beneficial area UK, with a preference for Jersey and Italy.

Abacus (C.I.) Limited, La Motte Chambers, St Helier, Jersey, Channel Islands JE1 1BJ

Tel. 01534 602000

Correspondent Karen Stoker

Trustees *Stephanie Berni; Catherine Rosa Cava; Abacus Limited.*

CC Number 264127

Information available Information was provided by the trust.

General These two trusts seem effectively to operate as one. Each grant awarded by the Mount A Charitable Trust is matched by the Mount B Charitable Trust and the individual accounts are more or less identical. In the past the trust has stated that 'only appeals from children's charities are considered by the trustees', however the current list of grants shows some deviation from this policy. Most grants awarded were for £1,000 or less.

In 2002/03 the Mount A Charitable Trust made 28 donations totalling £33,000. Larger grants included: £5,000 to St Thomas' Welcome Centre; £3,800 to Literacy Research Project; £2,800 to Brog Y Don Children's Home; £2,500 each to Flip's Fund and Shooting Star Trust Children's Hospice; £1,500 each to Family Nursing and Howard Davis Scholarship; £1,100 to durrell Wildlife Conservation Trust; and £1,100 to Gambia Schools Trust Fund.

Smaller grants included: £600 to Macmillan Cancer Relief; £500 each to Jersey Arts Centre, Jersey Christmas Appeal, Lions Club of Jersey and Wellbeing; £250 to Cystic Fibrosis Research Trust; £150 to Cancer BACUP; £130 to Royal CS for the Blind; and £100 each to Charterhouse–in–Southwark and Starlight Children's Foundation.

Applications In writing to the correspondent. Presumably a letter to either the Mount 'A' or Mount 'B' Charitable Trusts will be considered by both.

The Mount 'B' Charity Trust

General, children, arts

£33,000 (2002/03)

Beneficial area UK, with a preference for Jersey and Italy.

Abacus (CI) Limited, La Motte Chambers, St Helier, Jersey, Channel Islands JE1 1BJ

Tel. 01534 6020000

Correspondent Karen Stoker

Trustees *Stephanie Berni; Catherine Rosa Cava; Abacus Limited.*

CC Number 264129

Information available Information was provided by the trust.

General These two trusts seem effectively to operate as one. Each grant awarded by the Mount A Charitable Trust is matched by the Mount B Charitable Trust and the individual accounts are more or less identical. In the past the trust has stated that 'only appeals from children's charities are considered by the trustees', however the current list of grants shows some deviation from this policy. Most grants awarded were for £1,000 or less.

In 2002/03 the Mount B Charitable Trust made 28 donations totalling £33,000. Larger grants included: £5,000 to St Thomas' Welcome Centre; £3,800 to Literacy Research Project; £2,800 to Brog Y Don Children's Home; £2,500 each to Flip's Fund and Shooting Star Trust Children's Hospice; £1,500 each to Family Nursing and Howard Davis Scholarship; £1,100 to Durrell Wildlife Conservation Trust; and £1,100 to Gambia Schools Trust Fund.

Smaller grants included: £600 to Macmillan Cancer Relief; £500 each to Jersey Arts Centre, Jersey Christmas Appeal, Lions Club of Jersey and Wellbeing; £250 to Cystic Fibrosis Research Trust; £150 to Cancer BACUP; £130 to Royal CS for the Blind; and £100 each to Charterhouse–in–Southwark and Starlight Children's Foundation.

Applications In writing to the correspondent. Presumably a letter to either the Mount 'A' or Mount 'B' Charitable Trusts will be considered by both.

Mountbatten Festival of Music

Royal Marines and Royal Navy charities

£88,000 (2000/01)

Beneficial area UK.

The Corps Secretariat, HMS Excellent, Whale Island, Portsmouth PO2 8ER

Tel. 02392 547 201

Correspondent Capt. S D Orr, Royal Marines

Trustees *Commandant General Royal Marines; Director of Royal Marines; Chief Staff Officer Personnel.*

CC Number 1016088

Information available Information was on file at the Charity Commission.

General The trust was set up in 1993 and is administered by the Royal Marines. It raises funds from band concerts, festivals of music and beating retreat. Unsurprisingly, the main beneficiaries are service charities connected with the Royal Marines and Royal Navy. The only other beneficiaries are those hospitals or rehabilitation centres etc. which have recently directly aided a Royal Marine in some way and Sargent Cancer Care for Children. Both one-off and recurrent grants are made.

In 2003/04 the trust had an income of £262,000 and a total expenditure of £232,000. Further information for this year was not available.

In 2001/02 it had assets of £125,000 and an income of £239,000, mainly from fundraising. It made donations totalling £78,000 and spent £132,000 on fundraising expenses. The trust has two major fundraising events which raise the bulk of the trust's annual income: a concert in Royal Albert Hall in mid-February each year and the Beat Retreat Ceremony on Horse Guards Parade, which is held every three to five years.

Grants, ranging from £500 to £18,000, were made, most of which were supported in the previous year. The largest grants were £18,000 to Malcolm Sargent Cancer Fund, £16,000 to The 1939 War Fund and £10,000 to RN Benevolent Fund.

Other larger grants included those to RM Museum (£9,000), Mission to Seaman RM Benevolent Fund, Royal Marines Association, SE Dunstans and SSAFA – Lord Roberts Workshop (£4,000 each), Metropolitan Police Benevolent Trust and Mountbatten Trust (£3,000 each), Band Services Amenities Fund (£2,000) and BLESMA, Hearing Concern, Forces Mental Welfare, Pembroke House, RBL, Scottish Veterans Residence and Wrens Benevolent Fund (£1,000 each).

Grants of £500 each included those to Erskine Hospital and Royal Sailors Rest.

Exclusions Charities/organisations unknown to the trustees.

Applications Unsolicited applications are not considered as the trust's income is dependent upon the running and success of various musical events. Any money raised by this means is then disbursed to a set of regular beneficiaries.

The Mountbatten Memorial Trust

Technological research in aid of disabilities

£32,000 (2001/02)

Beneficial area Worldwide.

The Estate Office, Broadlands, Romsey, Hampshire SO51 9ZE

Tel. 01794 518885

Correspondent John Moss, Secretary

Trustees *HRH The Prince of Wales, Chair; Lord Brabourne; Lady Pamela Hicks; Hon. Michael-John Knatchbull; Countess Mountbatten of Burma; Lord Romsey.*

CC Number 278691

Information available Full accounts were on file at the Charity Commission, with a detailed description of the trust's grant policy.

General This trust is notable for its set of aristocratic trustees. It has filed full accounts with the Charity Commission, with a detailed description of its grant policy.

The trust was set up in 1979 to honour the ideals of the Admiral of the Fleet, the Earl Mountbatten of Burma. It supports charities and causes 'working to further the humanitarian purposes with which he was associated in his latter years'. The trust mainly focuses on making grants towards the development of technical aids for people with disabilities. A previous focus has also been to support the United World Colleges movement, which has the aim of providing a broad education to students from around the world and grants continue to be given to Atlantic College.

The trustees state that they 'wish to provide grants as seed money acting in the form of a catalyst for projects rather than to fund a given project in total'.

In 2001/02 the trust had assets of £563,000 with an income of £34,000 and grants totalling £29,500.

The Trust has provided a grants list with explanations on how the money awarded is to be utilized and is as follows:

£16,000 to Atlantic College – A commitment to fund a disabled student for another year at Atlantic College, one of the United World Colleges.

£10,000 to John Grooms – Donation to assist in the implementation of technology in specialist wheelchair-accessible housing.

£1,000 to Disability Aid Fund – Specific funding towards an adapted PC for an individual with multiple sclerosis.

Exclusions No grants are made towards the purchase of technology to assist people with disabilities.

Applications In writing to the correspondent, at any time.

The Edwina Mountbatten Trust

Medical

£227,000 (2000)

Beneficial area UK and overseas.

Estate Office, Broadlands, Romsey, Hampshire SO51 9ZE

Tel. 01794 518885

Correspondent John Moss, Secretary

Trustees *Countess Mountbatten of Burma, Chair; Noel Cunningham-Reid; Lord Faringdon; Lord Romsey; Peter H T Mimpriss; Mrs Mary Fagan.*

CC Number 228166

Information available Full accounts were on file at the Charity Commission.

General This trust was established in 1960 to honour the causes Edwina, Countess Mountbatten of Burma was involved with during her lifetime. Each year support is given to St John Ambulance (of which she was superintendent-in-chief) for work in the UK and its Commonwealth, and Save the Children (of which she was president) for the relief of children who are sick, distressed or otherwise in need. Nursing organisations are also supported, as she was the patron or vice-president of a number of nursing organisations. Grants, even to the core beneficiaries, are only given towards specific projects rather than core costs.

In 2001 the trust had an income of £78,000 with an expenditure of £78,500. No further information was available.

It 2000 it made grants totalling £227,000, including a special one-off grant of £100,000 to St John Ophthalmic Hospital for a 40th Anniversary capital project. St John Ambulance and Save the Children each received £35,000. Other grants were £10,000 each to Countess

Brecknock Hospice, Demelza Hospice, Edwina Mountbatten House and Pilgrims House, £5,000 each to Changing Faces, Sargent Cancer Care and Soma Project and £2,000 to Ashram Project.

Exclusions No grants for research or to individual nurses working in the UK for further professional training.

Applications In writing to the correspondent. The trustees meet once a year, generally in September/October.

The F H Muirhead Charitable Trust

Hospitals, medical research institutes

£56,000 (2003)

Beneficial area UK

51 Perrymount Road, Haywards Heath, West Sussex RH16 3BN

Tel. 01403 214500 **Fax** 01403 241457

Email teca@argonet.co.uk

Correspondent S J Gallico

Trustees *M J Harding; S J Gallico; C N Mallinson.*

CC Number 327605

Information available Information was provided by the trust.

General This trust makes grants for specific items of medical equipment for use in hospitals and medical research institutes. Priority is given to applications from smaller organisations.

In 2002/03 the trust had assets of £461,000, an income of £23,000 and £56,000. Grant beneficiaries included Defeating Deafness (£11,000), Cystic Fibrosis Trust (£9,300), Bath Institute of Medical Engineering (£9,100), Ehlers-Danlos Support Group (£8,000), The David Tolkien Trust for Stoke Mandeville NBIC (£7,700), Covent Garden Cancer Research Trust (£6,400) and High Blood Pressure Foundation (£4,700).

Exclusions No grants to non-charitable bodies. No grants for equipment for diagnostic or clinical use.

Applications On a form available from the address below. This should be returned with details of specific items of equipment for which a grant is required. Trustees meet twice a year in March and October. Application forms to be received at least three weeks before the meeting.

The Edith Murphy Foundation

General

£1.2 million (2002/03)

Beneficial area UK.

c/o Crane & Walton, 113–117 London Road, Leicester LE2 0RG

Tel. 01263 515650

Correspondent D L Tams, Solicitor

Trustees *Edith A Murphy; David L Tams; Pamela M Breakwell; Freda Kesterton; Jack Kesterton; Jean Twiggs*

CC Number 1026062

Information available Accounts were on file at the Charity Commission.

General This trust was established in 1993 and it supports organisations helping medical causes and people who are poor or in need. There is a strong preference for animal charities.

In 2002/03 this trust had assets of £570,000 and a total income of £43,000. Grants totalled £1.2 million, a significant increase from 2001/02 when grants totalled £421,000.

By far the largest grant was £580,000 to National Kidney Research Fund. Two other substantial grants went to De Montfort University (£350,000) and Glenfield Hospital (£104,000).

Other grants went to Compassion in World Farming (£55,000), Headway – The Brain Injury Association and Leicester & Leicestershire Animal Aid Association (£25,000 each), Parish of the Resurrection (£20,000), RSPCA (£10,000), County Air Ambulance, Guide Dogs for the Blind, PDSA and St Bridgid's – Kilcurry (£5,000 each).

Applications In writing to the correspondent.

Murphy-Newmann Charity Company Limited

People who are older, very young have disabilities

£26,000 (2003/2004)

Beneficial area UK, predominantly the south, the south east and the Midlands.

Hayling Cottage, Upper Street, Stratford-St-Mary, Colchester, Essex CO7 6JW

Tel. 01206 323685 **Fax** 01206 323686

Correspondent Mrs T R Lockett, Director

Trustees *M J Lockett; Mrs T R Lockett; M Richman.*

CC Number 229555

Information available Full accounts and narrative were provided by the trust.

General The trustees state that: the objects of the charity are to support projects aimed at helping those in society who suffer economic or social disadvantages; aid charities working to alleviate chronic illness and disabling diseases among all age groups; and help fund research into medical conditions for which there is not yet a cure.

In 2003/04 the trust had assets of £612,000, an income of £33,000 and made grants totalling £26,000. Beneficiaries included Contact the Elderly (£2,000), Evening Argus Christmas Appeal (£1,750), Haemophilia Society and Invalids at Home Trust (£1,500 each), British Home & Hospital for Incurables, Hospice in the Weald, Malcom Sargent Cancer Fund for Children, North London Hospice, Norwood Children & Families Trust and Winged Fellowship Trust (£1,000 each).

In the year 2004/05 the Murphy Neumann Charity will make 42 grants ranging between £250 and £2,500 totalling £27,000.

Exclusions No grants to individuals.

Applications In writing to the correspondent, in a letter outlining the purpose of the required charitable donation. Telephone calls are not welcome. There are no application forms, guidelines or deadlines. No sae required. Grants are usually given in November and December.

The Mushroom Fund

General

About £22,000 (2003/04)

Beneficial area UK and overseas, with a preference for St Helens.

Liverpool Council of Social Services (Inc.), 14 Castle Street, Liverpool L2 ONJ

Tel. 0151 236 7728

Correspondent Marjorie Staunton

Trustees *Liverpool Council of Social Services (Inc.); D F Pilkington; Mrs R Christian; Mrs J Wailing.*

CC Number 259954

Information available Information was on file at the Charity Commission.

General The trust has general charitable purposes, usually supporting causes known to the trustees. In 2003/04 it had an income of £27,000 and a total expenditure of £23,000, most of which was probably distributed in grants.

In 2001/02 the trust had assets of £815,000 generating an income of £28,000. Grants totalled £33,000.

Grants of £1,000 or more were listed in the annual report. These were: Intermediate Technology Development Group Ltd, Northlands Creative Glass Centre and Refugee Education Trust (£5,000 each), Médicines Sans Frontierés (£2,000), Walesby Village Hall (£1,500), Bristol Cancer Help Centre and St Ann's Church (Millennium Centre) – Rainhill (£1,000 each)

Grants under £1,000 totalled £12,500.

Exclusions No grants to individuals, or to organisations which are not registered charities.

Applications The trust does not respond to unsolicited applications.

The Music Sales Charitable Trust

Children and youth, musical education; see below

£36,000 (2001)

Beneficial area UK, but mostly Bury St Edmunds and London.

Music Sales Ltd, Newmarket Road, Bury St Edmunds, Suffolk IP33 3YB

Tel. 01284 702600

Correspondent The Clerk

Trustees *Robert Wise; Frank Johnson; Ian Morgan; Malcolm Graham; Christopher Butler; David Rockberger; Mrs Mildred Wise.*

CC Number 1014942

Information available Accounts were on file at the Charity Commission, but without a list of grants.

General The trust was established in 1992 by the company Music Sales Ltd. It supports registered charities benefiting children and young adults, musicians, people who are disabled and people disadvantaged by poverty. The trust is particularly interested in helping to promote music and musical education.

In 2001 it had an income of £102,000. A total of £36,000 was given in 40 donations. Unfortunately, no list of grants was on file with the accounts.

Exclusions No grants to individuals.

Applications In writing to the correspondent. The trustees meet quarterly, generally in March, June, September and December.

The Music Sound Foundation

Music education

£193,000 (2002/03)

Beneficial area UK.

27 Wrights Lane, London W8 5SW

Tel. 020 7795 7000 **Fax** 020 7795 7296

Email orrj@emigroup.com

Website www.musicsoundfoundation.com

Correspondent Ms Janie Orr, Administrator

Trustees *Eric Nicoli, Chair; Jim Beach; Jason Berman; John Deacon; Leslie Hill; David Hughes; Rupert Perry; Richard Holland; John Hutchinson.*

CC Number 1055434

Information available Information was provided by the trust.

General Established in 1997 by EMI Records, this foundation is an independent charity dedicated to the improvement of music education. Grants are given to individuals and schools for the purchase of instruments and equipment and for music courses for teachers.

Assistance with sponsorship for performing art college status can be provided, although this is co-ordinated through the Specialist Schools Trust.

The foundation has sponsored 24 schools to date to become art colleges, totalling £1.5 million. Six colleges have also received funds from the foundation for bursaries to music students. These are: Royal Scottish Academy of Music & Drama – Glasgow; Royal Welsh College of Music & Drama - Cardiff; Royal Academy – London; Institute of Popular Music – University of Liverpool; Birmingham Conservatoire; Drumtech, Vocaltech and Guitar X; and Percussion School – London.

In 2002/03 it had assets totalling £6.1 million and an income of £372,000. Grants totalled £193,000, with a further £162,000 given in miscellaneous grants, presumably directly to individuals.

Exclusions Community projects, student fees/living expenses and music therapy are not funded.

Applications On a form available from the correspondent. Applications from students are considered by the colleges themselves. Applicants must come from the UK and be able to show evidence of severe financial hardship.

The Mutual Trust Group

Religion, education

Possibly about £70,000 a year

Beneficial area UK.

12 Dunstan Road, London NW11 8AA

Tel. 020 8458 7549

Correspondent B Weisz, Trustee

Trustees *A Weisz; B Weisz; M Weisz.*

CC Number 1039300

Information available Very brief accounts were on file at the Charity Commission, up to 1999, with no narrative report or list of grants.

General In 2002 the trust had an income of £69,000 and a total expenditure of £102,000. Unfortunately no further information was available for view in the public files at the Charity Commission.

Applications In writing to the correspondent.

MYA Charitable Trust

Jewish

£147,000 (1999/2000)

Beneficial area Worldwide.

4 Amhurst Parade, Amhurst Park, London N16 5AA

Tel. 020 8800 3582

Correspondent M Rothfield, Trustee

Trustees *M Rothfeld; Mrs E Rothfeld; Mrs H Schraiber.*

CC Number 299642

Information available Accounts were on file at the Charity Commission.

General In 2002/03 the trust had an income of £62,000 and a total expenditure of £92,000. No further information was available on file at the Charity Commission.

In 1999/2000 this trust had assets of £540,000 and an income of £272,000. Grants totalled £147,000. There were 22 grants listed in the accounts. Beneficiaries included Torah Ve-emuno (£20,000), Beis Avrohom Trust, Society of Friends of the Torah and Torah Vachesed Leezrah Vesaad (£10,000 each), Friends of Nachalas Osher and Yad Eliezer (£7,000 each), Friends of Ponevezh (£6,100), Beis Ruzin Trust (£6,000), Beis Yaakov Institution and Dushinsky Trust (£5,000 each), Keren Association (£1,000) and CM Trust (£500).

Applications In writing to the correspondent.

The Nadezhda Charitable Trust

Christian

£54,000 (2002/03)

Beneficial area UK and worldwide, particularly Russia and the Ukraine.

c/o Ballard Dale Syree LLP, 11a Kingswood Road, Hampton Lovett, Droitwich Spa, Worcestershire WR9 0GH

Correspondent The Trustees

Trustees *William M Kingston; Mrs Jill M Kingston; Anthony R Collins.*

CC Number 1007295

Information available Information was provided by the trust.

General The trust makes grants to projects for the advancement of Christianity in the UK and overseas. A number of churches, drug rehabilitation centres and street children's projects in Russia and the Ukraine are supported.

In 2001/02 the trust had an income of £37,000 and an expenditure of £54,000, all of which was given in grants to organisations.

The most recent other information available was from 1996/97, when the trust had an income of £53,000 mainly comprised of donations. Grants totalled about £61,000 and the deficit for this year balanced out a surplus in the previous year. Assets totalled only £8,000 at the year end.

Donations were categorised in the trust's accounts as follows:

	Organisations	*Individuals*	*Total*
Unrestricted	£8,500	£7,400	£15,900
Restricted	£31,000	£14,000	£45,000
Total	£39,500	£21,400	£60,900

Exclusions No grants to individuals.

Applications The trust states; 'The majority of funds are directed to supporting the Christian Church in the Ukraine'. It does not, therefore, respond to unsolicited applications.

The Willie Nagel Charitable Trust

Jewish, general

£74,000 (2001/02)

Beneficial area UK.

Lubbock Fine, Russell Bedford House, City Forum, 250 City Road, London EC1V 2QQ

Tel. 020 7490 7766

Correspondent A L Sober, Trustee

Trustees *W Nagel; A L Sober.*

CC Number 275938

Information available Accounts were available at the Charity Commission, but without a full narrative report or a grants list.

General The trust makes grants to registered charities, committing its income before the funds have been generated.

In 2001/02 it had assets of £17,000. Total income was £77,000. Grants were made totalling £74,000. No further information on the size or type of grants, or any details of the beneficiaries, was available.

The most recent grants information available was for 1989/90, when grants generally ranged from £20 to £2,000, but were mostly for £100 or less. There were five larger grants made, one of which was for £20,000, the others for £5,000 or less. These went to Board of Deputies Charitable Trust, Friends of Wiznitz, Israel Music Foundation, National Children's Home, and Victoria and Albert Museum.

Applications In writing to the correspondent.

The Naggar Charitable Trust

Jewish, general

£157,000 (2002/03)

Beneficial area Worldwide.

15 Grosvenor Gardens, London SW1W 0BD

Tel. 020 7834 8060

Correspondent Mr & Mrs Naggar, Trustees

Trustees *Guy Naggar; Hon. Marion Naggar.*

CC Number 265409

Information available Accounts were on file at the Charity Commission.

General The trust mainly supports Jewish organisations and a few medical charities. Arts organisations also receive some support.

In 2002/03 the trust had assets of £35,000, an income of £93,000 and a grant total of £157,000.

Grant beneficiaries included CHABAD Charities Fund (£68,400), Society of the Friends of Torah (£19,000), AISH Ha Torah UK Limited, Community Security Trust and Jerusalem Foundation (£10,000 each), BFAMI (£9,900), UK Friends of AWIS (£7,000), Tate Gallery Foundation (£5,500) and Israel Museum Jerusalem and Pro Natura (£3,000 each).

Applications In writing to the correspondent.

The Elani Nakou Foundation

Education, international understanding

£34,000 (2000/01)

Beneficial area Worldwide, mostly Continental Europe.

c/o Kleinwort Benson Trustees, PO Box 191, 10 Fenchurch Street, London EC3M 3LB

Tel. 020 7475 5093

Correspondent Dr E Holm, Trustee

Trustees *E Holm; Y A Sakellarakis; L St John T Jackson; H Moller.*

CC Number 803753

Information available Full accounts were on file at the Charity Commission.

General The main aim of the trust is to advance the education of the people of Europe in each other's culture. The four trustees include two Danish people, one Briton and one Greek.

In 2000/01 the foundation had assets of £6,000 with an income of £56,000 and grants totalling £34,000.

The grants include £13,000 to Danish Institute at Athens, £7,200 to Archanes Museum, £3,600 to Danish Greek Cultural Association Copenhagen, £3,500 to Greek Notos Theatre Company, £3,000 to University Copenhagen, £2,400 to Ny Carlsberg Glyptotek Copenhagen and £1,800 to Institute of Mediterranean Studies.

Applications In writing to the correspondent. Applications are considered in May.

The Janet Nash Charitable Trust

Medical, general

£131,000 to organisations (2001/02)

Beneficial area UK.

Ron Gulliver and Co. Ltd, The Old Chapel, New Mill, Eversley, Hampshire RG27 0RA

Tel. 0118 973 0300 **Fax** 0118 973 0022

Correspondent R Gulliver, Trustee

Trustees *Ronald Gulliver; M S Jacobs; Miss C E Nash.*

CC Number 326880

Information available Full accounts were on file at the Charity Commission.

General This trust has general charitable purposes, although it mostly supports medical causes. Warwickshire and West Midlands' organisations are usually well represented in the grants list.

In 2001/02 the trust had an income of £327,000, almost all of which came in donations from an electrical firm. It had assets of £158,000 and made grants to 14 organisations totalling £131,000.

Grants of £1,000 or more were £30,000 to Shirley Medical Centre, £25,000 to Royal Air Force Museum – Hendon, £18,000 to Vail Valley Foundation, £10,000 each to Acorn's Children's Hospice Trust and London Immunotherapy Cancer Trust, £4,000 to Dyslexia Institute, £2,500 to Leukaemia Research and £2,000 to Crimestoppers.

Applications In writing to the correspondent. The trustees meet monthly.

Nathan Charitable Trust

Christianity

£221,000 (2001/02)

Beneficial area UK and overseas.

The Copse, Sheviock, Torpoint, Cornwall PL11 3EL

Correspondent T R Worth, Trustee

Trustees *T R Worth; Mrs P J Worth; G A Jones.*

CC Number 251781

Information available Information provided by the trust.

General In 2001/02 the trust had an income of £82,000. Grants were made to 17 organisations totalling £221,000. Beneficiaries included Open Doors and Operation Mobilisation (£50,000 each); Bridges for Peace, Care, Leprosy Mission and Mission Aviation Fellowship (£20,000); Carrot Tops (£10,000); Riding Lights (£6,000) and Christian Friends of Israel and Christian Outreach (£5,000 each).

Applications In writing to the correspondent including an sae, although please note, most of the trust's funds are already fully allocated.

National Committee of The Women's World Day of Prayer for England, Wales, and Northern Ireland

Christian education and literature

£137,000 (2001/02)

Beneficial area UK and worldwide.

Commercial Road, Tunbridge Wells, Kent TN1 2RR

Tel. 01892 541411 **Fax** 01892 541745

Email office@wwdp-natcomm.org

Correspondent Mrs Lynda Lynam, Administrator

Trustees *Mrs Marlene Moore; Mrs Emma Wilcock.*

CC Number 233242

Information available Annual report was provided by the trust.

General The trust makes grants to charitable Christian educational projects and Christian organisations publishing literature and audio-visual material designed to advance the Christian faith.

The main object of the trust is to unite Christians in prayer, focused in particular on a day of prayer in March each year. The trust's income is mainly from donations collected at this event. After the trust's expenses, including the costs of running the day of prayer, the income can be used for grantmaking.

Themes for the Day of Prayer have been set as:

2003	Lebanon	Holy Spirit, Fill Us
2004	Panama	In Faith, Women Shape The Future
2005	Poland	Let Our Light Shine
2006	South Africa	Signs Of The Times
2007	Paraguay	United Under God's Tent

In 2002 the organisation had an income of £320,000. Grants and 'international donations' totalled £137,000.

Ongoing grants were made to 16 organisations. The beneficiaries were Bible Society, Feed the Minds and United Society for Christian Literature (£18,000 each), Scripture Gift Mission (£13,000), Society for Promoting Christian Knowledge (£4,000), Scripture Union (£3,000), Royal National Institute for the Blind, St John's Guild for the Blind, Leprosy Mission, Salvation Army for the Missionary Literature Fund and Cafod (£2,000 each), Northern Ireland Bible Society (£1,500), Royal National Mission to Deep Sea Fishermenfor the Scriptures for Deep Sea Fishermen Scheme and United Christian Broadcasters (£1,000 each).

Two 'International donations' were made to World Day of Prayer International (£11,000) and World Day of Prayer European Committee (£200).

Grants were made by the Committee for Welsh Speaking Churches for £700 or less, all made to Welsh branches. These were to Sunday School Council (£700), Christian Aid, Fellowship of Reconciliation and Christians Against Torture (£500 each), Alcohol and Drug Council and Society for the Blind in Wales (£400 each), Cytun (£300), Cafod (£200) and Bible Society (£100).

Six one-off grants were made to Youth For Christ for evangelistic literature (£5,000), International Fellowship of Evangelical Students and Project Romania (£4,000 each), Feed the Minds for bibles for Romania, Bible Society for bibles for Romania (£2,500 each) and Loaves and Fishes (£2,000).

Exclusions No grants to individuals.

Applications In writing to the correspondent, before the end of June. Grants are made in November.

The National Gardens Scheme Charitable Trust

Nursing, welfare, gardening

£1.8 million (2004)

Beneficial area UK.

Hatchlands Park, East Clandon, Guildford, Surrey GU4 7RT

Tel. 01483 211535

Email ngs@ngs.org.uk

Website www.ngs.org.uk

Correspondent The Chief Executive

Trustee *Mrs Daphne Foulsham, Chair.*

CC Number 279284

Information available Information was available on the trust's website.

General This trust has, since 1927, raised funds by 'opening gardens of quality, character and interest to the public' and through the sale of a publication called *The Gardens of England and Wales*, known as *The Yellow Book.*

In 2004 grants totalled £1.8 million. Beneficiaries were Macmillan Cancer Relief (£550,000), Marie Curie Cancer Care (£490,000), National Trust for NGS gardeners' bursaries (£192,000), Nurses Welfare Service (£90,000), Queen's Nursing Institute (£85,000), Crossroads Caring for Carers and Help the Hospices (£62,000 each), Perennial Gardeners' Royal Benevolent Society and Royal Gardeners' Orphan Fund (£48,000 each), county nursing associations (£28,000) and Royal Horticultural Society for its bicentenary year (£25,000) with £162,000 given in smaller grants to additional charities nominated by the owners of gardens.

Applications The trust's website states: 'The National Gardens Scheme head office donates money only to beneficiaries pre-selected by the NGS Council. These recipients are reviewed every three years. We would appreciate it [if] you did not send us speculative applications for funding as we regret we will not be able to acknowledge them'.

The National Manuscripts Conservation Trust

Conserving manuscripts

£76,000 (2001)

Beneficial area UK.

c/o The National Archives, Kew, Surrey TW9 4DU

Tel. 020 8392 5218

Email sue.barclay@nationalarchives.gov.uk

Correspondent The Secretary

Trustees *Lord Egremont; B Naylor; C Sebag-Montefiore.*

CC Number 802796

Information available Annual report and accounts were provided by the trust.

General The object of the trust is to make grants towards the costs of conserving manuscripts and archives that are of historic or educational value, and of national importance.

Grants are available to record offices, libraries and other similar publicly funded institutions including local authority, university and specialist record repositories, as well as to owners of manuscript material which is conditionally exempt from capital taxation or owned by a charitable trust. Grants are made towards the cost of repair, binding and other preservation measures, including reprography and may cover the cost of contract preservation and conservation or the salaries and related expenses of staff specially employed for the project, as well as expendable materials required for the project.

In 2002 the trust had both an income and total expenditure of £98,000.

Previous beneficiaries have included Berkeley Castle to complete the conservation and microfilming of the Berkeley Castle muniments, University of Nottingham Library towards the conservation of the Wollaton Antiphonal, a service book from the fifteenth century, Staffordshire and Stoke-on-Trent Archive Service towards a project to conserve the Staffordshire Tithe maps, London Metropolitan Archives towards the conservation of architectural plans of three London theatres: the Theatre Royal at Drury Lane, the Savoy and the Gaiety, The

Royal Institute of British Architects Architectural Library towards the Architects' Papers Conservation Project, York City Archives towards the repair and rebinding of volume A/Y, which contains material from the fourteenth to the sixteenth centuries on the life and customs of York, University of Surrey Library towards the conservation of the manuscript letters of E H Shepard, D'Oyly Carte Opera Company to conserve their archives, Glasgow University Archive Services towards the conservation of the Blackhouse charters.

The trust is administered by The National Archives.

Exclusions The following are not eligible: public records within the meaning of the Public Records Act; official archives of the institution or authority applying except in the case of some older records; loan collections unless exempt from capital taxation or owned by a charitable trust; and photographic, audio-visual or printed materials.

Applications Applicants must submit six copies of the application form including six copies of a detailed description of the project. The applicant should also submit one copy of their most recent annual reports and accounts and details of its constitution.

Nazareth Trust Fund

Christian, in the UK and developing countries

£32,000 to organisations (2002/03)

Beneficial area UK and developing countries.

Barrowpoint, 18 Millennium Close, Salisbury, Wiltshire SP2 8TB

Tel. 01722 349322

Correspondent Mrs E M Hunt, Trustee

Trustees *Robert Gainer Hunt; Eileen Mary Hunt; David Gainer Hunt; Elma Lilburn Hunt; Philip Hunt; Nicola Mhairi Hunt.*

CC Number 210503

Information available Accounts were provided by the trust.

General This trust funds churches, Christian missionaries, Christian youth work and overseas aid. Grants are only made to people or causes known personally to the trustees.

In 2002/03 the trusts assets totalled £29,000 and it had an income of £31,000, mainly from Gift Aid donations. Grants to organisations totalled £32,000, with a further £3,900 given to 11 individuals.

Donations included: £10,000 to Harnham Free Church; £6,100 to IREF; £2,600 to Durham Road Baptist Church; £1,700 to SAT 7; £1,000 to Crusaders; £700 each to London Bible College and Tearfund; £480 to World Vision; and £250 to Christians in Sport.

Exclusions No support for individuals not known to the trustees.

Applications In writing to the correspondent, although the trust tends to only support organisations it is directly involved with.

Nesswall Ltd

Jewish

£63,000 (2002/03)

Beneficial area Worldwide.

28 Overlea Road, London E5 9BG

Tel. 020 8806 2965

Correspondent Mrs R Teitelbaum, Trustee

Trustees *I Teitelbaum, Chair; Mrs R Teitelbaum; I Chersky.*

CC Number 283600

Information available Accounts were on file at the Charity Commission but without a recent list of grants.

General In 2002/03 the trust's assets totalled £472,000 and it had an income of £64,000. Total number of grants given totalled £63,000. Further information was not available for that year.

In 1992/93, the most recent year for which a list of grants was available, 22 donations were made totalling £92,000, all to Jewish organisations. The largest grants were to Friends of Horim Establishments (£36,000), Torah Vochesed L'Ezra Vesaad (£21,000) and Emunah Education Centre (£10,000). The other grants ranged from £18 to £3,600.

Applications In writing to the correspondent, at any time.

The New Durlston Trust

Christian, overseas development

£31,000 to individuals and organisations (2002/03)

Beneficial area UK and developing countries.

95 Fleet Road, Fleet, Hampshire GU51 3PJ

Tel. 01252 620444 **Fax** 01252 622292

Correspondent N A H Pool, Trustee

Trustees *Nigel Austen Hewitt Pool; Alister John Mogford; Alexandra Louise Mayne.*

CC Number 1019028

Information available Full accounts were provided by the trust.

General The trust supports charities and individuals involved in Christian-based projects. In 2002/03 it had assets of £119,000 and an income of £26,000. Grants were made totalling £31,000.

The largest grants were £5,000 to The Triangle, £2,500 to Gateway Charity, £1,000 each to Caring for Life and Handsworth International Mission and £500 each to Beacon Centre Trust, Bible Society, Breakout Trust, Elam Ministries, Highlands and Islands Youth for Christ and Project Denqke. A further £18,000 was paid in smaller grants, including at least £1,000 to individuals.

Exclusions No grants for work other than for Christian-based work. Overseas grants are only given through UK-based charities.

Applications In writing to the correspondent.

Newby Trust Limited

Welfare

£150,000 to organisations (2002/03)

Beneficial area UK.

Hill Farm, Froxfield, Petersfield, Hampshire GU32 1BQ

Tel. 01730 827557 **Fax** 01730 827938

Website www.newby-trust.org.uk

Correspondent Miss W Gillam, Secretary

Trustees *Mrs S A Charlton; Mrs J M Gooder; Dr R D Gooder; Mrs A S Reed; R B Gooder; Mrs A L Foxell.*

CC Number 227151

Information available Full accounts and report were provided by the trust.

General This trust has a specific theme for its funding for organisations each year, usually within social welfare. In recent years these have been:

2005/06	Development, education and activities for teenagers within the UK
2004/05	Mobility for the physically disabled
2003/04	The homeless
2002/03	Supporting families with health care problems
2001/02	Regeneration of the urban community
2000/01	Children under the age of 11 with particular educational needs

Please note that the years above refer to the financial year of 6 April to 5 April. Grants range from £100 to £10,000 each.

In addition to the funding for organisations, it also provides welfare grants to individuals for medical or relief of need purposes and funding to postgraduate students. These are made generally regardless of the theme for organisations. (Full details of the funding available to individuals can be found on the trust's website.)

In 2002/03 it had assets of £9.2 million, which generated an income of £419,000. Grants were made totalling £302,000, broken down as follows:

Medical welfare

Grants to 57 organisations totalled £114,000, and to 84 individuals totalling £16,000. By far the largest was £15,000 to Rhys Daniels Trust. Other beneficiaries included I-Can and Refresh (£5,000 each), Sense (£3,500), Barnet Carers Centre and Honeypot (£3,000 each), Edinburgh Young Carers and Living Paintings Trust (£2,500 each), Carers Association – South Staffordshire and Hackney Cares Centre (£2,000 each) and Arthritis Research Campaign and MedicAlert Foundation (£1,000 each).

Education, training and research

Grants to 20 organisations totalled £23,000, while 130 grants to individuals totalled £70,000. The largest were £5,000 each to Academy of Ancient Music Trust, Bedales Grants Trust Fund and Winchester College Development Appeal and £3,000 to Royal Academy of Arts.

Relief of poverty

Grants to 15 organisations totalled £14,000, whilst grants to 277 individuals totalled £66,000. By far the largest was £10,000 to Beild Housing Trust.

Sundry gifts

Grants to nine organisations under this heading totalled £1,700.

Applications In writing to the correspondent, on no more than two sides of A4 with costings and amount raised so far. An sae and a copy of the latest annual report/account must also be enclosed. Applications need to be received by the end of September or January for consideration in November or March respectively. Applicants are advised of the outcome approximately three weeks after the meeting. (There is a separate application procedure for individuals, please see their website if further information is needed.)

The Richard Newitt Fund

Education

£75,000 (2002/03)

Beneficial area UK.

Kleinwort Benson Trustees Ltd, PO Box 191, 10 Fenchurch Street, London EC3M 3LB

Tel. 020 7475 5093

Correspondent Chris Gilbert

Trustees *Kleinwort Benson Trustees Ltd; D A Schofield; Prof. D Holt; Baroness Diana Maddock.*

CC Number 276470

Information available Full accounts were on file at the Charity Commission.

General In 2002/03 the trust had assets of £1.6 million, an income of £71,000 and made grants totalling £75,000. Grant donations were made to University of Southampton – £45,000 towards new bursaries and £20,000 towards existing bursaries (£65,000), Bristol Old Vic Theatre School and Royal Northern College of Music (£5,000 each).

Exclusions No grants to individuals.

Applications Requests for application forms should be submitted by 1 April in any one year; applicants will be notified of the results in August. Unsolicited applications are unlikely to be considered, educational institutional applications by invitation only.

Mr and Mrs F E F Newman Charitable Trust

Christian, overseas aid and development

£43,000 (2001/02)

Beneficial area UK, Republic of Ireland and overseas.

Bircham Dyson Bell, 50 Broadway, London SW1H 0BL

Correspondent The Trustees

Trustees *G S Smith; F E F Newman.*

CC Number 263831

Information available Full accounts were on file at the Charity Commission.

General In 2001/02 the trust had assets of £142,000 and an income of £37,000, of which £24,000 was received through Gift Aid Donations. Grants totalling £43,000 were made from two funds: the 'A' fund (£5,600) and the 'B' fund (£37,000).

Grants from the 'A' fund were mostly for less than £200 each. Examples of grants are as follows: £1,000 to Old Leysian Benevolent Fund, £450 in two donations to Christian Aid, £400 to Thal Village Project, £300 to Guildford Samaritans, £200 each to Care International and Tear Fund, and £100 each to Active for Kids, Church Housing Trust, National Trust and Voluntary Service Overseas.

There were 34 grants made from the 'B' fund. Larger grants were £3,000 each to Bible Society, Children's Society, CMS and Tearfund, £2,500 to Anglican Renewal Ministries, £2,000 each to Adoption Now, African Enterprise and Children's Society and £1,000 each to Barnabas Fund, Church Mission to the Jews, Keston Trust, Riding Lights Trust and Traidcraft Exchange. The rest of the beneficiaries received either £600 or £500.

Exclusions No grants to individuals.

Applications In writing to the correspondent.

Newpier Charity Ltd

Jewish, general

£129,000 (1998/99)

Beneficial area UK.

Wilder Coe, Auditors, 233–237 Old Marylebone Road, London NW1 5QT

Correspondent Charles Margulies, Trustee & Secretary

Trustees *C Margulies; H Knopfler; R Margulies; S Margulies; M Margulies.*

CC Number 293686

Information available Accounts were on file at the Charity Commission, but without a list of grants.

General The main objectives of the charity are the advancement of the orthodox Jewish faith and the relief of poverty.

In 2002/03 the trust had an income of £572,000 and a total expenditure of £335,000. Further information for this year was not available.

In 2000/01 it had an income of £526,000 and a total expenditure of £431,000. Unfortunately no further details were available for this year. In 1998/99 it had an income of £412,000 including donations totalling £271,000 and rent received totalling £124,000. Grants totalled £129,000.

No grants list was included in the 1998/99 accounts. The last available list was from 1997/98 when grants were made to 23 organisations totalling £80,000. All the beneficiaries were Jewish organisations and nine had also received a grant the year before. The largest donation was to SOFT for redistribution to other charities (£23,000 was given in 1996/97).

Other larger grants were £17,000 to KID (£14,000 in 1996/997), £7,000 to Mesdos Wiznitz, £6,100 to BML Benityashvut, £5,000 to Friends of Biala (£1,500 in 1996/97) and £3,000 to Gateshead Yeshiva.

Applications In writing to the correspondent. The address given is effectively a PO Box, from where letters are passed on to the trustees and telephone calls are not invited.

The Chevras Ezras Nitzrochim Trust

Jewish

About £190,000 (2001)

Beneficial area UK, with a preference for London.

53 Heathland Road, London N16 5PQ

Tel. 020 8800 5187

Correspondent H Kahan, Trustee

Trustees *H Kahan; J Stern.*

CC Number 275352

Information available Full acounts were on file at the Charity Commission.

General 'The objects of the charity are the relief of the poor, needy and sick and the advancement of Jewish religious education.'

There is a preference for Greater London, but help is also given further afield. Grants can also be made to individuals.

In 2001 the trust had an income of £197,000, which was raised by the trustees and voluntary helpers. The previous year assets stood at just £4,700. Total expenditure was £195,000, most of which would have been given in grants.

Grants included £3,000 to Yad Eliezer Trust, £2,900 to Beis Chinuch Lebonos, £2,600 to Rehabilliation Trust, £2,200 to Yeshivo Horomo, £2,100 to Yesodey Harotah Schools, £1,600 to Gerer Shtibel Synagogue, £1,400 to Lubavitch Foundation, £1,200 to Bobov Trust and £1,000 each to Bnos Yerushalaim and Gur Trust.

Applications In writing to the correspondent.

The Noel Buxton Trust

Child and family welfare, penal matters, Africa

£82,000 (2001)

Beneficial area UK, eastern and southern Africa.

PO Box 393, Farnham, Surrey GU9 8WZ

Correspondent Ray Waters, Secretary

Trustees *Richenda Wallace, Chair; Joyce Morton; Simon Buxton; Paul Buxton; David Birmingham; Angelica Mitchell; Jon Snow; Jo Tunnard, Vice Chair; John Littlewood; Brendan Gormley.*

CC Number 220881

Information available Full accounts and guidelines for applicants were provided by the trust.

General Grants are made for the following:

- The welfare of children in disadvantaged families and of children in care. This will normally cover families with children of primary school age and younger, although work with children in care will be considered up to the age at which they leave care. (Grants are NOT given for anything connected with physical or mental disability or any medical condition.)
- The prevention of crime, especially work with young people at risk of offending; the welfare of prisoners' families and the rehabilitation of prisoners (housing of any kind is excluded).
- Education and development in eastern and southern Africa.

The trust seldom gives grants of more than £2,000 and often considerably less. Applications for recurrent funding over several years and for core running costs are considered. Due to the size of grants, contributions are not normally made towards salary costs. The trust does not respond to appeals from large, well-supported UK charities, but welcomes appeals from small local groups throughout England, Scotland and Wales. Preference is given to areas outside London and south east England.

In 2001 the trust had assets of £2.1 million and an income of £119,000. Donations were made to 89 organisations totalling £82,000, broken down as follows:

Education and development in eastern and southern Africa – 25 grants totalling £29,000 (35% of fund)

APT Enterprise Development – Zimbabwe (£4,000), WaterAid – Tanzania (£3,300), Harvest Help – Zambia (£2,500), Farm Africa – Tanzania and Intermediate Technology Development Group (£2,000 each), Book Aid International (£1,500). Beneficiaries receiving £1,000 each included African Initiatives – Tanzania, Books Abroad – Zimbabwe, Busoga Trust – Uganda, Lewa Water Conservancy – Kenya, Tools for Self Reliance – Africa.

Penal matters – 27 grants totalling £27,000 (33% of fund)
Howard League for Penal Reform (£3,000), Centre for Crime and Justice Studies and Prisoners Abroad (£2,500 each), Consett Churches Detached Youth Project, New Bridge and Prisoners' Advice Service (£2,000). Grants of £1,000 each went to Inside Out Trust, Prisoners' Education Trust, Waterville Projects for Children & Young People and Wood End and Bell Green Truancy & Exclusion Group.

Welfare of disadvantaged children (UK) – 37 grants totalling £26,000 (32% of fund)
Family Rights Group (£4,000) and Asylum Aid (£2,000). Grants of £1,000 each went to bfriends, Birmingham Settlement, Family Meditation Scotland, Family Welfare Association, National Family Meditation, Playbus Scotland, Respect, Space for Parents and Children to Enjoy, Thamesmead Family Service Unit and Think Children. Smaller grants included those to Central Community Group – Crewe, Hansworth Community Nursery, Home-Start Telford & Wrekin and Quaker Social Action.

The trust was able to give grants to about 16% of applicants. Four organisations were offered the possibility of repeat grants during the year but did not reply to the offer.

Exclusions The trust does not give to: academic research; advice centres; animals; the arts of any kind; buildings; conferences; counselling; development education; drug and alcohol work; the elderly; the environment; expeditions, exchanges, study tours, visits, and so on, or anything else involving fares; housing and homelessness; human rights; anything medical or connected with illness or mental or physical disability; anywhere overseas except eastern and southern Africa; peace and disarmament; race relations; youth (except for the prevention of offending); and unemployment. Grants are not made to individuals for any purpose.

Applications There is no application form and applications may be submitted at any time. They should include the organisation's charity registration number and the name of the organisation to which grants should be paid if different from that at the head of the appeal letter. The following should be included with applications: budget for current and following year; details of funding already received, promised, or applied for from other sources and the last available annual report/accounts in their shortest available form.

In order to reduce administration costs the trust does not acknowledge receipt of applications or reply to unsuccessful appeals. Every effort is made to communicate a decision on successful appeals as soon as possible (normally within six months).

The Noon Foundation

General, education, relief of poverty, community relations, alleviation of racial discrimination

£102,000 to organisations (2000)

Beneficial area England and Wales.

25 Queen Anne's Gate, St James' Park, London SW1H 9BU

Tel. 020 7654 1600

Correspondent The Trustees

Trustees *Gulam Kanderbhoy Noon; Akbar Shirazi; Mrs Zeenat Harnal; Mrs Zarmin Noon Sekhon; Jehangir Jamshed Mehta.*

CC Number 1053654

Information available Information was provided by the foundation.

General This trust was set up in 1996 by Gulam Kaderbhoy Noon, the founder of Noon Products. In 2002 the trust had an income of £63,000 and a total expenditure of £168,000.

In the previous year beneficiaries included Tower Hamlets College, British Prince's Trust, Ethnic Median Group, Memorial Gates Trust- Hyde Park, Commonwealth Youth Exchange Council, National Osteoporosis Society, Sunrise Orphan Trust.

Applications In writing to the correspondent.

The Norman Family Charitable Trust

General

£272,000 (2002/03)

Beneficial area Primarily south west England.

14 Fore Street, Budleigh Salterton, Devon EX9 6NG

Tel. 01395 446699 **Fax** 01395 446698

Email enquiries@nfct.org

Website www.nfct.org

Correspondent R J Dawe, Chairman of the Trustees

Trustees *R J Dawe, Chairman; Mrs M H Evans; M B Saunders; Mrs M J Webb; Mrs C E Houghton.*

CC Number 277616

Information available Full accounts were provided by the trust.

General This trust has general charitable purposes, with a preference for organisations in the south west of England.

In 2002/03 the trust had assets of £5.8 million and an income of £1.4 million. In total 280 grants were made totalling £272,000 and were broken down as follows (only donations of £1,000 or over were listed):

Animal welfare – 14 grants totalling £6,100
Only one donation of £1,000 was made to Dogs for the Disabled, while the remaining 13 donations of less than £1,000 totalled £5,100.

Blind welfare – 21 grants totalling £11,000
Five grants of £1,000 each were made to Devon County Association for the Blind, Exmouth and District Handicraft Show, Royal Blind Society, Royal London Society for the Blind and SENSE South West.

Children's welfare – 42 grants totalling £26,000
Grants included: £2,500 each to Bristol Hospital for Sick Children, Children's Hospice South West and Foundation for the Study of Infant Death and £1,000 each to Action for Kids, Happy Ways Children's Charity and St Olave's Trust.

Teenagers and youths – 29 grants totalling £26,000
These included: £5,000 to Sports Aid South West; £2,000 each to British

Schools Exploring Society, Raleigh International and Sail Training; and £1,000 each to Friends of Milwater School, GAP Activity Projects and Yeovil College.

Social services – 1 grant totalling £500

Drugs – 6 grants totalling £4,800

Grants included: £2,000 to Terrence Higgins Trust and £1,000 to Addaction.

Mental disability – 13 grants totalling £7,600

Four recipents received grants of £1,000, these were Brainwave, DASS, Leonard Cheshire Foundation and Mencap – Falmouth.

Physical disability – 25 grants totalling £17,000

Grants included: £5,000 each to Ellen Tinkham School and £1,000 each to BREAK, David Tolkein Trust and Dawlish Gardens Trust.

Medical other – 32 grants totalling £64,000

The largest grants were: £20,000 to Hospicecare Exmouth and Lympstone; £10,000 each to FORCE and North Devon Hospice; £5,000 to ELF and; £2,500 to Marie Curie Cancer Care. Beneficiaries of £1,000 each included: Headway – Devon, League of Friends of Tiverton Hospital, Pain Relief Foundation and Spinal Injuries Association.

Senior citizens – 10 grants totalling £13,000

Resthaven Residential Home received £10,000 and Age Concern – Kingsbridge received £1,000.

Research – 9 grants totalling £50,000

The largest grant in this category was £25,000 to Fountain Foundation. Other donations included: £7,500 each to Dr Hadwens Trust and Humane Research; £5,000 to Diabetes Research and Education Centre; £2,500 to Prostate Research Campaign; and £1,000 to Dermatrust.

Homeless – 5 grants totalling £4,000

Centrepoint received £1,500 and Youth Enquiry Service received £1,000.

Miscellaneous – 73 grants totalling £43,000

The largest grants included: £5,000 to Exeter Women's Aid; £2,500 each to Devon Air Ambulance, Devon Red Cross and Torbay Coast and Countryside Trust and; £2,000 to Open Door Centre – Exmouth. Beneficiaries of £1,000 each included: Cornwall Domestic Violence Forum, Home-Start – Torbay, Samaritans – Exeter and Sidmouth Inshore Rescue Service.

Exclusions No support will be given to projects involving experiments on live animals or the maintenance of churches, or to overseas projects. No grants to individuals.

Applications In writing to the trustees, who meet regularly to discuss the distribution of grants.

The Duncan Norman Trust Fund

General

£33,000 (2001/02)

Beneficial area UK, with a preference for Merseyside.

Liverpool Council of Social Service (Inc.), 14 Castle Street, Liverpool L2 0NJ

Tel. 0151 236 7728

Correspondent The Trustees

Trustees *J A H Norman; R K Asser; Mrs V S Hilton; Mrs C E Lazar; W Stothart.*

CC Number 250434

Information available Information was on file at the Charity Commission.

General This trust has general charitable purposes, particularly supporting Merseyside organisations. In 2002/03 it had an income of £66,000 and a total expenditure of £73,000.

In 2001/02 it had assets of £1.8 million, generating an income of £60,000. Grants totalled £33,000.

The fund made seven grants of £1,000 or more. These were to Cancer Research Campaign (£5,000), Oundle School's Foundation and Rydal Youth Centre (£2,000 each), Retail Trust (£1,500), After Adoption, Foundation for the Prevention of Blindness and Liverpool Family Service Unit (£1,000 each).

Other smaller grants totalled £19,000.

Exclusions No grants to individuals.

Applications The trust states that it only makes grants to charities known to the settlor and unsolicited applications are not considered.

The Alderman Norman's Foundation

Education

£206,000 (2002/03)

Beneficial area Norwich and Old Catton.

Brown & Co, Old Bank of England Court, Queen Street, Norwich NR2 4TA

Tel. 01603 629871

Correspondent N F Saffell, Clerk

Trustees *Revd J Boston, Chair; C D Brown; C I H Mawson; R Sandall; D Armes; Mrs T Hughes; Rev Canon M Smith; S Slack; Dr J Leach.*

CC Number 313105

Information available Accounts were on file at the Charity Commission.

General The trust was originally founded by the terms of the will of Alderman Norman dated February 1720. It is currently regulated by schemes from 1972 and 1973. All grants are for educational purposes. The main beneficiaries are the descendants of Alderman Norman and also other young people living in the parish of Old Catton. Local schools and other educational organisations established for charitable purposes can also receive grants.

In 2002/03 the trust had assets of £4.4 million, an income of £232,000 and made grants totalling £206,000. Grant beneficiaries included How Hill Trust – Centenary Appeal 2004 (£20,000), Norwich Cathedral Chair Endowment Fund (£5,000), Hand Partnership, Norfolk Pupil Attendance Service (Norwich) – Activity Fund and Young Citizens Guild (£3,000 each), Norfolk Splash (£2,400), Falcon Middle School and Norfolk and Norwich Association for the Blind (£2,000 each), and Build and Claimants Unity (£1,000 each).

Exclusions No grants to non-registered charities. No applications from outside Norwich and Old Catton will be considered.

Applications In writing to the correspondent. The trustees meet twice each year, in June and October.

The Normanby Charitable Trust

Social welfare, disability, general

£485,000 (2001/02)

Beneficial area UK, with a special interest in north east England.

Morgan Intakes, Great Fryup Dale, Lealholm, Whitby, North Yorkshire YO21 2AT

Correspondent Lady Henrietta Burridge

Trustees *The 5th Marquis of Normanby; The Dowager Marchioness of Normanby; Lady Lepel Kornicka; Lady Evelyn Buchan; Lady Peronel Phipps de Cruz; Lady Henrietta Burridge.*

CC Number 252102

Information available Information was on file at the Charity Commission.

General The trust supports social welfare, disability and the arts, with a special interest in north east England. The trust will occasionally consider giving grants for the preservation of religious and secular buildings of historical or architectural interest in the north east of England.

In 2002/03 the trust had an income of £264,000 and a total expenditure of £257,000. No further details were available for this year and the following is taken from the 2001/02 accounts.

In 2001/02 the trust had assets of £7.6 million, which generated an income of £290,000. Grants were made to 57 organisations totalling £485,000.

There were 15 grants made over £1,000 each. The four largest donations were £65,000 to Whitby Literary and Philosophical Society, £50,000 each to Visceral and Yorkshire Agricultural Society Farmers' Fund and £46,000 to Cook Museum Trust. Other larger donations included £20,000 each to Lythe PCC, Northumberland Aged Mineworkers' Homes Association, Whitby Community College Private Fund and Worcester College, £15,000 to Landmark Trust and £10,000 each to Rainbow Trust and York Consortium for Conservation and Craftsmanship.

Other beneficiaries of smaller grants included British Red Cross Society – North Yorkshire (£5,000), Ryedale Festival (£3,000), Richmondshire District Scouts (£2,000), Whitby Sea Cadets (£1,000), Friends of Leeds University Library (£40), Whitby Trust for the Blind (£25) and Young NSPCC – Whitby branch (£15).

Exclusions No grants to individuals, or to non-UK charities.

Applications In writing to the correspondent. Only successful applications will be acknowledged. Telephone calls are not encouraged. There are no regular dates for trustees' meetings.

This entry was not confirmed by the trust but was correct according to information on file at the Charity Commission.

The Earl of Northampton's Charity

Welfare

£68,000 to unconnected charities (2002/03)

Beneficial area England, with a preference for London and the South East.

Mercers' Company, Mercers' Hall, Ironmonger Lane, London EC2V 8HE

Tel. 020 7726 4991 **Fax** 020 7600 1158

Email mail@mercers.co.uk

Website www.mercers.co.uk

Correspondent The Grants Manager

Trustees *Charles H Parker; Robert R Pope; Katherine A Payne.*

CC Number 210291

Information available Full accounts were on file at the Charity Commission.

General In 2002/03 it had assets of £13 million, which generated an income of £536,000. Grants were made totalling £168,000, of which £100,000 was for the benefit of individuals and the rest for organisations. Total expenditure totalled £276,000, mostly in the costs of running its almshouses.

The largest grant was of £100,000 to Charity of Sir Richard Whittington, which is a connected charity which makes relief in need grants.

The remaining grants were £12,000 to Trinity Hospital – Castle Rising, £10,000 each to Abbeyfield Society branches in Eastbourne and North Down, £5,000 each to Abbeyfield Ballachulish Society, Cheltenham Old People's Housing Society, Gurkha Welfare Trust, Seckford Foundation and St Mary's Convent and Nursing Home, £4,000 to Trinity Hospital – Clun, £2,500 to Roundabout, £2,000 each to Jubilee Almshouses, Save the Church Barn Fund and £250 to St Michael's Framlingham.

Applications In writing to the correspondent.

The Norton Foundation

Young people under 25 years of age

£34,000 to organisations (2003/04)

Beneficial area UK, with a preference for Birmingham, Coventry and Warwickshire.

PO Box 10282, Redditch, Worcestershire B97 5ZA

Email correspondent@nortonfoundation.org

Website www.nortonfoundation.org

Correspondent The Clerk to the Trustees

Trustees *R H Graham Suggett, Chair; Peter Adkins; Parminder Singh Birdi; Mrs Erica Corney; John Gardener; Mrs Jane Gaynor; Mrs Sarah V Henderson; John R Kendrick; Brian W Lewis; David F Perkins; Mrs Liza Singh; Michael R Bailey.*

CC Number 702638

Information available Information was provided by the trust.

General The trust was created in 1990. Its objects are to help children and young people under 25 who are in 'need of care or rehabilitation or aid of any kind, particularly as a result of delinquency, deprivation, maltreatment or neglect or who are in danger of lapsing or relapsing into delinquency'.

In 2003/04 it had assets of £3.1 million, which generated an income of £110,000. Grants were made to 28 organisations totalling £34,000, with a further £64,000 given in total to 466 individuals. Grants to organisations were broken down as follows:

	2003/04		*2002/03*	
	No.	Total	No.	Total
Education and training	8	£9,800	5	£16,000
Housing	1	£2,000	–	–
Leisure activities	4	£5,300	4	£9,000
Medical	–	–	1	£5,000
Social work	7	£8,000	1	£1,000
Holidays	8	£9,200	6	£17,000

Grants of £1,000 or more were: £2,500 to Warwickshire Crimebeat; £2,000 each to Geese Theatre Company, Sail Training Association West Midlands and Warwickshire, St Matthew's Holiday Playscheme and Warwickshire Domestic Violence Support Service; £1,500 each to 870 House, Double R Playscheme, Home Start – Northfield and E R Mason Youth Centre; £1,400 to Harvest Trust; £1,300 to Training Ship Sutton Coldfield; £1,000 each to BAAF Adoption & Fostering, Bangladeshi Community Development, Birmingham Young Volunteers' Adventure Camps, Coventry Boys' Club, Edwards Trust, Fairbridge West Midlands, Katie Foxon's Holidays for Sick Children, Kids, React, Sea Cadets, Trescott Primary School, UK Youth and Youth Wise.

From time to time a substantial grant is awarded to an institution and applications are invited for such a grant to be awarded in February 2005. Current expectations are that the next grant could be at least £600,000. The previous major grant awarded in January was £100,000 to Sydenham Community Project.

Exclusions No grants for the payment of debts that have already been incurred. Grants are not made for further education (except in very exceptional circumstances).

Applications By letter which should contain all the information required as detailed in the guidance notes for applicants. Guidance notes are available from the correspondent or the website. Applications from organisations are normally processed by the trustees at their meeting in July each year and should be sent by the end of April. The ideal period for receipt of applications is in the period 1 January to 30 April. The 30 April closing date is rigorously enforced. The trust's website contains guidance notes and other useful information for applicants.

Norwood & Newton Settlement

Christian

£240,000 (2001/02)

Beneficial area England and Wales.

126 Beauly Way, Romford, Essex RM1 4XL

Tel. 01708 723670

Correspondent David M Holland, Trustee

Trustees *P Clarke; D M Holland; W W Leyland.*

CC Number 234964

Information available Full accounts were on file at the Charity Commission.

General The trust supports Methodist and other mainline Free Churches and some other smaller UK charities in which the founders had a particular interest. As a general rule, grants are for capital building projects which aim to improve the worship, outreach and mission of the church.

Where churches are concerned, the trustees take particular note of the contribution and promised contributions towards the project by members of the church in question.

In 2001/02 the trust had assets of £6.6 million and an income of £285,000. Grants totalling £240,000 were given in 53 grants ranging from £1,500 to £10,000. Over 70% of grants (38) were to Methodist churches engaged in the building of new premises, or in making improvements to their existing premises. Other grants were made to various other churches. Grants were given throughout the UK in areas ranging from Isle of Man to Essex and Middlesbrough to Wiltshire.

Exclusions Projects will not be considered where an application for National Lottery funding has been made or is contemplated. No grants to individuals, rarely to large UK charities and not for staff/running costs, equipment, repairs or general maintenance.

Applications In writing to the correspondent. In normal circumstances, the trustees' decision is communicated to the applicant within seven days (if a refusal), and if successful, immediately after the trustees' quarterly meetings.

The Sir Peter O'Sullevan Charitable Trust

Animals worldwide

£120,000 (2000/01)

Beneficial area Worldwide.

Hope Cottage, 26 The Green, West Drayton, Middlesex UB7 7PQ

Website www.thevoiceofracing.com

Correspondent Nigel Payne

Trustees *Christopher Spence; Lord Oaksey; Sir Peter O'Sullevan.*

CC Number 1078889

Information available Accounts were on file at the Charity Commission.

General Registered with the Charity Commission in January 2000, in its first year of operation it had an income of £187,000 mainly derived from fundraising events and donations, and made grants totalling £120,000. Six organisations, mostly related to animals (particularly horses), received £20,000 each including: Brooke Hospital for Animals, Compassion in World Farming, International League for the Protection of Horses and Thoroughbred Rehabilitation Centre.

In 2001/02 this trust had an income of £239,000 and a total expenditure of £231,000. Unfortunately more up-to-date information was not available.

Applications In writing to the correspondent.

The Oak Trust

General

£30,000 (2002/03)

Beneficial area UK.

Birkett Long, Red House, Colchester Road, Halstead, Essex CO9 2DZ

Correspondent Richard Long, Clerk

Trustees *Revd A C C Courtauld; J Courtauld; Dr E Courtauld.*

CC Number 231456

Information available Information was provided by the trust.

General The trust has a preference for supporting those charities which it has a special interest in, knowledge of or association with.

In 2002/03 the trust's assets totalled £522,000, it had an income of £29,000 and made grants totalling £30,000.

The largest grants were £3,000 each to Cordan Sailing Trust and Save the Children and £2,000 to Prader-Willi Syndrome Association (UK).

Exclusions No support to individuals.

Applications In writing to the correspondent. Trustees meet twice a year. Unsuccessful applications are not replied to.

The Oakdale Trust

Social work, medical, general

£202,000 (2002/03)

Beneficial area Worldwide, especially Wales.

Tansor House, Tansor, Oundle, Peterborough PE8 5HS

Email oakdale@tanh.demon.co.uk

Correspondent Rupert Cadbury

Trustees *B Cadbury; Mrs F F Cadbury; R A Cadbury; F B Cadbury; Mrs O Tatton-Brown; Dr R C Cadbury.*

CC Number 218827

Information available Full accounts were provided by the trust.

General This trust's main areas of interest include:

- Welsh-based social and community projects
- medical – support groups operating in Wales and UK-based research projects
- UK-based charities working in the third world
- environmental conservation in the UK and overseas
- penal reform.

Some support is also given to the arts, particularly where there is a Welsh connection.

In 2002/03 the trust had assets of £3.4 million and an income of £244,000, including a donation of £122,000. Management and administration costs were very low at just £610. Grants were made to 199 organisations and totalled £202,000.

The largest grants were £18,000 to Tai Hafan, £15,000 in two grants to Concern Universal, £10,000 each to CARAD and International Children's Trust and £5,000 each to CARE International, F P W P Hibiscus, Howard League for Penal Reform and Medical Foundation for the Care of Victims of Torture.

Around a quarter of the beneficiaries were identifiably based in Wales. Grants to these included £1,000 each to Age Concern Montgomeryshire, Arthritis Care Wales, Brecon Mountain Rescue and Prince's Trust – Cymru, £750 to Welsh Initiative for Conductive Education, £500 to Aberystwyth Arts Centre, Bobarth Cymru, Merthyr Tydfil Children's Contact Centre, Mid Wales Opera, Mind – Neath, Newport Action for the Single Homeless, St Celynnin Church – Llangelynnin and YMCA Bridgend and £250 to Carmarthen Family Centre, Glamorgan Federation of Young Farmers Clubs, Llandeilo Summer Okay Scheme, Play Montgomeryshire, Rhayader and District Community Support, St Erfyl Church – Llanerfyl and St John Ambulance in Wales.

Amongst the smaller overseas grants were £2,000 to International Childcare Trust, £1,000 each to Angels International, Cape Town Quaker Peace Centre, Ockenden International and Wulungu Project, £500 each to Books Abroad, Chernobyl Children in Need, Prisoners Abroad and Rainbow Development in Africa and £250 to African Aids Action.

Other grants included £2,000 each to Cambridge Female Education Trust and Irish Seal Sanctuary, £1,200 to Quaker Peace and Social Witness, £1,000 each to Mental Health Foundation, MS Action and Staffordshire Wildlife Trust, £750 to Spinal Injuries Association, £500 each to Barnardos, Devon Wildlife Trust, Hartington Grove Meeting, Headway Devon, Hearing Dogs for Deaf People, Nottingham Quaker Meeting Roof Fund and People's Trust for Endangered Species, Pesticide Action Network UK, Sunderland Kidney Patients Group, £300 to The Pace Centre and £250 each to Crimestoppers Trust, Gay Youth Line Project and Trinity Methodist and United Reform Church.

Exclusions No grants to individuals, holiday schemes, sport activities or expeditions.

Applications An application form is available from the trust; however, applicants are free to submit requests in any format, providing they are clear and concise, covering aims, achievements, plans and needs, and supported by a budget. Applications for grants in excess of £1,000 are asked to submit a copy of a recent set of audited accounts (these can be returned on request). The trustees meet twice a year in April and October to consider applications. The deadline for these meetings is 1 March and 1 September respectively; no grants are awarded between meetings. Unsuccessful applicants are not normally notified and similarly applications are not acknowledged even when accompanied by an sae.

The Odin Charitable Trust

General

£135,000 (2001/02)

Beneficial area UK.

PO Box 1898, Bradford-on-Avon, Wiltshire BA15 1YS

Correspondent Mrs M Mowinckel, Trustee

Trustees *Mrs S G P Scotford; Mrs A H Palmer; Mrs M Mowinckel.*

CC Number 1027521

Information available Annual report and accounts were provided by the trust.

General In 2001/02 the trust had assets of £4.2 million and an income of £123,000. Grants were made to 40 organisations, some of whom have been awarded recurrent grants up to 2004. A total of £135,000 was given during the year, with a further £100,000 to be distributed between six of the beneficiaries up to 2004.

Although the objects of the charity are wide, the trust has a preference for making grants towards: furthering the arts; providing care for people who are disabled and disadvantaged; supporting hospices, the homeless, prisoners' families, refugees, gypsies and 'tribal groups'; and furthering research into false memories and dyslexia.

The trustees are more likely to support small organisations and those that by the nature of their work, find it difficult to attract funding.

Beneficiaries receiving recurrent grants were Crisis Fairshare (£9,000 in total to 2003), Dorothy House (£15,000 in total to 2004), Helen Arkell Dyslexia Centre (£17,000 in total to 2004), Mustard Tree (£9,000 in total to 2003) and New Bridge (£15,000 in total to 2003).

Other beneficiaries included Crisis, Detention Advice Centre, Karten CTEC Centre and Naomi House (£5,000 each), Finsbury Park Street Drinkers Initiative

(£4,000), Bath Recital Artists' Trust and Crossroads – Caring for Carers (£3,000 each), Edinburgh Young Carers Project (£2,000), Harvest Trust, Pearson's Holiday Fund and Primrose Cancer Help Centre (£1,500 each), Bag Books, Geese Theatre Company and Jessie's Fund (£1,000 each), Neighbourly Care Southall and Southwark Children's Foundation (£500); Friends of Style Acre and the PACE Centre also received grants.

Exclusions Applications from individuals are not considered.

Applications In writing to the correspondent.

The Ogle Christian Trust

Evangelical Christianity

£116,000 (2003)

Beneficial area Worldwide.

43 Woolstone Road, Forest Hill, London SE23 2TR

Tel. 020 8699 1036

Email ogletrust@rockuk.net

Correspondent Mrs F J Putley, Trustee

Trustees *D J Harris, Chair; C Fischbacher; R J Goodenough; S Proctor; Mrs F J Putley; Mrs L M Quanrud.*

CC Number 1061458

Information available Accounts were provided by the trust, but without a list of grants.

General This trust mainly directs funds to new initiatives in evangelism worldwide, support of missionary enterprises, publication of Scriptures and Christian literature, pastor training and famine and other relief work. This trust receives approximately 300 applications per year of which around 75% are rejected.

In 2003 it had assets of £2.3 million and an income of £107,000. Grants totalled £116,000, broken down as follows:

Regular beneficiaries – individuals	£2,500
Regular beneficiaries – organisations	£59,000
Occasional beneficiaries	£55,000

Exclusions Applications from individuals are discouraged; those granted require accreditation by a sponsoring organisation. Grants are rarely made for building projects. Funding will not be offered in response to general appeals from large national organisations.

Applications In writing to the correspondent, accompanied by documentary support and an sae. Trustees meet in May and November, but applications can be made at any time.

The Oikonomia Trust

Christian

£33,000 (2001/02)

Beneficial area UK and overseas.

Westoaks, St John's Close, Sharow, Ripon, North Yorkshire HG4 5BB

Tel. 01765 602829

Correspondent D H Metcalfe, Trustee

Trustees *D H Metcalfe; R H Metcalfe; S D Metcalfe; C Mountain; R O Owens.*

CC Number 273481

Information available Full accounts were on file at the Charity Commission.

General The trust supports evangelical work, famine and other relief through Christian agencies. The trust is not looking for new outlets as those it has knowledge of are sufficient to absorb its available funds.

In 2001/02 it had assets of £532,000 and an income of £56,000. Grants were made to 18 organisations and totalled £33,000.

The largest were £7,000 to Bethel Church, £4,000 to Africa Inland Mission, £3,000 to Association of Evangelists, £2,500 to Leeds City Mission and £2,000 each to Asia Link, Caring for Life, Japan Mission and Prospects.

Other grants were £1,500 each to Drumchapel Church, Faith Mission and Slavic Gospel Association, £1,000 to Arab World Ministries and Outreach Worker Fund, £500 each to David House Fellowship, IDOS, Oriental Missionary Society and Soldiers' and Sailors' Scripture RA and £250 to People International.

Exclusions No grants made in response to general appeals from large national organisations.

Applications In writing to the correspondent, although the trust has previously stated that known needs are greater than the trust's supplies. If an applicant desires an answer, an sae should be enclosed. Applications should arrive in January.

The Old Broad Street Charity Trust

General

£52,000 to organisations (2002/03)

Beneficial area UK and overseas.

Eagle House, 110 Jermyn Street, London SW1Y 6RH

Tel. 020 7451 9000 **Fax** 020 7451 9090

Correspondent S P Jennings, Secretary to the Trustees

Trustees *Mrs Evelyn J Franck; Mrs Martine Cartier-Bresson; Adrian T J Stanford; Peter A Hetherington; Christopher J Sheridan.*

CC Number 231382

Information available Full accounts were provided by the trust.

General The objects of the trust are general, although most of the funds are given towards the arts. It was the wish of Louis Franck, the founder, that part of the income should be used to fund scholarships, preferably for UK citizens to reach the highest levels of executive management in banking and financial institutions. It gives around half of its grant total each year to the Louis Franck Scholarship Fund for this purpose.

In 2002/03 it had assets of £1.8 million, which generated an income of £84,000. Grants totalling £52,000 were made to 12 organisations, three-quarters of which were also supported in the previous year.

The largest grant went to one of these new beneficiaries and was £19,000 to Fondation Henri Cartier-Bresson for initial start-up and operation costs. The only newcomers to the grants list were Chichester Cathedral Restoration Fund and Square Rigger Trust, both of which received £2,500.

Other beneficiaries were L'Hopital Intercommunal de Creteil (£9,600), Bezirksfursorge – Saanen (£8,700), Royal Academy of Arts and Victoria and Albert Museum Trust (£2,500 each), Fondation de Bellerive (£2,200), Serpentine Gallery Trust and Tate Gallery Foundation (£650 each), Whitechapel Art Gallery Trust (£460) and Artangel (£390).

Exclusions The trustees only support organisations of which they personally have some knowledge.

Applications In writing to the correspondent. Unsolicited applications are not considered.

Old Possum's Practical Trust

General

£218,000 (2001/02)

Beneficial area UK and overseas.

Baker Tilly, 5th Floor, Exchange House, 446 Midsummer Boulevard, Milton Keynes MK9 2EA

Tel. 01908 687800 **Fax** 01908 687801

Correspondent Judith Hooper, Trustee

Trustees *Mrs Esme Eliot; Judith Hooper; Brian Stevens.*

CC Number 328558

Information available Full accounts were on file at the Charity Commission.

General The trust supports a wide range of causes, with an interest in literacy and the arts. Children's, educational, animal, welfare and medical research charities are also supported.

In 2001/02 the trust had assets of £1.5 million, an income of £1.5 million and made grants totalling £218,000.

The largest grants were £10,000 each to Chelsea Physic Garden, Victoria and Albert Museum, Motor Neurone Disease, Newham College, Friends of the National Library, Wordsworth Trust and Poetry Book Society Prize, £7,000 to Action for Kids, £5,000 each to Radlett Church Appeal, Home Start, English PEN Society, Unicorn Theatre, Blue Cross, PDSA, Extra Care, Trinity Hospice, Share our Care, Guide Dogs for the Blind, Beds and Northants MS Centre, RNIB, Camphill Village Trust, Brainwave, Stepping Stones, Marie Curie Cancer Care, Royal School for the Blind, Tiny Tims Centre, British Heart Foundation, Great Ormond Street Hospital and MS Nerve Centre.

Grants of £2,000 or less were awarded to MS Therapy Centre, Disfigurement Guidance Centre, Haven Trust, National Literacy Trust, Workforce, Operation New World, Books Abroad, Royal Society of Literature, Refuge, Dreams Come True, Derbyshire Children's Holidays, Hope and Homes for Children, East Anglian Childrens Hospice and South Devon Healthcare.

Exclusions No grants towards sports or to students for academic studies or overseas trips, unless special circumstances apply.

Applications In writing to the correspondent. The 2000/01 annual report stated: 'The trustees wish to continue the policy of using the trust's income to support a few carefully chosen cases, generally located in the UK, rather than make a large number of small grants. The emphasis will be on continued support of those institutions and individuals who have received support in the past. Unfortunately we have to disappoint the great majority of applicants who nevertheless continue to send appeal letters. The trustees do not welcome telephone calls from applicants soliciting funds.'

The John Oldacre Foundation

Research and education in agricultural sciences

£80,000 (2001/02)

Beneficial area UK.

Hazleton House, Hazleton, Cheltenham, Gloucestershire GL54 4EB

Tel. 01453 835486

Correspondent Henry Shouler, Trustee

Trustees *H B Shouler; S J Charnock; D G Stevens.*

CC Number 284960

Information available Full accounts were on file at the Charity Commission.

General Grants are made to universities and agricultural colleges towards the advancement and promotion, for public benefit, of research and education in agricultural sciences and the publication of useful results.

In 2001/02 it had assets of £3.2 million and an income of £102,000. Grants were made to eight organisations totalling £80,000.

Beneficiaries were Royal Agricultural College (£35,000), Arable Research Centre (£12,000), Harper Adams University College (£10,000), Nuffield Farming Scholarship Trust and Nuffield Trust (£7,500 each), University of Leicester (£6,000), Nuffield News (£2,000) and Moreton Show (£100).

Exclusions No grants towards tuition fees.

Applications In writing to the correspondent.

This entry was not confirmed by the trust, but was correct according to information on the Charity Commission database.

Onaway Trust

General

£170,000 income (2003)

Beneficial area UK, USA and worldwide.

275 Main Street, Shadwell, Leeds LS17 8LH

Tel. 0113 265 9611

Email david@onaway.org

Website www.onaway.org

Correspondent David Watters, Trust Administrator

Trustees *J Morris; Ms B J Pilkinton; A Breslin; Annie Smith; Elaine Fearnside; C Howles; D Watters.*

CC Number 268448

Information available Information was on file at the Charity Commission.

General This trust's objects are stated on its website as follows:

'To relieve poverty and suffering amongst indigenous peoples by providing seed grants for (small) self-help, self-sufficiency and environmentally sustainable projects.

This is expressed in many areas and includes the protection of the environment, the support of children and adults with learning difficulties, the assistance of smaller charities whose aim is to safeguard the sick, injured, threatened or abandoned animals and emergency relief for victims of disaster.'

In 2003 the trust had an income of £178,000 and a total expenditure of £194,000. Although an actual grant total was unavailable, the trust's website details extensive narrative regarding the support it distibutes including:

Indigenous projects:

- Druk White Lotus School, India
- Native American Rights Fund
- Pygmies of the Democratic Republic of Congo
- The Taino People of Cuba.

Environmental projects:

- Compassion in World Farming
- ICT SEEDS Project
- Indus Valley, India
- The Woodland Trust – In 2003, a grant of £5,000 was made for the PAWS restoration work at Nidd Gorge and the pilot planting scheme at

Cleatop Wood, both situated in the Yorkshire Dales, UK.

Animal Welfare projects:

- Farm Animal Sanctuary
- Skye View Animal Home
- Society for the Welfare of Horses and Ponies
- Support Dogs.

General projects:

- Bradford Family Service Unit
- British Red Cross
- Jeel Al Amal Home for Boys in Palestine
- Opera North (Children with Learning Difficulties)
- Oxfam.

Exclusions No grants for administration costs, travel expenses or projects considered unethical or detrimental to the struggle of indigenous people.

Applications In writing to the correspondent, enclosing an sae.

Oppenheim Foundation

General

£116,000 (2001/02)

Beneficial area UK.

39 King Street, London EC2V 2DQ

Tel. 020 7623 9021

Correspondent Peter Smith, Trustee

Trustees *J N Oppenheim; T S Oppenheim; P A Smith.*

CC Number 279246

Information available Accounts were on file at the Charity Commission, but without a description of its grant-making practice.

General In 2001/02 the foundation had assets of £132,000 with an income of £1,200 and grants totalling £115,500. Unfortunately no grant list was available for this period.

Applications The trust stated that it does not consider applications from organisations with whom it has had no previous contact.

Oppenheimer Charitable Trust

General

£64,000 (2003)

Beneficial area UK.

17 Charterhouse Street, London EC1N 6RA

Tel. 020 7404 4444

Correspondent The Secretary to the Trust

Trustees *Sir Christopher Collet; Michael Farmiloe; G I Watson.*

CC Number 200395

Information available Information was provided by the trust.

General This trust has general charitable purposes for the well-being and benefit of people living in areas where companies of the De Beers group operate. The following areas are particularly supported: medicine and health; children and youth; older people; general welfare; and the arts.

In 2003 grants totalling £64,000 were made to 58 charitable bodies. Unfortunately further information was unavailable.

Exclusions No educational grants are given.

Applications In writing to the correspondent. Trustees meet in January, April, July and October.

The Ormsby Charitable Trust

General

£28,000 (2002/03)

Beneficial area UK, London and the South East.

85 Ravenscourt Road, London W6 0UJ

Tel. 0118 981 9663

Correspondent Mrs K McCrossan, Trustee

Trustees *Rosemay Ormsby David; Angela Ormsby Chiswell; Katrina Ormsby McCrossan.*

CC Number 1000599

Information available Full accounts were on file at the Charity Commission.

General In 2002/03 the trust had assets of £933,000, an income of £131,000 and made grants totalling £28,000. Beneficiaries included ARK Facility Appeal (£4,000), Hammersmith & Fulham Carers Centre, Honeypot and In Kind Direct (£2,500 each), Broadway (£2,000) and Haven Trust, Cancer Relief Macmillan Trust, Galapogos Conservation Trust and Send a Cow (£1,000 each).

Exclusions No grants to individuals, animals or religious causes.

Applications In writing to the correspondent.

The Ouseley Trust

Choral services of the Church of England, Church in Wales and Church of Ireland, choir schools

£80,000 (2002)

Beneficial area England, Wales and Ireland.

127 Coleherne Court, London SW5 0EB

Tel. 020 7373 1950 **Fax** 020 7341 0043

Email clerk@ouseleytrust.org.uk

Website www.ouseleytrust.org.uk

Correspondent Martin Williams, Clerk

Trustees *Dr Christopher Robinson, Chair; Dr J A Birch; Rev Canon Mark Boyling; Dr R J Shephard; N E Walker; Revd A F Walters; Mrs Gillian Perkins; Sir David Willcocks; N A Ridley; Dr S M Darlington; Dr J Rutter.*

CC Number 527519

Information available Information was provided by the trust.

General The trust administers funds made available from trusts of the former St Michael's College, Tenbury. Its object is 'projects which promote and maintain to a high standard the choral services of the Church of England, the Church in Wales and the Church of Ireland', including contributions to endowment funds, courses, fees and the promotion of religious, musical and secular education for pupils connected to the churches and observing choral liturgy.

In 2002 the trust had assets of £2.5 million and an income of £117,000. 21 grants were made totalling £80,000, broken down as follows:

Endowments – 3 grants totalling £43,000
Grants awarded will usually be paid in one sum to provide an immediate contribution to an endowment fund. Beneficiaries were Guildford Cathedral (£20,000), St Peter's Brighton Choral Foundation (£13,000) and St Woolo's Cathedral (£10,000).

Fees for individuals – 12 grants totalling £25,000
Applications must be submitted by an institution. Grants awarded will be paid in one sum as an immediate contribution. The trustees may require an assurance that the sum offered will achieve the purpose for which help has been requested.

Organs – 3 grants totalling £6,000
Grants are only made in exceptional circumstances, where the organ is of particular significance and an integral element in a place of worship where there is a well-established and musically accomplished choir. Recipients, of £2,000 each, were All Saints' – Warlington, St George's – Upper Cam and St Mary the Virgin – St Neots.

Other – one grant of £5,000
This went to St Michael's – Tenbury.

Music – 1 grant of £880
Grants will be awarded only where the replacement of old, or the purchase of new music will render specific assistance to the promotion or maintenance of high choral standards. The only beneficiary was St Mary and St Michael's – Great Malvern.

Courses – 1 grant of £350
Grants will be awarded only where there is a clear indication that an already acceptable standard of choral service will be raised. Under certain circumstances grants may be awarded for organ tuition. The only donation went to Royal Hospital – Chelsea.

Each application will be considered on its merits, keeping in mind the specific terms of the trust deed. Unique, imaginative ventures will receive careful consideration.

The trust does not normally award further grants to successful applicants within a two-year period. The trustees' policy is to continue making grants to cathedrals, choral foundations and parish churches throughout England, Wales and Ireland.

Exclusions Grants will not be awarded to help with the cost of fees for ex-choristers, for chant books, hymnals or psalters. Grants will not be made for the purchase of new instruments nor for the installation of an instrument from another place of worship where this involves extensive reconstruction. Under normal circumstances, grants will not be awarded for buildings, cassettes, commissions, compact discs, furniture, pianos, robes, tours or visits. No grants are made towards new organs or the installation of one which involves extensive reconstruction.

Applications Applicants are strongly advised to obtain a copy of the trust's guidelines (either from the correspondent or their website, currently under construction at the time of writing) before drafting an application. Applications must be submitted by an institution on a form available from the correspondent. Closing dates for applications are 31 January for the March meeting and 30 June for the October meeting.

The Owen Family Trust

Christian, general

£162,000 (2002/03)

Beneficial area UK, with a preference for West Midlands.

Mill Dam House, Mill Lane, Aldridge, Walsall WS9 0NB

Tel. 0121 526 3131

Correspondent A D Owen, Trustee

Trustees *Mrs H G Jenkins; A D Owen.*

CC Number 251975

Information available Information and accounts provided by the trust.

General Grants are given to independent and church schools, Christian youth centres, churches, community organisations, arts, conservation and medical charities. Support is given throughout the UK, with a preference for the West Midlands.

In 2002/03 it had assets of £1.2 million and an income of £70,000. Grants were made to 34 organisations and totalled £162,000.

The largest grant was of £85,000 to Ironbridge Gorge Museum. Other beneficiaries included Frink School of Figurative Sculpture, Frontier Youth Trust, Black Country Museum Development Trust, Lichfield Cathedral Trust Music Campaign, St John & St Peter's Church Ladywood, Students Exploring Marriage Trust, The Pioneer Centre NAYC and Sutton Coldfield YMCA (£5,000 each) and Lazarica a Serbian Orthodox Church (£4,500).

Exclusions The trust states 'no grants to individuals unless part of a charitable request'.

Applications In writing to the correspondent including annual report, budget for project and general information regarding the application. Organisation needs to be a registered charity, however an 'umbrella' body which would hold funds would be acceptable. Only a small number of grants can be given each year and unsuccessful applications are not acknowledged unless an sae is enclosed. The trustees meet quarterly.

Padwa Charitable Foundation

Education, religion, general

£39,000 (2001/02)

Beneficial area UK.

Walpole Group Plc, 18 Rosebery Avenue, London EC1R 4TD

Tel. 020 7843 1635

Correspondent John A Benns, Secretary

Trustees *Meyer Padwa; K O'Sullivan; J Randall; N A Fulton; T Chandler.*

CC Number 1019274

Information available Accounts were on file at the Charity Commission, but without a list of beneficiaries.

General The trust has the following aims:

- the relief of poverty
- the advancement of religion and education
- charitable purposes beneficial to the community.

Donations are given to both individuals and organisations.

It is the policy of the trust wherever possible, if a donation is made to another charity, to identify an individual or group that will benefit directly as a result of the donation.

In 2001/02 the foundation had assets of £36,000 with an income of £43,000 and grants totalling £39,000. Unfortunately no grant list was available for this period.

Applications In writing to the correspondent.

The Pallant Charitable Trust

Church music

£50,000 (2002/03)

Beneficial area UK, with a preference for areas within 50 miles of Chichester.

c/o Thomas Eggar, The Corn Exchange, Baffins Lane, Chichester, West Sussex PO19 1GE

Tel. 01243 786111 **Fax** 01243 532001

Correspondent The Clerk to the Trustees

Trustees *A J Thurlow; S A E Macfarlane; C Smyth; C J Henville.*

CC Number 265120

Information available Information provided by the trust.

General The trust's objective is to promote mainstream church music both in choral and instrumental form. Consideration will be given for schemes which provide training and opportunities for children or adults in the field of church music and with an emphasis on traditional services. Such schemes may include:

- vocal or instrumental (in particular organ) training
- choral work in the context of church services
- the training of choir leaders, organists or directors
- the provision and the purchase of equipment necessary for the above.

In 2002/03 the trust had an income of £51,000 and an expenditure of £70,000. Grants were made totalling £50,000. No further information was available for this year.

Previous beneficiaries have included: Sarum College for a church musician, Church Music Advisor Project towards salary costs, Prebendal School for chorister's scholarships, St Peter's Brighton Choral Foundation and Dean and Chapter of Chichester for awards to the organ scholar.

Exclusions No grants to:

- individuals
- computer equipment
- sponsorship for concerts

Applications In writing to the correspondent. (The trust states that applications should be submitted by recognised organisations such as churches, schools, colleges or charities working in the field of church music).

The Gerald Palmer Trust

Education, medical research, religion

£148,000 (2000/01)

Beneficial area UK, especially Berkshire.

Eling Estate Office, Hermitage, Thatcham, Berkshire RG18 9UF

Tel. 01635 200268 **Fax** 01635 201077

Correspondent The Clerk

Trustees *J M Clutterbuck; D R W Harrison; J N Abell; R Broadhurst.*

CC Number 271327

Information available Accounts were on file at the Charity Commission.

General The trust's main activity is the management of its Eling Estate, but it also gives grants to organisations. In 2001/02 it had an income of £764,000 and a total expenditure of £642,000. Further information for this year was not available.

In 2000/01 the trust had assets of over £16 million and an income of £712,000 comprising mainly income from the estate and woodland. Expenditure on the estate and woodlands totalled £472,000 and £148,000 was given in grants.

The trust tends to support mainly UK education, medical and health-related charities together with a range of local organisations in Berkshire. Grants were given to 59 organisations ranging from £50 to £10,000. The two largest donations were £10,000 each to GAP and Ripon College – Cuddesdon. Other larger grants included those to Abbeyfield House Appeal, Advance Housing and Support Ltd, Enham Trust, Guideposts Trust, Heritage Education Trust, Hermitage Primary School, Iris Fund, National Star Centre, Newbury and District Agricultural Society, Newbury Spring Festival, Riding for the Disabled Association, St John Ambulance, Sobell House Hospice Charity, Thames Valley Jubilee Sailing Trust, Toynbee Hall and West Berkshire Mencap.

Exclusions No grants to individuals or to local charities outside Berkshire.

Applications In writing to the correspondent.

The Panacea Society

Christian religion, relief of sickness

Around £250,000 (2003)

Beneficial area UK, with a preference for Bedford and its immediate region.

14 Albany Road, Bedford MK40 3PH

Tel. 01234 359737

Email admin@panacea-society.org

Website www.panacea-society.org

Correspondent D McLynn

Trustees *J Powell; J L Coghill; R Klien; L Aston; Revd Jane Shaw.*

CC Number 227530

Information available Information is available on the society's website.

General The work of this Christian charity, established in 1926, is informed by the teachings of Joanna Southcott. In recent years, in conjunction with the Charity Commission, it has undergone a significant modernisation of its constitution and a broadening of its activities. In meeting its charitable objects the society from time to time makes grants out of its income.

Grant criteria

For the present, the trustees have agreed the following basic criteria. The purpose of the grant should be:

- to advance and promote the religious beliefs of the Society and the Christian religion generally
- for all aspects relating to the relief of sickness for the benefit of people living within the town of Bedford and its immediate region
- the advancement of education both generally and in the production, publication and dissemination of religious works.

Grants awarded must be for charitable purposes and are made to UK-based organisations only. Priority will usually be given to grants that:

- will promote the religious aims of the Panacea Society
- can benefit large numbers of people
- will have a lasting impact
- are of a capital nature
- are to organisations rather than individuals
- operate in Bedfordshire.

In 2003 the society had an income of £574,000 and a total expenditure of £506,000. Grants totalled around £250,000. Beneficiaries were Bedfordshire & Northamptonshire Multiple Sclerosis Therapy Centre, Book – Joanna Southcott's Box of Sealed Prophecies, Deafblind UK, Department of Theology – Oxford University, Macmillan Cancer Relief, Guild House – Bedford, Multiple Sclerosis Society – Bedfordshire branch, Sight Concern – Bedfordshire, St Paul's Parish Church – Bedford and Sue Ryder Care – St John's Hospice, Bedfordshire.

Exclusions The society will not make grants:

- to political parties or political lobbying
- to pressure groups
- which support commercial ventures
- which could be paid out of central or local government funds.

Applications Please note that in September 2004 the trust stated that it receives many applications that they are unable or unwilling to support. Please read the grant criteria carefully before submitting an application. Unsolicited applications are not responded to.

Any organisation wishing to apply to be considered for a grant should write in the first instance to the society's administrator setting out briefly the purpose for which the grant is required, showing how it falls within the criteria and complies with the other requirements stated above and giving an indication of the amount being requested. This letter should provide details of the organisation applying with details of the contact person, postal address, telephone number, and email address (if available).

Where the society is interested in considering an application, the applicant organisation will be sent an application form to complete and where appropriate the Administrator will contact the applicant to ascertain further information. The trustees consider applications at their meetings which take place two or three times per year, but not at set dates.

Panahpur Charitable Trust

Missionaries, general

£762,000 (2002/03)

Beneficial area UK, overseas.

Jacob Cavenagh and Skeet, 5 Robin Hood Lane, Sutton, Surrey SM1 2SW

Tel. 020 8643 1166

Correspondent The Trust Department

Trustees *P East; Miss D Haile; A E Perry; R Moffett.*

CC Number 214299

Information available Accounts were on file at the Charity Commission.

General The trust's 2000/01 accounts stated: 'The trust was established for the distribution of funds to Christian charities and other Christian organisations and individuals, both in the UK and overseas. In particular, the trust has sought to support a wide range of Christian missionary organisations.'

In 2002/03 it had assets of £3.4 million, which generated an income of £168,000. Grants totalling £762,000 were made. Grants were broken down as follows:

Geographic area

Africa	£19,400
United Kingdom	£53,000
Far East	£13,000
India	£25,000
Middle East	£250
Others	£651,000

Distribution categories

Relief work	£38,000
Missionary work (UK)	£9,700
Missionary work (overseas)	£51,000
Direct preaching of the gospel	£9,100
Sundries	£3,000
Others	£651,000

The largest grants were £520,000 to Benjamin Trust, £131,000 to Lois Perry Charitable Trust, £12,00 to Interserve, £11,000 to EHA UK, £10,000 to All Nations Christian College, £9,600 to SIM United Kingdom, £8,000 each to Oasis International and Penhurst Retreat Centre.

Other grants of over £1,000 each included those to Cord (£6,000), Word For Life Trust (£5,000), Relationships Foundation International (£4,500), South Asian Concern (£4,000), Outlook Trust (£3,000) and Dr M F Foyle and London Bible College (£2,000 each).

Smaller grants included those to Holy Trinity Brompton (£960), New Life Centre (£750), UCCF (£600), PFCS Trust (£500), SMTA (£500), CWR and St. Andrew's Church (£300 each), L Clemence Dipti, Mission Without Orders and United Christian Broadcasters (£200 each) and Anglican Pacifist Fellowship (£50).

Applications In writing to the correspondent, although the trust informed us that applicants will not be successful unless they are already known to the trust.

Panton Trust

Animal wildlife worldwide; environment UK

£27,000 (2002/03)

Beneficial area UK and overseas.

Ramsay House, 18 Vera Avenue, Grange Park, London N21 1RB

Tel. 020 8370 7700

Correspondent Laurence Slavin, Trustee

Trustees *L M Slavin; R Craig.*

CC Number 292910

Information available Full accounts were on file at the Charity Commission.

General The trust states that it is 'concerned with any animal or animals or with wildlife in any part of the world, or with the environment of the UK or any part thereof. The trustees consider applications from a wide variety of sources and favour smaller charities which do not have the same capacity for large-scale fundraising as major charities in this field.'

In 2002/03 the trust had assets of £202,000 with an income of £36,000 and grants totaling £27,000.

Grants include £4,000 each to William Ellis School, St Tiggywinkles Wildlife Hospital and Whale and Dolphin Conservation Society, £3,000 to Flora and Fauna, £2,000 each to Gonville and Caius College Cambridge, IPPL and New Hall Cambridge, £1,750 to Emmanuel College Cambridge, £1,000 each to Tree for London, Wroxton Duck Fund, Royal Botanic Gardens, Kew and University of Glasgow and £450 to London Borough of Barnet School Prizes.

Applications In writing to the correspondent.

The Paragon Trust

General

£98,000 (2001/02)

Beneficial area UK.

c/o Thomson Snell & Passmore, Solicitors, 3 Lonsdale Gardens, Tunbridge Wells, Kent TN1 1NX

Tel. 01892 510000

Correspondent Kathy Larter

Trustees *Rt Hon. J B B Wrenbury; Revd Canon R F Coppin; Miss L J Whistler; P Cunningham; P Bagwell-Purefoy; Dr F E Cornish.*

CC Number 278348

Information available Full accounts were on file at the Charity Commission.

General In 2001/02 the trust had assets of £1.8 million with an income of £220,000 and grants totalling £98,000.

The largest grants were £4,000 to Age Concern East Sussex, £3,000 to British Red Cross and £2,000 to Medecins sans Frontieres.

Grants of £1,000 were awarded to Friends of the National Libraries, Divert Trust, Prison Reform Trust, Crisis, YMCA, Newham College, Sussex Bells Restoration Fund, Council for the Protection of Rural England, St Luke's Hospice, Mildmay Mission Hospital, Macmillan Fund for Cancer Relief, National Aids Trust, Camphill Village Trust, Home Farm Trust, L'Arche Kent Community, Sussex Housing Association for the Aged and Church Army.

Grants of less than £1,000 include Medical Foundation (Victims of Torture), Fellowship of St Nicholas, South London Industrial Mission, Church Housing Trust, Winged Fellowship, Leonard Cheshire Foundation, Send a Cow, Amnesty International, Christian Aid, Canon Collins Educational Trust for Southern Africa, Action Health, DGAA Homelife, L'Arche, National Autistic Society, RNIB, Arthritis Care, Leprosy Relief Association, Greenpeace Trust and The Children's Family Trust.

Applications The trust states that it does not respond to unsolicited applications; all beneficiaries 'are known personally to the trustees and no attention is paid to appeal literature, which is discarded on receipt. Fundraisers are therefore urged to save resources by not sending literature.'

The Park Hill Trust

Older people

£49,000 (2002/03)

Beneficial area UK.

Miller Centre, 30 Godstone Road, Caterham, Surrey CR3 6RA

Correspondent A M Pilch, Trustee

Trustees *A M Pilch; Mrs B C Pilch; Mrs R A Gill; Ms N D G Pendrigh; Mrs I J Creffield; R F Price; M A Swain.*

CC Number 258420

Information available Limited information was provided by the trust.

General The trust supports imaginative new projects which aim to improve the quality of life of older people in retirement, and to relieve loneliness by helping them to use their knowledge and experience for the benefit of the community. Charities aided particularly are those working in the fields of community facilities, conservation, the arts, support and self-help groups, health-related volunteer schemes and health promotion. The trust does not restrict grants to registered charities.

Grants are one-off for a specific project or start up costs. Funding for one year or less will be considered.

In 2002/03 the trust's assets totalled £469,000 and it received an income of £51,000. Grants totalled £49,000.

The trust does not publish a list of beneficiaries. Unless this is because all donations were less than £1,000 each then it is failing to met its statutory obligation to disclose how it spends its funds. If it is because the grants are small, then a note confirming this should appear in its accounts to avoid such uncertainity.

Exclusions The trust aims to encourage new ideas rather than existing work. No project will be considered unless older people play an active rather than a passive role. Funding is not available to meet the costs of paid staff or professional contractors.

Applications No applications can be considered unless they satisfy the criteria above. Applications falling outside these guidelines will not be acknowledged. Apply in writing to the correspondent. There is no application form.

The Park House Charitable Trust

Education, social welfare, ecclesiastical

£166,000 (2003)

Beneficial area UK and overseas, with a preference for the Midlands, particularly Coventry and Warwickshire.

Dafferns, Queen's House, Queen's Road, Coventry CV1 3DR

Tel. 024 7622 1046

Correspondent Paul Varney

Trustees *N P Bailey; M M Bailey; P Bailey; J Hill; M F Whelan.*

CC Number 1077677

Information available Information was provided by the trust.

General This trust was established in September 1999. In 2003 it had assets of £973,000 and a total income of £408,000, mostly in funds added by the settlor. A total of 24 grants were made totalling £166,000.

Arts – 1 grant totalling £1,000

One grant for £1,000 was made to St James the Greater Organ Appeal

Ecclesiastical – 3 grants totalling £49,000

Beneficiaries were the Ark of the Covenant (£25,000), Equestrian Order of the Holy Sephulchre of Jerusalem (£23,000 towards the building of a church) and Rosary Church Kowloon (£1,000).

Education – 6 grants totalling £84,000

The largest grants were £36,700 to Equestrian Order of the Holy Sepulchre of Jerusalem (£20,000 towards extension of Students Home in Bethlehem, £10,000 for science laboratories in Gaza and £6,700 to sewerage system improvements for a school in Ramallah) and £25,000 to Cambridge Nazareth Trust (£20,000 for provision of laboratory equipment in Jordon and £5,000 for costs of fitting out classrooms in Beit Sahour). Other beneficiaries were Batemans Trust (£15,000), Friends of Bethlehem University (£4,000), Operation New World (£2,000), Association of Christian Counsellors (£1,000).

Medical – 1 grant totalling £2,000

One grant for £2,000 was made to Baby Lifeline.

Social welfare – 10 grants totalling £30,000
Beneficiaries were Society for the Protection of Unborn Children (£10,000), Malawi Link Trust (£5,000), National Association for People Abused in Childhood (£4,000), Autism West Midlands, Baby Alive, Calcutta Rescue and Salvation Army (£2,000 each) and Action for Leisure, East Anglia Children's Hospice and Family Project – Coventry (£1,000 each).

Exclusions No grants to individuals.

Applications In writing to the correspondent. The trust stated in June 2004 that it did not expect to have surplus funds available to meet the majority of applications.

The Samuel & Freda Parkinson Charitable Trust

General

£100,000 (2003)

Beneficial area UK.

Thomson Wilson Pattinson, Trustees' Solicitors, Stonecliffe, Lake Road, Windermere, Cumbria LA23 3AR

Tel. 01539 442233 **Fax** 01539 488810

Correspondent J R M Crompton, Solicitor

Trustees *D E G Roberts; Miss J A Todd; J F Waring.*

CC Number 327749

Information available Information was provided by the trust.

General This trust was established in 1987 with £100. The fund stayed at this level until 1994/95 when £2.1 million worth of assets were placed in the trust on the death of the settlor. It supports the same eight beneficiaries each year, although for varying amounts.

In 2002/03 it had an income of £104,000. Grants were made totalling £100,000. These were: £30,000 to Leonard Cheshire Foundation; £20,000 each to Church Army and Salvation Army; £10,000 to RNLI; £7,500 to RSPCA; £5,000 each to Animal Rescue and Animal Concern; and £2,500 to Animal Welfare (Furness).

Applications The founder of this charity restricted the list of potential beneficiaries to named charities of his choice and accordingly the trustees do not have discretion to include further beneficiaries, although they do have complete discretion within the stated beneficiary list.

The Constance Paterson Charitable Trust

Medical research, health, welfare of children, older people, service people

£28,000 (2002/03)

Beneficial area UK.

Royal Bank of Canada Trust Corporation Limited, 71 Queen Victoria Street, London EC4V 4DE

Tel. 020 7653 4756

Email anita.carter@rbc.com

Correspondent Miss Anita Carter

Trustee *Royal Bank of Canada Trust Corporation Ltd.*

CC Number 249556

Information available Full accounts were on file at the Charity Commission.

General The trust makes grants in support of medical research, healthcare, welfare of elderly people and children (including accommodation and housing) and service people's welfare.

In 2002/03 the trust had assets of £836,000 and an income of £37,000. Grants totalled £28,000. Beneficiaries included Heartline and Kids Cut (£5,000 each), National Eczema Society and Tower Hamlets Mission (£3,500 each), Arthritis Research Campaign, 3H Fund and The Rainbow Centre (£3,000 each) and The Queen's Nursing Institute (£2,000).

Exclusions No grants to individuals.

Applications In writing to the correspondent, including covering letter and latest set of annual report and accounts. The trust does not have an application form. Deadlines for applications are June and December.

Arthur James Paterson Charitable Trust

Medical research, welfare of older people and children

£39,000 (2003/04)

Beneficial area UK.

Royal Bank of Canada Trust Corporation Limited, 71 Queen Victoria Street, London EC4V 4DE

Tel. 020 7653 4756

Email anita.carter@rbc.com

Correspondent Miss Anita Carter

Trustee *Royal Bank of Canada Trust Corporation Ltd.*

CC Number 278569

Information available The information for this entry was previously provided by the trust.

General In 2003/04 the trust had assets of £1.1 million with an income of £69,000 and grants totalling £38,500.

Grants include £10,000 each to Glenalmond College and Worcester College, £4,500 to Defeating Deafness, £4,000 each to West London Action for Children and Universal Beneficent Society, £3,500 to Contact the Elderly and £2,500 to Bromley Advocacy Alliance.

Applications There are no application forms. Send your application with a covering letter and include latest set of report and accounts. Deadlines are February and August. This entry was not confirmed by the trust, but the information was correct according to the trust's file at the Charity Commission.

The Late Barbara May Paul Charitable Trust

Older people, young people, medical care and research, preservation of buildings

£33,000 (2001/02)

Beneficial area East Anglia and UK-wide.

Lloyds TSB Private Banking Ltd, UK Trust Centre, The Clock House, 22–26 Ock Street, Abingdon, Oxfordshire OX14 5SW

Tel. 01235 232731

Correspondent C Shambrook, Trust Manager

Trustee *Lloyds TSB Bank plc.*

CC Number 256420

Information available Accounts were on file at the Charity Commission, but without a list of grants.

General Lloyds TSB Bank plc is the sole trustee for this and two other trusts, each founded by a different sister from the Paul family. This trust is the largest and makes larger grants but they all appear to have very similar grant-making policies. There is a preference throughout the trusts for Suffolk and some organisations have been supported by all three trusts.

This trust has stated in recent years that it is increasingly focusing its grant-making on local organisations in East Anglia, and East Anglian branches of UK charities. UK-wide organisations can, and do, receive funding, although local groups outside of East Anglia are not.

In 2001/02 the trust had an income of £84,000 and gave grants totalling £33,000. No further information was available for this year.

Previous beneficiaries have included Bus Project, Cancer Research Campaign, Essex County Youth Service, East Suffolk Mines, Essex Voluntary Association for the Blind, Ipswich Disabled Advice, Ipswich Scouts & Guides Council, Malcolm Sargent Cancer Fund, Norfolk Millennium Trust for Carers, Norfolk & Norwich Scope, One-to-One, Queen Elizabeth's Foundation for Disabled People, Rotary Club of Ipswich, Shelter, Suffolk Association for Youth, Suffolk Preservation Society, Tannington Church and Whizz-Kidz. Previously, grants have ranged from £500 to £5,000.

Exclusions No grants to overseas charities.

Applications In writing to the correspondent at any time.

The Susanna Peake Charitable Trust

General

£86,000 (2001/02)

Beneficial area UK, with a preference for the south west of England.

Rathbone Trust Company Limited, 159 New Bond St, London W1S 2UD

Tel. 020 7399 0820 **Fax** 020 7399 0050

Email linda.cousins@rathbones.com

Correspondent The Secretary

Trustees *Susanna Peake; David Peake.*

CC Number 283462

Information available Full accounts were on file at the Charity Commission.

General This is one of the Kleinwort family trusts. It was set up by Susanna Peake in 1981 for general charitable purposes and has a preference for charities based in the Gloucestershire area. In addition, non-local appeals when received are accumulated and considered by the trustees annually. Although grants ranged from £100 to £5,000, most grants were between £1,000 and £2,000.

In 2001/02 the trust had assets of £1.9 million and an income of £145,000. Grants totalled £86,000. Donations included: £9,000 to PCC St James' Church – Longborough; £5,000 to Condicote New Village Hall Fund; £3,000 each to Chipping Norton Theatre Trust and PCC Blockey with Aston Magna; £2,500 to Samaritans; £2,000 each to Heythrop Hunt Charitable Trust and Woodstock Trust; £1,000 each to Cotswold Victim Support, Citizen's Advice Bureau – Cirencester and Gloucestershire Society; £500 to Vauxhall City Farm; and £200 each to Parents and Friends Association and Longborough Church of England.

Exclusions No grants to individuals.

Applications In writing to the correspondent.

Pearson's Holiday Fund

Young people who are disadvantaged

£65,000 to groups (2003)

Beneficial area UK.

PO Box 3017, South Croydon CR2 9PN

Tel. 020 8657 3053

Website www.pearsonsholidayfund.org

Correspondent The General Secretary

Trustees *A John Bale, Chair; David P Golder; John S Bradley; Revd Noel Cooper; John F Gore; Mrs Christine B Graham; Ian M Halliwell; Mark A Hutchings; Michael P A Longworth; Andrew Noble.*

CC Number 217024

Information available Full accounts and guidelines were provided by the trust.

General The following is taken from the trust's guidelines:

'Pearson's Holiday Fund provides financial grants towards helping disadvantaged children and young people to have holidays, outings or take part in group respite activities, that take them away for a little while from their otherwise mundane or restricted environment which would not be possible without some external financial support.

'We regard children and young people as being disadvantaged who may have:

(a) learning difficulties

(b) physical disabilities or other heath related problems

(c) experienced abuse or violence in the home or are regarded as being at risk

(d) disabled or elderly parents to care for

(e) other problems, e.g. living in the poverty trap, refugees, homeless, etc.

'The following conditions must also be met in all cases:

(a) The child/children/young person(s) must live in the United Kingdom

(b) The holiday, outing or group activity must be in the United Kingdom

(c) The child/children/young person(s) must be aged 4 to 16 years (inclusive) at the time of the holiday or activity.

'Where a family with disadvantaged child/young person are taking a holiday together, we normally regard all the children/young people in the family, within our age range, participating in the holiday as meeting our criteria for grants.'

These grants can go to individuals or to groups and are to a maximum of £75 per person and £750 per group.

In 2003 it had assets of £154,000 and an income of £98,000, mostly from various donations received. Grants were made totalling £120,000, of which £65,000 went to 94 group activities (2,600 individual beneficiaries) and £55,000 went directly to 449 families (1,100 individual beneficiaries).

Applications In writing to the correspondent. Full guidelines are available from the correspondent (upon receipt of an sae) or downloadable from the website. Completed forms must be returned with an sae. Applications must include evidence the criteria and conditions of the fund are being met, the number of children/young people expected to benefit from the activity, the amount requested and details of who the cheque should be made payable to. Applications for individuals must be supported by a referring agency, such as social workers, health visitors, teachers, doctors, ministers of religion and so on.

The Pedmore Trust

Christian

£36,000 (2000/01)

Beneficial area Worldwide.

10 Falmouth Close, Veille Park, Torquay TQ2 7SE

Correspondent Ms Suzanne Wesley

Trustees *W R Cossham; D R Meek; J Hutchinson; D M John; L R Meek; W E John; A M Fordyce.*

CC Number 266644

Information available Full accounts were on file at the Charity Commission.

General This trust supports Christian causes throughout the world. In 2000/01 the trust made grants totalling £36,000 and it had assets totalling £600,000.

Further information was not available for this year.

Previous grants have ranged from £1,000 to £5,000 with beneficiaries including African Enterprise, Christian Alliance Exeter, Mission Aviation Fellowship, New English Orchestra, Scripture Union and Youth for Christ.

Exclusions No support for students on short-term projects (gap years).

Applications Please note, the trust states that it carries out its own research and is unable to accept any applications for grants.

Peltz Trust

Arts and humanities, education and culture, health and welfare, Jewish

£77,000 (2003/04)

Beneficial area UK and Israel.

Berwin Leighton Paisner, Adelaide House, London Bridge, London EC4R 9HA

Tel. 020 7760 1000

Correspondent M D Paisner, Trustee

Trustees *M D Paisner; Daniel Peltz; Elizabeth Julia Natasha Wolfson Peltz.*

CC Number 1002302

Information available Information was provided by the trust.

General In 2003/04 the trust had an income of £77,000, all of which was given in grants. Donations included £5,000 each to British Friends of the Jaffa Institute, Central Synagogue General Charities Fund and Lubavitch Foundation, £1,500 to Saatchi Synagogue and £1,000 to Royal Academy.

Exclusions No grants to individuals for research or educational awards.

Applications In writing to the correspondent. The trustees meet at irregular intervals during the year to consider appeals from appropriate organisations.

Elizabeth Wolfson Peltz Trust

Arts and humanities, education and culture, health and welfare, Jewish in the Uk and Israel

£85,000 (2003/04)

Beneficial area UK and Israel.

Berwin Leighton Paisner, Adelaide House, London Bridge, London EC4R 9HA

Tel. 020 7760 1000

Correspondent M D Paisner, Trustee

Trustees *M D Paisner; Daniel Peltz; Elizabeth Wolfson Peltz; Lord Wolfson of Marylebone.*

CC Number 1070064

Information available Information was provided by the trust.

General In 2003/04 the trust had an income of £2,100, although it brought forward a further £94,000 from its surplus from the previous year. Grants were made to three organisations totalling £85,000. Beneficiaries were Magen David Adom (£50,000), Norwood (£25,000) and Jewish Care (£10,000).

Exclusions No grants to individuals for research or educational awards.

Applications In writing to the correspondent. The trustees meet at irregular intervals during the year to consider appeals from appropriate organisations.

The Penny Charitable Trust

Photographic archival projects

£48,000 (2000/01)

Beneficial area UK.

Bryan Cave, Watling House, 33 Cannon Street, London EC4M 5TE

Correspondent Mrs Dyke Davies, Trustee

Trustees *Mrs Dyke M Davies; Dr Ilse Sternberg; Dr Judith Neaman.*

CC Number 1053800

Information available Accounts were on file at the Charity Commission.

General Established in March 1996, this trust supports photographic archival projects at institutions open to the public. In 2002/03 the trust had an income of £30,500 and a total expenditure of £2,700. Although submitted to the Charity Commission, the 2002/03 accounts were not available to view on file.

In 2000/01 it had an income of £57,000, mainly from donations, and made grants totalling £48,000. The trust gives ongoing support to the Original Photographs Project at the British Library; in the year £47,500 was given to this project. The trust also made a donation of £750 to CATCH to support the purchase of medical dictionaries.

Applications In writing to the correspondent.

Penny in the Pound Fund Charitable Trust

Hospitals, health-related charities

£91,000 (2003)

Beneficial area Northern England, southern Scotland, Wales and Northern Ireland, but mostly around the Merseyside area.

Medicash Health Benefits Limited, Merchants Court, 2–12 Lord Street, Liverpool L2 1TS

Tel. 0151 702 0202 **Fax** 0151 702 0250

Email karnold@medicash.org

Website www.medicash.org

Correspondent K Arnold, Finance Officer

Trustees *P B Teare; K W Monti; K Arnold; W Gaywood; J E Brown.*

CC Number 257637

Information available Information was provided by the trust.

General This trust was established in 1968 by a health benefits insurance company, from which the trust continues to receive donations each year. The objects of the trust are to provide amenities to patients in hospital or under the care of health-related charities by reimbursing them with the cost of facilities purchased to make their patients stays more comfortable and enjoyable. Grants are given in Wales, Northern Ireland, southern Scotland and the north of England, although they are centred around the north-west of England, especially Merseyside.

In 2002 the trust had assets of £119,000. Total income was £74,000, of which £60,000 came from donations and gifts. During the year £51,000 in grants was made to hospitals and charities, with a further £91,000 committed in grants in 2003.

The 2002 accounts included details of the grant commitments for 2003, broken down as follows:

Health authorities – 26 grants totalling £68,000

The largest grants were given on Merseyside, with £16,000 to Aintree Hospitals NHS Trust, £15,000 to Royal Liverpool & Broadgreen University Hospitals NHS Trust and £10,000 to Wirral Hospitals NHS Trust. Other beneficiaries included Southport & Ormskirk Hospital NHS Trust (£4,300), Countess of Chester Hospital NHS Trust (£4,000), Liverpool Women's Hospital NHS Trust and Blackpool, Wrye & Fylde Community NHS Trust (£2,000 each), Lancashire Teaching Hospital (£1,500) and Conwy & Denbighshire NHS Trust (£1,000). Grants of less than £1,000 each included those to Blackburn, Hyndburn & Ribble Valley Health Care NHS Trust, Dumfries & Galloway NHS Trust, Newcastle, North Tyneside & Northumberland NHS Trust and West Lancashire NHS Trust.

Charities – 32 grants totalling £23,000

Beneficiaries included Forge Road Surgery (£3,500), Marie Curie Cancer Care (£1,500), British Stammering Association and Community Integrated Care (£1,000 each). Most beneficaries in this category received less than £1,000 each, including Bolton Coronary Care Appeal, David Lewis Centre for Epilepsy, Granby Toxteth Activity Club, Merseyside Association of Leagues of Friends, The Extra Care Foundation and Whizz-Kidz.

Exclusions No grants towards medical equipment.

Applications There is a seperate application form for hospitals and charities available from the trust.

Applications need to be received by the end of September and trustees meet in October. Successful applicants are notified in November.

The Pennycress Trust

General

£53,000 (2002/03)

Beneficial area UK, with a preference for Cheshire and Norfolk.

15d Millman Street, London WC1N 3EP

Tel. 020 7404 0145

Correspondent Mrs Doreen Howells, Secretary to the Trustees

Trustees *Lady Aline Cholmondeley; Anthony J M Baker; C G Cholmondeley; Miss Sybil Sassoon.*

CC Number 261536

Information available Accounts were provided by the trust.

General The trust's policy is to make donations to smaller charities and especially those based in Cheshire and Norfolk, with some donations to UK organisations.

In 2002/03 the assets stood at £1.7 million and the income was £79,000. Management and administration came to £11,000. Grants were made to 175 organisations totalling £53,000, mainly of sums between £100 and £500, but with one of £1,000 and one of £2,500.

Beneficiaries of the two largest grants were Chester Cathedral Song School Appeal (£2,500) and Royal Academy of Arts (£1,000). Other beneficiaries included: All Saints' Church – Beeston Regis, Brain Research Trust, Brighton and Hove Parent's and Children's Group, British Red Cross, Crusaid, Depaul Trust, Elimination of Leukemia Fund, Eyeless Trust, Genesis Appeal, Help the Aged, Matthew Project, RUKBA, St Peter's – Eaton Square Appeal, Salvation Army, Tibet Relief Fund, West Suffolk Headway, Women's Link and Youth Federation.

Exclusions No support for individuals.

Applications In writing to the correspondent. 'No telephone applications please.' Trustees meet twice during the year, usually in July and December. Applications need to be received by June or November.

The Mrs C S Heber Percy Charitable Trust

General

£126,000 (2001/02)

Beneficial area Worldwide, with a preference for Gloucestershire.

Rathbones, 159 New Bond Street, London W1S 2UD

Tel. 020 7399 0823

Correspondent Miss L J Cousins

Trustees *Mrs C S Heber Percy; Mrs J A Prest.*

CC Number 284387

Information available Information was provided by the trust.

General The trust has a stated preference for Gloucestershire. In addition to local appeals, non-local applications are accumulated and considered annually by the trustees. In 2001/02 the trust had assets of around £1.6 million and an income of £70,000. It gave donations totalling £126,000. Grants were in the range of £200 to £10,000, but were mostly for £1,000 or less. No further information was available for the year.

Previous beneficiaries include Royal Shakespeare Company, University of Kent, Friends of Aphcodicias, Institute of Policy Research, St Gregory's Special Orphanage, Sport Horse Breeding of Great Britian, Royal Agricultural Benevolent Institute, Hopes and Homes for Children, St Peter's Church – Upper Slaughter, League of Friends of MacIntyre Tall Trees, Cotswold Canals Trust, Friends of St Petersburgh, Royal Ballet School and The Sobell House Hospice.

Exclusions No grants to individuals.

Applications The correspondent stated that unsolicited applications are not required.

B E Perl Charitable Trust

Jewish, general

Unknown

Beneficial area UK.

Fofoane House, 35–37 Brent Street, Hendon, London NW4 2EF

Correspondent B Perl, Chair

Trustees *B Perl, Chair; Mrs S Perl; S Perl; J Koval; Jonathan Perl; Mrs R Reidel; Joseph Perl.*

CC Number 282847

Information available Accounts were on file at the Charity Commission, but without a list of grants.

General The trust says it makes grants for the advancement of the Orthodox Jewish faith as well as for other charitable purposes.

In 2003/04 the trust had an income of £968,000 and a total expenditure of £298,000. In recent years the income has been well over £1 million with a much lower expenditure so it may be that the trust is building up its funds and will in future have much more money available. The last grant total available comes from 1998/99 when grants totalled £25,000.

Applications In writing to the correspondent.

The Persula Foundation

Homeless, disability, human and animal welfare, visual impairment, criminal injustice, youth issues, mental health, hearing difficulties

£206,000 (2002)

Beneficial area Predominantly UK; overseas grants are given, but this is rare.

Unit 3/4 Gallery Court, Hankey Place, London SE1 4BB

Tel. 020 7357 9298 **Fax** 020 7357 8685

Email info@persula.org

Website www.persula.org

Correspondent Mrs Fiona Brown, Chief Executive

Trustees *Julian Richer; David Robinson; David Highton; Mrs R Richer; Mrs H Oppenheim.*

CC Number 1044174

Information available Information was provided by the trust.

General 'The trust works in collaboration with organisations to support projects that are innovative and original, national in application and fall with the following areas: multiple sclerosis, blindness and visual impairment, animal welfare, physical disabilities and spinal injuries, bullying, homelessness, human rights, criminal injustice, deafness, mental health and youth issues.'

The foundation also has access to many resources such as marketing, design and strategic consultation and prefers to use these resources to provide an added value aspect to its collaboration with organisations. It also offers support in the form of time and resources.

In 2002 the trust's income was £290,000 and grants were made totalling £206,000. A list of beneficiaries was not provided, however previous recipients have included Bridge Housing Association for a rent deposit scheme for homeless people, Kidscape for assertiveness training for bullied children, Irwell Valley Housing Association for Gold Service project, League Against Cruel Sports, Mayhew Animal Home for a neutering project, National Information Forum towards a conference and brochure, National Missing Persons Helpline towards a case manager for Message Home service, New Forest Drag Hunt, Royal National Institute for the Deaf for the safer sound campaign and Wandle Valley Animal Hospital for new enclosures for wildlife.

Exclusions No grants to individuals, including sponsorship, for core costs, buildings/building work or to statutory bodies.

Applications In writing to the correspondent.

The Pestalozzi Overseas Children's Trust

Children

£79,000 (2002)

Beneficial area Worldwide, especially Asia and Africa.

Pestalozzi Village, Cottage Lane, Sedlescombe, Battle, East Sussex TN33 0RR

Tel. 01424 871098

Correspondent Joanna Nair

Trustees *Lady Butler; J J Dilger; S P Pahlson-Moller; F Von Hurter.*

CC Number 1046599

Information available Full accounts were on file at the Charity Commission.

General The 2000 accounts stated: 'Our mission is to provide a practical secondary education (age about 10 onwards) to disadvantaged children in some of the poorest countries in Africa and Asia. It focuses on the brightest children, especially girls. The uniqueness of the programme is that the children once educated by Pestalozzi help provide education for other children similar to themselves. This produces an ongoing ripple effect.

'With the help of Pestalozzi US Children's Charity Link, the trust focussed its activities on Nepal and Zambia as well as working with the alumni foundations from India, Thailand, Tibet and Vietnam.

'The construction of a workshop at the Pestalozzi skills centre in Nepal enabled the scholars to acquire additional skills. It also provides a forum for them to work with the alumni in establishing the new foundation.

'A summer camp was held for the first time at Bhudanilkatha School for scholars at the school and those sponsored by Pestalozzi in the far west Doti District.

'The trust supported over 250 scholars during the year, either by paying their fees and living expenses directly to the school they attend or through the Pestalozzi alumni foundations.

'The Pestalozzi alumni foundations held a reunion in Chiang-mai Thailand. The trustees assisted with the cost of the reunion and were most encouraged by the dedication of members. The Thai Pestalozzi Foundation has already helped more than 100 children with their education and hope to establish a centre in the north of Thailand before too long.'

The accounts went on to provide the following information on its work in Zambia:

'Zambia is one of the poorest countries in the world. Services continue to deteriorate and education is limited with teachers' salaries being paid well in arrears and lagging behind the inflation rate (the exchange rate rose from K3,000=1 in March to K5,000=1 in December).

'Pestalozzi established the centre at Kaisi to provide a boarding education with skills training for poor but bright girls from the remote area. A new Pestalozzi Zambian Children's Society will be established next year to provide a local decision-making group for the centre which now houses over 60 girls.'

In 2002 the trust had assets of £226,000. Its total income was £120,000 and the total expenditure was £103,000. Grants totalled £79,000, of which £59,000 was given towards school fees and £2,150 for capital projects.

Exclusions The trust emphasised that funding is not available to individuals, including students.

Applications Applications cannot be made to this trust. It works in partnerships with schools it identifies through its own research and networks and are given proactively by the trust. The trust will contact organisations it wants to support proactively.

The Pet Plan Charitable Trust

Dogs, cats and horses

£563,000 (2000/01)

Beneficial area UK.

Great West Road, Brentford, Middlesex TW8 9EG

Tel. 020 8580 8013 **Fax** 020 8580 8186

Email roz-hb-petplanct@allianzcornhill.co.uk

Correspondent Roz Hayward-Butt, Administrator

Trustees *David Simpson, Chair; Clarissa Baldwin; Patsy Bloom; John Bower; Dave Bishop; Nicholas Mills; George Stratford; Michael Tucker.*

CC Number 1032907

Information available Information was provided by the trust.

General This trust was established by a pet insurance company by adding an optional £1 a year to the premiums paid by its members. The trust provides grants towards the welfare of dogs, cats and horses by funding clinical veterinary investigation, education and welfare projects. Funding is sometimes given for capital projects. Educational grants are given to fund projects aimed at both the general public and the welfare industry.

In 2000/01 the trust had assets of £850,000. Its income was £488,000 and administration costs were high at £69,000. Grants were made totalling £563,000.

Beneficiaries included Animal Health Trust for research into the cause of cancer in dogs (£39,000), University of Cambridge Veterinary School to investigate joint disease in horses (£21,000), Royal Veterinary College for a study investigating insulin resistance in diabetic cats (£20,000), Paws for Kids for its pet-fostering service (£12,000) and Ada Cole Rescue Stables for a replacement van and Ty-Agored Animal Sanctuary for neutering and veterinary assistance (£8,000 each).

Exclusions No grants to individuals or non-registered charities. The trust does not support or condone invasive procedures, vivisection or experimentation of any kind.

Applications In writing, or by telephone or e-mail, to the correspondent. Closing dates for scientific and welfare applications vary so please check first. Grants are generally announced at the end of the year.

The Philanthropic Trust

Homelessness, developing world, welfare (human and animal), environment, human rights

£167,000 (2002/03)

Beneficial area UK, Africa, Asia.

Trustee Management Limited, 19 Cookridge Street, Leeds LS2 3AG

Tel. 0113 243 6466

Correspondent The Trust Administrator

Trustees *Paul H Burton; Jeremy J Burton; Amanda C Burton.*

CC Number 1045263

Information available Full accounts were provided by the trust.

General Although the trust has general charitable purposes, special consideration is given to institutions relating to homelessness, the developing world, human and animal welfare, the environment and human rights.

In 2002/03 the trust had assets of £1.6 million. The total income was

£294,000 including £170,000 in Gift Aid donations. Grants totalled £167,000 and were allocated to the following sectors:

	No.	Total
Health	17	£17,500
Social and welfare including helping the homeless	69	£93,500
Third World and overseas aid to the developing world	29	£37,500
Animal Welfare	11	£3,400
Environmental and conservation	6	£4,000
Disability	11	£11,000

Beneficiaries in the UK included Centrepoint and Medical Foundation for Victims of Torture (£10,000 each), St Basils', Prisoners of Conscience Appeals Fund (£3,000 each), Refugee Council (£2,500) and Age Concern, Association for Mentally Infirm & Elderly, Children with Aids Charity, Beecan Housing Project and Help the Aged.

Beneficiaries working overseas included Oxfam (£5,000), Cambodia Trust (£2,000) and African Medical & Research Foundation, Anti-Slavery International, Appropriate Technology Asia, Children in Crisis, Civis Trust, FARM Africa, Find Your Feet, Friends of Seva Mandir (£1,000 each).

Exclusions No grants for the arts, education, religious organisations, expeditions or individuals. Grants are given to UK registered charities only.

Applications In writing to the correspondent. Unsuccessful appeals will not necessarily be acknowledged.

The Ruth & Michael Phillips Charitable Trust

General, Jewish

£132,000 (2002/03)

Beneficial area UK.

Berkeley Square House, Berkeley Square, London W1X 5PB

Tel. 020 7491 3763 **Fax** 020 7491 0818

Correspondent M L Phillips, Trustee

Trustees *M L Phillips; Mrs R Phillips; M D Paisner.*

CC Number 260378

Information available Full accounts were on file at the Charity Commission.

General The trust supports a wide range of causes, including medical research, education, disability, old age, poverty, sheltered accommodation and the arts. In practice, almost all the grants are made to Jewish/Israeli organisations.

In 2002/03 the trust had assets of £809,000. Total income was £188,000, including £150,000 donated by J B Rubens Charitable Foundation which is, alongside The Phillips Family Charitable Trust, connected to this trust through a common trustee.

Grants were made totalling £132,000 with beneficiaries including Community Security Trust (£20,000), United Jewish Israel Appeal (£13,000), Chief Rabbi Charitable Fund, Friends of Nightgale House and Jreusalem Foundation (£10,000 each), Norwood Children and Families First (£8,000), Royal Opera House Benevolent Fund (£7,750) and British ORT, Lubavitch Foundation and Maccabi GB (£5,000 each).

Exclusions No grants are made to individuals.

Applications In writing to the correspondent at any time.

The Phillips Family Charitable Trust

Jewish charities, welfare, general

£74,000 (2002/03)

Beneficial area UK.

Berkeley Square House, Berkeley Square, London W1J 6BY

Tel. 020 7491 3763 **Fax** 020 7491 0818

Email psphillipsbsh@aol.com

Correspondent Paul S Phillips, Trustee

Trustees *M L Phillips; Mrs R Phillips; M D Paisner; P S Phillips; G M Phillips.*

CC Number 279120

Information available Information was provided by the trust.

General This trust stated that it makes grants to Jewish organisations and to a range of other organisations, including elderly, children and refugee charities and educational establishments.

In 2002/03 it had assets of £205,000 and an income of £75,000. Grants were made totalling £74,000.

In previous years grants have mostly ranged from £100 to £750 each. They have mostly gone to various types of Jewish charities, while other welfare causes are regularly supported. However, around three quarters of the grants go to regular beneficiaries with around five to ten new organisations supported each year.

Exclusions No grants to individuals.

Applications In writing to the correspondent. Please note, the trust informed us that there is not much scope for new beneficiaries.

The David Pickford Charitable Foundation

Christian, general

£46,000 (2002/03)

Beneficial area UK (with a preference for Kent and London) and overseas.

Elm Tree Farm, Mersham, Ashford, Kent TN25 7HS

Tel. 01233 720200 **Fax** 01233 720522

Correspondent D M Pickford, Trustee

Trustees *D M Pickford; Mrs E G Pickford.*

CC Number 243437

Information available Full accounts provided by the foundation.

General The general policy is to make gifts to Christian organisations especially those helping youth, and with special needs in overseas countries.

In 2002/03 the trust had assets of £786,000 and an income of £42,000. The trustees gave grants totalling £46,000. Many beneficiaries are evangelical Christian organisations. Other grants are given for general welfare purposes.

The largest grant was £7,500 to Philo Trust. Other grants included £6,500 to Oasis Trust, £5,000 to Willesborough Baptist Church, £2,000 to CARE Trust, £2,500 to The Chasah Trust, £1,500 to Luis Palau Evangelistic Association and Prison Fellowship and £1,000 each to Alpha, Evangelical Alliance and Kent Baptist Association.

Exclusions No grants to individuals. No building projects.

Applications In writing to the correspondent. Trustees meet every other month from January. Applications will not be acknowledged. The correspondent states: 'It is our general policy only to give to charities to whom we are personally known'. Those falling outside the criteria mentioned above will be ignored.

The Bernard Piggott Trust

General

£49,000 (2003/04)

Beneficial area North Wales and Birmingham.

4 Streetsbrook Road, Shirley, Solihull, West Midlands B90 3PL

Tel. 0121 744 1695 **Fax** 0121 744 1695

Correspondent Miss J P Whitworth

Trustees *D M P Lea; N J L Lea; R J Easton.*

CC Number 260347

Information available Information was provided by the trust

General This trust provides one-off grants for Church of England, Church of Wales, educational, medical, drama and youth organisations in Birmingham and North Wales only. Grants range from £250 to £4,000 although they do not often exceed £1,000.

In 2003/04 the trust had assets of £1 million. Grants were made to 39 organisations totalling £49,000.

Beneficiaries included St Hynwyn, Aberdaron, St Matthew, Borth, St Martin in the Bull Ring, MacMillan Cancer Relief, Elizabeth Dowell's Trust and 2nd Shirley Scout Group.

Exclusions No grants to individuals.

Applications The trustees meet in May/June and November. Applications should be in writing to the secretary including annual accounts and details of the specific project including running costs and so on. General policy is not to consider any further grant to the same institution within the next two years.

The Cecil Pilkington Charitable Trust

Conservation, medical research, general on Merseyside

£158,000 (2000/01)

Beneficial area UK, particularly Sunningwell in Oxfordshire and St Helens.

PO Box 8162, London W2 1JG

Tel. 0118 959 7111

Correspondent A P Pilkington, Trustee

Trustees *A P Pilkington; R F Carter Jones; M R Feeney.*

CC Number 249997

Information available Accounts were on file at the Charity Commission.

General This trust supports conservation and medical research causes across the UK, supporting both national and local organisations. It also has general charitable purposes in Sunningwell in Oxfordshire and St Helens.

In 2002/03 the trust had an income of £181,000 and a total expenditure of £139,000. Further information from this year was unavailable.

In 2000/01 the trust had assets of £5.9 million, which generated an income of £173,000. Grants to 42 organisations totalled £158,000.

The largest grants went to Psychiatry Research Trust – Deperonalisation Research Unit (£45,000), Covent Garden Cancer Research Trust (£24,000) and Royal Agricultural Benevolent Institution (£20,000).

Other beneficiaries included Handel House Trust (£5,000), Richmond Fellowship (£4,000), BTCV, British Trust for Ornithology and Rare Breeds Survival Trust (£3,000 each), Alzheimer's Research Trust (£2,500), Royal School for the Blind – Liverpool (£2,000), Liverpool PSS, Oxfordshire Woodland Project and St Helens' Deaf Society (£1,000 each), Department of Plant Sciences – University of Oxford (£600) and Oxford Festival of Contemporary Music (£500).

Exclusions No grants to individuals or non-registered charities.

Applications In writing to the correspondent. The trust does not respond to unsolicited appeals.

The Elsie Pilkington Charitable Trust

Equine animals, welfare

£240,000 (2002/03)

Beneficial area UK.

Taylor Wessing, Carmelite, 50 Victoria Embankment, London EC4Y 0DX

Correspondent Lord Brentford

Trustees *Mrs Caroline Doulton; Mrs Tara Economakis; Richard Scott.*

CC Number 278332

Information available Information was provided by the trust.

General This trust supports small specific projects of a capital nature which benefit equines and older people in need. In 2002/03 its assets totalled £2.1 million and its income was £99,000 (£96,000). Grants totalled £240,000, broken down as follows (2001/02 in brackets):

- to prevent cruelty to equine animals – £67,000 (£95,000)
- to relieve suffering and distress amongst such equine animals and to care for and protect such equines in need of care and protection – £29,000 (£60,000)
- to provide social services and help for the relief of older people, and people who are infirm and poor – £46,000 (£85,000).

A grants list was not available for the year, although the trust stated that 7 grants were made under the final object heading above, with the remaining 12 grants made in the other two categories.

Applications In writing to the correspondent.

The Sir Harry Pilkington Trust

General

£128,000 (2002/03)

Beneficial area UK and Merseyside, with a preference for the St Helens area.

Liverpool Council of Social Service (Inc.), 14 Castle Street, Liverpool, Merseyside L2 0NJ

Tel. 0151 236 7728 **Fax** 0151 258 1153

Correspondent The Trustees

Trustee *Liverpool Council of Social Service (Inc.).*

CC Number 206740

Information available Full accounts were provided by the trust.

General This trust has general charitable purposes, giving most of its grants in and around St Helens.

In 2002/03 it had assets of £3.9 million, which generated an income of £131,000. Grants were made totalling £128,000.

Two substantial grants were made, namely £50,000 to The Extra Care Charitable Trust and £40,000 to Liverpool Council of Social Service (Inc) – the corporate trustee.

Other beneficiaries included Barnardos and Millennium Centre – St Helens (£10,000), Southport Flower Show (£6,000), The Theatre Trust (£5,000), Merseyside Development Fund (£3,000), Worcestershire County Council (£1,400) and Association for the History of Glass and ROC (£1,000 each).

Applications In writing to the correspondent.

The Austin & Hope Pilkington Trust

Music, arts, overseas (2005); community, disability (2006)

£350,000 (2001/02)

Beneficial area Unrestricted, but see below.

PO Box 124, Stroud, Gloucestershire GL6 7YN

Email admin@austin-hope-pilkington.org.uk

Website www.austin-hope-pilkington.org.uk

Correspondent Karen Frank, Administrator

Trustees *Jennifer Jones; Deborah Nelson; Penny Shankar.*

CC Number 255274

Information available Annual reports and accounts.

General The trust usually gives about 100 grants to mainly national organisations through its regular programme. In a refreshing change from conventional practice, this changes to new fields each year as follows:

2003	Community, poverty and religion
2004	Children, youth, elderly, medical
2005	Music and the arts; overseas
2006	Community, disability

'The trustees welcome applications for projects within the [above] areas for the next three years. These categories are then repeated in a three-year rotation. Please note that the trustees have decided no longer to consider applications that deal solely with religion or poverty.'

In 2001/02 it had an income of £220,000 and a total expenditure of £411,000. Grants are usually in the region of £350,000. Grants are usually between £1,000 and £10,000, with most being for £5,000 or less. Exceptionally, grants for up to £20,000 can be made for medical research projects. Grants are usually one-off.

The trust's website gives examples of charities that have been supported during the last three years as follows:

Community and disability

Royal Albert Dock Trust to fund an additional instructor for local young people at a rowing centre, and Mind towards a resource centre providing advice and training for workers dealing with mental health in rural areas (£5,000 each). Other recent beneficiaries include Barnado's, Federation of Prisoners' Families' Support Groups and National Missing Persons Helpline.

Religion

Lincoln Theological Institute for the Study of Religion and Society towards a research project to see why 'so many leave ordained ministry' (£3,000). Other beneficiaries include Gather in the Isles, Lisburn Methodist Church and University of Warwick.

Children and youth

Brandon Centre towards a behavioural programme for persistent young offenders, and National Family Mediation Centre for a child support project (£5,000 each). Other recent beneficiaries in this area include Bethnal Green Museum of Chilldhood, Howard League for Penal Reform and AMP Youth Development Project.

Elderly

Beneficiaries include Action on Elder Abuse (£3,000), UBS Survival Income and Age Concern Bath and N E Somerset (£1,000 each).

Medical

National Asthma Campaign for a research project into the causes of asthma (£20,000) and Diabetes UK for research (£10,000). Other recent beneficiaries include Maternity Alliance (£5,000), Arthritis Care and Pain Research Institute (£3,000 each).

Music and the arts

Sir John Soane Museum towards the development of 14 Lincoln's Inn Fields including a children's education centre (£5,000), Imaginate to enable children with special needs to participate in an international children's theatre festival, and Royal Liverpool Philharmonic to provide teachers'packs in preparation for school visits (£3,000 each). Smaller beneficiaries include Live Music Now! and Scottish Opera.

Overseas

Recent beneficiaries included Save the Children for programmes in Africa (£10,000), Children in Crisis for a day care centre in Afghanistan and Mildmay towards work with AIDS patients in Uganda (£5,000 each), Book Aid International for library books in Zambia (£3,000) and Concern International for a project helping girls at risk in Brazil (£1,000).

Exclusions Grants only to registered charities. No grants to individuals, including individuals embarking on a trip overseas with an umbrella organisation. Overseas projects can only be supported in the stated year.

National organisations are more likely to be supported than purely local organisations.

Applications In writing to the correspondent. There is no application form. Applications should include an A4 summary of the project, a budget for the project and the applicant's most recent annual report and accounts. Necessary supporting information should be kept to a minimum as the trust will request further information if required.

Grants are made twice a year, with deadlines for applications being 1 June and 1 November. All applicants will be contacted.

The Col W W Pilkington Will Trusts – The General Charity Fund

Welfare

£33,000 (2001/02)

Beneficial area UK, with a preference for Merseyside.

Rathbones, Port of Liverpool Building, Pier Head, Liverpool L3 1NW

Correspondent A P Pilkington

Trustees *Arnold Pilkington; Hon. Mrs Jennifer Jones; Neil Pilkington Jones.*

CC Number 234710

Information available Accounts were on file at the Charity Commission.

General The trust gives grants to registered charities only, with a preference for the Merseyside area.

In 2001/02 the trust had assets of £1.3 million and an income of £43,000. Grants totalled £33,000. Donations of £1,000 or more included £2,500 to Handel House Museum and £1,000 each to Childline North West, Drug Scope, Fairbridge, Henshaw's Society for the Blind, Mental Health Foundation, St Helens District Council for Voluntary Service, Soil Association, Marie Stopes International, Talking Newspapers and Worklink.

Other beneficiaries of grants for either £500 or £600 each included Deysbrook Community Dance School – Liverpool, Lancashire Youth Clubs Association, Liverpool Somali Association, Merseyside Society for Deaf People, St Helens Bereavement Service, St Helens District CVS and Toxteth CAB.

Exclusions No support for non-registered charities, building projects, animal charities or individuals.

Applications In writing to the correspondent. Grant distributions are made in January and July.

A M Pilkington's Charitable Trust

General

£130,000 (2003)

Beneficial area UK, with a preference for Scotland.

Carters, Chartered Accountants, Pentland House, Saltire Centre, Glenrothes, Fife KY6 2AH

Tel. 01592 630055 **Fax** 01592 623200

Email info@cartersca.co.uk

Correspondent The Trustees

SC Number SC000282

Information available Information was provided by the trust.

General The trust supports a wide variety of causes in the UK, with few causes excluded. In practice there is a preference for Scotland – probably half the grants are given in Scotland. There is a preference for giving recurring grants, which normally range from £500 to £1,500.

In 2003 the trust told us that it supports around 300 mainly recurrent organisations each year and grants totalled about £130,000 annually.

In 1999/2000 the trust had assets of £3.1 million and an income of £172,000. It gave grants to 146 charities totalling £130,000. Details on the beneficiaries were not available.

Exclusions Grants are not given to overseas projects or political appeals.

Applications The trustees state that, regrettably, they are unable to make grants to new applicants since they already have more than enough causes to support. Trustees meet in June and December.

The Platinum Trust

Disability

About £300,000 (2001/02)

Beneficial area UK.

Russels Solicitors, 5 Offa Road, St Albans AL3 4QR

Tel. 01727 375301

Correspondent The Secretary

Trustees *G K Panayiotou; A D Russell; C D Organ.*

CC Number 328570

Information available A report was on file at the Charity Commission with no grants list.

General This trust gives grants in the UK for the relief of children with special needs and adults with mental or physical disabilities 'requiring special attention'.

In 2001/02 the trust had an income of £336,000. Total expenditure was £304,000. Further information was unavailable.

In 1999/2000 grants to eight organisations came to £122,000, as well as a cheque of £500,000 to Kosovo Appeal. Beneficiaries were BCODP (£39,000), Alliance for Inclusive Education and Parents for Inclusion (£20,000 each), CSIE (£18,000), DPPI (£11,000) with £5,000 each to Disability Equality in Education, Regard and Muscle Power.

Exclusions No grants for services run by statutory or public bodies, or from mental-health organisations. No grants for: medical research/treatment or equipment; mobility aids/wheelchairs; community transport/disabled transport schemes; holidays/exchanges/holiday playschemes; special-needs playgroups; toy and leisure libraries; special Olympic and Paralympics groups; sports and recreation clubs for people with disabilities; residential care/sheltered housing/respite care; carers; conservation schemes/city farms/horticultural therapy; sheltered or supported employment/ community business/social firms; purchase/construction/repair of buildings; and conductive education/ other special educational programmes.

Applications The trust does not accept unsolicited applications; all future grants will be allocated by the trustees to groups they have already made links with.

G S Plaut Charitable Trust

Sickness, disability, Jewish, elderly, Christian, general

£34,000 (2001/02)

Beneficial area Predominantly UK.

c/o 3 Princess Gardens, Grove, Wantage, Oxfordshire OX12 0QN

Correspondent Dr R Speirs

Trustees *Dr G S Plaut, Chair; Mrs A D Wrapson; Dr H M Liebeschuetz; K A Sutcliffe; W E Murfett; Miss T A Warburg.*

CC Number 261469

Information available Information was provided by the trust.

General This trust appears to make grants across the whole spectrum of the voluntary sector, however it may have some preference for charities in those fields listed above. In 2002/03 the trust's assets totalled £520,000, it had an income of £33,000 and grants to 141 organisations totalled £34,000.

The largest grants were £750 to both C M Jacobs Home and Friends of Meals on Wheels Service (Liverpool) and £600 to Nightingale Home for Aged Jews, RNIB Talking Book Services and St Dunstan's. Most grants were for £100 or £200.

A number of national sickness and disability charities received grants including British Deaf Association and Down's Syndrome Association.

Jewish beneficiaries included Friendships' Way and Hull Jewish Community Care.

Grants to elderly organisations included those to Friends of the Elderly and Methodist Homes for the Aged.

Other beneficiaries included Book Aid International, Gurkha Welfare Trust, Liverpool School of Tropical Medicine, Rehearsal Orchestra, St George's Crypt – Leeds, Southend Riding Club for the Disabled, TOC H and VSO.

Exclusions No grants to individuals or for repeat applications.

Applications In writing to the correspondent. Applications are reviewed twice a year. An sae should be enclosed. Applications will not be acknowledged.

The J S F Pollitzer Charitable Settlement

General

£67,000 (2002/03)

Beneficial area UK and overseas.

c/o H W Fisher & Co., 11–15 William Road, London NW1 3ER

Tel. 020 7388 7000

Correspondent P Samuel, Accountant

Trustees *Mrs J F A Davis; Mrs S C O'Farrell; R F C Pollitzer; J S Challis.*

CC Number 210680

Information available Full accounts were on file at the Charity Commission.

General The trust supports a range of UK and local charities. In 2002/03 it had an income of £32,000 and a grant total of £67,000. Donations of £1,000 were given to 67 organisations. Beneficiaries included Alone in London, Bath Recital Artists Trust, Brainwave, Chicken Shed Theatre Company, The Extra Care Charitable Trust, Hearing Dogs for Deaf People, Hertfordshire Sclerosis Therapy Centre, Royal School for the Blind Liverpool, RSPB and The Yehudi Menuhin School. One organisation Art From Under Your Bed received a smaller sum of £300.

Exclusions No grants to individuals or students, i.e. those without charitable status.

Applications In writing to the correspondent. Grants are distributed twice a year, usually around April/May and November/December.

The George & Esme Pollitzer Charitable Settlement

Jewish, health, social welfare, general

£358,000 (2002/03)

Beneficial area UK.

Saffery Champness, Beausort House, 2 Beausort Road, Clifton, Bristol B58 2AE

Tel. 0117 915 1617

Correspondent J Barnes, Trustee

Trustees *J Barnes; B G Levy; R F C Pollitzer.*

CC Number 212631

Information available Full accounts were on file at the Charity Commission.

General This trust has general charitable purposes with no exclusions. Most funds are given to Jewish causes. In 2002/03 it had assets of £262,000, which generated an income of £105,000. Grants were made totalling £358,000.

The largest grants were £250,000 to Sunridge Endowment Fund, £25,000 each to The Big Issue and Sunridge Housing Association. A grant of £5,000 went to Nightengale House, £3,000 each to Deafblind UK and Starlight Children's Foundation, £2,000 each went to Break Through Breast Cancer, Breast Cancer Care, Norwood Ravenswood, Outside the Box, Royal College of Surgeons of England, Speech Language & Hearing Centre and VSO.

Further grants were for £1,000 each, some beneficiaries included Alzheimer's Research Trust, Barnardo's, Cancer BACUP, Fight for Sight, Iris Fund, Listening Books, Motability, Royal National Institute for the Blind, Sequal Trust The Samaritans and Whizz Kidz.

Applications In writing to the correspondent.

Edith & Ferdinand Porjes Charitable Trust

Jewish, general

£145,000 (2003)

Beneficial area UK and overseas.

Adelaide House, London Bridge, London EC4R 9HA

Tel. 020 7353 0299 **Fax** 020 7583 8621

Correspondent M D Paisner, Trustee

Trustees *M D Paisner; A H Freeman; A S Rosenfelder.*

CC Number 274012

Information available Full accounts were on file at the Charity Commission.

General Although the trust has general charitable purposes, the trust is inclined to support applications from the Jewish community in the UK and overseas. It has a British Friends of the Art Museums of Israel Endowment Fund and in 2000 provisionally designated a fund for London School of Jewish Studies out of proceeds from the sale of manuscripts which had been on loan to the school.

In 2003 the trust had assets of £1.5 million and an income of £63,000 with grants totalling £145,000.

The largest grants were £90,000 to London School of Jewish Studies, £25,000 to Jewish Museum and 3 grants of £18,000 to Oxford Centre for Hebrew Jewish Studies.

Other beneficiaries include £17,000 to Jerusalem Foundation, £10,000 each to Friends of Hebrew University, Jewish Book Council and Royal Academy Trust, £7,500 each to Worcester College, Council of Christians and Jews, St Anne's College, and Queen Mary and Westfield College, £2,500 to Finchley Road Synagogue Limited and £1,500 to British Friend of Ohel Sarah.

Applications In writing to the correspondent.

The David and Elaine Potter Charitable Foundation

The advancement of education and scientific research

£166,000 (2000)

Beneficial area UK and other countries with particular emphasis on the developing world.

10 Park Crescent, London W1B 1PQ

Correspondent Ms Dharmista Pancholi

Trustees *M S Polonsky; T Laub; M Langley.*

CC Number 1078217

Information available Accounts were on file at the Charity Commission.

General This foundation was registered with the Charity Commission in November 1999.

In 2003 the trust had an income of £752,000 and a total expenditure of £501,000. Further information for this year was not available.

In 2000 its assets stood at £17 million and it had income from investments of £421,000. A further £28 million was received in a donation from its founder. Grants to organisations were made totalling £166,000 with £3,700 going to individuals. By far the largest grants in the year were £50,000 to Howard League for Penal Reform, £26,000 to International Centre for Child Studies, £25,000 to SANE and £10,000 to Nuffield College. Beneficiaries of smaller grants included: UK Friends of the Johannesburg Child Welfare Society (£7,000), Westminster School (£5,600), Cancer Bacup and Philharmonic Orchestra Trust Ltd (£5,000 each), and Elizabeth Finn Trust (£3,000).

Applications In writing to the correspondent.

This entry was not confirmed by the trust. The information is derived from the trust's annual reports and accounts on file at the Charity Commission.

The Powell Foundation

People who are elderly or mentally or physically disabled

£109,000 (2003/04)

Beneficial area Within the Milton Keynes Unitary Council area.

c/o Milton Keynes Community Foundation, Acorn House, 381 Midsummer Boulevard, Central Milton Keynes MK9 3HP

Tel. 01908 304432

Email information@mkcommunityfoundation.co.uk

Website www.mkcommunityfoundation.co.uk

Correspondent Julia Seal, Chief Executive

Trustees *R W Norman; R Hill.*

CC Number 1012786

Information available Full accounts were on file at the Charity Commission.

General The foundation supports general charitable purposes; however, according to the wishes of Margaret Powell, the trustees restrict the activities of the trust to providing grants for the benefit of people who are older or disabled living in the Milton Keynes area.

In 2003/04 the trust had assets of £3 million and an income of £135,000. Grants totalled £109,000, of which £100,000 was designated to Milton Keynes Community Foundation, an annual grant for distribution to voluntary groups that meet the Foundation's criteria of benefiting older people or people who are physically or mentally disabled, regardless of age. Direct grants can be considered for groups. Small grants can be considered for disabled individuals in exceptional circumstances; they must be residents of Milton Keynes.

Other beneficiaries in the year were Drake Music Project to fund a new 3-year post (£53,500), Milton Keynes Theatre Pantomine Trip to purchase an entire matinee performance (£12,800), Workbridge to establish job clubs to support people with disabilities wishing to return to work (£7,500) and Bucks Association for the Blind to establish an information centre for visually impaired people (£5,000).

Applications In writing to the correspondent.

Prairie Trust

Third world development, the environment, conflict prevention

£102,000 (2003/04)

Beneficial area Worldwide.

83 Belsize Park Gardens, London NW3 4NJ

Tel. 020 7722 2105 **Fax** 020 7483 4228

Correspondent The Administrator

Trustees *Dr R F Mulder; Fenella Rouse.*

CC Number 296019

Information available Information was provided by the trust.

General The trust does not consider unsolicited applications and instead develops its own programme to support a small number of organisations working on issues of third world development, the environment and conflict prevention, particularly to support policy and advocacy work in these areas. The trustees are also interested in supporting innovative and entrepreneurial approaches to traditional problems.

In 2003/04 the trust's assets totalled £346,000, its income was £37,000 and grants to 13 organisations totalled £102,000. The largest grants were £24,000 in three grants to Funding Network, £22,000 to Linacre College and £20,000 to Centre for Social Markets. Other beneficiaries included Network for Social Change (£7,000), FINCA (£6,000), Nicol Society and Oxfam (£5,000 each),

Action for ME (£3,500), New Economics Foundation (£2,500), Salts of the Earth (£1,000) and RESULTS Education (£250).

Exclusions No grants to individuals, for expeditions or for capital projects.

Applications The trust states: 'As we are a proactive trust with limited funds and administrative help, we are unable to consider unsolicited applications'.

The W L Pratt Charitable Trust

General

£35,000 (2003/04)

Beneficial area UK, particularly York, and overseas.

Messrs Grays, Duncombe Place, York YO1 7DY

Tel. 01904 634771 **Fax** 01904 610711

Email christophergoodway@grayssolicitors.co.uk

Correspondent C C Goodway, Trustee

Trustees *J L C Pratt; C M Tetley; C C Goodway.*

CC Number 256907

Information available Information was provided by the trust

General In 2003/04 the trust had assets of £1.4 million and an income of £47,000. Grants were made totalling £35,000. The trust divides its grant-giving between overseas charities, local charities in the York area and UK national charities. UK and overseas grants are restricted to well-known registered charities.

The largest grants included £3,900 to York Diocesan Board of Finance for the ministry of the Church of England, £2,100 to St Leonard's Hospice, £2,000 each to Christian Aid for overseas aid and Sight Savers International and Wilberforce Home for the Multiple Handicapped, £1,700 each to York Minister Fund and Save the Children Overseas Aid, £1,300 each to York Samaritans and Yorkshire Cancer Relief and £1,000 each to Barnardo's, Soundseekers, Salvation Army and York CVS.

Exclusions No grants to individuals. No grants for buildings or for upkeep and preservation of places of worship.

Applications In writing to the correspondent. Applications will not be acknowledged unless an sae is supplied. Telephone applications are not accepted.

Premierquote Ltd

Jewish, general

£457,000 (2002/03)

Beneficial area Worldwide.

Harford House, 101–103 Great Portland Street, London W1N 6BH

Tel. 020 8203 0665

Correspondent D Last, Trustee

Trustees *D Last; Mrs L Last; H Last; M Weisenfeld.*

CC Number 801957

Information available Accounts were on file at the Charity Commission, but without a list of grants.

General The trust was established in 1985 for the benefit of Jewish organisations, the relief of poverty and general purposes. In 2001/02 it had an income of £848,000 and its total assets were £42,000. Grants were given to the amount £457,000.

Grants paid out were £144,200 to Belz Yeshiva Trust, £52,800 to Friends of Senet Wiznitz, £30,000 to Meadowgold Limited, £18,500 to Friends of the United Institutions of Arad, £15,180 to North West London Communal Mikvah, £11,055 to Beth Jacob Grammar School for Girls Ltd, and £10,000 to Friends of Ohel Moshe.

Other grants were given between £1,000 and £9,500 to charities such as Kehal Chasidel Bobov (£9,500), Menorah Primary School (£7,930), British Friends of Shuvu (£5,000), A.V. Truzi (£4,000), Achisomoch (£2,250), Yarchei Kalla (£1,500) and Torah Vedaas Primary School (£1,120).

Applications In writing to the correspondent.

Premishlaner Charitable Trust

Jewish

£47,000 (1999/2000)

Beneficial area UK and worldwide.

186 Lordship Road, London N16 5ES

Correspondent C M Margulies, Trustee

Trustees *H C Freudenberger; S Honig; C M Margulies.*

CC Number 1046945

Information available A grants list was provided by the trust. Accounts were on file at the Charity Commission, without a full grants list.

General This trust was founded in 1995; its principal objects are:

- to advance orthodox Jewish education
- to advance the religion of the Jewish faith in accordance with the Orthodox practice
- the relief of poverty.

In 2002/03 the trust had an income of £57,000 and a total expenditure of £59,000. Further information for this year was not available.

In 1999/2000 it had an income of £75,000 and awarded 24 grants totalling £80,000, although one grant of £34,000 was returned. Grants paid included £20,000 to a Jewish educational organisation, £1,600 to Lev Efraim, £1,000 to Beth Jacob Primary School, two grants of £750 each to SOFT, two grants totalling £620 to Yeshuos Chaim Synagogue and £250 to Beis Ruzhin Trust. Many of these organisations were also beneficiaries in the previous year.

No other financial information for this year as available, although in 1998/99 the trust had assets of £428,000 and an income of £90,000, £51,000 of which came from donations and gifts.

Applications In writing to the correspondent.

The Simone Prendergast Charitable Settlement

General

£32,000 (2002/03)

Beneficial area UK, Israel.

Flat C, 52 Warwick Square, London SW1V 2AJ

Tel. 020 7821 7653

Correspondent Dame Simone Prendergast, Trustee

Trustees *Dame Simone Prendergast; Christopher H Prendergast; Mrs Jennifer Skidmore.*

CC Number 242881

Information available Full accounts were provided by the trust.

General The trust states that it does not have a specific grant-making policy. Particular preference is given to charities working in the fields of: religion, arts, culture and recreation, hospices, immunology, historic buildings, pre-school education, theatres and opera houses, crime prevention schemes, playschemes, campaigning for racial equality and against discrimination. As it can be seen, the trust supports a wide range of organsations.

In 2002/03 it had assets of £478,000, which generated an income of £26,000. Grants totalling £32,000 were made to 58 organisations.

The largest grants were £4,000 to Westminster Children's Society, £3,000 to Council of Christians and Jews and £2,000 each to Age Concern Westminster, Anglo-Israel Association, British WIZO, Jewish Lads' and Girls' Brigade, Royal College of Surgeons of England and World Jewish Relief.

Most of the grants were for small amounts. They included £650 to Westminster Synagogue, £500 each to Alzheimer's Research Trust, Holocaust Educational Trust and Royal Opera House Foundation, £350 to National Theatre, £300 to UKJAID, £250 to British ORT, CRISIS, Central School of Ballet, Heritage of London Trust, Magen David Adom UK, Meningitis Research Foundation, Mental Health Foundation and YWCA, £200 each to Activenture, Counsel and Care of the Elderly, Delamere Forest School, Migraine Trust, St Marylebone Health Society and Stoneham Memorial Trust, £100 each to Blond McIndoe centre, Greater London Fund for the Blind, Limbless Association and Westminster Tree and Preservation trust and £25 to Ben Uri Gallery.

Exclusions No grants to non-registered charities or to individuals.

Applications In writing to the correspondent, at any time. Trustees meet twice a year. Clear details of the project are required – no acknowledgements will be sent.

The Nyda and Oliver Prenn Foundation

Arts, education, health

£78,000 (2002)

Beneficial area UK, with a preference for London.

Moore Stephens, Chartered Accountants, 1 Snow Hill, London EC1A 2EN

Correspondent T Cripps

Trustees *O S Prenn; Mrs N M McDonald Prenn; S Lee; Mrs C P Cavanagh; A D S Prenn; N C N Prenn.*

CC Number 274726

Information available Information was provided by the trust.

General This trust supports arts, education and health organisations, usually based in London, which have been identified by the trustees through their own research.

In 2002 the foundation had assets of £559,000. Total income was £24,000. After low administration costs of £2,500, grants totalling £78,000 were made to 26 organisations, of which 22 were supported in the previous year.

UCL Development received £15,000. Other beneficiaries were Union Dance Trust (£10,000), Contempary Art Society (£7,500), British Red Cross (£5,000), Speech, Language and Hearing Centre (£4,000), Amadeus Scholarship Fund, Royal National Theatre and SOS Poland (£3,000 each) and British Heart Foundation, Hearing Dogs for the Deaf and Motability (£2,500 each).

Smaller grants included those to The Serpentine Trust (£650), National Asthma Campaign and Streatham Youth Centre (£500 each).

Exclusions Local projects outside London are unlikely to be considered.

Applications Unsolicited applications are not acknowledged.

The Primrose Hill Trust

Prison welfare

£42,000 (2002/03)

Beneficial area UK and worldwide.

Sayers Butterworth, 18 Bentink Street, London W1U 2AR

Tel. 020 7935 8504 **Fax** 020 7487 5621

Correspondent Stuart G Kemp, Trustee

Trustees *Richard Astor; Mrs Sarah Astor; Stuart Kemp.*

CC Number 326957

Information available Full accounts were provided by the trust.

General This trust currently supports matters relating to prison welfare.

In 2002/03 it had assets of £72,000. Its income was £52,000, of which £50,000 came from a donation given by The Avenue Charitable Trust, which shares the same trustees. Grants were made to four organisations totalling £42,000.

Prisons Video Trust received by far the largest grant, of £30,000. The accounts stated that it also had £20,000 committed to the charity, dependent on it receiving match funding.

Other beneficiaries were Emmaus UK and Eritrean Relief Association (£5,000 each) and Comeback (£2,000).

Applications In writing to the correspondent.

The Primrose Trust

General

£211,000 (2001/02)

Beneficial area UK.

5 South View, Horton, Wiltshire SN10 3NA

Tel. 01380 860 794

Correspondent M Clark, Trustee

Trustees *M G Clark; Susan Boyes-Korkis.*

CC Number 800049

Information available Full accounts were on file at the Charity Commission.

General The trust was established in 1986 with general charitable purposes.

In 2001/02 the trust had assets of £3.2 million and an income of £139,000 with grants totalling £211,000.

The largest grants were £30,000 each to Swan Rescue Sanctuary, Raptor Rescue and Langford Trust and £25,000 each to Bluebell Charitable Trust and National Federation Badger Groups.

Other grants include £10,000 each to Youth Action Group Wiltshire, WANHS, Victim Support Wiltshire and KASH and

£5,000 each to Action on Homelessness, Gloucestershire Wildlife Rescue, London Narrow Boat Project, Mustard Tree and YMCA Cardiff.

Exclusions Grants are given to registered charities only.

Applications In writing to the correspondent, including a copy of the most recent accounts. The trust does not wish to receive telephone calls.

Princess Anne's Charities

Children, medical, welfare, general

£114,000 (2001/02)

Beneficial area UK.

Buckingham Palace, London SW1A 1AA

Correspondent Capt. N Wright

Trustees *Hon. M T Bridges; Commodore T J H Laurence; B Hammond.*

CC Number 277814

Information available Accounts were on file at the Charity Commission, but without a list of grants.

General This trust has general charitable purposes, with a preference for charities or organisations in which The Princess Royal has a particular interest.

In 2001/02 the trust had assets of £3.9 million, which generated an income of £107,000. After high management and administration costs of £148,000, grants were made totalling £114,000.

No information was contained in the accounts as to which organisations were supported, although they were broken down as follows (2000/01 figures in brackets):

	2001/02	*2000/01*
Children and youth	£34,000	£54,000
Environment	£16,500	£5,000
Medical	£20,000	£23,000
Social welfare	£41,000	£48,000
Education	nil	£23,000
Animals	nil	£7,000
Armed forces	nil	£6,500
General	£2,000	£2,000

Exclusions No grants to individuals.

Applications Trustees meet to consider applications in January, and applications need to be received by November. 'The trustees are not anxious to receive unsolicited general applications as these are unlikely to be successful and only increase the cost of administration of the charity.'

The Priory Foundation

Health and social welfare, especially children

£198,000 (1998)

Beneficial area UK.

20 Thayer Street, London W10 2DD

Correspondent The Trustees

Trustees *N W Wray; L E Wray; M Kelly; T W Bunyard.*

CC Number 295919

Information available Accounts were on file at the Charity Commission.

General The trust was established in 1987 to make donations to charities and appeals that directly benefit children.

In 2003 the trust had an income of £61,000 and a total expenditure of £363,000. Further information for this year was not available.

In 2001 it had an income of £209,000 and a total expenditure of £340,000. Unfortunately no further details were available for this year. In 1998 it had assets of £4.5 million, having increased from £2.1 million in 1995 following realised and unrealised gains on investments. Over 600 grants were given, totalling £198,000.

The largest grants were to the London Borough of Barnet for social needs cases (over £30,000), and over £5,000 each to ABCD, Birthright and MEP.

Most of the remaining grants were under £1,000 with beneficiaries including Action for Sick Children, ChildLine, Disability Aid Fund, East Belfast Mission, Sandy Gall's Afghanistan Appeal, Teenage Trust Cancer Appeal and Training Ship Broadsword. Most grants were one-off and given to UK organisations.

Applications In writing to the correspondent.

Prison Service Charity Fund

General

About £70,000 (2001)

Beneficial area UK.

68 Hornby Road, Walton, Liverpool L9 3DF

Tel. 0151 524 0537

Correspondent The Trustees

Trustees *A N Joseph, Chair; D Magill; C F Smith; Revd P Beaman; P McFall; R Howard.*

CC Number 801678

Information available Accounts were on file at the Charity Commission.

General The trust's accounts included the following narrative, describing how the trust was started: 'Having started a cash collection to assist in the treatment of a very sick local child, Liverpool's [prison] staff were obliged to seek help from other prisons nationwide, in order to achieve their financial goal. This resulted in us receiving considerably more money than we needed for our appeal and we used the spare cash to launch the Prison Service Charity Fund.' The charity is now an established fundraiser and grant-making trust.

In 2003 the fund had an income of £150,000 and a total expenditure of £122,000. No further information for this year was available on file at the Charity Commission.

In 2001 the fund had assets totalling around £430,000, an income of £116,000 and a total expenditure of £83,000. Most of the fund's income is raised through various fundraising efforts by prison staff. Grants totalled around £70,000.

The trust stated that the fund is 'for the staff, run by the staff'; the staff comprises 5–6,000 members of the Prison Service. The trust does not accept outside applications, and the person making the application has got to be a member of staff.

During the previous financial year, grants were made to almost 100 organisations, mostly local charities nationwide. Grants were mainly for less than £1,000 each.

Previous beneficiaries include: Donna Rose Appeal – Frankland, Jim McDermott Heart Foundation – Wetherby, ACROSS Trust – Frankland, Prison Service Special Games – Grendon, Joshua Walter Trust – Nottinghamshire, Spirit of Freedom – Lindholm, Dr

Naquis Heart Fund Appeal – Manchester, Leeds Prison Service, Leicester Oncology Cancer Unit and Susan White Appeal – Dartmoor.

Applications The trust does not accept outside applications – the person making the application has to be a member of staff.

The Privy Purse Charitable Trust

General

£259,000 (2002/03)

Beneficial area UK.

Buckingham Palace, London SW1A 1AA

Tel. 020 7930 4832

Email privypurse@royal.gov.uk

Correspondent Ian McGregor, Trustee

Trustees *Sir M C Peat; G N Kennedy; I McGregor; P A Reid.*

CC Number 296079

Information available Accounts were on file at the Charity Commission, but with only a brief narrative report and without a full grants list.

General This trust supports a wide range of causes, giving grants to UK-wide and local charities.

In 2002/03 the trust had assets of £1.4 million with an income of £113,000 and grants totalling £259,000.

The trust has broken down its grant distribution and below is a small example:

Aged
£500 to Sandringham Seniors Club, £300 each to Ballater Day Centre and Parish of Upper Donside, £200 each to Age Concern, Dersingham Seniors Club and Ballater Day Centre, £150 each to Royal Surgical Aid Society and Dersingham Meals on Wheels and £100 to Dersingham Day Centre for the Elderly.

Animals
£450 to Battersea Dogs Home, £300 each to Animal Health Trust and Cleveland Bay Horse Society, £250 to International League for the Protection of Horses and £150 each to Royal Veterinary College, Royal Society for the Prevention of Cruelty to Animals and Fell Pony Society.

Armed Services
£650 to Not Forgotten Association, £300 each to Royal British Legion, King George's Fund for Sailors, Army Benevolent Fund, RAF Benevolent Fund and SSAFA, £150 each to Royal School Hampstead, Royal School Bath and Portsmouth Royal Sailors Club, £100 each to Argyll & Sutherland Highlanders Regimental Association, Blues and Royals Comrades Association and Royal Artillery Association.

Children and Youth
£500 to Crathie School Sport Fund, £400 to Friends of the Sandcastle Children's Home, £300 each to Barnardo's, First Dersingham Scout Group and First Sandringham Guide Company, £200 each to Church Lads and Church Girls Brigade, Prince's Trust & Royal Jubilee Trusts and National Council of YMCA's and £150 each to British and Foreign School Society, Gordon Boys School and Children's Country Holidays Fund.

Cultural
£500 to Royal Academy Trust: Art World, £400 to Royal Geographical Society, £250 to Haddo House Hall Arts Trust, £150 each to GLC Royal Female School of Art, Queen Mary's London Needlework Guild, Royal Academy of Dancing, Royal College of Music and Royal Commonwealth Society.

Disabilities
£600 to Park House, £500 to Guide Dogs for the Blind Association, £250 each to Shaw Trust, Norfolk and Norwich Association for the Blind and Royal Aberdeen Workshop for the Blind, £150 each to Shaftesbury Society and Riding for the Disabled and £100 to Saving Sight in Grampian.

Ecclesiastical
£45,000 to Chapel Royal St James's Palace, £41,000 to Chapel Royal Hampton Court Palace, £9,000 to Chapel Royal Windsor Great Park, £200 each to Anmer Church and Bircham Church.

Education
£33,000 to Chorister School Fees.

Environments
£3,000 to Upper Deeside Access Trust, £300 each to Game Conservancy Trust and Game Conservancy (Scottish Grouse Research) and £100 each to Royal Windsor Rose & Horticultural Society and Royal South Bucks Agricultural Association.

Family Welfare
£300 each to RELATE and Military Knights Widows Benevolent Fund, £200 to Family Welfare Association and £150 to National Association for Maternal and Child Welfare.

Applications The trust makes donations to a wide variety of charities, but does not respond to applications.

The John Pryor Charitable Trust

Medical research, homelessness

£38,000 (2001/02)

Beneficial area UK.

The Old Cricketers, Passfield, Nr Liphook, Hampshire GU30 7RU

Correspondent Mrs J H Pryor, Trustee

Trustees *Mrs J H Pryor; M F Cook; A W Cook; Mrs E Dixon.*

CC Number 275605

Information available Information was provided by the trust. Accounts were on file at the Charity Commission, but without a list of grants.

General The trust has a preference for medical charities, but supports other causes, including a few homeless charities. Both one-off and ongoing grants can be made. In 2001/02 it had assets of £728,000 and an income of £21,000. Grants were made totalling £38,000. Further information was not available.

Exclusions No grants to individuals.

Applications The trust advises that no applications from new charities can be considered as all funds are going to charities already supported, and therefore sending expensive literature is a waste of resources. Telephone calls are not welcome.

The Puebla Charitable Trust

Community development work, relief of poverty

£90,000 (2002/03)

Beneficial area Worldwide.

Ensors, Cardinal House, 46 St Nicholas Street, Ipswich IP1 1TT

Tel. 01473 220 022

Correspondent The Clerk

Trustees *J Phipps; M A Strutt.*

CC Number 290055

Information available Accounts were on file at the Charity Commission.

General The trust has stated that: 'At present, the council limits its support to charities which assist the poorest sections of the population and community development work – either of these may be in urban or rural areas, both in the UK and overseas.'

Grants are normally in the region of £5,000 to £20,000, with support given over a number of years where possible. Most of the trust's income is therefore already committed, and the trust rarely supports new organisations.

In 2002/03 the trust had assets of £2.1 million with an income of £105,000 and grants totalling £90,000.

Grants include £20,000 to Wandsworth & Merton Law Centre, £15,000 each to Child Poverty Action Group and Shelter and £10,000 each to Medical Foundation for the Victims of Torture, Action on Disability & Development, Cambodian Trust and Immigrants Aid.

Exclusions No grants for capital projects, religious institutions, research or institutions for people who are disabled. Individuals are not supported and no scholarships are given.

Applications In writing to the correspondent. The trustees meet in July. The trust is unable to acknowledge applications.

The Pyke Charity Trust

Prisoners and disadvantaged communities

£89,000 (2003)

Beneficial area UK.

The Shieling, St Agnes, Cornwall TR5 0SS

Tel. 01871 553822

Correspondent Martin Ward, Administrator

Trustees *J Macpherson; T Harvie Clark.*

CC Number 296418

Information available Accounts were provided by the trust.

General The trustees have recently reviewed the aims and objectives of the trust. The trust will now concentrate the grants it awards to assisting small UK charities whose work does not readily attract popular support and where a grant from the trust can make a significant difference. The charities which will be considered for grants include those working for the rehabilitation of prisoners, before and after release and support for prisoners' families. The trust will also consider small local charities whose primary aim should be to improve the quality of life for the most severely disadvantaged communities or individuals.

Because of the size of the charity they are not usually able to help with the funding of a complete project and preference is given where the charity applying for help has less than six months running costs. Grants are not normally given to charities whose income is in excess of £400,000.

In 2003 it had assets of £2.9 million and an income of £112,000. Grants totalled £89,000 and were broken down as follows:

	Total 2003	*%*	*Total 2002*	*%*
Disabled	£17,000	12%	£4,000	7%
General	£50,000	23%	£21,000	3%
Medical	£1,500	2%	£3,000	6%
Old people	£3,000	3%	£500	1%
Youth	£7,500	7%	–	–
Individuals	£500	1%	£1,000	2%
School fees	£8,900	7%	£24,000	45%

Awards of £1,000 or more were listed in the accounts. The largest grants were £7,000 to Samaritans – North Devon, £5,500 to Elizabeth Finn Trust and £5,000 each to Samaritans of Cornwall and St John's Memorial Hall Project. Other grants over £1,000 included Active 8, Detainees Support Unit, Hopscotch, St Teath Church Hall Project and West Sussex Association for the Disabled (£3,000 each), North Devon Housing Association (£2,500), Family Mediation Scotland, Greenwich Toy Library, Music Alive and Universal Beneficent Society (£2,000 each) and Spires (£1,500).

Grants of £1,000 went to Ace of Clubs, Arthritis Care – Woking, Cornwall Mobility Centre, Crossover Family Project, Family and Carers Trust, Grenleg Village Hall, Inneland and Toward Family Project, Multiple Sclerosis Therapy Centre, Positive Youth, Prisoners Advice Service and Woking Gallaries.

Please note: The trust has recently reviewed its giving policy and the grant breakdown and examples of individual grants includes beneficiaries that may no longer be supported.

Exclusions The trust no longer accepts applications from individuals, applications for assistance with school fees, charities involved in medical projects, animal welfare or those whose aim is soley to promote religious beliefs.

Applications The trust has previously stated that 'normally the trustees approach charities that they know well and respect to offer support, occasionally they consider applications received from small local charities where a grant, if approved, can be seen to be used for direct charitable expenditure in support of the aims laid down by the applicant charity'.

Quercus Trust

Arts, general

£133,000 (2002/03)

Beneficial area UK.

Chantrey Vellacott, Russell Square House, 10–12 Russell Square, London WC1B 5LF

Tel. 020 7509 9000

Correspondent A C Langridge, Trustee

Trustees *Lord Bernstein of Craigwell; A C Langridge; Kate E Bernstein; Lady Bernstein.*

CC Number 1039205

Information available Full accounts were on file at the Charity Commission.

General In February 1999 the trustees declared by deed that distributions would in future be directed principally (but not exclusively) to the arts and any other objects and purposes which seek to further public knowledge, understanding and appreciation of any matters of artistic, aesthetic, scientific or historical interest.

In 2002/03 the trust had assets of £38 million and an income of £116,000. Grants totalled £133,000 with the beneficiary of the largest grant being the Royal National Theatre who received £54,000. Other beneficiaries included Siobhan Davies Dance Company (£21,000), Royal Court Theatre (£12,000), Artangel (£10,000), Dance Umbrella Limited and Stowe Collection of Contemporary Sculpture (£5,000 each), Wigmore Hall Trust (£3,700), Royal Opera House Foundation (£3,400), Roundhouse Trust (£3,000) and Guggenheim UK Charitable Trust (£2,800).

Exclusions No grants to individuals.

Applications In writing to the correspondent, but please note, the trust states: 'All of the trust's funds are currently earmarked for existing projects. The trust has a policy of not making donations to individuals and the trustees regret that, in order to keep administrative costs to a minimum, they are unable to reply to any unsuccessful applicants.'

R S Charitable Trust

Jewish, welfare

£159,000 (2002)

Beneficial area UK.

138 Stamford Hill, London N16 6QT

Correspondent Max Freudenberger, Trustee

Trustees *M Freudenberger; Mrs M Freudenberger; H C Freudenberger; S N Freudenberger; C Margulies.*

CC Number 1053660

Information available Accounts were on file at the Charity Commission.

General Established in 1996, this trust states that it supports Jewish organisations and other bodies working towards the relief of poverty.

In 2002/03 the trust had an income of £519,000 and a total expenditure of £457,000. Although submitted to the Charity Commission, further account information was not available on file.

In 2002 the trust had assets of £1.4 million, an income of £675,000 and made grants totalling £166,000. Grant beneficiaries included British Friends of Tzhenoble (£50,000), Yeshiva Horomo (£16,000), Society of the Friends of the Torah and Torah Vechesed Leezra Vesad (£15,000 each), Torah Learning Centre (£12,000), Friends of Horim Establishments (£6,000), Beis Rochel Institution (£5,500) and Beis Aharon Institution, The Rehabilitation Trust and Vayoel Moshe Charitable Trust (£5,000 each).

Applications In writing to the correspondent.

The R V W Trust

Music education and appreciation, relief of need for musicians

£287,000 (2002)

Beneficial area UK.

16 Ogle Street, London W1W 6JA

Tel. 020 7255 2590 **Fax** 020 7255 2591

Correspondent Helen Faulkner, Secretary/Administrator

Trustees *Michael Kennedy, Chair; Lord Armstrong of Ilminster; Sir John Manduell; Mrs Ralph Vaughan Williams; Hugh Cobbe.*

CC Number 1066977

Information available Information was provided by the trust.

General The trust's current grant-making policies are as follows:

- to give assistance to British composers who have not yet achieved a national reputation
- to give assistance towards the performance and recording of music by neglected or currently unfashionable 20th century British composers, including performances by societies and at festivals which include works by such composers in their programmes
- to assist UK organisations that promote public knowledge and appreciation of 20th and 21st century British music
- to assist education projects in the field of music.

In 2002 the trust had assets of £1.4 million and an income of £291,000. Grants were made totalling £287,000.

In 2001 the trust had assets of £1.4 million and an income of £332,000, mainly from royalties from the musical works of Ralph Vaughan Williams paid through the Performing Rights Society. Grants were paid to 106 beneficiaries and totalled £387,000. They were broken down in the following categories:

	No.	*Total*
Public performance	63	£127,000
Music festivals	15	£49,000
Public education	13	£161,000
Education grants	15	£50,000

The largest grants were given to British Music Information Centre (£87,500), Society for the Promotion of New Music (£60,000), BBC Philharmonic Orchestra (£22,000), Huddersfield Contemporary Music Festival (£20,000), Royal Philharmonic Society (£18,000) and Sinfonia 21 (£15,000).

Grants ranging from £1,200 to £8,000 were given to beneficiaries including Oxford Bach Choir, Classico Records, Almeida Theatre, Between the Notes, London Guildhall University, Lichfield Cathedral Special Choir, Brighton Festival, Bournemouth Symphony Orchestra, Dartington International Summer School, Hampstead and Highgate Festival, Hereford Choral Society, York Late Music Festival, Birmingham Ensemble and Contemporary Music Making for Amateurs.

Smaller grants below £1,000 totalled £41,000.

Exclusions No grants for local authority or other government-funded bodies, nor degree courses, except first Masters' degrees in musical composition. No support for dance or drama courses. No grants for workshops without public performance, private vocal or instrumental tuition or the purchase or repair of musical instruments. No grants for concerts that do not include music by 20th and 21st century composers or for musicals, rock, pop, ethnic, jazz or dance music. No grants for the construction or restoration of buildings.

Applications In writing to the correspondent, giving project details, at least two months before the trustees meet. Trustees' meetings are held in February, June and October. Masters in Music Composition applicants will only be considered at the June meeting; applications must be received by the middle of April. Further details are available from the trust.

The Monica Rabagliati Charitable Trust

Human and animal welfare, education and medical care and research in the UK

£54,000 (2001/02)

Beneficial area UK.

S G Hambros Trust Company Limited, S G House , 41 Tower Hill, London EC3N 4SG

Tel. 020 7597 3000 **Fax** 020 7597 9263

Correspondent Mrs Shirley Baines

Trustees *S G Hambros Trust Company Limited; R C McLean*

CC Number 1086368

Information available Accounts were on file at the Charity Commission.

General This trust was registered with the Charity Commission in April 2001. In 2001/02 it had assets amounting to £1.7 million. It had an income of £59,000 and out of a total expenditure of £80,000, grants totalled £54,000. The sum of £26,000 was spent on management and administration costs.

There were 30 grants made in the range of £500 and £10,000. Beneficiaries included: RNLI (£10,000); Ironmongers' Company (£6,000), Jubilee Appeal for Commonwealth Veterans (£5,000); Hereford Cathedral and Salvation Army (£2,500 each); DEBRA (£2,000); Helen Arkell Dyslexia Centre (£1,500); Army Benevolent Fund, Atlantic Council for Peace, Centrepoint, Children with Leukaemia Trust, Gurkha Welfare Trust and Treloar Trust (£1,000 each); and Battersea Dogs' Home, Sight Savers international, Spitalfield's Festival and Trinity Hospice (£500 each).

Applications 'The charity does not solicit applications, but considers all relevant applications and the the trustees give such applications fair consideration.'

The Radcliffe Trust

Music, crafts, conservation

£281,000 (2001/02)

Beneficial area UK.

5 Lincoln's Inn Fields, London WC2A 3BT

Tel. 020 7405 1234

Correspondent John Burden, Secretary to the Trustees

Trustees *Lord Cottesloe, Chair; Lord Quinton; Lord Balfour of Burleigh; Christopher J Butcher; Dr Ivor F Guest.*

CC Number 209212

Information available Full accounts were provided by the trust.

General The trust's annual report has stated: 'The Radcliffe Trust was founded in 1714 by the will of Dr John Radcliffe, the most prominent physician of his day, who left his residuary estate for the income to be applied for general charitable purposes.

'The trustees' present grant-making policy is concentrated in two main areas – music and the crafts – but they may consider applications which do not fall within those two categories provided that they do not come with the exclusions listed below.

'In the area of music they operate a scheme under which the Allegri Quartet make regular visits to a selected number of universities and other centres, master-classes and teaching sessions. As a further development of this scheme the trustees have appointed John Cooney as composer-in-association with the Allegri Quartet. The trustees have also initiated a highly successful series of specialist seminars in double-reed playing and on the technology of pianos. In addition the trustees make grants for classical music education, but they do not accept applications from individuals .

'In the area of crafts, the main thrust is the support of craft training among young people both at the level of apprenticeships (mostly, but not exclusively, in cathedral workshops) and also at the postgraduate and post-experience levels. This can be by way of direct grants to employers, contributions to bursaries or other awards on offer to students or interns at appropriate training establishments, or support for the setting up of relevant new posts or courses at such institutions. For other grants, the trustees' main concern is to achieve a standard of excellence in crafts related particularly to conservation. The trustees monitor the progress of projects for which grants are made, particularly those which are spread over a period of more than one year, in which cases satisfactory progress reports are required as a condition of later instalments being paid .

'The trustees make small grants for the repair and conservation of church furniture, including bells and monuments. Such grants are made in England through the Council for the Care of Churches and in Scotland through the Scottish Churches Architectural Heritage Trust; direct applications are not accepted. Grants are not made for structural repairs to church buildings, nor for organs.

'Miscellaneous applications which do not fall within the above categories may be considered subject to availability of surplus income, but the following categories are excluded:

- construction, conversion, repair or maintenance of buildings
- grants directly to individuals for education fees or maintenance
- sponsoring of musical and theatrical performances
- medical research
- social welfare
- support of excellence.

'The trustees are only empowered to make grants to bodies with charitable status, and do not make grants to clear or reduce past deficits.'

In 2001/02 it had assets of £9.9 million, which generated an income of £379,000. Grants were made totalling £281,000, broken down as follows:

Crafts – 23 grants totalling £161,000

The largest grants were £20,000 to Scottish Lime Centre Trust for a training manager, £17,000 to Scottish Maritime Museum for shipwright apprenticeship training, £13,000 to Council for the Care of Churches for conservation grants to seven places of worship, £11,000 to Meridian Trust Association for shipwright apprenticeship training and £10,000 each to Leather Conservation Centre for student placements and Textile Conservation Centre for student bursaries.

Other beneficiaries included Weald and Downland Open Air Museum towards an adult conservation office (£8,000), Historic Chapels Trust for the conservation and repair of stained glass windows (£6,000), Lincoln Cathedral Preservation Council for graduate training in conservation studies (£3,200), Edward Barnsley Educational Trust for an apprenticeship in cabinet making (£3,000), Orton Trust for tutorial fees and course bursaries (£2,500) and Dean and Chapter of Carlisle for an apprenticeship in stonemasoning (£1,500).

Music – 24 grants totalling £99,000

The largest grants were £11,000 to Allegri String Quartet for residency costs and £10,000 to Royal College of Music towards researching and editing a performance of Haydn string quartets.

Other recipients included City of Birmingham Symphony Orchestra for a choral programme for young people (£6,000), Scottish Borders Community Orchestra for instruments (£5,000), London Sinfornia for bursaries for young composers (£3,500), Youth Music Centre – Barnet for bursaries for summer and weekend courses (£3,000), Yorke Trust for an educational composition project in Norfolk (£2,500), Council for Music in Hospital for a series of live concerts (£2,000) and Opera Group towards an education workshop with performances (£1,000).

Miscellaneous – 8 grants totalling £20,000

The largest grant, of £10,000, went to Cumbria Community Foundation in response to the foot and mouth epidemic. Other recipients were Sir Ralph Verney Memorial Fund (£5,000), Oxford University Chest and Barbara Whatmore Charitable Trust (£2,000 each), Victoria and Albert Museum (£750), St Bart's Hospital (£600), PCC St Mary's and St Giles' (£25) and Ratcliffe School Welfare Fund for science prizes (£15).

Exclusions No grants to individual applicants. No grants to non-registered charities, or to clear or reduce past debts.

Applications 'Applications for music grants are short-listed for consideration by a panel of musicians who make recommendations, where appropriate; recommended applications are then placed before the trustees for decision. The music panel usually meets in March and October in advance of the trustees' meetings in June and December, and applications should be submitted by the end of January and the end of August respectively to allow time for any further particulars (if so required) to be furnished.'

Applications for miscellaneous grants should be in writing and received by the end of April for consideration at the June meeting, or by October for consideration at the December meeting.

The Ragdoll Foundation

Children and the arts

£60,000 (2002/03)

Beneficial area UK and worldwide.

Timothy's Bridge Road, Stratford upon Avon, Warwickshire CV37 9NQ

Tel. 01789 404100

Email info@ragdollfoundation.org.uk

Website www.ragdollfoundation.org.uk

Correspondent The Trustees

Trustees *Anne Wood; Mark Hollingsworth; Katherine Wood; Peter Thornton.*

CC Number 1078998

Information available Information was provided by the foundation and is available on its website.

General The foundation's website states:

'The Ragdoll Foundation is dedicated to developing the power of imaginative responses in children through the arts. It owns 15% of its parent company and springs from the same philosophical roots. This can be summed up by the quotation from Sylvia Ashton-Warner in her book *Teacher* which has greatly influenced Anne's work:

"I see the mind of a five year old as a volcano with two vents; destructiveness and creativeness. And I can see that to the extent that we widen the creative channel, we atrophy the destructive one".

'The foundation is governed by a board of trustees, chaired by Katherine Wood, and administered by one Ragdoll member of staff with some additional professional support from Ragdoll the company. It is funded entirely from its share of the profits of the company.'

Ragdoll Foundation Guidelines

'The primary purpose is to make grants for charitable purposes around the world that:

- 'promote the development of children through children's imaginative thinking
- 'encourage innovation and innovative thinking and influence good practice elsewhere
- 'offer creative solutions that deal with the causes of problems in childhood
- 'ensures effective evaluation of projects to promote sharing and learning
- 'above all demonstrate how the voices of children can be heard.

'Furthermore the Ragdoll Foundation aims to:

- 'provide a space for alternative thinking, voices and practices. A factory of creative ideas, that is self confident, not afraid to take risks, where people can innovate, be creative, demonstrate and share ideas
- 'seek new creative solutions problems, promote new approaches to creativity and innovation. Combining perspectives, cultures and disciplines
- 'work on all stages in the creative process, generating ideas and following through on implementation.
- 'collaborate and share knowledge - Create connections and maintain the ability to be responsive. Seek partners to help in achieving their aims develop meaningful relationships with the funded groups that are based on shared values.
- 'promote a culture of innovation and creativity, identify exemplary cases of innovation, fund pilot projects, showing how and where it made a difference.
- 'invest in research, supporting the groups in their learning.
- 'support co-operative ventures across sectors.

'Preference will be given to original projects which are in the spirit and share the same values of the Ragdoll Foundation being imaginative, creative and innovative. In particular those projects which show a true understanding of how to listen to children and allow the voices of children themselves to be heard.

'We will focus mainly on applications which involve children during their early years, but appropriate projects for older children will not be dismissed without consideration.

'The trustees wish to make a range of grants available. We will consider a large scale grant, but it is anticipated that the majority will range from £500 - £20,000.'

It goes on to state:

'Grants will also be made to projects, organisations or individuals through personal recommendation or knowledge of those connected with the foundation.'

Models and methodologies

'We wish to encourage and promote new ways of working, people who want to:

- 'seek to facilitate new partnerships
- 'share ideas and contacts
- 'working across boundaries
- 'support pilot projects.

'We will be highlighting good examples of this work on our website [www.ragdollfoundation.org.uk] next year [2005].'

Research and advocacy

'We wish to develop our advocacy role and will therefore take an active role in projects where appropriate. We also wish to:

- 'pioneer new research
- 'support innovative ideas
- 'support learning and new ways of thinking
- 'work with hard to reach children.'

In 2002/03 it had assets of £311,000 and an income of £72,000, mostly through donations, gifts and legacies. Grants were made totalling £60,000.

The largest grants were £10,000 to Hearts and Minds for a roving unit of flying clown doctors for children in hospices and residential care across Britian, £8,000 to The Forge for a creative collaboration in Durham for pre-school children involving nurseries and creative artists and £6,000 each to Elmhurst Ballet School – London for student development and Side by Side – London for an inclusive therapeutic arts programme for two to eight year olds.

Other grants listed in the accounts were £5,000 each to Bath Opportunity Playgroup for a one-year pilot programme for art therapy for pre-school children with special needs and Young Carers – South Gloucestershire for a series of group activity days and creative workshops for young carers, £4,900 to Clown Doctors to develop training, videos and workshops which will lead to an accepted way of working and a standard of excellence, £2,900 to Northern Ballet Theatre for a summer school offering places to children who have not had the opportunity to participate in ballet before, £2,000 to Burton Street Arts Project for a creative arts programme for children and £400 to Radyr and Morganstown Brass Band for the purchase of ensemble format music, mouth pieces and equipment.

Exclusions Grants are not given for:

- replacement of statutory funding
- work that has already started or will have been completed whilst the application is being considered
- promotion of religion
- animal welfare charities
- vehicles
- emergency relief work
- general fundraising or marketing appeals
- open ended funding arrangements
- loans or business advice
- charities which are in serious deficit
- holidays
- any large capital, endowment or widely distributed appeal.

Applications On a short form available from the correspondent, preferably by e-mail if possible (sent to karenn@ragdollfoundation.org.uk). Completed forms should be submitted with an inspirational paragraph summarising the project (one side of A4 maximum). Once these appeals have been successful there are other short stages to overcome before the grant is approved. Further information on these stages are available on receipt of the application form, or from the foundation's website.

The Rainford Trust

Social welfare, general

£101,000 (2001/02)

Beneficial area Worldwide, with a preference for areas in which Pilkington plc have works and offices, especially St Helens and Merseyside.

c/o Pilkington plc, Prescot Road, St Helens, Merseyside WA10 3TT

Tel. 01744 20574 **Fax** 01744 20574

Correspondent W H Simm, Secretary

Trustees *Mrs J Graham; A L Hopkins; Mrs A J Moseley; H Pilkington; Lady Pilkington; R E Pilkington; R G Pilkington; Mrs I Ratiu.*

CC Number 266157

Information available Full accounts were provided by the trust.

General The trust confirmed that its current policy is as follows:

'To consider applications from organisations that aim to enhance the quality of community life. To help initiate and promote special projects by charitable organisations which seek to provide new kinds of employment. To assist programmes whose objects are the provision of medical care, including holistic medicine, the advancement of education and the arts, and the improvement of the environment. Applications from religious bodies and individuals will be considered if they fall within the scope of these aims.

'Although the trust will continue to give preference to applications from St Helens (as stated in the trust deed), and from other main Pilkington UK areas, this does not prejudice the trustees' discretion to help charities that operate outside these areas.'

In 2001/02 the trust had assets of £4.7 million and an income of £283,000. Grants were made to 118 organisations, totalling £101,000.

The largest grants were £6,000 to Clonter Opera for All, £5,000 to Citadel Arts Centre, £2,000 each to Foundation for the Prevention of Blindness and VSO, £1,300 to Dumfries and Galloway Action and £1,200 to Farm Africa.

Other grants in St Helens included £1,000 to Rainford Carers; Support Group, St Helens Choral Society, St Helens and District Mencap Society, St Helens and District Women's Aid and St Helens and Knowsley Cystic Fibrosis Support Group, £750 to Knowsley Carers' Centre, £500 to 1st Rainford (10th St Helens) Scout Group, Pilkington Rec ARLFC and St Helens Group of Advanced Motorists and £100 to St Helens Metropolitan Borough Council for the Rainford Gallery.

Beneficiaries elsewhere on Merseyside included Royal Liverpool Philharmonic Society, Royal School for the Blind – Liverpool and Weston Spirit (£1,000 each), Merseyside and Deeside Outward Bound Association, Merseyside Police and High Sheriff's Charitable Trust and Wirral Society of the Blind and Partially Sighted (£500 each) and Royal Tank Regiment – Merseyside branch (£250)

Overseas recipients included ApTibeT, Leprosy Mission, Mission Aviation Fellowship (£1,000 each), Tibet Relief Fund for the United Kingdom (£750) and ADFAM International and International Community Trust for Health and Educational Services (£500 each).

Other grants included £1,000 each to British Deaf Association and University of Southampton School of Medicine, £750 to Sheffield Cathedral and £500 each to Bath Institute of Medical Engineering, Canine Partners for Independence, CommunicAbility and In Kind Direct.

Exclusions Funding for the arts is restricted to St Helens only. Applications from individuals for grants for educational purposes will be considered only from applicants who are normally resident in St Helens.

Applications On a form available from the correspondent. Applications should be accompanied by a copy of the latest accounts and cost data on projects for which funding is sought. Applicants may apply at any time. Only successful applications will be acknowledged.

The Peggy Ramsay Foundation

Writers and writing for the stage

£116,000 to organisations (2001)

Beneficial area British Isles.

Harbottle & Lewis Solicitors, Hanover House, 14 Hanover Square, London W1S 1HP

Tel. 020 7667 5000 **Fax** 020 7667 5100
Email laurence.harbottle@harbottle.com
Website www.peggyramsayfoundation.org
Correspondent G Laurence Harbottle, Trustee

Trustees *Laurence Harbottle; Simon Cowell; Michael Codron; Sir David Hare; Baroness (Genista) McIntosh of Hudnall; John Tydeman; Harriet Walker; John Welch.*

CC Number 1015427

Information available Full accounts were provided by the trust.

General This trust exists to help writers and writing for the stage. It was established from Peggy Ramsay's personal estate in accordance with her will. The objectives of the foundation are:

- the advancement of education by the encouragement of the art of writing
- the relief of poverty among those practising the arts, together with their dependants and relatives, with special reference to writers
- any charitable purpose which may, in the opinion of the trustees, achieve, assist in, or contribute to, the achievement of these objectives.

Grants are made to:

- writers who have some writing experience who need time to write and cannot otherwise afford to do so
- companies which might not otherwise be able to find, develop or use new work
- projects which may facilitate new writing for the stage.

In 2001 the trust had assets totalling £5 million and an income of £357,000. Grants were made to 54 beneficiaries, divided equally between organisations (27) and individuals (27), totalling £202,000. Grants to organisations amounted to £116,000, while individuals received £86,000. Management and administration costs totalled £57,000.

Grants made to organisations were mainly for initiatives to help individual writers to create new work. The foundation continues to support certain prizes such as the Alfred Fagon Award, the George Devine Award and the Society of Authors. There is a preference for concentrating more on encouraging new writing than rewarding success. All grants to individuals are made in cases of need to established writers of stage plays.

During the year the foundation created a new award to replace the Peggy Ramsay Play Award. While the Play Award supported new work, this was not an essential factor in its production, and so the new award requires managers to submit a project that they consider would encourage creative writing for the theatre. This was won by Paines Plough, which became entitled to £50,000 and received the first instalment of £10,000 in 2001. (In 2002 this award was given to Bush Theatre and amounted to £30,000.)

Apart from the Project Award, the largest grant was £20,000 to Theatre Centre Limited. Other beneficiaries included Contact Theatre (£6,500), Eastern Angles Theatre Company Limited (£6,000), Warehouse Theatre Company Limited (£6,000 in total), UK Arts Explore/Festcep, TAPS and The George Devine Memorial Fund (£5,000 each), The Ashton Group Contemporary Theatre Limited and Magnetic North Theatre Productions Limited (£4,000 each), Wilson Wilson Company and Production Line (£3,000), Artists in Exile – Gog Theatre, New Perspectives Theatre Company, PMA Award, Stellar Quines, Theatre & Beyond and Union Theatre (£2,000 each).

Exclusions No grants are made for productions or writing not for the theatre. Commissioning costs are often considered as part of production costs. Course fees are not considered. Aspiring writers without some production record are not usually considered.

Applications Applications should be made by writing a short letter, when there is a promising purpose not otherwise likely to be funded and which will help writers or writing for the stage. Grants are considered at four or five meetings during the year, although urgent appeals can be considered at other times. All appeals are usually acknowledged.

The Joseph & Lena Randall Charitable Trust

General

£105,000 (2002/03)

Beneficial area Worldwide.

Europa Residence, Place des Moulins, Monte-Carlo
Tel. 00 377 93 50 03 82 **Fax** 00 377 93 25 82 85
Correspondent D A Randall, Trustee

Trustees *D A Randall; B Y Randall.*

CC Number 255035

Information available Information was provided by the trust.

General It is the policy of this trust to provide regular support to a selection of charities.

In 2002/03 the trust's assets totalled £1.7 million, it had an income of £96,000 and 34 grants were made totalling £105,000. Beneficiaries included Aldenham School 400 Development Appeal, Diabetes UK, Glyndebourne Festival Opera, Imperial Cancer Research Campaign, London School of Economics and Political Science, and Royal Opera House Development Fund.

Exclusions No grants to individuals.

Applications In writing to the correspondent. The trust stated that funds were fully committed and that it was 'unable to respond to the many worthy appeals'.

Ranworth Trust

General

£211,000 (2001/02)

Beneficial area UK and developing countries, with a preference for Norfolk.

The Old House, Ranworth, Norwich NR13 6HS
Tel. 01603 270300
Correspondent Hon. Mrs J Cator, Trustee

Trustees *Hon. Mrs J Cator; F Cator; Mrs E A Thistlewayte; C F Cator.*

CC Number 292633

Information available Full accounts were on file at the Charity Commission.

General The trust has previously stated that the scope of charitable causes benefiting from the trust is varied and has covered such areas as medical research, local community, health and welfare and social charities in the Norfolk area, and national and international charities.

In 2001/02 the trust had assets of £4.3 million, due to the receipt of a donation of £2.9 million from one of the trustees in the form of shares in 1999/2000, and an income of £178,000. After administration costs of only £4,700, grants totalled £211,000. As in previous years the largest donation was made to Jubilee Sailing Trust for £25,000. Other larger grants included: £15,000 each to Intermediate Technology and Medicins Sans Frontier; £10,000 each to Cancer Research and Tree Aid; and £7,500 to Norfolk Wildlife Trust and Ormiston Trust Norwich Prison Visitors Centre.

Other donations included: £5,000 each to Eating Disorder Association and Norfolk and Norwich Association for the Blind; £4,100 to Aldburgh Poetry Trust; £3,000 each to Game Conservancy Trust, Norfolk and Families House and Rhino Rescue; £2,500 to Red Poll Cattle Society; £2,000 to Interfaith Centre and Raynaud's and Scleroderma Association; £1,500 to Fairhaven Church of England Primary School; £1,000 each to Jazzangles and S.A.N.D.S.; £500 to National Gardens Scheme; and £250 to VSO.

Applications In writing to the correspondent.

The Fanny Rapaport Charitable Settlement

Jewish, general

£71,000 (2002/03)

Beneficial area North west England.

Kuit Steinart Levy, 3 St Mary's Parsonage, Manchester M3 2RD

Tel. 0161 832 3434 **Fax** 0161 832 6650

Email janfidler@kuits.com

Correspondent J S Fidler, Trustee

Trustees *J S Fidler; N Marks.*

CC Number 229406

Information available Information was provided by the trust.

General The trust supports mainly, but not exclusively, Jewish charities and health and welfare organisations, with preference for the north west of England. As a result of the diminishing income of the trust, donations are almost always restricted to those charities which the trustees have supported in the last five to ten years. In 2002/03 the trust had an income of £32,000 and made grants totalling £71,000. Unfortunately a breakdown of this total was not provided by the trust. However we do know that previous beneficiaries have included Christie Hospital NHS Trust, Delamere Forest School, Manchester Charitable Trust, Disabled Living and Derian House Children's Hospice.

Exclusions No grants to individuals.

Applications Trustees hold meetings twice a year in March/April and September/October with cheques for donations issued shortly thereafter. If the applicant does not receive a cheque by the end of April or October, the application will have been unsuccessful. No applications acknowledged.

The Ratcliff Foundation

General

£181,000 (2001/02)

Beneficial area UK, with a preference for local charities in the Midlands, North Wales and Gloucestershire.

c/o Clement Keys, 39/40 Calthorpe Road, Edgbaston, Birmingham B15 1TS

Tel. 0121 456 4456 **Fax** 0121 200 1614

Email chris.gupwell@feltonandco.co.uk

Correspondent C J Gupwell, Secretary

Trustees *Miss C M Ratcliff; E H Ratcliff; D M Ratcliff; J M G Fea; Mrs G M Thorpe; C J Gupwell.*

CC Number 222441

Information available Full accounts were on file at the Charity Commission.

General The trust was established in 1961, by Martin Rawlinson Ratcliff. In 2001/02 it had assets of £3 million, with an income of £212,000 from investments and an additional £69,000 from the F R Ratcliff Charitable Settlement. Management and administration costs were high at £33,000, over 10% of the income.

A total of £181,000 was given in 73 grants in the range of £1,000 to £23,000. Major grants included £23,000 to Holy Trinity Belfry Appeal – Conwy, £11,000 to CRAB Appeal for Cancer Research – Birmingham and £10,000 to Birmingham Parish Church Renewal Campaign.

Other larger grants included £6,300 to Acorn Children's Hospice Trust, £5,000 each to Cancer Research Campaign – Kemerton and St Nicholas' Church – Kemerton, £4,000 to YMCA Birmingham, £3,500 to British Blind Sport, £3,300 to Birmingham Federation of Clubs for Young People and £3,000 each to Extra Care, Hearing Dogs for Deaf People, Myton Hamlet Hospice, Soil Association, Tewkesbury Welfare & Volunteer Centre and Warwickshire Wildlife Trust.

The accounts show the grants grouped under the name of each individual trustee. This may be due to the trustees preferring particular causes and living in different areas. Grants have shown an interest in health/disability, social welfare, children/youth, wildlife/conservation/environment and education causes. The trustees have a preference for Worcester/Gloucester, Birmingham/Midlands, Warwickshire and Wales.

Organisations to benefit include Avoncroft Museum of Historic Buildings, British Blind Sport, CBSO Society Ltd, Devon Wildlife Trust, Dogs for the Disabled, Elgar School of Music, Motability, Pershore Theatre Arts Association, Roundabout, St David's Hospice, Tewkesbury Hospital League of Friends, Well Trust and YMCA Birmingham.

Exclusions No grants to individuals.

Applications In writing to the correspondent, by 30 November for consideration by trustees in following January. Grants made once a year only, by 31 March.

The Ratcliffe Charitable Trust

General

£37,000 (1999/2000)

Beneficial area UK.

Messrs Barlows, 55 Quarry Street, Guildford, Surrey GU1 3UE

Tel. 01483 562901

Correspondent The Trustees

Trustees *James Arthur Brett; Timothy Christopher James Adams.*

CC Number 802320

Information available Accounts were on file at the Charity Commission.

General This trust makes grants for general charitable purposes. In 2003/04 it had an income of £19,000 and a total expenditure of £51,000. Further information for this year was not available.

In 1999/2000 it had assets of £816,000 and gave grants totalling £37,000. A list of beneficiaries was not available for the year.

However, in 1998/99 the trust gave grants of £1,500 each to Barnardos, Family Holiday Association, New Martin Community Youth Trust, Motor Neurone Disease Association, Orchdale Vale Trust Limited, VSO, Cancer Care Dorset, GUTS, British Council for the Prevention of Blindness, British Laser Appeal, Save the Children, Brainwave, Compaid Trust, Chicks (camping for inner city kids) and South West Thames Kidney Fund.

Applications In writing to the correspondent.

The E L Rathbone Charitable Trust

Education and welfare of women, alleviation of poverty

£73,000 (2002/03)

Beneficial area UK, with a strong preference for Merseyside.

Rathbones, Port of Liverpool Building, Pier Head, Liverpool L3 1NW

Tel. 0151 236 6666

Correspondent The Trustees

Trustees *Miss E J Cotton; Mrs S K Rathbone; Mrs V P Rathbone; R S Rathbone.*

CC Number 233240

Information available Accounts were on file at the Charity Commission, without a list of grants.

General There is a strong preference for Merseyside with local beneficiaries receiving the major funding. The trust has a special interest in social work charities. In 2002/03 it had assets of £1.4 million, an income of £69,000 and gave grants totalling £73,000. Further information for this year was not available.

Previous beneficiaries have included Action for ME, Brunswick Boys' Club, Crosby Victim Support, FWAG, Garston CAB, Sheila Kay Fund, Liverpool Deaf Children's Society, Liverpool Playhouse, LPSS, Rathbone Society, River Mersey Inshore Rescue, St John's Hospice, Walton & District Family Support Group and YMCA.

Exclusions No grants to individuals seeking support for second degrees.

Applications In writing to the correspondent.

The Eleanor Rathbone Charitable Trust

Merseyside, women, unpopular causes

£223,000 (2003/04)

Beneficial area UK, with the major allocation for Merseyside; also women-focused international projects.

3 Sidney Avenue, Wallasey, Merseyside CH45 9JL

Email eleanor.rathbone.trust@tinyworld.co.uk

Website www.eleanorrathbonetrust.org

Correspondent Lindsay Keenan, Administrator

Trustees *W Rathbone; Ms Jenny Rathbone; A Rathbone; Lady Morgan.*

CC Number 233241

Information available Information was provided by the trust.

General The trust concentrates its support largely on the following:

- charities and charitable projects focused on Merseyside (52% of beneficiaries in 2002/03)
- charities benefiting women and unpopular and neglected causes but avoiding those with a sectarian interest
- special consideration is given to charities with which any of the trustees have a particular knowledge or association or in which it is thought Eleanor Rathbone or her father William Rathbone VI would have had a special interest.
- a small number of grants are made to charities providing holidays for disadvantaged people from Merseyside

A note on international grants

Due to a large increase in the number of applications from organisations working overseas, in autumn 2003, trustees undertook a policy review. They agreed that for 2004 they will only consider projects from Africa, the Indian subcontinent, plus exceptionally Iraq and Palestine. Projects must be sponsored and monitored by a UK-based charity.

In addition, projects must meet one or more of the following criteria; they will:

- benefit women or orphan children
- demonstrate local involvement in scoping and delivery, except where skills required are not currently available, such as eye surgeons in remote rural areas
- aim to repair the damage in countries recently ravaged by international or civil war
- deliver clean water.

Most grants are made on a one-off basis, although requests for commitments over two or more years are considered.

In 2003/04 the trust had assets of £5.5 million and an income of £221,000. Grants were made during the year totalling £223,000.

Grants were made, ranging from £100 to £5,000. They were broken down as follows: Merseyside charities (£113,850), International charities (£67,600), Other UK/regional charities (£34,300) and Holiday Fund (£7,600). A further breakdown of grant beneficiaries was not available.

Exclusions Grants are not made in support of:

- any activity which relieves a statutory authority of its obligations
- individuals, unless (and only exceptionally) it is made through a charity and it also fulfils at least one of the other positive objects mentioned above
- overseas organisations without a sponsoring charity based in the UK.

The trust does not generally favour grants for running costs, but prefers to support specific projects, services or to contribute to specific developments.

Applications There is no application form. The trust asks for a brief proposal for funding including costings, accompanied by the latest available accounts and any relevant supporting material. It is useful to know who else is supporting the project.

To keep administration costs to a minimum, receipt of applications is not usually acknowledged. Applicants requiring acknowledgement should enclose an sae.

Trustees currently meet three times a year on varying dates.

The Rawlings Charitable Trust

General

£35,000 (2002/03)

Beneficial area UK.

Rathbone Trust Company Limited, 159 New Bond Street, London W1S 2UD

Tel. 020 7399 0823

Correspondent The Administrator

Trustee *Rathbone Trust Company Limited.*

CC Number 287483

Information available Information was provided by the trust.

General This trust gives support to certain charities annually, although no commitment is given to the recipients for future grants.

In 2002/03 it had assets of £152,000, which generated an income of £30,000. Grants totalling £35,000 were made to 19 organisations.

The largest were £6,000 to Prince's Trust, £5,000 each to British Epilepsy Foundation and Epilepsy Research Foundation. Other grants were mostly of £500 each and recipients included Cystic Fibrosis Trust, Friends of Holy Trinity, Rehab UK, Samaritans and UCL Friends Development Trust.

Exclusions No grants to individuals.

Applications In writing to the correspondent.

The Raydan Charitable Trust

Jewish

£64,000 (2002/03)

Beneficial area UK.

9 Harley Street, London W1G 9QF

Tel. 020 7436 3323

Correspondent Clive Raydan, Trustee

Trustees *S Raydan; C Raydan; P Raydan.*

CC Number 294446

Information available Accounts were on file at the Charity Commission, but without a list of grants.

General In 2002/03 the trust had assets of £16,000 with an income of £67,000 and grants totalling £64,000.

Unfortunately no grants list was available for this period.

A list of beneficiaries was available with the 1999/2000 accounts, when grants totalled £39,000. Mainly Jewish causes were supported. Larger grants were £7,800 to Or Chadash, £7,300 to Naima JPS, £4,100 to UK Friends for Further Education in Israel, £2,500 to Western Marble Arch Synagogue, £2,000 to Nightingale House, £1,600 to Yesoday Hatorah School, £1,400 each to LWCJDS and Norwood Ravenswood and £1,300 to L'Chaim Society. A further 73 grants were made of £1,000 or less.

Applications In writing to the correspondent.

The Roger Raymond Charitable Trust

Older people, education, medical

£205,000 (2001/02)

Beneficial area UK (and very occasionally large, well-known overseas organisations).

Suttondene, 17 South Border, Purley, Surrey CR8 3LL

Tel. 020 8660 9133

Email russell@pullen.cix.co.uk

Correspondent R W Pullen, Trustee

Trustees *R W Pullen; P F Raymond; M G Raymond.*

CC Number 262217

Information available Information was provided by the trust.

General In 2001/02 the trust had assets of £7 million and an income of £231,000. After management and administration costs of £25,000, grants were made to about 50 organisations totalling £205,000.

The principal beneficiary during the year, as in previous years, was Bloxham School, which received a donation of £126,000. Other grants ranged up to £5,000, although most were for £1,000 or less. Many beneficiaries are regularly supported.

Beneficiaries during the year included King Edward VII Hospital and Macmillan Cancer Relief (£5,000 each), National Trust and Royal Commonwealth Society for the Blind (£3,000 each), Putney Animal Hospital and Salvation Army (£2,000 each), Huntington's Disease Society, Defeating Deafness and Children with Leukaemia (£1,000 each).

Previous beneficiaries include Leonard Cheshire Foundation, Barnardo's, British Heart Foundation, British Wheelchair Sports Foundation, ChildLine, Handy 1 Robotic Appeal, Isle of Purbeck Club, MIND, National Asthma Campaign, NSPCC, RNLI, Save the Children Fund, WaterAid, Woodlands Trust, WWF, Girl Guides Association, Scout Association and College of Law.

Exclusions Grants are rarely given to individuals.

Applications The trust stated that applications are considered throughout the year, although funds are not always available.

The Rayne Trust

Jewish, general

£167,000 (2000/01)

Beneficial area UK.

33 Robert Adam Street, London W1U 3HR

Tel. 020 7935 3555

Correspondent Robert Dufton, Director

Trustees *Lady Rayne; Hon. R A Rayne.*

CC Number 207392

Information available Full accounts were previously provided by the trust. More up-to-date information was not available.

General This trust supports the welfare of young and older people. Nearly all of the grants are made to Jewish organisations. There are connections between this trust and the much larger Rayne Foundation.

In 2000/01 the trust had assets of £2.2 million. Income was £234,000, including £125,000 in donations received, the same level of donations as in the previous year. Management and administration costs were very low at just £3,300. Grants totalled £167,000. Of the 29 organisations receiving £1,000 or more, 13 were also supported in the previous year.

The largest grants were £25,000 to Home for Aged Jews, £20,000 to Yehudi Menuhin School, £15,000 to Centre for Jewish–Christian Relations and £10,000 each to Community Security Trust,

Jewish Care and Royal Academy of Dramatic Art.

Other beneficiaries included Royal Opera House and West London Synagogue (£6,000 each), Jewish Association for the Mentally Ill (£5,600), Finchley Reformed Synagogue (£5,200), Arnott Cato Foundation and Edinburgh House (£5,000 each), Otto Schiff Housing Association (£2,500), Leo Baeck Institute and British Red Cross (£2,000 each), Jewish Museum London (£1,500), British Friends of the Art Museums of Israel (£1,300), with £1,000 each to British Friends of the Israel Philharmonic Orchestra Foundation, The Holocaust Centre, Institute for Jewish Policy Research, Emile Littler Foundation, The Reform Foundation Trust and Wizo Charitable Foundation.

Exclusions No grants to individuals or non-registered charities.

Applications In writing to the correspondent at any time, enclosing annual report and accounts.

The John Rayner Charitable Trust

General

£30,000 (2001/02)

Beneficial area England, with a preference for Merseyside.

Manor Farmhouse, Church St, Gt Bedwyn, Marlborough, Wiltshire SN8 3PE

Tel. 01672 870362 **Fax** 01672 870750

Correspondent Mrs J Wilkinson, Trustee

Trustees *Mrs J Wilkinson; Dr J M H Rayner; Mrs A L C de Boinville.*

CC Number 802363

Information available Information was on file at the Charity Commission.

General This trust has general charitable purposes in the UK, with a preference for Merseyside. Support is given to small organisations.

In 2002/03 the trust had an income of £29,000 and a total expenditure of £41,000. Further information for this year was not available.

In the previous year the trust had assets of £1.6 million, an income of £32,000 and gave grants totalling £30,000. Beneficiaries included Action for Kids, Combat Stress, Live Music Now! North West, Merseyside Drugs Council and Prospect Cancer Charity.

Exclusions No grants to individuals or non-registered charities.

Applications In writing to the correspondent by 31 January each year. Trustees meet to allocate donations in February/March. Only successful applicants will be contacted. There are no application forms or guidelines.

The Albert Reckitt Charitable Trust

General

£63,000 (2003/04)

Beneficial area UK.

Southwark Towers, 32 London Bridge Street, London SE1 9SY

Correspondent J Barrett, Secretary

Trustees *Mrs S C Bradley, Chair; Sir Michael Colman; Mrs G M Atherton; D F Reckitt; J Hughes-Reckitt; P C Knee; Dr A Joy; W Russell.*

CC Number 209974

Information available Information was provided by the trust.

General The trust states its objects are 'to make grants to a wide variety of registered charities, including non-political charities connected with the Society of Friends'. It tends to support UK organisations rather than local groups, giving grants of £250 to £750 each.

In 2003/04 it had assets of £1.9 million, which generated an income of £70,000. Grants totalled £63,000, given as £43,000 in subscriptions (annual grants), the rest in donations (one-off grants). No further information for the year was available.

Exclusions No support to individuals. No grants for political or sectarian charities, except for non-political charities connected with the Society of Friends.

Applications In writing to the correspondent. Trustees meet in June/July and applications need to be received by the end of March.

The Red Rose Charitable Trust

People who are elderly, disability

£40,000 to organisations and individuals (2001/02)

Beneficial area UK with a preference for Lancashire and Merseyside.

c/o Rathbones, Port of Liverpool Building, Pier Head, Liverpool L3 1NW

Tel. 0151 236 6666 **Fax** 0151 243 7003

Correspondent J N L Packer, Trustee

Trustees *Miss Olwen Seddon; J N L Packer; Lesley Eileen Allison.*

CC Number 1038358

Information available Accounts were on file at the Charity Commission.

General This trust was registered with the Charity Commission in June 1994. It has a preference for supporting charities working with people who are elderly and people who are physically or mentally disabled. Grants are also made to individuals within these categories.

In 2001/02 it had assets amounting to £1 million, an income of £33,000 and made grants totalling £40,000.

Grants included 19 of £2,000 each and 15 of £1,000 each. Beneficiaries included Brain Research Trust, Demand, Dystonia Society, Hope House, Make-A-Wish Foundation, Royal School for the Blind and Royal School for the Deaf (£2,000 each) and Dale Farm Development, British Deaf Association, Help the Aged, Leprosy Mission, Motor Neurone Disease Association and Schizophrenia Fellowship.

Grants were also made to three individuals.

Applications In writing to the correspondent.

The C A Redfern Charitable Foundation

General

£189,000 (2001/02)

Beneficial area UK.

PricewaterhouseCoopers, 9 Greyfriars Road, Reading, Berkshire RG1 1JG

Tel. 0118 959 7111

Correspondent The Trustees

Trustees *C A G Redfern; T P Thornton; S R Ward; Sir R A Clark; D S Redfern.*

CC Number 299918

Information available Accounts were on file at the Charity Commission.

General This trust supports a wide range of organisations with some preference for those concerned with health and welfare.

In 2002/03 the trust had an income of £215,000 and a total expenditure of £239,000. Further information for this year was not available.

Previous grant beneficiaries have included South Buckinghamshire Riding for the Disabled, Saints and Sinners Club, Motor and Allied Trades Benevolent Fund, Cancer Support Centre Wandsworth, Canine Partners for Independence, Seven Springs Play and Support Centre, Farms for City Children, Campus Children's Holidays, CRUSE, RNIB, The De Paul Trust, British Red Cross, Help the Aged, Northwick Park Institute for Medical Research and NSPCC – Berkshire.

Exclusions No grants for building works or individuals.

Applications The trust does not accept unsolicited applications.

The Sir Steve Redgrave Charitable Trust

Children and young people up to the age of 18 worldwide

£400,000 available (2004)

Beneficial area UK.

PO Box 200, Petersfield, Hampshire GU32 2ZX

Correspondent Adrian Milne

Trustees *Paul Richardson, Chair; Sir Steve Redgrave; Dr Lady Ann Redgrave; Wallace Dobbin; Andrew Wigmore; Athole Still; Lizzy Pearce; Adrian Milne; Ian Holder.*

CC Number 1086216

Information available Information was provided by the trust.

General This trust was established in 2001 by Britain's greatest ever Olympian after his retirement from rowing. The original reason for the creation of the trust was to raise £5 million for children's charities through Sir Steve participating in the London Marathon three times, in 2001, 2003 and 2005. The trust has also been raising funds through over sponsored events, corporate sponsorship and fundraising from other individuals. In 2004 fundraising events included achieving world records in the biggest 100 metres ever lasting 24 hours, the fastest four-player round of golf, dragon-boat races and various charity balls. This raised over £400,000 in 2004. The intention for 2005 was to break the world record for most money raised in a marathon of £1.1 million, which would be donated through the trust, although this record attempt has been postponed until 2006 to avoid clashing with public fundraising ventures concerned with the Asian tsunami appeal. However, it is still likely that the trust will be well financed during the year.

Projects receiving support should:

- be children/youth/community-based
- be UK-based
- have low administrative costs: less than 25 per cent of revenues per annum
- have income of less than £200,000 per annum
- have low public profile
- have a tangible outcome/be 'making a real difference': for example, for buildings/equipment, research, drugs/ crime prevention
- be nationwide
- benefit children and young people up to age 18.

Recent beneficiaries have included Children's Hospice Association of Scotland (£50,000), Tommy's (£35,000), Winston's Wish (£25,000) and Naomi House (£15,000).

Applications In writing to the correspondent. The recipient shall report within six months of receipt of the grant detailing how the money was used and the difference it has made. This will be published in the Sir Steve Redgrave Charitable Trust's annual report/website.

The Max Reinhardt Charitable Trust

Deafness, fine arts promotion

£87,000 (2002/03)

Beneficial area UK.

Flat 2, 43 Onslow Square, London SW7 3LR

Correspondent The Secretary

Trustees *Joan Reinhardt; Veronica Reinhardt; Belinda McGill.*

CC Number 264741

Information available Information was provided by the trust.

General The trust supports organisations benefiting people who are deaf and fine arts promotion. In 2003 grants to five organisations totalled £87,000. St George's Medical School was given the largest grant, of £85,000. Volunteer Reading Help received £1,000 with smaller grants made to DeafPlus, Deafway, Paintings in Hospital and Sense.

Exclusions No grants to individuals.

Applications In writing to the correspondent.

REMEDI

Research into disability

£189,000 (2003/04)

Beneficial area UK.

14 Crondace Road, London SW6 4BB

Tel. 020 7384 2929 **Fax** 020 7731 8240

Email rosie.wait@remedi.org.uk

Website www.remedi.org.uk

Correspondent Mrs Rosie Wait, Director

Trustees *Brian Winterflood, President; Dr A K Clarke, Chair; Alan Line; Dr A H M Heagerty; Dr I T Stuttaford; David Hume; Michael Hines; Dr Anthony Ward.*

CC Number 1063359

Information available Information was provided by the trust.

General REMEDI supports pioneering research into all aspects of disability in the widest sense of the word, with special emphasis on the way in which disability limits the activities and lifestyle of all ages.

The trust receives most of its income from companies and other trusts, which is then given towards researchers carrying out innovative and original work who find it difficult to find funding from larger organisations. Grants are generally for one year, although funding for the second year is considered sympathetically and for a third year exceptionally. There is a preference for awarding a few sizeable grants rather than many smaller grants. The priority funding area for 2005 is cerebral palsy in children.

In 2003/04 the trust made grants totalling £189,000, however no information was available to suggest who the beneficiaries of these grants were.

Previous information provided stated that in 2001/02 the largest grants were £54,000 to the research project 'Can functional magnetic resonance imaging (MRI) studies help to develop effective therapy interventions for stroke patients?' at King's College, London; £49,000 for research into the underlying cause of autism at the Newcomen Centre at Guy's Hospital; and £40,000 towards research into prostate cancer at St Mary's Hospital, London.

Other large grants included £38,000 towards early intensive home-based intervention for the treatment of autism and the analysis of tutor performance at the University of Southampton; £32,000 towards further development of intensive single-case methods for investigation of recovery after stroke at the University of Nottingham; £26,000 towards the clinical trial of ossointegrated prostheses for transfemoral amputees at Queen Mary's Hospital, Roehampton; and £25,000 towards research in the control of prosthetic wrist rotation from residual rotation of the amputated forearm at the University of Salford.

Smaller grants included those towards research into caregiver strain in spouses of stroke patients at University of Nottingham (£10,000); an anal sphincter rupture repair study at North Staffordshire Hospital and Keele University (£9,000); and courses for carers at The Research Institute for the Care of the Elderly, Bath (£3,800).

Exclusions Cancer and cancer-related diseases are not supported.

Applications By e-mail to the correspondent. Applications are received throughout the year. They should initially include a summary of the project on one side of A4 with costings. The Chair normally considers applications on the third Tuesday of each month with a view to inviting applicants to complete an application form by e-mail.

The Rest Harrow Trust

Jewish, general

£97,000 (2002/03)

Beneficial area UK.

c/o Portrait Solicitors, 1 Chancery Lane, London WC2A 1LF

Tel. 020 7320 3890

Correspondent Mr T Miles

Trustees *Mrs J B Bloch; Miss J S Portrait; HON & V Trustee Limited.*

CC Number 238042

Information available Full accounts were provided by the trust.

General In 2002/03 it had assets of £612,000 and an income of £55,000, which included a donation received of £23,000. Grants were made to 224 organisations totalling £97,000. Management and administration charges were high for the year at £13,000, possibly due to the high number of grants made although this includes payments to a firm in which one of the trustees is a payment. Whilst wholly legal, these editors always regret such payments unless, in the words of the Charity Commission, 'there is no realistic alternative'.

By far the largest grant, of £20,000, went to Nightingale House. The next in size were £2,000 each to Jewish Care and World Jewish Relief, £1,500 to Canon Collins Educational Trust for Southern Africa and £1,000 each to Assembly of Masorti Synagogues, British Technion Society, Hebrew University of Jerusalem, Friends of Israel Educational Trust, Institute for Jewish Policy Research, Jewish Blind and Disabled, The Jewish Museum, JNF Charitable Trust, Oxford Jewish Centre for a building appeal, Shaare Zedek UK, Trinity House, The Wiener Library and Weizmann Institute of Science.

Most of the other grants were for amounts much smaller than this. They included £700 to Sight Savers International, £600 to Action for Blind People, £500 each to Amnesty International, European Association for Jewish Culture, Inter Faith Network for the UK and Spiro Ark, £400 each to Aid for the Aged in Distress, Centerpoint, Church Housing Trust, Depaul Trust, Friends of the Earth, Howard League for Penal Reform, Kings Cross Homelessness Project, Martha Project, MS Society, Prison Reform Trust, Prisoners of Conscience, Re-Solv, Salvation Army, Shaftesbury Society and Tzedek and £200 each to Ace Centre Advisory Trust, Allotments Regeneration Initiative, Book Aid International, British Blind Sport, British Heart Foundation, Camphill Village Trust, Care International UK, ChildLine, Church Army, Community Security Trust, Defeating Deafness, Family Welfare Association, Hearing Concern, Jubilee Sailing Trust, Marfan Trust, Meningitis Trust, Motability, New Avenues Youth and Community Project, One Parent Families, Royal Blind Society, Shelter, Spires, Staffordshire University, Threshold Housing Advice and Weston Spirit.

Exclusions No grants to non-registered charities or to individuals.

Applications In writing to the correspondent. Appeals are considered quarterly. Only applications from eligible bodies are acknowledged.

The Rhododendron Trust

Welfare, overseas aid and development, culture, wildlife

£36,000 (2003)

Beneficial area UK and overseas.

Lewis House, 12 Smith Street, Rochdale OL16 1TX

Tel. 01706 355505

Correspondent The Trustees

Trustees *Peter Edward Healey; Dr Ralph Walker; Mrs Sarah Ray; Mrs Sarah Oliver.*

CC Number 267192

Information available Information was provided by the trust.

General This trust gives half of its grant total for development work overseas and the remaining half to UK welfare or cultural organisations. Grants of £500 or £1,000 are made generally to charities which have been supported in the past although a few new beneficiaries are included each year. In 2003 grants totalled £36,000.

UK beneficiaries included Brandon Centre, Camphill Village Trust, Historic Churches Preservation Fund, NACRO, Refugee Support Centre and WWF. Overseas beneficiaries included Ashram International, Nepal Leprosy Trust, Ockenden International and Sight Savers International.

Exclusions No grants to individuals, churches, expeditions, scholarships or research work (including medical research).

Applications In writing to the correspondent. The majority of donations are made in February. Applications are not acknowledged.

Daisie Rich Trust

General

£36,000 to organisations (2003/04)

Beneficial area UK, with a priority for the Isle of Wight.

The Hawthorns, School Lane, Arreton, Isle of Wight PO30 3AD

Tel. 07866 449855

Email daisierich@yahoo.co.uk

Correspondent Mrs Lyn Mitchell, Administrator/Secretary

Trustees *M R Oatley; A H Medley; D G Creighton; Mrs M Creighton.*

CC Number 236706

Information available Full accounts were on file at the Charity Commission.

General This trust has a priority for supporting organisations and individuals on the Isle of Wight, with any available surplus given in the UK or elsewhere.

In 2003/04 it had assets of £2.1 million, which generated an income of £106,000. Grants to organisations totalled £36,000. Grants to 56 individuals totalled £42,000.

The largest grants were £2,000 to RSPB, £1,500 to Douglas Haig House, Isle of Wight Muscular Dystrophy Group, Isle of Wight Youth Trust and Isle of Wight Rural Community Council, £1,200 to SSAFA Forces Help and £1,000 each to Carisbrooke Castle Museum, Carisbrooke Priory Trust, Isle of Wight Foot Beagles, Hampshire and Wight Trust for Maritime Archaeology, Hampshire and Wight Wildlife Trust, Macmillan Cancer Relief, Earl Mountbatten Hospice, Porchfield Youth Club, Portsmouth Hospitals Rocky Appeal, Shanklin Town Brass, St Helens Youth Club and YMCA.

Smaller grants included £500 each to Cathedral Camps, Isle of Wight Society for the Blind, NCH Action for Children and RoRO Sailing Project, £250 to Isle of Wight Deaf Children's Association, Medina Marching Band, Samaritans, £200 to St Helens Carnival, £150 to Rope Walk Social Club and £35 to Mouth and Foot Painting Artists.

Applications In writing to the correspondent.

The Sir Cliff Richard Charitable Trust

Spiritual and social welfare

£150,000 (2001/02)

Beneficial area UK.

Harley House, 94 Hare Lane, Claygate, Esher, Surrey KT10 0RB

Tel. 01372 467752 **Fax** 01372 462352

Correspondent Bill Latham, Trustee

Trustees *William Latham; Malcolm Smith.*

CC Number 1096412

Information available Accounts were on file at the Charity Commission, but without a detailed breakdown of all donations, or a full narrative report.

General This trust has general charitable purposes, with a preference for causes seeking to improve spiritual and social welfare.

In 2001/02 it had assets of £994,000 and an income of £127,000. Grants were made totalling £150,000.

In the previous year grants totalled £192,000, of which £81,000 was given in sundry donations not listed in the accounts. £50,000 each to British Lung Foundation and Cliff Richard Tennis Development Trust. The other two donations listed were £6,500 to Genesis Art Trust and £5,000 to Arts Centre Group.

Exclusions Capital building projects, church repairs and renovations are all excluded. No support for individuals.

Applications Applications should be from registered charities only, in writing, and for one-off needs. All applications are acknowledged. Grants are made quarterly in January, April, July and October.

The Violet M Richards Charity

Older people, sickness, medical research and education

£68,000 (2002/03)

Beneficial area UK, with a preference for East and West Sussex and Kent.

c/o Wedlake Bell (ref CAH), 16 Bedford Street, London WC2E 9HF

Tel. 020 7395 3000 **Fax** 020 7395 3118

Correspondent Charles Hicks

Trustees *Mrs E H Hill; G R Andersen; C A Hicks; Miss M Davies; Mrs M Burt; Dr J Clements.*

CC Number 273928

Information available Full accounts were provided by the trust.

General The trust's objects are relief of age and sickness, through advancement of medical research (particularly into geriatric problems), medical education, homes and other facilities for people who are elderly or sick. The trustees are happy to commit themselves to funding a research project over a number of years, including 'seedcorn' projects. Applications from Kent and East or West Sussex are especially favoured by the trustees.

In 2002/03 it had assets of £1.6 million, which generated an income of £78,000. Management and administration costs were high at £14,000, which equated to nearly 20% of the trust's income. This included a payment of £8,300 plus VAT (£9,800) to a firm of solicitors one of the trustees is a partner in. Whilst wholly legal, these editors always regret such payments unless, in the words of the Charity Commission, 'there is no realistic alternative'.

Grants were made to five organisations and totalled £68,000. Grants went to University of Cambridge for a

Huntington's Disease project (£27,000), Brain Research Trust (£25,000) and University College London for a motor neurone disease project (£10,000), all of which were also supported in the previous year. The only two new recipients were Hospice in the Weald (£5,000) and Hope and Homes for Children (£1,000).

Exclusions No support for individuals.

Applications In writing to the correspondent. There is no set format for applying. The trustees generally meet to consider grants approximately twice a year. Only successful applications are acknowledged.

The Clive Richards Charity Ltd

Disability, poverty

£65,000 (2001/02)

Beneficial area UK, with a preference for Herefordshire.

40 Great James Street, London WC1N 3HB

Tel. 020 7831 3310

Correspondent Clive Richards

Trustees *W S C Richards; Mrs S A Richards.*

CC Number 327155

Information available Full accounts were on file at the Charity Commission.

General The area of this trust's interest is people with disabilities and those disadvantaged by poverty. Priority has been given to education, arts and sport.

In 2001/02 the trust had assets of £409,000, an income of £21,000 and it gave grants totalling £65,000.

Grants included £11,000 to Everest 2000 Reserve Forces North Ridge Expedition, £10,000 to Premanda Orphanage Centre, £5,840 to Royal Opera House Trust, £4,000 to Bromyard Sports Foundation and £2,500 to Rural Britain 2006.

Exclusions No grants for political causes.

Applications In writing to the correspondent. However, the trust states that 'due to the generally low interest rates that have been available over the last few months, the charity's resources are fully committed and thus it is extremely selective in accepting any requests for funding'.

The Muriel Edith Rickman Trust

Medical research, education

£122,000 (2000/01)

Beneficial area UK.

12 Fitzroy Court, 57–59 Shepherds Hill, London N6 5RD

Correspondent H P Rickman, Trustee

Trustees *H P Rickman, Chair; M D Gottlieb; Raymond Tallis.*

CC Number 326143

Information available Information was provided by the trust.

General The trust makes grants to medical research organisations towards equipment. The trust prefers to support physical disabilities rather than mental illnesses.

In 2002/03 it had assets of £66,000 and an income of £76,000. Grants to nine organisations totalled £122,000.

Beneficiaries were King's College London (£56,000), Ataxia Telangiectasia Society (£17,000), British Heart Foundation (£16,000), University of Manchester (£10,000), Canniesburn Research Trust (£8,000), National Asthma Campaign (£5,800), Sheffield Kidney Research Foundation (£4,700), Meningitis Research Foundation (£4,500) and Guide Dogs for the Blind (£250).

Exclusions The trustees will not respond to individual students, clubs, community projects or expeditions.

Applications There are no guidelines for applications and the trust only replies if it is interested at first glance; it will then ask for further details. Trustees meet as required.

The Ripple Effect Foundation

General

£61,000 (2000/01)

Beneficial area UK.

Marlborough Investment Consultants Ltd, Wessex House, Oxford Road, Newbury, Berkshire RG14 1PA

Tel. 01635 814470

Correspondent Miss Caroline D Marks, Trustee

Trustees *Miss Caroline D Marks; I R Marks; I S Wesley.*

CC Number 802327

Information available Accounts were on file at the Charity Commission.

General The 2000/01 accounts stated: 'The objectives of the trustees are to support a range of charitable causes over a few years that meet their funding criteria. They proactively seek out projects that meet their criteria and do not respond to unsolicited applications. The Ripple Effect continued its policy of making donations towards effective charities working in the broad fields of environmental work, Third World development and empowering young people in the UK. However, it is now beginning to focus on local community projects based in the south west of England.'

In 2003/04 the foundation had an income of £29,000 and a total expenditure of £9,000. Further information including a grant total and beneficiaries for this year was not available on file at the Charity Commission.

In 2000/01 the trust had assets of £1.5 million, which generated a low income of £30,000. Three payments were made (£50,000 to Network Foundation, £12,000 to Devon Community and £250 to Breakthrough), mostly to be passed on to smaller organisations.

Network Foundation received £50,000, which was passed on to other charities. Funding for environmental projects centred around growing issues in the UK, particularly genetically modified food. Soil Association received £1,000 through Network Foundation, while Global Commons Institute was also supported. Third World work supported included Oxford Research Group's work towards developing peaceful resolutions between warring factions.

Numerous young people's organisations were also supported from the funds given to Network Foundation. The foundation also worked with Devon Community Foundation to identify youth homeless projects and problems in rural areas. £5,000 went to a small community project improving social, sport and leisure facilities for young people, while £6,600 went towards the community foundation's core costs. An emerging Exeter group was also identified as a potential beneficiary once the organisation is fully established.

Applications The trust states that it does not respond to unsolicited applications.

The John Ritblat Charitable Trust No. 1

Jewish, general

£36,000 (2002/03)

Beneficial area UK.

Baker Tilly, Chartered Accountants, 46 Clarendon Road, Watford WD17 1JJ

Tel. 01923 816400 **Fax** 01923 353402

Correspondent The Clerk

Trustees *J H Ritblat; N S J Ritblat; C B Wagman; Miss S C Ritblat; J W J Ritblat.*

CC Number 262463

Information available Full accounts were on file at the Charity Commission.

General In 2002/03 the trust had assets of £261,000 and an income of £76,000. Grants to 12 organisations totalled £36,000. Grants were £20,000 to Skiers Trust, £10,000 to Weizmann Institute Foundation, £1,800 to United Synagogue, £1,000 each to King Edward VII Hospital for Officers and UCL Development Fund, £500 to Tate Gallery Foundation, £450 to Artangel, £380 to Central Synagogue and £100 each to Friends of St Mary's Church, Friends of War Memorials and Norwood.

The trust makes grants primarily to long-established organisations.

Exclusions No grants to individuals.

Applications Please do not apply as all funds are committed.

The Rivendell Trust

Sickness, disability, family problems, education, music

£33,000 to organisations (2002/03)

Beneficial area UK.

PO Box 19375, London W4 2GH

Correspondent Jayne Buchanan

Trustees *Mrs S D Caird; Miss M J Verney; E R Verney; A W Layton; Dr I Laing; S P Weil; G Caird.*

CC Number 271375

Information available Full accounts were on file at the Charity Commission.

General The trust aims to 'enable those with disadvantages to receive benefits which would not usually come their way'. It achieves this by providing grants for groups working with people of any age who are sick, disabled or have special learning difficulties, as well as schoolchildren and students with personal or family difficulties. Musically and artistically gifted people who are unable to fulfil their potential can be directly supported (for further information, please see *The Educational Grants Directory*, also published by DSC).

In 2002/03 it had assets of £625,000 and an income of £27,000. Grants were made totalling £34,000.

As in previous years, the largest grant was £31,000 to University of Edinburgh for the Simpson Memorial Hospital for Neo-Natal Research. This was the final payment of a three-year commitment and as such the trust stated in its accounts that it would be in a position to give more money in future years than had been available to other organisations. There were only two other beneficiaries during the year; these were BACO (£2,000) and an individual (£1,000).

Exclusions Applications for the construction, restoration or purchase of buildings are not normally considered. Grants to individuals are limited to those in the above categories, and children and bona fide students within the UK in connection with education in music. Further grants to charities or individuals will normally be considered once every three years.

Applications Charities should send comprehensive details including a statement of the previous two years' accounts. Individuals apply in writing with an sae to the correspondent for an application form. Because of the number of grants received, failure to supply an sae could result in an application failing. Trustees meet three times a year (usually March, July and November) to consider applications. The list of applications is closed six weeks before the date of each meeting, and any applications received after the closing date are carried forward.

This entry was not confirmed by the trust, but was correct according to information on file at the Charity Commission.

The River Trust

Christian

£161,000 (2001/02)

Beneficial area UK, with a preference for Sussex.

c/o Kleinwort Benson Trustees Ltd, PO Box 191, 10 Fenchurch Street, London EC3M 3LB

Tel. 020 7475 5093

Correspondent Chris Gilbert, Secretary

Trustee *Kleinwort Benson Trustees Ltd.*

CC Number 275843

Information available Full accounts were provided by the trust.

General Gillian Warren formed the trust in 1977 with an endowment mainly of shares in the merchant bank Kleinwort Benson. It is one of the many Kleinwort trusts. The River Trust is one of the smaller of the family trusts. It supports Christian causes.

In 2001/02 the trust had assets of £410,000 and an income of £126,000. Grants to 49 organisations totalled £161,000. Donations ranged from between £250 to £20,000. Over half of the beneficiaries had been supported in previous years. Grants were broken down into the following categories:

Advancement of the Christian faith – 18 grants totalling £53,000

Grants included those to: Youth with a Mission (£18,000); Timothy Trust (£11,000); Sovereign Giving (£4,000); Ashburnham Christian Trust and Tear Fund (£3,000 each); Prison Fellowship and Relationship Foundation (£2,000 each); Bourne Trust and Release International (£1,000 each); Beauty from Ashes (£750); and Interhealth (£500).

Religious education – 10 grants totalling £44,000
Beneficiaries included: London Bible College (£11,000); Care Trust, Genesis Arts Trust and Scripture Union (£8,000 each); Chasah Trust (£5,000); Bible Society (£1,500); Arts Group Centre (£1,000); Focus Radio (£600); and Civitas (£250).

Church funds – 8 grants totalling £46,000
Beneficiaries were: Barcombe Parochial Church Council (£20,000); St Peter's & James' Hospice (£10,000); St Luke's Prestonville Church (£6,000); Westborough URC (£4,000); St Andrew's Church (£2,800); All Souls' Church Eastbourne (£1,500); St Barnabas' Church (£1,000); and Woodberry Down Church (£500).

Missionary work – 7 grants totalling £8,700
Beneficiaries were: Olive Tree Christian (£2,000); On the Move and St Stephen's Society (£1,500 each); ICCOWE (£1,200); Indian Christian Mission Centre – Tamilnadu (£1,000); African Enterprise and Storm Ministries (£750 each).

Religious welfare work – 6 grants totalling £10,000
Recipients were: Care for the Family (£5,000); Marriage Resource (£3,000); Mercy Ships UK (£1,000); Stewardship Services (£750); St Patrick's Trust (£500); and Fountain Gate Trust (£100).

Exclusions Only appeals for Christian causes will be considered. No grants to individuals. The trust does not support 'repairs of the fabric of the church' nor does it give grants for capital expenditure.

Applications In writing to the correspondent. Unsolicited appeals are considered as well as causes which have already been supported and are still regarded as commitments of the trust. Only successful applicants are notified of the trustees' decision. Some charities are supported for more than one year, although no commitment is usually given to the recipients.

Riverside Charitable Trust Limited

Health, welfare, older people, education, general

£186,000 (2001/02)

Beneficial area Mainly Lancashire.

c/o E Suttons & Sons, Riverside, New Church Road, Bacup, Lancashire OL13 0DT

Tel. 01706 874961

Correspondent Jackie Davidson, Trustee

Trustees *B J Lynch; I B Dearing; J A Davidson; F Drew; H Francis; A Higginson; G Maden; L Clegg.*

CC Number 264015

Information available Accounts were on file at the Charity Commission.

General The trust's objects are to support the following: poor, sick and older people; education; healthcare; the relief of poverty of people employed or formerly employed in the shoe trade; and other charitable purposes.

In 2001/02 the trust had assets of £2.1 million and an income of £97,000. A total of £186,000 was distributed in 231 grants which were mostly recurrent.

The largest donation of £10,000 went to a branch of Macmillan Cancer Relief in Burnley. Other beneficiaries of larger grants included Cancer Research UK (£6,200), St Mary's Hospice for Furness (£6,000), Derwen College for the Disabled, Rossendale Society for the Blind and Rossendale Valley Domestic Violence Forum (£5,000 each), British Dyslexics Association (£4,200), Derian House Hospice – Bolton and East Lancashire Contact Centre (£2,500 each), Stacksteads Junior Band (£2,000) and NSPCC – South Cumbria Appeal (£1,000).

Smaller grants included those to Furness Rotary Club (£750), Furness MS Action, Rawtenstall Players, Rawtenstall Public Welfare Committee, St Mary's RC Church – Bacup, Salvation Army – Clitheroe, Rossendale General Hospital Radio (£500 each) and Furness Osteoporosis Support Group and Wallbank Family Centre (£250 each).

Exclusions No grants for political causes.

Applications In writing to the correspondent.

The Daniel Rivlin Charitable Trust

Jewish, general

£55,000 (2002/03)

Beneficial area UK.

Manor House, Northgate Lane, Linton, Wetherby, West Yorkshire LS22 4HN

Tel. 07785 381928

Correspondent D R Rivlin, Trustee

Trustees *D R Rivlin; N S Butler; M Miller.*

CC Number 328341

Information available Full accounts were available on file at the Charity Commission.

General In 2002/03 this trust had an income of £50,000 and made grants totalling £55,000. Assets totalled £14,000 at the year end.

Grants in this year were as follows: £35,000 to Beth Shalom, £13,000 to UJIA, £3,000 to CIS Development Fund, £1,800 to Donisthorpe, £1,500 to Holly Bank Trust, £400 Makor Charitable Trust, £300 to Beth Hamedrash Synagogue, £50 to Welfare Care and £25 to Blue & White Bazaar.

Applications The trust states that funds are fully committed and does not welcome unsolicited applications.

The Alex Roberts-Miller Foundation

See below

£54,000 (2002 to December 2003)

Beneficial area UK.

PO Box 104, Dorking, Surrey RH5 6YN

Fax 01306 741356

Email alexrmfoundation@mac.com

Website www.alexrmfoundation.org.uk

Correspondent The Trustees

Trustees *R A Roberts-Miller; F M Roberts-Miller; J M Roberts-Miller; E D Roberts-Miller.*

CC Number 1093912

Information available Information was on the foundation's website.

General The foundation was established in 2002. Its main goal is to help provide educational, sporting and social opportunities for disadvantaged young people. It aims to target funds where they will have a direct and significant impact on the lives of the people we are trying to help. The foundation also promotes road safety and its education.

The foundation hopes to build up a substantial permanent endowment which will ensure that it can continue to support charitable causes far into the future. To December 2003 grants totalling £54,000 have been made to Afasic, Back-Up Trust, British Blind Sport, RoadPeace and SeeAbility.

Exclusions No grants to individuals.

Applications The foundation researches its own beneficiaries.

Edwin George Robinson Charitable Trust

Medical research

£49,000 (2002/03)

Beneficial area UK and developing countries.

71 Manor Road South, Hinchley Wood, Surrey KT10 0QB

Tel. 020 8398 6845

Correspondent E C Robinson, Trustee

Trustees *E C Robinson; Mrs S C Robinson.*

CC Number 1068763

Information available Information was provided by the trust. Full accounts were on file at the Charity Commission.

General The trust makes grants for specific research projects. Grants are not usually made to fund general operating costs. In 2002/03 it had an income of £16,000 and gave £49,000 in grants.

In 2000/01, when it had an income of £21,000, 30 grants were made totalling £49,000. The largest were £5,000 each to British Red Cross, Marie Curie Cancer Care, Diabetes UK and National Society for Epilepsy and £2,500 each to Brainwave, Spencer Dayman Meningitis Laboratory, Elimination of Leukaemia Fund, Fight for Sight, Research into Ageing and RNLI.

Exclusions No grants to individuals or for general running costs for small local organisations.

Applications In writing to the correspondent.

The Rock Foundation

Christian ministries, see below

£242,000 (2001/02)

Beneficial area Worldwide.

Park Green Cottage, Barhatch Road, Cranleigh, Surrey GU6 7DJ

Tel. 01483 274 556

Correspondent The Trustees

Trustees *Richard Borgonon; Andrew Green; Irene Spreckley; Kevin Locock; Jane Borgonon; Colin Spreckley.*

CC Number 294775

Information available Accounts were on file at the Charity Commission.

General Formed in 1986, this charity seeks to support charitable undertakings which are built upon a clear biblical basis and which, in most instances, receive little or no publicity. It is not the intention of the foundation to give widespread support, but rather to specifically research and invest time and money in the work of a few selected Christian ministries. As well as supporting six such ministries, grants are also made to registered charities.

In 2001/02 The foundation had assets of £286,000 with an income of £260,000 and grants totalling £242,000.

The largest grants were £14,000 to St Luke's Church, £10,000 each to Cranleigh Baptist Church, Prostate Research Campaign UK and Cornhill Training Courses Bursary Fund, £8,500 to International Student Christian Society, £3,500 to Hospice in the World, £2,700 to Priors Field School, £1,200 to Cloverfield Community Church and £1,000 to Christian Heritage.

Applications The trust identifies its beneficiaries through its own networks, choosing to support organisations it has a working relationship with. This allows the trust to verify that the organisation is doing excellent work in a sensible manner in a way which cannot be conveyed from a written application. As such, all appeals from charities the foundation do not find through their own research are simply thrown in the bin. If an sae is included in an application, it will merely end up in the foundation's waste-paper bin rather than a post box.

The Rock Solid Trust

Christian worldwide

£214,000 (2001)

Beneficial area Worldwide.

7 Belgrave Place, Clifton, Bristol B58 3DD

Correspondent J D W Pocock, Trustee

Trustees *J D W Pocock; A J Pocock; T P Wicks; T G Bretell.*

CC Number 1077669

Information available Accounts were on file at the Charity Commission.

General This trust supports:

- Christian charitable institutions and the advancement of Christian religion
- the maintenance, restoration and repair of the fabric of Christian church
- the education and training of individuals
- relief of need.

In 2001 it had assets of £842,000 and an income of £948,000, from which £930,000 was received in donations. Grants to 6 organisations totalled £214,000. The largest donations were £93,000 in three grants to Hope Community Church and £50,000 each to Alpha International and Emmuas House.

Other beneficiaries were: Beacon Centre Project and Christ Church School (£10,000 each) and Highfield Church (£1,000). A further £750 was given in one grant to an individual.

Applications In writing to the correspondent.

Rofeh Trust

General, religious activities

£53,000 (2001/02)

Beneficial area UK.

44 Southway, London NW11 6SA

Correspondent The Trustees

Trustees *Martin Dunitz; Ruth Dunitz; Vivian Wineman; Henry Eder.*

CC Number 1077682

Information available Accounts were on file at the Charity Commission, but without a list of grants.

General In 2001/02 this trust had assets of £703,000, an income of £82,000 and made grants totalling £53,000. Unfortunately no list of grants was included with accounts on file at the Charity Commission.

Applications In writing to the correspondent.

Richard Rogers Charitable Settlement

Housing, homelessness

£122,000 (2001/02)

Beneficial area UK.

Lee Associates, 5 Southampton Place, London WC1A 2DA

Tel. 020 7831 3609

Correspondent K A Hawkins

Trustees *Lord R G Rogers; P Rogers; G H Camamile.*

CC Number 283252

Information available Accounts were on file at the Charity Commission, but without a grants list or a description of the trust's grant-making policy.

General In 2001/02 the trust's assets totalled £655,000 and it received an income of £186,000. Grants totalled £122,000. Grants were given to four beneficiaries: £50,400 to the National Tenants Resource Centre, £30,000 to Refuge, £15,000 to Education Extra and £8,300 to Medical Foundation for the Care of Victims of Torture.

Applications In writing to the correspondent.

Rokach Family Charitable Trust

Jewish, general

£103,000 (2000/01)

Beneficial area UK.

20 Middleton Road, London NW11 7NS

Tel. 020 8455 6359

Correspondent Norman Rokach, Trustee

Trustees *N Rokach; Mrs H Rokach; Mrs E Hoffman; Mrs M Feingold; Mrs A Gefilhaus; Mrs N Brenig.*

CC Number 284007

Information available Full accounts were on file at the Charity Commission.

General This trust supports Jewish and general causes in the UK. In 2002/03 it had an income of £647,000 and a total expenditure of £716,000. Further information for this year was not available.

In 2000/01 its assets totalled £1.3 million and it had an income of £155,000, mainly from rent on its properties. Grants totalled £103,000.

The accounts listed 51 grants made over £100 each. The beneficiary of the largest grant was Finchley Road Synagogue (£33,000). Seven further grants of over £1,000 were made, to Beth Hamedrash Ponovez (£21,000), Adath Israel Synagogue and Woodstock Sinclair Trust (£10,000 each), Cosmon Belz Ltd (£7,600), Moreshet Hatorah Ltd (£2,400), Jewish Education Trust (£2,000) and Institute of Rabbinical Studies D'Chasidei Belz London (£1,500).

Other smaller donations included those to Before Trust, Beis Yaakov Primary School, CMZ Trust, British Friends of Laniado Hospital, CMZ Trust, Friends of Mir, Gertner Trust and Pardes House School.

Unlisted smaller grants under £100 each totalled £3,100.

Applications In writing to the correspondent.

The Sir James Roll Charitable Trust

General

£149,000 (2000/01)

Beneficial area UK.

5 New Road Avenue, Chatham, Kent ME4 6AR

Tel. 01634 830111 **Fax** 01634 408891

Correspondent N T Wharton, Trustee

Trustees *N T Wharton; B W Elvy; J M Liddiard.*

CC Number 1064963

Information available Full accounts were on file at the Charity Commission, although in December 2004 they were only available for those up to 2000/01.

General The trust's main objects are the:

- promotion of mutual tolerance, commonality and cordiality in major world religions
- furtherance of access to computer technology as a teaching medium at primary school levels
- promotion of improved access to computer technology in community based projects other than political parties or local government
- funding of projects aimed at early identification of specific learning disorders.

In 2000/01 the trust had assets totalling £3.8 million and an income of £179,000. Grants were made to 117 beneficiaries totalling £149,000. Grants ranged from £500 to £15,000, although over half were for £500.

Beneficiaries included: DEC India Earthquake Appeal (£15,000), CRISIS at Christmas (£10,000), Howard League for Penal Reform and Prison Reform Trust (£6,000 each), The Community Self Build Agency and Frontline Community Project (£5,000 each), National Missing Persons Helpline and Mission in Houndslow (£3,000 each), The National Autistic Society and The Dyslexia Institute (£2,000 each).

Grants of £1,000 included those to Alzheimer's Disease Society, Battersea Dogs Home, Children's Aid Foundation and Great Ormond Street Hospital. Beneficiaries receiving £500 each included ACE Centre Advisory Trust, Africa NOW, Barnado's, British Red Cross, Combat Stress, Dermatrust, Five

Ways School, MIND, NatureWatch, Vision Aid and YMCA Swansea.

Applications In writing to the correspondent.

The Helen Roll Charitable Trust

General

£82,000 (2002/03)

Beneficial area UK.

Manches, 3 Worcester Street, Oxford OX1 2PZ

Correspondent F R Williamson, Trustee

Trustees *Jennifer Williamson; Dick Williamson; Paul Strang; Christine Chapman; Terry Jones; Christine Reid.*

CC Number 299108

Information available Full accounts were provided by the trust.

General 'One of the trustees' aims is to support work for charities which find it difficult or impossible to obtain funds from other sources. Some projects are supported on a start-up basis, others involve funding over a longer term.'

The charities supported are mainly those whose work is already known to the trustees and who report on both their needs and achievements. Each year a handful of new causes are supported. However the trust states that 'the chances of success for a new application are about 100–1'.

In 2002/03 it had assets of £1.3 million, which generated an income of £70,000. Grants totalling £82,000 were made to 20 organisations, only a quarter of which were not supported in the previous year.

The largest grants were £10,000 to Pembroke College – Oxford, £8,000 to Friends of Home Farm Trust, £6,500 to European Men's Health Development Foundation, £6,000 each to Purcell School and Trinity College of Music, £5,500 to Stroud Court Community Trust and £5,000 to Greenhouse Trust.

Other beneficiaries included Carthusian Trust (£4,000), Winged Fellowship Trust (£3,100), RSPB (£3,000), Friends of Animal League (£2,500), Playhouse Theatre Trust (£2,100), Royal Scottish Academy of Music (£1,000) and Susy Lamplugh Trust (£500).

Exclusions No support for individuals or non–registered charities.

Applications In writing to the correspondent during the first fortnight in February. Applications should be kept short, ideally on one sheet of A4. Further material will then be asked of those who are short-listed. The trustees normally make their distribution in March.

The Rootstein Hopkins Foundation

Arts

£74,000 to organisations (2002)

Beneficial area UK.

PO Box 14720, London W3 7ZG

Tel. 020 8746 2136

Correspondent The Secretary

Trustees *M J Southgate, Chair; G L Feldman; Ms J Hartwell; Mrs D Hopkins; Mrs J Morreau.*

CC Number 1001223

Information available Information was provided by the trust.

General The trust's objects are described as follows:

- To promote fine and applied arts by providing grants, bursaries and other financial assistance to schools of art, other art educational establishments, arts organisations, artists or groups of artists, and students or groups of them, art teachers and lecturers and groups of them, and any body which runs a school or arts school or otherwise promotes or develops for public benefit the development, study, research and practice of art in all its branches, but in particular painting, drawing, sculpture, photography and fine and applied art.
- To promote and develop the study and research of fine arts in all branches (particularly painting and drawing).
- To promote and develop the study and research into improved methods of display and visual mechanisms.

In 2002 it had assets of £1.5 million and an income of £155,000. Grants to organisations totalled £74,000.

Applications On a form available from the correspondent, to be returned by December.

The Cecil Rosen Foundation

Welfare, especially older people, infirm, people who are mentally or physically disabled

£267,000 (2001/02)

Beneficial area UK.

118 Seymour Place, London W1H INP

Tel. 020 7262 2003

Correspondent M J Ozin, Trustee

Trustees *Mrs L F Voice; M J Ozin; J A Hart.*

CC Number 247425

Information available Accounts were on file at the Charity Commission, but without a list of grants and only a limited review of activities.

General Established in 1966, the charity's main object is the assistance and relief of the poor, especially older people, the infirm or people who are disabled.

The correspondent has previously stated that almost all the trust's funds are (and will always continue to be) allocated between five projects. The surplus is then distributed in small donations between an unchanging list of around 200 organisations. 'Rarely are any organisations added to or taken off the list.'

In 2001/02 the trust had assets of £3.9 million and an income of £304,000. Grants were made totalling £267,000. As in recent years, no grants list was included in the accounts. However, the accounts stated that the charity made a donation of £100,000 to Jewish Blind and Disabled and £60,000 was given to The Cecil Rosen Charitable Trust (a charity with the same trustees as this foundation).

Exclusions No grants to individuals.

Applications The correspondent stated that 'no new applications can be considered'. Unsuccessful applications are not acknowledged.

The Rothermere Foundation

Education, general

£338,000 (2002/03)

Beneficial area UK and overseas.

Associated Newspapers, Northcliffe House, 2 Derry Street, London W8 5TT

Tel. 020 7938 6682

Correspondent V P W Harmsworth, Director of Corporate Affairs

Trustees *Rt Hon. Viscount Rothermere; V P W Harmsworth; J G Hemingway; Hon. Esme Countess of Cromer.*

CC Number 314125

Information available Information was on file at the Charity Commission.

General This trust was set up for: the establishment and maintenance of 'Rothermere Scholarships' to be awarded to graduates of the Memorial University of Newfoundland to enable them to undertake further periods of study in the UK; and general charitable causes.

In 2002/03 the foundation had assets of £608,000 and an income of £509,000 with grants totalling £338,000.

The largest grants were £58,000 to Royal Naval Division and £50,000 to London Symphony Orchestra.

Other grants include £13,000 to Bristol Cathedral, £12,000 to Dr Johnson House, £10,000 each to Stationers' and Newspaper Makers' Benevolent Fund and St Paul's Cathedral Foundation, £5,000 each to Weston Spirit and Prince of Wales Charitable Foundation, £2,100 to Royal Academy of Dramatic Art and £1,600 to Maccabi Union JCG Games.

Applications In writing to the correspondent.

Rowanville Ltd

Orthodox Jewish

£552,000 (2002/03)

Beneficial area UK and Israel.

8 Highfield Gardens, London NW11 9HB

Tel. 020 8458 9266

Correspondent J Pearlman, Governor

Trustees *J Pearlman; Mrs R Pearlman; M Neuberger; M D Frankel.*

CC Number 267278

Information available Full accounts were on file at the Charity Commission.

General The objectives of the trust are 'to advance religion in accordance with the orthodox Jewish faith' and to support 'philanthropic religious and educational activities'. Only 'established institutions' are supported.

In 2002/03 the trust carried assets of £3.8 million and had an income of £745,000. Grants totalled £552,000. The trust tends to make a large number of recurrent grants each year, giving all of its support to Jewish organisations.

By far the largest grant was £100,000 to Friends of Ohel Moshe. Other large grants went to Menorah Grammar School (£36,000), Yeshuas Chaim Synagogue (£35,000), Yeshivas Shaarei Torah (£24,600), Achisomoch Aid Co., Gateshead Jewish Academy for Girls, Telz Academy Trust and Torah 5759 Ltd. (£20,000 each), Beth Jacob Youth Movement (£15,300), Union of Hebrew Congregations (£13,800), Emuno Educational Centre (£13,000), Sefer Torah - HaSofer (M.Flumenbaum) (£12,000), British Friends of Kerem Be Yavneh and Yesodi HaTorah School (£11,000 each) and London Jewish Girl's High School (£10,000).

Smaller grants range from £120 to £8,000 some beneficiaries are BCG CT, Edgware Yeshiva, Emuno Educational Centre, Friends of Beis Eliyohu Trust, J.L.E., Kollel Rabbi Yechiel, Od Yoseph Chai, SOFOT, Yad Toiva Trust and Yeshivo Ho Romo.

Applications The trust states that applications are unlikely to be successful unless one of the trustees has prior personal knowledge of the cause, as this charity's funds are already very heavily committed.

Joshua and Michelle Rowe Charitable Trust

Jewish

£341,000 (2002/03)

Beneficial area UK and worldwide.

84 Upper Park Road, Salford M7 4JA

Tel. 0161 720 8787

Correspondent J Rowe, Trustee

Trustees *J Rowe; Mrs M B Rowe.*

CC Number 288336

Information available Accounts were on file at the Charity Commission.

General In 2002/03 the trust had assets of £132,000 with an income of £434,000 and grants totalling £341,000.

The largest grants were £180,000 to UJIA, £57,000 to King David School, £20,000 to Manchester Kashrus Authority, £11,000 to Aish Hatorah and £10,000 each to Tel Hai Fund and Office of the Chief Rabbi.

Other grants include £6,000 to Shaarei Torah, £5,000 each to Matono Ezra and Friends of Bnei Triva, £3,000 each to Community Security Trust and Stenecourt Charity, £2,000 each to Yeshevat Keren Byavneh and Higher Crumpsall Hebrew Congregation.

Grants of £1,000 or less were awarded to Academy for Rabbanical Research, Ahaves Chessed Charity, El-Ami, BAAR Hatorah, Broome Foundation, Friends of Beis Eliyahu Trust, JNF Charitable Trust, Ziv Hatorah, Yenham Centre for Torah Education, Rabbi Lieb, Our Lady's High School, Migdal, Neive Casall Synagogue and Purim Fund Rabbi Bamberger.

Applications In writing to the correspondent.

The Rowing Foundation

Water sports

£30,000 (2003)

Beneficial area UK.

2 Roehampton Close, Roehampton, London SW15 5LU

Tel. 020 8878 3723 **Fax** 020 8878 3723

Email pbr@tesco.net

Website www.ara-rowing.org/development/foundation

Correspondent Pauline Churcher, Secretary

Trustees *David Parry, Chair; John Buchan; Helen Foord; Phil Phillips; Pat Sherwin; Anne Gregory-Jones; Pauline Churcher.*

CC Number 281688

Information available Information was available on the foundation's website.

General The Rowing Foundation was set up in 1981 to generate and administer funds for the aid and support of young people (those under 18 or still in full-time education) and people who are disabled of all ages, through their participation in sport and games, particularly water sports. Its income is mainly dependent on donations from the rowing fraternity. Grants in 2003 totalled £30,000.

Grants are made in the range of £500 and £2,000 to pump-prime projects. The foundation is anxious to help organisations and clubs whose requirements may be too small or who may be otherwise ineligible for an approach to the National Lottery or other similar sources of funds. It has also helped to get rowing started in areas where it did not exist or was struggling. Beneficiaries have included: Headington School – Oxford to purchase single sculling boats, designed specifically for juniors; Doncaster Schools Rowing Association to help provide equipment; Merchant Taylors' School – Crosby with their joint scheme with the Birkdale School for the Hearing Impaired; the Rees Thomas School – Cambridge for children with special needs; and Iffley Mead School – Oxford.

Grants have also been made towards the purchase of buoyancy aids, splash suits, canoes and the promotion of taster rowing courses for youth clubs, sailing and other water sports clubs.

Exclusions The foundation does not give grants to individuals, only to clubs and organisations, and for a specific purpose, not as a contribution to general funds.

Applications In writing to the correspondent.

The Rowlands Trust

General

£175,000 (2003)

Beneficial area UK, but primarily the West Midlands, South Midlands, and Gloucestershire.

c/o Wragge & Co., 55 Colmore Row, Birmingham B3 2AS

Tel. 0121 233 1000

Correspondent Ms N Fenn, Clerk to the Trustees

Trustees *A C S Hordern, Chair; G B G Hingley; K G Mason; Mrs A M I Harris; Mrs F J Burman.*

CC Number 1062148

Information available Information provided by the trust.

General This trust makes grants for 'research, education and training in the broadest sense so as to promote success' and to 'support charities providing for medical and scientific research, the sick, poor, handicapped, elderly, music, the arts and the environment'. The geographical area of benefit is the West Midlands and South Midlands, including Hereford and Worcester, Gloucester, South Shropshire and Birmingham.

In 2003 the trust had assets of £5.1 million, an income of £181,000 and made 85 grants totalling £175,000, broken down as follows:

Research, education and training areas – 28 grants totalling £86,000

City Technology College and Shenley Court received £15,000 each; Baverstock School (£14,000).

Medical and Scientific Research – 1 grant of £15,000

Motor Neurone Disease (£15,000)

The Services – 3 grants totalling £12,000

The Police Rehabilitation Trust and Royal British Legion recieved £5,000 each; Army Benevolent Fund (£2,000).

The Sick, the Poor, the Handicapped and the Elderly – 43 grants totalling £50,000

The largest grants were £5,000 to the Elizabeth Dowells Trust and Where Next Association, Sunfield Children's Homes (£3,000), Royal Midlands Counties Home for the Disabled (£2,500), Areley Kings Parish Room (£2,000).

Music – 1 grant of £1,000

Elgar School of Music (£1,000)

The Arts – 4 grants totalling £7,000

Belgrade Theatre Trust, Hereford Three Choirs, Leominster Folk Museum (£2,000 each), William Brookes School - Much Wenlock (£1,000).

The Environment – 5 grants totalling £4,000

Castle Bromwich Hall Gardens (£1,500), British Trust for Conservation Volunteers - Gloucester (£1,000), Cotswolds Canals Trust, Peoples' Trust for Endangered Species and Soil Association (£500 each).

Exclusions No support for individuals or to charities for the benefit of animals.

Applications On a form available from the correspondent, to be returned with a copy of the most recent accounts. The trustees meet to consider grants four times a year.

Royal Artillery Charitable Fund

Service charities

£54,000 to organisations (2003)

Beneficial area UK and overseas.

Front Parade, Royal Artillery Barracks, Woolwich, London SE18 4BH

Tel. 020 8781 3004 **Fax** 020 8654 3617

Email welfsec.rhgra@army.mod.uk.net

Correspondent The Welfare Secretary

CC Number 210202

Information available Information was provided by the trust.

General In 2003 it had assets of £14 million and an income of £1.2 million. Grants to organisations totalled £54,000. A further £586,000 was given in total to over 2,000 individuals.

Most of the grant total went to Army Benevolent Fund in various grants. Other beneficiaries included: King Edward VII Hospital (£2,000); and 'Not Forgotten' Association (£1,500).

Applications In writing to the correspondent.

Royal Masonic Trust for Girls and Boys

Children, young people

£109,000 to non-Masonic charities (2001)

Beneficial area UK.

31 Great Queen Street, London WC2B 5AG

Tel. 020 7405 2644 **Fax** 020 7831 4094

Website www.rmtgb.org

Correspondent Lt Col J C Chambers, Secretary

Trustees *Col G S H Dicker; Rt Hon. the Lord Swansea; M B Jones; P A Marsh.*

CC Number 285836

Information available Full accounts were on file at the Charity Commission.

General This trust was established in 1982. It predominantly makes grants to individual children of Freemasons who are in need. Grants are also made to UK non-Masonic organisations working with children and young people and it also supports bursaries at cathedrals and collegiate chapels.

In 2001 it had assets of £129 million and an income of £9.2 million. From a total expenditure of £8.8 million, grants totalled £272,000. Most of the grant total went to individuals, with choral bursaries totalling £174,000. The remaining £109,000 went in grants to 15 organisations.

These were £33,000 to Newman School – Rotherham, £15,000 to Winston's Wish, £12,000 to British Blind Sport, £10,000 each to Endeavour Training and Norman Laud Association, £8,200 to Side by Side, £5,000 each to Christ's Hospital Band, Nigel Clare Network, Plymouth Hospital School and Henry Spink Foundation, £100 to Fleet Air Arm Officers and £50 each to Ormskirk Grammar School, Reeds School, Royal Wolverhampton School and Wolverhampton Grammar School.

Applications In writing to the correspondent.

The J B Rubens Charitable Foundation

Mainly Jewish causes

£175,000 (2000/01)

Beneficial area UK, Israel, USA, India, Sri Lanka, Pakistan, South Africa, New Zealand, Australia, Canada.

Berkeley Square House, Berkeley Square, London W1J 6BY

Tel. 020 7491 3763 **Fax** 020 7491 0818

Correspondent Michael Phillips, Trustee

Trustees *Michael Phillips; J B Rubens Charity Trustees Limited.*

CC Number 218366

Information available Full accounts were on file at the Charity Commission.

General In 2002/03 this trust had an income and total expenditure of £377,000. Further information for this year was not available.

The 2000/01 accounts stated: 'The trustees receive applications from a wide variety of charitable institutions, including those engaged in medical and ancillary services (including medical research), education, helping the disabled and old aged, relieving poverty, providing sheltered accommodation, developing the arts, etc. The trustees consider all requests which they receive and make donations as they feel appropriate.'

The foundation is connected to two other charities, Ruth and Michael Phillips Charitable Trust and The Phillips Family Charitable Trust, sharing a common address and some of the trustees.

In 2000/01 the foundation had assets of £8.7 million, which generated an income of £371,000. Grants were made to five organisations totalling £175,000. Administration costs for the year were very high at £121,000.

The largest grants was £140,000 to Ruth and Michael Phillips Charitable Trust, a connected charity. Other beneficiaries were Simon Weisenthal Centre (£17,000), Charities Aid Foundation (£10,000), Jerusalem Foundation (£7,700) and Jewish Blind and Physically Handicapped Society (£500).

Exclusions No grants are made to individuals.

Applications In writing to the correspondent, at any time.

William Arthur Rudd Memorial Trust

General in the UK, and certain Spanish charities

£44,000 (2001/02)

Beneficial area In practice UK and Spain.

12 South Square, Gray's Inn, London WC1R 5HH

Tel. 020 7405 8932 **Fax** 020 7831 0011

Correspondent Miss A A Sarkis, Trustee

Trustees *Miss A A Sarkis; D H Smyth; R G Maples.*

CC Number 326495

Information available Full accounts were on file at the Charity Commission.

General This trust makes grants in practice to UK charities and certain Spanish charities. In 2001/02 the trust had assets of £661,000, an income of £47,000 and made grants totalling £44,000. The accounts state donations were made to registered charities in the UK and to certain spanish charities; however, no grants list was provided.

Applications As the trust's resources are fully committed, the trustees do not consider unsolicited applications.

The Rural Trust

Countryside

£30,000 (2003)

Beneficial area UK.

Fraser House, Albemarle Street, London W1S 4JB

Tel. 020 7409 1447 **Fax** 020 7409 1449

Correspondent Dr Charles Goodson-Wickes, Chairman

Trustees *Dr C Goodson-Wickes; The Earl of Stockton; H B E van Cutsem; R Matthew.*

CC Number 1060040

Information available Information was provided by the trust.

General The trust makes grants towards the protection, maintenance or preservation of the countryside, and to educate the public and promote any object that will benefit the countryside.

In 2003 the trust had an income of £51. It made grants totalling £30,000. Beneficiaries included the Barn Owl Trust (£500) and the Moorland Mousie Trust (£250). A further breakdown was not available, however we do know that in 1999/2000 beneficiaries included Centurion Press for an educational video 'Our Countryside Matters' (£9,000); Rural Buildings Trust for barn restoration in North Yorkshire (£2,000); Oxenhope Millennium Green for the creation of a green in the Pennines (£1,500); Blake Shield BNA Trust for conservation projects for 7–16 year olds, Second Chance towards angling for children with special needs, and Wildlife Trust Cumbria for red squirrel protection (£1,000 each); Chicks towards country holidays for inner city kids (£500 each); and Burnbake Trust for river bank restoration in Wiltshire, and North Wales Wildlife Trust for a water vole survey (£250 each).

Exclusions No support for individuals, non-charitable bodies or of new buildings works.

Applications In writing to the correspondent.

Willy Russell Charitable Trust

General, arts

£42,000 to organisations (2001/02)

Beneficial area Worldwide.

Malthouse & Co., America House, Rumford Court, Rumford Place, Liverpool L3 9DD

Tel. 0151 284 2000

Correspondent J Malthouse, Trustee

Trustees *William M Russell; Ann Russell; John C Malthouse.*

CC Number 1003546

Information available Full accounts were on file at the Charity Commission.

General Playwright and author Willy Russell, probably best known for his films *Educating Rita* and *Shirley Valentine*, created his eponymous trust in 1991.

In 2001/02 it had an income of £52,000, almost entirely from donations received. Grants to 14 organisations totalled £42,000 whilst educational support to five individuals totalled £5,100. Management and administration charges were high at £8,600 and included payments to a firm of accountants in which one of the trustees is a senior partner. Whilst wholly legal, these editors always regret such payments unless, in the words of the Charity Commission, 'there is no realistic alternative'.

Beneficiaries included Avron Foundation (£20,000), Brainwave (£6,000), National Student Drama Ltd (£5,000) and Cyril Taylor Trust Fund (£1,000).

Applications In writing to the correspondent.

The Frank Russell Charitable Trust

Not known

£37,000 (2000/01)

Beneficial area Not known.

Richard Anthony & Co., 13–15 Station Road, London N3 2SB

Tel. 020 8349 0353

Correspondent A Levy, Trustee

Trustees *F Russell; J Russell; A Levy.*

CC Number 327548

Information available Very brief accounts were on file at the Charity Commission, but without a list of grants or a description of the trust's grant-making policy.

General The trust's accounts are very brief and therefore we have limited information as to what type of causes it supports and the size of grants made.

In 2000/01 the trust had assets of £246,000, an income of £13,000 and made grants totalling £37,000. A list of grant beneficiaries was not available.

Applications In writing to the correspondent. Unsolicited applications are not considered.

The Russell Trust

General

£300,000 (2001/02)

Beneficial area UK, especially Scotland.

Markinch, Glenrothes, Fife KY7 6PB

Tel. 01592 753311

Email russelltrust@trg.co.uk

Correspondent Mrs Cecilia Croal, Secretary

Trustees *Mrs Cecilia Croal; Fred Bowden; Duncan Ingram; David Erdal; Mrs Margaret Russell Granelli; Graeme Crombie.*

SC Number SC004424

Information available Accounts were provided by the trust, without full grants list.

General This family trust was established in 1947 in memory of Capt. J P O Russell who was killed in Italy during the Second World War. The trustees prefer to make grants to pump-prime new projects, rather than giving on an ongoing basis. Grants of up to £10,000 can be distributed; however, generally the amounts given are for between £250 and £2,000. Three or four larger grants of up to £20,000 may be awarded annually.

In 2001/02 it had assets of £7.4 million and an income of £271,000. Grants totalled £300,000, broken down as follows:

	2001/02	*2000/01*
St Andrew's University	£112,000	£58,000
Archaeology	£14,000	£9,200
National Trust for Scotland	£20,000	£20,000
Church	£6,000	£19,000
Music and the Arts	£33,000	£40,000
Education	£23,000	£14,000
Youth work	£7,000	£5,000
Preservation work	£30,000	£8,500
Iona Community	£1,700	£500
Local	£9,700	£18,000
General	£15,000	£13,000
Health and Welfare	£29,000	£27,000

Exclusions Only registered charities or organisations with charitable status are supported.

Applications On a form available from the correspondent. A statement of accounts must be supplied. Trustees meet quarterly, although decisions on the allocation of grants are made more regularly.

Ryklow Charitable Trust 1992 (also known as A B Williamson Charitable Trust)

Education, health and welfare

£73,000 (1998/99)

Beneficial area Worldwide.

Robinsons Solicitors, 83 Friar Gate, Derby DE1 1FL

Tel. 01332 291431 **Fax** 01332 291461

Email info@robinsons-solicitors.co.uk

Correspondent Stephen F Marshall

Trustees *A B Williamson; Mrs K Williamson; J B Nickols; J V Woodward; A Williamson; E J S Cannings.*

CC Number 1010122

Information available Accounts were on file at the Charity Commission.

General The trust says that its notes for applicants: 'have been compiled to help applicants understand how best it is felt the trust can be operated and the constraints of time under which the (unpaid) trustees must work. It will help enormously if you try to ensure that your application follows these guidelines if at all possible.'

Applications will only be considered for activities if they meet the following descriptions:

- medical research, especially that which benefits children
- assistance to students from overseas wishing to study in the UK or for UK students volunteering for unpaid work overseas
- projects in the developing world – especially those which are intended to be self-sustaining or concerned with education
- help for vulnerable families, minorities and the prevention of abuse or exploitation of children
- conservation of natural species, landscape and resources.

In 2002/03 the trust had an income of £38,000 and a total expenditure of £37,000. Further information for this year was not available.

In 2001/02 it had an income of £43,000 and a total expenditure of £68,000.

In 1998/99 the trust had assets of £1.5 million. Its income of £101,000 was made up of half donations and of half investment income. Grants totalling £73,000 were given to 61 organisations, 22 of which had been supported in the previous year.

Grants were in the range of £500 and £4,000. The two largest donations were £4,000 each to NSPCC and Plan International, while Gaumati (Nepal) High School Fund received £1,500.

The trust made 58 grants of £1,000 each. Education causes to receive grants included Mozambique Schools Fund, Tiger Kloot Educational Institution and The African Academy for CADD Training.

The trust gave to a wide variety of organisations including a number working in the areas of conservation, welfare and development. Recipients included Coral Cay Conservation, Galapagos Conservation Trust, Farm Africa, Aboriginal Support, Care International, Oxfam and Traidcraft.

An undisclosed number of grants were made to individuals in the year totalling £6,300.

Applications 'Applications should be brief. We are a small charity with few trustees and there is little time for all in turn to read numerous or long documents.

'A statement of your finances is a must, or better still, an audited financial report. Individual applicants unable to provide either should send details of the precise purpose for which help is required with reputable back-up evidence.

'The trustees read all applications (of which there are many) over the months of January and February because they feel that this is the only fair way of comparing the merits of one against another. To allow us to arrive at a fair distribution of available monies we ask that all applications reach us between 1 September and 31 December in any calendar year. Trustees can then devote January and February to the study of the needs before them. When decisions have been reached cheques are despatched at the end of March.

'Unfortunately we are unable to help every applicant no matter how deserving the cause may be. To keep down costs we do not write to unsuccessful applicants. Therefore if you have not heard from us before the end of April you will know that your application has been unsuccessful in that year.'

The Michael Sacher Charitable Trust

General

£161,000 (2000/01)

Beneficial area UK and Israel.

16 Clifton Villas, London W9 2PH

Tel. 020 7289 5873

Correspondent Mrs Irene Wiggins, Secretary

Trustees *Simon John Sacher; Jeremy Michael Sacher; Hon. Mrs Rosalind E C Sacher; Mrs Elisabeth J Sacher.*

CC Number 206321

Information available Full accounts were on file at the Charity Commission.

General This trust supports a wide range of organisations, with an interest in Jewish/Israeli organisations. In 2002 it had assets of £3.3 million and an income of £141,000. Grants were made totalling £135,000, broken down as follows:

Animal welfare – 1 grant of £6,700

This went to Whale and Dolphin Conservation Society.

Arts, culture and heritage – 10 grants totalling £44,000

The largest grants were £13,000 to Royal Opera House, £12,000 to Anglo-Russian Opera and Ballet Trust and £11,000 to Royal College of Music. The remaining beneficiaries were Pavilion Opera (£6,000), Royal National Theatre (£1,000), Nicholas Bear Charitable Trust (£700), Dorchester Arts Centre (£500), British Museum Development Trust and Friends of Jewish Arts and Culture (£200 each) and Glyndebourne Festival Society (£120).

Community and welfare – 4 grants totalling £8,500

Beneficiaries were Friends of the Hebrew University (£5,000), Community Security Trust (£3,300), RNLI (£100) and Zimbabwe Farmers' Trust Fund (£50).

Education – 3 grants totalling £69,000

By far the largest grant during the year was of £62,000 to Hebrew University Fund for Future Scientists. Other recipients were Flip's Fund (£5,000) and Emmaus South Lambeth Community Fund (£200).

General – 2 grants totalling £5,000

These were £3,000 to United Jewish Israel Appeal and £2,000 to New Israel Fund.

Medical and disability – 6 grants totalling £1,700

These went to Joseph Weld Hospice (£600), British Friends of Kishorit (£500), Brain Research Trust and Demelza House Children's Hospice (£200 each), Fergus Maclay Leukaemia Trust (£100) and Juvenile Diabetes Research Fund (£50).

Religious – 3 grants totalling £1,000

West London Synagogue received £600 whilst £200 each went to Jerusalem Foundation and Council for Christians and Jews.

Applications In writing to the correspondent at any time.

The Audrey Sacher Charitable Trust

Arts, medical, care

£75,000 (2002/03)

Beneficial area UK.

H W Fisher & Co, 11–15 William Road, London NW1 3ER

Tel. 020 7388 7000

Correspondent P Samuel

Trustees *Mrs Nicola Shelley Sacher; Michael Harry Sacher.*

CC Number 288973

Information available Accounts were on file at the Charity Commission, without a full list of grants.

General The trust states its main areas of work as the arts, medical and care. Grants are only made to charities known personally to the trustees and generally range from £250 to £30,000.

In 2002/03 the trust had assets of £1.3 million with an income of £52,500 and grants totalling £75,000.

The trust has broken down its grant distribution into these key areas:

Animals
£3,400 to Whale and Dolphin Conservation Society.

Children & Youth
£1,300 to KIDS, £1,000 to Norwood Ravenswood and £250 to NSPCC.

Community Care£2,000 to Community Security Trust.

Cultural
£25,000 to National Gallery Trust, £10,000 to British Friends of the Art Museums of Israel, £7,000 to Royal Opera House Foundation, £4,000 to Prince of Wales Charitable Foundation, £2,500 to Royal Academy Trust, £1,300 to English National Ballet School, £1,000 each to Royal Academy of Dance, Royal National Theatre and Tate Gallery Foundation, and £500 to Royal ballet School.

Education, Science and Technology
£3,500 to Insead UK Trust, £250 each to Weizmann Institute Foundation and British Friends of JCT.

Ethnic Organisations
£1,000 each to New Israel Fund and UK Friends of MDA.

Health£650 to Willow Foundation and £250 to Macmillan Cancer Relief.

Housing
£250 to Home Start

Overseas Aid
£500 to UK Friends of AWIS, £250 each to Flip's Fund and Venice in Peril Fund.

Religious Organisations
£2,000 to Jewish Care, £750 to Western Marble Arch Synagogue and £600 to West London Synagogue.

Other
£700 to J & J Sacher Charitable Trust.

Exclusions No grants to individuals or organisations which are not registered charities.

Applications In writing to the correspondent.

Dr Mortimer and Theresa Sackler Foundation

Arts, hospitals

£250,000 (2002)

Beneficial area UK.

15 North Audley Street, London W1K 6WZ

Tel. 020 7493 3842

Correspondent Christopher B Mitchell, Trustee

Trustees *Dr Mortimer Sackler; Theresa Sackler; Christopher Mitchell; Robin Stormonth-Darling; Raymond Smith.*

CC Number 327863

Information available Accounts were on file at the Charity Commission.

General The foundation was set up in 1985 by Mortimer Sackler of Rooksnest, Berkshire for general charitable purposes and 'the advancement of the public in the UK and elsewhere in the fields of art, science and medical research generally'.

The assets of the foundation stood at £5 million in December 2002 and it had an income of £1.2 million. Grants were made totalling £250,000. Grants made are as follows: £70,000 to Dulwich Picture Gallery Centre for Arts Education, £50,000 to National Gallery of Scotland-Sackler Sculpture Hall, £38,800 to World Monuments Fund in Britain, £30,000 to Reading University-Sackler Laboratories, £22,500 to The Louvre, £18,170 to Almeida Theatre Renovations and £10,000 each to Brain Research Trust and The Bradfield Foundation.

Applications To the correspondent in writing.

The Ruzin Sadagora Trust

Jewish

£210,000 (2001/02)

Beneficial area UK and Israel.

269 Golders Green Road, London NW11 9JJ

Correspondent I M Friedman, Trustee

Trustees *Israel Friedman; Sara Friedman.*

CC Number 285475

Information available Limited accounts were on file at the Charity Commission without a grants list since 1993/94.

General In 2001/02 the trust had assets of £500,000 with an income of £197,000 and grants totalling £210,000.

Grants include £165,000 to Friends of Ruzin Sadagora, £27,300 to Beth Israel Ruzin Sadagora, £10,000 to Knesset Mordechai Sadagora, £5,700 to Sundry Donations and £1,600 to Chayei Moshe Yeshivah.

Applications In writing to the correspondent.

This entry was not confirmed by the trust, but is correct according to information on file at the Charity Commission.

The Jean Sainsbury Animal Welfare Trust

Animal welfare

£171,000 (2002/03)

Beneficial area UK registered charities.

PO Box 469, London W14 8PJ

Tel. 020 7602 7948 **Fax** 020 7371 4918

Website www.jeansainsburyanimalwelfare.org.uk

Correspondent Mrs Madeleine Orchard, Administrator

Trustees *Jean Sainsbury; Colin Russell; Gillian Tarlington; James Keliher; Mark Spurdens; Evelyn Jane Winship.*

CC Number 326358

Information available Financial statements along with a grants list were provided by the trust.

General The trust was established in 1982 with the objective of benefiting and protecting animals from suffering. Around £3 million had been donated by 2001. The policy of the trustees is to support smaller charities concerned with animal welfare and wildlife. Some organisations receive regular donations. Seven overseas organisations were supported during the year.

In 2002/03 the trust had assets of £6.5 million with an income of £300,000 and grants totalling £171,000.

The largest grants were £8,000 to Animals in Need, £7,500 each to Royal Veterinary Society and All Creatures Great and Small Animal Sanctuary, and £7,000 each to Worcestershire Animal Rescue Shelter, North Clwyd Animal Rescue, Brent Lodge Bird & Wildlife Trust and Animals in Distress.

Other grants include £5,000 each to Great Dane Adoption Society, Animal Care and Bath Cats & Dogs Home, £4,500 to Animal Rescue Charity, £4,000 each to Willows Animal Sanctuary and SHEYA Greyhound and Lurcher Rescue, £3,500 each to Milstream Animal Shelter, National Canine Defence League, Easterleigh Animal Sanctuary and Hula Animal Rescue, £3,000 each to Barby Keel Animal Sanctuary, Lache Animal Sanctuary, Folly Wildlife Rescue and South West Equine Protection and £2,000 to Mountains Animal Sanctuary.

Grants of £1,000 or less were awarded to Worthing Animal Clinic, Waggy Tails Rescue, Dog Alert, Paws for Kids, Rotherham Dog Rescue, Island Farm Donkey Sanctuary, Vida Animal, Animal Lifeline, Save our Seabirds, Fife Cat Shelter, Environmental Animal Sanctuary, Hearing Dogs for Deaf People, Lord Whisky Sanctuary Fund, Compassion in World Farming, Gower Bird Hospital, Coventry City Farm, Skye View Animal Home, Cat Rescue and Greyhound Awareness League.

Exclusions No grants are made to individuals or non-registered charities and no loans can be given.

Applications In writing to the correspondent, including a copy of accounts. There are three trustees' meetings every year, usually in March, July and November. Application information is now available by visiting the website.

St Andrew Animal Fund Ltd

Animal welfare

£31,000 (2003)

Beneficial area UK and overseas, with a preference for Scotland.

10 Queensferry Street, Edinburgh EH2 4PG

Tel. 0131 225 2116 **Fax** 0131 220 6377

Email info@advocatesforanimals.org

Website www.advocatesforanimals.org

Correspondent Ross Minett

Trustees *Prof. Timothy Sprigge; Murray McGrath; Christopher Mylne; David Martin; Dr Jane Goodall; Heather Petrie; Rebecca Ford; Shona McManus; Stephen Blakeway; Emma Law, Audrey Fearn; Duchess of Hamilton; Virginia Hay*

SC Number SC005337

Information available Full accounts and policy information were provided by the trust.

General The fund was formed in 1969 to carry out charitable activities for the protection of animals from cruelty and suffering. Grants are awarded only to fund or to part-fund a specific project, e.g. building work, renovation, repairs and so on; an animal project – spaying/neutering, re-homing and so on; animal rescue/animal sanctuary – providing care for unwanted, ill or injured animals.

The activities during 2003 included making grants and awards to further animal welfare projects in the UK and overseas. The fund continued its involvement in a project dealing with the force feeding of ducks and geese in the production of foie gras, and with Focus on Alternatives, a group promoting the development, acceptance and use of humane alternatives to animals in research.

The trustees consider that the priorities for the charity in the next few years are support for the development of non-animal research techniques, funding farm animal and companion animal and wildlife projects to improve and enhance the welfare of animals.

In 2003 the assets of the fund stood at £608,000. Income totalled £71,000, including £31,000 from donations and legacies, £25,000 from investments and £16,000 from rent. Grants totalled £31,000 with other charitable expenditure amounting to £94,000.

There were 21 grants made in the year, the largest of which was £16,000 to Zimbabwe Horse Rescue Fund. There were six other grants of £1,000 or more; beneficiaries were Tinto Kennels (£3,000), Norwegian School of Veterinary Science (£1,200) and Fethiye Hayvan Dostlargi Dernegi - Turkey, Hwange Conservation Society - Zimbabwe, Monkey Guardians - Devon and Rhondda Valleys Animal Welfare (£1,000 each).

Beneficiaries of smaller grants included ATLA Abstracts, Dumfries & Galloway Canine Rescue Centre, Friends of the Ferals - Devon, Muirhead Animal Fund - Edinburgh, Rodent Rescue and Re-home - London, Stonehouse Animal Sanctuary - Carlisle and The Sanctuary - Morpeth.

Exclusions No support for routine day-to-day expenses.

Applications In writing to the correspondent. The trustees meet in April and applications must reach the fund by 28 February for consideration at the next meeting. Applications should include a copy of the latest accounts, the name and address of a referee (e.g. veterinary surgeon or an animal welfare organisation), the purpose for which any grant will be used and, where relevant, two estimates. Receipts for work carried out may be requested and the fund states that visits by representatives of the fund to those organisations receiving grants will be made at random.

St Gabriel's Trust

Higher and further religious education

£94,000 to organisations (2003)

Beneficial area Mainly in the UK.

Ladykirk, 32 The Ridgeway, Enfield, Middlesex EN2 8QH

Tel. 020 8363 6474

Correspondent Peter Duffell, Clerk

Trustees *General Secretary of the National Society; nine co-optative trustees and two nominated trustees.*

CC Number 312933

Information available Reports and financial statement were provided by the trust.

General The trust is concerned with the the advancement of higher and further education in one or more of the following ways:

- promotion of the education and training of people who are, or intend to become, engaged as teachers or otherwise in work connected with religious education
- promotion of research in, and development of, religious education
- promotion of religious education by the provision of instruction, classes, lectures, books, libraries and reading rooms
- granting of financial assistance to institutions of higher or further education established for charitable purposes only.

In 2003 the trust had assets of £5.1 million and an income of £228,000. Grants totalling £215,000 were made comprising £94,000 in corporate awards, £110,000 to St Gabriel's Programme (see below) and £12,000 in total to 14 individuals.

Six corporate grants were made, the largest being £60,000 to ACCT–RE Teachers Recruitment Initiative. Other beneficiaries were King's College – London (£21,000), Chruch House Symposium (£6,300), University of Exeter (£4,900), St Pierre International Youth Trust (£1,000) and University of East Anglia Conference (£490).

The trustees have committed funds for several corporate projects including:

(i) an initiative to recruit RE teachers, in conjunction with other trusts

(ii) the St Gabriel's Programme, an ongoing venture which has been run jointly with The Culham Institute, 'to develop thought and action in support of RE teachers'.

Awards to individuals are given towards course fees and expenses for teachers taking part-time RE courses whilst continuing their teaching jobs. Occasional grants have been given to those undertaking specialist research that will clearly benefit the religious education world.

Exclusions Grants are not normally available for: any project for which local authority money is available, or which ought primarily to be funded by the church – theological study, parish or missionary work – unless school RE is involved; and research projects where it will be a long time before any benefit can filter down into RE teaching. No grants are made to schools as such; higher and further education must be involved.

Applications In writing to the correspondent with an sae. Applicants are asked to describe their religious allegiance and to provide a reference from their minister of religion. Applications need to be received by the beginning of January, April or September as trustees meet in February, May and October.

St James' Trust Settlement

General

£313,000 (2002/03)

Beneficial area Worldwide.

44a New Cavendish Street, London W1G 8TR

Correspondent Edwin Green, Secretary

Trustees *Jane Wells; Cathy Ingram; Simon Taffler.*

CC Number 280455

Information available Full accounts were on file at the Charity Commission.

General The trust's main aims are to make grants to charitable organisations that respond to areas of concern which the trustees are involved or interested in. In the UK, the main concerns are health, education and social justice; in the USA the main areas are in education, especially to the children of very disadvantaged families, and in community arts projects.

Grants are made by the trustees through their involvement with the project. Projects are also monitored and evaluated by the trustees.

In 2002/03 the trust had assets of £3.9 million and an income of £113,000. Grants were paid totalling £313,000. Grants were made to 28 organisations the UK totalling £168,000 and 16 in the USA totalling £97,000. A further £337,000 was committed for future projects.

In the UK the largest single grant was £25,000 to Elizabeth House. Other large grants included Friends of Israel Educational Trust (£15,000), Lord Ashdown Charitable Settlement, Norwood and Soho Theatre and Writer's Centre (£10,000 each).

Smaller UK grants included those to Islington Music Centre (£7,000), Action for Kids Charitable Trust, Bath Institute of Medical Engineering, Caris Islington and Children of Chernobyl (£5,000 each).

In the USA, grants included those to Theatre for a New Audience (£44,000), Aspen Country Day School (£12,000), Human Rights Watch, International Women's Health Coalition and The McCarton School (£6,000 each).

Exclusions No grants to individuals.

Applications 'The trust does not seek unsolicited applications to grants, the trustees do not feel justified in allocating administrative costs to responding to applications. If you do send an application you must send a stamped addressed envelope.'

Joint Committee of St John & Red Cross Society

Human services

£400,000 to organisations (2000/01)

Beneficial area Worldwide

5 Grosvenor Crescent, London SW1X 7EH

Tel. 020 7201 5130 **Fax** 020 7235 9350

Email balwinder@jointcommittee.freeserve.co.uk

Correspondent Alan Baker

Trustees *Prof. Anthony Mellows; Miss Clare Dixon-Carter; Dr Gordon Paterson;*

Robert Clark Menzies; Roger De Lacy Holmes; Mrs Virginia Bearoshaw.

CC Number 225753

Information available Information was taken from the Charity Commission's database.

General Registered in 1964, this trust promotes the improvement of health, the prevention of disease and the relief of suffering throughout the world whether in peace or war. Its main activities are:

- providing help to war ex-servicemen who are disabled
- providing hospital libraries
- assisting medical and residential institutions
- providing help to the nursing profession
- assisting welfare work in service hospitals of HM Forces.

In 2000/01 it had assets of £6.3 million and an income of £928,000. Total expenditure was £1.6 million. Grants totalling £400,000 were made to organisations with a further £260,000 going to individuals.

Applications In writing to the correspondent.

Saint Luke's College Foundation

See below

About £50,000 a year

Beneficial area UK and overseas, with some preference for Exeter and Truro.

Heathayne, Colyton, Devon EX24 6RS

Tel. 01297 552281 **Fax** 01297 552281

Correspondent Professor Michael Bond

Trustees *The Bishop of Exeter; The Dean of Exeter; Diocesan Director of Education; Chairman of Diocesan Board of Finance; one nominated by the Bishop of Exeter; three nominated by the University of Exeter; four co-optative trustees.*

CC Number 306606

Information available Information was provided by the foundation.

General This foundation encourages original work and imaginative new projects by educational and training bodies. Postgraduate education and various study costs are also supported.

In 2003/04 it had an income of £150,000, of which about £50,000 is given in grants each year.

Exclusions Grants are not made for studies or research in fields other than religious studies, or for buildings or schools (except indirectly through courses or research projects undertaken by RE teachers). Block grants to support schemes or organisations are not made. Grants are not normally made for periods in excess of three years.

Applications Requests for application packs, and all other correspondence, should be sent to the correspondent. Applications are considered once a year and should be received by 1 May.

St Michael's and All Saints' Charities

Health, welfare

£108,000 (2002)

Beneficial area City of Oxford.

St Michael's Church Centre, St Michael at the North Gate, Cornmarket Street, Oxford OX1 3EY

Tel. 01865 240940

Correspondent P W Beavis

Trustees *C Burton; P Eldridge; R Hawes; M Lear; The Ven J Morrison; A Paine.*

CC Number 202750

Information available Full accounts were on file at the Charity Commission.

General 'Income of the charity is applied to relieve, either generally or individually, persons resident in the city of Oxford who are in conditions of need, hardship or distress. Grants may be made to institutions or organisations which provide services or facilities for such people.'

In 2002 the charities had assets of £468,000, an income of £109,000 and made a total of 48 grants amounting to £108,000. Grant beneficiaries included Marie Curie Cancer Care (£6,000), Oxford and District MENCAP (£5,500), Oxford Victim Support Scheme (£3,750), Friends of Ormerod School, Oxford and District Sports and Recreation Association for the Disabled – OXSRAD, Oxford OAP Club and RESTORE (£3,000 each), Abbeyfield Oxenford Extra Care Society, Cancer Relief Macmillan Nurses and Citizens Advice Bureau (£2,500 each).

Exclusions Individuals are very rarely supported.

Applications In writing to the correspondent.

The Late St Patrick White Charitable Trust

General

£72,000 (2002/03)

Beneficial area UK, with a possible preference for Hampshire.

HSBC Trust Co UK Ltd, Norwich House, Nelson Gate, Commercial Road, Southampton SO15 1GX

Tel. 023 8072 2217

Correspondent Barry Sims, Trust Manager

Trustee *HSBC Trusts Co. (UK) Ltd.*

CC Number 1056520

Information available information was provided by the trust.

General This trust has general charitable purposes, with most grants going to health, medical and welfare charities. In 2002/03 the trust gave grants totalling £72,000. Unfortunately no further information was available for this year.

In 2000/01 it had assets of £2 million, an income of £109,000 and gave grants to 57 organisations totalling £92,000. The largest grants included: £12,000 to Age Concern, £10,000 each to Dr Barnardo's and Royal National Institute for the Blind, £9,500 to Arthritis Research Campaign, £7,000 each to Cancer Research Campaign and Guide Dogs for the Blind Association, £6,000 to Institute of Cancer Research and £5,000 to Extracare Charitable Trust.

Other smaller donations included £2,000 to Action for Blind People and £1,000 each to Arthritis Care, Breakthrough Breast Cancer, Leukaemia Research Fund and National Library for the Blind. Many of the beneficiaries had been supported in previously years.

Applications In writing to the correspondent. Applications are considered in February, May, August and November.

Saint Sarkis Charity Trust

Armenian churches and welfare, disability, general

£303,000 (2002/03)

Beneficial area UK and overseas.

98 Portland Place, London W1B 1ET

Tel. 020 7636 5313

Correspondent Louisa Hooper, Secretary

Trustees *Mikhael Essayan; Boghos Parsegh Gulbenkian; Paul Curno; Robert Brian Todd.*

CC Number 215352

Information available Full accounts were provided by the trust.

General 'The principal objectives of the trust are the support of the Armenian Church of St Sarkis in London and Gulbenkian Library at the Armenian Patriarchate in Jerusalem. In addition, the trustees support other charities concerned with the Armenian Community in the UK and abroad, and to the extent that funds are available, grants are also made to small registered charities concerned with social welfare and disability.'

In 2002/03 it had assets of £5.5 million and an income of £241,000. Grants were made totalling £303,000.

As usual, the largest grants went to Armenian Church of St Sarkis (£79,000) and Surp Pirgic Hospital (£67,000). Other large grants went to Armenian Church of Great Britain (£23,000), Friends of Armenia (£21,000) and Kevork Tahtayan School (£20,000).

Other beneficiaries included Cafod and Sinfonietta Productions (£15,000 each), Elbow Room Dance Company (£10,000), London Armenian Poor (£7,500), Armenian Church for Information and Advice (£5,000), Field Land Foundation (£2,000) and Joseph Clarke School Trust and Gulbenkian Library at the Armenian Patriarchate – Jerusalem (£1,500).

Exclusions No grants to individuals.

Applications In writing to the correspondent. Trustees meet monthly.

The Saintbury Trust

General

£94,000 (2002)

Beneficial area Gloucestershire, West Midlands and Worcestershire; UK in exceptional circumstances.

Hawnby House, Hawnby, York YO62 5QS

Tel. 01439 798249

Correspondent Mrs V K Houghton, Trustee

Trustees *Victoria K Houghton; Anne R Thomas; Jane P Lewis; Amanda E Atkinson-Willes; Harry O Forrester.*

CC Number 326790

Information available Information on file at the Charity Commission.

General The trust gives grants for general charitable purposes, although the trust deed states that no grants can be given to animal charities. Grants are made to organisations in Gloucester, West Midlands and Worcestershire. They are only made in other parts of the UK in exceptional circumstances.

In 2002 the trust had assets of £5 million and an income of £194,000. Grants were made to 29 organisations totalling £94,000. Grants ranged from £2,000 to £25,000. Beneficiaries included University of Birmingham (£25,000), RAPt (£15,000), Batten Support and Research Trust, Cedar, Holy Trinity Church and The Friends of Woodlands (£5,000 each), Cherry Trees, Gloucestershire Family Mediation and Marie Curie Cancer Care (£4,000 each), Andover Mind (£2,000).

Exclusions No grants to individuals or to animal charities. The trust stated that they do not respond to 'cold-calling' from organisations outside its main beneficial area, and groups from other parts of the UK are only considered if personally known to one of the trustees.

Applications In writing to the correspondent. Applications are considered in April and November and should be received one month earlier.

The Saints & Sinners Trust

Welfare, medical

£87,000 (2002/03)

Beneficial area Mostly UK.

Lewis Golden & Co., 40 Queen Anne Street, London W1G 9EL

Tel. 020 7580 7313

Correspondent N W Benson, Trustee

Trustees *N W Benson; Sir Donald Gosling; P Moloney; N C Royds; I A N Irvine.*

CC Number 200536

Information available Full accounts were on file at the Charity Commission.

General This trust supports welfare and medical causes through the proceeds of its fundraising efforts.

In 2002/03 the trust had assets of £264,000 with an income of £68,000 and grants totalling £87,000.

The largest grants include £5,000 each to South Bucks Riding for the Disabled and White Ensign Association Limited, £4,000 each to Stroke Association, Sandy Gall's Afghanistan Appeal, Reform Foundation Trust, Marine Conservation Society, Manor House Trust, Cruisaid and AJET and £3,000 each to Motor & Allied Trade Benevolent Fund, Nuffield Orthopaedic Centre, Primary Immunodeficiency Association, Sight Savers International, Mike Ockrent Charitable Trust and Robert T Jones Memorial Trust.

Grants of £2,000 were awarded to Wild Camels Protection Fund, Police Rehabilitation Trust, British Limbless Ex-Service Men's Association, Stiftung Foundation, Refugio Aboim Ascensao, Refresh, NSPCC and Bud Flanagan Leukaemia Fund.

Grants of £1,000 or less include Action Against Hunger, Beverley's Appeal, Cystic Fybrosis, DeafPLUS, Foundation for the Study of Infant Deaths, St John Ambulance Berkshire, Caldecott Foundation, Lady Hoare Trust, Lord Taverners Limited, Pattaya Orphanage, Winged Fellowhip and 999 Club.

Exclusions No grants to individuals or non-registered charities.

Applications Applications are not considered unless nominated by members of the club.

The Salamander Charitable Trust

Christian, general

£79,000 (2002/03)

Beneficial area Worldwide.

Threave, 2 Brudenell Avenue, Canford Cliffs, Poole, Dorset BH13 7NW

Tel. 01202 706661

Correspondent John R T Douglas, Trustee

Trustees *J R T Douglas; Mrs Sheila M Douglas.*

CC Number 273657

Information available Full accounts were on file at the Charity Commission.

General Founded in 1977, the principal objects of the trust are the:

- relief and assistance of people who are poor or in need, irrespective of class, colour, race or creed
- advancement of education and religion
- relief of sickness and other exclusively charitable purposes beneficial to the community.

In 2002/03 the trust had assets of £1.3 million and an income of £64,000. Grants were made to 233 organisations totalling £79,000.

Grants of £1,000 or more totalled £16,000, beneficiaries included SAT- 7 Trust (£2,000), All Nations Christian College, All Saints in Branksome Park, Birmingham Christian College, Christian Aid, Churches Commission on overseas students, FEBA Radio, International Christian College, London Bible College, Middle East Media, Moorland College, St James PCC in Poole, SAMS, Trinity College and Wycliffe Bible Translators (£1,000 each).

Smaller grants were distributed to 211 beneficiaries totalling £63,000.

Exclusions No grants to individuals. Only registered charities are supported.

Applications The trust's income is fully allocated each year, mainly to regular beneficiaries. The trustees do not wish to receive any further new requests.

Salters' Charities

General

£155,000 (2003)

Beneficial area Greater London or UK.

The Salters' Company, Salters' Hall, 4 Fore Street, London EC2Y 5DE

Tel. 020 7588 5216 **Fax** 020 7638 3679

Email diane@salters.co.uk

Website www.salters.co.uk

Correspondent The Charities Administrator

Trustee *The Salters' Company: Master, Upper Warden and Clerk.*

CC Number 328258

Information available Information provided by the trust.

General The trust supports UK-wide charities concerned with children and young people, health, Christian aid, the developing world, the environment and members of the armed forces. Grants are also available to local charities connected with the City of London. As a livery company, the trust pays particular interest to charities a liveryman is involved with. In previous years, grants of around £2,000 have been given to around 80 charities each year where such sums can make a difference, placing less emphasis on giving small grants to large organisations. Many beneficiaries have received grants over a number of years.

In 2003 it had an income of £155,000, all of which was given in grants and was broken down as follows:

Children and youth – 13 grants totalling £28,000

Beneficiaries included Prince's Youth Business Trust – Northern Ireland Section (£4,000), Arkwright Scholarships, Federation of London Youth Clubs and Allan College Foundation (£3,000 each), Christ's Hospital, Hope and Homes for Children, King's Corner Project, Listening Books and Rainbow Trust (£2,000 each) and Just Ask – Counselling and Advisory Scheme and National Deaf Children's Society (£1,000 each).

Medical – 22 grants totalling £40,000

Only two grants were to a charity not supported the previous year. Recipients included Drugscope, Ability Net Thames Valley, Macmillan Cancer Relief, IRIS Fund, Parkinson's Disease Society and Home Farm Trust (£2,000 each) and British Diabetic Association and Westminster Pastoral Foundation (£1,000 each).

Christian aid – 3 grants totalling £6,000

These went to CARE, Church Urban Fund and St Botolph's Project (£2,000 each).

Environment/Developing World – 3 grants totalling £10,000

These went to World Conservation Monitoring Centre (£7,000) TEAR Fund (£2,000) and African Scholars' Fund (£1,000).

City – 10 grants totalling £22,000

These went to Lord Mayor's Appeal for 2002/03 (£5,000), Guildhall School Trust (£2,500), Community Links (£2,000), Mansion House Scholarship Scheme, Lord Mayor Treloar Trust (£2,000 each) and City University, St John Ambulance and Sheriffs' and Recorders' Fund (£1,000 each).

Armed forces – 5 grants totalling £5,000

Beneficiaries were Central London Sea Cadets Corps (£2,000), South West London Army Cadet Force, King's Royal Hussars Regimental Association (£1,500 each), Army Benevolent Fund (£1,000) and The Honourable Artillery Company (£500).

Homeless – 3 grants totalling £8,000

Beneficiaries included Centrepoint (£3,000) and Bryson House and Passage Appeal (£2,000 each).

Other donations – 17 grants totalling £19,000

Beneficiaries included Lord Todd Memorial Bursary (£3,000) and Sir Ralph Perring Senior Citizens Club and Royal British Legion – City of London poppy appeal (£2,000 each).

Exclusions Grants are not normally made to charities working with people who are homeless unless there is some connection with a liveryman of the company or with the Salters' City Foyer and the charities involved.

Applications In writing to the correspondent.

The Andrew Salvesen Charitable Trust

General

£100,000 (2000)

Beneficial area UK, with a preference for Scotland.

c/o Meston Reid & Co., 12 Carden Place, Aberdeen AB10 1UR

Tel. 01224 625554

Correspondent Mark Brown

Trustees *A C Salvesen; Ms K Turner; V Lall.*

SC Number SC008000

Information available Limited information was available from the trust.

General The trust gives grants for general charitable purposes, in particular it will support the arts, education/ training, medical sciences, and welfare of people who are young, elderly or ill.

In 2000 grants totalled £100,000. Unfortunately we were unable to obtain further up-to-date information.

In 1994 a total of £30,000 was awarded. Beneficiaries included Royal Zoological Society of Scotland (£7,500), Sick Kids Appeal (£5,000), Bield Housing Trust and Scottish Down's Syndrome Association (£3,500 each), Sail Training Association (£3,000) and MS Society in Scotland (£2,400). A number of miscellaneous distributions were also made, totalling £4,000.

Exclusions No grants to individuals.

Applications The trustees only support organisations known to them through their personal contacts. The address holders told us that all applications sent to them are thrown in the bin.

The Sammermar Trust

General

£238,000 (2002)

Beneficial area UK and overseas.

Swire House, 59 Buckingham Gate, London SW1E 6AJ

Tel. 020 7834 7717

Correspondent Mrs D Omar

Trustees *Lady Judith Swire; M Dunne; B N Swire; Sir Kerry St Johnson; Mrs M.V.Allfrey.*

CC Number 800493

Information available Accounts were on file at the Charity Commission.

General The trust, formerly known as The Adrian Swire Charitable Trust, was established in 1988 with general charitable purposes.

In 2002 the trust had assets of £3.5 million and an income of £135,000. Grants were made totalling £238,000.

The largest grants were £100,000 to Southampton University Development Trust, £13,000 to St Clement Danes Resident Chaplain's Discretionary Fund. The trust is also committed to making grants of approximately £12,000 to The Cystic Fibrosis Trust over the next three years (stated in 2002).

Five grants of £10,000 were given to Blond McIndoe Centre, British Empire & Commonwealth Museum, Griffin Hall Trust, Head & Neck Cancer Research Trust and ss Great Britain. Eight grants of £5,000 went to charities such as Royal Air Force Museum, Vivat Trust and Yehudi Menuhin School.

Further smaller grants between £1,000 and £4,000 were made to such charities as Amber Foundation, Glydebourne Festival, Spitfire Society, Waterford School Trust, Worcestershire Association for the Blind and Wordsworth Trust.

Applications In writing to the correspondent. The trustees meet monthly.

Coral Samuel Charitable Trust

General, health, the arts

£133,000 (2002/03)

Beneficial area UK.

c/o Great Portland Estates plc, Knighton House, 56 Mortimer Street, London W1N 8BD

Tel. 020 7580 3040

Correspondent Mrs Coral Samuel, Trustee

Trustees *Coral Samuel; P Fineman.*

CC Number 239677

Information available Full accounts were provided by the trust.

General This trust was established in 1962 by Coral Samuel, the wife of Basil Samuel, who has a larger charitable trust in his name.

It makes grants of £10,000 or more to educational, cultural and social welfare charities plus a number of smaller donations to other charities.

In 2002/03 the trust's assets totalled £4.2 million. The income was £209,000 and grants to charities totalled £133,000.

In total grants were made to 23 organisations, 7 of which were supported in the previous year. The two largest grants went to Imperial College of Science and Technology (£20,000) and Royal Opera House (£15,000). Recipients of £10,000 each were Save Britains's Heritage, Royal Academy Trust and The Wallace Collection.

The remaining, smaller grants ranged from £500 to £5,000. A wide variety of organisations were supported including National Portrait Gallery, DeafPlus, Jewish Museum, Wiltshire Air Ambulance and Royal College of Radiologists (£5,000 each); New West End Synagogue (£2,000); Alexandra Rose Day, Jewish Deaf Association, Music Therapy Charity and JMI (£1,000 each); and The Costume Society and British Wizo (£500 each).

Exclusions Grants are only made to registered charities.

Applications In writing to the correspondent.

The Peter Samuel Charitable Trust

Health, welfare, conservation, Jewish care

£112,000 (2002/03)

Beneficial area South Berkshire, Highlands of Scotland and East Somerset.

The Estate Office, Castle Road, Farley Hill, Berkshire RG7 1UL

Tel. 0118 973 0047 **Fax** 0118 973 0385

Correspondent Mrs Harriet Robbins, Trust Administrator

Trustees *Hon. Viscount Bearsted; Hon. Michael Samuel.*

CC Number 269065

Information available Accounts were on file at the Charity Commission, without a recent grants list.

General The trustees' report states: 'The trust seeks to perpetuate the family's interest in the medical sciences, the quality of life in the local areas, heritage and land/forestry restoration'.

In 2002/03 it had assets of £2.6 million, which generated an income of £126,000. Grants were made to organisations totalling £112,000.

By far the largest grants were £48,000 to Pippin and £20,000 to Union of Liberal and Progressive Synagogues. The next largest were £6,000 to Barkingside Jewish Youth Centre, £5,000 each to Child Bereavement Trust and Maidenhead Synagogue, £4,600 to Game Conservancy and £4,000 to University of Reading.

Other beneficiaries included Chicken Shed Theatre Company (£3,000), Jewish Care (£2,500), Weizman Institute of Science (£2,000), National Association of Gifted Children (£1,500), Oxford University Jewish Society and Woodland Trust (£500 each) and BBONT (£200).

Exclusions No grants to purely local charities outside Berkshire or to individuals.

Applications In writing to the correspondent. Trustees meet twice-yearly.

The Camilla Samuel Fund

Medical research

£36,000 (2001/02)

Beneficial area UK.

Upton Viva, Banbury, Oxfordshire OX15 6HT

Correspondent The Secretary to the Trustees

Trustees *Sir Ronald Grierson; Hon. Mrs Waley-Cohen; Dr Hon. J P H Hunt; J Grierson.*

CC Number 235424

Information available Information was supplied by the trust.

General The trust supports medical research projects in a discipline agreed by the trustees at their annual meetings.

In 2001/02 the trust had assets of £611,000, an income of £23,000 and made grants totalling £36,000. Grant beneficiaries were Imperial Cancer Research Fund (£30,000) and EORTC (£6,000).

Exclusions No grants to individuals, general appeals or any other charitable institution.

Applications The trustees will request written applications following the recommendation of a suitable project by the medical trustees. However, please note that as all the money available, together with the fund's future income, has been earmarked for four years for an important research project, the fund will not be in a position to consider any applications for grants during this period.

Jimmy Savile Charitable Trust

General

£33,000 (2002/2003)

Beneficial area UK.

Stoke Mandeville Hospital, Mandeville Road, Aylesbury, Buckinghamshire HP21 8DL

Correspondent The Trustees

Trustees *Sir James Savile; James Collier; Harold Gruber; Luke Lucas.*

CC Number 326970

Information available Full accounts were on file at the Charity Commission.

General The trust's 2002/03 annual report states that the objects of the charity are 'to provide funds for the relief of poverty, the relief of sickness and other charitable purposes beneficial to the community including the provision of recreational and other facilities for people with disability'.

In 2002/03 it had assets of £2.9 million, an income of £153,000 and made grants totalling £33,000.

Grant beneficiaries included Across Scotland Trust (£7,500), Leukaemia Research Fund (£5,000), Around the World in 80 (£3,000), Disability Aid Fund (£1,500), Children's Charity, Garel Vale Fund, Glencoe Mountain Rescue, Leukaemia Fund and Little Sisters of the Poor (£1,000 each) and Children's Fire & Burns Unit (£500).

Applications The trust does not respond to unsolicited applications.

The Scarfe Charitable Trust

Environment, churches, arts

£67,000 (2003/04)

Beneficial area UK, with an emphasis on Suffolk.

Salix House, Falkenham, Ipswich, Suffolk IP10 0QY

Tel. 01394 448 339 **Fax** 01394 448 339

Email ericmaule@hotmail.com

Correspondent Eric Maule

Trustees *N Scarfe; E E Maule.*

CC Number 275535

Information available Information was provided by the trust.

General The trust was established in 1978 by W S N Scarfe. In 2003/04 it had assets of £1 million and an income of £71,000. Grants totalled £67,000.

The largest was £20,000 to Institute of Neurology for research into multiple sclerosis, which has also been the largest beneficiary in previous years although this relationship has now ceased. Other recipients included Aldeburgh Productions (£8,000), Green Light Trust (£3,000) and Cultural Village of Europe (£2,500).

Applications In writing to the correspondent.

The Schapira Charitable Trust

Jewish

£54,000 (2002)

Beneficial area UK.

2 Dancastle Court, 14 Arcadia Avenue, Finchley, London N3 2JU

Tel. 020 8371 0381

Correspondent The Trustees

Trustees *Issac Y Schapira; Michael Neuberger; Suzanne L Schapira.*

CC Number 328435

Information available Accounts were on file at the Charity Commission, but without a narrative report.

General This trust appears to make grants exclusively to Jewish charities.

In 2001 the trust had assets of £34,000, an income of £411,000 and made grants totalling £54,000. Beneficiaries included SOFT (£8,800), NWLC (£5,000), Beis Trane and BHHS (£4,000 each), UTA (£3,000), Friends of Wizttitz (£2,800), GUR (£2,700), Gateshead of Talmudical College (£2,000), Finchley Road Synagogue (£2,200) and PH Grammar (£1,800).

Applications In writing to the correspondent.

The Annie Schiff Charitable Trust

Orthodox Jewish education

£72,000 (2001/02)

Beneficial area UK, overseas.

8 Highfield Gardens, London NW11 9HB

Tel. 020 8458 9266

Correspondent J Pearlman, Trustee

Trustees *J Pearlman; Mrs R Pearlman.*

CC Number 265401

Information available Full accounts were on file at the Charity Commission.

General The trust's objectives are:

- relief of poverty, particular amongst the Jewish community
- advancement of education, particularly the study and instruction of Jewish religious literature
- advancement of religion, particularly Judaism.

In 2001/02 it had assets of £256,000 and an income of £62,000, which included £28,000 in donations received. Grants were made to 15 organisations totalling £72,000.

These were £11,000 to Beis Yaacov Primary School (£11,000), Be'er Avrohom (UK) Trust (£8,000), Friends of Nachalat Osher Charitable Trust (£7,500), Gevurath Ari Torah Academy Trust (£7,000), Telz Talmudical Academy and Talmud Torah Trust (£6,000), Torah Teminah Primary School (£5,500), Friends of Beis Yisroel Trust (£5,000), Friends of Ohel Moshe (£4,000), Choshen Mishpat Centre (£2,000), Yeshivo Horomo Talmudical College (£1,500) with £1,000 each to Gateshead Beis Hatalmud Scholarship Fund, Institute for Higher Rabbinical Studies, Mechinoh L'Yeshiva and Yesodey Hatorah Schools.

Exclusions No support for individuals and non-recognised institutions.

Applications In writing to the correspondent, but grants are generally made only to registered charities. The trust states that presently all funds are committed.

The Schmidt-Bodner Charitable Trust

Jewish, general

£57,000 (2002/03)

Beneficial area Worldwide.

5 Fitzhardinge Street, London W1H 6ED

Tel. 020 7486 3111

Correspondent Harvey Rosenblatt

Trustees *Mrs E Schmidt-Bodner; Marion Diner; Linda Rosenblatt.*

CC Number 283014

Information available Full accounts were on file at the Charity Commission.

General This trust mainly supports Jewish organisations though it has also given a few small grants to medical and welfare charities. In 2002/03 it had assets of £1.1 million, an income of £198,000 and made 16 grants totalling £57,000.

Of grants made in the year, 9 were for £1,000 or more. The largest donation was £11,000 to UJIA. Other beneficiaries included Friends of Lubavitch Uk and Jewish Care (£10,000 each), Community Security Trust, J F S Charitable Trust and Norwood Ravenswood (£5,000 each), Simon Marks Jewish Primary School Trust (£1,250) and CHAI-Lifeline and Jerusalem Foundation (£1,000 each).

Smaller grants included £800 to British WIZO, £250 to Shaare Zedek UK and £110 to Friends of Bikur Cholim Hospital.

Applications In writing to the correspondent.

The R H Scholes Charitable Trust

Children and young people who are disabled or disadvantaged

£37,000 (2002/03)

Beneficial area England.

Fairacre, Bonfire Hill, Southwater, Horsham, West Sussex RH13 9BU

Email roger_pattison@msn.com

Correspondent R H C Pattison, Trustee

Trustees *R H C Pattison; Mrs A J Pattison.*

CC Number 267023

Information available Information was provided by the trust.

General This trust currently only supports organisations in which the trustees have a special interest, knowledge of or association with. Both recurrent and one-off grants are made depending upon the needs of the beneficiary. Core costs, project and research grants are made. Funding for more than three years will be considered.

In 2002/03 it had assets of £632,000 and a net income of £33,000. A total of £37,000 was given to 118 organisations, with 180 applications turned down during the year. This gave an overall success rate of less than 40%.

The largest grants, of £1,000 each, went to Children's Country Holidays Fund, Church of England Pensions Board, Historic Churches Preservation Trust, Friends of Lancing Chapel, St Catherine's Hospice and Southwater Parish Church.

Other grants ranged from £100 to £800 each and included those to Home Farm Trust (£800), Finchale Training College (£700), Chichester Cathedral Trust (£600), Impact Foundation and Jessie's Fund (£500 each), Martha Trust and Royal Commonwealth Society (£400 each), Mountbatten Community Trust and Weston Spirit (£300 each), Jubilee Sailing Trust and National Institute of Conductive Education (£250 each), Support Dogs and Tools for Self-Reliance (£200 each), David Tolkien Trust (£150) and Playway (£100).

Exclusions Grants only to registered charities. No grants to individuals, animal charities, expeditions or scholarships. The trust tries not to make grants to more than one charity operating in a particular field, and does not make grants to charities outside England.

Applications In writing to the correspondent, although due to a lack of funds it is not currently accepting unsolicited applications from organisations it is not already supporting. Replies are only sent to unsuccessful applicants if an sae or e-mail address is provided.

The Schreiber Charitable Trust

Jewish

£107,000 (2002/03)

Beneficial area UK.

PO Box 35547, The Exchange, 4 Brent Cross Gardens, London NW4 3WH

Correspondent G S Morris, Trustee

Trustees *Graham S Morris; David A Schreiber; Mrs Sara Schreiber.*

CC Number 264735

Information available Full accounts were on file at the Charity Commission.

General In 2002/03 the trust had assets of £2.5 million and an income of £234,000. Grants totalling £107,000 were made to 15 organisations, of which 7 were also supported in the previous year.

The largest grant was £23,000 to Friends of Rabbinical College Kol Torah. Other large donations were £7,500 to Gateshead Talmudical College, £7,000 each to Aish Hatorah UK and Conference of European Rabbis, £6,100 to Friends of Ohr Somayach and £5,470 to Friends of Ohr Torah Limited. Smaller grants went to British Friends of Israel Museums (£3,700), British Friends of Gesher (£3,500), Finchley Road Synagogue (£2,700), Yesodeh Hatorah Grammar School (£1,700), Society of Friends of the Torah (£1,300) with £1,000 each to Beth Hayeled, Collel Chibath Yerushalayim and Friends of the Bikur Cholim Hospital.

Applications The trust states that all funds are currently committed. No applications are therefore considered or replied to.

Scopus Jewish Educational Trust

Jewish education

£120,000 (2001/02)

Beneficial area UK.

52 Queen Anne Street, London W1G 8HL

Tel. 020 8906 4455

Correspondent The Trustees

Trustees *P Ohrenstein, Chair; J Kramer; S Cohen; Mrs B Hyman.*

CC Number 313154

Information available Information was on file at the Charity Commission.

General This trust makes grants to Jewish day schools, associations, societies and institutions, calculated to benefit directly or indirectly Jewish education.

In 2001/02 the trust had assets of £2 million, an income of £129,000 and made grants totalling £120,000. Simon Marks Jewish Primary School received a grant of £31,000 and a further £89,000 was distributed towards the cost of the depreciation of school buildings.

Applications In writing to the address below.

The Scott Bader Commonwealth Ltd

See below

£134,000 (2003)

Beneficial area UK and overseas.

Wollaston, Wellingborough, Northamptonshire NN29 7RL

Tel. 01933 666755 **Fax** 01933 666608

Email commonwealth_office@scottbader.com

Website www.scottbader.com

Correspondent Denise Sayer, Secretary

Trustees *The Board of Management: S Carter; N Kegg; J Deamer; J Legg; P Dembicki; M Maille; R Coxon.*

CC Number 206391

Information available Information was provided by the trust.

General This commonwealth supports projects, activities or charities which: find difficulty raising funds; are innovative, imaginative and pioneering; or are initiated and/or supported by local people. Each year there is a particular area of focus, so applicants should check current focus before applying.

Grants are given for the assistance of distressed and needy people of all nationalities and the establishment and support of charitable institutions whose objects may include the advancement of education. The commonwealth looks for projects, activities or charities which: respond to the needs of those who are most underprivileged, disadvantaged, poor or excluded; encourage the careful use and protection of the earth's resources (those which assist poor rural people to become self reliant are particularly encouraged); or promote peace-building and democratic participation. The commonwealth also supports the research, development and advancement of education and advancement of education in industrial participation of a nature beneficial to the community.

In 2003 it had assets of £207,000, an income of £108,000 and made 394 grants totalling £134,000, including £38,000 in charity nomination scheme donations.

Larger grants in the UK included £8,000 to Family Care – Northampton, £5,000 each to Rugmark UK and Tools for Self Reliance – Milton Keynes, £4,700 to Volunteer Reading Help – Northampton, £4,000 to Shadwell Pre-School – Leeds, £3,100 to Hope Project – Wellingborough, £2,000 to Caring and Sharing Trust – Cogenhoe, £1,000 to Greens Norton Jubilee – Northampton and £75 to Oasis Coffee Shop – Wollaston.

Larger international donations included £5,000 each to Fulton School for the Deaf – South Africa and Rakitovo Self-Sufficiency Fund – Bulgaria, £4,900 to Phoenix – India, £4,200 to Sardeo – Zimbabwe, £3,400 to Abaseen Foundation – Pakistan, £2,500 to Children of Fiji – Fiji Islands, £2,100 to Arauna Ark Ministries – South Africa, £2,000 to Themba Lethu – South Africa, £1,700 to Deva Organisation Rural Development Society – India and £900 to Peace Child International.

Exclusions No support for charities concerned with the well-being of animals, individuals in need or organisations sending volunteers abroad. It does not respond to general appeals or support the larger well-established national charities. It does not provide educational bursaries or grants for academic research. It does not make up deficits already incurred, or support the arts, museums, travel/adventure, sports clubs or the construction, renovation or maintenance of buildings.

Applications In writing or by e-mail to the correspondent. Trustees meet quarterly in January, April, July and October.

Sir Samuel Scott of Yews Trust

Medical research

£121,000 (2003/04)

Beneficial area UK.

c/o Currey & Co, 21 Buckingham Gate, London SW1E 6LS

Tel. 020 7802 2700 **Fax** 020 7828 5049

Correspondent The Secretary

Trustees *Lady Phoebe Scott; Sir Oliver Scott; Hermione Stanford; Edward Perks.*

CC Number 220878

Information available Accounts were provided by the trust.

General In 2003/04 the trust had assets of £4.3 million and an income of £147,000. Grants totalled £121,000. The beneficiary of the largest grant was The Kathleen Trust who received a grant of £45,000. Other beneficiaries included University of Warwick (£10,000), Tommy's The Baby Charity (£6,000), Lepra, Leukaemia Research Fund, Royal Brompton and Harefield Charitable Fund, Royal College of Surgeons of England and University of Oxford (£5,000 each) and Epilepsy Research Foundation and University of Bristol (£4,000 each).

Exclusions • No core funding
- no support for purely clinical work
- no grants to individuals (although research by an individual may be funded if sponsored by a registered charity through which the application is made)
- no support for research leading to higher degrees (unless the departmental head concerned certifies that the work is of real scientific importance)
- no grants for medical students' elective periods
- no grants for expeditions (unless involving an element of genuine medical research).

Applications In writing to the correspondent. Trustees hold their half-yearly meetings in April and October and applications have to be submitted two months before. There are no special forms, but applicants should give the following information:

- the nature and purpose of the research project or programme
- the names, qualifications and present posts of the scientists involved
- reference to any published results of their previous research
- details of present funding
- if possible, the budget for the next 12 months or other convenient period.

All applications are acknowledged and both successful and unsuccessful applicants are notified after each meeting of the trustees. No telephone calls.

The Scouloudi Foundation

General

£191,000 (2003/04)

Beneficial area UK charities working domestically or overseas.

c/o Haysmacintyre, Fairfax House, 15 Fulwood Place, London WC1V 6AY

Tel. 020 7969 5500 **Fax** 020 7969 5529

Correspondent The Administrators

Trustees *Miss Sarah E Stowell, Chair; David J Marnham; James R Sewell.*

CC Number 205685

Information available Full accounts were provided by the trust.

General The foundation has three types of grants:

- Historical grants are made each year to the Institute of Historical Research at University of London for research and publications, to reflect the interests of the settlor, Irene Scouloudi, who was a historian
- Regular grants, generally of £1,000 each, are made to organisations on a five-year cycle

In 2003/04 the foundation had assets of £4.7 million, which generated an income of £200,000. Management and administration charges for the year were high at £26,000. Grants were made to 134 charities, totalling £191,000 and broken down as shown in the table below.

Institute of Historical Research at University of London, which received £60,000 as the historical award, also received a regular donation of £5,000. Aside from a further £5,000 to British Red Cross Disaster Fund and £1,500 to British Museum, the other 92 regular donations were of £1,000 each. Recipients included Arthritis Research Campaign, Barnardo's, British and International Sailors' Society, British Records Association, Cathedral Camps, Centrepoint, Crossroads Caring for Carers, CORDA, Environment Council, Family Welfare Association, Habitat Scotland, Help the Hospices, Historical Association, London Topographical Society, Mental Health Foundation, National Art Collections Fund, NSPCC, Professional Classes Aid Council, Reed's School, Royal Commonwealth Society for the Blind, Samaritans and UK Youth.

Special, one-off grants went to 18 organisations. British Red Cross Disaster Fund received £6,000. All other grants were of £1,000 each with beneficiaries including 3H Fund, Action for Blind People, Coram Family, JoLt, Marfan Trust, St Christopher's Hospice, Queen's Nursing Institute and Wisdom Hospice.

Exclusions Donations are not made to individuals, and are not normally made for welfare activities of a purely local nature.

THE SCOULOUDI FOUNDATION
Grants in 2003/04

Category	*Historical*	*Regular*	*Special*	*Total*	*%*
Aged	-	£7,000	£1,000	£8,000	4%
Children & youth	-	£9,000	£5,000	£14,000	7%
Environment	-	£10,000	-	£10,000	5%
Famine relief & overseas aid	-	£10,000	£6,000	£16,000	8%
Handicapped & disability	-	£17,000	£4,000	£21,000	12%
Humanities	£64,000	£14,000	–	£78,000	41%
Medicine & health	-	£19,000	£7,000	£26,000	14%
Social welfare	-	£11,000	£1,000	£12,000	6%
Welfare of armed forces & sailors	-	£6,000	–	£6,000	3%
Total	£64,000	£103,000	£24,000	£191,000	100%

The trustees do not make loans or enter into deeds of covenant.

Applications Copies of the regulations and application forms for 'Historical Awards' can be obtained from: The Secretary, The Scouloudi Foundation Historical Awards Committee, c/o Institute of Historical Research, University of London, Senate House, London WC1E 7HU.

Seamen's Hospital Society

Seafarers

£324,000 to organisations (2003)

Beneficial area UK.

29 King William Walk, Greenwich, London SE10 9HX

Tel. 020 8858 3696

Email shs@btconnect.com

Website www.seahospital.org.uk

Correspondent Peter Coulson, General Secretary

Trustees *Capt. S T Smith, Chair; A P J Lydekker; J C Jenkinson; J Allen; J D Guthrie; Capt. P M Hambling; P McEwan; Capt. G W S Miskin; A R Nairne; Capt. A G Russell; T Santamera; Capt. A J Speed; A F D Williams; G P Ellis; Dr J F Leonard; Capt. A J R Tyrrell.*

CC Number 231724

Information available Information was taken from the trust's website.

General This trust makes grants to medical, care and welfare organisations working with seafarers and to individual seafarers and their dependants. In 2003 the society distributed over £324,000 to organisations helping seafarers, with a further £80,000 to individuals.

Beneficiaries were Glasgow Veterans' Association for welfare services for seafarers, Merchant Seaman's War Memorial Society for holidays and towards disabled access, NUMAST John Davies Memorial Home for nursing costs and replacement of beds, Royal Alfred Seafarers' Society for nursing costs, Royal National Mission to Deep Sea Fishermen for transport of sick and injured seafarers, Royal Merchant Navy School Foundation for costs of transport and medical items for foundationers, Queen Victoria Seamen's Rest for welfare services for seafarers and Yarmouth International Seafarers' Centre for transport of sick and injured seafarers.

The society also operates the Seafarers' Benefits Advice Line, which provides free confidential advice and information on welfare benefits, housing, consumer problems, legal matters, credit and debt, matrimonial and tax. In 2003 they raised over £110,000 for their seafaring clients.

Applications On a form available from the correspondent. Grants are awarded in November of each year.

Search

Medical research, medicine, health

£104,000 (2002)

Beneficial area UK, with a possible preference for the south of England.

22 City Business Centre, 6 Brighton Road, Horsham, West Sussex RH13 5BB

Tel. 01403 211252 **Fax** 01403 271553

Email search@snowdonawardscheme.org.uk

Correspondent A Farquhar

Trustees *Dr R Leach; Prof. H Wolff; Prof S Glickman.*

CC Number 1038477

Information available Information was provided by the trust.

General This trust supports established medical research institutions and organisations benefiting people who are sick and disabled. Children and young adults may be considered.

In 2002 the trust had assets of £253,000 and an income of £115,000. Grants totalled £104,000. Major grants were £40,000 to the Institute of Child Health and £29,000 to Brunel University.

Exclusions No grants to individuals or students.

Applications Application forms are available from the correspondent. However, the trust states that all funds are currently committed.

The Searchlight Electric Charitable Trust

General

£67,000 (2002/03)

Beneficial area UK, with a preference for Manchester.

Searchlight Electric Ltd, 900 Oldham Road, Manchester M40 2BS

Tel. 0161 203 3300

Correspondent The Trustees

Trustees *H E Hamburger; D M Hamburger; M E Hamburger; J S Fidler.*

CC Number 801644

Information available Full accounts were on file at the Charity Commission.

General This trust has general charitable purposes, although most grants are given to Jewish organisations. A large number of grants are made in the Manchester area.

In 2002/03 the trust had assets of £550,000. The total income for the year was £44,000. Grants were made totalling £67,000.

The largest grants were £31,950 to UJIA, £3,500 to Manchester Jewish Federation and £3,300 to Lubavitch. Other grants were £2,000 to Young Israel Synagogue, £1,770 to Holy Law Synagogue, £1,400 to Vaad Haztsadaka. There were 5 grants of £1,000 which went to charities like Hillel House, British Friends of Laniado Hospital and Manchester Great and New Synagogue.

Smaller grants between £250 and £600 went to charities such as Heathlands Home for the Aged, Jewish National Fund, Manchester Chaplaincy Board, Manchester Charitable Trust and Manchester Beth Din.

Exclusions No grants for individuals.

Applications In writing to the correspondent, but note that in the past the trustees have stated that it is their policy to only support charities already on their existing list of beneficiaries or those already known to them.

The Searle Charitable Trust

Sailing

£56,000 (2000/01)

Beneficial area UK.

20 Kensington Church Street, London W8 4EP

Tel. 020 7761 7207

Correspondent A D Searle, Trustee

Trustees *Andrew D Searle; Victoria C Searle.*

CC Number 288541

Information available Full accounts were on file at the Charity Commission.

General This trust was established in 1982 by Joan Wynne Searle. Following the death of the settlor in 1995 the trust was split into two. One half is administered by the son of the settlor (Searle Charitable Trust) and the other half by her daughter (Searle Memorial Trust).

The Searle Charitable Trust only supports projects/organisations for youth development within a nautical framework.

In 2002/03 the trust had an income of £66,000 and a total expenditure of £60,000. Further information for this year was not available on file. The trust's assets were valued at almost £3 million in 2000/01 and the income totalled £75,000. Grants totalled £56,000. By far the largest grant was £53,000 to RONA Trust, also a major beneficiary in previous years. Four small grants were made to Wooden Spoon Society (£500), Cancer Research Campaign (£360) and ICRF and Scope (£250 each). A further two grants of £600 and £250 were made to individuals.

Exclusions No grants for individuals or for appeals not related to sailing.

Applications In writing to the correspondent.

The Helene Sebba Charitable Trust

Disability, medical, Jewish

£77,000 (2002/03)

Beneficial area UK, Canada and Israel.

PO Box 326, Bedford MK40 3XU

Tel. 01234 266657

Correspondent David L Hull

Trustees *Mrs N C Klein; Mrs J C Sebba; L Sebba.*

CC Number 277245

Information available Full accounts were provided by the trust.

General The trust supports disability, medical and Jewish organisations and in the past has made grants to causes in the UK, Canada and Israel.

In 2002/03 it had assets of £4.1 million, which generated an income of £81,000. Grants totalling £77,000 were made to 23 organisations, only 9 of which were not supported in the previous year.

The largest grants were £15,000 each to AKIM for Ruchama Home and Ehlers-Danlos and Connective Tissue Disorders Research Fund and £13,000 to Friends of Israel Sports Centre for the Disabled.

Other welfare, health and medical research beneficiaries included Ferring Country Centre (£5,000), MS Society (£3,000), Jewish Care (£2,800), Jewish Care and Mencap (£2,500), Alzheimer's Society, North London Hospice and Scope (£2,000 each), Hasmonean High School (£1,000) and BIBIC and Prostate Cancer Charity (£500 each).

Two other grants were listed under the 'other' category; £1,500 to Royal Geographical Society and £500 to National Jewish Chaplaincy.

Applications In writing to the correspondent.

The Seedfield Trust

Christian, relief of poverty

£85,000 (2002)

Beneficial area Worldwide.

Regent House, Heaton Lane, Stockport, Cheshire SK4 1BS

Tel. 0161 477 4750

Correspondent David Ryan, Trustee

Trustees *John Atkins; Keith Buckler; David Ryan; Revd Lionel Osborn; Janet Buckler; D Heap.*

CC Number 283463

Information available Information was provided by the trust.

General The trust's main objects are the furthering of Christian work and the relief of poverty. In 2002 the trust had assets of £1.9 million and an income of £104,000. Grants total of £85,000.

During the year the trust made 35 grants. A number of the beneficiaries had been supported at the same or similar levels in the previous year, these included some of the recipients of the largest grants: European Christian Mission (£14,000), Dorothea Trust (£11,000) and Overseas Missionary Fellowship (£10,000). Other larger grants included those to Gideons International (£7,000), Muller Homes (£6,000), Operation Mobilisation and New English Orchestra (£5,000 each) and Pentecostal Child Care Association (£4,000).

Recipients of grants of £500 or £1,000 included The Message (Manchester), Prison Fellowship, Amos Trust, Innovista, Youth for Christ and Arab Vision Trust.

Exclusions No grants to individuals.

Applications In writing to the correspondent, for consideration by the trustees who meet twice each year. Please enclose an sae for acknowledgement.

Leslie Sell Charitable Trust

Uniformed youth groups

£148,000 (2001/02)

Beneficial area UK and worldwide.

Ground Floor Offices, 52/58 London Road, St Albans, Hertfordshire AL1 1NG

Tel. 01727 843603 **Fax** 01727 843663

Correspondent J Byrnes

Trustees *P S Sell, Chair; Mrs M R Wiltshire; A H Sell.*

CC Number 258699

Information available Accounts were provided by the trust.

General Established in 1969 by the late Leslie Baden Sell, the trust supports youth groups, mainly Scouts and Guides, but also community groups.

In 2001/02 the trust had an income of £178,000 and assets totalling £2.3 million. Grants were made totalling £148,000, which included modest donations to Ivinghoe Aston Village Hall, Chalton Barn and Cottesloe School, and £128,000 to Scout and Guide groups.

A total of 202 grants were made to Scout and Guide groups (including Rangers, Brownies and sea Scouts groups) throughout the UK, with some grants to overseas guide associations. Grants to individual Scout or Guide groups were mostly for £500 or less, with some larger grants up to £4,000 also being given.

Applications In writing to the correspondent. Applications should include clear details of the project or purpose for which funds are required, together with an estimate of total costs and total funds raised by the group or individual for the project.

Sellata Ltd

Jewish, welfare

£94,000 (2000/01)

Beneficial area UK.

29 Fontayne Road, London N16 7EA

Correspondent E S Benedikt, Trustee

Trustees *E S Benedikt; Mrs N Benedikt; P Benedikt.*

CC Number 285429

Information available Accounts were on file at the Charity Commission, but without a list of grants.

General The trust says it supports the advancement of religion and the relief of poverty.

In 2000/01 the trust's assets totalled £87,000 and its income was £146,000. Grants totalled £94,000.

Applications In writing to the correspondent.

SEM Charitable Trust

Disability, general, Jewish

£110,000 (2000/01)

Beneficial area Mainly South Africa, Israel and UK.

Reeves and Neylan, 37 St Margaret's Street, Canterbury, Kent CT1 2TU

Tel. 01227 768231

Correspondent The Trustees

Trustees *Mrs Sarah E Radomir; Michael Radomir.*

CC Number 265831

Information available Infomation was provided by the trust.

General The trust makes grants mainly to disability-related organisations. In 2000/01 its assets totalled £776,000, it had an income of £73,000 and grants were made totalling £110,000. Grants included £17,000 to Together in Notre Dame, £10,000 each to Beth Shalon, CET, HAFAD, KWA Zulu National Philharmonic Orchestra and £8,000 to Sea World.

Exclusions No grants to individuals.

Applications In writing to the correspondent.

The Ayrton Senna Foundation

Children's health and education

£290,000 (2002)

Beneficial area Worldwide, with a preference for Brazil.

34–43 Russell Square, London WC2B 5HA

Tel. 020 7078 1400

Correspondent Julian Jakobi, Trustee

Trustees *Viviane Lalli, President; Milton Guerado Theodoro da Silva; Neyde Joanna Senna da Silva; Leonardo Senna da Silva; Fabio da Silva Machado; Christopher Bliss; Julian Jakobi.*

CC Number 1041759

Information available Accounts were on file at the Charity Commission.

General The trust was established in 1994 by the father of the late Ayrton Senna, in memory of his son, the racing driver. The trust was given the whole issued share capital of Ayrton Senna Foundation Ltd, a company set up to license the continued use of the Senna trademark and copyrights.

In 2002 the foundation had assets of £2.5 million with an income of £500,000 and grants totalling £290,000.

The Instituto Ayrton Senna (Brazil) received 3 grants totalling £290,000. This was the only grant awarded for the year 2002.

Exclusions No grants to individuals.

Applications In writing to the correspondent.

Servite Sisters' Charitable Trust Fund

Women, refugees

£108,000 (2003)

Beneficial area UK and worldwide.

Parkside, Coldharbour Lane, Dorking, Surrey RH4 3BN

Tel. 01306 875756 **Fax** 01306 889339

Email m@servite.demon.co.uk

Correspondent Michael J W Ward, Secretary

Trustees *Sister Joyce Mary Fryer OSM; Sister Ruth Campbell OSM; Sister Eugenia Geraghty OSM; Sister Catherine Ryan OSM.*

CC Number 241434

Information available Full information was provided by the trust.

General This trust is run by the English province of the international religious Order of The Servants of Mary (known as Servites). The province has 60 members, most of whom have given their working lives to the charitable activities of the order. When any of the members carry out any work independently of the charity, any earnings are covenanted to the charity.

The trust was set up in 1993 and makes grants principally to support:

- activities intended primarily to help women who are exploited or marginalised physically, spiritually or morally
- activities intended to alleviate the distress of refugees and other disadvantaged migrants.

The funds may also be used to help:

- the Servite family in the developing world/Eastern Europe
- students and youth groups the Servites are associated with.

In 2003 grants were made totalling £108,000, of which £44,000 was given in the UK.

Grants included capital for a women's small livestock business in Uganda (£800), for a female outreach worker for women with disabilities in Cambodia (£1,000), training and livestock for women's small business in Malawi (£800) and rehabilitation and development grants for women with disabilities in Bangladesh (£1,600).

Exclusions No grants to individuals. No grants towards building projects and no recurring grants.

Applications In writing to the correspondent with brief details of your organisation, project and needs with a full copy of your most recent audited accounts.

The Seven Fifty Trust

Christian

£69,000 (2001/02)

Beneficial area UK and worldwide.

All Saints Vicarage, Chapel Green, Crowborough, East Sussex TN6 1ED

Tel. 01892 667384

Correspondent Revd Andrew C J Cornes, Trustee

Trustees *Revd Andrew C J Cornes; Katherine E Cornes; Peter N Collier; Susan M Collier.*

CC Number 298886

Information available Full accounts were on file at the Charity Commission.

General This trust is for the advancement of the Christian religion in the UK and throughout the world.

In 2001/02 the trust had assets of £1.3 million and an income of £42,000. 18 grants totalled £69,000, the largest being £15,000 to Aquila and £11,000 to All Saints Church in Crowbridge (Faith in the Future Fund). All Saints Church also received a further donation of £8,000. Other beneficiaries included Aicmar (£5,000), St Matthew's in Fulham (£4,000), CS Lewis Institute and Universities and Colleges Christian Fellowship (£3,000 each), and Christians Solidarity Worldwide, Church Mission Society, International Fellowship of Evangelical Students and Kaduna Diocese Fund (£2,000 each).

Exclusions No support for unsolicited requests.

Applications It should be noted that the trust's funds are fully committed and unsolicited requests are not entertained. No reply is sent unless an sae is included with the application, but even then the reply will only say that the trust does not respond to unsolicited applications.

SFIA Educational Trust

Education

£95,000 (2002/03)

Beneficial area UK.

39 Queen Street, Maidenhead, Berkshire SL6 1NB

Tel. 01628 502040 **Fax** 01628 502049

Email admin@plans-ltd.demon.co.uk

Website www.plans-ltd.co.uk/trusts

Correspondent Mrs Anne Feek, Chief Executive

Trustee *SFIA (Trustees) Ltd.*

CC Number 313659

Information available Information was provided by the trust.

General Associated with charity S.F.I.A. Educational Trust Limited, since 1959 over £13 million has been paid out in grants.

Grants are only awarded to schools/ educational organisations towards bursaries to cover part fees for pupils with the following needs:

- special learning difficulties
- social deprivation
- emotional/behavioural difficulties
- physical disabilities
- gifted in a specialist area
- boarding need.

Grants are also given towards educational projects, books, equipment and school trips to promote the advancement of learning. Grants will only be considered for specific projects. Recipients will be asked to complete a declaration confirming that the funds will be used for the nominated purpose. No applications will be considered from individuals or from schools/ organisations in respect of pupils/ students over the age of 18.

In 2002/03 the trust had assets of £3.3 million and an income of £331,000. Grants totalled £95,000 and ranged from £1,000 to £30,000.

The largest grants was made to Combined Trusts Scholarship Trust (£30,000). Other beneficiaries included: Learning Through Action and Sense (£10,000 each), Small School (£8,000), Choir Schools Association, IAPS Orchestra and Pro Corda (£5,000 each), St Joseph's Catholic High School (£1,000).

Grants were also made to four statutory bodies, the education authorities of Cardiff, Glasgow and Liverpool (£7,000 each).

Exclusions No applications will be considered from individuals or from schools/organisations in respect of pupils/students over the age of 18.

Applications Application forms are available on the trust's website. All applications should be received by 31 January accompanied by the most recent set of audited accounts. Applications are considered in March/April each year. After the meeting, all applicants will be informed of the outcome as soon as possible.

SFIA Educational Trust Limited

Education

£144,000 (2002/03)

Beneficial area UK.

39 Queen Street, Maidenhead, Berkshire SL6 1NB

Tel. 01628 502040 **Fax** 01628 502049

Email admin@plans-ltd.demon.co.uk

Website www.plans-ltd.co.uk/trusts

Correspondent Mrs Anne Feek, Chief Executive

Trustees *Beatrice Roberts; Anthony Hastings; John Rees; Hugh Monro.*

CC Number 270272

Information available Information was provided by the trust.

General Associated with charity S.F.I.A. Educational Trust , grants are only awarded to schools/educational organisations towards bursaries to cover part fees for pupils with the following needs:

- special learning difficulties
- social deprivation
- emotional/behavioural difficulties
- physical disabilities
- gifted in a specialist area
- boarding need.

Grants are also given towards educational projects, books, equipment and school trips to promote the advancement of learning. Grants will only be considered for specific projects. Recipients will be asked to complete a declaration confirming that the funds will be used for the nominated purpose. No applications will be considered from individuals or from schools/ organisations in respect of pupils/ students over the age of 18.

In 2002/03 the trust had assets of £2.3 million and an income of £26,000. Grants in the range of £500 to £15,000 were made totalling £144,000.

The largest grants was made to Dyslexia Institute (£15,000), King Edwards, Kingham Hill, Lord Wandsworth, Reeds and Royal Wolverhampton (£10,000 each), Buttle, Purcell and Stanbridge Earls (£8,000 each) and Arkwright Scholarships and Disability Aid Fund (£6,000 each).

Exclusions No applications will be considered from individuals or from schools/organisations in respect of pupils/students over the age of 18.

Applications Application forms are availble on the trust's website. All applications should be received by 31 January accompanied by the most recent set of audited accounts. Applications are considered in March/April each year. After the meeting, all applicants will be informed of the outcome as soon as possible.

The Cyril Shack Trust

Jewish, general

£67,000 (2001/02)

Beneficial area UK.

c/o Lubbock Fine, Chartered Accountants, Russell Bedford House, City Forum, 250 City Road, London EC1V 2QQ

Tel. 020 7490 7766

Correspondent The Clerk

Trustees *J Shack; C C Shack.*

CC Number 264270

Information available Accounts were on file at the Charity Commission, but without a description of the trust's grant-making policy.

General In 2001/02 the trust's assets totalled £537,000. It had an income of £325,000 and made grants totalling £67,000. Mainly Jewish organisations are supported.

There was no grants list available for that year. The most recent list of beneficiaries in the public files at the Charity Commission was from 1996/97 when grants totalled £33,000. The largest 10 grants made, of £1,000 or more, were all to Jewish organisations, with the exception of one grant of £2,500 to an individual. Other grants ranged from £25. Jewish beneficiaries included Finchley Road Synagogue (four grants totalling £9,600), St John's Wood Synagogue (five grants totalling £3,100) and Nightingale House (four grants totalling £1,300). A range of other organisations benefited, including Breakthrough Breast Cancer, Crisis, Golf Aid, Hampstead Theatre, Hartsbourne Ladies Charity, London Library, Prisoners of Conscience, Samaritans, St John's Hospice and University of the Third Age – London.

Exclusions No grants for expeditions, travel bursaries, scholarships or to individuals.

Applications In writing to the correspondent.

The Shanti Charitable Trust

General, Christian, international development

£58,000 (2002/03)

Beneficial area UK, with preference for West Yorkshire, and developing countries (especially Nepal).

Parkside, Littlemoor, Queensbury, Bradford BD13 1DB

Tel. 01535 65311

Correspondent J E Brown

Trustees *Miss J B Gill; T F X Parr; R K Hyett.*

CC Number 1064813

Information available Accounts were on file at the Charity Commission.

General This trust's main interest is in supporting International Nepal Fellowship, although plenty of other funding is given. The trust states that most of the beneficiaries are those which the trustees already have links with and this priority also influences them in giving to local branches of national organisations.

In 2002/03 it had assets of £129,000 and an income of £38,000 (of which £36,000 came in donations received). Grants were made totalling £58,000, of which £21,000 went to International Nepal Fellowship.

Other beneficiaries were University of Edinburgh for the Nepali Church archives (£9,400), CBRS and Tearfund (£5,000 each), All Nations' Christian College (£4,000), Columbian Commission, Marie Curie Cancer Care, Sue Ryder Foundation and St John's Church (£3,000 each) and CLIC and Frame FM (£1,500 each).

Exclusions No grants to gap year students, or political or animal welfare causes.

Applications In writing to the correspondent. Please note, most beneficiaries are those the trustees already has contact with.

The Sharon Trust

Christian

£44,000 (2001/02)

Beneficial area England, Scotland and overseas.

1 Mount Pleasant, Lowestoft, Suffolk NR32 4JB

Tel. 01502 574849

Correspondent Miss M Warnes

Trustees *F W Warnes; Mrs H G Taylor; Miss M H Warnes; W R Warnes.*

CC Number 268742

Information available Accounts were on file at the Charity Commission, but without a list of grants.

General In 2001/02 the trust had assets of £472,000 and an income of £35,000. Grants were made totalling £44,000. There was no grants list in the accounts, although the following is taken from the annual report:

'During this year substantial gifts were made to missions, both at home and abroad, young people's camps and Bible conferences, upkeep of gospel halls, old people's homes and distributions of Bibles and Christian literature, etc.

'During the year, the trustees met to approve a number of gifts as attuned in our trust deed, including donations to help provide a home for street children in Africa, Christian radio work and foreign missionaries support etc.'

Exclusions No grants to individuals.

Applications In writing to the correspondent. The trustees meet to consider applications in January.

The Linley Shaw Foundation

Conservation

£63,000 (2003)

Beneficial area UK.

National Westminster Bank plc, NatWest Private Banking, 153 Preston Road, Brighton BN1 6BD

Tel. 01273 545035 **Fax** 01273 545075

Correspondent The Trust Section

Trustee *National Westminster Bank plc.*

CC Number 1034051

Information available Non-financial information was provided by the trust.

General The trust supports charities working to conserve, preserve and restore the natural beauty of the UK countryside for the public benefit.

Generally the trust prefers to support a specific project, rather than give money for general use. In his will, Linley Shaw placed particular emphasis on those charities which organise voluntary workers to achieve the objects of the trust. This may be taken into account when considering applications. Grants can be given towards any aspect of a project. Previous examples include the cost of tools, management surveys and assistance with the cost of land purchase.

In 2003 it had an income of £51,000 and gave grants totalled £63,000. Grants were made to 9 Charitable Bodies as follows: Wiltshire Wildlife Trust, Nottinghamshire Wildlife, John Muir Trust, Norfolk Wildlife, Stroud Valleys Project, London Wetland Centre, Marston Vale Trust, Gala Trust and Bedfordshire Wildlife Trust.

Exclusions No grants to non-charitable organisations, or to organisations whose aims or objects do not include conservation, preservation or restoration of the natural beauty of the UK countryside, even if the purpose of the grant would be eligible. No grants to individuals.

Applications In writing to the correspondent. All material will be photocopied by the trust so please avoid sending 'bound' copies of reports and so on. Evidence of aims and objectives are needed, usually in the forms of accounts, annual reports or leaflets, which cannot be returned. Applications are considered in February/early March and should be received by December/early January.

The Sheldon Trust

General

£162,000 (2002/03)

Beneficial area West Midlands.

White Horse Court, 25c North Street, Bishop's Stortford, Hertfordshire CM23 2LD

Fax 01279 657626

Email charities@pothecary.co.uk

Correspondent The Trust Administrator

Trustees *A Bidnell; Revd R S Bidnell; R V Wiglesworth; J C Barratt; Mrs R M Bagshaw.*

CC Number 242328

Information available Full accounts were provided by the trust, with a very informative trustees' report.

General The trust's geographical area of giving is the West Midlands, with particular emphasis on the areas of Birmingham, city of Coventry, Dudley, Sandwell, Solihull, Warwickshire and Wolverhampton. The main aims continue to be relieving poverty and distress in society, concentrating grants on community projects as well as those directed to special needs groups, especially in deprived areas. The trustees review their policy and criteria regularly. 'Although they have a central policy, a certain flexibility is ensured in reacting to changes in the environment and the community alike.'

In 2002/03 it had assets of £2.6 million, which generated an income of £162,000. Management and administration costs were high at £23,000 and included payments totalling £16,000 to firms in which members of the trustees had an interest. Whilst wholly legal, these editors always regret such payments unless, in the words of the Charity Commission, 'there is no realistic alternative'. Grants were made to 54 organisations totalling £162,000.

Grants were broken down in the accounts as follows [with values added where known]:

Grants to individuals

'To regionalise their interest in the Midlands, the trustees have continued to make an annual grant of £13,000 to Birmingham Money Advice and Grants (Personal Services) in Birmingham, who make many small grants to individuals for clothing, furniture and travel expenses for visiting the sick, as well as providing a debt counselling service.

Holiday

'An annual sum of £6,000 is allocated for holiday projects and during the year grants were awarded to: Peak National Asthma Joint Holidays (£5,000); Second City Lone Parents Group (£2,000); 3H Fund, Break, Warwickshire Association of Youth Clubs, Bethany Christian Fellowship, Bugs- Comic Kids Adventure, The Over the Wall Gang Camp and Winged Fellowship, The Harvest Trust (£600 each).

Grants for special needs groups

'Organisations supported during the year included: The Norman Laud Association (£3,500), Age Concern Warwickshire

(£2,500), Heart of England Care (£2,500), West Birmingham Crossroads Care (£4,000) and Warley Leisure and Enabling Services (£3,000).

Community projects
'Organisations supported during the year included: St Basil's (£5,000), Living Springs (£3,000), Birmingham Habitat for Humanity, Beginagain Community Project and St Oswalds's Community Advice Centre (£2,000 each).

Continuing grants
'Several continuing grants came to an end during the year and therefore the new awards were approved by the trustees for a period of two or three years: Frankley Youth Affairs Forum, Wolverhampton Clubs for Young People, St George's House Charity, Contact the Elderly and The Haven Wolverhampton.'

Exclusions 'The trustees will not consider appeals in respect of the cost of buildings, but will consider appeals where buildings have to be brought up-to-date to meet health, safety and fire regulations. The trustees will not consider general appeals from national organisations or individual appeals.'

Applications On a form available from the correspondent. The trustees meet three times a year, in March, July and November, making 10 to 15 grants depending on income. The trust's report stated that they will 'for the present be committing a good proportion of their income to continuing grants which means that they will have less income for other charitable purposes'.

The Patricia and Donald Shepherd Trust

General

£125,000 to organisations (2001/02)

Beneficial area Worldwide, particularly the north of England and Scotland.

PO Box 10, York YO1 1XU

Correspondent Mrs Patricia Shepherd, Trustee

Trustees *Mrs P Shepherd; Mrs J L Robertson; Patrick M Shepherd; D R Reaston; I O Robertson; Mrs C M Shepherd.*

CC Number 272948

Information available Full accounts were on file at the Charity Commission.

General The trust makes grants through charitable organisations to benefit people in need and society in general. There is a preference for supporting charities in the north of England and Scotland, or those connected with the trustees, particularly those involving young people.

In 2001/02 it had assets of £482,000 and an income of £97,000. Grants were made to 188 organisations totalling £125,000, with a further £4,800 given in total to 20 individuals.

By far the largest grant, of £50,000, went to St Peter's Foundation. Other large grants were £7,600 to United Response, £5,000 each to Clan Beck Children's Farm and St Leonard's Hospice, £4,000 to York Festival Trust, £2,500 to York Early Music Festival, £2,000 each to York Amateur Operatic and Dramatic Society and £1,000 to SNAPPY.

Other grants averaged £250. Previous beneficiaries of grants of this size are Catholic Youth Services, Dermatrust, Caring for Life, Books Abroad, Swaledale Festival, Filey Sea Cadets, National Playing Fields Association, Yorkshire Agoonoree, Durham Victim Support Scheme, York Scout Activity Centre, Sheffield Association for People with Cerebral Palsy and The Missing Persons Helpline.

Applications In writing to the correspondent.

The Archie Sherman Cardiff Charitable Foundation

Health, education, Jewish

£135,000 (2002/03)

Beneficial area UK, Canada, Australia, New Zealand, Pakistan, Sri Lanka, South Africa, India, Israel, USA and other parts of the British Commonwealth.

Archie Sherman Administration Limited, 27 Berkeley House, Hay Hill, London W1J 8NS

Correspondent The Trustees

Trustee *Rothschild Trust Corporation Ltd.*

CC Number 272225

Information available Full accounts were provided by the trust.

General Established in 1976, this trust supports health and educational charities. Most of the beneficiaries are Jewish or Israeli organisations. In 2002/03 it had assets of £1.8 million, which generated an income of £129,000. Grants were made totalling £135,000.

Beneficairies were UJIA (£97,000), Friends of the Hebrew University of Jerusalem (£30,000) and Tel Aviv Foundation (£8,400).

Exclusions No grants to individuals.

Applications In writing to the correspondent.

The Bassil Shippam and Alsford Trust

Young and older people, health, education, learning disabilities, Christian

£158,000 to organisations (2002/03)

Beneficial area UK, with a preference for West Sussex.

Messrs Thomas Eggar, The Corn Exchange, Baffins Lane, Chichester, West Sussex PO19 1GE

Tel. 01243 786111 **Fax** 01243 775640

Correspondent A MacFarlane, Clerk to the Trustees

Trustees *J H S Shippam; C W Doman; S A E MacFarlane; S W Young; Mrs M Hanwell; R Tayler; Mrs S Trayler.*

CC Number 256996

Information available Full accounts were provided by the trust.

General This is basically a Christian trust and the trustees mainly support charities active in the fields of care for younger and older people, health, education and religion. Many of the organisations supported are in West Sussex.

In 2002/03 it had assets of £3.1 million and an income of £188,000. Grants to 126 organisations totalled £158,000, with a further £6,500 given in total to 23 individuals (for further information, see *The Educational Grants Directory*, also published by DSC).

The largest grants were £25,000 to Aldingbourne Trust, £12,000 to Chichester Eventide Housing Association, £7,200 to Outset Youth Action – South West Sussex, £5,000 each to ACET, Chichester Counselling Service, St Wilfred's Hospice and Weald and Downland Open Air Museum, £3,500 to Schools Outreach, £2,500 to Abernethy Trust, £2,400 to West Sussex County Council Voluntary Fund and £2,000 each to Bishop Otter Centre for Theology and Ministry, Christian Care Association, Eartham PCC, Life Education Centre and Raleigh International.

The next largest were £1,800 to Chichester District Council for the Elderly, £1,700 to Sail Training Association, £1,600 to West Sussex Probation Service for the Social Skills Fund, £1,500 to Tearfund, £1,400 to Operation Wallacea, £1,300 to Chichester City Division Guides, £1,200 each to Abinger Hammer Village School and Shippams Retirement Association and £1,000 each to Chichester Cathedral Restoration and Development Trust, Chichester District Association for the Elderly, Cokehole Bridges, Crohn's Disease in Childhood Research Association, Fordwater School, HUTS, L'Arche, Living Options, Dame Vera Lynn Trust for Children with Cerebral Palsy, Mothers Unions – Chichester, Ravenscourt Trust, St Richard's Hospital Appeal, Ann Sutton Foundation and West Sussex Learning Links.

Other grants included £900 to Shippams Retirement Association, £750 each to Fittleworth District Playgroup and Worthing MIND, £500 each to Chestnut Tree House, Chichester Youth Wing, Eastergate Sportsfield and Petworth Festival, £400 to Sussex Association of Clubs for Young People, £350 to Positive Parenting, £300 to City Lights Theatre Company, £250 each to Bognor Regis Swimming Club, Chichester Stroke Club, Cued Speech Association UK, Liverpool School of Tropical Medicine, West Sussex Guitar Club and Willow Nursery, £200 each to Action Research, British and Foreign Bible Society, Church Pastoral Aid Society, Elizabeth Finn Trust and £100 each to Oxmarket Centre of Arts and Friends of Wrenford.

Applications In writing to the correspondent, including a copy of the latest set of accounts. Applications are considered in May and November.

The Shipwrights' Company Charitable Fund

Maritime or waterborne connected charities

£123,000 (2003/04)

Beneficial area UK.

Ironmongers' Hall, Barbican, London EC2Y 8AA

Tel. 020 7606 2376 **Fax** 020 7600 8117

Email clerk@shipwrights.co.uk

Website www.shipwrights.co.uk

Correspondent Rear Admiral D J Anthony

Trustee *The Worshipful Company of Shipwrights*

CC Number 262043

Information available Information was provided by the trust.

General The Shipwrights' Company is a Livery Company of the City of London and draws its members from all the various aspects of marine commerce and industry in the UK. Its charitable interests therefore focus on the maritime, with an emphasis on young people and the City. There is a preference for salt water over fresh.

In 2003/04 the fund had assets of £1.3 million. Total income was £140,000, including £90,000 from donations received. Grants totalled £123,000.

The company considers that getting young people afloat, especially with the various sail training organisations, is the best way of demonstrating the value of cooperation and teamwork, besides often giving disadvantaged young people an opportunity to realise themselves in an environment in which everyone starts off at the same point. It therefore supports a programme in which members may nominate candidates for sail training or Outward Bound-type courses (47 people for £21,000 in 2003/04) but also makes an indirect contribution to this aim by making grants to the sea cadets (HQ and units), sea scouts (HQ and groups), sail training organisations, Royal Hospital School and Fairbridge.

It maintains its London connections both with local youth groups and with grants for City churches: it supplies a Governor for George Green's School in the Isle of Dogs and financial support for activities not funded by the tax payer. It helps all the major maritime charities, including the seafarers' missions and especially the Royal Merchant Navy School Foundation.

Applications from individuals or, for example, schools to join sail training voyages are considered. It supports sailing for people with disabilities, with both the Jubilee Sailing Trust and the Challenger class.

Exclusions Any application without a clear maritime connection.

Applications In writing to the correspondent. Applications are considered in February, June and November.

The Charles Shorto Charitable Trust

General

£66,000 (2002/03)

Beneficial area UK.

Lancaster House, 67 New Hall Street, Birmingham B3 1NR

Tel. 0121 233 6900

Correspondent T J J Baxter

Trustees *Joseph A V Blackham; Brian M Dent.*

CC Number 1069995

Information available Full accounts were on file at the Charity Commission.

General This trust was established under the will of Edward Herbert Charles Shorto with general charitable purposes. Whilst welcoming applications, the trustees also like to identify causes that they know Charles Shorto had an interest in.

In 2002/03 the trust had assets of £3.1 million, which generated an income of £164,000. Management and administration expenses were high at £66,000. Grants were made totalling £66,000.

Beneficiaries included St Teresa's Residential Home in Fisguard (£31,000), Oxford Youth Works (£15,000), Devon Air Ambulance Fund and St Paul's and St Peters RC Parish (£5,000 each), ExtraCare (£4,000), St Mary in Bicton (£2,000) and Llhamlach Restoration Fund (£1,000).

Applications In writing to the correspondent at any time.

The Barbara A Shuttleworth Memorial Trust

Disability

£45,000 (2001/02)

Beneficial area UK, with a preference for West Yorkshire.

Baty Casson Long, Shear's Yard, 21 Wharf Street, The Calls, Leeds LS2 7EQ

Tel. 0113 242 5848 **Fax** 0013 247 0342

Email baty@btinternet.com

Correspondent John Baty, Chair

CC Number 1016117

Information available Accounts were on file at the Charity Commission.

General The trust gives grants to organisations which aim to improve the circumstances of people who are disabled generally and particularly children. Grants are given for equipment to facilitate the work of qualified professionals in treating the problems.

In 2002/03 the trust had an income of £21,000 and a total expenditure of £31,000. Further information for this year was not available, however previous information gathered stated that in 2001/02 the trust had an income of £23,000 and a total expenditure of £51,000. Grants totalled about £45,000.

Previous beneficiaries include Heaton Royds School, Shipley Leisure, Friends of Airedale Child Development Centre, Meanwood Valley Urban Farm, Haaris Qureshi Appeal, Bradford City Farm and Bradford Toy Library.

Applications In writing to the correspondent.

L H Silver Charitable Trust

Jewish, general

£222,000 (2002/03)

Beneficial area UK, but mostly West Yorkshire.

Wilson Braithwaite Scholey, 21–27 St Paul's Street, Leeds LS1 2ER

Tel. 0113 244 5451 **Fax** 0113 242 6308

Correspondent I J Fraser, Trustee

Trustees *Leslie H Silver; Mark S Silver; Ian J Fraser.*

CC Number 1007599

Information available Information was provided by the trust.

General This trust principally supports Jewish-based charities and appeal funds launched in the West Yorkshire area.

The trustees' report for 2002/03 stated that major donations have been made to educational institutions and Jewish charities. Most of the smaller donations were made to charities and appeal funds operating in the Leeds area.

In 2002/03 the trust had assets of £792,000, generating an income of £287,000. Grants totalling £222,000 went to 14 organisations.

The largest grants were to Donisthorpe Hall (£125,000), Cancer Research UK (£38,000) and UJIA (£27,000). Other beneficiaries included Leeds Friends of Laniado Hospital (£9,000), Imperial Cancer Research Fund (£6,000), British Friends of Jerusalem College of Technology and Learning Parnerships (£2,000 each) and Variety Club, One to One Children Fund and Leeds Jewish Welfare Board (£1,000 each).

Exclusions No grants to individuals or students.

Applications The trustees state that 'the recipients of donations are restricted almost exclusively to the concerns in which the trustees take a personal interest and that unsolicited requests from other sources, although considered by the trustees, are rejected almost invariably'.

The Simpson Education & Conservation Trust

Environmental conservation, with a preference for the neotropics (South America)

£72,000 (2001/02)

Beneficial area UK and overseas, with a preference for the neotropics (South America).

Honeysuckle Cottage, Tidenham Chase, Chepstow, Gwent NP16 7JW

Tel. 01291 689423 **Fax** 01291 689803

Correspondent N Simpson, Acting Chair

Trustees *Dr R N F Simpson, Chair; Prof. D M Broom; Dr J M Lock; Prof. S Chang; Dr K A Simpson.*

CC Number 1069695

Information available Full and detailed accounts were on file at the Charity Commission.

General Established in 1998, the trust produced a detailed annual report for 1998/99 giving a full description of its activities. Its main objectives were listed as follows:

a) the advancement of education in the UK and overseas, including medical and scientific research

b) the conservation and protection of the natural environment and endangered species of plants and animals with special emphasis on the protection of forests and endangered avifauna in the neotropics (South America).

The trust receives its income from Gift Aid donations, which totalled £78,000 in 2001/02. Its priority for that year was to support the Jocotoco Conservation Foundation (JCF) in Equador. This charity is dedicated to the conservation of endangered special birds through the acquisition of forest habitat. The chair of this trust, an expert in ornithology and conservation, is also on the board of trustees for Jocotoco Conservation Foundation.

In 2001/02 JCF received a grant of $80,000 (about £56,000) from the trust. Other grants were: $10,000 (about £7,000) to Association Armonia for a conservation project in Bolivia; £3,000 each to World Lands Trust towards a training and education project to encourage sustainable use of tropical forests in Costa Rica and BirdLife International; and £1,000 each to Caius College Cambidge University, Sound Seekers – Royal Commonwealth Institute for the Deaf and Treloar Trust.

Exclusions No grants to individuals.

Applications In writing to the correspondent. The day-to-day activities of this trust are carried out by e-mail, telephone and circulation of documents, since the trustees do not all live in the UK.

The Huntly & Margery Sinclair Charitable Trust

Medical, general

£30,000 (2002/03)

Beneficial area UK.

c/o Vernor-Miles & Noble Solicitors, 5 Raymond Buildings, Gray's Inn, London EC1R 5DD

Tel. 020 7423 8000 **Fax** 020 7423 8001

Email wilfridvm@vmn.org.uk

Correspondent Wilfrid Vernor-Miles

Trustees *Mrs A M H Gibbs; Mrs M A H Windsor; Mrs J Floyd.*

CC Number 235939

Information available Full accounts were provided by the trust.

General This trust has general charitable purposes at the discretion of the trustees, although it does not respond to unsolicited applications.

In 2002/03 it had assets of £982,000, which generated an income of £47,000. Grants were made to 20 organisations totalling £30,000.

The largest grant, of £15,000, went to Rencombe School. Other grants were £2,400 to University of Greenwich, £2,000 each to Foundation and Friends of the Royal Botanical Gardens – Kew and St Anne's Church – Kew, £1,000 each to Alzheimer's – Scotland and High Blood Pressure Foundation, £500 each to Abbeyfield Society, Elsktone Church PCC, ELVAS British Cemetery, Colesbourne Church PCC, Council for the Protection of Rural England, Friends of Insch Hospital, Mare and Foal Society, Priors Court Foundation, Racing Welfare, Rare Breeds Survival Trust, Friends of Turiff Hospital, World Cancer Research Fund and World Wildlife Fund and £100 to Cats Protection League.

Applications This trust does not respond to unsolicited applications.

Sinclair Charitable Trust

Jewish learning, welfare

£200,000 (2002)

Beneficial area UK.

4th Floor , 9 McIndeville Place, London WIL1 3AT

Tel. 020 7034 1940

Correspondent Dr M J Sinclair, Trustee

Trustees *Dr M J Sinclair; Mrs P K Sinclair; E J Gold.*

CC Number 289433

Information available Accounts were on file at the Charity Commission, but without a list of grants.

General The objects of the trust are to support organisations concerned principally, although not necessarily exclusively, with Jewish learning and welfare. Most of the income derives from substantial donations received from a company controlled by two of the trustees.

In 2000 the trust had an income of £223,000, all of which came from donations and gifts. Grants were made totalling £200,000, although details of the beneficiaries and the types of size of grants made were not included in the accounts.

Applications In writing to the correspondent.

Sino-British Fellowship Trust

Education

£410,000 (2003)

Beneficial area UK and China.

23 Bede House, Manor Fields, London SW15 3LT

Correspondent Mrs Anne Ely

Trustees *Prof. H D R Baker; P Ely; Mrs A E Ely; Prof. Sir Brian Heap; Dr J A Langton; Prof. M N Naylor; Prof. Sir David Todd; Lady Pamela Youde.*

CC Number 313669

Information available Information was provided by the trust.

General The trust makes grants to institutions benefiting individual postgraduate students. It does this through: scholarships to Chinese citizens to enable them to pursue their studies in Britain; grants to British citizens in China to educate/train Chinese citizens in any art, science, profession or handicraft; grants to Chinese citizens associated with charitable bodies to promote their education and understanding of European methods. In 2003 it had an income of £342,000 and a total expenditure of £410,000.

Applications On a form available by writing to the correspondent.

The Charles Skey Charitable Trust

General

£55,000 (2002/03)

Beneficial area UK.

Flint House, Park Homer Road, Colehill, Wimborne, Dorset BH21 2SP

Correspondent J M Leggett, Trustee

Trustees *C H A Skey, Chair; J M Leggett; C B Berkeley; Revd J H A Leggett.*

CC Number 277697

Information available Full accounts were provided by the trust.

General The trust's 2002/03 annual report states: 'The trustees support causes on an annual basis, irregularly and on a one-off basis. For those charities receiving annual donations, the amount to be given is reviewed annually. For those receiving periodic donations, the trustees are the judge of when a further grant should be made. For one-off donations, the trustees examine the requests which have been received and have sole authority as to which to support. In general, the trust supports those causes where the grant made is meaningful to the recipient'.

In 2002/03 it had assets of £1.7 million and an income of £209,000, including donations received of £135,000. Grants totalling £55,000 were made to 22 organisations, only five of which had not been supported in the previous year.

The largest grants were £10,000 to Lloyds Patriotic Fund, £8,000 to Trinity Hospice, £4,500 each to Careforce and Stepping Stones Trust, £3,000 each to Camphill Village Trust and St James' Church – Ryde, £2,500 to Cleft Lip and Palate Trust Fund and Joint Educational Trust, £2,000 each to Christian Care Association, Roses Charitable Trust, St Dunstan's and Water Aid.

Other grants were £1,000 each to Heritage of London Trust, Institute of Cancer Research, King Edward VII Hospital for Officers, Old Rugbeian Trust, Royal Naval Division Memorial Appeal, St George Beacontree

Community Worker Project, St Philip's Community Worker Project and Speech, Language and Hearing Centre and £500 to Trinity Church – Buxton.

Applications No written or telephoned requests for support will be entertained.

The John Slater Foundation

Medical, animal welfare, general

About £200,000 a year

Beneficial area UK, with a strong preference for the north west of England especially West Lancashire.

HSBC Trust Services, Norwich House, Nelson Gate, Commercial Road, Southampton SO15 1GX

Tel. 023 8072 2230

Correspondent Colin Bould

Trustee *HSBC Trust Co. Ltd.*

CC Number 231145

Information available Information was on file at the Charity Commission.

General The trust gives grants for £1,000 to £5,000 to a range of organisations, particularly those working in the fields of medicine or animal welfare.

In 2002/03 it had an income of £159,000 and a total expenditure of £215,000. Further information for this year was not available.

Grants have previously totalled around £200,000 and past beneficiaries have included Bispham Parish Church, Blackpool and Fylde Society for the Blind, Blue Cross Hospital, Duchess of York Hospital for Babies and Wildlife Hospital Trust, Guide Dogs for the Blind, Liverpool School of Tropical Medicine, RNLI and Samaritans.

Exclusions No grants to individuals.

Applications In writing to the correspondent, including accounts. Applications are considered twice a year, on 1 May and 1 November.

The Ernest William Slaughter Charitable Trust

Health, older people

£49,000 (2001/02)

Beneficial area Worldwide.

c/o Ozannes, PO Box 186, 1 Le Marchant Street, St Peter Port, Guernsey GY1 4HP

Tel. 01481 723466 **Fax** 01481 713491

Correspondent R A R Evans

Trustees *Mrs J Harris; Mrs M A Matthews.*

CC Number 256684

Information available Accounts were on file at the Charity Commission, but without a grants list in the most recent accounts.

General The trust states a preference for supporting organisations working with older people and people who are 'chronically sick'. In practice a number of beneficiaries have a focus on developing countries.

In 2001/02 the trust had assets in the region of £1.3 million with an income of £52,000 and grants totalling £49,000. Unfortunately no charity list was provided for recent years.

Exclusions No grants for explorations or expeditions.

Applications In writing to the correspondent.

Rita and David Slowe Charitable Trust

General

£38,000 (2002/03)

Beneficial area UK and overseas.

32 Hampstead High Street, London NW3 1JQ

Correspondent R L Slowe, Trustee

Trustees *R L Slowe; Mrs E H Douglas; J L Slowe; G Weinberg.*

CC Number 1048209

Information available Full accounts were provided by the trust.

General The trust makes grants to a range of registered charities. In 2002/03 it had assets of £317,000 and an income of £75,000, mostly from donations received. Grants were made to four charities totalling £38,000.

Beneficiaries were Schumacher Centre for Technology and Development and Shelter (£13,000 each), Motivation Charitable Trust (£8,000) and Books Abroad (£5,000).

Exclusions No grants are made to individuals (including gap year students) or religious bodies.

Applications In writing to the correspondent.

The SMB Charitable Trust

Christian, general

£166,000 (2002/03)

Beneficial area UK and overseas.

15 Wilman Rd, Tunbridge Wells, Kent TN4 9AJ

Tel. 01892 537301 (after 6pm)
Fax 01892 618202

Correspondent Mrs B M O'Driscoll, Trustee

Trustees *E D Anstead; P J Stanford; Mrs B O'Driscoll; J A Anstead.*

CC Number 263814

Information available Information was provided by the trust.

General The trust supports charities which meet one of the following criteria:

- support of the Christian faith
- provision of social care in the UK and abroad
- provision of famine or emergency aid
- protection of the environment and wildlife
- support of education or medical research.

Grants are generally of £1,000 each, although this can vary. The founder's preferences are taken into account when deciding which of the applicants will be supported.

In 2002/03 it had assets of £4.4 million and an income of £204,000. 136 grants were made totalling £166,000, of which 53 were recurrent.

The largest grants were £4,000 to London City Mission, Pilgrim Homes, £3,000 to Salvation Army, £2,500 to Baptist Missionary Society, British Red Cross, Hope Now, £2,000 to All Nations' Christian College, Barnabas Fund, Bible Society, Hospice of Hope – Romania, Leprosy Mission, Mildmay Mission Hospital, Mission Aviation Fellowship, Oasis Trust, Tearfund and World Medical Fund for relief work in Malawi.

More typical grants included £1,500 each to Dentaid and Worldwide Evangelism Crusade, £1,000 each to Arab Vision Trust Fund, Breadline, Cambodia Trust, Church Army, Elimination of Leukaemia, Glasgow City Mission, Home Evangelism, International Community Trust for Healthy Educational Services, Micro Loan Foundation, Motor Neurone Disease Association, National Missing Person's Helpline, Parenthood, Prostate Research Campaign, Royal School for the Blind, Treloar Trust, Victim Support London and Wells for India and £500 each to Fairtrade Foundation and Traidcraft Exchange.

Exclusions Grants to individuals are not normally considered, unless the application is made through a registered charity which can receive the cheque.

Applications In writing to the correspondent, including the aims and principal activities of the applicant, the current financial position and details of any special projects for which funding is sought. Application forms are not used. Trustees met in March, June, September and December and applications should be received before the beginning of the month in which meetings are held. Because of the volume of appeals received, unsuccessful applicants will only receive a reply if they enclose an sae. However, unsuccessful applicants are welcome to reapply.

SMILES (Slimmers Making it a Little Easier for Someone)

Children, young people

£169,000 (2002/03)

Beneficial area UK.

c/o Slimming World, Clover Nook Industrial Estate, Clover Nook Road, Derbyshire DE55 4RF

Tel. 01773 546010

Correspondent D Rathbone, Trustee

Trustees *Margaret Whittaker; Ronald Whittaker; David Rathbone.*

CC Number 1061429

Information available Accounts were on file at the Charity Commission.

General This trust receives its funds from donations by members of Slimming World. In 2002/03 it received an income of £140,000. No donations were made during the year, with the largest expenditure being £1,500 to purchase a bond for places in the London Marathon which will no doubt be a valuable source of fundraising. However, there was a grant of £169,000 given just after the year end, from the funds raised during 2002/03. In the previous financial year, its only donation was of £86,000 to Barnardo's, so it appears that it just makes one very large grant each year.

Applications In writing to the correspondent.

The Amanda Smith Charitable Trust

General

£125,000 (2001/02)

Beneficial area UK.

c/o Manro Haydan Trading, 1 Knightsbridge, London SW1X 7LX

Tel. 020 7823 2200

Correspondent Christopher Smith, Chair

Trustees *C Smith, Chair; P Bennett; Ms A Smith.*

CC Number 1052975

Information available Accounts were on file at the Charity Commission.

General This trust was established in 1996. The trust's income is derived mainly from the rent of a shopping centre and a housing estate. The trust stated that this is gradually decreasing. The trust makes grants irregularly.

In 2001/02 the trust had assets of £1.4 million with an income of £176,000 and grants totalling £125,000.

There were two substantial grants made for this period, they were £75,000 to Cedar School and £50,000 to Nordoff Robbins Music Therapy.

Applications In writing to the correspondent.

The N Smith Charitable Trust

General

£96,000 (2002/03)

Beneficial area Worldwide.

Bullock Worthington & Jackson, 1 Booth Street, Manchester M2 2HA

Tel. 0161 833 9771 **Fax** 0161 832 0489

Email bulworjac@compuserve.com

Correspondent Anne E Merricks

Trustees *T R Kendal; P R Green; J H Williams-Rigby; G Wardle.*

CC Number 276660

Information available Accounts were on file at the Charity Commission.

General In 2002/03 the trust had assets of £2.6 million. The income was £124,000, with management and administration costs totalling £24,000. Grants were made to organisations totalling £96,000, as follows:

Medical research charities – 22 grants totalling £16,000

There were 18 grants of £750 each and 4 grants of £500 each. Beneficiaries included Arthritis Research Campaign – arc, BackCare, The Iris Fund, The Migraine Trust, Prostate Research Campaign UK, The University of Nottingham and WellBeing.

Social work – 42 grants totalling £21,000

These were all for £500 each. Recipients included After Adoption, The British Polio Fellowship, Douglas House, The Honeypot Charity, Meningitis Trust, Neglect Child, Shaftesbury Youth Club.

Education – 13 grants totalling £7,000

These were all for £500 except for one of £1,000 to Barnstondale. Other beneficiaries were Boilerhouse Theatre Company Ltd., Enable, Endeavour Training, Punch and Judy Family Centre and Wessex Autistic Society.

Environmental work and animals – 8 grants totalling £4,000
All these grants were for £500 each and included those to Environmental Animal Sanctuary & Education – EASE, The Gala Trust, Plantlife, Tusk Trust and WWF - UK.

Arts – 8 grants totalling £4,000
These were all for £500 each and sample beneficiaries were Fleet Arts, The National Youth Orchestra of Great Britain, Northern Ballet Theatre, Rehearsal Orchestra and Scottish Storytelling Centre.

Overseas aid – 36 grants totalling £23,000
Grants were for £625 each. Recipients included Action for People in Conflict, Child Advocacy International, Christian Mission Blind CBM, The Esther Benjamins Trust, Farm Africa, Mission Without Borders (UK) Ltd, Operation Smile United Kingdom, Religious Society of Friends in Britain – Quakers, and World Jungle.

Exclusions Grants are only made to registered charities and not to individuals.

Applications In writing to the correspondent. The trustees meet in October and March.

Harold Smith Charitable Trust

General

£58,000 (2002/03)

Beneficial area UK.

Keepers, 3 Oakland Close, Horsham, West Sussex RH13 6RU

Tel. 01403 249112

Correspondent Mrs S E Norgan, Trustee

Trustees *Mrs S E Norgan; Mrs E C Selby.*

CC Number 277172

Information available Full accounts were on file at the Charity Commission.

General In 2002/03 the trust held assets totalling £529,000 and received an income of £20,000. Grants totalled £58,000.

Larger grants were: £5,000 to Lord's Taverners, £2,500 to NSPCC, £2,000 each to CHASE Children's Hospice Service and Lewis-Manning House Cancer Trust, £1,750 to David Adams Leukaemia Appeal Fund, £1,500 to Royal National College for the Blind, £1,250 each to King Edward VII Hospital and Royal College of Sugeons of England, £1,000 each to Cherry Trees, KIDS, King George's Fund for Sailors – KGFS and SSAFA Forces Help.

The remaining grants were between £100 and £700 and included those to Cancer Research UK, Children Nationwide, Deafblind UK, Macmillan Nurses, Phoenix Sheltered Workshop and Young Minds.

Applications In writing to the correspondent.

The Smith Charitable Trust

General

£39,000 (2002/03)

Beneficial area UK and overseas.

Messrs Moon Beever, Solicitors, 24 Bloomsbury Square, London WC1A 2PL

Tel. 020 7637 0661

Correspondent Paul Shields

Trustees *A G F Fuller; J W H Carey; C R L Coubrough; R I Turner.*

CC Number 288570

Information available Accounts were on file at the Charity Commission.

General The trust supports registered charities, which are usually larger well-known UK organisations. Beneficiaries are chosen by the settlor and he has a set list of charities which are supported twice a year. Other charities are unlikely to receive a grant.

In 2002/03 the trust had assets of £1.7 million with an income of £52,000 and grants totalling £38,500.

Grants include £9,000 to Sue Ryder Foundation, £3,500 to St Mary's Convent & Nursing Home, £3,000 each to Royal National Institute for the Blind and Research Institute for the Care of the Elderly, £2,000 each to League of Friends of Chiswick Lodge Hospital, NHC Action for Children, Royal National Lifeboat Association, MacMillan Cancer Relief, YMCA England, British Red Cross, Providence Row Charity and Artists General Benevolent Fund, £1,500 each to Sea Cadets Association and Salvation Army and £1,000 to Sight Savers International.

Exclusions No grants to animal charities or to individuals.

Applications In writing to the correspondent. Unsolicited applications are not considered.

The E H Smith Charitable Trust

General

About £93,000 (2002/03)

Beneficial area UK, some preference for the Midlands.

1 Sherbourne Road, Acocks Green, Birmingham B27 6AB

Tel. 0121 706 6100

Correspondent K H A Smith, Trustee

Trustees *K H A Smith; Mrs B M Hodgskin-Brown; D P Ensell.*

CC Number 328313

Information available Full accounts were on file at the Charity Commission.

General This trust supports a wide and varied range of causes throughout the UK, concentrating mainly on the Midlands. It tends to give a large number of smaller grants, which average around £250 each, although they have been made of over £1,000 to £2,000 each on average. In 2002/03 the trust had an income of £69,000 and grant expenditure of £93,000. The trust's assets came to £180,000.

One large donation was given to Christadelphin Bible Mission at £25,000. Other donations have been £5,000 to Kidderminster Railway Museum, £1,700 to Three Peaks Challenge, £1,400 to Kingsleigh House, £650 to Betel, £350 to County Air Ambualnce, £250 to Children's Heart Federation, £200 each to BAYC and Jubilee Sailing Trust, £100 to David Tolkien Trust, £150 each to The Association for Post-Natal Illness and St Clare Hospice, £30 to Sir John Moore School and £20 to Hobs Moat Centre.

Exclusions No grants to political parties. Grants are not normally given to individuals.

Applications In writing to the correspondent. Apply at any time.

The Leslie Smith Foundation

General

£179,000 (2002/03)

Beneficial area UK.

The Old Coach House, Sunnyside, Bergh Apton, Norwich NR15 1DD

Correspondent M D Willcox, Trustee

Trustees *M D Willcox; H L Young Jones.*

CC Number 250030

Information available Full accounts were on file at the Charity Commission.

General In 2002/03 the trust had assets of £2.9 million and an income of £125,000. Grants totalled £179,000.

The foundation, which regularly reviews its grant–making policy, is currently focusing on:

- children's hospices and bereavement counselling for children
- education
- matrimonial counselling
- children with disabilities
- welfare of retired clergy.

Beneficiaries of the largest grants were Gaddum Centre, Joseph Weld Hospice, Paul Strickland Scanner Centre Appeal, Wessex Children's Hospice Trust and Wiltshire Community Foundation (£20,000 each).

Other beneficiaries of smaller grants included Barnardo's and Cystic Fibrosis Holiday Fund for Children (£15,000 each), Relate (£12,000), Norfolk Accident Rescue Serive and Theatre Royal in Norwich (£5,000 each).

Exclusions Grants are given to registered charities only; no grants are available to individuals.

Applications In writing to the correspondent. Only successful applications are acknowledged.

WH Smith Group Charitable Trust

General

£86,000 (2001/02)

Beneficial area UK.

WH Smith plc, Nations House, 103 Wigmore Street, London W1H 0WH

Correspondent Orla Kilgallon, Secretary

Trustees *L Tribe, Chair; J Woodcock; M Taylor; P Whitelock; A Finch; S Preece; C Clarke; A Walker.*

CC Number 1013782

Information available Full accounts were on file at the Charity Commission.

General This trust is unusual in that although it is connected to a company, it is totally independent and controlled by the employees rather than the management. Employees of WH Smith Group have effectively established their own trust for which they raise funds, making grants to the organisations which inspired them to solicit those donations.

In 2001/02 the trust had assets of £100,000 and an income of £92,000. Grants totalled £86,000, with £66,000 going to Royal National Institute for the Deaf which was the 'charity of the year'. Donations £1,000 and over were made to Evolution Appeal (£10,000), Medina Marching Band (£1,800) and Cancer Research UK, Copthorne Guide Units, Isle of Wight Hospital Radio and St Catherine's Hospice (£1,000). Donations below £1,000 totalled £13,000.

Applications Due to the proactive nature of the trust, it is a waste of time applying for a grant.

The Stanley Smith UK Horticultural Trust

Horticulture

£121,000 to organisations (2002/03)

Beneficial area UK and, so far as it is charitable, outside the UK.

Cory Lodge, PO Box 365, Cambridge CB2 1HR

Tel. 01223 336299 **Fax** 01223 336278

Correspondent James Cullen, Director

Trustees *John Norton; Christopher Brickell; John Dilger; Lady Renfrew; J B E Simmons.*

CC Number 261925

Information available Accounts were on file at the Charity Commission.

General Established by deed in 1970, the trust's objects are the advancement of horticulture. In particular, the trustees have power to make grants for the following purposes:

- horticultural research
- the creation, development, preservation and maintenance of public gardens
- the promotion of the cultivation and wide distribution of plants of horticultural value/other value to mankind
- the promotion of the cultivation of new plants
- publishing books and work related to horticultural sciences.

In 2002/03 the trust's assets totalled £2.5 million and it had an income of £123,000. Grants were made to 23 organisations and totalled £121,000. Five scholarships totalling £41,000 were also awarded.

Beneficiaries from the general fund included Metropolitan Public Garden Association and European Orchid Conference and Show (£5,000 each), Garden & Heritage Landscape Working Group – University of York (£3,000), Museum of Garden History and Royal Botanic Gardens Kew Foundation (£2,500 each), Blackpool Borough Council and Silver End Memorial Garden (£2,000 each), Eden Project and Wiltshire Gardens Trust (£1,000 each) and Friends of Rock Park – Llandrindod Wells (£500).

Three grants totalling £76,000 were given out from the approved grants fund. Beneficiaries were Lucy Cavendish College (£35,000), Royal Botanic Garden Edinburgh (£31,000) and Chelsea Physic Garden Education Programme (£10,000).

The director continues to provide advice to actual and potential applicants, and to established projects which have already received grants. Any grant provided by the trust bears the condition that the recipient should provide within six months, or some other agreed period, a report on the use of the grant.

Exclusions Grants are not made for projects in commercial horticulture (crop production) or agriculture, nor are they made to support students taking academic or diploma courses of any kind, although educational institutions are supported.

Applications In writing to the correspondent. Detailed *Guidelines for Applicants* are available from the trust. The director is willing to give advice on how applications should be presented.

Grants are awarded twice a year, in spring and autumn. To be considered in the spring allocation, applications should reach the director before 15 February of each year; for the autumn allocation the equivalent date is 15 August. Potential recipients are advised to get their applications in early.

Philip Smith's Charitable Trust

Welfare, older people, children

£91,000 (2003)

Beneficial area UK.

50 Broadway, Westminster, London SW1H 0BL

Tel. 020 7227 7039 **Fax** 020 7222 3480

Correspondent M Wood

Trustees *Hon. P R Smith; Mrs M Smith.*

CC Number 1003751

Information available Information was provided by the trust.

General The trust makes grants to UK-wide charities, prinicipally in the fields of welfare, older people and children.

In 2003 the trust had an income of £29,000 from assets of £821,000. Grants totalled £91,000. Beneficiaries of the largest grants included G.R.C.C, Sir Baptist Hicks Almshouses Trust and the University of Gloucestershire whom received £10,000 each. Other beneficiaries included Chipping Campden School Charity and Gloucester Cathedral & 900 Year Fund (£5,000 each) and The National Galleries of Scotland (£2,500). Smaller grants went to The Spring Centre Trust Fund and Campden PCC (£500 each) and Royal Green Jackets (£100).

Applications In writing to the correspondent. The trustees meet regularly to consider grants. A lack of response can be taken to indicate that the trust does not wish to contribute to an appeal.

Social Education Trust

See below

£48,000 (2001/02)

Beneficial area UK.

PO Box 47, St Albans AL1 4ZN

Tel. 01727 836624 **Fax** 01727 836624

Email mike@tidball.com

Correspondent Michael Tidball

Trustees *Phill Warrilow, Chair; David Crimmens; Jim Hyland; Kathleen Lane; Erinna McNeil.*

CC Number 297605

Information available Information was provided by the trust.

General This trust supports charities and not for profit organisations concerned with young people. Grants are made to projects concerned with residential care and exploring alternative approaches from other countries such as the social pedagogy model. Support is given to help young people who have been in the public care to participate and communicate.

In 2001/02 the trust had assets of £450,000 and an income of £24,000. Grants were made totalling £48,000.

Grant commitments included: £30,000 to fund a national survey of residential childcare to ascertain morale and job satisfaction; £25,000 to a charity to develop an electronic youth club; £9,600 to enable the development of a website and boost an advocacy service; £7,500 to to enable young people to attend a Parliamentary Group.

A total of 40 bursaries of up to £500 a year were made from the Travel Bursary Fund.

Exclusions Support to individual young people – other than through the Travel Bursary Fund.

Applications In writing to the correspondent. E-mail applications are welcomed. For details of the Travel Bursary Scheme see website: www.childrenuk.co.uk.

Society for the Assistance of Ladies in Reduced Circumstances

Women in need in the British Isles

£56,000 (2002)

Beneficial area UK.

Lancaster House, 25 Hornyold Road, Malvern WR14 1QQ

Tel. 01684 574645 **Fax** 01684 577212

Email mail@salrc.org.uk

Website www.salrc.org.uk

Correspondent John Sands, General Secretary

Trustees *Mrs O M Wickens, Chair; M J Andrews; S D Ginn; Revd D F Gutteridge;*

CC Number 205798

Information available Accounts were provided by the trust, but without a list of grants.

General This trust mainly makes grants to individual women living on their own, who are on a low income, but grants are also made to organisations supporting 'needy females'.

In 2002 it had assets of £17 million, which generated an income of £1.2 million. Grants were made to organisations totalling £56,000. A further £527,000 was paid in total to 747 individuals. No further information was available.

Applications In writing to the correspondent. The trust stated in February 2004 that it would not be likely to enter into any more grants to organisations during 2004 since it already had many commitments to honour.

Solev Co Ltd

Jewish charities

£313,000 (1996/97)

Beneficial area UK.

Romeo House, 160 Bridport Road, London N18 1SY

Correspondent O Tager, Trustee

Trustees *M Grosskopf; A E Perelman; R Tager.*

CC Number 254623

Information available Accounts were on file at the Charity Commission, but without a grants list.

General In 2002/03 the trust had an income of £874,000 and a total expenditure of £746,000. Further information for this year was not available.

In 2000/01 it had an income of £345,000 and an expenditure of £524,000. Unfortunately further information for this year was not available.

In 1996/97 the trust had assets of £1.6 million, which generated an income of £489,000. Grant giving was £313,000 and management and administrative costs were £10,000.

Only two donations are mentioned in the annual report: '£100,000 to the Dina Perelmam Trust Ltd, a charitable company of which Mr Perelman and Mr Grosskopf are governors; and £40,000 to Songdale Ltd, a charity of which Mr M Grosskopf is an governor.'

No grants list has been included in the accounts since 1972/73, when £14,000 was given to 52 Jewish charities. Examples then included Society of Friends of the Torah (£3,900), Finchley Road Synagogue (£2,300), NW London Talmudical College (£1,500), Yesodey Hatorah School (£700), and Gateshead Talmudical College (£400).

Applications In writing to the correspondent.

The Solo Charitable Settlement

Jewish, general

£30,000 (2001/02)

Beneficial area UK and Israel.

Rawlinson & Hunter, Eagle House, 110 Jermyn Street, London SW1Y 6RH

Tel. 01483 230440

Correspondent The Trustees

Trustees *P D Goldstein; Edna Goldstein; P Goldstein; D Goldstein; J Goldstein; Tammy Ward.*

CC Number 326444

Information available Accounts were on file at the Charity Commission up to 1998/99.

General The trust was established in 1983, by Peter David Goldstein. The trustees can hold the capital and income for 21 years to increase the trust's assets.

In 2001/02, the trust had assets of £4.5 million and an income of £151,000. Grants were made to organisations totalling £30,000. Grants ranged from £75 to £8,250, although most were for £650 or under. Some organisations have previously been supported.

Beneficiaries receiving over £1,000 were Norwood Ravenswood (£8,250), Community Security Trust and Nightingale House (the home for aged Jews) (£5,000 each), Dulwich College Bursary Appeal (£1,500), Weizmann Institute Foundation (£1,450), English Stage Company Limited (£1,250) and The City Charity (£1,000).

Beneficiaries receiving £650 or under included After Adoption, British WIZO, Cancer Research UK, Chelsea Synagogue, Conran Foundation, JNF Charitable Trust, MDA UK, North Bristol NHS Trust, St Luke's Hospice, United Synagogue and World Jewish Relief.

Applications In writing to the correspondent.

David Solomons Charitable Trust

Disability

£48,000 (2000/01)

Beneficial area UK.

81 Chancery Lane, London WC2A 1DD

Tel. 020 7911 7209 **Fax** 020 7911 7105

Email glynis.jones@offsol.qsi.gov.uk

Correspondent Miss Glynis Jones, Administrator

Trustees *Mrs B J Taylor; J J Rutter; W H McBryde; J L Drewitt; Dr R E B Solomons; Dr Y V Wiley; M T Chamberlayne.*

CC Number 297275

Information available Accounts were on file at the Charity Commission, but without a list of grants.

General This trust supports research into the treatment and care of people with mental disabilities, with a preference for smaller or localised charities. Most grants range from £1,000 to £2,000, although larger and smaller amounts are given. Administrative expenses and large building projects are not usually funded, although grants can be made towards furnishing or equipping rooms.

In 2000/01 the trust had an income of £64,000 and gave grants totalling £48,000. No recent information was available.

In the previous year, when there was a similar income, grants were made to 49 organisations totalling £77,000. The largest grants were £8,000 to Down's Syndrome Association, £5,000 to Ysgol Grug Glas, £3,500 to Keighley Mental Health and £3,000 each to the Roy Kinnear Charitable Foundation and the Development Trust. Other beneficiaries included The Aidis Trust, Autism London, Break and White Lodge Children's Centre.

Exclusions No grants to individuals.

Applications In writing to the correspondent. Meetings are in May and November and applications should be received the previous month.

Songdale Ltd

Jewish

£182,000 (2002/03)

Beneficial area UK and Israel.

6 Spring Hill, London E5 9BE

Correspondent M Grosskopf, Governor

Trustees *M Grosskopf; Mrs M Grosskopf; Y Grosskopf.*

CC Number 286075

Information available Accounts were on file at the Charity Commission.

General In 2002/03 the trust had assets of £2.2 million, an income of £228,000 and made grants totalling £182,000.

Previous beneficiaries receiving £1,000 or more in 2001 were Cosmon Belz Limited (£44,500), Kedushas Zion and Nevey Eretz (£25,000 each), Toldos Avraham Bet Sh. (£10,500), Bnos Yroshalayim, B'H Govoha Lakewood and Yad Romoh (£7,000 each), Yeshiva Belz, Jerusalem (£6,000), C W C T and Tora Vemuma (£4,000 each), Ezras Yitchock Yisoe (£3,500), N W L Talmundical College and Yad Eliezer (£3,000 each), Ponovez Rabbi Pinter Memorial (£1,500) and New Rachmestriuke Trust (£1,000).

Grants of under £500 included those to Alexandra Institution, Belz Synagogue, Collel Yirey Hashem, Ezer Mitzion,

Friends of Yeshivas Chevron, Glasgow Kollel, Keshev for Deaf, Miepi Ollelim, Mondos Shaarei, Noam Shabbos, Rambam Foundation and Yeshivas Midrash Shmuel.

Applications In writing to the correspondent.

This entry was not confirmed by the trust, but is correct according to information on file at the Charity Commission.

The E C Sosnow Charitable Trust

Arts, education

£48,000 (2002/03)

Beneficial area UK, overseas.

110 Cannon Street, London EC4N 6AR

Correspondent Ellis S Birk, Trustee

Trustees *E S Birk; E R Fattal; Mrs F I M Fattal.*

CC Number 273578

Information available Full accounts were on file at the Charity Commission.

General The trust informed us that it makes grants mainly to educational charities, including arts organisations. Other areas mentioned in its annual report are welfare, education, the arts, the underprivileged, healthcare and emergency relief.

In 2002/03 the trusts had assets of £1.3 million and an income of £58,000 with grants totalling £48,000.

The largest grants were £7,000 to Christ's College Cambridge and £5,000 each to UJLA and Weizman Institute Foundation.

Other beneficiaries include £2,500 to Griffins Society, £2,000 each to Chicken Shed, RNIB, Daneford Trust, CST and Breast Cancer Care, £750 to Spanish and Portuguese Congregation, £1,000 each to MHJP, London Youth, ILE and Jewish Care, £500 each to Skiers Trust of Great Britain, Royal Court Theatre, Nightingale House and Medical Aid Poland.

Exclusions No grants are made to individuals.

Applications In writing to the correspondent.

This entry was not confirmed by the trust, but the address was correct according to information according to the Charity Commission.

The South Square Trust

General

£175,000 to organisations (2001/02)

Beneficial area UK, with a preference for London and the Home Counties.

PO Box 67, Heathfield, East Sussex TN21 9ZR

Tel. 01435 830778 **Fax** 01435 830778

Correspondent Mrs Nicola Chrimes, Clerk to the Trustees

Trustees *C R Ponter; A E Woodall; W P Harriman; C P Grimwade; D B Inglis.*

CC Number 278960

Information available Full accounts were provided by the trust.

General General donations are made to registered charities working in the fields of the arts, culture and recreation, health, social welfare, medical, disability and conservation and environment.

The trust also gives grants to students for full-time postgraduate or undergraduate courses within the UK connected with the fine and applied arts, including drama, dance, music, but particularly related to gold and silver work. Students should be over 18 years old. Courses have to be of a practical nature. Help is given to various colleges in the form of bursary awards. A full list is available from the correspondent. Where a school is in receipt of a bursary, no further assistance will be given to individuals as the school will select candidates themselves.

In 2001/02 it had assets of £3.3 million, which generated an income of £171,000. Grants were made totalling £199,000, broken down as follows:

Annual donations to charities – £26,000

These consisted of 15 grants of £1,000 each and 22 grants of £500 each. Further information was not available.

General charitable donation – £51,000

A total of 53 grants were made. Those over £1,000 each went to Yale University Press for *Silver in Society* (£7,500), Loros Hospice and Unicef for Children in Conflict (£5,000 each) and Shooting Star Trust (£1,500).

Bursaries and scholarships to schools/colleges – £98,000

20 institutions were supported by these schemes. The largest payments were £21,000 to St Paul's School, £11,000 to West Dean College and £10,000 to Textile Conservation Centre. Other recipients included Royal Academy Schools (£6,500), Sir John Cass Department of Art and Frink School of Sculpture (£4,000 each), Guildhall School of Music and Drama (£3,200), Royal College of Art (£3,000), Bristol Old Vic Theatre School (£2,700), Slade School of Fine Art (£2,000), London Contemporary Dance School (£2,000) and St George's Cathedral – Southwark (£1,000).

Directly aided students and single payment grants – £23,000

These were made to 50 individuals. For further information, please see *The Educational Grants Directory*, also published by DSC.

Exclusions No grants given to individuals under 18 or those seeking funding for expeditions, travel, courses outside UK, short courses or courses not connected with fine and applied arts.

Applications Registered charities

In writing to the correspondent with details about your charity, the reason for requesting funding, and enclosing a condensed copy of your accounts. Applications are considered three times a year, in spring, summer and winter. It is advisable to telephone the correspondent for up-to-date information about the criteria for funding.

Individuals

Standard application forms are available from the correspondent. Forms are sent out between January and April only, to be returned by the end of April for consideration for the following academic year.

The Stephen R and Philippa H Southall Charitable Trust

General

£56,000 (2001/02)

Beneficial area UK, but mostly Herefordshire.

Porking Barn, Clifford, Hereford HR3 5HE

Correspondent Mrs P H Southall, Trustee

Trustees *S R Southall; Mrs P H Southall; Anna Catherine Southall; Candia Compton.*

CC Number 223190

Information available Full accounts were on file at the Charity Commission.

General This trust has general charitable purposes, with a large number of grants made in Herefordshire.

In 2001/02 it had assets of £1.9 million, which generated an income of £48,000. Grants were made totalling £56,000.

By far the largest grant was of £30,000 and went to Hereford Waterworks Museum Trust. The accounts stated that there is a £500,000 project in progress at the museum and the trust will be making a substantial contribution towards these costs in the near future.

Other large grants were £5,500 to National Museums and Galleries of Wales, £5,100 to Royal Agricultural Benevolent Fund, £5,000 to ARC Addington Fund, £1,300 to Oxfam and £1,000 each to Assist U and National Trust.

Beneficiaries of smaller grants included Hereford Lifestyles and Quaker Peace and Service (£250 each), Herefordshire Historic Churches Trust (£200), Disabled Living Foundation (£150), Black Country Museum, Clifford PCC, Hay and District Dial-a-Ride, Hereford Nature Trust, Outward Bound – Hereford and Shuttleworth Collection (£100 each), British Red Cross (£25) and Denham College (£10).

Applications The trust has previously stated: 'No applications can be considered or replied to.'

R H Southern Trust

Education, disability, relief of poverty, environment, conservation

£296,000 (2002/03)

Beneficial area Worldwide.

23 Sydenham Road, Cotham, Bristol BS6 5SJ

Tel. 0117 942 5834

Correspondent The Trustees

Trustees *Marion Valiant Wells; Charles Sebastian Rivett Wells; Charles James Long Brugel; Avon Executor and Trustee Co. Ltd.*

CC Number 1077509

Information available Accounts were on file at the Charity Commission.

General This trust was registered with the Charity Commission on 31 March 1999. In 2000 substantial funds were settled totalling £6.9 million. Its objects are:

- the advancement of education (including medical and scientific research)
- the relief of poverty
- disability
- the preservation, conservation and protection of the environment.

In 2002/03 the trust had assets of £3.8 million with an income of £137,000 and grants totalling £296,000.

The largest grants were £47,000 to Oxford University, £33,000 to Friends of the Earth, £30,000 each to Natural Step and Brunel University – Design for Life Centre, £20,000 each to Just Change (Oxfam) and Motivation, £19,000 to SCAD, £15,000 each to New Economics and Sustrans and £10,000 each to Action Vilage India, FEASTA and Soil Association.

Other grants include £8,500 to Europe/ India Rural Links, £6,000 to Religious Society of Friends and £5,000 each to Tree Aid and World Development Movement.

Applications In writing to the correspondent.

Spar Charitable Fund

Children

£234,000 (2002/03)

Beneficial area UK.

Mezzanine Floor, Hygeia Building, 66 – 68 College Road, Harrow, Middlesex HA1 1BE

Correspondent P W Marchant, Director and Company Secretary

Trustee *The National Guild of Spar Ltd.*

CC Number 236252

Information available Full accounts were on file at the Charity Commission.

General This trust tends to choose one main beneficiary which receives most of its funds, with smaller grants being made to the same beneficiaries each year. In 2002/03 the main beneficiary was Macmillan Cancer Relief, as it was in the previous year.

In 2002/03 the trust had assets of £704,000. The total income was £213,000, of which £39,000 was generated from investment income and £174,000 was received in donations. Grants were made to four organisations totalling £234,000.

The main beneficiary was Macmillan Cancer Relief, which received £216,000. Business in the Community was given £10,000. The other two grants were made to Caravan NGBF (£6,000) and SGBF (£1,500).

Applications In writing to the correspondent.

The Spear Charitable Trust

General

£78,000 to organisations (2002)

Beneficial area UK.

Roughground House, Old Hall Green, Ware, Hertfordshire SG11 1HB

Tel. 01920 823071 **Fax** 01920 823071

Correspondent Hazel E Spear, Secretary

Trustees *P N Harris; F A Spear; H E Spear; N Gooch.*

CC Number 1041568

Information available Full accounts were provided by the trust.

General Established in 1994 with general charitable purposes, this trust has particular interest in helping employees and former employees of J W Spear and Sons plc and their families and dependants.

In 2002 the assets totalled £3.6 million and generated an income of £142,000. Grants were made to 73 organisations totalling £178,000, whilst ex-employees received £52,000 in total. Management and administration charges were high at £19,000 and included payments to two firms in which a member of the trustees is a partner. Whilst wholly legal, these editors always regret such payments unless, in the words of the Charity Commission, 'there is no realistic alternative'.

The largest grants were £10,000 each to Demelza House, Jewish Care and Southgate and District Reform Synagogue; £7,500 to RSPCA Enfield; £6,500 to Imagine; and £5,000 each to Animals in War Memorial Fund, International Performers' Aid Trust and The Woodland Trust.

Other beneficiaries included Family Welfare Association and Motor Neurone Disease (£2,500 each), Friends of the Hebrew University of Jerusalem and Russian Immigrants Aid Fund (£2,000 each); with £1,500 each to Pekinese Rescue, British Jewish Heritage Society, National Animal Welfare Trust, NSPCC for a tennis tournament and Oneg Shabbos Youth Club; £1,000 each to Ballet West, Cats Protection League, Diabetes UK, Exmoor Search and Rescue Team.

Exclusions Appeals from individuals are not considered.

Applications In writing to the correspondent.

Roama Spears Charitable Settlement

Welfare causes

£69,000 (2002/03)

Beneficial area Worldwide.

Silver Altman, Chartered Accountants, 8 Baltic Street East, London EC1Y 0UP

Tel. 020 7251 2200

Correspondent Robert Ward

Trustees *Mrs R L Spears; P B Mendel.*

CC Number 225491

Information available Full accounts were on file at the Charity Commission.

General This trust states that it makes grants to organisations towards the relief of poverty worldwide. In practice it appears to support a range of organisations including a number of museums and arts organisations. It has some preference for Jewish causes.

In 2002/03 the trust's assets totalled £1.8 million, generating an income of £23,000. After management and administration costs of £33,000, grants were made totalling £69,000.

Donations of over £1,000 included £20,000 to Cancer Macmillan Fund, £15,000 to Royal Opera House, £8,300 to Royal College of Music, £7,000 to Ackerman Institute for the Family, £5,400 to Wellbeing and £1,000 to North West London Jewish Day School.

Applications In writing to the correspondent.

The Worshipful Company of Spectacle Makers Charity

Visual impairment, City of London, general

£30,000 (2000/01)

Beneficial area Worldwide.

Apothecaries Hall, Blackfriars Lane, London EC4V 6EL

Tel. 020 7236 2932

Correspondent John Salmon

Trustee *Christine Tomkins, Paul Southworth, Michael Barton, John Marshall.*

CC Number 1072172

Information available Accounts were on file at the Charity Commission.

General Registered with the Charity Commission in October 1998, this livery company stated that it tends to support causes related to visual impairment and City of London, however it has supported a wide range of projects worldwide. No grants are made to individuals.

In 2003/04 the trust had an income of £138,000 and a total expenditure of £30,000. Further information from this year was unavailable. Past information collated from the Charity Commission stated that in 2000/01 the trust had an income of £161,000 and a total expenditure of £30,000 all of which was given in grants.

Previous beneficiaries have included Blind in Business, Royal National College for the Blind and Vision Aid Overseas.

Applications The trustees do their own research; unsolicited applications are unlikely to be successful.

The Jessie Spencer Trust

General

£95,000 (2002/03)

Beneficial area UK, with a preference for Nottinghamshire.

1 Royal Standard Place, Nottingham NG1 6FZ

Tel. 0115 950 7000 **Fax** 0115 950 7111

Correspondent The Trustees

Trustees *V W Semmens; Mrs E K M Brackenbury; R S Hursthouse; Mrs J Galloway.*

CC Number 219289

Information available Information was provided by the trust.

General The trust supports a range wide of causes, including welfare, religion and the environment amongst others. Whilst grants are made UK-wide, there is a preference for work in Nottinghamshire.

In 2002/03 it had assets of £2.5 million, which generated an income of £129,000. Grants were made totalling £95,000, broken down as follows:

Accommodation – 5 grants totalling £2,500

The Dovecoat Trust Limited, The Haven Housing Trust, Newark Emmaus Trust, Penrose Housing Association Limited and St Mungo's received £500 each.

Arts – 5 grants totalling £2,100

Cambridge Handel Opera Group, Koestler Award Trust and The Rehearsal Orchestra received £500 each, Youngchoirs.net was given £350 while The Magdala Opera Trust received £250.

Churches – 12 grants totalling £9,700
Grants included £5,000 to Nottinghamshire Historic Churches Trust, £1,000 each to St Margaret's Church (Kings Lynn) and St Mary's Church (Nottingham), £500 each to St Peter's Church (Flawborough), New Cross Community Church, Ollerton Methodist Church, The Parish of St Mary (Arnold) and St Paul's Church (Wilford Hill) and £200 to Clifton Methodist Church.

Education – 6 grants totalling £12,800
The largest grant was £10,000 to Portland Training College for the Disabled. Other beneficiaries were Zibby Garnett Travelling Fellowship (£1,000), Christians of Nottingham Training and Studying Together, The Countryside Foundation for Education and Schools Outreach (£500 each) and Arnold Methodist Playgroup and Edwinstowe Pre-School Playgroup (£125 each).

Environment – 4 grants totalling £1,800
These went to FWAG, The Woodland Trust, York Foundation for Conservation and Craftmanship (£500 each) and The Barn Owl Trust (£250).

Groups/clubs – 5 grants totalling £2,500
These were £500 each to The Acorn Project (Skegby), Notts County Guide Association, Oliver Hind Group, Nottingham Youth Orchestra and St John's Day Centre for the Elderly.

Individuals – 7 grants totalling £1,500

Medical/disabled – 26 grants totalling £42,000
The largest grants were £10,000 to Nottingham City Hospital for the Breast Unit Fund and £5,000 each to Alzheimer's Research Trust, Autonomic Disorders Association the Sarah Matheson Trust and Nottinghamshire Dyslexia Association. Other grants included £2,000 to the National Kidney Research Fund and £1,000 each to Nottingham Royal Society for the Blind and Cystic Fibrosis Trust.

Other – 3 grants totalling £850
National Playing Fields Association received £500, Prevented Unwanted Pets £250 and Linby & Papplewick PCC £100.

Welfare – 25 grants totalling £20,000
The largest grants were £2,500 to NSPCC Nottinghamshire Appeal, £2,300 to Southwell Care Project and £1,000 each to Apex Trust, Barnardos, Fundays in Nottinghamshire, Lenton Care Link and Jonathan Young Memorial Trust. Other beneficiaries recieved £500 each, including All Saints Community Care Project, Dream Holidays, East Midlands Open Minds and Northern Ireland Children's Holiday Scheme.

Exclusions Grants are rarely made for the repair of parish churches outside Nottinghamshire.

Applications In writing to the correspondent, including the latest set of audited accounts, at least three weeks before the trustees' meetings in March, June, September and December. Unsuccessful applications will not be notified.

The Moss Spiro Will Charitable Foundation

Jewish welfare

£438,000 (2001/02)

Beneficial area UK.

Crowndean House, 26 Bruton Lane, London W1J 6JH

Tel. 020 7491 9817 **Fax** 020 7499 6850

Correspondent Trevor Spiro, Trustee

Trustees *Trevor David Spiro; Geoffrey Michael Davis; David Jeremy Goodman.*

CC Number 1064249

Information available Full accounts were on file at the Charity Commission.

General The trust makes grants towards Jewish welfare. In 2001/02 the foundation had assets of £1.2 million with an income of £64,000. A grants list was not provided but total grants amounted to £438,000.

In 1999/2000 the trust made grants totalling £53,000 as follows: £20,000 to American Friends of Yershivas Birchas Ha Torah, £16,000 to Lubavitch Foundation (the only beneficiary which was also supported in the previous year, with a grant of £27,000), £10,000 to J T Tannenbaum Jewish Cultural Centre, £4,000 to Friends of Neve Shalom, £2,500 to Jewish Care and £500 to HGS Emunah.

Applications In writing to the correspondent.

W W Spooner Charitable Trust

General

£91,000 (2001/02)

Beneficial area UK, with a preference for Yorkshire especially West Yorkshire.

Addleshaw Goddard, PO Box 8, Sovereign House, Sovereign Street, Leeds LS1 1HQ

Tel. 0113 209 2000

Correspondent Liz Jones

Trustees *M H Broughton, Chair; Sir James F Hill; J C Priestley; T J P Ramsden; Mrs J M McKiddie; J H Wright.*

CC Number 313653

Information available Accounts were on file at the Charity Commission.

General The trust will support charities working in the following areas:

- Youth – for example, welfare, sport and education including school appeals and initiatives, clubs, scouting, guiding, adventure training, individual voluntary service overseas and approved expeditions
- Community – including churches, associations, welfare and support groups
- Healing – including care of people who are sick, disabled or underprivileged, welfare organisations, victim support, hospitals, hospices and selected medical charities and research
- The countryside – causes such as the protection and preservation of the environment including rescue and similar services and preservation and maintenance of historic buildings
- The arts – including museums, teaching, performing, musical and literary festivals and selective support for the purchase of works of art for public benefit.

It has a list of regular beneficiaries which receive grants each year and also supports around 40 to 50 one-off applications. Grants can range from £200 to £2,000, although they are usually for £250 to £350.

In 2001/02 the trust had assets of £1.8 million and an income of £76,000. Grants were given to about 100 regular beneficiaries and 40 one-off applications and totalled £91,000.

The largest grants went to Wordsworth Trust – Grasmere (£5,000), Parish of Tong and Holme Wood (£2,500), Guide

Dogs for the Blind (£1,700), St Margaret's PCC – Ilkley (£1,500) with £1,000 each to Abbeyfield Society, All Saints' Church – Ilkley, Ardenlea, Hawksworth Church of England School, Leith School of Art, Martin House Hospice, North of England Christian Healing Trust, St Gemma's Hospice, St George's Crypt, Wheatfield House and Yorkshire Ballet Seminar.

Exclusions 'No grants for high-profile appeals seeking large sums.' Most donations are for less than £500.

Applications In writing to the correspondent.

Stanley Spooner Deceased Charitable Trust

Children, general

£38,000 (2001/02)

Beneficial area UK.

The Public Trustee Ref 65361, Official Solicitor and Public Trustee, 81 Chancery Lane, London WC2A 1DD

Tel. 020 7911 7068 **Fax** 020 7911 7230

Correspondent G Owen, Trust Officer

CC Number 1044737

Information available Full accounts were on file at the Charity Commission.

General The trust mainly makes grants to charities listed in the trust deed and only a small part of its grant-making is discretionary. In 2001/02 it had assets of £641,000 and an income of £43,000. Grants were made totalling £38,000.

The three regular beneficiaries are The Children's Society, Docklands Settlement and Metropolitan Police Courts Poor Boxes (Drinan Bequest). Each of these beneficiaries received three-tenths of the income. The remaining tenth was divided equally between Barnardo's and National Children's Home. It appears as if both of these charities also receive grants on an ongoing basis.

Applications In writing to the correspondent.

Rosalyn and Nicholas Springer Charitable Trust

Welfare, Jewish, education, general

£130,000 (2002/03)

Beneficial area UK.

Flat 27, Berkeley House, 15 Hay Hill, London W1J 8NS

Tel. 020 7493 1904

Correspondent Nicholas Springer, Trustee

Trustees *Mrs R Springer; N S Springer; J Joseph.*

CC Number 1062239

Information available Full accounts were on file at the Charity Commission.

General This trusts supports the relief and assistance of people in need, for the advancement of education, religion and other purposes.

In 2002/03 it had assets of £34,000 and an income of £125,000, almost all of which were received in donations. Grants were made to 65 organisations totalling £130,000. In addition to this, the accounts stated that £19,000 was donated towards the school fees of the grandchildren of two of the trustees, which was 'approved by the independent trustee'. Whilst wholly legal, these editors always regret such payments, believing trustees should not receive personal benefit from their positions.

The largest grants were £31,000 to UJIA, £19,000 to London Jewish Cultural Centre and £13,000 to UK Friends of MDA.

Other beneficiaries included Royal Opera House (£6,700), Cancerkin (£3,600), British Friends of the Jaffa Trust (£3,000), Youth Aliyah Child Rescue (£2,000), West London Synagogue (£1,200), Almeida Theatre (£1,000), Family Housing Association (£750), London String Quartet (£500), British Friends of Shalva (£250), Institute of Jewish Policy Research (£200) and Philharmonia Orchestra (£150).

In addition to this, the accounts stated that £19,000 was donated towards the school fees of the grandchildren of two of the trustees, with the accounts showing that payments to family members of the trustees has been a regular feature of this trust's work.

Whilst the 2002/03 accounts state that these payments were 'approved by the independent trustee', questions must be asked about whether these payments were made in the best interests of the trust or the trustees. If the payments were agreed with no input from the related trustees and following guidelines of the trust which unrelated individuals could apply under, then this would be a satisfactory practice. If this was not the case, however, then the trust could be seen as allowing the trustees to transfer money through the tax-efficient medium of charitable donations to enable their private payments for school fees to be subsidised by the tax payer. Such payments could be seen as harming the public perception of the trust world. These editors regret that the accounts do not offer sufficient evidence that this was not the case.

Applications The trust states that it only supports organisations it is already in contact with. 99% of unsolicited applications are unsuccessful and because of the volume it receives, the trust is unable to reply to such letters. It would therefore not seem appropriate to apply to this trust.

The Spurrell Charitable Trust

General

£74,000 (2003/04)

Beneficial area UK, with some preference for Norfolk.

16 Harescroft, Moat Farm, Tunbridge Wells, Kent TN2 5XE

Tel. 01892 541565

Correspondent A T How, Trustee

Trustees *Alan T How; Richard J K Spurrell; Mrs Inge H Spurrell.*

CC Number 267287

Information available Full accounts were provided by the trust.

General This trust's funds are only distributed to charities known personally to the trustees. There appears to be a preference for supporting causes in Norfolk. The trust states that funds are fully committed.

In 2003/04 it had assets of £1.8 million which generated an income of £69,000. Grants totalling £74,000 were made to 72 organisations, only 7 of which were not also supported in the previous year.

The largest grants were £5,500 to East Anglian Air Ambulance, £5,000 each to Friends of Norwich Cathedral, Number One Community Trust and Parkinson's Disease Society and Royal Agricultural Benevolent Institute and £3,000 to Break (including £2,000 for the Long Stratton Project).

Other grants included £2,500 to Injured Jockeys Fund, £1,400 to John Grooms Association – Norwich, £1,000 each to Animal Health Trust, RAF Benevolent Fund, Roughton PCC and Salvation Army – Norwich, £750 each to Connection at St Martins and Disability Aid Fund, £500 each to Bessingham Church PCC, Church Mission Society, Corrymeela Community, Felbrigg PCC, Listening Books, National Animal Welfare Trust, Norfolk Deaf Association, PDSA, Riding for the Disabled – North Norfolk and St John Ambulance and £250 each to Felbrigg Crusaders and Sustead Village Hall Fund.

Applications Unsolicited applications are not considered.

The Geoff and Fiona Squire Foundation

General in the UK

£125,000 (2001/02)

Beneficial area UK.

Home Farm House, Hursley, Winchester, Hampshire SO21 2JL

Correspondent Fiona Squire, Trustee

Trustees *G W Squire; F P Squire; B P Peerless.*

CC Number 1085553

Information available Accounts were on file at the Charity Commission.

General Registered with the Charity Commission in March 2001, in 2001/02, its first year of operation £11 million was settled with the foundation. Out of a total expenditure of £148,000, the sum of £125,000 was distributed in 11 grants.

Beneficiaries were: Save the Children (£56,000); Sense – holiday fund (£52,000); Make a Wish Foundation (£5,600); BBC Children in Need Appeal (£5,000); Starlight Children's Foundation (£3,000); Breakthrough Breast Cancer Appeal and Children's County Holiday's Fund (£1,000 each); and Canine Partners for independence, Friends of Hampshire County Youth Orchestra, Lord Taverners and Thames Valley & Chiltern Air Ambulance Trust.

Applications 'The trustees have in place a well-established donations policy and we do not therefore encourage unsolicited grant applications, not least because they take time and expense to deal with properly.'

Miss Doreen Stanford Trust

General

£27,000 (2003)

Beneficial area UK.

26 The Mead, Beckenham, Kent BR3 5PE

Tel. 020 8650 3368

Correspondent Mrs G M B Borner, Secretary

Trustees *T Carter; R S Borner; T Butler.*

CC Number 1049934

Information available Accounts were on file at the Charity Commission.

General The trust states that its aims are to provide grants to individuals in need through charities, to further their education and help them or the public in the appreciation of the learned arts or sciences, to help towards holidays and to help those in conditions of hardship or distress. Grant size depends on the requirements of each case, but is rarely above £2,000.

In 2003 the trust had assets of £658,000 and an income of £32,000. Grants totalled £27,000. Donations included: £3,000 each to Deafblind UK and Motor Neurone Disease Association; £2,500 to Kent Association for the Blind; £2,000 each to Aidis Trust and Church Army; £1,500 each to Aged in Distress, Charity Search, Harvest Trust, Invalids-at-Home and Neuromuscular Centre; and £1,000 to Talking Newspapers Association.

Exclusions No grants are given towards building repairs, alterations to property, electrical goods, floor coverings, holidays for individuals or towards household furniture or equipment.

Applications In writing to the correspondent, enclosing an sae. Allocations of grants are made once a year in March at the trustees' meeting.

The Stanley Charitable Trust

Jewish

About £90,000 (2002/03)

Beneficial area UK, with a preference for Greater Manchester.

32 Waterpark Road, Salford M7 4ET

Correspondent David Adler

Trustees *A M Adler; I Adler; J Adler.*

CC Number 326220

Information available Brief accounts for 1990/91 were in the public files at the Charity Commission.

General The trust supports Jewish religious charities, with a preference for those in Greater Manchester and for projects and people known to the trustees.

In 2002/03 the trust had an income of £143,000 and a total expenditure of £95,000. Further information for this year was not available.

In 1998/99 it had an income of £90,000 and an expenditure of £110,000. Further up-to-date information was not available.

In 1990/91 it owned 30% of Nailsea Estate Co. and also had £204,000 in property. Its income of £113,000 included £36,000 from rent, £33,000 loan interest and £41,000 share of surplus joint venture. Expenditure totalled £39,000, including £31,000 on a bank overdraft. This left a net income of £74,000 out of which £65,000 was given in unspecified donations.

Exclusions Only registered charities are supported.

Applications The trust has said that it gives regular donations and does not consider new applications.

This entry was not confirmed by the trust, but was correct according to information on file at the Charity Commission.

The Stanley Foundation Ltd

Older people, medical, education, social welfare

£106,000 (2002/03)

Beneficial area UK.

Flat 3, 19 Holland Park, London W11 3TD

Correspondent The Secretary

Trustees *Nicholas Stanley, Chair; D J Aries; S R Stanley; Albert Rose; Mrs E Stanley; C Shale.*

CC Number 206866

Information available Full accounts were on file at the Charity Commission.

General The trust has traditionally supported charities helping older people and medical, educational and social welfare charities. In 2002/03 it had assets of £2.3 million and an income of £77,000. Grants were made to 50 organisations totalled £106,000.

The largest grants were £15,000 to COS Biography, £7,500 to St John Ambulance, £6,000 to Grange Park Opera and £5,000 each to Cancer BACUP, Flips Fund, National Gallery, St Joseph's and WWVOL.

Other beneficiaries included Headway (£2,600), Elizabeth Finn Trust (£2,500), Prisoners Educational Trust (£2,000), Aid International and Royal Geographical Society (£1,000 each), Eating Disorders Association and Feathers Club Association (£500 each), Juvenile Diabetes Research (£300), Crisis (£250) and Kensington Day Centre (£200).

Exclusions No grants to individuals.

Applications In writing to the correspondent.

The Star Charitable Trust

General

£145,000 (2001/02)

Beneficial area UK.

94 Saffron Hill, London EC1N 8PT

Tel. 020 7404 2222 **Fax** 020 7404 2950

Correspondent The Trustees

Trustees *D D Fiszman; P I Propper.*

CC Number 266695

Information available Accounts were on file at the Charity Commission, without a list of grants.

General Connected to the star Diamond Group of companies, this trust was established in March 1974. In 2001/02 it had assets amounting to £663,000 and an income of £41,000. Grants to 12 organisations totalled £145,000.

Unfortunately, no list of beneficiaries was included with the accounts on file at the Charity Commission.

Applications In writing to the correspondent.

Star Foundation Trust

General in the UK

£78,000 to organisations and individuals (2001/02)

Beneficial area UK.

Flat 23, Manor Fields, Putney Heath, London, SW15 3LT

Correspondent J D Hewens, Trustee

Trustees *Mrs J Cameron; R A Griffiths; J D Hewens; Mrs J S McCreadie; Dr David Spalton.*

CC Number 257711

Information available Accounts were on file at the Charity Commission.

General Registered with the Charity Commission in February 1969, in 2001/02 the trust had assets amounting to £3.3 million and an income of £165,000. Grants totalled £78,000 with £19,000 being spent on administration.

There were 15 grants made in the year including those to: John Muir Trust (£15,000), National Trust for Scotland and Sir John Soames Museum (£10,000 each), 3H Fund and Cystic Fibrosis Holiday Fund for Children (£5,000 each), Abbeyfield North London Society Ltd, Alzheimer's Society and Crimestoppers Trust (£2,500 each) and Accord Hospice (£1,600).

Applications In writing to the correspondent. Trustees meet twice a year.

The Educational Charity of the Stationers' and Newspaper Makers' Company

Printing education

£77,000 to organisations (2002/03)

Beneficial area UK.

The Old Dairy, Adstockfields, Adstock, Buckingham MK18 2JE

Tel. 01296 714886 **Fax** 01296 714711

Correspondent P Thornton, Secretary

Trustee *Stationers' and Newspaper Makers' Company.*

CC Number 312633

Information available Accounts were provided by the trust, but without a list of grants.

General This trust was set up in 1985 primarily to support the education of people under 25 wishing to enter the stationers' or newspaper makers' trades. It has close links with Reeds School and King Edward's School – Witley. However, possibly reflecting the changing technological nature of the business, the trust also funds the installation of printing departments at schools. The trust stated that grants to schools towards fitting out a printing department vary from year to year and may be for more than £30,000 a year.

In 2002/03 the trust's assets totalled £2.1 million and it had an income of £88,000. 50 grants were made totalling £133,000, of which £77,000 went to organisations and £55,000 to individuals.

Grants were made to Reeds School for desktop publishing equipment, St Peter and Paul RC Primary School, Bootham School and Central Foundation Boys' School for running costs of its desktop publishing suite. King Edward's School – Witley and Reeds School both received bursaries to be paid to pupils, with two PhD students also supported.

Exclusions No grants towards anything not related to printing, stationery or papermaking.

Applications Application forms can be obtained from the correspondent. They are considered monthly.

The Peter Stebbings Memorial Charity

General

£28,000 (2002/03)

Beneficial area UK and developing countries.

45 Pont Street, London SW1X 0BX

Tel. 020 7591 3333

Correspondent Andrew Stebbings, Secretary to the Trustees

Trustees *Mrs P M Cosin; N F Cosin; Mrs J A Clifford.*

CC Number 274862

Information available Information was provided by the trust.

General The trust makes grants for a range of charitable purposes and the objects of the trust are to fund, in particular, medical research and education, and the welfare of those who are poor, old or sick.

In 2002/03 it had assets of £735,000 and an income of £54,000. Grants totalled £28,000.

Age Concern received £2,000, whilst £1,000 each went to Alzheimer's Disease Society, Amnesty International, Brent Family Service Unit, Camden Society, MIND, Mozambique Flood Appeal, National Schizophrenic Society, SOS Children's Villages, Wellcome Brent and Westminster School PHAB.

Exclusions No grants to individuals, non-registered charities or for salaries.

Applications This trust states that it does not respond to unsolicited applications and that its funds are fully committed.

The Cyril & Betty Stein Charitable Trust

Jewish causes

£209,000 (2001/02)

Beneficial area UK and Israel.

c/o Clayton Stark & Co., 5th Floor, Charles House, 108–110 Finchley Road, London NW3 5JJ

Tel. 020 7935 4999

Correspondent The Trustees

Trustees *Cyril Stein; Betty Stein; David Clayton.*

CC Number 292235

Information available Accounts were on file at the Charity Commission.

General The trust makes a small number of substantial grants each year, primarily for the advancement of the Jewish religion and the welfare of Jewish people.

In 2001/02 the trust had an income of £220,000 and the total number of assets was £337,000. Grants were donated to the amount of £209,000.

The beneficiaries included The Institute for the Advancement of Education in Jaffa (£96,828), Friends of Bnei David (£40,250), Project Seed (£11,250), Lubavitch Foundation (£10,000), Chief Rabbinate Charitable Trust (£7,500), British Friends of Machon Meir (£7,000), The Hebrew University of Jerusalem (£5,300), The Hope Charity (£5,500), British Friends of Ariel (£2,500), Friends of El Ami (£1,400), Enncounter, Manchester Jewish Foundation and Tsad Kadima (£1,000 each).

Other grants below £1,000 came to £2,200.

Applications In writing to the correspondent.

The Steinberg Family Charitable Trust

Jewish, health

£243,000 (2001/02)

Beneficial area UK, with a preference for Greater Manchester.

Stanley House, 151 Dale Street, Liverpool L2 2JW

Correspondent L Steinberg, Trustee

Trustees *D Burke, Chairman; Ms B Steinberg; J Steinberg; Ms L R Ferster; D K Johnston; M Sampson; B Davidson.*

CC Number 1045231

Information available Full accounts were on file at the Charity Commission.

General This trust has general charitable purposes, with a preference for Jewish or health organisations in the north west of England.

In 2001/02 it had an income of £1.5 million, much higher than in previous years due to the receipt of a donation of £1.2 million. Grants were made to 66 organisations totalling £243,000, typical of the amount given each year. After minimal management and administration fees of just £15, the remaining funds from the donation were transferred to assets, which stood at £5.8 million at the year end.

The largest grants were £50,000 to Hale and District Hebrew Congregation, £25,000 to Manchester Jewish Federation, £20,000 each to Friends of Lubavitch UK and United Synagogue, £15,000 to Heathlands Village, £11,000 to Magen David Adom UK and £10,000 each to Cayo Foundation, Crimestoppers Trust and HaMesorah Institution.

Beneficiaries in the Greater Manchester area included Christie's Against Cancer (£5,000), Yeshivas Lubavitch Manchester (£2,200), Hale Adult Education Trust (£2,000), Encounter Conference Manchester (£1,000), Manchester Talmud Torah (£250) and Manchester Jewish School for Special Education (£100).

Other recipients included Centre for Torah Education Trust (£6,000), Gust-Etzion Emergency Appeal (£5,000), Wingate Institute for Physical Education and Sport (£2,000), UJIA (£1,500), Nightingale Trust (£1,000), Bryson House and Reality at Work in Scotland (£500 each), Jewish Museum (£400), Action for Blind People and St Gregory's Youth and Community Initiative – Liverpool (£250 each), Meningitis Research Foundation (£200), Reshet (£150) and Bournemouth Jewish Day School Charitable Trust and Liverpool Daughters of Zion (£100 each)

Applications In writing to the correspondent.

The Sir Sigmund Sternberg Charitable Foundation

Jewish, inter-faith causes, general

£314,000 (2002/03)

Beneficial area Worldwide.

Star House, Grafton Road, London NW5 4BD

Tel. 020 7485 2538

Correspondent Sir S Sternberg, Trustee

Trustees *Sir S Sternberg; V M Sternberg; Lady Sternberg.*

CC Number 257950

Information available Full accounts were on file at the Charity Commission.

General This trust supports Jewish and Israeli charities, with a preference for organisations that address inter-faith issues and cooperation. It makes a small number of large grants, generally of £10,000 to £50,000 each, and a large number of smaller grants.

In 2002/03 the foundation had assets of £3.9 million and a total income of £1.2 million, including £940,000 in donations received. Management and administration costs appear high at £175,000, but this includes charitable activities carried out by the trust, particularly concerning the promotion of education between the Christian, Islamic and Jewish faiths. Grants were made totalling £314,000 and were broken down as follows.

	No.	*Total*
Education	82	£69,000
Religious activities	47	£95,000
Promotion of interfaith understanding	47	£94,000
Medical Care and care of elderly/disabled	40	£40,000
Relief of poverty	15	£1,900
Arts and culture	10	£5,200
Bereavement care	2	£6,000
Communal	7	£2,900

The largest grants were £50,000 to Reform Synagogues of Great Britain, £45,000 to Friends of the Hebrew University of Jerusalem, £32,000 to the Reform Education Trust, £21,000 to Manor House Trust, £15,000 to United Jewish Israel Appeal, £12,000 to Centre fo Jewish Christian Relations, £11,000 to Dartmouth Street Trust and £10,000 each to Board of Deputies Charitable Foundation, Institute of Business Ethics and Interreligious Coordinating Council in Israel.

Smaller grants included those to International Council for Christians and Jews (£7,600), Cruse Bereavement Care (£6,000), Oxford Centre for Hebrews and Jewish Studies (£5,000), Queen's College Cambridge (£4,500), Israel Diaspora Trust (£3,000), World Jewish Relief (£2,500) and St Ethelburga's Centre for Reconciliation and Peace (£2,000).

Exclusions No grants to individuals.

Applications The foundation stated in April 2004 that its funds are fully committed.

Stervon Ltd

Jewish

£149,000 (2000)

Beneficial area UK.

c/o Stervon House, 1 Seaford Road, Salford, Greater Manchester M6 6AS

Tel. 0161 737 5000

Correspondent A Reich, Secretary

Trustees *A Reich; G Rothbart.*

CC Number 280958

Information available Accounts were on file at the Charity Commission.

General 'The principal objective of the company is the distribution of funds to Jewish, religious, educational and similar charities.'

In 2003 this trust had an income of £248,000 and a total expenditure of £222,000. Unfortunately no further information was available for this year.

In 2000 the trust had assets of £133,000 and an income of £181,000, £74,000 of which came from donations. Grants totalled £149,000.

Beneficiaries included Chasdei Yoel and Machzikei Hadass (£14,000 each), Chessed Lyisroel (£12,000), Bnos Yisroel (£9,300), Yetev Lev (£6,500), Yeshivas Ponives (£5,700), Beis Ruchel (£5,000), Craven Walk Trust and Sheves Achim (£3,500 each), BHST (£2,000) and Satmar (£1,000).

Applications In writing to the correspondent.

The Stewards' Charitable Trust

Rowing

£91,000 (2002/03)

Beneficial area Principally the UK.

Regatta Headquarters, Henley-on-Thames, Oxfordshire RG9 2LY

Tel. 01491 572153 **Fax** 01491 575509

Correspondent R S Goddard, Secretary

Trustees *M A Sweeney; C G V Davidge; C L Baillieu; R C Lester.*

CC Number 299597

Information available Full accounts were provided by the trust.

General The trust makes grants to organisations and clubs benefiting boys and girls involved in the sport of rowing. It supports rowing at all levels, from grassroots upwards; beneficiaries should be in full-time education or training. Support is also given to related medical and educational research projects. Grants range from £1,000 to £60,000. They are preferably one-off and are especially made where matched funds are raised elsewhere.

In 2002/03 the trust had assets of £2.7 million and an income of £390,000, including £299,000 in donations received from various aspects of the Henley Regatta and Henley Festival. Grants were made to three organisations totalling £91,000.

Beneficiaries were ARA Scholarships to allow five individuals to obtain coaching qualifications at academic institutions (£50,000), a biodynamics research project into rowing and back injuries at Imperial College of Science, Technology and Medicine (£31,000) and Rowing Foundation to distribute to small-scale charitable projects (£10,000).

Exclusions No grants to individuals or for building or capital costs.

Applications In writing to the correspondent. Applications are usually first vetted by Amateur Rowing Association.

The M J C Stone Charitable Trust

General

£277,000 (2001)

Beneficial area UK.

Estate Office, Ozleworth Park, Wotton-under-Edge, Gloucestershire GL12 7QA

Tel. 01453 845591

Correspondent M J C Stone, Trustee

Trustees *M J C Stone; Mrs L Stone; C R H Stone; A J Stone; N J Farquhar.*

CC Number 283920

Information available Full accounts were on file at the Charity Commission.

General While the trust has general charitable objects, giving to a range of causes, it stated that its main area of interest is the advancement of education.

In 2001 the trust had assets of £971,000 and an income of £29,000. Grants made totalled £277,000. Grants ranged from £100 to £25,000. Some beneficiaries were supported in the previous year.

The largest beneficiaries were Game Conservancy Trust (£52,400), University of Gloucester (£50,000), Bradfield Foundation and Rare Breeds Survival Trust (£25,000 each) and Covent Garden Cancer Research Trust and Jubilee Sailing Trust (£10,000 each). Other beneficiaries included Action for Dysphasic Adults, ARC Addington, Brain Research Trust, County Durham Foundation and Rubka/SSAFA Namib Desert Challenge (£5,000 each), Blue Coat C of E School (£4,000), British Wheelchair Sports Foundation (£1,750), Aberlour House Ltd (£1,500) and Cancer Research Campaign (£1,200).

Grants of £1,000 each included those to Atlantic Council of the United Kingdom, Friends of the Elderly, HML Projects Central & Eastern Europe, National Osteoporosis Society, Royal Horticultural Society, Society for Environmental Improvement, Treloar Trust and World Pheasant Association.

Beneficiaries receiving under £1,000 included Altnaharra Primary School, British Diabetic Association, Cumbria Wildlife Trust, Hawkwood College, Raleigh International Trust and North Atlantic Salmon Trust.

Applications 'Unsolicited applications will not be replied to.'

The Stone-Mallabar Charitable Foundation

Medical, education

£181,000 (2002/03)

Beneficial area UK.

41 Orchard Court, Portman Square, London W1H 6LF

Correspondent Jonathan M Stone, Trustee

Trustees *Jonathan Stone; Thalia Stone; Robin Paul.*

CC Number 1013678

Information available Annual report and accounts on file at the Charity Commission.

General In 2002/03 the foundation had an income of £340,000. Grants were made totalling £181,000. The largest grants went to Centrepoint Soho, Motor Neurone Disease Association, Pelecan Cancer Foundation and the University of Wales (£25,000), Wigmore Hall Trust (£16,000) and the University of Bristol (£10,000).

Other beneficiaries included Prostate Research Campaign UK (£7,000), Hardman Trust and Oxford University Development Trust Fund (£5,000 each) and CFS Research Foundation (£2,500).

Exclusions No grants to individuals.

Applications The trustees regret that they cannot respond to applications as all funds have been allocated.

The Samuel Storey Family Charitable Trust

General

£119,000 (2002/03)

Beneficial area UK, with a preference for Yorkshire.

21 Buckingham Gate, London SW1E 6LS

Tel. 020 7802 2700 **Fax** 020 7828 5049

Correspondent Hon. Sir Richard Storey, Trustee

Trustees *Hon. Sir Richard Storey; Wren Hoskyns Abrahall; K Storey.*

CC Number 267684

Information available Full accounts were on file at the Charity Commission.

General This trust has general charitable purposes, supporting a wide range of causes, including the arts, gardens and churches. The grants list shows a large number of beneficiaries in Yorkshire.

In 2002/03 the trust had assets of £3.1 million with an income of £127,000 and grants totalling £119,000.

The largest grants were £20,000 to York University and £13,000 to Sunderland University Development Trust.

Other grants include £5,000 to Thare Machi, Settrington PCC and Norton Trinity Methodist Church, £4,000 to Museum of Garden History, £3,000 each to Abba Light Foundation, North East Helplink, St Gregory's Foundation, Ryedale District Council, Royal Horticultural Society and North Yorkshire Fire & Rescue Service, £2,000 each to Thomas Morley Trust, Help Tibet and Brooke Hospital for Animals.

Grants of £1,000 or less were awarded to All Saints Church (Brompton Organ Appeal), Anglican Centre in Rome, Breast Cancer Campaign, Brompton Hall School, Butterfly Conservation, Defeating Deafness, Friends of Summer Music, International Bible Society UK, Lambeth Fund, Maggie's Centre, Martin House, National Botanic Gardens of Wales, Plantlife, Spinal Injuries Association, Theatre Royal Appeal and York Minster.

Exclusions The trust does not support non-registered charities or individuals.

Applications In writing to the correspondent.

Peter Stormonth Darling Charitable Trust

Heritage, medical research, sport

£53,000 (1997)

Beneficial area UK.

33 King William Street, London EC4R 9AS

Correspondent Peter Stormonth Darling, Trustee

Trustees *Tom Colville; J F M Rodwell; Peter Stormonth Darling.*

CC Number 1049946

Information available Full accounts were on file at the Charity Commission.

General The trust makes grants towards heritage, education, healthcare and sports facilities.

In 2003 it had an income of £47,000 and a total expenditure of £48,000. Further information for this year was not available.

In 2001 the trust had an income of £48,000 and a total expenditure of £31,000. This information was taken from the Charity Commission's website; unfortunately no further information was available.

In 1997, the trust's assets totalled £1.4 million, it had an income of £42,000 and grants were made totalling £53,000 (up from £20,000 in the previous year). Beneficiaries were Winchester College (£35,000 – it had also received £10,000 in the previous year), King Edward VII Hospital for Officers (£8,000), Royal Medical Benevolent Fund (£5,000), National Trust for Scotland (£3,000) and Martin and Barry's Trust (£2,500).

Applications This trust states that it does not respond to unsolicited applications.

Peter Storrs Trust

Education

£103,000 (2002/03)

Beneficial area UK.

Fordyce Curry & Co., 91–93 Charterhouse Street, London EC1M 6PN

Tel. 020 7253 3757

Correspondent J A Fordyce, Trustee

Trustees *G V Adams; A R E Curtis; J A Fordyce.*

CC Number 313804

Information available Accounts were on file at the Charity Commission, but without a list of beneficiaries.

General The trust makes grants to registered charities working for the advancement of education in the UK. In 2002/03 the trust had assets of £1.6 million, an income of £327,000 and made grants totalling £103,000. Further information including a list of grant beneficiaries was not available.

Applications In writing to the correspondent. Applications are considered every three to six months. Please note, the trust receives far more applications than it is able to support, many of which do not meet the criteria outlined above. This results in a heavy waste of time and expense for both applicants and the trust itself.

The A B Strom & R Strom Charitable Trust

Jewish, general

£79,000 (2000/01)

Beneficial area UK.

c/o 11 Gloucester Gardens, London NW11 9AB

Tel. 020 8455 5949

Correspondent Mrs R Strom, Trustee

Trustees *Mrs R Strom; M Weissbraun.*

CC Number 268916

Information available Only very brief information was on file at the Charity Commission for this trust for 2000/01.

General According to the correspondent 'the trust only supports a set list of charities working with elderly people, schools/colleges, hospitals and Christian causes. It does not have any money available for any charities not already on the list.'

In 2000/01 the trust had assets of £228,000 with an income of £53,000 and grants totalling £79,000. Unfortunately a grants list was unavailable for recent years.

Applications In writing to the correspondent. Please note that the same organisations are supported each year.

This entry was not confirmed by the trust, but the address was correct according to the Charity Commission database.

Sueberry Ltd

Jewish, welfare

£117,000 (2002/03)

Beneficial area UK and overseas.

11 Clapton Common, London E5 9AA

Correspondent Mrs M Davis, Trustee

Trustees *J Davis, Chair; Mrs H Davis; Mrs M Davis; D S Davis; C Davis.*

CC Number 256566

Information available Accounts were on file at the Charity Commission but without a list of beneficiaries.

General The trust makes grants to Jewish organisations and also to other UK welfare, educational and medical organisations benefiting children and young adults, at risk groups, people who are disadvantaged by poverty, or socially isolated people.

In 2002/03 the trust had assets of £10,000 and an income of £81,000. Grants totalled £117,000. A list of beneficiaries was not available. In previous years the trust has supported educational, religious and other charitable organisations.

Applications In writing to the correspondent.

The Alan Sugar Foundation

Jewish charities, general

£273,000 (2002/03)

Beneficial area UK.

Brentwood House, 169 Kings Road, Brentwood, Essex CM14 4EF

Tel. 01277 201333 **Fax** 01277 208006

Correspondent Colin Sandy

Trustees *Sir Alan Sugar; Colin Sandy; Simon Sugar; Daniel Sugar; Mrs Louise Baron.*

CC Number 294880

Information available Full accounts are on file at the Charity Commission with grants list but with no narrative report.

General This trust was established by the well-known ex-chair of Tottenham Hotspur FC, and gives a small number of substantial grants each year. Grants are made to registered charities that are of current and ongoing interest to the trustees.

In 2002/03 the trust had assets of £21,000 with an income of £238,000 and grants totaling £273,000.

Grants include £200,000 to Jewish Care, £40,000 to Chigwell School Appeal, £10,000 each to PiggyBank Kids and Leukaemia Research Fund, £5,000 each to 4 Kids Sake and Rhys Daniels Trust, £2,000 to Prostate Cancer Charitable Fund and £1,000 to Disability Foundation.

Exclusions No grants for individuals or to non-registered charities.

Applications This trust states that it does not respond to unsolicited applications. All projects are initiated by the trustees.

The Adrienne and Leslie Sussman Charitable Trust

Jewish, general

£51,000 (2001/02)

Beneficial area UK, in practice Greater London, particularly Barnet.

25 Tillingbourne Gardens, London N3 3JJ

Correspondent Mrs A H Sussman

Trustees *A H Sussman; L Sussman; M D Paisner.*

CC Number 274955

Information available Accounts are on file at the Charity Commission.

General The trust supports a variety of Jewish, medical and social welfare organisations, including many in the Greater London area. In 2001/02 the trust had assets of £1.3 million and an income of £54,000. Grants totalling £51,000 were made in the year.

Previous beneficiaries have included BF Shvut Ami, Chai – Lifeline and B'nai B'rith Hillel Fund, Child Resettlement, Children and Youth Aliyah, Finchley Synagogue, Jewish Care, Nightingale House, Norwood, Sidney Sussex CLL.

Exclusions No grants to branches of UK charities outside Barnet, non-registered charities and individuals.

Applications In writing to the correspondent.

The Sutasoma Trust

Education, general

£121,000 (2001/02)

Beneficial area UK and overseas.

Kett House, Station Road, Cambridge CB1 2JY

Tel. 01223 355933

Correspondent Emma Drayson

Trustees *Dr A R Hobart; M A Burgauer; J M Lichtenstein.*

CC Number 803301

Information available Full accounts were on file at the Charity Commission up until 1996/97.

General The trust's objects are 'to advance education in particular by providing grants to graduate students in the social sciences and humanities' and general charitable purposes.

In 2001/02 the trust had assets of £2 million with an income of £99,000 and grants totalling £121,000.

The largest grants were £25,000 to Westminster Pastoral Foundation, £21,600 to Scott Polar Research institute and £15,000 to Lucy Cavendish College Fellowship.

Other grants include £5,000 each to British Museum, School of Oriental & African Studies and NW Brown (Natalie Clein Instrument Scheme), £4,000 to Emslie Horniman Fund, £2,000 each to Cambodia Trust, Stiftung Basel Dankt, ITDG, Lewa Wildlife – General Conservancy, Ailenn Alleyne and European Children's Trust.

Grants of £1,000 or less were awarded to Cambridge Regional College, Mmabana Primary School (Link Africa), Afghan Appeal and Hawks Charitable Trust.

Applications In writing to the correspondent.

The Swan Trust

General, arts, culture

£65,000 (2002/03)

Beneficial area Overseas and the UK, with a preference for East Sussex, Kent, Surrey and West Sussex.

Pollen House, 10–12 Cork Street, London W1S 3LW

Tel. 020 7439 9061

Correspondent A J Winborn

Trustee *The Cowdray Trust Limited.*

CC Number 261442

Information available Information was provided by the trust.

General The trust makes grants to a range of organisations including a number that are arts and culture related. Priority is given to grants for one year or less; grants for up to two years are considered.

In 2002/03 its assets totalled £708,000, it had an income of £59,000 and 55 grants were made totalling £65,000. Grants were in the range of £20 and £20,000.

The two largest grants were £20,000 to British Museum Development Trust and £11,000 to Magdalen College Development Trust. There were a further 12 grants of £1,000 or more including those to: Caldicott Foundation and Yehudi Menuhin School Ltd (£5,000 each); National Trust (£3,700); Painshill Park Trust (£3,000); Friends of Covent Garden (£1,500); Royal Academy Trust (£1,300); and Aldeburgh Productions, Charles Darwin Trust, National Portrait Gallery, Royal National Theatre and Withyham Parochial Church Council (£1,000 each).

Beneficiaries of smaller grants included 999 Club Trust, British Agencies for Adoption & Fostering, Chelsea Old Church, English National Opera, Family Welfare Association, Hospice in the Weald, Live Music Now!, National Art Collections Fund, Shelterand World Monuments Fund in Britain. A quarter of the beneficiaries had been supported in the previous year.

Exclusions No grants to individuals or non-registered charities.

Applications In writing to the correspondent. Acknowledgements will only be sent if a grant is being made.

The John Swire (1989) Charitable Trust

General

£279,000 (2002)

Beneficial area UK.

John Swire & Sons Ltd, Swire House, 59 Buckingham Gate, London SW1E 6AJ

Tel. 020 7834 7717

Correspondent B N Swire, Trustee

Trustees *Sir John Swire; J S Swire; B N Swire; M C Robinson; Lady Swire.*

CC Number 802142

Information available Full accounts were on file at the Charity Commission.

General Established in 1989 by Sir John Swire of John Swire & Sons Ltd, merchants and ship owners, the trust supports a wide range of organisations including some in the area of arts, welfare, education, medicine and research.

In 2002 the trust had assets of £8 million and an income £303,000. Grants were made totalling £279,000. Grants of over £1,000 were made to St Anthony's College towards scholarship (£17,000) and The Durrell Institute of Conservation and Ecology (£13,000).

Grants of £1,000 were made to Kent Wildlife Trust, King Edward VII Hospital, Leighton Buzzard PCC, London Cycle Campaign, Macmillan Fund, National Back Pain Association, National Meningitis Trust, Pilgrims Hospices in East Kent, Riding for the Disabled and St John Eye Hospital.

Applications In writing to the correspondent.

The Swire Charitable Trust

General

£391,000 (2002)

Beneficial area Worldwide.

John Swire & Sons Ltd, Swire House, 59 Buckingham Gate, London SW1E 6AJ

Tel. 020 7834 7717

Correspondent B N Swire, Trustee

Trustees *Sir J Swire; Sir Adrian Swire; B N Swire; M J B Todhunter; P A Johansen; J S Swine.*

CC Number 270726

Information available Full accounts were on file at the Charity Commission.

General In 2002 the trust had assets of £36,000 and an income of £242,000 with grants totalling £391,000.

The largest grants were St George's Hospital Medical School (£100,000) and British Urological Foundation (£75,000).

Other beneficiaries included Southampton University Development Trust (£25,000), Queen's Golden Jubilee Weekend Trust (£20,000), Air League Educational Trust (£18,000), BESO (£12,000), Book Aid International and Moorefields Eye Hospital Development Fund (£10,000 each), Voluntary Service Overseas (£8,000), Macmillan Cancer Relief (£6,000), Project Trust (£5,500), Eton College (£3,000), Link-Overseas (£1,500) and Cheshire Military Museum, Gurkha Welfare Trust and Phyllis Tuckwell Memorial Hospice (£1,000 each).

Applications In writing to the correspondent. Applications are considered throughout the year.

The Hugh & Ruby Sykes Charitable Trust

General, medical, education, employment

£270,000 (2002/03)

Beneficial area Principally South Yorkshire, also Derbyshire.

Bamford Hall Holdings Ltd, Bamford Hall, The Hollow, Bamford, Hope Valley S33 0AU

Tel. 01433 651190

Correspondent Sir Hugh Sykes, Trustee

Trustees *Sir Hugh Sykes; Lady Sykes.*

CC Number 327648

Information available Accounts were on file at the Charity Commission.

General This trust was set up in 1987 for general charitable purposes by Sir Hugh Sykes and his wife Lady Sykes. It supports local charities in South Yorkshire and Derbyshire, some major UK charities and a few medical charities.

In 2002/03 the trust had assets of £1.7 million. Total income was £108,000, including £60,000 generated by assets and £48,000 in rents. Sundry expenses and audit fees for the year were kept low at £1,400. Grants totalled £270,000. A grants list was not included in the accounts.

Exclusions No grants are made to individuals. Most grants are made to organisations which have a connection to one of the trustees.

Applications Applications can only be accepted from registered charities and should be in writing to the correspondent. In order to save administration costs, replies are not sent to unsuccessful applicants. If the trustees are able to consider a request for support, they aim to express interest within one month.

The Sylvanus Charitable Trust

Animal welfare, Roman Catholic

£65,000 in Europe (2002)

Beneficial area Europe and North America.

Vernor Miles & Noble, 5 Raymond Buildings, Gray's Inn, London WC1R 5DD

Tel. 020 7242 8688

Correspondent John C Vernor Miles, Trustee

Trustees *John C Vernor Miles; Alexander D Gemmill; Wilfred E Vernor Miles; Gloria Taviner.*

CC Number 259520

Information available Full accounts were on file at the Charity Commission.

General This trust was established in 1968 by the Countess of Kinnoull, who spent the last 40 years of her life in California, and supports the animal welfare, prevention of animal cruelty and the teachings and practices of the Roman Catholic Church. Organisations in North America and Europe are supported, with the trust spliting its finances into two sections, the sterling section (Europe) and the Dollar section (North America) to avoid currency troubles.

As the dollar section focusses on US giving only (and information on it was unavailable) only the sterling section is described here. It had assets of £1.3 million, which generated an income of £54,000. Grants were made to 20 organisations totalling £65,000.

These were £30,000 to Fraternity of Saint Pius X, £8,000 to Mauritian Wildlife Foundation, £7,500 to University College Oxford, £3,000 to FRAME, £2,000 each to Environmental Investigation Agency, Fauna & Flora International, SPCA Zimbabwe, and World Society for the Protection of Animals, £1,500 each to Help in Suffering and Lynx Educational Trust. There were also 6 donations of £1,000, beneficiaries included Associaco Felinos e Caninos Todos Unidos, Blue

Cross Brooke Hospital for Animals and PDSA.

Exclusions No grants for expeditions, scholarships or individuals.

Applications In writing to the correspondent. The trustees meet once a year.

The Tabeel Trust

Evangelical Christian

£78,000 (2002)

Beneficial area Worldwide.

Dairy House Farm, Great Holland, Frinton-on-Sea, Essex CO13 0EX

Tel. 01255 812130

Correspondent D K Brown, Secretary

Trustees *K A Brown, Chair; D K Brown; Mrs P M Brown; Mrs B J Carter; Dr M P Clark; Mrs J A Richardson; N T Davey; Mrs H M Corteen.*

CC Number 266645

Information available Full accounts were on file at the Charity Commission.

General In 2002 this trust had assets amounting to £907,000 and an income of £46,000. Grants were made totalling £78,000.

Beneficiaries included Shenandoah University (£11,000), Bible Society, Careline and CLC (£4,000 each), Latin Link, MAF and St Paul's with Emmanuel Church (£3,000 each), Association of Christian Teachers, Barnado's, SFI and TWR (£2,000 each) and Ambassadors in Sport and Evangelical Alliance (£1,500 each).

Over half of the grants were for £1,000 or £500 each, including Children for Christ, Faith Mission, Hand in Hand, On the Move, Prospects and Tear Fund (£1,000) and Emmanus Bible School, Gideons, London City Mission and Salvation Army (£500 each).

Applications In writing to 'the trustee who has an interest in the project', i.e. only charities with which a trustee already has contact should apply. Grants are considered at trustees' meetings in May and November.

Talteg Ltd

Jewish, welfare

£153,000 (2001)

Beneficial area UK, with a preference for Scotland.

90 Mitchell Street, Glasgow G1 3NQ

Tel. 0141 221 3353

Correspondent F S Berkeley, Trustee

Trustees *F S Berkeley; M Berkeley; A Berkeley; A N Berkeley; M Berkeley; Miss D L Berkeley.*

CC Number 283253

Information available Accounts were on file at the Charity Commission, but without a grants list or a narrative report.

General In 2002 the trust had an income of £349,000 and a total expenditure of £178,000. Most of the expenditure usually goes towards grants. In 2001 grants totalled £153,000 but no grants list was available.

A grants list has not been available since 1993 when the trust had an income of £175,000 (£134,000 from donations) and gave £92,000 in grants. Of the 48 grants made in the year, 34, including the larger grants, were to Jewish organisations. British Friends of Laniado Hospital received £30,000 and £20,000 each was given to Centre for Jewish Studies and Society of Friends of the Torah. Other larger grants were to JPAIME (£6,000), Glasgow Jewish Community Trust (£5,000), National Trust for Scotland (£2,300) and Friends of Hebrew University of Jerusalem (£1,000).

The remaining grants were all for less than £1,000 with several to Scottish charities, including Ayrshire Hospice (£530), Earl Haig Fund – Scotland (£200) and RSSPCC (£150). Other small grants went to welfare organisations, with an unusual grant of £780 to Golf Fanatics International.

Applications In writing to the correspondent.

The Tangent Charitable Trust

Jewish, general

£183,000 (2002/03)

Beneficial area UK.

21 South Street, London W1 2XB

Tel. 020 7663 6402

Correspondent Beverley Matthews

Trustees *M P Green; Mrs T M Green; R S Wolfson Green; C V Wolfson Green.*

CC Number 289729

Information available Accounts were on file at the Charity Commission.

General The trust makes grants to Jewish causes as well as for general charitable purposes. In 2002/03 the trust had an income of £11,000 and assets of £253,000. Grants totalled £183,000.

Beneficiaries included Westminster Synagogue (£100,000), Imperial College, London (£45,000), Central Synagogue General Charities Fund and Community Security Trust (£10,000 each) Institute for Jewish Policy Research and Maccabi G B (£5,000 each), Eastern Grey Parochial Church Council (£2,000) and Adelburgh Productions (£1,000).

Applications In writing to the correspondent.

The Lady Tangye Charitable Trust

Catholic, overseas aid, general

£31,000 (2001/02)

Beneficial area UK and worldwide, with some preference for the Midlands.

55 Warwick Crescent, Arthur Road, Birmingham B15 2LH

Correspondent The Clerk

Trustees *Gitta Clarisse Gilzean Tangye; Colin Ferguson Smith.*

CC Number 1044220

Information available Accounts are on file at the Charity Commission, but without a full narrative report.

General This trust has general charitable purposes, with a preference for work in the Midlands or developing world. Christian and environmental causes are well- represented in the grants list.

In 2001/02 it had assets of £459,000, which generated an income of £32,000. Grants were made to 21 organisations totalling £31,000.

The largest grants were £3,000 to West Midlands Wildlife Trust and £2,000 each to Aid to the Church in Need, ChildLine Midlands, Father O'Mahoney Memorial

Trust, Friends of the Royal Botanic Gardens (Kew), Spana and Tettenhall Horse Santuary.

Other beneficiaries in the West Midlands included Dudley Zoo Development and St Giles Hospice (£1,500 each), Middlemore Homes and Walsall and District Urban Wildlife Trust (£1,000 each) and St Saviour's Church (£500).

Recipients working in developing countries included Amnesty International (£1,500) and European Children's Trust and VSO (£1,000).

Other beneficiaries included Priest Training Fund (£1,500) and WWF (£1,000).

Applications In writing to the correspondent.

This entry was not confirmed by the trust, but the address was correct according to the Charity Commission database.

The Tanner Trust

General

£228,000 (2002/03)

Beneficial area UK, with a slight preference for the south of England, and overseas.

Blake Lapthorn Linnell, Seacourt Tower, West Way, Oxford OX2 0FB

Tel. 01865 248607

Correspondent Robert Foster, Trust Administrator

Trustees *Lucie Nottingham; Robert Foster; Alice Williams.*

CC Number 1021175

Information available Full accounts were on file at the Charity Commission.

General This trust has general charitable purposes, supporting organisations worldwide. The grants list shows no cause or geographical regions favoured or missing, although there appears to be many organisations concerned with youth, welfare and relief work.

In 2002/03 the trust had an income of £321,000 and a total expenditure of £235,000. Grants totalled £228,000.

The largest grant was £15,000 to Countryside Restoration Trust.

Other beneficiaries included British Homeopathic Association (£9,000), Corporation London Burnham Beeches (£6,000), BESO, British Red Cross - Ethiopian Appeal, British Retinitis Pigmentosa Society and DEC Southern Africa Crisis Appeal (£5,000 each), Oxfordshire Army Cadet Force League (£4,000) and Historic Chapels Trust and Parkinsons Society (£3,000 each),

Exclusions No grants to individuals.

Applications The trust states that unsolicited applications are, without exception, not considered. Support is only given to charities personally known to the trustees.

The Lili Tapper Charitable Foundation

Jewish

£33,000 (2002/03)

Beneficial area UK.

KPMG Tax, St James' Square, Manchester M2 6DS

Tel. 0161 246 4608

Correspondent Robert Luty

Trustees *Mrs L Tapper; M Webber; J Webber.*

CC Number 268523

Information available Accounts were on file at the Charity Commission.

General The trust supports organisations benefiting Jewish people.

In 2002/03 it had assets of £2.4 million, which generated an income of £99,000. Grants were made to seven organisations totalling £33,000. After administration, management and sundry expenses, there was a surplus for the year of £57,000.

Grants were £10,000 each to Impetus and UJIA, £5,000 each to East London Schools Fund and UNHCR, £1,000 each to Cheltenham Hebrew Congregation and Manchester Jewish Community Care and £250 to Jewish Representative Council.

Exclusions No grants to individuals.

Applications The trust states that it does not respond to any unsolicited applications.

The Tay Charitable Trust

General

£190,000 (2002/03)

Beneficial area UK, with a preference for Scotland, particularly Dundee.

6 Douglas Terrace, Broughty Ferry, Dundee DD5 1EA

Correspondent Mrs Elizabeth A Mussen, Trustee

Trustees *Mrs E A Mussen; Mrs Z C Martin; G C Bonar.*

SC Number SC001004

Information available Accounts were provided by the trust.

General This trust has general charitable purposes and supports a wide range of causes. Grants are generally made to UK-wide charities or organisations benefiting Scotland or Dundee, although local groups elsewhere can also be supported.

In 2002/03 the trust had assets of £3.6 million and an income of £192,000. Management and administration for the year was very low at just £1,700. Grants were made to 227 charities totalling £190,000, including 117 smaller grants of less than £1,000 totalling £60,000.

The largest grant was £10,000 to Ninewells Cancer Campaign. Other beneficiaries in the city included St Stephen's & West Church (£5,500), Broughty Ferry Scouts, Dundee Heritage Trust, Link, Maritime Volunteer, RNLI, TICR and Waterways Trust (£5,000 each), Dermatrust (£3,000) and Byre Theatre (£1,000).

Grants given outside Scotland included £2,000 to York Minster Fund and £1,000 each to Great Ormond Street Hospital, Lincoln Cathedral and Lincoln Theological Institute.

Exclusions Grants are only given to charities recognised by the Inland Revenue. No grants to individuals.

Applications No standard form; applications in writing to the correspondent, including a financial statement. An sae is appreciated.

C B & H H Taylor 1984 Trust

Quaker, general

£155,000 (2002/03)

Beneficial area West Midlands, Ireland and overseas.

c/o Home Farm, Abberton, Worcestershire WR10 2NR

Correspondent W J B Taylor, Trustee

Trustees *Mrs C H Norton; Mrs E J Birmingham; J A B Taylor; W J B Taylor; Mrs C M Penny; T W Penny; R J Birmingham; S B Taylor.*

CC Number 291363

Information available Full accounts and guidelines were provided by the trust.

General The trust's geographical areas of benefit are:

- organisations serving Birmingham and the West Midlands
- organisations outside the West Midlands where the trust has well-established links
- organisations in Ireland
- UK-based charities working overseas.

The general areas of benefit are:

- the Religious Society of Friends (Quakers) and other religious denominations
- healthcare projects
- social welfare: community groups; children and young people; older people; disadvantaged people; people with disabilities; homeless people; housing initiatives; counselling and mediation agencies
- education: adult literacy schemes; employment training; youth work
- penal affairs: work with offenders and ex-offenders; police projects
- the environment and conservation work
- the arts: museums and art galleries; music and drama
- Ireland: cross-community health and social welfare projects
- UK charities working overseas on long-term development projects.

75% of grants are for the work and concerns of the Religious Society of Friends (Quakers). The trust favours specific applications. It does not usually award grants on an annual basis for revenue costs. Applications are encouraged from minority groups and woman-led initiatives. Grants, which are made only to or through registered charities, range from £500 to £3,000. Larger grants are seldom awarded.

In 2002/03 it had assets of £5.2 million and an income of £209,000. Grants were made to 111 organisations and totalled £155,000.

As usual the largest grant went to Warwickshire Monthly Meeting, which was of £33,000. Other beneficiaries included Quaker Peace and Service (£6,000), Money for Madagascar (£5,000), Cape Town Quaker Peace Centre, Woodlands (£4,000 each) and CYPC Britain YM, BIA Quaker Social Action, Birmingham Family Service Unit, Swanirvar, Ulster Quaker Service and Royal School for the Deaf (£3,000 each).

Exclusions The trust does not fund: individuals (whether for research, expeditions, educational purposes and so on); local projects or groups outside the West Midlands; or projects concerned with travel or adventure.

Applications There is no formal application form. Applicants should write to the correspondent giving the charity's registration number, a brief description of the charity's activities, and details of the specific project for which the grant is being sought. Applicants should also include a budget of the proposed work, together with a copy of the charity's most recent accounts. Trustees will also wish to know what funds have already been raised for the project and how the shortfall will be met.

The trust states that it receives more applications than it can support. Therefore, even if work falls within its policy it may not be able to help, particularly if the project is outside the West Midlands.

Trustees meet twice-yearly in May and November.

Applications will be acknowledged if an sae is provided.

The Cyril Taylor Charitable Trust

Education

About £40,000 (2001/02)

Beneficial area In practice, mainly Greater London.

Penningtons, 83 Cannon Street, London EC4N 8PE

Tel. 020 7457 3000

Correspondent Christopher Lintott

Trustees *Sir Cyril Taylor; Clifford D Joseph; Robert W Maas; Peter A Tcherepnine; M Stephen Rasch; Christopher Lintott.*

CC Number 1040179

Information available Accounts were on file at the Charity Commission.

General This trust makes grants to organisations benefiting students in particular those studying at Richmond College and the American International University in London.

In 2001/02 it had an income of £45,000 and a total expenditure of £46,000. Beneficiaries have included British Friends of Harvard Business School, Trinity Hall – Cambridge and Institute of Economic Affairs.

Applications In writing to the correspondent. The trust advises that it is not in a position to receive applications for grants at present.

Rosanna Taylor's 1987 Charity Trust

General

£60,000 (2003/04)

Beneficial area UK and overseas, with a preference for Oxfordshire and West Sussex.

Pollen House, 10–12 Cork Street, London W1S 3LW

Tel. 020 7439 9061 **Fax** 020 7437 2680

Correspondent A J Winborn

Trustee *The Cowdray Trust Limited.*

CC Number 297210

Information available Information was provided by the trust.

General This trust has general charitable purposes, including support for medical, cancer, child development and environmental charities.

In 2003/04 it had assets of £999,000, which generated an income of £28,000. Grants were made totalling £60,000.

Beneficiaries were Pearson Taylor Trust (£28,000), Charities Aid Foundation (£24,000) and Oxfam and Plantlife International (£4,000 each).

Exclusions No grants to individuals or non-registered charities.

Applications In writing to the correspondent. Acknowledgements are not sent to unsuccessful applicants.

Tegham Limited

Orthodox Jewish faith, welfare

£163,000 (2001/02)

Beneficial area UK.

1 Hallswelle Road, London NW11 0DH

Tel. 020 8209 1535

Correspondent Mrs S Fluss, Trustee

Trustees *Mrs S Fluss; Miss N Fluss.*

CC Number 283066

Information available Accounts were on file at the Charity Commission but without a list of grants.

General This trust supports the promotion of the Jewish Orthodox faith and the relief of poverty.

In 2001/02 the trust had assets of £1.5 million, an income of £285,000 and made grants totaling £163,000. Unfortunately no grants list was available for this period.

Applications In writing to the correspondent, although the trust stated that it has enough causes to support and does not welcome other applications.

Thackray Medical Research Trust

History of medical products and of their supply trade

£150,000 available (2002/03)

Beneficial area Worldwide.

c/o Thackray Museum, Beckett Street, Leeds LS9 7LN

Website www.tmrt.org

Correspondent Martin Schweiger, Chair of the Trustees

Trustees *Martin Schweiger, Chair; Richard Keeler; Christin Thackray; Stanley Warren; Matthew Wrigley.*

CC Number 702896

Information available Full accounts were provided by the trust.

General This trust is concerned with two aspects of medical products: their history with particular emphasis on the medical supplies trade; and their charitable supply and development for third world countries. The trust initiated and supported the establishment of the award-winning Thackray Museum in Leeds, one of the largest medical museums in the world, and continues to support the research resource there, to provide a unique information centre for the history of medical products and the medical supplies trade worldwide. Now that the museum is fully operational, the trust is looking to support its other areas of interest. Current programmes are:

Medical supply grants

Grants of up to £10,000 a year are available to charitable organisations specialising in the supply of medical equipment to charities working in developing countries, especially those which show the best 'value for money' (for instance, those interested in reusing equipment rather than buying new). Support is generally given towards pump-priming and start-up costs rather than for equipment purchases.

Conference organisers

Grants of up to £1,500 are available towards conferences, symposia and lecture series where the content relates in part to the history of medical products and supplies.

Research into the history of medicinal products and supplies

Support is given to researchers whose work is wholly or partly related to that aspect of medical history. Researchers or their supervisors must have demonstrated experience in this particular field. Grants of up to £2,000 are available for the reimbursement of expenses (excluding books) and subsistence grants for up to three years may be awarded with an upper limit of £20,000.

In November 2002 the trust had assets of £4.1 million. This was expected to generate £150,000 during the 2002/03 financial year, all of which was available for distribution.

Applications In writing to the correspondent, in duplicate. The trustees meet quarterly, in January, April, July and October; applications should be submitted no later than the start of the preceding month. Projects which are not supported cannot be resubmitted. All applications must include:

- names and addresses of applicant(s), with brief CVs
- a description of the activity to be supported
- a timetable against which progress can be measured
- a breakdown of the expected costs, with details of how any balance will be paid
- details of requests made to other sources of funding
- names and addresses of referees.

For medical supply grants, accounts for the last three years, a copy of the trust deed, and a summary of the operational policy must be provided.

For conference organisers' grants, details must be provided of the applicant's experience in organising similar events and details of the intended speakers.

For research grants, a list of any previously published work, details of intended publication and/or dissemination of the results of the research and, where appropriate, a letter from a supervisor confirming the details of the application and their support for the research must be included.

The Thames Wharf Charity

General

£203,000 (2001/02)

Beneficial area UK.

Lee Associates, 5 Southampton Place, London WC1A 2DA

Tel. 020 7025 4600

Correspondent K Hawkins

Trustees *P H Burgess; G H Camamile; J M Young; A Lotay.*

CC Number 1000796

Information available Full accounts are on file at the Charity Commission.

General In 2001/02 the charity had assets of £306,000 with an income of £178,000 and grants totalling £203,000.

The largest grants were £10,000 each to Brookfield School Association and Friends of St Giles the Abbott, £9,000 to NSPCC and £7,000 to SENSE.

Other beneficiaries include £5,000 to Medical Foundation for the Care of Victims of Torture, £4,000 each to Kent Air Ambulance trust and Architectural Association Scholarship Programme, £3,000 each to Friends of Pirbright

School, Amnesty International and Imperial Cancer Research Fund, £2,000 each to Breast Cancer Care, Cancer Research, MIND, Oxfam and Shelter.

Grants of £1,000 or less went to Accord hospice, Addison Pre-School, Anti-Bullying Campaign, Breakthrough Centre, Centre for Democratic Development, Children in Crisis Aid for Children in Nepal, Corpus Christi College Parker Library Appeal, Everychild, Fight for Sight, Foresight, Friends of the Earth, Pilgrims Hospice, Orbis Charitable trust and RNLI.

Exclusions No grants for the purchase of property, motor vehicles or holidays.

Applications In writing to the correspondent.

Lisa Thaxter Trust

Children and adolescents with cancer in the UK

£70,000 (2001/02)

Beneficial area UK.

1 Betjeman Close, Coulson, Surrey CR5 2LU

Website www.lisathaxter.org

Correspondent The Trustees

Trustees *Colin Reynolds; Anthony James Kirk; Mrs Denise Clarke; Geoffrey Gordon Thaxter; Mrs Gillian Lesley Thaxter; Dr Michael Charles Garston Stevens.*

CC Number 1056017

Information available Accounts are available on the trust's website.

General Established in 1996, the trust provides grants to organisations that provide support to children and adolescents with cancer and their families.

In 2001/02 the trust had assets of £135,000. Its income was £103,000, of which 42% came from It's A Wrap charity gift-wrapping service. Other sources of income included monies from fundraising, sponsorship and Gift Aid. Grants totalled £70,000.

The trust specialises in 'pump-priming' programmes that advance both treatment and care. Grants of up to £20,000 per annum are considered. Organisations who may apply can include research and hospital units, or other organisations helping children and adolescents with cancer, for example parent groups.

Beneficiaries in 2001/02 included: UKCCSG/Leicester University (£28,000 for a contact magazine for families); Over the Wall Gang (£5,000 for camp sponsorship); NACCPO (£3,000 for its annual conference); UKCCSG (£2,000 for conference sponsorship); Rainbow Trust (£1,100 for bereavement support); Royal Marsden CCU Parent's Association (£1,000 for parent and family support); Martin House (£1,600 for palliative care); Sargent Cancer Care (£500 for support costs); and Parents Helping Parents (£350 for support costs).

Programmes need to be able to demonstrate an end result, or be capable of continuation beyond the grant period. The trust will not normally consider requests to support individual treatment or hardship grants.

Applications In writing to the correspondent.

The Theodore Trust

Christian education

£6,300 (1995)

Beneficial area UK.

3 Upper King Street, Norwich NR3 1RL

Correspondent G W Woolsey Brown, Trustee

Trustees *Revd D J Baker, Chair; Revd J E Barnes; Right Hon. J S Gummer MP; G W Woolsey Brown.*

CC Number 1008532

Information available Accounts were on file at the Charity Commission, but only up to 1996 on the public screen and up to 1995 in the public files.

General The trust aims to support the advancement of Christianity by way of education.

The trust previously told us that its income is around £40,000 each year. It did not state its grant total, but said that during the three years 1999 to 2001 grants had included: £30,000 in three grants to Sarum College for Institute of Liturgy; £15,000 each to Anglican Centre in Rome for their library and to Catholic Central Library; £10,000 to Let the Children Live to help fund a Christian television station in South America; £5,000 to St Dimitry's Orphanage in Moscow; £3,000 to Catholic Student Council; £2,500 to International Theological Institute; and £1,400 to Newman Conference at Oxford for attenders' expenses.

This list of grants shows that the grant total must have risen considerably since 1995, when grants totalled £6,300.

Exclusions No grants to individuals.

Applications In writing to the correspondent.

The Thistle Trust

Arts, general

£31,000 (2003/04)

Beneficial area UK.

PO Box 191, 10 Fenchurch Street, London EC3M 3LB

Tel. 020 7475 6246 **Fax** 020 7475 5558

Email nick.kerr-sheppard@kbpb.co.uk

Correspondent Nicholas Robert Kerr-Sheppard, Secretary

Trustees *Madeleine, Lady Kleinwort; Nigel Porteous; Neil Derek Morris; Donald James McGilvray; Nicholas Robert Kerr-Sheppard*

CC Number 1091327

Information available Information was provided by the trust.

General This trust was established in 2002, and during the following year it received a £1 million endowment from the settlor. Its annual report states the objects of the trust as follows:

- to further public education in all aspects of the arts including the development of artistic taste and the knowledge, understanding and appreciation of the arts in such manner as the trustees shall think fit including the award of scholarships, exhibitions, bursaries or maintenance, or allowances tenable at any school, university or other educational establishment
- such other charitable purposes as the trustees shall in their absolute discretion think fit.

In 2003/04 the trust had assets of £1.1 million and an income of £78,000 including a donation of £50,000. Grants were made to Almeida Theatre (£25,000) and Royal Academy of Music (£6,000) resulting in a grant total of £31,000.

Exclusions No grants to individuals.

Applications In writing to the correspondent including most recent report and financial accounts. The trustees meet at least once a year with only successful applicants notified of the trustees' decision.

The Loke Wan Tho Memorial Foundation

Environment, medical

£55,000 (2001/02)

Beneficial area Worldwide.

c/o PricewaterhouseCoopers, 9 Greyfriars Road, Reading RG1 1JG

Correspondent David McMahon

Trustees *Lady Y P McNeice; Mrs T S Tonkyn; A Tonkyn.*

CC Number 264273

Information available Full accounts were on file at the Charity Commission.

General In 2001/02 the trust had assets of £1.9 million and an income of £62,000. Grants totalled £55,000. The trust supports environment/conservation organisations, medical causes and overseas aid organisations.

In total 17 grants were made, with the two largest going to Bird Life International for £13,000 (also the major beneficiary in previous years) and Flora and Fauna International for £12,000. Other grants were in the range of £1,000 to £5,000. Beneficiaries included World Wildlife Fund (£5,000), Global Cancer Concern (£4,000), Liverpool School of Tropical Medicine (£3,000), Scottish Seabird Centre (£1,500) and DEBRA (£1,000).

Applications In writing to the correspondent.

The Thompson Family Charitable Trust

Medical, veterinary, education, general

£117,000 (2002/03)

Beneficial area UK.

Hillsdown Court, 15 Totteridge Common, London N20 8LR

Tel. 020 8445 4343

Correspondent Roy Copus

Trustees *D B Thompson; P Thompson; K P Thompson.*

CC Number 326801

Information available Accounts were provided by the trust

General This trust has general charitable purposes. There appear to be preferences for educational, medical and veterinary organisations.

In 2002/03 the trust had assets of £36.7 million, which generated an income of £2.1 million. Grants were made to 31 organisations totalling £117,000. It regularly builds up its reserves to enable it to make large donations in the future, for example towards the construction of new medical or educational facilities.

The largest grants were £20,000 to All the Queen's Horses, £15,000 to Racing Welfare Charities and £10,000 to Break Caring Homes for Special Children. Other large grants went to Cancer BACUP (£7,500), Parish Church of St Andrew Totteridge (£6,700), Animal Health Trust (£5,500), Essex Voluntary Association for the Blind, Save the Children, Score – Serving Sport Through Chaplaincy, Spinal Injuries Association and St Nicholas' Hospice (£5,000 each).

Other beneficiaries included Royal Opera House Foundation (£3,800), Macmillan Cancer Relief (£2,000), British Blind Sport, Canine Partners, HEAL Cancer Charity, North London Hospice and Rainbow Trust Children's Charity (£1,000 each), Cancer Research Campaign (£100) and Noah's Ark Children's Hospice (£50).

Exclusions No grants to individuals.

Applications In writing to the trustees.

The Thompson Fund

Medical, welfare, education, general

£62,000 (2003/04)

Beneficial area UK, with a preference for Sussex and the Brighton and Hove area.

PO Box 104, Hove, East Sussex BN3 2XP

Tel. 01273 562110

Correspondent The Trustees

Trustees *P G Thompson; Patricia Thompson; M H de Silva.*

CC Number 327490

Information available Full accounts were on file at the Charity Commission.

General In 2003/04 the trust had assets of £927,000, an income of £62,000 and gave grants totalling £62,000. Grants ranged from £200 to £2,500. The trust showed a strong preference for locally based organisations in Sussex.

The largest grants in the year were £2,500 each to Martlets Hospice, Scope and Stroke Association. Other large grants included: £2,250 to Chichester Cathedral Restoration & Development Trust; £2,000 each to Motor Neurone Disease Association and SENSE; £1,700 to Hearing Research Trust; £1,600 to Churches Commission for International Students; and £1,500 each to Cancer Research UK, Dial UK and Foundation for Conductive Education.

Those receiving smaller grants included: £1,250 to Arthritis Care, Lewes & District Mencap Society and RUKBA; £1,000 each to Augustinian Care, Calibra, Horder Centre for Arthritis, LUPUS UK and Retail Trust; and £500 each to Disability Aid Fund, Horsham Volunteer Bureau, Nightstop UK, Royal Blind Society, Shaftesbury Society and Stroke Association.

Exclusions No personal applications; grants only to other charitable and similar organisations.

Applications In writing to the correspondent. The trustees meet approximately every six to eight weeks.

The Sue Thomson Foundation

Christ's Hospital School, education

£139,000 (2002/03)

Beneficial area UK.

Furners Keep, Furners Lane, Henfield, West Sussex BN5 9HS

Tel. 01273 493461 **Fax** 01273 495139

Correspondent Mrs S M Mitchell, Trustee

Trustees *Mrs S M Mitchell; C L Corman; J Gillham.*

CC Number 298808

Information available Full accounts were provided by the trust.

General The foundation exists to support children in need in the UK, mainly by helping Christ's Hospital and the school in Horsham which caters specifically for children in need. Other areas of support include medical, educational and self-help organisations and projects.

In 2002/03 it had assets of £1.8 million and an income of £180,000. Grants were made totalling £139,000.

The majority of the funds went to Christ's Hospital, which received £118,000, partly as the fourth of five annual payments to support five pupils at the school and partly towards its programme of providing help to children unable to afford the school's fees.

Other beneficiaries were Cardinal Hume Centre (£15,000), Bridewell Royal Hospital (£1,600), Publishing Training Centre for dissertation awards (£750), Benevolent Society of Blues and Stationers' Benevolent Fund (£500 each), Handicapped Children's Aid Committee and Open Door Project (£250 each) and Nicholas Boas Charitable Trust, Brighton and Hove Unwaged Centre and KME Appeal (£100 each). A further £1,600 went to individual students.

Exclusions No grants to large charities or individuals, except as part of a specific scheme.

Applications Applications are acknowledged only if an sae is enclosed.

The Thornton Foundation

General

£357,000 (2001/02)

Beneficial area UK.

Stephenson Harwood, 1 St Paul's Churchyard, London EC4M 8SH

Tel. 020 7329 4422

Correspondent Richard Thornton, Chair

Trustees *R C Thornton, Chair; A H Isaacs; H D C Thornton; Mrs S J Thornton.*

CC Number 326383

Information available Full accounts were provided by the trust.

General The object of the foundation is to make grants to charities selected by the trustees. The principal guideline of the trust is to use the funds to further charitable causes where their money will, as far as possible, act as 'high powered money', in other words be of significant use to the cause. Only causes that are known personally to the trustees and/or that they are able to investigate thoroughly are supported. The trust states it is proactive rather than reactive in seeking applicants.

In 2001/02 the trust had assets of £3.6 million, which generated an income of £159,000. Grants totalling £357,000 were made to 16 organisations, of which 10 were also supported in the previous year.

The largest grant of £110,000 was given to an exceptional project. Other large grants were £60,000 to Peper Harrow Foundation, £35,000 to St Christopher's Hospice, £30,000 each to 21st Learning Initiative and HMS Trincomlee Trust and £20,000 to Mary Rose Trust.

The other recipients were Stowe House Preservation Trust (£10,000), St Peter's Trust (£7,500), Helen House and Keble College – Oxford (£5,000 each), Prisoners of Conscience (£2,000) and Museum of London (£1,500), with £1,000 each to Break, Hope House and Scope. A further grant of £32,000 was also given to another capital project.

Applications The trust strongly emphasises that it does not accept unsolicited applications, and, as it states above, only organisations that are known to one of the trustees will be considered for support. Any unsolicited applications will not receive a reply.

The Thornton Trust

Evangelical Christianity, education, relief of sickness and poverty

£180,000 (2002/03)

Beneficial area UK and overseas.

Hunters Cottage, Hunters Yard, Debden Road, Saffron Walden, Essex CB11 4AA

Correspondent D H Thornton, Trustee

Trustees *D H Thornton; Mrs B Y Thornton; J D Thornton.*

CC Number 205357

Information available Information was provided by the trust.

General This trust was created in 1962 for 'the promotion of and furthering of education and the Evangelical Christian faith, and assisting in the relief of sickness, suffering and poverty'.

In 2002/03 it had assets of £1.2 million and an income of £91,000. Grants were made totalling £180,000. Further information for this year was not available.

In 2001/02, when grants totalled £152,000, the largest were £24,000 to Africa Inland Mission, £15,000 to Saffron Walden Baptist Church, £7,000 to Redcliffe Missionary College and £5,000 each to Bible Society, Keswick Convention and London City Mission.

Smaller grants have included £3,300 to Tearfund, £2,900 to Dugdale Trust, £2,500 to Scripture Union, £1,500 to Salisbury Baptist Church, £1,000 each to Christians in Sport and Send a Cow, £500 each to Cog Wheel Trust and RAF Benevolent Fund, £250 to Spring Harvest Trust, £100 to London Institute for Contemporary Christianity, £70 to Hertford Baptist Church, £50 to Christians in Property and £25 to Chartered Institute of Building Benevolent Fund.

Applications The trust states: 'Our funds are fully committed and we regret that we are unable to respond to the many unsolicited calls for assistance we are now receiving.'

The Three Oaks Trust

Welfare

£155,000 to organisations (2001/02)

Beneficial area Overseas, UK, with a preference for West Sussex.

The Three Oaks Family Trust Co. Ltd, PO Box 243, Crawley, West Sussex RH10 6YB

Website www.thethreeoakstrust.co.uk

Correspondent The Trustees

Trustee *The Three Oaks Family Trust Co. Ltd.*

CC Number 297079

Information available Full accounts were taken from the trust's website.

General The trust regularly supports the same welfare organisations in the UK and overseas each year. A small number of grants have also been made to individuals via statutory authorities or voluntary agencies, although the trust's 2001/02 annual report stated that it 'does not intend to expand the scope of donations made for the benefit of individuals. Currently all the applications made on behalf of individuals receive a repsonse, but this would cease to be the case if applications came from further afield'.

In 2001/02 the trust gave £154,000 to UK charities in grants larger than £1,000 and a further £1,100 in donations of less than £1,000. A total of £18,000 was donated to charities whose focus of work is overseas and £38,000 was distributed to support individuals and families living in the community. Grants were given under the following programmes:

Within the UK

Projects that aid people with psychological or emotional difficulties

The largest grants were £12,000 to Horsham Counselling Service and £10,000 to Crawley Open House. Other donations included £5,000 to Coventry Day Centre for Norton House and £3,000 to Information Shop for Young People. All donations were given for running costs.

Welfare – Illness

Raynaud's and Scleroderma Association received their annual donation of £15,000 towards the salary of a welfare support worker while Visceral received £5,000 as a research grant towards the study of gastro-intestinal disorders.

Support to individuals and families living in the community

A psychotherapeutic service for children was given £40,000 in a grant through West Sussex County Council. Grants totalling £38,000 were also given directly to individuals, through Surrey and West Sussex county councils.

Overseas aid

Donations included £6,500 to Ceco – Sri Lanka for computer equipment and student tuition to provide job opportunities for young people and £5,000 each to Kaloko Trust – Zambia to develop the livelihood of people who might otherwise be without work or food and Health Help International to help an area of Zambia which was affected by famine.

The accounts also listed the following two future commitments: £45,000 to 2005 to Raynauds and Scleroderma Association and £5,000 to Parkinson's Disease Society.

Applications The trust's 2001/02 annual report stated: 'The directors intend to continue supporting the organisations that they have supported in the past and are not planning to fund any new projects in the near future. To save administration costs, the directors do not respond to requests, unless they are considering making a donation.

'Requests from organisations for donations that exceed £2,000 are considered on a quarterly basis in meetings held in January, April, July and October.'

The Thriplow Charitable Trust

Higher education and research

£67,000 (2002/03)

Beneficial area Preference for British institutions.

PO Box 243, Cambridge CB3 9PQ

Correspondent Mrs E Mackintosh, Secretary

Trustees *Sir Peter Swinnerton-Dyer; Dr Harriet Crawford; Prof. Karen Sparck Jones; Prof. Christopher Bayly.*

CC Number 1025531

Information available Information was provided by the trust.

General The charity was established by a trust deed in 1983. Its main aims are the furtherance of higher and further education and research, with preference given to British institutions.

Projects that have generally been supported in the past include contributions to research study funds, research fellowships, academic training schemes, computer facilities and building projects. Specific projects are preferred rather than contributions to general running costs. The trust prefers to support smaller projects where grants can 'make a difference'.

In 2002/03 it had an income of £93,000 and gave 17 grants totalling £67,000. The largest were £7,500 each to Daphne Jackson Trust for a research fellowship and University of St Andrews for archaeological research and £5,000 each to National Gallery for conservation equipment, Royal Botanical Gardens – Kew, University of Sunderland towards a digital media centre and Women's Library.

Other grants included £4,000 each to Churches' Commission for International Students for a hardship fund and University of North London for the TUC library collection, £2,000 each to University of Cambridge for the Fitzwilliam Museum and University of Glasgow Exploration Society and £1,000 to Cambridge NW Ecuador Butterfly Expedition.

Exclusions Grants can only be made to charitable bodies or component parts of charitable bodies. In no circumstances can grants be made to individuals.

Applications There is no application form. A letter of application should specify the purpose for which funds are sought and the costings of the project. It should be indicated whether other applications for funds are pending and, if the funds are to be channelled to an individual or a small group, what degree of supervision over the quality of the work would be exercised by the institution. Trustee meetings are held twice a year – in spring and in autumn.

The Tillett Trust

Classical music

£39,000, mostly to individuals (2003/04)

Beneficial area UK.

Courtyard House, Neopardy, Crediton, Devon EX17 5EP

Tel. 01363 777844 **Fax** 01363 777845

Email tilletttrust@tiscali.co.uk

Website www.thetilletttrust.org.uk

Correspondent Miss K Avey, Secretary to the Trust

Trustees *Paul Strang, Chair; Miss Fiona Grant; Miss Yvonne Minton; David Stiff; Miss Clara Taylor; Howard Davis; Paul Harris.*

CC Number 257329

Information available Information was provided by the trust.

General The trust supports young classical musicians of outstanding ability in the UK. Funds are directed at the start of their professional careers to help them obtain performing experience. It is not normally available to individuals for the support of study courses, either undergraduate or postgraduate, although postgraduate bursaries are awarded annually to nominees from each of the main UK conservatoires. Grants are also made to two organisations which provide opportunities for young performers (YCAT and Young Songmakers) and money is put into the trust's own performance scheme, Young Artists' Platform.

In 2003/04 it had an income of £39,000, all of which was given in grants, including £12,000 through its Young Artists' Platform Recital Scheme. The largest grants were £12,000 to YCAT for performances by young artists under their management and £11,000 awarded through the colleges as bursaries for a second or subsequent year of postgraduate study.

Exclusions Funding for the purchase of musical instruments, for study courses, for commercial recordings or for the commissioning of new works. Applications for ordinary subsistence costs are also not considered.

Applications In writing to the correspondent. No application form is used and there are no deadlines. Enclose a CV or biography and references, also a performance cassette and budget for the project.

The Tisbury Telegraph Trust

Christian, overseas aid, general

£98,000 (2002/03)

Beneficial area UK and overseas.

35 Kitto Road, Telegraph Hill, London SE14 5TW

Email ttt@howzatt.demon.co.uk

Correspondent Mrs E Orr, Trustee

Trustees *John Davidson; Alison Davidson; Eleanor Orr; Roger Orr; Sonia Phippard.*

CC Number 328595

Information available Full accounts were provided by the trust.

General In 2002/03 it had assets of £88,000 and an income of £117,000, mostly from Gift Aid donations. This was slightly down on the previous year when the income included, interestingly, wedding presents. Grants were made to 55 organisations totalling £98,000. Administration costs were very low at just £40.

The largest grants were £23,000 to Tearfund, £11,000 to Crisis and £10,000 each to Romania Care and World Vision.

The next largest were £5,400 to Shaftesbury Society, £5,000 to Help the Aged, £4,100 to St Mary's PCC, £2,500 each to Agape Trust – Uganda and Christian Aid, £2,000 each to British Red Cross and Community of Celebration, £1,200 to Church Mission Society and £1,000 each to Crosslinks, Maple School Association, Shelter and Traidcraft Exchange.

Most of the donations were for amounts much lower than these. They included £800 to Oasis Trust, £600 each to St David's Cathedral, Salvation Army and Scripture Union, £500 to Bible Society, £400 each to Chinese Church Support Mission, Mission Aviation Fellowship, Prisoners of Conscience Appeal and 2 Tim 2 Trust, £300 each to Farm Africa, Leprosy Mission, Manna Society and RSPCA and £250 to National Trust.

Exclusions Grants are only made to registered charities. No applications from individuals for expeditions or courses can be considered.

Applications In writing to the correspondent. However, it is extremely rare that unsolicited applications are successful and the trust does not respond to applicants unless an sae is included. No telephone applications please.

TJH Foundation

General

£498,000 (2001/02)

Beneficial area England and Wales with some preference for organisations based in the north west of England.

Gleadhill House, Dawbers Lane, Euxton, Chorley, Lancashire PR7 6EA

Tel. 01257 269400 **Fax** 01257 269997

Correspondent J C Kay, Trustee

Trustees *T J Hemmings, Chair; Mrs M Catherall; J C Kay.*

CC Number 1077311

Information available Accounts were on file at the Charity Commission.

General The TJH Foundation was established in 1999. In 2001/02 it had assets of £2.2 million generating an income of £122,000. Grants to 13 organisations totalled £498,000.

By far the largest grants were £200,000 to NSPCC, £190,000 to Princess Royal Trust for Carers and £50,000 to British Red Cross – Lancashire.

Other beneficiaries included Juvenile Diabetes Research Foundation (£21,000), Animal Health Trust, Royal Veterinary College Animal Care Trust and Zoe's Place Baby Hospice (£10,000 each), Royal Agricultural Benevolent Institution (£2,500), Cancer Bacup and Club Children's Charity (£1,000 each) and WellBeing (£250).

Applications In writing to the correspondent.

Tomchei Torah Charitable Trust

Jewish educational institutions

£850,000 (2002/03)

Beneficial area UK.

Harold Everett Wreford, Second Floor, 32 Wigmore Street, London W1U 2RP

Tel. 020 7535 5900

Correspondent A Frei, Trustee

Trustees *I J Kohn; S M Kohn; A Frei.*

CC Number 802125

Information available Full accounts were on file at the Charity Commission.

General This trust supports Jewish educational institutions. Grants usually average about £5,000.

In 2002/03 the trust's assets were £251,000 and it had an income of £1.2 million from Gift Aid donations. Grants totalled £850,000 and were made to mainly Jewish organisations.

By far the largest grant was £333,000 to British Friends of Gesher, closely followed by £250,000 to British Friends of Nehora. Other large grants were £66,000 to Friends of Mir, £29,400 to United Talmudical Association Ltd, £21,500 to Yeshiva L'zeirim Gateshead, £15,000 to Schapiro Charitable Trust, £12,300 to WST Charity, £12,230 to Menorah Primary School and £10,000 each to Chesed Trust and Menorah Grammar School.

Other grants made ranged from £2,200 to £8,000 and example beneficiaries were Gertner Charitable Trust, North West London Communal Mikveh and Yeshiva Ezras Torah.

Applications In writing to the correspondent at any time.

The Tory Family Foundation

Education, Christian, medical

£56,000 (2001/02)

Beneficial area Worldwide, but principally Folkestone.

The Estate Office, Etchinghill Golf, Folkestone, Kent CT18 8FA

Tel. 01303 862280

Correspondent P N Tory, Trustee

Trustees *P N Tory; J N Tory; Mrs S A Rice.*

CC Number 326584

Information available Full accounts were on file at the Charity Commission.

General The trust's 2001/02 annual report stated: 'The charity was formed to provide financial help to a wide variety of charitable needs. It is currently supporting causes principally in the locality of Folkestone. These causes include education, religious, social and medical subjects and the donees themselves are often registered charities.'

In 2000/01 it was stated that: 'The charity does not normally aim to fund the whole of any given project, and thus applicants are expected to demonstrate a degree of existing and regular support.'

In 2001/02 assets totalled £2.4 million, which generated an income of £112,000. Grants were made totalling £56,000 and were broken down as follows:

Local – 20 grants totalling £31,000

Beneficiaries included: Battle of Britain Memorial Trust (£15,000); Etchinghall Village Hall (£3,000); FHODS, Folkstone Rainbow Centre and Kent Wildlife Trust (£2,000 each); Ashford Sea Scouts and Vale of Elham Trust for the tea room appeal (£1,000); Shepway Volunteer Centre for an outreach vehicle (£500); and Boughton Aluph Group (£100).

Education – 14 grants totalling £14,000

Recipients included: Augustine Order for computer funding (£1,800); Canterbury Oast Trust, Fairbridge – Kent and Lyminge Primary School (£1,000 each); Compaid Trust and Disability Aid Fund for computer funding (£500 each); and Aldis Trust (£250). Two individuals also received grants totalling £700.

Overseas – 8 grants totalling £7,300

Beneficiaries included: Prisoners Abroad (£2,000); Marie Stopes International, Population Concern and Sight Savers (£1,000 each); and Project Trust (£250). One individual also received a donation of £250.

Health – 6 grants totalling £1,800

Beneficiaries included: Huntington's Disease Association (£500); The Royal Marsden Hospital for a cancer project (£250); Teenage Cancer Trust (£200); and K and C Paediatric Department for a special baby unit (£50).

Churches – 3 grants totalling £1,000

Recipients were Dover Parish Church (£500), Postling Church and St Stephen's Canterbury (£250 each).

Other – 2 grants totalling £1,200

Beneficiaries were RABI for the farming community (£1,000) and South Bank Foundation for the Royal Festival Hall (£200).

Exclusions Grants are given to registered charities only. Applications outside Kent are unlikely to be considered. No grants are given for further education.

Applications In writing to the correspondent. Applications are considered throughout the year. To keep costs down, unsuccessful applicants will not be notified.

The Toy Trust

Children

£245,000 (2002)

Beneficial area UK.

British Toy & Hobby Association, 80 Camberwell Road, London SE5 0EG

Tel. 020 7701 7271

Correspondent Ms Karen Baxter

Trustees *The British Toy and Hobby Association; T G Willis; A Munn; J D Hunter; B Ellis.*

CC Number 1001634

Information available Full accounts were on file at the Charity Commission.

General This trust was registered in 1991 to centralise the giving of the British Toy and Hobby Association. Prior to this, the association raised money from the toy industry, which it pledged to one charity on an annual basis. It was felt that the fundraising activities of the association were probably more than matched by its individual members, and that the charitable giving of the toy industry to children's charities was going unnoticed by the public. The trust still receives the majority of its income from fundraising activities, donating the proceeds to children's charities and charitable projects benefiting children.

In 2002 the trust had assets of £160,000 and an income of £194,000, mostly in donations received. Grants were made totalling £245,000.

The largest grants were £10,000 each to Kidscape and Toy Box Charity, £9,700 to Medical Engineering Resource Unit and £5,000 each to Haven House Foundation, Lancing College for a Malawi expedition, Pace, Ryder Cheshire, Rose Road Children's Appeal and Toby Henderson Trust.

Other beneficiaries included Zambian Ecumenical Link (£4,300), Disfigurement Guidance Centre and Parents for Children (£4,000 each), Exmouth Community College Association (£3,400), Camp Quality UK (£3,200) and Mary Hare Foundation (£3,100). A further £145,000 was given in grants of less than £3,000 each.

Applications In writing to the correspondent.

Annie Tranmer Charitable Trust

General, young people

£63,000 to organisations (2001/02)

Beneficial area UK, particularly Suffolk and adjacent counties.

51 Bennett Road, Ipswich IP1 5HX

Tel. 01473 743694

Correspondent Mrs M R Kirby

Trustees *J F F Miller; V A Lewis.*

CC Number 1044231

Information available Accounts were on file at the Charity Commission.

General This trust mainly supports charities recognised by Annie Tranmer within her lifetime.

In 2003/04 the trust had an income of £114,000 and a total expenditure of £104,000. Further information for this year was unavailable.

In 2001/02 it had assets of £3 million and an income of £121,000. Grants totalled £67,000 of which £63,000 went to organisations and the remainder to 11 individuals.

Donations included those of £10,000 to Cancer Research UK, £5,000 each to East Anglia's Children's Hospice, Felixstowe Ferry Youth Sailing and Guide Association, £2,500 to Motor Neurone Disease, £2,000 to Winged Fellowship, £1,000 each to Centre for Brain Injury, Raynaud's & Scleroderma Association and Sparks Appeal, £800 to Clopton Village Hall, £340 to First Melton Guides and £300 to Children Nationwide Medical Research.

Applications This trust does not accept unsolicited applications.

The Constance Travis Charitable Trust

General

£262,000 (2001/02)

Beneficial area UK (national charities only); Northamptonshire (all sectors).

Quinton Rising, Quinton, Northampton NN7 2EF

Tel. 01604 862296

Correspondent A Travis

Trustees *Mrs C M Travis; E R A Travis.*

CC Number 294540

Information available Accounts were on file at the Charity Commission, but without a full list of grants.

General This trust has general charitable purposes, supporting local organisations in Northamptonshire as well as organisations working UK-wide.

In 2001/02 the trust had assets of £12 million. Its income was £2.2 million, mostly from a donation of £2 million which was transferred to assets. Grants totalling £262,000 were made to 37 organisations, 11 of which were also supported in the previous year.

The largest grants were £30,000 each to Extra Care Charitable Trust and NSPCC, £25,000 to Imperial Cancer Research Fund, £20,000 to Macmillan Cancer Relief, £15,000 to Age Concern and £10,000 each to DDS, Stroke Association and YMCA Northampton.

Other grants included £5,000 each to Brain Research Trust, Colon Cancer Care, Mental Health Foundation, National Kidney Research Fund, Northamptonshire Association of Youth Clubs, Sulgrave Manor Trust and Youth UK, £3,000 each to Crimestoppers, Prince's Trust, Shaftesbury Society and Workbridge Centre – Northampton and £2,000 each to All Saints' Church – Kettering, Life Education Centres, Northamptonshire Rape and Incest Centre and Relate.

Exclusions No grants to individuals or non-registered charities.

Applications In writing to the correspondent.

The Treeside Trust

General

£74,000 (2002/03)

Beneficial area UK, but mainly local.

4 The Park, Grasscroft, Oldham OL4 4ES

Tel. 01457 876422

Correspondent John Roger Beresford Gould, Trustee

Trustees *C C Gould; J R B Gould; J R W Gould; D M Ives; R J Ives; B Washbrook.*

CC Number 1061586

Information available Accounts were provided by the trust, but without a list of grants.

General The trust supports mainly small local charities, and a few UK-wide charities which are supported on a regular basis. It states: 'In the main the trustees' policy is to make a limited number of substantial grants each year, rather than a larger number of smaller ones, in order to make significant contributions to some of the causes supported.'

In 2002/03 the trust had assets of £762,000 and an income of £107,000. Grants totalled £74,000. No further information was available.

Applications In writing to the correspondent, but unsolicted applications are unlikely to be supported.

Triodos Foundation

Overseas development, organics, community development

£120,000 (1999)

Beneficial area UK and developing countries.

Brunel House, 11 The Promenade, Clifton, Bristol BS8 3NN

Tel. 0117 973 9339

Correspondent The Trustees

Trustees *P Blom; M Robinson; M Bierman.*

CC Number 1052958

Information available Full accounts were on file at the Charity Commission.

However, in December 2004 they were only available up to those for 1999.

General This trust, registered in 1996, makes grants both nationally and overseas, through its own networks. Wherever possible it prefers to act in partnership with existing charitable organisations to provide benefits.

The objectives of the foundation are to support charitable needs which have been identified through, but which are unable to be fully supported by, the work of Triodos Bank in the UK. It works closely with individuals, organisations and depositors of the bank to support projects that work in charitable areas.

Donations in 2002 included a grant to a leading micro-finance institution, K-Rep Bank in Kenya and support for the first organic research conference in the UK, in Aberystwyth.

In 1999 the trust had an income of £162,000, comprised mainly of donations. It made grants totalling £120,000 and, after further management and administration expenses of £2,000, transferred the surplus of £40,000 to the capital account, resulting in assets at the year end totalling £199,000.

Exclusions No grants to individuals or students.

Applications In writing to the correspondent. Initial telephone enquiries are welcome.

The True Colours Trust

Special needs, sensory disabilities and impairments, palliative care, young carers, HIV/Aids

£278,000 (2003/04)

Beneficial area Mostly UK and Africa.

Allington House, 1st Floor, 150 Victoria Street, London SW1E 5AE

Tel. 020 7410 0330 **Fax** 020 7410 0332

Email info@sfct.org.uk

Correspondent Michael Pattison, Director

Trustees *Miss L A Sainsbury; D M Flynn.*

CC Number 1089893

Information available Full accounts were provided by the trust.

General Established in 2001, this is the newest of the 18 Sainsbury family charitable trusts, which collectively give over £54 million a year. It is interested in supporting:

- services for people with special needs
- hearing impairment in children and adults
- speech and language disorders
- hospice and palliative care for children
- services which support young careers
- support for people with HIV/Aids in Africa.

The 2003/04 accounts includes the following statement, which appears to be generic across the Sainsbury trusts:

'Grants are likely to be made to a small number of pilot projetcts which have the potential to develop into larger programmes. The trustees are also likely to consider support for projects that assist in raising awareness and the development of high quality educational materials. The trustees prefer to support innovative schemes that can be successfully replicated or become self-sustaining.

'Proposals are generally invited by the trustees or initiated at their request. Unsolicited applications are not encouraged and are unlikely to be successful. Grants are not normally made to individuals.'

In 2003/04 it had assets of £755,000 and an income of £41,000. Management and administration costs were high at £14,000, including payments totalling £4,600 to a firm of solicitors in which one of the trustees is a partner. Whilst wholly legal, these editors always regret such payments unless, in the words of the Charity Commission, 'there is no realistic alternative'. In total 76 grants were approved totalling £278,000, broken down as follows:

Special needs – 2 grants totalling £139,000

Children's Express received £79,000 towards an action research project for children who are deaf to produce an overview of the experience to gain personal development and skills in journalism, research, running a project and teamwork. National Blind Children's Society was given £60,000 to produce set texts as part of the CustomEyes programme.

Children and young careers

No grants were approved during the year under this category, although there were three grants paid which were approved, and accounted for, in the previous financial year.

HIV/Aids in Africa – 1 grant of £10,000

This went to Nairobi Hospice towards a palliative-care training programme.

Small grants for disadvantaged children – 72 grants totalling £76,000

The majority of grants in this category were of less than £1,000 each; 58 such grants were made totalling £11,000. Larger grants included £10,000 each to Coleraine and District Riding for Disabled Association towards new premises and Maplewood School for a new hydrotherapy pool, £7,600 to Special Toys Educational Postal Service for switches and specially adapted toys for use by 50 children, £5,000 to Jessie May Trust for palliative care, £4,000 to Park Lane Special School for a sensory lighting system, £2,000 to Chester and Ellesmere Port Young Carers Project for the holiday programme and £1,000 to Winkleigh Pre-School for resources.

General – 1 grant of £30,000

This went to BBC World Service Trust to assist in raising awareness of Down's Syndrome in Russia.

Applications The 18 Sainsbury Family Charitable Trusts are jointly administered and follow the same application precedure. An application to one trust is considered as an application to them all. However, 'applications' are probably not the best way forward to gaining funding from these trusts. More sensible might be to write briefly and say what is being done or planned, on the assumption that, if one or more of the trusts is indeed interested in that area of work, they will want to know about what you are doing. A telephone call to do the same is fine. Staff are polite, but wary of people seeking to talk about money rather than issues.

More generally, the trusts are involved in a number of networks, with which they maintain long-term contact. Charities doing work relevant to the interests of these trusts may find that if they are not a part of these networks (which may not be inclusive and most of which are probably London-based) they may get limited Sainsbury attention.

The most inappropriate approach would often be from a fundraiser. Staff, and in many cases trustees, are knowledgeable and experienced in their fields, and expect to talk to others in the same position.

Truedene Co. Ltd

Jewish

£547,000 (2001/02)

Beneficial area UK and overseas.

Cohen Arnold & Co., 1075 Finchley Road, London NW11 0PU

Tel. 020 8731 0777 **Fax** 020 8731 0778

Correspondent The Trustees

Trustees *M Gross; S Berger; S Laufer; S Berger; Mrs Sarah Klein; Mrs Z Sternlicht.*

CC Number 248268

Information available Accounts were on file at the Charity Commission up until 1996/97, but without a grants list.

General In 2001/02 this trust had assets of £4.2 million and an income of £313,000, including £90,000 in donations received. Grants were made totalling £547,000.

By far the largest grant was £150,000 to United Talmudical Associates. Other large grants included £45,000 to Congregation Mosdos Toldos Aharon Institution, £35,000 each to Machene Sva Rotzohn and V'yoel Moshe Charitable Trust, £28,000 to Machaneh Rav Tov, £22,000 to Kollel Avreichim of UTA, £18,000 to Gemach Zichron Aron Velya, £13,000 to Yeshiva Horomo Talmudical College and £10,000 each to Friends of Horim Establishments, Mesifta Talmusical College and Yesodei Hatorah School.

Beneficiaries receiving under £10,000 included Congregation V'Joel Moshe (£7,500), Beer Avrohum, Gur Trust and Satmar Nursery Trust (£5,000 each), Beth Hamedrash Satmar Trust and Friends of the Torah Study Centre Trust (£3,000 each), Oizer Dalim Trust (£2,000), Yeshiva Horomo Talmudical College (£1,500) and Craven Walk Charitable Trust (£1,000).

Applications In writing to the correspondent.

The Truemark Trust

General

£195,000 (2002/03)

Beneficial area UK only.

PO Box 2, Liss, Hampshire GU33 6YP

Correspondent Mrs Judy Hayward

Trustees *Sir Thomas Lucas; Wendy Collett; Michael Collishaw; Stuart Neil; Michael Meakin; Richard Wolfe.*

CC Number 265855

Information available Full accounts were provided by the trust.

General The trust favours small organisations with a preference for innovatory projects, particularly neighbourhood-based community projects and less popular groups. Current main areas of interest are: disability, older people and people otherwise disadvantaged, including counselling and community support groups in disadvantaged areas and alternative or complementary health projects.

Grants are usually one-off for a specific project or part of a project. Core funding and/or salaries are rarely considered. The average size of grants is £1,000.

In 2002/03 it had assets of £4.6 million which generated an income of £229,000 (after rental expenses). Grants were made to 123 organisations totalling £195,000.

The largest were £5,000 each to EATA – London and Yoga of the Heart Trust – London, £3,500 to Quiet Mind Centre – Exmouth, £3,000 each to Clover House – Bristol, Katoe Foxons Holiday for Sick Children – Leicester, Lewisham Churches for Asylum Seekers, Mandala Yoga Ashram – Carmarthenshire, National ME Centre – Romford, Prince of Wales's Foundation for Integrated Health – London, Prison Phoenix Trust – Oxford and Rowley Regis Committee for the Welfare of the Physically Handicapped – Cradley Heath and £2,500 each to Aston Community Youth Project, Beth Hayeled – London, Clouds (Alcohol and Drug Dependency) – Salisbury, Holiday Endeavour for Lone Parents (HELP) – Gainsborough, Marches Family Network – Leominster, Kennet Furniture Recycling Scheme and Pines School – Birmingham.

Other grants included £2,000 to East Kilbride Befriending Project, Taunton Dean Association for Neighbourhood Care and West Midlands Quaker Peace Education Project – Dudley, £1,500 each to Newton and District Dial-a-Ride, Peterborough Shopmobility and Scamp - Swindon, £1,000 each to Ark of Hope Chambers – Hastings, Clouds Trust – Liss, Kerbside – Hebden Bridge, Mountain Rescue Council – Stokesley, SVP Furniture Store – Sheffield, Talking Pictures – Aldridge and Tukes – Aberystwyth and £500 to Bradford Police Club for Young People.

Exclusions Grants are made to registered charities only. Applications from individuals, including students, are ineligible. No grants are made in response to general appeals from large national charities. Grants are seldom available for churches or church buildings or for scientific or medical research projects.

Applications In writing to the correspondent, including the most recent set of accounts, clear details of the need the project is designed to meet and an outline budget. Trustees meet four times a year. Only successful applicants receive a reply.

Truemart Limited

General, Judaism, welfare

£83,000 (2001/02)

Beneficial area UK-wide and overseas, with a preference for Greater London.

34 The Ridgeway, London NW11 8QS

Correspondent Mrs S Heitner, Secretary

Trustees *I Heitner; I M Cymerman: Mrs S Heitner.*

CC Number 1090586

Information available Accounts were on file at the Charity Commission.

General The trust was set up to promote:

- the advancement of religion in accordance with the Orthodox Jewish faith
- the relief of poverty
- general charitable purposes.

In 2001/02 it had assets of £29,000 and an income of £143,000. Grants totalled £83,000. Unfortunately a list of beneficiaries was not available in the accounts.

Applications In writing to the correspondent.

Trumros Limited

Jewish

£139,000 (2000)

Beneficial area UK.

182 Finchley Road, London NW3 7AD

Correspondent Mrs H Hofbauer, Trustee

Trustees *R S Hofbauer; Mrs H Hofbauer.*

CC Number 285533

Information available Full accounts were on file at the Charity Commission.

General This trust appears to support Jewish organisations only. In 2003 it had an income of £585,000 and a total expenditure of £77,000. Further information for this year was not available.

In 2000 the trust had assets of £2.5 million and an income of £539,000, of which £446,000 came from rental income. A total of £139,000 was given in grants; unfortunately a list of donations was not included with the accounts that were on file at the Charity Commission.

In 1999 a total of £212,000 was distributed in 128 grants. Over 40% of donations were for £1,000 or more, with the remainder being mainly for £500 or less. The three largest grants were: £20,000 each to Menorah Primary School, Centre for Torah Education Zichron Yaacov and Beis Yoseph Zvi Institutions. Other larger grants went to SOFOT (£11,000), General Cherra Kadish Jerusalem (£5,800), Oldos Aharon (£4,800), Jewish learning Exchange (£2,000) and Gateshead Jewish Academy for Girls (£1,000).

Smaller grants included: Beis Avrohom Synagogue (£600), London Jerusalem Academy, Friends of Ohr Someach and YMER (£500 each), Achiezer Assia (£200) and Israel Settlement Fund (£100).

Applications In writing to the correspondent, but note that the trust states it is already inundated with applications.

Trust Sixty Three

Disability, overseas aid, famine relief, general

£96,000 to organisations (2001/02)

Beneficial area UK and overseas, with a preference for Bedfordshire and Hertfordshire.

3 The Compasses, High Street, Clophill, Bedfordshire MK45 4AF

Tel. 01525 860777 **Fax** 01525 862246

Correspondent The Trustees

Trustees *M W Tait; Mrs A F Tait; C G Nott; Mrs J Hobbs; Mrs D Staines.*

CC Number 1049136

Information available Full accounts were provided by the trust.

General This trust has general charitable purposes, although usually grants are only made towards disability causes, overseas aid and famine relief.

In 2001/02 it had assets of £413,000 and an income of £21,000. Grants were made to 118 organisations totalling £96,000. The largest grants were: £7,400 to Brandles School; £6,200 to Bedfordshire County Council; £5,000 to Pasque Hospice; £4,900 to St Mary's Church; £3,700 to Home Start Hitchin; £3,500 to Mobility Trust; and £3,000 to SCOPE.

Other local donations included: £1,000 to Clophill Churches Aid Appeal; £950 to Botton Village; £450 to North Hertfordshire Sanctuary; £400 to Bedfordshire Cargen Carers; £250 to Hertfordshire Community Foundation; £200 to Bedfordshire Scope Holidays Scheme; £100 to St Mary's School – Clophill; and £50 to North Hertfordshire Breast Cancer.

Grants elsewhere included: £1,300 to Shelter; £1,100 to Great Ormond Street Hospital; £800 to MIND; £710 to SENSE; £500 each to BREAK and British Red Cross; £300 each to Prison Phones Trust and Starlight Foundation; £100 to British Heart Foundation; £50 to Woodland Trust; and £45 to Riding for the Disabled.

Overseas donations included: £5,000 to Churches Together – Bosnia; £3,000 to Kanyike Project Uganda; £1,400 to 'Taller' Nerja; and £250 to Rotary International.

Exclusions No grants to individuals.

Applications In writing to the correspondent.

Tudor Rose Ltd

Jewish

£82,000 (2000/01)

Beneficial area UK.

Martin and Heller, Accountants, 5 North End Road, London NW11 7RJ

Tel. 020 8455 6789

Correspondent Samuel Taub, Secretary

Trustees *M Lehrfield; M Taub; A Taub; S Taub; S L Taub.*

CC Number 800576

Information available Full accounts were on file at the Charity Commission.

General This trust works for the promotion of the Orthodox Jewish faith and the relief of poverty.

In 2002/03 the trust had an income of £521,000 and a total expenditure of £186,000. Further information for this year was not available on file at the Charity Commission.

In 2000/01 it had assets of £704,000. Total income was £254,000, including £8,300 from donations and £208,000 from property income. £110,000 was spent during the year on these properties and listed as expenditure. Grants were made totalling £82,000.

The eight grants of £1,000 or over were listed in the accounts. These were £29,000 to Ponovex, £18,000 to CWCT, £13,000 to Yetev Lev, £12,000 to Yad Eliezer, £4,100 to Torah Study Centre, £3,000 to Rihiliation Trust, £1,600 to NWL Synagogue and £1,000 to Gur Trust. Smaller grants totalled £1,100.

Applications In writing to the correspondent.

The Tufton Charitable Trust

Christian

£336,000 (2003)

Beneficial area UK.

Slater Maidment, 7 St James's Square, London SW1Y 4JU

Tel. 020 7930 7621

Correspondent C Sadlow

Trustees *Sir Christopher Wates; Lady Wates; J R F Lulham.*

CC Number 801479

Information available Accounts were provided by the trust.

General This trust supports Christian organisations, by providing grants as well as allowing them to use premises leased by the trust for retreats.

In 2003 the trust had assets of £1.3 million and an income of £310,000. Grants totalled £336,000. Unfortunately a breakdown of the grant total was unavailable, however we do have a list of the grants from 2002 (collated from the Charity Commission). Grants were made totalling £268,000. The largest grant was given to the Church of England (eight grants totalling £28,000). Other beneficiaries included Wealdon Youth for Christ (£7,500), Oasis Trust-St John Ambulance, Gooderough College (three grants totalling £4,500), Treloar Trust (£2,500), London Institute for Contemporary Christianity and Acton Institute for the Study of Religion and Liberty (£2,000 each), Vines Centre Trust (£1,500), Regeneration Trust Gap activity projects, Medical Support in Romania, Prayer for the Nation and 1st Northian Scout Group (£1,000 each). £4,000 was distributed in 12 smaller grants.

Exclusions No grants for repair or maintenance of buildings.

Applications In writing to the correspondent, including an sae.

The Tunnell Trust

Chamber music

£29,000 (2003/04)

Beneficial area UK, with a preference for Scotland.

4 Royal Terrace, Edinburgh EH7 5AB

Tel. 0131 556 4043 **Fax** 0131 556 3969

Email tunnelltrust@aol.com

Website www.tunnelltrust.org.uk

Correspondent The Secretary

Trustees *C J Packard, Chair; C Abram; T D Chadwick; Carol Colburn Høgel; M Hunter; D McLellan; D Nicholson; K Robb; K Thompson; D W S Todd; O W Tunnell; P Tunnell.*

SC Number SC021739

Information available Information was provided by the trust.

General The trust was set up in 1988 as a tribute to John Tunnell, who was leader of the Scottish Chamber Orchestra from its foundation in 1974 until his death in 1988.

The trust aims to promote chamber music, advance the education of young professional chamber musicians and provide performance opportunities for talented chamber musicians. Modest fees are paid to British groups of two to eight young professional chamber music players aged 27 or under.

Its main programme is to support Scottish chamber music clubs and societies for tours of Scotland. Other fees are paid, usually for residential chamber music courses and concerts elsewhere in the UK.

In 2003/04 it had an income of £52,000 and made awards totalling £29,000. Beneficiaries included Trio Belle Epoque and Pavao String Quartet. In making these awards, the trust sponsored a total of 15 concerts in 15 different music clubs and societies through Scotland and a chamber music course at Strathgarry House – Perthshire.

Exclusions Awards are not available to singers or vocal groups, nor to instrumental duos consisting of a soloist with accompanist. Duos in which the players are equal partners, for example in violin and piano, or cello and piano sonatas, are eligible.

Applications Application forms are available from the trust's website. The deadline is 30 June each year, with auditions for potential recipients held in November.

The R D Turner Charitable Trust

General

£150,000 (2001/02)

Beneficial area UK, with a preference for Worcestershire.

1 The Yew Trees, High Street, Henley-in-Arden B95 5BN

Tel. 01564 793085

Correspondent J E Dyke, Administrator

Trustees *W S Ellis; D P Pearson; T J Lunt; Sir Christopher Stuart-White.*

CC Number 263556

Information available Information was provided by the trust.

General In 2001/02 the trust had assets of £15 million, and an income of £344,000. Grants were made to 22 organisations totalling £150,000.

The largest grant was £50,000 to Acorns Children's Hospice for the Worcester Appeal. Other large grants were £10,000 each to Cambridge Foundation, Ironbridge Gorge Museum Development Trust, Pioneer Centre and Worcester and Dudley Historic Churches Trust and £5,000 each to Royal Agricultural Benevolent Institution, Sunfield School, Worcester Rural Stress Support Network and Worcester Three Choirs Festival.

Other beneficiaries included Pattaya Orphanage and St John Ambulance – Hereford and Worcester (£3,000 each), DISCS and Sail Training Association – Worcester (£2,000 each), Royal National Lifeboat Institution – Kidderminster (£1,500), Worcester Regiment Museum Trust (£1,000) and Bishampton Village Hall (£500).

Exclusions No grants to non-registered charities or to individuals.

Applications In writing to the correspondent with a copy of your latest annual report and accounts. There are no application forms. The trustees meet in February, May, August and October to consider applications, which should be submitted in the month prior to each meeting. Telephone enquiries may be made before submitting an appeal.

The Florence Turner Trust

General

£129,000 (2002/03)

Beneficial area UK, but with a strong preference for Leicestershire.

c/o Harvey Ingram Owston, 20 New Walk, Leicester LE1 6TX

Tel. 0116 254 5454 **Fax** 0116 255 3318

Correspondent The Trustees

Trustees *Roger Bowder; Allan A Veasey; Caroline A Macpherson.*

CC Number 502721

Information available Full accounts were provided by the trust.

General This trust has general charitable purposes, giving most of its support in Leicestershire. The grants list shows many grants to children's and welfare organisations.

In 2002/03 it had assets of £3.3 million, which generated an income of £140,000.

Grants were made to 122 organisations and totalled £129,000.

The largest grants were £27,000 to Leicester Grammar School for bursaries, library and prizes and £12,000 to Leicester Charity Organisation Society.

In all there were 30 grants of £1,000 or over. The only beneficiaries not identifiably in Leicestershire were CARE Fund for the Mentally Handicapped, Mosaic and VISTA (£2,200 each), Army Benevolent Fund, Macmillan Cancer Relief, Marie Curie Cancer Care, PDSA and Royal National Lifeboat Institution (£1,800 each) and Barnardos (£1,500).

Other beneficiaries included Leicester Learning Zone (£5,000), Age Concern Leicester (£3,000) and Leicestershire Historic Churches Preservation Trust (£2,600). There were a further 92 grants under £1,000.

Exclusions The trust does not support individuals for educational purposes.

Applications In writing to the correspondent. Trustees meet every eight or nine weeks.

Miss S M Tutton Charitable Trust

Music

£26,000 (2002/03)

Beneficial area UK.

BDO Stoy Hayward, 8 Baker Street, London W1U 3LL

Tel. 020 7893 2439

Correspondent Peter Raddenbury

Trustees *Susan Diane Dolton; Peter G G Miller; Rosemary Pickering; Richard Van Allen.*

CC Number 298774

Information available Information was provided by the trust.

General The trust provides financial support to young singers (through the Sybil Tutton Awards) for postgraduate opera studies and selected music colleges, charities and training opera companies benefiting adults aged 20 to 30. Assistance is generally provided only where students are recommended by organisations with which the trust has a close working relationship.

In 2002/03 the trust had assets of £543,000 and an income of £40,000. Grants were made totalling £26,000.

The main focus of the funds was towards the Sybil Tutton Awards, with £16,000 given for this purpose. Other beneficiaries, all also supported in the previous year, were National Opera Studio (£5,000), Clonter Farm Music Trust (£3,000), Aldeburgh Foundation for Britten-Pears School (£1,500) and Young Concert Artists Trust (£1,000).

Applications Individuals seeking grants for opera studies should consider applying directly to the Musicians' Benevolent Fund (charity no: 228089) which administers the Sybil Tutton Awards. Organisations should submit full details of projects to the address below. The trust has some funds available for occasional discretionary grants, but they are very limited. Assistance is generally provided only where students are recommended by organisations with which the trust has a close working relationship.

The TUUT Charitable Trust

General, but with a bias towards trade-union-favoured causes

£73,000 (2002/03)

Beneficial area Worldwide.

Congress House, Great Russell Street, London WC1B 3LQ

Tel. 020 7637 7116 **Fax** 020 7637 7087

Email info@tufm.co.uk

Correspondent Ann Smith, Secretary

Trustees *Lord Christopher; J Monks; A Tuffin; M Walsh; M Bradley; E Chapman.*

CC Number 258665

Information available Accounts and a newsletter were provided by the trust.

General Established in 1969 by the trade-union movement to ensure the profits of the company would go to good causes rather than individual schareholders. In previous years, the trust has had no particular areas of interest, with the trust deed requiring all trustees to be trade unionists so the giving of the funds represents the interests of the membership. Due to the large number of applications the trust is receiving but are unable to support, it has now decided to have specific areas of interest to enable it to make fewer, but more worthwhile, grants than it has been able to in recent years.

Preference is given to:

- charities established by the TUC or an affiliated trade union for the benefit of its members
- charities formally supported by the TUC or an individual trade union at national or branch level
- charities demonstrating a direct and active link with one or more unions (for instance, those that recognise an individual union for bargaining purposes)
- overseas applications accompanied by a letter of support on behalf of the ICFTU, CTUC, ETUC or a member organisation.

The trustees still also consider applications outside these categories from small to medium-sized non-religious charities in the UK that benefit a wide range of people, with reference to one of the following:

- medical research
- support for victims of war or natural disaster
- relief of poverty, age or mental or physical illness or disability
- influencing public policy on human rights, welfare or employment issues
- education
- promoting economic and social development in developing countries.

In 2002/03 the trust had assets of £1.4 million million and an income of £108,000. Grants were made totalling £73,000. A Fellowship Award was also made worth £1,900.

The largest grants were £25,000 to NACRO, £10,000 to TUC Aid and £5,000 to Fabian Society. Other beneficiaries included Maternity Alliance (£3,000), Mental Health Foundation (£2,500), Banner Theatre Company, CWUHA (£2,000 each), Apex Trust, Chaucer Clinic, Hearing Dogs for Deaf People and Seaview Projects (£1,000 each).

Beneficiaries receiving under £1,000 include CARES, Evelina Childrens Hospital and Tyddyn Bach Trust (£500 each), 999 Club, British Retinus Pigmentosa Society, Contact the Elderly, National ME Centre and TECSAT (£250 each), Macmillan Cancer Relief and Mayor of Merton's Charities (£100 each).

Exclusions No grants to individuals.

Applications In writing to the correspondent. Applications should be submitted from a head office (where appropriate) and include latest accounts, purpose for donation and details of trade-union links. Trustees meet three times a year.

Ulting Overseas Trust

Theological training

£100,000 (2003/04)

Beneficial area The developing world (mostly, but not exclusively, Asia, Africa and South and Central America).

2 Bristol Avenue, Ashby-de-la-Zouch, Leicestershire LE65 2PA

Tel. 01530 417426 **Fax** 01530 417426

Email sue.brown22@btopenworld.com

Correspondent Dr Sue Brown, Projects Officer

Trustees *Dr J A B Kessler; J C Heyward; J S Payne; A J Bale; Dr D G Osborne; Mrs M Brinkley; D Ford; N W H Sylvester; T B Warren; Revd J Kapolyo.*

CC Number 294397

Information available Information was provided by the trust.

General The trust exists solely to provide bursaries, normally via grants to Christian theological training institutions or organisations with a training focus, for those in the developing world who wish to train for the Christian ministry, or for those who wish to improve their ministry skills. It gives priority to the training of students in their home countries or continents.

In 2002/03 it had assets of £2.8 million and an income of £95,000. Grants totalled £100,000, as is budgeted each year. They included £16,000 to Scripture Union, £6,000 to Nairobi Evangelical Graduate School of Theology – Kenya, £1,100 to Nagaland Bible College – India and £1,000 each to Christian Service College – Kumasi in Ghana and Higher Institute of Theology – Sucuani in Peru.

Exclusions No grants are given for capital projects such as buildings or library stock, nor for training in subjects other than Biblical, theological and missionary studies. Grants are only made to institutions to pass on to their students; direct grants to individuals cannot be made.

Applications The funds of the trust are already committed. Unsolicited applications cannot be supported.

The Ulverscroft Foundation

People who are sick and visually impaired, ophthalmic research

£213,000 to organisations (2002/03)

Beneficial area Worldwide.

1 The Green, Bradgate Road, Anstey, Leicester LE7 7FU

Tel. 0116 236 4325 **Fax** 0116 234 0205

Email foundation@ulverscroft.co.uk

Website www.ulverscroft.co.uk

Correspondent Joyce Sumner

Trustees *Allan Leach, chair; P H Carr; M K Down; A W Price; D Owen; R Crooks.*

CC Number 264873

Information available Full accounts were provided by the trust.

General A non-profit organisation, Ulverscroft Large Print Books Limited, was formed in 1964 to meet the needs of people who had difficulty reading due to sight problems. The company republished existing books in large type to sell to libraries and donate the profits to sight-related charitable causes. In 1972 The Ulverscroft Foundation was created, which acquired the company to protects its trade and the charitable donations of profits. The company has since expanded, owning its own print works to cut its publication costs and gain the custom of other publishers and in 2001 integrated an audio tape publishing business.

The foundation's aim is to help improve the quality of life for people who are blind and partially sighted (visually impaired). The foundation finances:

- eye clinics
- eye treatment departments in hospitals
- eye operating theatres
- ophthalmic diagnostic equipment
- research into eye diseases and their treatment
- library services for people who are visually impaired or housebound
- improvements in the quality of life for people who are visually impaired.

All financial help given by the foundation is made through channels such as NHS Trusts, hospitals, schools, libraries and groups for the visually impaired.

In 2002/03 the trust had assets of £8.8 million. Ulverscroft Group (as the trading company is known) generated an income of £19.5 million, which produced an income of £1.5 million. From this, grants were made totalling £213,000.

The largest grants were £50,000 each to St Mary's and Deafblind UK, £29,000 to University of Leicester, £11,000 to UMRA and £10,000 to Royal Australian College. Other beneficiaries included Great Ormnand Street Children's Hospital Ophlthalmology Unit (£6,000), Swinfen Charitable Trust (£4,000), Talking Newspaper Association (£3,000), Royal London Society for the Blind (£2,800), Action for Blind People, Calibre, Joseph Clarke School and Soundaround (£2,000 each), Rochdale Special Needs Cycling (£1,600) and Blind in Business, Diabetes UK, Grampian Society for the Blind, Living Options Devon, Oxfam and RNCB (£1,000 each). A further £6,700 was given in grants of less than £1,000.

Exclusions Applications from individuals are not encouraged. Generally, assistance towards salaries and general running costs are not given.

Applications In writing to the correspondent. Applicants are advised to make their proposal as detailed as possible, to include details of the current service to people who are visually impaired, if any, and how the proposed project will be integrated or enhanced. If possible the trust asks for an estimate of how many people who are visually impaired use/will use the service, the amount of funding obtained to date, if any, and the names of other organisations to whom they have applied. The success of any appeal is dependent on the level of funding at the time of consideration. The trustees meet four times a year to consider applications.

The Union of Orthodox Hebrew Congregation

Jewish

£171,000 (1998)

Beneficial area UK.

140 Stamford Hill, London N16 6QT

Tel. 020 8802 6226

Correspondent J R Conrad, Acting Administrator

Trustees *B S F Freshwater; I Cymerman; C Konig; Rabbi A Pinter.*

CC Number 249892

Information available Accounts were on file at the Charity Commission.

General The trust works to protect and to further the interests of traditional Judaism in Great Britain and to establish and support such institutions as will serve this object. In 2003 it had an income of £1 million and a total expenditure of £979,000. Further information for this year was not available.

In 2001 it had an income of £723,000 and a total expenditure of £520,000.

In 1998 it had assets of £772,000. The total income is £791,000 and grants totalled £171,000.

Applications In writing to the correspondent.

Unity Charitable Trust

General

Around £68,000 (2002/03)

Beneficial area UK.

5 Accommodation Road, London NW11 8ED

Correspondent Elaine Abrahams, Project Coordinator

Trustees *J Endfield; R Baron; R Woolich.*

CC Number 1057710

Information available Information was provided by the trust. Accounts were on file at the Charity Commission, but without a list of grant beneficiaries.

General This trust tends to give one large grant each year rather than making a number of smaller grants; as such it stated that it has no extra funds to give. In 2002/03 it had an income of £68,000 and a total expenditure of £71,000. No further information was available as regards the recipient of the funds or how much was given.

Applications In writing to the correspondent. Unsolicited applications are not considered.

The David Uri Memorial Trust

Jewish, general

£57,000 (2001/02)

Beneficial area Worldwide.

Suite 511, 78 Marylebone High Street, London W1U 5AP

Correspondent The Trustees

Trustees *Mrs S Blackman; Mrs B Roden; B Blackman.*

CC Number 327810

Information available Accounts were on file at the Charity Commission, but without a list of grants since that for 1991/92.

General In 2001/02 the trust's assets totalled £1.8 million, it had an income of £190,000 including £180,000 from rents and made grants to organisations totalling £57,000. Other expenditure included £100,000 spent on earning rent from trust properties and £3,400 on management and administration costs.

Unfortunately, no grants list or information was available on the beneficiaries of the trust since 1991/92. In that year, grants totalled £28,000, with most grants to Jewish organisations. The largest were £15,000 to Yakar Education Foundation and £2,500 to the National Jewish Chaplaincy Board. All the other grants to Jewish organisations were under £500.

Grants to non-Jewish organisations included £5,000 to the Jefferies Research Wing Trust, with all the others receiving under £500, including Age Concern, Crisis at Christmas and NSPCC.

Exclusions No grants to individuals.

Applications In writing to the correspondent.

This entry was not confirmed by the trust, but the address was correct according to the Charity Commission database.

The Albert Van Den Bergh Charitable Trust

Medical/disability, welfare

£68,000 (2002/03)

Beneficial area UK and overseas.

Triggs Wilkinson Mann, Broadoak House, Horsham Road, Cranleigh, Surrey GU6 8DJ

Tel. 01483 273515

Correspondent G R Oliver, Trustee

Trustees *P A Van Den Bergh; G R Oliver; Mrs J M Hartley.*

CC Number 296885

Information available Full accounts were on file at the Charity Commission.

General The trust was established in 1987. In 2002/03, its assets were valued at £1.6 million, invested in property, a wide range of investments and cash at the bank. It had an income of £64,000 and the trust gave £68,000 in grants. Unfortunately there was no grants list on file at the Charity Commission for that year.

However, in 1996/97, £38,000 was given in grants with the largest being: £5,000 to United Charities Fund – Liberal Jewish Synagogue, £2,100 to Care for the Elderly, £2,000 to Parentline Surrey, £1,200 to both Counsel & Care for the Elderly and Riding for the Disabled – Cranleigh, and £1,000 to both Age Concern and St John Ambulance.

Smaller grants were generally of £500 and were given to charities such as: Bishop of Guildford's Charity, BLISS, British Heart Foundation, CSV, Leukaemia Research Trust, Multiple Sclerosis Society, National Osteoporosis Society, RNID and SSAFA.

Most grants went to national charities in the fields of health, welfare and disability. Some went to Jewish organisations and some to Surrey-based charities. A few grants went to local charities elsewhere, but mainly in the London area.

Applications In writing to the correspondent, including accounts and budgets.

Bernard van Leer Foundation

Development of young children who are disadvantaged

€414,000 in the UK, €21 million worldwide (2003)

Beneficial area Brazil, Colombia, Czech Republic, Egypt, El Salvador, Germany, Greece, Guatemala, Hungary, India, Indonesia, Israel, Jamaica, Kenya, Malaysia, Mexico, Morocco, Mozambique, the Netherlands, Nicaragua, Nigeria, Peru, Poland, Slovakia, South Africa, Tanzania, Thailand, Trinidad and Tobago, Turkey, Uganda, United Kingdom, United States of America, Venezuela and Zimbabwe.

The Royal Bank of Scotland plc, Private Trust and Taxation, 2 Festival Square, Edinburgh EH3 9SU

Tel. 0131 523 2657 **Fax** 0131 228 9889

Website www.bernardvanleer.org

Correspondent The Trustees

Trustee *The Royal Bank of Scotland plc.*

CC Number 265186

Information available Information was provided by the trust. Accounts were on file at the Charity Commission.

General The objectives of the foundation are 'to enhance opportunities for children aged zero to seven years of age, growing up in circumstances of social and economic disadvantage to optimally develop their innate potential'. Support is generally given to projects lasting three years rather than general appeals, and is concentrating on the 40 countries where the Van Leer Group is established. The following information is taken from the trust's website:

'Programming in early childhood development is about meeting the multi-faceted needs and rights of young children and their community. Every child has the fundamental right to be given the best possible start in life, and supported in fully developing his or her potential.

'To maximise our effectiveness in support of work that furthers the holistic development of young children, the Bernard van Leer Foundation avoids spreading its resources too thinly. Grantmaking is guided by thematic and programmatic priorities. Our geographical criteria emanate from the Foundation's legacy, and from our programme development principles.

'We organise our grantmaking in two ways:

1. on a country and, to a lesser extent, regional basis; and
2. through thematic initiatives, which may include partners from countries where we do not otherwise have a grantmaking programme.

'A grantmaking programme is a set of projects that responds to national and local contexts and realities.

'A thematic initiative explores one specific topic of interest. Current topics are: children affected by HIV/AIDS; respect for diversity, and; growing up in indigenous societies. Each initiative seeks to have an impact that reaches beyond individual projects and across borders. Within these initiatives, the Foundation invests in activities that will disclose, and deepen its understanding of, key programmatic experiences.

Criteria for funding:

- 'Public, private or community-based organisations are eligible for grantmaking partnerships. Individuals are not eligible.
- 'Proposals may be considered for funding if they fit within the programme strategy of a country eligible for grantmaking or because they are part of a thematic or regional initiative.
- 'Grants are only made for projects concerned with the development of children aged 0 to 8 years in socially and economically disadvantaged circumstances, principally in countries where we have a grantmaking programme.

The Foundation funds:

Projects that promote:

- 'a holistic approach to early childhood development;
- 'the enhancement of parents' capacity to support their children's development
- 'a development strategy that is rooted in the local context and is culturally, socially and economically appropriate;
- 'the building of capacity, local ownership and working in partnership.

Projects that aim to:

- 'have a preventive and lasting effect; and
- 'generate tangible benefits to young children and their environments.

The Foundation does not fund:

- 'applications for support to individual children
- 'projects that concentrate solely on one aspect of children's development or learning
- 'projects that specifically focus on children with special needs such as mental and/or physical handicap;
- 'proposals for the construction and maintenance of buildings, or the purchase of equipment and materials;
- 'isolated requests for scholarships, conferences, media or theatre events;
- 'general support to organisations, or requests to cover recurrent costs or deficits.'

In 2003 the foundation had an income of €24 million, mostly in donations received. Grants were made totalling €21 million.These were distributed widely across the areas of benefit, with the five countries receiving the most funds being as follows:

Israel	€1.2 million
Mexico	€1.1 million
Germany	€1.0 million
South Africa	€1.0 million
Colombia	€0.9 million

A total of €414,000 was given in five grants in the UK. Respecting Diversity in Scotland and CAF received €143,000 to gather policy and practice information relating to respect for diversity, social inclusion and integration in Scotland and the rest of Europe. Listening to Young Children and Coram Family were given €125,000 to inspire and enable adults to listen and respond appropriately to children under the age of eight, and to enable young children to participate routinely in matters that are important to them. Children in Europe and Children in Scotland recevied €99,850 to provide a forum for childcare practitioners in various European countries for the exchange of ideas, practice and information. Publication of Alliance and Allavida received €30,000 to continue publishing for three years, expand its circulation, explore new roles it can play and develop a model for long-term financial sustainability. Spaces to Play and Thomas Coram Research Unit were given €17,000 to develop, apply and evaluate a method for listening to, and involving, preschool children aged 3 to 5 years in the process of changing outdoor spaces.

Exclusions Grants are not made to individuals, nor for the general support of organisations such as staffing/ administrative costs. The foundation does not provide study, research or travel grants. No grants are made in response to general appeals.

Applications On a form available from the correspondent, which requires a brief, 50-word description of the project. Applications are considered in March and September. Due to the large number of applications received, no acknowledgements are given and unsuccessful appeals will not receive a reply.

The Van Neste Foundation

Welfare, Christian, developing world

£182,000 (2003/04)

Beneficial area UK, especially the Bristol area, and overseas.

15 Alexandra Road, Clifton, Bristol BS8 2DD

Correspondent Fergus Lyons, Secretary

Trustees *M T M Appleby, Chair; F J F Lyons; G J Walker; J F J Lyons; B M Appleby.*

CC Number 201951

Information available Full accounts were provided by the trust.

General The trustees currently give priority to the following:

1. Developing world

2. People who have disabilities or are elderly

3. Advancement of religion and respect for the sanctity and dignity of life

4. Community and Christian family life

These objectives are reviewed by the trustees from time to time but applications falling outside them are unlikely to be considered.

In 2003/04 the trust had assets of £4.5 million and an income of £186,000. Grants for the year totalled £182,000 and were given to 25 organisations. They were broken down as follows:

	No.	*Total*
Developing world	5	£34,000
Disability/older people	4	£9,000
Advancement of religion and respect for the sanctity and dignity of life	4	£70,000
Community Projects	12	£69,000

The largest grants were to Alabore Christian Care Centres for support for ex-prisoners and those at high risk, Downside School and Prior Park School (£25,000 each); Home-Start Bristol (£15,000); Ammerdown Centre, CAFOD towards food production in Southern Sudan, Prinknash Abbey for restoration of the retreat house, St Bede's School Bristol, St Joseph's Society Mill Hill for a health centre and school in Southern Sudan (£10,000 each).

The remainder were between £250 and £5,000. Beneficiaries included Appropriate Technology Asia towards a health care project for the elderly in Cameroon, Bristol & District Tranquiliser Project to aid recovery from prescribed drugs and Bristol Urological Institute received a contribution to building a new centre (£5,000 each); McHenry Rural Health Centre for a health care project for the elderly in Cameroon (£3,500), Air Cadets towards cost of minibus (£3,000); and Little Sisters of the Poor received a contribution towards transport for older people (£1,000).

Smaller grants under £1,000 each included those to St John's Residents Association for a lunch club, SSAFA towards support costs (£500 each); and Colston Society (£250).

Exclusions No grants to individuals or to large, well-known charities. Applications are only considered from registered charities.

Applications Applications should be in the form of a concise letter setting out the clear objectives to be obtained, which must be charitable. Information must be supplied concerning agreed funding from other sources together with a timetable for achieving the objectives of the appeal and a copy of the latest accounts. The foundation does not normally make grants on a continuing basis. To keep overheads to a minimum, only successful applications are acknowledged. Even then it may be a matter of months before any decision can be expected, depending on the dates of trustees' meetings.

Mrs Maud Van Norden's Charitable Foundation

General

£40,000 (2002)

Beneficial area UK.

Messrs Payne Hicks Beach, 10 New Square, Lincoln's Inn, London WC2A 3QG

Tel. 020 7465 4300 **Fax** 020 7465 4393

Correspondent N J Wingerath, Trustee

Trustees *F C S Tufton; Mrs E M Dukler; Mrs E A Humphryes; N J Wingerath.*

CC Number 210844

Information available Full accounts were provided by the trust.

General In 2002 the trust's income totalled £43,000 and it made grants totalling £40,000. At the year end the trust's assets totalled £95,000.

Grant beneficiaries included House of St Barnabas in Soho, Marie Curie Cancer Care, Royal Hospital for Neuro-disability and Society for the Relief of the Poor (£2,000 each) and Bishop Creighton House Settlement, Break, Carers National Association, Changing Faces, Child Victims of Crime and Christian Family Concern (£1,000 each).

The trust has a list of charities which it regularly supports and the list is reviewed annually at the trustees' meeting. Surplus income is distributed to other charities during the year. The 2002 annual report and accounts stated the trust's aim is to make a charitable distribution of £40,000 per annum with donations being made at the trustees' discretion.

Exclusions No grants to individuals, expeditions or scholarships.

Applications The trustees will only consider applications if accompanied by a copy of the applicant's latest reports and accounts. The trustees make donations to registered charities only. The trustees meet to consider applications in May each year.

The Vandervell Foundation

General

£288,000 to organisations (2001)

Beneficial area UK.

Bridge House, 181 Queen Victoria Street, London EC4V 4DZ

Tel. 020 7248 9045

Correspondent Ms Sheila Lawler

Trustee *The Vandervell Foundation Limited Trustee Company.*

CC Number 255651

Information available Accounts were on file at the Charity Commission, but without a narrative report or grants list.

General This trust has general charitable purposes, supporting both individuals and organisations. A wide range of causes has been supported, include schools, educational establishments, hospices and other health organisations, with the trust stating there are no real preferences or exclusions. Grants generally range from £1,000 to £5,000 each.

In 2000 the trust had assets of £4.9 million. Total income was £826,000, including £676,000 received from G A Vandervell Deceased Will Trust. Management and administration totalled £75,000. Grants totalled £186,000 whilst donations totalled £345,000, although no explanation was given in the accounts explaining the difference between the two.

Applications In writing to the correspondent. Trustees meet every two months to consider major grant applications; smaller grants are considered more frequently.

Roger Vere Foundation

General

£939,000 to organisations and individuals (2001/02)

Beneficial area UK and worldwide, with a special interest in High Wycombe.

19 Berwick Road, Marlow, Buckinghamshire SL7 3AR

Tel. 01628 471702

Correspondent Peter Allen, Trustee

Trustees *Mrs Rosemary Vere, Chair; Mrs Marion Lyon; Peter Allen.*

CC Number 1077559

Information available Information was provided by the trust. However no recent accounts were available.

General This trust was established in September 1999 and it supports, worldwide:

- the relief of financial hardship in and around, but not restricted to, High Wycombe
- advancement of education
- advancement of religion
- advancement of scientific and medical research
- conservation and protection of the natural environment and endangered plants and animals
- relief of natural and civil disasters
- general charitable purposes.

In 2001/02 the trust had an income of £34,000 and an expenditure of £948,000. Donations totalled £939,000. No further information was available for this year, however in November 2003 the trust stated that their funds are depleting and applications are not encouraged at the present time.

In 1999/2000 it had an income of £7.6 million and made grants totalling £551,000. Two substantial grants were made during the year, these were £200,000 to Trent Vineyard and £100,000 to Jubilee 2000 Coalition. National Star Centre and YMCA each received £50,000. Other large grants were £20,000 each to Disaster Emergency Committee and Stepping Stones Trust, £15,000 to USPG and £10,000 to CARE International.

Other grants included £7,000 to Church Army, £6,000 each to BTCV and Marlow Pastoral Foundation, £5,500 to Children's Country Holidays and Rescue Foundation, £5,000 each to Action for Blind People, British Wireless for the Blind, Elimination of Leukaemia, Fauna and Flora International, Prince's Trust and Young Minds, £3,500 to Greening Brill School and £2,500 to National Missing Persons Helpline.

Applications Please see the comments in the general section.

The Nigel Vinson Charitable Trust

General

£66,000 (2003/04)

Beneficial area UK, with a preference for north east England.

Messrs Hoare Trustees, 37 Fleet Street, London EC4P 4DQ

Tel. 020 7353 4522

Correspondent Chris Durrant

Trustees *Rt Hon. Lord Vinson of Roddam Dene; Hon. Mrs Bettina Claire Witheridge; M F Jodrell; Mrs Rowena A Cowan; Thomas O C Harris.*

CC Number 265077

Information available Full accounts were on file at the Charity Commission.

General This trust was established in 1972. It makes grants towards the encouragement and development of business and industry, the arts and education.

In 2003/04 the trust had assets of £2.6 million and an income of £185,000. Grants were made totalling £66,000. The largest were £14,000 to Civitas, £11,000 to Institute of Economic Affairs, £8,000 to Institute for Policy Research, £7,000 to Hampden Trust and £3,000 to Chillingham Wild Cattle Association. Smaller grants of less than £1,000 were made to various charities amounting to £23,000.

Applications In writing to the correspondent. Applications are considered throughout the year.

The William and Ellen Vinten Trust

Industrial education, training and welfare

£75,000 (2001/02)

Beneficial area UK, but mostly Bury St Edmunds.

Greene & Greene Solicitors, 80 Guildhall Street, Bury St Edmunds, Suffolk IP33 1QB

Tel. 01284 762211

Correspondent D J Medcalf, Chair

Trustees *D J Medcalf, Chair; J V Crosher; M Shallow; A C Leacy; P M Tracey; A Grigg.*

CC Number 285758

Information available Accounts were on file at the Charity Commission, but without a list of beneficiaries.

General The 2001/02 accounts stated: 'During the year, the trust has largely completed its initiative with the upper schools in the Bury St Edmunds area and the West Suffolk College, enhancing the facilities for the teaching of science and technology subjects leading towards careers in industry. Over the years in which this project has been pursued, the environment for students in these subjects and the facilities available to their teachers have been radically improved, on a jointly funded basis.

'The trust has continued to give smaller grants to middle schools, when particularly meritorious cases have been presented [relating] to the acquisition of scientific and information technology equipment.

'With the winding down of the Upper Schools' Initiative, the trust has embarked upon two new inititatives. The first, which started during the year, was a modern craft apprenticeship scheme, involving the giving of grants to encourage engineering companies to engage and train apprentices. The second inititative is a scheme of bursaries and scholarships awarded within the upper schools to students pursuing sixth form and university courses leading towards careers in engineering. This project is aimed to run for a trial period of five years.

'The trust has continued to provide grants for university students and, when cases have come to light, to provide welfare grants to people employed in industry.'

In 2001/02 the trust had assets of £1.8 million and an income of £89,000. Grants totalled £75,000 and broken down as follows:

Education	£71,000
Training	£3,600
Welfare	£620

Applications The trust stated that as a proactive charity it does not seek unsolicited applications. Such applications are now so significant in number that the trust has decided not to respond to them, however discourteous this may seem.

Vision Charity

Children who are blind, visually impaired or dyslexic

£199,000 (2002/03)

Beneficial area UK.

PO Box 260, Dorking, Surrey RH5 6WL

Tel. 01306 731781 **Fax** 01306 731791

Website www.visioncharity.co.uk

Correspondent Mrs G Fitzpatrick

Trustees *Ian Myhill, Chair; David Coupe; Peter Davies; David Pacy.*

CC Number 1075630

Information available Full accounts were provided by the trust.

General The objects of the charity are to combine the fundraising efforts of companies and individuals who use or benefit from, or work in, the visual communications industry for the benefit of children who are blind, visually impaired or dyslexic.

In 2002/03 it had assets of £201,000 and an income of £338,000, most of which came from donations received and various fundraising events organised by the charity (see their website for further details). A total of £165,000 was spent on organising these events. Grant were made totalling £199,000.

The largest were: £27,000 each, both for minibuses, to Neatherlea Respite Home – Dumfries and Royal National Institute for the Blind – Cardiff; £15,000 each to Blind in Business for specialist software for teenagers who are visually impaired and SeeAbility – Leatherhead towards a minibus; and £14,000 to University of York Dyslexia Centre for audio-visual equipment for education and training.

Other beneficiaries included National Blind Children's Society for a large print book project (£9,700), Royal Blind Society – Kent for a specialist holiday scheme for students who are blind (£8,100), PACE Centre – Aylesbury for video, photography and computer equipment (£7,300), Christian Blind Mission for children's cataract operations (£5,000), Radio Academy for a training scheme for people with visual impairments (£3,000) and Oldham Visual Impairment Unit for equipment and software (£2,400).

Applications A brief summary of the request should be sent to the correspondent. If the request is of interest to the trustees, further details will be requested. If the request has not been acknowledged within three months of submission, the applicant should assume that it has not been successful. The charity is interested to receive such applications but regrets that it is not able to acknowledge every unsuccessful submission.

Vivdale Ltd

Jewish

£46,000 (1998/99)

Beneficial area UK.

17 Cheyne Walk, London NW4 3QH

Correspondent D H Marks, Trustee

Trustees *D H Marks; L Marks; F Z Sinclair.*

CC Number 268505

Information available Accounts were available at the Charity Commission, but without a full narrative report or a grants list.

General In 2003/04 the trust had an income of £112,000 and a total expenditure of £62,000. Further information for this year was not available.

In 1998/99, the trust's assets totalled £421,000, it had an income of £83,000 and donations totalled £46,000. Further information was not available.

The most recent list of grants on file for this trust at the Charity Commission was for 1994/95, when 16 grants were given to Jewish organisations, ranging from £32 to £3,600, with the exception of a grant of £22,000 to Friends of Harim Establishments Ltd. Grants of £20 and below totalled £240.

Applications In writing to the correspondent.

The Viznitz Foundation

General

£104,000 (2001/02)

Beneficial area Worldwide.

23 Overlea Road, London E5 9BG

Tel. 020 8557 9557

Correspondent H Feldman, Trustee

Trustees *H Feldman; E Kahan; E S Margulies.*

CC Number 326581

Information available Accounts were on file at the Charity Commission.

General In 2001/02 the foundation had assets of £1.3 million with an income of £170,000 and grants totalling £104,000. Unfortunately no grant list was available for this period.

Applications In writing to the correspondent.

The Scurrah Wainwright Charity

Social reform, root causes of poverty and injustice

£64,000 (2002/03)

Beneficial area Preference for Yorkshire, South Africa and Zimbabwe.

16 Blenheim Street, Hebden Bridge, West Yorkshire HX7 8BU

Tel. 01422 845085

Email kerry@waintrust.fsnet.co.uk

Correspondent Kerry McQuade, Administrator

Trustees *J M Wainwright; H A Wainwright; M S Wainwright; T M Wainwright; P Wainwright; H Scott; R Bhaskar.*

CC Number 1002755

Information available Information was provided by the trust.

General The trust supports a wide range of charitable projects with an emphasis on social reform and tackling the root causes of poverty and injustice. Applications from the north of England, particularly Yorkshire, will generally be given strong priority; the trustees also have an interest in Zimbabwe.

Grants have ranged from less than £100 to over £25,000, but there is no minimum or maximum. Support may be given in stages, for example a £30,000 grant over three years via three annual payments of £10,000. A brief progress report must be sent within a year of receiving a grant.

In 2002/03 the trust had an income of £42,000. A total of £64,000 was given in 31 grants.

Beneficiaries included Ovenden Community Credit Union (£10,000), Avsed (£4,600), Youth Base and Bradford Community Environment Project (£4,000 each), Together for Peace (£3,700), Public Concern at Work and East Manchester Community Forum (£2,000 each), Harehills Irish Music Project (£1,800), Futuresonic (£1,500), Education for Democracy in South Africa (£1,300), Power of Women and Children, West Yorkshire Youth Association, African Scholars UK Fund, Caring for Life, Keighley Community Transport, Leeds Action to Create Homes and Brathay Hall Trust (£1,000 each).

Grants of less than £1,000 each were made to 13 institutions and totalled £5,000.

Exclusions No grants for individuals, buildings, medical research or the welfare of animals.

Applications In writing to the correspondent. Applicants are expected to provide background information about their organisation, the work they wish to pursue and their plans for its practical implementation, which will involve an outline budget and details of any other sources of finance. The most recent income and expenditure and balance sheets should be included. Trustees meet in March, July and November. Applications should be received by the first day of the preceding month.

The Wakefield Trust

General

£242,000 (2001/02)

Beneficial area UK, with a preference for Devon.

Yarner Farm House, Dartington, Devon TQ9 6JH

Tel. 01803 840681

Correspondent C E White

Trustees *Mrs M P Mitchell; Anne N Brain; C D Torlesse; A H Harrison; M B Shaw.*

CC Number 800079

Information available Full accounts were on file at the Charity Commission.

General The trust's annual report stated: 'The current policy of the trustees is to endow further and much needed Almshouses in the Totnes area' and to 'continue to make grants to projects in Devon and for the restoration of churches'.

In 2001/02 the trust had an income of £19,000 and gave grants totalling £242,000. No further information was available for this year.

In 2000/01 when it had assets of £639,000 and an income of £31,000, grants totalled £284,000. Further significant grants were made to Wakefield Almshouses Trust totalling £280,000. Other beneficiaries included Dartington Summer School, Birmingham Parish Church and Ways with Words (£1,000 each) and St John the Baptist – Skelgate (£500).

Exclusions No grants to individuals.

Applications In writing to the correspondent.

Wakeham Trust

Community development, education, community service by young people

£37,000 (1999/2000)

Beneficial area UK.

Wakeham Lodge, Rogate, Petersfield, Hampshire GU31 5EJ

Tel. 01730 821748 **Fax** 01730 821748

Email julie@wakehamtrust.demon.co.uk

Website www.wakehamtrust.org

Correspondent Mrs Julie Austin

Trustees *Harold Carter; Barnaby Newbolt; Tess Silkstone.*

CC Number 267495

Information available Full accounts were on file at the Charity Commission.

General The trust makes grants to a wide range of community organisations, and for educational purposes. This includes grants towards community service carried out by young people.

In 1999/2000 the trust's assets totalled £2.2 million, its income from investments was £46,000 and grants to 121 organisations were made totalling £37,000. In addition £5,700 was spent on administration costs.

Larger grants were £3,700 to Glebe Charitable Trust, £2,500 to Liverpool Council of Social Service and £1,000 to each of the following: Find Your Feet, Inner City Music, International Service, Lansalian Developing World Projects and Zion Congregational Church. The remaining grants were all for less, mostly for under £500. Beneficiaries included Barnstaple Youth House, Elim Church Centre, Frontier Youth Trust, Halton Pentacostal Church, Katie's Ski Tracks, Leicester Volunteer Centre, Mission in Hounslow and Warrington Mencap.

Exclusions No grants to individuals or large, well-established charities, or towards buildings and transport.

Applications In writing to the correspondent.

The F J Wallis Charitable Settlement

General

£45,000 (2002/03)

Beneficial area UK, with some interest in Hampshire and Surrey.

c/o Bridge House, 11 Creek Road, Hampton Court, East Molesey, Surrey KT8 9BE

Correspondent F H Hughes, Trustee

Trustees *F H Hughes; A J Hills; J J A Archer.*

CC Number 279273

Information available Full accounts were provided by the trust.

General The trust supports:

- UK charities related to health and welfare
- local charities and support groups in Hampshire and Surrey
- international disaster relief appeals
- causes in which the trustees have a specific interest.

In 2002/03 the settlement had assets of £921,000 and an income of £52,000. Grants were made to 48 organisations totalling £45,000.

The majority of grants were £1,000 each. The beneficiaries included Action for Blind People, Association for Spina Bifida and Hydrocephalus, BackCare (National Back Pain Association), Barnardos, Buckmore Park, COMPAID Trust, Contact the Elderly, Cruse Bereavement Care, Parentline Plus and St John Ambulance. Beneficiaries of £500 were Hope Worldwide, Street Child Africa and Treborth RDA Group.

Exclusions No grants to individuals or to local charities except those in Surrey or in Hampshire. The same organisation is not supported twice within a 24-month period.

Applications In writing to the correspondent. No telephone calls. Applications are not acknowledged and unsuccessful applicants will only be contacted if an sae is provided. Trustees meet in March and September and applications need to be received the month prior to the trustees' meeting.

Warbeck Fund Ltd

Jewish, the arts, general

£179,000 (2000/01)

Beneficial area UK, with a preference for London.

2nd Floor, Pump House, 10 Chapel Place, Rivington Street, London EC2A 3DQ

Tel. 020 7739 2224 **Fax** 020 7739 5544

Correspondent The Secretary

Trustees *Michael Brian David; Jonathan Gestetner; Neil Sinclair.*

CC Number 252953

Information available Accounts were on file at the Charity Commission.

General This fund has general charitable purposes, with preferences for Jewish, Israeli and arts organisations. The grants list indicates a preference for London, especially the West End.

In 2000/01 the fund had assets of £189,000. Total income was £257,000, of which £250,000 came from donations received. Management and administration costs amounted to just £1,800. Grants totalling £179,000 were made to 129 organisations, just under half of which were also supported in the previous year.

The largest grants were £26,000 to Westminster Society for People with Learning Difficulties and £21,000 each to Royal National Theatre and United Jewish Israel Appeal.

Other large grants were £10,000 each to British ORT and Hampstead Theatre Trust, £7,000 to British Friends of Haifa University, £6,900 to West London Synagogue and £5,300 to Wiezmann Institute Foundation.

Other London beneficiaries included London Symphony Orchestra (£2,500), Heritage of London Trust (£1,000), Friends of Covent Garden (£750), Worshipful Company of Information Technologists (£250) and Chelsea and Westminster Hospital and West London Action for Children (£25 each).

Smaller grants included those to Chicken Shed Theatre Company (£4,300), Red Hot Aids Charitable Trust (£1,300), British Friends of the Art Museums of Israel and International Centre for Child Studies (£1,000 each), Jewish Museum (£570), Scopus Jewish Educational Trust (£500), Tibet Foundation (£430), English National Opera (£350), After Adoption (£150), Chamber Orchestra of Europe and Macmillan Cancer Relief (£100 each), Friends of Tate Gallery (£60), Jewish Historical Society of England (£30) and National Coastwatch Institute (£15).

Exclusions No grants to individuals or non-UK registered charities.

Applications According to the correspondent, it is not worth applying as unsolicited applications tend to be unsuccessful.

The Ward Blenkinsop Trust

Medicine, social welfare, general

£220,000 to organisations (1999/2000)

Beneficial area UK, with a special interest in Merseyside and surrounding counties.

PO Box 28840, London SW13 0WZ

Tel. 020 8878 9975

Correspondent Charlotte Blenkinsop, Trustee

Trustees *A M Blenkinsop; J H Awdry; S J Blenkinsop; C A Blenkinsop; A F Stormer; H E Millin.*

CC Number 265449

Information available Accounts had been filed with the Charity Commission.

General The trust currently supports charities in the Merseyside area and charities of a medical nature, but all requests for funds are considered.

In 2001/02 the trust had an income of £237,000 and a total expenditure of £234,000. This information was taken from the Charity Commission database, no further details were available for this year. In 1999/2000 the trust had an income of £238,000 and gave grants to: 50 charities totalling £220,000; 15 ex-employees totalling £7,200 and £4,400 in Christmas boxes for people of pensionable age.

Two-thirds of all grants are given to organisations in the Merseyside area for general charitable purposes, including Clatterbridge Cancer Research Trust (£45,000). Grants were given to other organisations in north-west England including Cheshire County Council, which received £25,000 for its Youth Art

Initiative, and £20,000 for its South Africa Initiative. Other beneficiaries included Wade Deacon High School (£12,000), Manchester Youth Theatre (£6,000) and Robson Street Clinic District Nurses (£3,000).

UK groups were supported with a preference for medical charities, especially those connected with cancer. Beneficiaries in the previous year included Royal Academy of Dancing Special Needs Programme (£17,000), International Spine Research Trust (£5,000), St John Ambulance (£4,000), National Asthma Campaign (£3,000), Roy Castle Lung Cancer Foundation (£1,500), Age Concern and British Polio Fellowship (£750 each) and Cancer Research Campaign (£50).

Exclusions No grants to individuals.

Applications In writing to the correspondent.

The Barbara Ward Children's Foundation

Children, mental disability

£243,000 (2002/03)

Beneficial area England and Wales.

5 Great College Street, London SW1P 3SJ

Correspondent Chris Banks

CC Number 1089783

Information available Full accounts and information were provided by the trust.

General This charity's aims are primarily geared towards children's charities. Its primary objects are to carry out exclusively charitable purposes in relation to children and adults who are mentally disabled.

In 2002/03, the foundation had assets of £7.3 million and an income of £382,000. Grants totalled £243,000 and were donated to organisations to benefit children who were seriously or terminally ill, disadvantaged or otherwise. The largest grants were made to Rainbow Trust Children's Charity (£60,000), EveryChild (£43,000), Meru (£28,000) and Debra (£23,000). Beneficiaries of smaller grants included Break, Chicks, Delta, Disability Challengers, Lisa Thaxter Trust, Martin House (£5,000 each).

Applications In writing to the correspondent including latest set of audited financial statements. The trustees usually meet quarterly.

Mrs Waterhouse Charitable Trust

Medical, health, welfare, environment, wildlife, churches, heritage

£254,000 (2002/03)

Beneficial area UK, with an interest in Lancashire.

25 Clitheroe Road, Whalley, Clitheroe BB7 9AD

Correspondent D H Dunn, Trustee

CC Number 261685

Information available Information was provided by the trust.

General Support is given to organisations working in the Lancashire area or UK-wide. It mostly makes small recurrent grants towards core costs of small organisations to enable them to maintain and improve their services. Larger grants can also be made towards capital projects.

In 2002/03 the trust had assets of £5.2 million, which generated an income of £275,000. Grants were made to 61 organisations, including 59 recurrent grants from the previous year, and totalled £254,000. Grants included £106,000 to Lancashire charities and £40,000 to Lancashire branches of UK-wide organisations and were broken down as follows:

	No.	*Total*
Medical and health		
– general	13	£63,000
– research	10	£53,000
– children	8	£28,000
Welfare in the community		
– children	10	£32,000
– people who are deaf or blind	5	£19,000
– general	6	£14,000
Environment and wildlife	5	£21,000
Church and heritage	4	£24,000

The largest grants were £15,000 to Whalley Abbey Restoration Fund and £10,000 each to Christie Hospital NHS Trust, East Lancashire Hospice Fund and National Trust for the Lake District Appeal. Marie Curie Cancer Care and Macmillan Cancer Relief both received £8,000. Grants of £5,000 each were made to 20 organisations which included Arthritis Research Campaign, Mary Cross Trust, Down's Syndrome Association, Fight for Sight and Leukaemia Research Fund.

Beneficiaries of smaller grants included Accrington and District Blind Society, After Adoption, Brainwave, East Lancashire Scout Council, I-Can, Friends of the Lake District, Mencap, Mires Beck Nursery and Salvation Army – Blackburn Citadel.

Exclusions No grants to individuals.

Applications In writing to the correspondent. There is no set time for the consideration of applications, but donations are normally made in March each year.

G R Waters Charitable Trust 2000

General

£186,000 (1999/2000)

Beneficial area UK. Also North and Central America.

Finers Stephens Innocent, 179 Great Portland Street, London W1W 5LS

Tel. 020 7323 4000 **Fax** 020 7344 7689

Correspondent Michael Lewis

CC Number 1091525

Information available Full accounts (for the previous trust) were on file at the Charity Commission.

General This trust was registered with the Charity Commission in 2002, replacing Roger Waters 1989 Charitable Trust (Charity Commission number 328574), which transferred its assets to this new trust. (The 2000 in the title refers to when the declaration of trust was made.) Like the former trust, it receives a share of Pink Floyd's royalties as part of its annual income. It has general charitable purposes throughout the UK, as well as North and Central America.

The following financial information (as well as the list of trustees) refer to the former, now extinct, trust. As the new trust stated that it will work in exactly the same manner as the one it has replaced, it can be assumed it is typical of how this trust will operate.

In 1999/2000 the trust had assets of £734,000. Total income was £68,000, including £45,000 as a share of the band's income. Grants were made to 20 organisations totalling £186,000.

The largest grant was £100,000 to Rhys Daniels Trust, a regular beneficiary. Ovingdean Hall School received £25,000. Other large grants were US$10,000 each to Barbados Welfare Charities, Millennium Kids Foundation and Robin Hood Foundation and £5,000 each to Chicks, Dove Cottage Day Hospice, Happy Days Children's Charity, NSPCC and React.

Other beneficiaries included Croydon Playcare Company (£3,000 in three grants), Lambourn Open Day and Racing Welfare Charities (£2,000 each), Louise Gibson Medical Fund (£1,800), Morley School (£1,000) and Young Vic Company (£500).

Applications In writing to the correspondent.

Blyth Watson Charitable Trust

General, UK based humanitarian organisations

£85,000 (2002/03)

Beneficial area UK.

50 Broadway, Westminster, London SW1H 0BL

Correspondent The Trustees

Trustees *Edward Nicholas William Brown; Ian Hammond McCulloch.*

CC Number 1071390

Information available Accounts were on file at the Charity Commission.

General The trust dedicates its grant-giving policy in the area of humanitarian causes based in the UK.

In 2002/03 the trust had assets of £84,500 and an income of £73,000. Grants totalled £84,500. There was no grants list available within the accounts.

Previous beneficiaries have included Seaford College, Brain Research Trust, Cancer BACUP, Development Foundation, Jessie May Trust, St John's Hospice, RUKBA, Brent Adolescent Centre, English Concert and Christina Noble Children's Foundation.

Applications In writing to the correspondent. Trustees usually meet twice during the year.

The Weavers' Company Benevolent Fund

Young people at risk from criminal involvement, young offenders and rehabilitation of prisoners and ex-prisoners

£145,000 (2001/02)

Beneficial area UK.

The Worshipful Company of Weavers', Saddlers' House, Gutter Lane, London EC2V 6BR

Tel. 020 7606 1155 **Fax** 020 7606 1119

Email charity@weaversco.co.uk

Correspondent John Snowdon, Clerk

Trustee *The Worshipful Company of Weavers.*

CC Number 266189

Information available Full accounts and a detailed report and grants list were made available by the trust, along with a copy of their *Guidelines for Applicants.*

General This benevolent fund was set up in 1973 with funds provided by the Worshipful Company of Weavers, the oldest of the City of London Livery Companies.

The company has selected three particular areas of need which it wishes to support and grants are mainly restricted to projects working within these categories. These are:

- young people who for any reason are at risk from criminal involvement
- young offenders
- the rehabilitation of prisoners and ex-prisoners.

The following advice is given to applicants:

- it only supports specific projects
- it does not provide long-term funding to any one organisation, and it would wish to be assured that all other possible sources of finance had been explored and that efforts were being made to obtain long-term funding from statutory and voluntary sources
- it prefers to support small or new, community-based organisations rather than long-established, large or national organisations, and to support projects where the company's grant would form a substantial part of the funds required
- it is particularly interested in innovative projects that are trying to get off the ground, that would be evaluated and that could act as a catalyst for other similar projects elsewhere
- it is willing to consider applications for equipment and capital projects, as well as salaries and running costs, subject to the overall policy not to provide long-term funding.

Grants ordinarily range from £5,000 to £15,000, but the trust states that it welcomes applications for smaller amounts from small or new organisations.

In 2001/02 the trust had assets of £4.6 million, an income of £225,000 and made grants totalling £145,000.

Grant beneficiaries included HMYOI Portland–Resettlement Workshops 2nd Year (£15,000), New Horizon Youth Centre–ICT Programme (£8,100), Foundation Training Company, The HMP and YOI Styal in Cheshire (£6,000), Centre for Crime and Justice Studies (CCJS) (£5,800) and Fakenham Baptist Church–The Ekklesia Project, HMYOI Portland–Training Projects Year 2 and Inside Out Trust–Training Projects in HMYOI Portland Year 2 (£5,000 each).

Exclusions No grants to individuals, or to non-registered charities – unless they are intending to apply for charitable status. Grants are not normally made in response to general appeals from large, well-established charities whose work does not fall within one of the company's chosen areas of interest.

It does not often support central or umbrella bodies, but prefers assisting projects directly working in its chosen fields.

It is not the company's policy to provide for running costs or deficit funding for established projects, nor to provide grants to replace start-up funding provided by other statutory or charitable funds.

Applications Detailed *Guidelines for Applicants* are available from the trust and applicants are urged to obtain these before making any appeal.

Applicants should write in the first instance to the correspondent with details of their requirements and include a set of their most recent accounts. If an application is accepted for further consideration, an application form will be issued. Before an application goes to the trustees an assessment visit is always made. The company uses its own members, who live throughout the country, to do this. The trustees meet three times a year in February, June and October. Applications may be submitted at any time and will be put to the next appropriate committee. 'Applicants should take into account the time it takes to process an application, raise queries and organise an assessment visit.'

Successful applicants are required to provide regular reports on progress.

Webb Memorial Trust

Higher education (particularly economic and social sciences), the furthering of democracy and human rights, and development in Eastern Europe

About £30,000 to organisations

Beneficial area UK and Eastern Europe.

Mount Royal, Allendale Road, Hexham, Northumberland NE46 2NJ

Fax 01434 601846

Correspondent Michael J Parker, Honorary Secretary

Trustees *M D Bailey; D Gladwin; D Hayter; J Miller; M J Parker; R N Rawes.*

CC Number 313760

Information available Information was provided by the trust.

General This trust was set up to run a conference centre for the 'advancement of education and learning with respect to the history and problems of government and social policy'. In the 1950s and 1960s it became an important base for education and discussion for bodies such as the Fabian Society and many trade unions. However, following the decline in demand for such a facility, the trust decided to sell the house; the proceeds provided the funds for the trust's present grant-making activities.

The trust's grants policy reflects its original values and grants are made in the areas of higher education (particularly economic and social sciences), the furthering of democracy and human rights, and development in Eastern Europe. Grants are made to both individuals and universities. Other projects can also be supported, 'including international conferences and think tanks to increase the understanding of individuals and groups resident in Eastern Europe of democracy and how its institutions and political parties function and behave, as well as the development of social and economic policies within the UK'.

Beneficiaries have included Ruskin College, Fabian Society, Institute of Contemporary British History, Socialist Health Association, Transport 2000, Westminster Foundation for Democracy and Unison. Amounts awarded by the trust in the past have ranged between £500 and £10,000 for a single project.

The trust states that it distributes about £60,000 to £65,000 each year in grants, half of which goes towards funding students from Eastern Europe attending Ruskin College – Oxford to study courses relevant to the trust's objects. The rest goes on projects either within the UK or overseas in Europe.

Exclusions No grants in support of any political party.

Applications On a form available from the correspondent, outlining the nature of the project – costs, timing and how the project fits in with the trust's objectives as outlined above. Applications for grants in the trust's financial year, which begins on 1 August, must be submitted by 31 January in the previous financial year (i.e. in the same calendar year). A copy of your latest annual report and accounts should be submitted with the application form.

The Mary Webb Trust

General

£68,000 (2002/03)

Beneficial area UK and overseas.

Cherry Cottage, Hudnall Common, Berkhamsted HP4 1QN

Correspondent Mrs C M Nash, Trustee

Trustees *Martin Ware; Mrs Jacqueline Fancett; Mrs Cherry Nash.*

CC Number 327659

Information available Accounts were provided by the trust.

General The trust states that it generally supports only smaller charities and will continue to do so. In 2002/03 the trust had assets of £676,000 generating an income of £24,000. Grants totalled £68,000.

The trust broke down its grant giving as follows:

	2002/03	*2001/02*
Health	£17,000	£17,000
Social Services	£14,000	£15,000
Environment	£11,000	£10,000
International	£11,000	£8,000
Culture & recreation	£7,000	£8,000
Religion	£5,000	£5,000
Education & research	£4,000	£3,000

Beneficiaries included The National Trust for Bre Pen (£5,000), NSRA for Apeldoorn Blind Shooting (£4,000), Fenland Archaeological Trust (£2,000) and Jubilee Appeal for Commenwealth Veterans (£1,000). Grants below £1,000 were distributed to 211 various other charities.

Exclusions No grants to individuals or non-registered charities.

Applications The trust's annual report says that the trustees are: 'concerned by the large number of appeals received during the year. They prefer to make their own enquiries and find it difficult to handle the large volume of documents and unsolicited accounts sent to them'. Trustees normally meet quarterly, in March, May, August and December; applications need to be received by the month prior to the trustees' meeting.

The Weinberg Foundation

General

£242,000 (2002/03)

Beneficial area UK and overseas.

2nd Floor , Manfield House, 1 Southampton Street, London WC2R 0LR

Tel. 020 7845 7500

Correspondent N A Steinberg

Trustees *N H Ablitt; C L Simon.*

CC Number 273308

Information available Accounts were on file at the Charity Commission, but without a list of grants or a narrative report.

General In 2002/03 the trust had assets of £1.6 million, which generated an income of £62,000. Grants were made totalling £242,000.

The last accounts to contain such information were those for 1996, when grants ranged from £150 to £10,000, although they were mostly for £500 or less. The grants list showed many health and welfare charities as well as numerous Jewish charities amongst its varied beneficiaries.

Applications In writing to the correspondent.

The Weinstein Foundation

Jewish, medical, welfare

£116,000 (2001/02)

Beneficial area Worldwide.

32 Fairholme Gardens, Finchley, London N3 3EB

Tel. 020 8346 1257

Correspondent M L Weinstein, Trustee

Trustees *E Weinstein; Mrs S R Weinstein; M L Weinstein; P D Weinstein; Mrs L A F Newman.*

CC Number 277779

Information available Full accounts were on file at the Charity Commission.

General This trust mostly supports Jewish organisations, although it does have general charitable purposes and supports a wide range of other causes, notably medical-related charities.

In 2001/02 the foundation had assets of £1.4 million with an income of £46,000 and grants totalling £116,000.

The largest grants were £25,000 to Beis Hrucha, £10,000 to British Friends of Laniado Hospital, £9,000 to Chevras Ezras Nitzroehim Trust, £7,500 to Friends of Mir, £5,000 to Woodstock Sinclair Charitable Trust and £3,000 to Chesed Charitable Trust.

Grants of less than £1,000 include Ahavas Chesed, Ahavas Yisrael Synagogue, Alzheimers Foundation, Baer Hatorah Ltd, Barnardo's, Boys Tower Jerusalem, Bolton Village, Bristol University Library, British Friends of Shaare Zedek, British Friends of the Israel Guide Dogs Centre, British Heart Foundation, British Lung Foundation, CMZ, Craven Walk Charitable Trust, CST, Delaville Ltd, English National Opera, Gesher, Golders Charitable Trust, Hagers, Hendon Synagogue, Jewish Care, Jewish Child's Day, Jewish Institute for the Blind, Jewish Marriage Council, Lepra, London Jewish Academy, Marie Curie Cancer Care, Mind, National Autistic Society, National Deaf Children's Society, NSPCC, Rav Chesed Trust, St. John's Ambulance, Talmuid Torah Tashbar, Tiferes Shlomo, United Jewish Israel Appeal, World Jewish Relief, Youth Aliyah and ZSV Trust.

Exclusions No grants to individuals.

Applications In writing to the correspondent.

The Weinstock Fund

General

£260,000 (2002/03)

Beneficial area Unrestricted, but with some local interest in the Wiltshire and Newbury area.

PO Box 17734, London SW18 3ZQ

Correspondent Miss Jacqueline Elstone

Trustees *Susan Lacroix; Michael Lester; Laura Weinstock.*

CC Number 222376

Information available Annual report and accounts were provided by the trust.

General In 2002/03 the fund had assets of £8.1 million and an income of £335,000. Grants totalled £260,000, with the beneficary of the largest grant being Seven Springs Foundation which received £20,000. Other beneficiaries included United Jewish Israel Appeal and Friends of the Ravenna Festival (£10,000 each); National Society for Epilepsy (£7,000); Institute for Policy Research (£6,000); Cystic Fibrosis Trust, Friends of the Hebrew University, Royal National Theatre, and Worldwide Fund for Nature (£5,000 each); and Blind in Business (£3,000).

Exclusions No grants to individuals or unregistered organisations.

Applications In writing to the correspondent. There are no printed details or applications forms. Previous information received stated 'Where nationwide charities are concerned, the trustees prefer to make donations centrally.' Donations can only be made to registered charities, and details of the registration number are required before any payment can be made.

The James Weir Foundation

Welfare, education, general

£162,000 (2002)

Beneficial area UK, with a preference for Ayrshire and Glasgow.

84 Cicada Road, London SW18 2NZ

Tel. 020 8870 6233 **Fax** 020 8870 6233

Correspondent Louisa Lawson, Secretary

Trustees *Simon Bonham; William J Ducas; Elizabeth Bonham.*

CC Number 251764

Information available Accounts were on file at the Charity Commission.

General The foundation has general charitable purposes, giving priority to schools and educational institutions; Scottish organisations, especially local charities in Ayrshire and Glasgow; and charities with which either James Weir or the trustees are particularly associated. These preferences, however, do not appear to be at the expense of other causes, UK-wide charities or local organisations outside of Scotland. The following six charities are listed in the trust deed as potential beneficiaries:

The Royal Society

The British Association for Advancement of Science

The RAF Benevolent Fund

The Royal College of Surgeons

The Royal College of Physicians

The University of Strathclyde.

In 2003 the trust had an income of £172,000 and a total expenditure of £177,000. Further details from this year were not available.

In the previous year the trust had assets of £4.7 million and an income of £168,000. Grants ranging from £250 to £3,000 were made to 85 organisations and totalled £162,000.

The largest grants were for £3,000 each, given to the six organisations listed in the trust deed. Grants of £2,000 each went to 66 organisations, including Age

Concern – Scotland, Barnardos, Capacity Scotland, David Tolkien Trust for Stoke Mandeville, I Can, Listening Books, Meningitis Trust, Roses Charitable Trust, Sargent Cancer Care for Children in Scotland and Winton's Wish.

Exclusions Grants are given to recognised charities only. No grants to individuals.

Applications In writing to the correspondent. Distributions are made twice-yearly in June and November when the trustees meet. Applications should be received by May or October.

The Barbara Welby Trust

Animal welfare, medical, general

£31,000 (2002/03)

Beneficial area UK, with a small preference for Lincolnshire.

9 New Square, Lincoln's Inn, London WC2A 3QN

Tel. 0207 412 0050 **Fax** 020 7421 4850

Email legal@dawsons-legal.com

Correspondent C N Robertson

Trustees *N J Barker; C W H Welby; C N Robertson.*

CC Number 252973

Information available Full accounts were provided by the trust.

General The trust states that it considers supporting a range of charities but has a preference for those of which the founder had special knowledge and for charities which have objects of which she was especially associated. This was not defined any further by the trust, but from the list of grant beneficiaries it would appear that support is given mainly to animal welfare and medical charities. A number of beneficiaries were based in Lincolnshire.

In 2002/03 it had assets of £673,000, which generated an income of £35,000. Grants were made to 38 organisations totalling £31,000. A payment of £6,100 was made to a firm of solicitors one of the trustees is a partner in. Whilst wholly legal, these editors always regret such payments unless, in the words of the Charity Commission, 'there is no realistic alternative'.

The largest grant, of £3,500, went to Lincoln Cathedral Fabric Fund. Grants of £1,000 each went to 17 organisations, including CAFOD, Children's Brain Tumour Research, De Paul Trust, Kesteven Children in Need, Ponies Association – UK, St Luke's Hospital for the Clergy, St Matthews' Church Restoration Appeal, Strut and Wytham Hall.

Grants of £500 each went to 20 organisations including Action for Kids, Brooke Hospital for Animals, Colesterworth PCC, FRAME, Jubilee Sailing Trust, King's School New Trust, PHAB, St Barnabas' Hospice, St John Ambulance, Salvation Army and Samaritans – Grantham.

Exclusions Applications for individual assistance are not normally considered unless made through an established charitable organisation.

Applications In writing at any time to the above address, although the trustees meet to consider grants in March and October.

The Weldon UK Charitable Trust

Major arts-related projects

£69,000 (2000)

Beneficial area UK.

4 Grosvenor Place, London SW1X 7HJ

Tel. 020 7235 6146 **Fax** 020 7235 3081

Correspondent J M St J Harris, Trustee

Trustees *J M St J Harris; H J Fritze.*

CC Number 327497

Information available Full accounts were on file at the Charity Commission.

General In 2002 the trust had assets of £9,000, an income of £30,000 and a total expenditure of £149,000.

Previous beneficiaries have included Royal Opera House Theatre, Yehudi Menuhin School, National Portrait Gallery, Royal College of Music Development Fund, B'nac B'rith Leo Baeck (London) Lodge Trust Funds and Great Ormond Street Children's Hospital.

Exclusions No grants to individuals.

Applications In writing to the correspondent, although the trust stated that it is fully committed with existing projects.

The Wesleyan Charitable Trust

General

£61,000 (2003/04)

Beneficial area Some preference for the Midlands.

Colmore Circus, Birmingham B4 6AR

Tel. 0121 200 9050 **Fax** 0121 200 9779

Email ian.farquharson@wesleyan.co.uk

Correspondent The Secretary to the Trustees

Trustees *Derek Byfield, Chair; Clive Ward; Raymond Lowe; Joe Roderick; Neil Boast; Miss Chris Gibbons.*

CC Number 276698

Information available Information was provided by the trust.

General The trust was set up in 1978 by the Wesleyan Assurance Society, a financial services company based in Birmingham. It is funded by the society on the basis of £200 for every £1 million of the society's total premium income each year, and the society also pays the trust's administration costs.

The trust particularly supports causes associated with the society's business, policyholders, staff and special local appeals 'considered to be of outstanding merit to the community'. Medical, health and welfare charities are often amongst the beneficiaries. Grants range from £50 to £15,000, although they are usually around £250.

In 2003/04 the trust had an income of £66,000. Grants totalled £61,000. Beneficiaries included Foundation for Conductive Education (£10,000), BBC Children in Need (£3,000), Dreamaway (£2,500), Teenage Cancer Trust (£2,000) and Birmingham Women's Hospital NHS Trust, Heartcare, Home-Start Winson Green, Insurance Charities, Sense and St Basil's (£1,000 each).

Applications In writing to the correspondent including accounts. The trustees meet quarterly.

The Earl & Countess of Wessex Charitable Trust

General

£127,000 (2001/02)

Beneficial area Worldwide.

Farrer & Co, 66 Lincoln's Inn Fields, London WC2A 3LH

Tel. 020 7242 2022

Correspondent Jenny Cannon

Trustees *Mark Foster-Brown; Abel Hadden; Denise Poulton; Sir Henry Boyd-Carpenter; Malcolm Cockren.*

CC Number 1076003

Information available Accounts on file at The Charity Commission

General This trust was established by Prince Edward and Sophie Rhys-Jones shortly after their marriage in 1999 and was initially named The Bagshot Park Charity after their Surrey home. It has general charitable purposes, although there are preferences for organisations working with young people, self-help organisations, applications that will open extra fundraising opportunities to the charity, as well as where the Earl or Countess of Wessex have a personal connection or interest. Most grants are one-off, although substantial grants may be made for up to five years.

In 2001/02 the trust had an assets of £242,000 and an income of £17,000. Grants totalled £127,000. A list of beneficiaries was unavailable.

Previous beneficiaries have included A R C Addington, Delta, East Anglia's Children's Hospices 2000, Family Heart Association, Four Lanes Regeneration Group, International Care and Relief, Learning for Life, London Narrow Boat Project, Northwick Park Hospital Children's Centre Appeal, Michael Palin Centre for Stammering Children, Royal Liverpool Philharmonic Society, Rural Stress Network, Sadler's Wells Trust, St George's School – Windsor Castle and Side by Side.

The accounts stated: 'The Charities [sic] Commission has been supplied with details of amounts given to each charity together with an explanation of the reasons for the non-disclosure of individual amounts in the financial statements.' Non-disclosure of grants information should only be made where the information being made public may be potentially harmful to the trust or its recipients; failing to disclose information without providing an explanation in the public sphere may prompt unjustified speculation about the nature of grants made.

Exclusions No grants are made to:

- non-registered charities or causes
- individuals, including to people who are undertaking fundraising activities on behalf of a charity
- organisations whose main objects are to fund or support other causes
- organisations whose accounts disclose substantial financial resources and that have well-established and ample fundraising capabilities
- fund research that can be supported by government funding or that is popular among trusts.

Applications In writing to the correspondent in the first instance. A response will be made within two weeks in the form of an application form and guidelines to eligible applicants or a letter of rejection if more appropriate. Completed forms, which are not acknowledged upon receipt, need to be submitted by 1 May or 1 November, for consideration by the end of the month. Clarity of presentation and provision of financial details are among the qualities which impress the trustees. Successful applicants will receive a letter stating that the acceptance of the funding is conditional on an update being received before the next meeting. The trust's criteria state other correspondence cannot be entered into, and organisations cannot reveal the size of any grants they receive.

West London Synagogue Charitable Fund

Jewish, general

£52,000 (2002)

Beneficial area UK.

33 Seymour Place, London W1H 5AU

Tel. 020 7723 4404

Email k.colton@wls.org.uk

Correspondent Mrs Kay Colton, Coordinator

Trustees *J Cutter; F Epstein; V Feather; Rabbi M Winer; S Gluckstein; J Green; L Heath; P Levy; D Segal; C Marx; S Raperport; J Regen; M Ross; A Stewart.*

CC Number 209778

Information available Accounts on file at the Charity Commission.

General The trust stated that it makes grants to both Jewish and non-Jewish organisations. In 2002 the trust had assets of £18,000, an income of £66,000 and made grants totalling £52,000.

Grant beneficiaries included Canine Partners for Independence, CHICKS and Shooting Star Trust (£7,500 each), Synagogue (The) (£5,000), Berkeley Street Club and Rabbi Winer's Discretionary Fund (£2,000 each), Norwood (£1,500), Kehillah Kol Haneshama and UJIA (£1,000) and Akiva School (£500).

Exclusions No grants to individuals.

Applications In writing to the correspondent.

Mrs S K West's Charitable Trust

General

£30,000 (2002/03)

Beneficial area UK.

Davies & Crane Chartered Accountants, 5 Winckley Street, Preston PR1 2AA

Tel. 01772 253656 **Fax** 01772 202511

Correspondent P J Schoon, Trustee

Trustees *P Schoon; Chris Blakeborough; J Grandage.*

CC Number 294755

Information available Information available about this trust was limited.

General In 2002/03 the trust had assets of £433,000 with an income of £35,000 and grants totalling £30,000.

Grants include £9,000 to Tear Fund, £6,000 to Churchfields Hall, £2,000 each to BLESMA, Holme Christian Care Centre, Otley Meeting Room and Preston School Children's Fund and £1,000 each to Age Concern, Barnardo's, Bible Society, NSPCC, Salvation Army, Save the Children and Shaftesbury Society.

Applications The trust states that it does not respond to unsolicited applications.

The Westcroft Trust

International understanding, overseas aid, Quaker, Shropshire

£92,000 (2002/03)

Beneficial area Unrestricted, but with a special interest in Shropshire – causes of local interest outside Shropshire are rarely supported.

32 Hampton Road, Oswestry, Shropshire SY11 1SJ

Correspondent Mary Cadbury, Managing Trustee

CC Number 212931

Information available Full accounts were provided by the trust.

General Currently the trustees have five main areas of interest:

- international understanding, including conflict resolution and the material needs of the developing world
- religious causes, particularly social outreach, usually of the Society of Friends (Quakers) but also for those originating in Shropshire
- development of the voluntary sector in Shropshire
- needs of people with disabilities, primarily in Shropshire
- development of community groups and reconciliation between different cultures in Northern Ireland.

Medical education is only helped by support for expeditions overseas that include pre-clinical students. Medical aid, education and relief work in developing countries is mainly supported through UK-registered organisations. International disasters may be helped in response to public appeals.

The trust favours charities with low administrative overheads and that pursue clear policies of equal opportunity in meeting need. Grants may be one-off or recurrent; recurrent grants are rarely made for endowment or capital projects.

In 2002/03 it had assets of £1.8 million, which generated an income of £101,000. Grants were made totalling £92,000, broken down as follows:

Religious Society of Friends

Central Committees – 1 grant of £6,300

This went to Britain Yearly Meeting

Meeting Houses – 9 grants totalling £4,500

These were of £500 each and went to meeting houses in Aberystwyth, Barnsley, Bradford on Avon, Chesterfield, Harrington Grove, North Somerset and Wiltshire, Stourbridge, Pontefract and Watford.

Other funds, institutions and appeals – 13 grants totalling £11,000

The largest were £2,400 to Northern Friends Peace Board, £1,200 to Woodbrooke and £1,000 each to The Retreat – York and World Gathering of Young Friends. Others included £820 to Friends World Committee for Consultation, £780 to Quaker Peace Centre – Cape Town, £500 to Friends House Moscow, £400 to Quaker Social Action and £300 to Quaker Council for European Affairs.

Shropshire

Social Service in the county – 21 grants totalling £11,000

HOAP received two payments totalling £1,500. Other beneficiaries included Community Council of Shropshire and Home-Start North Shropshire and Oswestry (£1,000 each), Shropshire Youth Adventure Trust (£750), Citizen Advocacy (£600), West Midlands Rural Support Network (£500), Willowdene Farm (£450), Macintyre Charitable Trust (£350), Rainbow Nursery (£300), Cruse Bereavement Care – Shropshire (£280) and Shrewsbury Prison Chaplaincy (£180).

Education in the county – 2 grants totalling £550

These went to Second Chance – Oswestry (£420) and Shropshire Playbus (£130).

Disability, health and special needs – 7 grants totalling £4,500

These went to Robert Jones and Agnes Hunt Orthopaedic Hospital for a therapeutic swimming pool (£2,000), Macmillan Cancer Relief – Shropshire (£580), Hope House and Vision Homes Association (£550), Headway Shropshire (£350), No Panic (£270) and RSH Hummingbird Appeal (£250).

Medical and surgical

Research – 5 grants totalling £3,300

Recipients were Institute of Orthopaedics (£890), Remedi (£860), Liverpool School of Tropical Medicine (£660), Staffordshire University (£540) and Pain Relief Foundation (£390).

National

Disabilities and special needs – 7 grants totalling £4,200

By far the largest grant was £2,000 to British Epilepsy Association. Other beneficiaries were Mobility Information Service and Re-Solv (£480 each), SANDS (£400), Disability Aid Fund (£350), Cancer Bacup (£280) and Sequal Trust (£220).

Social Services (England, Wales and Scotland) – 9 grants totalling £5,100

The largest grant was £1,900 to Hoxton Hall. Other beneficiaries included London Connection (£610), Toynbee Hall (£520), Campus and Craven Citizen's Advice (£500 each), Two Saints (£270), Walton Prison Chaplaincy Fund (£250) and Liverpool One Parent Families (£220).

Social Services (Northern Ireland) – 5 grants totalling £2,400

These were £550 to Positive Ethos Trust, £500 each to action for Children in Conflict, Nexus – Ireland and Western Enterprise, Social, Legal and Educational Victims Trust and £350 to Cornerstone Community.

Overseas

Medical aid – 19 grants totalling £11,000

Beneficiaries included ChildHope and World Medical Fund (£1,000 each), Fourth World Action and Friends of the Centre for the Rehabilitation of the Paralysed (£750 each), Impact Foundation (£610), Orbis International (£590), Kings World Trust for Children and Operation Smile (£500 each), British Palawan Trust (£450), Marie Stopes International (£400) and Mission Romania (£350).

Education – 11 grants totalling £8,700

The largest were £2,500 to Budiriro Trust and £1,400 to Canon Collins Trust. Other recipients included Karuna Trust (£750), Harambee Educational Fund (£560), Books Abroad and Uganda Development Services (£500) and British Friends of Neve Shalom and Friends of Students' Education Trust (£400 each).

Relief work – 12 grants totalling £9,000

UNICEF received three grants totalling £2,400, including £1,000 each for the Children of Iraq Emergency Appeal and Malawi Famine Appeal. Other large grants went to Oxfam (£2,000), Miriam Dean Trust Fund (£1,100) and DEC South Africa Famine (£1,000). Smaller grants included £610 to Save the Children, £500 to Calcutta Rescue Fund, £380 to Village Service Trust and £250 to Anglo-Peruvian Child Care Mission.

International understanding – 12 grants totalling £10,000

By far the largest grant was £5,000 to University of Bradford Department of Peace Studies. Other recipients included Medical Foundation for the Victims of Torture (£780), Development Education Project (£660), Kurdish Human Rights Project and Survival for Tribal People (£500 each), Irish School of Ecumenics and World Development Movement Trust (£350 each) and Anti-Slavery International (£320).

Exclusions Grants are given to charities only. No grants to individuals or for medical electives, sport, the arts (unless specifically for people with disabilities in Shropshire) or armed forces charities. Requests for sponsorship are not supported. Annual grants are withheld if recent accounts are not available or do not satisfy the trustees as to continuing need.

Applications In writing to the correspondent. There is no application form or set format but applications should be restricted to a maximum of three sheets of paper, stating purpose, overall financial needs and resources together with previous years' accounts if appropriate. Printed letters signed by 'the great and good' and glossy literature do not impress the trustees, who prefer lower-cost applications. Applications are dealt with about every two months. No acknowledgement will be given. Replies to relevant but unsuccessful applicants will be sent only if a self-addressed envelope is enclosed. As some annual grants are made by Bank Telepay, details of bank name, branch, sort code, and account name and number should be sent in order to save time and correspondence.

The Whitaker Charitable Trust

Education, environment, music, personal development

£203,000 (2001/02)

Beneficial area UK, but mostly east Midlands, Northern Ireland and Scotland, particularly Bassetlaw.

c/o Currey & Co., 21 Buckingham Gate, London SW1E 6LB

Tel. 020 7828 4091

Correspondent Edward Perks, Trustee

Trustees *Edward Ronald Haslewood Perks; David W J Price; Lady Elizabeth Jane Ravenscroft Whitaker.*

CC Number 234491

Information available Accounts were provided by the trust.

General The trust has general charitable objects, although with stated preferences for music education, agricultural and silvicultural education, countryside conservation, spiritual matters and prison-related charities.

Grants are made to UK-wide organisations and local organisations in Scotland, Northern Ireland and Nottinghamshire and the east Midlands, with a large number of grants made in Bassetlaw.

In 2001/02 the trust had assets of £5.8 million, which generated an income of £209,000. Grants to 92 organisations totalled £203,000.

A substantial grant of £65,000 was made to Atlantic College. The next largest grants were £15,000 to Marlborough College and £12,000 to Bramcote School Limited. Remaining donations were mainly in the range of £500 to £2,000.

Beneficiaries in Bassetlaw included Focus on Bassetlaw Hospice, Bassetlaw Mencap and Youth in Bassetlaw (£2,000 each) and Bassetlaw CVS (£500). Other beneficiaries in the east Midlands included University of Nottingham (£5,000), Lincoln Cathedral Fabric Fund, Lincolnshire & Nottinghamshire Air Ambulance (£1,000), Mansfield Counselling and Nottinghamshire Community Transport (£1,000 each) and Nottinghamshire Bereavement Trust (£500).

Scottish beneficiaries included Leith School of Art (£3,000) and Game Conservancy Scottish Research Trust (£2,000).

Other recipients included Georgian Theatre (£2,500), Portland College (£2,000), Prison Phoenix Trust (£1,500), NSPCC and Winged Fellowship Trust (£1,000 each) and InKind Direct and Prison Arts Foundation (£500 each).

Exclusions Support is given to registered charities only. No grants are given to individuals or for the repair or maintenance of individual churches.

Applications In writing to the correspondent. Trustees meet half-yearly. Applications should include clear details of the need the intended project is designed to meet plus a copy of the latest accounts available and an outline budget. If an acknowledgement of the application, or notification in the event of the application not being accepted, is required, an sae should be enclosed.

The Simon Whitbread Charitable Trust

Education, family welfare, medicine, preservation

£72,000 (2003/04)

Beneficial area UK, with a preference for Bedfordshire.

Hunters, 9 New Square, Lincoln's Inn, London WC2A 3RZ

Fax 020 7412 0049

Correspondent E C A Martineau, Administrator

Trustees *Mrs H Whitbread; S C Whitbread; E C A Martineau.*

CC Number 200412

Information available Information was provided by the trust.

General The trust supports general causes in Bedfordshire, and education, family welfare, medicine, medical research and preservation UK-wide.

In 2003/04 the trust had assets of £2.6 million and an income of £90,000. Grants were made to 43 organisations totalling £72,000.

By far the largest grant, of £15,000, went to Bedford School Foundation. The next largest were £5,000 each to Chellington Project and St Luke's Hospital for Clergy, £3,000 each to St Peter's PCC and Telephones for the Blind, £2,500 to Mencap, £2,000 each to Army Benevolent Fund, Bedfordshire and Luton Community NHS Trust, Family Welfare Trust, Iris Fund, St Albans DBF, St John Ambulance and Spurgeons Child Care and £1,500 to Bedfordshire Housing Association Centre and Philharmonia Orchestra.

Other beneficiaries included Defeating Deafness and Northwell PCC (£1,000 each), Mayday Trust (£900), Friendship Group – Bedford (£600), Bedfordshire Garden Carers, Lavendon Baptist Church and Toddington St George Lower School (£500 each), Full House Theatre Company (£400) and Rainbow School – Bromham.

Exclusions Generally no support for local projects outside Bedfordshire.

Applications In writing to the correspondent. Acknowledgements are not given. Please do NOT telephone.

The Colonel W H Whitbread Charitable Trust

Health, welfare, general

£131,000 (2003)

Beneficial area UK, with an interest in Gloucestershire.

Fir Tree Cottage, Worlds End, Sinton Green, Worcestershire WR2 6NN

Tel. 020 7593 5000 **Fax** 020 7593 5099

Correspondent Mrs S Clifford-Smith

Trustees *M W Whitbread; J J Russell; R H J Steel; H F Whitbread.*

CC Number 210496

Information available Full accounts were on file at the Charity Commission.

General This trust has general charitable purposes in the UK. Although the trust does not have a stated policy, there is a particular emphasis on supporting applications from Gloucestershire. To keep administration costs low, the minimum grant the trust makes is £500. In some instances, more than one grant is made to an organisation in a year.

In 2003 the trust had assets of £5 million, which generated an income of £166,000. Grants were made to organisations totalling £131,000.

The largest grant was £12,000 in two payments to Household Cavalry Museum Appeal. Other recipients of larger grants were Breast Cancer Campaign and two payments each to Cheltenham & Gloucester Mencap Society and Gloucestershire Historic Churches Trust (£7,000 each), two payments to Noah's Ark Trust (£6,000), Burford Health Care Fund, County Air Ambulance, NSPCC and two payments to St John Ambulance (£5,000 each).

Other beneficiaries included Colbalt Unit Appeal Fund, Dyson Perrins School Friends Association and two payments to SCCWID (£3,000 each), British Red Cross, Halo Trust, Hunt Servent's Fund, Mark Davies' Injured Riders' Fund, Queen Mary's Clothing Guild, Royal Hospital for Neuro–Disability and SSAFA Forces Help (£2,000 each), two payments to Tree Aid (£1,500), Barnardo's, Battersea Dogs' Home, Elizabeth Finn Trust, Horseworld, Iris Fund, National Eye Research Centre, St. David's Foundation Hospice Care and Tommy's Baby Charity (£1,000 each) and Safehaven Parrot Refuge and Second Chances (£500 each).

Applications In writing to the correspondent. Trustees meet quarterly. Please note, successful applicants must cash their cheques within three months of receipt or, unless there are special circumstances, it is the trust's policy to cancel the cheque.

The Whitecourt Charitable Trust

Christian, general

£49,000 (2003/04)

Beneficial area UK and overseas, with a preference for Sheffield.

48 Canterbury Avenue, Fulwood, Sheffield S10 3RU

Tel. 0114 230 5555

Correspondent Mrs P W Lee, Trustee

Trustees *P W Lee; Mrs G W Lee; M P W Lee.*

CC Number 1000012

Information available Information was provided by the trust.

General Most of the grants given by the trust are recurrent and to Christian causes in the UK and overseas. Other grants are given to a few Christian and welfare causes in Sheffield.

In 2003/04 the trust had assets of £475,000 and an income of £51,000. Grants were made totalling £49,000

As in previous years a total of £10,000 was made to Christ Church Fulwood. Other large grants went to South Yorkshire Community Foundation (£10,000), Sheffield Cathedral Development Appeal (£2,500), Church Mission Society, Elam Ministries UK, Iran Earthquake Appeal and Sheffield Family Service Unit (£1,000 each).

All other beneficiaries received grants of £750 or less. Recipients included: Scripture Union, Frontier Youth Trust, Buxton Festival, Church Pastoral Aid Society, Greenhouse Trust, Jubilee Centre, Teen Ranch – Scotland, Oakes Trust, Yorkshire Cadet Corps and Youth for Christ.

Exclusions No support for animal or conservation organisations or for campaigning on social issues.

Applications In writing to the correspondent, at any time. However, the trust states very little money is available for unsolicited applications, due to advance commitments.

A H and B C Whiteley Charitable Trust

Art, environment, general

£78,000 (2001/02)

Beneficial area England, Scotland and Wales, with a special interest in Nottinghamshire.

Marchants, Regent Chambers, Regent Street, Mansfield, Nottinghamshire NG18 1SW

Tel. 01623 655111

Correspondent E G Aspley, Trustee

Trustees *E G Aspley; K E B Clayton.*

CC Number 1002220

Information available Full accounts were on file at the Charity Commission.

General The trust was established in 1990 and derives most of its income from continuing donations. The trust deed requires the trustees to make donations to registered charities in England, Scotland, and Wales but with particular emphasis on charities based in Nottinghamshire. Beneficiaries are varied, but the largest grant (which typically accounts for around 50% of the funds) usually goes to The Victoria and Albert Museum.

In 2003/04 the trust had an income of £43,000 and a total expenditure of £29,000. Further information for this year was unavailable.

In 2001/02 it had assets of £1.3 million and an income of £57,000, including £7,600 in donations received. Grants were made to 11 organisations totalling £78,000.

Beneficiaries were Hardwick Hall Trust and Portland College (£15,000 each), RNIB (£9,700), Terry Marsh Bird Rescue (£7,300), Mansfield and District Group

Cats Protection League (£6,000), Dr Kesham's Hospice, Liverpool Old Hebrew Congregation for Princes Road Synagogue and North West Cancer Research Fund (£5,000 each), Ravenshead Day Centre (£3,700) and St Paul's Trust Centre and Sherwood Forest Hospitals Charitable Fund (£3,000 each).

Applications The trust does not seek applications.

The Norman Whiteley Trust

Evangelical Christianity, welfare, education

£208,000 to organisations and individuals (2001/02)

Beneficial area Worldwide, although in practice mainly Cumbria.

Lane Cove, Grassgarth Lane, Ings, Cumbria LA8 9QF

Correspondent D Foster

Trustees *Mrs B M Whiteley; P Whiteley; D Dickson; J Ratcliff.*

CC Number 226445

Information available Full accounts were on file at the Charity Commission.

General This trust supports the furtherance of the Gospel, the relief of poverty and education. Grants can be made worldwide, but in practice are usually restricted to Cumbria and the surrounding areas.

In 2001/02 the trust had assets of £2 million, an income of £137,000 and made grants to organisations and individuals totalling £208,000.

There were 29 grants made to organisations in the year, of which 20 had been supported in the previous year. The largest grants were £50,000 to Bethsan Sheltered Housing Association, £23,000 to Osterreichische Allianz Evangelische, £16,000 to Kindersingkrien, £12,000 to Baptisten Gemeinde and £10,000 to Sport Reach.

Other beneficiaries included Millom Methodist Church (£9,000), Potteries Trust (£5,000), Littledale Trust (£3,000), Kendal Methodist Church (£1,000).

Exclusions Whilst certain overseas organisations are supported, applications from outside of Cumbria are not accepted.

Applications In writing to the correspondent. Trustees meet to consider applications twice a year.

The Whitley Animal Protection Trust

Protection and conservation of animals and their environments

£340,000 (2002)

Beneficial area UK and overseas, with a preference for Scotland.

Edgbaston House, Walker Street, Wellington, Telford, Shropshire TF1 1HF

Tel. 01952 641651 **Fax** 01952 247441

Email info@gwynnes.com

Correspondent Paul Rhodes

Trustees *E Whitley, Chair; Mrs P A Whitley; E J Whitley; J Whitley.*

CC Number 236746

Information available Full accounts were on file at the Charity Commission.

General This trust supports the prevention of cruelty to animals and the promotion of their conservation and environment. Grants are made throughout the UK and the rest of world, with about 20% of funds given in Scotland.

In 2002 the trust had assets of £7.5 million with an income of £365,000 and grants totalling £340,000.

Substantial grants were £125,000 to Whitley Laing Foundation, £60,000 to Fauna & Flora International, £30,000 to Shropshire Wildlife Trust and £20,000 to Edinburgh Zoo.

Other grants include £15,000 to The Wildlife Conservation Research Unit of the Department of Zoology in the University of Oxford and £10,000 each to Orangutan Foundation, Scottish Wildlife Trust and Tweed Foundation.

Grants of £5,000 were awarded to Western Isles Fisheries Trust, Wester Ross Fisheries Trust, Argyle Fisheries Trust, Galloway Fisheries Trust, West Sutherland Fisheries Trust, Ayrshire Rivers Trust, Lochaber & District Fisheries Trust, Clyde River Foundation, Eden Rivers Trust and RSPB Scotland.

Smaller grants include £4,000 to National Great Dane Rescue, £2,500 each to Deveron Bogie Isla and Wye & Usk Foundation and £1,000 to Pet Savers.

Exclusions No grants to non-registered charities.

Applications In writing to the correspondent. The correspondent stated: 'The trust honours existing commitments and initiates new ones through its own contacts rather than responding to unsolicited applications.'

The Lionel Wigram Memorial Trust

General

£63,000 to organisations (2001/02)

Beneficial area UK, with a preference for Greater London.

Highfield House, 4 Woodfall Street, London SW3 4DJ

Tel. 020 7730 6820 **Fax** 020 7730 6822

Correspondent A F Wigram, Chair

Trustees *A F Wigram, Chair; Mrs S A Wigram.*

CC Number 800533

Information available Accounts were provided by the trust.

General The trust makes grants to a wide range of organisations. Its annual report for 2001/02 stated the trustees 'have particular regard to projects which will commemorate the life of Major Lionel Wigram who was killed in action in Italy in 1944.'

In 2001/02 the trust's assets totalled £138,000 and it had an income of £49,000, comprised mainly of rental income. Grants included £9,300 to WAACIS fund, a project controlled by the trust.

Other grants totalled £53,000 and were made to 49 organisations. The largest grants were £23,000 to U Can Do It, £2,000 to Deafblind UK, £1,900 to Ability Net and £1,000 each to Philharmonia Ltd, Play for Peace Fund and Listening Books.

The remaining grants were small and given to a range of organisations, such as World Wildlife Fund, Changing Faces, Caring for Carers and St John's Hospice and some individuals.

Applications In writing to the correspondent.

The Felicity Wilde Charitable Trust

Children, medical research

£127,000 (2002/03)

Beneficial area UK.

Barclays Bank Trust Company Ltd, Executorship & Trustee Service, PO Box 15, Northwich, Cheshire CW9 7UR

Correspondent Miss M Bertenshaw

Trustee *Barclays Bank Trust Co Ltd.*

CC Number 264404

Information available Information was provided by the trust.

General The trust supports children's charities and medical research, with particular emphasis on research into the causes or cures of asthma.

In 2002/03 it had an income of £73,000 and gave grants totalling £127,000 to 70 organisations. By far the largest grants went to Asthma UK, which received two grants of £25,000 each.

Aside from the £5,000 each to British Lung Foundation and Southampton University Development Trust, all the remaining grants were of £1,000 each. Recipients included Action on Addiction, Bobath – Glasgow, Breakthrough Breast Cancer, British Epilepsy Association, ChildLine, Children's Liver Disease Foundation, Darlington Association on Disability, East Anglia Children's Hospices, Home-Start Leicester, Honeypot Charity, Kids Out, Meningitis Research Foundation, National Back Pain Association, National Eczema Society, Shooting Star Trust Children's Hospice, Sparks, Starlight Children's Foundation, West Midlands Post Adoption Service and Who Cares? Trust.

Exclusions No grants to individuals or non-registered charities.

Applications In writing to the correspondent at any time. Applications are usually considered quarterly.

The Wilkinson Charitable Foundation

Scientific research, education

£66,000 (2002/03)

Beneficial area UK.

Lawrence Graham, 190 Strand, London WC2R 1JN

Tel. 020 7379 0000

Correspondent B D S Lock, Trustee

Trustees *B D S Lock; Dr Anne M Hardy.*

CC Number 276214

Information available Full accounts were on file at the Charity Commission.

General The trust was set up for the advancement of scientific knowledge and education at Imperial College, University of London and for general purposes. Grants are only given to academic institutions.

The trustees have continued their policy of supporting research and initiatives commenced in the founder's lifetime and encouraging work in similar fields to those he was interested in.

In 2002/03 the foundation had assets of £1 million and an income of £49,000 with grants totalling £66,000.

The main beneficiaries were £36,000 to Wolfson College (Research in the Department of Humanities), £12,000 to University College of London, £2,500 to Imperial College of Science, Technology & Medicine (Prostate Cancer Reaserch fund), £1,000 each to Wellbeing, Blonde Melndoe and British Heart Foundation and £500 to Glasgow Science Centre.

Exclusions No grants to individuals.

Applications In writing to the correspondent. Applications from individuals will not be considered.

The Kay Williams Charitable Foundation

Medical research, disability, general

About £37,000 (2002/03)

Beneficial area UK.

BDO Stoy Hayward, Kings Wharf, 20–30 Kings Road, Reading, Berkshire RG1 3EX

Tel. 0118 925 4400

Correspondent R M Cantor, Trustee

Trustees *R M Cantor; D W Graham; Mrs M C Williams.*

CC Number 1047947

Information available Accounts were on file at the Charity Commission.

General The trust was established in 1995 and generally has about £50,000 available to be given in grants.

In 2002/03 the trust had an income of £19,000 and assets of £622,000. Charitable expenditure totalled £36,500. Twenty-five grants were made during the year. The largest grant was £3,750 to Royal Opera House Trust and £3,100 to Cancer Research Campaign. There were 9 grants for £2,000 each including those to Action for Blind People, Help the Aged, Cancer Relief Macmillan Fund, ITGD, NCH Action for Children, The River Thames Boat, The Samaritans and World Cancer Research Fund.

There were 8 grants of £1,000, some of which were to BACUP-helping people live with cancer, Royal National Institute for Deaf People and Shooting Star Children's hospice, and grants between £100 and £750 were made to, for example, Richmond Concert Society and Royal Academy of Art.

Applications In writing to the correspondent.

Dame Violet Wills Charitable Trust

Evangelical Christianity

£71,000 (2001/02)

Beneficial area UK and overseas, but there may be a preference for Bristol.

Ricketts Cooper & Co., Thornton House, Richmond Hill, Bristol BS8 1AT

Tel. 0117 973 8441

Correspondent H E Cooper, Secretary and Treasurer

Trustees *D G Cleave, Chair; H E Cooper; A J G Cooper; S Burton; Dr D M Cunningham; J R Dean; Miss J R Guy; R Hill; G J T Landreth; R D Spear; A W Down; Mrs M J Lewis; Prof A H Linton; Rev Dr E C Lucas; Rev J A Motyer; Mrs R E Peskett.*

CC Number 219485

Information available Full accounts were on file at the Charity Commission.

General The trust continues to operate within the original terms of reference, supporting evangelical Christian activities both within the UK and overseas. It is not the practice of the trustees to guarantee long-term support to any work, however worthy. The trust does not make a practice of supplying funds to individuals or non-registered charities.

Current categories of Christian work for trustee consideration are:

- training and bursaries
- mission – UK
- missions – other countries
- literature
- broadcasts.

The 2001/02 accounts states 'whilst a vast number of appeals are received each year, grants are more likely to be made to those which are personally known to one or more of the trustees',

In 2000/01 the trust had assets of £1.4 million, which generated an income of £90,000. Grants totalled £71,000 with the largest grant being given to Western Countries and SWE Trust Evangelists (£12,500), Echoes of Service–Bristol Missionaries (£5,100), Christian Ministries for general purposes (£2,000), Bristol International Students Centre (£1,800), FEBA Radio–Specialised English Programmes (£1,700), Living Waters Radio Ministry and UCCF–Oxford Mission (£1,600 each), Open Air Campaigners–Bristol (£1,500) All Nations–Bursary Fund Overseas Students (£1,300), AWM Media (£1,200) and Church's Ministry Among Jewish People (£1,100).

Exclusions Grants are not given to individuals.

Applications In writing to the correspondent. The trust states 'whilst a vast number of appeals are received each year, grants are more likely to be made to those which are personally known to one or more of the trustees'. Trustees meet in March and in September.

Sumner Wilson Charitable Trust

General

£172,000 (2001/02)

Beneficial area UK.

Munslows, Mansfield House, 2nd Floor, 1 Southampton Street, London WC2R 0LR

Tel. 020 7845 7500

Correspondent N A Steinberg

Trustees *J G Joffe; A M W Wilson; M S Wilson.*

CC Number 1018852

Information available Accounts were on file at the Charity Commission.

General This trust had general charitable purposes, with no preferences or exclusions. In 2001/02 the trust had an income of £54,000 and a grant total of £172,000.

Applications In writing to the correspondent, or to the trustees.

The Benjamin Winegarten Charitable Trust

Jewish

£103,000 to individuals and organisations (2001/02)

Beneficial area UK.

25 St Andrew's Grove, Stoke Newington, London N16 5NF

Correspondent B A Winegarten, Trustee

Trustees *B A Winegarten; Mrs E Winegarten.*

CC Number 271442

Information available Accounts were on file at the Charity Commission, but without a list of grants.

General This trust makes grants for the advancement of the Jewish religion and religious education. In 2001/02 it had assets of £383,000 and an income of £143,000. Grants to individuals and organisations totalled £103,000. Further information for this year was not available.

In 1998/99 the trust's assets totalled £147,000 and it had an income of £74,000, from Gift Aid donations and rent. Grants to individuals totalled £8,600 and to organisations £49,000. The largest grants for the year were £10,000 to Hechal Hatovah Institute, £8,000 to Merkaz Lechinuch Torani Zichron Ya'akov, £5,000 each to The Jewish Educational Trust and Ohr Someach Friends, £4,000 to Yeshivo Hovomo Talmudical College, and £3,000 each to The Mechinah School, Or Akiva Community Centre and ZSVT.

Applications In writing to the correspondent.

This entry was not confirmed by the trust, but was correct according to information on file at the Charity Commission.

The Francis Winham Foundation

Welfare of older people

£651,000 (2001/02)

Beneficial area England.

41 Langton Street, London SW10 0JL

Tel. 020 7795 1261 **Fax** 020 7795 1262

Email francinetrust@btopenworld.com

Correspondent Mrs J Winham

Trustees *Francine Winham; Dr John Norcliffe Roberts; Gwendoline Winham; Josephine Winham.*

CC Number 278092

Information available Accounts on file at the Charity Commission.

General The foundation makes around 150 grants a year, mostly for amounts under £5,000 and which can be as low as £75. Grants are given to both national organisations (including their local branches) and local charities. Many organisations are regular recipients, although not necessarily on an annual basis.

In 2001/02 the trust had assets of £3 million and an income of £320,000. Grants were made to 164 organisations totalling £651,000. Some organisations received many payments during the year, which are likely to have gone to local branches. Only 25 organisations received more than £5,000 each. Of these, three received more than £20,000 each in total. These were Age Concern (£73,500 in 45 donations), Care and Repair (£46,500 in 40 donations) and SSAFA (£22,000 in 25 donations).

Other beneficiaries of larger amounts included Camden Housebound Link Services (£17,500), Anchor Staying Put (£13,500), Electrical and Electronics Industries Benevolent Association (£12,000), Grimsby Agewell, Help the Hospice and Stroke Association (£10,000 each), and Jewish Care, Mast and Research into Ageing (£8,000 each).

Recipients of more typical grants in the £500 to £5,000 range included Activities for Blind People, Bentilee Volunteers, Burnley, Pendle & Rossendale CVS, Care Fund, Cleveland Volunteers Project, Cumbria Message in a Bottle Scheme, Devonshire Institute, Garfield Community Centre, Hartlepool District Hospice, Leicester Charity Link, Normandy Veterans' Association, The R & R Club, South Lambeth Neighbourhood Care Association, Stroke Association, Taste for Adventure Centre, Toynbee Hall and Wiltshire & Swindon Community Foundation.

Applications In writing to the correspondent. The trust regrets it cannot send replies to applications outside its specific field of help for older people. Applications should be made through registered charities or social services departments only.

Anona Winn Charitable Trust

Health, medical, welfare.

£132,000 (2001/02)

Beneficial area UK.

Flat 27, 56 Vincent Square, London SW1P 2NE

Tel. 020 7834 0403

Correspondent The Trustees

CC Number 1044101

Information available Accounts were on file at the Charity Commission.

General Registered with the Charity Commission in February 1995, the trustees maintain a list of charitable organisations which it supports; this list is reviewed periodically.

In 2003 the trust had an income of £39,000 and a total expenditure of £56,000. Further information for this year was not available.

In 2000/01 the trust had assets of £104,000 and an income of £54,000. Grants to 46 organisations totalled £132,000. Beneficiaries of the largest donations were: Sussex Snowdrop Trust (£27,000); Newmarket Day Centre (£26,000); and Charities Aid Foundation (£12,000). Smaller grants for amounts of £500, £1,000, £1,500 or £2,000 each included Arthritis Research, British Heart Foundation, Canine Partners for Independence, Centrepoint, Hope House, Macmillan Cancer Relief Fund, National Eye Research Centre and Riding for the Disabled.

Exclusions No applications are considered from individuals.

Applications Applications will only be considered if received in writing and accompanied by the organisation's latest report and full accounts.

The Michael and Anna Wix Charitable Trust

Older people, disability, education, medicine and health, poverty, welfare, Jewish

£78,000 (2002/03)

Beneficial area UK.

Portrait Solicitors, 1 Chancery Lane, London WC2A 1LF

Tel. 020 7320 3883

Correspondent The Trustees

CC Number 207863

Information available Full accounts were on file at the Charity Commission.

General In 2002/03 the trust had assets of £1.3 million and an income of £58,000. Grant Management and administration costs were high at £19,000, including payments to a firm of solicitors in which one of the trustees is a partner. Whilst wholly legal, these editors always regret such payments unless, in the words of the Charity Commission, 'there is no realistic alternative'. Grants were made to 174 organisations totalling £78,000.

The largest grants were: £7,000 to Nightingale Hospital; £4,000 to Friends of the Hebrew University – Jerusalem; £3,000 to British Technion Society; and £2,000 each to Federation of Women Zionists, Institute for Jewish Policy Research, Jewish Care, Norwood, Pinhas Rutenberg Educational Trust, Shaare Zedek UK, Wiener Library and World Jewish Relief.

Of the remaining grants, 7 were of £1,000, 5 of £500, 37 of £400 and 117 of £200. Beneficiaries included Ace of Clubs, Action for ME, Alone in London, Bosnian Support Centre, British Epilepsy Association, British Friends of Ohel Sarah, Care International UK, Delamere Forest School, Diabetes UK, Dystonia Society, Epilepsy Research Foundation, Greater London Fund for the Blind, Headway, Horder Centre for Arthritis, Jewish Museum King George's Fund for Sailors, Listening Books, Manacare Foundation, Motor Neurone Disease Association, National Ankyolosing Spondylitis Society, National Autistic Society, NCH Action for Children, Prostate Cancer Charity, Retail Trust, Shaftesbury Society, Soundaround, Spiro Ark, Stroke Association, Tzedek,and Who Cares? Trust.

Exclusions Applications from individuals are not considered. Grants are to national bodies rather than local branches or local groups.

Applications In writing to the trustees. Applications are considered half-yearly. Only applications from registered charities are acknowledged. Frequent applications by a single charity are not appreciated.

The Maurice Wohl Charitable Foundation

Jewish, health and welfare

£651,000 (2000/01)

Beneficial area UK and Israel.

1st Floor, 7–8 Conduit Street, London W1S 2XF

Tel. 020 7493 3777

Correspondent Joseph Houri

Trustees *Maurice Wohl; Mrs Vivienne Wohl; Mrs Ella Latchman; Prof. David Latchman; M D Paisner.*

CC Number 244519

Information available Accounts were on file at the Charity Commission.

General This foundation has general charitable purposes in the UK and Israel, with a preference for Jewish charities. A wide range of causes are supported, including medical treatment and research, education, disability and older people's organisations, sheltered accommodation, the arts, relief of poverty and so on.

In 2000/01 the foundation had assets of £18 million which generated an income of £914,000. Despite sharing its offices and certain administration services with two connected charities, administration costs for the year were high at £97,000. Grants were made to 29 organisations totalling £651,000.

Substantial grants were £175,000 to The Royal Academy and £143,000 to Kings College. Other large grants were £83,000 to JFS, £67,000 to Bikur Cholim Hospital and £50,000 each to Friends of Bar-Ilan University, Lord Jakobovits Centre and UCL.

Other grants of £5,000 or more went to Yeshivat Hakotel (£17,000), Medical Aid Trust (£12,000), Jewish Care and Joint Jewish Charitable Trust (£10,000), Jerusalem Great Synagogue (£6,800), Yeshivath Meor Hatalmud (£6,600) and FMRCU Charitable Trust and Helensea Charities (£5,000 each).

Other beneficiaries included Israel Museum (£2,100), Kisharon Day School (£1,000), Ohel Torah Beth David and TAL (£680 each), Holocaust Educational Trust (£500), British Friends of the Needy of Jerusalem (£250) and Brainwave and Chicken Shed Theatre Company (£100 each).

Exclusions The trustees do not in general entertain applications for grants for ongoing maintenance projects. The trustees do not administer any schemes for individual awards or scholarships and they do not, therefore, entertain any individual applications for grants.

Applications In writing to the correspondent. The trustees meet regularly throughout the year.

The Maurice Wohl Charitable Trust

Health, welfare, arts, education

£133,000 (2002/03)

Beneficial area UK and Israel.

1st Floor, 7–8 Conduit Street, London W1S 2XF

Tel. 020 7493 3777

Correspondent J Houri

Trustees *Maurice Wohl; Mrs Vivienne Wohl; Mrs Ella Latchman; Prof. David Latchman; Martin Paisner.*

CC Number 244518

Information available Full accounts were on file at the Charity Commission.

General This foundation has general charitable purposes in the UK and Israel, with a preference for Jewish charities. A wide range of causes are supported, including medical treatment and research, education, disability and older people's organisations, sheltered accommodation, the arts, relief of poverty and so on.

In 2002/03 the trust had assets of £2.8 million, which generated an income of £160,000. After administration charges of £35,000, grants were made to organisations totalling £133,000.

Large grants went to Communaute Israelite de Geneve (£11,000), Yeshivat Beth Abraham (£3,200), Israel Museum (£1,900), Jerusalem Great Synagogue (£1,300) and Friends of the Israel Aged, Friends of the Sick, Hope Charity, Yesodey Hatorah Schools (£1,000 each).

Beneficiaries receiving under £1,000 included Federation of Jewish Relief Organisation (£700), Council for a Beautiful Israel (£680), Yeshivat Beth Abraham (£650), Western Marble Arch Synagogue (£500), Friends of Bar Han University (£300), Friends of Lubavitch UK and Jewish Blind & Disabled (£250 each), AKIM, HASKEL, Initiation Society, Listening Books, Side by Side, Zion Orphanage Jerusalem (£100 each) and Invalids at Home (£50).

Exclusions The trustees do not administer any schemes for individual awards or scholarships, and they do not, therefore, entertain any individual applications for grants.

Applications To the correspondent in writing. Applications are regularly considered throughout the year.

The Aviezer Wolfson Charitable Trust

Jewish

Not known

Beneficial area UK.

c/o Clayton Stark & Co., 5th Floor, Charles House, 108–110 Finchley Road, London NW3 5JJ

Tel. 020 7431 4200

Correspondent D Clayton, Trustee

Trustees *I S J Wolfson; Mrs A Wolfson; D Clayton; Mrs R R Lauffer.*

CC Number 275927

Information available The information for this entry was provided by the trust.

General The trustees mainly give to Jewish charities and organisations. In 2002/03 the trust had an income of £34,000 and a total expenditure of £45,000. Further information for this year was not available.

In 1999/2000 the trust's income totalled £55,000. The trust's total expenditure was £438,000. It is not known how much of this was given in grants, although some examples of grants made were provided by the trust.

In 1999/2000 larger grants were: £10,000 to Yad Eliezev, £5,000 to British Friends of Laniado Hospital, £4,000 to British Friends of Ezra Lamarpeh, £3,300 to Arachim; and £3,000 to British Friends of Yad Sarah.

Applications In writing to the correspondent.

Women at Risk

Women

£78,000 (2002)

Beneficial area UK.

Flat 6 7 Sloane Street, London SW1X 9LE

Tel. 020 7201 9982

Email women.risk@reed.co.uk

Correspondent Alec Reed, Chair

Trustees *A Reed; A J Jewitt; Ms M Newham.*

CC Number 1059332

Information available Accounts were on file at the Charity Commission.

General The trust supports smaller projects that do not have well developed fundraising campaigns, and which benefit women and people disadvantaged by poverty, psychological abuse, emotional distress and infringement of human rights. Its grantmaking is particularly focused on the relief of poverty and sickness, the preservation of health and advancement of education among women who are in need.

The trust seeks projects that meet its charitable objects, to work in partnership to fundraise and to then distribute the money raised to the partners.

In 2002 the trust had assets of £51,000 and an income of £182,000. After management and administration costs of £30,000, grants were made totalling £78,000.

Beneficiaries were Womankind Worldwide (£18,000), Refuge (£12,000), Centre for Filipinos and Family Focus (£11,000), Ockenden International (£7,700), Shooting Star Trust (£7,000), Action for Elder Abuse (£6,500) and Bangladesh Acid Survivors Trust and Cleveland Rape & Sexual Abuse (£3,000 each).

Exclusions No grants to individuals. Only charitable/not-for-profit organisations are supported on a long-term basis.

Applications In writing to the correspondent.

The Woo Charitable Foundation

Education in the arts

£368,000 (2000/01)

Beneficial area UK.

277 Green Lanes, London N13 4XS

Tel. 07974 570475 **Fax** 020 7383 5004

Correspondent The Administrator

Trustees *Nelson Woo, Chair; Countess Benckendorff; Nigel Kingsley; Michael Trask; Jackson Woo.*

CC Number 1050790

Information available Accounts were provided by the trust.

General 'The Woo Charitable Foundation was established for the advancement of education through supporting, organising, promoting or assisting the development of the arts in England, together with the specific aim of helping children, young people and those less able to help themselves.'

In autumn 2000 the trust introduced a bursary scheme giving £5,000 each to artists who have finished formal education but are yet to establish meaningful careers. The first bursary awards were made in autumn 2000 with two further awards made in 2001. It is likely that the bursary scheme will become the main funding focus of the foundation.

In 2000/01 the trust had an income of £406,000 mostly from voluntary income and donations. After administration expenses of £25,000, grants were made totalling £368,000. The trust largely funds smaller projects that aim to restore arts education. Grants ranged between £800 and £15,000.

Grants over £10,000 included: £15,000 to Chicken Shed Theatre; £12,000 to Serpentine Gallery for educational activities focusing on the under-12 age group; £11,000 to the Royal Academy towards intensive education projects based on a specific exhibition; and £10,000 each to London Academy of Music and Dramatic Art for the student hardship fund, Greenwich Chinese School towards providing five extra teachers and classes and Opera North towards workshops in primary and secondary schools.

Beneficiaries of smaller grants included: Citizens Theatre towards its youth group (£8,500); Centre for Arts and Disability towards the salary of a sculptor tutor (£7,500); The Orchestra towards expenses for volunteers, New Addington Musical Project, Poetry Archive and SPEC Jewish Youth & Community Orchestra (£5,000 each); Stagecoach Youth Theatre (£1,000); and The Cedar Foundation (£800).

Exclusions No grants for travel, building work and fundraising activities, especially abroad. Support is very rarely given to individuals, but note the above.

Applications In writing to the correspondent.

Woodlands Green Ltd

Jewish

£221,000 (2001/02)

Beneficial area Worldwide.

19 Green Walk, London NW4 2AL

Tel. 020 8203 1947

Correspondent A Ost, Trustee

Trustees *A Ost; E Ost; D J A Ost; J A Ost; A Hepner.*

CC Number 277299

Information available Accounts were on file at the Charity Commission, but without a list of grants.

General The trust's objectives are the advancement of the Orthodox Jewish faith and the relief of poverty. It mostly gives large grants to major educational projects being carried out by orthodox Jewish charities.

In 2001/02 the trust had an income of £182,000 and a total amount of grants came to £221,000. The assets in that year totalled £1.5 million.

Grants to beneficiaries are as follows: the largest was £56,000 to Friends of Toldos Avrohom Yitzchok, then £40,000 went to TYY Square, £25,000 to JET, £20,000 to Friends of Seret Wiznitz, £12,000 to Kahal Imrei Chaim, £10,000 each to Beis Soro Schneirer, NWLCM, Oizer Dalim Trust and UTA.

Smaller grants between £1,000 and £6,900 went to charities such as Achisomoch Aid Co, Friends of Beis Yisroel Trust, Friends of Mir and LJGH.

Exclusions No grants to individuals, or for expeditions or scholarships.

Applications In writing to the correspondent.

The Woodroffe Benton Foundation

General

£138,000 (2003)

Beneficial area UK.

16 Fernleigh Court, Harrow, London HA2 6NA

Tel. 020 8421 4120

Email alan.king3@which.net

Correspondent Alan King

Trustees *James Hope; Mrs Sheila Dickson; Colin Russell; Miss Celia Clout; Peter Foster; Tony Shadrack.*

CC Number 1075272

Information available Information was provided by the trust.

General This trust makes grants towards:

- people in need, primary care of people who are sick or elderly or those effected by the results of a local or national disaster
- promotion of education
- conservation and improvement of the environment

The trust rarely donates more than £2,000 and does not normally make more than one grant to the same charity in a 12 month period.

In 2003 it had assets of £4.7 million and an income of £186,000. Grants totalled £138,000.

In 2001 a total of £101,000 was given in ongoing grants to 19 organisations and £101,000 in 149 one-off grants. Charities receiving ongoing grants included Calibre, Community Links, Queen Elizabeth's Grammar School – Ashbourne and Victim Support.

Exclusions Grants are not made outside the UK and are only made to registered charities. No grants to individuals. Branches of UK charities should not apply as grants, if made, would go to the charity's headquarters.

Applications On a form available from the correspondent. Full guidance notes on completing the form and procedures for processing applications are sent with the form.

The Geoffrey Woods Charitable Foundation

Young people, education, disability, health

£67,000 (2001/02)

Beneficial area UK and overseas.

The Girdlers Company, Girdlers Hall, Basinghall Avenue, London EC2V 5DD

Tel. 020 7638 0488

Correspondent The Clerk

Trustees *The Girdlers Company; N K Maitland; A J R Fairclough.*

CC Number 248205

Information available Accounts were on file at the Charity Commission, but without a list of grants.

General In 2002/03 the trust had an income of £51,000 and a total expenditure of £73,000. Further information was not available.

In the previous year, the foundation had assets of £756,000, an income of £61,000 and made grants totalling £67,000.

The foundation is administered by the Girdlers Company and its objects are the advancement of education and religion and the relief of poverty. The trust is responsible for three funds as shown below:

The Masters Fund is allocated an amount each year for the master of the company to donate to charities of his or her own choice. This amounted to £1,600 in 2001/02

Christmas Court Donations allow members to nominate charities at Christmas time. Grants to 32 organisations totalled £14,000 in 2001/02.

The Jock French Charitable Fund encourages charitable donations from members of the livery of the company. The fund is allocated a sum that is three times the amount covenanted or donated to the foundation by the livery. The subscribing members are invited to nominate charities to receive donations. The total sum allocated is distributed in January and June each year, following ratification by the livery. In 2001/02 grants totalled £39,000.

Previous beneficiaries include All Saints Cathedral – Nairobi, Almshouse Association, Cordwainers College, Crown and Manor Boys Club, Garden School, Kings College Cambridge, LCCA initiative, London Federation of Clubs for Young People, National Spinal Injuries Unit, Surrey County Cricket Board, Queen Elizabeth Foundation for the Disabled and Westminster Abbey Choir School.

Applications 'Beneficiaries are nominated by members of the company and outside applications are no longer considered.'

The A & R Woolf Charitable Trust

General

£45,000 (2002/03)

Beneficial area Worldwide; UK, mainly in Hertfordshire.

2 Oak House, 101 Ducks Hill Road, Northwood, Middlesex HA6 2WQ

Tel. 01923 821385

Correspondent Mrs J D H Rose, Trustee

Trustees *Mrs J D H Rose; C Rose; Dr G L Edmonds; S Rose; A Rose.*

CC Number 273079

Information available Information was provided by the trust.

General The trust supports a range of causes, including Jewish organisations, animal welfare and conservation causes, children and health and welfare charities. Both UK and overseas charities (through a British-based office) receive support, together with local charities. Most of the grants are recurrent.

In 2002/03 the trust had an income of £55,000 and gave grants totalling £45,000. The majority of grants are of £100 or less, although some larger grants are made.

Larger grants of £500 and above included: £6,000 to UNICEF, which the trust has an ongoing commitment to support; £5,000 each to APEX, Diabetes UK, National Endometriosis Society and University of Hertfordshire; £1,200 to Zoological Society of London; £1,000 each to Council of Christians and Jews, Hampden Trust, Peace Hospital, RSPCC and WWF UK; and £500 to Hertfordshire Community Foundation.

Exclusions No grants to individuals or non-registered charities unless schools, hospices and so on.

Applications Support is only given to projects/organisations/causes personally known to the trustees. The trust does not respond to unsolicited applications.

This entry was not confirmed by the trust, but the information was correct according to the trust's file at the Charity Commission.

The Fred & Della Worms Charitable Trust

Jewish, education, arts

£187,000 (2001/02)

Beneficial area UK.

23 Highpoint, North Hill, London N6 4BA

Tel. 020 8342 5360 **Fax** 020 8342 5359

Email fred@worms5.freeserve.co.uk

Correspondent The Trustees

Trustees *Mrs D Worms; M D Paisner; F S Worms.*

CC Number 200036

Information available Full accounts were on file at the Charity Commission.

General In 2001/02 the trust had assets of £2 million, which generated an income of £86,000. After low administration fees of just £1,000, grants were made totalling £187,000.

The largest grants were £65,000 to British Friends of the Art Museums of Israel, £26,000 to Joint Jewish Charitable Trust, £21,000 to British Friends of the Hebrew University and £17,000 each to British Friends of Rabbi Steinsaltz and Moccali Union.

Other organisations receiving £1,000 or more were Child Resettlement Fund (£7,000), B'nai B'rith Hillel Foundation and European Jewish Publication Society (£5,000 each), Jewish National Fund (£1,300), United Synagogue Hampstead Garden Suburb (£1,200) and Duke of Edinburgh Award and Jewish Literacy Trust (£1,000 each).

Exclusions No grants to individuals.

Applications In writing to the correspondent. The trust stated that its funds are fully committed.

The Worshipful Company of Chartered Accountants General Charitable Trust (also known as CALC)

General, education

£114,000 (2001/02)

Beneficial area UK.

31 Oak Dene Park, Finchley, London N3 1EU

Tel. 01494 783402 **Fax** 01494 793306

Email michael_hardman@bigfoot.com

Correspondent M R Hardman

Trustees *D P J Ross; M N Peterson; J M Renshall; Sir Jeremy Hanley; Miss M A Yale; M J Richardson; A M C Staniforth; P Beenan.*

CC Number 327681

Information available Full accounts were on file at the Charity Commission.

General In general, the trust supports causes advancing education and/or benefiting disadvantaged people. It has a tendency to focus on a particular theme each year, as well as making grants to other causes and organisations of particular relevance to members of the company.

In 2001/02 the trust had assets of £775,000 and an income of £104,000, including £59,000 from donations received. Grants totalling £114,000 were made that year.

Under the heading '2002 Educational Project', grants totalling £50,000 were given to Bromley Branch M S Society (£20,000), Five Bridges Ltd and Notts Leukaemia Society (£10,000 each) and Prader-Willi Syndrome Association and Prisoners' Wives & Families Society (£5,000 each).

Under the heading '2001 Charitable Project', five grants were made totalling £50,200. These went to The Place to Be (£20,000), Beacon Community Cancer Palliative Care Centre (£10,000), Jubilee Primary School (£9,000), Royal Albert Dock Trust (£6,200) and Foxhill and Birley Carr Live at Home Scheme (£5,000).

Applications Applications must be sponsored by a liveryman of the company.

The Worwin UK Foundation

General

£177,000 (2002/03)

Beneficial area UK and overseas.

6 St Andrew Street, London EC4A 3LX

Tel. 020 7427 6400

Correspondent D J M Ward, Trustee

Trustees *William Hew John Hancock; Brian Moore; Mark Musgrave; Andrew Jonathan Hughes Penney; David John Marcus Ward.*

CC Number 1037981

Information available Full accounts were on file at the Charity Commission.

General In 2002/03 it had assets of £5,100 and an income of £282,000. Grants to 37 organisations totalled £177,000. Management and administration costs were high at £78,000.

The largest grants were £15,000 to Voice of the Poor Foundation, £14,000 to Evergreen, £13,000 each to Asper Centre for Entrepreneurship and Dominique Lapierre City of Joy Aid Charity, £11,000 to Bow Valley College and £10,000 each to Hospital for Sick Children Foundation and Therapeutic Clowns Canada Foundation.

Other beneficiaries included Light Up the Sky (£8,200), Thunder Bay Symphony Orchestra (£5,100), Children's Aid Society Foundation (£4,000), World Monuments Fund (£3,500), Mooreland's Camp (£2,600), Rideau High School (£1,300), Albert Park Elementary School (£880) and British Development Trust (£700).

Applications The foundation makes its own arrangements for making grants and does not seek applications.

The Diana Edgson Wright Charitable Trust

Animal conservation, welfare, general

£38,000 (2002)

Beneficial area UK with some preference for Kent.

2 Stade Street, Hythe, Kent CT21 6BD

Tel. 01303 262525

Correspondent R H V Moorhead, Trustee

Trustees *R H V Moorhead; P Edgson Wright; H C D Moorhead.*

CC Number 327737

Information available Full accounts were on file at the Charity Commission.

General This trust has general charitable purposes. The policy is to support a small number of charities. In 2002 it had assets of £956,000 and an income of £37,000. Grants totalled £38,000.

Donations included: £5,700 to Soroptimists of Ashford Charitable Trust; £4,800 to Kent Wildlife; £3,300 to Pluckley PCC; £2,000 to Pluckley Church of England Primary School; £1,500 each to Friends of Howletts and Port Lympre, Sellindge Parish Church – Kent and Sounds New; £1,200 to Little Chart Village Hall Management Committee; £1,000 each to Diabetes UK – Ashford and District Branch and The Major's Charity – Ashford; £850 to Hothfield Village Hall; £750 to Traditional Buildings Preservation Trust; £500 each to Action for the Blind and Artists' General Benevolent Institution; and £250 each to Channel Rotary Club of Folkestone, Friends of Kent Churches and Tomar Owl Sanctuary.

Applications In writing to the correspondent.

The Matthews Wrightson Charity Trust

Caring and Christian charities

£95,000 to organisations (2003)

Beneficial area UK and some overseas.

The Farm, Northington, Alresford, Hampshire SO24 9TH

Correspondent Adam Lee, Secretary & Administrator

Trustees *Miss Priscilla W Wrightson; Anthony H Isaacs; Guy D G Wrightson; Miss Isabelle S White.*

CC Number 262109

Information available Full accounts were provided by the trust.

General This trust has general charitable purposes, favouring innovation, Christian work and organisations helping disadvantaged people. Standard grants are of £400 and go to smaller charities or projects seeking to raise under £25,000. Large UK charities and those seeking to raise in excess of £250,000 are not generally supported, unless they have received funds in previous years. A few larger grants are also made, to organisations with a long connection to the trust.

In 2003 it had assets of £1.4 million and an income of £68,000. Grants to 186 organisations totalled £95,000. By far the largest grant was £14,000 to Royal College of Arts for the Hardship and Industrial Production Awards, which received the same amount in the previous year. Other exceptional grants were £1,200 to Peper Harow Foundation, £1,000 to FUN in Action for Children, £800 each to Children's Family Trust, Churches Together in Britain & Ireland for its hardship fund, The Daneford Trust and DEMAND and £500 each to Bible Society of Mongolia, CARE International and C.A.R.E. (Christian Action, Research & Education).

In 2003, in addition to the £13,000 given to individuals, grants were made to 186 organisations totalling £95,000 and were broken down as follows:

	No.	*Total*
Art causes	7	£17,000
Christian	20	£10,000
Disability	36	£14,500
Individuals	32	£13,000
Medical	9	£4,000
Older people	7	£3,000
Rehabilitation	17	£8,500
Worldwide	14	£7,000
Youth	44	£18,000

Exclusions No support for individuals (other than visitors from overseas) seeking education or adventure for personal character improvement. No support for unconnected local churches, village halls, schools and animal charities. Charities with a turnover of over £250,000 are generally not considered. Most grants are to organisations seeking, or with a turnover of less than, £25,000. Individuals seeking funding for 'self-improvement' education are not favoured.

Applications In writing to the correspondent. No special forms are used, although latest financial accounts are desirable. One or two sheets (usually the covering letter) are circulated monthly to the trustees, who meet every six months only for policy and administrative decisions. Replies are only sent to successful applicants; allow up to three months for an answer. Please include an sae if an answer to an unsuccessful application is required. The trust receives over 1,000 applications a year; 'winners have to make the covering letter more attractive than the 90 others received each month'.

Miss E B Wrightson's Charitable Settlement

Music education, inshore rescue, recreation

£45,000 to organisations and individuals (2000/01)

Beneficial area UK.

Swangles Farm, Cold Christmas, Hertfordshire SG12 7SP

Email norahhickman@henryhickman.com

Correspondent Mrs N Hickman

Trustees *A Callard; Mrs E Clarke; P Dorkings.*

CC Number 1002147

Information available Basic accounts were provided by the trust.

General The trust makes grants for general charitable purposes, with a preference for inshore rescue services, multiple sclerosis causes and young people with musical talent. It primarily supports individuals, but applications can also be made by groups and charities seeking funding for the advancement of music education and recreational charitable objects.

In 2002/03 the trust had an income of £36,000 and a total expenditure of £97,000. Further information for this year was not available.

In 2000/01 it had assets of £1.9 million and an income of £54,000. Out of a total expenditure of £98,000 the sum of £45,000 was distributed to 7 organisations and 51 individuals.

Three beneficiaries are mentioned in the trust's deed: The Musicians Benevolent Fund, Multiple Sclerosis Society and Royal National Lifeboat Institution.

Applications In writing to the correspondent. Trustees meet regularly to consider applications and 'all properly completed applications are acknowledged'. Guidelines are provided by the trust for applications by individuals, but not organisations.

Wychdale Ltd

Jewish

£126,000 (2002/03)

Beneficial area UK and abroad.

89 Darenth Road, London N16 6EB

Correspondent The Secretary

Trustees *C D Schlaff; J Schlaff; Mrs Z Schlaff.*

CC Number 267447

Information available Full accounts were on file at the Charity Commission.

General The objects of this charity are the advancement of the Orthodox Jewish religion and the relief of poverty in the UK and abroad. The charity stated in its 2000/01 accounts that it 'supports religious educational institutions in London, the provinces and further afield'.

In 2002/03 the trust had assets of £263,000 and an income of £146,000. Grants were made totalling £126,000.

The largest grants were £50,000 to Chevrath Torah Veyirah (Israel), £20,000 to Friends of Yeshivas Shaar Hashomayim (Israel), £11,000 to Kahal Chasidim Bobov and £10,000 to Torah Temimah (USA).

Other organisations receiving £1,000 or more: Medical Aid Trust (£7,000), Yeshiva Masoras Avos in USA (£6,000), Open Hand and Yeshivas Maalos Hatorah in Israel (£3,000 each), Bais Nadvorna (£2,800), Kollel Bnei Yisoschor (£2,500), Kollel Chibath Yerushlayim (£2,250), Beis Rochel d'Satmar (£1,500) and Society of Friends of the Torah (£1,000).

Exclusions Non-Jewish organisations are not supported.

Applications In writing to the correspondent.

Wychville Ltd

Jewish, education, general

£224,000 (2002/03)

Beneficial area UK.

44 Leweston Place, London N16 6RH

Correspondent Berisch Englander, Governor

Trustees *B Englander, Chair; Mrs S Englander; E Englander; Mrs B R Englander.*

CC Number 267584

Information available Accounts were on file at the Charity Commission, but without a list of grants.

General This trust support educational, Jewish and other charitable organisations. In 2002/03 the trust had assets of £61,000, an income of £230,000 and made grants totalling £224,000. No further information was available.

Applications In writing to the correspondent.

The Wyseliot Charitable Trust

Medical, welfare, general

£93,000 (2001/02)

Beneficial area UK.

17 Chelsea Square, London SW3 6LF

Correspondent J H Rose, Trustee

Trustees *E A D Rose; J H Rose; A E G Raphael.*

CC Number 257219

Information available Accounts were provided by the trust, but without a narrative report.

General In 2001/02 the trust had assets of £2.1 million, which generated an income of £89,000. Grants were made to 33 organisations totalling £93,000.

The largest grants were £5,000 each to Avenues Youth Project, Cystic Fibrosis Trust and Prostate Cancer Charity. Other grants were in the range of £1,000 to £4,000 and included those to: Enham Trust, St Mungo's Trust and Time and Talents Association (£4,000 each); Notting Hill Housing Trust (£3,500); Earls Court Homeless Families Trust, Queen Elizabeth Foundation for the Disabled, Trinity Hospice and Winged Fellowship (£3,000 each); Hackney Quest, Home Start, Musicians Benevolent Fund and Runnymede Trust (£2,000 each); and London Bereavement Network, Professional Classes Aid Council and Woodlarks Workshop (£1,000 each).

Exclusions Local charities are not supported. No support for individuals; grants are only made to registered charities.

Applications In writing to the correspondent; however, note that the trust states that the same charities are supported each year, with perhaps one or two changes. It is unlikely new charities sending circular appeals will be supported and large UK charities are generally not supported.

The Yamanouchi European Foundation

Medical

US$265,000 (2000/01)

Beneficial area Worldwide.

Yamanouchi House, Pyrford Road, West Byfleet, Surrey KT14 6RA

Tel. 01932 345535 **Fax** 01932 342404

Correspondent D Ferguson, Trustee

Trustees *Dr Toichi Takenaka, Chair; Yasuo Ishii; Joseph F Harford; Dudley H Ferguson; Prof. Peter van Brummeley; Toshinari Tamura; Shinji Usuda; Win Kockelkoren.*

CC Number 1036344

Information available Full accounts were on file at the Charity Commission.

General The objects of the foundation are:

- committing long-term support to basic medical and related scientific programmes through organisations such as the SIU (Societe Internationale D'Urologie).
- supporting selected short- medium- and long-term projects, aimed at integrating basic science and clinical research through interdisciplinary projects.
- providing facilities, promoting or sponsoring the exchange of ideas and views through lectures and discussions of an educational or cultural nature.
- promoting, assisting or otherwise supporting charitable institutions aimed at serving good causes.

The 2000/01 annual report stated: 'It is the long-term goal of the foundation to provide support for programmes and cultures that contribute to the advancement of an increasingly healthy society.

'The foundation's trustees believes this is best accomplished by providing funding for basic scientific research, for the examination of public health and environmental policy issues, and for the support of educational and cultural exchange programmes.'

The foundation administers The Yamanouchi Award and The Yamanouchi Lectureship, which are of US$30,000 given every three years to reward people significantly contributing to the medical and medicinal disciplines. The Yamanouchi Fellowship is a scholarship to people studying these disciplines worth up to US$150,000 as a two-year support programme, with people supported being eligible to reapply to a maximum of three years.

In 2000/01 the trust had assets of US$12 million, which generated an income of US$774,000. Direct scientific supported totalled US$194,000, with a further US$75,000 donated to charities.

The largest grants were both of US$75,000 as half of a US$150,000 two-year grant, to Departimento di Medicina Interna Universita di Pisa and the Department of Oncology at Helsinki University Central Hospital.

Other grants included US$10,000 each to Brauninger Stiftung GmbH Online Mouse Projekt, Connaître Les Syndromes Cérébelleux and Chase Children' Hospice and US$7,500 each to Foundation Sance at the Department of Hematooncology in Pediatric Faculty Hospital – Olomouc, Associacao De Amigos Da Criança E Da Familia for 'Chão Dos Meninos', Dyadis, Stichting VTV, Archipelago Cooperativa Sociale r.1. and Comitato Maria Letizia Verga.

Applications In writing to the correspondent.

The Yapp Charitable Trust

Social welfare

£222,000 (2002/03)

Beneficial area England and Wales

47a Paris Road, Scholes, Holmfirth HD9 1SY

Tel. 01484 683403 **Fax** 01484 683403

Email info@yappcharitabletrust.org.uk

Website www.yappcharitabletrust.org.uk

Correspondent Mrs Margaret Thompson, Administrator

Trustees *Revd Timothy C Brooke; Peter R Davies; Peter G Murray; Mrs Stephanie Willats; David Aeron-Thomas; Miss Sonya Richards.*

CC Number 1076803

Information available Information was provided by the trust.

General The Yapp Charitable Trust was formed in 1999 from the Yapp Welfare Trust (two-thirds share) and Yapp Education and Research Trust (one-third share). However, rather than combining the criteria for the two trusts, the trustees decided to focus on small charities, usually local rather than UK charities. The trust now accepts applications only from small charities and organisations with a turnover of less than £60,000 in the year of application. The objects are restricted to registered charities in the UK and cover work with:

1. older people

2. children and young people, aged 5 to 25

3. people with disabilities or mental health problems

4. moral welfare – people trying to overcome life-limiting problems such as addiction, relationship difficulties, abuse or a history of offending

5. education and learning (including lifelong learning) and scientific or medical research.

Applications from outside these areas cannot be considered. Grants are given towards running costs and salaries but not for capital equipment. The trust stated in 2004 that is concentrating on continuation funding for existing work and will not fund new organisations or new work.

The trust is proactive in ensuring its grants are made evenly across the areas of work. As such, its priorities are continually revised – current priorities and exclusions are publicised on the trust's website. A recent development has been the closure of grants to Scottish and Northern Irish charities, with the final deadline for application from these countries being 26 May 2005. Please note also that guidelines and exclusions change each year.

The trust is proactive in ensuring its grants are made evenly across the areas of work and the UK. In 2002, for instance, it used targeted publicity to increase its funding in Northern Ireland and Wales as well as to older people's organisations to increase funding in these areas. As such, its priorities are continually revised – current priorities and exclusions are publicised on the trust's website. Please note also that guidelines and exclusions change each year.

In 2002/03 the trust had assets of £4.8 million, generating an income of £286,000. Grants ranged between £6,000 and £500, although most were for £2,000 or less, and were made to 100 organisations totalling £222,000. Most grants are for one year, but recurrent grants for up to three years will be considered.

Examples of grants are broken down as follows:

Children and young people –34 grants totalling £65,000 (29%)

The largest grant in this category was £5,300 over three years to African Unite Against Child Abuse. Other organisations receiving funding over three years were Brandon Carrside Youth, Muslim Youth Helpline and Ruchill Church Outreach Project (£4,500 each). Other beneficiaries included Bognor Fun Bus Co Ltd and Edinburgh and Lothians Club for Young People (£3,000 each), Ledley Hall Boys' and Girls' Club Trust Ltd and Lower Wick Community & Youth Project (£2,500 each), East Cleveland Youth Housing Trust, Empower, Noonday and Teens in Crisis (£2,000 each) and Beckton Islamic Assoication, Eden Christian Trust and Sierra Leone War Trust for Children (£1,500 each) and Adventure Sailing Trust Ltd, Bromley Sea Cadets, Caister Youth and Community Centre, St Matthew's Special Needs Group and YWCA Coupar Angus (£1,000 each).

Disability – 29 grants totalling £57,000 (26%)

Organisations receiving grants over three years were Contact Community Care, Michael Roberts Charitable Trust, North Worcestershire Disability Information Advice Line and South Lakeland Carers' Association (£4,500 each). Other beneficiaries included Scope for Wellington – Helping Hands and Southwell Care Project (£3,000 each), Asian Deaf Women's Association and Western Isles Carers – Users and Supporters Network (£2,500 each), A Plus, City Centre Friends, Gwent Epilepsy Group and Norfolk Association for the Disabled (£2,000 each), Special Needs Network and Woolverstone Project (£1,500 each) and Citizen's Advice – Solihull, Ezer North West Ltd, FOSTAR and North Herefordshire Shopmobility Scheme (£1,000 each).

Elderly people – 18 grants totalling £54,000 (24%)

The largest grants were £6,000 each over three years to Age Concern – Ledbury & District and Lenton Care Link. Other organisations to receive funding over two or three years were Ellesmere Port & Neston Live at Home Scheme, Frankley Church Community Project, Lydbrook Community Care and Oakley Rural Day Care Centre (£4,500 each over three years) and Age Concern – Frome (£4,000 over two years). Other beneificiaries included Age Concern – Syston and Tamil Welfare Association UK (£2,500 each), Drumgallon Area Community Association, South Leeds Live at Home Scheme and St Peter's Bengali Association (£2,000 each), Latin American Elderly Project and Third Age Arts (£1,500 each) and Wapping Bangladesh Association (£1,000).

Moral welfare – 12 grants totalling £36,000 (16%)

The largest grants were £6,000 each over three years to Ponthafren Association and Thetford Counselling Service and £4,500 over three years to Southampton Counselling & Therapy Centre. Other beneficiaries included Crisis Pregnancy Centre and Survivors – Hull & East Riding (£3,000 each), Hardman Trust (£2,500), Help Counselling Services (£2,000), Freeflow Counselling Service (£1,800) and Manna (£1,000).

Education – 7 grants totalling £11,000 (5%)

Grants went to Credo Arts Community (£2,100), MourneDerg Partnership and Sanaton Association (£2,000 each), Multi–Cultural Education & Youth Project (£1,500) and Birmingham Pen Trade Heritage Association, Complete Productions Limited and Kilcranny House (£1,000 each).

No research grants were awarded during year as the trust is in the process of selecting an area of interest to support. A total of £9,000 was accumulated during the year for research and applications will be considered once the area of interest has been selected.

Exclusions Grants are only made to organisations with charitable status. The following are not supported:

- individuals, including students undertaking research, expeditions or gap year projects and charities raising funds to purchase equipment for individuals
- groups that do not have their own charity registration number or exemption – students' hostels and youth hostels are therefore usually not eligible
- fundraising groups raising money to benefit another organisation such as a hospital or school.
- new organisations – organisations must have been operating for at least 3 years
- new work – funding is only provided for continuation funding for projects or work that is already happening
- capital expenditure, such as buildings, renovations, extentions, furnishings, equipment or minibuses.
- bereavement counselling
- childcare
- debt advice
- community safety initiatives
- holidays and holiday centres
- core funding of general community organisations – such as community associations, community centres, general advice centres as some of their work is outside the trust's objectives.
- medical and scientific research – funds are fully committe

Applications On a form available from the administrator. Applicants may request a form by e-mail in Word 2000 format if preferred, although all applications must be sent by post. The only document that will be read by all the trustees is the application form. It is therefore important that applicants complete every section. Applicants uncertain whether they are eligible or how to complete the form should contact the administrator for advice. Applications must include most recent accounts, and annual reports and newsletters are also appreciated. Closing dates for applications are 31 January, 26 May and 30 September for consideration about six weeks later, and notification around two weeks after this. Applications are all acknowledged, and all applicants hear the outcome after the trustees' meeting. In the case of successful applicants, this normally takes about two weeks as the letters are accompanied by grant cheques which take a little time to prepare and circulate for signature. Late applications will be considered at the following meeting.

The Dennis Alan Yardy Charitable Trust

General

£38,000 (2001/02)

Beneficial area Overseas and UK with a preference for the East Midlands.

PO Box 5039, Spratton, Northampton NN6 8YH

Correspondent The Secretary

Trustees *Dennis Alan Yardy, Chair; Mrs Christine Anne Yardy; Jeffrey Creek; Mrs Joanne Stoney.*

CC Number 1039719

Information available Accounts were on file at the Charity Commission, but without a list of grants.

General This trust was established in 1993. It supports major UK and international charities and those within the East Midlands area. In 2001/02 it had assets of £568,000, which generated an income of £36,000. Grants totalled £38,000. No further information was available.

Exclusions No grants to individuals or non-registered charities.

Applications In writing to the correspondent.

The John Young Charitable Settlement

Wildlife, general

£65,000 (2001/02)

Beneficial area UK and overseas.

c/o Lee Associates, 5 Southampton Place, London WC1A 2DA

Tel. 020 7025 4600

Correspondent K A Hawkins

Trustees *J M Young; G H Camamile.*

CC Number 283254

Information available Accounts were on file at the Charity Commission, but without a description of the trust's grant-making policy.

General In 2001/02 the trust had assets of £342,000 with an income of £136,000 and grants totalling £65,000.

Grants include £5,000 each to Voluntary Service Overseas, Tidy Britain Group, Wildfowl and Wetlands Trust, AA Foundation, Starlight Children's Foundation Austrailia, Sarah Matheson Trust, RSPB, Medical Foundation for the Care of Victims of Torture, Futures for Children, Forest Guardians and CAF-GFCT Special Donations Trust, £2,000 each to Architecture Foundation, Montana Aids Vaccine and Teenage Cancer Trust, £1,000 each to Memorial Arts Charity, Mencap Promotions and RIBA London Region.

Grants of less than £1,000 were awarded to Unit 17 The Bartlett, British Heart Foundation and Action Aid.

Applications In writing to the correspondent.

David Young Charitable Trust

Mainly Jewish

£48,000 (2002/03)

Beneficial area UK.

Harcourt House, 19 Cavendish Square, London W1M 9AB

Correspondent The Trustees

Trustees *M S Mishon; Lady L M Young of Graffham; The Rt Hon Lord Young of Graffham*

CC Number 265195

Information available Accounts were on file at the Charity Commission.

General The trust's 2002/03 accounts states it 'supports charitable institutions including those engaged in medical and ancillary services (including medical research), education, helping those who are disabled and older, relieving poverty, providing sheltered accomodation and developing the arts'.

In 2002/03 the trust had assets of £43,000, an income of £60,000 and made grants totalling £48,000.

Grant beneficiaries included United Jewish Appeal (£13,500), Jewish Care (£12,000), Community Security Trust (£6,500), Friends of Bar Ilan University (£5,000) and St John's Wood Synagogue, B'Nai Brith Foundation, Oxford Centre for Hebrew and Jewish Studies, Royal Academy Trust and UCL Development Fund (£1,000 each). Other donations less than £1,000 each totalled £5,700.

Applications In writing to the correspondent.

The William Allen Young Charitable Trust

General

£132,000 (2002/03)

Beneficial area UK, with a preference for south London.

The Ram Brewery, Wandsworth, London SW18 4JD

Tel. 020 8875 7000

Correspondent J A Young, Trustee

Trustees *J A Young; T F B Young; J G A Young.*

CC Number 283102

Information available Full accounts were on file at the Charity Commission.

General The trust supports humanitarian causes, with a large number of health organisations supported each year. Grants are made to local and national organisations throughout the UK, although there appears to be a preference for south London.

In 2002/03 the trust had assets of £3.7 million with an income of £116,000 and grants totalling £132,000.

The largest grants were £10,000 each to British Benevolent Fund of Madrid and Portsmouth Hospitals NHS Trust, £9,000 to Royal College of Surgeons, £5,000 to British Cemetery Foundation and £3,000 each to Ladies Samaritan Society, National Hospital Development Foundation and Royal Star & Garter Home.

Other grants include £2,000 each to Prospect Education (Technology) Trust and St Andrew's Church West Hatch Millennium Fund, £1,000 each to Bankside Gallery, Battersea District Scout Council, Breast Cancer Charity, British Blind Sailing Racing Association, Children's Hospice South-West, FAHOA, Imperial War Museum, Incorporated Brewers Benevolent Society, Jubilee Sailing Trust, Leukemia Research Fund, London Gardens Society, London Harness Horse Parade Society, Mayor's Charity Appeal (Wandsworth), Merton Medical Society, Multiple Sclerosis Society (Croydon), New Yeovil Hospice, Putney Recreation Rooms Trust, Royal Navy Historic Flight, St John Ambulance (Hampshire), St Andrew's Church, Royal War Widows Society, Trinity Hospice, and Victoria Cross and George Cross Association.

Grants of less than £1,000 were awarded to Wooden Spoon Society, Wimbledon High School, Streatham Youth Centre – John Corfield Memorial Fund, Swaffield Primary School, St Peter & St James Hospice, St George's Hospital Medical School, Shaftesbury Arethusa Homes, Royal Hospital for Neuro-Disability, Putney and Wandsworth Crime Prevention Panel, Police Foundation, Northcote Heavy Horse Centre, NACC, Marie Curie Cancer Care, London Choral Society, Greater London Fund for the Blind, Esher Friends of Cancer Research UK, City of London Migraine Clinic, Cancer Research UK, Cancer Research Centre, Bruce Trust, British Red Cross kingston Centre, Billinghurst Choral Society, Barnfield Riding for the Disabled Trust, Arts Express, Battersea Scout Centre and Action for Blind People.

Applications The trust stressed that all funds were committed and consequently unsolicited applications would not be supported.

Elizabeth & Prince Zaiger Trust

Welfare, health, general

£240,000 (2002/03)

Beneficial area UK, some preference for Somerset, Dorset and the south-west.

6 Alleyn Road, Dulwich, London SE21 8AL

Correspondent D W Parry, Trustee

Trustees *D W Parry; P J Harvey; D G Long.*

CC Number 282096

Information available Information was provided by the trust.

General As well as supporting general charitable causes, the trust has the following objects:

- relief of older people
- relief of people who are mentally and physically disabled
- advancement of education of children and young people
- provision of care and protection for animals.

In 2002/03 the trust had assets of £9 million and an income of £222,000. Donations totalled £240,000. The largest grants were £5,000 each to British Heart Foundation, Cystic Fibrosis Trust, Juvenile Diabetes Trust, Royal Hospital for Neuro-Disability and Variety Club of Great Britain, £4,000 each to ASBHA, National Animal Welfare Trust, Royal National Institute for the Blind and St Margaret – Somerset Hospice and £3,000 to British Institute for Brain-Injured Children.

Exclusions No grants to individuals.

Applications The trust does not respond to unsolicited applications, stating 'we have an ongoing programme of support for our chosen charities'.

Zephyr Charitable Trust

Housing, health, environment, third world

£29,000 (2003/04)

Beneficial area UK and worldwide.

New Guild House, 45 Great Charles Street, Queensway, Birmingham B3 2LX

Tel. 0121 212 2222 **Fax** 0121 212 2300

Correspondent R Harriman, Trust Administrator

Trustees *Elizabeth Breeze; Roger Harriman; David Baldock; Donald I Watson.*

CC Number 1003234

Information available Full accounts were provided by the trust.

General This trust provided help for organisations benefiting disabled people; homeless people; victims of famine, man-made or natural disasters, war and the environment.

In 2003/04 it had assets of £921,000, an income of £33,000 and made grants totalling £29,000. Grants included: £3,000 to Intermediate Technology; £2,100 to Pesticides Action Network UK; £2,000 each to CRISIS and Medical Foundation for the Care of Victims of Torture; £1,900 to Sandema Project; £1,800 to West Hampstead Community Association; £1,600 to Womankind UK; and £1,500 each to Friends of the Earth, Hearing Research Trust and Kings Cross Homelessness Project.

Exclusions No grants to individuals, expeditions or scholarships.

Applications In writing to the correspondent. The trustees meet to consider ongoing grants in June or July each year. Unsolicited applications are unlikely to be successful, since the trust makes annual donations to a list of beneficiaries. However, the trust stated that unsolicited applications are considered on a quarterly basis by the trustees and very occasional support is given.

Telephone applications are not accepted.

The I A Ziff Charitable Foundation

General, education, Jewish, arts, youth, older people, medicine

£181,000 (2001/02)

Beneficial area UK, with a preference for Yorkshire, especially Leeds and Harrogate.

Town Centre House, The Merrion Centre, Leeds LS2 8LY

Tel. 0113 222 1234 **Fax** 0113 242 1026

Correspondent B Rouse, Secretary

Trustees *I Arnold Ziff; Mrs Marjorie E Ziff; Michael A Ziff; Edward M Ziff; Mrs Ann L Manning.*

CC Number 249368

Information available Full accounts were on file at the Charity Commission.

General This trust likes to support causes that will provide good value for the money donated by benefiting a large number of people, as well as encouraging others to make contributions to the work. This includes a wide variety of schemes that involve the community at many levels, including education, public places, the arts and helping people who are disadvantaged. Capital costs and building work are particularly favoured by the trustees, as they feel projects such as these are not given the support they deserve from statutory sources.

In 2002/03 it had an income of £251,000 and a total expenditure of £286,000.

In 2001/02 the trust had assets of £2.3 million, which generated an income of £254,000. Grants were made totalling £181,000.

The 2001/02 trustees' report stated the current policies as follows:

'1. The University of Leeds. Funding has been agreed for a further five-year project to refurbish the fabric of certain buildings within the university to continue to provide the students with a sound working environment.

'2. A project to recreate gardens from seven different countries of the world. These gardens are located at the Canal Gardens Roundhay, which is the site of the already renowned Tropical World, attracting nearly one million visitors annually. The gardens project is supported by this charity and Leeds City Council and the second tranche of the charity's commitment will be paid when the council has made further progress with the project.

'3. The refurbishing of the main display room of the Leeds Art Gallery to improve the quality of the air conditioning and lighting in order to better preserve the valuable works on display. The release of funding has been delayed whilst Leeds City Council undertake necessary repairs to the roof of the art gallery.

'4. The Queenshill Estate Leeds. A five-year project to contribute to the refurbishment of the Queenshill Day Centre in Leeds.

'5. The Jewish Education Trust. A commitment to fund education for Jewish children in their own language and tradition.'

The largest grant paid during the year was £50,000 to University of Leeds for the project mentioned above.

A number of grants were made to Jewish organisations in Yorkshire, particularly Leeds. Leeds Jewish Welfare Board received £4,200, while other beneficiaries included Leeds Jewish Blind Society (£1,400), Leeds Talmund Torah (£150), Harrogate Hebrew Congregation (£90)

and Leeds Jewish Representative Council (£25).

Leeds International Piano Competition received £7,000 while Leeds Metropolitan University received £5,000. Other recipients in the Leeds area included Yorkshire Association of Boys' Clubs (£2,000), Yorkshire Film Archive (£1,000), Leeds Citizen's Advice Bureau (£250), Leeds City Council (£230), Leeds Diabetic Blindness Prevention Project and Samaritans of Leeds (£100) and Leeds Representative Council (£25).

UK Jewish organisations to benefit included United Jewish Israel Appeal (£21,000), the Jewish Museum (£3,500), United Hebrew Congregation (£1,300), Norwood (£1,100), Jewish Outreach Centre (£200) and Hadassa Women (£20).

St Gemma's Hospice received £7,400. Other beneficiaries included Scope (£1,000), Marie Curie Cancer Care (£580), St John Ambulance (£500), Gateways Educational Trust (£270), Community Shop Trust (£200), Action Research (£100), Cancer Bridge (£20) and North Lakeland Hospice (£10).

Exclusions No grants to individuals.

Applications In writing to the correspondent. Initial telephone calls are welcome, but please note the above comments.

Subject index

The following subject index begins with a list of the categories used. The categories are fairly wide-ranging to keep the index as simple as possible. There may be considerable overlap between some of these categories, particularly children, older people and young people with, for example, the social/moral welfare or medicine and health categories.

The list of categories is followed by the index itself. Before using the index, please note following:

How the index was compiled

1. The index aims to reflect the most recently recorded grant-making practice. It is therefore based on our interpretation of what each trust has actually given to, rather than what its policy statement says or its charitable objects allow it to do in principle. For example, where a trust states it has general charitable purposes, but its grants list shows a strong preference for welfare, we have indexed it as welfare.
2. We have tried to ensure that each trust has given significantly in the areas mentioned above (usually at least £30,000), therefore small, apparently untypical grants have been ignored for this classification.
3. The index has been compiled from the latest information available to us.

Limitations

1. It has not been possible to contact all 1,200 trusts specifically in regard to this index so policies may have changed.
2. Sometimes there will be a geographical restriction on the trust's grant giving which is not shown up in this index, or the trust may not give for the specific purposes you require under that heading. It is important to read the entry carefully, you will need to check:
   (a) The trust gives in your geographical area of operation.
   (b) The trust gives for the specific purposes you require.
   (c) There is no other reason to prevent you making an application to this trust.
3. We have omitted the General category as the number of trusts included would make it unusable.

Under no circumstances should the index be used as a simple mailing list. Remember that each trust is different and that often the policies or interests of a particular trust do not fit easily into the given categories. Each entry must be read individually and carefully before you send off an application. Indiscriminate applications are usually unsuccessful. They waste time and money and greatly annoy trusts.

The categories are as follows:

Arts, culture, sport and recreation *page 410*

A very wide category including performing, written and visual arts, crafts theatres, museums and galleries, heritage, architecture and archeology, sports.

Children and young people *page 411*

Mainly for welfare and welfare-related activities.

Community and economic development *page 413*

This includes employment.

Disadvantaged people *page 413*

This includes people who are:

- socially-excluded
- socially and economically disadvantaged
- unemployed
- homeless
- offenders
- educationally disadvantaged
- victims of social/natural occurrences, including refugees and asylum seekers.

Education/training *page 414*

Environment and animals *page 415*

This includes:

- agriculture and fishing
- conservation
- animal care
- environment and education
- transport
- sustainable environment.

Housing *page 416*

Ill or disabled people *page 417*

This includes people who are ill, or who have physical or mental disabilities, learning difficulties, or mental health problems.

Medicine and health *page 418*

Older people *page 420*

Religion general *page 420*

This includes inter-faith work and religious understanding.

Christianity page 421

Islam page 422

Judaism page 422

Rights, law, conflict *page 424*

This includes:

- citizen participation
- conflict resolution
- legal and advice services
- rights
- equilty and justice.

Arts, culture, sport and recreation

Children and young people

Community and economic development

Disadvantaged people

Education and training

Environment and animals

Housing

Ill or disabled people

Medicine and Health

Older People

Religion

Christianity

Islam

Judaism

Rights, law and conflict

Science and technology

Social sciences, and policy research

Social welfare

Voluntary sector management and development

Women

Geographical index

The following geographical index aims to highlight when a trust gives preference for, or has a special interest in, a particular area: county, region, city, town or London Borough. Please note the following:

1. Before using this index please read the following and the introduction to the subject index on page 408. We must emphasise that this index:
   (a) should not be used as a simple mailing list, and
   (b) is not a substitute for detailed research.

When you have identified trusts, using this index, please read each entry carefully before making an application. Simply because a trust gives in your geographical area does not mean that it gives to your type of work.

2. Most trusts in this list are not restricted to one area, usually the geographical index indicates that the trust gives some priority for the area(s).
3. Trusts which give throughout England, Northern Ireland, Scotland and Wales have been excluded as have those which give throughout the UK, unless they have a particular interest in one or more locality.
4. Each section is ordered alphabetically according to the name of the trust.

The categories for the overseas and UK indices are as follows:

England

We have divided England into the following nine categories:

Some trusts may be found in more than one category due to them providing grants in more than one area i.e. those with a preference for northern England.

These are listed in alphabetical order of continent.

The Middle East has been listed separately. Please note that most of the trusts listed are primarily for the benefit of Jewish people and the advancement of the Jewish religion.

England

North East

North West

Yorkshire and The Humber

East Midlands

West Midlands

Eastern England

South East

South West

London

Wales

Scotland

Northern Ireland

Developing world

Africa

Americas

Asia

Australasia

Europe

Middle East

Alphabetical index